Contents in Brief

Contents

Cognitive Psychology

5

Robert J. Sternberg
Tufts University

with contributions of the
Investigating Cognitive Psychology boxes by

Jeff Mio
California State University–Pomona

WADSWORTH
CENGAGE Learning

Australia • Brazil • Japan • Korea • Mexico • Singapore • Spain • United Kingdom • United States

WADSWORTH
CENGAGE Learning

Cognitive Psychology, Fifth Edition
Robert J. Sternberg

Psychology Editor: Jaime A. Perkins

Associate Development Editor:
Dan Moneypenny

Assistant Editor: Rachel Guzman

Editorial Assistant: Wilson Co

Sr. Technology Project Manager:
Bessie Weiss

Marketing Manager: Sara Swangard

Marketing Assistant: Melanie Cregger

Sr. Marketing Communications Manager:
Linda Yip

Sr. Content Project Manager: Pat Waldo

Creative Director: Rob Hugel

Sr. Art Director: Vernon Boes

Sr. Print Buyer: Becky Cross

Rights Acquisition Accounts Manager:
Scott Bragg

Production Service: Leah Bross, Graphic
World Publishing Services

Sr. Rights Acquisitions Accounts Manager,
Image: Deanna Ettinger

Photo Researcher: Terri Miller

Copy Editor: Graphic World Publishing
Services

Cover Designer: Hiroko K. Chastain, Cuttriss
& Hambleton

Cover Images: puzzle piece, key in lock, and
person checking watch, Corbis Images; all
others, Getty Images

Compositor: Graphic World Inc.

For product information and technology assistance, contact us at
Cengage Learning Customer & Sales Support, 1-800-354-9706

For permission to use material from this text or product,
submit all requests online at **cengage.com/permissions**
Further permissions questions can be e-mailed to
permissionrequest@cengage.com

Library of Congress Control Number: 2007941973

ISBN-13: 978-0-495-50629-4

ISBN-10: 0-495-50629-X

Wadsworth
10 Davis Drive
Belmont, CA 94002-3098
USA

Cengage Learning is a leading provider of customized learning solutions
with office locations around the globe, including Singapore, the United
Kingdom, Australia, Mexico, Brazil, and Japan. Locate your local office at
international.cengage.com/region.

Cengage Learning products are represented in Canada by Nelson
Education, Ltd.

For your course and learning solutions, visit **academic.cengage.com**

Purchase any of our products at your local college store or at our preferred
online store **www.ichapters.com**

20·06 003536

Printed in the United States of America
2   3   4   5   6   7   12   11   10   09   08

CHAPTER 2

Cognitive Neuroscience   33

CHAPTER 3

Perception   74

C H A P T E R 4

Attention and Consciousness   123

CHAPTER **5**

Memory: Models and Research Methods   176

CHAPTER **8**

Representation and Organization of Knowledge in Memory: Concepts, Categories, Networks, and Schemas   302

CHAPTER 9

Language: Nature and Acquisition   341

CHAPTER 10
Language in Context   380

CHAPTER 11
Problem Solving and Creativity   428

CHAPTER 13

Human and Artificial Intelligence   528

To the Instructor

Every year it was a gamble, and every year I lost: I had taught cognitive psychology a number of times during my years of teaching at Yale, and I had never used the same textbook twice. For whatever reason, my students were never taken with any of the books and neither was I. The book was too hard or too easy, too narrow or too broad, too dated or too trendy. They were decent books, just not the right books. Finally, I decided to stack the deck and write the book myself. In this preface, I describe my goals for both the fifth edition and for the original text in particular.

What's New in *Cognitive Psychology,* Fifth Edition

In *Cognitive Psychology,* fifth edition, you will find many changes. The biggest change reflects the explosion of knowledge in the field. There are more than 500 new references, greatly updating the coverage provided by the book. A second change, by popular demand, is that material on neurons and neurotransmitters that had been eliminated in the fourth edition is back and updated in the fifth edition. A third major change, also by popular demand, is that the order of Chapters 3 and 4 has been reversed, with attention now following perception. A fourth major change is that considerable cognitive-neuroscience material has been added to chapters throughout the book, including whole sections that have not appeared before. A fifth change is that additional practical examples relevant to students' everyday lives have been added to the book. A sixth general change is that "In the Lab" boxes have been updated, with many of the boxes being entirely new. And a seventh general change is that every sentence has been reviewed to ensure its complete readability.

There are also many specific changes:

Chapter 1

1. The usefulness of cognitive psychology is shown right from the start with the example of the availability heuristic applied to the 2008 presidential election.

2. The point is made that either/or thinking can be detrimental to science. For example, intelligence is not either heritable or environmental, but rather both.

3. A discussion of the importance of applied cognitive psychology is stressed in this chapter, giving aviation as an example.

4. I have added a discussion of the modularity of mind concept.
5. The discussion of statistical inference has been upgraded and clarified.
6. The discussion of experimental design and correlation has also been upgraded and clarified.
7. The subtraction method, now used in many studies in cognitive neuroscience, is explained.
8. Discussions of Genie and Phineas Gage have been added to explore the effects of trauma.
9. More material on the validity of self-reports has been added.
10. The discussion of artificial intelligence has been enhanced.

Chapter 2

1. The material on neurons and neural transmitters and their functioning, taken out of the last edition, is back by popular demand.
2. There is an enhanced and updated discussion of event-related potentials (ERP) methods.
3. There is now an improved discussion of functional magnetic resonance imaging (fMRI).
4. Material on positron emission tomography (PET) has been enhanced.
5. Pharmacological magnetic resonance imaging (phMRI) is now discussed.
6. Diffusion tensor imaging (DTI) is now discussed.
7. Magnetoencephalography (MEG) is now discussed.
8. More material on the amygdala has been added.
9. There is a discussion of autism and its brain bases.
10. Material on the hypothalamus has been enhanced.
11. Material on the lobes of the brain has been added.
12. Material on Brodmann areas has been added.

Chapter 3

1. There is now a discussion of the ways in which humans are superior to robots.
2. Substantial material has been added on vision.
3. Material on depth perception has been added.
4. Landmark-centered representation is now discussed.
5. Material on the structuralist approach was deleted at reviewers' request.
6. The neural bases of face recognition are discussed. In general, substantial information on face recognition has been added.
7. There is a new discussion on perception in autism.

8. The expert-individuation hypothesis is now presented.

9. The material contrasting bottom-up and top-down processing has been modified substantially and pared down at reviewers' request.

10. The lengthy discussion of Hubel and Wiesel's early findings has been pared down greatly because they are now out of date, and the discussion has been updated with recent findings.

11. Ataxias are now discussed.

12. Agnosias are mentioned.

13. Different forms of prosopagnosia are discussed.

14. The discussion of anomalies in color perception has been upgraded and updated.

15. Achromatopsia is now discussed.

Chapter 4

1. A discussion of visual priming has been added.

2. Material on the tip-of-the-tongue phenomenon has been added.

3. The potential effect of a stroke on the visual cortex is discussed.

4. Material on dyslexia has been added.

5. Tinnitus is now discussed in relation to auditory habituation.

6. Coverage of signal-detection theory (SDT) has been broadened to note that it can be applied in a variety of cognitive contexts.

7. The brain bases of vigilance are now discussed.

8. The discussion of movement-filter theory was deleted at reviewers' request.

9. Cherry's cocktail party phenomenon is related to working memory.

10. There is an enhanced discussion of the Stroop effect.

11. Talking on cell phones is discussed in terms of attentional theory.

12. Cultural differences in attentional processes are discussed.

13. Neural bases of attention deficit hyperactivity disorder (ADHD) are discussed in some detail.

Chapter 5

1. There is a new discussion of savings.

2. There is new material on the effects of informing students in advance of how their memory will be tested.

3. Implicit memory and explicit memory are compared across the life span.

4. There is new material on the role of the cerebellum in procedural memory.

5. There is new material on American Sign Language (ASL).

6. More practical material has been added, such as remembering street names from your childhood.

7. There is expanded discussion of the self-reference effect.

8. There is new material on subvocal rehearsal.

9. There is an added discussion of the episodic buffer.

10. There is further material on resource allocation in working-memory tasks.

11. There is further discussion of whether episodic memory and semantic memory comprise distinct stores of information.

12. There is further discussion of the role of relating new information to old information to facilitate learning of material.

13. There is inclusion of updated material on H. M.

14. There is further information on amnesia and its relation to procedural knowledge.

Chapter 6

1. Additional information is included on the relationship between stress and memory.

2. New material has been added on sleep and memory.

3. There is further discussion of the role of the hippocampus in attempts at learning during sleep.

4. There is a new discussion of reconsolidation.

5. There is new discussion of the relation between age and prospective memory.

6. There is an added discussion of probability models for separating storage from retrieval.

7. Proactive interference in alcoholic and nonalcoholic individuals is discussed, particularly in relation to Brodmann area 45.

8. There is a new discussion of the relation of self-esteem to autobiographical memory.

9. There is new material on the role of stress in eyewitness identification.

10. There is new material on memory development.

11. There is new material on how suggestion can influence memory.

12. There is new material on the Roediger-McDermott-Deese paradigm.

13. Spreading activation is now explained more clearly.

14. There is new material on flashbulb memory and emotional involvement, as well as on the potential for distortion of flashbulb memories.

15. Rehearsal is discussed in relation to ADHD.

16. There is new discussion of neuropsychological effects of aging on memory.

Chapter 7

1. There is a new discussion of mental imagery among children with Down syndrome.
2. There is further discussion of how analogue and propositional representations can coexist.
3. There is new material on how viewing an image or imagining it activates the same brain areas.
4. There is a new discussion of mental imagery in patients with schizophrenia.
5. The role of the motor cortex in mental rotation is discussed.
6. There is new material on sex differences in spatial imagery and the brain bases of the differences.
7. There is new material on how training can decrease sex differences in spatial visualization tasks.
8. There is an entirely new section on representational neglect.
9. There is new material on haptic imagery and its relation to visual imagery.
10. There is new material on mental models.
11. There is new material on neuropsychological bases of mental maps.

Chapter 8

1. There is new information on speed of assigning information to natural versus artifact categories.
2. There is further discussion of exemplar theories of categorization.
3. There is new information on semantic networks.
4. There is new information on cognitive impairments (e.g., semantic dementia) and how they affect categorization.
5. There is new information on cognitive impairment (e.g., schizophrenia) and scripts.
6. There is further information on spreading activation in mental representation.
7. Practical examples of proceduralization, such as air traffic control and learning phone numbers, are discussed.
8. Dyslexia is discussed in the context of parallel distributed processing (PDP) models.
9. Use of fMRI methods to study face recognition is discussed.

Chapter 9

1. A discussion of how language evolves over time has been added.
2. There is a new discussion of language extinction.

3. There is a new presentation of material on coarticulation.

4. There is a discussion of the use of phonological information by people with and without reading disabilities.

5. There is further discussion of the McGurk effect.

6. There is new discussion of denotation and connotation.

7. There is further discussion of syntactical priming.

8. There is new material on infants and how they respond to emotional information contained in communication.

9. There is a new presentation of material on cooing in children with cerebral palsy.

10. There is new material on babbling and ASL.

11. There is further material on innate language abilities.

12. There is new material on the role of imitation in language learning.

13. There is new information on child-directed speech.

14. New material appears on Koko the gorilla.

Chapter 10

1. There is more material on the sentence-superiority effect.

2. There is a discussion, in the context of linguistic relativity, of how familiarity with computers may breed more words for computer-associated concepts.

3. There is an enhanced discussion of how language choice affects other aspects of information processing.

4. There is now a discussion of how teachers may discourage bilingualism.

5. There is an added discussion of bilingualism and age of acquisition of second language.

6. There is a discussion of aphasia and how it affects bilingualism.

7. There is a discussion of how judgments of dialects can lead to biases in evaluating people.

8. There is a new discussion of personal space—both across cultures and in virtual-reality environments.

9. There is more material on indirect requests.

10. There is a discussion of language and autism, which includes the theory of executive dysfunction.

11. Gender differences in use of written language is discussed.

12. The relation of vocabulary size to other cognitive skills is discussed.

13. The role of Broca's area in sign production is discussed.

14. There is new material on neuropsychological analysis of language with fMRI and ERP.

Chapter 11

1. The relation of emotional intelligence to problem solving is discussed.
2. A better explanation is provided of types of errors in the hobbits and orcs problem.
3. Neuropsychological bases of insight are discussed.
4. The role of sleep in helping to produce insightful solutions is noted.
5. New material is presented on the relatively young age at which analogical thinking can be observed.
6. The effects of brain injury on problem solving are discussed in some detail.
7. As a real-world example, expert-novice differences are discussed in the context of tasting beers.
8. It is noted that expert mathematicians use visual imagery in problem solving even for problems that do not require it.
9. Further discussion has been added of the effects of verbal protocols on problem solving.
10. Preparation in problem solving is discussed in the context of ASL production.
11. There is new discussion of how knowledge helps creativity.
12. There is further discussion of the role of rewards in creative behavior.
13. A section has been added on the neuroscience of creativity.

Chapter 12

1. A new section on naturalistic decision making has been added.
2. A new section on group decision making has been added.
3. A new section on groupthink has been added.
4. A new section on antidotes for groupthink has been added.
5. An expanded discussion of the inclusion fallacy has been added.
6. A further discussion of fast and frugal heuristics has been added.
7. A section on the neuroscience of decision making has been added.
8. Evidence on the trainability of mental models has been added.
9. A further discussion of confirmation bias is included.
10. The use of analogy in politics is discussed.
11. A section on the neuroscience of reasoning has been added.

Chapter 13

1. New material on emotional intelligence has been added.
2. New material on cultural intelligence has been added.

3. The use of the Wechsler scale in neuropsychological assessment is discussed.

4. More material on the relationship of working memory to intelligence is included.

5. Crystallized intelligence is related to the brain and to brain damage.

6. More material on the relationship of intelligence to brain function has been included.

7. More material on cultural differences in thought processes is included.

8. New empirical material on using broad theories of intelligence to predict college success is included.

9. More material updating findings on the Abecedarian Project is included.

10. New material about the importance of students' beliefs on the malleability of intelligence is included.

11. New material on intelligent systems is included.

12. New material on modern applications of artificial intelligence is included.

The Original Goals of This Book

When I first undertook to write this textbook, I knew what I wanted in a textbook, and I knew what my students wanted; or at least I thought I did. We wanted a book that would achieve a number of objectives.

1. *Combine readability with integrity.* I have chosen books that were so chewy that only the strongest stomachs could digest their contents, and I have chosen ones that melted like cotton candy, with substance to match. I have tried to write a book that would give students something to chew on, but one that they could easily digest.

2. *Balance a clear presentation of the big questions of cognitive psychology with a respect for the important details of the field.* Perhaps in no course more than in cognitive psychology are both the forest and the trees important. The best and most lasting work in the field is driven by enduring and fundamental questions. However, that work also respects the details of methods and data analysis needed to produce meaningful results. In order to achieve the balance, I have opened each chapter with a preview of the big questions dealt with in that chapter and ended each chapter with a summary of what we have learned in the field that addresses each question. Within the chapters, the writing has been guided by the big questions, while conveying to students the kinds of details to which cognitive psychologists need to attend in both their theory and research.

3. *Balance the learning of subject matter with thinking about the subject matter.* An expert cognitive psychologist knows the discipline but can also use the knowledge. Knowledge without thought is useless, but thought without knowledge is empty. I have tried to balance a respect for

subject matter with an equal respect for its use. Every chapter ends with diverse questions that emphasize comprehension of the subject matter, as well as analytical, creative, and practical thinking with that subject matter. Students using this book will not only learn the basic ideas and facts of cognitive psychology, but also how to think with them.

4. *Recognize both the traditional and emerging trends in the field.* This book has all the traditional topics found in the chapters of the majority of textbooks, including the nature of cognitive psychology and how people think about issues in cognitive psychology (Chapter 1), perception (Chapter 3), attention and consciousness (Chapter 4), memory (Chapters 5 and 6), knowledge representation (Chapters 7 and 8), language (Chapters 9 and 10), problem solving and creativity (Chapter 11), and decision making and reasoning (Chapter 12).

   I have also included two chapters that are not typically included as chapters in other books. The chapter on cognitive neuroscience (Chapter 2) is included because the dividing line between cognitive psychology and psychobiology is becoming increasingly indistinct. A great deal of exciting work today is at the interface between the two fields, and so, whereas the cognitive psychologist of 20 years ago might have been able to get away without an understanding of biological foundations, I believe that today such a cognitive psychologist would be ill served.

   Human and artificial intelligence (Chapter 13) are becoming increasingly important to the field of cognitive psychology. Twenty years ago, the field of human intelligence was dominated by psychometric (test-based) approaches. The field of artificial intelligence was dominated by programs that were functionally rather remote from human thought processes. Today both fields of intelligence are more heavily influenced by cognitive models of how people process information. I include both human- and computer-based models in the same chapter because I believe that their goals are ultimately the same—namely, to understand human cognition.

   Although the book ends with the chapter on intelligence, intelligence also plays a major role in the beginning and the middle of the book because it is the organizing framework within which cognitive psychology is presented. This framework is not in terms of a traditional psychometric model of intelligence, but rather in terms of intelligence as the fundamental organizing framework for all of human cognition.

   I have tried not only to balance traditional and newer topics, but also older and more recent citations. Some books seem to suggest that almost nothing new has happened over the past decade, whereas others seem to suggest that cognitive psychology was invented in that decade. The goal of this book is to balance citation and description of classic studies with equal attention to recent, exciting contributions to the field.

5. *Show the basic unity of cognitive psychology.* On one hand, cognitive psychologists disagree about the extent to which the mechanisms of cognition are domain specific versus domain general. On the other hand, I believe that almost all cognitive psychologists believe that there is a fun-

damental functional unity to human cognition. This unity, I believe, is expressed through the concept of human intelligence.

The concept of intelligence can be seen as providing a unifying umbrella through which to understand the adaptive nature of human cognition. Through this single concept, society, as well as psychological science, acknowledges that as diverse as cognition may be, it comes together in providing us with a functionally unified way of making sense of and adapting to the environment. Thus, the unity of human cognition, as expressed by the concept of intelligence, serves as an integrating message for this book.

6. *Balance various forms of learning and instruction.* Students learn best when they learn material in a variety of ways and from different vantage points. To this end, I have sought to achieve a balance among a traditional presentation of text, a variety of kinds of questions about the material (factual, analytical, creative, practical), demonstrations of key ideas in cognitive psychology, and annotated suggested readings that students can consult if they wish for further information about a topic. A chapter outline at the beginning of each chapter also serves as an advance organizer for what is to come. The opening questions and closing answers help students appreciate the main questions in the field, as well as what progress we have made toward answering them. The text itself emphasizes how contemporary ideas have evolved from past ones, and how these ideas address the key questions cognitive psychologists have sought to answer in their research.

Acknowledgments

I am grateful to a number of reviewers who have contributed to the development of this book: Susan E. Dutch, Westfield State College; Jeremy Gottlieb, Carthage College; Andrew Herbert, Rochester Institute of Technology; Christopher B. Mayhorn, North Carolina State University; Padraig G. O'Seaghdha, Lehigh University; Thad Polk, University of Michigan; David Somers, Boston University.

I am grateful to Jessica Chamberland, Ph.D., Tufts University, for her invaluable assistance in producing this revision. I would also like to thank Dan Moneypenny, my developmental editor, and Leah Bross, my production editor.

To the Student

Why do we remember people whom we met years ago, but sometimes seem to forget what we learned in a course shortly after we take the final exam (or worse, sometimes right before)? How do we manage to carry on a conversation with one person at a party and simultaneously eavesdrop on another more interesting conversation taking place nearby? Why are people so often certain that they are correct in answering a question when in fact they are not? These are just three of the many questions that are addressed by the field of cognitive psychology.

Cognitive psychologists study how people perceive, learn, remember, and think. Although cognitive psychology is a unified field, it draws on many other fields, most notably neuroscience, computer science, linguistics, anthropology, and philosophy. Thus, you will find some of the thinking of all these fields represented in this book. Moreover, cognitive psychology interacts with other fields within psychology, such as psychobiology, developmental psychology, social psychology, and clinical psychology.

For example, it is difficult to be a clinical psychologist today without a solid knowledge of developments in cognitive psychology because so much of the thinking in the clinical field draws on cognitive ideas, both in diagnosis and in therapy. Cognitive psychology has also provided a means for psychologists to investigate experimentally some of the exciting ideas that have emerged from clinical theory and practice, such as notions of unconscious thought.

Cognitive psychology will be important to you not only in its own right, but also in helping you in all of your work. For example, knowledge of cognitive psychology can help you better understand how best to study for tests, how to read effectively, and how to remember difficult-to-learn material. However, to acquire this knowledge, you need to make use of the following pedagogical features of this book:

1. *Chapter outlines,* beginning each chapter, summarize the main topics covered and thus give you an advance overview of what is to be covered in that chapter.

2. *Opening questions* emphasize the main questions each chapter addresses.

3. *Boldface terms,* indexed at ends of chapters and defined in the glossary, help you acquire the vocabulary of cognitive psychology.

4. *End-of-chapter summaries* return to the questions at the opening of each chapter and show our current state of knowledge with regard to these questions.

5. *End-of-chapter questions* help you ensure both that you have learned the basic material and that you can think in a variety of ways (factual, analytical, creative, and practical) with this material.

6. *Annotated suggested readings* refer you to other sources that you can consult for further information on the topics covered in each chapter.

7. *"Investigating Cognitive Psychology"* demonstrations, appearing throughout the chapters, help you see how cognitive psychology can be used to demonstrate various psychological phenomena.

8. *"Practical Applications of Cognitive Psychology"* demonstrations show how you and others can apply cognitive psychology to your everyday lives.

9. *"In the Lab of . . . "* boxes tell you what it really is like to do research in cognitive psychology. Prominent researchers speak in their own words about their research—what research problems excite them most and what they are doing to address these problems.

10. *Key Themes sections,* near the end of each chapter, relate the content of the chapters to the key themes expressed in Chapter 1. These sections will help you see the continuity of the main ideas of cognitive psychology across its various subfields.

11. *CogLab,* an exciting series of laboratory demonstrations in cognitive psychology provided by the publisher of this textbook (Wadsworth), is available for purchase with this text. You can actively participate in these demonstrations and thereby learn firsthand what it is like to be involved in cognitive-psychological research.

This book contains an overriding theme that unifies all the diverse topics found in the various chapters: Human cognition has evolved over time as a means of adapting to our environment, and we can call this ability to adapt to the environment *intelligence.* Through intelligence, we cope in an integrated and adaptive way with the many challenges with which the environment presents us.

Although cognitive psychologists disagree about many issues, there is one issue about which almost all of them agree; namely, cognition enables us to successfully adapt to the environments in which we find ourselves. Thus, we need a construct such as that of *human intelligence,* if only to provide a shorthand way of expressing this fundamental unity of adaptive skill. We can see this unity at all levels in the study of cognitive psychology. For example, diverse measures of the psychophysiological functioning of the human brain show correlations with scores on a variety of tests of intelligence. Selective attention, the ability to tune in certain stimuli and tune out others, is also related to intelligence, and it has even been proposed that an intelligent person is one who knows what information to attend to and what information to ignore. Various language and problem-solving skills are also related to intelligence, pretty much without regard to how it is measured. In brief, then, human intelligence can be seen as an entity that unifies and provides direction to the workings of the human cognitive system.

I hope you enjoy this book, and I hope you see why I am enthusiastic about cognitive psychology and proud to be a cognitive psychologist.

About the Author

ROBERT J. STERNBERG

Robert J. Sternberg is Dean of the School of Arts and Sciences, Professor of Psychology, and Adjunct Professor of Education at Tufts University. He is also Honorary Professor of Psychology in the Department of Psychology at the University of Heidelberg, Heidelberg, Germany. Prior to accepting his positions at Tufts, he was IBM Professor of Psychology and Education in the Department of Psychology, Professor of Management in the School of Management, and Director of the Center for the Psychology of Abilities, Competencies, and Expertise at Yale. The Center, now relocated to Tufts, is dedicated to the advancement of theory, research, practice, and policy advancing the notion of intelligence as developing expertise—as a construct that is modifiable and capable, to some extent, of development throughout the life span. The Center seeks to have an impact on science, education, and society.

Sternberg was the 2003 President of the American Psychological Association (APA) and is the 2006–2007 President of the Eastern Psychological Association. He is President-Elect of the International Association for Cognitive Education and Psychology. He was on the Board of Directors of the APA (2002–2004) and on the Board of Trustees of the APA Insurance Trust (2004) and the American Psychological Foundation (2005–2007). He is on the Board of Directors of the Eastern Psychological Association (2005–2008) and the American Association of Colleges and Universities (2007–2009). He is also Chair of the Publications Committee of the American Educational Research Association (AERA). Sternberg has been President of the Divisions of General Psychology, Educational Psychology, Psychology and the Arts, and Theoretical and Philosophical Psychology of the APA.

Sternberg has been Acting Chair and Director of Graduate Studies in the Department of Psychology at Yale.

Sternberg received a Ph.D. from Stanford University in 1975 and a B.A. summa cum laude, Phi Beta Kappa, with honors with exceptional distinction in psychology, from Yale University in 1972. He also holds honorary doctorates from Complutense University of Madrid, Spain; University of Leuven, Belgium; University of Cyprus; University of Paris V, France; Constantine the Philosopher University, Slovakia; University of Durham, England; St. Petersburg State University in Russia; University of Tilburg in Holland; and Ricardo Palma University in Peru.

Sternberg is the author of about 1200 journal articles, book chapters, and books and has received over $20 million in government and other grants and contracts for his research. The central focus of his research is intelligence, creativity, and wisdom, and he also has studied love and close relationships, as well as hate. This research has been conducted on five different continents.

Sternberg is also a Fellow of the American Academy of Arts and Sciences, the American Association for the Advancement of Science, the APA (in 15 divisions), the American Psychological Society (APS), the Connecticut Psychological Association, the Royal Norwegian Society of Sciences and Letters, the International Association for Empirical Aesthetics, the Laureate Chapter of Kappa Delta Pi, and the Society of Experimental Psychologists. He has won many awards from APA, AERA, APS, and other organizations. These awards include the Arthur W. Staats Award from the American Psychological Foundation and the Society for General Psychology; the E. L.

Thorndike Award for Career Achievement in Educational Psychology Award from the Society for Educational Psychology of the APA; the Arnheim and Farnsworth Awards from the Society for the Psychology of Creativity, Aesthetics, and the Arts of the APA; the Boyd R. McCandless Award of the Society for Developmental Psychology of the APA; the Distinguished Award for an Early Career Contribution to Psychology from the APA; the Positive Psychology Network Distinguished Scientist and Scholar Award; the Palmer O. Johnson, Research Review, Outstanding Book, and Sylvia Scribner Awards from the AERA; the James McKeen Cattell Award from the APS; the Distinguished Lifetime Contribution to Psychology Award from the Connecticut Psychological Association; the Anton Jurovsky Award of the Slovak Psychological Society; the International Award of the Association of Portuguese Psychologists; the Distinguished Contribution Award and E. Paul Torrance Award of the National Association for Gifted Children; the Cattell Award of the Society for Multivariate Experimental Psychology; the Award for Excellence from the Mensa Education and Research Foundation; the Distinction of Honor SEK from the Institución SEK (Madrid); the Sidney Siegel Memorial Award of Stanford University; and the Wohlenberg Prize of Yale University. He has held a Fulbright Senior Specialist Fellowship to Slovakia, IREX Fellowship to Russia, Guggenheim Fellowship, and Yale University Senior and Junior Faculty Fellowships, as well as a National Science Foundation Graduate Fellowship. He also has held the Honored Visitor Fellowship of the Taiwan National Science Council and the Sir Edward Youde Memorial Visiting Professorship of the City University of Hong Kong.

Sternberg has been listed in the *APA Monitor on Psychology* as one of the top 100 psychologists of the twentieth century and is listed by the ISI as one of its most highly cited authors (top ½%) in psychology and psychiatry. He also was listed in the *Esquire* Register of Outstanding Men and Women under 40 and was listed as one of 100 top young scientists by *Science Digest*. He is currently listed in *Who's Who in America, Who's Who in the World, Who's Who in the East, Who's Who in Medicine and Healthcare,* and *Who's Who in Science and Engineering*. He has served as Editor of the *Psychological Bulletin* and of *The APA Review of Books: Contemporary Psychology* and as Associate Editor of *Child Development* and *Intelligence*.

Sternberg is most well known for his theory of successful intelligence, investment theory of creativity (developed with Todd Lubart), theory of thinking styles as mental self-government, balance theory of wisdom, WICS theory of leadership, and duplex theories of love and hate.

Introduction to Cognitive Psychology

EXPLORING COGNITIVE PSYCHOLOGY

1. What is cognitive psychology?

2. How did psychology develop as a science?

3. How did cognitive psychology develop from psychology?

4. How have other disciplines contributed to the development of theory and research in cognitive psychology?

5. What methods do cognitive psychologists use to study how people think?

6. What are the current issues and various fields of study within cognitive psychology?

Cognitive Psychology Defined

What will you be studying in a textbook about cognitive psychology?

1. *Cognition:* People think.
2. *Cognitive psychology:* Scientists think about how people think.
3. *Students of cognitive psychology:* People think about how scientists think about how people think.
4. *Professors who profess to students about cognitive psychology:* You get the idea.

To be more specific, **cognitive psychology** is the study of how people perceive, learn, remember, and think about information. A cognitive psychologist might study how people perceive various shapes, why they remember some facts but forget others, or how they learn language. Consider some examples:

- Why do objects look farther away on foggy days than they really are? The discrepancy can be dangerous, even deceiving drivers into having car accidents.
- Why do many people remember a particular experience (e.g., a very happy moment or an embarrassment during childhood), yet they forget the names of people whom they have known for many years?
- Why are many people more afraid of traveling in planes than in automobiles? After all, the chances of injury or death are much higher in an automobile than in a plane.
- Why do I often well remember people I met in my childhood but not people I met a week ago?
- Why do candidates spend so much money on television advertisements?

These are some of the kinds of questions that we can answer through the study of cognitive psychology.

Consider just the last of these questions: Why do candidates spend so much money on television advertisements? After all, how many people remember the details of their political positions, or how their positions are distinguished from others' political positions? One reason candidates spend so much is because of the *availability heuristic,* which you will study in Chapter 12. Using this heuristic, we make judgments on the basis of how easily we can call to mind what we perceive as relevant instances of a phenomenon (Tversky & Kahneman, 1973). One such judgment is the question of for whom one should vote in an election. We are much more likely to vote for someone whose name is familiar. Tom Vilsack, governor of the state of Iowa at the time of the 2008 primary campaign, entered and quickly dropped out of the contest for the Democratic candidacy for President of the United States. He dropped out not because his positions were incompatible with those of the party: On the contrary, many Democrats liked his positions. Rather, he dropped out because his lack of name recognition made it difficult to raise money. In the end, possible donors felt that his name was not "available" enough for people to vote for him when election day came. Mitt Romney, less well known than Republican primary competitors John McCain and Rudy Giuliani, spent large sums of money just to make his name psychologically available to the general public. The bottom line is that understanding cognitive psychology can help us understand much of what goes on in our everyday lives.

This chapter introduces the field of cognitive psychology. It describes some of the intellectual history of the study of human thinking. It particularly emphasizes some of the issues and concerns that arise when we think about how people think. Next is a brief overview of the major methods, issues, and content areas of cognitive psychology.

The ideas presented in this chapter will provide a foundation on which to build an understanding of the topics in cognitive psychology.

Why study the history of this field, or of any other field, for that matter? For one thing, if we know where we came from, we may have a better understanding of where we are heading. For another, we may learn from past mistakes. In this way, when we make mistakes they will be fresh, new mistakes and not the same old ones. Our ways of addressing fundamental issues have changed. But some of the fundamental questions remain much the same. Ultimately, we may learn something about how people think by studying how people have thought about thinking.

The progression of ideas often involves a *dialectic.* A dialectic is a developmental process whereby ideas evolve over time through a pattern of transformation. What is this pattern? In a dialectic:

- A thesis is proposed. A *thesis* is a statement of belief. For example, some people believe that human nature governs many aspects of human behavior (e.g., intelligence or personality; Sternberg, 1999). After a while, however, certain individuals notice apparent flaws in the thesis.

- Eventually, or perhaps even quite soon, an antithesis emerges. An *antithesis* is a statement that counters a previous statement of belief. For example, an alternative view is that our nurture (the environmental contexts in which we are reared) almost entirely determines many aspects of human behavior.

- Sooner or later, the debate between the thesis and the antithesis leads to a synthesis. A *synthesis* integrates the most credible features of each of two (or more) views. For example, in the debate over nature versus nurture, the interaction between our innate (inborn) nature and environmental nurture may govern human nature.

It is important to understand the dialectic because sometimes we may be tempted to think that if one view is right, another seemingly contrasting view must be wrong. For example, in my own field of intelligence, there has sometimes been a tendency to believe that intelligence is either all or mostly genetically determined, or else all or mostly environmentally determined. A similar debate has raged in the field of language acquisition. Often, though, we are better off posing such issues not as either/or questions, but rather as examinations of how different forces co-vary and interact with each other. Indeed, the most widely accepted current contention is that the "nature" and "nurture" views are both incomplete. Nature and nurture work together in our development.

If a synthesis seems to advance our understanding of a subject, it then serves as a new thesis. A new antithesis then follows it, then a new synthesis, and so on. Georg Hegel (1770–1831) observed this dialectical progression of ideas. He was a German philosopher who came to his ideas by his own dialectic. He synthesized some of the views of his intellectual predecessors and contemporaries.

Philosophical Antecedents of Psychology: Rationalism versus Empiricism

Where and when did the study of cognitive psychology begin? Historians of psychology usually trace the earliest roots of psychology to two different approaches to understanding the human mind:

- *Philosophy* seeks to understand the general nature of many aspects of the world, in part through *introspection,* the examination of inner ideas and experiences (from *intro-,* "inward, within," and *-spect,* "look").
- *Physiology* seeks a scientific study of life-sustaining functions in living matter, primarily through *empirical* (observation-based) methods.

Two approaches to the study of the mind are rationalism and empiricism. A **rationalist** believes that the route to knowledge is through logical analysis. In contrast, Aristotle (a naturalist and biologist as well as a philosopher) was an empiricist. An **empiricist** believes that we acquire knowledge via empirical evidence—that is, we obtain evidence through experience and observation (Figure 1.1).

Empiricism leads directly to empirical investigations of psychology. In contrast, rationalism is important in theory development. Rationalist theories without any connection to observations may not be valid. But mountains of observational data without an organizing theoretical framework may not be meaningful. We might see the rationalist view of the world as a thesis and the empirical view as an antithesis. Most psychologists today seek a synthesis of the two. They base empirical observations on theory. In turn, they use these observations to revise their theories.

FIGURE 1.1

(a)　　　　　　　　　　　　　　　　　　(b)

(a) According to the rationalist, the only route to truth is reasoned contemplation; (b) according to the empiricist, the only route to truth is meticulous observation. Cognitive psychology, like other sciences, depends on the work of both rationalists and empiricists.

The contrasting ideas of rationalism and empiricism became prominent with the French rationalist René Descartes (1596–1650) and the British empiricist John Locke (1632–1704). Descartes viewed the introspective, reflective method as being superior to empirical methods for finding truth. Locke, in contrast, had more enthusiasm for empirical observation (Leahey, 2003).

Locke believed that humans are born without knowledge and therefore must seek knowledge through empirical observation. Locke's term for this view was *tabula rasa* (meaning "blank slate" in Latin). The idea is that life and experience "write" knowledge on us. For Locke, then, the study of learning was the key to understanding the human mind. He believed that there are no innate ideas whatsoever. In the eighteenth century, German philosopher Immanuel Kant (1724–1804) dialectically synthesized the views of Descartes and Locke, arguing that both rationalism and empiricism have their place. Both must work together in the quest for truth. Most psychologists today accept Kant's synthesis.

Psychological Antecedents of Cognitive Psychology

Early Dialectics in the Psychology of Cognition

Structuralism

An early dialectic in the history of psychology is that between structuralism and functionalism (Leahey, 2003; Morawski, 2000). Structuralism was the first major school of thought in psychology. **Structuralism** seeks to understand the structure (configuration of elements) of the mind and its perceptions by analyzing those perceptions into their constituent components. Consider, for example, the perception of

Archives of the History of American Psychology—University of Akron

Wilhelm Wundt was no great success in school, failing time and again and frequently finding himself subject to the ridicule of others. However, Wundt later showed that school performance does not always predict career success because he is considered to be among the most influential psychologists of all time.

a flower. Structuralists would analyze this perception in terms of the constituent colors, geometric forms, size relations, and so on.

A German psychologist whose ideas later would contribute to the development of structuralism was Wilhelm Wundt (1832–1920). Wundt is often viewed as the founder of experimental psychology. Wundt used a variety of methods in his research. One of these methods was introspection. **Introspection** is a looking inward at pieces of information passing through consciousness. An example is the sensations experienced when looking at a flower. In effect, we analyze our own perceptions. Wundt advocated the study of sensory experiences through introspection.

Wundt had many followers. One was an American student, Edward Titchener (1867–1927). Titchener (1910) helped bring structuralism to the United States. Other early psychologists criticized both the method (introspection) and the focus (elementary structures of sensation) of structuralism.

Functionalism: An Alternative to Structuralism

An alternative to structuralism suggested that psychologists should focus on the *processes* of thought rather than on its contents. **Functionalism** seeks to understand what people *do* and *why* they do it. This principal question was in contrast to that of the structuralists, who had asked what the elementary contents (structures) of the human mind were. Functionalists held that the key to understanding the human mind and behavior was to study the processes of how and why the mind works as it does, rather than to study the structural contents and elements of the mind.

Functionalists were unified by the kinds of questions they asked but not necessarily by the answers they found or by the methods they used for finding those answers. Because functionalists believed in using whichever methods best answered a given researcher's questions, it seems natural for functionalism to have led to pragmatism. **Pragmatists** believe that knowledge is validated by its usefulness: What can you *do* with it? Pragmatists are concerned not only with knowing what people do; they want

Many cognitive psychologists continue to regard William James, a physician, philosopher, psychologist, and brother of author Henry James, as among the greatest psychologists ever, although James himself seems to have rejected psychology later in his life.

Archives of the History of American Psychology—University of Akron

PRACTICAL APPLICATIONS OF COGNITIVE PSYCHOLOGY

Take a moment right now to put the idea of pragmatism into use. Think about ways to make the information you are learning in this course more useful to you. Part of the work already has been done—notice that the chapter begins with questions that make the information more coherent and useful, and the chapter summary returns to those questions. Does the text successfully answer the questions posed at the beginning of the chapter? Come up with your own questions and try organizing your notes in the form of answers to your questions. Also, try relating this material to other courses or activities you participate in. For example, you may be called on to explain to a friend how to use a new computer program. A good way to start would be to ask that person if he or she has any questions. That way, the information you provide is more directly useful to your friend, rather than forcing this individual to search for the information he or she needs in a long, one-sided lecture.

to know what we can do with our knowledge of what people do. For example, pragmatists believe in the importance of the psychology of learning and memory. Why? Because it can help us improve the performance of children in school. It can also help us learn to remember the names of people we meet whose names we rapidly forget.

A leader in guiding functionalism toward pragmatism was William James (1842–1910). His chief functional contribution to the field of psychology was a single book: his landmark *Principles of Psychology* (1890/1970). Even today, cognitive psychologists frequently point to the writings of James in discussions of core topics in the field, such as attention, consciousness, and perception. John Dewey (1859–1952) was another early pragmatist who profoundly influenced contemporary thinking in cognitive psychology. Dewey is remembered primarily for his pragmatic approach to thinking and schooling.

Associationism: An Integrative Synthesis

Associationism, like functionalism, was less a rigid school of psychology than an influential way of thinking. **Associationism** examines how events or ideas can become associated with one another in the mind to result in a form of learning. For example, associations may result from *contiguity* (associating things that tend to occur together at about the same time), *similarity* (associating things with similar features or properties), or *contrast* (associating things that seem to show polarities, such as hot/cold, light/dark, day/night).

In the late 1800s, associationist Hermann Ebbinghaus (1850–1909) was the first experimenter to apply associationist principles systematically. Specifically, Ebbinghaus studied his own mental processes. He counted his errors and recorded his response times. Through his self-observations, Ebbinghaus studied how people learn and remember material through rehearsal. *Rehearsal* is the conscious repetition of to-be-learned material. Among other findings, he found that frequent repetition can fix mental associations more firmly in memory. Thus, repetition aids in learning (see Chapter 6).

Another influential associationist, Edward Lee Thorndike (1874–1949), held that the role of "satisfaction" is the key to forming associations. Thorndike termed this principle the *law of effect* (1905): A stimulus will tend to produce a certain response over time if an organism is rewarded for that response. Thorndike believed that an organism learns to respond in a given way (the *effect*) in a given situation if it is rewarded repeatedly for doing so (the *satisfaction*, which serves as a stimulus to future actions). Thus, a child given treats for solving arithmetic problems correctly learns to solve arithmetic problems accurately because he or she forms associations between valid solutions and treats.

From Associationism to Behaviorism

Other researchers who were contemporaries of Thorndike used animal experiments to probe stimulus-response relationships in ways that differed from those of Thorndike and his fellow associationists. These researchers straddled the line between associationism and the emerging field of behaviorism. **Behaviorism** is a theoretical outlook that psychology should focus only on the relation between observable behavior and environmental events or stimuli. The idea was to make physical whatever others might have called "mental" (Lycan, 2003). Some of these researchers, like Thorndike and other associationists, studied responses that were voluntary (although perhaps lacking any conscious thought, as in Thorndike's work). Others studied responses that were involuntarily triggered, in response to what appear to be unrelated external events.

In Russia, Nobel Prize–winning physiologist Ivan Pavlov (1849–1936) studied involuntary learning behavior of this sort. He began with the observation that dogs salivated in response to the sight of the lab technician who fed them. This response occurred before the dogs even saw whether the technician had food. To Pavlov, this response indicated a form of learning, classically conditioned learning, over which the dogs had no conscious control. In the dogs' minds, some type of involuntary learning linked the technician to the food (Pavlov, 1955). Pavlov's landmark work paved the way for the development of behaviorism. Classical conditioning involves more than just an association based on temporal contiguity (e.g., the food and the conditioned stimulus occurring at about the same time; Rescorla, 1967). Effective conditioning requires *contingency* (e.g., the presentation of food being contingent on the presentation of the conditioned stimulus; Rescorla & Wagner, 1972; Wagner & Rescorla, 1972).

Behaviorism may be considered an extreme version of associationism. It focuses entirely on the association between the environment and an observable behavior. According to strict, extreme ("radical") behaviorists, any hypotheses about internal thoughts and ways of thinking are nothing more than speculation.

Proponents of Behaviorism

The "father" of radical behaviorism is John Watson (1878–1958). Watson had no use for internal mental contents or mechanisms. He believed that psychologists should concentrate only on the study of observable behavior (Doyle, 2000). He dismissed thinking as subvocalized speech. Behaviorism also differed from previous movements in psychology by shifting the emphasis of experimental research from human to animal participants. Historically, much behaviorist work has been conducted (and still is) with laboratory animals, such as rats, because these animals allow for much greater behavioral control of relationships between the environment and the behavior emitted in reaction to it. One problem with using animals, however, is determining whether the research can be *generalized* to humans (i.e., applied more generally to humans instead of just to the kinds of animals that were studied).

B. F. Skinner (1904–1990), a radical behaviorist, believed that virtually all forms of human behavior, not just learning, could be explained by behavior emitted in reaction to the environment. Skinner conducted research primarily with nonhuman animals. He rejected mental mechanisms. He believed instead that *operant conditioning*— involving the strengthening or weakening of behavior, contingent on the presence or absence of reinforcement (rewards) or punishments—could explain all forms of human behavior. Skinner applied his experimental analysis of behavior to many psychological phenomena, such as learning, language acquisition, and problem solving. Largely because of Skinner's towering presence, behaviorism dominated the discipline of psychology for several decades.

Behaviorists Daring to Peek into the Black Box

Some psychologists rejected radical behaviorism. They were curious about the contents of the mysterious box. For example, Edward Tolman (1886–1959) thought that understanding behavior required taking into account the purpose of, and the plan for, the behavior. Tolman (1932) believed that all behavior is directed toward some goal. For example, the goal of a rat in a maze may be to try to find food in that maze. Tolman is sometimes viewed as a forefather of modern cognitive psychology.

Another criticism of behaviorism (Bandura, 1977b) is that learning appears to result not merely from direct rewards for behavior. It also can be social, resulting from observations of the rewards or punishments given to others. The ability to learn through observation is well documented and can be seen in humans, monkeys, dogs, birds, and even fish (Brown & Laland, 2001; Laland, 2004; Nagell, Olguin, & Tomasello, 1993). In humans this ability spans all ages; it is observed in both infants and adults (Mejia-Arauz, Rogoff, & Paradise, 2005). This view emphasizes how we observe and model our own behavior after the behavior of others. We learn by example. This consideration of social learning opens the way to considering what is happening inside the mind of the individual.

Gestalt Psychology

Of the many critics of behaviorism, Gestalt psychologists may be among the most avid. **Gestalt psychology** states that we best understand psychological phenomena when we view them as organized, structured wholes. According to this view, we cannot fully understand behavior when we only break phenomena down into smaller parts. For example, behaviorists tend to study problem solving by looking for subvocal processing—they are looking for the observable behavior through which problem solving can be understood. Gestaltists, in contrast, study insight, seeking to understand the unobservable mental event by which someone goes from having no idea about how to solve a problem to understanding it fully in what seems a mere moment of time.

The maxim "the whole differs from the sum of its parts" aptly sums up the Gestalt perspective. To understand the perception of a flower, for example, we would have to take into account the whole of the experience. We could not understand such a perception merely in terms of a description of forms, colors, sizes, and so on. Similarly, as noted in the previous paragraph, we could not understand problem solving merely by looking at minute elements of observable behavior (Köhler, 1927, 1940; Wertheimer, 1945/1959).

Emergence of Cognitive Psychology

A more recent approach is **cognitivism,** the belief that much of human behavior can be understood in terms of how people think. Cognitivism is, in part, a synthesis of earlier forms of analysis, such as behaviorism and Gestaltism. Like Gestaltism, it emphasizes internal mental processes. But like behaviorism, it has come to use precise quantitative analysis to study how people learn and think.

Early Role of Psychobiology

Ironically, one of Watson's former students, Karl Spencer Lashley (1890–1958), brashly challenged the behaviorist view that the human brain is a passive organ merely responding to environmental contingencies outside the individual (Gardner, 1985). Instead, Lashley considered the brain to be an active, dynamic organizer of behavior. Lashley sought to understand how the macro-organization of the human brain made possible such complex, planned activities as musical performance, game playing, and using language. None of these were, in his view, readily explicable in terms of simple conditioning.

In the same vein but at a different level of analysis, Donald Hebb (1949) proposed the concept of cell assemblies as the basis for learning in the brain. Cell assemblies are coordinated neural structures that develop through frequent stimulation. They develop over time as the ability of one neuron (nerve cell) to stimulate firing in a connected neuron increases. Behaviorists did not jump at the opportunity to agree with theorists like Lashley and Hebb. In fact, behaviorist B. F. Skinner (1957) wrote an entire book describing how language acquisition and usage could be explained purely in terms of environmental contingencies. This work stretched Skinner's framework too far, leaving Skinner open to attack. An attack was indeed forthcoming. Linguist Noam Chomsky

(1959) wrote a scathing review of Skinner's ideas. In his article, Chomsky stressed both the biological basis and the creative potential of language. He pointed out the infinite numbers of sentences we can produce with ease. He thereby defied behaviorist notions that we learn language by reinforcement. Even young children continually are producing novel sentences for which they could not have been reinforced in the past. Chomsky argued that our understanding of language is constrained not so much by what we have heard, but rather by an innate language acquisition device (LAD) that all humans possess. This device allows the infant to use what it hears to infer the grammar of its linguistic environment. In particular, the LAD actively limits the number of permissible grammatical constructions. Thus, it is the structure of the mind, rather than the structure of environmental contingencies, that guides our acquisition of language.

Add a Dash of Technology: Engineering, Computation, and Applied Cognitive Psychology

By the end of the 1950s some psychologists were intrigued by the tantalizing notion that machines could be programmed to demonstrate the intelligent processing of information (Rychlak & Struckman, 2000). Turing (1950) suggested that soon it would be hard to distinguish the communication of machines from that of humans. He suggested a test, now called the "Turing test," by which a computer program would be judged as successful to the extent that its output was indistinguishable, by humans, from the output of humans (Cummins & Cummins, 2000). In other words, suppose you communicated with a computer and you could not tell that it was a computer. The computer then passed the Turing test (Schonbein & Bechtel, 2003). By 1956 a new phrase had entered our vocabulary. **Artificial intelligence (AI)** is the attempt by humans to construct systems that show intelligence and, particularly, the intelligent processing of information (*Merriam-Webster's Collegiate Dictionary*, 1993). Chess-playing programs, which now can beat most humans, are examples of artificial intelligence.

Many of the early cognitive psychologists became interested in cognitive psychology through applied problems. For example, according to Berry (2002), Donald Broadbent (1926–1993) claimed to have developed an interest in cognitive psychology through a puzzle regarding AT6 aircraft. The planes had two almost identical levers under the seat. One lever was to pull up the wheels and the other to pull up the flaps. Pilots apparently regularly mistook one for the other, thereby crashing expensive planes upon take-off. During World War II, many cognitive psychologists, including one of my own advisors, Wendell Garner, consulted with the military in solving practical problems of aviation and other fields that arose out of warfare against enemy forces. Information theory, which sought to understand people's behavior in terms of how they process the kinds of bits of information processed by computers (Shannon & Weaver, 1963), also grew out of problems in engineering and informatics.

Applied cognitive psychology also has had great use in advertising. John Watson, after he left Johns Hopkins University as a professor, became an extremely successful executive in an advertising firm and used his knowledge of psychology to reach his success. Indeed, much of advertising has directly used principles from cognitive psychology to attract customers to products, sometimes dubious and sometimes not (Benjamin & Baker, 2004).

By the early 1960s developments in psychobiology, linguistics, anthropology, and artificial intelligence, as well as the reactions against behaviorism by many mainstream

Courtesy of Dr. Ulric Neisser

Ulric Neisser is professor emeritus at Cornell University. His book, Cognitive Psychology, *was instrumental in launching the cognitive revolution in psychology. He also has been a major proponent of an ecological approach to cognition and has shown the importance of studying cognitive processing in ecologically valid contexts.*

psychologists, converged to create an atmosphere ripe for revolution. Early cognitivists (e.g., Miller, Galanter, & Pribram, 1960; Newell, Shaw, & Simon, 1957b) argued that traditional behaviorist accounts of behavior were inadequate precisely because they said nothing about how people think. One of the most famous early articles in cognitive psychology was, oddly enough, on "the magic number seven." George Miller (1956) noted that the number seven appeared in many different places in cognitive psychology, such as in the literatures on perception and memory, and he wondered whether there was some hidden meaning in its frequent reappearance. For example, he found that most people can remember about seven items of information. In this work, Miller also introduced the concept of *channel capacity*, the upper limit with which an observer can match a response to information given to him or her. For example, if you can remember seven digits presented to you sequentially, your channel capacity for remembering digits is seven. Ulric Neisser's book *Cognitive Psychology* (Neisser, 1967) was especially critical in bringing cognitivism to prominence by informing undergraduates, graduate students, and academics about the newly developing field. Neisser defined *cognitive psychology* as the study of how people learn, structure, store, and use knowledge. Subsequently, Allen Newell and Herbert Simon (1972) proposed detailed models of human thinking and problem solving from the most basic levels to the most complex. By the 1970s cognitive psychology was recognized widely as a major field of psychological study, with a distinctive set of research methods.

In the 1970s, Jerry Fodor (1973) popularized the concept of the modularity of mind. He argued that the mind has distinct modules, or special-purpose systems, to deal with linguistic and possibly other kinds of information. Modularity implies that the processes that are used in one domain of processing, such as the linguistic (Fodor, 1973) or the perceptual (Marr, 1982), operate independently of processes in other domains. An opposing view would be one of domain-general processing, according to which the processes that apply in one domain, such as perception or language, apply in many other domains as well. Modular approaches are useful in studying some cognitive phenomena, such as language, but have proven less useful in studying other phenomena, such as intelligence, which seems to draw upon many different areas of the brain in complex interrelationships.

Curiously, the idea of the mind as modular goes back at least to phrenologist Franz-Joseph Gall (see Boring, 1950), who in the late eighteenth century believed that the pattern of bumps and swells on the skull was directly associated with one's pattern of cognitive skills. Although phrenology itself was not a scientifically valid technique, the practice of mental cartography lingered and eventually gave rise to ideas of modularity based on modern scientific techniques.

Research Methods in Cognitive Psychology

Goals of Research

To better understand the specific methods used by cognitive psychologists, one must first grasp the goals of research in cognitive psychology, some of which are highlighted here. Briefly, those goals include data gathering, data analysis, theory development, hypothesis formulation, hypothesis testing, and perhaps even application to settings outside the research environment. Often researchers simply seek to gather as much information as possible about a particular phenomenon. They may or may not have preconceived notions regarding what they may find while gathering the data. Their research focuses on describing particular cognitive phenomena, such as how people recognize faces or how they develop expertise.

Data gathering reflects an empirical aspect of the scientific enterprise. Once there are sufficient data on the cognitive phenomenon of interest, cognitive psychologists use various methods for drawing inferences from the data. Ideally, they use multiple converging types of evidence to support their hypotheses. Sometimes, just a quick glance at the data leads to intuitive inferences regarding patterns that emerge from those data. More commonly, however, researchers use various statistical means of analyzing the data.

Data gathering and statistical analysis aid researchers in describing cognitive phenomena. No scientific pursuit could get far without such descriptions. However, most cognitive psychologists want to understand more than the *what* of cognition; most also seek to understand the *how* and the *why* of thinking. That is, researchers seek ways to explain cognition as well as to describe it. To move beyond descriptions, cognitive psychologists must leap from what is observed directly to what can be inferred regarding observations.

Suppose that we wish to study one particular aspect of cognition. An example would be how people comprehend information in textbooks. We usually start with a theory. A **theory** is an organized body of general explanatory principles regarding a phenomenon, usually based on observations. We seek to test a theory and thereby to see whether it has the power to predict certain aspects of the phenomena with which it deals. In other words, our thought process is, "If our theory is correct, then whenever *x* occurs, outcome *y* should result." This process results in the generation of **hypotheses,** tentative proposals regarding expected empirical consequences of the theory, such as the outcomes of research.

Next, we test our hypotheses through experimentation. Even if particular findings appear to confirm a given hypothesis, the findings must be subjected to statistical analysis to determine their statistical significance. **Statistical significance** indicates the likelihood that a given set of results would be obtained if only chance factors were in operation. For example, a statistical significance level of .05 would mean that the likelihood of a given set of data would be a mere 5% if only chance factors were operating. Therefore, the results are not likely to be due merely to chance. Through this method we can decide to retain or reject hypotheses.

Once our hypothetical predictions have been experimentally tested and statistically analyzed, the findings from those experiments may lead to further work. For example, the psychologist may engage in further data gathering, data analysis, theory development, hypothesis formulation, and hypothesis testing. Based on the hypotheses that were retained and/or rejected, the theory may have to be revised. In addition, many cognitive psychologists hope to use insights gained from research to help people use cognition in real-life situations. Some research in cognitive psychology is applied from the start. It seeks to help people improve their lives and the conditions under which they live their lives. Thus, basic research may lead to everyday applications. For each of these purposes, different research methods offer differing advantages and disadvantages.

Photograph used courtesy of Carnegie Mellon University Archives

Herbert A. Simon was a professor of computer science and psychology at Carnegie-Mellon University. He is known for his pioneering work, with Allen Newell and others, on constructing and testing computer models that simulate human thought, and for his experimental tests of these models. He also was a major advocate of thinking-aloud protocols as a means of studying cognitive processing. Simon died in 2001.

IN THE LAB OF GORDON BOWER

By permission of G. Bower

CHUNKY EXPERTS WHO DIVIDE TO CONQUER

Growing up as a boy in small-town Ohio, I devoted hundreds of hours to playing baseball. My oldest coach, Dean Harrah, had the most prodigious memory for baseball games of anyone I ever knew. Dean could recall every significant play of a game, such as the inning, number of outs, pitch count, batter, and location of fielders as he flashed every hit-and-run sign in a game played 3 weeks ago. His recall of game details was just staggering. Yet he was notorious for forgetting most other things, such as his appointments, grocery shopping, and his wife's orders. I also had an amazing friend, Claude, a "chess freak," who played masterful chess and could remember, move by move, games he'd played several days before. Yet Claude couldn't remember worth beans school subjects like the periodic table for our chemistry class. Dean and Claude couldn't tell me a thing about how they did it, just that they "saw" significant events in their entirety as a game unfolded. Such prodigious memories, residing in the same head alongside such lousy memories, always fascinated me. It was one of the many puzzles of everyday life that got me interested in the psychology of human memory.

The puzzlement only deepened when academic psychologists told me just how limited everybody's memory usually is. Specifically, we are all severely limited in how many things we can take in and hold even briefly in memory, and consequently in how quickly we can put new information into a more permanent memory. But what are these "things" we take in? The psychologist George Miller (1956) called them "chunks of information" and proposed that people's immediate memory is limited in terms of the number of chunks they can quickly take in and recall. I wondered whether the prodigious memories of Dean and Claude were associated with their knowing how to chunk the information of especial significance for them.

Miller's proposal just led me to ask: What is a chunk of information? How big are chunks? What determines their size and properties? Are your chunks the same as mine? How do we measure chunks?

The intuitive notion is that a chunk is a pattern of more basic elements that a person has learned previously. These patterns can be recognized at several levels of complexity from small to large. For example, the phrase "happy new year" is for most English speakers a single chunk composed of 3 familiar sub-chunks (words), which are in turn composed of 12 familiar sub-chunks (letters) and two spaces—14 symbols in all. Suppose, however, that the 14 symbols were laid out on the page as "ha—ppyyne—wyear." That series now appears nonsensical and would be difficult to learn. Yet a foreign native without knowledge of the English alphabet would find both series equally nonsensical and difficult to remember. What a chunk is depends on an individual's past learning.

So, how hard it is to remember something depends on how we perceive it, how we divide it up into chunks. But what principles does our brain use to divide elements into perceptual groups?

A major grouping principle is how close together or bunched up they are in time or space. Thus, the empty spaces (dashes) in IC—BMIC—IAF—BI causes people to see the series as chunks of 2, 4, 3, and 2 letters, respectively. Those groupings capture perception and are copied into a person's immediate memory. Moreover, if students were to study and try to reproduce a number of such strings repeatedly, they would eventually recall the series in "all-or-none" chunks. That is, most of their recall errors would crop up as they tried to move in recall between chunks (at the C to B, the C to I, and the F to B transitions).

A second principle of grouping is that elements that look or sound alike will be grouped together. For example, letters similar in size, shape (font), and color will be grouped together and recalled as units.

Just as closeness in space and appearance influence visual grouping, so does closeness in time and quality of sounds influence grouping of spoken words and musical notes. Thus, hearing the above letter series spoken with pauses between groups will cause people to adopt that chunking and recall those groups. Similar groupings would arise if the chunks were similar in being spoken by different voices or in coming from different locations. Such auditory groupings are reflected in our habit of conveying telephone numbers

IN THE LAB OF GORDON BOWER—cont'd

in a 3-3-4 cadence, as in 555-123-4567, and are brought to masterful complexity in the sophisticated tempos and rhythms of music.

So, what's this chunking business got to do with learning and memory? Plenty. I hypothesized that the quickest way to learn something is to study and reproduce it repeatedly using the same chunk structure from one occasion to the next. Thus, to learn to reproduce IC—BMCI—AFB—I, it's best to study exactly those chunks in that order every time. Our experiments with college students found that they accumulate little or no learning of a collection of different sequences if we changed the groupings every time the students studied them. Thus, for our previous example series, students were likely to perceive a different grouping of the letters, such as I—CBM-CI—AF—BI or ICB—MC—IAFB—I, as a nearly novel sequence of letters, causing their immediate recall of it to be just as poor as when it was first presented. Was their failure due to being confused about where to put the spaces or pauses as they reproduced the series? Not at all, because they knew that only the letters needed to be recalled in their order, not the spaces. Moreover, the deficit was about the same when we simply counted correct letters regardless of the order in which students recalled them. In sum, repeated study helps mainly when the material is chunked in the same way from one occasion to the next.

An implication of this constant-chunking result is that people will readily recognize and reproduce any symbol sequence that conforms to chunks they already know, that are "familiar." For example, if our example letter sequence is grouped as ICBM—CIA—FBI, students easily recognize the familiar abbreviations and readily recall the series. (Some readers may have already recognized these acronyms.) This observation illustrates a simple, powerful principle: Human memory works most efficiently when it uses prior learning to recognize familiar chunks among the materials to be learned. By recognizing and exploiting familiar chunks, the expert greatly reduces the amount of new learning required to master the new material. A large part of expertise in many ability domains—from reading words to understanding chemical formulas, mathematical equations, musical fragments, computer-program subroutines, and, yes, even Dean's baseball events and Claude's chessboard positions—relies upon the brain's ability to recognize and exploit previously learned chunks and quickly assess the new situation confronting us. Such expertise develops slowly only from many hundreds of hours of concentrated study of the recurring patterns within particular domains. This benefit of very specific practice explains how expert memory in one domain, such as baseball for Dean or chess for Claude, can easily co-exist alongside poor memory in unrelated domains such as their daily appointments or chemistry lessons.

The value of consistent chunking applies to "reproductive learning," when we are trying to reproduce an arbitrary collection of items. Such learning is often required of us. In contrast, for mastery learning of conceptually richer domains, there are advantages of inter-relating groupings in cross-cutting classifications. For example, although constant groupings of facts about political, economic, and military categories may aid a student's recalling facts about the American Civil War, further understanding and memory likely would come by inter-relating and inter-associating facts across domains—for example, noting the political objectives served by a military campaign, such as General Sherman's famous "March to the Sea" through the southern states. The benefit of such conceptual inter-relations is a much-studied topic, but more on that later.

Distinctive Research Methods

Cognitive psychologists use various methods to explore how humans think. These methods include (a) laboratory or other controlled experiments, (b) psychobiological research, (c) self-reports, (d) case studies, (e) naturalistic observation, and (f) computer simulations and artificial intelligence. See Table 1.1 for descriptions and ex-

TABLE 1.1	Research Methods		

Cognitive psychologists use controlled experiments, psychobiological research, self-reports, case studies, naturalistic observation, and computer simulations and artificial intelligence when studying cognitive phenomena.

METHOD	**CONTROLLED LABORATORY EXPERIMENTS**	**PSYCHOBIOLOGICAL RESEARCH**	**SELF-REPORTS, SUCH AS VERBAL PROTOCOLS, SELF-RATING, DIARIES**
Description of method	Obtain samples of performance at a particular time and place	Study animal brains and human brains, using postmortem studies and various psychobiological measures or imaging techniques (see Chapter 2)	Obtain participants' reports of own cognition in progress or as recollected
Validity of causal inferences: random assignment of subjects	Usually	Not usually	Not applicable
Validity of causal inferences: experimental control of independent variables	Usually	Varies widely, depending on the particular technique	Probably not
Samples: size	May be any size	Often small	Probably small
Samples: representativeness	May be representative	Often not representative	May be representative
Ecological validity	Not unlikely; depends on the task and the context to which it is being applied	Unlikely under some circumstances	Maybe; see strengths and weaknesses
Information about individual differences	Usually de-emphasized	Yes	Yes
Strengths	Ease of administration, of scoring, and of statistical analysis make it relatively easy to apply to representative samples of a population; relatively high probability of drawing valid causal inferences	Provides "hard" evidence of cognitive functions by relating them to physiological activity; offers an alternative view of cognitive processes unavailable by other means; may lead to possibilities for treating persons with serious cognitive deficits	Access to introspective insights from participants' point of view, which may be unavailable via other means
Weaknesses	Not always possible to generalize results beyond a specific place, time, and task setting; discrepancies between real-life behavior and behavior in the laboratory	Limited accessibility for most researchers; requires access both to appropriate subjects and to equipment that may be extremely expensive and difficult to obtain; small samples; many studies are based on studies of abnormal brains or of animal brains, so generalizability of findings to normal human populations may be troublesome	Inability to report on processes occurring outside conscious awareness **Verbal protocols & self-ratings:** Data gathering may influence cognitive process being reported. **Recollections:** Possible discrepancies between actual cognition and recollected cognitive processes and products
Examples	David Meyer and Roger Schvaneveldt (1971) developed a laboratory task in which they very briefly presented two strings of letters (either words or nonwords) to subjects, and then they asked the subjects to make a decision about each of the strings of letters, such as deciding whether the letters made a legitimate word or deciding whether a word belonged to a predesignated category	Elizabeth Warrington and Tim Shallice (1972; Shallice & Warrington, 1970) have observed that lesions (areas of injury) in the left parietal lobe of the brain are associated with serious deficits in short-term (brief, active) memory but no impairment of long-term memory, but persons with lesions in the medial (middle) temporal regions of the brain show relatively normal short-term memory but grave deficits in long-term memory (Shallice, 1979; Warrington, 1982)	In a study of mental imagery, Stephen Kosslyn and his colleagues (Kosslyn, Seger, Pani, & Hillger, 1990) asked students to keep a weeklong diary recording all their mental images in each sensory modality

Case Studies	Naturalistic Observations	Computer Simulations and Artificial Intelligence
Engage in intensive study of single individuals, drawing general conclusions about behavior	Observe real-life situations, as in classrooms, work settings, or homes	**Simulations:** Attempt to make computers simulate human cognitive performance on various tasks **AI:** Attempt to make computers demonstrate intelligent cognitive performance, regardless of whether the process resembles human cognitive processing
Highly unlikely	Not applicable	Not applicable
Highly unlikely	No	Full control of variables of interest
Almost certain to be small	Probably small	Not applicable
Not likely to be representative	May be representative	Not applicable
High ecological validity for individual cases; lower generalizability to others	Yes	Not applicable
Yes; richly detailed information regarding individuals	Possible, but emphasis is on environmental distinctions, not on individual differences	Not applicable
Access to richly detailed information about individuals, including information about historical and current contexts, which may not be available via other means; may lead to specialized applications for groups of exceptional individuals (e.g., prodigies, persons with brain damage)	Access to rich contextual information, which may be unavailable via other means	Allows exploration of a wide range of possibilities for modeling cognitive processes; allows clear testing to see whether hypotheses accurately predicted outcomes; may lead to wide range of practical applications (e.g., robotics for performing dangerous tasks or for performing in hazardous environments)
Applicability to other persons; small sample size and nonrepresentativeness of sample generally limits generalizability to population	Lack of experimental control; possible influence on naturalistic behavior due to the presence of the observer	Limitations imposed by the hardware (i.e., the computer circuitry) and the software (i.e., the programs written by the researchers); distinctions between human intelligence and machine intelligence—even in simulations involving sophisticated modeling techniques, simulations may imperfectly model the way that the human brain thinks
Howard Gruber (1974/1981) conducted a case study of Charles Darwin, to explore in depth the psychological context for great intellectual creativity	Michael Cole (Cole, Gay, Glick, & Sharp, 1971) studied members of the Kpelle tribe in Africa, noting how the Kpelle's definitions of intelligence compared with traditional Western definitions of intelligence, as well as how cultural definitions of intelligence may govern intelligent behavior	**Simulations:** Through detailed computations, David Marr (1982) attempted to simulate human visual perception and proposed a theory of visual perception based on his computer models **AI:** Various AI programs have been written that can demonstrate expertise (e.g., playing chess), but they probably do so via different processes than those used by human experts

amples of each method. As the table shows, each method offers distinctive advantages and disadvantages.

Experiments on Human Behavior

In controlled experimental designs, an experimenter conducts research, typically in a laboratory setting. The experimenter controls as many aspects of the experimental situation as possible. There are basically two kinds of variables in any given experiment. **Independent variables** are aspects of an investigation that are individually *manipulated*, or carefully regulated, by the experimenter, while other aspects of the investigation are held constant (i.e., not subject to variation). **Dependent variables** are outcome responses, the values of which depend on how one or more independent variables influence or affect the participants in the experiment. When you tell some student research participants that they will do very well on a task, but you do not say anything to other participants, the independent variable is the amount of information that the students are given about their expected task performance. The dependent variable is how well both groups actually perform the task—that is, their score on the math test.

When the experimenter manipulates the independent variables, he or she controls for the effects of irrelevant variables and observes the effects on the dependent variables (outcomes). These irrelevant variables that are held constant are called *control variables*. Another type of variable is the confounding variable. *Confounding variables* are a type of irrelevant variable that has been left uncontrolled in a study. For example, imagine you want to examine the effectiveness of two problem-solving techniques. You train and test one group under the first strategy at 6 A.M. and a second group under the second strategy at 6 P.M. In this experiment, time of day would be a confounding variable. In other words, time of day may be causing differences in performance that have nothing to do with the problem-solving strategy. Obviously, when conducting research we must be careful to avoid the influence of confounding variables.

In implementing the experimental method, the experimenter must use a representative and random sample of the population of interest. He or she must exert rigorous control over the experimental conditions. The experimenter also must randomly assign participants to the treatment and control conditions. If those requisites for the experimental method are fulfilled, the experimenter may be able to infer probable causality. This inference is of the effects of the independent variable or variables (the treatment) on the dependent variable (the outcome) for the given population.

Many different dependent variables are used in cognitive-psychological research. Two common ones are percent correct (or its additive inverse, error rate) and reaction time. It is important to choose both kinds of variables with great care, because no matter what processes one is observing, what one can learn from an experiment will depend almost exclusively on the variables one chooses to isolate from the often complex behavior one is observing.

Psychologists who study cognitive processes with reaction time often use the *subtraction method*, which involves estimating the time a cognitive process takes by subtracting the amount of time information processing takes with the process from the time it takes without the process (Donders, 1868/1869). For example, if you are asked to scan the words *dog, cat, mouse, hamster, chipmunk* and to say whether the word *chip-*

munk appears in it, and then are asked to scan *dog, cat, mouse, hamster, chipmunk, lion,* and to say whether *lion* appears, the difference in the reaction times might be taken roughly to indicate the amount of time it takes to process each stimulus.

Suppose the outcomes in the treatment condition show a statistically significant difference from the outcomes in the control condition. The experimenter then can infer the likelihood of a causal link between the independent variable(s) and the dependent variable. Because the researcher can establish a likely causal link between the given independent variables and the dependent variables, controlled laboratory experiments offer an excellent means of testing hypotheses.

For example, suppose that we wanted to see whether loud, distracting noises influence the ability to perform well on a particular cognitive task (e.g., reading a passage from a textbook and responding to comprehension questions). Ideally, we first would select a random sample of participants from within our total population of interest. We then would randomly assign each participant to a treatment condition or a control condition. Then we would introduce some distracting loud noises to the participants in our treatment condition. The participants in our control condition would not receive this treatment. We would present the cognitive task to participants in both the treatment condition and the control condition. We then would measure their performance by some means (e.g., speed and accuracy of responses to comprehension questions). Finally, we would analyze our results statistically. We thereby would examine whether the difference between the two groups reached statistical significance. Suppose the participants in the treatment condition showed poorer performance at a statistically significant level than the participants in the control condition. We then might infer that loud distracting noises did, indeed, influence the ability to perform well on this particular cognitive task.

In cognitive-psychological research, the dependent variables may be quite diverse. But they often involve various outcome measures of accuracy (e.g., frequency of errors), of response times, or of both. Among the myriad possibilities for independent variables are characteristics of the situation, of the task, or of the participants. For example, characteristics of the situation may involve the presence versus the absence of particular stimuli or hints during a problem-solving task. Characteristics of the task may involve reading versus listening to a series of words and then responding to comprehension questions. Characteristics of the participants may include age differences, differences in educational status, or differences based on test scores.

On the one hand, characteristics of the situation or task may be manipulated through random assignment of participants to either the treatment or the control group. On the other hand, characteristics of the participant are not easily manipulated experimentally. For example, suppose the experimenter wants to study the effects of aging on speed and accuracy of problem solving. The researcher cannot randomly assign participants to various age groups because people's ages cannot be manipulated (although participants of various age groups can be assigned at random to various experimental conditions). In such situations researchers often use other kinds of studies. Examples are studies involving *correlation* (a statistical relationship between two or more attributes, such as characteristics of the participants or of a situation). Correlations are usually expressed through a correlation coefficient known as Pearson's r. Pearson's r is a number that can range from -1.00 (a negative correlation) to 0 (no correlation) to 1.00 (a positive correlation).

A correlation is a description of a relationship. The correlation coefficient describes the strength of the relationship. The closer the coefficient is to 1 (either positive or negative), the stronger the relationship between the variables is. The sign (positive or negative) of the coefficient describes the direction of the relationship. A positive relationship indicates that as one variable increases (e.g., vocabulary size), another variable also increases (e.g., reading comprehension). A negative relationship indicates that as the measure of one variable increases (e.g., fatigue), the measure of another decreases (e.g., alertness). No correlation—that is, when the coefficient is 0—indicates that there is no pattern or relationship in the change of two variables (e.g., intelligence and earlobe length). In this final case, both variables may change, but the variables do not vary together in a consistent pattern.

Findings of statistical relationships are highly informative. Their value should not be underrated. Also, because correlational studies do not require the random assignment of participants to treatment and control conditions, these methods may be applied flexibly. However, correlational studies generally do not permit unequivocal inferences regarding causality. As a result, many cognitive psychologists strongly prefer experimental data to correlational data.

Psychobiological Research

Through *psychobiological research*, investigators study the relationship between cognitive performance and cerebral events and structures. Chapter 2 describes various specific techniques used in psychobiological research. These techniques generally fall into three categories. The first category is that of techniques for studying an individual's brain *postmortem* (after the death of an individual), relating the individual's cognitive function prior to death to observable features of the brain. The second category is techniques for studying images showing structures of or activities in the brain of an individual who is known to have a particular cognitive deficit. The third is techniques for obtaining information about cerebral processes during the normal performance of a cognitive activity.

Postmortem studies offered some of the first insights into how specific *lesions* (areas of injury in the brain) may be associated with particular cognitive deficits. Such studies continue to provide useful insights into how the brain influences cognitive function. Recent technological developments also have increasingly enabled researchers to study individuals with known cognitive deficits *in vivo* (while the individual is alive). The study of individuals with abnormal cognitive functions linked to cerebral damage often enhances our understanding of normal cognitive functions.

In addition, psychobiological researchers study some aspects of normal cognitive functioning by studying cerebral activity in animal participants. Researchers often use animal participants for experiments involving neurosurgical procedures that cannot be performed on humans because such procedures would be difficult, unethical, or impractical. For example, studies mapping neural activity in the cortex have been conducted on cats and monkeys (e.g., psychobiological research on how the brain responds to visual stimuli; see Chapter 3).

Can cognitive and cerebral functioning of animals and of abnormal humans be generalized to apply to the cognitive and cerebral functioning of normal humans? Psychobiologists have responded to these questions in various ways. Most of them go beyond the scope of this chapter (see Chapter 2). As just one example, for some kinds of cognitive activity, the available technology permits researchers to study the dynamic cerebral activity of normal human participants during cognitive processing (see the brain-imaging techniques described in Chapter 2).

Self-Reports, Case Studies, and Naturalistic Observation

Individual experiments and psychobiological studies often focus on precise specification of discrete aspects of cognition across individuals. To obtain richly textured information about how particular individuals think in a broad range of contexts, researchers may use other methods. These methods include *self-reports* (an individual's own account of cognitive processes), case studies (in-depth studies of individuals), and *naturalistic observation* (detailed studies of cognitive performance in everyday situations and nonlaboratory contexts). On the one hand, experimental research is most useful for testing hypotheses. On the other hand, research based on self-reports, case studies, and naturalistic observation is often particularly useful for the formulation of hypotheses. These methods are also useful to generate descriptions of rare events or processes that we have no other way to measure.

In very specific circumstances, these methods may provide the only way to gather information. An example is the case of Genie, a girl who was locked in a room until the age of 13 and thus provided with severely limited social and sensory experiences. As a result of her imprisonment, Genie had severe physical impairments and no language skills. Through case-study methods, information was collected about how she later began to learn language (Fromkin & associates, 1974; Jones, 1995; LaPointe, 2005). It would have been unethical experimentally to deny a person any language experience for the first 13 years of life. Therefore, case-study methods are the only reasonable way to examine the results of someone's being denied language and social exposure.

Similarly, traumatic brain injury cannot be manipulated in humans in the laboratory. Therefore, when traumatic brain injury occurs, case studies are the only way to gather information. For example, consider the case of Phineas Gage, a railroad worker who, in 1848, had a large metal spike driven through his frontal lobes in a freak accident (Damasio & associates, 1994). Surprisingly, Mr. Gage survived. His behavior and mental processes were drastically changed by the accident, however. Obviously, we cannot insert large metal rods into the brains of experimental participants. Therefore, in the case of traumatic brain injury we must rely on case-study methods to gather information.

The reliability of data based on various kinds of self-reports depends on the candor of the participants when providing the reports. A participant may misreport information about his or her cognitive processes for a variety of reasons. These reasons can be intentional or unintentional. Intentional misreports can include trying to edit out unflattering information. Unintentional misreports may involve not understanding the question or not remembering the information accurately. For example, when a participant is asked about the problem-solving strategies he or she used in high school, the participant may not remember. The participant may try to be completely truthful in his or her reports. But reports involving recollected information (e.g., diaries, retrospective accounts, questionnaires, and surveys) are notably less reliable than reports provided during the cognitive processing under investigation. The reason is that participants sometimes forget what they did. In studying complex cognitive processes, such as problem solving or decision making, researchers often use a verbal protocol. In a *verbal protocol,* the participants describe aloud all their thoughts and ideas during the performance of a given cognitive task (e.g., "I like the apartment with the swimming pool better, but I can't really afford it, so I might choose.").

An alternative to a verbal protocol is for participants to report specific information regarding a particular aspect of their cognitive processing. Consider, for example, a study of insightful problem solving (see Chapter 11). Participants were asked at 15-second intervals to report numerical ratings indicating how close they felt they were to reaching a solution to a given problem. Unfortunately, even these methods of self-reporting have their limitations. As one example, cognitive processes may be altered by the act of giving the report (e.g., processes involving brief forms of memory; see Chapter 5). As another example, cognitive processes may occur outside of conscious awareness (e.g., processes that do not require conscious attention or that take place so rapidly that we fail to notice them; see Chapter 4). To get an idea of some of the difficulties with self-reports, carry out the following "Investigating Cognitive Psychology" tasks. Reflect on your experiences with self-reports.

INVESTIGATING COGNITIVE PSYCHOLOGY	1. Without looking at your shoes, try reporting aloud the various steps involved in tying your shoe. 2. Recall aloud what you did on your last birthday. 3. Now, actually tie your shoe (or something else, such as a string tied around a table leg), reporting aloud the steps you take. Do you notice any differences between task 1 and task 3? 4. Report aloud how you pulled into consciousness the steps involved in tying your shoe or your memories of your last birthday. Can you report exactly how you pulled the information into conscious awareness? Can you report which part of your brain was most active during each of these tasks?

Ask half of your friends individually one of the following series of questions and the other half the other series. Ask them to respond as quickly as they can.

Set 1:

What do silkworms weave?

What is a popular material for clothing that comes from silkworms?

What do cows drink?

Set 2:

What do bees make?

What grows in fields that eventually is made into material for clothing?

What do cows drink?

For many of your friends, when they get to question 3 in set 1, they will say "milk" when we all know that cows drink water. Most of your friends responding to set 2 will say "water," not "milk." You have just conducted an experiment. The experimental method divides people into two equal groups, changes one aspect between the two groups (in your case, you asked a series of questions before asking the critical question), then measures the difference between the two groups. The number of mistakes is what you are measuring, and it is likely that your friends in group 1 will make more mistakes than your friends in group 2 because they have established the wrong set of expectations for answering the question.

Case studies (e.g., the study of exceptionally gifted individuals) and naturalistic observations (e.g., the observation of individuals operating in nuclear power plants) may be used to complement findings from laboratory experiments. These two methods of cognitive research offer high **ecological validity,** the degree to which particular findings in one environmental context may be considered relevant outside of that context. As you probably know, *ecology* is the study of the interactive relationship between an organism (or organisms) and its environment. Many cognitive psychologists seek to understand the interactive relationship between human thought processes and the environments in which humans are thinking. Sometimes, cognitive processes that commonly are observed in one setting (e.g., in a laboratory) are not identical to those observed in another setting (e.g., in an air-traffic control tower or a classroom).

Computer Simulations and Artificial Intelligence

Digital computers played a fundamental role in the emergence of the study of cognitive psychology. One kind of influence is indirect—through models of human cognition based on models of how computers process information. Another kind is direct—through computer simulations and artificial intelligence.

In *computer simulations*, researchers program computers to imitate a given human function or process. Examples are performance on particular cognitive tasks (e.g., manipulating objects within three-dimensional space) and performance of particular cognitive processes (e.g., pattern recognition). Some researchers even have attempted to create computer models of the entire cognitive architecture of the human mind. Their models have stimulated heated discussions regarding how the human mind may function as a whole (see Chapter 8). Sometimes the distinction between simulation and artificial intelligence is blurred. An example would be certain programs that are designed to simulate human performance and to maximize functioning simultaneously.

Consider, for example, a program that plays chess. There are two entirely different ways to conceptualize how to write such a program. One is known as brute force: One constructs an algorithm that considers extremely large moves in a very short time, potentially beating human players simply by virtue of the number of moves it considers and the future potential consequences of these moves. The program would be viewed as successful to the extent that it beat the best humans. This kind of artificial intelligence does not seek to represent how humans function, but done well it can produce a program that plays chess at the highest possible level. An alternative approach, that of simulation, looks at how chess grandmasters solve chess problems and then seeks to function the way they do. The program would be viewed as successful if it chose, in a sequence of moves in a game, the same moves that the grandmaster would choose. It is also possible to combine the two approaches, producing a program that, say, generally simulates human performance but can use brute force as necessary to win games.

Putting It All Together

Cognitive psychologists often broaden and deepen their understanding of cognition through research in cognitive science. **Cognitive science** is a cross-disciplinary field that uses ideas and methods from cognitive psychology, psychobiology, artificial intelligence, philosophy, linguistics, and anthropology (Nickerson, 2005; Von Eckardt, 2005). Cognitive scientists use these ideas and methods to focus on the study of how humans acquire and use knowledge. Cognitive psychologists also profit from collaborations with other kinds of psychologists. Examples are social psychologists (e.g., in the cross-disciplinary field of social cognition), psychologists who study motivation and emotion, and engineering psychologists (i.e., psychologists who study human-machine interactions).

Key Issues and Fields within Cognitive Psychology

Throughout this chapter, we have alluded to some of the key themes that arise in the study of cognitive psychology. Because these themes appear again and again in the various chapters of this textbook, a summary of these themes follows. Some of these questions go to the very core of the nature of the human mind.

Underlying Themes in the Study of Cognitive Psychology

If we review the important ideas in this chapter, we discover some of the major themes that underlie all of cognitive psychology. What are some of these themes? Here are seven of them, viewed dialectically:

1. *Nature versus nurture:*
   a. *Thesis/Antithesis:* Which is more influential in human cognition—nature or nurture? If we believe that innate characteristics of human cognition are more important, we might focus our research on studying innate characteristics of cognition. If we believe that the environment plays an important role in cognition, we might conduct research exploring how distinctive characteristics of the environment seem to influence cognition.
   b. *Synthesis:* How can we learn about co-variations and interactions in the environment, such as how an impoverished environment adversely affects someone whose genes otherwise might have led to success in a variety of tasks?
2. *Rationalism versus empiricism:*
   a. *Thesis/Antithesis:* How should we discover the truth about ourselves and about the world around us? Should we do so by trying to reason logically,

based on what we already know? Or should we do so by observing and testing our observations of what we can perceive through our senses?

    b. *Synthesis:* How can we combine theory with empirical methods to learn the most we can about cognitive phenomena?

3. *Structures versus processes:*

    a. *Thesis/Antithesis:* Should we study the structures (contents, attributes, and products) of the human mind? Or should we focus on the processes of human thinking?

    b. *Synthesis:* How do mental processes operate on mental structures?

4. *Domain generality versus domain specificity:*

    a. *Thesis/Antithesis:* Are the processes we observe limited to single domains, or are they general across a variety of domains? Do observations in one domain apply also to all domains, or do they apply only to the specific domains observed?

    b. *Synthesis:* Which processes might be domain-general, and which domain-specific?

5. *Validity of causal inferences versus ecological validity:*

    a. *Thesis/Antithesis:* Should we study cognition by using highly controlled experiments that increase the probability of valid inferences regarding causality? Or should we use more naturalistic techniques, which increase the likelihood of obtaining ecologically valid findings but possibly at the expense of experimental control?

    b. *Synthesis:* How can a variety of methods be combined, including laboratory ones and more naturalistic ones, so as to converge on findings that hold up, regardless of method of study?

6. *Applied versus basic research:*

    a. *Thesis/Antithesis:* Should we conduct research into fundamental cognitive processes? Or should we study ways in which to help people use cognition effectively in practical situations?

    b. *Synthesis:* Can the two kinds of research be combined dialectically so that basic research leads to applied research, which leads to further basic research, and so on?

7. *Biological versus behavioral methods:*

    a. *Thesis/Antithesis:* Should we study the brain and its functioning directly, perhaps even scanning the brain while people are performing cognitive tasks? Or should we study people's behavior in cognitive tasks, looking at measures such as percentage correct and reaction time?

    b. *Synthesis:* How can biological and behavioral methods be synthesized so that we understand cognitive phenomena at multiple levels of analysis?

Note that these questions can be posed in the "either/or" form of thesis/antithesis, or in the both/and form of a synthesis of views or methods, which often proves more useful than one extreme position or another. For example, our nature may provide an inherited framework for our distinctive characteristics and patterns of thinking and acting. But our nurture may shape the specific ways in which we flesh out that framework. We may use empirical methods for gathering data and for testing hypotheses. But we may use rationalist methods for interpreting data, constructing theories, and formulating hypotheses based on theories. Our understanding of cognition deepens when we consider both basic research into fundamental cognitive processes and applied research regarding effective uses of cognition in real-world settings. Syntheses constantly are evolving. What today may be viewed as a synthesis may tomorrow be viewed as an extreme position or vice versa.

Key Ideas in Cognitive Psychology

Certain key ideas seem to keep emerging in cognitive psychology, regardless of the particular phenomenon one studies. Here are what might be considered five major ideas.

1. *Data in cognitive psychology can be fully understood only in the context of an explanatory theory, but theories are empty without empirical data.*

   Science is not merely a collection of empirically collected facts. Rather, it comprises such facts that are explained and organized by scientific theories. Theories give meaning to data. For example, suppose that we know that people's ability to recognize information that they have seen is better than their ability to recall such information. As an example, they are better at recognizing whether they heard a word said on a list than they are at recalling the word without the word's being given. This is an interesting empirical generalization. But science requires us not only to be able to make the generalization but also to understand why memory works this way. For one thing, an important goal of science is explanation. An empirical generalization does not, in the absence of an underlying theory, provide *explanation*. For another thing, theory helps us understand the limitations of empirical generalizations and when and why they occur. For example, a theory proposed by Tulving and Thomson (1973) suggested that, in fact, recognition should not always be better than recall. An important goal of science is also *prediction*. Tulving and Thomson's theory led them to predict the circumstances under which recall should be better than recognition. Subsequent data collection proved them to be right. Under some circumstances, recall is indeed better than recognition. Theory therefore suggested under which circumstances, among the many circumstances one might examine, limitations to the generalization should occur. Theory thus assists both in explanation and prediction.

   At the same time, theory without data is empty. Almost anyone can sit in an armchair and propose a theory—even a plausible-sounding one. Science, however, requires empirical testing of such theories. Without such testing, theories remain merely speculative. Thus, theories and data depend on each other. Theories generate data collections, which help correct theories, which then lead to further data collections, and so forth. It is through this iteration of and interaction between theory and data that we increase scientific understanding.

2. *Cognition is generally adaptive but not in all specific instances.*

   When we consider all the ways in which we can make mistakes, it is astonishing how well our cognitive systems operate. Evolution has served us well in shaping the development of a cognitive apparatus that is able accurately to decode environmental stimuli. It also can understand internal stimuli that make the most of the information available to us. We can perceive, learn, remember, reason, and solve problems with great accuracy. And we do so even though we constantly are barraged by a plethora of stimuli. Any of the stimuli easily could distract us from processing information properly. The same processes, however, that lead us to perceive, remember, and reason accurately in most situations also can lead us astray. Our memories and reasoning processes, for example, are susceptible to certain well-identified, systematic errors. For example, as we saw when we learned about the availability heuristic, we tend to overvalue information that is easily available to us. We do this even when this information is not optimally relevant to the problem at hand. In general, all systems—natural or artificial—are based on tradeoffs. The same characteristics that make them highly efficient in a large variety of circumstances can render them inefficient in specialized circumstances. A system that would be extremely efficient in each specialized circumstance would be inefficient across a wide variety of circumstances simply because it would become too cumbersome and complex. Humans thus represent a highly efficient, but imperfect, adaptation to the environments they face.

Consider, as an example of availability, college admissions. Most admissions officers would like to know a lot about students' leadership skills, their creativity, their ethics, and other characteristics such as these. But such information is not readily available, and when it is, it is often available only for some students. In contrast, test scores and grade-point averages are more easily available for all applications. So the college admissions officers may rely more heavily on test scores and grades than they otherwise might if the information on characteristics such as creativity and ethics were more readily available.

3. *Cognitive processes interact with each other and with noncognitive processes.*

Although cognitive psychologists try to study and often to isolate the functioning of specific cognitive processes, they know that these processes work together. For example, memory processes depend on perceptual processes. What you remember depends in part on what you perceive. Similarly, thinking processes depend in part on memory processes: You cannot reflect on what you do not remember. But noncognitive processes also interact with cognitive ones. For example, you learn better when you are motivated to learn. However, your learning likely will be reduced if you are upset about something and cannot concentrate on the learning task at hand. Cognitive psychologists therefore seek to study cognitive processes not only in isolation but also in their interactions with each other and with noncognitive processes.

One of the most exciting areas of cognitive psychology today is at the interface between cognitive and biological levels of analysis. In recent years, for example, it has become possible to localize activity in the brain associated with various kinds of cognitive processes. One has to be careful about assuming that the biological activity is causal of the cognitive activity, however. Research shows that learning that causes changes in the brain—in other words, cognitive processes—can affect biological structures just as biological structures can affect cognitive processes. So the interactions between cognition and other processes occur at many levels. The cognitive system does not operate in isolation. It works in interaction with other systems.

4. *Cognition needs to be studied through a variety of scientific methods.*

There is no one right way to study cognition. Naïve researchers sometimes seek the "best" method by which to study cognition. Their search inevitably will be in vain. All cognitive processes need to be studied through a variety of converging operations. That is, varied methods of study seek a common understanding. The more different kinds of techniques that lead to the same conclusion, the higher the confidence one can have in that conclusion. For example, suppose studies of reaction times, error rates, and patterns of individual differences all lead to the same conclusion. Then one can have much more confidence in the conclusion than if only one method led to that conclusion.

Cognitive psychologists need to learn a variety of different kinds of techniques to do their job well. All these methods, however, must be *scientific*. Scientific methods differ from other methods in that they provide the basis for the self-correcting nature of science. Eventually we correct our errors. The reason is that scientific methods enable us to disconfirm our expectations when those expectations are wrong. Nonscientific methods do not have this feature. For example, methods of inquiry that simply rely on faith or authority to determine truth may have value in our lives. But they are not scientific and hence are not self-correcting. Indeed, the words of one authority may be replaced by the words of another authority tomorrow without anything new being learned about the phenomenon to which the words apply. As the world learned long ago, important dignitaries stating that the Earth is at the center of the universe do not make it so.

5. *All basic research in cognitive psychology may lead to applications, and all applied research may lead to basic understandings.*

Politicians, and sometimes even scientists, like to draw tidy distinctions between basic and applied research. But the truth is, the distinction often is not clear at all. Research that seems like it will be basic often leads to immediate applications. Similarly, research that seems like it will be applied sometimes leads quickly to basic understandings, whether or not there are immediate applications. For example, a basic finding from research on learning and memory is that learning is superior when it is spaced out over time rather than crammed into a short time interval. This basic finding has an immediate application to study strategies. At the same time, research on eyewitness testimony, which seems on its face to be very applied, has enhanced our basic understanding of memory systems and of the extent to which humans construct their own memories. It does not merely reproduce what happens in the environment.

Before closing this chapter, think about some of the fields of cognitive psychology, described in the remaining chapters, to which these key themes and issues may apply.

Chapter Previews

Cognitive psychologists have been involved in studying a wide range of psychological phenomena. This range includes not only perception, learning, memory, and thinking but also seemingly less cognitively oriented phenomena, such as emotion and motivation. In fact, almost any topic of psychological interest may be studied from a cognitive perspective. Nonetheless, there are some main areas of interest to cognitive psychologists. In this textbook we attempt to describe some of the preliminary answers to questions asked by researchers in the main areas of interest.

- Chapter 2 *Cognitive Neuroscience*—What structures and processes of the human brain underlie the structures and processes of human cognition?

- Chapter 3 *Perception*—How does the human mind perceive what the senses receive? How does the human mind distinctively achieve the perception of forms and patterns?

- Chapter 4 *Attention and Consciousness*—What basic processes of the mind govern how information enters our minds, our awareness, and our high-level processes of information handling?

- Chapter 5 *Memory: Models and Research Methods*—How are different kinds of information (e.g., our experiences related to a traumatic event, the names of U.S. presidents, or the procedure for riding a bicycle) represented in memory?

- Chapter 6 *Memory Processes*—How do we move information into memory, keep it there, and retrieve it from memory when needed?

- Chapter 7 *Representation and Manipulation of Knowledge in Memory: Images and Propositions*—How do we mentally represent information in our minds? Do we do so in words, in pictures, or in some other form representing meaning? Alternatively, do we have multiple forms of representation?

- Chapter 8 *Representation and Organization of Knowledge in Memory: Concepts, Categories, Networks, and Schemas*—How do we mentally organize what we know? How do we manipulate and operate on knowledge—do we do so serially, through parallel processing, or through some combination of processes?

- Chapter 9 *Language: Nature and Acquisition*—How do we derive and produce meaning through language? How do we acquire language—both our primary language and any additional languages?

- Chapter 10 *Language in Context*—How does our use of language interact with our ways of thinking? How does our social world interact with our use of language?

- Chapter 11 *Problem Solving and Creativity*—How do we solve problems? What processes aid and impede us in reaching solutions to problems? Why are some of us more creative than others? How do we become and remain creative?

- Chapter 12 *Decision Making and Reasoning*—How do we reach important decisions? How do we draw reasonable conclusions from the information we have available? Why and how do we so often make inappropriate decisions and reach inaccurate conclusions?

- Chapter 13 *Human and Artificial Intelligence*—Why do we consider some people more intelligent than others? Why do some people seem better able to accomplish whatever they want to accomplish in their chosen fields of endeavor?

In this book I try to emphasize the underlying common ideas and organizing themes across various aspects of cognitive psychology, rather than simply to state the facts. I follow this path to help you perceive large, meaningful patterns within the domain of cognitive psychology. I also try to give you some idea of how cognitive psychologists think and how they structure their field in their day-to-day work. I hope that this approach will help you to contemplate problems in cognitive psychology at a deeper level than might otherwise be possible. Ultimately, the goal of cognitive psychologists is to understand not only how people may think in their laboratories but also how they think in their everyday lives.

Summary

1. **What is cognitive psychology?**   Cognitive psychology is the study of how people perceive, learn, remember, and think about information.

2. **How did psychology develop as a science?**   Beginning with Plato and Aristotle, people have contemplated how to gain understanding of the truth. Plato held that rationalism offers the clear path to truth, whereas Aristotle espoused empiricism as the route to knowledge. Centuries later, Descartes extended Plato's rationalism, whereas Locke elaborated on Aristotle's empiricism. Kant offered a synthesis of these apparent opposites. Decades after Kant proposed his synthesis, Hegel observed how the history of ideas seems to progress through a *dialectical* process.

3. **How did cognitive psychology develop from psychology?**   By the twentieth century, psychology had emerged as a distinct field of study. Wundt focused on the structures of the mind (leading to *structuralism*), whereas James and Dewey focused on the processes of the mind (*functionalism*).

   Emerging from this dialectic was *associationism*, espoused by Ebbinghaus and Thorndike. It paved the way for behaviorism by underscoring the importance of mental associations. Another step toward behaviorism was Pavlov's discovery of the principles of classical conditioning. Watson and later Skinner were the chief proponents of *behaviorism*. It focused entirely on observable links between an organism's behavior and particular environmental contingencies that strengthen or weaken the likelihood that particular behaviors will be repeated. Most behaviorists dismissed entirely the notion that there is merit in psychologists' trying to understand what is going on in the mind of the individual engaging in the behavior.

   However, Tolman and subsequent behaviorist researchers noted the role of cognitive processes in influencing behavior. A convergence of developments across many fields led to the emergence of *cognitive psychology* as a discrete discipline, spearheaded by such notables as Neisser.

4. **How have other disciplines contributed to the development of theory and research in cognitive psychology?**   Cognitive psychology has roots in philosophy and physiology. They merged to form the mainstream of psychology. As a discrete field of psychological study, cognitive psychology also profited from cross-disciplinary investigations.

   Relevant fields include linguistics (e.g., How do language and thought interact?), biological psychology (e.g., What are the physiological bases for cognition?), anthropology (e.g., What is the importance of the cultural context for cognition?), and technological advances like artificial intelligence (e.g., How do computers process information?).

5. **What methods do cognitive psychologists use to study how people think?** Cognitive psychologists use a broad range of methods, including experiments, psychobiological techniques, self-reports, case studies, naturalistic observation, and computer simulations and artificial intelligence.

6. **What are the current issues and various fields of study within cognitive psychology?** Some of the major issues in the field have centered on how to pursue knowledge. Psychological work can be done

- by using both *rationalism* (which is the basis for theory development) and *empiricism* (which is the basis for gathering data);
- by underscoring the importance of cognitive structures and of cognitive processes;
- by emphasizing the study of domain-general and of domain-specific processing;

- by striving for a high degree of experimental control (which better permits causal inferences) and for a high degree of *ecological validity* (which better allows generalization of findings to settings outside of the laboratory);
- by conducting basic research seeking fundamental insights about cognition and applied research seeking effective uses of cognition in real-world settings.

Although positions on these issues may appear to be diametrical opposites, often apparently antithetical views may be synthesized into a form that offers the best of each of the opposing viewpoints.

Cognitive psychologists study biological bases of cognition as well as attention, consciousness, perception, memory, mental imagery, language, problem solving, creativity, decision making, reasoning, developmental changes in cognition across the life span, human intelligence, artificial intelligence, and various other aspects of human thinking.

Thinking about Thinking: Factual, Analytical, Creative, and Practical Questions

1. Describe the major historical schools of psychological thought leading up to the development of cognitive psychology.

2. Describe some of the ways in which philosophy, linguistics, and artificial intelligence have contributed to the development of cognitive psychology.

3. Compare and contrast the influences of Plato and Aristotle on psychology.

4. Analyze how various research methods in cognitive psychology reflect empiricist and rationalist approaches to gaining knowledge.

5. Design a rough sketch of a cognitive-psychological investigation involving one of the research methods described in this chapter. Highlight both the advantages and the disadvantages of using this particular method for your investigation.

6. This chapter describes cognitive psychology as the field is now. How might you speculate that the field will change in the next 50 years?

7. How might an insight gained from basic research lead to practical uses in an everyday setting?

8. How might an insight gained from applied research lead to deepened understanding of fundamental features of cognition?

Key Terms

artificial intelligence (AI)
associationism
behaviorism
cognitive psychology
cognitive science
cognitivism
dependent variables

ecological validity
empiricist
functionalism
Gestalt psychology
hypotheses
independent variables
introspection

pragmatists
rationalist
statistical significance
structuralism
theory

Annotated Suggested Readings

Nadel, L. (Ed.). (2003). *Encyclopedia of cognitive science* (4 vols.). London, England: Nature Publishing Group. A detailed analysis of topics in the full range of cognitive sciences. Entries are graded for difficulty.

Wilson, R. A., & Keil, F. C. (Eds.). (1999). *The MIT encyclopedia of cognitive sciences*. Cambridge, MA: MIT Press. Entries on the full range of topics that constitute the study of cognitive science.

Cognitive Neuroscience

EXPLORING COGNITIVE PSYCHOLOGY

1. **What are the fundamental structures and processes of the cells within the brain?**

2. **How do researchers study the major structures and processes of the brain?**

3. **What have researchers found as a result of studying the brain?**

An ancient legend from India (Rosenzweig & Leiman, 1989) tells of Sita. She marries one man but is attracted to another. These two frustrated men behead themselves. Sita, bereft of them both, desperately prays to the goddess Kali to bring the men back to life. Sita is granted her wish. She is allowed to reattach the heads to the bodies. In her rush to bring the two men back to life, Sita mistakenly switches their heads. She attaches them to the wrong bodies. Now, to whom is she married? Who is who?

The mind–body issue has long interested philosophers and scientists. Where is the mind located in the body, if at all? How do the mind and body interact? How are we able to think, speak, plan, reason, learn, and remember? What are the physical bases for our cognitive abilities? These questions all probe the relationship between cognitive psychology and neurobiology. Some cognitive psychologists seek to answer such questions by studying the biological bases of cognition. Cognitive psychologists are especially concerned with how the anatomy (physical structures of the body) and the physiology (functions and processes of the body) of the nervous system affect and are affected by human cognition.

Cognitive neuroscience is the field of study linking the brain and other aspects of the nervous system to cognitive processing and, ultimately, to behavior. The **brain** is the organ in our bodies that most directly controls our thoughts, emotions, and motivations (Gloor, 1997; Rockland, 2000; Shepherd, 1998). We usually think of the brain as being at the top of the body's hierarchy—as the boss, with various other organs responding to it. Like any good boss, however, it listens to and is influenced by its subordinates, the other organs of the body. Thus, the brain is reactive as well as directive.

A major goal of present work on the brain is to study localization of function. **Localization of function** refers to the specific areas of the brain that control specific skills or behaviors. Before we focus on the brain, however, we will consider how it fits into the overall organization of the nervous system.

From Neuron to Brain: Organization of the Nervous System

The **nervous system** is the basis for our ability to perceive, adapt to, and interact with the world around us (Gazzaniga, 1995, 2000; Gazzaniga, Ivry, & Mangun, 1998). Through this system we receive, process, and then respond to information from the environment (Pinker, 1997a; Rugg, 1997). In this brief section, we first consider the basic building block of the nervous system—the neuron. We will examine in detail how information moves through the nervous system at the cellular level. Then we consider the various levels of organization within the nervous system. In later sections, we will focus on the supreme organ of the nervous system—the brain—paying special attention to the cerebral cortex, which controls many of our thought processes. For now, let's consider how information processing occurs at the cellular level.

Neuronal Structure and Function

To understand how the entire nervous system processes information, we need to examine the structure and function of the cells that constitute the nervous system. Individual neural cells, called **neurons,** transmit electrical signals from one location to another in the nervous system (Carlson, 2006; Shepherd, 2004). The greatest concentration of neurons is in the neocortex of the brain. The neocortex is the part of the brain associated with complex cognition. This tissue can contain as many as 100,000 neurons per cubic millimeter (Churchland & Sejnowski, 2004). The neurons tend to be arranged in the form of networks, which provide information and feedback to each other within various kinds of information processing (Vogels, Rajan, & Abbott, 2005).

Neurons vary in their structure, but almost all neurons have four basic parts, as illustrated in Figure 2.1. These include a soma (cell body), dendrites, an axon, and terminal buttons.

The **soma,** which contains the nucleus of the cell (the center portion that performs metabolic and reproductive functions for the cell), is responsible for the life of the neuron and connects the dendrites to the axon. The many **dendrites** are branch-like structures that receive information from other neurons, and the soma integrates the information. Learning is associated with the formation of new neuronal connections. Hence, it occurs in conjunction with increased complexity or ramification in the branching structure of dendrites in the brain. The single **axon** is a long, thin tube that extends (and sometimes splits) from the soma and responds to the information, when appropriate, by transmitting an electrochemical signal, which travels to the terminus (end), where the signal can be transmitted to other neurons.

Axons are of two basic, roughly equally occurring kinds, distinguished by the presence or absence of myelin. **Myelin** is a white fatty substance that surrounds some of the axons of the nervous system, which accounts for some of the whiteness of the white matter of the brain. Some axons are myelinated (in that they are surrounded by a myelin sheath). This sheath, which insulates and protects longer axons from electrical interference by other neurons in the area, also speeds up the conduction of information. In fact, transmission in myelinated axons can reach 100 meters per second (equal to about 224 miles per hour). Moreover, myelin is not distributed continuously along the axon. It is distributed in segments broken up by nodes of Ranvier. **Nodes of Ranvier** are small gaps in the myelin coating along the axon, which serve to increase conduction speed even more. The second kind of axon lacks the myelin coat altogether. Typically, these unmyelinated axons are smaller and shorter (as well as slower) than the myelinated axons. As a result, they do not need the increased conduction velocity myelin provides for longer axons. Multiple sclerosis, an autoim-

FIGURE 2.1

Terminal buttons

Soma

Dendrites

Axon

© Omikron/Science Source/
Photo Researchers, Inc.

The shape of a neuron is determined by its function. Each neuron, however, has the same structure: soma, dendrites, an axon, and terminal buttons.

mune disease, is associated with the degeneration of myelin sheaths along axons in certain nerves. It results in impairments of coordination and balance. In severe cases this disease is fatal.

The **terminal buttons** are small knobs found at the ends of the branches of an axon that do not directly touch the dendrites of the next neuron. Rather, there is a very small gap, the synapse. The **synapse** serves as a juncture between the terminal buttons of one or more neurons and the dendrites (or sometimes the soma) of one or more other neurons (Carlson, 2006; see Figure 2.1). Synapses are important in cognition. Rats show increases in both the size and the number of synapses in the brain as a result of learning (Turner & Greenough, 1985). Decreased cognitive functioning, as in Alzheimer's disease, is associated with reduced efficiency of synaptic transmission of nerve impulses (Selkoe, 2002). Signal transmission between neurons occurs when the terminal buttons release one or more neurotransmitters at the synapse. These **neurotransmitters** serve as chemical messengers for transmission of information across the synaptic gap to the receiving dendrites of the next neuron (von Bohlen und Halbach & Dermietzel, 2006).

Although scientists already know of more than 50 transmitter substances, it seems likely that more remain to be discovered. Medical and psychological researchers are working to discover and understand neurotransmitters. In particular, they wish to understand how the neurotransmitters interact with drugs, moods, abilities, and perceptions. We know much about the mechanics of impulse transmission in nerves. But we still know relatively little about how the nervous system's chemical activity relates to psychological states. Despite the limits on present knowledge, we have gained some insight into how several of these substances affect our psychological functioning.

At present, it appears that three types of chemical substances are involved in neurotransmission:

1. The *monoamine neurotransmitters*, each of which is synthesized by the nervous system through enzymatic actions on one of the amino acids (constituents of proteins, such as choline, tyrosine, and tryptophan) in our diet (e.g., acetylcholine, dopamine, and serotonin);
2. *Amino-acid neurotransmitters*, which are obtained directly from the amino acids in our diet without further synthesis (e.g., gamma-aminobutyric acid, or GABA); and
3. *Neuropeptides*, which are peptide chains (molecules made from the parts of two or more amino acids).

Table 2.1 lists some examples of neurotransmitters, together with their typical functions in the nervous system and their associations with cognitive processing.

Acetylcholine is associated with memory functions, and the loss of acetylcholine with Alzheimer's disease has been linked to impaired memory functioning in Alzheimer's patients (Hasselmo, 2006). Acetylcholine also plays an important role in sleep and arousal. When someone awakens, there is an increase in the activity of so-called cholinergic neurons in the basal forebrain and the brainstem (Rockland, 2000).

Dopamine is associated with both attention and learning. Dopamine also is involved in motivational processes, such as reward and reinforcement. Schizophrenics show very high levels of dopamine. This fact has led some researchers to believe that high levels of dopamine may be partially responsible for schizophrenic conditions. Drugs used to combat schizophrenia often inhibit dopamine activity (von Bohlen und Halbach & Dermietzel, 2006). In contrast, patients with Parkinson's disease show very low dopamine levels. With dopamine treatment, patients with Parkinson's disease sometimes show an increase in pathological gambling. When dopamine treatment is suspended, these patients no longer exhibit this behavior (Drapier & associates, 2006; Voon & associates, 2007). These findings support the role of dopamine in motivational processes.

Serotonin plays an important role in eating behavior and body-weight regulation. It is involved, as well, in aggression and regulation of impulsivity (Rockland, 2000).

TABLE 2.1	Neurotransmitters

Neurotransmitters are responsible for intercellular communication in the nervous system. This table lists only a subset of known neurotransmitters.

NEUROTRANSMITTERS	DESCRIPTION	GENERAL FUNCTION	SPECIFIC EXAMPLES
Acetylcholine (Ach)	Monoamine neurotransmitter synthesized from choline	Excitatory in brain and either excitatory (at skeletal muscles) or inhibitory (at heart muscles) elsewhere in the body	Believed to be involved in memory because of high concentration found in the hippocampus (Squire, 1987)
Dopamine (DA)	Monoamine neurotransmitter synthesized from tyrosine	Influences movement, attention, and learning; mostly inhibitory but some excitatory effects	Parkinson's disease, characterized by tremors and limb rigidity, results from too little DA; some schizophrenia symptoms are associated with too much DA
Epinephrine and norepinephrine	Monoamine neurotransmitter synthesized from tyrosine	Hormones (also known as adrenaline and noradrenaline) involved in regulation of alertness	Involved in diverse effects on body related to fight-or-flight reactions, anger, and fear
Serotonin	Monoamine neurotransmitter synthesized from tryptophan	Involved in arousal, sleep and dreaming, and mood; usually inhibitory but some excitatory effects	Normally inhibits dreaming; defects in serotonin system are linked to severe depression
GABA (gamma-aminobutyric acid)	Amino acid neurotransmitter	General neuromodulatory effects resulting from inhibitory influences on presynaptic axons	Currently believed to influence certain mechanisms for learning and memory (Izquierdo & Medina, 1997)
Glutamate	Amino acid neurotransmitter	General neuromodulatory effects resulting from excitatory influences on presynaptic axons	Currently believed to influence certain mechanisms for learning and memory (Izquierdo & Medina, 1997)
Neuropeptides	Peptide chains serving as neurotransmitters	General neuromodulatory effects resulting from influences on postsynaptic membranes	Endorphins play a role in pain relief. Neuromodulating neuropeptides sometimes are released to enhance the effects of Ach

Drugs that block serotonin tend to result in an increase in aggressive behavior. High serotonin levels play a role in some types of anorexia. Specifically, serotonin seems to play a role in the types of anorexia resulting from illness or treatment of illness. For example, patients suffering from cancer or undergoing dialysis often experience a severe loss of appetite (Agulera & associates, 2000; Davis & associates, 2004). This loss of appetite is related, in both cases, to high serotonin levels.

The preceding description drastically oversimplifies the intricacies of constant neuronal communication. Such complexities make it difficult to understand what is happening in the normal brain when we are thinking, feeling, and interacting with our environment. Many researchers seek to understand the normal information processes of the brain. They wish to determine what is going wrong in the brains of people affected by neurological and psychological disorders. Perhaps if we can understand what has gone awry—what chemicals are out of balance—we can figure out how to put things back into balance. One way of doing so might be by providing needed neurotransmitters or by inhibiting the effects of overabundant neurotransmitters.

Receptors and Drugs

Receptors in the brain that normally are occupied by the standard neurotransmitters can be hijacked by psychopharmacologically active drugs, legal or illegal. In such cases, the molecules of the drugs enter into receptors that normally would be for neurotransmitter substances endogenous in (originating in) the body.

When people stop using the drugs, withdrawal symptoms arise. Once a user has formed narcotic dependence, for example, the form of treatment differs for *acute toxicity* (the damage done from a particular overdose) versus *chronic toxicity* (the damage done by long-term drug addiction). Acute toxicity is often treated with naloxone or related drugs. Naloxone (as well as a related drug, naltrexone) occupies opiate receptors in the brain better than the opiates themselves occupy those sites; thus, it blocks all effects of narcotics. In fact, naloxone has such a strong affinity for the endorphin receptors in the brain that it actually displaces molecules of narcotics already in these receptors and then moves into the receptors itself. Naloxone is not addictive, however. Even though it binds to receptors, it does not activate them. Although naloxone can be a life-saving drug for someone who has overdosed on opiates, its effects are short lived. Thus, it is a poor long-term treatment for drug addiction.

In narcotic detoxification, methadone often is substituted for the narcotic (typically, heroin). Methadone binds to endorphin receptor sites in a similar way to naloxone and reduces the heroin cravings and withdrawal symptoms of addicted persons. After the substitution, gradually decreasing dosages are administered to the patient until he or she is drug free. Unfortunately, the usefulness of methadone is limited by the fact that it is, itself, addictive.

Viewing the Structures and Functions of the Brain

Scientists can use many methods for studying the human brain. These methods include both postmortem (from Latin, "after death") studies and *in vivo* (from Latin, "living") techniques on both humans and animals. Each technique provides important information about the structure and function of the human brain. Even some of the earliest postmortem studies still influence our thinking about how the brain performs certain functions. However, the recent trend is to focus on techniques that provide information about human mental functioning as it is occurring. This trend is in contrast to the earlier trend of waiting to find people with disorders and then studying their brains after they died. Because postmortem studies are the foundation for later work, we discuss them first before moving on to the more modern *in vivo* techniques.

Postmortem Studies

For centuries investigators have been able to dissect a brain after a person has died. Even today dissection often is used for studying the relation between the brain and behavior. Researchers look carefully at the behavior of people who show signs of brain damage while they are alive (Wilson, 2003). The researchers document behavior in these case studies of patients as thoroughly as possible (Fawcett, Rosser, & Dunnett, 2001). Later, after the patients die, the researchers examine the patients' brains for *lesions*—areas where body tissue has been damaged, such as from injury or disease. Then the researchers infer that the lesioned locations may be related to the behavior that was affected. The case of Phineas Gage, discussed in Chapter 1, was explored through these methods.

In this way, researchers may trace a link between an observed type of behavior and anomalies in a particular location in the brain. An early example is Paul Broca's (1824–1880) famous patient, Tan (so named because that was the only syllable he was capable of uttering). Tan had severe speech problems. These problems were linked to lesions in an area of the frontal lobe now called *Broca's area*. This area is involved in certain functions of speech production. In more recent times, postmortem examinations of victims of Alzheimer's disease (an illness that causes devastating losses of memory; see Chapter 5) have led researchers to identify some of the brain structures involved in memory (e.g., the hippocampus, described in a subsequent subsection of this chapter). These examinations also have identified some of the microscopic aberrations associated with the disease process (e.g., distinctive tangled fibers in the brain tissue). Although lesioning techniques provide the basic foundation for understanding the relation of the brain to behavior, they are limited in that they cannot be performed on the living brain. As a result, they do not offer insights into more specific physiological processes of the brain. For this kind of information, we need *in vivo* techniques such as, but not limited to, those described next.

Animal Studies

Scientists also want to understand the physiological processes and functions of the living brain. To study the changing activity of the living brain, scientists must use *in vivo* research. Many early *in vivo* techniques were performed exclusively on animals. For example, Nobel Prize–winning research on visual perception arose from *in vivo* studies investigating the electrical activity of individual cells in particular regions of the brains of animals (Hubel & Wiesel, 1963, 1968, 1979; see Chapter 3).

In these kinds of studies, microelectrodes are inserted into the brain of an animal (usually a monkey or cat). They obtain *single-cell recordings* of the activity of a single neuron in the brain. In such recordings, researchers insert a very thin electrode next to a single neuron. They then record the changes in electrical activity that occur in the cell. This technique can be used only in laboratory animals, not in humans, because no safe way has yet been devised to perform such recordings in humans. In this way, scientists can measure the effects of certain kinds of stimuli, such as visually presented lines, on the activity of individual neurons. Other animal studies include selective lesioning—surgically removing or damaging part of the brain—to observe resulting functional deficits (Al'bertin, Mulder, & Wiener, 2003; Mohammed, Jonsson, & Archer, 1986). Obviously, these techniques cannot be used on human participants. Moreover, we cannot simultaneously record the activity of every neuron. Generalizations based on these studies are somewhat limited. Therefore an array of less invasive imaging techniques for use with humans has been developed. These techniques are described in the following section.

Electrical Recordings

Event-Related Potentials

Researchers and practitioners (e.g., psychologists and physicians) often record electrical activity in the brain. This activity appears as waves of various widths (frequencies) and heights (intensities). **Electroencephalograms (EEGs)** are recordings of the electrical frequencies and intensities of the living brain, typically recorded over relatively long periods (Picton & Mazaheri, 2003). Through EEGs, it is possible to study brainwave activity indicative of changing mental states such as deep sleep or dreaming. To obtain EEG recordings, electrodes are placed at various points along the surface of the scalp. The electrical activity of underlying brain areas is then recorded. Therefore, the information is not well localized to specific cells. Rather, it is very sensitive to changes over time. For example, EEG recordings taken during sleep reveal changing patterns of electrical activity involving the whole brain. Different patterns emerge during dreaming versus deep sleep.

To relate electrical activity to a particular event or task (e.g., seeing a flash of light or listening to sentences), EEG waves can be averaged over a large number (e.g., 100) of trials to reveal event-related potentials (ERPs). An **event-related potential** is the record of a small change in the brain's electrical activity in response to a stimulating event. The fluctuation typically lasts a mere fraction of a second. ERPs provide very good information about the time-course of task-related brain activity by averaging out activity that is not task related. ERPs are identified by placing a series of electrodes on a person's head and then recording the electrical activity of the brain through the electrodes. The resulting wave forms show characteristic spikes related to the timing of electrical activity, but they reveal only very general information about the location of that activity (because of low spatial resolution, limited by the placement of scalp electrodes).

The ERP technique has been used in a wide variety of studies. For example, some studies of intelligence have attempted to relate particular characteristics of ERPs to scores on intelligence tests (e.g., Caryl, 1994). The examination of language processing has also benefited from the use of ERP methods. In studies examining reading, researchers' ability to measure brain changes during specific time intervals has allowed us to learn about how we understand sentences (Kuperberg & associates, 2006). Developmental changes in cognitive abilities have also been examined through ERP methods. These experiments have led to a more nearly complete understanding of the relationship between brain and cognitive development (Taylor & Baldeweg, 2002). Furthermore, the high degree of temporal resolution afforded by ERPs can be used to complement other techniques. For example, ERPs and positron emission tomography (PET; discussed next) were used to pinpoint areas involved in word association (Posner & Raichle, 1994). Using ERPs, the investigators found that participants showed increased activity in certain parts of the brain (left lateral frontal

Michael Posner is a professor of psychology emeritus at the University of Oregon. His ground-breaking research has provided strong evidence of links between cognitive operations and localized brain activity. His work has helped to establish joint cognitive experimental and biological approaches to higher brain function.

cortex, left posterior cortex, and right insular cortex) when they made rapid associations to given words. Another study showed that decreases in electrical potentials are twice as great for tones that are attended to as for tones that are ignored (see Phelps, 1999). As with any technique, EEGs and ERPs provide only a glimpse of brain activity. They are most helpful when used in conjunction with other techniques to converge on particular brain areas involved in cognition.

Static Imaging Techniques

Psychologists also use various techniques for obtaining still images revealing the structures of the brain (Buckner, 2000a; Posner & Raichle, 1994; Rosen, Buckner, & Dale, 1998; Figure 2.2 and Table 2.2). These techniques include angiograms, computed tomography (CT) scans, and magnetic resonance imaging scans. The X-ray–based techniques (angiogram and CT scan) allow for the observation of large abnormalities of the brain, such as damage resulting from strokes or tumors. However, they are limited in their resolution and cannot provide much information about smaller lesions and aberrations.

Probably the still-image technique of greatest interest to cognitive psychologists is the **magnetic resonance imaging (MRI)** scan, a technique for revealing high-resolution images of the structure of the living brain by computing and analyzing magnetic changes in the energy of the orbits of nuclear particles in the molecules of the body. It facilitates the detection of lesions *in vivo*, such as lesions associated with particular disorders of language use. In MRI, a strong magnetic field is passed through the brain of a patient. A scanner detects various patterns of electromagnetic changes in the atoms of the brain (Malonek & Grinvald, 1996; Ugurbil, 1999). These molecular changes are analyzed by a computer to produce a three-dimensional picture of the brain. This picture includes detailed information about brain structures. For example, MRI has been used to show that musicians who play string instruments such as the violin or the cello tend to have an expansion of the brain in an area of the right hemisphere that controls left-hand movement (because control of hands is contralateral, with the right side of the brain controlling the left hand, and vice versa) (Münte, Altenmüller, & Jäncke, 2002). We sometimes tend to view the brain as controlling what we can do. This study is a good example of how what we do—our experience—can affect the development of the brain. The MRI technique is relatively expensive, however. Moreover, it does not provide much information about physiological processes (Figure 2.3). The final two techniques, discussed in the following section, do provide such information.

Metabolic Imaging

Metabolic imaging techniques rely on changes that take place within the brain as a result of increased consumption of glucose and oxygen in active areas of the brain. The basic idea is that active areas in the brain consume more glucose and oxygen than do inactive areas during some tasks. An area specifically required by one task ought to be more active during that task than during more generalized processing. Scientists attempt to pinpoint specialized areas for a task by using the subtraction method. This method involves subtracting activity during a more general task from activity during the task of interest. The resulting activity then is analyzed statistically.

FIGURE 2.2

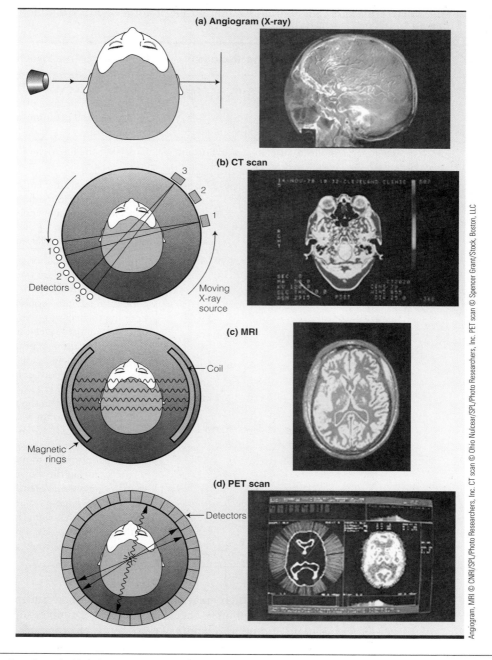

Various techniques have been developed to picture the structures—and sometimes the processes—of the brain. (a) A brain angiogram highlights the blood vessels of the brain. (b) A CT image of a brain uses a series of rotating scans (one of which is pictured here) to produce a three-dimensional view of brain structures. (c) A rotating series of MRI scans (one of which is pictured here) shows a clearer three-dimensional picture of brain structures than CT scans show. (d) These still photographs of PET scans of a brain show different metabolic processes during different activities. PET scans permit the study of brain physiology.

TABLE 2.2	Major Structures and Functions of the Brain

The forebrain, midbrain, and hindbrain contain structures that perform essential functions for survival, as well as for high-level thinking and feeling.

REGION OF THE BRAIN	MAJOR STRUCTURES WITHIN THE REGIONS	FUNCTIONS OF THE STRUCTURES
Forebrain	**Cerebral cortex** (outer layer of the cerebral hemispheres)	Involved in receiving and processing sensory information, thinking, other cognitive processing, and planning and sending motor information
	Basal ganglia (collections of nuclei and neural fibers)	Crucial to the function of the motor system
	Limbic systems (hippocampus, amygdala, and septum)	Involved in learning, emotions, and motivation (in particular, the hippocampus influences learning and memory, the amygdala influences anger and aggression, and the septum influences anger and fear)
	Thalamus	Primary relay station for sensory information coming into the brain; transmits information to the correct regions of the cerebral cortex through projection fibers that extend from the thalamus to specific regions of the cortex; comprises several nuclei (groups of neurons) that receive specific kinds of sensory information and project that information to specific regions of the cerebral cortex, including four key nuclei for sensory information: (1) from the visual receptors, via optic nerves, to the visual cortex, permitting us to see; (2) from the auditory receptors, via auditory nerves, to the auditory cortex, permitting us to hear; (3) from sensory receptors in the somatic nervous system, to the primary somatosensory cortex, permitting us to sense pressure and pain; and (4) from the cerebellum (in the hindbrain) to the primary motor cortex, permitting us to sense physical balance and equilibrium

This analysis determines which areas are responsible for performance of a particular task above and beyond the more general activity. For example, suppose the experimenter wishes to determine which area of the brain is most important for something like retrieval of word meanings. The experimenter would have to subtract activity during a task involving reading of words from activity during a task involving the physical recognition of the letters of words. The difference in activity would be presumed to reflect retrieval of meaning. There is one important caveat to remember about these techniques, however. It is that scientists have no way of determining

TABLE 2.2	Major Structures and Functions of the Brain (cont.)	
REGION OF THE BRAIN	**MAJOR STRUCTURES WITHIN THE REGIONS**	**FUNCTIONS OF THE STRUCTURES**
	Hypothalamus	Controls the endocrine system; controls the autonomic nervous system, such as internal temperature regulation, appetite and thirst regulation, and other key functions; involved in regulation of behavior related to species survival (in particular, fighting, feeding, fleeing, and mating); plays a role in controlling consciousness (see reticular activating system); involved in emotions, pleasure, pain, and stress reactions
Midbrain	*Superior colliculi* (on top)	Involved in vision (especially visual reflexes)
	Inferior colliculi (below)	Involved in hearing
	Reticular activating system (also extends into the hindbrain)	Important in controlling consciousness (sleep arousal), attention, cardiorespiratory function, and movement
	Gray matter, red nucleus, substantia nigra, ventral region	Important in controlling movement
Hindbrain	*Cerebellum*	Essential to balance, coordination, and muscle tone
	Pons (also contains part of the RAS)	Involved in consciousness (sleep and arousal); bridges neural transmissions from one part of the brain to another; involved with facial nerves
	Medulla oblongata	Serves as juncture at which nerves cross from one side of the body to opposite side of the brain; involved in cardiorespiratory function, digestion, and swallowing

whether the net effect of this activity is excitatory or inhibitory (because some neurons are inhibited by other neurons' neurotransmitters). Therefore, the subtraction technique reveals net brain activity for particular areas. It cannot show whether the area's effect is positive or negative. Moreover, the method assumes that activation is purely additive—that it can be discovered through a subtraction method. This description greatly oversimplifies the subtraction method. But it shows at a general level how scientists determine physiological functioning of particular areas using the imaging techniques described next.

FIGURE 2.3

An MRI machine can provide data that show what areas of the brain are involved in different kinds of cognitive processing.

Positron emission tomography (PET) scans measure increases in oxygen consumption in active brain areas during particular kinds of information processing (Buckner & associates, 1996; O'Leary & associates, 2007; Raichle, 1998, 1999). To track their use of oxygen, participants are given a mildly radioactive form of oxygen that emits positrons as it is metabolized. (Positrons are particles that have roughly the same size and mass as electrons, but that are positively rather than negatively charged.) Next, the brain is scanned to detect positrons. A computer analyzes the data to produce images of the physiological functioning of the brain in action. For example, PET scans have been used to show that blood flow increases to the occipital lobe of the brain during visual processing (Posner & associates, 1988). PET scans also have been used for comparatively studying the brains of people who score high versus low on intelligence tests. When high-scoring people are engaged in cognitively demanding tasks, their brains seem to use glucose more efficiently, in highly task-specific areas of the brain. The brains of people with lower scores appear to use glucose more diffusely, across larger regions of the brain (Haier & associates, 1992; see Chapter 13).

Consider PET-based work that illustrates integration of information from various parts of the cortex (Petersen & associates, 1988, 1989; Posner & associates, 1988). Specifically, this work used PET scans to study regional cerebral blood flow during several activities involving the reading of single words. When participants looked at a word on a screen, areas of their visual cortex showed high levels of activity. When they spoke a word, their motor cortex was highly active. When they heard a word spoken, their auditory cortex was activated. When they produced words related to the words they saw (requiring high-level integration of visual, auditory, and motor information), the relevant areas of the cortex showed the greatest amount of activity.

PET scans are not highly precise. The reason is that they require a minimum of about half a minute to produce data regarding glucose consumption. If an area of the brain shows different amounts of activity over the course of time measurement, the activity levels are averaged, potentially leading to conclusions that are less than precise.

Another technique, **functional magnetic resonance imaging (fMRI),** is a neuroimaging technique that uses magnetic fields to construct a detailed representation in three dimensions of levels of activity in various parts of the brain at a given moment in time. This technique builds on MRI (discussed earlier), but it uses increases in oxygen consumption to construct images of brain activity. The basic idea is the same as in PET scans. The fMRI technique does not require the use of radioactive particles. Rather, the participant performs a task while placed inside an MRI machine. This machine typically looks like a tunnel. When someone is wholly or partially inserted in the tunnel, he or she is surrounded by a donut-shaped magnet. Functional MRI creates a magnetic field that induces changes in the particles of oxygen atoms. More active areas draw more oxygenated blood than do less active areas in the brain. The differences in the amounts of oxygen consumed form the basis for fMRI measurements. These measurements then are computer analyzed to provide the most precise information currently available about the physiological functioning of the brain's activity during task performance.

This technique is less invasive than PET. It also has higher temporal resolution—measurements can be taken for activity lasting fractions of a second, rather than only for activity lasting minutes to hours. One major drawback, however, is the expense and novelty of fMRI. Relatively few researchers have access to the required machinery. Moreover, testing of participants is very time consuming. See Figure 2.4 for a direct comparison of various brain imaging techniques in terms of spatial and temporal resolution.

The fMRI technique has been used to identify regions of the brain active in many areas, such as vision (Engel & associates, 1994), attention (Cohen & associates, 1994), language (Gaillard & associates, 2003), and memory (Gabrieli & associates, 1996). For example, fMRI has been used to show that the lateral prefrontal cortex is essential for

FIGURE 2.4

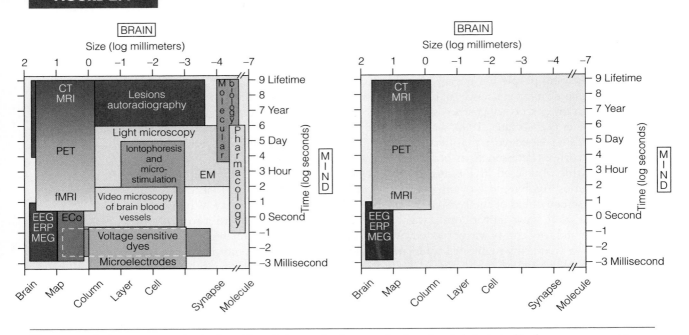

We can view the brain at various levels of spatial resolution ranging from a molecule to the whole brain itself, whereas we can envision the mind as events occurring over times as brief as a few milliseconds—the time it takes one neuron to communicate with another—or as long as a lifetime. Over the past decade or two, scientists have developed a remarkable array of techniques capable of addressing the relationship between brain and mind. Here we graphically summarize the potential contribution of these various techniques to an understanding of this relationship by plotting, logarithmically, the brain on the horizontal axis and the mind on the vertical axis. The techniques then are positioned according to their spatial and temporal precision. Into the left graph we have placed all the available techniques, including X-ray CT, MRI, PET, EEG, ERP, electrocorticography (ECo; EEGs recorded from the brain surface at surgery), and electron microscopy (EM). In the right graph we have eliminated all the techniques that cannot be applied to human subjects. Although the study of the mind–brain relationship in humans clearly will depend on brain-imaging techniques like MRI, PET, and CT in conjunction with electrical techniques, our ultimate understanding of that relationship will require the integration of information from all levels of inquiry. Brain illustration at various levels of spatial resolution from IMAGES OF MIND by Michael I. Posner and Marcus E. Raichle. Copyright 1994, 1997 by Scientific American Library. Reprinted by permission of Henry Holt and Company, LLC.

working memory. This is a part of memory that is used to process information that is actively in use at a given time (McCarthy & associates, 1994). Also, fMRI methods have been applied to the examination of brain changes in patient populations, including persons with schizophrenia and epilepsy (Detre, 2004; Weinberger & associates, 1996).

A related procedure is pharmacological MRI (phMRI). The phMRI combines fMRI methods with the study of psychopharmacological agents. These studies examine the influence and role of particular psychopharmacological agents on the brain. They have allowed the examination of the role of agonists (which strengthen responses) and antagonists (which weaken responses) on the same receptor cells. Furthermore, these studies have allowed for the examination of drugs used for treatment. This examination permits the investigators to predict the responses of patients to neurochemical treatments through examination of the person's brain makeup. Overall, these methods aid in the understanding of brain areas and the effects of psycho-

FIGURE 2.5

Harvard University Gazette photo by Jon Chase

Transcranial magnetic stimulation (TMS).

pharmacological agents on brain functioning (Baliki & associates, 2005; Easton & associates, 2007; Honey & Bullmore, 2004; Kalisch & associates, 2004).

Another procedure related to fMRI is diffusion tensor imaging (DTI). Diffusion tensor imaging enables one to examine the restricted dispersion of water in tissue. This technique has been useful in the mapping of the white matter of the brain and in examining neural circuits. Some applications of this technique include examination of traumatic brain injury, schizophrenia, brain maturation, and multiple sclerosis (Ardekani & associates, 2003; Beyer, Ranga, & Krishnan, 2002; Ramachandra & associates, 2003; Sotak, 2002; Sundgren & associates, 2004).

A recent technique for studying brain activity bypasses some of the problems with other techniques (Walsh & Pascual-Leone, 2005). This new technique is **transcranial magnetic stimulation (TMS),** which temporarily disrupts the normal activity of the brain in a limited area. TMS requires placing a coil on a person's head and then allowing an electrical current to pass though it (Figure 2.5). The current generates a magnetic field. This field disrupts the small area (usually no more than a cubic centimeter) beneath it. The researcher can then look at cognitive functioning when the particular area is disrupted.

Another recent technique is **magnetoencephalography (MEG),** which measures activity of the brain from outside the head by picking up magnetic fields emitted by changes in brain activity. This technique allows localization of brain signals so that it is possible to know what different parts of the brain are doing at different times. It is one of the most precise of the measuring methods. MEG is used to help surgeons locate pathological structures in the brain (Baumgartner, 2000). A recent application of MEG involved patients who reported phantom limb pain. In cases of phantom limb pain, a patient reports pain in a body part that has been removed, for example, a missing foot. It has been noted that when certain areas of the brain are stimulated, phantom limb pain is reduced. MEG has been used to examine the changes in brain activity before, during, and after electrical stimulation. These changes in brain activity corresponded with changes in the experience of phantom limb pain (Kringelbach & associates, 2007).

Current techniques still do not provide unambiguous mappings of particular functions to particular brain structures, regions, or even processes. Rather, we have found that some discrete structures, regions, or processes of the brain appear to be involved in particular cognitive functions. Our current understanding of how particular cognitive functions are linked to particular brain structures or processes allows us only to infer suggestive indications of some kind of relationship. Through sophisticated analyses, we can infer increasingly precise relationships. But we are not yet at a point where we can determine the specific cause–effect relationship between a given brain structure or process and a particular cognitive function. Particular functions may be influenced by multiple structures, regions, or processes of the brain. Finally, these techniques provide the best information only in conjunction with other experimental techniques for understanding the complexities of cognitive functioning. These combinations generally are completed with human participants. However, some researchers have combined *in vivo* studies in animals with brain-imaging techniques (Dedeogle & associates, 2004; Kornblum & associates, 2000; Logothetis, 2004).

Cognition in the Brain: Cerebral Cortex and Other Structures

So far, we have discussed how scientists determine the structure and function of the brain using various postmortem and *in vivo* techniques. Now we discuss what scientists have discovered about the supreme organ of the nervous system, the human brain. The brain can be viewed as being divided into three major regions: forebrain, midbrain, and hindbrain (Figure 2.6; see Table 2.2). These labels do not correspond exactly to locations of regions in an adult's or even a child's head. Rather, the terms come from the front-to-back physical arrangement of these parts in the nervous system of a developing embryo. Initially, the *forebrain* is generally the farthest forward, toward what becomes the face. The *midbrain* is next in line. And the *hindbrain* is generally farthest from the forebrain, near the back of the neck (Figure 2.7 *a*). In development, the relative orientations change so that the forebrain is almost a cap on top of the midbrain and hindbrain. Nonetheless, the terms still are used to designate areas of the fully developed brain. Figure 2.7 *b* and *c* shows the changing locations and relationships of the forebrain, the midbrain, and the hindbrain over the course of development of the brain. You can see how they develop, from an embryo a few weeks after conception to a fetus of 7 months of age.

FIGURE 2.6

What does a brain actually look like? Here you can see side (a) and top (b) views of a human brain. Subsequent figures and schematic pictures (i.e., simplified diagrams) point out in more detail some of the main features of the brain.

Gross Anatomy of the Brain: Forebrain, Midbrain, Hindbrain

Forebrain

The forebrain is the region of the brain located toward the top and front of the brain (Figure 2.8). It comprises the cerebral cortex, the basal ganglia, the limbic system, the thalamus, and the hypothalamus. The cerebral cortex is the outer layer of the cerebral hemispheres. It plays a vital role in our thinking and other mental processes. It therefore merits a special section. This section follows the present discussion of the major structures and functions of the brain. The basal ganglia (singular, ganglion) are collections of neurons crucial to motor function. Dysfunction of the basal ganglia can result in motor deficits. These deficits include tremors, involuntary movements, changes in posture and muscle tone, and slowness of movement. Deficits are observed in Parkinson's disease and Huntington's disease. Both these diseases entail severe motor symptoms (Rockland, 2000; Shepherd, 1998).

The **limbic system** is important to emotion, motivation, memory, and learning. Animals such as fish and reptiles, which have relatively undeveloped limbic systems, respond to the environment almost exclusively by instinct. Mammals and especially humans have relatively more developed limbic systems. They seem to allow us to suppress instinctive responses (e.g., the impulse to strike someone who accidentally causes us pain). Our limbic systems make us better able to adapt our behaviors flexibly in response to our changing environment. The limbic system comprises three central interconnected cerebral structures. They are the amygdala, the septum, and the hippocampus.

FIGURE 2.7

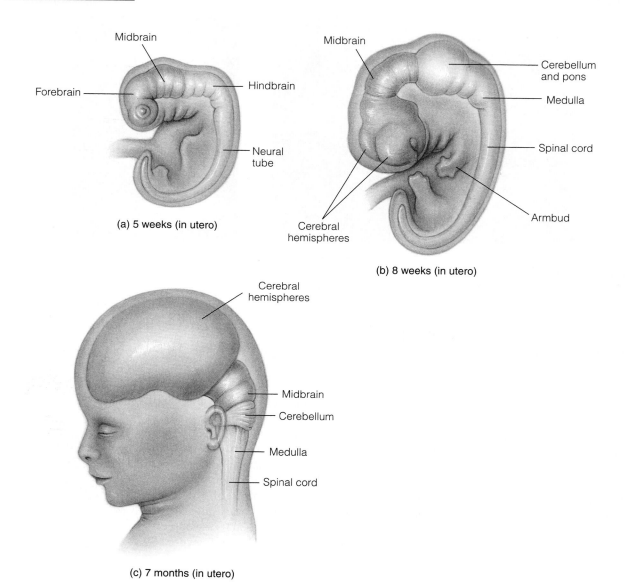

(a) 5 weeks (in utero)

Midbrain

Forebrain

Hindbrain

Neural
tube

(b) 8 weeks (in utero)

Midbrain

Cerebellum
and pons

Medulla

Spinal cord

Armbud

Cerebral
hemispheres

(c) 7 months (in utero)

Cerebral
hemispheres

Midbrain

Cerebellum

Medulla

Spinal cord

Over the course of embryonic and fetal development, the brain becomes more highly specialized and the locations and relative positions of the hindbrain, the midbrain, and the forebrain change from conception to term. From In Search of the Human Mind *by Robert J. Sternberg, copyright © 1995 by Harcourt Brace & Company. Reproduced by permission of the publisher.*

The **amygdala** plays an important role in emotion, especially in anger and ag-gression (Adolphs, 2003). The **septum** is involved in anger and fear. Stimulation of the amygdala commonly results in fear. It can be evidenced in various ways, such as through palpitations, fearful hallucinations, or frightening flashbacks in memory

FIGURE 2.8

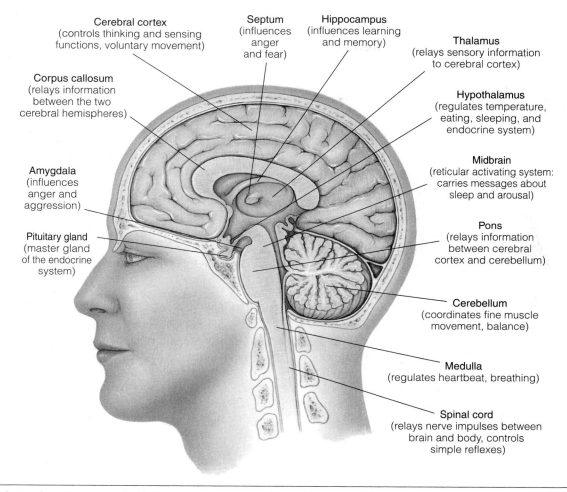

The forebrain, the midbrain, and the hindbrain contain structures that perform essential functions for survival and for high-level thinking and feeling. From In Search of the Human Mind *by Robert J. Sternberg, copyright © 1995 by Harcourt Brace & Company, reproduced by permission of the publisher.*

(Frackowiak & associates, 1997; Gloor, 1997; Rockland, 2000). Damage to (lesions) or removal of the amygdala can result in maladaptive lack of fear. In the case of lesions to the animal brain, the animal approaches potentially dangerous objects without hesitation or fear (Adolphs & associates, 1994; Frackowiak & associates, 1997). The amygdala also has an enhancing effect for the perception of emotional stimuli. In humans, lesions to the amygdala negate this enhancement (Anderson & Phelps, 2001). Additionally, persons with autism display limited activation in the amygdala. A resulting theory of autism suggests that the disorder involves dysfunction of the amygdala (Baron-Cohen & associates, 2000; Howard & associates, 2000; Adolphs, Sears, & Piven, 2001). Two other effects of lesions to the amygdala can

IN THE LAB OF JOHN GABRIELI

Courtesy of Dr. John Gabrieli

Everything we know is either in our genes or learned through experience. Only some experiences, however, are remembered. We quickly forget a great deal of our lives. Selection of what we remember and what we forget is, therefore, important for who we become, what we believe in, and what we are good at. The memories we keep from the past shape our futures.

How does our brain let us selectively remember experiences? I became fascinated with this question when, as a graduate student, I had the opportunity to perform research with perhaps the most famous neuropsychological patient of the twentieth century, H.M. Due to surgery in 1953 intended to treat his epilepsy, H.M. became a globally amnesic patient who could not remember any new events or facts. After a few seconds, he forgot all his new experiences, including materials encountered in laboratory experiments, the most famous public events, and the most important of personal events, such as the deaths of his parents.

H.M.'s surgery involved removal of a number of structures located in the medial, or inner, aspects of the temporal lobes. From his case, it was difficult to know what roles these different structures played in normal memory and whether they played a critical role in the initial recording (encoding) of memories (as opposed to retaining or later retrieving those memories). With noninvasive imaging of brain activity via functional magnetic resonance imaging, we could examine these issues in the normal human brain.

During the imaging session of normal human brains, people saw pictures of indoor or outdoor scenes while we recorded their brain response to each scene. Next, they received an unexpected memory test with scenes from the brain-scanning session and new scenes. Sometimes they correctly recognized a previously presented scene (a remembered experience), but other times they failed to recognize a scene previously viewed (a forgotten experience). The level of brain activity in the parahippocampal cortex, one particular area in the medial temporal lobe, as a person saw each scene predicted whether he or she would later remember or forget that scene. Thus, we could visualize brain activity in a specific brain structure that determined whether current experience was fated to be well remembered in the future or doomed to be forgotten in a few moments. In a way, we could see the birth of a memory and the selective recording of experiences destined to be remembered and influence future behavior.

be visual agnosia (inability to recognize objects) and hypersexuality (Steffanaci, 1999).

The **hippocampus** plays an essential role in memory formation (Eichenbaum, 1999, 2002; Gluck, 1996; Manns & Eichenbaum, 2006; O'Keefe, 2003). It gets its name from the Greek word for "seahorse," its approximate shape. People who have suffered damage to or removal of the hippocampus still can recall existing memories—for example, they can recognize old friends and places—but they are unable to form new memories (relative to the time of the brain damage). New information—new situations, people, and places—remain forever new. **Korsakoff's syndrome** produces loss of memory function. This loss is believed to be associated with deterioration of the hippocampus. The syndrome can result from excessive alcohol use. The case of H.M., to be discussed in Chapter 5, is another illustration of the resulting problems with memory formation due to hippocampus damage. The hippocampus also appears to keep track of where things are and how these things are spatially related to each other. In other words, it monitors what is where (Cain, Boon, & Corco-

TABLE 2.3	Four Major Nuclei of the Thalamus*		
Four key thalamic nuclei relay visual, auditory, somatosensory, and equilibrium-related information			
NAME OF NUCLEUS†	**RECEIVES INFORMATION FROM**	**PROJECTS (TRANSMITS INFORMATION) PRIMARILY TO**	**FUNCTIONAL BENEFIT**
Lateral geniculate nucleus	The visual receptors, via optic nerves	The visual cortex	Permits us to see
Medial geniculate nucleus	The auditory receptors, via auditory nerves	The auditory cortex	Permits us to hear
Ventroposterior nucleus	The somatic nervous system	The primary somatosensory cortex	Permits us to sense pressure and pain
Ventrolateral nucleus	The cerebellum (in the hindbrain)	The primary motor cortex	Permits us to sense physical balance and equilibrium

*Other thalamic nuclei also play important roles.

†The names refer to the relative location of the nuclei within the thalamus: *lateral*, toward the right or left side of the medial nucleus; *ventral*, closer to the belly than to the top of the head; *posterior*, toward the back, behind; *ventroposterior*, bellyward and in the back; *ventrolateral*, bellyward and on the side. Also, *geniculate* means "knee-shaped."

ran, 2006; McClelland, McNaughton, & O'Reilly, 1995; Tulving & Schacter, 1994). Disruption in the hippocampus appears to result in deficits in declarative memory (i.e., memory for pieces of information), but it does not result in deficits in procedural memory (i.e., memory for courses of action) (Rockland, 2000).

The exact role of the hippocampus in memory and memory formation is yet to be determined. One hypothesis is that the hippocampus provides a cognitive map of sorts. The map represents the space an organism needs to navigate (O'Keefe & Nadel, 1978). Another view is that the hippocampus is essential for flexible learning and for seeing the relations among items learned (Eichenbaum, 1997; Squire, 1992). We return to the role of the hippocampus in Chapter 5.

The **thalamus** relays incoming sensory information through groups of neurons that project to the appropriate region in the cortex. Most of the sensory input into the brain passes through the thalamus. It is located approximately in the center of the brain, at about the level of the eyes. To accommodate all the different types of information that must be sorted out, the thalamus is divided into a number of nuclei (groups of neurons of similar function). Each nucleus receives information from specific senses. The information is then relayed to corresponding specific areas in the cerebral cortex. (Table 2.3 includes the names and roles of the various nuclei.) The thalamus also helps in the control of sleep and waking. When the thalamus malfunctions, the result can be pain, tremor, amnesia, impairment of language, and disruptions in waking and sleeping (Rockland, 2000; Steriade, Jones, & McCormick, 1997). In cases of schizophrenia, imaging and *in vivo* studies reveal abnormal changes in the thalamus (Clinton & Meador-Woodruff, 2004).

The **hypothalamus** regulates behavior related to species survival: fighting, feeding, fleeing, and mating. The hypothalamus also is active in regulating emotions and

TABLE 2.4	Cognitive Neuropsychological Methods for Studying Brain Functioning			
METHOD	**PROCEDURE**	**SUITABLE FOR HUMANS?**	**ADVANTAGES**	**DISADVANTAGES**
Single-cell recording	Very thin electrode is inserted next to a single neuron. Changes in electrical activity occurring in the cell are then recorded.	No	Rather precise recording of electrical activity	Cannot be used with humans
EEG	Changes in electrical potentials are recorded via electrodes attached to scalp.	Yes	Relatively noninvasive	Quite imprecise
ERP	Changes in electrical potentials are recorded via electrodes attached to scalp.	Yes	Relatively noninvasive	Does not show actual brain images
PET	Participants ingest a mildly radioactive form of oxygen that emits positrons as it is metabolized. Changes in concentration of positrons in targeted areas of the brain are then measured.	Yes	Shows images of the brain in action	Less useful for fast processes
fMRI	Creates magnetic field that induces changes in the particles of oxygen atoms. More active areas draw more oxygenated blood than do less active areas in the brain. The differences in the amounts of oxygen consumed form the basis for fMRI measurements.	Yes	Shows images of the brain in action; more precise than PET	Requires individual to be placed in uncomfortable scanner for some time
TMS	Involves placing a coil on a person's head and then allowing an electrical current to pass through it. The current generates a magnetic field. This field disrupts the small area (usually no more than a cubic centimeter) beneath it. The researcher can then look at cognitive functioning when the particular area is disrupted.	Yes	Enables researcher to pinpoint how disruption of a particular area of brain affects cognitive functioning	Potentially dangerous if misused
MEG	Involves measuring brain activity through detection of magnetic fields by placing a device over the head.	Yes	Extremely precise spatial and temporal resolution	Requires expensive machine not readily available to researchers

reactions to stress (Malsbury, 2003). It interacts with the limbic system. The small size of the hypothalamus (from Greek *hypo-*, "under"; located at the base of the forebrain, beneath the thalamus) belies its importance in controlling many bodily functions (see Table 2.4 for more information). The hypothalamus also plays a role in sleep. Dysfunction and neural loss within the hypothalamus are noted in cases of narcolepsy, whereby a person falls asleep often and at unpredictable times (Lodi & associates, 2004; Mignot, Taheri, & Nishino, 2002).

Midbrain

The midbrain helps to control eye movement and coordination. The midbrain is more important in nonmammals than in mammals. In nonmammals it is the main source of control for visual and auditory information. In mammals these functions are dominated by the forebrain. Table 2.2 lists several structures (and corresponding functions) of the midbrain. By far the most indispensable of these structures is the **reticular activating system (RAS;** also called the "reticular formation"), a network of neurons essential to the regulation of consciousness (sleep; wakefulness; arousal; attention, to some extent; and such vital functions as heartbeat and breathing) (Sarter, Bruno, & Berntson, 2003).

Actually, the RAS also extends into the hindbrain. Both the RAS and the thalamus are essential to our having any conscious awareness of or control over our existence. The **brainstem** connects the forebrain to the spinal cord. It comprises the hypothalamus, the thalamus, the midbrain, and the hindbrain. A structure called the *periaqueductal gray* (PAG) is in the brainstem. This region seems to be key for certain kinds of adaptive behaviors. Injections of small amounts of excitatory amino acids or, alternatively, electrical stimulation of this area results in any of several responses: an aggressive, confrontational response; avoidance or flight response; heightened defensive reactivity; or reduced reactivity as is experienced after a defeat, when one feels hopeless (Bandler & Shipley, 1994; Rockland, 2000).

Physicians make a determination of brain death based on the function of the brainstem. Specifically, a physician must determine that the brainstem has been damaged so severely that various reflexes of the head (e.g., the pupillary reflex) are absent for more than 12 hours, or the brain must show no electrical activity or cerebral circulation of blood (Berkow, 1992).

Hindbrain

The hindbrain comprises the medulla oblongata, the pons, and the cerebellum.

The **medulla oblongata** controls heart activity and largely controls breathing, swallowing, and digestion. The medulla is also the place at which nerves from the right side of the body cross over to the left side of the brain and nerves from the left side of the body cross over to the right side of the brain. The medulla oblongata is an elongated interior structure located at the point where the spinal cord enters the skull and joins with the brain. The medulla oblongata, which contains part of the RAS, helps to keep us alive.

The **pons** serves as a kind of relay station because it contains neural fibers that pass signals from one part of the brain to another. Its name derives from the Latin for "bridge," as it serves a bridging function. The pons also contains a portion of the RAS and nerves serving parts of the head and face. The **cerebellum** (from Latin, "little brain") controls bodily coordination, balance, and muscle tone, as well as some aspects of memory involving procedure-related movements (see Chapters 7 and 8) (Middleton & Helms Tillery, 2003). The prenatal development of the human brain within each individual roughly corresponds to the evolutionary development of the human brain within the species as a whole. Specifically, the hindbrain is evolutionarily the oldest and most primitive part of the brain. It also is the first part of the brain to develop prenatally. The midbrain is a relatively newer addition to the brain in evolutionary terms. It is the next part of the brain to develop prenatally. Finally, the forebrain is the most recent evolutionary addition to the brain. It is the last of the three portions of the brain to develop prenatally.

Additionally, across the evolutionary development of our species, humans have shown an increasingly greater proportion of brain weight in relation to body weight. However, across the span of development after birth, the proportion of brain weight to body weight declines. The brain weight of a newborn is proportionately much greater in relation to body weight than is the brain weight of an adult. From infancy through adulthood, the development of the brain centers chiefly on the organizational complexity of the connections within the brain. The individual's developmental increases in neural complexity are paralleled by the evolutionary development of our species. But the changing proportion of brain weight to body weight in evolution is not.

For cognitive psychologists, the most important of these evolutionary trends is the increasing neural complexity of the brain. The evolution of the human brain has offered us the increasing ability to exercise voluntary control over behavior. It has also increased our ability to plan and to contemplate alternative courses of action. These ideas are discussed in the next section with respect to the cerebral cortex.

Cerebral Cortex and Localization of Function

The **cerebral cortex** forms a 1- to 3-millimeter layer that wraps the surface of the brain somewhat like the bark of a tree wraps around the trunk. In human beings, the many convolutions, or creases, of the cerebral cortex comprise three different elements. *Sulci* (singular, sulcus) are small grooves. *Fissures* are large grooves. And *gyri* (singular, gyrus) are bulges between adjacent sulci or fissures. These folds greatly increase the surface area of the cortex. If the wrinkly human cortex were smoothed out, it would take up about 2 square feet. The cortex comprises 80% of the human brain (Kolb & Whishaw, 1990). The complexity of brain function increases with the cortical area. The human cerebral cortex enables us to think. Because of it, we can plan, coordinate thoughts and actions, perceive visual and sound patterns, and use language. Without it, we would not be human. The surface of the cerebral cortex is grayish. It is sometimes referred to as *gray matter*. This is because it primarily comprises the grayish neural-cell bodies that process the information that the brain receives and sends. In contrast, the underlying *white matter* of the brain's interior comprises mostly white, myelinated axons.

The cerebral cortex forms the outer layer of the two halves of the brain—the left and right cerebral hemispheres (Davidson & Hugdahl, 1995; Galaburda & Rosen, 2003; Gazzaniga & Hutsler, 1999; Hellige, 1993, 1995; Levy, 2000; Mangun & associates, 1994). Although the two hemispheres appear to be quite similar, they function differently. The left cerebral hemisphere is specialized for some kinds of activity. The right cerebral hemisphere is specialized for other kinds. For example, receptors in the skin on the right side of the body generally send information through the medulla to areas in the left hemisphere in the brain. The receptors on the left side generally transmit information to the right hemisphere. Similarly, the left hemisphere of the brain directs the motor responses on the right side of the body. The right hemisphere directs responses on the left side of the body. However, not all information transmission is **contralateral**—from one side to another (contra-, "opposite"; lateral, "side"). Some **ipsilateral** transmission—on the same side—occurs as well. For example, odor information from the right nostril goes primarily to the right side of the brain. About half the information from the right eye goes to the right side of the brain. In addition to this general tendency for contralateral specialization, the hemispheres also communicate directly with one another. The **corpus callosum** is a dense aggregate of neural fibers connecting the two cerebral hemispheres (see Witelson, Kigar, & Walter, 2003). It allows transmission of information back and forth. Once information has reached one hemisphere, the corpus callosum transfers it to the other hemisphere. If the corpus callosum is cut, the two **cerebral hemispheres**—the two halves of the brain—cannot communicate with each other. Although some functioning, like language, is highly lateralized, most functioning—even language—depends in large part on integration of the two hemispheres of the brain.

Hemispheric Specialization

How did psychologists find out that the two hemispheres have different responsibilities? The study of hemispheric specialization in the human brain can be traced back to Marc Dax, a country doctor in France. By 1836, Dax had treated more than 40 patients suffering from *aphasia*—loss of speech—as a result of brain damage. Dax noticed a relationship between the loss of speech and the side of the brain in which damage had occurred. Dax saw, in studying his patients' brains after death, that in every case there had been damage to the left hemisphere of the brain. He was not able to find even one case of speech loss resulting from damage to the right hemisphere only.

In 1861, French scientist Paul Broca claimed that an autopsy revealed that an aphasic stroke patient had a lesion in the left cerebral hemisphere of the brain. By 1864, Broca was convinced that the left hemisphere of the brain is critical in speech, a view that has held up over time. The specific part of the brain that Broca identified, now called *Broca's area*, contributes to speech (Figure 2.9). Broca's area also plays a pivotal role in imitation (Heiser & associates, 2003). Another important early researcher, German neurologist Carl Wernicke, studied language-deficient patients who could speak but whose speech made no sense. Like Broca, he traced language ability to the left hemisphere. He studied a different precise location, now known as *Wernicke's area*, which contributes to language comprehension (see Figure 2.9).

Karl Spencer Lashley, often described as the father of neuropsychology, started studying localization in 1915. He found that implantations of crudely built electrodes in apparently identical locations in the brain yielded different results. Different locations sometimes paradoxically yielded the same results (e.g., see Lashley, 1950). Subsequent researchers, using more sophisticated electrodes and measurement procedures, have found that specific locations do correlate with specific motor responses across many test sessions. Apparently, Lashley's research was limited by the technology available to him at the time.

Despite the valuable early contributions by Broca, Lashley, and others, the individual most responsible for modern theory and research on hemispheric specialization was Nobel Prize–winning psychologist Roger Sperry. Sperry (1964) argued that each hemisphere behaves in many respects like a separate brain. In a classic experiment

FIGURE 2.9

Strangely, although people with lesions in Broca's area cannot speak fluently, they can use their voices to sing or shout. From Introduction to Psychology, *11/e, by Richard Atkinson, Rita Atkinson, Daryl Bem, Ed Smith, and Susan Nolen Hoeksema, copyright © 1995 by Harcourt Brace & Company, reproduced by permission of the publisher.*

that supports this contention, Sperry and his colleagues severed the corpus callosum connecting the two hemispheres of a cat's brain. They then proved that information presented visually to one cerebral hemisphere of the cat was not recognizable to the other hemisphere. Similar work on monkeys indicated the same discrete performance of each hemisphere (Sperry, 1964).

Some of the most interesting information about how the human brain works, and especially about the respective roles of the hemispheres, has emerged from studies of humans with epilepsy in whom the corpus callosum has been severed. Surgically severing this neurological bridge prevents epileptic seizures from spreading from one hemisphere to another. This procedure thereby drastically reduces the severity of the seizures. However, this procedure also results in a loss of communication between the two hemispheres. It is as if the person has two separate specialized brains processing different information and performing separate functions.

Split-brain patients are people who have undergone operations severing the corpus callosum. Split-brain research reveals fascinating possibilities regarding the ways we think. Many in the field have argued that language is localized in the left hemisphere. Spatial visualization ability appears to be largely localized in the right hemisphere (Farah, 1988a, 1988b; Gazzaniga, 1985; Zaidel, 1983). Spatial-orientation tasks also seem to be localized in the right hemisphere (Vogel, Bowers, & Vogel, 2003). It appears that roughly 90% of the adult population has language functions that are predominantly localized within the left hemisphere. More than 95% of right-handers and about 70% of left-handers have left-hemisphere dominance for language. In people who lack left-hemisphere processing, language development in the right hemisphere retains phonemic and semantic abilities, but it is deficient in syntactic competence (Gazzaniga & Hutsler, 1999). Jerre Levy (one of Sperry's students) and her colleagues (Levy, Trevarthen, & Sperry, 1972) have probed the link between the cerebral hemispheres and visuospatial versus language-oriented tasks using participants who have undergone split-brain surgery.

The left hemisphere is important not only in language but also in movement. People with *apraxia*—disorders of skilled movements—often have had damage to the left hemisphere. Such people have lost the ability to carry out familiar purposeful movements (Gazzaniga & Hutsler, 1999). Another role of the left hemisphere is to examine past experiences to find patterns. Finding patterns is an important step in the generation of hypotheses. Therefore, the left hemisphere also plays an important role in this function (Wolford, Miller, & Gazzaniga, 2000).

The right hemisphere is largely "mute" (Levy, 2000). It has little grammatical or phonetic understanding. But it does have very good semantic knowledge. It also is involved in practical language use. People with right-hemisphere damage tend to have deficits in following conversations or stories. They also have difficulties in making inferences from context and in understanding metaphorical or humorous speech (Levy, 2000). The right hemisphere also plays a primary role in self-recognition. In particular, the right hemisphere seems to be responsible for the identification of one's own face (Platek & associates, 2004).

In studies such as the one shown in Figure 2.10, split-brain patients typically are unaware that they saw conflicting information in the two halves of the picture. When asked to give an answer about what they saw in words, they report that they saw the image in the right half of the picture. Recall the contralateral association between hemisphere and side of the body. Given this, it seems that the left hemisphere is controlling their verbal processing (speaking) of visual information. Consider in contrast what happens when they are asked to use the fingers of the left hand (which contralaterally sends and receives information to and from the right hemisphere) to point to what they saw. Participants then choose the image from the left half of the picture. This finding indicates that the right hemisphere appears to control spatial processing (pointing) of visual information. Thus, the task that the participants are asked to perform is crucial in determining what image the participant thinks was shown.

FIGURE 2.10

Research on split-brain patients reveals that each hemisphere of the brain processes images and other information distinctively. (a) A composite photograph of two different faces is flashed before a split-brain subject. (b) When shown a group of photographs and asked to pick out a person shown in the composite, the subject will say it is the face from the right half of the composite. (c) However, if asked to point out which one the subject originally saw, she will indicate the picture from the left side of the composite. (After Levy, Trevarthen, & Sperry, 1972)

(a)

"Whom did you see?"
"It was Cher."   (b)

"Point to the person you saw"   (c)

© Kobal Collection

In one study, the participant is asked to focus his or her gaze on the center of screen. Then a chimeric face (a face showing the left side of the face of one person and the right side of another) is flashed on the screen. The participant then is asked to identify what he or she saw, either by speaking or by pointing to one of several normal (not chimeric) faces.

Michael Gazzaniga—another of Sperry's students—has dissociated himself from the position of his former teacher, Sperry, and of his colleagues, such as Levy. Gazzaniga disagrees with their assertion that the two hemispheres function completely independently. Nonetheless, he still holds that each hemisphere serves a complementary role. For instance, according to Gazzaniga, there is no language processing in the right hemisphere (except in rare cases of early brain damage to the left hemisphere). Rather, only visuospatial processing occurs in the right hemisphere. As an example, Gazzaniga has found that before split-brain surgery, people can draw three-dimensional representations of cubes with each hand (Gazzaniga & LeDoux, 1978). After surgery, however, they can draw a reasonable-looking cube only with the left hand. In each patient, the right hand draws pictures unrecognizable either as cubes or as three-dimensional objects. This finding is important because of the contralateral association between each side of the body and the opposite hemisphere of the brain. Recall that the right hemisphere controls the left hand. The left hand is the only one that a split-brain patient can use for drawing recognizable figures. This experiment thus supports the contention that the right hemisphere is dominant in our comprehension and exploration of spatial relations.

Gazzaniga (1985) argues that the brain, and especially the right hemisphere of the brain, is organized into relatively independent functioning units that work in parallel.

According to Gazzaniga, each of the many discrete units of the mind operates relatively independently of the others. These operations are often outside of conscious awareness. While these various independent and often subconscious operations are taking place, the left hemisphere tries to assign interpretations to these operations. Sometimes the left hemisphere perceives that the individual is behaving in a way that does not intrinsically make any particular sense. It still finds a way to assign some meaning to that behavior.

In addition to studying hemispheric differences in language and spatial relations, researchers have tried to determine whether the two hemispheres think in ways that differ from one another. Levy (1974) has found some evidence that the left hemisphere tends to process information analytically (piece-by-piece, usually in a sequence). She argues that the right hemisphere tends to process it holistically (as a whole).

Lobes of the Cerebral Hemispheres

For practical purposes, four **lobes** divide the cerebral hemispheres and cortex into four parts. These lobes are not distinct units. Rather, they are largely arbitrary anatomical regions. Particular functions have been identified with each lobe. But the lobes also interact. The four lobes, named after the bones of the skull lying directly over them (Figure 2.11), are the frontal, parietal, temporal, and occipital lobes. The naming of the lobes is a function of bones in the skull that encase them, so their names and even the particular division are both fairly arbitrary. The lobes are involved in numerous functions. Our discussion of them here describes only part of what they do.

The **frontal lobe,** toward the front of the brain, is associated with motor processing and higher thought processes, such as abstract reasoning, problem solving, planning, and judgment (Stuss & Floden, 2003). It tends to be involved when sequences of thoughts or actions are called for. It is critical in producing speech. The *prefrontal cortex,* the region toward the front of the frontal lobe, is involved in complex motor

FIGURE 2.11

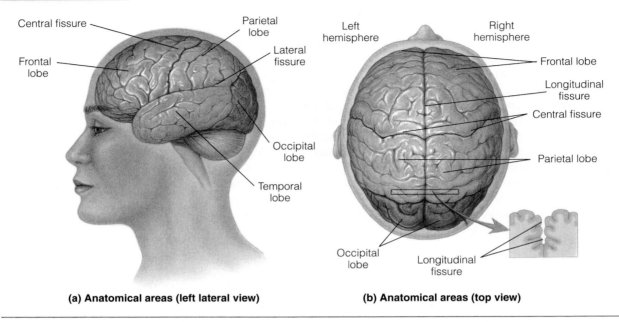

(a) Anatomical areas (left lateral view)   **(b) Anatomical areas (top view)**

The cortex is divided into the frontal, parietal, temporal, and occipital lobes. The lobes have specific functions but also interact to perform complex processes. From In Search of the Human Mind *by Robert J. Sternberg, copyright © 1995 by Harcourt Brace & Company, reproduced by permission of the publisher.*

control and tasks that require integration of information over time (Gazzaniga, Ivry, & Mangun, 2002).

The **parietal lobe,** at the upper back portion of the brain, is associated with somatosensory processing. It receives inputs from the neurons regarding touch, pain, temperature sense, and limb position when you are perceiving space and your relationship to it—how you are situated relative to the space you are occupying (Culham, 2003; Gazzaniga, Ivrey, & Mangun, 2002). The parietal lobe is also involved in consciousness and paying attention. If you are paying attention to what you are reading, your parietal lobe is activated.

The **temporal lobe,** directly under your temples, is associated with auditory processing (Murray, 2003) and comprehending language. It is also involved in your retention of visual memories. For example, if you are trying to keep in memory Figure 2.11, then your temporal lobe is involved. The temporal lobe also matches new things you see to what you have retained in visual memory.

The **occipital lobe** is associated with visual processing (De Weerd, 2003b). The occipital lobe contains numerous visual areas, each specialized to analyze specific aspects of a scene, including color, motion, location, and form (Gazzaniga, Ivrey, & Mangun, 2002). As you read this text, your occipital lobe is involved in your perception of the words in front of you.

Projection areas are the areas in the lobes in which sensory processing occurs. This name reflects the fact that the nerves contain sensory information going to the thalamus. It is from here that the sensory information is projected to the appropriate area in the relevant lobe. Similarly, the projection areas project motor information downward through the spinal cord to the appropriate muscles via the peripheral nervous system (PNS). Now let us consider the lobes, and especially the frontal lobe, in somewhat more detail.

The frontal lobe, located toward the front of the head (the face), plays a role in judgment, problem solving, personality, and intentional movement. It contains the **primary motor cortex,** which specializes in the planning, control, and execution of movement, particularly of movement involving any kind of delayed response. If your motor cortex were electrically stimulated, you would react by moving a corresponding body part. The nature of the movement would depend on where in the motor cortex your brain had been stimulated. Control of the various kinds of body movements is located contralaterally on the primary motor cortex. A similar inverse mapping occurs from top to bottom. The lower extremities of the body are represented on the upper (toward the top of the head) side of the motor cortex, and the upper part of the body is represented on the lower side of the motor cortex.

Information going to neighboring parts of the body also comes from neighboring parts of the motor cortex. Thus, the motor cortex can be mapped to show where and in what proportions different parts of the body are represented in the brain (Figure 2.12).

The three other lobes are located farther away from the front of the head. These lobes specialize in various kinds of sensory and perceptual activity. For example, in the parietal lobe, the **primary somatosensory cortex** receives information from the senses about pressure, texture, temperature, and pain. It is located right behind the frontal lobe's primary motor cortex. If your somatosensory cortex were electrically stimulated, you probably would report feeling as if you had been touched (Figure 2.13).

From looking at the homunculi (see Figures 2.12 and 2.13), you can see that the relationship of function to form applies in the development of the motor and somatosensory cortex regions. The more need we have for use, sensitivity, and fine control in a particular body part, the larger the area of cortex generally devoted to that part. For example, we humans are tremendously reliant on our hands and faces in our interactions with the world. We show correspondingly large proportions of the cerebral cortex devoted to sensation in, and motor response by, our hands and face. Conversely, we rely relatively little on our toes both for movement and information gathering. As a result, the toes represent a relatively small area on both the primary motor and somatosensory cortices.

The region of the cerebral cortex pertaining to hearing is located in the temporal lobe, below the parietal lobe. This lobe performs complex auditory analysis. This kind of analysis is needed, for example, in understanding human speech or listening to a symphony. The lobe also is specialized. Some parts are more sensitive to sounds of higher pitch, others to sounds of lower pitch. The auditory region is primarily contralateral, although both sides of the auditory area have at least some representation from each ear. If your auditory cortex were stimulated electrically, you would report having heard some sort of sound.

The visual region of the cerebral cortex is primarily in the occipital lobe. Some neural fibers carrying visual information travel ipsilaterally from the left eye to the left

FIGURE 2.12

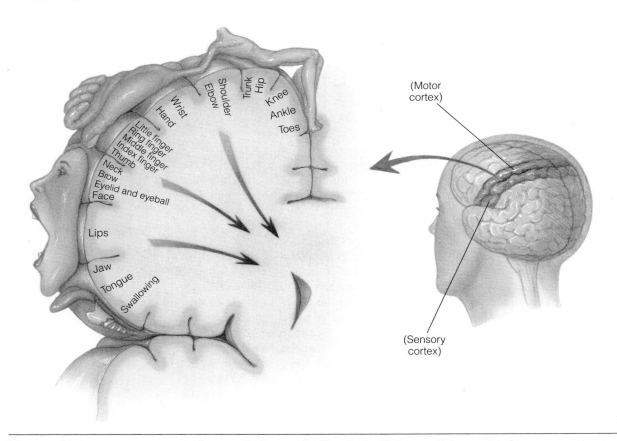

This map of the primary motor cortex is often termed a homunculus (from Latin, "little person") because it is drawn as a cross section of the cortex surrounded by the figure of a small upside-down person whose body parts map out a proportionate correspondence to the parts of the cortex.

cerebral hemisphere and from the right eye to the right cerebral hemisphere. Other fibers cross over the *optic chiasma* (from Greek, "visual X" or "visual intersection") and go contralaterally to the opposite hemisphere (Figure 2.14). In particular, neural fibers go from the left side of the visual field for each eye to the right side of the visual cortex. Complementarily, the nerves from the right side of each eye's visual field send information to the left side of the visual cortex.

The brain typically makes up only one fortieth of the weight of an adult human body. Nevertheless, it uses about one fifth of the circulating blood, one fifth of the available glucose, and one fifth of the available oxygen. It is, however, the supreme organ of cognition. Understanding both its structure and function, from the neural to the cerebral levels of organization, is vital to an understanding of cognitive psychology. The recent development of the field of cognitive neuroscience, with its focus on localization of function, reconceptualizes the mind–body question discussed in the beginning of this chapter. The question has changed from "Where is the mind located in the body?" to

FIGURE 2.13

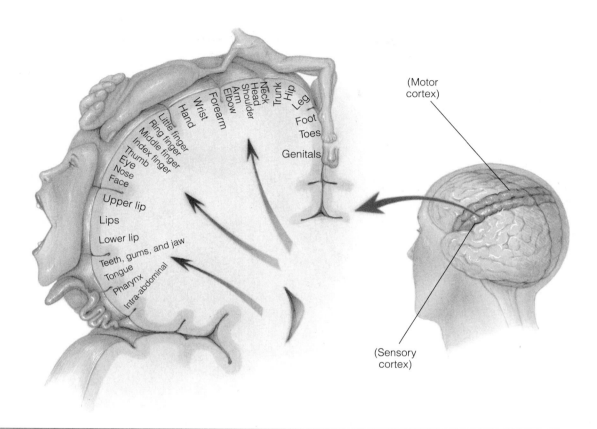

As with the primary motor cortex in the frontal lobe, a homunculus of the somatosensory cortex maps, in inverted form, the parts of the body from which the cortex receives information. From In Search of the Human Mind by Robert J. Sternberg, copyright © 1995 by Harcourt Brace & Company, reproduced by permission of the publisher.

"Where are particular cognitive operations located in the nervous system?" Throughout the rest of the text, we return to these questions in reference to particular cognitive operations as these operations are discussed in more detail in subsequent chapters.

Brodmann Areas

The cerebral cortex can be divided into different modules referred to as *Brodmann's areas*. These areas, applying to other species besides humans, can provide convenient ways of localizing cortical function. In humans, there are 52 such areas. For example, area 4 encompasses primary motor cortex, and area 17, the primary visual cortex.

Brain Disorders

A number of brain disorders can impair cognitive functioning. The summary here is based in part on the work of Gazzaniga, Ivrey, and Mangun (2002).

FIGURE 2.14

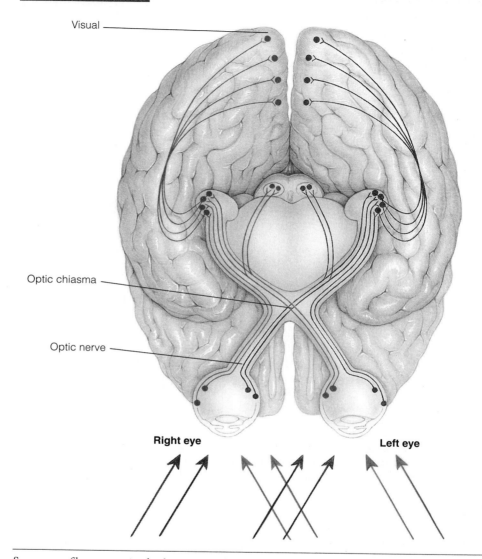

Visual

Optic chiasma

Optic nerve

Right eye

Left eye

Some nerve fibers carry visual information ipsilaterally from each eye to each cerebral hemisphere; other fibers cross the optic chiasma and carry visual information contralaterally to the opposite hemisphere. From In Search of the Human Mind *by Robert J. Sternberg, copyright © 1995 by Harcourt Brace & Company, reproduced by permission of the publisher.*

Stroke

Vascular disorder is a brain disorder caused by a stroke. Strokes occur when the flow of blood to the brain undergoes a sudden disruption. People who experience stroke typically show marked loss of cognitive functioning. The nature of the loss depends on the area of the brain that is affected by the stroke. There may be paralysis, pain, numbness, a loss of speech, a loss of language comprehension, impairments in thought processes, a loss of movement in parts of the body, or other symptoms.

Two different kinds of stroke may occur (*NINDS stroke information page*, 2004). The first kind is an *ischemic stroke*. Usually such a stroke occurs when a buildup of fatty tissue occurs in blood vessels over a period of years, and a piece of this tissue breaks off and gets lodged in arteries of the brain. Ischemic strokes can be treated by clot-busting drugs. The second kind of stroke is a *hemorrhagic stroke*, which occurs when a blood vessel in the brain suddenly breaks. Blood then spills into surrounding tissue. As the blood spills over, brain cells in the affected areas begin to die. This death is either from the lack of oxygen and nutrients or from the rupture of the vessel and the sudden spilling of blood. Symptoms of stroke occur immediately on the occurrence of stroke.

Typical symptoms include:

- Numbness or weakness in the face, arms, or legs (especially on one side of the body)
- Confusion, difficulty speaking or understanding speech
- Vision disturbances in one or both eyes
- Dizziness, trouble walking, loss of balance or coordination
- Severe headache with no known cause
  (*NINDS stroke information page*, 2004)

The prognosis for stroke victims depends on the type and severity of damage.

Brain Tumors

Brain tumors, also called *neoplasms*, can affect cognitive functioning in very serious ways. Tumors can occur in either the gray or white matter of the brain. Tumors of the white matter are more common (Gazzaniga, Ivrey, & Mangun, 2002). Consider some basic facts about brain tumors (*What you need to know about brain tumors*, 2004).

Two types of brain tumors can occur. Primary brain tumors start in the brain. Most childhood brain tumors are of this type. Secondary brain tumors start somewhere else in the body, such as in the lungs. Brain tumors can be either benign or malignant. Benign tumors do not contain cancer cells. They typically can be removed and will not grow back. Cells from benign tumors do not invade surrounding cells or spread to other parts of the body. However, if they press against sensitive areas of the brain, they can result in serious cognitive impairments. They also can be life threatening, unlike benign tumors in most other parts of the body. Malignant brain tumors, unlike benign ones, contain cancer cells. They are more serious and usually threaten the victim's life. They often grow quickly. They also tend to invade surrounding healthy brain tissue. In rare instances, malignant cells may break away and cause cancer in other parts or the body. Following are the most common symptoms of brain tumors:

- Headaches (usually worse in the morning)
- Nausea or vomiting
- Changes in speech, vision, or hearing
- Problems balancing or walking

- Changes in mood, personality, or ability to concentrate
- Problems with memory
- Muscle jerking or twitching (seizures or convulsions)
- Numbness or tingling in the arms or legs
  (*What you need to know about brain tumors*, 2004)

The diagnosis of brain tumor is typically made through neurological examination, CT scan, and/or MRI. The most common form of treatment is a combination of surgery, radiation, and chemotherapy.

Head Injuries

Head injuries result from many causes, such as car accident, contact with a hard object, and bullet wound. Head injuries are of two types (Gazzaniga, Ivrey, & Mangun, 2002). In *closed-head injuries*, the skull remains intact but there is damage to the brain, typically from the mechanical force of a blow to the head. Slamming one's head against a windshield in a car accident might result in such an injury. In *open-head injuries*, the skull does not remain intact but rather is penetrated, for example, by a bullet.

Head injuries are surprisingly common. Roughly 700,000 North Americans suffer such injuries each year. Between 70,000 and 90,000 are left permanently disabled (*The anatomy of a head injury*, 2004). Loss of consciousness is a sign that there has been some degree of damage to the brain as a result of the injury. Damage resulting from head injury can include spastic movements, difficulty in swallowing, and slurring of speech, among many other cognitive problems. Immediate symptoms of a head injury include:

- Unconsciousness
- Abnormal breathing
- Obvious serious wound or fracture
- Bleeding or clear fluid from the nose, ear, or mouth
- Disturbance of speech or vision
- Pupils of unequal size
- Weakness or paralysis
- Dizziness
- Neck pain or stiffness
- Seizure
- Vomiting more than two to three times
- Loss of bladder or bowel control
  (*Head injuries*, 2004)

In summary, brain damage can result from multiple causes, only a few of which are listed here. Others are listed throughout the book. When brain damage occurs, it always should be treated by a medical specialist at the earliest possible time. A neuropsychologist may be called in to assist in diagnosis, and rehabilitation psychologists can be helpful in bringing the patient to the optimal level of psychological functioning possible under the circumstances.

Key Themes

In Chapter 1, we reviewed seven key themes that pervade cognitive psychology. Several of them are relevant here.

One is relative emphases on biological and behavioral mechanisms. The mechanisms described in this chapter are primarily biological, but a major goal of biological researchers is to discover how behavior relates to these biological mechanisms. For example, they study how the hippocampus enables learning. Thus, biology and behavior work together. They are not in any way mutually exclusive.

A second relevant theme is the nature-nurture distinction. One comes into the world with many biological structures and mechanisms in place. But nurture acts to develop them and enable them to reach their potential. The existence of the cerebral cortex is a result of nature, but the memories stored in it derive from nurture. As stated in Chapter 1, nature does not act alone. Rather, its marvels unfold through the interventions of nurture.

A third relevant theme is basic versus applied research. Much of the research in biological approaches to cognition is basic. But this basic research later enables us, as cognitive psychologists, to make applied discoveries. For example, to understand how to treat and, hopefully, help individuals with brain damage, cognitive neuropsychologists first must understand the nature of the damage and its pervasiveness. Many modern antidepressants, for example, affect the reuptake of serotonin in the nervous system. By inhibiting reuptake, they increase serotonin concentrations and ultimately increase feelings of well-being. Interestingly, applied research can help basic research as much as basic research can help applied research. In the case of antidepressants, for example, scientists knew the drugs worked before they knew exactly how they worked. Applied research in creating the drugs helped the scientists understand the biological mechanisms underlying the success of the drugs in relieving symptoms of depression.

People who have strokes on the left side of their brain have some difficulties in language, whereas those who have strokes on the right side typically have minimal language interferences. Readers who know people who have had strokes might have noticed this. This is because our language center is generally located on the left side of our brain.

Summary

1. **What are the fundamental structures and processes of the human brain?** The nervous system, governed by the brain, is divided into two main parts: the central nervous system, consisting of the brain and the spinal cord, and the peripheral nervous system, consisting of the rest of the nervous system (e.g., the nerves in the face, legs, arms, and viscera).

2. **How do researchers study the major structures and processes of the brain?** For centuries scientists have viewed the brain by dissecting it. Modern dissection techniques include the use of electron microscopes and sophisticated chemical analyses to probe the mysteries of individual cells of the brain. Additionally, surgical techniques on animals (e.g., the use of selective lesioning and

single-cell recording) often are used. On humans, studies have included electrical analyses (e.g., electroencephalograms and event-related potentials), studies based on the use of X-ray techniques (e.g., angiograms and computed tomograms), studies based on computer analyses of magnetic fields within the brain (magnetic resonance imaging), and studies based on computer analyses of blood flow and metabolism within the brain (positron emission tomography and functional magnetic resonance imaging).

3. **What have researchers found as a result of studying the brain?**   The major structures of the brain may be categorized as those in the forebrain (e.g., the all-important cerebral cortex and the thalamus, the hypothalamus, and the limbic system, including the hippocampus), the midbrain (including a portion of the brainstem), and the hindbrain (including the medulla oblongata, the pons, and the cerebellum). The highly convoluted cerebral cortex surrounds the interior of the brain and is the basis for much of human cognition. The cortex covers the left and right hemispheres of the brain. They are connected by the corpus callosum. In general, each hemisphere contralaterally controls the opposite side of the body. Based on extensive split-brain research, many investigators believe that the two hemispheres are specialized: In most people, the left hemisphere seems primarily to control language. The right hemisphere seems primarily to control visuospatial processing. The two hemispheres also may process information differently. Another way to view the cortex is identify differences among four lobes. Roughly speaking, higher thought and motor processing occur in the frontal lobe. Somatosensory processing occurs in the parietal lobe. Auditory processing occurs in the temporal lobe, and visual processing occurs in the occipital lobe. Within the frontal lobe, the primary motor cortex controls the planning, control, and execution of movement. Within the parietal lobe, the primary somatosensory cortex is responsible for sensations in our muscles and skin. Specific regions of these two cortices can be mapped to particular regions of the body.

Thinking about Thinking: Factual, Analytical, Creative, and Practical Questions

1. How have views of the nature of the relation between the brain and cognition changed over time?

2. Briefly summarize the main structures and functions of the brain.

3. What are some of the reasons that researchers are interested in finding out the localization of function in the human brain?

4. In your opinion, why have the hindbrain, the midbrain, and the forebrain evolved (across the human species) and developed (across human prenatal development) in the sequence mentioned in this chapter? Include the main functions of each in your comments.

5. Researchers already are aware that a deficit of a neurotransmitter, acetylcholine, in the hippocampus is linked to Alzheimer's disease. Given the difficulty of reaching the hippocampus without causing other kinds of brain damage, how might researchers try to treat Alzheimer's disease?

6. In your opinion, why is it that some discoveries, such as that of Marc Dax, go unnoticed? What can be done to maximize the possibility that key discoveries will be noticed?

7. Given the functions of each of the cortical lobes, how might a lesion in one of the lobes be discovered?

8. What is an area of cognition that could be studied effectively by viewing the structure or function of the human brain? Describe how a researcher might use one of the techniques mentioned in this chapter to study that area of cognition.

Key Terms

amygdala

axon

brain

brainstem

cerebellum

cerebral cortex

cerebral hemispheres

contralateral

corpus callosum

dendrites

electroencephalograms (EEGs)

event-related potential

frontal lobe

functional magnetic resonance imaging (fMRI)

hippocampus

hypothalamus

ipsilateral

Korsakoff's syndrome

limbic system

lobes

localization of function

magnetic resonance imaging (MRI)

magnetoencephalography (MEG)

medulla oblongata

myelin

nervous system

neurons

neurotransmitters

nodes of Ranvier

occipital lobe

parietal lobe

pons

positron emission tomography (PET)

primary motor cortex

primary somatosensory cortex

reticular activating system (RAS)

septum

soma

split-brain patients

synapse

temporal lobe

terminal buttons

thalamus

transcranial magnetic stimulation (TMS)

Explore CogLab by going to **http://coglab.wadsworth.com.** To learn more, examine the following experiments:

Brain Asymmetry

Annotated Suggested Readings

Anderson, A. K., & Phelps, E. A. (2001). Lesions of the human amygdala impair enhanced perception of emotionally salient events. *Nature, 411,* 305–309. An interesting paper covering the effects of damage to the amygdala on perception.

Gazzaniga, M. (Ed.). (2000). *The new cognitive neuroscience* (2nd ed.). Cambridge, MA: MIT Press. Probably the most comprehensive review of cog-

nitive neuroscience currently available. The level of writing is high.

Taylor, M. J., & Baldeweg, T. (2002). Application of EEG, ERP and intracranial recordings to the investigation of cognitive functions in children. *Developmental Science, 5*(3), 318–334. A combination of behavioral and neurological changes in childhood are covered.

Perception

EXPLORING COGNITIVE PSYCHOLOGY

1. How do we perceive stable objects in the environment given variable stimulation?

2. What are two fundamental approaches to explaining perception?

3. What happens when people with normal visual sensations cannot perceive visual stimuli?

Have you ever been told that you "can't see something that's right under your nose"? How about that you "can't see the forest for the trees"? Have you ever listened to your favorite song over and over, trying to decipher the lyrics? In each of these situations, we call on the complex construct of perception. **Perception** is the set of processes by which we recognize, organize, and make sense of the sensations we receive from environmental stimuli (Epstein & Rogers, 1995; Goodale, 2000a, 2000b; Kosslyn & Osherson, 1995; Marr, 1982; Pomerantz, 2003). Perception encompasses many psychological phenomena. In this chapter, we focus on visual perception. It is the most widely recognized and the most widely studied perceptual modality (system for a particular sense, e.g., touch or smell). To find out about some of the phenomena of perception, psychologists often study situations that pose problems in making sense of our sensations.

Consider, for example, the image displayed in Figure 3.1. To most people, the figure initially looks like a blur of meaningless shadings. A recognizable creature is staring them in the face, but they may not see it. When people finally realize what is

FIGURE 3.1

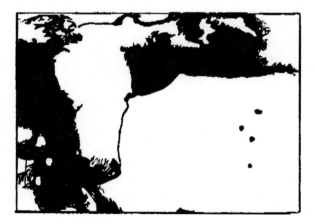

What do you learn about your own perception by trying to identify the object staring at you from this photo? From Dallenbach, K. M. (1951). A puzzle-picture with a new principle of concealment. American Journal of Psychology, 54, 431–433.

FIGURE 3.2

What perceptual changes would make it easier for you to identify the figure depicted here?

in the figure, they rightfully feel "cowed." In Figure 3.1, the figure of the cow is hidden within the continuous gradations of shading that constitute the picture. Before you recognized the figure as a cow, you correctly sensed all aspects of the figure. But you had not yet organized those sensations to form a mental *percept*—that is, a mental representation of a stimulus that is perceived. Without such a percept of the cow, you could not meaningfully grasp what you previously had sensed. In Figure 3.2, you will see shadings as well. These shadings, however, are discrete. In many instances, they are nothing more than dots. Again, there is a hidden object. If you are dogged in your pursuit of the hidden object, you will no doubt find it.

The preceding examples show that sometimes we cannot perceive what does exist. At other times, however, we perceive things that do not exist. For example, notice the black triangle in the center of the left panel of Figure 3.3. Also note the white triangle in the center of the right panel of Figure 3.3. They jump right out at you. Now look very closely at each of the panels. You will see that the triangles are not really all there. The black that constitutes the center triangle in the left panel looks darker, or blacker, than the surrounding black. But it is not. Nor is the white central triangle in the right panel any brighter, or whiter, than the surrounding white. Both central triangles are optical illusions. They involve the perception of visual information not physically present in the visual sensory stimulus. So, sometimes we do not perceive what is there. Other times, we perceive what is not there. And at still other times, we perceive what cannot be there. Consider, for example, the winding staircase

FIGURE 3.3

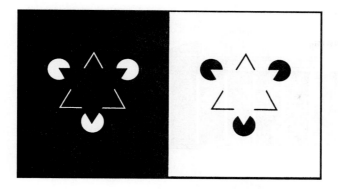

You easily can see the triangles in this figure—or are the triangles just an illusion? From In Search of the Human Mind *by Robert J. Sternberg, copyright © 1995 by Harcourt Brace & Company. Reproduced by permission of the publisher.*

FIGURE 3.4

How can you reach the top of the staircase depicted here?

in Figure 3.4. Follow it around until you reach the top. Are you having trouble reaching the top? This illusion is called a "perpetual staircase." It seems always to go up, although this feat is impossible.

The existence of perceptual illusions suggests that what we sense (in our sensory organs) is not necessarily what we perceive (in our minds). Our minds must be taking the available sensory information and manipulating that information somehow to create mental representations of objects, properties, and spatial relationships of our environments (Peterson, 1999). Moreover, the way we represent these objects will depend in part on our viewpoint in perceiving the objects (Edelman & Weinshall, 1991; Poggio & Edelman, 1990; Tarr, 1995; Tarr & Bülthoff, 1998). For millennia,

FIGURE 3.5

Early in the first century A.D., *Roman architect Marcus Vitruvius Polio wrote* De Architectura, *in which he documented the genius of the Greek architects Ictinus and Callicrates, who designed the Parthenon (dedicated in 438* B.C.*). The columns of the Parthenon actually bulge slightly in the middle (b) to compensate for the visual tendency to perceive that straight parallel lines (a) seem to curve inward. Similarly, the horizontal lines of the beams crossing the top of the columns and the top step of the porch bulge slightly upward to counteract the tendency to perceive that they curve slightly downward. In addition, the columns lean ever so slightly inward at the top to compensate for the tendency to perceive them as spreading out as we gaze upward at them. Vitruvius also described many optical illusions in his treatise on architecture, and contemporary architects consider these distortions of visual perception in their designs today.*

people have recognized that what we perceive often differs from the rectilinear sensory stimuli that reach our sense receptors. An example is the use of optical illusions in the construction of the Parthenon (Figure 3.5). Were the Parthenon actually constructed the way it appears to us perceptually (with strictly rectilinear form), its appearance would be bizarre.

Even though we humans have limited vision and are subject to illusions, we still are much better able than robots to encode visual displays and make sense of them. Given the sophistication of current-day robots, what is the source of our superiority? There may be several, but one is certainly knowledge. We simply know much more about the environment and sources of regularity in the environment than do robots. Our knowledge gives us a great advantage that robots, at least of the current day, are unable to bridge.

Architects are not the only ones to have recognized some fundamental principles of perception. For centuries, artists have known how to lead us to perceive three-dimensional (3-D) percepts when viewing two-dimensional (2-D) images. What are some of the principles that guide our perceptions of both real and illusory percepts? First, we consider some of the perceptual information that leads us to perceive 3-D space from 2-D sensory information. Then we discuss some of the ways in which we perceive a stable set of percepts. Such stable perception occurs despite constant changes in the size and shape of what we observe. Then, we move on to theoretical approaches to perception. Finally, we consider some rare failures in normal visual perception among people with brain injuries.

From Sensation to Representation

Basics of Vision

Vision begins when light passes through the protective covering of the eye. This covering, *the cornea,* is a clear dome that protects the eye. The light then passes through the *pupil,* the opening in the center of the *iris.* Light then passes through the *crystalline lens* and the *vitreous humor.* The crystalline lens is a transparent membrane located behind the iris. This membrane can flex or relax to allow one to view objects both close and at a distance. The vitreous humor is a gel-like substance that comprises the majority of the eye. The major role of the vitreous humor is to provide support for the eye. This process results in the *refraction,* a change in direction and speed, of the light entering the eye. Refracted light focuses on the **retina,** a network of neurons extending over most of the back (posterior) surface of the interior of the eye. The retina is where electromagnetic light energy is transduced—that is, converted—into neural electrochemical impulses (Blake, 2000). Although the retina is only about as thick as a single page in this book, it nevertheless consists of three main layers of neural tissue.

The first layer of neuronal tissue—closest to the front, outward-facing surface of the eye—is the layer of **ganglion cells,** whose axons constitute the **optic nerve.** The second layer consists of three kinds of interneuron cells. **Amacrine cells** and **horizontal cells** make single lateral connections among adjacent areas of the retina in the middle layer of cells. **Bipolar cells** make dual connections forward and outward to the ganglion cells, as well as backward and inward to the third layer of retinal cells.

The third layer of the retina contains the **photoreceptors,** which transduce light energy into electrochemical energy. This energy then can be transmitted by neurons to the brain. The transmission enables the eye to detect visual stimulation. Ironically, the photoreceptor cells are the retinal cells farthest from the light source. Light must pass through the other two layers first. Messages are then passed back outward toward the front of your eye before traveling to the brain. There are two kinds of photoreceptors. The **rods** are long and thin photoreceptors. They are more highly concentrated in the periphery of the retina than in the foveal region of the retina, where vision is most acute. The **cones** are short and thick photoreceptors. They are more highly concentrated in the foveal region of the retina than in the periphery. The **fovea** is a small, thin region of the retina, the size of the head of a pin that is most directly in the line of sight. In fact, when you look straight at an object, your eyes rotate so that the image falls directly onto the fovea. The visual receptive field of the fovea is approximately as big as the size of a grape held at arm's length.

Each cone in the fovea typically has its own ganglion cell, but the rods on the *periphery* (outer boundary area) of the retina share ganglion cells with other rods. Thus, each ganglion cell collecting information from the periphery gathers information from many rods. But each ganglion cell from the fovea gathers information from only one cone, perhaps because of the more complex function of cones with regard to the processing of color.

Each eye contains roughly 120 million rods and 8 million cones. Rods and cones differ not only in shape but also in their compositions, locations, and responses to light. Within the rods and cones are **photopigments,** chemical substances that react to light. The photopigments start the complex transduction process that transforms physical electromagnetic energy into an electrochemical neural impulse that can be understood by the brain.

The rods, cones, and photopigments within them could not do their work were they not somehow hooked up to the brain (Sandell, 2000). The neurochemical messages processed by the rods and cones of the retina travel via the bipolar cells to the ganglion cells (see Goodale, 2000a, 2000b). As noted earlier, the axons of the ganglion cells in the eye collectively form the optic nerve for that eye. The optic nerves of the two eyes join at the base of the brain to form the optic chiasma. At this point, the ganglion cells from the inward, or nasal, part of the retina—the part closer to your nose—cross through the optic chiasma and go to the opposite hemisphere of the brain. The ganglion cells from the outward, or temporal, area of the retina closer to your temple, go to the hemisphere on the same side of the body. The lens of each eye naturally inverts the image of the world as it projects the image onto the retina. In this way, the message sent to your brain is literally upside-down and backward.

After being routed via the optic chiasma, the ganglion cells then go to the thalamus. From the thalamus, neurons carry information to the primary visual cortex in the occipital lobe of the brain. The visual cortex contains several processing areas. Each area handles different kinds of visual information relating to intensity and quality, including color, location, depth, pattern, and form. Let us consider in more detail how the cortex processes color information through the workings of the rods and the cones.

We have two separate visual systems. One, responsible for vision in dim light, depends on the rods. The other, responsible for vision in brighter light, depends on the cones (Durgin, 2000).

Some Basic Concepts of Perception

If a tree falls in the forest and no one is around to hear it, or, for that matter, to see it, does it make a sound? An answer to this old riddle can be found by placing the riddle in the context of perception. In his influential and controversial work, James Gibson (1966, 1979) provided a useful framework for studying perception. He introduced the concepts of distal (external) object, informational medium, proximal stimulation, and perceptual object.

The distal (far) object is the object in the external world. In this case, it is the falling tree. This event imposes a pattern on an informational medium. The informational medium is the reflected light, sound waves (here, the sound of the falling tree),

TABLE 3.1	Perceptual Continuum		
Perception occurs as environmental objects impart the structure of the informational medium that ultimately impinges on sensory receptors, leading to internal object identification.			
DISTAL OBJECT	**INFORMATIONAL MEDIUM**	**PROXIMAL STIMULATION**	**PERCEPTUAL OBJECT**
Vision—sight (e.g., Grandma's face)	Reflected light from Grandma's face (visible electromagnetic waves)	Photon absorption in the rod and cone cells of the retina, the receptor surface in the back of the eye	Grandma's face
Audition—sound (e.g., a falling tree)	Sound waves generated by the tree's fall	Sound wave conduction to the basilar membrane, the receptor surface within the cochlea of the inner ear	A falling tree
Olfaction—smell (e.g., sizzling bacon)	Molecules released by frying bacon	Molecular absorption in the cells of the olfactory epithelium, the receptor surface in the nasal cavity	Bacon
Gustation—taste (e.g., a bite of ice cream)	Molecules of ice cream both released into the air and dissolved in water	Molecular contact with taste buds, the receptor cells on the tongue and soft palate, combined with olfactory stimulation (see previous entry)	Ice cream
Touch (e.g., a computer keyboard)	Mechanical pressure and vibration at the point of contact between the surface of the skin (epidermis) and the keyboard	Stimulation of various receptor cells within the dermis, the innermost layer of skin	Computer keys

chemical molecules, or tactile (relating to touch) information coming from the environment. Thus, the prerequisites for perception of objects in the external world begin early. They start even before sensory information impinges on our sense receptors (neural cells that are specialized to receive particular kinds of sensory information). When the information comes into contact with the appropriate sensory receptors of the eyes, ears, nose, skin, or mouth, proximal (near) stimulation occurs. Finally, perception occurs when an internal perceptual object in some way reflects the properties of the external world.

Table 3.1 summarizes this framework for the occurrence of perception. It lists the various properties of distal objects, informational media, proximal stimuli, and perceptual objects involved in perceiving the environment. To return to the original question, if a tree falls in the forest and no one is around to hear it, it makes no perceived sound. But it does make a sound. So the answer is yes or no, depending on how you look at the question.

The question of where to draw the line between perception and cognition, or even between sensation and perception, arouses much debate. Instead, to be more productive we should view these processes as part of a continuum. Information flows through the system. Different processes address different questions. Questions of sensation focus on qualities of stimulation. Is that shade of red brighter than the red of an apple? Is the sound of that falling tree louder than the sound of thunder? How well do one person's impressions of colors or sounds match someone else's impressions of those same colors or sounds? This same color or sound information answers different questions for perception. These are typically questions of identity and of form, pattern, and movement. Is that red thing an apple? Did I just hear a tree falling? Finally, cognition occurs as this information is used to serve further goals. Is that apple edible? Should I get out of this forest?

We never can experience through vision, hearing, taste, smell, or touch exactly the same set of stimulus properties we have experienced before. Therefore, one fundamental question for perception is "How do we achieve perceptual stability in the face of this utter instability at the level of sensory receptors?" Indeed, given the nature of our sensory receptors, variation seems necessary for perception.

In the phenomenon of sensory adaptation, receptor cells adapt to constant stimulation by ceasing to fire until there is a change in stimulation. Through sensory adaptation, we may stop detecting the presence of a stimulus. This mechanism ensures that sensory information is changing constantly. Because of sensory adaptation in the retina (the receptor surface of the eye), our eyes constantly are making tiny rapid movements. These movements create constant changes in the location of the projected image inside the eye. To study visual perception, scientists devised a way to create stabilized images. Such images do not move across the retina because they actually follow the eye movements. The use of this technique has confirmed the hypothesis that constant stimulation of the cells of the retina gives the impression that the image disappears (Ditchburn, 1980; Martinez-Conde, Macknik, & Hybel, 2004; Riggs & associates, 1953). Thus, stimulus variation is an essential attribute for perception. It paradoxically makes the task of explaining perception more difficult.

Perceptual Constancies

The perceptual system deals with variability by performing a rather remarkable analysis regarding the objects in the perceptual field. For example, picture yourself walking across campus to your cognitive psychology class. Suppose that two students are standing outside the door. They are chatting as you approach. As you get closer to the door, the amount of space on your retina devoted to images of those students becomes increasingly large. On the one hand, this proximal sensory evidence suggests that the students are becoming larger. On the other hand, you perceive that the students have remained the same size. Why?

Your classmates' perceived constancy in size is an example of perceptual constancy. **Perceptual constancy** occurs when our perception of an object remains the same even when our proximal sensation of the distal object changes (Gillam, 2000). The physical characteristics of the external distal object are probably not changing. But because we must be able to deal effectively with the external world, our perceptual system has mechanisms that adjust our perception of the proximal stimulus. Thus, the perception remains constant although the proximal sensation changes. Of the several kinds of perceptual constancies, here we consider two of the main constancies: size and shape constancies.

Size constancy is the perception that an object maintains the same size despite changes in the size of the proximal stimulus. The size of an image on the retina depends directly on the distance of that object from the eye. The same object at two different distances projects different-sized images on the retina. Some striking illusions can be achieved when our sensory and perceptual systems are misled by the very same information that usually helps us to achieve size constancy. For example, look at Figure 3.6. Here we see the Ponzo illusion. In this illusion, two objects that appear to be of different sizes are actually of the same size. The Ponzo illusion stems from the depth cue provided by the converging lines. Equivalent image sizes at different depths usually indicate different-sized objects. Another example is the Müller-Lyer illusion, illustrated in Figure 3.7. Here, two line segments that are of the same length appear to be of different lengths. Finally, compare the two center circles in the pair of circle patterns in Figure 3.8. Both center circles are actually the same size. But the size of the center circle relative to the surrounding circles affects perception of the center circle's size.

Like size constancy, shape constancy relates to the perception of distances but in a different way. *Shape constancy* is the perception that an object maintains the same shape despite changes in the shape of the proximal stimulus. For example, Figure 3.9 is an illustration of shape constancy. An object's perceived shape remains the same despite changes in its orientation and hence in the shape of its retinal image. As the actual shape of the pictured door changes, some parts of the door seem to be changing differentially in their distance from us. It is possible to use

FIGURE 3.6

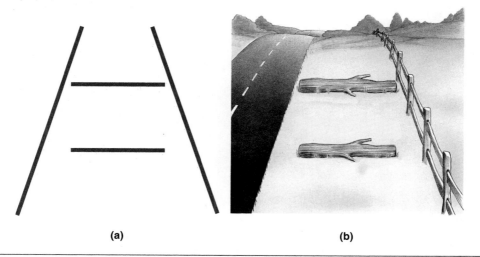

(a)   (b)

We perceive the top line and the top log in a and b as being longer than the bottom line and the bottom log, respectively, although the top and bottom figures are identical in length. We do so because in the real three-dimensional world, the top line and the log would be larger.

FIGURE 3.7

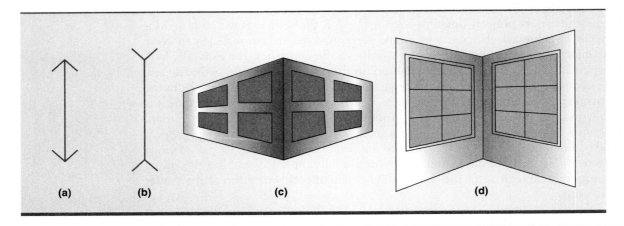

(a)   (b)   (c)   (d)

In this illusion, too, we tend to view two equally long line segments as being of different lengths. In particular, the vertical line segments in panels a and c appear shorter than the line segments in panels b and d, although all the line segments are the same size. Oddly enough, we are not certain why such a simple illusion occurs. Sometimes, the illusion we see in the abstract line segments (panels a and b) is explained in terms of the diagonal lines at the ends of the vertical segments. These diagonal lines may be implicit depth cues similar to the ones we would see in our perceptions of the exterior and interior of a building (Coren & Girgus, 1978). In panel c, a view of the exterior of a building, the sides appear to recede into the distance (with the diagonal lines angling toward the vertical line segment, as in panel a), whereas in panel d, a view of the interior of a building, the sides appear to come toward us (with the diagonal lines angling away from the vertical line segment, as in panel b).

FIGURE 3.8

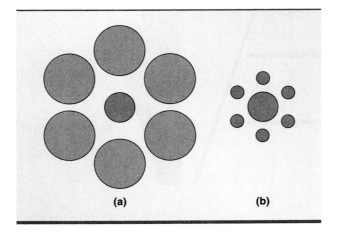

(a)   (b)

Guess which center circle is larger (a or b) and then measure the diameter of each one.

FIGURE 3.9

Here, you see a rectangular door and door frame, showing the door as closed, slightly opened, more fully opened, or wide open. Of course, the door does not appear to be a different shape in each panel. Indeed, it would be odd if you perceived a door to be changing shapes as you opened it. Yet, the shape of the image of the door sensed by your retinas does change as you open the door. If you look at the figure, you will see that the drawn shape of the door is different in each panel.

neuropsychological imaging to localize parts of the brain that are used in this shape analysis. They are in the extrastriate cortex (Kanwisher & associates, 1996, 1997). Points near the outer edge of the door seem to move more quickly toward us than do points near the inner edge. Nonetheless, we perceive that the door remains the same shape.

Depth Perception

As you move in your environment, you constantly look around. You visually orient yourself in 3-D space. As you look forward into the distance, you look into the third dimension of depth. **Depth** is the distance from a surface, usually using your own body as a reference surface when speaking in terms of depth perception. Consider what happens when you transport your body, reach for or manipulate objects, or otherwise position yourself in your 3-D world. You must use information regarding depth. This use of depth information even extends beyond the range of your body's reach. When you drive, you use depth to assess the distance of an approaching automobile. When you decide to call out to a friend walking down the street, you determine how loudly to call. Your decision is based on how far away you perceive your friend to be. How do you manage to perceive 3-D space when the proximal stimuli on your retinas comprise only a 2-D projection of what you see?

Refer back to the impossible staircase (see Figure 3.4). Look also at other impossible configurations in Figure 3.10. They are confusing because there is contradictory depth information in different sections of the picture. Small segments of these impossible figures look reasonable to us because there is no inconsistency in their individual depth cues (Hochberg, 1978). However, it is difficult to make sense of the figure as a whole. The reason is that the cues providing depth information in various segments of the picture are in conflict.

Generally, depth cues are either monocular (mon-, "one"; ocular, "related to the eyes") or binocular (bin-, "both," "two"). **Monocular depth cues** can be represented in just two dimensions and observed with just one eye. Figure 3.11 illustrates several of the monocular depth cues defined in Table 3.2. They include texture gradients, relative size, interposition, linear perspective, aerial perspective, location in the picture plane, and motion parallax. Before you read about the cues in either the table or the figure caption, look just at the figure. See how many depth cues you can decipher for yourself simply by observing the figure carefully.

Table 3.2 also describes motion parallax, the only monocular depth cue not shown in the figure. Motion parallax requires movement. It thus cannot be used to judge depth within a stationary image, such as a picture. Another means of judging depth involves **binocular depth cues,** based on the receipt of sensory information in

FIGURE 3.10

What cues may lead you to perceive these impossible figures as entirely plausible?

FIGURE 3.11

In The Annunciation *(left), Carlo Crivelli masterfully illustrated at least five monocular depth cues: (1, 2) Texture gradients and relative size: The floor tiles appear similar both in front of and behind the figures in the forefront of the corridor, but the tiles at the front of the corridor are larger and are spread farther apart than the tiles at the rear. (3) Interposition: The peacock partially blocks our view of the frieze on the wall to the right of the corridor. (4) Linear perspective: The sides of the wall seem to converge inward toward the rear of the corridor. (5) Location in the picture plane: The figures at the rear of the corridor are depicted higher in the picture plane than are the figures at the front of the corridor. M. C. Escher used his mastery of visual perception to create paradoxical depictions such as in his drawing* Waterfall *(right). Can you see how he used various monocular depth cues to lead us to perceive the impossible?*

three dimensions from both eyes (Parker, Cumming, & Dodd, 2000). Table 3.2 also summarizes some of the binocular cues used in perceiving depth.

Binocular depth cues utilize the relative positioning of your eyes. Your two eyes are positioned far enough apart to provide two kinds of information to your brain: binocular disparity and binocular convergence. In *binocular disparity*, your two eyes send increasingly disparate (differing) images to your brain as objects approach you. Your brain interprets the degree of disparity as an indication of distance from you. In addition, for objects we view at relatively close locations, we use depth cues based on binocular convergence. In *binocular convergence*, your two eyes increasingly turn inward as objects approach you. Your brain interprets these muscular movements as

TABLE 3.2	Monocular and Binocular Cues for Depth Perception

Various perceptual cues aid in our perception of the three-dimensional world. Some of these cues can be observed by one eye alone, whereas others require the use of both eyes.

CUES FOR DEPTH PERCEPTION	APPEARS CLOSER	APPEARS FARTHER AWAY
Monocular Depth Cues		
Texture gradients	Larger grains, farther apart	Smaller grains, closer together
Relative size	Bigger	Smaller
Interposition	Partially obscures other object	Is partially obscured by other object
Linear perspective	Apparently parallel lines seem to diverge as they move away from the horizon	Apparently parallel lines seem to converge as they approach the horizon
Aerial perspective	Images seem crisper, more clearly delineated	Images seem fuzzier, less clearly delineated
Location in the picture plane	Above the horizon, objects are higher in the picture plane; below the horizon, objects are lower in the picture plane	Above the horizon, objects are lower in the picture plane; below the horizon, objects are higher in the picture plane
Motion parallax	Objects approaching get larger at an ever-increasing speed (i.e., big and moving quickly closer)	Objects departing get smaller at an ever-decreasing speed (i.e., small and moving slowly farther away)
Binocular Depth Cues		
Binocular convergence	Eyes feel tug inward toward nose	Eyes relax outward toward ears
Binocular disparity	Huge discrepancy between image seen by left eye and image seen by right eye	Minuscule discrepancy between image seen by left eye and image seen by right eye

indications of distance from you. Figure 3.12 illustrates how these two processes work. The brain contains neurons that specialize in the perception of depth. These are, as one might expect, referred to as *binocular neurons*. These neurons integrate incoming information from both eyes to form information about depth. The binocular neurons are found in the visual cortex (Parker, 2007).

Depth perception may depend upon more than just the distance or depth at which an object is located relative to oneself. Proffitt and associates (2003, 2006) reported that the perceived distance to a target is influenced by the effort required to walk to the location of the target, and that perceived distance to a target location is greater for people wearing a heavy backpack than for those not wearing such a backpack. In other words, there can be an interaction between the perceptual result and the perceived effort required to reach the object perceived (see also Wilt, Proffitt, & Epstein, 2004). The more effort one requires to reach something, the farther away it is perceived to be.

The role of effort is not limited to walking toward something. When they play well, tennis players report that a tennis ball looks relatively large. Similarly, golfers say that the cup looks bigger (Wilt & Proffitt, 2005). In both these cases, perceptions

FIGURE 3.12

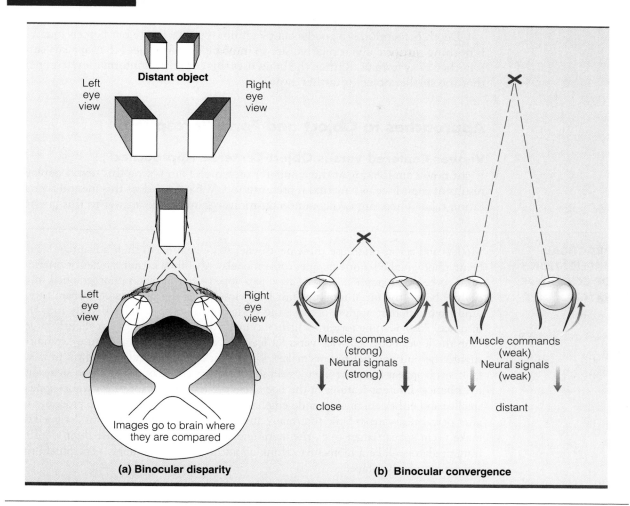

(a) Binocular disparity

(b) Binocular convergence

(a) Binocular disparity: The closer an object is to you, the greater the disparity between the views of it as sensed in each of your eyes. You can test these differing perspectives by holding your finger about an inch from the tip of your nose. Look at it first with one eye covered, then the other: It will appear to jump back and forth. Now do the same for an object 20 feet away, then 100 yards away. The apparent jumping, which indicates the amount of binocular disparity, will decrease with distance. Your brain interprets the information regarding disparity as a cue indicating depth. (b) Binocular convergence: Because your two eyes are in slightly different places on your head, when you rotate your eyes so that an image falls directly on the central part of your eye, in which you have the greatest visual acuity, each eye must turn inward slightly to register the same image. The closer the object you are trying to see, the more your eyes must turn inward. Your muscles send messages to your brain regarding the degree to which your eyes are turning inward, and these messages are interpreted as cues indicating depth.

are in part a function of the quality of performance. Investigators confirmed this phenomenon (Wilt & Proffitt, 2005). They found that batters who hit well perceived the ball to be bigger than did participants who batted less well.

Depth perception is a good example of how cues facilitate our perception. There is nothing intrinsic about relative size to indicate that an object that appears smaller is farther away from us. Rather, the brain uses this contextual information to conclude that the smaller object is farther away.

Approaches to Object and Form Perception

Viewer-Centered versus Object-Centered Approaches

Right now I am looking at the computer on which I am typing this text. I depict the results of what I see as a mental representation. What form does this mental representation take? There are two common positions regarding the answer to this question.

PRACTICAL APPLICATIONS OF COGNITIVE PSYCHOLOGY	Models and actors often use these depth cues of perception to their advantage while being photographed. For example, some models only allow certain angles or orientations to be photographed. A long nose can appear shorter when photographed from slightly below the facial midline (just look closely at some pictures of Barbara Streisand from different angles) because the bridge of the nose recedes slightly into the distance. Also, leaning forward a little can make the upper body appear slightly larger than the lower body, and vice versa for leaning backward. In group pictures, standing slightly behind another person makes you appear smaller; standing slightly in front makes you appear larger. Women's swimsuit designers create optical-illusion swimsuits to enhance different features of the body, making legs appear longer or waists appear smaller and either enhancing or de-emphasizing bustlines. Some of these processes to alter perceptions are so basic that many animals have special adaptations designed to make them appear larger (e.g., the fanning peacock tail) or to disguise their identity from predators. Take a moment to think about how you could apply perceptual processes to your advantage.

One position, **viewer-centered representation,** is that the individual stores the way the object looks to him or her. Thus, what matters is the appearance of the object to the viewer, not the actual structure of the object. The second position, **object-centered representation,** is that the individual stores a representation of the object, independent of its appearance to the viewer. The key similarity between these two positions is that both can account for how I represent a given object and its parts. The key difference is in whether I represent the object and its parts in relation to me (viewer-centered) or in relation to the entirety of the object itself, independent of my own position (object-centered).

Consider, for example, my computer. It has different parts: a screen, a keyboard, a mouse, and so forth. Suppose I represent the computer in terms of viewer-centered representation. Then its various parts are stored in terms of their relation to me. I see the screen as facing me at perhaps a 20-degree angle. I see the keyboard facing me horizontally. I see the mouse off to the right side and in front of me. Suppose, instead, that I use an object-centered representation. Then I would see the screen at a 70-degree angle relative to the keyboard. And the mouse is directly to the right side of the keyboard, neither in front of it nor in back of it.

One potential reconciliation of these two approaches to mental representation suggests that people may use both kinds of representations. According to this approach, recognition of objects occurs on a continuum (Burgund & Marsolek, 2000; Tarr, 2000; Tarr & Bülthoff, 1995). At one end of this continuum are cognitive mechanisms that are more viewpoint-centered. At the other end of the continuum are cognitive mechanisms that are more object-centered. For example, suppose you see a picture of car that is inverted. How do you know it is a car? Object-centered mechanisms would recognize the object as a car, but viewpoint-centered mechanisms would recognize the car as inverted. In general, decomposition of objects into parts will be useful for recognizing the differences between, say, a Mercedes and a Hyundai but may not be so useful for recognizing that two different views of a Mercedes are views of the same car. In the latter case, viewpoint-centered perception may be more important, as shown in Figure 3.13.

FIGURE 3.13

(a)

(c)

(b)

Viewpoint-centered mechanisms may be more important in distinguishing two different models of Mercedes-Benz (a and b), whereas object-centered mechanisms may be more important in distinguishing the Hyundai (c) from either Mercedes model.

A third orientation in representation is landmark-centered. In landmark-centered representation, information is characterized by its relation to a well-known or prominent item. Imagine visiting a new city. Each day you leave your hotel and go on short trips. It is easy to imagine that you would represent the area you explore in relation to your hotel. Back to the desk example, in the landmark-centered representation, the desk may be described in terms of a computer monitor. For example, the keyboard is arranged in front of the monitor and the mouse is situated to the right of the monitor.

Evidence indicates that, in the laboratory, participants can switch between these three strategies. There are, however, differences in brain activation among these strategies (Committeri & associates, 2004).

The Gestalt Approach

Perception does much more for us than maintain size and shape constancy in depth. It also organizes objects in a visual array into coherent groups. Kurt Koffka (1886–1941), Wolfgang Köhler (1887–1968), and Max Wertheimer (1880–1943) founded the **Gestalt approach to form perception.** It was based on the notion that the whole differs from the sum of its individual parts (see Chapter 1). The Gestalt approach has proved to be useful particularly for understanding how we perceive groups of objects or even parts of objects to form integral wholes (Palmer, 1999a, 1999b, 2000; Palmer & Rock, 1994; Prinzmetal, 1995). According to the Gestalt **law of Prägnanz,** we tend to perceive any given visual array in a way that most simply organizes the disparate elements into a stable and coherent form. Thus, we do not merely experience a jumble of unintelligible, disorganized sensations. For example, we tend to perceive a focal figure and other sensations as forming a background for the figure on which we focus.

Consider what happens when you walk into a familiar room. You perceive that some things stand out (e.g., faces in photographs or posters). Others fade into the background (e.g., undecorated walls and floors). A figure is any object perceived as being highlighted. It is almost always perceived against or in contrast to some kind of receding, unhighlighted (back)ground. Figure 3.14 *a* illustrates the concept of **figure-ground**—what stands out from versus what recedes into the background. You probably first will notice the light-colored lettering of the word *figure;* we perceive this light-colored lettering as the figure against the darker-lettered surrounding ground of the word *ground.* Similarly, in Figure 3.14 *b,* you can see either a white vase against a black background or two silhouetted faces peering at each other against a white ground. It is virtually impossible to see both sets of objects simultaneously. Although you may switch rapidly back and forth between the vase and the faces, you cannot see them both at the same time.

One of the reasons suggested as to why each figure makes sense is that both figures conform to the Gestalt principle of symmetry. Symmetry requires that features appear to have balanced proportions around a central axis or a central point. Table 3.3 and Figure 3.15 summarize a few of the Gestalt principles of form perception. They include figure-ground perception, proximity, similarity, continuity, closure, and symmetry. Each of these principles supports the overarching law of Prägnanz. Each thereby illustrates how we tend to perceive visual arrays in ways that most simply organize the disparate elements into a stable and coherent form. Stop for a moment

FIGURE 3.14

(a)

(b)

Courtesy of Kaiser Porcelain, Ltd.

In these two Gestalt images (a and b), find which is the figure and which is the ground.

and look at your environment. You will perceive a coherent, complete, and continuous array of figures and background. You do not perceive holes in objects where your textbook occludes (i.e., covers up) your view of them. If your book obscures part of the edge of a table, you still perceive the table as a continuous entity. You do not see it as having gaping holes. In viewing the environment, we tend to perceive groupings. We see groupings of nearby objects (proximity) or of like objects (similarity). We also see groupings of complete objects rather than partial ones (closure), continuous lines rather than broken ones (continuity), and symmetrical patterns rather than asymmetrical ones.

People tend to use Gestalt principles even when they are confronted with novel stimuli. Palmer (1977) showed participants novel geometric shapes that served as targets. He then showed them fragments of the shapes. For each fragment, the par-

TABLE 3.3	Gestalt Principles of Visual Perception	
The Gestalt principles of proximity, similarity, continuity, closure, and symmetry aid in our perception of forms.		
GESTALT PRINCIPLES	**PRINCIPLE**	**FIGURE ILLUSTRATING THE PRINCIPLE**
Figure-ground	When perceiving a visual field, some objects (figures) seem prominent, and other aspects of the field recede into the background (ground).	Figure 3.14 shows a figure-ground vase, in which one way of perceiving the figures brings one perspective or object to the fore, and another way of perceiving the figures brings a different object or perspective to the fore and relegates the former foreground to the background.
Proximity	When we perceive an assortment of objects, we tend to see objects that are close to each other as forming a group.	In Figure 3.15 a, we tend to see the middle four circles as two pairs of circles.
Similarity	We tend to group objects on the basis of their similarity.	In Figure 3.15 b, we tend to see four columns of xs and os, not four rows of alternating letters.
Continuity	We tend to perceive smoothly flowing or continuous forms rather than disrupted or discontinuous ones.	Figure 3.15 c shows two fragmented curves bisecting, which we perceive as two smooth curves, rather than as disjointed curves.
Closure	We tend to perceptually close up, or complete, objects that are not, in fact, complete.	Figure 3.15 d shows only disjointed, jumbled line segments, which you close up to see a triangle and a circle.
Symmetry	We tend to perceive objects as forming mirror images about their center.	For example, when viewing Figure 3.15 e, a configuration of assorted brackets, we see the assortment as forming four sets of brackets, rather than eight individual items, because we integrate the symmetrical elements into coherent objects.

ticipants had to say whether it was part of the original novel geometric shape. Participants were quicker to recognize the fragments as part of the original target if they conformed to Gestalt principles. Consider, for example, a triangle. It exhibits closure. It was recognized more quickly as part of the original novel figure than were three line segments that were comparable to the triangle except that they were not closed. They thus did not conform to the Gestalt principle. In sum, we seem to use Gestalt principles in our everyday perception. We use them whether the figures to which we apply the principles are familiar or not.

The Gestalt principles of form perception are remarkably simple. Yet they characterize much of our perceptual organization (Palmer, 1992). The Gestalt principles provide valuable descriptive insights into form and pattern perception. But they offer few or no explanations of these phenomena. To understand how or why we perceive forms and patterns, we need to consider explanatory theories of perception.

FIGURE 3.15

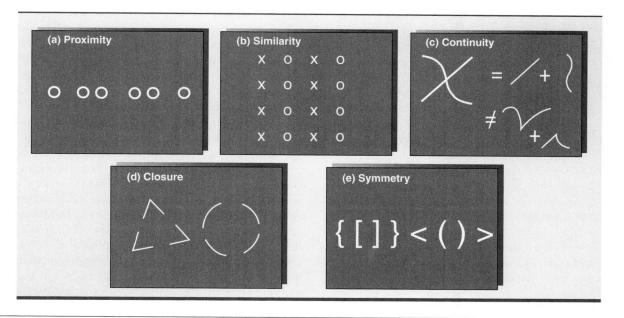

The Gestalt principles of form perception include perception of figure-ground, (a) proximity, (b) similarity, (c) continuity, (d) closure, and (e) symmetry. Each principle demonstrates the fundamental law of law of Prägnanz, which suggests that through perception, we unify disparate visual stimuli into a coherent and stable whole.

Pattern-Recognition Systems

How do we recognize patterns? For example, how do we recognize faces? One proposal is that humans have two systems for recognizing patterns (Farah, 1992, 1995; Farah & associates, 1998). The first system specializes in recognition of parts of objects and in assembling those parts into distinctive wholes. For example, when you are in a biology class and notice the elements of a tulip—the stamen, the pistil, and so forth—you look at the flower through this first system. The second system specializes in recognizing larger configurations. It is not well equipped to analyze parts of objects or the construction of the objects. But it is especially well equipped to recognize configurations. For example, if you look at a tulip in a garden and admire its distinctive beauty and form, you look at the flower through the second system.

The second system would typically be most relevant to the recognition of faces. So when you spot a friend whom you see on a daily basis, you recognize him or her using the configurational system. So dependent are you on this system in everyday life that you might not even notice some major change in your friend's appearance, such as his or her having longer hair or having put on new glasses. But the first system can also be used in face recognition. Suppose you see someone whose face looks vaguely familiar, but you are not sure who it is. You start analyzing features and then realize it is a friend

IN THE LAB OF STEPHEN PALMER

One important topic that is largely ignored in current cognitive psychology studies is aesthetics: the psychological dimension anchored at the positive end by the experience of beauty and the sublime and at the negative end by ugliness. One might suppose that aesthetics is only important in people's appreciation of the arts (painting, music, dance, etc.), but it actually permeates our lives. Our choices in clothes, movies, home furnishings, vacation spots, and even other people are all strongly influenced by our aesthetic reactions to them.

In my lab, we have recently begun to study visual aesthetics scientifically. In examining the aesthetics of spatial composition, for example, we show participants two pictures that differ only in the placement of a sin-gle object within a rectangular frame and ask them to tell us which one they prefer aesthetically. Figure *a* shows three such pairs depicting a side view of a wolf against a plain background. (Before reading further, please decide which of each pair you find more aesthetically pleasing.) We record people's choices for all such pairs of positions and facing directions and then compute the percentage of times each position and direction is chosen in comparison with all others.

The pattern of results we found is shown in Figure *b*, plotting separate curves for the left-facing and right-facing objects. It exhibits three important effects: a strong *center bias*, a strong *inward bias*, and a weaker *rightward bias*. The *center bias* refers to the preference for the object to be at or near the center of the frame. It is reflected in the graph by the fact that both curves are generally higher near the central position than near the sides of the frame. This is the reason why you probably preferred the left picture in the top pair of Figure *a*. The *inward bias* refers to the fact that people generally prefer a directed object to face into the frame rather than out of it. It is reflected in the graph by the asymmetry of the left-facing and right-facing curves: If the object is off-center on the left side of the frame, people prefer the right-facing object, but if it is off-center on the right side of the frame, they prefer the left-facing object. This is the reason you probably chose the right picture in the middle pair of Figure *a* as more pleasing; they have the same off-center location, but the wolf faces inward in the right picture and outward in the left one. The *rightward bias* refers to the fact that people generally prefer a directed object to face to the right rather than to the left. It is reflected in the graph by the fact that the curve for the right-facing objects is slightly higher than that for the left-facing objects, the difference being most noticeable at the central position. This is the reason you may have preferred the left picture in the bottom pair of Figure *a*; they have the same central location in the frame, but the wolf faces rightward in the left picture.

The center, inward, and rightward biases were also evident when we gave people a camera and a set of objects and asked them to take the most aestheti-

(a)

IN THE LAB OF STEPHEN PALMER—cont'd

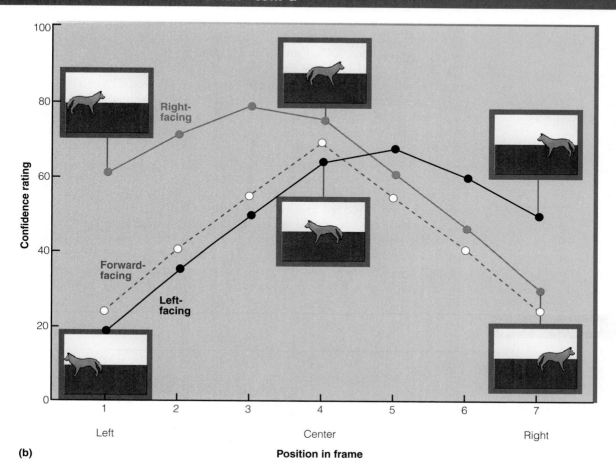

(b)   **Position in frame**

cally pleasing picture they could. If they decided to place a right-facing object off-center in the frame, for example, they were much more likely to position it on the left side of the frame than on the right side. We find the same biases were present when we gave people a computer display in which they could control the position of the object and asked them to place it in the aesthetically most pleasing position. We are now examining the framing decisions made by photographers and painters by measuring the position and direction of pictures with a single focal object in real photographs and real paintings sampled from databases on the Internet.

We are also in the process of studying preferences for the vertical position and size of objects in pictures of a single focal object. Once we have done that, we will begin to study the more complex compositional issues that arise when two or more objects are depicted in the same picture. The main point of our results thus far, however, is that aesthetic preferences can be studied scientifically. Beauty is indeed in the eye of the beholder, as the old saying goes, but as cognitive scientists, we can understand the perception of beauty just like any other perceptual phenomenon: by isolating the important variables and determining how they combine in the mind of the beholder.

you have not seen for 10 years. In this case, you were able to make the facial recognition only after you analyzed the face by its features. In the end, both configurational and feature analysis may help in making difficult recognitions and discriminations.

Face recognition occurs, at least in part, in the fusiform gyrus of the temporal lobe (Gauthier & associates, 2003; Kanwisher, McDermott, & Chun, 1997; Tarr & Cheng, 2003). There is good evidence that there is something special about recognition of faces, even from an early age. For example, infants track movements of a photograph of a human face more rapidly than they track movements of stimuli of similar complexity that are not, however, faces (Farah, 2000a). In one study, experimental participants were shown sketches of two kinds of objects, faces and houses (Farah & associates, 1998). In each case, the face was paired with the name of the person whom the face represented and the house was paired with the name of the house's owner. There were six pairings per trial. After learning the six pairings, participants were asked to recognize parts of either the faces or the houses or to recognize the faces or houses as a whole. For example, they might see just a nose or ear, or just a window or a doorway. Or they might see a whole face or house. If face recognition is somehow special and especially dependent on the second, configurational system, then people should have more difficulty recognizing parts of faces than parts of houses. The data are shown in Figure 3.16.

People generally were better at recognizing houses, whether they were presented in parts or in wholes. But more important, people had relatively more difficulty in

FIGURE 3.16

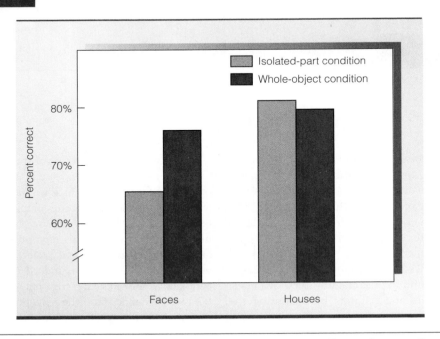

People have more trouble recognizing parts of faces than whole faces. They recognize parts of houses about as well as they recognize whole houses, however. From J. W. Tanaka and M. J. Farah, "Parts and Wholes in Face Recognition," Quarterly Journal of Experimental Psychology, 46A, pp. 225–245, Fig. 6. Reprinted by permission of the Experimental Psychology Society.

FIGURE 3.17

Normal (center) and distorted faces.

recognizing parts of faces than they had in recognizing whole faces. In contrast, they did about the same, whether they had to recognize parts of houses or whole houses. Face recognition, therefore, appears to be special. Presumably, it is especially dependent on the configurational system.

An interesting example of a configurational effect in face recognition occurs when people stare at distorted faces. If you stare at a distorted face for a while (Figure 3.17) and then stare at a normal face, the normal face will look distorted in the opposite direction. For example, if you stare at a face where the eyes are too close together, when you look at a normal face the eyes will appear too far apart (Leopold & associates, 2001; Webster & associates, 2004; Zhao & Chubb, 2001). Your knowledge of faces normally tells you what is a normal face and what is a distorted one, but in this case, that knowledge is very briefly overridden by your having accustomed yourself to the distorted face.

Cognitive processing of faces and the emotion of the face can interact. Indeed, there is some evidence of an age-related "face positivity" effect. In one study, older but not younger adults were found to show a preference for looking at happy faces and away from sad or angry faces (Isaacowitz & associates, 2006a, 2006b). Furthermore, happy faces are rated as more familiar than are either neutral or negative faces (Lander & Metcalfe, 2007).

There is evidence that emotion increases activation within the fusiform gyrus when people are processing faces. In one study, participants were shown a face and asked either to name the person or to name the expression. When asked to name the expression, participants show increased activation of the fusiform gyrus compared with when the participants were asked to name the person (Ganel & associates, 2005). Examination of patients with autism provides additional evidence for the processing of emotion within the fusiform gyrus. Patients with autism have impaired emotional recognition. Scanning the brains of persons suffering from autism reveals that the fusiform gyrus is less active then in nonpatient populations.

Patients with autism can learn to identify emotions through an effortful process. However, this training does not allow identification of emotion to become an automatic process in this population, nor does it increase the activation within the fusiform gyrus (Bolte & associates, 2006; Hall, Szechtman, & Nahmias, 2003).

In another study, participants looked either at houses or faces. The fusiform gyrus was activated when people looked at the faces but not when they looked at the houses. Thus, there seems to be true localization of perception in this area for faces as opposed to other objects that might be perceived (Yovel & Kanwisher, 2004).

Researchers do not all agree that the fusiform gyrus is specialized for face perception, in contrast to other forms of perception. Another point of view is that this area is that of greatest activation in face perception, but that other areas also show activation, albeit at lower levels. Similarly, this or other brain areas that respond maximally to faces or anything else may still show some activation when perceiving other objects. In this view, areas of the brain are not all-or-none in what they perceive, but rather, may be differentially activated, in greater or lesser degrees, depending on what is perceived (Haxby & associates, 2001; Haxby, Gobbini, & Montgomery, 2004; O'Toole & associates, 2005).

Another theory concerning the role of the fusiform gyrus is called the expert-individuation hypothesis. According to this theory, the fusiform gyrus is activated when one examines items with which one has visual expertise. Imagine that you are an expert on birds and spend much of your time studying birds. It is expected that you would be able to differentiate among very similar birds and would have much practice at such differentiation. As a result, if you are shown five robins, you would likely be able to tell birds apart. A person without this expertise would likely not be able to discern among these birds. If your brain was scanned during this activity, activation in the fusiform gyrus, specifically the right one, would be seen. Such activation is seen in persons who are experts concerning cars and birds. Even when people are taught to differentiate among very similar abstract figures, activation of the fusiform gyrus is observed (Gauthier & associates, 1999, 2000; Rhodes & associates, 2004; Xu, 2005). This theory is able to account for the activation of the fusiform gyrus when people view faces because we are, in effect, experts at identifying and examining faces.

Prosopagnosia—the inability to recognize faces—would imply damage of some kind to the configurational system. But other disabilities, such as an early reading disability in which a beginning reader has difficulty in recognizing the features that comprise unique words, might stem from damage to the first, element-based system. Moreover, processing can move from one system to another. A typical reader may learn the appearances of words through the first system—element by element—and then come to recognize the words as wholes. Indeed, some forms of reading disability might stem from the inability of the second system to take over from the first.

Theoretical Approaches to Perception

Several different theoretical approaches to perception have been described.

Direct Perception

How do you know the letter A when you see it? Easy to ask, hard to answer. Of course, it's an A because it looks like an A. What makes it look like an A, though, instead of like an H? Just how difficult it is to answer this question becomes apparent when you

FIGURE 3.18

When you read these words, you probably have no difficulty differentiating the A from the H. Look more closely at each of these two letters. What features differentiate them?

look at Figure 3.18. You probably will see the image in Figure 3.18 as the words "THE CAT." Yet the *H* of "THE" is identical to the *A* of "CAT." What subjectively feels like a simple process of pattern recognition is almost certainly quite complex. How do we connect what we perceive to what we have stored in our minds? Gestalt psychologists referred to this problem as the *Hoffding function* (Köhler, 1940). It was named after nineteenth-century Danish psychologist Harald Hoffding. He questioned whether perception can be reduced to a simple view of associating what is seen with what is remembered. An influential and controversial theorist who also questioned associationism is James J. Gibson (1904–1980).

According to Gibson's theory of **direct perception,** the array of information in our sensory receptors, including the sensory context, is all we need to perceive anything. In other words, we do not need higher cognitive processes or anything else to mediate between our sensory experiences and our perceptions. Existing beliefs or higher-level inferential thought processes are not necessary for perception.

Gibson believed that, in the real world, sufficient contextual information over time usually exists to make perceptual judgments. He claimed that we need not appeal to higher-level intelligent processes to explain perception. For example, Figure 3.19 shows that we do not need to have prior experience with particular shapes to perceive apparent shapes. Gibson (1979) believed that we use this contextual information directly. In essence, we are biologically tuned to respond to it. According to Gibson, we often observe depth cues such as texture gradients. Those cues aid us to perceive directly the relative proximity or distance of objects and of parts of objects. Based on our analysis of the stable relationships among features of objects and settings in the real world, we directly perceive our environment (Gibson, 1950, 1954/1994; Mace, 1986). We do not need the aid of complex thought processes.

Such contextual information might not be readily controlled in a laboratory experiment. But such information is likely to be available in a real-world setting. Gibson's model sometimes is referred to as an ecological model (Turvey, 2003). This is because of Gibson's concern with perception as it occurs in the everyday world (the ecological environment) rather than in laboratory situations, where less contextual information is available. Ecological constraints apply not only to initial perceptions but also to the ultimate internal representations (such as concepts) that are formed from those perceptions (Hubbard, 1995; Shepard, 1984). Continuing to wave the

FIGURE 3.19

The perception of these apparent amorphous shapes is consistent with James Gibson's direct-perception view that contextual information alone is sufficient for perception to occur, without additional knowledge or high-level thinking. Prior knowledge about the contexts does not lead to our perception of the triangle or the pear. From The Legacy of Solomon Asch: Essays in Cognition and Social Psychology *by Irving Rock. Copyright © 1990 by Lawrence Erlbaum Associates. Reprinted by permission.*

Gibsonian banner was Eleanor Gibson (1991, 1992). She conducted landmark research in infant perception. She observed that infants (who certainly lack much prior knowledge and experience) quickly develop many aspects of perceptual awareness, including depth perception.

Bottom-Up and Top-Down Theories

Theories starting with processing of low-level features are termed **bottom-up theories,** which are data-driven (i.e., stimulus-driven) theories. Not all theorists focus on the sensory data of the perceptual stimulus, however. Many theorists prefer **top-down theories,** which are driven by high-level cognitive processes, existing knowledge, and prior expectations that influence perception (Clark, 2003). These theories then work their way down to considering the sensory data, such as the perceptual stimulus. Expectations are important. When people expect to see something, they may see it even if it is not there or is no longer there. For example, suppose people expect to see a certain person in a certain location. They may think they see that person, even if they are actually seeing someone else who looks only vaguely similar (Simons, 1996). Top-down and bottom-up approaches have been applied to virtually every aspect of cognition. As applied to perception, there are two major theories of perception. They manifest the bottom-up and top-down approaches. These theories usually are presented in opposition to each other. But to some extent they deal with different aspects of the same phenomenon. Ultimately, a complete theory of perception will need to encompass both bottom-up and top-down processes.

Bottom-Up Theories

The four main bottom-up theories of form and pattern perception are template theories, prototype theories, feature theories, and structural-description theories.

Template Theories

One theory says that we have stored in our minds myriad sets of templates. **Templates** are highly detailed models for patterns we potentially might recognize. We recognize a pattern by comparing it with our set of templates. We then choose the exact template that perfectly matches what we observe (Selfridge & Neisser, 1960). We see examples of template matching in our everyday lives. Fingerprints are matched in this way. Machines rapidly process imprinted numerals on checks by comparing them to templates. Increasingly, products of all kinds are identified with universal product codes (UPCs or "bar codes"). They can be scanned and identified by computers at the time of purchase. Chess players who have knowledge of many games use a matching strategy in line with template theory to recall previous games (Gobet & Jackson, 2002).

In each of the aforementioned instances, the goal of finding one perfect match and disregarding imperfect matches suits the task. You would be alarmed to find that your bank's numeral-recognition system failed to register a deposit to your account. Such failure might occur because it was programmed to accept an ambiguous character according to what seemed to be a best guess. For template matching, only an exact match will do. This is exactly what you want from a bank computer. However, consider your perceptual system at work in everyday situations. It rarely would work if you required exact matches for every stimulus you were to recognize. Imagine, for example, needing mental templates for every possible percept of the face of someone you love. Imagine one for each facial expression, each angle of viewing, each addition or removal of makeup, each hairdo, and so on.

Letters of the alphabet are simpler than faces and other complex stimuli. Yet template-matching theories also fail to explain some aspects of the perception of letters. For one thing, such theories cannot easily account for our perception of the letters and words in Figure 3.18. We identify two different letters (*A* and *H*) from only one physical form. Hoffding (1891) noted other problems. We can recognize an *A* as an *A* despite variations in the size, orientation, and form in which the letter is written. Are we to believe that we have mental templates for each possible size, orientation, and form of a letter? Storing, organizing, and retrieving so many templates in memory would be unwieldy. Moreover, how could we possibly anticipate and create so many templates for every conceivable object of perception (Figure 3.20)?

Prototype Theories

The unwieldiness and rigidity of template theories soon led to an alternative explanation of pattern perception: prototype-matching theory. A **prototype** is a sort of average of a class of related objects or patterns, which integrates all the most typical (most frequently observed) features of the class. That is, a prototype is highly representative of a pattern, but it is not intended as a precise, identical match to any pattern or all other patterns for which it is a model. A great deal of research has been found to support the prototype-matching approach (e.g., Franks & Bransford, 1971). The prototype model seems to explain perception of configurations. Examples include arrays of dots, a triangle, a diamond, an *F*, an *M*, or a random array (Posner, Goldsmith, &

FIGURE 3.20

Template matching will distinguish between different bar codes but will not recognize that different versions of the letter A written in different scripts are indeed both As.

Welton, 1967; Posner & Keele, 1968) and highly simplified line drawings of faces (Reed, 1972). Prototypes even include rather well-defined faces created by the police with Identikits, which are often used for witness identification (Solso & McCarthy, 1981; Figure 3.21).

Surprisingly, we seem to be able to form prototypes even when we have never seen an exemplar that exactly matches the prototype. That is, the prototypes we form seem to integrate all the most typical features of a pattern. This occurs even when we have never seen a single instance in which all the typical features are integrated at

FIGURE 3.21

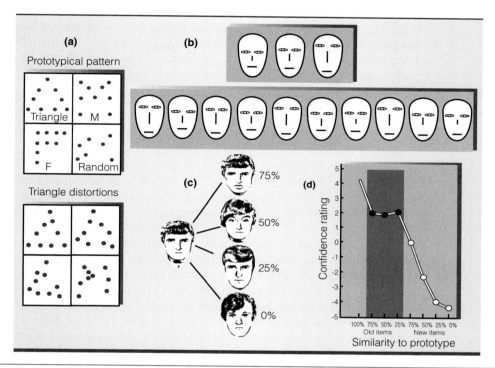

(a) Prototypical pattern

Triangle | M

F | Random

Triangle distortions

(b)

(c) 75% 50% 25% 0%

(d)

Confidence rating

100% 75% 50% 25% 75% 50% 25% 0%
Old items   New items
Similarity to prototype

(a) These dot configurations are similar to those used in the experiment by Michael Posner and his colleagues. Michael I. Posner, Ralph Goldsmith, and Kenneth E. Welton, Jr. (1967), "Perceived Distance and the Classification of Distorted Patterns," from Journal of Experimental Psychology, *73(1):28–38. Copyright © 1967 by the American Psychological Association. Reprinted with permission. (b) These highly simplified drawings of faces are similar to those used by Stephen Reed. Stephen K. Reed (1972), "Pattern Recognition and Categorization,"* Cognitive Psychology, *July 1972, 3(3):382–407. Reprinted by permission of Elsevier. (c) These faces are similar to those created in the experiment by Robert Solso and John McCarthy (1981). Robert Solso and Judith McCarthy (1981), "Prototype Formation of Faces: A Case of Pseudomemory,"* British Journal of Psychology, *November 1981, Vol. 72, No. 4, pp. 499–503. Reprinted by permission of The British Psychological Society. (d) This graph illustrates Solso and McCarthy's findings, indicating the confidence rating for perceived recognition of each face, including the recognition of a prototypical face never observed by the subjects.*

one time (Neumann, 1977). Consider an illustration of this point. Some researchers generated various series of patterns, such as the patterns in Figure 3.21 *a* and *c,* based on a prototype. They then showed participants the series of generated patterns. They did not show the prototype on which the patterns were based. Later, they again showed participants the series of generated patterns. They also showed some additional patterns, including both distracters and the prototype pattern. Under these conditions, participants not only identified the prototype pattern as being one they had seen previously (e.g., Posner & Keele, 1968). They also gave particularly high ratings of their confidence in having seen the prototype previously (Solso & McCarthy, 1981).

Feature Theories

Yet another alternative explanation of pattern and form perception may be found in *feature-matching theories*. According to these theories, we attempt to match features of a pattern to features stored in memory, rather than to match a whole pattern to a template or a prototype (Stankiewicz, 2003). One such feature-matching model has been called *pandemonium*. In it, metaphorical "demons" with specific duties receive and analyze the features of a stimulus (Selfridge, 1959). Figure 3.22 shows this model.

Oliver Selfridge's pandemonium model describes "image demons." They pass on a retinal image to "feature demons." Each feature demon calls out when there are matches between the stimulus and the given feature. These matches are yelled out at demons at the next level of the hierarchy, the "cognitive (thinking) demons." They shout out possible patterns stored in memory that conform to one or more of the features noticed by the feature demons. A "decision demon" listens to the pandemonium of the cognitive demons. It decides on what has been seen, based on which cognitive demon is shouting the most frequently (i.e., which has the most matching features).

Although Selfridge's model is one of the most widely known, other feature models have been proposed. Most also distinguish not only different features but also different kinds of features, such as global versus local features. Local features constitute the small-scale or detailed aspects of a given pattern. There is no consensus as to what exactly constitutes a local feature. Nevertheless, we generally can distinguish such features from global features, the features that give a form its overall shape. Consider, for example, the stimuli depicted in Figure 3.23 *a* and *b*. These are of the type used in some research on pattern perception (Navon, 1977). Globally, the stimuli in panels *a* and *b* form the letter H. In panel *a*, the local features (small Hs) correspond to the global ones. In panel *b*, comprising many local letter Ss, they do not.

In one study, participants identified the stimuli at either the global or the local level (Navon, 1977). Consider what happened when the local letters were small and positioned close together. Participants could identify stimuli at the global level more quickly than at the local level. Moreover, when participants were required to identify stimuli at the global level, whether the local features matched the global ones did not matter. They responded equally rapidly whether the global H was made up of local Hs or of local Ss. However, now consider what happened when participants were asked to respond at the local level. They responded more quickly if the global features agreed with the local ones. In other words, they were slowed down if they had to identify local Ss combining to form a global H instead of identifying local Hs combining to form a global H. This pattern of results is called the *global precedence effect*.

In contrast, when letters are more widely spaced, as in panels *a* and *b* of Figure 3.24, the effect is reversed. Then a *local-precedence effect* appears. That is, the participants more quickly identify the local features of the individual letters than the global ones, and the local features interfere with the global recognition in cases of contradictory stimuli (Martin, 1979). Other limitations (e.g., the size of the stimuli) hold as well, and other kinds of features also influence perception.

Some support for feature theories comes from neurological and physiological research. Researchers used single-cell recording techniques with animals (Hubel & Wiesel, 1963, 1968, 1979). They carefully measured the responses of individual neu-

FIGURE 3.22

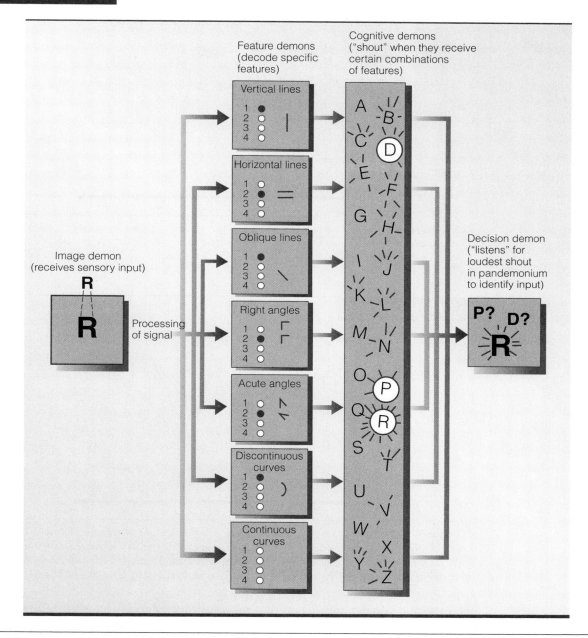

According to Oliver Selfridge's feature-matching model, we recognize patterns by matching observed features to features already stored in memory. We recognize the patterns for which we have found the greatest number of matches.

FIGURE 3.23

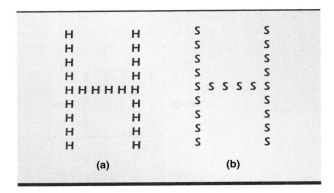

Compare panel a (global Hs made of local Hs) with panel b (global Hs made of local Ss). All the local letters are tightly spaced. From D. Navon, "Forest Before Trees: The Precedence to Global Features in Visual Perception," Cognitive Psychology, *July 1977, Vol. 9, No. 3, pp. 353–382. Reprinted by permission of Elsevier.*

FIGURE 3.24

Compare panels a and b, in which the local letters are widely spaced. In which figure (Figure 3.22 or Figure 3.23) do you note the global-precedence effect, and in which figure do you note the local-precedence effect? D. Navon, "Forest Before Trees: The Precedence to Global Features in Visual Perception," *Cognitive Psychology, July 1977, Vol. 9, No. 3, p. 353–382. Reprinted by permission of Elsevier.*

rons in the visual cortex. Then they mapped those neurons to corresponding visual stimuli for particular locations in the visual field (see Chapter 2). Their research showed that specific neurons of the visual cortex in the brain respond to varying stimuli presented to specific regions of the retina corresponding to these neurons. Each individual cortical neuron, therefore, can be mapped to a specific receptive field on the retina. A disproportionately large amount of the visual cortex is devoted to neurons mapped to receptive fields in the foveal region of the retina.

FIGURE 3.25

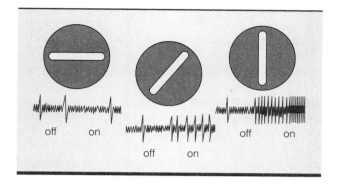

David Hubel and Torsten Wiesel discovered that cells in our visual cortex become activated only when they detect the sensation of line segments of particular orientations. From In Search of the Human Mind by Robert J. Sternberg, copyright © 1995 by Harcourt Brace & Company. Reproduced by permission of the publisher.

Most of the cells in the cortex do not respond simply to spots of light. Rather, they respond to "specifically oriented line segments" (Hubel & Wiesel, 1979, p. 9). What's more, these cells seem to show a hierarchical structure in the degree of complexity of the stimuli to which they respond, somewhat in line with the ideas behind the Pandemonium model. Consider what happens as the stimulus proceeds through the visual system to higher levels in the cortex. In general, the size of the receptive field increases, as does the complexity of the stimulus required to prompt a response. As evidence of this hierarchy, there were once believed to be just two kinds of visual cortex neurons (Figure 3.25), *simple cells* and *complex cells* (Hubel & Wiesel, 1979), which were believed to differ in the complexity of the information about stimuli they processed. This view proved to be oversimplified.

Based on Hubel and Wiesel's work, other investigators have found feature detectors that respond to corners and angles (DeValois & DeValois, 1980; Shapley & Lennie, 1985). In some areas of the cortex, highly sophisticated complex cells fire maximally only in response to very specific shapes, regardless of the size of the given stimulus. Examples would be a hand or a face. As the stimulus decreasingly resembles the optimal shape, these cells are decreasingly likely to fire.

We now know the picture is rather more complex than Hubel and Wiesel imagined. Multiple kinds of cells serve multiple functions. These cells operate partially in parallel, although we are not conscious of their operation. For example, spatial information about locations of perceived objects was found to be processed simultaneously with information about how contours of the objects are integrated. In other words, quite complex judgments about what is perceived are made quite early in information processing, and in parallel (Dakin & Hess, 1999).

Other work on visual perception has identified separate neural pathways in the cerebral cortex for processing different aspects of the same stimuli (De Yoe & Van Essen, 1988; Köhler & associates, 1995). They are termed the "what" and "where" pathways. The "what" pathway descends from the primary visual cortex in the oc-

Irving Biederman is the William M. Keck professor of cognitive neuroscience at the University of Southern California. He is best known for his work in high-level vision and in shape recognition in particular. His theory of geons shows a possible way in which various images of objects can be decomposed into a set of fundamental units.

cipital lobe (see Chapter 2) toward the temporal lobes. It is mainly responsible for processing the color, shape, and identity of visual stimuli. The "where" pathway ascends from the occipital lobe toward the parietal lobe. It is responsible for processing location and motion information. Thus, feature information feeds into at least two different systems for identifying objects and events in the environment.

Once discrete features have been analyzed according to their orientations, how are they integrated into a form we can recognize as particular objects?

Structural-Description Theory

Consider a means by which we may form stable 3-D mental representations of objects, based on the manipulation of a few simple geometric shapes (Biederman, 1987). This means is a set of 3-D geons (for geometrical ions). They include objects such as bricks, cylinders, wedges, cones, and their curved axis counterparts (Biederman, 1990/1993b). According to Biederman's **recognition-by-components (RBC) theory,** we quickly recognize objects by observing the edges of them and then decomposing the objects into geons. The geons also can be recomposed into alternative arrangements. You know that a small set of letters can be manipulated to compose countless words and sentences. Similarly, a small number of geons can be used to build up many basic shapes and then myriad basic objects (Figure 3.26).

The geons are simple and are viewpoint-invariant (i.e., discernible from various viewpoints). The objects constructed from geons thus are recognized easily from many perspectives, despite visual noise. According to Biederman (1993a), his RBC theory parsimoniously explains how we are able to recognize the general classification for multitudinous objects quickly, automatically, and accurately. This recognition occurs despite changes in viewpoint. It occurs even under many situations in which the stimulus object is degraded in some way. Biederman's RBC theory explains how we may recognize general instances of chairs, lamps, and faces, but it does not adequately explain how we recognize particular chairs or particular faces. An example would be your own face or your best friend's face.

Biederman himself has recognized that aspects of his theory require further work, such as how the relations among the parts of an object can be described (Biederman, 1990/1993b). Another problem with Biederman's approach, and the bottom-up approach in general, is how to account for the effects of prior expectations and environmental context on some phenomena of pattern perception.

Top-Down Approaches

In contrast to the bottom-up approach to perception is the top-down, constructive approach (Bruner, 1957; Gregory, 1980; Rock, 1983; von Helmholtz, 1909/1962). In **constructive perception,** the perceiver builds (constructs) a cognitive understanding (perception) of a stimulus. He or she uses sensory information as the foundation for the structure but also using other sources of information to build the perception. This viewpoint also is known as *intelligent perception* because it states that higher-order thinking plays an important role in perception. It also emphasizes the role of learning in perception (Fahle, 2003). Some investigators have pointed out that not only does the world affect our perception but also the world we experience is actually formed by our perception (Goldstone, 2003). These ideas go back to the philosophy of Immanuel Kant. In other words, perception is reciprocal with the world we experience. Perception both affects and is affected by the world as we experience it.

Irvin Rock was an adjunct professor of psychology at the University of California at Berkeley. He is well known for his championing of the role of problem solving in perception and the claim that perception is indirect. He also originated the study of one-trial learning and has made major contributions to the study of the moon and other perceptual illusions.

FIGURE 3.26

(a)

(b)

Irving Biederman amplified feature-matching theory by proposing a set of elementary components of patterns (a), which he based on variations in three-dimensional shapes derived in large part from a cone (b).

For example, picture yourself driving down a road you have never traveled before. As you approach a blind intersection, you see an octagonal red sign with white lettering. It bears the letters "ST_P." An overgrown vine cuts between the *T* and the *P*. Chances are, you will construct from your sensations a perception of a stop sign. You thus will respond appropriately. Similarly, constructivists would suggest that our perceptions of size and shape constancy indicate that high-level constructive processes are at work during perception. Another type of perceptual constancy can be viewed as illustrating top-down construction of perception. In color constancy, we perceive that the color of an object remains the same despite changes in lighting that alter the hue. Consider lighting that becomes so dim that color sensations are virtually absent. We still perceive bananas as yellow, plums as purple, and so on.

According to constructivists, during perception we quickly form and test various hypotheses regarding percepts. The percepts are based on three things. The first is what we sense (the sensory data). The second is what we know (knowledge stored in memory). The third is what we can infer (using high-level cognitive processes). In perception, we consider prior expectations. An example would be expecting to see an approaching friend whom we had arranged to meet. We also use what we know about the context. Here, an example would be that trains often ride on railroad tracks, but airplanes and automobiles usually do not. And we also may use what we reasonably can infer, based both on what the data are and on what we know about the data. According to constructivists, we usually make the correct attributions regarding our visual sensations. The reason is that we perform unconscious inference, the process by which we unconsciously assimilate information from a number of sources to create a perception (Snow & Mattingley, 2003). In other words, using more than one source of information, we make judgments that we are not even aware of making.

In the stop-sign example, sensory information implies that the sign is a meaningless assortment of oddly spaced consonants. However, your prior learning tells you something important—that a sign of this shape and color posted at an intersection of roadways and containing these three letters in this sequence probably means that you should stop thinking about the odd letters. Instead, you should start slamming on the brakes. Successful constructive perception requires intelligence and thought in combining sensory information with knowledge gained from previous experience.

One reason for favoring the constructive approach is that bottom-up (data-driven) theories of perception do not fully explain context effects. **Context effects** are the influences of the surrounding environment on perception (e.g., our perception of "THE CAT" in Figure 3.18). Fairly dramatic context effects can be demonstrated experimentally (Biederman, 1972; Biederman & associates, 1974; Biederman, Glass, & Stacy, 1973; De Graef, Christiaens, & D'Ydewalle, 1990). In one study, people were asked to identify objects after they had viewed the objects in either an appropriate or an inappropriate context for the items (Palmer, 1975). For example, participants might see a scene of a kitchen followed by stimuli such as a loaf of bread, a mailbox, and a drum. Objects that were appropriate to the established context, such as the loaf of bread in this example, were recognized more rapidly than were objects that were inappropriate to the established context. The strength of the context also plays a role in object recognition (Bar, 2004).

Perhaps even more striking is a context effect known as the *configural-superiority effect* (Bar, 2004; Pomerantz, 1981), by which objects presented in certain configurations are easier to recognize than the objects presented in isolation, even if the objects in the configurations are more complex than those in isolation. Suppose you show a participant four stimuli, all of them diagonal lines. Three of the lines are slanting one way, and one line is slanting the other way. The participant's task is to identify which stimulus is unlike the others (Figure 3.27 a). Now suppose that you show participants four stimuli. All of them comprise three lines (Figure 3.27 c). Three of the stimuli are shaped like triangles. One is not. In each case, the stimulus is a diagonal line (see

FIGURE 3.27

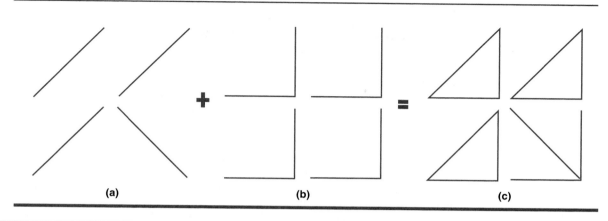

(a)   (b)   (c)

Subjects more readily perceive differences among integrated configurations comprising multiple lines (c) than they do solitary lines (a). In this figure, the lines in panel b are added to the lines in panel a to form shapes in panel c, thereby making panel c more complex than panel a.

Figure 3.27 a) plus other lines (Figure 3.27 b). Thus, the stimuli in this second condition are more complex variations of the stimuli in the first condition. Participants can more quickly spot which of the three-sided figures is different from the others than they can spot which of the lines is different from the others.

In a similar vein, there is an object-superiority effect, in which a target line that forms a part of a drawing of a 3-D object is identified more accurately than a target that forms a part of a disconnected 2-D pattern (Lanze, Weisstein, & Harris, 1982; Weisstein & Harris, 1974). These findings parallel findings in the study of letter and word recognition.

The viewpoint of constructive or intelligent perception shows the central relation between perception and intelligence. According to this viewpoint, intelligence is an integral part of our perceptual processing. We do not perceive simply in terms of what is "out there in the world." Rather, we perceive in terms of the expectations and other cognitions we bring to our interaction with the world. In this view, intelligence and perceptual processes interact in the formation of our beliefs about what it is that we are encountering in our everyday contacts with the world at large.

An extreme top-down position would drastically underestimate the importance of sensory data. If it were correct, we would be susceptible to gross inaccuracies of perception. We frequently would form hypotheses and expectancies that inadequately evaluated the sensory data available. For example, if we expected to see a friend and someone else came into view, we might inadequately consider the perceptible differences between the friend and a stranger. Thus, an extreme constructivist view of perception would be highly error-prone and inefficient. However, an extreme bottom-up position would not allow for any influence of past experience or knowledge on perception. Why store knowledge that has no use for the perceiver? Neither extreme is ideal for explaining perception. It is more fruitful to consider ways in which bottom-up and top-down processes interact to form meaningful percepts.

Synthesizing Bottom-Up and Top-Down Approaches

Both theoretical approaches have been able to garner empirical support (cf. Cutting & Kozlowski, 1977, vs. Palmer, 1975). So how do we decide between the two? On one level, the constructive-perception theory, which is more top-down, seems to contradict direct-perception theory, which is more bottom-up. Constructivists emphasize the importance of prior knowledge in combination with relatively simple and ambiguous information from the sensory receptors. In contrast, direct-perception theorists emphasize the completeness of the information in the receptors themselves. They suggest that perception occurs simply and directly. Thus, there is little need for complex information processing.

Instead of viewing these theoretical approaches as incompatible, we may gain deeper insight into perception by considering the approaches to be complementary. Sensory information may be more richly informative and less ambiguous in interpreting experiences than the constructivists would suggest. But it may be less informative than the direct-perception theorists would assert. Similarly, perceptual processes may be more complex than hypothesized by Gibsonian theorists. This would be particularly true under conditions in which the sensory stimuli appear only briefly or are degraded. Degraded stimuli are less informative for various reasons. For example, the stimuli may be partially obscured or weakened by poor lighting. Or they may be incomplete, or distorted by illusory cues or other visual "noise" (distracting visual stimulation analogous to audible noise). We likely use a combination of information from the sensory receptors and our past knowledge to make sense of what we perceive. Some experimental evidence supports this integrated view (Treue, 2003; van Zoest & Donk, 2004; Wolfe & associates, 2003).

Recent work suggests that, whereas the very first stage of the visual pathway represent only what is in the retinal image of an object, very soon, color, orientation, motion, depth, spatial frequency, and temporal frequency are represented. Later-stage representations emphasize the viewer's current interest or attention. In other words, the later-stage representations are not independent of our attentional focus. On the contrary, they are directly affected by it (Maunsell, 1995). Moreover, vision for different things can take different forms. Visual control of action is mediated by cortical pathways that are different from those involved in visual control of perception (Ganel & Goodale, 2003). In other words, when we merely see an object, such as a cell phone, we process it differently than if we intend also to pick up the object. In general, according to Ganel and Goodale (2003), we perceive objects holistically. But if we plan to act on them, we perceive them more analytically so that we can act in an effective way.

To summarize, current theories concerning the ways we perceive patterns explain some, but not all, of the phenomena we encounter in the study of form and pattern perception. Given the complexity of the process, it is impressive that we understand as much as we do. At the same time, clearly a comprehensive theory is still some way off. Such a theory would need to account fully for the kinds of context effects described here.

Deficits in Perception

Agnosias and Ataxias

In general, what are the visual pathways in the brain? One hypothesis is that there are two distinct visual pathways, one for identifying objects, the other for pinpointing where objects are located in space (Ungerleider & Haxby, 1994; Ungerleider & Mishkin, 1982). The investigators referred to this as the *what/where hypothesis*. This division is based on research that was carried out with monkeys. In particular, a group of monkeys with lesions in the temporal lobe were able to indicate where things were but seemed unable to recognize what they were. In contrast, monkeys with lesions in the parietal lobe were able to recognize what things were but not where they were.

An alternative interpretation of the visual pathways has suggested that the two pathways refer not to what things are and to where they are, but rather to what they are and how they function. This is known as the *what/how hypothesis* (Goodale & Milner, 2004; Goodale & Westwood, 2004). This hypothesis argues that spatial information about where something is located in space is always present in visual information processing. What differs between the two pathways is whether the emphasis is on identifying what an object is or, instead, on how we can situate ourselves so as to grasp the objects. Thus, the question here is whether it is more important to know what the object is or how to reach for it.

Two kinds of processing deficits support the what/how hypothesis. Consider first the "what." Clearly, cognitive psychologists learn a great deal about normal perceptual processes by studying perception in normal participants. In addition, however, we also often gain understanding of perception by studying people whose perceptual processes differ from the norm (Farah, 1990; Weiskrantz, 1994). An example would be people who suffer from an **agnosia,** a severe deficit in the ability to perceive sensory information (Moscovitch, Winocur, & Behrmann, 1997). There are many kinds of agnosias. Not all of them are visual. Here we focus on a few specific inabilities to see forms and patterns in space. People with visual agnosia have normal sensations of what is in front of them, but they cannot recognize what they see. Agnosias often are caused by brain lesions (Farah, 1990, 1999). Another major cause of agnosia is restricted oxygen to areas of the brain. Oxygen depravation is frequently the result of traumatic brain injury (Zoltan, 1996). Agnosias are associated with damage to the border of the temporal and occipital lobes. People with these deficits have trouble with the "what" pathway.

Sigmund Freud (1953), who specialized in neurology in his medical practice before he developed his psychodynamic theory of personality, observed that some of his patients were unable to identify familiar objects. Nevertheless, they seemed to have no particular psychological disturbance or discernible damage to their visual abilities. In fact, people who suffer from visual-object agnosia can sense all parts of the visual field, but the objects they see do not mean anything to them (Kolb & Whishaw, 1985). For example, one agnosic patient, on seeing a pair of eyeglasses, noted first that there was a circle, then that there was another circle, then that there was a crossbar, and finally guessed that he was looking at a bicycle. A bicycle does, indeed, comprise two circles and a crossbar (Luria, 1973). Lesions in particular visual areas of the cortex may be responsible for visual-object agnosia.

Disturbance in the temporal region of the cortex can lead to simultagnosia. In *simultagnosia*, an individual is unable to pay attention to more than one object at a time. For instance, if you were simultagnosic and you were to look at Figure 3.28 *a,* you would not be able to see each of the objects depicted. Rather, you might report seeing the hammer but not the other objects (Williams, 1970). In *spatial agnosia,* a person has severe difficulty in negotiating the everyday environment. For example, a spatial agnosic can get lost at home, make wrong turns en route to familiar locations, and fail to recognize even the most familiar landmarks. Such individuals also seem to have great difficulty drawing the symmetrical features of symmetrical objects (Heaton, 1968). This disorder seems to stem from lesions in the parietal lobe of the brain. *Prosopagnosia,* mentioned earlier, results in a severely impaired ability to recognize human faces (Farah & associates, 1995; Feinberg & associates, 1994; McNeil & Warrington, 1993; Young, 2003). A prosopagnosic, for example, might not even be able to recognize her or his own face in the mirror. Furthermore, there are even extremely rare cases of prosopagnosics who cannot recognize human faces but who can recognize the faces of their farm animals. The problem thus appears to be extremely specific to human faces (McNeil & Warrington, 1993). This fascinating disorder has spawned much research on face identification. It has become the latest "hot topic" in visual perception (Damasio, 1985; Farah & associates, 1995; Farah, Levinson, & Klein, 1995; Haxby & associates, 1996). The functioning of the right-hemisphere fusiform gyrus is strongly implicated in prosopagnosia. In particular, the disorder is associated with damage to the right temporal lobe of the brain. To complicate things, prosopagnosia can take different forms. Sometimes, other domains of expertise, such as names of familiar animals, are affected, rather than human faces. So the disorder may not be exclusively in failure of face recognition, as once was thought. Prosopagnosia in particular and agnosia in general are obstacles that persist over time. In one particular

FIGURE 3.28

When you view this figure, you see various objects overlapping. People with simultagnosia cannot see more than one of these objects at any one time. From Sensation and Perception by Stanley Coren and Lawrence M. Ward, copyright © 1989 by Harcourt Brace & Company. Reproduced by permission of the publisher.

case, a woman who sustained carbon-monoxide toxicity began to suffer from agnosia, including prosopagnosia. After 40 years, this woman was reevaluated and still demonstrated these deficits. These findings reveal the lasting nature of agnosia (Sparr & associates, 1991).

There are other types of agnosias as well. One type is *auditory agnosia,* which is an impairment in the ability to recognize certain sounds. One patient, C.N., was reported to be unable to distinguish different types of music. She could not recognize melodies from her own collection of records and also could not tell whether two melodies were the same or different (Peretz & associates, 1994).

Recent research has suggested that auditory agnosia may be neurologically different from music agnosia (Ayotte & associates, 2000; Peretz, 1996). Behaviorally, auditory and music agnosia can be dissociated (Vignolo, 2003). In some patients, the ability to recognize known music is impaired. In others, the ability to recognize specific nonmusical sounds is impaired.

Two other kinds of agnosias pertain to object recognition (Gazzaniga, Ivry, & Mangun, 2002). *Apperceptive agnosia* is a failure in object recognition that is linked to a failure in perceptual processing. *Associative agnosia* is the ability to represent objects visually but not to be able to use this information to recognize things. Thus, in associative agnosia, the problem is not in perceptual processing but rather in associative cognitive processes operating on perceptual representations (Anaki & associates, 2007). A final type of agnosia to be described here is *color agnosia.* Color agnosia is the inability to name colors without a corresponding loss in the ability to perceive the colors (Nijboer & associates, 2007; Nijboer, van Zandvoort, & de Haan, 2007; Woodward & associates, 1999).

A different kind of perceptual deficit is associated with damage to the "how" pathway. This deficit is **optic ataxia,** which is an impairment in the ability to use the visual system to guide movement (Himmelbach & Karnath, 2005). People with this deficit have trouble reaching for things. All of us have had the experience of trying to grab something in the dark. For example, I dread leaving off the lights on my house because then when I get home, I cannot see the keyhole and have to grope with my key for the keyhole, often taking quite a while to find it. Someone with optic ataxia has this problem even with a fully lit visual field. The "how" pathway is impaired.

This kind of extreme specificity of deficits leads to questions about specialization. Specifically, are there distinct processing centers or modules for particular perceptual tasks? This question goes beyond the separation of perceptual processes along different sensory modalities (e.g., the differences between visual and auditory perception). Modular processes are those that are specialized for particular tasks. They may involve only visual processes (as in color perception), or they may involve an integration of visual and auditory processes (as in certain aspects of speech perception that are discussed in Chapter 10).

Jerry Fodor, an influential modern philosopher, has written a book entirely devoted to the delineation of the necessary characteristics of modular processes. For some processes to be truly modular, the following properties must exist. First, the modules must work fast and their operation must be mandatory. Second, modules have characteristically shallow outputs (i.e., yielding basic categorizations). Central access to the module's computations is limited. It is not subject to conscious attentional influences. Third, modules are domain specific. They are fine-tuned with respect to the kinds of information used. Information does not necessarily flow freely across various modules. It is sometimes referred to as "encapsulated." Finally, modules are supported by fixed neural architectures and therefore suffer characteristic break-down patterns. Thus, for face perception to be considered a truly modular process, we would need to have further evidence of domain specificity and informational encap-sulation. That is, other perceptual processes should not contribute to, interfere with, or share information with face perception. Moreover, the neurological basis of prosop-agnosia is not well understood.

Although cognitive psychologists are intrigued by the fact that a few people are prosopagnosic, they are even more fascinated by the fact that most of us are not. Just how do you recognize your mother or your best friend? In addition, how do you rec-ognize the much simpler and less dynamic forms and patterns of the letters and words in this sentence? This chapter has considered just a few of the many aspects of percep-tion that interest cognitive psychologists. Of particular note are the cognitive pro-cesses by which we form mental representations of what we sense. These representa-tions use prior knowledge, inferences, and specialized cognitive operations to make sense of our sensations.

Anomalies in Color Perception

Another kind of deficit in perception is a deficit in color perception. This deficit is much more common in men than in women. It is genetically linked. This deficit is different than color agnosia. In color agnosia, previously discussed, the person can still perceive a color; however, he or she cannot name it. When a deficit in color perception exists, one cannot detect differences in colors. Deficits in color perception are generally lifelong and do not, as color agnosia does, develop as a result of injury.

There are several kinds of color deficiency, which are sometimes referred to as kinds of "color blindness." However, only one kind represents true color blindness—that in which people cannot see any color at all. People suffering from this most se-vere difficulty have what is referred to as *monochromacy*. Persons who suffer from deficits in color perception to a lesser degree than monochromacy have what is re-ferred to as *dichromacy*. In dichromacy, one of the mechanisms for color perception is malfunctioning. The result of this malfunction is one of the following color percep-tion deficits. The most common is red-green color blindness. People with this form of color-blindness have difficulty in distinguishing red from green, although they may be able to distinguish, say, dark red from light green. People with this form of color blind-ness experience either of two syndromes (*Visual disabilities: Color-blindness*, 2004).

One kind is *protanopia*, which is the extreme form of red-green color blindness. People with this syndrome have trouble seeing the very long wavelengths—namely, reds. These reds appear to them more as beiges, but darker than they really are. The greens look similar to the reds. *Protanomaly* is a less extreme form of red-green color blindness. The second kind of red-green color blindness is *deuteranopia*. People with this syndrome have trouble seeing medium wavelengths—namely, greens. *Deuteranomaly* is a less serious form of this condition. Although people with deuteranomaly do not see reds and greens the way normal people do, they still usually can distinguish them.

Much less common than red-green color blindness is blue-yellow color blindness. People with this form of color blindness have difficulty distinguishing between blues and yellows. *Tritanopia* is insensitivity to short wavelengths—the blues. Blues and greens can be confused, but yellows also can seem to disappear or to appear as light shades of reds.

Least common of all is *rod monochromacy*, also called *achromacy*. People with this condition have no color vision at all. It is thus the only true form of pure color blindness. People with this condition have cones that are nonfunctional. They see only shades of gray, as a function of their vision through the rods of the eye.

Akinetopsia and Achromatopsia

Akinetopsia is a selective loss of motion perception (Gazzaniga, Ivry, & Mangun, 2002). In this disorder, an individual is unable to perceive motion. Rather, motion appears instead as a series of snapshots. The deficit appears to be extremely rare (Zihl, von Cramon, & Mai, 1983). The deficit appears to occur only in cases of severe bilateral damage to the temporoparietal cortices. It is a result of a lesion in the prestriate cortex.

Achromatopsia is a hereditary disorder that results in the absence of cones in the retina. People with this syndrome rely on rods for their vision. They lack color vision and have trouble seeing details. The incidence is estimated at roughly 1 in 33,000 people (*What is achromatopsia?* 2007).

Key Themes

Several key themes, as outlined in Chapter 1, emerge in our study of perception. The first theme is that of rationalism versus empiricism. How much of the way we perceive can be understood as due to some kind of order in the environment that is relatively independent of our perceptual mechanisms? In the Gibsonian view, much of what we perceive derives from the structure of the stimulus, independent of our experience with it. In contrast, in the view of constructive perception, we construct what we perceive. We build up mechanisms for perceiving based on our experience with the environment. As a result, our perception is influenced at least as much by our intelligence as it is by the structure of the stimuli we perceive.

The second important theme is that of basic versus applied research. Research on perception has many applications, such as in understanding how we can construct machines that perceive. The United States Postal Service, for example, relies heavily on machines that read zip codes on mailed items. To the extent that the machines are inaccurate, mail risks going astray. These machines cannot rely on strict template matching because people write numbers in different ways. So the machines must do at least some feature analysis. A second example of an application of perception research is in human factors. Human-factors researchers design machines and user interfaces to be user-friendly. An automobile driver or airplane pilot sometimes needs to make split-second decisions. The cockpits thus must have instrument panels that are well lighted, easy to read, and accessible for quick action.

The third theme is that of domain generality versus domain specificity. Perhaps nowhere is this theme better illustrated than in research on face recognition. Is there something special about face recognition? It appears so. Yet many of the mechanisms that are used for face recognition are used for other kinds of perception as well. Thus, it appears that perceptual mechanisms may be mixed—some general across domains, others specific to domains such as face recognition.

Stand at one end of a room and hold your thumb up to your eye so that it is the same size as the door on the opposite side of the room. Do you *really* think that your thumb is as large as a door? No. You know that your thumb is close to you, so it just *looks* as large as the door. There are numerous cues in the room to tell you that the door is farther away from you than your thumb is. In your mind, you make the door much larger to compensate for the distance away from you. Consistent with a theme mentioned at the beginning of the chapter, knowledge is a key to perception. You know that your thumb and the door are not the same size, so you are able to use this knowledge to correct for what you know is not so.

Summary

1. **How do we perceive stable objects in the environment, given variable stimulation?** Perceptual experience involves four elements: distal object, informational medium, proximal stimulation, and perceptual object. Proximal stimulation is constantly changing because of the variable nature of the environment and physiological processes designed to overcome sensory adaptation. Perception therefore must address the fundamental question of constancy.

   Perceptual constancies (e.g., size and shape constancy) result when our perceptions of objects tend to remain constant. That is, we see constancies even as the stimuli registered by our senses change. Some perceptual constancies may be governed by what we know about the world. For example, we have expectations regarding how rectilinear structures usually appear. But constancies also are influenced by invariant relationships among objects in their environmental context.

   One reason we can perceive 3-D space is the use of binocular depth cues. Two such cues are binocular disparity and binocular convergence. Binocular disparity is based on the fact that each of two eyes receives a slightly different image of the same object as it is being viewed. Binocular convergence is based on the degree to which our two eyes must turn inward toward each other as objects get closer to us. We also are aided in perceiving depth by monocular depth cues. These cues include texture gradients, relative size, interposition, linear perspective, aerial perspective, height in the picture plane, and motion parallax. One of the earliest approaches to form and pattern perception is the Gestalt approach to form perception. The Gestalt law of Prägnanz has led to the explication of several principles of form perception. These principles include figure-ground, proximity, similarity, closure, continuity, and symmetry. They characterize how we perceptually group together various objects and parts of objects.

2. **What are two fundamental approaches to explaining perception?** Perception is the set of processes by which we recognize, organize, and make sense of stimuli in our environment. It may be viewed from either of two basic theoretical approaches: top-down, constructive perception, or bottom-up, direct perception. The viewpoint of constructive (or intelligent) perception asserts that the perceiver essentially constructs or builds up the stimulus that is perceived. He or she does so by using prior knowledge, contextual information, and sensory information. In contrast, the viewpoint of direct perception asserts that all the information we need to perceive is in the sensory input (such as from the retina) that we receive.

Three of the main bottom-up theoretical approaches to pattern perception include template-matching theories, prototype-matching theories, and feature-matching theories. Some support for feature-matching theories comes from neurophysiological studies identifying what are called "feature detectors" in the brain. It appears that various cortical neurons can be mapped to specific receptive fields on the retina. Differing cortical neurons respond to different features. Examples of such features are line segments or edges in various spatial orientations. Visual perception seems to depend on three levels of complexity in the cortical neurons. Each level of complexity seems to be further removed from the incoming information from the sensory receptors. Another bottom-up approach, the recognition-by-components (RBC) theory, more specifically delineates a set of features involved in form and pattern perception.

Bottom-up approaches explain some aspects of form and pattern perception. Other aspects require approaches that suggest at least some degree of top-down processing of perceptual information. For example, top-down approaches better but incompletely explain such phenomena as context effects, including the object-superiority effect and the word-superiority effect.

An alternative to both these approaches integrates features of each. It suggests that perception may be more complex than direct-perception theorists have suggested, yet perception also may involve more efficient use of sensory data than constructive-perception theorists have suggested. Specifically, a computational approach to perception suggests that our brains compute 3-D perceptual models of the environment based on information from the 2-D sensory receptors in our retinas.

3. **What happens when people with normal visual sensations cannot perceive visual stimuli?** Agnosias, which are usually associated with brain lesions, are deficits of form and pattern perception.

They cause afflicted people to be insufficiently able to recognize objects that are in their visual fields, despite normal sensory abilities. People who suffer from visual-object agnosia can sense all parts of the visual field. But the objects they see do not mean anything to them. Individuals with simultagnosia are unable to pay attention to more than one object at a time. People with spatial agnosia have severe difficulty in comprehending and handling the relationship between their bodies and the spatial configurations of the world around them. People with prosopagnosia have severe impairment in their ability to recognize human faces, including their own. These deficits lead to the question of whether specific perceptual processes are modular—specialized for particular tasks. Other perception deficits include various types of color blindness and the inability to perceive motion (akinetopsia).

Thinking about Thinking: Factual, Analytical, Creative, and Practical Questions

1. Briefly describe each of the monocular and binocular depth cues listed in this chapter.

2. Describe bottom-up and top-down approaches to perception.

3. How might deficits of perception, such as agnosia, offer insight into normal perceptual processes?

4. Compare and contrast the Gestalt approach to form perception and the theory of direct perception.

5. Design a demonstration that would illustrate the phenomenon of perceptual constancy.

6. Design an experiment to test either the prototype-matching theory of pattern perception or the feature-matching theory.

7. To what extent does perception involve learning? Why?

Key Terms

agnosia

amacrine cells

binocular depth cues

bipolar cells

bottom-up theories

cones

constructive perception

context effects

depth

direct perception

figure-ground

fovea

ganglion cells

Gestalt approach to form perception

horizontal cells

law of Prägnanz

monocular depth cues

object-centered representation

optic ataxia

optic nerve

perception

perceptual constancy

photopigments

photoreceptors

prototype

recognition-by-components (RBC) theory

retina

rods

templates

top-down theories

viewer-centered representation

 Explore CogLab by going to **http://coglab.wadsworth.com.** Answer the questions required by your instructor from the student manual that accompanies CogLab.

Mapping the Blind Spot

Receptive Fields

Apparent Motion

Metacontrast Masking

Müller-Lyer Illusion

Signal Detection

Visual Search

Lexical Decision

Annotated Suggested Readings

Gauthier, I., Skudlarski, P., Gore, J. C., & Anderson, A. W. (2000). Expertise for cars and birds recruits brain areas involved in face recognition. *Nature Neuroscience, 3,* 191–197. An examination of the role of expertise on the fusiform gyrus.

Palmer, S. E. (1999). *Vision science.* Cambridge, MA: Bradford Books. A very complete and penetrating analysis of all aspects of the cognitive-scientific study of vision.

Sparr, S. A., Jay, M., Drislane, F. W., & Venna, N. (1991). A historical case of visual agnosia revisited after 40 years. *Brain, 114*(2), 789–790. An examination of agnosia over the life of a patient.

Xu, Y. (2005). Revisiting the role of the fusiform face area in visual expertise. *Cerebral Cortex, 15*(8), 1234–1242. An examination of visual expertise.

Attention and Consciousness

EXPLORING COGNITIVE PSYCHOLOGY

1. Can we actively process information even if we are not aware of doing so? If so, what do we do, and how do we do it?

2. What are some of the functions of attention?

3. What are some theories cognitive psychologists have developed to explain what they have observed about attentional processes?

4. What have cognitive psychologists learned about attention by studying the human brain?

The Nature of Attention and Consciousness

[Attention] is the taking possession of the mind, in clear and vivid form, of one out of what seem several simultaneously possible objects or trains of thoughts. . . . It implies withdrawal from some things in order to deal effectively with others.

—William James, *Principles of Psychology*

Attention is the means by which we actively process a limited amount of information from the enormous amount of information available through our senses, our stored memories, and our other cognitive processes (De Weerd, 2003a; Duncan, 1999; Motter, 1999; Posner & Fernandez-Duque, 1999; Rao, 2003). It includes both conscious and unconscious processes. Conscious processes are relatively easy to study in many cases. Unconscious processes are harder to study simply because you are not conscious of them (Jacoby, Lindsay, & Toth, 1992; Merikle, 2000). For example, you always have available to you your memory of where you slept when you were 10 years old, but you probably do not often process that information actively. Similarly, you usually have available a wealth of sensory information (e.g., in your body and in your peripheral vision at this very moment). But you attend to only a limited amount of the available sensory information at a given time (Figure 4.1). Moreover, you have very little reliable information about what happens when you sleep. Additionally, the contents of attention can reside either within or outside of awareness (Davies, 1999; Davies & Humphreys, 1993; Metzinger, 1995).

There are many advantages to having attentional processes of some sort. There seem to be at least some limits to our mental resources. There are limits as well to the amount of information on which we can focus those mental resources at any one time. The psychological phenomenon of attention allows us to use our limited mental resources judiciously. By dimming the lights on many stimuli from outside (sensations) and inside (thoughts and memories), we can highlight the stimuli that interest us. This heightened focus increases the likelihood that we can respond speedily and accurately to interesting stimuli. Heightened attention also paves the way for memory

FIGURE 4.1

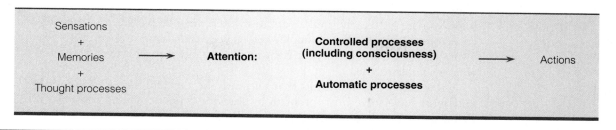

Attention acts as a means of directing mental resources toward the information and cognitive processes that are most salient at a given moment.

processes. We are more likely to remember information to which we paid attention than information we ignored.

Consciousness includes both the feeling of awareness and the content of awareness, some of which may be under the focus of attention (Block, Flanagan, & Güzeldere, 1997; Bourguignon, 2000; Chalmers, 1995, 1996; Cohen & Schooler, 1997; Farthing, 1992, 2000; Marcel & Bisiach, 1988; Nelkin, 1996; Peacocke, 1998; Taylor, 2002; Velmans, 1996). Therefore, attention and consciousness form two partially overlapping sets (DiGirolamo & Griffin, 2003). At one time, psychologists believed that attention was the same thing as consciousness. Now, however, they acknowledge that some active attentional processing of sensory information, and the remembered information, proceeds without our conscious awareness (Shear, 1997; Tye, 1995). For example, at this time in your life, writing your own name requires no conscious awareness. You may write it while consciously engaged in other activities—although not if you are completely unconscious. In contrast, writing a name that you have never encountered requires attention to the sequence of letters.

The benefits of attention are particularly salient when we refer to conscious attentional processes. In addition to the overall value of attention, conscious attention serves three purposes in playing a causal role for cognition. First, it helps in monitoring our interactions with the environment. Through such monitoring, we maintain our awareness of how well we are adapting to the situation in which we find ourselves. Second, it assists us in linking our past (memories) and our present (sensations) to give us a sense of continuity of experience. Such continuity may even serve as the basis for personal identity. Third, it helps us in controlling and planning for our future actions. We can do so based on the information from monitoring and from the links between past memories and present sensations.

Preconscious Processing

Some information that currently is outside our conscious awareness still may be available to consciousness or at least to cognitive processes. Information that is available for cognitive processing but that currently lies outside conscious awareness exists at the preconscious level of awareness. Preconscious information includes stored memories that we are not using at a given time but that we could summon when needed. For example, when prompted, you can remember what your bedroom looks like. But obviously you are not always consciously thinking about your bedroom (unless, perhaps, you are extremely tired). Sensations, too, may be pulled from preconscious to conscious awareness. For example, before you read this sentence, were you highly aware of the sensations in your right foot? Probably not. However, those sensations were available to you.

How can we study things that currently lie outside conscious awareness? Psychologists have solved this problem by studying a phenomenon known as priming. **Priming** occurs when recognition of certain stimuli is affected by prior presentation of the same or similar stimuli (Neely, 2003). Suppose, for example, someone is talking to you about how much he has enjoyed watching television since buying a satellite dish. He speaks at length about the virtues of satellite dishes. Later, you hear the word *dish*. You are probably more likely to think of a satellite dish, as opposed to a dish served at dinner, than is someone who did not hear the prior conversation about satellite dishes. Most priming is positive. Prior presentation of stimuli facilitates later recognition. But priming on occasion may be negative. It may impede later recognition. Sometimes we are aware of the priming stimuli. For example, you are now primed to read descriptions of studies involving priming. However, priming occurs even when the priming stimulus is presented in a way that does not permit its entry into conscious awareness. In such a case, it is presented at too low an intensity, in too "noisy" a background (i.e., too many other stimuli divert conscious attention from it), or too briefly to be registered in conscious awareness.

For example, in a set of studies Marcel observed processing of stimuli that were presented too briefly to be detected in conscious awareness (Marcel, 1983a, 1983b). In these studies, words were presented to participants very briefly (as measured in milliseconds, or thousandths of a second). After presentation, each word was replaced by a visual mask. The mask blocks the image of the word from remaining on the retina (the rear surface of the eye, comprising the sensory receptors of vision). Marcel timed the presentations to be very brief (20–110 milliseconds). In this way, he was sure that participants could not detect their presence consciously. When participants were asked to guess the word they had seen, their guesses were no better than chance.

In one such study, Marcel presented participants with a series of words to be classified into various categories. Examples would be *leg—body part* and *pine—plant*. In this study, the priming stimuli were words having more than one meaning. For example, a palm can be either a tree or a part of the hand. In one condition, participants consciously were aware of seeing a priming word that had two meanings. For these participants, the mental pathway for only one of the two meanings seemed to become activated. In other words, one of the two meanings of the word showed the priming effect. It facilitated (speeded up) the classification of a subsequent related word. However, the other of the two meanings showed a sort of negative priming effect. It actually inhibited (slowed down) the classification of a subsequent unrelated word. For example, if the word *palm* was presented long enough so that the participant was consciously aware of seeing it, the word either facilitated or inhibited the classification of the word *wrist*, which it did depending on whether the participant associated *palm* with *hand* or with *tree*. Apparently, if the participant was consciously aware of seeing the word *palm*, the mental pathway for only one meaning was activated. The mental pathway for the other meaning was inhibited. In contrast, if the word *palm* was presented so briefly that the person was unaware of seeing the word, both meanings of the word appeared to be activated. This procedure facilitated subsequent classification of the new words, such as *wrist*.

Marcel's results were controversial and in need of replication by independent investigators using stringent controls. Such a replication was indeed performed (Cheesman & Merikle, 1984). The investigators used a color-identification task. They found that the occurrence of subliminal perception depended on how one defined the threshold of awareness. If one defined the threshold below which perception is subliminal in terms of the level at which participants report a word occurring half the time, then subliminal perception could be said to occur. If, however, one defined subliminal perception in terms of an objective threshold that applies for everyone, then subliminal perception did not occur. This study points out the importance of a precise definition in any cognitive-psychological investigation. Whether a phenomenon occurs sometimes depends on exactly how that phenomenon is defined.

Another example of possible priming effects and preconscious processing can be found in a study described as a test of intuition. This study used a "dyad of triads" task (Bowers & associates, 1990). Participants were presented with pairs (dyads) of three-word groups (triads). One of the triads in each dyad was a potentially coherent grouping. The other triad contained random and unrelated words. For example, the words in Group A, a coherent triad, might have been *playing, credit*, and *report*. The words in Group B, an incoherent triad, might have been *still, pages*, and *music*. After presentation of the dyad of triads, participants were shown various possible choices for a fourth word related to one of the two triads. The participants then were asked to identify two things. The first was which of the two triads was coherent and related to a fourth word. The second was which fourth word linked the coherent triad. In the preceding example, the words in Group A can be meaningfully paired with a fourth word—*card* (playing card, credit card, report card). The words in Group B bear no such relationship.

Some participants could not figure out the unifying fourth word for a given pair of triads. They were nevertheless asked to indicate which of the two triads was coherent. When participants could not ascertain the unifying word, they still were able to identify the coherent triad at a level well above chance. They seemed to have some preconscious information available to them. This information led them to select one triad over the other. They did so even though they did not consciously know what word unified that triad.

The examples described above involve visual priming. Priming, however, does not have to be visual. Priming effects can be demonstrated using aural material as well. Experiments exploring auditory priming reveal the same behavioral effects as visual priming. Using neuroimaging methods, investigators have discovered that similar brain areas are involved in both types of priming (Badgaiyan, Schacter, & Alpert, 1999; Bergerbest, Ghahremani, & Gabrieli, 2004; Schacter & Church, 1992).

An interesting application of auditory priming was used with patients under anesthesia. While under anesthesia, these patients were presented lists of words. After awakening from anesthesia, the patients were asked yes/no questions and word-stem completion questions about the words they heard. The patients performed at chance on the yes/no questions. They reported no conscious knowledge of the words. However, on the word-stem completion task, patients showed evidence of priming. The patients frequently completed the word-stems with the items they were presented while they were under anesthesia. These findings reveal that, even when the patient has absolutely no recollection of an aural event, it can still affect performance (Deeprose & associates, 2005).

Unfortunately, sometimes pulling preconscious information into conscious awareness is not easy. For example, most of us have experienced the **tip-of-the-tongue phenomenon,** in which we try to remember something that is known to be stored in memory but that cannot readily be retrieved. Psychologists have tried to come up with experiments that measure this phenomenon. For example, they have sought to find out how much people can draw from information that seems to be stuck at the preconscious level. In one study (Brown & McNeill, 1966), participants were read a large number of dictionary definitions. They then were asked to identify the corresponding words having these meanings. This procedure constituted a game similar to the television show *Jeopardy*. For example, they might have been given the clue, "an instrument used by navigators to measure the angle between a heavenly body and a horizon."

In the study, some participants could not come up with the word but thought they knew it. They then were asked various questions about the word. For example, they might be asked to identify the first letter, indicate the number of syllables, or approximate the word's sounds. The participants often answered these questions accurately. They might have been able to indicate some properties of the appropriate word for the aforementioned instrument. For example, it begins with an *s*, has two syllables, and sounds like *sextet*. Eventually, some participants realized that the sought-after word was *sextant*. These results indicate that particular preconscious information, although not fully accessible to conscious thinking, is still available to attentional processes.

The tip-of-the-tongue phenomenon is apparently universal. It is seen in speakers of many different languages. It is also seen in people with limited or no ability to read (Brennen, Vikan, & Dybdahl, 2007). The tip-of-the-tongue phenomenon is affected by the person's age and the difficulty of the question. Older adults have more tip-of-the-tongue experiences compared with younger adults (Gollan & Brown, 2006). The anterior cingualate-prefrontal cortices are involved when one is experiencing the tip-of-the-tongue phenomenon. This is likely due to high-level cognitive mechanisms being activated in order to resolve the retrieval failure (Maril, Wagner, & Schacter, 2001).

Preconscious perception also has been observed in people who have lesions in some areas of the visual cortex (Ro & Rafal, 2006). Typically, the patients are blind in areas of the visual field that correspond to the lesioned areas of the cortex. Some of these patients, however, seem to show **blindsight**—traces of visual perceptual ability in blind areas (Kentridge, 2003). When forced to guess about a stimulus in the "blind" region, they correctly guess locations and orientations of objects at above-chance levels (Weiskrantz, 1994). Similarly, when forced to reach for objects in the blind area, "cortically blind participants . . . will nonetheless preadjust their hands appropriately to size, shape, orientation and 3-D location of that object in the blind field" (Marcel, 1986, p. 41). Yet they fail to show voluntary behavior, such as reaching for a glass of water in the blind region, even when they are thirsty. Some visual processing seems to occur even when participants have no conscious awareness of visual sensations.

An interesting example of blindsight can be found in a case study of a patient called D. B. (Weiskrantz, 1986). The patient was blind on the left side of his visual field as an unfortunate result of an operation. That is, each eye had a blind spot on the left side of its visual field. Consistent with this damage, D. B. reported no awareness of any objects placed on his left side or of any events that took place on this side. But despite his unawareness of vision on this side, there was evidence of vision. The investigator would present objects to the left side of the visual field and then present D. B. with a forced-choice test in which the patient had to indicate which of two objects had been presented to this side. D. B. performed at levels that were significantly better than chance. In other words, he "saw" despite his unawareness of seeing.

Another study was completed on a patient who had, as a result of a stroke, suffered damage to his visual cortex. The experimenters repeatedly paired a visual stimulus with an electric shock. After multiple pairings, the patient began to experience fear when the visual stimulus was presented, even though he could not explain why he was afraid. Thus, the patient was processing visual information, although he could not see (Hamm & associates, 2003).

The preceding examples show that at least some cognitive functions can occur outside of conscious awareness. We appear able to sense, perceive, and even respond to many stimuli that never enter our conscious awareness (Marcel, 1983a). Just what kinds of processes do or do not require conscious awareness?

Repeatedly write your name on a piece of paper while you picture everything you can remember about the room in which you slept when you were 10 years old. While continuing to write your name and picturing your old bedroom, take a mental journey of awareness to notice your bodily sensations, starting from one of your big toes and proceeding up your leg, across your torso, to the opposite shoulder, and down your arm. What sensations do you feel—pressure from the ground, your shoes, or your clothing or even pain anywhere? Are you still managing to write your name while retrieving remembered images from memory and continuing to pay attention to your current sensations?	**INVESTIGATING COGNITIVE PSYCHOLOGY**

Controlled versus Automatic Processes

Many cognitive processes also may be differentiated in terms of whether they do or do not require conscious control (Schneider & Shiffrin, 1977; Shiffrin & Schneider, 1977). **Automatic processes** involve no conscious control (see Palmeri, 2003). For the most part, they are performed without conscious awareness. Nevertheless, you may be aware that you are performing them. They demand little or no effort or even intention. Multiple automatic processes may occur at once, or at least very quickly, and in no particular sequence. Thus, they are termed *parallel processes*. In contrast, **controlled processes** are accessible to conscious control and even require it. Such processes are performed serially. In other words, they occur sequentially, one step at a time. They take a relatively long time to execute, at least as compared with automatic processes.

Three attributes characterize automatic processes (Posner & Snyder, 1975). First, they are concealed from consciousness. Second, they are unintentional. Third, they

IN THE LAB OF JOHN F. KIHLSTROM

Courtesy of Yale University

John Kihlstrom is a professor in the Department of Psychology at the University of California, Berkeley. He is also a member of two interdisciplinary groups, the Institute for Cognitive and Brain Sciences and the Institute for Personality and Social Research. He currently directs the interdisciplinary undergraduate program in cognitive science. His article in Science *magazine on "The Cognitive Unconscious" (Kihlstrom, 1987) is widely credited with sparking renewed scientific interest in unconscious mental life after almost a century of Freudianism.*

A major goal of my research is to use the methods of cognitive psychology to understand the phenomena of hypnosis, a special state of consciousness in which subjects may see things that aren't there, fail to see things that are there, and respond to posthypnotic suggestions without knowing what they are doing or why. Afterward, they may be unable to remember the things they did while they were hypnotized—the phenomenon of posthypnotic amnesia, which has been a major focus of my research (Kihlstrom, 2007).

First, however, we have to find the right subjects. There are big individual differences in hypnotizability, or the ability to experience hypnosis. Although hypnotizable individuals have a proclivity for other sorts of imaginative and absorbing experiences, there is no personality questionnaire that can predict reliably who can experience hypnosis and who cannot. The only way to find out who is hypnotizable is to try hypnosis and see if it works. For this purpose, we rely on a set of standardized scales of hypnotic susceptibility, which are performance-based tests much like tests of intelligence. Each scale begins with an induction of hypnosis in which the subjects are asked to relax, focus their eyes, and pay close attention to the voice of the hypnotist. Then the subjects receive a series of suggestions for various hypnotic experiences. Their response to each of these suggestions is evaluated according to standardized, behavioral criteria, yielding a total score representing the person's ability to experience hypnosis.

From this point on, however, our experiments on cognition look just like anyone else's—except that our subjects are hypnotized. In one study using a familiar verbal-learning paradigm (Kihlstrom, 1980), the subjects memorized a list of 15 familiar words, such as *girl* or *chair*, and then received a suggestion for posthypnotic amnesia: "You will not be able to remember that you learned any words while you were hypnotized....You will have no memory that I told you these words, or what the words were." As part of this suggestion, we set up a "reversibility cue" ("Now you can remember everything") to cancel the amnesia suggestion. After coming out of hypnosis, highly hypnotizable subjects remembered virtually none of the list, whereas insusceptible subjects, who had gone through the same procedures, remembered the list almost perfectly. This shows that the occurrence of posthypnotic amnesia is highly correlated with hypnotizability.

Then we gave all subjects a word-association test, in which they were presented with cues and asked to report the first word that came to mind. Some of these cues were words like *boy* and *table*, which were known to have a high probability of producing the "critical targets" on the study list. Others were control cues, like *lamp* and *dogs*, which had an equally high probability of producing neutral targets like *light* and *cats*, which had not been studied. Despite their inability to remember the words they had just studied, the hypnotizable, amnesic subjects produced critical targets as free associates at the same rate as the insusceptible, nonamnesic subjects. This shows that posthypnotic amnesia is a disruption of episodic, but not semantic, memory. In fact, Endel Tulving (1983) cited this experiment as one of the few convincing studies of the difference between these two kinds of memory.

Even more important, the subjects were more likely to generate critical rather than neutral targets on the free-association test. This is a phenomenon of semantic priming, in which a previous experience, such as studying a list of words, facilitates performance on a subsequent task, such as generating words on a free-

IN THE LAB OF JOHN F. KIHLSTROM—cont'd

association test (Meyer & Schvaneveldt, 1971). The magnitude of the priming effect was the same in the hypnotizable, amnesic subjects as it was in the insusceptible, nonamnesic subjects. In other words, posthypnotic amnesia entails a dissociation between explicit and implicit memory (Schacter, 1987).

While explicit and implicit memory is dissociated in other forms of amnesia, the dissociation observed in posthypnotic amnesia has some features that make it special. Most studies of implicit memory in neurologically intact subjects employ highly degraded encoding conditions, such as shallow processing, to impair explicit memory. But in posthypnotic amnesia, encoding is not by any means degraded: The subjects deliberately memorized the list to a strict criterion of learning before the amnesia suggestion was given, and they remembered the list perfectly well after the amnesia suggestion was reversed. Thus, the phenomenon shows that implicit memory can be dissociated from explicit memory even under deep processing conditions. More important, most studies of implicit memory in amnesia (and normal memory, too) concern repetition priming, as exemplified by stem-completion and fragment-completion tests. Repetition priming can be mediated by a perception-based representation of the prime—and, accordingly, the most popular theories of implicit memory focus on perceptual representation systems in the brain. But in this study, the priming is semantic in

nature and must be mediated by a meaning-based representation of the prime. In this way, studies of hypnosis remind us that a comprehensive theory of implicit memory is going to have to go beyond repetition priming and beyond perceptual representation systems.

References

Kihlstrom, J. F. (1980). Posthypnotic amnesia for recently learned material: Interactions with "episodic" and "semantic" memory. *Cognitive Psychology, 12*, 227–251.

Kihlstrom, J. F. (1987). The cognitive unconscious. *Science, 237*(4821), 1445–1452.

Kihlstrom, J. F. (2007). Consciousness in hypnosis. In P. D. Zelazo, M. Moscovitch, & E. Thompson (Eds.), *Cambridge handbook of consciousness* (pp. 445–479). Cambridge, U.K.: Cambridge University Press.

Meyer, D. E., & Schvaneveldt, R. W. (1971). Facilitation in recognizing pairs of words: Evidence of a dependence between retrieval operations. *Journal of Experimental Psychology, 90*, 227–234.

Schacter, D. L. (1987). Implicit memory: History and current status. *Journal of Experimental Psychology: Learning, Memory, and Cognition, 13*, 501–518.

Tulving, E. (1983). *Elements of episodic memory.* Oxford, U.K.: Oxford University Press.

consume few attentional resources. An alternative view of attention suggests a continuum of processes between fully automatic processes and fully controlled processes. For one thing, the range of controlled processes is so wide and diverse that it would be difficult to characterize all the controlled processes in the same way (Logan, 1988). Similar difficulties arise with characterizing automatic processes. Some automatic processes truly cannot be retrieved into conscious awareness, despite any amount of effort to do so. Examples are preconscious processing and priming. Other automatic processes, such as tying your shoes, can be controlled intentionally. But they rarely are handled in this way. For example, you seldom may think about all the steps involved in executing many automatic behaviors. Automatic behaviors, regardless of whether they can be called into consciousness, require no conscious decisions regarding which muscles to move or which actions to take. For example, when you dial a familiar telephone number or drive a car to a familiar place, you do not think about

TABLE 4.1	Controlled versus Automatic Processes

There is probably a continuum of cognitive processes from fully controlled processes to fully automatic ones; these features characterize the polar extremes of each.

CHARACTERISTICS	CONTROLLED PROCESSES	AUTOMATIC PROCESSES
Amount of intentional effort	Require intentional effort	Require little or no intention or effort (and intentional effort may even be required to avoid automatic behaviors)
Degree of conscious awareness	Require full conscious awareness	Generally occur outside of conscious awareness, although some automatic processes may be available to consciousness
Use of attentional resources	Consume many attentional resources	Consume negligible attentional resources
Type of processing	Performed serially (one step at a time)	Performed by parallel processing (i.e., with many operations occurring simultaneously or at least in no particular sequential order)
Speed of processing	Relatively time-consuming execution, as compared with automatic processes	Relatively fast
Relative novelty of tasks	Novel and unpracticed tasks or tasks with many variable features	Familiar and highly practiced tasks, with largely stable task characteristics
Level of processing	Relatively high levels of cognitive processing (requiring analysis or synthesis)	Relatively low levels of cognitive processing (minimal analysis or synthesis)
Difficulty of tasks	Usually difficult tasks	Usually relatively easy tasks, but even relatively complex tasks may be automatized, given sufficient practice
Process of acquisition	With sufficient practice, many routine and relatively stable procedures may become automatized, such that highly controlled processes may become partly or even wholly automatic; naturally, the amount of practice required for automatization increases dramatically for highly complex tasks	

the muscles you move to do so. However, their identities can be pulled into conscious awareness and controlled relatively easily. (Table 4.1 summarizes the characteristics of controlled versus automatic processes.)

In fact, many tasks that start off as controlled processes eventually become automatic ones. For example, driving a car is initially a controlled process. Once we master driving, however, it becomes automatic under normal driving conditions. Such conditions involve familiar roads, fair weather, and little or no traffic. Similarly, when you first learn to speak a foreign language, you need to translate word-for-word from your native tongue. Eventually, however, you begin to think in the second language. This thinking enables you to bypass the intermediate-translation stage. It also allows the process of speaking to become automatic. Your conscious attention can revert to the content, rather than the process, of speaking. A similar shift from conscious control to automatic processing occurs when acquiring the skill of reading.

However, when conditions change, the same activity may again require conscious control. In the driving example, if the roads become icy, you will likely need to pay attention to when you need to brake or accelerate. Both tasks usually are automatic when driving.

You may notice that the procedures you learned early in life often are more highly automatic and less accessible to conscious awareness than are procedures acquired later. Examples are tying your shoes, riding a bicycle, or even reading. In general, more recently acquired routine processes and procedures are less fully automatic. At the same time, they are more accessible to conscious control. **Automatization** (also termed *proceduralization*) is the process by which a procedure changes from being highly conscious to being relatively automatic. As you may have guessed based on your own experience, automatization occurs as a result of practice. Highly practiced activities can be automatized (LaBerge, 1975, 1976, 1990; LaBerge & Samuels, 1974).

How does automatization occur? A widely accepted view has been that during the course of practice, implementation of the various steps becomes more efficient. The individual gradually combines individual effortful steps into integrated components. These components then are further integrated. Eventually the entire process is a single highly integrated procedure, rather than an assemblage of individual steps (Anderson, 1983; LaBerge & Samuels, 1974). According to this view, people consolidate various discrete steps into a single operation. This operation requires few or no cognitive resources, such as attention. This view of automatization seems to be supported by one of the earliest studies of automatization (Bryan & Harter, 1899). This study investigated how telegraph operators gradually automatized the task of sending and receiving messages. Initially, new operators automatized the transmission of individual letters. However, once the operators had made the transmission of letters automatic, they automatized the transmission of words, phrases, and then other groups of words.

An alternative explanation, called "instance theory," has been proposed. Logan (1988) suggested that automatization occurs because we gradually accumulate knowledge about specific responses to specific stimuli. For example, when a child first learns to add or subtract, he or she applies a general procedure—counting—for handling each pair of numbers. Following repeated practice, the child gradually stores knowledge about particular pairs of particular numbers. Eventually, the child can retrieve from memory the specific answers to specific combinations of numbers. Nevertheless, he or she still can fall back on the general procedure (counting) as needed. Similarly, when learning to drive, the person can draw on an accumulated wealth of specific experiences. These experiences form a knowledge base from which the person quickly can retrieve specific procedures for responding to specific stimuli, such as oncoming cars or stoplights. Preliminary findings suggest that Logan's instance theory may better explain specific responses to specific stimuli, such as calculating arithmetic combinations. The prevailing view may better explain more general responses involving automatization (Logan, 1988).

The effects of practice on automatization show a negatively accelerated curve. In such a curve, early practice effects are great. A graph of improvement in performance would show a steeply rising curve early on. Later practice effects make less and less difference in the degree of automatization. On a graph showing improvement, the curve would eventually level off (Figure 4.2). Clearly, automatic processes generally

FIGURE 4.2

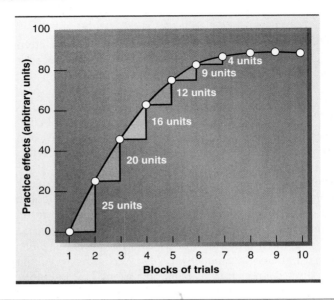

The rate of improvement caused by practice effects shows a pattern of negative acceleration. The negative acceleration curve attributed to practice effects is similar to the curve shown here, indicating that the rate of learning slows down as the amount of learning increases, until eventually learning peaks at a stable level.

govern familiar, well-practiced tasks. Controlled processes govern relatively novel tasks. In addition, most automatic processes govern relatively easy tasks. Most difficult tasks require controlled processing. With sufficient practice, however, even many extremely complex tasks, such as reading, can become automatized. Because highly automatized behaviors require little effort or conscious control, we often can engage in multiple automatic behaviors. But we rarely can engage in more than one labor-intensive controlled behavior. Although automatic processes do not require conscious control, they are subject to such control. For example, skilled articulation (speaking) and skilled typing can be stopped almost immediately on signal or in response to detection of an error. However, skilled performance of automatic behaviors often is impaired by conscious control. Try riding a bicycle while consciously monitoring your every movement. It will be extremely difficult to succeed.

Automatization of tasks like reading is not guaranteed, even with practice. Much research has indicated that, in cases of dyslexia, automatization is impaired. More specifically, persons who have dyslexia frequently have difficulty completing tasks, in addition to reading, that are normally automated (Brambati & associates, 2006; Ramus & associates, 2003; van der Leij, de Jong, & Rijswijk-Prins, 2001; Yap & van der Leij, 1994). It is not necessary that all tasks that involve automatization are impaired in people with dyslexia. In some studies, some degree of automatization has been noted in persons with dyslexia (Kelly, Griffths, & Frith, 2002).

It is important to automate various safety practices (Norman, 1976). This is particularly true for people engaging in high-risk occupations, such as pilots, undersea divers, and firefighters. For example, novice divers often complain about the frequent repetition of various safety procedures within the confines of a swimming pool. An example would be releasing a cumbersome weight belt. However, the practice is important, as the novices will learn later. Experienced divers recognize the value of being able to rely on automatic processes in the face of potential panic should they confront a life-threatening deep-sea emergency.

In some situations, automatic processes may be life saving. But in others, they may be life threatening (Langer, 1997). Consider an example of what Langer (1989) calls "mindlessness." In 1982, a pilot and copilot went through a routine checklist prior to takeoff. They mindlessly noted that the anti-icer was "off," as it should be under most circumstances. But it should not have been off under the icy conditions in which they were preparing to fly. The flight ended in a crash that killed 74 passengers. Typically, our absentminded implementation of automatic processes has far less lethal consequences. For example, when driving, we may end up routinely driving home instead of stopping by the store, as we had intended to do. Or we may pour a glass of milk and then start to put the carton of milk in the cupboard rather than in the refrigerator.

An extensive analysis of human error notes that errors can be classified either as mistakes or as slips (Reason, 1990). Mistakes are errors in choosing an objective or in specifying a means of achieving it. Slips are errors in carrying out an intended means for reaching an objective. Suppose, for example, you decided that you did not need to study for an examination. Thus, you purposely left your textbook behind when leaving for a long weekend. But then you discovered at the time of the exam that you should have studied. In Reason's terms, you made a mistake. However, suppose instead you fully intended to bring your textbook with you. You had planned to study extensively over the long weekend, but in your haste to leave, you accidentally left the textbook behind. That would be a slip. In sum, mistakes involve errors in intentional, controlled processes. Slips often involve errors in automatic processes (Reason, 1990).

There are several kinds of slips (Norman, 1988; Reason, 1990; see Table 4.2). In general, slips are most likely to occur when two circumstances occur. First, when we must deviate from a routine and automatic processes inappropriately override intentional, controlled processes. Second, when our automatic processes are interrupted. Such interruptions are usually a result of external events or data, but sometimes they are a result of internal events, such as highly distracting thoughts. Imagine that you are typing a paper after an argument with a friend. You may find yourself pausing in your typing as thoughts about what you should have said interrupt your normally automatic process of typing. Automatic processes are helpful to us under many circumstances. They save us from needlessly focusing attention on routine tasks, such as tying our shoes or dialing a familiar phone number. We are thus unlikely to forgo them just to avoid occasional slips. Instead, we should attempt to minimize the costs of these slips.

How can we minimize the potential for negative consequences of slips? In everyday situations, we are less likely to slip when we receive appropriate feedback from the environment. For example, the milk carton may be too tall for the cupboard shelf, or a passenger may say, "I thought you were stopping at the store before going home."

| TABLE 4.2 | Slips Associated with Automatic Processes |

Occasionally, when we are distracted or interrupted during implementation of an automatic process, slips occur. However, in proportion to the number of times we engage in automatic processes each day, slips are relatively rare events (Reason, 1990).

TYPE OF ERROR	DESCRIPTION OF ERROR	EXAMPLE OF ERROR
Capture errors	We intend to deviate from a routine activity we are implementing in familiar surroundings, but at a point where we should depart from the routine we fail to pay attention and to regain control of the process; hence, the automatic process captures our behavior, and we fail to deviate from the routine.	Psychologist William James (1890/1970, cited in Langer, 1989) gave an example in which he automatically followed his usual routine, undressing from his work clothes, then putting on his pajamas and climbing into bed—only to realize that he had intended to remove his work clothes to dress to go out to dinner.
Omissions*	An interruption of a routine activity may cause us to skip a step or two in implementing the remaining portion of the routine.	When going to another room to retrieve something, if a distraction (e.g., a phone call) interrupts you, you may return to the first room without having retrieved the item.
Perseverations*	After an automatic procedure has been completed, one or more steps of the procedure may be repeated.	If, after starting a car, you become distracted, you may turn the ignition switch again.
Description errors	An internal description of the intended behavior leads to performing the correct action on the wrong object.	When putting away groceries, you may end up putting the ice cream in the cupboard and a can of soup in the freezer.
Data-driven errors	Incoming sensory information may end up overriding the intended variables in an automatic action sequence.	While intending to dial a familiar phone number, if you overhear someone call out another series of numbers, you may end up dialing some of those numbers instead of the ones you intended to dial.
Associative-activation errors	Strong associations may trigger the wrong automatic routine.	When expecting someone to arrive at the door, if the phone rings, you may call out, "Come in!"
Loss-of-activation errors	The activation of a routine may be insufficient to carry it through to completion.	All too often, each of us has experienced the feeling of going to another room to do something and getting there only to ask ourselves, "What am I doing here?" Perhaps even worse is the nagging feeling, "I know I should be doing something, but I can't remember what." Until something in the environment triggers our recollection, we may feel extremely frustrated.

*Omissions and perseverations may be considered examples of errors in the sequencing of automatic processes. Related errors include inappropriately sequencing the steps, as in trying to remove socks before taking off shoes.

If we can find ways to obtain useful feedback, we may be able to reduce the likelihood that harmful consequences will result from slips. A particularly helpful kind of feedback involves forcing function. These are physical constraints that make it difficult or impossible to carry out an automatic behavior that may lead to a slip (Norman, 1988). As an example of a forcing function, some modern cars make it difficult or impossible to drive the car without wearing a seatbelt. You can devise your own forcing functions. You may post a small sign on your steering wheel as a reminder to run an errand on the way home. Or you may put items in front of the door. In this way, you block your exit so that you cannot leave without the items you want.

Over a lifetime, we automatize countless everyday tasks. However, one of the most helpful pairs of automatic processes first appears within hours after birth: habituation and its complementary opposite, dishabituation.

Habituation and Adaptation

Habituation involves our becoming accustomed to a stimulus so that we gradually pay less and less attention to it. The counterpart to habituation is dishabituation. In **dishabituation,** a change in a familiar stimulus prompts us to start noticing the stimulus again. Both processes occur automatically. They involve no conscious effort. The relative stability and familiarity of the stimulus govern these processes. Any aspects of the stimulus that seem different or novel (unfamiliar) either prompt dishabituation or make habituation less likely to occur in the first place. For example, suppose that a radio is playing instrumental music while you study your cognitive psychology textbook. At first the sound might distract you. But after a while you become habituated to the sound and scarcely notice it. If the loudness of the noise were suddenly to change drastically, however, immediately you would dishabituate to it. The once familiar sound to which you had been habituated would become unfamiliar. It thus

---

PRACTICAL APPLICATIONS OF COGNITIVE PSYCHOLOGY

Habituation is not without faults. Becoming bored during a lecture or while reading a textbook is a sign of habituation. Your attention may start to wander to the background noises, or you may find that you have read a paragraph or two with no recollection of the content. Fortunately, you can dishabituate yourself with very little effort. Here are a few tips on how to overcome the negative effects of boredom.

1. Take a break or alternate between different tasks if possible. If you do not remember the last few paragraphs of the text, it is time to stop for a few minutes. Go back and mark the last place in the text you do remember and put the book down. If you feel like a break is a waste of valuable time, do some other work for a while.

2. Take notes while reading or listening. Most people already do so. Note-taking focuses attention on the material more than does simply listening or reading. If necessary, try switching from script to printed handwriting to make the task more interesting.

3. Adjust your attentional focus to increase stimulus variability. Is the instructor's voice droning on endlessly so that you cannot take a break during lecture? Try noticing other aspects of your instructor, like hand gestures or body movements, while still paying attention to the content. Create a break in the flow by asking a question—even just raising your hand can make a change in a lecturer's speaking pattern. Change your arousal level. If all else fails, you may have to force yourself to be interested in the material. Think about how you can use the material in your everyday life. Also, sometimes just taking a few deep breaths or closing your eyes for a few seconds can change your internal arousal levels.

TABLE 4.3	Differences between Sensory Adaptation and Habituation

Responses involving physiological adaptation take place mostly in our sense organs, whereas responses involving cognitive habituation take place mostly in our brains (and relate to learning).

ADAPTATION	HABITUATION
Not accessible to conscious control (*Example:* You cannot decide how quickly to adapt to a particular smell or a particular change in light intensity.)	Accessible to conscious control (*Example:* You can decide to become aware of background conversations to which you had become habituated.)
Tied closely to stimulus intensity (*Example:* The more the intensity of a bright light increases, the more strongly your senses will adapt to the light.)	Not tied very closely to stimulus intensity (*Example:* Your level of habituation will not differ much in your response to the sound of a loud fan and to that of a quiet air conditioner.)
Unrelated to the number, length, and recency of prior exposures (*Example:* The sense receptors in your skin will respond to changes in temperature in basically the same way no matter how many times you have been exposed to such changes and no matter how recently you have experienced such changes.)	Tied very closely to the number, length, and recency of prior exposures (*Example:* You will become more quickly habituated to the sound of a chiming clock when you have been exposed to the sound more often, for longer times, and on more recent occasions.)

would enter your awareness. Habituation is not limited to humans. It is found in organisms as simple as the mollusk *Aplysia* (Castellucci & Kandel, 1976).

We usually exert no effort whatsoever to become habituated to our sensations of stimuli in the environment. Nonetheless, although we usually do not consciously control habituation, we can do so. In this way, habituation is an attentional phenomenon that differs from the physiological phenomenon of sensory adaptation. **Sensory adaptation** is a lessening of attention to a stimulus that is not subject to conscious control. It occurs directly in the sense organ, not in the brain. We can exert some conscious control over whether we notice something to which we have become habituated, but we have no conscious control over sensory adaptation. For example, we cannot consciously force ourselves to smell an odor to which our senses have become adapted. Nor can we consciously force our pupils to adapt—or not adapt—to differing degrees of brightness or darkness. In contrast, if someone asked us, "Who's the lead guitarist in that song?" we can once again notice background music. Table 4.3 provides some of the other distinctions between sensory adaptation and habituation.

Two factors that influence habituation are stimulus internal variation and subjective arousal. Some stimuli involve more internal variation than do others. For example, background music contains more internal variation than does the steady drone of an air conditioner. The relative complexity of the stimulus (e.g., an ornate, intricate Oriental rug versus a gray carpet) does not seem to be important to habituation. Rather, what matters is the amount of change within the stimulus over time. For example, a mobile involves more change than does an ornate but rigid sculpture. Thus, it is relatively difficult to remain continually habituated to the frequently changing noises coming from a television. But it is relatively easy to become habituated to a constantly running fan. The reason is that the voices typically speak animatedly and with great inflectional expression. They are constantly changing, whereas the sound a fan makes remains constant with little to no variation.

Psychologists can observe habituation occurring at the physiological level by measuring our degree of arousal. **Arousal** is a degree of physiological excitation, responsivity, and readiness for action, relative to a baseline. Arousal often is measured in terms of heart rate, blood pressure, electroencephalograph (EEG) patterns, and other physiological signs. Consider what happens, for example, when an unchanging visual stimulus remains in our visual field for a long time. Our neural activity (as shown on an EEG) in response to that stimulus decreases (see Chapter 2). Both neural activity and other physiological responses (e.g., heart rate) can be measured. These measurements detect heightened arousal in response to perceived novelty or diminished arousal in response to perceived familiarity. In fact, psychologists in many fields use physiological indications of habituation to study a wide array of psychological phenomena in people who cannot provide verbal reports of their responses. Examples of such people are infants and comatose patients. Physiological indicators of habituation tell the researcher whether the person notices changes in the stimulus. Such changes might occur in the color, pattern, size, or form of a stimulus. These indicators signal whether the person notices the changes at all, as well as what specific changes the person notices in the stimulus.

Among other phenomena, psychologists have used habituation to study visual discrimination (detection of differences among stimuli) in infants. First, they habituate the infant to a particular visual pattern. They do so by presenting it until the infant no longer pays attention to it. Then they introduce a visual pattern that only slightly differs from the one to which the infant has become habituated. If the infant is able to discriminate the difference, the infant will not habituate to (i.e., will notice) the new pattern. If the infant cannot discriminate the difference, however, the infant will appear to be habituated to the new pattern as well.

Habituation definitely gives much more to our attentional system than it receives. That is, habituation itself requires no conscious effort and few attentional resources. Despite its negligible use of attentional resources, it offers a great deal of support to attentional processes. It allows us easily to turn our attention away from familiar and relatively stable stimuli and toward novel and changing stimuli. We might conjecture about the evolutionary value of habituation. Without habituation, our attentional system would be much more greatly taxed. How easily would we function in our highly stimulating environments if we could not habituate to familiar stimuli? Imagine trying to listen to a lecture if you could not habituate to the sounds of your own breathing, the rustling of papers and books, or the faint buzzing of fluorescent lights.

An example of the failure to habituate can be seen in persons who suffer from tinnitus. Tinnitus is a ringing in the ears. People who complain of having tinnitus seem to have problems habituating to auditory stimuli. Many people have ringing in their ears, and if they are placed in a quiet room, will report a buzzing or other sounds. However, people who chronically suffer from tinnitus have difficulty adapting to the noise (Walpurger & associates, 2003). Evidence also indicates that people with attention deficit hyperactivity disorder (ADHD), which will be discussed later in this chapter, have difficulty habituating to many types of stimuli. This difficulty helps to explain why ordinary stimuli, such as the buzzing of fluorescent lights, can be distracting to a person with ADHD (Jansiewicz & associates, 2004).

Attention

Signal Detection

Habituation supports our attentional system, but this system performs many functions other than merely tuning out familiar stimuli and tuning into novel ones. Conscious attention has four main functions. First, in **signal detection,** we detect the appearance of a particular stimulus. We try to detect a signal, through *vigilance,* even after we begin to feel fatigue as a result of long-term absence of a signal. Second, in **selective attention,** we choose to attend to some stimuli and to ignore others (Cohen, 2003; Duncan, 1999). Third, in **divided attention,** we prudently allocate our available attentional resources to coordinate our performance of more than one task at a time. Fourth, in search, we try to find a signal amidst distractors. These four functions are summarized in Table 4.4.

First consider signal detection. What factors contribute to your ability to detect important events in the world? How do people search the environment to detect important stimuli? Understanding this function of attention has immediate practical importance. A lifeguard at a busy beach must be ever vigilant. Similarly, an air-traffic controller must be highly vigilant. Many other occupations require vigilance. Examples are those involving communications and warning systems and quality control in almost any setting. Even the work of police detectives, physicians, and research psychologists requires vigilance. We also must search out from among a diverse array of items those that are more important. In each of these settings, people must remain alert to detect the appearance of a stimulus. But each setting also involves the presence of distracters, as well as prolonged periods during which the stimulus is absent.

The Nature of Signal Detection

Signal-detection theory (SDT) involves four possible outcomes of the presence or absence of a stimulus and our detection or nondetection of a stimulus. It characterizes our attempts to detect a **signal,** a target stimulus (Table 4.5). First, in *hits* (also called "true positives"), we correctly identify the presence of a target. Second, in *false alarms* (also called "false positives"), we incorrectly identify the presence of a target that is actually absent. Third, in *misses* (also called "false negatives"), we fail to observe the presence of a target. Fourth, in *correct rejections* (also called "true negatives"), we correctly identify the absence of a target. Usually, the presence of a target is difficult to detect. Thus, we make detection judgments based on inconclusive information with some criteria for target detections. The number of hits is influenced by where you place your criteria for considering something a hit. In other words, how willing are you to make false alarms? For example, sometimes the consequences of making a miss are so grave that we lower the criteria for considering something as a hit. In this way, we increase the number of false alarms we make to boost hit detection. This trade-off often occurs with medical diagnoses. For example, it might occur with highly sensitive screening tests where positive results lead to further tests. Thus, overall sensitivity to targets must reflect the placement of a flexible criterion and is measured in terms of hits minus false alarms. SDT often is used to measure sensitivity to a target's

TABLE 4.4		Four Main Functions of Attention

Cognitive psychologists have been particularly interested in the study of divided attention, vigilance and signal detection, search, and selective attention.

FUNCTION	DESCRIPTION	EXAMPLE
Vigilance and signal detection	On many occasions, we vigilantly try to detect whether we did or did not sense a signal, a particular target stimulus of interest. Through vigilant attention to detecting signals, we are primed to take speedy action when we do detect signal stimuli.	In a research submarine, we may watch for unusual sonar blips; in a dark street, we may try to detect unwelcome sights or sounds; or following an earthquake, we may be wary of the smell of leaking gas or of smoke.
Selective attention	We constantly are making choices regarding the stimuli to which we will pay attention and the stimuli that we will ignore. By ignoring or at least deemphasizing some stimuli, we thereby highlight particularly salient stimuli. The concentrated focus of attention on particular informational stimuli enhances our ability to manipulate those stimuli for other cognitive processes, such as verbal comprehension or problem solving.	We may pay attention to reading a textbook or to listening to a lecture while ignoring such stimuli as a nearby radio or television or latecomers to the lecture.
Divided attention	We often manage to engage in more than one task at a time, and we shift our attentional resources to allocate them prudently, as needed.	Experienced drivers easily can talk while driving under most circumstances, but if another vehicle seems to be swerving toward their car, they quickly switch all their attention away from talking and toward driving.
Search	We often engage in an active search for particular stimuli.	If we detect smoke (as a result of our vigilance), we may engage in an active search for the source of the smoke. In addition, some of us are constantly in search of missing keys, sunglasses, and other objects; my son often "searches" for missing items in the refrigerator (often without much success—until someone else points them out to him).

TABLE 4.5		Signal Detection Matrix Used in Signal-Detection Theory

Signal-detection theory was one of the first theories to suggest an interaction between the physical sensation of a stimulus and cognitive processes such as decision making.

SIGNAL	DETECT A SIGNAL	DO NOT DETECT A SIGNAL
Present	Hit	Miss
Absent	False alarm	Correct rejection

presence. Measurement can occur under conditions of both vigilance and the search for targets. It also is used in memory research to control for effects of guessing.

Signal-detection theory can be covered in the context of attention, perception, or memory. It is relevant in the context of attention in terms of whether one is paying enough attention to perceive objects that are there. It is relevant in the context of perception in terms of whether one is able to perceive faint signals that may or may not be beyond one's perceptual range (such as a very high-pitched tone). It is relevant in the context of memory in terms of whether one indicates one has or has not been exposed to a stimulus before, such as a word that may or may not have appeared on a list that was to be memorized.

Consider a practical example of signal-detection theory relevant to attention—detecting a box cutter in hand-carried luggage. Airport screeners generally are capable of perceiving such objects. The question is whether they attend carefully enough. A hit would involve recognizing a box cutter in a passenger's luggage. A miss would involve failing to see a box cutter that is there. A false alarm would involve thinking one sees a box cutter when there is none, and a correct rejection would be recognizing that there is no box cutter when there is none.

In a disturbing finding, on September 11, 2001, the 9/11 hijackers were screened at airports as they prepared to board their flights, and several of them were pulled aside because they set off metal detectors. After further screening, they were let onto their planes anyway, although they were carrying box cutters. The results of what constituted a "miss" for the screeners were disastrous. As a result of this fiasco, the rules for screening were tightened up considerably. But the tightening of rules created many false alarms. Babies, grandmothers, and other relatively low-risk passengers started to get second and sometimes even third screenings. So the rules were modified to profile passengers by computer. For example, those who bought one-way tickets or changed their flight plans at the last moment became more likely to be subjected to extra screening. This procedure, in turn, has inconvenienced those travelers who need to change their travel plans frequently, such as business travelers. The system for screening passengers is constantly evolving in order to minimize both misses and false alarms (Figure 4.3).

Vigilance

Vigilance refers to a person's ability to attend to a field of stimulation over a prolonged period, during which the person seeks to detect the appearance of a particular target stimulus of interest. When being vigilant, the individual watchfully waits to detect a signal stimulus that may appear at an unknown time. Typically, vigilance is needed in settings where a given stimulus occurs only rarely but requires immediate attention as soon as it does occur. Military officers watching for a sneak attack are engaged in a high-stakes vigilance task.

In one study, participants watched a visual display that looked like the face of a clock (Mackworth, 1948). A clock hand moved in continuous steps. Every once in a while, the clock hand would take a double step. The participants' task was to press a button as soon as possible after observing a double step. Participants' performance began to deteriorate substantially after just half an hour of observation. Indeed, after a half hour, participants were missing close to one fourth of the double steps. It ap-

FIGURE 4.3

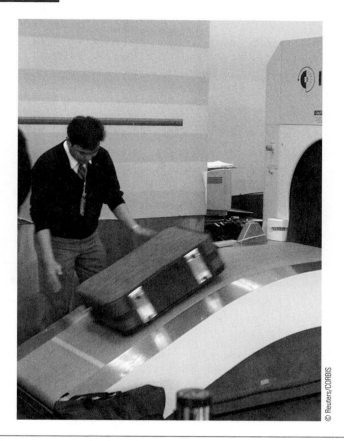

© Reuters/CORBIS

Screening hand luggage is an example of signal-detection theory at work in everyday life. Screeners learn techniques to enable them to maximize "hits" and "correct rejections" and to minimize "false alarms" and "misses."

pears that decreases in vigilance are not primarily a result of participants' decreased sensitivity. Rather, they are due to their increased doubtfulness about their perceived observations (Broadbent & Gregory, 1965). To relate these findings to SDT, over time it appears that participants become less willing to risk reporting false alarms. They err instead by failing to report the presence of the signal stimulus when they are not sure they detect it. They thereby show higher rates of misses. Training can help to increase vigilance (Fisk & Schneider, 1981). But in tasks requiring sustained vigilance, fatigue hinders performance. So there may be no substitute for frequent rest periods to enhance signal detection.

Attentional processes governing signal detection also appear to be highly localized and strongly influenced by expectation (Motter, 1999; Posner, Snyder, & Davidson, 1980). Neurological studies show that signal detection of a visual stimulus is greatest at the point where a signal is expected to appear. Accuracy of signal detection

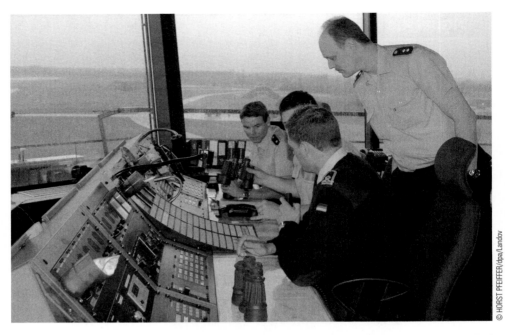

© HORST PFEIFFER/dpa/Landov

For some jobs, vigilance is a matter of life and death.

falls off sharply as the appearance of the stimulus occurs farther from the locus of attention (LaBerge & Brown, 1989; LaBerge, Carter, & Brown, 1992; Mangun & Hillyard, 1990, 1991). Thus, a busy lifeguard or air-traffic controller may respond quickly to a signal within a narrow radius of where a signal is expected to appear. But signals appearing outside the concentrated range of vigilant attention may not be detected as quickly or as accurately.

In vigilance tasks, expectations regarding location strongly affect response efficiency. In this case, efficiency involves the speed and accuracy of detecting a target stimulus. However, expectations regarding the form of the stimulus do not (Posner, Snyder, & Davidson, 1980). Here, form refers to what shape or letter may appear in a visual field. Suppose, now, that a participant is cued to look for a target stimulus in two distant locations. This cueing does not enhance vigilance performance for both locations. Various studies suggest that visual attention may be (very roughly) likened to a spotlight. Stimuli within the region of the attentional spotlight are detected readily, but stimuli outside the spotlight are not detected as well (Eckstein, Shumozaki, & Abbey, 2000; Norman, 1968; Palmer, 1990; Posner, Snyder, & Davidson, 1980). Furthermore, like a spotlight, the beam of focused attention can be narrowly concentrated on a small area or widened to embrace a larger, more diffuse area (Palmer, 1990). However, the abrupt onset of a stimulus (i.e., the sudden appearance of a stimulus) captures our attention. This effect occurs even when factors such as degree of illuminance (brightness) are controlled (Yantis, 1993). Thus, we seem to be predisposed to notice the sudden appearance of stimuli in our visual field. We might speculate about the adaptive advantage this feature of attention may have offered to our ancestral hunter-gatherer forebears. They presumably needed to avoid various predators. They also had to catch various prey.

Increased vigilance is seen in cases where emotional stimuli are used. The amygdala plays a pivotal role in the recognition of emotional stimuli. Thus, the amygdala appears to be an important brain structure in the regulation of vigilance (Phelps, 2004, 2006; Whalen, 1998).

Vigilance is extremely important in warding off terrorist attacks of various kinds. For example, repeating announcements at airports often ask travelers to be vigilant in looking for unattended baggage, which may contain explosives. Because luggage is such a common site at airports, it is difficult to spot bags that are lying unattended, not seeming to belong to anyone. Similarly, in many countries, pedestrians are asked to be vigilant for cars or trucks that seem to be unattended and parked in odd places because they may contain explosives that can be detonated at a distance. The costs of failure of vigilance, in today's world, can be great loss of life as well as property.

Search

Whereas vigilance involves passively waiting for a signal stimulus to appear, search involves actively and often skillfully seeking out a target (Pashler, 1998; Posner & DiGirolamo, 1998; Posner, DiGirolamo, & Fernandez-Duque, 1997; Wolfe, 1994). Specifically, **search** refers to a scan of the environment for particular features— actively looking for something when you are not sure where it will appear. Trying to locate a particular brand of cereal in a crowded aisle at the grocery store—or a particular key term in a crowded textbook—is an example of search. As with vigilance, when we are searching for something, we may respond by making false alarms. Airport screeners look at X-rays of hand luggage, trying to determine whether there are any sharp objects in the baggage that might pose a danger in flight. Search is made more difficult by **distracters,** nontarget stimuli that divert our attention away from the target stimulus. In the case of search, false alarms usually arise when we encounter such distracters while searching for the target stimulus. For instance, consider searching for a product in the grocery store. We often see several distracting items that look something like the item we hope to find. Package designers take advantage of the effectiveness of distracters when creating packaging for products. For example, if a container looks like a box of Cheerios, you may pick it up without realizing that it's really Tastee-Oh's.

As you may have expected, the number of targets and distracters affects the difficulty of the task. For example, try to find the *T* in panel *a* of Figure 4.4 *a*. Then try to find the *T* in panel *b* of Figure 4.4 *a*. *Display size* is the number of items in a given visual array. (It does not refer to the size of the items or even the size of the field on which the array is displayed.) The display-size effect is the degree to which the number of items in a display hinders (slows down) the search process. When studying visual-search phenomena, investigators often manipulate the display size. They then observe how various contributing factors increase or decrease the display-size effect.

Distracters cause more trouble under some conditions than under others. Suppose we look for some distinctive features. Examples might be color, size, proximity to like items, distance from unlike items, or orientation, such as vertical, horizontal, or oblique. We are able to conduct a **feature search,** in which we simply scan the envi-

FIGURE 4.4A

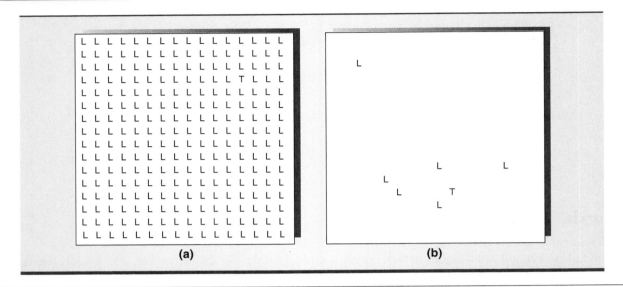

(a)   (b)

Compare the relative difficulty in finding the T in panels a and b. The display size affects your ease of performing the task.

Anne Treisman is a professor of psychology at Princeton University. She is well known for her work in a variety of areas of attention and perception, especially her theory that incoming signals are attenuated rather than filtered when they make their way through the cognitive-processing system.

ronment for that feature or those features (Treisman, 1986, 1992, 1993). Distracters play little role in slowing our search in that case. For example, try to find the O in panel c of Figure 4.4 b. The O has some distinctive features, as compared with the L distracters in the display. The O thus seems to pop out of the display. Featural singletons, which are items with distinctive features, stand out in the display (Yantis, 1993). When featural singletons are targets, they seem to grab our attention. They make search virtually impossible to avoid. Unfortunately, any featural singletons grab our attention. This includes featural singletons that are distracters. When we are searching for a featural-singleton target stimulus, a featural-singleton distracter stimulus seems to distract us from finding the target (Theeuwes, 1992). For example, find the T in panel d of Figure 4.4 b. The T is a featural singleton. But the presence of the black (filled) circle probably slows you down in your search.

A problem arises, however, when the target stimulus has no unique or even distinctive features. An example might be a particular boxed or canned item in a grocery aisle. In these situations, the only way we can find it is to conduct a conjunction search (Treisman, 1991). In a **conjunction search,** we look for a particular combination (conjunction—joining together) of features. For example, the only difference between a T and an L is the particular integration (conjunction) of the line segments. The difference is not a property of any single distinctive feature of either letter. Both letters comprise a horizontal line and a vertical line. So a search looking for either of these features would provide no distinguishing information. In Figure 4.4 a, you had to perform a conjunction search to find the T. So it probably took you longer to find it than to find the O in Figure 4.4 b.

FIGURE 4.4B

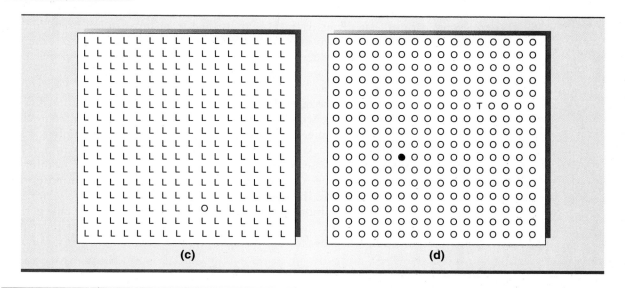

In panel c, find the O, and in panel d, find the T.

As we age, our ability to perform an efficient visual search declines. Researchers have noted that this decline is associated with areas that are responsible for processing visual information (Madden & associates, 2007). These findings highlight the importance of the visual system in search.

Feature-Integration Theory

According to Anne Treisman, **feature-integration theory** explains the relative ease of conducting feature searches and the relative difficulty of conducting conjunction searches. Consider Treisman's (1986) model of how our minds conduct visual searches. For each possible feature of a stimulus, each of us has a mental map for representing the given feature across the visual field. For example, there is a map for every color, size, shape, or orientation (e.g., p, q, b, d) of each stimulus in our visual field. For every stimulus, the features are represented in the feature maps immediately. There is no added time required for additional cognitive processing. Thus, during feature searches, we monitor the relevant feature map for the presence of any activation anywhere in the visual field. This process can be done in parallel (all at once). It therefore shows no display-size effects. However, during conjunction searches, an additional stage of processing is needed. During this stage, we must use our attentional resources as a sort of mental "glue." It conjoins two or more features into an object representation at a particular location. This attentional process can only conjoin the features one object at a time. This stage must be carried out sequentially, conjoining each object one by one. Effects of display size (i.e., a larger number of objects with features to be conjoined) therefore appear.

Sometimes people search for information quite effectively, although their attention is divided. How can they do this? One way is through a feature inhibition mechanism (Treisman & Sato, 1990). Here, inhibition or suppression occurs of irrelevant features that might distract an individual from being able to search for a target. There is some neuropsychological support for Treisman's model. For example, Nobel laureates David Hubel and Torsten Wiesel (1979) have identified specific neural feature detectors. These are cortical neurons that respond differentially to visual stimuli of particular orientations. Examples of such orientations would be vertical, horizontal, or diagonal. More recently, investigators have identified additional cortical processes involved in the various distinct steps of feature integration required for a variety of tasks (Bachevalier & Mishkin, 1986; Mishkin & Appenzeller, 1987; Mishkin, Ungerleider, & Macko, 1983). These tasks include object recognition and visual discrimination. The researchers observed that during visual search, differing neural activity appears to be involved in the relatively low-level identification of features. This is in contrast to the neural activity during relatively high-level featural integration and synthesis. Today we know that processing is more complex than Hubel and Wiesel originally thought. There is parallel processing of color, orientation, motion, depth, and other features (Maunsell, 1995).

Similarity Theory

Not everyone agrees with Treisman's model, however. According to *similarity theory*, Treisman's data can be reinterpreted. In this view, the data are a result of the fact that as the similarity between target and distracter stimuli increases, so does the difficulty in detecting the target stimuli (Duncan & Humphreys, 1989, 1992). Thus, targets that are highly similar to distracters are hard to detect. Targets that are highly disparate from distracters are easy to detect. For example, try to find the black (filled) circle in Figure 4.4 c. The target is highly similar to the distracters (black squares or white circles). It is therefore very difficult to find.

According to this theory, another factor that facilitates the search for target stimuli is similarity (uniformity) among the distracters (Duncan & Humphreys, 1989). Searching for target stimuli against a background of relatively uniform (highly similar) distracters is fairly easy. But searching for target stimuli against a background of highly diverse distracters is quite difficult. Furthermore, the difficulty of search tasks depends on the degree of similarity between the targets and the distracters and on the degree of disparity among the distracters. But it does not depend on the number of features to be integrated. For instance, one reason that it is easier to read long strings of text written in lowercase letters than text written in capital letters is that capital letters tend to be more similar to one another in appearance. Lowercase letters, in contrast, have more distinguishing features. However, as in the initial letter of a sentence or of a word in a title, capital letters are quite distinctive from lowercase letters. You can get an idea of how highly dissimilar distracters impede visual search. Try to find the capital letter R in panels f and g of Figure 4.4 d.

In addition, some findings do not fit well with Treisman's theory. For example, some features (e.g., size and color) may be conjoined easily even without attentional processes. Search for these integrated features appears to occur about as rapidly as does search for some discrete features (He & Nakayama, 1992; Nakayama, 1990). It

FIGURE 4.4C

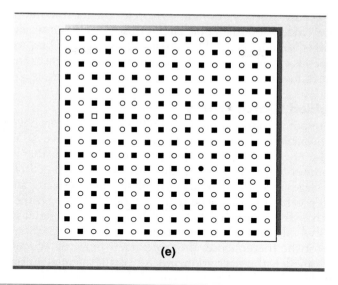

(e)

In panel e, find the black circle.

FIGURE 4.4D

(f)   (g)

In panels f and g, find the R.

would be about as easy to search for objects with conjoined features of size and color as it would be to search for objects of a distinctive color alone. For instance, it would be as easy to search for large red circles (target stimuli) versus small red circles, large blue circles, and small blue circles (distracters) as it would be to search for red circles (target stimuli) versus blue circles (distracters). Thus, the difficulty of visual search depends not only on whether discrete features must be integrated. It also depends on which features must be integrated in a given search.

Guided Search Theory

In response to these and other findings, investigators have proposed an alternative to Treisman's model. They call it *guided search* (Cave & Wolfe, 1990). According to these researchers, the guided-search model suggests that all searches, whether feature searches or conjunction searches, involve two consecutive stages. The first is a parallel stage. In it, the individual simultaneously activates a mental representation of all the potential targets. The representation is based on the simultaneous activation of each of the features of the target. In a subsequent serial stage, the individual sequentially evaluates each of the activated elements, according to the degree of activation. He or she then chooses the true targets from the activated elements. According to this model, the activation process of the parallel initial stage helps to guide the evaluation and selection process of the serial second stage of the search.

Let's see how guided search might work. Try to find the white circles in panel *h* of Figure 4.4 *e*. In this case, the targets are all white circles. The distracters are all black squares. Thus, we have a feature search. So the parallel stage will activate all the circles, but it will activate none of the squares. Therefore, the serial stage quickly will be able to select all the targets. However, look at panel *i* of Figure 4.4 *e*. Try to find the black circle. The distracters include white squares, white circles, and black squares. Hence, the parallel stage will activate a mental map for the target black circle. This is the top-priority activation because of the conjunction of features. For the distracter, it will activate black squares and white circles. During the serial stage, you first will evaluate the black circle, which was highly activated. But then you will evaluate the black squares and the white circles, which were less highly activated. You then will dismiss them as distracters.

Cave and Wolfe's guided-search model predicts that some conjunction searches are easier than others. In particular, those involving more items with features similar to those of the target are easier than those involving fewer items with features similar to those of the target. These researchers found support for their model by creating computer simulations. They then compared the performance of the simulations with the actual performance of participants carrying out searches. Under most circumstances, the simulations of their model produced results that were very similar to those of the actual participants.

Final Considerations

Suppose we know in advance the general area in which to expect a stimulus to be located. We then can find the stimulus much more readily (Posner, Snyder, & Davidson, 1980). For example, consider panel *j* of Figure 4.4 *f*. Once we detect the spatial pattern regarding where to expect the target stimulus, our search becomes easier. Prior

FIGURE 4.4E

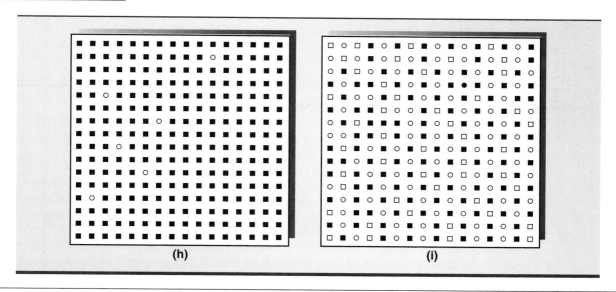

In panel h, find the white (hollow) circles, and in panel i, find the black circle.

FIGURE 4.4F

In panel j, find the deviant stimulus in each subarray. In panels k and l, find all instances of the letters p and a.

knowledge also influences our ability to use various strategies for conjunctive searches. For example, for most people over age 7 years, it will be relatively easy to find the instances of the letters *a* and *p* in panel *k* of Figure 4.4 *f*. Similarly, anyone who is experienced at touch-typing can readily find the instances of those letters in panel *l* of Figure 4.4 *f*. In both cases, prior knowledge may facilitate visual search.

Selective and Divided Attention

Basic Paradigms for Studying Selective Attention

Suppose you are at a dinner party. It is just your luck that you are sitting next to a salesman. He sells 110 brands of vacuum cleaners. He describes to you in excruciating detail the relative merits of each brand. As you are listening to this blatherer, who happens to be on your right, you become aware of the conversation of the two diners sitting on your left. Their exchange is much more interesting. It contains juicy information you had not known about one of your acquaintances. You find yourself trying to keep up the semblance of a conversation with the blabbermouth on your right, but you are also tuning in to the dialogue on your left.

The preceding vignette describes a naturalistic experiment in selective attention. It was inspired by the research of Colin Cherry (1953). Cherry referred to this phenomenon as the **cocktail party problem,** the process of tracking one conversation in the face of the distraction of other conversations. He observed that cocktail parties are often settings in which selective attention is salient. The preceding is a good example.

Cherry did not actually hang out at numerous cocktail parties to study conversations. He studied selective attention in a more carefully controlled experimental setting. He devised a task known as shadowing. In *shadowing,* you listen to two different messages. You are required to repeat back only one of the messages as soon as possible after you hear it. In other words, you are to follow one message (think of a detective "shadowing" a suspect) but ignore the other. For some participants, he used **binaural presentation,** presenting the same two messages or sometimes just one message to both ears simultaneously. For other participants, he used **dichotic presentation,** presenting a different message to each ear. (Figure 4.5 illustrates how these listening tasks might be presented.)

Cherry's participants found it virtually impossible to track only one message during simultaneous binaural presentation of two distinct messages. It is as though in attending to one thing, we divert attention from another (Desimone & Duncan, 1995; Duncan, 1996). His participants much more effectively shadowed distinct messages in dichotic-listening tasks. In such tasks they generally shadowed messages fairly accurately. During dichotic listening, participants also were able to notice physical, sensory changes in the unattended message—for example, when the message was changed to a tone or the voice changed from a male to a female speaker. However, they did not notice semantic changes in the unattended message. They failed to notice even when the unattended message shifted to English or German or was played backward. Conversely, about one third of people, when their name is presented during these situations, will switch their attention to their name. Some researchers have

FIGURE 4.5

Colin Cherry discovered that selective attention was much easier during dichotic presentation than during binaural presentation of differing messages.

noted that those who hear their name in the unattended message tend to have limited working-memory capacity. As a result, they are easily distracted (Conway, Cowan, & Bunting, 2001). Infants will also shift their attention to one of two messages if their name is said (Newman, 2005).

Think of being at a cocktail party or in a noisy restaurant. Three factors help you to selectively attend only to the message of the target speaker to whom you wish to listen. The first is distinctive sensory characteristics of the target's speech. Examples of such characteristics are high versus low pitch, pacing, and rhythmicity. A second is sound intensity (loudness), and a third is location of the sound source (Brungard & Simpson, 2007). Attending to the physical properties of the target speaker's voice has its advantages. You can avoid being distracted by the semantic content of messages from nontarget speakers in the area. Clearly, the sound intensity of the target also helps. In addition, you probably intuitively can use a strategy for locating sounds. This changes a binaural task into a dichotic one. You turn one ear toward and the other ear away from the target speaker. Note that this method offers no greater total sound intensity. The reason is that with one ear closer to the speaker, the other is farther away. The key advantage is the difference in volume. It allows you to locate the source of the target sound.

Filter and Bottleneck Theories of Selective Attention

Models of selective attention can be of several different kinds (Bundesen, 1996, 2000; Logan, 1996). The models differ in two ways. First, do they have a distinct "filter" for incoming information? Second, if they do, where in the processing of information does the filter occur (Pashler, 1998)?

Broadbent's Model

According to one of the earliest theories of attention, we filter information right after it is registered at the sensory level (Broadbent, 1958; Figure 4.6). In Broadbent's view, multiple channels of sensory input reach an attentional filter. It permits only one channel of sensory information to proceed through the filter to reach the processes of perception. We thereby assign meaning to our sensations. In addition to the target stimuli, stimuli with distinctive sensory characteristics may pass through the attentional system. Examples would be differences in pitch or in loudness. They thereby reach higher levels of processing, such as perception. However, other stimuli will be filtered out at the sensory level. They may never pass through the attentional filter to reach the level of perception. Broadbent's theory was supported by Colin Cherry's findings that sensory information may be noticed by an unattended ear. Examples of such material would be male versus female voices or tones versus words. But information requiring higher perceptual processes is not noticed in an unattended ear. Examples would be German versus English words or even words played backward instead of forward.

FIGURE 4.6

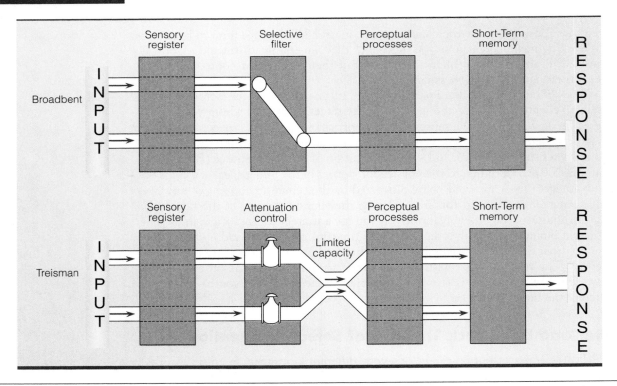

Various mechanisms have been proposed suggesting a means by which incoming sensory information passes through the attentional system to reach high-level perceptual processes.

Moray's Selective Filter Model

Not long after Broadbent's theory, evidence began to suggest that Broadbent's model must be wrong (e.g., Gray & Wedderburn, 1960). First, an investigator found that even when participants ignore most other high-level (e.g., semantic) aspects of an unattended message, they frequently still recognize their names in an unattended ear (Moray, 1959). He suggested that the reason for this effect is that powerful, highly salient messages may break through the filter of selective attention. But other messages may not. To modify Broadbent's metaphor, one could say that, according to Moray, the selective filter blocks out most information at the sensory level. But some highly salient, or personally important, messages are so powerful that they burst through the filtering mechanism.

Treisman's Attenuation Model

While a participant is shadowing a coherent message in one ear and ignoring a message in the other ear, something interesting occurs. If the message in the attended ear suddenly is switched to the unattended ear, participants will pick up the first few words of the old message in the new ear (Treisman, 1960). This finding suggests that context briefly will lead the participants to shadow a message that should be ignored.

Moreover, if the unattended message was identical to the attended one, all participants noticed it. They noticed even if one of the messages was slightly out of temporal synchronization with the other (Treisman, 1964a, 1964b). Participants typically recognized the two messages to be the same when the shadowed message was as much as 4.5 seconds ahead of the unattended one. They also recognized it if it was as far as 1.5 seconds behind the unattended one. Treisman also observed fluently bilingual participants. Some of them noticed the identity of messages if the unattended message was a translated version of the attended one.

Moray's modification of Broadbent's filtering mechanism was clearly not sufficient to explain Treisman's (1960, 1964a, 1964b) findings. Her findings suggested to Treisman that at least some information about unattended signals is being analyzed. Treisman also interpreted Moray's findings as indicating that some higher-level processing of the information reaching the supposedly unattended ear must be taking place. Otherwise, participants would not recognize the familiar sounds to realize that they were salient. That is, the incoming information cannot be filtered out at the level of sensation. If it were, we would never perceive the message to recognize its salience.

Based on these findings, Treisman proposed a theory of selective attention. It involves a different kind of filtering mechanism. Recall that in Broadbent's theory the filter acts to block stimuli other than the target stimulus. In Treisman's theory, however, the mechanism merely attenuates (weakens the strength of) stimuli other than the target stimulus. For particularly potent stimuli, the effects of the attenuation are not great enough to prevent the stimuli from penetrating the signal-weakening mechanism. Figure 4.6 illustrates Treisman's signal-attenuating mechanism.

According to Treisman, selective attention involves three stages. In the first stage, we preattentively analyze the physical properties of a stimulus. Examples would be loudness (sound intensity) and pitch (related to the "frequency" of the sound waves). This preattentive process is conducted in parallel (simultaneously) for all incoming sensory stimuli. For stimuli that show the target properties, we pass the signal on to the next stage. For stimuli that do not show these properties, we pass on only a weakened version of the stimulus. In the second stage, we analyze whether a given stimulus has a pattern, such as speech or music. For stimuli that show the target pattern, we pass the signal on to the next stage. For stimuli that do not show the target pattern, we pass on only a weakened version of the stimulus. In the third stage we focus attention on the stimuli that make it to this stage. We sequentially evaluate the incoming messages. We assign appropriate meanings to the selected stimulus messages.

Deutsch and Deutsch's Late Filter Model

Consider an alternative to Treisman's attenuation theory. It simply moves the location of the signal-blocking filter to follow, rather than precede, at least some of the perceptual processing needed for recognition of meaning in the stimuli. In this view, the signal-blocking filter occurs later in the process. It has its effects after sensory analysis. Thus, it occurs after some perceptual and conceptual analysis has occurred (Deutsch & Deutsch, 1963; Norman, 1968; Figure 4.7). This later filtering would allow people to recognize information entering the unattended ear. For example, they might recognize the sound of their own names or a translation of attended input (for bilinguals). If the information does not perceptually strike some sort of chord, people will throw it out at the filtering mechanism shown in Figure 4.7. If it does, however, as with the sound of an important name, people will pay attention to it. Note that proponents of both the early and the late filtering mechanisms propose that there is an attentional bottleneck through which only a single source of information can pass. The two models differ only in terms of where they hypothesize the bottleneck to be positioned.

The Multimode Theory

Multimode theory (Johnston & Heinz, 1978) proposes that attention is flexible. Selection of one message over another message can be made at any of various different points in the course of information processing. According to this theory, processing

---

FIGURE 4.7

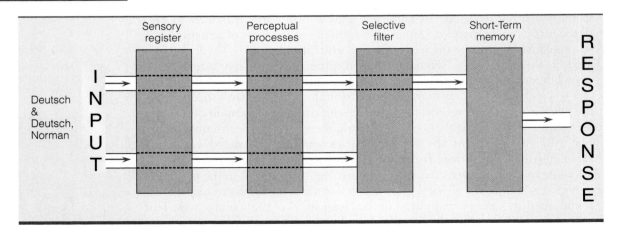

According to some cognitive psychologists, the attentional filtering mechanisms follow, rather than precede, preliminary perceptual processes.

occurs in three stages. In Stage 1, the individual constructs sensory representations of stimuli. In Stage 2, the individual constructs semantic representations. Neither of these stages is fully conscious. In Stage 3, the representations of Stages 1 and 2 become conscious. Early selection (Broadbent) would be associated with Stage 1, whereas late selection would be associated with Stage 3. The difficulty of a task requiring selection depends, in part, upon when selection takes place. More effort is required in later than in earlier stages.

Neisser's Synthesis

In 1967, Ulric Neisser synthesized the early-filter and the late-filter models in a way different from Johnston and Heinz (1978). He proposed that there are two processes governing attention: preattentive and attentive processes. Preattentive, automatic processes are rapid and occur in parallel. They can be used to notice only physical sensory characteristics of the unattended message. But they do not discern meaning or relationships. Attentive, controlled processes occur later. They are executed serially and consume time and attentional resources, such as working memory. They also can be used to observe relationships among features. They serve to synthesize fragments into a mental representation of an object. More recent work in attention builds on Neisser's distinction between preattentive and attentive processes. It focuses only on the consciously controlled aspects of attention (Cowan, 1995).

Consider a different view of the two processes (McCann & Johnston, 1992). According to these researchers, physical analysis of sensory data occurs continually, but semantic analysis of stimuli occurs only when cognitive capacity (in the form of working memory) is not already overtaxed; the capacity also must be sufficient to permit such analysis. Supportive evidence is that people show much faster reaction times when responding to physically discriminable stimuli than to semantically discriminable stimuli.

A two-step model of some sort could account for Cherry's, Moray's, and Treisman's data. Evidence of fully automatic versus fully controlled processes also seems to support this model. Automatic processes may be governed only by the first step of attentional processing. Controlled processes additionally may be governed by the second of the two steps. The model also nicely incorporates aspects of Treisman's signal-attenuation theory and of her subsequent feature-integration theory. According to this latter theory, discrete processes for feature detection and for feature integration occur during searches. Again, Treisman's feature-detection process may be linked to the former of the two processes (i.e., speedy, automatic processing). Her feature-integration process may be linked to the latter of the two processes (i.e., slower, controlled processing). Unfortunately, however, the two-step model does not do a good job of explaining the continuum of processes from fully automatic ones to fully controlled ones. Recall, for example, that fully controlled processes appear to be at least partially automatized (Spelke, Hirst, & Neisser, 1976). How does the two-process model explain the automatization of processes in divided-attention phenomena? For example, how can one read for comprehension while writing dictated, categorized words?

Attentional-Resource Theories of Selective Attention

More recent theories have moved away from the notion of signal-blocking or signal-attenuating filters. They have instead moved toward the notion of apportionment of limited attentional resources. Attentional-resource theories help to explain how we

FIGURE 4.8

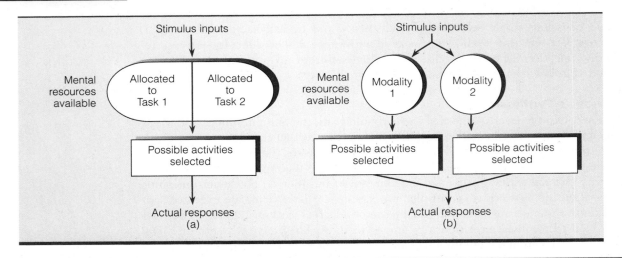

Attentional resources may involve either a single pool or a multiplicity of modality-specific pools. Although the attentional resources theory has been criticized for its imprecision, it seems to complement filter theories in explaining some aspects of attention.

can perform more than one attention-demanding task at a time. They posit that people have a fixed amount of attention that they can choose to allocate according to what the task requires. Figure 4.8 shows two examples of such a theory. In panel *a*, the system has a single pool of resources that can be divided up, say, among multiple tasks (Kahneman, 1973).

However, it now appears that such a model represents an oversimplification. People are much better at dividing their attention when competing tasks are in different modalities. At least some attentional resources may be specific to the modality in which a task is presented. For example, most people easily can simultaneously listen to music and concentrate on writing. But it is harder to listen to the news station and concentrate on writing at the same time. The reason is that both are verbal tasks. The words from the news interfere with the words you are thinking about. Similarly, two visual tasks are more likely to interfere with each other than are a visual task coupled with an auditory one. Panel *b* of Figure 4.8 shows a model that allows for attentional resources to be specific to a given modality (Navon & Gopher, 1979). For someone trying to write while listening to music, the use of two distinctive modality-specific attentional resources probably would not pose serious attentional difficulties. An example would be auditory for music, writing for visual.

Attentional-resources theory has been criticized severely as overly broad and vague (e.g., S. Yantis, personal communication, December 1994). Indeed, it may not stand alone in explaining all aspects of attention, but it complements filter theories quite well. Filter and bottleneck theories of attention seem to be more suitable metaphors for competing tasks that appear to be attentionally incompatible. Examples would be selective-attention tasks or simple divided-attention tasks involving the psychological refractory period (PRP) effect (Pashler, 1994). For these kinds of tasks, it appears that some preattentive processes may occur simultaneously, but processes requiring attention must be handled sequentially, as if passing one-by-one through an attentional bottleneck.

Resource theory seems to be a better metaphor for explaining phenomena of divided attention on complex tasks. In these tasks, practice effects may be observed. According to this metaphor, as each of the complex tasks becomes increasingly automatized, performance of each task makes fewer demands on the limited-capacity attentional resources. Additionally, for explaining search-related phenomena, theories specific to visual search (e.g., models proposing guided search [Cave & Wolfe, 1990] or similarity [Duncan & Humphreys, 1989]) seem to have stronger explanatory power than do filter or resource theories. However, these two kinds of theories are not altogether incompatible. Although the findings from research on visual search do not conflict with filter or resource theories, the task-specific theories more specifically describe the processes at work during visual search.

Additional Considerations in Selective Attention

The Role of Task, Situation, and Person Variables

The existing theoretical models of attention may be too simplistic and mechanistic to explain the complexities of attention. For example, both trait-based anxiety (a personality characteristic) and situation-related anxiety have been found to affect attention (Eysenck & Byrne, 1992; Eysenck & Calvo, 1992; Eysenck & Graydon, 1989). Both types of anxiety tend to place constraints on attention. Other considerations enter in as well. The first is overall arousal. One may be tired, drowsy, or drugged, which may limit attention. Being excited sometimes enhances it. A second consideration is specific interest in a target task and stimuli, compared with interest in distracters. A third is the nature of the task. For example, it may be highly difficult, complex, or novel. Such tasks require more attentional resources than do easy, simple, or highly familiar tasks. Task difficulty particularly influences performance during divided attention. A fourth consideration is amount of practice in performing a given task or set of tasks. Related to this is the skill of utilizing attentional resources for a task or tasks. Increased practice and skill enhance attention (Spelke, Hirst, & Neisser, 1976). A fifth consideration is the stage of processing at which attentional demands are needed. This stage may be before, during, or after some degree of perceptual processing.

In sum, certain attentional processes occur outside our conscious awareness. Others are subject to conscious control. The psychological study of attention has included diverse phenomena, such as vigilance, search, selective attention, and divided attention during the simultaneous performance of multiple tasks. To explain this diversity of attentional phenomena, current theories emphasize that a filtering mechanism appears to govern some aspects of attention. Limited modality-specific attentional resources appear to influence other aspects of attention. Clearly, findings from cognitive research have yielded many insights into attention, but additional understanding also has been gained through the study of attentional processes in the brain.

The Stroop Effect

Much of the research on selective attention has focused on auditory processing, but selective attention also can be studied through visual processing. One of the tasks most frequently used for this purpose was first formulated by John Ridley Stroop (1935). The Stroop effect is named after him. The task works as follows:

Quickly read aloud the following words: brown, blue, green, red, purple. Easy, isn't it? Now quickly name aloud the colors shown in part *a* of the top figure on the back endpaper of this book. In this figure, the colored ink matches the name of the color word. This task, too, is easy. Now, look at part *c* of the same figure. Here, the colors of the inks differ from the color names that are printed with them. Again, name the ink colors you see, out loud, as quickly as possible.

You probably will find the task very difficult: Each of the written words interferes with your naming the color of the ink. The **Stroop effect** demonstrates the psychological difficulty in selectively attending to the color of the ink and trying to ignore the word that is printed with the ink of that color. One explanation of why the Stroop test may be particularly difficult is that, for you and most other adults, reading is now an automatic process. It is not readily subject to your conscious control (MacLeod, 1991, 1996). For that reason, you find it difficult intentionally to refrain from reading and instead to concentrate on identifying the color of the ink, disregarding the word printed in that ink color. An alternative explanation is that the output of a response occurs when the mental pathways for producing the response are activated sufficiently (MacLeod, 1991). In the Stroop test, the color word activates a cortical pathway for saying the word. In contrast, the ink-color name activates a pathway for naming the color. But the former pathway interferes with the latter. In this situation, it takes longer to gather sufficient strength of activation to produce the color-naming response and not the word-reading response.

A number of variations of the Stroop effect exist, including the number Stroop, the directional Stroop, the animal Stroop, and the emotional Stroop. Theses tasks are very similar to the standard Stroop. For example, in the number Stroop, number words are used. Thus, the word *two* might be written three times, *two two two,* and the participant be asked to count the number of words. As with the standard Stroop task, reading sometimes interferes with the counting task (Girelli & associates, 2001; Kaufmann & Nuerk, 2006). One of the most extensively used Stroop variations is the emotional Stroop. In this task, the standard task is modified so that the color words are replaced with either emotional or neutral words. Participants are asked to name the colors of the words. Researchers find that there is a longer delay in color naming for emotional words as compared with neutral words. These findings suggest that the automatic reading of emotional words causes more interference than reading of neutral words (Borkenau & Mauer, 2006; Larsen, Mercer, & Balota, 2006; Phaf & Kan, 2007; Thomas, Johnstone, & Gonsalvez, 2007).

Divided Attention

In signal detection and selective attention, the attentional system must coordinate a search for the simultaneous presence of many features. This is a relatively simple, if not easy, task. At times, however, the attentional system must perform two or more discrete tasks at the same time. Early work in this area was done by Ulric Neisser and

Robert Becklen (1975). They had participants view a videotape in which the display of one activity was superimposed on the display of another activity. The first activity was a three-person basketball game; the second, two people playing a hand-slapping game. Initially, the task was simply to watch one activity and ignore the other. The participant pressed a button whenever key events occurred in the attended activity. Essentially, this first task required only selective attention.

However, the two researchers then asked participants to attend to both activities simultaneously. They were to signal key events in each of the two activities. Even when the researchers presented the two activities dichoptically (i.e., not in a single visual field, but rather with one activity observed by one eye and the other activity observed by the other eye), participants had great difficulty performing both tasks simultaneously. Neisser and Becklen hypothesized that improvements in performance would have occurred eventually as a result of practice. They also hypothesized that the performance of multiple tasks was based on skill resulting from practice. They believed it not to be based on special cognitive mechanisms.

The following year, investigators used a dual-task paradigm to study divided attention during the simultaneous performance of two activities (Spelke, Hirst, & Neisser, 1976). The dual-task paradigm involves two tasks (Task A and Task B) and three conditions (Task A only, Task B only, and both Tasks A and B). The idea was that the researchers would compare and contrast the latency (response time) and accuracy of performance in each of the three conditions. Of course, higher latencies mean slower responses. Previous research had shown that the speed and accuracy of simultaneous performance of two tasks was quite poor for the simultaneous performance of two controlled processes. There are rare instances in which people demonstrate high levels of speed and accuracy for the simultaneous performance of two tasks. In those instances, at least one of the tasks generally involves automatic processing, and usually both tasks involve such processing.

As expected, initial performance was indeed quite poor for the two controlled tasks they chose. These two tasks were reading for detailed comprehension and writing down dictated words. However, Spelke and her colleagues continued to have the two participants in their study perform these two tasks 5 days a week for many weeks (85 sessions in all). To the surprise of many, given enough practice, the participants' performance improved on both tasks. They showed improvements in their speed of reading and accuracy of reading comprehension, as measured by comprehension tests. They also showed increases in their recognition memory for words they had written during dictation. Eventually, participants' performance on both tasks reached the same levels that the participants previously had shown for each task alone.

The authors then introduced sublists of related words within the full word-dictation lists. Examples would be sublists of words that formed a sentence or rhymed. They asked the participants to report any of the words that had been dictated, or any general properties of the particular list that they remembered. The participants initially recalled very few words and no relationships among any of the words. After repeated practice, however, they noticed words related in various ways. One was by superordinate categories. A second was by rhyming sounds. A third was by strings of words that formed sentences. And a fourth was by parts of speech. They included grammatical classes, such as verbs and plural nouns. Furthermore, simultaneous performance of the more complex dictation task initially led to a dip in performance on the reading-comprehension task. With continued practice, performance on that task soon returned to previous high levels.

Next, the authors modified the word-dictation task. Now, the participants sometimes wrote the dictated words and sometimes wrote the correct one of two categories (e.g., animals versus furniture) to which the dictated words belonged. At the same time, they still engaged in the reading-comprehension task. As with previous modifications, initial performance on the two tasks dropped. But performance returned to high levels after practice. Spelke and her colleagues suggested that these findings showed that controlled tasks can be automatized so that they consume fewer attentional resources. Further, two discrete controlled tasks may be automatized to function together as a unit. These authors were quick to point out that the tasks do not, however, become fully automatic. For one thing, they continue to be intentional and conscious. For another, they involve relatively high levels of cognitive processing.

An entirely different approach to studying divided attention has focused on extremely simple tasks that require speedy responses. When people try to perform two overlapping speeded tasks, the responses for one or both tasks are almost always slower (Pashler, 1994). When a second task begins soon after the first task has started, speed of performance usually suffers. The slowing resulting from simultaneous engagement in speeded tasks, as mentioned earlier in the chapter, is the PRP effect. Findings from PRP studies indicate that people can accommodate fairly easily perceptual processing of the physical properties of sensory stimuli while engaged in a second speeded task (Pashler, 1994). However, they cannot readily accommodate more than one cognitive task requiring them to choose a response, retrieve information from memory, or engage in various other cognitive operations. When both tasks require performance of any of these cognitive operations, one or both tasks will show the PRP effect.

Consider driving a car, for example. You need constantly to be aware of threats to your safety. Suppose you fail to select one such threat, such as a car that runs a red light and is headed directly at you as you enter an intersection. The result is that you may become an innocent victim of a horrible car accident. Moreover, if you are unsuccessful in dividing your attention, you may cause an accident. Most automobile accidents are caused by failures in divided attention. A study of 2700 crashes in the state of Virginia between June and November of 2002 investigated causes of accidents (Warner, 2004). According to the study, rubbernecking (viewing accidents that have already occurred) was the cause of 16% of accidents, followed by driver fatigue (12%); looking at scenery or landmarks (10%); distractions caused by passengers or children (9%); adjusting a radio, tape, or CD player (7%); and cell phone use (5%). On average, distractions occurring inside the vehicle accounted for 62% of the distractions reported. Distractions outside the vehicle accounted for 35%. The other 3% were of undetermined cause. The causes of accidents differed somewhat for rural versus urban areas. Accidents in rural areas were more likely to be due to driver fatigue, insects entering or striking the vehicle, or pet distractions. In urban areas, crashes were more likely to result from rubbernecking, traffic, or cell-phone use. Overall, this study and others suggested that cell phones are somewhat less responsible for accidents than some people had expected (Cohen & Graham, 2003; Figure 4.9).

As many as 21% of accidents and near-accidents involve at least one driver talking on a cell phone, although the conversation may or may not have been the cause of the accident (Seo & Torabi, 2004). Other research has indicated that, when time

FIGURE 4.9

© Troy Freeman/PhotoEdit

Illustrating a failure of divided attention, drivers who rubberneck at the scene of an accident are a major cause of further accidents.

on task and driving conditions are controlled for, the effects of talking on a cell phone can be as detrimental to driving as intoxication (Strayer, Drews, & Crouch, 2006). Still other research has found that, compared with people not on a cell phone, people talking on a cell phone exhibit more anger, through honking and facial expressions, when presented with a frustrating situation (McGarva, Ramsey, & Shear, 2006). Increased aggression has been linked with increased accidents (Deffenbacher & associates, 2003). Therefore, it is likely that people who talk on the phone while driving are more prone to anger and, as a result, more accidents. These findings, combined with those on the effects of divided attention, help to explain why an increase in accidents is seen when cell phones are involved.

There are many ways to study divided attention (Egeth, 2000; Luck & associates, 1996; Moore & Egeth, 1997; Pashler, 1998; Pashler & Johnston, 1998; Van der Heijden, 1992). One of the simplest starts with our own set of everyday experiences. One widely used paradigm makes use of a simulation of the driving situation (Strayer & Johnston, 2001). Researchers had participants perform a tracking task. The participants had control of a joystick, which moved a cursor on a computer screen. The participants needed to keep the cursor in position on a moving target. At various times, the target would flash either green or red. If the color was green, the participants were to ignore the signal. If the color was red, however, the participants were to push a simulated brake. The simulated brake was a button on the joystick.

In one condition, participants did the task singly—that is, by itself. In another condition, participants were involved in a second task. This procedure created a dual-

FIGURE 4.10

In the top panel, dual-task performance significantly increased the probability of a miss in the cell-phone condition but not in the radio-control condition. In the bottom panel, reaction time increased significantly for a dual task in the cell-phone condition but not in the radio-control condition. From Strayer, D. L., & Johnston, W. A. (2001). Driven to distraction: Dual-task studies of simulated driving and conversing on a cellular telephone. Psychological Science, 12, 463. *Reprinted by permission of Blackwell Publishing.*

task situation. The participants either listened to a radio broadcast while doing the task or talked on a cell phone to an experimental confederate. Participants talked roughly half the time and also listened roughly half the time. Two different topics were used to ensure that the results were not due to the topic of conversation. The results of the study are shown in Figure 4.10.

As shown in Figure 4.10, the probability of a miss in the face of the red signal increased substantially in the cell-phone dual-task condition relative to the single-task condition. Reaction times were also substantially slower in this condition than in the single-task condition. In contrast, there was no significant difference between probabilities of a miss in the single-task and radio dual-task condition, nor was there a significant difference in reaction time in this condition. Thus, use of cell phones appears to be substantially more risky than listening to the radio while driving.

Consciousness of Complex Mental Processes

No serious investigator of cognition believes that people have conscious access to very simple mental processes. For example, none of us has a good idea of the means by which we recognize whether a printed letter such as A is an uppercase or lowercase one. But now consider more complex processing. How conscious are we of our complex mental processes? Cognitive psychologists have differing views on how this question is best answered.

One view (Ericsson & Simon, 1984) is that people have quite good access to their complex mental processes. Simon and his colleagues, for example, have used *protocol analysis* in analyzing people's solving of problems, such as chess problems and so-called cryptarithmetic problems, in which one has to figure out what numbers substitute for letters in a mathematical computation problem. These investigations have suggested to Simon and his colleagues that people have quite good conscious access to their complex information processes.

A second view is that people's access to their complex mental processes is not very good (e.g., Nisbett & Wilson, 1977). In this view, people may think they know how they solve complex problems, but their thoughts are frequently erroneous. According to Nisbett and Wilson, we typically are conscious of the products of our thinking, but only vaguely conscious, if at all, of the processes of thinking. For example, suppose you decide to buy one model of bicycle over another. You certainly will know the product of the decision—which model you bought. But you may have only a vague idea of how you arrived at that decision. Indeed, according to this view, you may believe you know why you made the decision, but that belief is likely to be flawed. Advertisers depend on this second view. They try to manipulate your thoughts and feelings toward a product so that, whatever your conscious thoughts may be, your unconscious ones will lead you to buy their product over that of a competitor.

The essence of the second view is that people's conscious access to their thought processes, and even their control over their thought processes, is quite minimal (Wegner, 2002; Wilson, 2002). Consider the problem of getting over someone who has terminated an intimate relationship with you. One technique that is sometimes used to get over someone is thought suppression. As soon as you think of the person, you try to put the individual out of your mind. There is one problem with this technique, but it is a major one: It often does not work. Indeed, the more you try not to think about the person, the more you may end up thinking about him or her and having trouble getting the person off your mind. Research has actually shown that trying not to think about something usually does not work (Wegner, 1997a, 1997b). Ironically, the more you try not to think about someone or something, the more "obsessed" you may become with the person or object.

Change Blindness

Adaptive behavior requires us to be attentive to changes in our environment because changes cue us to both opportunities and dangers. Evolutionarily, the ability to spot predators suddenly appearing in the visual field would have been a great advantage for the survival of organisms and, ultimately, their genes. It thus may be surprising to discover that people can show remarkable levels of **change blindness,** the inability to detect changes in objects or scenes that are being viewed (O'Regan, 2003; Simons, 2000).

In one study, a stranger asks a bystander for directions. As the interaction proceeds, two workers carrying a wooden door walk between the stranger and the bystander. When the workers have passed by, the original stranger has been replaced by a different stranger (one of the workers). The interaction then continues as before. How likely do you think it is that the bystander would notice that the person to whom he or she is talking is no longer the same person? Oddly enough, only about half of the bystanders notice that a switch has been made. Many do not even notice the change when they are explicitly told that the person to whom they are talking is not the one with whom they originally were conversing (Simons & Levin, 1997, 1998).

In another paradigm, participants see pairs of pictures, separated by brief intervals. Changes are made in the pictures in the interval. For the most part, people have difficulty recognizing the changes. They are more likely to recognize them when they are important to the scene than when they are unimportant. Even when told explicitly to look for changes, people have trouble finding them (Levin & Simons, 1997; Rensink, O'Regan, & Clark, 1997; Shore & Klein, 2000; Simons, 2000; Simons & Ambinder, 2005).

There do seem to be cultural differences in the areas that we observe changes. In American participants, central items are recognized more readily than peripheral changes. However, in East Asian participants, changes in peripheral information are more promptly identified compared with central changes (Masuda & Nisbett, 2006). The right parietal cortex plays a significant role in change blindness. Electrical stimulation to this area increases the time it takes to identify a change in a scene (Beck & associates, 2006).

Change blindness is not limited to visual information. The inability to detect a change can be observed in auditory and tactile stimuli (Gallace & associates, 2006; Vitevitch, 2003). However, as in visual stimuli, a brief delay must be present between the original and changed stimuli.

These results suggest that people are much less astute in recognizing changes in their environments than we might expect. Even fairly blatant changes, such as the identity of a person to whom we speak, may pass us by. When we admire Sherlock Holmes for his astuteness, we probably give him too little credit. In the fictional detective stories in which he plays a role, he notices extremely unobvious things. Often we tend not to notice even things that are obvious.

Attention Deficit Hyperactivity Disorder

Most of us take for granted our ability to pay attention and to divide our attention in adaptive ways. But not everyone can do so. People with *attention deficit hyperactivity disorder* (ADHD) have difficulties in focusing their attention in ways that enable them to adapt in optimal ways to their environment (*Attention deficit hyper-activity disorder,* 2004, upon which this section is largely based; see also Swanson & associates, 2003). This condition typically first displays itself during the preschool or early school years. It is estimated that 3% to 5% of children have the disorder, meaning that in the United States roughly 2 million children exhibit symptoms. Some studies have suggested that the rate of ADHD is much higher, affecting up to 12% of children worldwide (Biederman & Faraone, 2005). The disorder does not typically end in adulthood, although it may vary in its severity, becoming either more or less severe.

The condition was first described by Dr. Heinrich Hoffman in 1845. Today, it has been widely investigated. No one knows for sure the cause of ADHD. It may be a partially heritable condition. There is some evidence of a link to maternal smoking and drinking of alcohol during pregnancy (Hausknecht & associates, 2005; Rodriguez & Bohlin, 2005). Lead exposure on the part of the child may also be associated with ADHD. Brain injury is another possible cause, as are food additives—in particular, sugar and certain dyes (Cruz & Bahna, 2006). There are noted differences in the frontal-subcortical cerebellar catecholaminergic circuits and in dopamine regulation in people with ADHD (Biederman & Faraone, 2005).

There is some evidence that the incidence of ADHD has increased in recent years. During the period from 2000 to 2005, the prevalence of medicinal treatment increased by more than 11% each year (Castle & associates, 2007). The reasons for this increase are not clear. Various hypotheses have been put forward, including increased watching of fast-paced television shows, use of fast-paced video games, additives in foods, and increases in unknown toxins in the environment.

The three primary characteristics of ADHD are inattention, hyperactivity (i.e., levels of activity that exceed what is normally shown by children of a given age), and impulsiveness. There are three main types. One is predominantly hyperactive-impulsive. The second is predominantly inattentive. The third combines inattentive-ness with hyperactivity and impulsiveness. I describe the inattentive type here because it is most relevant to the topic of this chapter.

Children with the inattentive type of ADHD show several distinctive symptoms. First, they are easily distracted by irrelevant sights and sounds. Second, they often fail to pay attention to details. Third, they are susceptible to making careless mistakes in their work. Fourth, they often fail to read instructions completely or carefully. Fifth, they are susceptible to forgetting or losing things they need for tasks, such as pencils or books. Finally, they tend to jump from one incompleted task to another.

ADHD is most often treated with a combination of psychotherapy and drugs. Some of the drugs currently used to treat ADHD are Ritalin (methylphenidate), Metadate (methylphenidate), and Strattera (atomoxetine). This last drug differs from other drugs used to treat ADHD in that it is not a stimulant. Rather, it affects the neurotransmitter norepinephrine. The stimulants, in contrast, affect the neurotrans-mitter dopamine. Interestingly, in children, the rate of boys who are given medication for treatment of ADHD is more than double that of girls. However, in adults, the use of ADHD medication is approximately equal for both sexes (Castle & associates, 2007). A number of studies have noted that, although medication is a useful tool in the treatment of ADHD, it is best used in combination with behavioral interventions (Corcoran & Dattalo, 2006; Rostain & Tamsay, 2006).

Cognitive Neuroscientific Approaches to Attention and Consciousness

The neuroscience of attention has an ever-growing body of literature. Consider an attempt to synthesize diverse studies investigating attentional processes in the brain (Posner, 1992; Posner & Dehaene, 1994; Posner & Raichle, 1994). Is attention a function of the entire brain, or is it a function of discrete attention-governing modules in the brain? According to Posner, the attentional system in the brain "is neither a property of a single brain area nor of the entire brain" (Posner & Dehaene, 1994, p. 75).

Posner and Rothbart (2007) completed a review of neuroimaging studies in the area of attention. What at first seemed like an unclear pattern of activation can be effectively organized into areas associated with the three subfunctions of attention. The researchers define these functions as alerting, orienting, and executive attention. The researchers organized the findings to describe each of these functions in terms of the brain areas involved, the neurotransmitters that modulate the changes, and the results of dysfunction within this system. The following section is closely based on the comprehensive review by Posner and Rothbart (2007).

Alerting is defined as being prepared to attend to some incoming event. Alerting also includes the process of getting to this state of preparedness. The brain areas involved in alerting are the superior parietal, temporal parietal junction, frontal eye field, and superior colliculus. The neurotransmitter that modulates alerting is acetylcholine. Dysfunction of the alerting system is related to attentional changes as we age and to ADHD.

The second function of attention is orienting. Orienting is defined as the selection of stimuli to attend to. The brain areas involved in the orienting function are the locus coeruleus, right frontal, and parietal cortex. The modulating neurotransmitter for orienting is norephinephrine. Dysfunction within this system is related to autism.

The final function defined within attention is executive attention. Executive attention includes processes for monitoring and resolving conflicts that arise among internal processes. These processes include thoughts, feelings, and responses. The brain areas involved in this final and highest order of attentional process are anterior cingulated, lateral ventral, prefrontal, and basal ganglia. The neurotransmitter most involved in the executive attention process is dopamine. Dysfunction within this system is associated with Alzheimer's disease, borderline personality disorder, and schizophrenia.

Spatial Neglect

Spatial neglect or just *neglect* is an attentional dysfunction in which participants ignore the half of their visual field that is contralateral, on the opposite side, to the hemisphere of the brain that has a lesion. It is due mainly to unilateral lesions in the parietal lobes. Research reveals that the problem may be a result of the interaction of systems that mutually inhibit one another. When only one of the pair involved in the system is damaged, as is the case with neglect patients, patients become locked in to one side of the visual field. The reason is that the inhibition normally provided by the other half of the system is no longer working. Spatial neglect has been examined by a number of experimenters (Luaute & associates, 2006; Schindler & associates, 2006).

One way to test for neglect is to give patients who are suspected of suffering from neglect a sheet of paper with a number of horizontal lines. Patients are then asked to bisect the lines precisely in the middle of each. Patients with lesions in the right hemisphere tend to bisect the lines to the right of the midline. Patients with lesions in the left hemisphere tend to bisect the lines to the left of the midline. The reason is that the former group of patients does not see all of the lines to the left, whereas the latter group does not see all of the lines to the right. Sometimes patients miss the lines altogether (patients who neglect the entire visual field).

Attentional Systems

Posner (1995) has identified an anterior (frontward) attention system (attentional network) within the frontal lobe and a posterior (toward the rear) attention system within the parietal lobe. The anterior attention system becomes increasingly activated during tasks requiring awareness. An example would be tasks in which participants must attend to the meanings of words. This system also is involved in "attention for action." Here, the participant is planning or selecting an action from among alternative courses of action. In contrast, the posterior attention system involves the parietal lobe of the cortex, a portion of the thalamus, and some areas of the midbrain related to eye movements. This system becomes highly activated during tasks involving visuospatial attention. In these tasks, the participant must disengage and shift attention (e.g., visual search or vigilance tasks) (Posner & Raichle, 1994). Attention also involves neural activity in the relevant visual, auditory, motor, and association areas of the cortex involved in particular visual, auditory, motor, or higher order tasks (Posner & associates, 1988). The anterior and posterior attention systems appear to enhance attention across various tasks. This suggests that they may be involved in regulating the activation of relevant cortical areas for specific tasks (Posner & Dehaene, 1994).

Another question has arisen regarding the activity of the attentional system. This activity occurs as a result of enhanced activation of attended items, inhibition or suppressed activation of unattended items, or both processes. Apparently, it depends on the particular task and on the area of the brain under investigation (Posner & Dehaene, 1994). The task at hand is to determine which processes occur in which areas of the brain during the performance of which tasks. For mapping the areas of the brain involved in various tasks, cognitive neuropsychologists often use positron emission tomography (PET). This technique maps regional cerebral blood flow (see Chapter 2 for a more in-depth discussion of this technique). In one such PET study (Corbetta & associates, 1993), researchers found increased activation in areas responsible for each of the distinct attributes of various search tasks. These include features such as motion, color, and shape and selected versus divided attentional conditions.

Using Event-Related Potentials to Measure Attention

An alternative way of studying attention in the brain is to focus on studying event-related potentials (ERPs; see Chapter 2). They indicate minute changes in electrical activity in response to various stimuli. Both the PET and ERP techniques offer information on the geography (localization) of cerebral activity and on the chronology of cerebral events. However, the PET technique provides higher resolution for spatial localization of cerebral function. The ERP provides much more sensitive indications of the chronology of responses (within milliseconds; Näätänen, 1988a, 1988b, 1990, 1992). Thus, through ERP studies, even extremely brief responses to stimuli may be noticed.

The ERP's sensitivity to very brief responses has allowed Näätänen and his colleagues (e.g., Cowan & associates, 1993; Näätänen, 1988a, 1988b; Paavilainen & associates, 1993) to examine the specific conditions in which target versus distracter stimuli do or do not prompt attentional responses. For example, Näätänen has found that at least some response to infrequent, deviant auditory stimuli (e.g., peculiar changes in pitch) seems to be automatic. It occurs even when the participant is focusing attention on a primary task and is not consciously aware of the deviant stimuli. These automatic, preconscious responses to deviant stimuli occur whether the stimuli are targets or distracters. The responses occur whether the deviants are widely different from the standard stimuli or are only slightly different from the standard stimuli (Cowan & associates, 1993; Paavilainen & associates, 1993). There is no performance decrement in the controlled task as a result of the automatic response to deviant stimuli (Näätänen, 1990). So it seems that some automatic superficial analysis and selection of stimuli may occur without taxing attentional resources.

Many of the foregoing studies have involved normal participants. But cognitive neuropsychologists also have learned a great deal about attentional processes in the brain by studying people who do not show normal attentional processes, such as people who show specific attentional deficits and who are found to have either lesions or inadequate blood flow in key areas of the brain. Overall attention deficits have been linked to lesions in the frontal lobe and in the basal ganglia (Lou, Henriksen, & Bruhn, 1984); visual attentional deficits have been linked to the posterior parietal cortex and the thalamus, as well as to areas of the midbrain related to eye movements (Posner & Petersen, 1990; Posner & associates, 1988). Work with split-brain patients (e.g., Ladavas & associates, 1994; Luck & associates, 1989) also has led to some interesting findings regarding attention and brain function, such as the observation that the right hemisphere seems to be dominant for maintaining alertness and that the attentional systems involved in visual search seem to be distinct from other aspects of visual attention. Using the variety of methods described here enables researchers to study attention in a way that any one method would not permit (Stuss & associates, 1995).

Another neuroimaging technique that has been used to examine attention is functional magnetic resonance imaging (fMRI; see Chapter 2 for more information). As with other methods, both patient and nonpatient populations have been examined through these methods (Madden & associates, 2007; Weaver & Stevens, 2007).

A Psychopharmacological Approach

Another approach to understanding attentional processes is psychopharmacological research, which evaluates changes in attention and consciousness associated with various chemicals (e.g., neurotransmitters such as acetylcholine or GABA [see Chapter 2], hormones, and even central nervous system stimulants ["uppers"] or depressants ["downers"]; Wolkowitz, Tinklenberg, & Weingartner, 1985). In addition, researchers study physiological aspects of attentional processes at a global level of analysis. For example, overall arousal can be observed through such responses as pupillary dilation, changes in the autonomic (self-regulating) nervous system (see Chapter 2), and distinctive EEG patterns. An area that has long been recognized as crucial to overall arousal is the reticular activating system (RAS; see Chapter 2). Changes in the RAS and in specific measures of arousal have been linked to habituation and dishabituation, as well as to the orienting reflex, in which an individual reflexively responds to sudden changes by reorienting the position of the body toward the source of the sudden change (e.g., sudden noise or a flash of light).

Key Themes

Consider one psychologist's view of how consciousness and perception interact. Anthony Marcel (1983a) has proposed a model for describing how sensations and cognitive processes that occur outside our conscious awareness may influence our conscious perceptions and cognitions. According to Marcel, our conscious representations of what we perceive often differ qualitatively from our nonconscious representations of sensory stimuli. Outside of conscious awareness, we continually try to make sense of a constant flow of sensory information. Also outside of awareness are perceptual hypotheses regarding how the current sensory information matches with various properties and objects we have encountered previously in our environment. These hypotheses are inferences based on knowledge stored in long-term memory. During the matching process, information from differing sensory modalities is integrated.

According to Marcel's model, once there is a suitable match between the sensory data and the perceptual hypotheses regarding various properties and objects, the match is reported to conscious awareness as "being" particular properties and objects. Consciously, we are aware only of the reported objects or properties; we are not aware of the sensory data, the perceptual hypotheses that do not lead to a match, or even the processes that govern the reported match. Thus, before a given object or property is detected consciously (i.e., is reported to conscious awareness by the nonconscious matching process), we will have chosen a satisfactory perceptual hypothesis and excluded various possibilities that less satisfactorily matched the incoming sensory data to what we already know or can infer.

According to Marcel's model, the sensory data and the perceptual hypotheses are available to and used by various nonconscious cognitive processes in addition to the matching process. Sensory data and cognitive processes that do not reach awareness still exert influence on how we think and how we perform other cognitive tasks. It is widely held that we have limited attentional capacity (e.g., see Norman, 1976). According to Marcel, we accommodate these limitations by making use of nonconscious information and processes as much as possible, while limiting the information and processing that enter our conscious awareness. In this way, our limited attentional capacity is not constantly overtaxed. Hence, our processes of attention are intimately intertwined with our processes of perception. In this chapter, we have described many functions and processes of attention. In the following chapter, we focus on various aspects of perception.

The study of attention and consciousness highlights several key themes in cognitive psychology, as described in Chapter 1.

The first theme is the respective roles of structures and processes. The brain contains various structures and systems of structures, such as the reticular activating system, that generate the processes that contribute to attention. Sometimes, the relationship between structure and process is not entirely clear, and it is the job of cognitive psychologists to better understand it. For example, blindsight is a phenomenon in which a process occurs—sight—in the absence of the structures in the brain that would seem to be necessary for the sight to take place.

A second theme is the relation between biology and behavior. Blindsight is a case of a curious and as yet poorly understood link. The biology does not appear to be there to generate the behavior. Another interesting example is attention deficit hyperactivity disorder. Physicians now have available a number of drugs that treat ADHD. These treatments enable children as well as adults better to focus on tasks that they need to get done. But the mechanisms by which the drugs work are still poorly understood. Indeed, somewhat paradoxically, most of the drugs used to treat ADHD are stimulants, which, when given to children with ADHD, appear to calm them down.

A third theme is validity of causal inference versus ecological validity. Where should one study, say, vigilance? One can study it in a laboratory, of course, to achieve careful experimental control. But if one is studying high-stakes vigilance situations, such as those in which military officers are examining radar screens for possible attacks against the country, one must insist on having a high degree of ecological validity to ensure that the results apply to the actual situation in which the military officers find themselves. The stakes are too high to allow slippage. Yet, when one studies vigilance in the actual-life situation, one cannot and would not want to make attacks against the country happen. So one needs simulations that are as realistic as possible. In this way, one tries to ensure ecological validity of conclusions drawn.

Get two friends to help you with this demonstration. Ask one friend to read something very softly into your other friend's ear (it can be anything—a joke, a greeting card, or a cognitive psychology textbook), and have your other friend try to "shadow" what the other friend is saying. (Shadowing is repeating all the words that another person is saying.) In your friend's other ear, say "animal" very softly. Later, ask your friend what you said. Most likely, your friend will not be able to identify what you said. Try this again, but this time say your friend's name. Your friend will most likely be able to recall that you said his or her name. This demonstrates Triesman's attenuation model.

Summary

1. **Can we actively process information even if we are not aware of doing so? If so, what do we do, and how do we do it?** Whereas attention embraces all the information that an individual is manipulating (a portion of the information available from memory, sensation, and other cognitive processes), consciousness comprises only the narrower range of information that the individual is aware of manipulating. Attention allows us to use our limited active cognitive resources (e.g., because of the limits of working memory) judiciously, to respond quickly and accurately to interesting stimuli, and to remember salient information.

   Conscious awareness allows us to monitor our interactions with the environment, to link our past and present experiences and thereby sense a continuous thread of experience, and to control and plan for future actions.

   We actively can process information at the preconscious level without being aware of doing so. For example, researchers have studied the phenomenon of priming, in which a given stimulus increases the likelihood that a subsequent related (or identical) stimulus will be readily processed (e.g., retrieval from long-term memory). In contrast, in the tip-of-the-tongue phenomenon, another example of preconscious processing, retrieval of desired information from memory does not occur, despite an ability to retrieve related information.

   Cognitive psychologists also observe distinctions in conscious versus preconscious attention by distinguishing between controlled and automatic processing in task performance. Controlled processes are relatively slow, sequential in nature, intentional (requiring effort), and under conscious control. Automatic processes are relatively fast, parallel in nature, and for the most part outside of conscious awareness. Actually, a continuum of processing appears to exist, from fully automatic to fully controlled processes. Two automatic processes that support our attentional system are habituation and dishabituation, which affect our responses to familiar versus novel stimuli.

2. **What are some of the functions of attention?** One main function involved in attention is identifying important objects and events in the environment. Researchers use measures from signal-detection theory to determine an observer's sensitivity to targets in various tasks. For example, vigilance refers to a person's ability to attend to a field of stimulation over a prolonged period, usually with the stimulus to be detected occurring only infrequently. Whereas vigilance involves passively waiting for an event to occur, search involves actively seeking out a stimulus.

   People use selective attention to track one message and simultaneously to ignore others. Auditory selective attention (such as in the cocktail party problem) may be observed by asking participants to shadow information presented dichotically. Visual selective attention may be observed in tasks involving the Stroop effect. Attentional processes also are involved during divided attention, when people attempt to handle more than one task at once; generally, the simultaneous performance of more than one automatized task is easier to handle than the simultaneous performance of more than one controlled task. However, with practice, individuals appear to be capable of handling more than one controlled task at a time, even engaging in tasks requiring comprehension and decision making.

3. **What are some of the theories cognitive psychologists have developed to explain what they have observed about attentional processes?** Some theories of attention involve an attentional filter or bottleneck, according to which information is selectively blocked out or attenuated as it passes from one level of processing to the next. Of the bottleneck theories, some suggest that the signal-blocking or signal-attenuating mechanism occurs just after sensation and prior to any perceptual processing; others propose a later mechanism, after at least some perceptual processing has

occurred. Attentional-resource theories offer an alternative way of explaining attention; according to these theories, people have a fixed amount of attentional resources (perhaps modulated by sensory modalities) that they allocate according to the perceived task requirements. Resource theories and bottleneck theories actually may be complementary. In addition to these general theories of attention, some task-specific theories (e.g., feature-integration theory, guided-search theory, and similarity theory) have attempted to explain search phenomena in particular.

4. **What have cognitive psychologists learned about attention by studying the human brain?**   Early neuropsychological research led to the discovery of feature detectors, and subsequent work has explored other aspects of feature detection and integration processes that may be involved in visual search. In addition, extensive research on attentional processes in the brain seems to suggest that the attentional system primarily involves two regions of the cortex, as well as the thalamus and some other subcortical structures; the attentional system also governs various specific processes that occur in many areas of the brain, particularly in the cerebral cortex. Attentional processes may be a result of heightened activation in some areas of the brain, of inhibited activity in other areas of the brain, or perhaps of some combination of activation and inhibition. Studies of responsivity to particular stimuli show that even when an individual is focused on a primary task and is not consciously aware of processing other stimuli, the brain of the individual automatically responds to infrequent, deviant stimuli (e.g., an odd tone). By using various approaches to the study of the brain (e.g., PET, ERP, lesion studies, and psychopharmacological studies), researchers are gaining insight into diverse aspects of the brain and also are able to use converging operations to begin to explain some of the phenomena they observe.

Thinking about Thinking: Factual, Analytical, Creative, and Practical Questions

1. Describe some of the evidence regarding the phenomena of priming and preconscious perception.

2. Why are habituation and dishabituation of particular interest to cognitive psychologists?

3. Compare and contrast the theories of visual search described in this chapter.

4. Choose one of the theories of attention and explain how the evidence from signal detection, selective attention, or divided attention supports or challenges the theory you chose.

5. Design one task likely to activate the posterior attentional system and another task likely to activate the anterior attentional system.

6. Design an experiment for studying divided attention.

7. Describe some practical ways in which you can use forcing functions and other strategies for lessening the likelihood that automatic processes will have negative consequences for you in some of the situations you face.

8. How could advertisers use some of the principles of visual search or selective attention to increase the likelihood that people will notice their messages?

Key Terms

arousal

attention

automatic processes

automatization

binaural presentation

blindsight

change blindness

cocktail party problem

conjunction search

consciousness

controlled processes

dichotic presentation

dishabituation

distracters

divided attention

feature-integration theory

feature search

habituation

multimode theory

priming

search

selective attention

sensory adaptation

signal

signal detection

signal-detection theory (SDT)

Stroop effect

tip-of-the-tongue phenomenon

vigilance

 Explore CogLab by going to **http://coglab.wadsworth.com.** To learn more, examine the following experiments:

Prototypes   Implicit Learning

Absolute Identification

Annotated Suggested Readings

Pashler, H. (1998). *The psychology of attention.* Cambridge, MA: MIT Press. An excellent review of the literature on attention.

Posner, M. I., & Rothbart, M. K. (2007). Research on attention networks as a model for the integration of psychological science. *Annual Review of Psychology, 58,* 1–23. A comprehensive review of neurological systems and attention.

Memory: Models and Research Methods

EXPLORING COGNITIVE PSYCHOLOGY

1. **What are some of the tasks used for studying memory, and what do various tasks indicate about the structure of memory?**

2. **What has been the prevailing traditional model for the structure of memory?**

3. **What are some of the main alternative models of the structure of memory?**

4. **What have psychologists learned about the structure of memory by studying both exceptional memory and the physiology of the brain?**

Who is the president of the United States? What is today's date? What does your best friend look like, and what does your friend's voice sound like? What were some of your experiences when you first started college? How do you tie your shoelaces?

INVESTIGATING COGNITIVE PSYCHOLOGY

How do you know the answers to the preceding questions, or to any questions for that matter? How do you remember any of the information you use every waking hour of every day? **Memory** is the means by which we retain and draw on our past experiences to use that information in the present (Tulving, 2000b; Tulving & Craik, 2000). As a process, memory refers to the dynamic mechanisms associated with storing, retaining, and retrieving information about past experience (Bjorklund, Schneider, & Hernández Blasi, 2003; Crowder, 1976). Specifically, cognitive psychologists have identified three common operations of memory: encoding, storage, and retrieval (Baddeley, 1998, 1999, 2000b; Brown & Craik, 2000). Each operation represents a stage in memory processing. In encoding, you transform sensory data into a form of mental representation. In storage, you keep encoded information in memory. In retrieval, you pull out or use information stored in memory. These memory processes are discussed at length in Chapter 6.

This chapter introduces some of the tasks used for studying memory. It then discusses the traditional model of memory. This model includes the sensory, short-term, and long-term storage systems. Although this model still influences current thinking about memory, we consider some interesting alternative perspectives and models of memory before moving on to discuss exceptional memory and insights provided by neuropsychology.

Tasks Used for Measuring Memory

In studying memory, researchers have devised various tasks that require participants to remember arbitrary information (e.g., numerals or letter strings) in different ways. Because this chapter includes many references to these tasks, we begin this section with an advance organizer—a basis for organizing the information to be given. In this way, you will know how memory is studied. The tasks described in the following section involve recall versus recognition memory and implicit versus explicit memory.

Recall versus Recognition Tasks

In **recall,** you produce a fact, a word, or other item from memory. Fill-in-the-blank and most essay tests require that you recall items from memory. In **recognition,** you select or otherwise identify an item as being one that you learned previously. (See Table 5.1 for examples and explanations of each type of task.) Multiple-choice and true-false tests involve some degree of recognition. Three main types of recall tasks are used in experiments (Lockhart, 2000). The first is *serial recall,* in which you recall items in the exact order in which they were presented (Crowder & Green, 2000). The second is *free recall,* in which you recall items in any order you choose. The third is *cued recall,* in which you are first shown items in pairs, but during recall you are cued with only one member of each pair and are asked to recall each mate. Cued recall is also called "paired-associates recall" (Lockhart, 2000). Psychologists also can measure *relearning,* which is the number of trials it takes to learn once again items that were learned at some time in the past. Relearning has also been referred to as savings and can be observed in adults, children, and animals (Bauer, 2005; Lynne, Yukako, &

TABLE 5.1	Types of Tasks Used for Measuring Memory

Some memory tasks involve recall or recognition of explicit memory for declarative knowledge. Other tasks involve implicit memory and memory for procedural knowledge.

TASKS REQUIRING EXPLICIT MEMORY FOR DECLARATIVE KNOWLEDGE	DESCRIPTION OF WHAT THE TASKS REQUIRE	EXAMPLE
Explicit-memory tasks	You must consciously recall particular information.	Who wrote *Hamlet?*
Declarative-knowledge tasks	You must recall facts.	What is your first name?
Recall tasks	You must produce a fact, a word, or other item from memory.	Fill-in-the-blank tests require that you recall items from memory. For example, "The term for persons who suffer severe memory impairment is _____."
Serial-recall task	You must repeat the items in a list in the exact order in which you heard or read them.	If you were shown the digits 2-8-7-1-6-4, you would be expected to repeat "2-8-7-1-6-4," in exactly that order.
Free-recall task	You must repeat the items in a list in any order in which you can recall them.	If you were presented with the word list "dog, pencil, time, hair, monkey, restaurant," you would receive full credit if you repeated "monkey, restaurant, dog, pencil, time, hair."
Cued-recall task	You must memorize a list of paired items; then when you are given one item in the pair, you must recall the mate for that item.	Suppose that you were given the following list of pairs: "time-city, mist-home, switch-paper, credit-day, fist-cloud, number-branch." Later, when you were given the stimulus "switch," you would be expected to say "paper," and so on.

McKinney, 2002; Monk & associates, 1996). The relearning effect was also observed in fetal rats. These rats demonstrated shorter learning times for motor movements they had previously learned (Robinson, 2005). This effect is clearly extensively generalizable to many situations and participants.

Recognition memory is usually much better than recall (although there are some exceptions, which are discussed in Chapter 6). For example, in one study, participants could recognize close to 2000 pictures in a recognition-memory task (Standing, Conezio, & Haber, 1970). It is difficult to imagine anyone recalling 2000 items of any kind they were just asked to memorize. As you will see later in the section on exceptional memory, even with extensive training the best measured recall performance is around 80 items.

Informing participants of the type of future test can influence the amount of learning that occurs. Specifically, recall tasks generally elicit deeper levels of information processing than recognition ones. Imagine studying for an exam. You will likely, when preparing for an essay exam, aim to relate concepts to one another. However, when preparing for a multiple-choice exam, you will likely try to remember facts. It

TABLE 5.1	Types of Tasks Used for Measuring Memory (cont.)	
TASKS REQUIRING EXPLICIT MEMORY FOR DECLARATIVE KNOWLEDGE	**DESCRIPTION OF WHAT THE TASKS REQUIRE**	**EXAMPLE**
Recognition tasks	You must select or otherwise identify an item as being one that you learned previously.	Multiple-choice and true-false tests involve recognition. For example, "The term for people with outstanding memory ability is (1) amnesics, (2) semanticists, (3) mnemonists, or (4) retrograders."
Implicit-memory tasks	You must draw on information in memory without consciously realizing that you are doing so.	Word-completion tasks tap implicit memory. You would be presented with a word fragment, such as the first three letters of a word; then you would be asked to complete the word fragment with the first word that comes to mind. For example, suppose that you were asked to supply the missing three letters to fill in these blanks and form a word: _e_or_. Because you had recently seen the word *memory*, you would be more likely to provide the three letters m-m-y for the blanks than would someone who had not recently been exposed to the word.
Tasks involving procedural knowledge	You must remember learned skills and automatic behaviors, rather than facts.	If you were asked to demonstrate a "knowing-how" skill, you might be given experience in solving puzzles or in reading mirror writing, and then you would be asked to show what you remember of how to use those skills. Or you might be asked to master or to show what you already remember about particular motor skills (e.g., riding a bicycle or ice skating).

is likely that, after studying for the essay exam, you would remember more details about the information. As mentioned before, the essay exam resembles the recall task and the multiple-choice exam resembles the recognition task, although of course they are not identical. Some psychologists refer to recognition-memory tasks as tapping *receptive* knowledge. Recall memory tasks, in which you have to produce an answer, instead require *expressive* knowledge. Differences between receptive and expressive knowledge also are observed in areas other than that of simple memory tasks (e.g., language, intelligence, and cognitive development).

Implicit versus Explicit Memory Tasks

Memory theorists distinguish between explicit memory and implicit memory (Mulligan, 2003). Each of the tasks previously discussed involves **explicit memory,** in which participants engage in conscious recollection. For example, they might recall or recognize words, facts, or pictures from a particular prior set of items. A related phenomenon is **implicit memory,** in which we use information but are not consciously aware that we are doing so (McBride, 2007; Roediger & McDermott, 1993; Schacter, 1995a, 2000; Schacter, Chiu, & Ochsner, 1993; Schacter & Graf, 1986a, 1986b). Every day you engage in many tasks that involve your unconscious recollection of information. Even as you read this book, you unconsciously are remembering various things. They include the meanings of particular words, some of the cognitive-psychological concepts you read about in earlier chapters, and even how to read. These recollections are aided by implicit memory. There are differences in explicit memory over the life span; however, implicit memory does not show the same changes. Specifically, infants and older adults often tend to have relatively poor explicit memory but implicit memory that is comparable to that of young adults (Carver & Bauer, 2001; Murphy, McKone, & Slee, 2003). In certain patient groups you also see differences in explicit memory with spared implicit memory; these groups will be discussed later in the chapter.

In the laboratory, implicit memory is sometimes examined by having people perform word-completion tasks. In a word-completion task, participants receive a word fragment, such as the first three letters of a word. They then complete it with the first word that comes to mind. For example, suppose that you are asked to fill in the blanks with the five missing letters to form a word: imp_ _ _ _ _. Because you recently have seen the word *implicit,* you would be more likely to provide the five letters "l-i-c-i-t" for the blanks than would someone who had not recently been exposed to the word. You have been primed. *Priming* is the facilitation of your ability to utilize missing information. In general, participants perform better when they have seen the word on a recently presented list, although they have not been explicitly instructed to remember words from that list (Tulving, 2000a). Priming even works in situations where you are not aware that you have seen the word before—that is, if the word was presented for a fraction of a second or in some other degraded form.

Procedural memory, or memory for processes, is a subtype of nondeclarative memory (Tulving, 1985). Examples of procedural memory include the procedures involved in riding a bike or driving a car. Consider when you drive to the mall: You probably put the car into gear, use your blinkers, and stay in your lane without actively thinking about the task. Nor do you need consciously to remember what you should do at a red light. Many of the activities that we do every day fall under the purview of procedural memory; these can range from brushing your teeth to writing a paper.

The cerebellum of the brain seems to be centrally involved in procedural memory. The neuropsychological and cognitive evidence supporting a discrete procedural memory has been quite well documented (Cohen & associates, 1985; Cohen & Squire, 1980; Rempel-Clower & associates, 1996; Squire, 1987; Squire, Knowlton, & Musen, 1993). In the laboratory, procedural memory is frequently examined with the rotary-pursuit task. The rotary-pursuit task requires participants to maintain contact between an L-shaped stylus and a small rotating disk (Costello, 1967). The disk is generally the size of a nickel, less than an inch in diameter. This disk is placed on a quickly rotating platform. The participant must track the small disk with the wand as it quickly spins around on a platform. After learning with a specific disk and speed of rotation, participants are asked to complete the task again, either with the same disk and the same speed or with a new disk or speed. Verdolini-Marston and Balota (1994) noted that when a new disk or speed is used, participants do relatively poorly. But with the same disk and speed, participants do as well as they had after learning the task, even if they don't remember previously completing the task.

Another task used to examine procedural memory is mirror tracing. In the mirror-tracing task, a plate with the outline of a shape drawn on it is put behind a barrier where it cannot be seen. Beyond the barrier in the participant's line of sight is a mirror. When the participant reaches around the barrier, his or her hand and the plate with the shape are within view. Participants then take a stylus and trace the outline of the shape drawn on the plate. When first learning this task, participants have difficulty staying on the shape. Typically, there are many points at which the stylus leaves the outline. Moreover, it takes a relatively long time to trace the entire shape. With practice, however, participants become quite efficient and accurate with this task. Participants' retention of this skill gives us a way to study procedural memory (Gabrieli & associates, 1997; Rodrigue, Kennedy, & Raz, 2005).

The methods for measuring both implicit and explicit memory described here and in Table 5.1 assume that implicit and explicit memory are separate and can be measured by different tasks. Some researchers have challenged this assumption. Instead, they assume that implicit and explicit memory both play a role in every response, even if the task at hand is intended to measure only one type of memory. Thus, cognitive psychologists have developed models that assume that both implicit and explicit memory influence almost all responses.

One of the first and most widely recognized models in this area is the *process-dissociation model* (Jacoby, 1991). The model assumes that implicit and explicit memory both have a role in virtually every response. Thus, only one task is needed to measure both these processes. However, two different tasks can be used within the process-dissociation framework.

In one of these tasks, participants learn a list of words and are then presented with word fragments. At this point, they are given either inclusive instructions, in which they are to use the information they previously learned to complete the words; or the instructions are exclusive, in which the participant is told not to use the items from the previous list to fill in the word fragments. By subtracting the number of times that a word from the list is used in the exclusion condition from the same event in the inclusion condition Jacoby was able to estimate the effect of explicit memory. A few more steps allowed Jacoby to estimate implicit memory on the same task. The process-dissociation task has been used extensively (Memon, Holliday, & Hill, 2006; Yonelinas, 2001). However, this procedure is not without criticisms. These criticisms include that process dissociation produces biased estimates when guessing occurs and when participants use a strategy that involves evaluating and second guessing their responses (McBride & Dosher, 2002; McKenzie & Tiberghien, 2004; Yu & Bellezza, 2000).

Traditional Model of Memory

There are several different major models of memory (Murdock, 2003; Roediger, 1980b). In the mid-1960s, based on the data available at the time, researchers proposed a model of memory distinguishing two structures of memory first proposed by William James (1890/1970): primary memory, which holds temporary information currently in use, and secondary memory, which holds information permanently or at least for a very long time (Waugh & Norman, 1965). Three years later, Richard Atkinson and Richard Shiffrin (1968) proposed an alternative model that conceptualized memory in terms of three memory stores: (1) a **sensory store,** capable of storing relatively limited amounts of information for very brief periods; (2) a **short-term store,** capable of storing information for somewhat longer periods but also of relatively limited capacity; and (3) a **long-term store,** of very large capacity, capable of storing information for very long periods, perhaps even indefinitely (Richardson-Klavehn & Bjork, 2003).

The model differentiates among structures for holding information, termed *stores*, and the information stored in the structures, termed *memory*. Today, however, cognitive psychologists commonly describe the three stores as sensory memory, short-term memory, and long-term memory. Also, Atkinson and Shiffrin were not suggesting that the three stores are distinct physiological structures. Rather, the stores are **hypothetical constructs**—concepts that are not themselves directly measurable or observable but that serve as mental models for understanding how a psychological phenomenon works. Figure 5.1 shows a simple information-processing model of these stores (Atkinson & Shiffrin, 1971). As this figure shows, the Atkinson-Shiffrin model emphasizes the passive receptacles in which memories are stored. But it also alludes to some control processes that govern the transfer of information from one store to another.

The three-store model is, however, not the only way to conceptualize memory. The following sections first present what we know about memory in terms of the three-store model. Then some alternative ways in which to conceptualize memory are described. Let's begin with the sensory store in the three-store model.

Sensory Store

The *sensory store* is the initial repository of much information that eventually enters the short- and long-term stores. Strong (although not undisputed; see Haber, 1983) evidence argues in favor of the existence of an iconic store. The **iconic store** is a discrete visual sensory register that holds information for very short periods. Its name derives from the fact that information is stored in the form of icons. These in turn are

FIGURE 5.1

Richard Atkinson and Richard Shiffrin proposed a theoretical model for the flow of information through the human information processor. Illustration by Allen Beechel, adapted from "The Control of Short-Term Memory," by Richard C. Atkinson and Richard M. Shiffrin. Copyright © 1971 by Scientific American, Inc. All rights reserved. Reprinted with permission.

visual images that represent something. Icons usually resemble whatever is being represented.

If you have ever "written" your name with a lighted sparkler (or stick of incense) against a dark background, you have experienced the persistence of a visual memory. You briefly "see" your name, although the sparkler leaves no physical trace. This visual persistence is an example of the type of information held in the iconic store.

Sperling's Discovery

The initial discovery regarding the existence of the iconic store came from a doctoral dissertation by a graduate student at Harvard named George Sperling (1960). He addressed the question of how much information we can encode in a single, brief glance at a set of stimuli. Sperling flashed an array of letters and numbers on a screen for a mere 50 milliseconds (thousandths of a second). Participants were asked to report the identity and location of as many of the symbols as they could recall. Sperling could be sure that participants got only one glance because previous research had shown that 0.050 seconds is long enough for only a single glance at the presented stimulus.

Sperling found that when participants were asked to report on what they saw, they remembered only about four symbols. The finding confirmed an earlier one made by Brigden in 1933. The number of symbols recalled was pretty much the same, without regard to how many symbols had been in the visual display. Some of Sperling's participants mentioned that they had seen all the stimuli clearly. But while reporting what they saw, they forgot the other stimuli. Sperling then conceived an ingenious idea for how to measure what the participants saw. The procedure used by Brigden and in the first set of studies by Sperling is a *whole-report procedure*. In this procedure, participants report *every* symbol they have seen. Sperling then introduced a *partial-report procedure*. Here, participants need to report only part of what they see.

Sperling found a way to obtain a sample of his participants' knowledge. He then extrapolated from this sample to estimate their total knowledge. His logic was similar to that of school examinations, which also are used as samples of an individual's total knowledge of course material. Sperling presented symbols in three rows of four symbols each. Figure 5.2 shows a display similar to one that Sperling's participants might have seen. Sperling informed participants that they would have to recall only a single row of the display. The row to be recalled was signaled by a tone of high, medium, or low pitch. The pitches corresponded to the need to recall the top, middle, or bottom row, respectively.

To estimate the duration of iconic memory, Sperling manipulated the interval between the display and the tone. The range of the interval was from 0.10 seconds *before* the onset of the display to 1.0 second *after* the offset of the display. The partial-report procedure dramatically changed how much participants could recall. Sperling then multiplied the number of symbols recalled with this procedure by three. The reason was that participants had to recall only one third of the information presented but did not know beforehand which of the three lines they would be asked to report.

Using this partial-report procedure, Sperling found that participants had available roughly 9 of the 12 symbols if they were cued immediately before or immediately after the appearance of the display. However, when they were cued 1 second later, their recall was down to 4 or 5 of the 12 items. This level of recall was about the same as that obtained through the whole-report procedure. These data suggest that the iconic store can hold about 9 items. They also suggest that information in this store decays very rapidly (Figure 5.3). Indeed, the advantage of the partial-report procedure

FIGURE 5.2

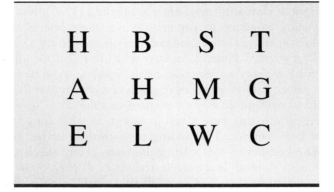

This symbolic display is similar to the one used for George Sperling's visual-recall task. From Psychology, Second Edition *by Margaret W. Matlin, copyright © 1995 by Holt, Rinehart and Winston. Reproduced by permission of the publisher.*

FIGURE 5.3

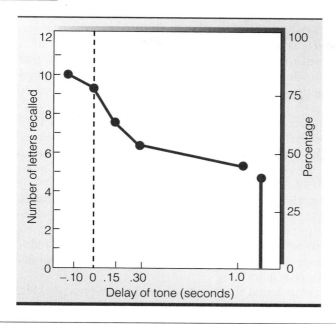

The figure shows the average number of letters recalled (left axis; percentage equivalents indicated on right axis) by a subject, based on using the partial-report procedure, as a function of the delay between the presentation of the letters and the tone signaling when to demonstrate recall. The bar at the lower-right corner indicates the average number of letters recalled when subjects used the whole-report procedure. (After Sperling, 1960.)

is reduced drastically by 0.3 seconds of delay. It essentially is obliterated by 1 second of delay for onset of the tone.

Sperling's results suggest that information fades rapidly from iconic storage. Why are we subjectively unaware of such a fading phenomenon? First, we rarely are subjected to stimuli such as the ones in his experiment. They appeared for only 50 milliseconds and then disappeared before participants needed to recall them. Second and more important, however, we are unable to distinguish what we see in iconic memory from what we actually see in the environment. What we see in iconic memory is what we take to be in the environment. Participants in Sperling's experiment generally reported that they could still see the display up to 150 milliseconds after it actually had been terminated.

Elegant as it was, Sperling's use of the partial-report procedure was imperfect. It still suffered, at least to some small extent, from the problem inherent in the full-report procedure: Participants had to report multiple symbols. They may have experienced fading of memory during the report. Indeed, a distinct possibility of output interference exists. In this case, the production of output interferes with the phenomenon being studied. That is, verbally reporting multiple symbols may interfere with reports of iconic memory.

Subsequent Refinement

In subsequent work, participants were shown displays of two rows of eight randomly chosen letters for a duration of 50 milliseconds (Averbach & Coriell, 1961). In this investigation, a small mark appeared just above one of the positions where a letter had appeared (or was about to appear). Its appearance was at varying time intervals before or after presentation of the letters. In this research, then, participants needed to report only a single letter at a time. The procedure thus minimized output interference. These investigators found that when the bar appeared immediately before or after the stimulus display, participants could report accurately on about 75% of the trials. Thus, they seemed to be holding about 12 items (75% of 16) in sensory memory. Sperling's estimate of the capacity of iconic memory, therefore, may have been conservative. The evidence in this study suggests that when output interference is greatly reduced, the estimates of the capacity of iconic memory may greatly increase. Iconic memory may comprise as many as 12 items.

A second experiment (Averbach & Coriell, 1961) revealed an additional important characteristic of iconic memory: It can be erased. The erasable nature of iconic memory definitely makes our visual sensations more sensible. We would be in serious trouble if everything we saw in our visual environment persisted for too long. For example, if we are scanning the environment at a rapid pace, we need the visual information to disappear quickly.

The investigators found that when a stimulus was presented after a target letter in the same position that the target letter had occupied, it could erase the visual icon (Averbach & Coriell, 1961). This interference is called backward visual masking. *Backward visual masking* is mental erasure of a stimulus caused by the placement of one stimulus where another one had appeared previously. If the mask stimulus is presented in the same location as a letter and within 100 milliseconds of the presentation of the letter, the mask is superimposed on the letter. For example, *F* followed by *L* would be *E*. At longer intervals between the target and the mask, the mask erases the original stimulus. For example, only the *L* would remain if *F* and then *L* had been presented. At still longer intervals between the target and the mask, the mask no longer interferes. This noninterference is presumably because the target information already has been transferred to more durable memory storage.

To summarize, visual information appears to enter our memory system through an iconic store. This store holds visual information for very short periods. In the normal course of events, this information may be transferred to another store. Or it may be erased. Erasure occurs if other information is superimposed on it before there is sufficient time for the transfer of the information to another memory store. Erasure or movement into another store also occurs with auditory information that is in echoic memory.

Short-Term Store

Most of us have little or no introspective access to our sensory memory stores. Nevertheless, we all have access to our short-term memory store. It holds memories for matters of seconds and, occasionally, up to a couple of minutes. For example, can you remember the name of the researcher who discovered the iconic store? What about the names of the researchers who subsequently refined this work? If you can recall those names, you used some memory-control processes for doing so. According to the Atkinson-Shiffrin model, the short-term store holds not only a few items. It also has available some control processes that regulate the flow of information to and from the long-term store. Here, we may hold information for longer periods. Typically, material remains in the short-term store for about 30 seconds, unless it is rehearsed to retain it. Information is stored acoustically (by the way it sounds) rather than visually (by the way it looks).

How many items of information can we hold in short-term memory at any one time? In general, our immediate (short-term) memory capacity for a wide range of items appears to be about seven items, plus or minus two (Miller, 1956). An item can be something simple, such as a digit, or something more complex, such as a word. If we chunk together a string of, say, 20 letters or numbers into 7 meaningful items, we can remember them. We could not, however, remember 20 items and repeat them immediately. For example, most of us cannot hold in short-term memory this string of 21 numbers: 101001000100001000100. Suppose, however, we chunk it into larger units, such as 10, 100, 1000, 10000, 1000, and 100. We probably will be able to re-produce easily the 21 numerals as 6 items (Miller, 1956).

Other factors also influence the capacity for temporary storage in memory. For example, the number of syllables we pronounce with each item affects the number of items we can recall. When each item has a larger number of syllables, we can recall fewer items (Baddeley, Thomson, & Buchanan, 1975; Naveh-Benjamin & Ayres, 1986; Schweickert & Boruff, 1986). In addition, any delay or interference can cause our seven-item capacity to drop to about three items. Indeed, in general the capacity limit may be closer to three to five than it is to seven (Cowan, 2001). Some estimates are even lower (e.g., Waugh & Norman, 1965).

Most studies have used verbal stimuli to test the capacity of the short-term store, but people can also hold visual information in short-term memory. For example, they can hold information about shapes as well as their colors and orientations. What is the capacity of the short-term store of visual information? Is it less, the same, or perhaps greater?

A team of investigators set out to discover the capacity of the short-term store for visual information (Luck & Vogel, 1997; Vogel, Woodman, & Luck, 2001). They presented experimental participants with two visual displays. The displays were presented in sequence, one following the other. The stimuli were of three types: colored squares, black lines at varying orientations, and colored lines at different orientations. Thus, the third kind of stimulus combined the features of the first two. The kind of stimulus was the same in each of the two displays. For example, if the first display contained colored squares, so did the second. The two displays could be either the same or different from each other. If they were different, then it was by only one feature. The participants needed to indicate whether the two displays were the same or different from each other. The investigators found that participants could hold roughly four items in memory, within the estimates suggested by Cowan (2001). The results were the same whether just individual features were varied (i.e., colored squares, black lines at varying orientation) or pairs of features were varied (i.e., colored lines at different orientations). Thus, storage seems to depend on numbers of objects rather than numbers of features.

This work contained a possible confound (i.e., other responsible factor that cannot be easily disentangled from the supposed causal factor). In the stimuli with colored lines at different orientations, the added feature was at the same spatial location as the original one. That is, color and orientation were, with respect to the same object, in the same place in the display. A further study thus was done to separate the effects of spatial location from number of objects (Lee & Chun, 2001). In this research, stimuli comprising boxes and lines could be either at separate locations or at overlapping locations. The overlapping locations thus separated the objects from the fixed locations. The research would enable one to determine whether people can remember four objects, as suggested in the previous work, or four spatial locations. The results were the same as in the earlier research. Participants still could remember four objects, regardless of spatial locations. Therefore, memory was for objects, not spatial locations. Further, using American Sign Language, researchers have found that short-term memory can hold approximately four items for signed letters. This finding is consistent with earlier work on visual-spatial short-term memory. The finding makes sense, given the visual nature of these items (Bavelier & associates, 2006; Wilson & Emmorey, 2006).

Long-Term Store

We constantly use short-term memory throughout our daily activities. When most of us talk about memory, however, we usually are talking about long-term memory. Here we keep memories that stay with us over long periods, perhaps indefinitely. All of us rely heavily on our long-term memory. We hold in it information we need to get us by in our day-to-day lives. Examples are what people's names are, where we keep things, how we schedule ourselves on different days, and so on. We also worry when we fear that our long-term memory is not up to snuff.

How much information can we hold in long-term memory? How long does the information last? The question of storage capacity can be disposed of quickly because the answer is simple. We do not know. Nor do we know how we would find out. We can design experiments to tax the limits of short-term memory. But we do not know how to test the limits of long-term memory and thereby find out its capacity. Some theorists have suggested that the capacity of long-term memory is infinite, at least in practical terms (Bahrick, 1984a, 1984b, 2000; Bahrick & Hall, 1991; Hintzman, 1978). It turns out that the question of how long information lasts in long-term memory is not easily answerable. At present, we have no proof even that there is an absolute outer limit to how long information can be stored.

What is stored in the brain? Wilder Penfield addressed this question while performing operations on the brains of conscious patients afflicted with epilepsy. He used electrical stimulation of various parts of the cerebral cortex to locate the origins of each patient's problem. In fact, his work was instrumental in plotting the motor and sensory areas of the cortex described in Chapter 2 of this text.

During the course of such stimulation, Penfield (1955, 1969) found that patients sometimes would appear to recall memories from way back in their childhoods. These memories may not have been called to mind for many, many years. (Note that the patients could be stimulated to recall episodes such as events from their childhood, not facts such as the names of U.S. presidents.) These data suggested to Penfield that long-term memories might be permanent.

Some researchers have disputed Penfield's interpretations (e.g., Loftus & Loftus, 1980). For example, they have noted the small number of such reports in relation to

Courtesy of Dr. Harry Bahrick

Harry Bahrick is a research professor of psychology at Ohio Wesleyan University. He is best known for his studies of the lifetime retention of information in semantic memory. He has shown that unrehearsed knowledge can remain in memory for a quarter of a century or even longer, as, for example, in the case of recognizing fellow students known during the high school years but not seen or thought of since.

the hundreds of patients on whom Penfield operated. In addition, we cannot be certain that the patients actually were recalling these events. They may have been inventing them. Other researchers, using empirical techniques on older participants, found contradictory evidence.

Some researchers tested participants' memory for names and photographs of their high-school classmates (Bahrick, Bahrick, & Wittlinger, 1975). Even after 25 years, there was little forgetting of some aspects of memory. Participants tended to recognize names as belonging to classmates rather than to outsiders. Recognition memory for matching names to graduation photos was quite high. As you might expect, recall of names showed a higher rate of forgetting. The term *permastore* refers to the very long-term storage of information, such as knowledge of a foreign language (Bahrick, 1984a, 1984b; Bahrick & associates, 1993) and of mathematics (Bahrick & Hall, 1991).

Schmidt and associates (2000) studied the permastore effect for names of streets near one's childhood homes. Indeed, I just returned to my childhood home of more than 40 years ago and perfectly remembered the names of the nearby streets. These findings indicate that permastore can occur even for information that you have passively learned. Some researchers have suggested that permastore is a separate memory system. Others, such as Neisser (1999), have argued that one long-term memory system can account for both. There is to date no resolution of the issue.

The Levels-of-Processing Model

A radical departure from the three-stores model of memory is the **levels-of-processing framework,** which postulates that memory does not comprise three or even any specific number of separate stores but rather varies along a continuous dimension in terms of depth of encoding (Craik & Lockhart, 1972). In other words, there are theoretically an infinite number of levels of processing (LOP) at which items can be encoded. There are no distinct boundaries between one level and the next. The emphasis in this model is on processing as the key to storage. The level at which information is stored will depend, in large part, on how it is encoded. Moreover, the deeper the level of processing, the higher, in general, is the probability that an item may be retrieved (Craik & Brown, 2000).

A set of experiments seemed to support the LOP view (Craik & Tulving, 1975). Participants received a list of words. A question preceded each word. Questions were varied to encourage three different levels of processing. In progressive order of depth, they were *physical, phonological,* and *semantic*. Samples of the words and the questions are shown in Table 5.2. The results of the research were clear. The deeper the level of processing encouraged by the question, the higher the level of recall achieved. Similar results emerged independently in Russia (Zinchenko, 1962, 1981). Words that were logically (e.g., taxonomically) connected (e.g., *dog* and *animal*) were recalled more easily than were words that were concretely connected (e.g., *dog* and *leg*). At the same time, concretely connected words were more easily recalled than were words that were unconnected.

The levels-of-processing framework can also be applied to nonverbal stimuli. Melinda Burgess and George Weaver (2003) noted that faces that were deeply pro-

TABLE 5.2	Levels-of-Processing Framework

Among the levels of processing proposed by Fergus Craik and Endel Tulving are the physical, phonological, and semantic levels, as shown in this table.

LEVEL OF PROCESSING	BASIS FOR PROCESSING	EXAMPLE	
Physical	Visually apparent features of the letters	Word:	TABLE
		Question:	Is the word written in capital letters?
Phonological	Sound combinations associated with the letters (e.g., rhyming)	Word:	CAT
		Question:	Does the word rhyme with "MAT"?
Semantic	Meaning of the word	Word:	DAFFODIL
		Question:	Is the word a type of plant?

cessed were better recognized on a subsequent test than those that were studied at a lower level of processing. A level-of-processing (or depth-of-processing) benefit can be seen for a variety of populations, including in patients with schizophrenia (Ragland & associates, 2003).

An even more powerful inducement to recall has been termed the self-reference effect (Rogers, Kuiper, & Kirker, 1977). In the *self-reference effect,* participants show very high levels of recall when asked to relate words meaningfully to themselves by determining whether the words describe them. Even the words that participants assess as not describing themselves are recalled at high levels. This high recall is a result of considering whether the words do or do not describe the participants. However, the highest levels of recall occur with words that people consider self-descriptive. Similar self-reference effects have been found by many other researchers (e.g., Bower & Gilligan, 1979; Brown, Keenan, & Potts, 1986; Ganellen & Carver, 1985; Halpin & associates, 1984; Katz, 1987; Reeder, McCormick, & Esselman, 1987).

Surprisingly, the type of information that is being learned can influence the self-reference effect. When comparing positive and negative traits, investigators found the self-reference effect for the positive but not the negative traits (D'Argembeau, Comblain, & Van der Linden, 2005). Thus, we are better able to associate positive than negative descriptors with ourselves.

Some researchers suggest that the self-reference effect is distinctive, but others suggest that it is explained easily in terms of the LOP framework or other ordinary memory processes (e.g., Mills, 1983). Specifically, each of us has a very elaborate self-schema. This self-schema is an organized system of internal cues regarding our attributes, our personal experiences, and ourselves. Thus, we can richly and elaborately encode information related to ourselves much more so than information about other topics (Bellezza, 1984, 1992). Also, we easily can organize new information pertaining to ourselves. When other information is also readily organized, we may recall non–self-referent information easily as well (Klein & Kihlstrom, 1986). Finally, when we generate our own cues, we demonstrate much higher levels of recall than when someone else generates cues for us to use (Greenwald & Banaji, 1989).

Despite much supporting evidence, the LOP framework as a whole has its critics. For one thing, some researchers suggest that the particular levels may involve a circular definition. On this view, the levels are defined as deeper because the information is retained better. But the information is viewed as being retained better because the levels are deeper. In addition, some researchers noted some paradoxes in retention. For example, under some circumstances, strategies that use rhymes have produced better retention than those using just semantic rehearsal. For example, focusing on superficial sounds and not underlying meanings can result in better retention than focusing on repetition of underlying meanings. Specifically, consider what happens when the context for retrieval involves attention to phonological (acoustic) properties of words (e.g., rhymes). Here, performance is enhanced when the context for encoding involves rehearsal based on phonological properties, rather than on semantic properties of words (Fisher & Craik, 1977, 1980). Nonetheless, consider what happened when semantic retrieval, based on semantic encoding, was compared with acoustic (rhyme) retrieval, based on rhyme encoding. Performance was greater for semantic retrieval than for acoustic retrieval (Fisher & Craik, 1977).

In light of these criticisms and some contrary findings, the LOP model has been revised. The sequence of the levels of encoding may not be as important as the match between the type of elaboration of the encoding and the type of task required for retrieval (Morris, Bransford, & Franks, 1977). Furthermore, there appear to be two kinds of strategies for elaborating the encoding. The first is within-item elaboration. It elaborates encoding of the particular item (e.g., a word or other fact) in terms of its characteristics, including the various levels of processing. The second kind of strategy is between-item elaboration. It elaborates encoding by relating each item's features (again, at various levels) to the features of items already in memory. Thus, suppose you wanted to be sure to remember something in particular. You could elaborate it at various levels for each of the two strategies.

Elaboration strategies have practical applications: In studying, you may wish to match the way in which you encode the material to the way in which you will be expected to retrieve it in the future. Furthermore, the more elaborately and diversely you encode material, the more readily you are likely to recall it later in a variety of task settings. Just looking over material again and again in the same way is less likely to be productive for learning the material than is finding more than one way in which to learn it. If the context for retrieval will require you to have a deep understanding of the information, you should find ways to encode the material at deep levels of processing, such as by asking yourself meaningful questions about the material.

PRACTICAL APPLICATIONS OF COGNITIVE PSYCHOLOGY

An Integrative Model: Working Memory

The working-memory model is probably the most widely used and accepted today. Psychologists who use it view short-term and long-term memory from a different perspective (e.g., Baddeley, 1990a, 1995; Cantor & Engle, 1993; Daneman & Carpenter, 1980; Daneman & Tardif, 1987; Engle, 1994; Engle, Cantor, & Carullo, 1992). Table 5.3 shows the contrasts between the Atkinson-Shiffrin model and an alternative perspective. Note the semantic distinctions, the differences in metaphorical representation, and the differences in emphasis for each view. The key feature of the alternative view

TABLE 5.3	Traditional versus Nontraditional Views of Memory

Since Richard Atkinson and Richard Shiffrin first proposed their three-stores model of memory (which may be considered a traditional view of memory), various other models have been suggested.

	TRADITIONAL THREE-STORES VIEW	**ALTERNATIVE VIEW OF MEMORY***
Terminology: definition of memory stores	Working memory is another name for short-term memory, which is distinct from long-term memory.	Working memory (active memory) is that part of long-term memory that comprises all the knowledge of facts and procedures that recently has been activated in memory, including the brief, fleeting short-term memory and its contents.
Metaphor for envisioning the relationships	Short-term memory may be envisioned as being distinct from long-term memory, perhaps either alongside it or hierarchically linked to it.	Short-term memory, working memory, and long-term memory may be envisioned as nested concentric spheres, in which working memory contains only the most recently activated portion of long-term memory and short-term memory contains only a very small, fleeting portion of working memory.
Metaphor for the movement of information	Information moves directly from long-term memory to short-term memory and then back—never in both locations at once.	Information remains within long-term memory; when activated, information moves into long-term memory's specialized working memory, which actively will move information into and out of the short-term memory store contained within it.
Emphasis	Distinction between long- and short-term memory.	Role of activation in moving information into working memory and the role of working memory in memory processes.

*Examples of researchers holding this view: Cantor & Engle, 1993; Engle, 1994; Engle, Cantor, & Carullo, 1992.

is the role of working memory. **Working memory** holds only the most recently activated, or conscious, portion of long-term memory, and it moves these activated elements into and out of brief, temporary memory storage (Dosher, 2003).

Alan Baddeley has suggested an integrative model of memory (Baddeley, 1990b, 1992, 1993, 1997; Baddeley & Hitch, 1974). It synthesizes the working-memory model with the LOP framework. Essentially, he views the LOP framework as an extension of, rather than as a replacement for, the working-memory model.

Baddeley originally suggested that working memory comprises four elements. The first is a **visuospatial sketchpad,** which briefly holds some visual images. The second is a **phonological loop,** which briefly holds inner speech for verbal comprehension and for acoustic rehearsal. We use the phonological loop for a number of everyday tasks, including sounding out new and difficult words and solving word problems. There are two critical components of this loop. One is phonological storage, which holds information in memory. The other is subvocal rehearsal, which is used to put the information into memory in the first place. The role of subvocal rehearsal can be seen in the following example. Consider trying to learn a list of words while repeating the number five. In this case subvocal rehearsal is inhibited and you would be unable to rehearse the new words. When subvocal rehearsal is inhibited, the new information is not stored. This is called *articulatory suppression*. Articulatory suppression is more pronounced when the information is presented visually versus aurally.

The amount of information that can be manipulated within the phonological loop is limited. Thus, we can remember fewer long words compared with short words (Baddeley, 2000b). Without this loop, acoustic information decays after about 2 seconds. The third element is a **central executive,** which both coordinates attentional activities and governs responses. The central executive is critical to working memory because it is the gating mechanism that decides what information to process further and how to process it. It decides what resources to allocate to memory and related tasks, and how to allocate them. It is also involved in higher-order reasoning and comprehension and is central to human intelligence. The fourth element is a number of other *"subsidiary slave systems"* that perform other cognitive or perceptual tasks (Baddeley, 1989, p. 36). Recently, another component, the **episodic buffer,** has been added to working memory (Baddeley, 2000a, 2001). The episodic buffer is a limited-capacity system that is capable of binding information from the subsidiary systems and from long-term memory into a unitary episodic representation. This component integrates information from different parts of working memory—that is, visual spatial and phonological—so that they make sense to us. This incorporation allows us to solve problems and reevaluate previous experiences with more recent knowledge.

Neuropsychological methods, and especially brain imaging, can be very helpful in understanding the nature of memory (Buckner, 2000a, 2000b; Cabeza & Nyberg, 1997; Markowitsch, 2000; Nyberg & Cabeza, 2000; Rosenzweig, 2003; Rugg & Allan, 2000; Ungerleider, 1995). Support for a distinction between working memory and long-term memory comes from neuropsychological research. Neuropsychological studies have shown abundant evidence of a brief memory buffer. The buffer is used for remembering information temporarily. It is distinct from long-term memory, which is used for remembering information for long periods (Rudner & associates, 2007; Schacter, 1989a; Smith & Jonides, 1995; Squire, 1986; Squire & Knowlton, 2000). Furthermore, through some promising new research using positron emission tomography (PET) techniques, investigators have found evidence for distinct brain areas involved in the different aspects of working memory. The phonological loop, maintaining speech-related information, appears to involve bilateral activation of the frontal and parietal lobes (Cabeza & Nyberg, 1997). It is interesting that the visuospatial sketchpad appears to activate slightly different areas. Which ones it activates depends on the length of the retention interval. Shorter intervals activate areas of the occipital and right frontal lobes. Longer intervals activate areas of the parietal and left frontal lobes (Haxby & associates, 1995). The central executive functions appear to involve activation mostly in the frontal lobes (Roberts, Robbins, & Weiskrantz, 1996). Finally, the episodic buffer operations seem to involve the bilateral activation of the frontal lobes and portions of the temporal lobes, including the left hippocampus (Rudner & associates, 2007). Whereas the three-store view emphasizes the structural receptacles for stored information, the working-memory model underscores the functions of working memory in governing the processes of memory. These processes include encoding and integrating information. Examples are integrating acoustic and visual information through cross-modality, organizing information into meaningful chunks, and linking new information to existing forms of knowledge representation in long-term memory.

Courtesy of Dr. Alan Baddeley

Alan Baddeley is past director of the MRC Applied Psychology Unit, Cambridge, England, and is a professor of cognitive psychology at York University in England. Baddeley is best known for his work on the concept of working memory, which has shown that working memory can be viewed as an interface among many of the varied aspects of cognition.

We can conceptualize the differing emphases with contrasting metaphors. For example, we can compare the three-store view to a warehouse in which information is passively stored. The sensory store serves as the loading dock. The short-term store comprises the area surrounding the loading dock. Here, information is stored temporarily until it is moved to or from the correct location in the warehouse. A metaphor for the working-memory model might be a multimedia production house. It continuously generates and manipulates images and sounds. It also coordinates the integration of sights and sounds into meaningful arrangements. Once images, sounds, and other information are stored, they still are available for reformatting and reintegration in novel ways, as new demands and new information become available. Different aspects of working memory are represented in the brain differently. Figure 5.4 shows some of these differences.

Working memory can be measured through a number of different tasks. The most commonly used are shown in Figure 5.5.

Task a is a retention delay task. It is the simplest task shown in the figure. An item is shown—in this case, a geometric shape. (The + at the beginning is merely a focus point to indicate that the series of items is beginning.) There is then a retention interval, which may be filled with other tasks, or unfilled; in which case time passes without any specifically designed intervening activity. The participant is then presented with a stimulus and must say whether it is old or new. In the figure, the stimulus being tested is new. So "new" would be the correct answer.

Task b is a temporally ordered working memory load task. A series of items is presented. After a while, the series of asterisks indicates that a test item will be presented. The test item is presented, and the participant must say whether the item is old or new. Because "4," the number in the figure, has not been presented before, the correct answer is "new."

Task c is a temporal order task. A series of items is presented. Then the asterisks indicate a test item will be given. The test item shows two previously presented items, 3 and 7. The participant must indicate which of the two numbers, 3 or 7, appeared more recently. The correct answer is 7 because 7 occurred after 3 in the list.

Task d is an n-back task. Stimuli are presented. At specified points, one is asked to repeat the stimulus that occurred n presentations back. For example, one might be asked to repeat the digit that occurred 1 back—or just before (as with the 6). Or one might be asked to repeat the digit that occurred 2 back (as with the 7).

Task e is a temporally ordered working memory load task. It can also be referred to simply as a digit-span task (when digits are used). One is presented with a series of stimuli. After they are presented, one repeats them back in the order they were presented. A variant of this task has the participant repeat them back in the order opposite to that in which they were presented—from the end to the beginning.

Finally, Task f is a temporally ordered working memory load task. One is given a series of simple arithmetic problems. For each problem, one indicates whether the sum or difference is correct. At the end, one repeats the results of the arithmetic problems in their correct order.

Each of the tasks described here and in Figure 5.5 allows for the examination of how much information we can manipulate in memory. Frequently, these tasks are paired with a second task (called, appropriately, a *secondary task*) so that researchers can learn more about the central executive. The central executive is responsible for allocating attentional and other resources to ongoing tasks. By having participants do more than one task at once, we can examine how mental resources are assigned (Bau-

FIGURE 5.4

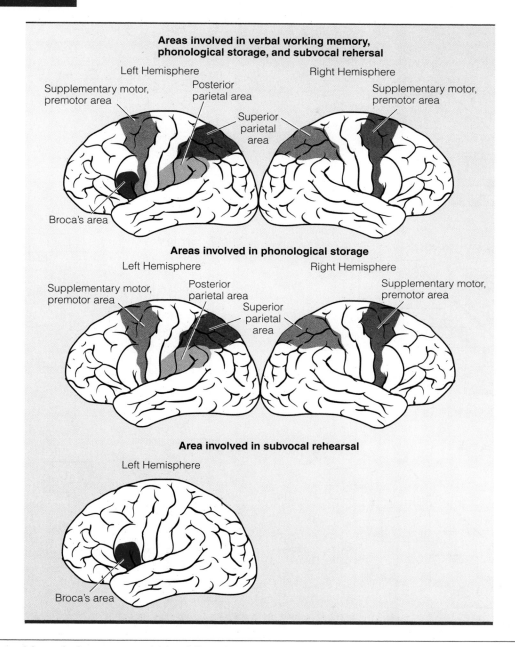

Different areas of the cerebral cortex are involved in different aspects of working memory. The figure shows those aspects involved primarily in the articulatory loop, including phonological storage and subvocal rehearsal. From E. Awh et al. (1996). Dissociation of storage and rehearsal in verbal working memory: Evidence from positron emission tomography. Psychological Science, 7, 25–31. Copyright 1996 by Blackwell, Inc. Reprinted by permission.

FIGURE 5.5

Tasks and working memory. From Encyclopedia of Cognitive Science, *Vol. 4, p. 571. Copyright © 2003. Reproduced with permission of B. Dosher.*

douin & associates, 2006; D'Amico & Guarnera, 2005). A task that often is paired with those listed in Figure 5.5 is a random-number generation task. In this task, the participant has to try to generate a random series of numbers while completing a working memory task (Rudkin, Pearson, & Logie, 2007).

Multiple Memory Systems

The working-memory model is consistent with the notion that multiple systems may be involved in the storage and retrieval of information. Recall that when Wilder Penfield electrically stimulated the brains of his patients, the patients often asserted that they vividly recalled particular episodes and events. They did not, however, recall semantic facts that were unrelated to any particular event. These findings suggest that there may be at least two separate explicit memory systems. One would be for organizing and storing information with a distinctive time referent. It would address questions such as, "What did you eat for lunch yesterday?" or "Who was the first person you saw this morning?" The second system would be for information that has no particular time referent. It would address questions such as, "Who were the two psychologists who first proposed the three-stores model of memory?" and "What is a mnemonist?"

Based on such findings, Endel Tulving (1972) proposed a distinction between two kinds of explicit memory. **Semantic memory** stores general world knowledge. It is our memory for facts that are not unique to us and that are not recalled in any particular temporal context. **Episodic memory** stores personally experienced events or episodes. According to Tulving, we use episodic memory when we learn lists of words or when we need to recall something that occurred to us at a particular time or in a particular context. For example, suppose I needed to remember that I saw Harrison Hardimanowitz in the dentist's office yesterday. I would be drawing on an episodic memory. But if I needed to remember the name of the person I now see in the waiting room ("Harrison Hardimanowitz"), I would be drawing on a semantic memory. There is no particular time tag associated with the name of that individual being Harrison. But there is a time tag associated with my having seen him at the dentist's office yesterday.

Tulving (1983, 1989) and others (e.g., Shoben, 1984) provide support for the distinction between semantic and episodic memory. It is based on both cognitive research and neurological investigation. The neurological investigations have involved electrical-stimulation studies, studies of patients with memory disorders, and cerebral blood flow studies. For example, lesions in the frontal lobe appear to affect recollection regarding *when* a stimulus was presented. But they do not affect recall or recognition memory *that* a particular stimulus was presented (Schacter, 1989a).

It is not clear that semantic and episodic memories are two distinct systems. Nevertheless, they sometimes appear to function in different ways. Many cognitive psychologists question this distinction (e.g., Baddeley, 1984; Eysenck & Keane, 1990; Humphreys, Bain, & Pike, 1989; Johnson & Hasher, 1987; Ratcliff & McKoon, 1986; Richardson-Klavehn & Bjork, 1988). They point to blurry areas on the boundary between these two types of memory. They also note methodological problems with some of the supportive evidence. Perhaps episodic memory is merely a specialized form of semantic memory (Tulving, 1984, 1986). Some neurological evidence suggests that

IN THE LAB OF M. K. JOHNSON

Courtesy of Dr. M. K. Johnson

A memory is a mental experience that is taken to be a veridical (truthful) representation of an event from one's past. Memories can be false in relatively minor ways (e.g., believing one last saw the car keys in the kitchen when they were in the living room) and in major ways that have profound implications for oneself and others (e.g., mistakenly believing one is the source or originator of an idea, or believing that one was sexually abused as a child when one was not). Such memory distortions reflect errors arising from imperfect source monitoring processes—the processes by which we make attributions about the origin of activated information in mental experience. Source monitoring errors include both confusions between internal and external sources of information and between various external sources (e.g., attributing something that was imagined to perception, an intention to an action, something one heard about to something one witnessed, something read in a tabloid to a television program, an incident that occurred in place A or time A to place B or time B). The integration of information across individual experiences from different sources is necessary for all higher-order, complex thought. But this very creativity makes us vulnerable to having false memories because we sometimes misattribute the sources of the information that comes to mind. Several types of evidence indicate that the prefrontal cortex (PFC) plays a key role in identifying the sources of mental experiences. Damage to the PFC produces deficits in source memory. Source memory deficits are more likely in children (whose frontal lobes are slow to develop) and in older adults (who are likely to show increased neuropathology in the PFC with age). PFC dysfunction may play a role in schizophrenia, which sometimes includes severe source monitoring deficits in the form of delusions.

My lab currently is using functional magnetic resonance imaging (fMRI) to help clarify the brain regions involved in source monitoring. In one type of study, participants saw a series of items of two types (pictures and words). Later they were given a memory test in which they were shown some words that corresponded to the items seen earlier (old items) intermixed with some that did not correspond to any of the items seen earlier (new items). We compared the brain activity when participants were asked to make source judgments (e.g., say "yes" to items previously seen as pictures) with brain activity when they were simply asked to decide whether a test item was familiar (say "yes" to any previously presented item). We found greater activity in the left PFC in the source identification compared with the old/new test condition (and sometimes greater activity in the right PFC as well). Furthermore, several other labs have reported related findings providing converging evidence that the left PFC is recruited in monitoring the origin of memories. Other studies suggest that the right PFC is engaged when judgments can be made on the basis of more global, less specific information such as familiarity or recency. It appears that processes subserved by both the right and left PFC contribute to evaluating the origin of mental experiences, possibly in different ways, and interactions between right and left hemispheres are likely important. Thus, one goal for future research is to more specifically relate component processes of memory to patterns of activity across various regions of the PFC and to specify how PFC regions interact with other brain regions in producing the subjective experiences we take to be memories.

Suggested Readings

Johnson, M. K. (2006). Memory and reality. *American Psychologist, 61,* 760–771.

Johnson, M. K., & Raye, C. L. (1998). False memories and confabulation. *Trends in Cognitive Sciences, 2,* 137–145.

Johnson M. R., Mitchell K. J., Raye C. L., D'Esposito M., & Johnson M. K. (2007). A brief thought can modulate activity in extrastriate visual areas: Top-down effects of refreshing just-seen visual stimuli. *NeuroImage, 37,* 290–299.

Lyle, K. B., & Johnson, M. K. (2006). Importing perceived features into false memories. *Memory, 14,* 197–213.

Mitchell, K. J., Johnson, M. K., Raye, C. L., & Greene, E. J. (2004). Prefrontal cortex activity associated with source monitoring in a working memory task. *Journal of Cognitive Neuroscience, 16,* 921–934.

Ranganath, C., Johnson, M. K., & D'Esposito, M. (2000). Left anterior prefrontal activation increases with demands to recall specific perceptual information. *Journal of Neuroscience, 20*(RC 108), 1–5.

these two types of memory are separate, however. Through neuropsychological methods, investigators found dissociations in brain areas for semantic versus episodic memory retrieval (Prince, Tsukiura, & Cabeza, 2007). Further research on patients with specific types of memory loss found the patients with a loss of semantic memory but no impairment of episodic memory (Temple & Richardson, 2004), again suggesting separate systems for episodic and semantic memory. Other researchers examining a different type of memory loss noted an impairment of episodic memory but intact semantic memory (Vargha-Khadem & associates, 1997). These findings all support the conclusion that there are separate episodic and semantic memory systems.

Other findings, however, suggest that the neural processes involved in these memories overlap (Rajah & McIntosh, 2005). Clearly, there is substantial evidence that there are differences between these two types of memory, both behavioral and neurological. Most researchers agree, however, that there is, at the very least, a great deal of interaction between these two types of memory. As a result, the question of whether these forms of memory are separate is still open.

A neuroscientific model attempts to account for differences in hemispheric activation for semantic versus episodic memories. According to this model, *HERA* (hemispheric encoding/retrieval asymmetry), there is greater activation in the left than in the right prefrontal hemisphere for tasks requiring retrieval from semantic memory (Nyberg, Cabeza, & Tulving, 1996; Tulving & associates, 1994). In contrast, there is more activation in the right than in the left prefrontal hemisphere for episodic-retrieval tasks. This model, then, proposes that semantic and episodic memories must be distinct because they draw on separate areas of the brain. For example, if one is asked to generate verbs that are associated with nouns (e.g., "drive" with "car"), this task requires semantic memory. It results in greater left-hemispheric activation (Nyberg, Cabeza, & Tulving, 1996). In contrast, if people are asked to freely recall a list of words, an episodic-memory task, they show more right-hemispheric activation.

A taxonomy of the memory system in terms of the dissociations described in the previous sections is shown in Figure 5.6 (Squire, 1986, 1993). It distinguishes de-

FIGURE 5.6

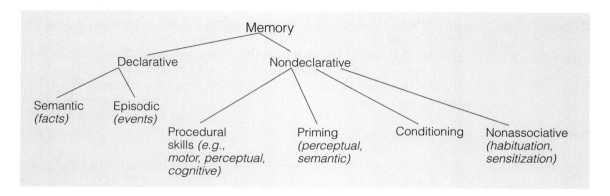

Based on extensive neuropsychological research, Larry Squire has posited that memory comprises two fundamental types: declarative (explicit) memory and various forms of nondeclarative (implicit) memory, each of which may be associated with discrete cerebral structures and processes.

clarative (explicit) memory from various kinds of nondeclarative (implicit) memory. Nondeclarative memory comprises procedural memory, priming effects, simple classical conditioning, habituation, sensitization, and perceptual aftereffects. In yet another view, there are five memory systems in all: episodic, semantic, perceptual (i.e., recognizing things on the basis of their form and structure), procedural, and working (Schacter, 2000).

A Connectionist Perspective

The network model provides the structural basis for *connectionist* parallel distributed processing (PDP) model (Frean, 2003; Sun, 2003). According to the PDP model, the key to knowledge representation lies in the connections among various nodes, not in each individual node (Feldman & Shastri, 2003). Activation of one node may prompt activation of a connected node. This process of spreading activation may prompt the activation of additional nodes. The PDP model fits nicely with the notion of working memory as comprising the activated portion of long-term memory. In this model, activation spreads through nodes within the network. This spreading continues as long as the activation does not exceed the limits of working memory. A **prime** is a node that activates a connected node. A priming effect is the resulting activation of the node. The **priming effect** has been supported by considerable evidence. Examples are the aforementioned studies of priming as an aspect of implicit memory. In addition, some evidence supports the notion that priming is due to spreading activation (McClelland & Rumelhart, 1985, 1988). But not everyone agrees about the mechanism for the priming effect (see McKoon & Ratcliff, 1992b).

Connectionist models also have some intuitive appeal in their ability to integrate several contemporary notions about memory: *Working memory* comprises the *activated* portion of long-term memory and operates through at least some amount of *parallel processing*. *Spreading activation* involves the simultaneous (parallel) activation (*priming*) of multiple links among *nodes* within the *network*. Many cognitive psychologists who hold this integrated view suggest that part of the reason we humans are as efficient as we are in processing information is that we can handle many operations at once. Thus, the contemporary cognitive-psychological conceptions of working memory, network models of memory, spreading activation, priming, and parallel processes mutually enhance and support one another.

Some of the research supporting this connectionist model of memory has come directly from experimental studies of people performing cognitive tasks in laboratory settings. Connectionist models effectively explain priming effects, skill learning (procedural memory), and several other phenomena of memory. Thus far, however, connectionist models have failed to provide clear predictions and explanations of recall and recognition memory that occurs following a single episode or a single exposure to semantic information.

In addition to using laboratory experiments on human participants, cognitive psychologists have used computer models to simulate various aspects of information processing. The three-stores model is based on serial (sequential) processing of information. Serial processing can be simulated on individual computers that handle only one operation at a time. In contrast, the parallel-processing model of working memory, which involves simultaneous processing of multiple operations, cannot be simulated on a single computer. Parallel processing requires neural networks. In these networks, multiple computers are linked and operate in tandem. Alternatively, a single special computer may operate with parallel networks. Many cognitive psychologists now prefer a parallel-processing model to describe many phenomena of memory. The parallel-processing model was actually inspired by observing how the human brain seems to process information. Here, multiple processes go on at the same time. In addition to inspiring theoretical models of memory function, neuropsychological research has offered specific insights into memory processes. It also has provided evidence regarding various hypotheses of how human memory works.

Not all cognitive researchers accept the connectionist model. Some believe that human thought is more systematic than connectionist models will allow (Fodor & Pylyshyn, 1988; Matthews, 2003). They believe that complex behavior displays a degree of orderliness and purposefulness that connectionist models cannot incorporate. Connectionist modelers dispute this claim. The issue will be resolved as cognitive psychologists explore the extent to which connectionist models can reproduce and even explain complex behavior.

Memory in the Real World

How is memory used in everyday situations, and what is memory for? Some researchers believe we should study memory in more real-world settings, in addition to laboratory settings (Cohen, 1989; Neisser, 1978, 1982). The basic idea is that memory research should have ecological validity and apply to natural memory phenomena in natural settings. The techniques used therefore examine naturalistic settings using self-reports and questionnaires. Although this approach has been criticized for its lack of control and generalizability (Banaji & Crowder, 1989), it has generated some interesting new conceptualizations into the nature of memory research in general.

For example, one set of researchers has called for a change in the metaphor used in conceptualizing memory, rather than a change in the research setting. The traditional *storehouse* metaphor of memory, in which memory is conceived of as a repository of information and events, inevitably leads to questions of quantity. The question thus becomes: How many items can be remembered from or used in a particular occasion (Koriat & Goldsmith, 1996a, 1996b)? The laboratory setting is most congenial to this approach, allowing for control over the variables of quantity. In contrast, the everyday or real-world approach calls for more of a *correspondence* metaphor. Here, memory is conceived of as a vehicle for interaction with the real world. Thus, the questions shift toward accuracy in representing past events. How closely does memory correspond to particular events? Here, memory would be viewed as a structure fulfilling a particular purpose in our interactions with the world.

We may see this new trend broadening as more researchers become increasingly interested in the functional properties of memory. Already some promising new insights into the question of what memory is for offer some concrete proposals into the structure of memory. For example, one view calls for a memory system centered around bodily interactions with the environment (Glenberg, 1997). Thus, correspondence with the real world is achieved via representations that reflect the structural relationship between the body and the external world, rather than the encoding of abstract symbolic representations.

Whether this approach will take the lead in memory research or be overcome by the impetus of the laboratory-storehouse metaphor remains to be seen. Whatever the case may be, new metaphors and controversies are essential for the survival of the field. Without a constant flow of new ideas or rethinking of old ideas, science would stagnate and die. Another approach that already is beginning to dominate much of memory research is the neuropsychological study of memory. It developed in part from the study of people with exceptional memory.

Exceptional Memory and Neuropsychology

Up to this point, the discussion of memory has focused on tasks and structures involving normally functioning memory. However, there are rare cases of people with exceptional memory (either enhanced or deficient) that provide some interesting insights into the nature of memory in general. The study of exceptional memory leads directly to neuropsychological investigations of the physiological mechanisms underlying memory.

Outstanding Memory: Mnemonists

Imagine what your life would be like if you had outstanding memory abilities. Suppose, for example, you were able to remember every word printed in this book. In this case, you would be considered an **mnemonist,** someone who demonstrates extraordinarily keen memory ability, usually based on using special techniques for memory enhancement. Perhaps the most famous of mnemonists was a man called "S."

Russian psychologist Alexander Luria (1968) reported that one day S. appeared in his laboratory and asked to have his memory tested. Luria tested him. He discovered that the man's memory appeared to have virtually no limits. S. could reproduce extremely long strings of words, regardless of how much time had passed since the words had been presented to him. Luria studied S. over 30 years. He found that even when S.'s retention was measured 15 or 16 years after a session in which S. had learned words, S. still could reproduce the words. S. eventually became a professional entertainer. He dazzled audiences with his ability to recall whatever was asked of him.

What was S.'s trick? How did he remember so much? Apparently, he relied heavily on the mnemonic of visual imagery. He converted material that he needed to remember into visual images. For example, he reported that when asked to remember the word *green*, he would visualize a green flowerpot. For the word *red*, he visualized a man in a red shirt coming toward him. Even numbers called up images. For example, *1* was a proud, well-built man. The number *3* was a gloomy person. The number *6* was a man with a swollen foot, and so on.

For S., much of his use of visual imagery in memory recall was not intentional. Rather, it was the result of a rare psychological phenomenon. This phenomenon, termed *synesthesia,* is the experience of sensations in a sensory modality different from the sense that has been physically stimulated. For example, S. automatically would convert a sound into a visual impression. He even reported experiencing a word's taste and weight. Each word to be remembered evoked a whole range of sensations. They automatically would come to S. when he needed to recall that word.

Other mnemonists have used different strategies. V. P., a Russian immigrant, could memorize long strings of material such as rows and columns of numbers (Hunt & Love, 1972). Whereas S. relied primarily on visual imagery, V. P. apparently relied more on verbal translations. He reported memorizing numbers by transforming them into dates. Then he would think about what he had done on that day.

Another mnemonist, S. F., remembered long strings of numbers by segmenting them into groups of three or four digits each. He then encoded them into running times for different races (Ericsson, Chase, & Faloon, 1980). An experienced long-distance runner, S. F. was familiar with the times that would be plausible for different races. S. F. did not enter the laboratory as a mnemonist. Rather, he had been selected to represent the average college student in terms of intelligence and memory ability.

S. F.'s original memory for a string of numbers was about seven digits, average for a college student. After 200 practice sessions distributed over a period of 2 years, however, S. F. had increased his memory for digits more than 10-fold. He could recall up to about 80 digits. His memory was impaired severely, however, when the experimenters purposely gave him sequences of digits that could not be translated into running times. The work with S. F. suggests that a person with a fairly typical level of memory ability can, at least in principle, be converted into one with quite an extraordinary memory. At least, this is possible in some domains, following a great deal of concerted practice.

Many of us yearn to have memory abilities like those of S. or V. P. In this way, we may believe we could ace our exams virtually effortlessly. However, we should consider that S. was not particularly happy with his life, and part of the reason was his exceptional memory. He reported that his synesthesia, which was largely involuntary, interfered with his ability to listen to people. Voices gave rise to blurs of sensations. They in turn interfered with his ability to follow a conversation. Moreover, S.'s heavy reliance on imagery created difficulty for him when he tried to understand abstract concepts. For example, he found it hard to understand concepts such as *infinity* or *nothing.* These concepts do not lend themselves well to visual images. He also sometimes was overwhelmed when he read. Earlier memories also sometimes intruded on later ones. Of course, we cannot say how many of S.'s problems in life were caused by his exceptional memory. But clearly S. believed that his exceptional memory had a downside as well as an upside. It was often as likely to be a hindrance as a help.

These exceptional mnemonists offer some insight into processes of memory. Each of the three described here did more or less the same thing—consciously or almost automatically. Each translated arbitrary, abstract, meaningless information into more meaningful or more sensorially concrete information. Whether the translated information was racing times, dates and events, or visual images, the key was their meaning for the mnemonist.

Like the mnemonists, we more easily encode information into our long-term memory that is similar to the information already stored there. Because we have information in long-term memory that pertains to our interests, it is easier to learn new information that is in line with these interests and that we can relate to the old information (De Beni & associates, 2007). Thus, you may be able to remember the lyrics of your favorite songs from years ago but not be able to recall the definitions of new terms that you have just learned. You can improve your memory for new information if you can relate the new information to old information already stored in long-term memory.

If you are unable to retrieve a memory that you need, does it mean that you have forgotten it? Not necessarily. Cognitive psychologists have studied a phenomenon called **hypermnesia,** which is a process of producing retrieval of memories that would have seem to have been forgotten (Erdelyi & Goldberg, 1979; Holmes, 1991; Turtle & Yuille, 1994). Hypermnesia is sometimes loosely referred to as "unforgetting," although the terminology cannot be correct because, strictly speaking, the memories that are retrieved were never unavailable (i.e., forgotten), but rather, inaccessible (i.e., hard to retrieve). Hypermnesia is usually achieved by trying many and diverse retrieval cues to unearth a memory. Psychodynamic therapy, for example, is sometimes used to try to achieve hypermnesia. This therapy also points out the risk of trying to achieve hypermnesia. The individual may create a new memory, believing it is an old one, rather than retrieving a genuine old memory.

We usually take for granted the ability to remember, much like the air we breathe. However, just as we become more aware of the importance of air when we do not have enough to breathe, we are less likely to take memory for granted when we observe people with serious memory deficiencies.

Deficient Memory

Several different syndromes are associated with memory loss. The most well known is amnesia.

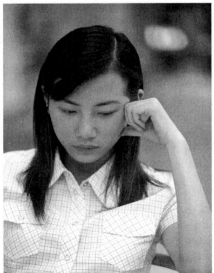

If the patient uses hypermnesia to dredge up what has seemed to be a forgotten memory, we often cannot be certain that the memory is genuine, rather than one newly created by suggestion.

Amnesia

Amnesia is severe loss of explicit memory (Mayes & Hunkin, 2003). One type is retrograde amnesia, in which individuals lose their purposeful memory for events prior to whatever trauma induces memory loss (Squire, 1999). Mild forms of **retrograde amnesia** can occur fairly commonly when someone sustains a concussion. Usually, events immediately prior to the concussive episode are not well remembered.

W. Ritchie Russell and P. W. Nathan (1946) reported a more severe case of retrograde amnesia. A 22-year-old greenkeeper was thrown from his motorcycle in August 1933. A week after the accident, the young man was able to converse sensibly. He seemed to have recovered. However, it quickly became apparent that he had suffered a severe loss of memory for events that had occurred prior to the trauma. On questioning, he gave the date as February 1922. He believed himself to be a schoolboy. He had no recollection of the intervening years. Over the next several weeks, his memory for past events gradually returned. The return started with the least recent and proceeded toward more recent events. By 10 weeks after the accident, he had recovered his memory for most of the events of the previous years. He finally was able to recall everything that had happened up to a few minutes prior to the accident. In retrograde amnesia, the memories that return typically do so starting from the more distant past. They then progressively return up to the time of the trauma. Often events right before the trauma are never recalled.

Another kind of amnesia is one that almost all of us experience. It is **infantile amnesia,** the inability to recall events that happened when we were very young (Spear, 1979). Generally, we can remember little or nothing that has happened to us before the age of about 5 years. It is extremely rare for someone to recall many memories before age 3 years. The few reports of childhood memories that are recorded usually involve memories of significant events. Examples are the birth of a sibling or the death of a parent (Fivush & Hamond, 1991). For example, some adults have recalled their own hospitalization or the birth of a sibling as far back as age 2 years. The death of a parent or a family move may be recalled from as far back as age 3 years (Usher & Neisser, 1993). The probability that an early event will be recalled is affected by intelligence, education, and language ability (Pillemer & White, 1989). Furthermore, asking adults to recall events from their preschool years results in many more remembered events than when adults are asked to report their earliest memory (Nelson & Fivush, 2004).

The accuracy of reported childhood memories has come into question recently, however. In fact, many psychologists suggest that the accuracy of children's recollections of events may be questionable even shortly after these events occurred (e.g., Ceci & Bruck, 1993). The memories are particularly suspect if the children are exposed to covert or overt suggestions regarding the remembered material. (The unreliability of our memories for events is discussed more fully in the next chapter.)

One of the most famous cases of amnesia is the case of H. M. (Scoville & Milner, 1957). H. M. underwent brain surgery to save him from continual disruptions due to uncontrollable epilepsy. The operation took place on September 1, 1953. It was largely experimental. The results were highly unpredictable. At the time of the operation, H. M. was 29 years old. He was above average in intelligence. After the operation, his recovery was uneventful with one exception. He suffered severe **anterograde amnesia,** the inability to remember events that occur after a traumatic event.

However, he had good (although not perfect) recollection of events that had occurred before his operation. H. M.'s memory loss severely affected his life. H.M. has been extensively studied through behavioral and neurological methods. On one occasion, he remarked, "Every day is alone in itself, whatever enjoyment I've had, and whatever sorrow I've had" (Milner, Corkin, & Teuber, 1968, p. 217). Many years after the surgery, H.M. still reported that the year was 1953. He also could not recall the name of any new person he met after the operation, regardless of the number of times they interacted. Apparently, H. M. lost his ability purposefully to recollect any new memories of the time following his operation. As a result, he lives suspended in an eternal present.

The examination of H.M.'s memory is ongoing, with recent work examining changes in H.M.'s memory and brain as he ages. These recent studies have noted additional memory and cognitive declines. In particular, H. M. exhibited new problems with comprehension and generation of new sentences (MacKay, 2006; MacKay & associates, 2006; Salat & associates, 2006; Skotko & associates, 2004).

Amnesia and the Explicit-Implicit Memory Distinction

Research psychologists study amnesia patients in part to gain insight into memory functioning in general. One of the general insights gained by studying amnesia victims highlights the distinction between explicit and implicit memories. Explicit memory is typically impaired in amnesia. Implicit memory, such as priming effects on word-completion tasks and procedural memory for skill-based tasks, is typically not impaired. Apparently two kinds of abilities need to be distinguished. The first is the ability to reflect consciously on prior experience, which is required for tasks involving explicit memory of declarative knowledge. The second is the ability to demonstrate remembered learning in an apparently automatic way, without conscious recollection of the learning (Baddeley, 1989). Amnesia victims perform extremely poorly on most explicit memory tasks, but they may show normal or almost-normal performance on tasks involving implicit memory, such as cued-recall tasks (Warrington & Weiskrantz, 1970) and word-completion tasks (Baddeley, 1989). Consider what happens following word-completion tasks. When amnesics were asked whether they previously had seen the word they just completed, they were unlikely to remember the specific experience of having seen the word (Graf, Mandler, & Haden, 1982; Tulving, Schacter, & Stark, 1982). Furthermore, these amnesics do not explicitly recognize words they have seen at better than chance levels. Although the distinction between implicit memory and explicit memory has been readily observed in amnesics, both amnesics and normal participants show the presence of implicit memory.

Likewise, amnesia victims also show paradoxical performance in another regard. Consider two kinds of tasks. As previously described, *procedural-knowledge* tasks involve "knowing how." They involve skills such as how to ride a bicycle, whereas *declarative-knowledge* tasks involve "knowing that." They tap factual information, such as the terms in a psychology textbook. On the one hand, amnesia victims may perform extremely poorly on the traditional memory tasks requiring recall or recognition memory of declarative knowledge. On the other hand, they may demonstrate improvement in performance resulting from learning—remembered practice—when engaged in tasks that require procedural knowledge. Such tasks would include solving puzzles, learning to read mirror writing, or mastering motor skills (Baddeley, 1989).

Consider an example of this spared procedural knowledge. Patients with amnesia, when asked to drive in a normal situation, were able to operate and control the car as a normal driver would (Anderson & associates, 2007). However, the investigators also exposed the patients to a simulation in which a complex accident sequence was experienced. In this situation, the patients with amnesia showed significant impairment. They could not recall the proper response to this situation. This finding is in line with the fact that in patients with amnesia, implicit, procedural knowledge is spared while explicit knowledge is impaired. Most drivers do not have extensive experience with complex accident-avoidance scenarios and therefore would have to rely more on their declarative memory to make decisions about how to respond.

Amnesia and Neuropsychology

Studies of amnesia victims have revealed much about the way in which memory depends on the effective functioning of particular structures of the brain. By looking for matches between particular lesions in the brain and particular deficits of function, researchers come to understand how normal memory functions. Thus, when studying different kinds of cognitive processes in the brain, neuropsychologists frequently look for dissociations of function. In *dissociations*, normal individuals show the presence of a particular function (e.g., explicit memory). But people with specific lesions in the brain show the absence of that particular function. This absence occurs despite the presence of normal functions in other areas (e.g., implicit memory).

By observing people with disturbed memory function, we know that memory is volatile. A blow to the head, a disturbance in consciousness, or any number of other injuries to or diseases of the brain may affect it. We cannot determine, however, the specific cause-effect relationship between a given structural lesion and a particular memory deficit. The fact that a particular structure or region is associated with an interruption of function does not mean that the region is solely responsible for controlling that function. Indeed, functions can be shared by multiple structures or regions. A broad physiological analogy may help to explain the difficulty of determining localization based on an observed deficit. The normal functioning of a portion of the brain—the reticular activating system (RAS)—is essential to life. But life depends on more than a functioning brain. If you doubt the importance of other structures, ask a patient with heart or lung disease. Thus, although the RAS is essential to life, a person's death may be the result of malfunction in other structures of the body. Tracing a dysfunction within the brain to a particular structure or region poses a similar problem.

For the observation of simple dissociations, many alternative hypotheses may explain a link between a particular lesion and a particular deficit of function. Much more compelling support for hypotheses about cognitive functions comes from observing double dissociations. In *double dissociations*, people with different kinds of neuropathological conditions show opposite patterns of deficits. For some functions and some areas of the brain, neuropsychologists have managed to observe the presence of a double dissociation. For example, some evidence for distinguishing brief memory from long-term memory comes from just such a double dissociation (Schacter, 1989b). People with lesions in the left parietal lobe of the brain show profound inability to retain information in short-term memory, but they show no impairment of long-term memory. They continue to encode, store, and retrieve information in long-term memory, apparently with little difficulty (Shallice & Warrington, 1970; Warrington & Shallice, 1972). In contrast, persons with lesions in the medial (middle) temporal regions of the brain show relatively normal short-term memory of verbal materials, such as letters and words, but they show serious inability to retain new verbal materials in long-term memory (Milner, Corkin, & Teuber, 1968; Shallice, 1979; Warrington, 1982).

Double dissociations offer strong support for the notion that particular structures of the brain play particular vital roles in memory (Squire, 1987). Disturbances or lesions in these areas cause severe deficits in memory formation. But we cannot say that memory—or even part of memory—resides in these structures. Nonetheless, studies of brain-injured patients are informative and at least suggestive of how memory works. At present, cognitive neuropsychologists have found that double dissociations support several distinctions. These distinctions are those between brief memory and long-term memory and between declarative (explicit) and nondeclarative (implicit) memory. There also are some preliminary indications of other distinctions.

Alzheimer's Disease

Although amnesia is the syndrome most associated with memory loss, it is often less devastating than a disease that includes memory loss as one of many symptoms. **Alzheimer's disease** is a disease of older adults that causes dementia as well as progressive memory loss (Kensinger & Corkin, 2003). Dementia is a loss of intellectual function that is severe enough to impair one's everyday life. The memory loss in Alzheimer's disease can be seen in comparative brain scans of individuals with and without Alzheimer's disease. Note in Figure 5.7 that as the disease advances, there is diminishing cognitive activity in the areas of the brain associated with memory function.

The disease was first identified by Alois Alzheimer in 1907. It is typically recognized on the basis of loss of intellectual function in daily life. Formally, a definitive diagnosis is possible only after death. The brains of people with the disease show plaques and tangles that are not found in normal brains. Plaques are dense deposits found outside the nerve cells of the brain. They are spherical structures with a dense core of amyloid β-protein (Kensinger & Corkin, 2003). Tangles are pairs of filaments that become twisted around each other. They are found in the cell body and dendrites of neurons and often are shaped like a flame (Kensinger & Corkin, 2003). Alzheimer's disease is diagnosed when memory is impaired and there is at least one other area of dysfunction in the domains of language, motor, attention, executive function, personality, or object recognition. The symptoms are of gradual onset, and the progression is continuous and irreversible.

Although the progression of disease is irreversible, it can be slowed somewhat. The main drug currently being used for this purpose is Aricept (donepezil). Research evidence is mixed (Fischman, 2004). It suggests that, at best, Aricept may slightly slow progression of the disease, but that it cannot reverse it. A more recent drug, memantine (sold as Namenda or Ebixa), can supplement Aricept and slow progression of the disease somewhat more. The two drugs have different mechanisms. Aricept slows destruction of the neurotransmitter acetylcholine in the brain. Memantine inhibits a chemical that overexcites brain cells and leads to cell damage and death (Fischman, 2004).

The incidence of Alzheimer's increases exponentially with age (Kensinger & Corkin, 2003). The incidence at ages 70 to 75 is about 1% per year. But between ages

FIGURE 5.7

(a)

(b)

NORMAL   DEMENTIA

BRAIN METHIONINE METABOLISM

S.N.F.J. ORSAY

(c)

Brain scans of (a) a normal individual, (b) an individual with early-stage Alzheimer's, and (c) an individual with late-stage Alzheimer's. As the disease progresses, cognitive activity in the brain associated with memory function decreases.

80 and 85, the incidence is more than 6% a year. By age 70, 30% to 50% of adults have Alzheimer's symptoms, and after 80 years, the percentage is in excess of 50%.

A special kind of Alzheimer's disease is familial, known as early-onset Alzheimer's disease. It has been linked to a genetic mutation. People with the genetic mutation always develop the disease. It results in the disease exhibiting itself early, often before even 50 years of age and sometimes as early as the 20s (Kensinger & Corkin, 2003). Late-onset Alzheimer's, in contrast, appears to be complexly determined and related to a variety of possible genetic and environmental influences, none of which have been conclusively identified.

The earliest signs of Alzheimer's disease typically include impairment of episodic memory. People have trouble remembering things that were learned in a temporal or spatial context. As the disease progresses, semantic memory also begins to go. Whereas people without the disease tend to remember emotionally charged information better than they remember non–emotionally charged information, people with the disease show no difference in the two kinds of memory (Kensinger & associates, 2002). Most forms of nondeclarative memory are spared in Alzheimer's disease until near the very end of its course. The end is inevitably death unless the individual dies first of other causes.

Role of the Hippocampus and Other Structures

Where in the brain are memories stored, and what structures and areas of the brain are involved in memory processes, such as encoding and retrieval? Many early attempts at localization of memory were unfruitful. For example, after literally hundreds of experiments, renowned neuropsychologist Karl Lashley reluctantly stated that he could find no specific locations in the brain for specific memories. In the decades since Lashley's admission, psychologists have been able to locate many cerebral structures involved in memory. For example, they know of the importance of the hippocampus and other nearby structures. However, the physiological structure may not be such that we will find Lashley's elusive localizations of specific ideas, thoughts, or events. Even Penfield's findings regarding links between electrical stimulation and episodic memory of events have been subject to question.

Some studies show encouraging, although preliminary, findings regarding the structures that seem to be involved in various aspects of memory. First, specific sensory properties of a given experience appear to be organized across various areas of the cerebral cortex (Squire, 1986). For example, the visual, spatial, and olfactory (odor) features of an experience may be stored discretely in each of the areas of the cortex responsible for processing of each type of sensation. Thus, the cerebral cortex appears to play an important role in memory in terms of the long-term storage of information (Zola & Squire, 2000; Zola-Morgan & Squire, 1990).

In addition, the hippocampus and some related nearby cerebral structures appear to be important for explicit memory of experiences and other declarative information. The hippocampus also seems to play a key role in the encoding of declarative information (Squire & Zola-Morgan, 1991; Thompson, 2000; Thompson & Krupa, 1994; Zola-Morgan & Squire, 1990). Its main function appears to be in the integration and consolidation of separate sensory information (Moscovitch, 2003). Most important, it is involved in the transfer of newly synthesized information into long-term structures supporting declarative knowledge. Perhaps such transfer provides a means of cross-referencing information stored in different parts of the brain (Reber, Knowlton, & Squire, 1996; Squire, 1986; Squire, Cohen, & Nadel, 1984). Additionally, the hippocampus seems to play a crucial role in complex learning (McCormick & Thompson, 1984). The amygdala also appears to play an important role in memory consolidation, especially where emotional experience is involved (Cahill & associates, 1995; Cahill & McGaugh, 1996; Ledoux, 1996; McGaugh, 1999; McGaugh, Cahill, & Roozendaal, 1996; Packard, Cahill, & McGaugh, 1994). Finally, the hippocampus also has a significant role in the recollection of information (Gilboa & associates, 2006).

In evolutionary terms, the aforementioned cerebral structures (chiefly the cortex and the hippocampus) are relatively recent acquisitions. Declarative memory also may be considered a relatively recent phenomenon. At the same time, other memory structures may be responsible for nondeclarative forms of memory. For example, the basal ganglia seem to be the primary structures controlling procedural knowledge (Mishkin & Petri, 1984). But they are not involved in controlling the priming effect

(Heindel, Butters, & Salmon, 1988), which may be influenced by various other kinds of memory (Schacter, 1989b). Furthermore, the cerebellum also seems to play a key role in memory for classically conditioned responses and contributes to many cognitive tasks in general (Cabeza & Nyberg, 1997; Thompson, 1987). Thus, various forms of nondeclarative memory seem to rely on differing cerebral structures.

In addition to these preliminary insights regarding the macro-level structures of memory, we are beginning to understand the micro-level structure of memory. For example, we know that repeated stimulation of particular neural pathways tends to strengthen the likelihood of firing. In particular, at a particular synapse, there appear to be physiological changes in the dendrites of the receiving neuron. These changes make the neuron more likely to reach the threshold for firing again.

We also know that some neurotransmitters disrupt memory storage. Others enhance memory storage. Both serotonin and acetylcholine seem to enhance neural transmission associated with memory. Norepinephrine also may do so. High concentrations of acetylcholine have been found in the hippocampus of normal people (Squire, 1987), but low concentrations are found in people with Alzheimer's disease. In fact, Alzheimer's patients show severe loss of the brain tissue that secretes acetylcholine.

Memory tests may be given to assess whether an individual has Alzheimer's disease. However, definitive diagnosis is possible only through analysis of brain tissue, which, as mentioned earlier, shows plaques and tangles in cases of disease. In one test, individuals see a sheet of paper containing four words (Buschke & associates, 1999). Each word belongs to a different category. The examiner says the category name for one of the words. The individual must point to the appropriate word. For example, if the category is animal, the individual might point to a picture of a cow. A few minutes after the words have been presented, individuals make an attempt to recall all the words they saw. If they cannot recall a word, they are given the category to which the word belongs. Some individuals cannot remember the words, even when prompted with the categories. Alzheimer's patients score much worse on this test than do other individuals.

Researchers have been better able to track down the cause of another form of memory dysfunction, but they have not devised a way to eliminate this preventable deficit. Alcohol consumption has been shown to disrupt the activity of serotonin. It thereby impairs the formation of memories (Weingartner & associates, 1983). In fact, severe or prolonged abuse of alcohol can lead to Korsakoff's syndrome, a devastating form of anterograde amnesia. This syndrome is often accompanied by at least some retrograde amnesia (Clark & associates, 2007; Parkin, 1991; Shimamura & Squire, 1986). Korsakoff's syndrome has been linked to damage in the diencephalon (the region comprising the thalamus and the hypothalamus) of the brain (Jernigan & associates, 1991; Langlais, Mandel, & Mair, 1992). It also has been linked to dysfunction or damage in other areas (Jacobson & Lishman, 1990), such as in the frontal (Parsons & Nixon, 1993; Squire, 1982) and the temporal (Blansjaar & associates, 1992) lobes of the cortex.

Other physiological factors also affect memory function. Some of the naturally occurring hormones stimulate increased availability of glucose in the brain, which enhances memory function. These hormones are often associated with highly arousing events. Examples of such events are traumas, achievements, first-time experiences (e.g., first passionate kiss), crises, or other peak moments (e.g., reaching a major decision). They may play a role in remembering these events.

The amygdala is often associated with emotional events, so a natural question to ask is whether, in memory tasks, there is involvement of the amygdala in memory for emotionally charged events. In one study, participants saw two video presentations presented on separate days (Cahill & associates, 1996). Each presentation involved 12 clippings, half of which had been judged as involving relatively emotional content and the other half as involving relatively unemotional content. As participants watched the video clippings, brain activity was assessed by means of PET (see Chapter 2). After a gap of 3 weeks, the participants returned to the lab and were asked to recall the clips. For the relatively emotional clips, amount of activation in the amygdala was associated with recall; for the relatively unemotional clips, there was no association. This pattern of results suggests that when memories are emotionally charged, level of amygdala activation is associated with recall. In other words, the more emotionally charged the emotional memory, the greater the probability the memory will later be retrieved. There also may be a sex difference with regard to recall of emotional memories. There is some evidence that women recall emotionally charged pictures better than do men (Canli & associates, 2002).

Some of the most fascinating work has focused more on the strategies used in regard to memory. Memory strategies and memory processes are the subject of the following chapter.

Key Themes

This chapter illustrates some of the key themes noted in Chapter 1.

First, it shows how basic and applied research can interact. An example is research on Alzheimer's disease. At the present time, the disease is not curable, but it is treatable. It can be treated with drugs and with guidance provided in a structured living environment. Basic research into the biological structures (e.g., tangles and plaques) and cognitive functions (e.g., impaired memory) associated with Alzheimer's may one day help us better understand and treat the disease.

Second, the chapter shows the interaction of biology with behavior. The hippocampus has become one of the most carefully studied parts of the brain. Current functional magnetic resonance imaging (fMRI) research is showing how the hippocampus and other parts of the brain, such as the amygdala (in the case of emotionally based memories) and the cerebellum (in the case of procedural memories) function to enable us to remember what we need to know.

Third, the chapter shows how structure and function are both important to understanding human memory. The Atkinson-Shiffrin model proposed control processes that operate on three structures: a very short-term store, a short-term store, and a long-term store. The more recent working-memory model proposes how executive function controls and activates portions of long-term memory to provide the information needed to solve tasks at hand.

After you use an ATM with a friend, ask him or her to fill in the blank: A_M. Your friend will most likely say "ATM." If you were to do this without visiting an ATM, most people will likely say "ARM." The first response is an example of implicit memory.

Ask some friends or family members to help you with a memory experiment. Give half of them the instruction to count the number of letters in the words you are about to recite. Give the other half the instruction to think of three words related to the words you are about to recite. Recite the following words about 5 seconds apart: *beauty, ocean, competitor, bad, decent, happy, brave, beverage, artistic, dejected.* About 5 or 10 minutes later, ask your friends to write down as many of the 10 words as they can remember. In general, those who were asked to think of three related words to the words you read will remember more than those who were asked to count the number of letters in the words. This is a demonstration of levels of processing. Those friends who thought of three related words processed the words more deeply than those who merely counted up the number of letters in the words. Words that are processed more deeply are remembered better.

Summary

1. **What are some of the tasks used for studying memory, and what do various tasks indicate about the structure of memory?** Among the many tasks used by cognitive psychologists, some of the main ones have been tasks assessing explicit recall of information (e.g., free recall, serial recall, and cued recall) and tasks assessing explicit recognition of information. By comparing memory performance on these explicit tasks with performance on implicit tasks (e.g., word-completion tasks), cognitive psychologists have found evidence of differing memory systems or processes governing each type of task (e.g., as shown in studies of amnesics).

2. **What has been the prevailing traditional model of the structure of memory?** Memory is the means by which we draw on our knowledge of the past to use this knowledge in the present. According to one model, memory is conceived as involving three stores. A sensory store is capable of holding relatively limited amounts of information for very brief periods. A short-term store is capable of holding small amounts of information for somewhat longer periods. And a long-term store is capable of storing large amounts of information virtually indefinitely. Within the sensory store, the iconic store refers to visual sensory memory.

3. **What are some of the main alternative models of the structure of memory?** An alternative model uses the concept of working memory, usually defined as being part of long-term memory and also comprising short-term memory. From this perspective, working memory holds only the most recently activated portion of long-term memory. It moves these activated elements into and out of short-term memory. A second model is the levels-of-processing framework, which hypothesizes distinctions in memory ability based on the degree to which items are elaborated during encoding. A third model is the multiple memory systems model, which posits not only a distinction between procedural memory and declarative (semantic) memory but also a distinction between semantic and episodic memory. In addition, psychologists have proposed other models for the structure of memory. They include a parallel distributed processing (PDP; connectionist) model. The PDP model incorporates the notions of working memory, semantic memory networks, spreading activation, priming, and parallel processing of information. Finally, many psychologists call for a complete change in the conceptualization of memory, focusing on memory functioning in the real world. This call leads to a shift in memory metaphors from the traditional storehouse to the more modern correspondence metaphor.

4. **What have psychologists learned about the structure of memory by studying exceptional memory and the physiology of the brain?** Among other findings, studies of mnemonists have shown the value of imagery in memory for concrete information. They also have demon-

strated the importance of finding or forming meaningful connections among items to be remembered. The main forms of amnesia are anterograde amnesia, retrograde amnesia, and infantile amnesia. The last form of amnesia is qualitatively different from the other forms and occurs in everyone.

Through the study of the memory function of people with each form of amnesia, it has been possible to differentiate various aspects of memory. These include long-term versus temporary forms of memory, procedural versus declarative memory processes, and explicit versus implicit memory.

Although specific memory traces have not yet been identified, many of the specific structures involved in memory function have been located. To date, the subcortical structures involved in memory appear to include the hippocampus, the thalamus, the hypothalamus, and even the basal ganglia and the cerebellum. The cortex also governs much of the long-term storage of declarative knowledge.

The neurotransmitters serotonin and acetylcholine appear to be vital to memory function. Other physiological chemicals, structures, and processes also play important roles, although further investigation is required to identify these roles.

Thinking about Thinking: Factual, Analytical, Creative, and Practical Questions

1. Describe two characteristics each of sensory memory, short-term memory, and long-term memory.

2. What are double dissociations, and why are they valuable to understanding the relationship between cognitive function and the brain?

3. Compare and contrast the three-stores model of memory with one of the alternative models of memory.

4. Critique one of the experiments described in this chapter. What problem do you see regarding the interpretation given? How could subsequent research be designed to enhance the interpretation of the findings?

5. How would you design an experiment to study some aspect of implicit memory?

6. Imagine what it would be like to recover from one of the forms of amnesia. Describe your impressions of and reactions to your newly recovered memory abilities.

7. How would your life be different if you could greatly enhance your own mnemonic skills in some way?

Key Terms

Alzheimer's disease
amnesia
anterograde amnesia
central executive
episodic buffer
episodic memory
explicit memory
hypermnesia
hypothetical constructs

iconic store
implicit memory
infantile amnesia
levels-of-processing framework
long-term store
memory
mnemonist
phonological loop
prime

priming effect
recall
recognition
retrograde amnesia
semantic memory
sensory store
short-term store
visuospatial sketchpad
working memory

Explore CogLab by going to **http://coglab.wadsworth.com.**
To learn more, examine the following experiments:

Memory Span	Modality Effect
Partial Report	Position Error
Absolute Identification	Irrelevant Speech
Operation Span	Phonological Similarity
Implicit Learning	Levels of Processing

Annotated Suggested Reading

Tulving, E., & Craik, F. I. M. (Eds.). (2000). *The Oxford handbook of memory.* New York: Oxford University Press. This handbook provides perhaps the most comprehensive account of memory phenomena that is currently available.

Memory Processes

EXPLORING COGNITIVE PSYCHOLOGY

1. **What have cognitive psychologists discovered regarding how we encode information for storing it in memory?**

2. **What affects our ability to retrieve information from memory?**

3. **How does what we know or what we learn affect what we remember?**

4. **How does memory develop with age?**

> *The procedure is actually quite simple. First you arrange items into different groups. Of course one pile may be sufficient depending on how much there is to do. If you have to go somewhere else due to lack of facilities that is the next step; otherwise, you are pretty well set. It is important not to overdo things. That is, it is better to do too few things at once than too many. In the short run this may not seem important but complications can easily arise. A mistake can be expensive as well. At first, the whole procedure will seem complicated. Soon, however, it will become just another facet of life. It is difficult to foresee any end to the necessity for this task in the immediate future, but then, one can never tell. After the procedure is completed one arranges the materials into different groups again. Then they can be put into their appropriate places. Eventually they will be used once more and the whole cycle will then have to be repeated. However, that is part of life.*

John Bransford and Marcia Johnson (1972, p. 722) asked their participants to read the preceding passage and to recall the steps involved. To get an idea of how easy it was for their participants to do so, try to recall those steps now yourself. Bransford and Johnson's participants (and probably you, too) had a great deal of difficulty understanding this passage and recalling the steps involved. What makes this task so difficult? What are the mental processes involved in this task?

As mentioned in the previous chapter, cognitive psychologists generally refer to the main processes of memory as comprising three common operations: encoding, storage, and retrieval. Each one represents a stage in memory processing. **Encoding** refers to how you transform a physical, sensory input into a kind of representation that can be placed into memory. **Storage** refers to how you retain encoded information in memory. **Retrieval** refers to how you gain access to information stored in memory. Our emphasis in discussing these processes will be on recall of verbal and pictorial material. Remember, however, that we have memories of other kinds of stimuli as well, such as odors (Herz & Engen, 1996).

Encoding, storage, and retrieval often are viewed as sequential stages. You first take in information. Then you hold it for a while. Later you pull it out. However, the processes interact with each other and are interdependent. For example, you may have found the text in the chapter-opening paragraph difficult to encode, thereby also making it hard to store and to retrieve the information. However, a verbal label can facilitate encoding and hence storage and retrieval. Most people do much better with the passage if given its title, "Washing Clothes." Try now to recall the steps described in the passage. The verbal label helps us to encode, and therefore to remember, a passage that otherwise seems incomprehensible.

Encoding and Transfer of Information

Forms of Encoding

Short-Term Storage

When you encode information for temporary storage and use, what kind of code do you use? Participants were visually presented with several series of six letters at the rate of 0.75 seconds per letter (Conrad, 1964). The letters used in the various lists were B, C, F, M, N, P, S, T, V, and X. Immediately after the letters were presented, participants had to write down each list of six letters in the order given. What kinds of errors did participants make? Despite the fact that letters were presented visually, errors tended to be based on acoustic confusability. In other words, instead of recalling the letters they were supposed to recall, participants substituted letters that sounded like the correct letters. Thus, they were likely to confuse F for S, B for V, P for B, and so on. Another group of participants simply listened to single letters in a setting that had noise in the background. They then immediately reported each letter as they heard it. Participants showed the same pattern of confusability in the listening task as in the visual memory task (Conrad, 1964). Thus, we seem to encode visually presented letters by how they sound, not by how they look.

The Conrad experiment shows the importance in short-term memory of an acoustic code rather than a visual code. But the results do not rule out the possibility that there are other codes. One such code would be a *semantic code*—one based on word meaning. One researcher argued that short-term memory relies primarily on an acoustic rather than a semantic code (Baddeley, 1966). He compared recall performance for lists of acoustically confusable words—such as *map*, *cab*, *mad*, *man*, and *cap*—with that for lists of acoustically distinct words—such as *cow*, *pit*, *day*, *rig*, and *bun*. He found that performance was much worse for the visual presentation of acoustically similar words.

He also compared performance for lists of semantically similar words—such as *big*, *long*, *large*, *wide*, and *broad*—with performance for lists of semantically dissimilar words—such as *old*, *foul*, *late*, *hot*, and *strong*. There was little difference in recall between the two lists. Suppose performance for the semantically similar words had been much worse. It would have indicated that participants were confused by the semantic similarities and hence were processing the words semantically. However, performance for the semantically similar words was only *slightly* worse than that for the semantically dissimilar words.

Subsequent work investigating how information is encoded in short-term memory has shown clear evidence of at least some semantic encoding in short-term memory (Shulman, 1970; Wickens, Dalezman, & Eggemeier, 1976). Thus, encoding in short-term memory appears to be primarily acoustic, but there may be some secondary semantic encoding as well. In addition, we sometimes temporarily encode information visually as well (Posner, 1969; Posner & associates, 1969; Posner &

Keele, 1967). But visual encoding appears to be even more fleeting (about 1.5 seconds). It also is more vulnerable to decay than acoustic encoding. Thus, initial encoding is primarily acoustic in nature, but other forms of encoding may be used under some circumstances.

Long-Term Storage

As mentioned, information stored temporarily in working memory is encoded primarily in acoustic form. Hence, when we make errors in retrieving words from short-term memory, the errors tend to reflect confusions in sound. How is information encoded into a form that can be transferred into storage and available for subsequent retrieval?

Most information stored in long-term memory seems to be primarily semantically encoded. In other words, it is encoded by the meanings of words. Consider some relevant evidence.

Participants learned a list of 41 different words (Grossman & Eagle, 1970). Five minutes after learning took place, participants were given a recognition test. Included in the recognition test were distracters. These are items that appear to be legitimate choices but that are not correct alternatives. That is, they were not presented previously. Nine of the distracters were semantically related to words on the list. Nine were not. The data of interest were false alarms to the distracters. These are responses in which the participants indicated that they had seen the distracters, although they had not. Participants falsely recognized an average of 1.83 of the synonyms but only an average of 1.05 of the unrelated words. This result indicated a greater likelihood of semantic confusion.

Another way to show semantic encoding is to use sets of semantically related test words, rather than distracters. Participants learn a list of 60 words that included 15 animals, 15 professions, 15 vegetables, and 15 names of people (Bousfield, 1953). The words were presented in random order. Thus, members of the various categories were intermixed thoroughly. After participants heard the words, they were asked to use free recall to reproduce the list in any order they wished. The investigator then analyzed the order of output of the recalled words. Did participants recall successive words from the same category more frequently than would be expected by chance? Indeed, successive recalls from the same category did occur much more often than would be expected by chance occurrence. Participants were remembering words by clustering them into categories.

Levels of processing, discussed in Chapter 5, also influences encoding in long-term memory. When learning lists of words, participants move more information into long-term memory when using a semantic encoding strategy than when using a non-semantic strategy. Interestingly, in people with autism, this advantage is not seen. This finding suggests that, in persons with autism, information may not be encoded semantically, or at least, not to the same extent as in people who do not have autism (Toichi & Kamio, 2002).

Encoding of information in long-term memory is not exclusively semantic. There also is evidence for visual encoding. Participants received 16 drawings of objects, including four items of clothing, four animals, four vehicles, and four items of furniture (Frost, 1972). The investigator manipulated not only the semantic category but also the visual category. The drawings differed in visual orientation. Four were angled to the left, four angled to the right, four horizontal, and four vertical. Items were presented in random order. Participants were asked to recall them freely. The order of participants' responses showed effects of both semantic and visual categories. These results suggested that participants were encoding visual as well as semantic information.

In addition to semantic and visual information, acoustic information can be encoded in long-term memory (Nelson & Rothbart, 1972). Thus, there is considerable flexibility in the way we store information that we retain for long periods. Those who seek to know the single correct way we encode information are seeking an answer to the wrong question. There is no one correct way. A more useful question involves asking, "In what *ways* do we encode information in long-term memory?" From a more psychological perspective, however, the most useful question to ask is, "*When* do we encode in *which* ways?" In other words, under what circumstances do we use one form of encoding, and under what circumstances do we use another? These questions are the focus of present and future research.

Transfer of Information from Short-Term Memory to Long-Term Memory

Given the problems of decay and interference, described later in this chapter, how do we move information from short-term memory to long-term memory? The means of moving information depend on whether the information involves declarative or nondeclarative memory. Some forms of nondeclarative memory are highly volatile and decay quickly. Examples are priming and habituation. Other nondeclarative forms are maintained more readily, particularly as a result of repeated practice (of procedures) or repeated conditioning (of responses). Examples are procedural memory, such as tying one's shoes, and simple classical conditioning, such as phobias.

Entrance into long-term declarative memory may occur through a variety of processes. One method of accomplishing this goal is by deliberately attending to information to comprehend it. Another is by making connections or associations between the new information and what we already know and understand. We make connections by integrating the new data into our existing schemas of stored information. **Consolidation** is this process of integrating new information into stored information. In humans, the process of consolidating declarative information into memory can continue for many years after the initial experience (Squire, 1986). Stress generally impairs the memory functioning. However, stress also can help enhance the consolidation of memory through the release of hormones (Roozendaal, 2002, 2003). The disruption of consolidation has been studied effectively in amnesics. Studies have particularly examined people who have suffered brief forms of amnesia as a consequence of electroconvulsive therapy (ECT; Squire, 1986). For these amnesics, the source of the trauma is clear. Confounding variables can be minimized. A patient history before the trauma can be obtained, and follow-up testing and supervision after the trauma are more likely to be available. A range of studies suggests that during the process of consolidation, our memory is susceptible to disruption and distortion.

To preserve or enhance the integrity of memories during consolidation, we may use various metamemory strategies (Koriat & Goldsmith, 1996a, 1996b; Metcalfe, 2000; Nelson & Narens, 1994; Schwartz & Metcalfe, 1994). **Metamemory** strategies involve reflecting on our own memory processes with a view to improving our memory. Such strategies are especially important when we are transferring new information to long-term memory by rehearsing it. Metamemory strategies are just one component of **metacognition,** our ability to think about and control our own processes of thought and ways of enhancing our thinking.

Rehearsal

One technique people use for keeping information active is **rehearsal,** the repeated recitation of an item. The effects of such rehearsal are termed *practice effects*. Rehearsal may be *overt*, in which case it is usually aloud and obvious to anyone watching. Or it may be *covert*, in which case it is silent and hidden. Just repeating words over and over again to oneself is not enough to achieve effective rehearsal (Tulving, 1962). One needs also to think about the words and, possibly, their inter-relationships. Whether rehearsal is overt or covert, what is the best way to organize your time for rehearsing new information?

More than a century ago, Hermann Ebbinghaus (1885, cited in Schacter, 1989a) noticed that the distribution of study (memory rehearsal) sessions over time affects the consolidation of information in long-term memory. Much more recently, researchers have offered support for Ebbinghaus's observation as a result of their studies of people's long-term recall of Spanish vocabulary words the subjects had learned 8 years earlier (Bahrick & Phelps, 1987). They observed that people's memory for information depends on how they acquire it. Their memories tend to be good when they use **distributed practice,** learning in which various sessions are spaced over time. Their memories for information are not as good when the information is acquired through **massed practice,** learning in which sessions are crammed together in a very short space of time. The greater the distribution of learning trials over time, the more the participants remembered over long periods. This effect is termed the *spacing effect*.

Research has linked the spacing effect to the process by which memories are consolidated in long-term memory (Glenberg, 1977, 1979; Leicht & Overton, 1987). That is, the spacing effect may occur because at each learning session, the context for encoding may vary. The individuals may use alternative strategies and cues for encoding. They thereby enrich and elaborate their schemas for the information. The principle of the spacing effect is important to remember in studying. You will recall information longer, on average, if you distribute your learning of subject matter and you vary the context for encoding. Do not try to cram it all into a short period. Imagine studying for an exam in several short sessions over a 2-week period. You will remember much of the material. However, if you try to study all the material in just one night, you will remember very little and the memory for this material will decay relatively quickly.

Why would distributing learning trials over days make a difference? One possibility is that information is learned in variable contexts. These diverse contexts help strengthen and begin to consolidate it. Another possible answer comes from studies of the influences of sleep on memory. Of particular importance is the amount of rapid eye movement (REM) sleep, a particular stage of sleep characterized by dreaming and increased brainwave activity (Karni & associates, 1994). Specifically, disruptions in REM sleep patterns the night after learning reduced the amount of improvement on a visual discrimination task that occurred relative to normal sleep. Furthermore, this lack of improvement was not observed for disrupted stage-three or stage-four sleep patterns (Karni & associates, 1994). Other research also shows better learning with increases in the proportion of REM-stage sleep after exposure to learning situations (Ellenbogen, Payne, & Stickgold, 2006; Smith, 1996). The positive influence of sleep on memory consolidation is seen across age groups (Hornung & associates, 2007). People who suffer from insomnia, a disorder that deprives the sufferer of much-needed sleep, have trouble with memory consolidation (Backhaus & associates, 2006). These findings highlight the importance of biological factors in the consolidation of memory. Thus, a good night's sleep, which includes plenty of REM-stage sleep, aids in memory consolidation.

Is there something special occurring in the brain that could explain why REM sleep is so important for memory consolidation? Neuropsychological research on animal learning may offer a tentative answer to this question. Recall that the hippocampus has been found to be an important structure for memory. In recording studies of rat hippocampal cells, researchers have found that cells of the hippocampus that were activated during initial learning are reactivated during subsequent periods of sleep. It is as if they are replaying the initial learning episode to achieve consolidation into long-term storage (Scaggs & McNaughton, 1996; Wilson & McNaughton, 1994). This effect has also been observed in humans. After learning routes within a virtual town, participants slept. Increased hippocampal activity was seen during sleep after the person had learned the spatial information. In the people with the most hippocampal activation, there was also an improvement in performance when they needed to recall the routes (Peigneux & associates, 2004). During this increased activity, the hippocampus also shows extremely low levels of the neurotransmitter acetylcholine. When patients were given acetylcholine during sleep, they showed impaired memory consolidation, but only for declarative information. Procedural memory consolidation was not affected by acetylcholine levels (Gais & Born, 2004).

In a recent review, investigators have proposed that the hippocampus acts as a rapid learning system (McClelland, McNaughton, & O'Reilly, 1995). It temporarily maintains new experiences until they can be appropriately assimilated into the more gradual neocortical representation system of the brain. Such a complementary system is necessary to allow memory to represent more accurately the structure of the environment. McClelland and his colleagues have used connectionist models of learning to show that integrating new experiences too rapidly leads to disruptions in long-term memory systems. Thus, the benefits of distributed practice seem to occur because we have a relatively rapid learning system in the hippocampus. It becomes activated during sleep. Repeated exposure on subsequent days and repeated reactivation during subsequent periods of sleep help learning. These rapidly learned memories become integrated into our more permanent long-term memory system.

A topic related to consolidation is reconsolidation. The process of consolidation makes memories less likely to undergo either interference or decay. However, after a memory is called back into consciousness, it may return to a more unstable state. In this state, the memory that was consolidated may again fall victim to interference or decay. To prevent this loss, a process of reconsolidation takes place. Reconsolidation has the same effect that consolidation does but is completed on previously encoded information. Reconsolidation does not necessarily occur with each memory we recall but does seem to occur with relatively newly consolidated material (Walker & associates, 2003).

The spacing of practice sessions affects memory consolidation. However, the distribution of learning trials within any given session does not seem to affect memory. According to the *total-time hypothesis*, the amount of learning depends on the amount of time spent mindfully rehearsing the material. This relation occurs more or less without regard to how that time is divided into trials in any one session. The total-time hypothesis does not always hold, however. Moreover, the total-time hypothesis of rehearsal has at least two apparent constraints (Cooper & Pantle, 1967). First, the full amount of time allotted for rehearsal actually must be used for that purpose. Second, to achieve beneficial effects, the rehearsal should include various kinds of elaboration or mnemonic devices that can enhance recall.

To move information into long-term memory, an individual must engage in elaborative rehearsal. In *elaborative rehearsal*, the individual somehow elaborates the items to be remembered. Such rehearsal makes the items either more meaningfully integrated into what the person already knows or more meaningfully connected to one another and therefore more memorable. Consider, in contrast, maintenance rehearsal. In *maintenance rehearsal*, the individual simply repetitiously rehearses the items to be repeated. Such rehearsal temporarily maintains information in short-term memory without transferring the information to long-term memory. Without any kind of elaboration, the information cannot be organized and transferred.

Organization of Information

Stored memories are organized. One way to show this organization is through the measurement of subjective organization in free recall. This refers to our individually determined ways of organizing our memories. To measure subjective organization, researchers may give participants a multi-trial free-recall task. Participants have multiple trials during which to learn to recall in any order they choose a list of unrelated words. Recall that if sets of test words can be divided into categories (e.g., names of fruits or of furniture), participants spontaneously will cluster their recall output by these categories. They do so even if the order of presentation is random (Bousfield, 1953). Similarly, participants will tend to show consistent patterns of word order in their recall protocols, even if there are no apparent relations among words in the list (Tulving, 1962). In other words, participants create their own consistent organization. They then group their recall by the subjective units they create. Although most adults spontaneously tend to cluster items into categories, categorical clustering also may be used intentionally as an aid to memorization.

You can use these memory strategies to help you study for exams:
1. Study throughout the course rather than cram the night before an exam. This distributes the learning sessions, allowing for consolidation into more permanent memory systems.
2. Link new information to what you already know by rehearsing new information in meaningful ways. Organize new information to relate it to other coursework or areas of your life.
3. Use the various mnemonic devices shown in Table 6.1.

PRACTICAL APPLICATIONS OF COGNITIVE PSYCHOLOGY

Mnemonic devices are specific techniques to help you memorize lists of words (Best, 2003). Essentially, such devices add meaning to otherwise meaningless or arbitrary lists of items. As Table 6.1 shows, a variety of methods—categorical clustering, acronyms, acrostics, interactive imagery among items, pegwords, and the method of loci—can help you to memorize lists of words and vocabulary items. Although the techniques described in Table 6.1 are not the only available ones, they are among the most frequently used.

- In *categorical clustering*, one organizes a list of items into a set of categories. For example, one might organize one's shopping list by the types of foods to be bought (e.g., fruits, vegetables, meats).
- In *interactive images*, one imagines (as vividly as possible) the objects represented by words one has to remember interacting with each other in some active way. For example, suppose you have to remember to buy socks, apples, and a pair of scissors. You might imagine cutting with a pair of scissors a sock that has an apple stuffed in it.

TABLE 6.1	Mnemonic Devices: Assorted Techniques

Of the many mnemonic devices available, the ones described here rely either on organization of information into meaningful chunks, such as categorical clustering, acronyms, and acrostics, or on visual images, such as interactive images, a pegword system, and the method of loci.

TECHNIQUE	EXPLANATION/DESCRIPTION	EXAMPLE
Categorical clustering	Organize a list of items into a set of categories	If you needed to remember to buy apples, milk, bagels, grapes, yogurt, rolls, Swiss cheese, grapefruit, and lettuce, you would be better able to do so if you tried to memorize the items by categories: *fruits*—apples, grapes, grapefruit; *dairy products*—milk, yogurt, Swiss cheese; *breads*—bagels, rolls; *vegetables*—lettuce.
Interactive images	Create interactive images that link the isolated words in a list	Suppose, for example, that you need to remember a list of unrelated words: *aardvark, table, pencil, book, radio, Kansas, rain, electricity, stone, mirror*. You might better remember these words by generating interactive images. For example, you might imagine an *aardvark* sitting on a *table* holding a *pencil* in its claws and writing in a *book*, with *rain* pouring over *Kansas* (as pictured on a map) that lands on a *radio* that is sitting on a *stone*, which generates *electricity* reflected in a *mirror*.
Pegword system	Associate each new word with a word on a previously memorized list, and form an interactive image between the two words	One such list is from a nursery rhyme: One is a bun. Two is a shoe. Three is a tree. Four is a door. Five is a hive. Six is a stick. Seven is heaven. Eight is a gate. Nine is a dime. Ten is a hen. To recall the list of words you used for the interactive images system, you might visualize an *aardvark* eating a delicious *bun*. You might imagine a *shoe* atop a tall *table*. You might visualize one large branch of a *tree* that ends with a sharp *pencil* point. Then you would go on forming interactive images for each of the words in the list. When you need to remember the words, you first recall the numbered images and then recall the words as you visualize them in the interactive images.

- In the *pegword system,* one associates each word with a word on a previously memorized list and forms an interactive image between the two words. For example, you might memorize a list such as "One is a bun," "Two is a shoe," "Three is a tree," and so on. To remember that you need to buy socks, apples, and a pair of scissors, you might imagine an apple between two buns, a sock stuffed inside a shoe, and a pair of scissors cutting a tree.

- In the *method of loci,* one visualizes walking around an area with distinctive landmarks that one knows well. One then links the various landmarks to specific items to be remembered. For example, suppose you have three landmarks on your route to school—a strange-looking house, a tree, and a baseball diamond. You might imagine a big sock on top of the house in place of the chimney, the pair of scissors cutting the tree, and apples replacing bases on the baseball diamond.

- In using *acronyms,* one devises a word or expression in which each of its letters stands for a certain other word or concept. An example is UK for the United Kingdom.

TABLE 6.1	Mnemonic Devices: Assorted Techniques (cont.)	
Technique	**Explanation/Description**	**Example**
Method of loci	Visualize walking around an area with distinctive landmarks that you know well, and then link the various landmarks to specific items to be remembered	When you need to memorize a list of words, mentally walk past each of the distinctive landmarks, depositing each word to be memorized at one of the landmarks. Visualize an interactive image between the new word and the landmark. For example, if you wished to remember the list of items mentioned previously, you might envision an *aardvark* nibbling at the roots of a familiar tree, a *table* sitting on the sidewalk in front of an empty lot, a *pencil*-shaped statue in the center of a fountain, and so on. When you wished to remember the list, you would take your mental walk and pick up the words you had linked to each of the landmarks along the walk.
Acronym	Devise a word or expression in which each of its letters stands for a certain other word or concept (e.g., USA, IQ, and laser)	Suppose that you want to remember the names of the mnemonic devices described in this chapter. The acronym "IAM PACK" might prompt you to remember Interactive images, Acronyms, Method of loci, Pegwords, Acrostics, Categories, and Keywords. Of course, this technique is more useful if the first letters of the words to be memorized actually can be formed into a word phrase, or something close to one, even if the word or phrase is nonsensical, as in this example.
Acrostic	Form a sentence rather than a single word to help you remember the new words	Music students trying to memorize the names of the notes found on lines of the treble clef (the higher notes; specifically E, G, B, D, and F above middle C) learn that "Every Good Boy Does Fine."
Keyword system	Form an interactive image that links the sound and meaning of a foreign word with the sound and meaning of a familiar word	Suppose that you needed to learn that the French word for *butter* is *beurre.* First, you would note that *beurre* sounds something like "bear." Next, you would associate the keyword *bear* with *butter* in an image or sentence. For instance, you might visualize a bear eating a stick of butter. Later, *bear* would provide a retrieval cue for *beurre.*

- In using *acrostics*, one forms a sentence rather than a single word to help one remember new words. For example, one might remember that "every good boy does fine" to recall the names of notes found on the lines of the treble clef in music.
- In using the *keyword system*, one forms an interactive image that links the sound and meaning of a foreign word with the sound and meaning of a familiar word. To remember the word *libro*, for example, which means "book" in Spanish, one might associate *libro* with *liberty*. Then think of the Statue of Liberty holding up a large book instead of a torch.

What is the comparative effectiveness of various mnemonic strategies, including verbal elaborative rehearsal, mental imagery for isolated items, interactive images (linking a sequence of items), the method of loci, and the pegword system (Table 6.2)? The relative effectiveness of the methods for encoding is influenced by the kind of task (free recall versus serial recall) required at the time of retrieval (Roediger, 1980a). Thus, when choosing a method for encoding information for subsequent recall, one should consider the purpose for recalling the information. The individual should choose not only strategies that allow for effectively encoding the information (moving it into long-term memory). He or she also should choose strategies that offer appropriate cues for facilitating subsequent retrieval when needed. For example, prior to taking an exam in cognitive psychology, using a strategy for retrieving an alphabetical list of prominent cognitive psychologists would probably be relatively ineffective. Using a strategy for linking particular theorists with the key ideas of their theories is likely to be more effective.

The use of mnemonic devices and other techniques for aiding memory involves metamemory. Most adults spontaneously use categorical clustering. So its inclusion in this list of mnemonic devices is actually just a reminder to use this common memory strategy. In fact, each of us often uses various kinds of *reminders*—external memory aids—to enhance the likelihood that we will remember important information. For example, by now you have surely learned the benefits of various external memory aids. These include taking notes during lectures, writing shopping lists for items to purchase, setting timers and alarms, and even asking other people to help you remember things. In addition, we can design our environment to help us remember important information through the use of *forcing functions* (Norman, 1988). These are physical constraints that prevent us from acting without at least considering the key information to be remembered. For example, to ensure that you remember to take your notebook to class, you might lean the notebook against the door through which you must pass to go to class.

Most of the time, we try to improve our *retrospective memory*—our memory for the past. At times we also try to improve our *prospective memory*—memory for things we need to do or remember in the future. For example, we may need to remember to call someone, to buy cereal at the supermarket, or to finish a homework assignment due the next day. We use a number of strategies to improve prospective memory. Examples are keeping a to-do list, asking someone to remind us to do something, or tying a string around our finger to remind us that we need to do something. Research suggests that having to do something regularly on a certain day does not necessarily improve

TABLE 6.2	Mnemonic Devices: Comparative Effectiveness

Henry Roediger conducted a study of recall memory, in which initial recall of a series of items was compared with recall following brief training in each of several memory strategies. For both free recall and serial recall, training in interactive imagery, the method of loci, and the pegword system was more effective than either elaborative (verbal) rehearsal or imagery for isolated items. However, the beneficial effects of training were most pronounced for the serial-recall condition. In the free-recall condition, imagery of isolated items was modestly more effective than elaborative (verbal) rehearsal, but for serial recall, elaborative (verbal) rehearsal was modestly more effective than imagery for isolated items.

		FREE-RECALL CRITERION			SERIAL-RECALL CRITERION		
		Average number of items recalled correctly following training			*Average number of items recalled correctly following training*		
Condition (type of mnemonic training)	*Number of participants*	*Number of correct items recalled on practice list, prior to training*	*Immediate recall*	*Recall following a 24-hour delay*	*Number of correct items recalled on practice list, prior to training*	*Immediate recall*	*Recall following a 24-hour delay*
Elaborative rehearsal (verbal)	32	13.2	11.4	6.3	7.0	5.8	1.3
Isolated images of individual items	25	12.4	13.1	6.8	6.8	4.8	1.0
Interactive imagery (with links from one item to the next)	31	13.0	15.6	11.2	7.6	9.6	5.0
Method of loci	29	12.6	15.3	10.6	6.8	13.6	5.8
Pegword system	33	13.1	14.2	8.2	7.7	12.5	4.9
Mean performance across conditions	—	12.9	13.9	8.6	7.2	9.4	3.6

H. L. Roediger (1980), "The Effectiveness of Four Mnemonics in Ordering Recall," *Journal of Experimental Psychology: HLM*, 6(5): 558–567. Copyright © 1980 by the American Psychological Association. Adapted with permission.

prospective memory for doing that thing. However, being monetarily reinforced for doing the thing does tend to improve prospective memory (Meacham, 1982; Meacham & Singer, 1977).

Prospective memory, like retrospective memory, is subject to declines as we age. Over the years, we retain more of our prospective memory than of our retrospective memory. This retention is likely the result of the use of the external cues and strategies that can be used to bolster prospective memory. In the laboratory, older adults show a decline in prospective memory; however, outside the laboratory they show better performance than young adults. This difference may be due to greater reliance on strategies to aid in remembering as we age (Henry & associates, 2004).

Retrieval

Once we have stored information, how do we retrieve it when we want to do so? If we have problems retrieving information, how do we know whether we even stored the information in the first place?

Retrieval from Short-Term Memory

Once information is encoded and stored in short-term memory, how do people retrieve that information?

INVESTIGATING COGNITIVE PSYCHOLOGY	Memorize the following list of numbers: 6, 3, 8, 2, 7. Now, was 8 on the list? How do people make decisions such as this one?

In one study, participants received a short list including from one to six digits (Sternberg, 1966). They were expected to be able to hold it in short-term memory. After a brief pause, a test digit was flashed on a screen. Participants had to say whether this digit appeared in the set that they had been asked to memorize. Thus, if the list comprised the digits 4, 1, 9, 3, and the digit 9 flashed on the screen, the correct response would be "yes." If, instead, the test digit was 7, the correct response would be "no." The digits that were presented are termed the *positive set*. Those that were not presented are termed the *negative set*. Results are shown in Figure 6.1.

Are items retrieved all at once (parallel processing) or sequentially (serial processing)? If retrieved serially, the question then arises, "Are all items retrieved, regardless of the task (exhaustive retrieval), or does retrieval stop as soon as an item seems to accomplish the task (self-terminating retrieval)?"

Parallel versus Serial Processing

As mentioned previously, parallel processing refers to the simultaneous handling of multiple operations. As applied to short-term memory, the items stored in short-term memory would be retrieved all at once, not one at a time. The prediction in Figure 6.1 *a* shows what would happen if parallel processing were the case in the memory scanning task. Response times should be the same, regardless of the size of the positive set. This is because all comparisons would be done at once.

Serial processing refers to operations being done one after another. In other words, on the digit-recall task, the digits would be retrieved in succession, rather than all at once (as in the parallel model). According to the serial model, it should take longer to retrieve four digits than to retrieve two digits (as shown in Figure 6.1 *b*).

Exhaustive versus Self-Terminating Processing

Suppose information processing were serial. Then there would be two ways in which to gain access to the stimuli: exhaustive or self-terminating processing. *Exhaustive serial processing* implies that the participant always would check the test digit against *all* digits in the positive set, even if a match were found partway through the list.

FIGURE 6.1

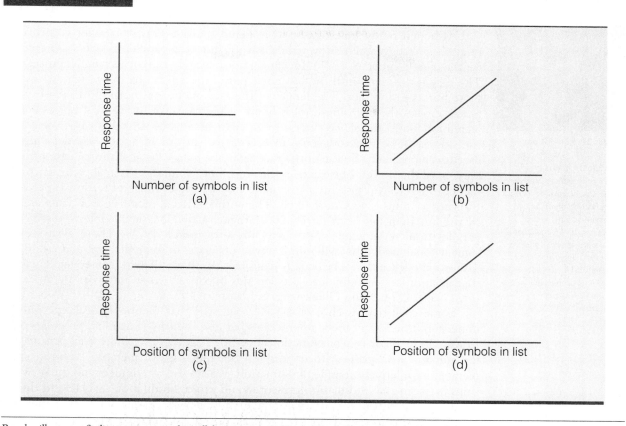

Panel a illustrates findings suggestive of parallel processing; b illustrates serial processing; c shows exhaustive serial processing; and d shows self-terminating serial processing. Based on S. Sternberg (1966), "High Speed in S. Sternberg's Short-Term Memory-Scanning Task," Science, Vol. 153, pp. 652–654. Copyright © 1966 American Association for the Advancement of Science.

Exhaustive processing would predict the pattern of data shown in Figure 6.1 c. Note that positive responses all would take the same amount of time, regardless of the serial position of a positive test probe. In other words, in an exhaustive search, you would take the same amount of time to find any digit. Where in the list it was located would not matter.

Self-terminating serial processing implies that the participant would check the test digit against only those digits needed to make a response. Consider Figure 6.1 d. It shows that response time now would increase linearly as a function of where a test digit was located in the positive set. The later the serial position, the longer is the response time.

The Winner—a Serial Exhaustive Model—with Some Qualifications

The actual pattern of data was crystal clear. The data looked like those in Figures 6.1 b and c. Response times increased linearly with set size, but they were the same, regardless of serial position. Later, this pattern of data was replicated (Sternberg, 1969).

Gordon H. Bower is professor emeritus of psychology at Stanford University. His earlier contributions were in mathematical learning theories. Later, with John Anderson, he developed a theoretical framework for linking laboratory studies of verbal memory with psycholinguistic theories of memory. He also has investigated how people's emotional states influence memory storage and retrieval.

Moreover, the mean response times for positive and negative responses were essentially the same. This fact further supported the serial exhaustive model. Comparisons took roughly 38 milliseconds (0.038 seconds) apiece (Sternberg, 1966, 1969).

Although many investigators considered the question of parallel versus serial processing to have been answered decisively, in fact, a parallel model could account for the data (Corcoran, 1971). Imagine a horse race that involves parallel processing. The race is not over until the last horse passes the finish line. Now suppose we add more horses to the race. The length of the race (from the start until the last of the horses crosses the finishing line) is likely to increase. For example, if horses are selected randomly, the slowest horse in an eight-horse race is likely to be slower than the slowest horse in a four-horse race. That is, with more horses, a wider range of speeds is more likely. So the entire race will take longer because the race is not complete until the slowest horse crosses the finish line. Similarly, when applying a parallel model to a retrieval task involving more items, a wider range of retrieval speeds for the various items is also more likely. The entire retrieval process is not complete until the last item has been retrieved. Mathematically, it is impossible to distinguish parallel from serial models unequivocally (Townsend, 1971). There always exists some parallel model that will mimic any serial model in its predictions and vice versa. The two models may not be equally plausible, but they still exist. Moreover, it appears that what processes individuals use depends in part on the stimuli that are processed (e.g., Naus, 1974; Naus, Glucksberg, & Ornstein, 1972).

Some cognitive psychologists have suggested that we should seek not only to understand the *how* of memory processes but also the *why* of memory processes (e.g., Bruce, 1991). That is, what functions does memory serve for individual persons and for humans as a species? To understand the functions of memory, we must study memory for relatively complex information. We also need to understand the relationships between the information presented and other information available to the individual, both within the informational context and as a result of prior experience.

Retrieval from Long-Term Memory

It is difficult to separate storage from retrieval phenomena. Participants in one study were tested on their memory for lists of categorized words (Tulving & Pearlstone, 1966). Participants would hear words within a category together in the list. They even would be given the name of the category before the items within it were presented. For example, the participants might hear the category "article of clothing" followed by the words, "shirt, socks, pants, belt." Participants then were tested for their recall.

The recall test was done in one of two ways. In the free-recall condition, participants merely recalled as many words as they could in any order they chose. In a cued-recall condition, however, participants were tested category by category. They were given each category label as a cue. They then were asked to recall as many words as they could from that category. The critical result was that cued recall was far better, on average, than free recall. Had the researchers tested only free recall, they might have concluded that participants had not stored quite so many words. However, the comparison to the cued-recall condition demonstrated that apparent memory failures were largely a result of retrieval rather than storage failures.

Categorization dramatically can affect retrieval. Investigators had participants learn lists of categorized words (Bower & associates, 1969). Either the words were presented in random order or they were presented in the form of a hierarchical tree that showed the organization of the words. For example, the category "minerals" might be at the top, followed by the categories of "metals and stones," and so on. Participants given hierarchical presentation recalled 65% of the words. In contrast, recall was just 19% by participants given the words in random order.

A number of studies have used probability models to try to separate storage and retrieval. These models find probabilities that an item was stored or retrieved, based on participants' responses to a number of questions (Chechile 2004; Chechile & Soraci, 1999). The models tend to be quite complex and require many hundreds of trials to be accurate. Therefore, these models tend to be limited in application to use of memory outside the laboratory. In one study described by Chechile, participants learned three words and then were tested on these words. Chechile was able to show differences in retrieval by changing how much time the participant had to recall the item. When there was very little time per item, fewer items were recalled. When the participant had more time, more of the items were recalled (Chechile, 2004). Participants could not retrieve items quickly enough in the "little-time" condition.

Another problem that arises when studying memory is figuring out why we sometimes have trouble retrieving information. Cognitive psychologists often have difficulty finding a way to distinguish between availability and accessibility of items. **Availability** is the presence of information stored in long-term memory. **Accessibility** is the degree to which we can gain access to the available information. Memory performance depends on the accessibility of the information to be remembered. Ideally, memory researchers would like to assess the availability of information in memory. Unfortunately, they must settle for assessing the accessibility of such information.

Processes of Forgetting and Memory Distortion

Why do we so easily and so quickly forget phone numbers we have just looked up or the names of people whom we have just met? Several theories have been proposed as to why we forget information stored in working memory. The two most well-known theories are interference theory and decay theory. **Interference** occurs when competing information causes us to forget something; **decay** occurs when simply the passage of time causes us to forget.

Interference versus Decay Theory

Interference theory refers to the view that forgetting occurs because recall of certain words interferes with recall of other words. Evidence for interference goes back many years (Brown, 1958; Peterson & Peterson, 1959). In one study, participants to recall *trigrams* (strings of three letters) at intervals of 3, 6, 9, 12, 15, or 18 seconds after the presentation of the last letter (Peterson & Peterson, 1959). The investigator used

FIGURE 6.2

The percentage of recall of three consonants (a trigram) drops off quickly if participants are not allowed to rehearse the trigrams. G. Keppel and B. J. Underwood (1962), "Proactive Inhibition in Short-Term Retention of Single Items," Journal of Verbal Learning and Verbal Behavior, Vol. 1, pp. 153–161. Reprinted by permission of Elsevier.

only consonants so that the trigrams would not be easily pronounceable—for example, "K B F." Figure 6.2 shows percentages of correct recalls after the various intervals of time. Why does recall decline so rapidly? Because after the oral presentation of each trigram, participants counted backward by threes from a three-digit number spoken immediately after the trigram. The purpose of having the participants count backward was to prevent them from rehearsing during the *retention interval*. This is the time between the presentation of the last letter and the start of the recall phase of the experimental trial.

Clearly, the trigram is almost completely forgotten after just 18 seconds if participants are not allowed to rehearse it. Moreover, such forgetting also occurs when words rather than letters are used as the stimuli to be recalled (Murdock, 1961). Thus, counting backward interfered with recall from short-term memory, supporting the interference account of forgetting in short-term memory. At that time, it seemed surprising that counting backward with numbers would interfere with the recall of letters. The previous view had been that verbal information would interfere only with verbal (words) memory. Similarly, it was thought that quantitative (numerical) information would interfere only with quantitative memory.

Although the foregoing discussion has construed interference as though it were a single construct, at least two kinds of interference figure prominently in psychological theory and research: retroactive interference and proactive interference. **Retroactive interference** (or retroactive inhibition) is caused by activity occurring *after* we learn something but *before* we are asked to recall that thing. The interference in the Brown-Peterson task appears to be retroactive because counting backward by threes occurs after learning of the trigram. It interferes with our ability to remember information we learned previously.

A second kind of interference is proactive interference (or proactive inhibition). **Proactive interference** occurs when the interfering material occurs *before*, rather than *after*, learning of the to-be-remembered material. Proactive as well as retroactive interference may play a role in short-term memory (Keppel & Underwood, 1962). Thus, retroactive interference appears to be important (Reitman, 1971; Shiffrin, 1973; Waugh & Norman, 1965), but not the only factor.

Some early psychologists recognized the need to study memory retrieval for connected texts and not just for unconnected strings of digits, words, or nonsense syllables. In one study, participants learned a text and then recalled it (Bartlett, 1932). Participants in Britain learned what was to them a strange and difficult-to-understand North American Indian legend called "The War of the Ghosts." (The text is depicted in its entirety in Table 6.3.)

Participants distorted their recall to render the story more comprehensible to themselves. In other words, their prior knowledge and expectations had a substantial effect on their recall. Apparently, people bring into a memory task their already existing schemas, or organized relevant knowledge structures, which affect the way in which they recall what they learn. The later work using the Brown-Peterson paradigm confirms the notion that prior knowledge has an enormous effect on memory, sometimes leading to interference or distortion.

Yet another method often used for determining the causes of forgetting draws inferences from a serial-position curve: The serial-position curve represents the probability of recall of a given word, given its serial position (order of presentation) in a list. Suppose that you are presented with a list of words and are asked to recall them. You even might try it on yourself with the "Investigating Cognitive Psychology" box.

Say the following list of words once to yourself, and then, immediately thereafter, try to recall all the words, in any order, without looking back at them: *Table, Cloud, Book, Tree, Shirt, Cat, Light, Bench, Chalk, Flower, Watch, Bat, Rug, Soap, Pillow.*	**INVESTIGATING COGNITIVE PSYCHOLOGY**

If you are like most people, you will find that your recall of words is best for items at and near the end of the list. Your recall will be second best for items near the beginning of the list and poorest for items in the middle of the list. A typical serial-position curve is shown in Figure 6.3.

The **recency effect** refers to superior recall of words at and near the end of a list. The **primacy effect** refers to superior recall of words at and near the beginning of a list. As Figure 6.3 shows, both the recency effect and the primacy effect seem to influence recall. The serial-position curve makes sense in terms of interference theory. Words at the end of the list are subject to proactive but not to retroactive interference. Words at the beginning of the list are subject to retroactive but not to proactive interference. And words in the middle of the list are subject to both types of interference. Hence, recall would be expected to be poorest in the middle of the list. Indeed, it is poorest.

The amount of proactive interference generally climbs with increases in the length of time between when the information is presented (and encoded) and when

| **TABLE 6.3** | Bartlett's Legend |

Read the legend described in this table, and then turn the page and try to recall the legend in its entirety.

(A) ORIGINAL INDIAN MYTH	(B) TYPICAL RECALL BY A STUDENT IN ENGLAND
The War of the Ghosts	*The War of the Ghosts*
One night two young men from Egulac went down to the river to hunt seals, and while they were there it became foggy and calm. Then they heard war-cries, and they thought: "Maybe this is a war-party." They escaped to the shore, and hid behind a log.　Now canoes came up, and they heard the noise of paddles, and saw one canoe coming up to them. There were five men in the canoe, and they said:　"What do you think? We wish to take you along. We are going up the river to make war on the people."　One of the young men said, "I have no arrows."　"Arrows are in the canoe," they said.　"I will not go along. I might be killed. My relatives do not know where I have gone. But you," he said, turning to the other, "may go with them."　So one of the young men went, but the other returned home.　And the warriors went on up the river to a town on the other side of Kalama. The people came down to the water, and they began to fight, and many were killed. But presently the young man heard one of the warriors say: "Quick, let us go home; that Indian has been hit." Now he thought: "Oh, they are ghosts." He did not feel sick, but they said he had been shot.　So the canoes went back to Egulac, and the young man went ashore to his house, and made a fire. And he told everybody and said: "Behold I accompanied the ghosts, and we went to fight. Many of our fellows were killed, and many of those who attacked us were killed. They said I was hit, and I did not feel sick."　He told it all, and then he became quiet.　When the sun rose he fell down. Something black came out of his mouth. His face became contorted. The people jumped up and cried.　He was dead.	Two men from Edulac went fishing. While thus occupied by the river they heard a noise in the distance.　"It sounds like a cry," said one, and presently there appeared some in canoes who invited them to join the party of their adventure. One of the young men refused to go, on the ground of family ties, but the other offered to go.　"But there are no arrows," he said.　"The arrows are in the boat," was the reply.　He thereupon took his place, while his friend returned home. The party paddled up the river to Kaloma, and began to land on the banks of the river. The enemy came rushing upon them, and some sharp fighting ensued. Presently someone was injured, and the cry was raised that the enemy were ghosts.　The party returned down the stream, and the young man arrived home feeling none the worse for his experience. The next morning at dawn he endeavored to recount his adventures. While he was talking something black issued from his mouth. Suddenly he uttered a cry and fell down. His friends gathered round him.　But he was dead.

"The War of the Ghosts," from *Remembering: A Study in Experimental and Social Psychology* by F. C. Bartlett. Copyright © 1932 by Cambridge University Press. Reprinted with permission of Cambridge University Press.

the information is retrieved (Underwood, 1957). Also as you might expect, proactive interference increases as the amount of prior—and potentially interfering—learning increases (Greenberg & Underwood, 1950).

Proactive interference seems to be associated with activation in the frontal cortex. In particular, it activates Brodmann area 45 in the left hemisphere (Postle, Brush, & Nick, 2004). In alcoholic patients, proactive interference is seen to a lesser degree

FIGURE 6.3

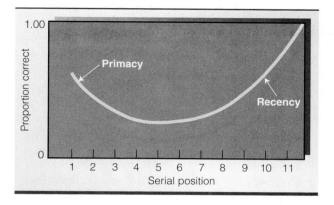

When asked to recall a list of words, we show superior recall of words close to the end of a list (the recency effect), pretty good recall of words close to the beginning of the list (primacy effect), and relatively poor recall of words in the middle of the list.

than in nonalcoholic patients. This finding suggests that the alcoholic patients have difficulty integrating past information with new information. Thus, alcoholic patients may have difficulty binding together unrelated items in a list (De Rosa & Sullivan, 2003). Taken together, these findings suggest that Brodmann area 45 is likely involved in the binding of items into meaningful groups. When more information is gathered, an attempt to relate them to one another can occupy much of the available resources, leaving limited processing ability for new items.

All information does not equally contribute to proactive interference. For instance, if you are learning a list of numbers, your performance in learning the list will gradually decline as the list continues. If, however, the list switches to words, your performance will rebound. This enhancement in performance is known as release from proactive interference (Bunting, 2006). The effects of proactive interference appear to dominate under conditions in which recall is delayed. However, proactive and retroactive interference now are viewed as complementary phenomena.

Yet another theory for explaining how we forget information is decay theory. **Decay theory** asserts that information is forgotten because of the gradual disappearance, rather than displacement, of the memory trace. Thus, decay theory views the original piece of information as gradually disappearing unless something is done to keep it intact. This view contrasts with interference theory, just discussed, in which one or more pieces of information block recall of another.

Decay theory turns out to be exceedingly difficult to test. Why? First, under normal circumstances, preventing participants from rehearsing is difficult. Through rehearsal, participants maintain the to-be-remembered information in memory. Usually participants know that you are testing their memory. They may try to rehearse the information or they may even inadvertently rehearse it to perform well during testing. However, if you do prevent them from rehearsing, the possibility of interference arises. The task you use to prevent rehearsal may interfere retroactively with the original memory.

For example, try not to think of white elephants as you read the next two pages. When instructed not to think about them, you actually find it quite difficult not to. The difficulty persists even if you try to follow the instructions. Unfortunately, as a test of decay theory, this experiment is itself a white elephant because preventing people from rehearsing is so difficult.

Despite these difficulties, it is possible to test decay theory. Such a test involves using a task intervening between learning and testing that (1) prevents rehearsal and (2) presents no interfering learning. In one such study, the intervening task, involving tone detection, required a great deal of effort and attention but no new learning (Reitman, 1971, 1974). Participants heard a very faint tone presented through earphones. They were to press a button each time they heard the tone. Of course, there was no guarantee that participants would not rehearse at all. Nor was there any guarantee that all information would be blocked from entering short-term memory. However, the test was about as close to ideal as one could realistically produce.

Participants saw five words (Reitman, 1974). The display lasted for 2 seconds. As soon as the display went off, participants engaged in the tone-detection task for 15 seconds, after which they tried to recall as many of the five words as they could. Recall declined by about 24% over the 15 seconds. Reitman interpreted this decline as evidence of decay.

To conclude, evidence exists for both interference and decay, at least in short-term memory. The evidence for decay is not airtight, but it is certainly suggestive. The evidence for interference is rather strong. However, the extent to which the interference is retroactive, proactive, or both is unclear. In addition, interference also affects material in long-term memory, leading to memory distortion.

The Constructive Nature of Memory

An important lesson about memory is that memory retrieval is not just **reconstructive,** involving the use of various strategies (e.g., searching for cues, drawing inferences) for retrieving the original memory traces of our experiences and then rebuilding the original experiences as a basis for retrieval (see Kolodner, 1983, for an artificial-intelligence model of reconstructive memory). Rather, in real-life situations, memory is also **constructive,** in that prior experience affects how we recall things and what we actually recall from memory (Grant & Ceci, 2000; Sutton, 2003). Think back to the Bransford and Johnson (1972) study, cited at the opening of this chapter. In this study, participants could remember a passage about washing clothes quite well but only if they realized that it was about washing clothes.

In a further demonstration of the constructive nature of memory, participants read an ambiguous passage that could be interpreted meaningfully in two ways (Bransford & Johnson, 1973). Either it could be viewed as being either about watching a peace march from the fortieth floor of a building or about a space trip to an inhabited planet. Participants omitted different details, depending on what they thought the passage was about. Consider, for example, a sentence mentioning that the atmosphere did not require the wearing of special clothing. Participants were more likely to remember it when they thought the passage was about a trip into outer space than when they thought it was about a peace march.

Consider a comparable demonstration in a different domain (Bower, Karlin, & Dueck, 1975). Investigators showed participants 28 different *droodles*—nonsense pictures that can be given various interpretations (see also Chapter 10). Half of the participants in their experiment were given an interpretation by which they could label what they saw. The other half did not receive an interpretation prompting a label. Participants in the label group correctly reproduced almost 20% more droodles than did participants in the control group.

Autobiographical Memory

Autobiographical memory refers to memory of an individual's history. Autobiographical memory is constructive. One does not remember exactly what has happened. Rather, one remembers one's construction or reconstruction of what happened. People's autobiographical memories are generally quite good. Nevertheless, they are subject to distortions (as will be discussed later). They are differentially good for different periods of life. Middle-aged adults often remember events from their youthful and early-adult periods better than they remember events from their more recent past (Rubin, 1982, 1996).

One way of studying autobiographical memory is through diary studies. In such studies, individuals, often researchers, keep detailed autobiographies (e.g., Linton, 1982; Wagenaar, 1986). One investigator, for example, kept a diary for a 6-year period (Linton, 1982). She recorded at least two experiences per day on index cards. Then, each month she chose two cards at random and tried to recall the events she had written on the cards as well as the dates of the events. She further rated each memory for its salience and its emotional content. Surprisingly, her rate of forgetting of events was linear. It was not curvilinear, as is usually the case. In other words, a typical memory curve shows substantial forgetting over short time intervals and then a slowing in the rate of forgetting over longer time intervals. Linton's forgetting curve, however, did not show any such pattern. Her rate of forgetting was about the same over the entire 6-year interval. She also found little relationship between her ratings of the salience and emotionality of memories, on the one hand, and their memorability, on the other. Thus, she surprised herself in what she did and did not remember.

In another study of autobiographical memory, a researcher attempted to recall information regarding performances attended at the Metropolitan Opera over a period of 25 years (Sehulster, 1989). A total of 284 performances comprised the data for the study. The results were more in line with traditional expectations. Operas seen near the beginning and end of the 25-year period were remembered better (serial-position effect). Important performances also were better recalled than less important ones.

Recent work has illustrated the importance of self-esteem in the formation and recall of autobiographical memory. People with positive self-esteem remember more positive events, whereas people with negative self-esteem remember more negative events (Christensen, Wood, & Barrett, 2003).

Memory Distortions

People have tendencies to distort their memories (Ayers & Reder, 1998; Balota & associates, 1999; Garry & associates, 1996; Goff & Roediger, 1998; Heaps & Nash, 1999; Johnson & Raye, 1998; Norman & Schacter, 1997; Roediger & McDermott,

2000; Schacter, 1995b; Schacter & Curran, 2000). For example, just saying something has happened to you makes you more likely to think it really happened. This is true whether the event happened or not (Ackil & Zaragoza, 1998). These distortions tend to occur in seven specific ways, which Schacter (2001) refers to as the "seven sins of memory." Here are Schacter's "seven sins":

1. *Transience*. Memory fades quickly. For example, although most people know that O. J. Simpson was acquitted of criminal charges in the murder of his wife, they do not remember how they found out about his acquittal. At one time they could have said, but they no longer can.

2. *Absent-mindedness*. People sometimes brush their teeth after already having brushed them or enter a room looking for something only to discover that they have forgotten what they were seeking.

3. *Blocking*. People sometimes have something that they know they should remember, but they can't. It's as though the information is on the tip of their tongue, but they cannot retrieve it. For example, people may see someone they know but the person's name escapes them. Or they may try to think of a synonym for a word, knowing that there is an obvious synonym but are unable to recall it.

4. *Misattribution*. People often cannot remember where they heard what they heard or read what they read. Sometimes people think they saw things they did not see or heard things they did not hear. For example, eyewitness testimony is sometimes clouded by what we think we should have seen, rather than what we actually saw.

5. *Suggestibility*. People are susceptible to suggestion, so if it is suggested to them that they saw something, they may think they remember seeing it. For example, in Holland, when asked whether they had seen a television film of a plane crashing into an apartment building, many people said they had seen it. There was no such film.

6. *Bias*. People often are biased in their recall. For example, people who currently are experiencing chronic pain in their lives are more likely to remember pain in the past, whether or not they actually experienced it. People who are not experiencing such pain are less likely to recall pain in the past, again with little regard to their actual past experience.

7. *Persistence*. People sometimes remember things as consequential that, in a broad context, are inconsequential. For example, someone with many successes but one notable failure may remember the single failure better than the many successes.

What are some of the specific ways in which memory distortions are studied?

The Eyewitness Testimony Paradigm

A survey of U.S. prosecutors estimated that about 77,000 suspects are arrested each year after being identified by eyewitnesses (Dolan, 1995). Studies of more than 1000 known wrongful convictions have pointed to errors in eyewitness identification as being "the single largest factor leading to those false convictions" (Wells, 1993, p. 554). What proportion of eyewitness identifications are mistaken? The answer to that question varies widely ("from as low as a few percent to greater than 90%"; Wells, 1993, p. 554), but even the most conservative estimates of this proportion suggest frightening possibilities.

Consider the story of a man named Timothy. In 1986, Timothy was convicted of brutally murdering a mother and her two young daughters (Dolan, 1995). He was then sentenced to die, and for 2 years and 4 months, Timothy lived on death row. Although the physical evidence did not point to Timothy, eyewitness testimony placed him near the scene of the crime at the time of the murder. Subsequently, it was discovered that a man who looked like Timothy was a frequent visitor to the neighborhood of the murder victims, and Timothy was given a second trial and was acquitted.

Some of the strongest evidence for the constructive nature of memory has been obtained by those who have studied the validity of eyewitness testimony. In a now classic study, participants saw a series of 30 slides in which a red Datsun drove down a street, stopped at a stop sign, turned right, and then appeared to knock down a pedestrian crossing at a crosswalk (Loftus, Miller, & Burns, 1978). As soon as the participants finished seeing the slides, they had to answer a series of 20 questions about the accident. One of the questions contained information that was either consistent or inconsistent with what they had been shown. For example, half the participants were asked: "Did another car pass the red Datsun while it was stopped at the stop sign?" The other half of the participants received the same question, except with the word *yield* replacing the word *stop*. In other words, the information in the question given this second group was inconsistent with what the participants had seen.

Later, after engaging in an unrelated activity, all participants were shown two slides and asked which they had seen. One had a stop sign, the other had a yield sign. Accuracy on this task was 34% better for participants who had received the consistent question (stop sign question) than for participants who had received the inconsistent question (yield sign question). This experiment and others (e.g., Loftus, 1975, 1977) have shown people's great susceptibility to distortion in eyewitness accounts. This distortion may be due, in part, to phenomena other than just constructive memory. But it does show that we easily can be led to construct a memory that is different from what really happened. As an example, you might have had a disagreement with a roommate or a friend regarding an experience in which both of you were in the same place at the same time. But what each of you remembers about the experience may differ sharply. And *both* of you may feel that you are truthfully and accurately recalling what happened.

There are serious potential problems of wrongful conviction when using eyewitness testimony as the sole or even the primary basis for convicting accused people of crimes (Loftus & Ketcham, 1991; Loftus, Miller, & Burns, 1987; Wells & Loftus, 1984). Moreover, eyewitness testimony is often a powerful determinant of whether a jury will convict an accused person. The effect particularly is pronounced if eyewitnesses appear highly confident of their testimony. This is true even if the eyewitnesses can provide few perceptual details or offer apparently conflicting responses. People sometimes even think they remember things simply because they have imagined or thought about them (Garry & Loftus, 1994). It has been estimated that as many as 10,000 people per year may be convicted wrongfully on the basis of mistaken eyewitness testimony (Cutler &

Elizabeth Loftus is a professor of psychology at the University of California, Irvine. She has made major contributions to the study of human memory, particularly in the areas of eyewitness testimony and so-called repressed memories, which she has argued can be planted in the minds of unwitting individuals so that the individuals believe they are remembering events that they never actually experienced.

Penrod, 1995; Loftus & Ketcham, 1991). In general, then, people are remarkably susceptible to mistakes in eyewitness testimony. In general, they are prone to imagine that they have seen things they have not seen (Loftus, 1998).

Lineups can lead to faulty conclusions (Wells, 1993). Eyewitnesses assume that the perpetrator is in the lineup. This is not always the case, however. When the perpetrator of a staged crime was not in a lineup, participants were susceptible to naming someone other than the perpetrator as the perpetrator. In this way, they can recognize *someone* in the lineup as having committed the crime. The identities of the nonperpetrators in the lineup also can affect judgments (Wells, Luus, & Windschitl, 1994). In other words, whether a given person is identified as a perpetrator can be influenced simply by who the others in the lineup are. So the choice of the "distracter" individuals is important. Police may inadvertently affect the likelihood of whether an identification occurs or not and also whether a false identification is likely to occur.

Eyewitness identification is particularly weak when identifying people of a race other than the race of the witness (e.g., Bothwell, Brigham, & Malpass, 1989; Brigham & Malpass, 1985; Pezdek, Blandon-Gitlin, & Moore, 2003; Shapiro & Penrod, 1986). Evidence suggests that this is not a result of problems remembering stored

IN THE LAB OF ELIZABETH LOFTUS

Courtesy of Dr. Elizabeth Loftus

Remember the time when you were a kid and your family went to Disneyland? The highlight of your trip was meeting Mickey Mouse, who shook your hand? Remember that? Marketers use autobiographical advertising like this to create nostalgia for their products. Several years ago, we wondered whether such referencing could cause people to believe that they had experiences as children that are mentioned in the ads (Braun, Ellis, & Loftus, 2002). In our first study, participants viewed an ad for Disneyland that suggested that as a child they shook hands with Mickey Mouse. Later on they answered questions about their childhood experiences at Disneyland. Relative to controls, the ad increased their confidence that as a child they personally had shaken hands with Mickey at Disneyland.

Of course we realized that the increased confidence could be due to either (1) a revival of a true memory or (2) the creation of a new, false one. Because some people could have actually met Mickey at Disney, both are possibilities. So, we conducted a second study in which our participants viewed a fake

ad for Disneyland that suggested that they shook hands with an impossible character: Bugs Bunny. Of course, Bugs is a Warner Brothers character and would not be found at a Disney resort. Again, relative to controls, the ad increased confidence that they personally had shaken hands with the impossible character as a child at Disneyland. Although this could not possibly have happened because Bugs Bunny is a Warner Brothers character and would not be caught dead at a Disney property, about 16% of the subjects later said that they remembered or knew that the event actually had happened to them. In another study, we showed that having a picture of Bugs mattered. Even more people claimed to have met Bugs when a picture of Bugs was included in the ad than when Bugs was only described verbally. False memories of Bugs in one condition were as high as 48% (Braun-LaTour & associates, 2004).

We wondered whether it was the advertisement itself that was producing the false memory, or whether any recent exposure to Bugs Bunny would produce a similar effect. For example, if people recently had seen Bugs in a Bugs Bunny cartoon, would they also claim later that they had met Bugs on a childhood trip to Disneyland? In one series of studies, people did not faces of people from other races, but rather, of encoding these faces (Walker & Tanaka, 2003). Even infants seem to be influenced by post-event information when recalling an experience, as shown through their behavior in operant-conditioning experiments (Rovee-Collier & associates, 1993).

Eyewitness identification and recall are also affected by the witness's level of stress. As stress increases, the accuracy of both recall and identification declines (Deffenbacher & associates, 2004; Payne & associates, 2002). These findings further call into question the accuracy of eyewitness testimony because most crimes occur in highly stressful situations.

Not everyone views eyewitness testimony with such skepticism, however (e.g., see Zaragoza, McCloskey, & Jamis, 1987). It is still not clear whether the information about the original event actually is displaced by, or is simply competing with, the subsequent misleading information. Some investigators have argued that psychologists need to know a great deal more about the circumstances that impair eyewitness testimony before impugning such testimony before a jury (McKenna, Treadway, & McCloskey, 1992). At present, the verdict on eyewitness testimony is still not in. The same can be said for repressed memories, considered in the next section.

IN THE LAB OF ELIZABETH LOFTUS—cont'd

claim to have met Bugs if they had recently seen a large cardboard cutout of him; they only claimed to have done so if exposed to the doctored ad (Pickrell, 2005).

It's one thing to plant a false memory of meeting Bugs Bunny, but quite another to plant a false memory of an unpleasant experience with another character. So with Shari Berkowitz and other colleagues, we tried to plant a false belief that people had had an unpleasant experience with the Pluto character while on a childhood trip to Disney (Berkowitz & associates, 2008). We succeeded with about 30% of the subjects. Moreover, those who were seduced by the suggestion did not want to pay as much for a Pluto souvenir. This finding shows that false beliefs can have consequences—they can affect later thoughts and behaviors.

These studies are part of a larger program of research on the malleability of human memory (Loftus, 2005). But more specifically, these findings suggest that advertisements that contain autobiographical referencing can tamper with our personal childhood memories. Although advertisers are probably not mentioning false details, they do mention details that could be true. However, they are not true for everyone. You may have seen a picture of Mickey Mouse when you were at Disneyland, but you never actually met him or shook hands with him. An ad may make you think you did. Because we view thousands of advertisements in the course of a typical month, could we all be unwitting subjects in a mass experiment on memory distortion?

References
Berkowitz, S. R., Laney, C., Morris, E. K., Garry, M., & Loftus, E. F. (2008). Pluto behaving badly: False beliefs and their consequences. *American Journal of Psychology*, in press.

Braun, K. A., Ellis, R., & Loftus, E. F. (2002). Make my memory: How advertising can change our memories of the past. *Psychology and Marketing, 19*, 1–23.

Braun-LaTour, K. A., LaTour, M. S., Pickrell, J., & Loftus, E.F. (2004). How (and when) advertising can influence memory for consumer experience. *Journal of Advertising, 33,*7–25.

Loftus, E. F. (2005). A 30-year investigation of the malleability of memory. *Learning and Memory, 12*, 361–366.

Pickrell, J. E. (2005). *What's up doc? Factors involved in the acceptance of false information.* Unpublished doctoral dissertation, University of Washington.

Whatever may be the validity of eyewitness testimony for adults, it clearly is suspect for children (Ceci & Bruck, 1993, 1995). Children's recollections are particularly susceptible to distortion. Such distortion is especially likely when the children are asked leading questions, as in a courtroom setting. Consider some relevant facts (Ceci & Bruck, 1995). First, the younger the child is, the less reliable the testimony of that child can be expected to be. In particular, children of preschool age are much more susceptible to suggestive questioning that tries to steer them to a certain response than are school-age children or adults. Second, when a questioner is coercive or even just seems to want a particular answer, children can be quite susceptible to providing the adult with what he or she wants to hear. Given the pressures involved in court cases, such forms of questioning may be unfortunately prevalent. For instance, when asked a yes-or-no question, even if they don't know the answer, most children will give an answer. If the question has an explicit "I don't know" option, most children, when they do not know an answer, will admit they do not know rather than speculate (Waterman, Blades, & Spencer, 2001). Third, children may believe that they recall observing things that others have said they observed. In other words, they hear a story about something that took place and then believe that they have observed what allegedly took place. If the child has some intellectual disability, memory for the event is even more likely to be distorted, at least when a significant delay has occurred between the time of the event and the time of recall (Henry & Gudjonsson, 2003). Perhaps even more than eyewitness testimony from adults, the testimony of children must be interpreted with great caution.

Steps can be taken to enhance eyewitness identification (e.g., using methods to reduce potential biases, to reduce the pressure to choose a suspect from a limited set of options, and to ensure that each member of an array of suspects fits the description given by the eyewitness, yet offers diversity in other ways; described in Wells, 1993). Research also indicates that suggestive interviews can cause biases in memory (Melnyk & Bruck, 2004). This is especially likely when these interviews take place close in time to the actual event. After a crime, the witnesses are generally interviewed as soon as possible. Therefore, steps must be taken to ensure that the questions asked of witnesses are not leading questions, especially when the witness is a child. This caution can decrease the likelihood of distortion of memory. In addition, some psychologists (e.g., Loftus, 1993a, 1993b) and many defense attorneys believe that jurors should be advised that the degree to which the eyewitness feels confident of her or his identification does not necessarily correspond to the degree to which the eyewitness is actually accurate in her or his identification of the defendant as being the culprit. At the same time, some psychologists (e.g., Egeth, 1993; Yuille, 1993) and many prosecutors believe that the existing evidence, based largely on simulated eyewitness studies rather than on actual eyewitness accounts, is not strong enough to risk attacking the credibility of eyewitness testimony when such testimony might send a true criminal to prison, preventing the person from committing further crimes.

Repressed Memories

Might you have been exposed to a traumatic event as a child but have been so traumatized by this event that you now cannot remember it? Some psychotherapists have begun using hypnosis and related techniques to elicit from people what are alleged to be repressed memories. Repressed memories are memories that are alleged to have been pushed down into unconsciousness because of the distress they cause. Such memories, according to the view of psychologists who believe in their existence, are very inaccessible, but they can be dredged out (Briere & Conte, 1993).

Do repressed memories actually exist? Many psychologists strongly doubt their existence (Ceci & Loftus, 1994; Lindsay & Read, 1994; Loftus & Ketcham, 1994; Pennebaker & Memon, 1996; Roediger & McDermott, 1995, 2000). Others are at least highly skeptical (Bowers & Farvolden, 1996; Brenneis, 2000). There are many reasons for this skepticism, which are provided in the following section. First, some therapists may be inadvertently planting ideas in their clients' heads. In this way, they may be creating false memories of events that never took place. Indeed, creating false memories is relatively easy, even in people with no particular psychological problems. Such memories can be implanted by using ordinary, nonemotional stimuli (Roediger & McDermott, 1995). Second, showing that implanted memories are false is often extremely hard to do. Reported incidents often end up, as in the case of childhood sexual abuse, merely pitting one person's word against another (Schooler, 1994). At the present time, no compelling evidence points to the existence of such memories. But psychologists also have not reached the point where their existence can be ruled out definitively. Therefore, no clear conclusion can be reached at this time.

The Roediger-McDermott (1995) paradigm, which is adapted from work of Deese (1959), is able to show the effects of memory distortion in the laboratory. Participants receive a list of 15 words strongly associated with a critical but nonpresented word. For example, the participants might receive 15 words strongly related to the word *sleep* but never receive the word *sleep*. The recognition rate for the nonpresented word (in this case, *sleep*) was comparable to that for presented words. This result has been replicated multiple times (McDermott, 1996; Schacter, Verfaellie, & Pradere, 1996; Sugrue & Hayne, 2006). Even when shorter lists were used, there was an increased level of false recognition for nonpresented items. In one experiment, lists as short as three items revealed this effect, although to a lesser degree (Coane & associates, 2007). Embedding the list in a story can increase this effect in young children. This strategy strengthens the shared context and increases the probability of a participant's falsely recognizing the nonpresented word (Dewhurst, Pursglove, & Lewis, 2007).

Why are people so weak in distinguishing what they have heard from what they have not heard? One possibility is a *source-monitoring error,* which occurs when a person attributes a memory derived from one source to another source. Research by Marcia Johnson and her colleagues (Johnson, 1996; Johnson, Hashtroudi, & Lindsay, 1993; Lindsay & Johnson, 1991) suggests that people frequently have difficulties in *source monitoring,* or figuring out the origins of a memory. They may believe they read an article in a prestigious newspaper, such as the *New York Times,* when in fact they saw it in a tabloid on a supermarket shelf while waiting to check out. When people hear a list of words not containing a word that is highly associated with the other words, they may believe that their recall of that central word is from the list rather than from their minds.

Another possible explanation of this increased false recognition is spreading activation. In spreading activation, every time an item is studied, you think of the items related to that item. Imagine a metaphorical spider web with a word in the middle. Branching out from that word are all the words relating to that word. There will of course be individual differences in the construction of these webs, but there will also be a lot of overlap. For instance, when you read the word *nap*, words like *sleep*, *bed*, and *cat* may be activated in your mind. In this way, activation branches out from the original word *nap*. If you see 15 words, all of which activate the word *sleep*, it is likely that, via a source-monitoring error, you may think you had been presented the word *sleep*. Some recent work supports the spreading-activation theory of errors in this paradigm (Dodd & MacLeod, 2004; Hancock & associates, 2003; Roediger, Balota, & Watson, 2001). This theory is not, however, universally accepted (Meade & associates, 2007).

Context Effects on Encoding and Retrieval

As studies of constructive memory show, our cognitive contexts for memory clearly influence our memory processes of encoding, storing, and retrieving information. Studies of expertise also show how existing schemas may provide a cognitive context for encoding, storing, and retrieving new information. Specifically, experts generally have more elaborated schemas than do novices in regard to their areas of expertise (e.g., Chase & Simon, 1973; Frensch & Sternberg, 1989). These schemas provide a cognitive context in which the experts can operate. The use of schemas makes integration and organization relatively easy. They fill in gaps when provided with partial or even distorted information and visualize concrete aspects of verbal information. They also can implement appropriate metacognitive strategies for organizing and rehearsing new information. Clearly, expertise enhances our confidence in our recollected memories.

Another factor that enhances our confidence in recall is the perceived clarity— the vividness and richness of detail—of the experience and its context. When we are recalling a given experience, we often associate the degree of perceptual detail and intensity with the degree to which we are accurately remembering the experience (Johnson & associates, 1988; Johnson, Hashtroudi, & Lindsay, 1993; Johnson, Nolde, & De Leonardis, 1996; Johnson & Raye, 1981). We feel greater confidence that our recollections are accurate when we perceive them with greater richness of detail. Although this heuristic for reality monitoring is generally effective, there are some situations in which factors other than accuracy of recall may lead to enhanced vividness and detail of our recollections (Neisser, 1982). When you can recall the context of the learning experience, there is an increased activation of the hippocampus (Eldridge & associates, 2000). Events that involve emotional stimuli also produce an increased activation in the amygdala. This activation leads to an enhancement of explicit memory (Milner, Squire, & Kandel, 1998; Roberson-Nay & associates, 2006). Interestingly, electrical stimulation of either the hippocampus or the amygdala can lead to recall and even hallucinations of autobiographical memories (Vignal & associates, 2007).

In particular, an oft-studied form of vivid memory is the **flashbulb memory**—a memory of an event so powerful that the person remembers the event as vividly as if it were indelibly preserved on film (Brown & Kulik, 1977). People old enough to recall the assassination of President John Kennedy may have flashbulb memories of this event. Some people also have flashbulb memories for the explosion of the space shuttle *Challenger*, the destruction of the World Trade Center on 9/11, or momentous events in their personal lives. The emotional intensity of an experience may enhance the likelihood that we will recall the particular experience (over other experiences) ardently and perhaps accurately (Bohannon, 1988). A related view is that a memory is most likely to become a flashbulb memory under three circumstances. These are that the memory trace is important to the individual, is surprising, and has an emotional effect on the individual (Conway, 1995).

Some investigators suggest that flashbulb memories may be more vividly recalled because of their emotional intensity. Other investigators, however, suggest that the vividness of recall may be the result of the effects of rehearsal. The idea here is that we frequently retell, or at least silently contemplate, our experiences of these momentous events. Perhaps our retelling also enhances the perceptual intensity of our recall (Bohannon, 1988). Other findings suggest that flashbulb memories may be perceptually rich (Neisser & Harsch, 1993). In this view, they may be recalled with relatively greater confidence in the accuracy of the memories (Weaver, 1993) but not actually be any more reliable or accurate than any other recollected memory (Neisser & Harsch, 1993; Weaver, 1993). Suppose flashbulb memories are indeed more likely to be the subject of conversation or even silent reflection. Then perhaps, at each retelling of the experience, we reorganize and construct our memories such that the accuracy of our recall actually diminishes while the perceived vividness of recall increases over time. At present, researchers heatedly debate whether studies of such memories as a special process are a flash in the pan (e.g., Cohen, McCloskey, & Wible, 1990) or a flash of insight into memory processes (e.g., Schmidt & Bohannon, 1988).

Some interesting effects of flashbulb memory involve the role of emotion. The more a person is emotionally involved in an event, the better the person's memory for that event is. Also, over time, memory for the event degrades (Smith, Bibi, & Sheard, 2004). In one study, more than 70% of people questioned reported seeing on September 11, 2001, the day of the World Trade Center attacks, the first plane hit the first tower. However, this footage was not available until the next day (Pezdek, 2003, 2006). Thus, they could not have seen on September 11 the footage of the plane hitting the tower. These distortions illustrate the constructive nature of flashbulb memories. These findings further indicate that flashbulb memories are not immune to distortion, as once was thought.

The emotional intensity of a memorable event is not the only way in which emotions, moods, and states of consciousness affect memory. Our moods and states of consciousness also may provide a context for encoding that affects later retrieval of semantic memories. Thus, when we encode semantic information during a particular mood or state of consciousness, we may more readily retrieve that information when in the same state again (Baddeley, 1989; Bower, 1983). Regarding state of consciousness, something that is encoded when we are influenced by alcohol or other drugs may be retrieved more readily while under those same influences again (Eich, 1980, 1995). On the whole, however, the "main effect" of alcohol and many drugs is stronger than the interaction. In other words, the depressing effect of alcohol and many drugs on memory is greater than the facilitating effect of recalling something in the same drugged state as when one encoded it.

In regard to mood, some investigators have suggested a factor that may maintain depression. In particular, the depressed person can more readily retrieve memories of previous sad experiences, which may further the continuation of the depression (Baddeley, 1989). If psychologists or others can intervene to prevent the continuation of this vicious cycle, the person may begin to feel happier. As a result, other happy memories may be more easily retrieved, thus further relieving the depression, and so on. Perhaps the folk-wisdom advice to "think happy thoughts" is not entirely unfounded. In fact, under laboratory conditions, participants seem more accurately to recall items that have pleasant associations than they recall items that have unpleasant associations (Matlin & Underhill, 1979). Interestingly, people suffering from depression tend to have deficits in forming and recalling memories (Bearden & associates, 2006).

Emotions, moods, states of consciousness, schemas, and other features of our internal context clearly affect memory retrieval. In addition, even our external contexts may affect our ability to recall information. We appear to be better able to recall information when we are in the same physical context as the one in which we learned the material (Godden & Baddeley, 1975). In one experiment, 16 underwater divers were asked to learn a list of 40 unrelated words. Learning occurred either while the divers were on shore or while they were 20 feet beneath the sea. Later, they were asked to recall the words when either in the same environment as where they had learned them or in the other environment. Recall was better when it occurred in the same place as did the learning.

Even infants demonstrate context effects on memory. Consider an operant-conditioning experiment in which the infants could make a crib mobile move in interesting ways by kicking it. Three month olds (Butler & Rovee-Collier, 1989) and 6 month olds (Borovsky & Rovee-Collier, 1990) were given an opportunity to kick a distinctive crib mobile in the same context (i.e., surrounded by a distinctive bumper lining the periphery of the crib) in which they first learned to kick it or in a different context. They kicked more strongly in the same context. The infants showed much less kicking when in a different context or when presented with a different mobile.

From these results, such learning seems highly context dependent. However, in one set of studies, 3-month-olds (Rovee-Collier & DuFault, 1991) and 6-month-olds (Amabile & Rovee-Collier, 1991) were offered operant-conditioning experiences in multiple contexts for kicking a distinctive mobile. They were soon thereafter placed in a novel context. It was unlike any of the contexts for conditioning. The infants retained the memory. They kicked the mobile at high rates in the novel context. Thus, when information is encoded in various contexts, the information also seems to be retrieved more readily in various contexts. This effect occurs at least when there is minimal delay between the conditioning contexts and the novel context. However, consider what happened when the novel context occurred after a long delay. The infants did not show increased kicking. Nevertheless, they still showed context-dependent memory for kicking in the familiar contexts (Amabile & Rovee-Collier, 1991).

All of the preceding context effects may be viewed as an interaction between the context for encoding and the context for retrieval of encoded information. The results of various experiments on retrieval suggest that how items are encoded has a strong effect both on how and on how well items are retrieved. This relationship is called **encoding specificity**—what is recalled depends on what is encoded (Tulving & Thomson, 1973). Consider a rather dramatic example of encoding specificity. We know that recognition memory is virtually always better than recall. For example, recognizing a word that you have learned is easier than recalling it. After all, in recognition you have only to say whether you have seen the word. In recall, you have to generate the word and then mentally confirm whether it appeared on the list.

In one experiment, Watkins and Tulving (1975) had participants learn a list of 24 paired associates, such as *ground-cold* and *crust-cake*. Participants were instructed to learn to associate each response (such as *cold*) with its stimulus word (such as *ground*). After participants had studied the word pairs, they were given an irrelevant task. Then they were given a recognition test with distracters. Participants were asked simply to circle the words they had seen previously. Participants recognized an average of 60% of the words from the list. Then, participants were provided with the 24 stimulus words. They were asked to recall the responses. Their cued recall was 73%. Thus, recall was better than recognition. Why? According to the encoding-specificity hypothesis, the stimulus was a better cue for the word than the word itself. The reason was that the words had been learned as paired associates.

As mentioned previously (see Chapter 5), the link between encoding and retrieval also may explain the self-reference effect (Greenwald & Banaji, 1989). Specifically, the main cause of the self-reference effect is not due to unique properties of self-referent cues. Rather, it is due to a more general principle of encoding and retrieval: When individuals generate their own cues for retrieval, they are much more potent than when other individuals do so. Other researchers have confirmed the importance of making cues meaningful to the individual to enhance memory. For example, consider what happened when participants made up their own retrieval cues. They were able to remember, almost without errors, lists of 500 and 600 words (Mantyla, 1986). For each word on a list, participants were asked to generate another word (the cue) that to them was an appropriate description or property of the target word. Later, they were given a list of their cue words. They were asked to recall the target word. Cues were most helpful when they were both *compatible* with the target word and *distinctive,* in that they would not tend to generate a large number of related words. For example, if you are given the word *coat,* then *jacket* might be both compatible and distinctive as a cue. However, suppose you came up with the word *wool* as a cue. That cue might make you think of a number of words, such as *fabric* and *sheep,* that are not the target word.

To summarize, retrieval interacts strongly with encoding. Suppose you are studying for a test and want to recall well at the time of testing. Organize the information you are studying in a way that appropriately matches the way in which you will be expected to recall it. Similarly, you will recall information better if the level of processing for encoding matches the level of processing for retrieval (Moscovitch & Craik, 1976).

Memory Development

Many changes occur in memory with development (Bauer & Van Abbema, 2003). What are some of these changes?

Metacognitive Skills and Memory Development

Some researchers also have suggested that older children may have greater processing resources (Kail & Bisanz, 1992), such as attentional resources and working memory. These resources may underlie the overall greater speed of cognitive processing of older children. According to this view, the reason that older children seem able to process information more quickly than younger children may be because the older children can hold more information for active processing. Hence, in addition to being able to organize information into increasingly large and complex chunks, older children may be able to hold more chunks of information in working memory.

Children appear to develop and use increasing metamemory skills and various other kinds of metacognitive skills. These skills involve the understanding and control of cognitive processes. Examples are monitoring and modifying one's own cognitive processes while one is engaged in tackling cognitive tasks (Brown, 1978; Flavell & Wellman, 1977). Many information-processing researchers have been interested in the specific metacognitive skills of older children. An example is work on the understanding of appearance and reality. For example, 4- and 5-year-old children were shown imitation objects such as a sponge that looked exactly like a rock (Flavell, Flavell, & Green, 1983). The researchers encouraged the children to play with the imitations so they could become thoroughly familiar with the objects. In this way, the children would see clearly that the fakes were not what they appeared to be. Children then had to answer questions about the identity of the objects. Afterward, the children were asked to view the objects through a blue plastic sheet and to make color judgments about the objects. The sheet distorted the perceived hues of the objects. The children also were asked to make size judgments while viewing the objects through a magnifying glass. The children were fully aware that they were viewing the objects through these intermediaries.

The children's errors formed an interesting pattern. There were two fundamental kinds of errors. When asked to report reality (the way the object actually was), the children would sometimes report appearance (the way the object looked through the blue plastic or the magnifying glass). When asked to report appearance, they would sometimes report the reality. In other words, 4- and 5-year-old children did not yet clearly perceive the distinction between appearance and reality.

Actually, many scholars would agree with the observation that young children often fail to distinguish appearance from reality. Their failure to conserve quantity also may be attributed to their attention to the change in appearance, rather than to the stability of the quantity. Children also increasingly profit from and eventually even seek out feedback regarding the outcomes of their cognitive efforts. These changes in encoding, memory organization and storage, metacognition, and use of feedback seem to affect children's cognitive development across many specific domains. In addition, however, some cognitive-developmental changes seem to be domain specific.

The use of external memory aids, rehearsal, and many other memory strategies seems to come naturally to almost all of us as adults—so much so that we may take for granted that we have always done it; we have not. Lynne Appel and her colleagues (1972) designed an experiment to discover the extent to which young children spontaneously rehearse. They showed colored pictures of common objects to children at three grade levels: preschoolers, first-graders, and fifth-graders. Children were instructed either to "look at" the names of 15 pictures or to "remember" the names for a later test.

When children were instructed just to look at the pictures, almost no children exhibited rehearsal. In the memory condition, some of the young children showed some—but not much—rehearsal. Very few of the preschoolers seemed to know that rehearsing would be a good idea when they would later be asked to recall information. Moreover, the performance of the preschoolers was no better in the memory condition than in the looking condition.

Older children performed better. A major difference between the memory of younger and older children (as well as adults) is not in basic mechanisms, but in learned strategies, such as rehearsal (Flavell & Wellman, 1977). Young children seriously overestimate their ability to recall information. They rarely spontaneously use rehearsal strategies when asked to recall items. That is, young children seem not to know about many memory-enhancing strategies.

In addition, even when young children do know about such strategies, they do not always use them. For example, even when trained to use rehearsal strategies in one task, most do not transfer the use of that strategy. They do not carry over their learning from one task to other tasks (Flavell & Wellman, 1977; Jarrold, Baddeley, & Hewes, 2000). Thus, young children appear to lack not only the knowledge of strategies but also the inclination to use them when they do know about them. Older children understand that to retain words in short-term memory, they need to rehearse. Younger children do not have this understanding. In a nutshell, younger children lack metamemory skills.

Whether children rehearse is not just a function of age. Mentally retarded children are much less likely to rehearse spontaneously than are children of normal intelligence (Brown & associates, 1973). Indeed, if such children are trained to rehearse, their performance can be improved greatly (Belmont & Butterfield, 1971; Butterfield, Wambold, & Belmont, 1973). However, the mentally retarded performers will not always spontaneously transfer their learning to other tasks. For example, if the children are taught to rehearse with lists of numbers but then are presented with a list of animals, they may have to be taught all over again to rehearse for the new kinds of items, as well as for the old. In children with attention deficit hyperactivity disorder, where memory impairments are frequently observed, there also seems to be an underreliance on rehearsal (Kilingberg, Forssberg, & Westerberg, 2002).

Culture, experience, and environmental demands also affect the use of memory-enhancing strategies. For example, Western children generally have more formal schooling than do non-Western children. As a result, they are given much more practice using rehearsal strategies for remembering isolated bits of information. In contrast, Guatemalan children and Australian aboriginal children generally have many more opportunities to become adept at using memory-enhancing strategies that rely on spatial location and arrangements of objects (Kearins, 1981; Rogoff, 1986).

Another aspect of metamemory skill involves cognitive monitoring. In monitoring, the individual tracks and, as needed, readjusts an ongoing train of thought. Cognitive monitoring may consist of several related skills (Brown, 1978; see also Brown & DeLoache, 1978). For instance, you are realizing "what you know and what you do not know" (Brown, 1978, p. 82). You learn to be aware of your own mind and the degree of your own understanding (Holt, 1964). Other work on the development of cognitive monitoring proposes a distinction between self-monitoring and self-regulation strategies (Nelson & Narens, 1994). Self-monitoring is a bottom-up process of keeping track of current understanding, involving the improving ability to predict memory performance accurately. Self-regulation is a top-down process of central executive control over planning and evaluation. Children benefit from training in using such cognitive monitoring processes to enhance their use of appropriate strategies (see Schneider & Bjorklund, 1998).

Recall also that physiological maturation of the brain and increasing content knowledge may partially explain why adults and older children generally perform better on memory tests than do younger children. These physiological and experience-based changes augment the changes in memory processes. Examples are increased knowledge about and inclination to use metamemory strategies. The goal of such strategies is to be able eventually to retrieve stored information at will.

An important metacognitive development is the acquisition of a theory of mind—that is, an understanding of how the mind operates (Keil, 1999; Perner, 1998, 1999). As children grow older, their theory of mind becomes more sophisticated. Consider an example (Perner, 1999, p. 207): "Maxi puts his chocolate into the cupboard. He goes out to play. While he is outside he can't see that his mother comes and transfers the chocolate from the cupboard into the table drawer. She then leaves to visit a friend. When Maxi comes home to get his chocolate, where will he look for it?" Children below the age of 3 typically give the wrong answer, believing that Maxi will search for the chocolate in the drawer where it actually is. By age 3, some children start to get the problem right. By 4 years of age, most children solve the problem correctly, although even some 5 and 6 year olds still make errors (Ruffman & associates, 1998). Autistic children seem to lack or have a seriously defective theory of mind (Baron-Cohen, Leslie, & Frith, 1985; Perner, 1999).

Early development of theory of mind is related to verbal intelligence, communication abilities, and the number of siblings that a child has (McAlister & Peterson, 2007; Resches & Perez Pereira, 2007). This finding is not surprising, given that increased verbal and communication abilities and increased number of siblings are likely to increase the amount of interpersonal experience children have. Therefore, increased verbal abilities and number of siblings are likely to help the child to have increased ability to put himself or herself in another's shoes.

Throughout late childhood and most of adulthood, memory abilities remain relatively constant. However, in many older adults, memory abilities begin to decline. Many studies have noted a decrease in the amount of new material and skills that can be learned as we age (Collie & associates, 2001; Tunney & associates, 2002). It is apparent that memory decline in older adults occurs as a result in changes in the frontal-striatal system. These changes include changes in white matter and depletion in neurotransmitters (Buckner, 2004). Also, a decrease in hippocampal activity is associated with decline in memory (Cabeza & associates, 2004). These changes are different from the brain changes that are observed in patients with Alzheimer's disease (see Chapter 5).

This chapter and the previous chapter have indicated many situations in which knowledge and memory interact, such as when prior knowledge influences encoding and retrieval. The following two chapters describe how we represent knowledge. They emphasize the roles of mental imagery and semantic knowledge.

Key Themes

This chapter illustrates several of the key themes first presented in Chapter 1.

First, it highlights the issue of validity of causal inference versus ecological validity. Some researchers, such as Mahzarin Banaji and Robert Crowder, have argued that laboratory research yields findings that maximize not only experimental control but also ecological validity. Ulric Neisser has disagreed, suggesting that if one wishes to study everyday memory, one must study it in everyday settings. Ultimately, the two kinds of research together are likely to maximize our understanding of memory phenomena. Typically, there is no one right way to do research. Rather, we learn the most when we use a variety of methods that converge on a set of common findings.

Secondly, the chapter raises the issue of domain specificity versus domain generality. Mnemonics discussed in this chapter work better in certain domains than they do in others. For example, you may be able to devise mnemonics better if you are highly familiar with a domain, such as was the case for the runner studied by Chase, Ericsson, and Faloon (discussed in Chapter 5). In general, the more knowledge you have about a domain, the easier it will be to chunk information in that domain.

Thirdly, the chapter raises an interesting issue of rationalism versus empiricism. This issue is the extent to which courts should rely on empirical evidence from psychological research to guide what they do. To what extent should the credibility of witnesses be determined by rational considerations (e.g., were they at the scene of a crime, or are they known to be trustworthy) and to what extent by empirical considerations revealed by psychological research (e.g., being at the scene of a crime does not guarantee credible testimony, and people's judgments of trustworthiness are often incorrect)? Court systems often work on the basis of rational considerations—of what should be. Psychological research reveals what is.

Get some friends or family members to help you again. Tell them that you are going to read a list of words, and as soon as you finish, they are to write down as many words as they can remember in any order they wish. Read the following words to them about 1 second apart: *book, peace, window, run, box, harmony, hat, voice, tree, begin, anchor, hollow, floor, area, tomato, concept, arm, rule, lion, hope.* After giving them enough time to try to remember the words, total their number of recollections in the following groups of four: (1) *book, peace, window, run;* (2) *box, harmony, hat, voice;* (3) *tree, begin, anchor, hollow;* (4) *floor, area, tomato, concept;* (5) *arm, rule, lion, hope.* Most likely, your friends and family members will remember more from groups 1 and 5 than from groups 2, 3, and 4, with group 3 the least recalled group. This exercise demonstrates the serial-position curve. Save the recollections for a demonstration in Chapter 7.

Summary

1. **What have cognitive psychologists discovered regarding how we encode information for storing it in memory?** Encoding of information in short-term memory appears to be largely, although not exclusively, acoustic in form. Information in short-term memory is susceptible to acoustic confusability—that is, errors based on sounds of words. But there is some visual and semantic encoding of information in short-term memory. Information in long-term memory appears to be encoded primarily in a semantic form. Thus, confusions tend to be in terms of meanings rather than in terms of the sounds of words. In addition, some evidence points to the existence of visual encoding, as well as of acoustic encoding, in long-term storage.

Transfer of information into long-term storage may be facilitated by several factors. One is rehearsal of the information, particularly if the information is elaborated meaningfully. A second is organization, such as categorization of the information. A third is the use of mnemonic devices. And a fourth is the use of external memory aids, such as writing lists or taking notes. In addition, people tend to remember better when knowledge is acquired through distributed practice across various study sessions, rather than through massed practice. However, the distribution of time during any given study session does not seem to affect transfer into long-term memory. The effects of distributed practice may be due to a hippocampal-based mechanism that results in rapid encoding of new information to be integrated with existing memory systems over time, perhaps during sleep.

2. **What affects our ability to retrieve information from memory?** Studying retrieval from long-term memory is difficult due to problems of differentiating retrieval from other memory processes.

It also is difficult to differentiate accessibility from availability. Retrieval of information from short-term memory appears to be in the form of serial exhaustive processing. This implies that a person always sequentially checks all information on a list. Nevertheless, some data may be interpreted as allowing for the possibility of self-terminating serial processing and even of parallel processing.

3. **How does what we know or what we learn affect what we remember?** Two of the main theories of forgetting in short-term memory are decay theory and interference theory. Interference theory distinguishes between retroactive interference and proactive interference. Assessing the effects of decay, while ruling out both interference and rehearsal effects, is much harder. However, some evidence of distinctive decay effects has been found.

Interference also seems to influence long-term memory, at least during the period of consolidation. This period may continue for several years after the initial memorable experience.

Memory appears to be not only reconstructive—a reproduction of what was learned, based on recalled data and on inferences from only those data. It also is constructive—influenced by attitudes, subsequently acquired information, and schemas based on past knowledge. As shown by the effects of existing schemas on the construction of memory, schemas affect memory processes. So do other internal contextual factors, such as emotional intensity of a memorable experience, mood, and even state of consciousness. In addition, environmental context cues during encoding seem to affect later retrieval. Encoding specificity refers to the fact that what is recalled depends largely on what is encoded. How information is encoded at the time of learning will greatly affect how it is later recalled.

One of the most effective means of enhancing recall is for the individual to generate meaningful cues for subsequent retrieval.

4. **How does memory develop with age?** Memory generally improves with age up through adulthood and then declines in later life. The causes are many, but increased metacognitive skills seem to be essential for memory development to occur. Older children develop more advanced theories of mind. Children with autism may lack such theories.

Thinking about Thinking: Factual, Analytical, Creative, and Practical Questions

1. In what forms do we encode information for brief memory storage versus long-term memory storage?

2. What is the evidence for encoding specificity? Cite at least three sources of supporting evidence.

3. What is the main difference between two of the proposed mechanisms by which we forget information?

4. Compare and contrast some of the views regarding flashbulb memory.

5. Suppose that you are an attorney defending a client who is being prosecuted solely on the basis of eyewitness testimony. How could you demonstrate to members of the jury the frailty of eyewitness testimony?

6. Use the chapter-opening example from Bransford and Johnson as an illustration to make up a description of a common procedure without labeling the procedure. Try having someone read your description and then recall the procedure.

7. Make a list of 10 or more unrelated items you need to memorize. Choose one of the mnemonic devices mentioned in this chapter, and describe how you would apply the device to memorizing the list of items. Be specific.

8. What are three things you have learned about memory that can help you to learn new information so that you can effectively recall the information over the long term?

Key Terms

accessibility

autobiographical memory

availability

consolidation

constructive

decay

decay theory

distributed practice

encoding

encoding specificity

flashbulb memory

interference

interference theory

massed practice

metacognition

metamemory

mnemonic devices

primacy effect

proactive interference

recency effect

reconstructive

rehearsal

retrieval (memory)

retroactive interference

storage (memory)

 Explore CogLab by going to **http://coglab.wadsworth.com.** To learn more, examine the following experiments:

Brown-Peterson

False Memory

Serial Position

Sternberg Research

Von Restorff Effect

Encoding Specificity

Forgot It All Along

Remember/Know

Annotated Suggested Readings

Dewhurst, S. A., Pursglove, R. C., & Lewis, C. (2007). Story contexts increase susceptibility to the DRM illusion in 5-year-olds. *Developmental Science, 10*(3), 374–378. The use of the DRM in children is explored in this study. Many studies have explored ways to decrease the false-memory effect. This study exemplifies a way to increase the false-memory effect.

Pezdek, K. (2003). Event memory and autobiographical memory for the events of September 11, 2001. *Applied Cognitive Psychology, 17*(9), 1033–1045. A study examining flashbulb memory for September 11, 2001. Differences between personal and global memory are explored.

Schacter, D. L. (2002). *The seven sins of memory.* New York: Mariner. An interesting account of why people forget things they might otherwise remember. The book can be read by people with only a minimal background in cognitive psychology.

Representation and Manipulation of Knowledge in Memory: Images and Propositions

EXPLORING COGNITIVE PSYCHOLOGY

1. What are some of the major hypotheses regarding how knowledge is represented in the mind?

2. What are some of the characteristics of mental imagery?

3. How does knowledge representation benefit from both analogical images and symbolic propositions?

4. How may conceptual knowledge and expectancies influence the way we use images?

5. How do spatial skills develop?

Look carefully at the photos depicted in Figure 7.1. Describe to yourself what two of these people look like and sound like. Clearly, none of these people can truly exist in a physical form inside your mind. How are you able to imagine and describe them? You must have in your mind some form of *mental representation,* something that stands for something else, of what you know about them (Thagard, 1995; Von Eckardt, 1993, 1999). More generally, you use **knowledge representation,** the form for what you know in your mind about things, ideas, events, and so on that exist outside your mind.

Mental Representation of Knowledge

Ideally, cognitive psychologists would love to be able to observe directly how each of us represents knowledge. It would be as if we could take a videotape or a series of snapshots of ongoing representations of knowledge in the human mind. Unfortunately, direct empirical methods for observing knowledge representation are not available now. Moreover, such methods are unlikely to be available in the immediate future. When direct empirical methods are unavailable, several alternative methods remain. For one thing, we can ask people to describe their own knowledge representations and knowledge-representation processes. Unfortunately, none of us has conscious access to our own knowledge-representation processes, and self-reported information about these processes is highly unreliable (Pinker, 1985).

Another possibility is the rationalist approach. In this approach, we try to deduce logically the most reasonable account of how people represent knowledge. For centuries, philosophers have done exactly that. In classic epistemology—the study of the nature, origins, and limits of human knowledge—philosophers distinguished between two kinds of knowledge structures. The first is **declarative knowledge,** knowledge of facts that can be stated. Examples are the date of your birth, the name of your best friend, or the way a rabbit looks. The second kind of knowledge is **procedural knowledge,** knowledge of procedures that can be implemented. Examples are the steps in-

FIGURE 7.1

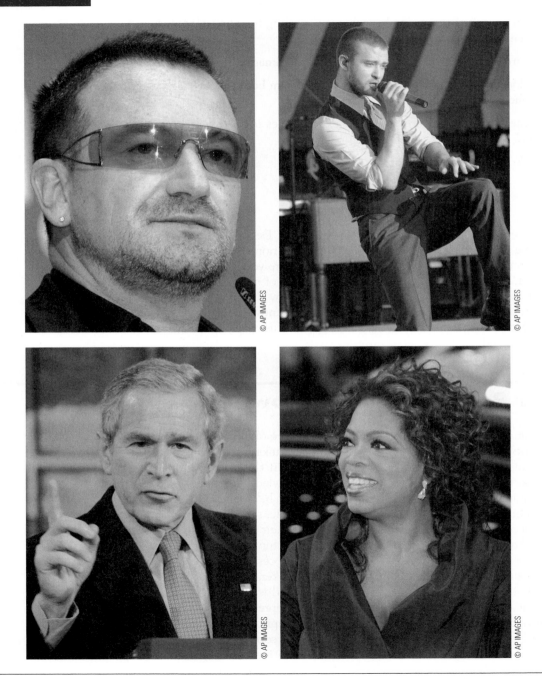

Look at each of these photos carefully. Next, close your eyes, and picture two of the people represented—people whom you recognize from reports in the media. Without looking again at the photos, mentally compare the appearances of the two people you have chosen.

volved in tying your shoelaces, adding a column of numbers, or driving a car. The distinction is between *knowing that* and *knowing how* (Ryle, 1949).

Cognitive psychologists have made extensive use of rationalist insights as a starting point for understanding cognition. But they rarely are content with rationalist descriptions alone. Instead, they seek some kind of empirical support for the insights proposed in rationalist accounts of cognition. There are two main sources of empirical data on knowledge representation. These are standard laboratory experiments and neuropsychological studies.

In experimental work, researchers indirectly study knowledge representation. They do so by observing how people handle various cognitive tasks that require the manipulation of mentally represented knowledge. In neuropsychological studies, researchers typically use one of two methods. One is to observe how the normal brain responds to various cognitive tasks involving knowledge representation. The other is to observe the links between various deficits in knowledge representation and associated pathologies in the brain.

External Representations: Pictures versus Words

In this chapter, we focus on the distinction between knowledge represented in mental pictures and knowledge represented in more symbolic forms, such as words or abstract propositions. Of course, cognitive psychologists chiefly are interested in our internal, mental representations of what we know. But to help our understanding, we consider first how external representations in words differ from such representations in pictures.

Some ideas are better and more easily represented in pictures and others in words. For example, suppose someone asks you, "What is the shape of a chicken egg?" You may find drawing easier than describing an egg. For many geometric shapes and concrete objects, pictures do seem to express myriad words about the object in an economical form. However, what if someone asks you, "What is justice?" Describing such an abstract concept in words would be very difficult. Doing so pictorially would be even harder.

As Figure 7.2 *a* and *b* shows, both pictures and words may be used to represent things and ideas. But neither form of representation actually retains all the characteristics of what is being represented. For example, neither the word *cat* nor the picture of the cat actually eats fish, meows, or purrs when petted. Both the word *cat* and the picture of this cat are distinctive representations of "catness." Each type of representation has distinctive characteristics.

As you just observed, the picture is relatively *analogous* to the real-world object it represents. The picture shows concrete attributes, such as shape and relative size. These attributes are similar to the features and properties of the real-world object the picture represents. Even if you cover up a portion of the figure of the cat, what remains is still analogous to a part of a cat. Under typical circumstances, most aspects of the picture may be grasped simultaneously. But you may scan the picture, zoom in for a closer look, or zoom out to see the big picture. Even when scanning or zooming, however, you do not have to follow any arbitrary rules for looking at features of the picture from top to bottom, left to right, and so on.

Unlike a picture of a cat, the word *cat* is a **symbolic representation,** meaning that the relationship between the word and what it represents is simply arbitrary. There is

FIGURE 7.2

(a)
(b) The cat is under the table.
(c) UNDER (CAT, TABLE)

We may represent things and ideas in pictures or in words. Neither pictures nor words capture all the characteristics of what they represent, and each more readily captures some kinds of information than other kinds. Some cognitive psychologists have suggested that we have (a) some mental representations that resemble pictorial, analogous images; (b) other mental representations that are highly symbolic, like words; and perhaps even (c) more fundamental propositional representations that are in a pure abstract "mentalese" that is neither verbal nor pictorial, which cognitive psychologists often represent in this highly simplified shorthand.

INVESTIGATING COGNITIVE PSYCHOLOGY	Observe Figure 7.2. What is the shape of the word *cat*? What is the shape of the picture of the cat? Cover part of the word. Now explain how what is left relates to the characteristics of a cat. Cover part of the picture. Now explain how what is left relates to the characteristics of a cat.

nothing inherently catlike about the word. Suppose you cover up part of the word. The remaining visible part no longer bears even a symbolic relationship to any part of the object it represents. Furthermore, because symbols are arbitrary, their use requires the application of rules. For example, in forming words, the sounds or letters also must be sequenced according to rules (e.g., "c-a-t," not "a-c-t" or "t-c-a"). In forming sentences, the words also must be sequenced according to rules. For example, one can say "the cat is under the table," not "table under cat the is."

Symbolic representations such as the word *cat* capture some kinds of information but not other kinds of information. The dictionary defines *cat* as "a carnivorous mammal (*Felis catus*) long domesticated as a pet and for catching rats and mice" (*Merriam-Webster's Collegiate Dictionary*, 1993). Suppose our own mental representations for the meanings of words resemble those of the dictionary. Then the word *cat* connotes an animal that eats meat ("carnivorous"), nurses its young ("mammal"), and so on. This information is abstract and general. It may be applied to any number of specific cats having any fur color or pattern. To represent additional characteristics, we must use additional words. Examples would be *black, Persian,* or *calico.*

The picture of the cat does not convey any of the abstract information conveyed by the word regarding what the cat eats, whether it nurses its young, and so on. However, the picture conveys a great deal of concrete information about this specific cat. For example, it communicates the exact position of the cat's legs, the angle at which we are viewing the cat, the length of the cat's tail, whether both of its eyes are open, and so on.

Pictures and words also represent relationships in different ways. The picture in Figure 7.2 *a* shows the spatial relationship between the cat and the table. For any given picture showing a cat and a table, the spatial (positional) relationship (e.g., beside, above, below, behind) will be represented concretely in the picture. In contrast, when using words, spatial relationships between things must be stated explicitly by a discrete symbol, such as a preposition. An example would be, "The cat is *under* the table." More abstract relationships, however, such as class membership, often are implied by the meanings of the words. Examples would be that cats are mammals or that tables are items of furniture. But abstract relationships rarely are implied through pictures.

To summarize, pictures aptly capture concrete and spatial information in a manner analogous to whatever they represent. Words handily capture abstract and categorical information in a manner that is symbolic of whatever they represent. Pictorial representations convey all features simultaneously. In general, any rules for creating or understanding pictures pertain to the analogous relationship between the picture and what it represents. They help ensure as much similarity as possible between the two. Representations in words usually convey information sequentially. They do so according to arbitrary rules that have little to do with what the words represent. But the words have a lot to do with the structure of the symbol system for using words. Each kind of representation is well suited to some purposes but not to others. For example, blueprints and identification photos serve different purposes than essays and memos do.

Now we have some preliminary ideas about external representations of knowledge. Let's turn to considering internal representations of knowledge. Specifically, how do we represent what we know in our minds? Do we have mental scenarios (pictures) and mental narratives (words)? In subsequent chapters on information processing and language, we discuss various kinds of symbolic mental representations. In this chapter, we focus on mental pictures.

Stephen M. Kosslyn is a professor of psychology at Harvard University. He is best known for his research showing that imagery is not a single, undifferentiated faculty but rather involves a number of distinct processes. He also has made major contributions to neuropsychology by identifying discrete areas of the brain associated with specific imagery processes.

Courtesy of Dr. Stephen M. Kosslyn

Mental Imagery

Imagery is the mental representation of things that are not currently being sensed by the sense organs (Behrmann, Kosslyn, & Jeannerod, 1996; Thomas, 2003). We often have images for objects, events, and settings. For example, recall one of your first experiences on a college campus. What were some of the sights, sounds, and even smells you sensed at that time? Might they have included cut grass, tall buildings, or tree-lined paths? These sensations are not immediately available to you at this moment. But you still can imagine them. In fact, mental imagery may represent things that have never been observed by your senses at any time. For example, imagine what it would be like to travel down the Amazon River. Mental images even may represent things that do not exist at all outside the mind of the person creating the image. For example, imagine how you would look if you had a third eye in the center of your forehead.

Imagery may involve mental representations in any of the sensory modalities, such as hearing, smell, or taste. Imagine the sound of a fire alarm, your favorite song, or your nation's anthem. Now imagine the smell of a rose, of fried bacon, or of an onion. Finally, imagine the taste of a lemon, of a pickle, or of your favorite candy. At least hypothetically, each form of mental representation is subject to investigation. Researchers have studied each of the sensory representations (e.g., Intons-Peterson, 1992; Intons-Peterson, Russell, & Dressel, 1992; Reisberg & associates, 1989; Reisberg, Wilson, & Smith, 1991; Smith, Reisberg, & Wilson, 1992).

Nonetheless, most research on imagery in cognitive psychology has focused on visual imagery. Such imagery includes the mental representation of visual knowledge such as objects or settings that are not presently visible to the eyes. Apparently, researchers are just like other people. Most of us are more aware of visual imagery than of other forms of imagery. When students kept a diary of their mental images, the students reported many more visual images than auditory, smell, touch, or taste images (Kosslyn & associates, 1990).

We use visual images to solve problems and to answer questions involving objects (Kosslyn, 1990; Kosslyn & Rabin, 1999). Which is darker red—a cherry or an apple? How many windows are there in your house or apartment? How do you get from your home to your first class of the day? How do you fit together the pieces of a puzzle or the component parts of an engine, a building, or a model? According to Kosslyn, to solve problems and answer questions such as these, we visualize the objects in question. In doing so, we mentally represent the images.

Many psychologists outside of cognitive psychology are interested in applications of mental imagery to other fields in psychology. Such applications include using guided-imagery techniques for controlling pain and for strengthening immune responses and otherwise promoting health. Such techniques are also helpful in overcoming psychological problems, such as phobias and other anxiety disorders. Design engineers, biochemists, physicists, and many other scientists and technologists use imagery to think about various structures and processes and to solve problems in their chosen fields. Not everyone is equally facile in creating and manipulating mental images, however. Research in applied settings and in the laboratory indicates that some of us are better able to create mental images than are others (Reisberg & associates, 1986). Research also indicates that the use of mental images can help to improve memory. In the case of persons with Down syndrome, the use of mental images when in conjunction with a story improved memory for the material as compared with just hearing the story (de la Iglesia, Buceta, & Campos, 2005; Kihara & Yoshikawa, 2001).

In just what form do we represent images in our minds? According to an extreme view of imagery, all images of everything we ever sense may be stored as exact copies of physical images. Realistically, to store every observed physical image in the brain seems impossible. The capacity of the brain and the structures and processes used by the brain would be inadequate to such a task (Kosslyn, 1981; Kosslyn & Pomerantz, 1977). Note the simple example in the following "Investigating Cognitive Psychology" box.

Dual-Code Theory: Analogical Images versus Symbols

According to dual-code theory, we use both imagined and verbal codes for representing information (Paivio, 1969, 1971). These two codes organize information into knowledge that can be acted on, stored somehow, and even later retrieved for subsequent use. According to Paivio, mental images are analogue codes. **Analogue codes** are a form of knowledge representation that preserves the main perceptual features of whatever is being represented for the physical stimuli we observe in our environment. For example, trees and rivers might be represented by analogue codes. Just as the movements of the hands on an analogue clock are analogous to the passage of time, the mental images we form in our minds are analogous to the physical stimuli we observe.

Look at your face in a mirror. Gradually turn your head from far right (to see yourself out of your left peripheral vision) to far left. Now tilt your head as far forward as you can then tilt it as far back as you can. All the while, make sure you still are seeing your reflection. Now make a few different expressions, perhaps even talking to yourself to exaggerate your facial movements. How could you possibly store a moving picture or even a series of separate images of your face or of other rotating objects?	**INVESTIGATING COGNITIVE PSYCHOLOGY**

In contrast, according to Paivio, our mental representations for words chiefly are represented in a symbolic code. A *symbolic code* is a form of knowledge representation that has been chosen arbitrarily to stand for something and that does not perceptually resemble whatever is being represented. Just as a digital watch uses arbitrary symbols (typically, numerals) to represent the passage of time, our minds use arbitrary symbols (words and combinations of words) to represent many ideas. A symbol may be anything that is arbitrarily designated to stand for something other than itself. For example, we recognize that the numeral "9" is a symbol for the concept of "nineness." It represents a quantity of nine of something. But nothing about the symbol in any way would suggest its meaning. Concepts like *justice* and *peace* would be represented symbolically. We arbitrarily have designated this symbol to represent the concept. But "9" has meaning only because we use it to represent a deeper concept.

To get an intuitive sense of how you may use each of the two kinds of representations, think about how you mentally represent all the facts you know about cats. Use your mental definition of the word *cat* and all the inferences you may draw from your mental image of a cat. Which kind of representation is more helpful for answering the following questions: Is a cat's tail long enough to reach the tip of the cat's nose if the cat is stretching to full length? Do cats like to eat fish? Are the back legs and the front legs of a cat exactly the same size and shape? Are cats mammals? Which is wider—a cat's nose or a cat's eye? Which kinds of mental representations were the most valuable for answering each of these questions?	**INVESTIGATING COGNITIVE PSYCHOLOGY**

IN THE LAB OF STEPHEN KOSSLYN

Courtesy of Dr. Stephen M. Kosslyn

If asked to decide what shape Mickey Mouse's ears are, most people report that they visualize the cartoon figure's ears and "see" that they are circular. Visual mental imagery hinges on such "seeing with the mind's eye" and is used not only to recall information that one has not thought about previously (such as the shape of that rodent's ears), but also in various forms of reasoning. For example, when considering how best to fit a bunch of backpacks, suitcases, and duffle bags into a trunk of a car, you might visualize each of them, and "see" how best to move them around and pack them efficiently—all before lifting a finger to heft a single bag into the trunk.

My lab has studied the nature of visual mental imagery for more than three decades now, and a considerable amount has been learned. First and foremost, visual mental imagery is a lot like visual perception, which occurs when one registers input from the eyes. That is, whereas imagery is a bit like playing a DVD and seeing the results on the screen, perception is more like seeing the input from a camera displayed on a screen (but this is just a metaphor; there's no little man in your head watching a screen—it's just signals being processed). In fact, when we asked participants to classify parts of visible (but degraded) objects and, in another part of the test, to classify parts of visualized objects, more than 90% of the same brain areas were activated in common (Ganis, Thompson, & Kosslyn, 2004).

However, there has been a controversy about just how low imagery goes in the brain. Specifically, is Area V1, the first part of the cortex to register input from the eyes, also used during visual mental imagery? Some neuroimaging studies find that this area is activated during visual imagery, but some do not. In a meta-analysis, considering the results from more than 50 such studies, Kosslyn and Thompson (2003) found that the variations in results reflected three factors: (1) If the task required "seeing" parts with relatively high resolution (e.g., as is necessary to use imagery to classify the shape of an animal's ears from memory), then the

first area is activated; (2) if the task is spatial (e.g., as required to decide in which arm the Statue of Liberty holds the torch), Area V1 is not activated, but parts of the parietal lobes are; and (3) if a more powerful scanning technique is used (e.g., using a more powerful magnet in a magnetic resonance imaging machine), then it is more likely that activation in Area V1 will be detected. However, the results from a meta-analysis are necessarily after the fact. Thus, we are now directly testing the inferences drawn from this analysis.

In addition, in order to use imagery in reasoning—such as in packing the trunk of a car—one must be able to transform the image (rotating objects in it, sliding them around, bending them, etc.). We have found that there are several distinct ways in which such processes occur. For example, you can imagine physically moving the objects in the images (e.g., twisting them by hand) or can imagine some external force moving them (e.g., watching a motor spin them around). In the former case, parts of the brain used to control actual movements are activated during mental imagery, but not when the same movement is imagined as a result of an external force's being at work (Kosslyn & associates, 2001).

In short, many questions about mental imagery that previously were purely in the realm of speculation now can be studied empirically, and each new discovery brings us a little closer toward understanding how we can "see" things that aren't there!

References

Ganis, G., Thompson, W. L., & Kosslyn, S. M. (2004). Brain areas underlying visual mental imagery and visual perception: an fMRI study. *Cognitive Brain Research, 20,* 226–241.

Kosslyn, S. M., & Thompson, W. L. (2003). When is early visual cortex activated during visual mental imagery? *Psychological Bulletin, 129,* 723–746.

Kosslyn, S. M., Thompson, W. L., Wraga, M., & Alpert, N. M. (2001). Imagining rotation by endogenous and exogenous forces: Distinct neural mechanisms for different strategies. *Neuroreport, 12,* 2519–2525.

Paivio also found some empirical support for his dual-code theory. He noted that verbal information seems to be processed differently than is imaginal information. For example, in one study, participants were shown both a rapid sequence of pictures and a sequence of words (Paivio, 1969). They then were asked to recall the words or the pictures in one of two ways. One way was at random so that they recalled as many as possible, regardless of the order in which the items were presented. The other way was in the correct sequence. Participants more easily recalled the pictures when they were allowed to do so in any order. But they more readily recalled the sequence in which the words were presented than the sequence for the pictures.

Other researchers also supported the notion that our minds use one system for representing verbal information and a different system for representing imaginal information. For example, it has been hypothesized that actual visual perception could interfere with simultaneous visual imagery. Similarly, the need to produce a verbal response could interfere with the simultaneous mental manipulation of words. A classic investigation tested this notion (Brooks, 1968). Participants performed either a visual task or a verbal task. The visual task involved answering questions requiring judgments about a picture that was presented briefly. The verbal task involved answering questions requiring judgments about a sentence that was stated briefly. Participants expressed their responses verbally (saying "yes" or "no" aloud), visually (pointing to an answer), or manually (tapping with one hand to agree and the other to disagree). The two interference conditions were a visual task requiring a visual (pointing) response and a verbal task requiring a verbal response. Interference was measured by slow-downs in response times. Brooks confirmed his hypothesis. Participants did show slower response times in performing the imaginal task when asked to respond using a competing visual display, as compared with when they were using a noninterfering response medium (i.e., either verbal or manual). Similarly, his participants showed more interference in performing the verbal task when asked to respond using a competing verbal form of expression, as compared with how they performed when responding manually or by using a visual display. Thus, a response involving visual perception can interfere with a task involving manipulations of a visual image. Similarly, a response involving verbal expression can interfere with a task involving mental manipulations of a verbal statement. These findings suggest the use of two distinct codes for mental representation of knowledge. The two codes are an imaginal (analogical) code and a verbal (symbolic) code.

Propositional Theory

Not everyone subscribes to the dual-code theory. An alternative theory of knowledge representation is sometimes termed a conceptual-propositional theory, or just a propositional theory (Anderson & Bower, 1973; Pylyshyn, 1973, 1978, 1981, 1984). According to this view, we do not store mental representations in the form of images. Rather, our mental representations (sometimes called "mentalese") more closely resemble the abstract form of a proposition. A proposition is the meaning underlying a particular relationship among concepts. According to this view, images are *epiphenomena*, secondary phenomena that occur as a result of other cognitive processes. Anderson and Bower have moved beyond their original conceptualization. Neither believes today in the idea that propositions are at the base of all mental representations. Others, such as Pylyshyn, however, still hold to this position.

How would a propositional representation work? Consider an example. To describe Figure 7.2 *a,* you could say, "The table is above the cat." You also could say, "The cat is beneath the table." Both these statements indicate the same relationship as "Above the cat is the table." With a little extra work, you probably could come up with a dozen or more ways of verbally representing this relationship. See this notion in Figure 7.2 *a.* Of course, imagery theorists would discount these explanations. They would explain the visual phenomena largely in terms of visual imagery and the neuropsychological mechanisms underlying it (Farah, 2000a, 2000b; Farah & Ratcliff, 1994; Hampson, Marks, & Richardson, 1990; Kosslyn, 1994a, 1994b; Kosslyn & Thompson, 2000; Logie & Denis, 1991).

Logicians have devised a shorthand means, called "predicate calculus," of expressing the underlying meaning of a relationship. It attempts to strip away the various superficial differences in the ways we describe the deeper meaning of a proposition:

[Relationship between elements]([Subject element], [Object element])

The logical expression for the proposition underlying the relationship between the cat and the table is shown in Figure 7.2 *c.* This logical expression, of course, would need to be translated by the brain into a format suitable for its internal mental representation.

Using Propositions

It is easy to see why the hypothetical construct of propositions is so widely accepted among cognitive psychologists. Propositions may be used to describe any kind of relationship. Examples of relationships include actions of one thing on another, attributes of a thing, positions of a thing, class membership of a thing, and so on, as shown in Table 7.1. In addition, any number of propositions may be combined to represent more complex relationships, images, or series of words. An example would be "The furry mouse bit the cat, who is now hiding under the table." The key idea is that the propositional form of mental representation is neither in words nor in images. Rather, it is in an abstract form representing the underlying meanings of knowledge. Thus, a proposition for a sentence would not retain the acoustic or visual properties of the words. Similarly, a proposition for a picture would not retain the exact perceptual form of the picture (Clark & Chase, 1972).

According to the propositional view (Clark & Chase, 1972), both images (e.g., of the cat and the table in Figure 7.2 *a*) and verbal statements (e.g., in Figure 7.2 *b*) are mentally represented in terms of their deep meanings. That is, they are represented as propositions, not as specific images or statements. According to propositional theory, imaginal and verbal information are encoded and stored as propositions. Then, when we wish to retrieve the information from storage, the propositional representation is retrieved. From it, our minds re-create the verbal or the imaginal code relatively accurately.

Some evidence suggests that these representations need not be exclusive. People seem to be able to employ both types of representations to increase their performance on cognitive tests (Talasli, 1990).

TABLE 7.1	Propositional Representations of Underlying Meanings

We may use propositions to represent any kind of relationship, including actions, attributes, spatial positions, class membership, or almost any other conceivable relationship. The possibility for combining propositions into complex propositional representational relationships makes the use of such representations highly flexible and widely applicable.

TYPE OF RELATIONSHIP	REPRESENTATION IN WORDS	PROPOSITIONAL REPRESENTATION*	IMAGINAL REPRESENTATION
Actions	A mouse bit a cat.	Bite [action] (mouse [agent of action], cat [object])	
Attributes	Mice are furry.	[external surface characteristic] (furry [attribute], mouse [object])	
Spatial positions	A cat is under the table.	[vertically higher position] (table, cat)	
Class membership	A cat is an animal.	[categorical membership] (animal [category], cat [member])	

*In this table, propositions are expressed in a shorthand form (known as "predicate calculus") commonly used to express underlying meaning. This shorthand is intended only to give some idea of how the underlying meaning of knowledge might be represented. It is not believed that this form is literally the form in which meaning is represented in the mind. In general, the shorthand form for representing propositions is this: [Relationship between elements] ([subject element], [object element]).

Analogical Limitations

Some evidence does suggest limits to analogical representation of images. For example, look quickly at Figure 7.3. Then look away. Does Figure 7.3 contain a *parallelogram* (a four-sided figure that has two pairs of parallel lines of equal length)? Participants in one study looked at figures such as this one. They had to determine whether particular shapes (e.g., a parallelogram) were or were not part of a given whole figure (as shown in Figure 7.3) (Reed, 1974). Overall performance was little better than chance. The participants appeared unable to call up a precise analogical mental image. They could not use a mental image to trace the lines to determine which component shapes were or were not part of a whole figure. To Reed, these findings suggested the use of a propositional code rather than an analogical one. Examples of a propositional code would be "a Star of David" or "two overlapping triangles, one of

FIGURE 7.3

Quickly glance at this figure and then cover it with your hand. Imagine the figure you just saw. Does it contain a parallelogram? From Cognition, *Third Edition, by Margaret W. Matlin. Copyright © 1994 by Holt, Rinehart and Winston. Reproduced by permission of the publisher.*

which is inverted." Another possible explanation is that people have analogical mental images that are imprecise in some ways.

There are additional limits to analogical representation (Chambers & Reisberg, 1985, 1992). Look now at Figure 7.4 *a*. Imagine the rabbit shown in the figure. Actually, the figure shown here is an *ambiguous figure*, meaning that it can be interpreted in more than one way. Ambiguous figures often are used in studies of perception. But these researchers decided to use such figures to determine whether mental representations of images are truly analogical to perceptions of physical objects. Without looking back at the figure, can you determine the alternative interpretation of Figure 7.4 *a*? When the participants in Chambers and Reisberg's study had difficulty, the researchers offered cues. But even participants with high visualization skills often were unable to conjure the alternative interpretation.

Finally, the investigators suggested to participants that they should call on their memory to draw their mental representations of the figures. Without looking again at the figure, briefly sketch Figure 7.4 *a*, based on your own mental representation of it. Once you have completed your sketch, try once more to see whether you can find an alternative interpretation of the figure. If you are like most of Chambers and Reisberg's participants, not until you have in front of you an actual *percept* (object of perception) of the figure can you guess at an alternative interpretation of the figure. These studies indicate that mental representations of figures are not the same as percepts of these figures. In case you have not yet guessed it, the alternative interpretation of the rabbit is a duck. In this interpretation, the rabbit's ears are the duck's bill.

One interpretation of Chambers and Reisberg's findings—an implausible one—is that there is no discrete imaginal code. An alternative and more plausible explana-

FIGURE 7.4

(a) (b)

(c)

(a) Look closely at the rabbit, then cover it with your hand and re-create it in your mind. Can you see a different animal in this image just by mentally shifting your perspective? (b) What animal do you observe in this figure? Create a mental image of this figure, and try to imagine the front end of this animal as the back end of another animal and the tail end of this animal as the front end of another animal. (c) Observe the animal in this figure, and create a mental image of the animal; cover the figure, and try to reinterpret your mental image as a different kind of animal (both animals probably are facing in the same direction). From D. Chambers and D. Reisberg (1985), "Can Mental Images be Ambiguous?" Journal of Experimental Psychology: Human Perception and Performance, 11, 317–328. *Copyright © 1985 by the American Psychological Association. Reprinted with permission. (b, c) Peterson, M. A., Kihlstrom, J. F., Rose, P. M., & Glisky, M. L. (1992). Mental images can be ambiguous: Reconstruals and reference-frame reversals.* Memory & Cognition, 20, 107–123. *Reprinted by permission of Psychonomic Society, Inc.*

tion is that a propositional code may override the imaginal code in some circumstances. That is, the initial interpretation of the figure in propositional code may override the imaginal code for the figure. Much earlier work suggested that semantic (verbal) information (e.g., labels for figures) tends to distort recall of visual images in the direction of the meaning of the images (Carmichael, Hogan, & Walter, 1932). For example, for each of the figures in the center column of Figure 7.5, observe the alternative interpretations for the figures recalled. Base your recall on the differing labels given for the figures.

Propositional Limits

In contrast to the work just discussed, there is some evidence that mental imagery may be manipulated directly, rather than via a propositional code (Finke, Pinker, & Farah, 1989). Participants in this study manipulated mental images by combining two

FIGURE 7.5

Reproduced figure	Verbal labels	Stimulus figures	Verbal labels	Reproduced figure
	Curtains in a window		Diamond in a rectangle	
	Seven		Four	
	Ship's wheel		Sun	
	Hourglass		Table	
	Kidney bean		Canoe	
	Pine tree		Trowel	
	Gun		Broom	
	Two		Eight	

Semantic labels clearly influence mental images, as shown here in the differing drawings based on mental images of objects given differing semantic (verbal) labels. (After Carmichael, Hogan, & Walter, 1932.)

distinct images to form a different mental image altogether. This manipulation of mental images may be viewed as an imaginal Gestalt experience. In the combined image, the whole of the two combined images differed from the sum of its two distinct parts. The study showed that in some situations, mental images can be combined effectively (e.g., the letter *H* and the letter *X*) to create mental images. They may be of geometric shapes (e.g., right triangles), of letters (e.g., *M*), or of objects (e.g., a bow tie). It appears that propositional codes are less likely to influence imaginal ones when participants create their own mental images, rather than when participants are presented with a picture to be represented. However, propositional codes may influence imaginal ones. This is especially likely when the picture used for creating an image is ambiguous (as in Figure 7.4 a–c) or rather abstract (as in Figure 7.3).

Other investigators have built on Finke's work regarding the construction of mental images (Finke, Pinker, & Farah, 1989). They presented an alternative view of Chambers and Reisberg's findings regarding the manipulation of ambiguous figures (see Figure 7.4 a) (Peterson & associates, 1992). They believe that the mental reinterpretation of ambiguous figures involves two manipulations. The first is a mental *realignment* of the reference frame. This would be a shift in the positional orientations of the figures on the mental "page" or "screen" on which the image is displayed. In Figure 7.4 a, the shift would be of the duck's back to the rabbit's front, and the duck's front to the rabbit's back. The second manipulation is a mental *reconstrual* (reinterpretation) of parts of the figure. This would be the duck's bill as the rabbit's ears. Participants may be unlikely to manipulate mental images spontaneously to reinterpret ambiguous figures. But such manipulations occur when participants are given the right context.

Under what conditions do participants mentally reinterpret their image of the duck-rabbit figure (see Figure 7.4 a) and some other ambiguous figures (Peterson & associates, 1992)? Some experiments differed in terms of the types of supporting hints.

Across experiments, from 20% to 83% of participants were able to reinterpret ambiguous figures, using one or more of the following hints:

1. *Implicit reference-frame hint*—in which participants first were shown another ambiguous figure involving realignment of the reference frame (e.g., see Figure 7.4 b; a hawk's head/a goose's tail, and a hawk's tail/a goose's head).

2. *Explicit reference-frame hint*—in which participants were asked to modify the reference frame by considering either "the back of the head of the animal they had already seen as the front of the head of some other animal" (Peterson & associates, 1992, p. 111; considered a conceptual hint) or "the front of the thing you were seeing as the back of something else" (p. 115; considered an abstract hint).

3. *Attentional hint*—in which participants were directed to attend to regions of the figure where realignments or reconstruals were to occur.

4. *Construals from "good" parts*—in which participants were asked to construe an image from parts determined to be "good" (according to both objective [geometrical] and empirical [inter-rater agreement] criteria), rather than from parts determined to be "bad" (according to similar criteria).

Additionally, some spontaneous reinterpretation of mental images for ambiguous figures may occur. This is particularly likely for images of figures that may be reinterpreted without realigning the reference frame. See, for example, Figure 7.4 c, which may be either a whole snail or an elephant's head, or possibly even a bird, a helmet, a leaf, or a seashell.

The investigators went on to suggest that the processes involved in constructing and manipulating mental images are similar to the processes involved in perceptual processes (Peterson & associates, 1992). An example would be the recognition of forms (discussed in Chapter 3). Not everyone agrees with this view. But some support for their views has been found by cognitive psychologists who hold that mental imagery and visual perception are functionally equivalent. Here, *functional equivalence* refers to individuals using about the same operations to serve about the same purposes for their respective domains. Overall, the weight of the evidence seems to indicate there are multiple codes rather than just a single code. But the controversy continues (Barsalou, 1994).

Mental Manipulations of Images

According to the **functional-equivalence hypothesis,** although visual imagery is not identical to visual perception, it is functionally equivalent to it. That is, as Paivio suggested decades ago, although we do not construct images that are exactly identical to percepts, we do construct images that are functionally equivalent to percepts. These functionally equivalent images are analogous to the physical percepts they represent. This view has many advocates (e.g., Farah, 1988b; Finke, 1989; Jolicoeur & Kosslyn, 1985a, 1985b; Rumelhart & Norman, 1988; Shepard & Metzler, 1971).

One investigator has suggested some principles of how visual imagery may be functionally equivalent to visual perception (Finke, 1989). These principles may be used as a guide for designing and evaluating research on imagery. Table 7.2 offers an idea of some of the research questions that may be generated, based on Finke's principles.

Evidence for functional equivalence can be seen in neuroimaging studies. In one study, participants either viewed or imagined an image. Activation of similar brain areas was noted, in particular in the frontal and parietal regions. However, there was no overlap in the areas associated with sensory processes, such as vision (Ganis, Thomspon, & Kosslyn, 2004).

Schizophrenia provides an interesting example of the similarities between perception and imagery. Many people who suffer from schizophrenia experience auditory hallucinations. Auditory hallucinations are the experience of "hearing" that occur in the absence of actual auditory stimuli. This "hearing" is the result of internally generated material. It is noted that these patients have difficulty discriminating between many different types of self-produced and externally provided stimuli (Blakemore & associates, 2000). Evidence from other researchers reveals that during auditory hallucinations there is abnormal activation of the auditory cortex (Lennox & associates, 2000). Additionally, activation of brain areas involved with receptive language is observed during auditory hallucinations (Ishii & associates, 2000). In sum, it is believed that auditory hallucinations occur at least in part because of malfunctions of auditory imaging system and problematic perception processes (Seal, Aleman, & McGuire, 2004). These challenges make it difficult for afflicted individuals to differentiate between internal images and the perception of external stimuli.

Mental Rotations

Basic Phenomena
Mental rotation involves rotationally transforming an object's visual mental image (Takano & Okubo, 2003). In a classic experiment, participants were asked to observe pairs of two-dimensional (2-D) pictures showing three-dimensional (3-D) geometric

TABLE 7.2	Principles of Visual Imagery: Questions

According to the functional-equivalence hypothesis, we represent and use visual imagery in a way that is functionally equivalent to that for physical percepts. Ronald Finke has suggested several principles of visual imagery that may be used to guide research and theory development.

PRINCIPLE	POSSIBLE QUESTIONS GENERATED FROM PRINCIPLES
1. Our mental transformations of images and our mental movements across images correspond to similar transformations of and movements across physical objects and percepts.	Do our mental images follow the same laws of motion and space that are observed in physical percepts? For example, does it take longer to manipulate a mental image at a greater angle of rotation than at a smaller one? Does it take longer to scan across a large distance in a mental image than across a smaller distance?
2. The spatial relations among elements of a visual image are analogous to those relations in actual physical space.	Are the characteristics of mental images analogous to the characteristics of percepts? For example, is it easier to see the details of larger mental images than of smaller ones? Are objects that are closer together in physical space also closer together in mental images of space?
3. Mental images can be used to generate information that was not explicitly stored during encoding.	After participants have been asked to form a mental image, can they answer questions that require them to infer information, based on the image, that was not specifically encoded at the time they created the image? For example, suppose that participants are asked to picture a tennis shoe. Can they later answer questions such as "How many lace-holes are there in the tennis shoe?"
4. The construction of mental images is analogous to the construction of visually perceptible figures.	Does it take more time mentally to construct a more complex mental image than a simpler one? Does it take longer to construct a mental image of a larger image than of a smaller one?
5. Visual imagery is functionally equivalent to visual perception in terms of the processes of the visual system used for each.	Are the same regions of the brain involved in manipulating mental imagery as are involved in manipulating visual percepts? For example, are similar areas of the brain activated when mentally manipulating an image, as compared with those involved when physically manipulating an object?

forms (Figure 7.6; Shepard & Metzler, 1971). As the figure shows, the forms were rotated from 0 to 180 degrees. The rotation was either in the picture plane (i.e., in 2-D space, as in Figure 7.6 *a*) or in depth (i.e., in 3-D space, as in Figure 7.6 *b*). In addition, participants were shown distracter forms. These were not rotations of the original stimuli (as in Figure 7.6 *c*). Participants then were asked to tell whether a given image was or was not a rotation of the original stimulus.

As shown in Figure 7.7, the response times for answering the questions about the figures formed a *linear function* of the degree to which the figures were rotated. For each increase in the degree of rotation of the figures, there was a corresponding increase in the response times. Furthermore, there was no significant difference between rotations in the picture plane and rotations in depth. These findings are functionally equivalent to what we might expect if the participants had been rotating physical objects in space. To rotate objects at larger angles of rotation takes longer. Whether the objects are rotated clockwise, counterclockwise, or in the third dimension of depth makes little difference. The finding of a relation between degree of angular

FIGURE 7.6

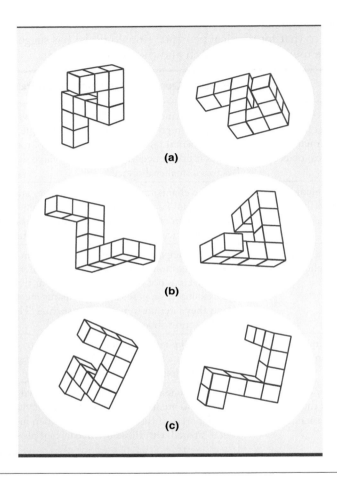

For which of these pairs of figures does the figure on the right show an accurate rotation of the figure on the left? Reprinted with permission from "Mental Rotation," by R. Shepard and J. Metzler. Science, *171(3972), 701–703. Copyright © 1971, American Association for the Advancement of Science.*

rotation and reaction time now has been replicated a number of times with a variety of stimuli (e.g., Jordan & Huntsman, 1990; Van Selst & Jolicoeur, 1994; see also Tarr, 1999).

To try your own hand at mental rotations, do the demonstration in the "Investigating Cognitive Psychology" box for yourself (based on Hinton, 1979).

Other researchers have supported these original findings in other studies of mental rotations. For example, they have found similar results in rotations of 2-D figures, such as letters of the alphabet (Jordan & Huntsman, 1990), cubes (Just & Carpenter, 1985), and body parts, in particular hands (Fiorio, Tinazzi & Aglioti, 2006; Fiorio & associates, 2007; Funk, Brugger, & Wilkening, 2005). In addition, response times are longer for *degraded stimuli*—stimuli that are blurry, incomplete, or otherwise less in-

FIGURE 7.7

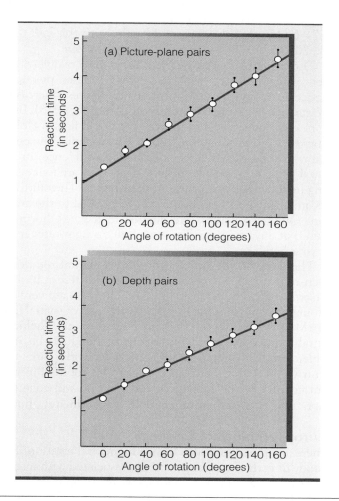

Response times to questions about mental rotations of figures show a linear relationship to the angle of rotation, and this relationship is preserved, whether the rotations are in the picture plane or are in depth. Reprinted with permission from "Mental Rotation," by R. Shepard and J. Metzler. Science, 171(3972), 701–703. Copyright © 1971, American Association for the Advancement of Science.

Imagine a cube floating in the space in front of you. Now, mentally grasp the left front bottom corner of the cube with your left hand. Also grasp the right back top corner of the cube with your right hand. While mentally holding those corners, rotate the cube so that the corner in your left hand is directly below the corner in your right hand (as if to form a vertical axis around which the cube would spin). How many corners of the imaginary cube are in the middle (i.e., not being grasped by your hands)? Describe the positions of the corners.

INVESTIGATING COGNITIVE PSYCHOLOGY

Roger N. Shepard is the Ray Lyman Wilbur professor emeritus of social science at Stanford University. Shepard is known best for his seminal work on the study of mental imagery, as well as his work on multidimensional scaling, on establishing general laws of cognition, and on visual thinking in general.

formative (Duncan & Bourg, 1983)—than for intact stimuli. Response times are also longer for complex items compared with simple items (Bethell-Fox & Shepard, 1988) and for unfamiliar figures compared with familiar ones (Jolicoeur, Snow, & Murray, 1987). Older adults have more difficulty with this task than younger adults (Band & Kok, 2000).

The benefits of increased familiarity also may lead to *practice effects*—improvements in performance associated with increased practice. When participants have practice in mentally rotating particular figures (increasing their familiarity), their performance improves (Bethell-Fox & Shepard, 1988). But this improvement appears not to carry over to rotation tasks for novel figures (Jolicoeur, 1985; Wiedenbauer, Schmid, & Jansen-Osmann, 2007). For example, few people have extensive experience with rotating actual geometrical cubes. Hence, in the demonstration with the mental cube, most people imagine that there are four remaining corners of the cube being held by the two corners in their hands. They further imagine that all four corners are aligned on a horizontal plane, parallel to the ground. In fact, six corners remain. Only two corners are aligned in a given horizontal plane (parallel to the ground) at any one time. Try it yourself, using whatever nonimaginary cube you can put your hands on.

The work of Shepard and others on mental rotation provides a direct link between research in cognitive psychology and research on intelligence. The kinds of problems studied by Shepard and his colleagues are very similar to problems that can be found on conventional psychometric tests of spatial ability. For example, the Primary Mental Abilities test of Louis Thurstone and Thelma Thurstone (1962) requires mental rotation of two-dimensionally pictured objects in the picture plane. Similar problems appear on other tests. Shepard's work points out a major contribution of cognitive research toward our understanding of intelligence. This contribution is the identification of the mental representations and cognitive processes that underlie adaptations to the environment and thus, ultimately, human intelligence.

Neuropsychological Evidence

Is there any physiological evidence for mental rotation? Researchers often are unable to study directly the cerebral activity associated with many cognitive processes in the living brain of a human. Sometimes we may gain insight into these processes by studying the brains of primates, animals whose cerebral processes seem most closely analogous to our own. Using single-cell recordings in the motor cortex of monkeys, investigators found some physiological evidence of mental rotations by the monkeys (Georgopoulos & associates, 1989). Each monkey had been trained to physically move a handle in a direction that was perpendicular and counterclockwise to a target light. This light was used as a reference point. Wherever the target light appeared, the monkeys were to use that point as a reference for the perpendicular and counterclockwise physical rotation of the handle. During these physical rotations, the monkey's cortical activity was recorded. Later, in the absence of the handle, the target light again was presented at various locations. The cortical activity again was recorded. During these presentations, activity in the motor cortex showed an interesting pattern. The same individual cortical cells tended to respond as if the monkeys were anticipating the movements of the particular rotations associated with particular locations of the target light. Another study examining metal-rotation indicates that the motor cortex is activated during this task. The areas associated with hand movement were particularly active during the mental-rotation task (Eisenegger, Herwig, & Jancke, 2007).

Preliminary findings based on primate research suggest that areas of the cerebral cortex have mappings that resemble the 2-D spatial arrangements of visual receptors in the retina of the eye (see Kosslyn, 1994b). These mappings may be construed as relatively depictive (Cohen & associates, 1996; Kosslyn & associates, 1995). Perhaps if these same regions of the cortex are active in humans during tasks involving mental imagery, mental imagery may be similarly depictive in representation. The rise of current brain-imaging techniques have allowed researchers to image human brain activity noninvasively to address such speculations. For example, in a study using functional magnetic resonance imaging, investigators found that the same brain areas involved in perception also are involved in mental-rotation tasks (Cohen & associates, 1996; see also Kosslyn & Sussman, 1995). Thus, not only are imagery and perception functionally equivalent in psychological studies but neuropsychological techniques verify the equivalence by demonstrating overlapping brain activity. However, does mental imagery involve the same mechanisms as memory processes? If so, the functional-equivalence hypothesis for perception would lose some ground. If imagery is "functionally equivalent" to everything, then it is really equivalent to nothing. A careful review cites many psychological studies that find differences between human-imagery and memory tasks (Georgopoulos & Pellizzer, 1995). Furthermore, this review addresses single-cell recording studies of primates performing analogous tasks to verify the distinction between imagery and memory. In sum, there is converging evidence, both from traditional and neuropsychological studies, to lend support to the hypothesis of functional equivalence between perception and mental imagery. Further neuropsychological work will be discussed later in the chapter.

Mental rotation has been extensively studied in addition to its application to the theories of imagery. A number of studies have highlighted an advantage for males over females in mental rotation tasks (De Lisi & Cammarano, 1996; Richardson, 1994; Roberts & Bell, 2000a, 2000b, 2003). Some researchers have speculated that this advantage has decreased since it was first observed. A number of other interesting features of this effect have been identified. First, in young children there is no gender difference either in performance or in neurological activation (Roberts & Bell, 2000a, 2000b). Second, there seems to be differences in the activation of the parietal regions between men and women. It has been noted that there is less parietal activation for women completing a mental rotation task, as compared with men completing the same task (Thomsen & associates, 2000; Roberts & Bell, 2000a, 2000b). This finding is taken to mean that in women spatial tasks involve both sides of the brain whereas in men the right side dominates this function (Blake, McKenzie, & Hamm, 2002). The differences in brain activation are also taken to mean that men and women use different strategies to solve mental rotation problems (Jordan & associates, 2002). Finally, training causes the gender difference to decrease or even disappear (Bosco, Longoni, & Vecchi, 2004; Kass, Ahlers, & Dugger, 1998; Roberts & Bell, 2000a, 2000b).

Image Scaling

The key idea underlying research on image size and scaling is that we represent and use mental images in ways that are functionally equivalent to our representations and uses of percepts. For example, in visual perception, there are limitations on *resolution*, our ability to distinguish individual elements, such as parts of an object or physically adjacent objects. There may also be limits on the clarity with which we perceive details in what we observe. In general, seeing featural details of large objects is easier than seeing such details of small ones. We respond more quickly to questions about large objects we observe than to questions about small ones we observe. Thus, if imaginal representation is functionally equivalent to perception, participants also should respond more quickly to questions about features of imaginally large objects than to questions about features of imaginally small ones.

However, what happens when we zoom in closer to objects to perceive featural details? Sooner or later we reach a point at which we can no longer see the entire object. To see the whole object once more, we must zoom out. See "Investigating Cognitive Psychology" to observe perceptual zooming for yourself.

INVESTIGATING COGNITIVE PSYCHOLOGY	Find a large bookcase (floor to ceiling, if possible; if not, observe the contents of a large refrigerator with an open door). Stand as close to the bookcase as you can while still keeping all of it in view. Now, read the smallest writing on the smallest book in the bookcase. Without changing your gaze, can you still see all of the bookcase? Can you read the title of the book farthest from the book on which you are focusing your perception?

Researchers fairly easily can control the sizes of percepts in perceptual research. However, for research on image size, controlling the sizes of people's mental images is more difficult. How do I know that the image of the elephant in my head is the same size as the image of the elephant in your head? There are some ways to get around this problem (Kosslyn, 1975).

One of the ways is to use relative size as a means of manipulating image size (Kosslyn, 1975). Specifically, participants imagine four different pairs of animals. They are an elephant and a rabbit, a rabbit and a fly, a rabbit and an elephant-sized fly, and a rabbit and a fly-sized elephant. Participants answer specific questions about the features of the rabbit and are timed in their responses. In such a situation, it takes longer to describe the details of smaller objects than to describe the details of the larger objects. That is, it takes longer to respond to rabbits paired with elephants or with elephant-sized flies than to respond to rabbits paired with flies or with fly-sized elephants. Consider a metaphor to explain this phenomenon (Kosslyn, 1983). Imagine we each have a mental screen for visual images. Our screen resolution is finer and more detailed for objects that take up a larger area of the mental screen than it is for objects taking up a smaller area (Kosslyn & Koenig, 1992).

In another study, children in the first and fourth grades and adult college undergraduates were asked whether particular animals can be characterized as having various physical attributes (Kosslyn, 1976). Examples would be "Does a cat have claws?" and "Does a cat have a head?" In one condition, participants were asked to visualize each animal. They were to use this mental image in answering the questions. In the other condition, they were not asked to use mental images. It was presumed that they used verbal-propositional knowledge to respond to the verbal questions.

In the imagery condition, all participants responded more quickly to questions about physical attributes that are larger than to questions about attributes that are smaller. For example, they might be asked about a cat's head (larger) and a cat's claws (smaller). Different results were found in the nonimagery condition. In the nonimagery condition, fourth graders and adults responded more quickly to questions about physical attributes based on the distinctiveness of the characteristic for the animal. For example, they responded more quickly to questions about whether cats have claws (which are distinctive) than to questions about whether cats have heads (which are not particularly distinctive to cats alone). The physical size of the features did not have any effect on performance in the nonimagery condition for either fourth graders or adults.

In contrast, first-graders constantly responded more quickly regarding larger attributes. They did so in both the imagery and the nonimagery conditions. Many of these younger children indicated that they used imagery even when not instructed to do so. Furthermore, in both conditions, adults responded more quickly than did children. But the difference was much greater for the nonimagery condition than for the imagery condition. These findings support the functional-equivalence hypothesis. The reason is that physical size influences perceptual-resolution ability. The findings also support the dual-code view in two ways. First, for adults and older children, responses based on the use of imagery (an imaginal code) differed from responses based on propositions (a symbolic code). Second, the development of propositional knowledge and ability does not occur at the same rate as the development of imaginal knowledge and ability. The distinction in the rate of development of each form of representation also seems to support Paivio's notion of two distinct codes.

Image Scanning

Kosslyn has found additional support for the use of imaginal representation in his studies of image scanning. The key idea underlying image-scanning research is that images can be scanned, in much the same way as physical percepts can be scanned. Furthermore, our strategies and responses for imaginal scanning are expected to be functionally equivalent to those we use for perceptual scanning. A means of testing the functional equivalence of imaginal scanning is to observe some aspects of performance during perceptual scanning. One then compares that performance with performance during imaginal scanning.

For example, in perception, to scan across longer distances takes longer than to scan across shorter ones (Denis & Kosslyn, 1999). In one of Kosslyn's experiments, participants were shown a map of an imaginary island, which you can see

Look at the rabbit and the fly in Figure 7.8. Close your eyes and picture them both in your mind. Now imaginally look only at the fly, and determine the exact shape of the fly's head. Do you notice yourself having to take time to zoom in to "see" the detailed features of the fly? If you are like most people, you are able to zoom the focus on your mental images to give the features or objects a larger portion of your mental screen, much as you might physically move toward an object you wanted to observe more closely.

Now, look at the rabbit and the elephant, and picture them both in your mind. Next, close your eyes and look at the elephant. Imagine walking toward the elephant, watching it as it gets closer to you. Do you find that there comes a point when you can no longer see the rabbit or even all of the elephant? If you are like most people, you will find that the image of the elephant will appear to overflow the size of your image space. To "see" the whole elephant, you probably have to mentally zoom out again.

FIGURE 7.8

Stephen Kosslyn (1983) asked participants to imagine either a rabbit and a fly (to observe zooming in to "see" details) or a rabbit and an elephant (to observe whether zooming in may lead to apparent overflow of the image space).

in Figure 7.9 (Kosslyn, Ball, & Reiser, 1978). The map shows various objects on the island, such as a hut, a tree, and a lake. Participants studied the map until they could reproduce it accurately from memory. At this point, they placed the locations of each of the six objects in the map no more than a quarter of an inch from their correct locations. Once the memorization phase of the experiment was completed, the critical phase began.

Participants were instructed that, on hearing the name of an object read to them, they should picture the map. They then should mentally scan directly to the men-

FIGURE 7.9

Stephen Kosslyn and his colleagues used a map of an imaginary island with various landmarks to determine whether mental scanning across the image of a map was functionally equivalent to perceptual scanning of a perceived map.

tioned object. Finally, they should press a key as soon as they arrived at the location of the named object. An experimenter then read to the participants the name of a first object. Five seconds later, the experimenter read to the participants the name of a second object. Participants again mentally had to scan to the proper location. They then pressed a button when they found the object. This procedure was repeated a number of times. In each case, the participants mentally moved between various pairs of objects on successive trials. The experimenter kept track of response times for participants on each trial. These response times indicated the amount of time it took participants to scan from one object to another. The critical finding was an almost perfect linear relation between the distances separating successive pairs of objects in the mental map and the amount of time it took participants to press the button. In other words, participants seem to have encoded the map in the form of an image. They actually scanned that image as needed for a response.

Findings supporting an imaginal code have been shown in several other domains. For example, the same pattern of results has been obtained for scanning objects in three dimensions (Pinker, 1980). Specifically, participants observed and then mentally represented a 3-D array of objects—toys suspended in an open box. Then they mentally scanned from one object to another.

Representational Neglect

Additional evidence for the similarity between perception and mental imagery can be seen in cases of representational neglect. Many patients suffering from spatial neglect (see Chapter 4) also suffer from a related impairment called representational neglect. In representational neglect a person is asked to imagine a scene and then describe it. In these cases, information that would be on the right visual field is fully described but information that would be on the left is ignored. Although these two types of neglect often occur together, they can also occur independently. Peru and Zapparoli (1999) describe a case of a woman who showed no evidence of spatial neglect while struggling with tasks that required the production of a mental image.

In another set of studies, an array was described to patients suffering from representational neglect. When the patients had to recall the array, they could not describe the left portion (Logie & associates, 2005). Similarly, when subjects with representational neglect are presented with an image, they can describe the entire image. However, when the image is removed and they are asked to describe the image from memory, they fail to describe the left portion (Denis & associates, 2002).

In scenes, representational neglect is only present when a vantage point is given (Rode & associates, 2004). For example, if a person with representational neglect was asked to describe his or her kitchen, he or she would do so accurately. However, if the same person was asked to describe the kitchen from the refrigerator, he or she would demonstrate neglect. It is likely that there exists complete knowledge of the scene, but it is sometimes not accessible when the patient generates a mental image.

Synthesizing Images and Propositions

In this chapter, we have discussed two opposing views of knowledge representation. One is a **dual-code theory,** suggesting that knowledge is represented both in images and in symbols. The second is a **propositional theory,** suggesting that knowledge is represented only in underlying propositions, not in the form of images or of words and other symbols. Before we consider some proposed syntheses of the two hypotheses, let's review the findings described thus far. We do so in light of Finke's principles of visual imagery (Table 7.3). In the discussion thus far, we have addressed the first three of Finke's criteria for imaginal representations. Mental imagery appears functionally equivalent to perception in many ways. This conclusion is based on studies of mental rotations, image scaling (sizing), and image scanning. However, the studies involving ambiguous figures and unfamiliar mental manipulations suggest that there are limits to the analogy between perception and imagery.

Epiphenomena and Demand Characteristics

Although there seems to be good evidence for the existence of both propositions and mental images (Kosslyn, 1994a, 1994b), the debate is not over. Perhaps some of the results found in image research could be the result of demand characteristics (Intons-Peterson, 1983). In this view, experimenters' expectancies regarding the

TABLE 7.3	Principles of Visual Imagery: Findings

How well did the studies reported in this chapter satisfy the criteria suggested by Ronald Finke's principles of visual imagery?

PRINCIPLE	**POSSIBLE QUESTIONS GENERATED FROM PRINCIPLES**
1. Our mental transformations of images and our mental movements across images correspond to similar transformations of and movements across physical objects and percepts.	Mental rotations generally conform to the same laws of motion and space that are observed in physical percepts (e.g., Shepard & Metzler, 1971), even showing performance decrements associated with degraded stimuli (Duncan & Bourg, 1983; see also Chapter 3, for comparisons with perceptual stimuli). However, it appears that for some mental images, mental rotations of imaginal objects do not fully and accurately represent the physical rotation of perceived objects (e.g., Hinton, 1979); hence, some nonimaginal knowledge representations or cognitive strategies appear influential in some situations. In image scanning, it takes longer to scan across a large distance in a mental image than across a smaller distance (Kosslyn, Ball, & Reiser, 1978).
2. The spatial relations among elements of a visual image are analogous to those relations in actual physical space.	It appears that cognitive manipulations of mental images are analogous to manipulations of percepts in studies involving image size. As in visual perception, there are limits to the resolution of the featural details of an image, as well as limits to the size of the image space (analogous to the visual field) that can be "observed" at any one time. To observe greater detail of individual objects or parts of objects, a smaller size or number of objects or parts of objects may be observed and vice versa (Kosslyn, 1975). In related work (Kosslyn, 1976), it appears easier to see the details of larger mental images (e.g., a cat's head) than of smaller ones (e.g., a cat's claws). It appears also that just as we perceive the physical proximity (closeness) of objects that are closer together in physical space, we also imagine the closeness of mental images in our mental image space (Kosslyn, Ball, & Reiser, 1978).
3. Mental images can be used to generate information that was not explicitly stored during encoding.	After participants have been asked to form a mental image, they can answer some kinds of questions that require them to infer information, based on the image, which was not specifically encoded at the time they created the image. The studies by Reed (1974) and by Chambers and Reisberg (1985) suggest that propositional representations may play a role; studies by Finke (1989) and by Peterson and associates (1992) suggest that imaginal representations are sometimes sufficient for drawing inferences.
4. The construction of mental images is analogous to the construction of visually perceptible figures.	Studies of lifelong blind people suggest that mental imagery in the form of spatial arrangements may be constructed from haptic, rather than visual, information. Based on the findings regarding cognitive maps (e.g., Hirtle & Mascolo, 1986; Saarinen, 1987b; Stevens & Coupe, 1978; Tversky, 1981), it appears that both propositional and imaginal knowledge representations influence the construction of spatial arrangements.
5. Visual imagery is functionally equivalent to visual perception in terms of the processes of the visual system used for each.	It appears that some of the same regions of the brain that are involved in manipulating visual percepts may be involved in manipulating mental imagery (e.g., see Farah & associates, 1988a, 1988b), but it also appears that spatial and visual imagery may be represented differently in the brain.

performance of participants on a particular task create an implicit demand for the participants to perform as expected.

Intons-Peterson (1983) manipulated experimenter expectancies by suggesting to one group of experimenters that task performance would be expected to be better for perceptual tasks than for imaginal ones. She suggested the opposite outcome to a second group of experimenters. She found that experimenter expectancies did influence participants' responses in three tasks: image scanning, mental rotations, and another task comparing perceptual performance with imaginal performance. When experimenters expected imaginal performance to be better than perceptual performance, participants responded accordingly and vice versa. This result occurred even when the experimenters were not present while participants were responding and when the cues were presented via computer. Thus, experimental participants performing visualization tasks may be responding in part to the demand characteristics of the task. These demand characteristics result from the experimenters' expectations regarding the outcomes.

Other investigators responded (Jolicoeur & Kosslyn, 1985a, 1985b). In one set of experiments, the researchers modified the procedure for the task. They completely omitted all instructions to scan the mental image. Furthermore, questions that involved responses requiring image scanning were intermixed with questions that did not require any image scanning. Even when image scanning was not an implicit task demand, participants' responses still showed that mental images were scanned in a manner analogous to perceptual scanning.

In another set of experiments, Jolicoeur and Kosslyn led experimenters to expect a pattern of responses that differed from the one analogous to perceptual scanning. Specifically, experimenters were led to expect that the pattern of responses would show a U-shaped curve, rather than a linear function. In this study, too, responses still showed a linear relation between distance and time. They did not show the U-shaped response pattern expected by the experimenters. The hypothesis regarding the functional equivalence of imagery and perception thus appears to have strong empirical support.

The debate between the propositional hypothesis and the functional-equivalence (analogical) hypothesis has been suggested to be intractable, based on existing knowledge (Keane, 1994). For each empirical finding that supports the view that imagery is analogous to perception, a rationalist reinterpretation of the finding may be offered. The reinterpretation offers an alternative explanation of the finding. Although the rationalist alternative may be a less parsimonious explanation than the empiricist explanation, the alternative cannot be refuted outright. Hence, the debate between the functional-equivalence view and the propositional view may boil down to a debate between empiricism and rationalism.

Johnson-Laird's Mental Models

An alternative synthesis of the literature suggests that mental representations may take any of three forms (Johnson-Laird, 1983, 1989, 1995, 1999; Johnson-Laird & Goldvarg, 1997). These forms are of propositions, mental models, or images. Here, propositions are fully abstracted representations of meaning that are verbally expressible. The criterion of verbal expressibility distinguishes Johnson-Laird's view from that of other cognitive psychologists. **Mental models** are knowledge structures that individuals construct to understand and explain their experiences (Brewer, 2003; Halford, 1993; Johnson-Laird, 2001; Schaeken, Johnson-Laird, & D'Ydewalle, 1996; Tversky, 2000). The models are constrained by the individuals' implicit theories about these experiences. These conceptions can be more or less accurate. For example, you may have a mental model to account for how planes fly into the air. But the model depends not on physical or other laws but rather on your beliefs about them. The same would apply to the creation of mental models from text or symbolic reasoning problems as from accounts of planes flying in the air (Byrne, 1996; Ehrlich, 1996; Garnham, 1987; Garnham & Oakhill, 1996; Rogers, Rutherford, & Bibby, 1992; Schwartz, 1996; Stevenson, 1993; Zwaan, Magliano, & Graesser, 1995).

Images are much more specific representations. They retain many of the perceptual features of particular objects, viewed from a particular angle, with the particular details of a given instantiation (Katz, 2000; Kunzendorf, 1991; Schwartz & Black, 1996). For example, "The cat is under the table" may be represented in several ways. It may be represented as a proposition (because it is verbally expressible), as a mental model (of any cat and table, perhaps resembling prototypical ones—see Chapter 4), or as an image (of a particular cat in a particular position under a particular table).

Consider an experiment (Mani & Johnson-Laird, 1982). Some participants received determinate descriptions for a spatial layout. It indicated a precise location for each object in the spatial array. Other participants received indeterminate descriptions for a spatial layout. They were given ambiguous locations for objects in the array. As an analogy, consider a relatively determinate description of the location of Washington, D.C. It lies between Alexandria, Virginia, and Baltimore, Maryland. An indeterminate description of the location is that it lies between the Pacific Ocean and the Atlantic Ocean. When participants were given determinate descriptions for the spatial layout of objects, they inferred additional spatial information not included in the descriptions, but they did not recall the verbatim details well. Their having inferred additional spatial information suggests that the participants formed a mental model of the information. That they then did not recall the verbatim descriptions very well suggests that they relied on the mental models. They did not rely on the verbal descriptions for their mental representations.

In contrast, consider what happened when participants were given indeterminate descriptions for the spatial layout of objects. They seldom inferred spatial information not given in the descriptions, but they remembered the verbatim descriptions better than the other participants did. The authors suggested that participants did not infer a mental model for the indeterminate descriptions because of the multitude of possibilities for mental models of the given information. Instead, the participants appear to have mentally represented the descriptions as verbally expressible propositions. The notion of mental models as a form of knowledge representation has been applied to a broad range of cognitive phenomena. These phenomena include visual perception, memory, comprehension of text passages, and reasoning (Johnson-Laird, 1983, 1989).

Perhaps the use of mental models may offer a possible explanation of some findings that cannot be fully explained in terms of visual imagery. A series of experiments studied people who were born blind (Kerr, 1983). Because these participants have never experienced visual perception, we may assume that they have never formed visual images. At least, they have not done so in the ordinary sense of the term. Some of Kosslyn's tasks were adapted to work comparably for sighted and for blind participants (Kerr, 1983). For example, for a map-scanning task, the experimenter used a board with topographical features and landmarks that could be detected by using touch. She then asked participants to form a mental image of the board.

For a task similar to Kosslyn's image-size tasks, Kerr asked participants to imagine various common objects of various sizes. The blind participants responded more slowly to all tasks than did the sighted participants. But Kerr's blind participants still showed similar response patterns to those of sighted participants. They showed faster response times when scanning shorter distances than when scanning longer distances. They also were faster when answering questions about images of larger objects than about images of smaller objects. At least in some respects, spatial imagery appears not to involve representations that are actual analogues to visual percepts. The use of haptic (touch-based) "imagery" suggests alternative modalities for mental imagery. Haptic imagery has been explored further by a number of researchers. These researchers have found that haptic imagery shares a number of features with visual imagery. For instance, similar brain areas are active during both types of imagery (James & associates, 2002; Zhang & associates, 2004).

Imaginal representation also may occur in an auditory modality (based on hearing). As an example, investigators found that participants seem to have auditory mental images, just as they have visual mental images (Intons-Peterson, Russell, & Dressel, 1992). Specifically, participants took longer mentally to shift a sound upward in pitch than downward. In particular, they were slower in going from the low-pitched purring of a cat to the high-pitched ringing of a telephone than in going from the cat's purring to a clock's ticking. The relative response times were analogous to the time needed physically to change sounds up or down in pitch. Consider what happened, in contrast, when individuals were asked to make psychophysical judgments involving discriminations between stimuli. Participants took longer to determine whether purring was lower-pitched than was ticking (two relatively close stimuli) than to determine whether purring was lower-pitched than was ringing (two relatively distant stimuli).

Psychophysical tests of auditory sensation and perception reveal findings analogous to these. In another study, participants listened to either familiar or unfamiliar songs with pieces of the song replaced with silence. Examining the brains of these participants revealed that there was more activation of the auditory cortex during silence when the song was familiar than when the song was unfamiliar (Kraemer & associates, 2005). These findings are taken to mean that when one generates an auditory image, the same brain areas involved in hearing are engaged.

Faulty mental models are responsible for many errors in thinking. Consider several examples (Brewer, 2003). One is that school children tend to think of heat and cold as moving through objects much as fluids do. These children also believe that plants obtain their food from the ground and that boats made of iron should sink. Even adults have trouble understanding the trajectory of an object dropped from a moving airplane.

Experience is a useful tool for the repair of faulty mental models (Greene & Azevedo, 2007). In one study, faulty mental models concerning the process of respiration were explored. A group of college students who made false predictions concerning the process of respiration participated in this study. These predictions were based on imprecise mental models. The experimenters set up a lab experience for the students to demonstrate and explore the process of respiration. One group stated their predictions before the experiment and another did not. Overall, participating in the activity improved the accuracy of the answers of participants to questions concerning respiration, compared with performance before the activity. However, when the students were required to state their predictions before the experiment, the improvement was even greater (Modell & associates, 2000). Thus, experience can help correct faulty mental models. However, it is most helpful when the faulty models are made explicit.

Neuropsychological Evidence for Multiple Codes

An argument can be made that experimenter expectancies and demand characteristics may influence performance on cognitive tasks. But it seems implausible that such factors would influence the results of psychobiological research. For example, suppose you remembered every word in Chapter 2 regarding which particular parts of your brain govern which kinds of perceptual and cognitive functions. (This is, of course, an unlikely assumption for you or for most participants in psychobiological research.) How would you go about conforming to experimenters' expectancies? You would have to control directly your brain's activities and functions so that you would simulate what experimenters expected in association with particular perceptual or cognitive functions. Likewise, brain-damaged patients do not know that particular lesions are supposed to lead to particular deficits. Indeed, the patients rarely know where a lesion is until after deficits are discovered. Thus, neuropsychological findings may circumvent issues of demand characteristics in resolving the dual-code controversy. However, this research does not eliminate experimenter biases regarding where to look for lesions or their corresponding deficits.

Lateralization of Function

Some investigators followed the longstanding tradition of studying patterns of brain lesions and relating them to cognitive deficits. They noted that lesions in particular areas of the brain seem to affect symbol-manipulation functions such as language (Luria, 1976; Milner, 1968). In contrast, lesions in other areas of the brain seem to affect imagery-manipulation functions such as the ability to recognize faces. Specifically, lesions in the right hemisphere are associated more strongly with impaired visual memory and visual perception. Lesions in the left hemisphere are associated more strongly with impaired verbal memory and verbal comprehension.

Initial psychobiological research on imagery came from studies of patients with identified lesions and from split-brain patients (see Chapter 2). Recall from Chapter 2 the studies of patients who underwent surgery that severed their right hemisphere from their left hemisphere. Researchers found that the right hemisphere appears to be more proficient in representing and manipulating knowledge of a visuospatial nature in a manner that may be analogous to perception (Gazzaniga & Sperry, 1967). In contrast, the left hemisphere appears to be more proficient in representing and manipulating verbal and other symbol-based knowledge.

One investigator has gone so far as to suggest that cerebral asymmetry has evolutionary origins (Corballis, 1989). As in the brains of other animals, the right hemisphere of the human brain represents knowledge in a manner that is analogous to our physical environment. Unlike the brains of other animals, however, the left

Martha Farah is a professor of psychology at the University of Pennsylvania. She is most well known for her seminal work on mental imagery and its relation to the brain. She has shown, for example, that imagery uses many of the same parts of the brain as does visual perception.

hemisphere of only the human brain has the ability to manipulate imaginal components and symbols and to generate entirely new information. Examples of such imaginal components would be consonant and vowel sounds and geometric shapes. According to Corballis, humans alone can conceive what they have never perceived. However, a recent review of the findings on lateralization has led to a modified view (Corballis, 1997). Specifically, recent neuropsychological studies of mental rotation in both animals and humans show that both hemispheres may be partially responsible for task performance. The apparent right hemisphere dominance observed in humans may be the result of the overshadowing of left hemisphere functions by linguistic abilities. Thus, it would be nice to have clear evidence of a cerebral hemispheric dissociation between analogue imagery functions and symbolic propositional functions. But scientists will have to look deeper into brain functioning before this issue is resolved completely.

Visual versus Spatial Images

In attempting to understand the nature of visual imagery, some investigators found evidence that visual and spatial imagery may be represented differently (Farah, 1988a, 1988b; Farah & associates, 1988a). Here, *visual imagery* refers to the use of images that represent visual characteristics such as colors and shapes. *Spatial imagery* refers to images that represent spatial features such as depth dimensions, distances, and orientations. Consider the case of L. H., a 36 year old who had a head injury at age 18 years. The injury resulted in lesions in the right and the left temporo-occipital regions, the right temporal lobe, and the right inferior frontal lobe. L. H.'s injuries implicated possible impairment of his ability to represent and manipulate both visual and spatial images. Figure 7.10 shows those areas of L. H.'s brain where there was damage.

Despite L. H.'s injuries, L. H.'s ability to see was intact. He was able satisfactorily to copy various pictures (Figure 7.11 *a* and *b*). Nonetheless, he could not recognize any of the pictures he copied. In other words, he could not link verbal labels to the objects pictured. He performed very poorly when asked to respond verbally to questions requiring visual imagery, such as those regarding color or shape. Surprisingly, however, L. H. showed relatively normal abilities in several kinds of tasks. These involved (1) rotations (2-D letters, 3-D objects); (2) mental scanning, size scaling, matrix memory, and letter corners; and (3) state locations (Figure 7.11 *c* and *d*).

The investigators also used event-related potential (ERP; see Chapter 2, Table 2.3) studies. They thereby compared brain processes associated with visual perception to brain processes associated with visual imagery (Farah & associates, 1988b). As you may recall, the primary visual cortex is located in the occipital region of the brain. During visual perception, ERPs generally are elevated in the occipital region. Suppose visual imagery were analogous to visual perception. We could expect that during tasks involving visual imagery, there would be analogous elevations of ERPs in the occipital region.

In this study, ERPs were measured during a reading task. In one condition, participants were asked to read a list of concrete words (e.g., *cat*). In the other condition,

FIGURE 7.10

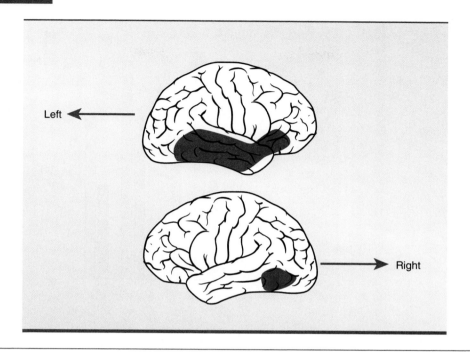

Regions in which the brain of L. H. was damaged: the right temporal lobe and right inferior frontal lobe, as shown in the figure at the top; and the temporo-occipital region, as shown in the figure at the bottom. From Robert Solso, Cognitive Psychology, *ed 6, p. 306. Copyright © 2000 Elsevier. Reprinted with permission.*

participants were asked to read a comparable list of concrete words. They also had to imagine the objects as they read the words. Each word was presented for 200 milliseconds. ERPs were recorded from the different sites in the occipital-lobe and temporal-lobe regions. The researchers found that the ERPs were similar during the first 450 milliseconds. After this time, however, participants in the imaginal condition showed greater neural activity in the occipital lobe than did participants in the non-imaginal (reading-only) condition.

According to the researchers, "Neurophysiological evidence suggests that our cognitive architecture includes both representations of the visual appearance of objects in terms of their form, color, and perspective and of the spatial structure of objects in terms of their three-dimensional layout in space" (Farah & associates, 1988a, p. 459). The knowledge of object labels (recognizing the objects by name) and attributes (answering questions about the characteristics of the objects) taps propositional, symbolic knowledge about the pictured objects. In contrast, the ability to manipulate the orientation (rotation) or the size of images taps imaginal, analogous knowledge of the objects. Thus, both forms of representation seem to answer particular kinds of questions for knowledge use.

FIGURE 7.11

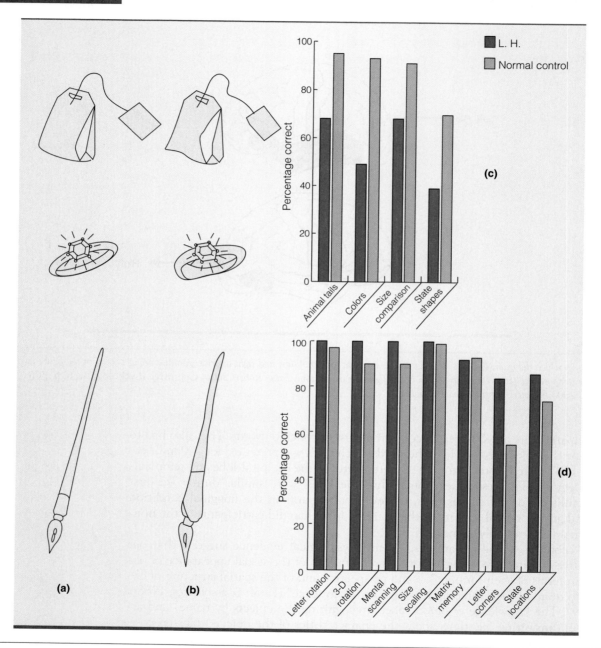

L. H. was able to draw accurately various objects. Panel a shows what he was shown, and panel b shows what he drew. However, he could not recognize the objects he copied. Despite L. H.'s severe deficits on visual-imagery tasks (panel c, regarding colors, sizes, shapes, etc.), L. H. showed normal ability on spatial-imagery tasks (panel d, regarding rotations, scanning, scaling, etc.). Reprinted from M. J. Farah, K. M. Hammond, D. N. Levine, & R. Calvanio. Visual and spatial mental imagery: Dissociable systems of representation. Cognitive Psychology, 20, 439–462, © 1988, with permission from Elsevier.

Spatial Cognition and Cognitive Maps

Rats, Bees, Pigeons, and Humans

Most of the studies described thus far have involved the way in which we represent imaginal knowledge. The studies are based on what we have perceived by looking at and then imagining visual stimuli. Other research suggests that we may form imaginal maps based solely on our physical interactions with and navigations through our physical environment. This is true even when we never have a chance to "see the whole picture," as from an aerial photograph or a map. **Cognitive maps** are internal representations of our physical environment, particularly centering on spatial relationships. Cognitive maps seem to offer internal representations that simulate particular spatial features of our external environment (Rumelhart & Norman, 1988).

PRACTICAL APPLICATIONS OF COGNITIVE PSYCHOLOGY

How do you benefit from having a dual code for knowledge representation? Although a dual code may seem redundant and inefficient, having a code for analogue physical and spatial features that is distinct from a code for symbolic propositional knowledge actually can be very efficient. Consider how you learn material in your cognitive psychology course. Most people go to the lecture. There they obtain information from an instructor. They also read material from a textbook, as you are doing now. If you had only an analogue code for knowledge representation, you would have a much harder time integrating the verbal information you received from your instructor in class with the printed information in your textbook. All your information would be in the form of auditory-visual images gleaned from listening to and watching your instructor in class and visual images of the words in your textbook. Thus, a symbolic code that is distinct from the analogue features of encoding is helpful for integrating across different modes of knowledge acquisition. Furthermore, analogue codes preserve important aspects of experience without interfering with underlying propositional information. For the purposes of performing well on a test, it is irrelevant whether the information was obtained in class or in the text. But later you may need to verify the source of information to prove that your answer is correct. In this case, analogical information might help.

Some of the earliest work on cognitive maps was done by Edward Tolman during the 1930s. At this time, it was considered almost unseemly for psychologists to try to understand cognitive processes that could not be observed or measured directly. In one study, the researchers were interested in the ability of rats to learn a maze, such as that shown in Figure 7.12 (Tolman & Honzik, 1930). Rats were divided into three groups:

1. In the first group, the rats had to learn the maze. Their reward for getting from the start box to the end box was food. Eventually, these rats learned to run the maze without making any errors. In other words, they did not make wrong turns or follow blind alleys.

2. A second group of rats also was placed in the maze, but these rats received no reinforcement for successfully getting to the end box. Although their performance improved over time, they continued to make more errors

FIGURE 7.12

Edward Tolman found that rats seemed to have formed a mental map of a maze during behavioral experiments.

than the reinforced group. These results are hardly surprising. We would expect the rewarded group to have more incentive to learn.

3. Finally, consider the third group. These rats received no reward for 10 days of learning trials. On the eleventh day, however, food was placed in the end box for the first time. With just one reinforcement, the learning of these rats improved dramatically. These rats ran the maze about as well as the rats in the first group in fewer trials.

What, exactly, were the rats in Tolman and Honzik's experiment learning? It seems unlikely that they were learning simply "turn right here, turn left there," and so on. Rather, according to Tolman, the rats were learning a cognitive map, an internal representation of the maze. Through this argument, Tolman became one of the earliest cognitive theorists. He argued for the importance of the mental representations that give rise to behavior.

Decades later, even very simple creatures were shown to appear able to form some cognitive maps. They may be able to translate imaginal representations into a primitive, prewired, analogical, and perhaps even symbolic form. For example, a Nobel Prize–winning German scientist studied the behavior of bees when they return to their hive after having located a source of nectar (von Frisch, 1962, 1967). Apparently, bees not only can form imaginal maps for getting to food sources. They also can use a somewhat symbolic form of communicating that information to other bees. Specifically, different patterns of dances can be used to represent different meanings. For example, a round dance indicates a source less than 100 yards from the hive. A figure-eight dance indicates a source at a greater distance. The details of the dance (e.g., in regard to wiggle patterns) differ from one species to another, but the basic dances appear to be the same across all species of bees. If the lowly bee appears able to imagine the route to nectar, what kinds of cognitive maps may be conceived in the minds of humans?

A set of animals noted for their excellent cognitive maps are homing pigeons. These birds are known for their ability to return to their home from distant locations. This quality made the birds useful for communication during earlier times. Extensive research has been completed on how pigeons form these maps. It has been noted that the hippocampus is integral to the process (Seigel, Nitz, & Bingman, 2005). Specifically, the left hippocampus plays a pivotal role in map formation. When the left hippocampus is lesioned, pigeons' ability to return to their homes is impaired. However, lesioning any part of the hippocampus impairs homing performance (Gagliardo & associates, 2001). Other research suggests that the right hippocampus is involved in sensitivity to global features of the environment (e.g., geometry of the space). The left hippocampus is crucial for the perception of landmarks within the environment (Bingman & associates, 2003). The hippocampus is also involved in the formation of cognitive maps in humans (Maguire, Frackowiak, & Frith, 1996).

Humans seem to use three types of knowledge when forming and using cognitive maps. The first is *landmark* knowledge, which is information about particular features at a location and which may be based on both imaginal and propositional representations (Thorndyke, 1981). The second is *route-road* knowledge, which involves specific pathways for moving from one location to another (Thorndyke & Hayes-Roth, 1982). It may be based on both procedural knowledge and declarative knowledge. The third is *survey* knowledge, which involves estimated distances between landmarks, much as they might appear on survey maps (Thorndyke & Hayes-Roth, 1982). It may be represented imaginally or propositionally (e.g., in numerically specified distances). Thus, people use both an analogical code and a propositional code for imaginal representations such as images of maps (McNamara, Hardy, & Hirtle, 1989; Russell & Ward, 1982).

Mental Shortcuts

When we use these three kinds of knowledge (landmark, route-road, and survey knowledge), we sometimes seem to take mental shortcuts that influence our estimations of distance. These mental shortcuts are cognitive strategies termed heuristics, often described as rules of thumb. For example, in regard to landmark knowledge, the density of the landmarks sometimes appears to affect our mental image of an area. Specifically, as the density of intervening landmarks increases, estimates of distances increase correspondingly. In other words, people tend to distort their mental images such that their mental estimates of distances increase in relation to the number of intervening landmarks (Thorndyke, 1981).

In estimations of distances between particular physical locations (e.g., cities), route-road knowledge appears often to be weighted more heavily than survey knowledge. This is true even when participants form a mental image based on looking at a map (McNamara, Ratcliff, & McKoon, 1984). Consider what happened when participants were asked to indicate whether particular cities had appeared on a map. They showed more rapid response times between names of cities when the two cities were closer together in route-road distance than when the two cities were physically closer together "as the crow flies" (Figure 7.13).

The use of heuristics in manipulating cognitive maps suggests that propositional knowledge affects imaginal knowledge (Tversky, 1981). This is so at least when people are solving problems and answering questions about images. In some situations, conceptual information seems to lead to distortions in mental images. In these situations, propositional strategies, rather than imaginal strategies, may better explain people's responses. In general, these distortions seem to reflect a tendency to regularize features of mental maps. Thus, angles, lines, and shapes are represented as more like pure abstract geometric forms than they really are.

1. *Right-angle bias:* People tend to represent intersections (e.g., street crossings) as forming 90-degree angles more often than the intersections really do (Moar & Bower, 1983).

2. *Symmetry heuristic:* People tend to represent shapes (e.g., states or countries) as being more symmetrical than they really are (Tversky & Schiano, 1989).

FIGURE 7.13

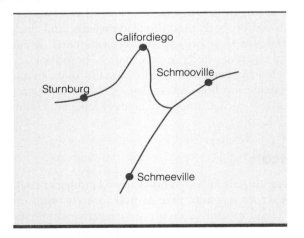

Which city is closer to Sturnburg: Schmeeville or Schmooville? It appears that our use of cognitive maps often emphasizes the use of route-road knowledge, even when it contradicts survey knowledge. Based on Timothy R. McNamara, Roger Ratcliff, and Gail McKoon (1984), "The Mental Representation of Knowledge Acquired from Maps," Journal of Experimental Psychology: LMC, 10(4), 723–732. *Copyright © 1984 by the American Psychological Association.*

3. *Rotation heuristic:* When representing figures and boundaries that are slightly slanted (i.e., oblique), people tend to distort the images as being either more vertical or more horizontal than they really are (Tversky, 1981).

4. *Alignment heuristic:* People tend to represent landmarks and boundaries that are slightly out of alignment by distorting their mental images to be better aligned than they really are (i.e., we distort the way we line up a series of figures or objects; Tversky, 1981).

5. *Relative-position heuristic:* People tend to represent the relative positions of particular landmarks and boundaries by distorting their mental images in ways that more accurately reflect their conceptual knowledge about the contexts in which the landmarks and boundaries are located, rather than reflecting the actual spatial configurations (Seizova-Cajic, 2003).

To see how the relative-position heuristic might work, close your eyes and picture a map of the United States. Is Reno, Nevada, west of San Diego, California, or east of it? In a series of experiments, investigators asked participants questions such as this one (Stevens & Coupe, 1978). They found that the large majority of people believe San Diego to be west of Reno. That is, for most of us, our mental map looks something like that in panel *a* of Figure 7.14. Actually, however, Reno is west of San Diego. See the correct map in panel *b* of Figure 7.14.

Some of these heuristics also affect our perception of space and of forms (see Chapter 3). For example, the symmetry heuristic seems to be equally strong in memory and in perception (Tversky, 1991). Nonetheless, there are differences between perceptual processes and representational (imaginal or propositional) processes. For example, the relative-position heuristic appears to influence mental representation much more strongly than it does perception (Tversky, 1991).

There is evidence of powerful influences of semantic or propositional knowledge (or beliefs) on imaginal representations of world maps (Saarinen, 1987b). Specifically, students from 71 sites in 49 countries were asked to draw a sketch map of the world. Most (even Asians) drew maps showing a Eurocentric view of the world. Many Americans drew Americentric views. A few others showed views centered on and highlighting their own countries. (Figure 7.15 shows an Australia-centered view of the world.) In addition, most students showed modest distortions that enlarged the more prominent, well-known countries. They also diminished the sizes of less well-known countries (e.g., in Africa).

Finally, further work suggests that propositional knowledge about semantic categories may affect imaginal representations of maps. In one study, the researchers studied the influence of semantic clustering on estimations of distances (Hirtle & Mascolo, 1986). Hirtle's participants were shown a map of many buildings and then were asked to estimate distances between various pairs of buildings. They tended to distort the distances in the direction of guessing shorter distances for more similar landmarks and longer distances for less similar landmarks. Investigators found similar distortions in students' mental maps for the city in which they lived (Ann Arbor, Michigan) (Hirtle & Jonides, 1985).

FIGURE 7.14

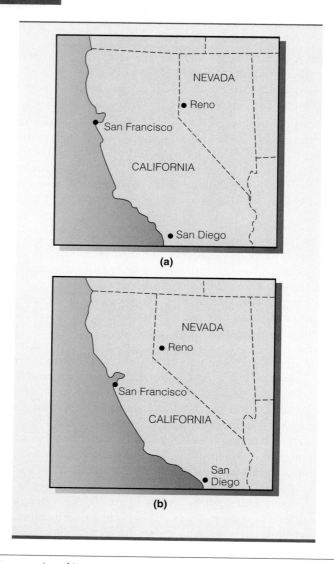

Which of these two maps (a or b) more accurately depicts the relative positions of Reno, Nevada, and San Diego, California?

The work on cognitive maps shows once again how the study of mental imagery can help elucidate our understanding of human adaptation to the environment—that is, of human intelligence. To survive, we need to find our way around the environment in which we live. We need to get from one place to another. Sometimes, to get between places, we need to imagine the route we will need to traverse. Mental imagery provides a key basis for this adaptation. In some societies (Gladwin, 1970), the

FIGURE 7.15

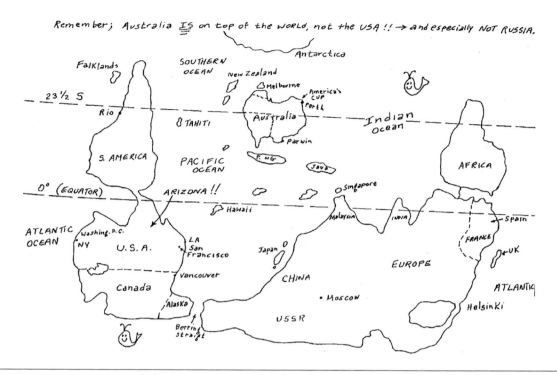

Based on this Australian student's map, can you infer that this student mentally represents the world in the same way you do? From Solso, Robert L., COGNITIVE PSYCHOLOGY, 8/e. Published by Allyn and Bacon, Boston, MA. Copyright © 2008 by Pearson Education. Reprinted by permission of the publisher.

ability to navigate with the help of very few cues is a life-or-death issue. If sailors cannot do so, they eventually get lost and potentially die of dehydration or starvation. Thus, our imagery abilities are potential keys to our survival and to what makes us intelligent in our everyday lives.

There are also sex differences in spatial and related skills. Women find it easier to remember where they saw things (spatial-location memory). Men find it easier to do mental rotation of spatial images (Silverman & Eals, 1992). Most tests of spatial abilities involve mental rotation, however, so men tend to perform better on common tests of spatial skills than do women.

Text Maps

Thus far we have discussed the construction of cognitive maps based on procedural knowledge (e.g., following a particular route, as a rat in a maze), on propositional information (e.g., using mental heuristics), and on observation of a graphic map. In addition, we may be able to create cognitive maps from a verbal description (Franklin

& Tversky, 1990; Taylor & Tversky, 1992a, 1992b). These cognitive maps may be as accurate as those created from looking at a graphic map. Others have found similar results in studies of text comprehension (Glenberg, Meyer, & Lindem, 1987).

Tversky noted that her research involved having the readers envision themselves in an imaginal setting as participants, not as observers, in the scene. She wondered whether people might create and manipulate images differently when envisioning themselves in different settings. Specifically, Tversky wondered whether propositional information might play a stronger role in mental operations when we think about settings in which we are participants, as compared with settings in which we are observers. As Item 4 in Table 7.3 indicates, the findings regarding cognitive maps suggest that the construction of mental imagery may involve both processes analogous to perception and processes relying on propositional representations.

Whether the debate regarding propositions versus imagery can be resolved in the terms in which it traditionally has been presented remains unclear. The various forms of mental representation sometimes are considered to be mutually exclusive. In other words, we think in terms of the question, "Which representation of information is correct?" Often, however, we create false dichotomies. We suggest that alternatives are mutually exclusive, when, in fact, they might be complementary. For example, models postulating mental imagery and those positing propositions can be seen as opposed to each other. However, this opposition does not inhere in the nature of things. Rather, it is in our construction of a relation. People possibly could use both representations. Propositional theorists might like to believe that all representations are fundamentally propositional. Quite possibly, though, both images and propositions are way stations toward some more basic and primitive form of representation in the mind of which we do not yet have any knowledge. A good case can be made in favor of both propositional and imaginal representations of knowledge. Neither is necessarily more basic than the other. The question we presently need to address is when we use which.

Development of Visuospatial Skills

Young children develop basic spatial understandings that form the basis for geometry. One such basic understanding is *spatial visualization*. This is our ability to orient ourselves in our surroundings and to manipulate images of objects mentally. Although many studies have examined spatial visualization in children (e.g., Huttenlocher, Hedges, & Duncan, 1991; Huttenlocher & Presson, 1973, 1979; Kail, 1991, 1997; Marmor, 1975, 1977; Van Garderen, 2006), consider just one typical example of this research (Kail, Pellegrino, & Carter, 1980).

Participants in grades 3, 4, and 6 and in college judged whether pairs of stimuli were identical or were mirror-image reversals of each other. One stimulus in each pair was presented in an upright position. The other was rotated 0, 30, 60, 90, 120, or 150 degrees from the standard upright position. The pairs comprising each stimulus item were either alphanumeric (alphabetic and/or numeric) symbols—such as 4, 5, F, and G—or unfamiliar abstract geometric forms. The speed of mental rotation increases with age and with the degree of familiarity of the objects (Kail, Pellegrino, & Carter, 1980). Thus, older participants can mentally rotate more quickly. All participants can rotate familiar objects more quickly than they can rotate unfamiliar ones.

The findings raised several questions, two of which particularly intrigued researchers. First, why might the speed of mental rotation improve with age? The researchers suggested that younger children must rotate the entire stimulus. Older children may rotate stimuli more analytically so that they rotate each component separately and may need only to rotate a part of the stimulus. Thus, the change in cognitive development may involve more than a simple change in processing speed. A second question is why participants encoded and rotated the unusual geometric forms more slowly than the familiar, alphanumeric ones. The difference might be because of the activation of an already existing, easily accessible pattern in memory for the familiar characters. This is in contrast to the requirement that the participants form a new representation for the unfamiliar stimuli.

Investigators also found that children and young adults showed speedier response times in mental-rotation tasks when given opportunities for practice (Kail & Park, 1990). The performance of both school-aged children and young adults on mental-rotation tasks is not impaired as a function of their engaging in simultaneous tasks involving memory recall (Kail, 1991). These findings suggest that mental rotation may be an automatic process for school-aged children and adults. Given that familiarity with the items and practice with mental rotation appear to enhance response times, his study suggests that mental rotation may be an automatic process. It may permit us to infer that enhanced response times may be the result of increasing automatization of the task across childhood and adolescence. Furthermore, such automatic processes may be a sign of more effective visuospatial skills because increased speed is associated with increased accuracy in spatial memory (Kail, 1997).

At the other end of the life span, two investigators studied whether processing speed or other factors may influence age-related changes in mental rotation by adults (Dror & Kosslyn, 1994). They found that older participants (55–71 years; mean 65 years) responded more slowly and less accurately than younger participants (18–23 years; mean 20 years) on mental-rotation tasks, a finding that frequently has been replicated (Band & Kok, 2000; Inagaki & associates, 2002). However, they also found that older and younger participants showed comparable response times and error rates on tasks involving image scanning. Based on these and other findings, these authors concluded that aging affects some aspects of visual imagery more than others.

The authors also analyzed their data for mental rotation, image scanning, and other imagery tasks. For example, participants were asked to generate or maintain a mental image within a visual region and then indicate whether the image would obscure a probe stimulus within that region. General effects of aging may lead to a reduction in response times across tasks. However, age differences in error rates may arise because of specific effects of aging. They may influence selectively particular aspects of mental imagery. The authors also speculated that if the participants had been urged to minimize their error rates, perhaps older people would have shown even slower response times to ensure lower error rates. However, other work directly testing that speculation failed to confirm the authors' hypothesis (Hertzog, Vernon, & Rypma, 1993). Other researchers have suggested that a factor contributing to task-specific differences in age-related decline in mental imagery is whether the task requires multiple simultaneous transformations or multiple sequential ones (Mayr & Kliegl, 1993).

Key Themes

This chapter illustrates some of the key themes mentioned in Chapter 1.

A first theme is that of structures and processes. The debate regarding whether images are phenomenal or epiphenomenal hinges upon what kinds of mental structures are used to process stimuli. For example, when people mentally rotate objects, is the structural representation imaginal or propositional? Either kind of mental representation could generate processes that would enable people to see objects at different angular viewpoints. But the kinds of processes would be different—either mental manipulation of images or mental manipulation of propositions. In order to understand cognition, we need to understand how structures and processes interact.

A second theme is that of validity of causal inferences versus ecological validity. Suppose you wish to hire air-traffic controllers. Can you assess their mental-imagery and spatial-visualization skills using paper-and-pencil tests of manipulation of geometric forms? Or do you need to test them in a setting that is more similar to that of air-traffic control, as through a simulation of the actual job? The paper-and-pencil test probably will yield more precise measurements, but will these measurements be valid? There is no final answer to the question. Rather, researchers are studying this kind of question in order to understand how best to assess people's real-life skills.

A third theme is biological and behavioral studies. As an example, early work by Stephen Kosslyn and his collaborators was all behavioral. The researchers investigated how people mentally manipulate various kinds of images. As time went by, the team started using biological techniques, such as functional magnetic resonance imaging (fMRI), to supplement their behavioral studies. But they never saw the two kinds of research as in opposition to each other. Rather, they viewed them as wholly complementary, and do even today.

Look at the list of words that your friends and family members recalled in the demonstration in Chapter 6. Add up the total number of recollections for every other word (i.e., book, window, box, hat, etc.—the words in odd-numbered positions in the list). Now add up the total number of recollections for the other words (i.e., peace, run, harmony, voice, etc.—the words in even-numbered positions in the list). Most people will recall more words from the first set than from the second set. This is because the first set is made up of words that are concrete, or those words that are easily visualizable. The second set of words is made up of words that are abstract, or not easily visualizable. This is a demonstration of the dual-coding hypothesis (or its more contemporary version, the functional-equivalence hypothesis).

Which is larger in land area, India or Germany? If you are used to seeing the world in terms of the popular Mercator map, in which the map is flat and the equator is in the bottom half of the map, you might think that India and Germany are about the same size. In fact, you might think that Germany may be a bit larger than India. Now look at a globe of the world. You will see that India is actually about five times as large as Germany. This is an example of how our cognitive maps may not be based in reality but rather in our exposure to the topic and to our constructions and heuristics.

Summary

1. **What are some of the major hypotheses regarding how knowledge is represented in the mind?** Knowledge representation comprises the various ways in which our minds create and modify mental structures that stand for what we know about the world outside our minds.

Knowledge representation involves both declarative (knowing that) and nondeclarative (knowing how) forms of knowledge. Through mental imagery, we create analogue mental structures that stand for things that are not presently being sensed in the sense organs. Imagery may involve any of the senses, but the form of imagery most commonly reported by laypeople and most commonly studied by cognitive psychologists is visual imagery. Some studies (e.g., studies of blind participants and some studies of the brain) suggest that visual imagery itself may comprise two discrete systems of mental representation. One system involves nonspatial visual attributes, such as color and shape. Another involves spatial attributes, such as location, orientation, and size or distance scaling.

According to Paivio's dual-code hypothesis, two discrete mental codes for representing knowledge exist. One code is for images and another for words and other symbols. Images are represented in a form analogous to the form we perceive through our senses. In contrast, words and concepts are encoded in a symbolic form, which is not analogical.

An alternative view of image representation is the propositional hypothesis. It suggests that both images and words are represented in a propositional form. The proposition retains the underlying meaning of either images or words, without any of the perceptual features of either. For example, the acoustic features of the sounds of the words are not stored. Nor are the visual features of the colors or shapes of the images. Furthermore, propositional codes, more than imaginal codes, seem to influence mental representation when participants are shown ambiguous or abstract figures. Apparently, unless the context facilitates performance, the use of visual images does not always readily lead to successful performance on some tasks requiring mental manipulations of either abstract figures or ambiguous figures.

2. **What are some of the characteristics of mental imagery?** Based on a modification of the dual-code view, Shepard and others have espoused a functional-equivalence hypothesis. It asserts that images are represented in a form functionally equivalent to percepts, even if images are not truly identical to percepts. Studies of mental rotations, image scaling, and image scanning suggest that imaginal task performance is functionally equivalent to perceptual task performance. Even performance on some tasks involving comparisons of auditory images seems to be functionally equivalent to performance on tasks involving comparisons of auditory percepts.

Propositional codes seem less likely to influence mental representation than imaginal ones when participants are given an opportunity to create their own mental images. For example, they might do so in tasks involving image sizing or mental combinations of imaginal letters.

Some researchers have suggested that experimenter expectancies may have influenced cognitive studies of imagery, but others have refuted these suggestions. In any case, psychobiological studies are not subject to such influences. They seem to support the functional-equivalence hypothesis by finding overlapping brain areas involved in visual perception and mental rotation.

3. **How does knowledge representation benefit from both analogical images and symbolic propositions?** Kosslyn has synthesized these various hypotheses to suggest that images may involve both analogous and propositional forms of knowledge representation. In this case, both forms influence our mental representation and manipulation of images. Thus, some of what we know about images is represented in a form that is analogous to perception. Other things we know about images are represented in a propositional

form. Johnson-Laird has proposed an alternative synthesis. He has suggested that knowledge may be represented as verbally expressible propositions, as somewhat abstracted analogical mental models, or as highly concrete and analogical mental images.

Studies of split-brain patients and patients with lesions indicate some tendency toward hemispheric specialization. Visuospatial information may be processed primarily in the right hemisphere. Linguistic (symbolic) information may be processed primarily in the left hemisphere of right-handed individuals. A case study suggests that spatial imagery also may be processed in a different region of the brain than the regions in which other aspects of visual imagery are processed. Studies of normal participants show that visual-perception tasks seem to involve regions of the brain similar to the regions involved in visual-imagery tasks.

4. **How may conceptual knowledge and expectancies influence the way we use images?** People tend to distort their own mental maps in ways that regularize many features of the maps. For example, they may tend to imagine right angles, symmetrical forms, either vertical or horizontal boundaries (not oblique ones), and well-aligned figures and objects. People also tend to employ distortions of their mental maps in ways that support their propositional knowledge about various landmarks.

They tend to cluster similar landmarks, to segregate dissimilar ones, and to modify relative positions to agree with conceptual knowledge about the landmarks. In addition, people tend to distort their mental maps. They increase their estimates regarding the distances between endpoints as the density of intervening landmarks increases.

Some of the heuristics that affect cognitive maps support the notion that propositional information influences imaginal representations. The influence of propositional information may be particularly potent when participants are not shown a graphic map. Instead, they are asked to read a narrative passage and to envision themselves as participants in a setting described in the narrative.

5. **How do spatial skills develop?** As children grow older, their spatial skills improve. For example, they are more rapid in performing mental rotations. Age differences can also appear during adulthood.

Thinking about Thinking: Factual, Analytical, Creative, and Practical Questions

1. Describe some of the characteristics of pictures versus of words as external forms of knowledge representation.

2. What factors might lead a person's mental model to be inaccurate with respect to how radio transmissions lead people to be able to hear music on a radio?

3. In what ways is mental imagery analogous (or functionally equivalent) to perception?

4. In what ways do propositional forms of knowledge representation influence performance on tasks involving mental imagery?

5. What are some strengths and weaknesses of ERP studies?

6. Some people report never experiencing mental imagery, yet they are able to solve mental-rotation problems. How might they solve such problems?

7. What are some practical applications of having two codes for knowledge representation? Give an example applied to your own experiences, such as applications to studying for examinations.

8. Based on the heuristics described in this chapter, what are some of the distortions that may be influencing your cognitive maps for places with which you are familiar (e.g., a college campus or your hometown)?

Key Terms

analogue codes

cognitive maps

declarative knowledge

dual-code theory

functional-equivalence hypothesis

imagery

knowledge representation

mental models

mental rotation

procedural knowledge

propositional theory

symbolic representation

 Explore CogLab by going to **http://coglab.wadsworth.com.** To learn more, examine the following experiments:

Mental Rotation

Link Word

Mental Scanning

Annotated Suggested Readings

Denis, M., Mellet, E., & Kosslyn, S. M. (2004). *Neuroimaging of mental imagery.* Philadelphia: Taylor & Francis. An up-to-date review of studies that seek to understand mental-imagery skills through the use of neuroimaging techniques.

Logie, R. H., Della Sala, S., Beschin, N., & Denis, M. (2005). Dissociating mental transformations and visuo-spatial storage in working memory: Evidence from representational neglect. *Memory,* *13*(3–4), 430–434. A description of representational neglect and the relationship of this disorder to cognitive processes.

Representation and Organization of Knowledge in Memory: Concepts, Categories, Networks, and Schemas

EXPLORING COGNITIVE PSYCHOLOGY

1. **How are representations of words and symbols organized in the mind?**

2. **How do we represent other forms of knowledge in the mind?**

3. **How does declarative knowledge interact with procedural knowledge?**

Once we have represented knowledge, how do we organize it so that we can retrieve and then use it? The preceding chapter described how knowledge may be represented in the form of propositions and images. In this chapter, we continue the discussion of knowledge representation. We expand this discussion to include various means of organizing declarative knowledge that can be expressed in words and other symbols (i.e., "knowing that"). Consider, for example, your knowledge of facts about cognitive psychology, about world history, about your personal history, and about mathematics. It relies on your mental organization of declarative knowledge. In addition, this chapter describes a few of the various models for representing procedural knowledge. This is knowledge about how to follow various procedural steps for performing actions (i.e., "knowing how"). For example, your knowledge of how to ride a bicycle, how to write your signature, how to drive a car to a familiar location, and how to catch a ball depends on your mental representation of procedural knowledge. Some theorists even have suggested integrative models for representing both declarative and procedural knowledge.

To get an idea of how declarative and procedural knowledge may interact, get out a piece of scrap paper and a pen or pencil. Try the demonstration in the "Investigating Cognitive Psychology" box.

In addition to seeking to understand the *what* (the form or structure) of knowledge representation, cognitive psychologists also try to grasp the *how* (the processes) of knowledge representation and manipulation. That is, what are some of the general processes by which we select and control the disorganized array of raw data available to us through our sense organs? How do we relate that sensory information

---

INVESTIGATING COGNITIVE PSYCHOLOGY

As quickly and as legibly as possible, write your normal signature, from the first letter of your first name to the last letter of your last name. Don't stop to think about which letters come next. Just write as quickly as possible.

Turn the paper over. As quickly and as legibly as possible, write your signature backward. Start with the last letter of your last name and work toward the first letter of your first name.

Now, compare the two signatures. Which signature was more easily and accurately created?

For both signatures, you had available extensive declarative knowledge of which letters preceded or followed one another. But for the first task, you also could call on procedural knowledge, based on years of knowing how to sign your name.

to the information we have available from internal sources of information (i.e., our memories and our thought processes)? How do we organize and reorganize our mental representations during various cognitive processes? Through what mental processes do we operate on the knowledge we have in our minds? To what extent are these processes domain general—common to multiple kinds of information, such as verbal and quantitative information? Conversely, to what extent are they domain specific—used only for particular kinds of information, such as verbal or quantitative information?

Knowledge representation and processing have been investigated by researchers from several different disciplines. Among these researchers are cognitive psychologists, computer scientists studying artificial intelligence (AI; attempts to program machines to perform intelligently), and neuropsychologists. Their diverse approaches to investigating knowledge representation promote exploration of a wide range of phenomena. They also encourage multiple perspectives of similar phenomena. Finally, they offer the strength of **converging operations**—the use of multiple approaches and techniques to address a problem.

Other than to satisfy their own idle curiosity, why do so many different researchers want to understand how knowledge is represented? The way in which knowledge is represented profoundly influences how effectively knowledge can be manipulated for performing any number of cognitive tasks. To illustrate the influence of knowledge representation through a very crude analogy, try the following multiplication task, using a representation in either Roman or Arabic numerals:

$$
\begin{array}{cc}
\text{CMLIX} & 959 \\
\underline{\times \text{ LVIII}} & \underline{\times\ 58}
\end{array}
$$

Organization of Declarative Knowledge

The fundamental unit of symbolic knowledge is the **concept**—an idea about something that provides a means of understanding the world (Bruner, Goodnow, & Austin, 1956; Fodor, 1994; Hampton, 1997b, 1999; Kruschke, 2003; Love, 2003). Often, a single concept may be captured in a single word, such as *apple*. Each concept relates to other concepts, such as *redness, roundness,* or *fruit*.

One way to organize concepts can be captured by the notion of a category. A **category** is a concept that functions to organize or point out aspects of equivalence among other concepts based on common features or similarity to a prototype; see Chapter 3 for more information on prototypes (Coley, Atran, & Medin, 1997; Hampton, 1995; Mayer, 2000b; Medin, 1998; Medin & Aguilar, 1999; Wattenmaker, 1995; Wisniewski & Medin, 1994). For example, the word *apple* can act as a category, as in a collection of different kinds of apples. But it also can act as a concept within the category *fruit*. We later discuss a number of different ways to organize concepts into categories. These ways include the use of defining features, prototypes and exemplars, and hierarchically organized semantic **networks.** Later in the chapter, we also discuss how concepts also may be organized into **schemas,** which are mental frameworks for representing knowledge that encompass an array of interrelated concepts in a meaningful organization (Bartlett, 1932; Brewer, 1999). For example, we might have a schema for a kitchen. It tells us the kinds of things one might find in a kitchen and where we might find them.

A problem with schemas is that they can give rise to stereotypes. We might, for example, have a schema for the kind of person we believe was responsible for the destruction of the World Trade Center on September 11, 2001. This schema can easily generate a stereotype of certain groups of people as likely terrorists.

Concepts and Categories

In general, concepts and categories can be divided in various ways. One commonly used distinction is that between natural categories and artifact categories (Medin & Heit, 1999; Medin, Lynch, & Solomon, 2000). **Natural categories** are groupings that occur naturally in the world. For example, birds or trees form natural categories. **Artifact categories** are groupings that are designed or invented by humans to serve particular purposes or functions. Examples of artifact categories are automobiles and kitchen appliances. The speed it takes to assign objects to categories seems to be about the same for both natural and artifact categories (VanRullen & Thorpe, 2001).

Natural and artifact categories are relatively stable. Moreover, people tend to agree on criteria for membership. A tiger is always a mammal, for example. A knife is always an implement used for cutting. But concepts are not always stable. They can change (Dunbar, 2003; Thagard, 2003). Some categories are referred to as *ad hoc categories*, which are categories that are formed with a particular purpose in mind (Barsalou, 1983; Little, Lewandowsky, & Heit, 2006). Whereas natural and artifact categories are likely to appear in a dictionary, ad hoc categories are not. An example would be "things you need to write a paper." If you are writing a paper for a course, you need certain things. But what are they? Well, they vary across persons, across subject matters, and across time. Similarly, "things you need to attract a romantic partner" may vary widely from one person to the next.

An additional kind of entity is a **nominal kind,** which is the arbitrary assignment of a label to an entity that meets a certain set of prespecified conditions or rules (Kloos & Sloutsky, 2004). In some cases, the features for nominal kinds are clear. For example, a widow is a woman whose husband is deceased. A quadrilateral is any four-sided figure. In other cases, the features are not so clear, as for "lover" or "annoyance." In these cases, it is particularly difficult to ascertain how meaning is constructed. Several theories have been proposed that attempt to do so.

Feature-Based Categories: A Defining View

The classic view of conceptual categories involves disassembling a concept into a set of featural components. These components are singly necessary and jointly sufficient to define the category (Katz, 1972; Katz & Fodor, 1963). In other words, each feature is an essential element of the category. Together, the properties uniquely define the category. These components may be viewed as defining features because they constitute the definition of a category, according to the feature-based, componential point of view. A **defining feature** is a necessary attribute: For a thing to be an "X," it must have that feature. Otherwise, it is not an "X."

Consider, for example, the term *bachelor*. In addition to being human, a bachelor can be viewed as comprising three features: male, unmarried, and adult. The features are each singly necessary. Even the absence of one feature makes the category inapplicable. Thus, an unmarried male who is not an adult would not be a bachelor. We would not refer to a 12-year-old unmarried boy as a bachelor because he is not an adult. Nor would we refer to just any male adult as a bachelor. If he is married, he is out of the running. An unmarried female adult is not a bachelor, either. Moreover, the three features are jointly sufficient. If a person has all three features, then he is automatically a bachelor. According to this view, you cannot be male, unmarried, and adult, and at the same time not be a bachelor. The feature-based view applies to more than bachelorhood, of course. For example, the term *wife* is made up of the features *married*, *female*, and *adult*. *Husband* comprises the features *married*, *male*, and *adult*.

The feature-based view is especially common among linguists, those who study language (Clark & Clark, 1977). This view is attractive because it makes categories of meaning appear so orderly. Unfortunately, it does not work as well as it appears to at first glance. Some categories do not readily lend themselves to featural analysis. *Game* is one such category. Finding anything at all that is a common feature of all games is actually difficult to do (Wittgenstein, 1953). Some are fun; some are not. Some involve multiple players; others, such as solitaire, do not. Some are competitive; others, such as children's circle games (e.g., ring-around-the-rosy), are not. The more you consider the concept of a game, the more you begin to wonder whether there is anything at all that holds the category together. It is not clear that there are any defining features of a game at all. Nonetheless, we all know what we mean, or think we do, by the word *game*.

Some things may seem to have clear defining features. Yet a violation of those defining features does not seem to change the category we use to define them. Consider a zebra (see Keil, 1989). We all know that a zebra is a black-and-white-striped horselike animal. However, suppose that someone were to paint a zebra all black. A zebra painted black is missing the critical attribute of stripes, but we still would call it a zebra. We run into the same problem with birds. We might think of the ability to fly as critical to being a bird. But certainly we would agree that a robin whose wings have been clipped is still a robin and still a bird. So is an ostrich, which does not fly.

The examples of the robin and the ostrich point out another problem with the feature-based theory. Both a robin and an ostrich share the same defining features of birds. They are, therefore, birds. However, loosely speaking, a robin seems somehow to be a better example of a bird than is an ostrich. Indeed, suppose people are asked to rate the typicality of a robin versus an ostrich as a bird. The former virtually always will get a higher rating than the latter (Malt & Smith, 1984; Mervis, Catlin, & Rosch, 1976; Rosch, 1975). Moreover, children learn typical instances of a category earlier than they learn atypical ones (Rosch, 1978). Table 8.1 shows some ratings of typicality for various instances of birds (Malt & Smith, 1984). Clearly, there are enormous differences. On the 7-point scale used by Malt and Smith for ratings of the typicality of birds, *bat* received a rating of 1.53. This rating is despite the fact that a bat, strictly speaking, is not even a bird at all.

In sum, the feature-based theory has some attractive features, but it does not seem to give a complete account of categories. Some specific examples of a category such as *bird* seem to be better examples than others. Yet they all have the same defining

TABLE 8.1	Typicality Ratings for Birds			

Barbara Malt and Edward Smith (1984) found enormous differences in the typicality ratings for various instances of birds (or birdlike animals). (After Malt & Smith, 1984.)

BIRD	RATING*	BIRD	RATING*
Robin	6.89	Vulture	4.84
Bluebird	6.42	Sandpiper	4.47
Seagull	6.26	Chicken	3.95
Swallow	6.16	Flamingo	3.37
Falcon	5.74	Albatross	3.32
Mockingbird	5.47	Penguin	2.63
Starling	5.16	Bat	1.53
Owl	5.00		

*Ratings were made on a 7-point scale, with 7 corresponding to the highest typicality.

features. However, the various examples may be differentially typical of the category of birds. Thus, we need a theory of knowledge representation that better characterizes how people truly represent knowledge.

Prototype Theory: A Characteristic View

The **prototype theory** suggests that categories are formed on the basis of a (prototypical, or averaged) model of the category. Crucial to this theory are **characteristic features,** which describe (characterize or typify) the prototype but are not necessary for it. Characteristic features commonly are present in exemplars of concepts. But they are not always present. For example, consider the prototype of a game. It might include that it usually is enjoyable, has two or more players, and presents some degree of challenge. But a game does not have to be enjoyable. It does not have to have two or more players. And it does not have to be challenging. Similarly, a bird usually has wings and flies. This theory introduces a new wrinkle into our attempt to understand knowledge organization by basing categorization on a prototype. A *prototype* is usually the original item on which subsequent models are based. But in this theory, the prototype may be whichever model best represents the class on which the category is based. This theory can handle the facts that (1) games seem to have no defining features at all and (2) a robin seems to be a better example of a bird than is an ostrich.

To understand how these problems are handled, you need to understand the concept of a characteristic feature. Whereas a defining feature is possessed by every instance of a category, a characteristic feature need not be. Instead, many or most instances possess each characteristic feature. Thus, the ability to fly is typical of birds. But it is not a defining feature of a bird. An ostrich cannot fly. It also lacks some other characteristic features of birds. According to prototype theory, it thus seems less birdlike than a robin, which can fly. Similarly, a typical game may be enjoyable; but it need not be so. Indeed, consider what happens when people are asked to list the features of a category, such as *fruit* or *furniture*. Most features that the people list are characteristic rather than defining (Rosch & Mervis, 1975). Suppose one lists the properties typical of a category such as *fruit* and then assesses how many of those properties a given instance has. One actually can compute a score of family resemblance that indicates how typical an instance is, overall, of the more general category (Rosch & Mervis, 1975).

Psychologists, in reflecting on how people seem to think about concepts and categories, came to differentiate two kinds of categories. These are called *classical concepts* and *fuzzy concepts*. Classical concepts are categories that can be readily defined through defining features, such as bachelor. Fuzzy concepts are categories that cannot be so easily defined, such as games. Their borders are, as their name implies, fuzzy. Classical concepts tend to be inventions that experts have devised for arbitrarily labeling a class that has associated defining features. Fuzzy concepts tend to evolve naturally (Smith, 1988, 1995a). Thus, the concept of a bachelor is an arbitrary concept we invented. Some experts may suggest that we use the word *fruit* to describe any part of a plant that has seeds, pulp, and skin. Nevertheless, our natural, fuzzy concept of fruit usually does not easily extend to tomatoes, pumpkins, and cucumbers. Check the dictionary definitions for tomatoes, pumpkins, and cucumbers if you doubt their fruitiness. All of them really belong to the superordinate (higher level) category, fruit. These examples are, however, rare subordinate (lower level) items within this category.

Classical concepts and categories—and the words that label them—may be built on defining features. Fuzzy concepts and categories are built around prototypes. According to the prototype view, an object will be classified as an instance of a category if it is sufficiently similar to the prototype. Exactly what is meant by similarity to a prototype can be a complex issue. There are actually different theories of how this similarity should be measured (Smith & Medin, 1981). For our purposes, we view similarity in terms of the number of features shared between an object and the prototype. Perhaps some features even should be weighed more heavily as being more central to the prototype than are other features (e.g., Komatsu, 1992).

Actually, some psychologists suggest that instead of using a single prototype for categorizing a concept, we use multiple exemplars. **Exemplars** are typical representatives of a category (Murphy, 1993; Ross, 2000; Ross & Spalding, 1994). For example, in considering birds, we might think of not only the prototypical songbird, which is small, flies, builds nests, sings, and so on. We might also think of exemplars for birds of prey, for large flightless birds, for medium-sized waterfowl, and so on. Some investigators use this approach in explaining how categories are both formed and used in speeded classification situations (Nosofsky & Palmeri, 1997; Nosofsky, Palmeri, & McKinley, 1994; see also Estes, 1994). In particular, categories are set up by creating a rule and then by storing exceptions as exemplars. Later during recognition, exemplars race in memory. The speed of each item is determined by similarity to the target item. Likely candidates then enter a selection process. Thus, the category is coherent and stable. Storing exceptions allows categories to remain flexible. Indeed, suppose we have multiple exemplars. Then when we see an instance of a bird we can more flexibly match this instance to an appropriate exemplar than to a single prototype (Ross & Spalding, 1994). Exemplar theories of categorization have also been criticized. One notable criticism questions the number and type of exemplars that are stored for each category (Smith, 2005). For instance, is every exception to the rule stored, or are only the most prominent ones saved? Some theorists contend that there are not enough resources within the mind for a representation of every rule and each exception to the rule for each category (Collier, 2005). Some work supports neither an exclusive exemplar theory nor an exclusive rule-based theory (Rouder, & Ratcliff, 2004, 2006). Rather, some combination of the two is thought to be more appropriate.

A Synthesis: Combining Feature-Based and Prototype Theories

It is interesting that even classical categories seem to have prototypes. Consider two classical concepts (Armstrong, Gleitman, & Gleitman, 1983): *odd number* and *plane geometry figure*. Both these concepts are defined easily. For example, an *odd number* is any integer not evenly divisible by 2. People found different instances of these categories to be more or less prototypical of their respective categories. For example, 7 and 13 are typical examples of odd numbers that are viewed as quite close to the prototype for an odd number. In contrast, 15 and 21 are not seen as so prototypically odd. In other words, people view 7 and 13 as better exemplars of odd numbers than 15 and 21. Nevertheless, all four numbers are actually odd. Similarly, a triangle is viewed as typical of plane geometry figures. In contrast, an ellipse is not. However, both figures are by definition, in a plane.

A full theory of categorization might need to combine both defining and characteristic features (see also Hampton, 1997a; Smith & associates, 1988; Smith, Shoben, & Rips, 1974; Wisniewski, 1997, 2000). According to this view, each category has both a prototype and a core. A **core** refers to the defining features something must have to be considered an example of a category. In contrast, the prototype encompasses the characteristic features that tend to be typical of an example but that are not necessary for being considered an example.

Consider the concept of a robber, for example. The core requires that someone labeled as a robber be a person who takes from others without permission. The prototype, however, tends to identify particular people as more likely to be robbers. Take, for example, white-collar criminals. Their crimes can include embezzling millions of dollars from their employers. These criminals are, however, difficult to catch. In part, the reason they are difficult to catch is that they do not look like our prototypes of robbers, no matter how much they may steal from other people. In contrast, unkempt denizens of our inner cities sometimes are arrested for crimes they did not commit. In part, the reason is that they more closely match the commonly held prototype of a robber, regardless of whether or not they steal.

Two researchers tested the notion that we come to understand the importance of defining features only as we grow older (Keil & Batterman, 1984). Younger children, they hypothesized, view categories largely in terms of characteristic features. The investigators presented children in the age range from 5 to 10 years with descriptions. Among them were two unusual individuals. The first was "a smelly, mean old man with a gun in his pocket who came to your house and took your TV set because your parents didn't want it anymore and told him he could have it." The second was "a very friendly and cheerful woman who gave you a hug, but then disconnected your toilet bowl and took it away without permission and with no intention to return it." Younger children often characterized the first description as a better depiction of a robber than the second description. It was not until close to age 10 years that children began to shift toward characterizing the second individual as more robberlike. In other words, the younger children viewed someone as a robber even if the person did not steal anything. What mattered was that the person had the characteristic features of a robber. However, the transition is never fully complete. We might suspect that the first individual would be at least as likely to be arrested as the second. Thus, the issue of categorization itself remains somewhat fuzzy, but it appears to include some aspects of defining features and some aspects of prototypicality.

Theory-Based View

A departure from feature-based, prototype-based, and exemplar-based views of meaning is a theory-based view of meaning, also sometimes called an explanation-based view. A **theory-based view of meaning** holds that people understand and categorize concepts in terms of implicit theories, or general ideas they have regarding those concepts (Markman, 2003). For example, what makes someone a "good sport"? In the componential view, you would try to isolate features of a good sport. In the prototype view, you would try to find characteristic features of a good sport. In the exemplar view, you might try to find some good examples you have known in your life. In the theory-based view, you would use your experience to construct an explanation for what makes someone a good sport. Such a theory might go something like this: A good sport is someone who, when he or she wins, is gracious in victory and does not mock losers or otherwise make them feel bad about losing. It is also someone who, when he or she loses, loses graciously and does not blame the winner or the referee or find excuses. Rather, he or she takes the defeat in stride, congratulates the winner, and then moves on. Note that in the theory-based view, it is difficult to capture the essence of the theory in a word or two. Rather, the view of a concept is more complex.

The theory-based view suggests that people can distinguish between essential and incidental, or accidental features of concepts because they have complex mental representations of these concepts. One study showed how such theories might manifest themselves in judgments about newly learned concepts (Rips, 1989). Participants received stories about hypothetical creature. The stimuli were presented under two experimental conditions.

In this study (Rips, 1989), one condition involved a birdlike creature called a sorp that, through an accident, came to look like an insect. It was never stated that the sorp was birdlike or insectlike. Rather, the circumstances of the transformation were described in some detail. The sorp was described as having a diet consisting of seeds and berries, as having two wings and two legs, and as nesting high in the branches of a tree. The nest, like that of a bird, was composed of twigs and similar materials. Moreover, the sorp was covered with bluish-gray feathers, like many birds. But a particular sorp had a misfortune. Its nest was near the burial place of hazardous chemicals. As the chemicals contaminated the vegetation that the sorp ate, its appearance gradually started to change. The sorp lost its feathers and instead grew a new pair of wings that had a transparent membrane. The sorp left its nest and developed an outer shell that was brittle and iridescent. It grew two more pairs of legs so that it now had six legs in all. It came to be able to hold on to smooth surfaces, and it started sustaining itself solely on the nectar of flowers. In due course, the sorp mated with another sorp, a normal female. The female laid the fertilized eggs that resulted from the mating in her nest and incubated them. Then, after 3 weeks, normal young sorps emerged from their shells. Note that, in this description, the fact of the sorp's being able to mate with a normal sorp to produce normal sorps shows that the unfortunate sorp never really changed its basic biological makeup. It remained, in essence, a sorp.

The second condition involved an essential change in the nature of a creature. In other words, the change was one of essence rather than of accident. The change involved a creature known as a doon. During an early stage of the doon's life, it is known as a sorp. It has all the characteristics of a sorp (as previously described). But after a few months, the doon sheds its feathers and then develops the same characteristics that resulted from the unfortunate sorp's accident. Note that in this second condition, there is a transformation identical to that of the sorp described in the first condition, but the transformation is represented as a natural biological one rather than an accidental one caused by proximity to hazardous chemicals.

A control group read only the description of sorps, but experimental participants in the study were asked to provide two ratings after reading about the sorp and the doon. The first rating was of the degree to which the sorp (in the sorp condition) or the doon (in the doon condition) fit into the category of "bird." The second rating was the similarity of the sorp or doon to birds. Thus, one rating was for category membership, and the other for similarity. Control-group participants were asked merely to rate the similarity of sorps to birds.

According to prototype and exemplar theories, there is no particular reason to expect the two sets of ratings from experimental participants to show different patterns. According to these theories, people categorize objects on the basis of their similarity to a prototype or an exemplar, so the results should be the same for both sets of ratings. Figure 8.1 shows the actual data.

The results for the categorization and similarity ratings are dramatically different. Note that in the accidental-change condition, category membership ratings are higher than in the essential-change condition. In other words, people were less likely to see the accidental change than the essential change as affecting fundamental category membership. In contrast, similarity ratings were lower in the accidental-change condition than in the essential-change condition. Control-group participants had no trouble recognizing the similarity of the sorp to a bird. The difference in patterns between the category-membership and similarity ratings is consistent with the theory-based view of meaning.

Further support for the theory-based view comes from work with children. A number of investigators have studied a view of meaning called *essentialism*. This view holds that certain categories, such as those of "lion" or "female," have an underlying reality that cannot be observed directly (Gelman, 2003, 2004). For example, someone could be, say, a female even if another individual were unable in his or her observations on the street to be able to detect that femaleness. One instance is having short hair. Having short hair might be more typical of males than females, yet females can have short hair. Gelman (2004) showed that even young children look beyond obvi-

FIGURE 8.1

Effects of Changes on Categorizing and Similarity Ratings

From L. J. Rips, "Similarity, Typicality, and Categorization," in S. Vosniadou & A. Ortony (Eds.), Similarity and Analogical Reasoning, pp. 21–59. Copyright © 1989 Cambridge University Press.

ous features to understand the essential nature of things. This view contradicts Piaget's theory of cognitive development. According to that theory, children in the age range from roughly 8 to 11 years are "concrete" thinkers. They cannot abstract features that are formal in nature. Yet, the work of psychologists studying essentialism suggests that young children can and do look for hidden features that are in no way obvious.

For example, in one study, 165 children ages 4 to 5 years were asked to make inferences about things like a tiger or gold (Gelman & Markman, 1986). They could use either category membership, which is abstract, or perceptual similarity, which is concrete, to make their inferences. The inferences they would make through these two means were different. The researchers found that even by the age of 4 years, children could make inferences using the abstract categories, even when these categories conflicted with appearances.

How people learn about concepts and categories depends, in part, on the task they will do with those concepts and categories. For example, people learn about categories one way if they need to make classifications (e.g., "Is this particular animal a cat or a dog?") and another way if they need to make inferences (e.g., "If this animal is a dog, how many toes will it have?") (Yamauchi & Markman, 1998). Learning, therefore, is strategically flexible, depending on the task that the individual will have to do; it does not occur with a "one-size-fits-all" rigidity (Markman & Ross, 2003; Ross, 1997).

What all this means is that meaning is not just a matter of a set of features or exemplars. From the time children are very young, they start to form theories about the nature of objects. These theories develop with age. For example, you probably have a theory about what makes a car a car. You could see cars looking all kinds of strange ways. As long as they conformed to your theory, you would nevertheless label them as cars. Theories enable us to view meaning deeply rather than just to assign meaning on the basis of superficial features of objects.

Semantic Network Models

An older model still in use today is that knowledge is represented in terms of a hierarchical semantic (related to meaning as expressed in language—i.e., in linguistic symbols) network. A semantic network is a web of interconnected elements of meaning (Collins & Quillian, 1969). **Nodes** are the elements of a network. In a semantic network, they typically represent concepts. The connections between nodes are *labeled relationships*. They might involve category membership (e.g., an "is a" relationship connecting "pig" to "mammal"), attributes (e.g., connecting "furry" to "mammal"), or some other semantic relationship. Thus, a network provides a means for organizing concepts. The exact form of a semantic network differs from one theory to another. But most networks look something like the highly simplified network shown in Figure 8.2. The labeled relationships form links that enable the individual to connect the various nodes in a meaningful way.

In a seminal study, the participants were given statements relating concepts, such as "A robin is a bird" and "A robin is an animal" (Collins & Quillian, 1969). They were asked to verify the truth of the statements. The participants received only *class-inclusion statements*, in which the subject was a single word. The *predicate*, describing the subject, took the form "is a [category noun]." Some of the statements were true. Others were not. As the conceptual category of the predicate became more hierarchically remote from the category of the subject of the statement, people generally took longer to verify a true statement. Thus, we could expect people to take longer to verify "A robin is an animal" than "A robin is a bird." The reason is that *bird* is an immediate superordinate category for *robin*. *Animal*, however, is a more remote super-

FIGURE 8.2

In a simple semantic network, nodes serve as junctures representing concepts linked by labeled relationships: (a) a basic network structure showing that relationship R links the nodes a and b; (b) a simple network diagram of the sentence "Mary hit the ball."

FIGURE 8.3

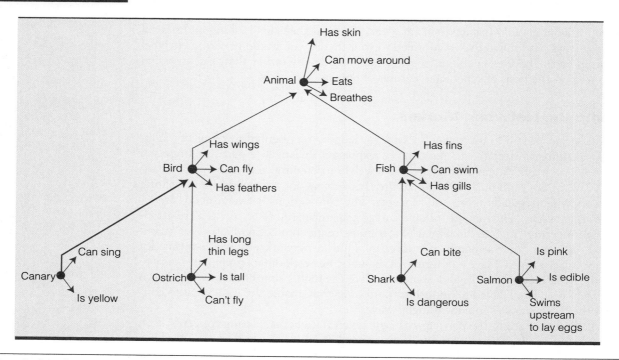

From In Search of the Human Mind *by Robert J. Sternberg. Copyright © 1995 by Harcourt Brace & Company. Reproduced by permission of the publisher.*

ordinate category. Collins and Quillian concluded that a hierarchical network representation, such as the one shown in Figure 8.3, adequately accounted for the response times in their study. According to this model, organized knowledge representation takes the form of a hierarchical tree diagram.

A hierarchical model seemed ideal to the investigators. Within a hierarchy we can efficiently store information that applies to all members of a category at the highest possible level in the hierarchy. We do not have to repeat the information at all of the lower levels in the hierarchy. Therefore, a hierarchical model contains a high degree of cognitive economy. The system allows for a maximum of efficient capacity use with a minimum of redundancy. Thus, if you know that dogs and cats are mammals, you store everything you know about mammals at the mammal level. For example, you might store that mammals have fur and give birth to live young whom they nurse. You do not have to repeat that information again at the hierarchically lower level for dogs and cats. Whatever was known about items at higher levels in a hierarchy was applied to all items at lower levels in the hierarchy. This concept of *inheritance* implies that lower-level items inherit the properties of higher-level items. This concept, in turn, is the key to the economy of hierarchical models. Computer models of the network clearly demonstrated the value of cognitive economy.

FIGURE 8.4

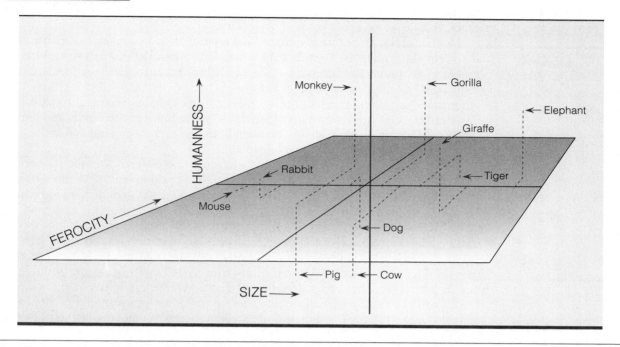

One alternative to hierarchical network models of semantic memory involves representations highlighting the comparison of semantic features. The features model, too, fails to explain all the data regarding semantic memory.

The Collins and Quillian study instigated a whole line of research into the structure of semantic networks. However, many of the psychologists who studied the Collins and Quillian data disagreed with Collins and Quillian's interpretations. For one thing, numerous anomalies in the data could not be explained by the model. For example, participants take longer to verify "A lion is a mammal" than to verify "A lion is an animal." Yet, in a strictly hierarchical view, verification should be faster for the mammal statement than for the animal one. After all, the category *mammal* is hierarchically closer to the category *lion* than is the category *animal*.

An alternative theory is that knowledge is organized based on a comparison of semantic features, rather than on a strict hierarchy of concepts (Smith, Shoben, & Rips, 1974). This theory differs from the feature-based theory of categorization in a key way. Features of different concepts are compared directly, rather than serving as the basis for forming a category.

Consider, for example, members of the set of mammal names. Mammal names can be represented in terms of a psychological space organized by three features: size, ferocity, and humanness (Henley, 1969). A lion, for example, would be high in all three. An elephant would be particularly high in size but not so high in ferocity. A rat would be small in size but relatively high in ferocity. Figure 8.4 shows how information might be organized within a nonhierarchical feature-based theory. Note that this representation, too, leaves a number of questions unanswered. For example, how does the word *mammal* itself fit in? It does not seem to fit into the space of mammal names. Where would other kinds of objects fit?

Neither of the preceding two theories of representation completely specifies how all information might be organized in a semantic network. Perhaps some kind of combination of representations is used (e.g., Collins & Loftus, 1975). Other network models tend to emphasize mental relationships that we think about more frequently rather than just any hierarchical relationships. For example, they might emphasize the link between birds and robins or sparrows or the link between birds and flying. They would not emphasize the link between birds and turkeys or penguins or the link between birds and standing on two legs.

Concepts appear to have a **basic level** (sometimes termed a natural level) of specificity, a level within a hierarchy that is preferred to other levels (Medin, Proffitt, & Schwartz, 2000; Rosch, 1978). Suppose I show you a red, roundish edible object that has a stem and that came from a tree. You might characterize it as a fruit, an apple, a Delicious apple, a Red Delicious apple, and so on. Most people, however, would characterize the object as an apple. The basic, preferred level is *apple*. In general, the basic level is neither the most abstract nor the most specific. Of course, this basic level can be manipulated by context or expertise (Tanaka & Taylor, 1991). Suppose the object were held up at a fruit stand that sold only apples. You might describe it as a Red Delicious apple to distinguish it from the other apples around it. Similarly, an apple farmer talking to a horticulture student might be more specific than would be a hurried shopper.

How can we tell what the basic level is? Why is the basic level the *apple*, rather than *Red Delicious apple* or *fruit?* Or why is it *cow*, rather than *mammal* or *Guernsey?* Perhaps the basic level is the one that has the largest number of distinctive features that set it off from other concepts at the same level (Rosch & associates, 1976). Thus, most of us would find more distinguishing features between an apple and a cow, say, than between a Red Delicious apple and a Pippin apple. Similarly, we would find few distinguishing features between a Guernsey cow and a Holstein cow. Again, not everyone necessarily would have the same basic level, as in the case of farmers. However, most people would. For our purposes, the basic level is the one that most people find to be maximally distinctive.

When people are shown pictures of objects, they identify the objects at a basic level more quickly than they identify objects at higher or lower levels (Rosch & associates, 1976). Objects appear to be recognized first in terms of their basic level. Only afterward are they classified in terms of higher- or lower-level categories. Thus, the picture of the roundish red edible object from a tree probably first would be identified as an apple. Only then, if necessary, would it be identified as a fruit or a Red Delicious apple.

A common method for examining semantic networks involves the use of word-stem completion. In this task, participants are presented a prime for a very short amount of time. Then the participant is given the first few letters of a word and told to complete the stem with the first word that comes to mind. The stems could be completed with a semantically related word or any number of unrelated words. Normally, participants complete these stems with a semantically related item. These findings are taken to mean that the activation of one node of the network increases the activation of related nodes. One study noted that, with the progression of Alzheimer's disease, the activation of related nodes is impaired. As a result, the word stems for patients with Alzheimer's disease more frequently are completed with words that are unrelated to the prime (Passafiume, Di Giacomo, & Carolei, 2006).

An interesting concept related to semantic networks is category-specific semantic impairments. These impairments may be caused by a number of syndromes, including, among others, semantic dementia and herpes simplex virus encephalitis (HSVE) (Capitani & associates, 2003). These category-specific impairments include, most commonly, difficulties with animate or inanimate categories. In cases of both semantic dementia and HSVE, damage to the anterior temporal lobes is observed (Ralph, Lowe, & Rogers, 2007). Damage to these areas seems to cause deficits in accessing semantic categories. Semantic networks were also explored with the patient H. M. (see Chapter 5 for general information on H. M). As you may recall, H. M.'s hippocampus was lesioned as a treatment for epilepsy. A side effect of this treatment was a great loss in the ability to form new memories. However, recent evidence suggests that H. M. is capable of learning at least some new semantic information. Although performance on semantic tasks was impaired in H. M., clearly there was some semantic learning (O'Kane, Kensinger, & Corkin, 2004). These findings indicate that, although semantic learning can occur without the involvement of the hippocampus, such learning is greatly improved by its use.

We may broaden our understanding of concepts further if we consider not only the hierarchical and basic levels of a concept (Komatsu, 1992). We also should take into account other relational information the concept contains. Specifically, we may better understand the ways in which we derive meanings from concepts by considering their relations with other concepts, as well as the relations among attributes contained within a concept.

Schematic Representations

Schemas

One main approach to understanding how concepts are related in the mind is through schemas. They are very similar to semantic networks except that schemas are often more task oriented. Recall that a schema is a mental framework for organizing knowledge. It creates a meaningful structure of related concepts. Of course, both concepts and schemas may be viewed at many levels of analysis. It all depends on the mind of the individual and the context (Barsalou, 2000). For example, most of us probably view *cow* as a fundamental concept within, perhaps, a more elaborate schema for farm animals. However, for a cattle breeder or a dairy farmer, *cow* may not be at all fundamental. Both the breeder and the farmer may recognize many different kinds of cows. Each one may have various distinctive characteristics. Similarly, most people do not have an elaborate schema for *cognitive psychology*. However, for most cognitive psychologists, the schema for *cognitive psychology* is richly elaborated. It encompasses many subschemas, such as subschemas for attention, memory, and perception.

Schemas have several characteristics that ensure wide flexibility in their use (Rumelhart & Ortony, 1977; Thorndyke, 1984):

1. Schemas can include other schemas. For example, a schema for animals includes a schema for cows, a schema for apes, and so on.
2. Schemas encompass typical, general facts that can vary slightly from one specific instance to another. For example, although the schema for mammals includes a general fact that mammals typically have fur, it allows for humans, who are less hairy than most other mammals. It also allows for porcupines, which seem more prickly than furry, and for marine mammals like whales that have just a few bristly hairs.
3. Schemas can vary in their degree of abstraction. For example, a schema for *justice* is much more abstract than a schema for *apple* or even a schema for *fruit*.

Schemas also can include information about relationships (Komatsu, 1992). Some of this information includes relationships among the following:

- Concepts (e.g., the link between trucks and cars)
- Attributes within concepts (e.g., the height and the weight of an elephant)
- Attributes in related concepts (e.g., the redness of a cherry and the redness of an apple)
- Concepts and particular contexts (e.g., fish and the ocean)
- Specific concepts and general background knowledge (e.g., concepts about particular U.S. presidents and general knowledge about the U.S. government and about U.S. history)

Relationships within schemas that particularly interest cognitive psychologists are causal ("if-then") relationships. For example, consider our schema for glass. It probably specifies that if an object made of glass falls onto a hard surface, the object may break. Schemas also include information that we can use as a basis for drawing inferences in novel situations. For instance, suppose that a 75-year-old woman, a 45-year-old man, a 30-year-old nun, and a 25-year-old woman are sitting on park benches surrounding a playground. A young child falls from some playground equipment. He calls out "Mama!" To whom is the child calling? Chances are, to determine your answer you would be able to draw an inference by calling on various schemas. They would include ones for mothers, for men and women, for people of various ages, and even for people who join religious orders.

Early conceptions of schemas centered on how we represent information in memory (e.g., Bartlett, 1932). They also focused on how children develop cognitive understandings of how the world works (Piaget, 1928, 1952, 1955). Researchers interested in AI have adapted the notion of schemas to fit various computer models of human intelligence. As a part of their overall interest in developing computer models of intelligence, these researchers devised computer models of how knowledge is represented and used.

Scripts

One notion about schematic representations is termed a script (Schank & Abelson, 1977). A **script** is

> *a structure that describes appropriate sequences of events in a particular context. A script is made up of slots and requirements about what can fill those slots. The structure is an interconnected whole, and what is in one slot affects what can be in another. Scripts handle stylized everyday situations. They are not subject to much change, nor do they provide the apparatus for handling totally novel situations. (Schank & Abelson, 1977, p. 41)*

Thus, scripts are much less flexible than are schemas in general. However, scripts include default values for the actors, the props, the setting, and the sequence of events expected to occur. These values taken together compose an overview of an event.

Consider the restaurant script. The script may be applied to one particular kind of restaurant—for example, a coffee shop. A script has several features. One is props. These include tables, a menu, food, a check, and money. A second is roles to be played. They include a customer, a waiter, a cook, a cashier, and an owner. A third feature is opening conditions for the script. For example, the customer is hungry and he or she has money. A fourth feature is scenes. These include entering, ordering, eating, and exiting. And a fifth feature is a set of results. The customer has less money. The owner has more money. The customer is no longer hungry. And sometimes the customer and the owner are pleased.

Various empirical studies have been conducted to test the validity of the script notion. In one, researchers presented their participants with 18 brief stories (Bower, Black, & Turner, 1979). Consider one of these, representing the doctor's office script, in the "Investigating Cognitive Psychology" box.

In the research, participants were asked to read 18 stories. Later, they were asked to perform one of two tasks. In a recall task, participants were asked to recall as much as

---

INVESTIGATING COGNITIVE PSYCHOLOGY

THE DOCTOR

John was feeling bad today, so he decided to go see the family doctor. He checked in with the doctor's receptionist and then looked through several medical magazines that were on the table by his chair. Finally the nurse came and asked him to take off his clothes. The doctor was very nice to him. He eventually prescribed some pills for John. Then John left the doctor's office and headed home.

Did John take off his clothes?

This "scripted" description of a visit to a doctor's office is fairly typical. Notice that in this description, as would probably happen in any verbal description of a script, some details are missing. The speaker (or scriptwriter, in this case) may have omitted mentioning these details. Thus, we do not know for sure that John actually took off his clothes. Moreover, the nurse probably beckoned John at some point. She or he then escorted him to an examination room. The nurse then probably took John's temperature and his blood pressure and weighed him. The doctor probably asked John to describe his symptoms, and so on. But we do not know any of these things for sure.

they could about each of the stories. Here, participants showed a significant tendency to recall, as parts of the stories, elements that were not actually in the stories but that were parts of the scripts that the stories represented. In the recognition task, participants were presented with sentences. They were asked to rate on a 7-point scale their confidence that they had seen each of the sentences. Some of the sentences were from the stories. Others were not. Of the sentences that were *not* from the stories, some were from the relevant scripts. Others were not from these scripts. Participants were more likely to characterize particular nonstory sentences as having come from the stories if the nonstory sentences were script relevant than if the nonstory sentences were not script relevant. The Bower, Black, and Turner research suggested that scripts seem to guide what people recall and recognize—ultimately, what people know.

Imaging studies reveal that the frontal and parietal lobes are involved in the generation of scripts (Godbout & associates, 2004). Generation of scripts requires a great deal of working memory. Further script generation involves the use of both temporal and spatial information.

A number of patient populations experience impaired script use. For instance, people with schizophrenia frequently have trouble recalling and sequencing scripts. Also, these people add events to a script that should not be included. Research indicates a relationship between difficulties with script processing and the positive symptoms of schizophrenia, on the one hand, and dysfunction of the frontal lobes, on the other hand (Matsui & associates, 2006). Another instance of malfunctioning scripts can be observed in people with attention deficit hyperactivity disorder. Impaired sequencing of scripts is observed in this population (Braun & associates, 2004). A decline in the ability to sequence events within a script is also seen as we age (Allain & associates, 2007), presumably as a result of disease processes in certain parts of the aging population. The role of the frontal lobes in script generation and use seems to be central.

An interesting effect seen in script learning is the typicality effect. In general, when a person is learning a script, if both typical and atypical actions are provided, the atypical information will be recalled more readily. This is likely due to the more effortful processing required for atypical information as compared with typical information. When someone suffers from a closed-head injury, the typicality effect disappears (Vakil & associates, 2002). In other words, people then have roughly equal recall of typical and atypical information.

In a related context, scripts also may come into play in regard to the ways in which experts converse with and write for one another. Certainly, experts share a **jargon**—specialized vocabulary commonly used within a group, such as a profession or a trade. In addition, however, experts share a common understanding of scripts that are known by insiders to the field of expertise. For example, after reading Chapter 2, you have a basic understanding of positron emission tomography (PET) methods. Therefore, when someone mentions that a PET scan was used to examine the brain, you have an idea of what happened. People outside the area of expertise do not share this understanding. In the PET example, a person who has never read or learned about PETs might know that the result was an image of the brain but would not know that the procedure involved the injection of a slightly radioactive form of oxygen. When trying to understand technical manuals and technical conversations outside your own area of expertise, you may run into vocabulary difficulties and information gaps. You lack the proper script for interpreting the language being spoken.

PRACTICAL APPLICATIONS OF COGNITIVE PSYCHOLOGY

Take a closer look at the scripts you use in your everyday life. Is your going-to-class script different from your going-to-meals script or other scripted activities? In what ways do your scripts differ—in structure or in details? Try making changes to your script, either in details or in structure. See how things work. For example, you may find that you rush in the morning to get to school or work and forget things or arrive late. Aside from the obvious adjustment of getting up earlier, analyze the structure of your script. See if you can combine or remove steps. You could try laying out your clothes and packing your backpack or briefcase the night before to simplify your morning routine. The bottom line? The best way to make your scripts work better for you is first to analyze what they are and then to correct them.

Despite the flaws in the script model, it has helped cognitive psychologists gain insight into knowledge organization. Scripts may enable us to use a mental framework for acting in certain situations when we must fill in apparent gaps within a given context. Without access to mental scripts, we probably would be at a loss the first time we entered a new restaurant or a new doctor's office. Imagine what it would be like if the nurse at the doctor's office had to explain each step to you. When everyone in a given situation follows a similar script, the day flows much more smoothly.

Whether we subscribe to the notion of categories, semantic networks, or schemas, the important issue is that knowledge is organized. These forms of organization can serve different purposes. The most adaptive and flexible use of knowledge would allow us to use any form of organization, depending on the situation. We need some means to define aspects of the situation, to relate these concepts to other concepts and categories, and to select the appropriate course of action given the situation. Next, we move on to discuss theories about how the mind represents procedural knowledge.

Representations of Procedural Knowledge

Some of the earliest models for representing procedural knowledge come from AI and computer-simulation research (see Chapter 1). With these models, researchers try to get computers to perform tasks intelligently, particularly in ways that simulate intelligent performance of humans. In fact, cognitive psychologists have learned a great deal about representing and using procedural knowledge. They have had to because of the distinctive problems posed in getting computers to implement procedures based on a series of instructions compiled in programs. Through trial-and-error attempts at getting computers to simulate intelligent cognitive processes, cognitive psychologists have come to understand some of the complexities of human information processing. As a result of their efforts, they have developed a variety of models for how information is represented and processed. Each of these models involves the **serial processing** of information, in which information is handled through a linear sequence of operations, one operation at a time. One way in which computers can represent and organize procedural knowledge is in the form of sets of rules governing a **production,** a generation and output of a procedure (Jones & Ritter, 2003). Specifically, computer simulations of productions follow production rules ("if-then" rules), comprising an "if" clause and a "then" clause (Newell & Simon, 1972). People may use this same form of organizing knowledge or something very close to it. For example, suppose your car is veering toward the left side of the road. Then you should steer toward the right side of the road if you wish to avoid hitting the curb. The "if" clause includes a set of conditions that must be met to implement the "then" clause. The "then" clause is an action or a series of actions that are a response to the "if" clause.

For a given clause, each condition may contain one or more variables. For each of these conditions, there may be one or more possibilities. For example, *if* you want to go somewhere by car, and *if* you know how to drive a car, and *if* you are licensed and insured to drive, and *if* you have a car available to you, and *if* you do not have other constraints (e.g., no keys, no gas, broken engine, dead battery), *then* you may execute the actions for driving a car somewhere.

When the rules are described precisely and all the relevant conditions and actions are noted, a huge number of rules are required to perform even a very simple task. These rules are organized into a structure of *routines* (instructions regarding procedures for implementing a task) and *subroutines* (instructions for implementing a subtask within a larger task governed by a routine). Many of these routines and subroutines are *iterative*, meaning that they are repeated many times during the performance of a task. The various routines and subroutines execute component tasks and subtasks required for implementing the main production. For the performance of a particular task or the use of a particular skill, knowledge representation involves a **production system** (Anderson, 1983; Newell & Simon, 1972). It comprises the entire set of rules (productions) for executing the task or using the skill (Anderson, 1993; Simon, 1999a, 1999b).

Consider an example of a simple production system for a pedestrian to cross the street at an intersection with a traffic light (Newell & Simon, 1972). It is shown here (with the "if" clauses indicated to the left of the arrows and the "then" clauses indicated to the right of the arrows):

traffic-light red → stop

traffic-light green → move

move and left foot on pavement → step with right foot

move and right foot on pavement → step with left foot

In this production system, the individual first tests to see whether the light is red. If it is red, the person stops and again tests to see whether the light is red. This sequence is repeated until the light turns green. At that point, the person starts moving. If the person is moving and the left foot is on the pavement, the person will step with the right foot. If the person is moving and the right foot is on the pavement, the person will step with the left foot.

Sometimes, production systems, like computer programs, contain bugs. *Bugs* are flaws in the instructions for the conditions or for executing the actions. For example, in the cross-the-street program, if the last line read "move and right foot on pavement → step with right foot," the individual executing the production system would get nowhere. According to the production-system model, human representations of procedural knowledge may contain some occasional bugs (VanLehn, 1990).

Until about the mid-1970s, researchers interested in knowledge representation followed either of two basic strands of research. AI and information-processing researchers were refining various models for representing procedural knowledge. Cognitive psychologists and other researchers were considering various alternative models for representing declarative knowledge. By the end of the 1970s, some integrative models of knowledge representation began to emerge.

Integrative Models for Representing Declarative and Nondeclarative Knowledge

Combining Representations: ACT-R

An excellent example of a theory that combines forms of mental representation is the **ACT** (adaptive control of thought) model of knowledge representation and information processing (Anderson, 1976, 1993; Anderson, Budiu, & Reder, 2001). In his ACT model, John Anderson synthesized some of the features of serial information-processing models and some of the features of semantic-network models. In ACT, procedural knowledge is represented in the form of production systems. Declarative knowledge is represented in the form of propositional networks. Anderson (1985) defined a proposition as being the smallest unit of knowledge that can constitute a separate assertion. Recall from Chapter 7 that propositions are abstracted underlying meanings of relationships among elements. ACT is an evolved form of earlier models (Anderson, 1972; Anderson & Bower, 1973).

Anderson intended his model to be so broad in scope that it would offer an overarching theory regarding the entire architecture of cognition. In Anderson's view, individual cognitive processes such as memory, language comprehension, problem solving, and reasoning are merely variations on a central theme. They all reflect an underlying system of cognition. The most recent version of ACT, **ACT-R** (where the R stands for *rational*), is a model of information processing that integrates a network representation for declarative knowledge and a production-system representation for procedural knowledge (Anderson, 1983; Figure 8.5).

In ACT-R, networks include images of objects and corresponding spatial configurations and relationships. They also include temporal information, such as relationships involving the sequencing of actions, events, or even the order in which items appear. Anderson referred to the temporal information as "temporal strings." He noted that they contain information about the relative time sequence. Examples would be before/after, first/second/third, and yesterday/tomorrow. These relative time sequences can be compared with absolute time referents, such as 2 P.M., September 4, 2004. The model is under constant revision and currently includes information about statistical regularities in the environment (Anderson, 1991, 1996; Anderson & Fincham, 1996).

Anderson's declarative network model, like many other network models (e.g., Collins & Loftus, 1975), contains a mechanism by which information can be retrieved and a structure for storing information. Recall that within a semantic network, concepts are stored at various nodes within the network. According to Anderson's model (and various other network models), the nodes can be either inactive or

John R. Anderson is a professor of psychology at Carnegie-Mellon University. He is best known for his ACT-R model of human cognition. Anderson also has made major contributions in his work on the application of psychology to real-world learning, such as in learning the computer language LISP.

FIGURE 8.5

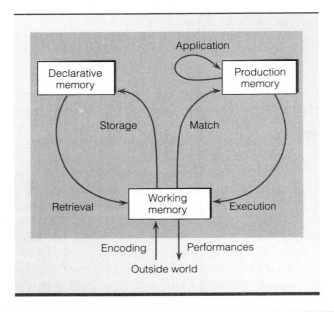

John Anderson's most recent version of ACT-R comprises declarative knowledge ("declarative memory"), procedural knowledge ("procedural memory"), and working memory (the activated knowledge available for cognitive processing, which has a limited capacity). From The Legacy of Solomon Asch: Essays in Cognition and Social Psychology *by Irwin Rock. Copyright © 1990 by Lawrence Erlbaum Associates. Reprinted by permission.*

active at a given time. An active node is one that is, in a sense, "turned on." A node can be turned on—activated—directly by external stimuli such as sensations, or it can be activated by internal stimuli, such as memories or thought processes. Also, it can be activated indirectly, by the activity of one or more neighboring nodes.

Given each node's receptivity to stimulation from neighboring nodes, activation easily can spread from one node to another. But there are limits on the amount of information (number of nodes) that can be activated at any one time. Within the limited capacity of the overall cognitive system, this **spreading activation** is excitation that fans out along a set of nodes within a given network (Shastri, 2003). Of course, as more nodes are activated and the spread of activation reaches greater distances from the initial source of the activation, the activation weakens. Therefore, the nodes closely related to the original node have a great deal of activation. However, nodes that are more remotely related are activated to a lesser degree. For instance, when the node for *mouse* is activated, the node for *cat* also is strongly activated. At the same time, the node for *deer* is activated, but to a much lesser degree. ACT-R also suggests means by which the network changes as a result of activation. For one thing, the more often particular links between nodes are used, the stronger the links become. In a complementary fashion, activation is likely to spread along the routes of frequently traveled connections. It is less likely to spread along infrequently used connections between nodes.

Consider an analogy. Imagine a complex set of water pipes interlinking various locations. When the water is turned on at one location, the water starts moving through various pipes. It is showing a sort of spreading activation. At various interconnections, a valve is either open or closed. It thus either permits the flow to continue through or diverts the flow (the activation) to other connections.

To carry the analogy a bit further, processes such as attention can influence the degree of activation throughout the system. Consider the water system again. The higher the water pressure in the system, the farther along the water will spread through the system of pipes. To relate this metaphor back to spreading activation, consider what happens when we are thinking about an issue and various associations seem to come to mind regarding that issue. We are experiencing the spread of activation along the nodes that represent our knowledge of various aspects of the problem and, possibly, its solution.

To help explain some aspects of spreading activation, picture the pipes as being more flexible than normal pipes. These pipes gradually can expand or contract. It all depends on how frequently they are used. The pipes along routes that are traveled frequently may expand to enhance the ease and speed of travel along those routes. The pipes along routes that are seldom traveled gradually may contract. Similarly, in spreading activation, connections that frequently are used are strengthened. Connections that are seldom used are weakened. Thus, within semantic networks, declarative knowledge may be learned and maintained through the strengthening of connections as a result of frequent use. The theory of spreading activation has been applied to a number of other cognitive concepts. These concepts include social cognition and bilingualism (Dixon & Maddox, 2005; Green, 1998).

How does Anderson explain the acquisition of procedural knowledge? Such knowledge is represented in production systems rather than in semantic networks. Knowledge representation of procedural skills occurs in three stages: cognitive, associative, and autonomous (Anderson, 1980). During the cognitive stage, we think about explicit rules for implementing the procedure. During the associative stage, we practice using the explicit rules extensively, usually in a highly consistent manner. Finally, during the autonomous stage, we use these rules automatically and implicitly. We show a high degree of integration and coordination, as well as speed and accuracy.

For example, while we are in the cognitive stage for learning how to drive a standard-shift car, we must explicitly think about each rule for stepping on the clutch pedal, the gas pedal, or the brake pedal. Simultaneously, we also try to think about when and how to shift gears. During the associative stage, we carefully and repeatedly practice following the rules in a consistent manner. We gradually become more familiar with the rules. We learn when to follow which rules and when to implement which procedures. Eventually, we reach the autonomous stage. At this time we have integrated all the various rules into a single, coordinated series of actions. We no longer need to think about what steps to take to shift gears. We can concentrate instead on listening to our favorite radio station. We simultaneously can think about going to our destination, avoiding accidents, stopping for pedestrians, and so on.

Our progress through these stages is proceduralization (Anderson & associates, 2004). *Proceduralization* is the overall process by which we transform slow, explicit information about procedures ("knowing that") into speedy, implicit, implementations of procedures ("knowing how"). (Recall the discussion of *automatization* in

Chapter 4. This is a term used by other cognitive psychologists to describe essentially the same process as proceduralization.) One means by which we make this transformation is through composition. During this stage, we construct a single production rule that effectively embraces two or more production rules. It thus streamlines the number of rules required for executing the procedure. For example, consider what happens when we learn to drive a standard-shift car. We may compose a single procedure for what were two separate procedures. One was for pressing down on the clutch. The other was for applying the brakes when we reach a stop sign. These multiple processes are combined together into the single procedure of driving.

Another aspect of proceduralization is "production tuning." It involves the two complementary processes of generalization and discrimination. We learn to generalize existing rules to apply them to new conditions. For example, we can generalize our use of the clutch, the brakes, and the accelerator to a variety of standard-shift cars. Finally, we learn to discriminate new criteria for meeting the conditions we face. For example, what happens after we have mastered driving a particular standard-shift car? If we drive a car with a different number of gears or with different positions for the reverse gear, we must discriminate the relevant information about the new gear positions from the irrelevant information about the old gear positions. Taatgen and Lee (2003) demonstrated that the learning of even extremely complex tasks—for instance, air-traffic controlling—can be described through these three processes.

Thus far, the models of knowledge representation presented in this chapter have been based largely on computer models of human intelligence. As the foregoing discussion shows, information-processing theories based on computer simulations of human cognitive processes have greatly advanced our understanding of human knowledge representation and information processing. An alternative approach to understanding knowledge representation in humans has been to study the human brain itself. Much of the research in psychobiology has offered evidence that many operations of the human brain do not seem to process information step-by-step, bit-by-bit. Rather, the human brain seems to engage in multiple processes simultaneously. It acts on myriad bits of knowledge all at once. Such models do not necessarily contradict step-by-step models. First, people seem likely to use both serial and parallel processing. Second, different kinds of processes may be occurring at different levels. Thus, our brains may be processing multiple pieces of information simultaneously. They combine into each of the steps of which we are aware when we process information step by step.

Models Based on the Human Brain

As mentioned previously, knowledge traditionally has been described as either declarative or procedural. Procedural knowledge usually involves some degree of skill. Examples would be skill in problem solving or numerical, linguistic, or musical operations. These skills increase as a result of practice. Eventually, performance requires little conscious attention, at least under most circumstances (see Chapter 4). For example, knowledge of a telephone number is declarative knowledge. Knowing how to memorize a phone number involves procedural knowledge. By now, you have become very skilled at knowing how to memorize information. As a result, you are no longer aware of many of the procedures you use for doing so. When you were a child, however, you were still learning how mentally to represent the procedural knowledge for memorizing simple facts. You were probably keenly conscious of learning to do so. For instance, when a child is trying to learn his or her own phone number, the child frequently is asked to recite and dial it. This repetition helps to form a permanent memory of the number. Now, when someone gives you his or her number, the individual probably does not ask you to recite it back. However, you likely recite the number silently to yourself, perhaps even imagining the numbers on a phone's keypad. You likely don't have to think about this process; rather, it has become automatic.

One can expand the traditional distinction between declarative and procedural knowledge to suggest that nondeclarative knowledge may encompass a broader range of mental representations than just procedural knowledge (Squire, 1986; Squire & associates, 1990). Specifically, in addition to declarative knowledge, we mentally represent the following forms of nondeclarative knowledge:

- Perceptual, motor, and cognitive skills (procedural knowledge)
- Simple associative knowledge (classical and operant conditioning)
- Simple nonassociative knowledge (habituation and sensitization)
- Priming (fundamental links within a knowledge network, in which the activation of information along a particular mental pathway facilitates the subsequent retrieval of information along a related pathway or even the same mental pathway; see Chapter 4)

According to Squire, all these nondeclarative forms of knowledge are usually implicit (unstated). They are not easily made explicit.

Squire's primary inspiration for his model came from three sources. The first was his own work. The second was a wide range of neuropsychological research done by others (e.g., Baddeley & Warrington, 1970; Milner, 1972). This range included studies of amnesic patients, animal studies, and studies of the *microanatomy* of the brain (using microscopes to study brain cells). The third source was human cognitive experiments. Consider an example: Work with amnesic patients reveals clear distinctions between the neural systems for representing declarative knowledge versus neural systems for some of the nondeclarative forms of knowledge. For instance, amnesic patients often continue to show procedural knowledge even when they cannot remember that they possess such knowledge. Often they show improvements in performance on tasks requiring skills. These improvements indicate some form of new knowledge representation despite an inability to remember ever having previous experience with the tasks. For example, an amnesic patient who is given repeated practice in reading mirror writing will improve as a result of practice, but he or she will not recall ever having engaged in the practice (Baddeley, 1989).

Nondeclarative knowledge representation occurs as a result of experience in implementing a procedure. It is not merely a result of reading, hearing, or otherwise acquiring information from explicit instructions. Once a mental representation of nondeclarative knowledge is constructed, that knowledge is implicit. It is not easily made explicit. In fact, the process of enhancing the mental representation of nondeclarative knowledge tends actually to decrease explicit access to that knowledge. For example, suppose you recently have learned how to drive a standard-shift car. You may find it easier to describe how to do so than may someone who learned that skill long ago. As your explicit access to nondeclarative knowledge decreases, however, your speed and ease of gaining implicit access to that knowledge increases. Eventually, most nondeclarative knowledge can be retrieved for use much more quickly than declarative knowledge can be retrieved.

Another paradox of human knowledge representation also is demonstrated by amnesics. Although amnesics do not show normal memory abilities under most circumstances, they do show the priming effect. Recall from Chapter 4 that, in priming, particular cues and stimuli seem to activate mental pathways. These pathways in turn enhance the retrieval or cognitive processing of related information. For example, if someone asks you to spell the word *sight,* you will probably spell it differently, depending on several factors. These factors include whether you have been primed to think about sensory modalities ("s-i-g-h-t"), about locations for an archaeological dig ("s-i-t-e"), or about lists of references ("c-i-t-e"). Consider what happens when the amnesic participants have no recall of the priming and cannot explicitly recall the experience during which priming occurred. Nevertheless, priming still affects their performance.

If you can recruit at least two (and preferably more) volunteers, try the experiment on priming in the "Investigating Cognitive Psychology" box. It requires you to draw on your store of declarative knowledge.

INVESTIGATING COGNITIVE PSYCHOLOGY	Separate your volunteers into two groups. For one group, ask them to unscramble the following anagrams (puzzles in which you must figure out the correct order of letters to make a sensible word): ZAZIP, GASPETHIT, POCH YUSE, OWCH MINE, ILCHI, ACOT. Ask the members of the other group to unscramble the following anagrams: TECKAJ, STEV, ASTEREW, OLACK, ZELBAR, ACOT. For the first group, the correct answers are *pizza, spaghetti, chop suey, chow mein, chili,* and a sixth item. The correct answers for the second group are *jacket, vest, sweater, cloak, blazer,* and a sixth item. The sixth item in each group may be either *taco* or *coat.* Did your volunteers show a tendency to choose one or the other answer, depending on the preceding list with which they were primed?

The preceding examples illustrate situations in which an item may prime another item that is somehow related in meaning. We actually may differentiate two types of priming: semantic priming and repetition priming (Posner & associates, 1988). In semantic priming, we are primed by a meaningful context or by meaningful information. Such information typically is a word or cue that is meaningfully related to the target that is used. Examples are fruits or green things, which may prime *lime.* In repetition priming, a prior exposure to a word or other stimulus primes a subsequent retrieval of that information. For example, hearing the word *lime* primes subsequent stimulation for the word *lime.* Both types of priming have generated a great deal of research, but semantic priming often particularly interests cognitive psychologists.

For example, there is evidence of priming from research on normal participants. In one study, participants received two short paragraphs (McKoon & Ratcliff, 1980). After reading the paragraphs, the participants took a recognition-memory test. Participants then stated whether they had seen a given word in one of the stories and were timed in their responses. Some of the words they saw were from one of the stories they had just read. Others were from neither story. The critical aspect of the experiment was whether a given test word was preceded by a word from the *same* story or by a word from the *other* story. The first kind of trial is a primed trial. The second kind is an unprimed control trial. Suppose priming does indeed occur. Then participants should respond more quickly to a test item if it has just been preceded by a test item from the same story than if it has just been preceded by a test item from the other story. The researchers verified this prediction in a series of experiments.

According to spreading-activation theories, the amount of activation between a prime and a given target node is a function of two things. The first is the number of links connecting the prime and the target. The second is the relative strengths of each connection. This view holds that increasing the number of intervening links tends to decrease the likelihood of the priming effect. But increasing the strength of each link between the prime and its target tends to increase the likelihood of the priming effect. This model has been well supported (e.g., McNamara, 1992). Furthermore, the occurrence of priming through spreading activation is taken by most psychologists as support for a network model of knowledge representation in memory processes. In particular, the notions of priming effects through spreading activation within a network model have led to the emergence of a newer model. It is called a connectionist model of knowledge representation.

Parallel Processing: The Connectionist Model

The computer-inspired information-processing theories assume that humans, like computers, process information serially. That is, information is processed one step after another. Some aspects of human cognition may indeed be explained in terms of serial processing, but psychobiological findings and other cognitive research seem to indicate other aspects of human cognition. These aspects involve **parallel processing,** in which multiple operations go on all at once. We have seen how the information processing of a computer has served as a metaphor for many models of cognition. Similarly, our increasing understanding of how the human brain processes information also serves as a metaphor for many of the recent models of knowledge representation in humans. The human brain seems to handle many operations and to process information from many sources simultaneously—in parallel. Thus, many contemporary models of knowledge representation emphasize the importance of parallel processing in human cognition. As a further result of interest in parallel processing, some computers have been made to simulate parallel processing, such as through so-called neural networks of interlinked computer processors.

At present, many cognitive psychologists are exploring the limits of parallel processing models. According to **parallel distributed processing (PDP) models** or **connectionist models,** we handle very large numbers of cognitive operations at once through a network distributed across incalculable numbers of locations in the brain (McClelland & Rogers, 2003; McClelland, Rumelhart, & the PDP Research Group,

James L. McClelland is a professor of psychology at Stanford University and is Director of the Center for Mind, Brain, and Computation. McClelland is best known for his seminal work with David Rumelhart on introducing PDP (connectionist) models into the mainstream of psychology and for the revelation that such models can be formulated, implemented, and tested in a number of different domains of cognitive functioning.

Courtesy of Dr. James L. McClelland

1986; McLeod, Plunkett, & Rolls, 1998; Plaut, 2000; Rumelhart, McClelland, & the PDP Research Group, 1986; Seidenberg & McClelland, 1989). A computer can begin responding to an input within nanoseconds (millionths of a second), but an individual neuron may take up to 3 milliseconds to fire in response to a stimulus. Consequently, serial processing in the human brain would be far too slow to manage the amount of information it handles. For example, most of us can recognize a complex visual stimulus within about 300 milliseconds. If we processed the stimulus serially, only a few hundred neurons would have had time to respond. Rather, according to PDP models, the distribution of parallel processes better explains the speed and accuracy of human information processing.

The mental structure within which parallel processing is believed to occur is the network. In connectionist networks, all forms of knowledge are represented within the network structure. Recall that the fundamental element of the network is the node. Each node is connected to many other nodes. These interconnected patterns of nodes enable the individual to organize meaningfully the knowledge contained in the connections among the various nodes. In many network models, each node represents a concept.

The network of the PDP model is different in key respects from the semantic network described earlier. In the PDP model, the network comprises neuronlike units (McClelland & Rumelhart, 1981, 1985; Rumelhart & McClelland, 1982). They do not, in and of themselves, actually represent concepts, propositions, or any other type of information. Thus, the pattern of connections represents the knowledge, not the specific units. The same idea governs our use of language. Individual letters (or sounds) of a word are relatively uninformative, but the pattern of letters (or sounds) is highly informative. Similarly, no single unit is very informative, but the pattern of interconnections among units is highly informative. Figure 8.6 illustrates how just six units (dots) may be used to generate many more than six patterns of connections between the dots.

The PDP model demonstrates another way in which a brain-inspired model differs from a computer-inspired one. Differing cognitive processes are handled by differing patterns of activation, rather than as a result of a different set of instructions from a computer's central processing unit. In the brain, at any one time a given neuron may be inactive, excitatory, or inhibitory.

- *Inactive* neurons are not stimulated beyond their threshold of excitation. They do not release any neurotransmitters into the synapse (the interneuronal gap).
- *Excitatory* neurons release neurotransmitters that stimulate receptive neurons at the synapse. They increase the likelihood that the receiving neurons will reach their threshold of excitation.
- *Inhibitory* neurons release neurotransmitters that inhibit receptive neurons. They reduce the likelihood that the receiving neurons will reach their threshold of excitation.

Furthermore, although the action potential of a neuron is all or none, the amounts of neurotransmitters and neuromodulators released may vary. (Neuromodulators are chemicals that can either increase or inhibit neural activation.) The fre-

FIGURE 8.6

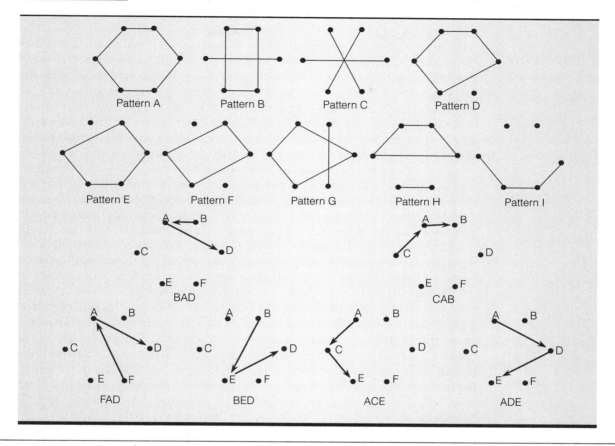

Each individual unit (dot) is relatively uninformative, but when the units are connected into various patterns, each pattern may be highly informative, as illustrated in the patterns at the top of this figure. Similarly, individual letters are relatively uninformative, but patterns of letters may be highly informative. Using just three-letter combinations, we can generate many different patterns, such as DAB, FED, and other patterns shown in the bottom of this figure.

quency of firing also may vary. This variation affects the degree of excitation or inhibition of other neurons at the synapse.

Similarly, in the PDP model, individual units may be inactive, or they may send excitatory or inhibitory signals to other units. That is not to say that the PDP model actually indicates specific neural pathways for knowledge representation. We are still a long way from having more than a faint glimmer of knowing how to map specific neural information. Rather, the PDP model uses the physiological processes of the brain as a metaphor for understanding cognition. According to the PDP model, connections between units can possess varying degrees of potential excitation or inhibition. These differences can occur even when the connections are currently inactive.

The more often a particular connection is activated, the greater is the strength of the connection, whether the connection is excitatory or inhibitory.

According to the PDP model, whenever we use knowledge, we change our representation of it. Thus, knowledge representation is not really a final product. Rather, it is a process or even a potential process. What is stored is not a particular pattern of connections. It is a pattern of potential excitatory or inhibitory connection strengths. The brain uses this pattern to re-create other patterns when stimulated to do so.

When we receive new information, the activation from that information either strengthens or weakens the connections between units. The new information may come from environmental stimuli, from memory, or from cognitive processes. The ability to create new information by drawing inferences and making generalizations allows for almost infinite versatility in knowledge representation and manipulation.

This versatility is what makes humans—unlike computers—able to accommodate incomplete and distorted information. Information that is distorted or incomplete is considered to be *degraded*. According to the PDP model, human minds are flexible. They do not require that all aspects of a pattern precisely match to activate a pattern. Thus, consider what happens when enough distinctive (but not all) aspects of a particular pattern have been activated by other attributes in the description. The degraded information does not prevent us from re-creating the correct pattern. This cognitive flexibility also greatly enhances our ability to learn new information.

By using the PDP model, cognitive psychologists attempt to explain various general characteristics of human cognition. These characteristics include our ability to respond flexibly, dynamically, rapidly, and relatively accurately, even when we are given only partial or degraded information. In addition, cognitive psychologists attempt to use the model to explain specific cognitive processes. Examples of such processes are perception, reasoning, reading, language comprehension, priming, and the Stroop effect, as well as other memory processes (Elman & associates, 1996; Hinton, 1991; Hinton & Shallice, 1991; Kaplan & associates, 2007; O'Reilly, 1996; Plaut & associates, 1996; Plaut & Shallice, 1994; Smolensky, 1999).

An example of the efforts to apply PDP models to specific cognitive processes can be seen through the exploration of dyslexia, or reading disability. A specific PDP model for the description of how we read was developed. This model involves pathways for both phonological and semantic representations (Plaut & associates, 1996). Computer simulations with this model have been able to mimic normal reading. When one of these two pathways is damaged, these simulations are able to imitate the behavioral manifestations of dyslexia (Welbourne & Ralph, 2007). These simulations help researchers understand what processes are malfunctioning in people with reading disabilities.

Although connectionist models of knowledge representation explain many phenomena of knowledge representation and processing, these models are not flawless. They explain many cognitive processes. These processes include, for example, those involving perception and memory. They may be learned gradually by our storing of knowledge through the strengthening of patterns of connections within the network. However, many aspects of the model are not yet well defined. For example, the model is less effective in explaining how people can remember a single event (Schacter, 1989a). For instance, how do we suddenly construct a whole new interconnected pattern for representing what we know about a memorable event, such as graduation day?

Similarly, connectionist models do not satisfactorily explain how we often quickly can unlearn established patterns of connections when we are presented with contradictory information (Ratcliff, 1990; Treadway & associates, 1992). For example, suppose that you are told that the criteria for classifying parts of plants as fruits are that they must have seeds, pulp, and skin. You also are told that whether they are sweeter than other plant parts is not important. Suppose now you are given the task of sorting various photos of plant parts into groups that are or are not fruits. You will sort tomatoes and pumpkins with apples and other fruits, even if you did not previously consider them to be fruits.

These shortcomings of connectionist systems can be bypassed. It may be that there are two learning systems in the brain (McClelland, McNaughton, & O'Reilly, 1995). One system corresponds to the connectionist model in resisting change and in being relatively permanent. The complementary system handles rapid acquisition of new information. It holds the information for a short time. It then integrates the newer information with information in the connectionist system. Evidence from neuropsychology and connectionist network modeling seem to corroborate this account (McClelland, McNaughton, & O'Reilly, 1995). Thus, the connectionist system is spared. But we still need a satisfactory account of the other learning system.

The preceding models of knowledge representation and information processing clearly have profited from technological advances in computer science, in brain imaging, and in the psychobiological study of the human brain in action. These are techniques that few would have predicted to have been so promising 40 years ago. Thus, it would be foolish to predict that specific avenues of research will lead us in particular directions. Nonetheless, particular avenues of research do hold promise. For example, using powerful computers, researchers are attempting to create parallel-processing models via neural networks. Increasingly sophisticated techniques for studying the brain offer intriguing possibilities for research. Case studies, naturalistic studies, and traditional laboratory experiments in the field of cognitive psychology also offer rich opportunities for further exploration. Some researchers are trying to explore highly specific cognitive processes, such as auditory processing of speech sounds. Others are trying to investigate fundamental processes that underlie all aspects of cognition. Which type of research is more valuable?

Comparing Connectionist with Network Representations

How do connectionist models compare with network models? Figure 8.7 shows the concept of a robin as represented by both a network model and a connectionist model.

In the network representation, an individual builds up a knowledge base about a robin over time as more and more information is acquired about robins. Note that information about robins is embedded in a general network representation that goes beyond just robins. One's understanding of robins partly depends on the relationship of the robin to other birds and even other kinds of living things. Indeed, perhaps the most fundamental feature of the robin is that it is a living thing. So this information is represented at the top to show that it is an extremely general characteristic of a robin. Living things are living and can grow, so this information is also represented at a very general level. As one moves down the network, information gets more and more specific. For example, we learn that a robin is a bird and that it is partly red.

FIGURE 8.7

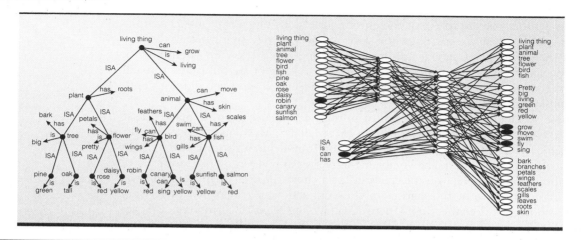

Network and connectionist representations of concepts relating to birds. From J. L. McClelland, "Connectionist Model of Memory," in E. Tulving & F. I. M. Craik (Eds.), The Oxford Handbook of Memory, pp. 583–596. Copyright © 2000 Oxford University Press. Reprinted by permission.

In contrast, the connectionist network represents patterns of activation. Here, too, the network shows knowledge that goes beyond just birds. The knowledge is in the connections rather than in the nodes. Through activation of certain connections, knowledge about a robin is built up. A strong connection is one that is activated many times, whereas a weak one is activated only on rare occasions.

How Domain General or Domain Specific Is Cognition?

Should cognitive psychologists try to find a set of mental processes that is common across all domains of knowledge representation and processing? Or should they study mental processes specific to a particular domain? In early AI research, investigators believed that the ideal was to write programs that were as domain general as possible. Although none of the programs truly worked in all domains, they were a good start. Similarly, in the broader field of cognitive psychology, the trend in the 1960s through the mid-1970s was to strive for domain-general understandings of cognitive processes (Miller, Galanter, & Pribram, 1960; Simon, 1976).

During the late 1970s and the 1980s, the balance shifted toward domain specificity. In part this was because of striking demonstrations regarding the role of specific knowledge in chess playing (Chase & Simon, 1973; De Groot, 1965; see Chapter 11). A key book, *The Modularity of Mind,* presented an argument for extreme domain specificity (Fodor, 1983). In this view, the mind is **modular,** divided into discrete modules that operate more or less independently of each other. According to Fodor, each independently functioning module can process only one kind of input, such as language (e.g., words), visual percepts (e.g., faces), and so on.

Further evidence for the domain specificity of face recognition can be observed in studies employing functional magnetic resonance imaging (fMRI) methods. In one

IN THE LAB OF JAMES L. MCCLELLAND

Courtesy of Dr. James L. McClelland

In my laboratory we attempt to understand the implications of the idea that human cognitive processes arise from the interactions of neurons in the brain. We develop computational models that directly carry out some human cognitive task using simple, neuron-like processing units.

Some psychologists and cognitive neuroscientists have supposed that worrying about the nature of the underlying hardware is a mistake.

According to their approach, human cognitive processes should be understood at a more abstract level of analysis. My collaborators and I believe, however, that the properties of the underlying hardware have important implications for the nature and organization of cognitive processes in the brain.

An important case in point is the process of assigning the past tense to a word in English. Consider the formation of the past tense of *like, take,* and *gleat.* (*Gleat* is not a word in English, but it might be. For example, we might coin the word *gleat* to refer to the act of saluting in a particular way.) In any case, most people agree that the past tense of *like* is *liked,* the past tense of *take* is *took,* and the past tense of *gleat* is *gleated.*

Before the advent of neural network models, everyone in the field assumed that to form the past tense of a novel verb like *gleat* one would need to use a rule (e.g., to form the past tense of a word, add -[e]d).

Also, developmental psychologists observed that young children occasionally made interesting errors like saying "taked" instead of "took," and they interpreted this as indicating that the children were (over)applying the past tense rule. They also assumed that to produce the past tense of an exception word like *take* correctly (e.g., to produce took) a child would need to memorize this particular item. For familiar but regular words like *like,* either the rule or the look-up mechanism might be used.

Dave Rumelhart and I (1986) thought about this issue and observed that neural network models have a tendency to be sensitive to both general regularities and specific exceptions. We thought based on this that in the brain a single mechanism might be used to produce the past tenses of both regular and exceptional items. To explore this possibility, we created a simple neural network model, as illustrated in the following figure. The model takes as its input a pattern of activity representing the present tense form of a word and produces on its output another pattern of activity representing the past tense form of the word. The network operates by propagating activation from the input units to the output units. What determines whether a unit will be active is the pattern of incoming connection activation to each unit. The incoming connections are modulated by weights like synapses between neurons that modulate the effect of an input on an output. If the overall effect of the input is positive, the unit comes on; if negative, it goes off.

Rumelhart and I trained this network with pairs of items representing the present and past tenses of familiar words. After we trained it with the 10 most frequent words (most of which are exceptions), the network knew how to produce the past tenses of these words, but it did not know how to deal with other words. We then trained it with the 10 frequent words plus 400 more words, most of which were regular, and we found that early in training, it tended to overregularize most of the exceptions (e.g., it said "taked" instead of "took"), even for those words that it had previously produced correctly. We trained it for a long time more, and at the end of training it recovered its ability to produce exceptions correctly, while still producing regular past tenses for regular words like *like* and for many novel items like *gleat.* Thus, to a first approximation the model accounted for the developmental pattern in which children first deal correctly with exceptions, then learn how to deal with regular words and novel words and overregularize exceptions, and then

Continues

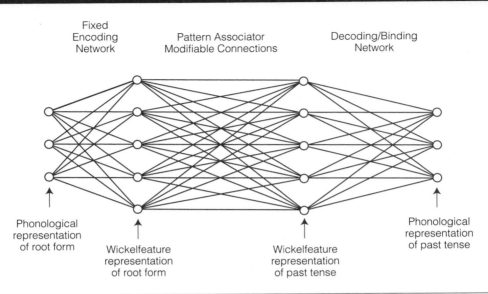

The neural network model used by Rumelhart and McClelland to model the formation of past tenses of English verbs. The fixed encoding network and fixed decoding network were used to encode and decode the patterns of activation corresponding to the present and past tenses of words. The connections in the pattern association were trained by presenting the encoded present tense of a word together with the encoded form of its past tense, then adjusting the connections so that the network would tend to produce the correct past tense on its own given the present tense as input. From D. E. Rumelhart & J. L. McClelland, 1986. On learning the past tenses of English verbs. In J. L. McClelland, et al. (Eds.), Parallel distribution processing. Explorations in the microstructure of cognition. Vol. 2. Psychological and biological models, p. 222. Reprinted with permission from MIT Press.

when they are older deal correctly with regular words, novel words, and exceptions.

Our model, then, illustrates that in a neural network, it is not necessary to have separate mechanisms to deal with rules and exceptions.

Furthermore, this illustrates the general point that the nature of the underlying processing machinery may have implications for higher-level characterizations of the cognitive processes. However, I should make clear that our initial work did not by any means settle the issue.

Several critics rushed to the defense of the two-process approach, criticizing several features of our models (Lachter & Bever, 1988; Pinker & Prince, 1988). Others responded to these criticisms with improved neural network models (MacWhinney & Leinbach, 1991; Plunkett & Marchman, 1991). Debate about these issues is still ongoing (McClelland and Patterson, 2002; Pinker and Ullman, 2002). Thus, our modeling work has not finally settled this issue. It simply has raised an alternative to earlier conceptualizations and suggested that we cannot ignore the nature of the underlying processing mechanisms whose activity gives rise to cognition.

References

Lachter, J., & Bever, T. G. (1988). The relation between linguistic structure and associative theories of language learning—constructive critique

IN THE LAB OF JAMES L. MCCLELLAND—cont'd

of some connectionist learning models. *Cognition*, 28, 195–247.

MacWhinney, B., & Leinbach, J. (1991). Implementations are not conceptualizations: Revising the verb learning model. *Cognition*, 39, 121–157.

McClelland, J. L., & Patterson, K. (2002). Rules or connections in past-tense inflections: What does the evidence rule out? *Trends in Cognitive Sciences*, 6, 465–472.

Pinker, S., & Prince, A. (1988). On language and connectionism: Analysis of a parallel distributed processing model of language acquisition. *Cognition*, 28, 73–193.

Pinker, S., & Ullman, M. T. (2002). The past and future of the past tense. *Trends in Cognitive Sciences*, 6, 456–463.

Plunkett, K., & Marchman, V. (1991). U-shaped learning and frequency effects in a multilayered perception: Implications for child language acquisition. *Cognition*, 38, 43–102.

Rumelhart, D. E., & McClelland, J. L. (1986). On learning past tenses of English verbs. In D. E. Rumelhart & J. L. McClelland (Eds.), *Parallel distributed processing: Vol. 2. Psychological and biological models*. Cambridge, MA: MIT Press.

study, it was observed that when subjects viewed faces and houses, different brain areas were active. It thus appears that there are both specialized brain and cognitive processes for the processing of faces. This is taken to suggest that there is domain specificity for facial recognition (Yovel & Kanwisher, 2004).

Fodor (1983) asserted the modularity of lower-level processes, such as the basic perceptual processes involved in lexical access (see Chapter 3). However, the application of modularity has been extended to higher intellectual processes as well (Gardner, 1983). Also, the book emphasized the modularity of specific cognitive functions, such as lexical access to word meanings, as distinct from word meanings derived from context. These functions primarily have been observed in cognitive experiments. However, issues of modularity also have been important in psychobiological research. For example, there are discrete pathological conditions associated with discrete cognitive deficits.

Recently, there has been more of an attempt to integrate domain-specific and domain-general perspectives in our thinking about knowledge representation and processing. In the chapters that follow, you may wish to reflect on whether the processes and forms of knowledge representation being described may be seen as primarily domain general or primarily domain specific.

Key Themes

This chapter brings out several of the key themes described in Chapter 1.

One theme is that of rationalism versus empiricism. How do we assign meaning to concepts? The featural view is largely a rationalistic one. Concepts have sets of features that are largely a priori and that are the same from one person to another. The underlying notion is that one could understand a concept by a detailed dictionary definition, pretty much without reference to people's experience. The prototype, exemplar, and theory-based views are much more empirically based. They assign a major role to experience. For example, theories may change with experience. The theory of a concept such as a "dog" that a 3-year-old child has may be very different from that of a 10-year-old child.

A second theme is that of the validity of causal inference versus ecological validity. Early research on concepts, such as that of Bruner, Goodnow, and Austin, used abstract concepts, such as geometric forms that could be of different colors, shapes, and sizes. But in her work, Eleanor Rosch called this approach into question. Rosch argued that natural concepts show few of the characteristics of artificial ones. Studying artificial concepts, therefore, might yield information that applied to those concepts but not necessarily to real-world ones. Modern researchers tend to study real-world concepts more than artificial ones.

A third theme is that of basic versus applied research. Basic research on concepts has generated a great deal of applied research. For example, market researchers are very interested in people's conceptualizations of commercial products. They use empirical and statistical techniques to understand how products are conceived. Often, then, advertising serves to reposition the products in customers' minds. For example, a car that is viewed as in the category of "economy cars" may be, through advertising, moved to a more "upscale car" category.

Ask a friend if he or she would like to win $20. The $20 can be won if your friend can recite the months of the year within 30 seconds—in alphabetical order. Go! In the years that we have offered this cash to the students in our courses, not a single student has ever won, so your $20 is probably safe. This demonstration shows how something as common and frequently used as the months of the year is bundled together in a certain order. It is very difficult to rearrange their names in an order that is different from their commonly used or more familiar order.

Summary

1. **How are representations of words and symbols organized in the mind?** The fundamental unit of symbolic knowledge is the concept. Concepts may be organized into categories, which may include other categories. They may be organized into schemas, which may include other schemas. They also may vary in application and in abstractness.

Finally, they may include information about relationships between concepts, attributes, contexts, and general knowledge and information about causal relationships. There are different general theories of categorization. They include feature-based definitional categories, prototype-based categories, and exemplar-based approaches. One of the forms for schemas is the script. An alternative model for knowledge organization is a semantic network, involving a web of labeled relations between conceptual nodes. An early network model was strictly hierarchical. It was based on the notion of cognitive economy. But subsequent ones have tended to emphasize the frequency with which particular associations are used.

2. **How do we represent other forms of knowledge in the mind?** Many cognitive psychologists have developed models for procedural knowledge.

These are based on computer simulations of such representations. An example of such a model is the production system.

3. How does declarative knowledge interact with procedural knowledge?   An important model in cognitive psychology is ACT, as well as its updated revision, ACT-R. It represents both procedural knowledge in the form of production systems and declarative knowledge in the form of a semantic network. In each of these models, the metaphor for understanding both knowledge representation and information processing is based on the way in which a computer processes information. For example, these models underscore the serial processing of information.

Research on how the human brain processes information has shown that brains, unlike computers, use parallel processing of information. In addition, it appears that much of information processing is not localized only to particular areas of the brain. Instead it is distributed across various regions of the brain all at once. At a microscopic level of analysis, the neurons within the brain may be inactive, or they may be excited or inhibited by the actions of other neurons with which they share a synapse. Finally, studies of how the brain processes information have shown that some stimuli seem to prime a response to subsequent stimuli so that it becomes easier to process the subsequent stimuli.

A model for human knowledge representation and information processing based on what we know about the brain is the parallel distributed processing (PDP) model. It is also called a connectionist model. In such models, it is held that neuronlike units may be excited or inhibited by the actions of other units, or they may be inactive. Further, knowledge is represented in terms of patterns of excitation or inhibition strengths, rather than in particular units. Most PDP models also explain the priming effect by suggesting the mechanism of spreading activation.

Many cognitive psychologists believe that the mind is at least partly modular. It has different activity centers that operate fairly independently of each other. However, other cognitive psychologists believe that human cognition is governed by many fundamental operations. According to this view, specific cognitive functions are merely variations on a theme. In all likelihood, cognition involves some modular, domain-specific processes and some fundamental, domain-general processes.

Thinking about Thinking: Factual, Analytical, Creative, and Practical Questions

1. Define *declarative knowledge* and *procedural knowledge*, and give examples of each.

2. What is a script that you use in your daily life? How might you make it work better for you?

3. Describe some of the attributes of schemas, and compare and contrast two of the schema models mentioned in this chapter.

4. In your opinion, why have many of the models for knowledge representation come from people with a strong interest in artificial intelligence?

5. What are some advantages and disadvantages of hierarchical models of knowledge representation?

6. How would you design an experiment to test whether a particular cognitive task was better explained in terms of modular components or in terms of some fundamental underlying domain-general processes?

7. What are some practical examples of the forms of nondeclarative knowledge in Squire's model? (For ideas on conditioning, see Chapter 1; for ideas on habituation or on priming, see Chapter 4.)

8. How might you use semantic priming to enhance the likelihood that a person will think of something you would like the person to think of (e.g., your birthday, a restaurant to visit, or a movie to view)?

Key Terms

ACT
ACT-R
artifact categories
basic level
category
characteristic features
concept
connectionist models
converging operations
core

defining feature
exemplars
jargon
modular
natural categories
networks
nodes
nominal kind
parallel distributed processing
(PDP) models

parallel processing
production
production system
prototype theory
schemas
script
serial processing
spreading activation
theory-based view of meaning

Explore CogLab by going to **http://coglab.wadsworth.com.**
To learn more, examine the following experiments:

Prototypes   Implicit Learning
Absolute Identification

Annotated Suggested Readings

Capitani, E., Laiacona, M., Mahon, B., & Caramazza, A. (2003). What are the facts of semantic category-specific deficits? A critical review of the clinical evidence. *Cognitive Neuropsychology, 20,* 213–261. A review of cases of deficits in the use of specific semantic categories. This article provides a comprehensive overview of this impairment.

McLeod, P., Plunkett K., & Rolls, E. T. (1998). *Introduction to connectionist modeling of cognitive processes.* New York: Oxford University Press. There is no simple introduction to connectionism, but this exposition is about as clear as one can find on the use of connectionist modeling to characterize a wide variety of cognitive processes.

Language: Nature and Acquisition

EXPLORING COGNITIVE PSYCHOLOGY

1. **What properties characterize language?**

2. **What are some of the processes involved in language?**

3. **How do we acquire the ability to use language?**

> I stood still, my whole attention fixed upon the motions of her fingers. Suddenly, I felt a misty consciousness as of something forgotten—a thrill of returning thought; and somehow the mystery of language was revealed to me.
>   I knew then that "w-a-t-e-r" meant the wonderful cool something that was flowing over my hand. That living word awakened my soul, gave it light, joy, set it free! . . . Everything had a name, and each name gave birth to a new thought. As we returned to the house every object which I touched seemed to quiver with life. . . . I learned a great many new words that day . . . words that were to make the world blossom for me.

—Helen Keller, *Story of My Life*

Helen Keller became both blind and deaf at 19 months of age after a severe childhood illness. She was first awakened to a sentient, thought-filled, comprehensible world through her teacher, Anne Sullivan. The miracle worker held one of Helen's hands under a spigot from which a stream of water gushed over Helen's hand. All the while she spelled with a manual alphabet into Helen's other hand the mind-awakening word "w-a-t-e-r."

Language is the use of an organized means of combining words in order to communicate. It makes it possible for us to communicate with those around us. It also makes it possible to think about things and processes we currently cannot see, hear, feel, touch, or smell. These things include ideas that may not have any tangible form. As Helen Keller demonstrated, the words we use may be written, spoken, or otherwise signed (e.g., via American Sign Language [ASL]). Even so, not all **communication**—exchange of thoughts and feelings—is through language. Communication encompasses other aspects. One such nonverbal means is gestures or facial expressions, which can be used, for example, to embellish or to indicate. A second aspect includes glances. Glances may serve many purposes. For example, sometimes they are deadly, other times, seductive. A third aspect includes touches, such as handshakes, hits, and hugs. These are only a few of the means by which we can communicate.

Psycholinguistics is the psychology of our language as it interacts with the human mind. It considers both production and comprehension of language (Gernsbacher & Kaschak, 2003a, 2003b; Indefrey & Levelt, 2000; Wheeldon, Meyer, & Smith, 2003). Four areas of study have contributed greatly to an understanding of psycholinguistics. One is linguistics, the study of language structure and change. A second is neurolinguistics, the study of the relationships among the brain, cognition, and language. A third is sociolinguistics, the study of the relationship between social behavior and language (Carroll, 1986). A fourth is computational linguistics and psycholinguistics, which is the study of language via computational methods (Coleman, 2003; Gasser, 2003; Lewis, 2003). This chapter first briefly describes some general properties of language. The next sections discuss the processes of language. These processes include how we understand the meanings of particular words and how we structure words into meaningful sentences. Then, the final section more fully elaborates the linguistic approach to language. It describes how each of us has acquired at least one language. As you might expect, this discussion brings up the nature-nurture debate that so often arises in regard to psychological issues. But it focuses on how acquired abilities interact with experience. Chapter 10 describes the broader context within which we use language. This context includes the psychological and social contexts of language.

Properties of Language

General Description

What properties characterize language? The answer to this question depends on whom you ask. Linguists may offer somewhat different answers than may cognitive psychologists. Nonetheless, there seems to be some consensus regarding six properties that are distinctive of language (Brown, 1965; Clark & Clark, 1977; Glucksberg & Danks, 1975). Specifically, language is:

1. *Communicative:* Language permits us to communicate with one or more people who share our language.
2. *Arbitrarily symbolic:* Language creates an arbitrary relationship between a symbol and its referent: an idea, a thing, a process, a relationship, or a description.
3. *Regularly structured:* Language has a structure; only particularly patterned arrangements of symbols have meaning, and different arrangements yield different meanings.
4. *Structured at multiple levels:* The structure of language can be analyzed at more than one level (e.g., in sounds, in meaning units, in words, in phrases).
5. *Generative, productive:* Within the limits of a linguistic structure, language users can produce novel utterances. The possibilities for creating new utterances are virtually limitless.
6. *Dynamic:* Languages constantly evolve.

The communicative property of language is listed first. Despite being the most obvious feature of language, it is also the most remarkable one. As an example, I can write what I am thinking and feeling so that you may read and understand my thoughts and feelings. This is not to say that there are not occasional flaws in the communicative property of language. Countless cognitive psychologists and others dedicate their lives to the study of how we fail to communicate through language.

Signs that resemble their referents in some way are termed icons. These pictographs are icons that were used in ancient Egyptian hieroglyphics. In contrast, most language involves the manipulation of symbols, which bear only an arbitrary relation to their referents.

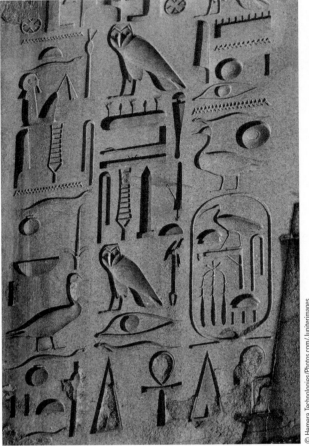

© Hemera Technologies/Photos.com/Jupiterimages

Despite the frustrations of miscommunications, however, for one person to be able to use language to communicate to another is impressive.

What may be more surprising is the second property of language. We communicate through our shared system of arbitrary symbolic reference to things, ideas, processes, relationships, and descriptions (Steedman, 2003). The arbitrary nature of the system alludes to the lack of any reason for choosing a particular symbol. Indeed, all words are symbols. In this context, a *symbol* is something that represents, indicates, or suggests something else. It refers, points, or alludes to a particular thing, process, or description, such as *professor, amuse,* or *brilliant.* By consensual agreement, a particular combination of letters or sounds may be meaningful to us. But the particular symbols do not themselves lead to the meaning of the word. The sound combination is arbitrary. This arbitrariness can be seen from the fact that different languages use very different sounds to refer to the same thing (e.g., *baum, árbol, tree*).

A convenient feature of symbols is that we can use them to refer to things, ideas, processes, relationships, and descriptions that are not currently present, such as the Amazon River. We even can use symbols to refer to things that never have existed, such as dragons or elves. And we can use symbols to refer to things that exist in a form that is not physically tangible, such as calculus, truth, or justice. Without arbitrary symbolic reference, we would be limited to symbols that somehow resembled the things they are supposed to symbolize. For example, we would need a treelike symbol to represent a tree. Two principles underlying word meanings are the *principle of conventionality* and the *principle of contrast* (Clark, 1993, 1995; Diesendruck, 2005). The first principle simply states that meanings of words are determined by conventions. In other words, words mean what conventions make them mean. According to the second principle, different words have different meanings. The point of having different words is precisely to have them symbolize things that are at least slightly different.

The third property is the regular structure of language. It makes possible this shared system of communication. Later in this chapter we describe more specifically the structure of language. For now, however, it suffices that you already know two things. The first is that particular patterns of sounds and of letters form meaningful words. Random sounds and letters, however, usually do not. The second is that particular patterns of words form meaningful sentences, paragraphs, and discourse. Most others make no sense.

The fourth property is the multiplicity of structure. Any meaningful utterance can be analyzed at more than one level. Subsequent sections describe several levels at which we can analyze the structure of language. These various levels convey varying degrees of meaningful content. For example, psycholinguists study language at the level of sounds, such as *p* and *t*. They also examine the level of words, such as "pat," "tap," "pot," "top," "pit," and "tip." They also analyze the level of sentences, such as "Pat said to tap the top of the pot, then tip it into the pit." Finally, they analyze things at the level of larger units of language, such as this paragraph or even this book.

A fifth property of language is productivity (sometimes termed *generativity*). *Productivity* refers here to our vast ability to produce language creatively. However, our use of language does have limitations. We have to conform to a particular structure and to use a particular shared system of arbitrary symbols. We can use language to produce an infinite number of unique sentences and other meaningful combinations of words. Although the number of sounds (e.g., *s* as in "hiss") used in a language may be finite, the various sounds can be combined endlessly to form new words and new sentences. Among them are many novel utterances. These are linguistic expressions that are brand new and never have been spoken before by anyone. Thus, language is inherently creative. None of us possibly could have heard previously all the sentences we are capable of producing and that we actually produce in the course of our everyday lives. Any language appears to have the potential to express any idea in it that can be expressed in any other language. However, the ease, clarity, and succinctness of expression of a particular idea may vary greatly from one language to the next. Thus, the creative potential of different languages appears to be roughly the same.

Finally, the productive aspect of language quite naturally leads to the dynamic, evolutionary nature of language. Individual language users coin words and phrases and modify language usage. The wider group of language users either accepts or rejects the modifications. Each year, recently coined words are added to the dictionary, signifying the extensive acceptance of these new words. Similarly, words that are no longer used are removed from the dictionary, further contributing to the evolution of language. To imagine that language would never change is almost as incomprehensible as to imagine that people and environments would never change. For example, the modern English we speak now evolved from Middle English. This language in turn evolved from Old English.

Although we can delineate various properties of language, it is important always to keep in mind the main purpose of language. Language facilitates our being able to construct a mental representation of a situation that enables us to understand the situation and communicate about it (Budwig, 1995; Zwaan & Radvansky, 1998).

In other words, ultimately, language is primarily about use, not just about one set of properties or another. For example, it provides the basis for linguistic encoding in memory. You are able to remember things better because you can use language to help you recall or recognize them.

To conclude, many differences exist among languages. Nevertheless, there are some common properties. Among them are communication, arbitrary symbolic reference, regularity of structure, multiplicity of structure, productivity, and change. Next, we consider how language is used in more detail. Then we observe some universal aspects of how we humans acquire our primary language.

Fundamental Aspects of Language

Essentially, there are two fundamental aspects of language. The first is receptive comprehension and decoding of language input. The second is expressive encoding and production of language output. *Decoding* refers to deriving the meaning from whatever symbolic reference system is being used (e.g., while listening or reading). In Chapters 5 and 6, we used the term *encoding* to refer to both semantic and nonsemantic encoding of information into a form that can be stored in both working memory and long-term memory (Waters & Caplan, 2003). As applied to language, encoding involves transforming our thoughts into a form that can be expressed as linguistic output (e.g., speech, signing, or writing). In this chapter, we use the terms *encoding* and *decoding* to describe only semantic encoding and decoding.

Related terms are verbal comprehension and verbal fluency. **Verbal comprehension** is the receptive ability to comprehend written and spoken linguistic input, such as words, sentences, and paragraphs (Starr & Rayner, 2003). **Verbal fluency** is the expressive ability to produce linguistic output. When we deal specifically with spoken communication, we can refer to vocal comprehension or fluency. Verbal comprehension and verbal fluency appear to be relatively distinct abilities (Thurstone, 1938). People may be able to understand language well but not produce it well or vice versa. The dissociation becomes particularly apparent in the case of second language. For example, many people around the world can understand substantial amounts of English without being able to read or write it adequately.

Language can be broken down into many smaller units. It is much like the analysis of molecules into basic elements by chemists. The smallest unit of speech sound is the *phone*, which is simply a single vocal sound. A given phone may or may not be part of the speech system of a particular language (Jusczyk, 2003; Meyer & Wheeldon, 2003; Munhall, 2003; Roca, 2003b). A click of your tongue, a pop of your cheek, or a gurgling sound are all phones. These sounds, however, are not used to form distinctive words in North American English. A **phoneme** is the smallest unit of speech sound that can be used to distinguish one utterance in a given language from another. In English, phonemes are made up of vowel and consonant sounds. For

TABLE 9.1	North American English Phonetic Symbols

The phonemes of a language constitute the repertoire of the smallest units of sound that can be used to distinguish one meaningful utterance from another in the given language. (After Clark & Clark, 1977.)

CONSONANTS				VOWELS		DIPTHONGS	
p	pill	θ	thigh	i	beet	Ay	bite
B	bill		thy		bit	Æw	about
M	mill	Š	shallow	e	bait	Oy	boy
T	till	Ž	measure		bet		
D	dill	Č	chip	Æ	bat		
N	nil		gyp	U	boot		
K	kill	L	lip	U	put		
G	gill	R	rip		but		
ŋ	sing	Y	yet	o	boat		
F	fill	W	wet		bought		
v	vat		whet	A	pot		
S	sip	h	hat	ə	sofa		
Z	zip				marry		

example, we distinguish among "sit," "sat," "fat," and "fit," so the /s/ sound, the /f/ sound, the /i/ sound, and the /Æ/ sound are all phonemes in English (as is the /t/ sound). These sounds are produced by alternating sequences of opening and closing the vocal tract. Different languages use different numbers and combinations of phonemes. Hawaiian has about thirteen phonemes. Some African dialects have up to sixty. North American English has about forty phonemes, as shown in Table 9.1. The following set of examples highlights the difference between phones and phonemes.

In English, the difference between the /p/ and the /b/ sound is an important distinction. These sounds function as phonemes in English because they comprise the difference between different words. For example, English speakers distinguish between "they bit the buns from the bin" and "they pit the puns from the pin" (a well-structured but meaningless sentence). At the same time, there are some phones that English speakers may produce but that do not function to distinguish words. They therefore do not serve as phonemes in English. These often are called *allophones*, which are sound variants of the same phoneme.

To illustrate the difference between the allophones of the phoneme /p/, try putting your open hand about 1 inch from your lips. Then say aloud, "Put the paper cup to your lip." If you are like most English speakers, you felt a tiny puff of air when you pronounced the /ph/ in "Put" and "paper." But you felt no puffs of air when you pronounced the /p/ in "cup" or "lip." If you somehow managed to stifle the puff of air when saying, "Put" or "paper" or to add a puff of air when saying "cup" or "lip," you would be producing different (allo)phones. But you would not be making a meaningful distinction in the phonemes of English. There is no meaningful difference between /ph/ut and /p/ut in English. In contrast, the difference between /k/ut and /g/ut is potentially meaningful. However, in some languages, such as Thai, a distinction considered irrelevant in English is meaningful. In these languages, the difference between /p/ and /ph/ is phonemic rather than merely allophonic (Fromkin & Rodman, 1988).

Phonemics is the study of the particular phonemes of a language. *Phonetics* is the study of how to produce or combine speech sounds or to represent them with written symbols (Roca, 2003a). Linguists may travel to remote villages to observe, record, and analyze different languages. The study of phonetic inventories of diverse languages is one of the ways linguists gain insight into the nature of language (Ladefoged & Maddieson, 1996). An obstacle for the exploration of language through these means is language extinction (or language death). Language death occurs for a variety of reasons, including members leaving tribal areas in favor of more urban areas, genocide, globalization, and the introduction of a new language to an area (Mufwene, 2004). Language death is occurring at an alarming rate, with some estimates suggesting that 90% of the world's languages will be extinguished within the next generation (Abrams & Strogatz, 2003). This trend clearly presents a problem for those who wish to study languages.

At the next level of the hierarchy is the **morpheme**—the smallest unit that denotes meaning within a particular language. English courses may have introduced you to two forms of morphemes. One is root words. Root words are the portions of words that contain the majority of meaning. These roots cannot be broken down into smaller meaningful units. They are the items that have entries in the dictionary (Motter & associates, 2002). We add the second form of morphemes, affixes, to these root words. Affixes include suffixes, which follow the root word, and prefixes, which precede the root word. The word *affixes* itself comprises the root "fix," a prefix, and a suffix. The prefix is "af-." This prefix is a variant of the prefix "ad-," meaning "toward," "to," or "near." The suffix is "-es," which indicates the plural form of a noun. The word *recharge* contains two morphemes, "re-" and "charge."

Linguists analyze the structure of morphemes and words in a way that goes beyond the analysis of roots and affixes. **Content morphemes** are the words that convey the bulk of the meaning of a language. **Function morphemes** add detail and nuance to the meaning of the content morphemes or help the content morphemes fit the grammatical context. Examples are the suffix "-ist," the prefix "de-," the conjunction "and," or the article "the." A subset of function morphemes are inflections, the common suffixes we add to words to fit the grammatical context. For example, most American kindergartners know to add special suffixes to indicate the following:

- *Verb tense:* You study often. You studied yesterday. You are studying now.
- *Verb and noun number:* The professor assigns homework. The teaching assistants assign homework.
- *Noun possession:* The student's textbook is fascinating.
- *Adjective comparison:* The wiser of the two professors taught the wisest of the three students.

The **lexicon** is the entire set of morphemes in a given language or in a given person's linguistic repertoire. The average adult speaker of English has a lexicon of about 80,000 morphemes (Miller & Gildea, 1987). Children in grade 1 in the United

States have somewhat more than 10,000 words in their vocabularies. By grade 3, they are at about 20,000. By grade 5, they have reached about 40,000, or half of their eventual adult level of attainment (Anglin, 1993). By combining morphemes, most adult English speakers have a vocabulary, a repertoire of hundreds of thousands of words. For example, by attaching just a few morphemes to the root content morpheme *study*, we have *student, studious, studied, studying,* and *studies.* Vocabulary is built up slowly. It develops through many diverse exposures to words and clues as to their meanings (Akhtar & Montague, 1999; Hoff & Naigles, 1999; Woodward & Markman, 1998). One of the ways in which English has expanded to embrace an increasing vocabulary is by combining existing morphemes in novel ways. Some suggest that a part of William Shakespeare's genius lay in his enjoying the creation of new words by combining existing morphemes. He is alleged to have coined more than 1700 words—8.5% of his written vocabulary—and countless expressions—including the word *countless* itself (Lederer, 1991).

The next level of analysis is termed syntax. **Syntax** refers to the way in which users of a particular language put words together to form sentences. Syntax plays a major role in our understanding of language. A sentence comprises at least two parts. The first is a **noun phrase,** which contains at least one noun (often the subject of the sentence) and includes all the relevant descriptors of the noun. The second is a **verb phrase,** which contains at least one verb and whatever the verb acts on, if anything. The verb phrase also may be termed the *predicate* because it affirms or states something about the subject. Typically, it is an action or a property of the subject. Linguists consider the study of syntax to be fundamental to understanding the structure of language. The syntactical structure of language specifically is addressed later in this chapter.

Identify which of the following are noun phrases: (1) the round, red ball on the corner; (2) and the; (3) round and red; (4) the ball; (5) water; (6) runs quickly. (*Hint:* Noun phrases can be the subject or object of a sentence, e.g., "_____[NP]_____ bounces _____[NP]_____.")

Identify which of the following are verb phrases: (1) the boy bounced the ball; (2) and the bouncing ball; (3) rolled; (4) ran across the room; (5) gave her the ball; (6) runs quickly. (*Hint:* Verb phrases contain verbs, as well as anything on which the verb acts [but not the subject of the action]. For example, "The psychology student _____[VP]_____.")

INVESTIGATING COGNITIVE PSYCHOLOGY

Complementary to syntax is **semantics,** the study of meaning in a language. A semanticist would be concerned with how words and sentences express meaning. The final level of analysis is that of **discourse,** which encompasses language use at the level beyond the sentence, such as in conversation, paragraphs, stories, chapters, and entire works of literature. Table 9.2 summarizes the various aspects of language. The next section discusses how we understand language through speech perception and further analysis. We will reserve discussion of discourse for Chapter 10 and the social context for language.

TABLE 9.2	Summary Description of Language

All human languages can be analyzed at many levels.

LANGUAGE INPUT			LANGUAGE OUTPUT

↓
D
e
c
o
d
i
n
g
↓
	Phonemes
	(distinctive subset of all possible phones)
	Morphemes
	(from the distinctive lexicon of morphemes)
	Words
	(from the distinctive vocabulary of words)
	Phrase:
	    Noun phrases (NP: a noun and its descriptors)
	    Verb phrases (VP: a verb and whatever it
	    acts on)
	Sentences
	(based on the language's syntax—
	syntactical structure)
	Discourse
		. . . /t/ + /ā/ + /k/ + /s/ . . .
		
		. . . take (content morpheme) + s (plural function
		morpheme) . . .
		It + takes + a + heap + of + sense + to + write
		+ good + nonsense.
		NP = It
		+
		VP = takes a leap of sense to write good nonsense.
		
		It takes a heap of sense to write good nonsense.
		
		"It takes a heap of sense to write good nonsense"
		was first written by Mark Twain (Lederer, 1991,
		p. 131) . . .
			↑
			E
			n
			c
			o
			d
			i
			n
			g
			↑

COMPREHEND LANGUAGE	PRODUCE LANGUAGE

Processes of Language Comprehension

How do we understand language, given its multifaceted encoding? One approach to this question centers on the psychological processes involved in speech perception (Hickok & Poeppel, 2000). It also considers how listeners deal with the peculiarities resulting from the acoustic (relating to sound) transmission of language. A second, more linguistically oriented approach focuses on descriptions of the grammatical structure of languages. Finally, a third approach examines the psycholinguistic processes involved in language comprehension at the discourse macro-level of analysis. All three approaches overlap to some degree and offer interesting insights into the nature of language and its use.

Speech Perception

Have you ever been in a situation where you needed to communicate with someone over the phone, but the speech you heard was garbled by a faulty telephone transmission? If so, you will agree that speech perception is fundamental to language use in our everyday lives. To understand speech is crucial to human communication. To understand speech perception, we consider some interesting phenomena of speech. We also reflect on the question of whether speech is somehow special among all the various kinds of sounds we can perceive.

We are able to perceive speech with amazing rapidity. On the one hand, we can perceive as many as fifty phonemes *per second* in a language in which we are fluent (Foulke & Sticht, 1969). On the other hand, we can perceive only about two thirds of a single phone per second of nonspeech sounds (Warren & associates, 1969). Consider why foreign languages are difficult to understand when we hear them. Even if we can read them, the sounds of their letters and letter combinations may be different from the sounds corresponding to the same letters and letter combinations in our native language. For example, my Spanish sounds "American" because I tend to reinterpret Spanish sounds in terms of the American English phonetic system rather than the Spanish one.

How are we able to perceive fifty phonemes per second if, paradoxically, we only can perceive less than one phone per second of nonspeech sounds? One answer to this question lies in the fact that speech sounds show coarticulation. **Coarticulation** occurs when phonemes or other units are produced in a way that overlaps them in time. One or more phonemes begin while other phonemes still are being produced. The articulations coincide. Not only do phonemes within a word overlap. The boundaries between words in continuous speech also tend to overlap. This overlapping of speech sounds may seem to create additional problems for perceiving speech, but coarticulation is viewed as necessary for the effective transmission of speech information, given the previously mentioned deficiencies in perceiving other sounds (Liberman & associates, 1967). Thus, speech perception is viewed as different from other perceptual abilities because of both the linguistic nature of the information and the particular way in which information must be encoded for effective transmission.

Coarticulation can be observed in nonverbal language as well. A number of studies have been completed that examine speech production in skilled signers. People who are skilled signers can convey many paragraphs worth of information in less than a minute (Lupton, 1998). A great deal of coarticulation occurs in skilled use of ASL (Jerde, Soechting, & Flanders, 2003). This coarticulation affects a number of aspects of the sign, both as it begins and as it leads into another sign. The affected aspects include hand shape, movement, and position (Yang & Sarkar, 2006). Coarticulation occurs more frequently with more informal forms of ASL (Emmorey, 1994). People who are just learning sign language are more likely to use the more formal form. Later, as people become more skillful, they typically begin to use the more informal forms. Therefore, as skill and fluency increase, so does the incidence of coarticulation. Coarticulation is a result of the anticipation of the next sign, much in the same way that verbal coarticulation is based on the anticipation of the next word. This coarticulation does not, however, typically impair understanding. These observations support the unique nature of language perception, regardless of whether its format is spoken or signed.

So how do we perceive speech with such ease? There are many alternative theories of speech perception to explain our facility. These theories differ mainly as to whether speech perception is viewed as special or ordinary with respect to other types of auditory perception.

The View of Speech Perception as Ordinary

One main approach equates processes of speech perception with processes of auditory perception of other sounds. These kinds of theories emphasize either template-matching or feature-detection processes. Such theories postulate that there are distinct stages of neural processing. In one stage speech sounds are analyzed into their components. In another stage these components are analyzed for patterns and matched to a prototype or template (Kuhl, 1991; Massaro, 1987; Stevens & Blumstein, 1981). One theory of this kind is the *phonetic refinement theory* (Pisoni & associates, 1985). It says that we start with an analysis of auditory sensations and shift to higher level processing. We identify words on the basis of successively paring down the possibilities for matches between each of the phonemes and the words we already know from memory. In this theory, the initial sound that establishes the set of possible words we have heard need not be the first phoneme alone. You may have observed this phenomenon yourself on a conscious level. Have you ever been watching a movie or listening to a lecture when you heard only garbled sound? It takes you a few moments to figure out what the speaker must have said. To decide what you heard, you may have gone through a conscious process of phonetic refinement. A similar theoretical idea is embodied by the TRACE model (McClelland & Elman, 1986). According to this model, speech perception begins with three levels of feature detection: the level of acoustic features, the level of phonemes, and the level of words. According to this theory, speech perception is highly interactive. Lower levels affect higher levels and vice versa.

One attribute these theories have in common is that they all require decision-making processes above and beyond feature detection or template matching. Thus, the speech we perceive may differ from the speech sounds that actually reach our ears. The reason is that cognitive and contextual factors influence our perception of the sensed signal. For example, the phonemic-restoration effect involves integrating what we know with what we hear when we perceive speech (Samuel, 1981; Warren, 1970; Warren & Warren, 1970).

Suppose that you were in an experiment. You are listening to a sentence having the following pattern: "It was found that the *eel was on the _____." For the final word, one of the following words is inserted: *axle, shoe, table,* or *orange.* In addition, the speaker inserts a cough instead of the initial sound where the asterisk appeared in "*eel." Virtually all participants are unaware that a consonant has been deleted. The sound they recall having heard differs according to the context. The participants recall hearing "the *wheel* was on the axle," "the *heel* was on the shoe," "the *meal* was on the table," or "the *peel* was on the orange." In essence, they restore the missing phoneme that best suits the context of the sentence.

Phonemic restoration is similar to the visual phenomenon of closure, which is based on incomplete visual information. Indeed, one main approach to auditory perception attempts to extend to various acoustic events, including speech, the Gestalt principles of visual perception (Bregman, 1990). These principles include, for example, symmetry, proximity, and similarity. Thus, theories that consider speech perception as ordinary use general perceptual principles of feature-detection and Gestalt psychology. They thereby attempt to explain how listeners understand speech. Other theorists, however, view speech perception as special.

The View of Speech Perception as Special

One phenomenon in speech perception that led to the notion of specialization was the finding of **categorical perception**—discontinuous categories of speech sounds. That is, although the speech sounds we actually hear comprise a continuum of variation in sound waves, we experience speech sounds categorically. This phenomenon can be seen in the perception of the consonant–vowel combinations *ba, da,* and *ga.* The acoustic difference between these syllables centers on distinct patterns of variation in the speech signal. Some patterns lead to perception of *ba.* Others lead to perception of *da.* And still others lead to perception of *ga.* Moreover, within each syllable category there are differences in the sound patterns for different instances that do not influence speech perception. The *ba* that you said yesterday differs from the *ba* you say today. But it is not perceived as different. This categorical form of perception does not apply to a non-speech sound, such as a tone. Here continuous differences in pitch (how high or low the tone is) are heard as continuous and distinct.

In a classic study, researchers used a speech synthesizer to mimic this natural variation in syllable acoustic patterns. By this means, they also were able to control the acoustic difference between the syllables (Liberman & associates, 1957). They created a series of consonant–vowel sounds that changed in equal increments from *ba* to *da* to *ga.* People who listened to the synthesized syllables, however, heard a sudden switch. It was from the sound category of *ba* to the sound category of *da* (and likewise from the category of *da* to that of *ga*). Furthermore, this difference in labeling the syllables led to poorer discrimination within a phoneme category. It also enhanced discrimination across phoneme boundaries. Thus, although the tokens were physically equal in acoustic distance from one another, people only heard the tokens that also differed in phonetic label as different. Discrimination of two neighboring *ba*s was poor, whereas discrimination of *ba* from its neighboring *da* was preserved. Normal perceptual processing should discriminate equally between all equally spaced pairs of the different tokens along the continuum, however. The researchers thus concluded that speech is perceived via specialized processes.

A number of studies have further examined categorical perception in people with reading disabilities. In illiterate adults, there are no differences in categorical perception between people with and without such disabilities (Serniclaes & associates, 2005). However, in children with learning disabilities, the perceptual ability to discrimination between categories is impaired. Conversely, the perceptual ability to discriminate *within* categories is enhanced in these same children (Breier & associates, 2005). That is, children at risk of reading disabilities, compared with children who are not at risk, utilize less phonological information even though they perceive more subtle acoustic (sound) differences when performing a categorical-perception task (Breier & associates, 2004).

These and other findings led the researchers to investigate the notion that speech perception relies on special processes. They also proposed the early but still influential motor theory of speech perception (Galantucci, Fowler, & Turvey, 2006; Liberman & associates, 1967; Liberman & Mattingly, 1985). The theory was developed to explain how listeners overcome the context sensitivity of phonetic segments that arises from coarticulation, resulting in categorical perception phenomena. To return to an earlier example, the /p/ spoken in the word *lip* differs acoustically from the /ph/ spoken in the word *put.* This largely results from the differences in the coarticulatory context of the two instances of the phoneme. The overlapping of /p/ with either *li-* or *-ut* causes the /p/ to sound different. Why do English speakers treat the /p/ and /ph/ as the same phoneme? According to the motor theory, speech perception depends on what we hear a speaker articulate (in this case, /p/ and /ph/). It also depends on what we infer as the intended articulations of the speaker (in this case, only /p/). Thus, the listener uses specialized processes involved in producing speech to perceive speech. He or she thereby overcomes the effects of coarticulation, which leads to categorical perception. Since the early work of Liberman and colleagues, the phenomenon of categorical perception has been extended to the perception of other kinds of stimuli, such as color and facial emotion. This extension weakens the claim that speech perception is special (Jusczyk, 1997). However, supporters of the speech-is-special position still maintain that other forms of evidence indicate that speech is perceived via specialized processes.

One such distinctive aspect of human speech perception can be seen in the so-called McGurk effect (McGurk & MacDonald, 1976). This effect involves the synchrony of visual and auditory perceptions. Imagine yourself watching a movie. As long as the soundtrack corresponds to the speakers' lip movements, you encounter no problems. However, suppose that the soundtrack indicates one thing, such as *da*. At the same time, the actor's lips clearly make the movements for another sound, such as *ba*. You are likely to hear a compromise sound, such as *tha*. It is neither what was said nor what was seen. You somehow synthesize the auditory and visual information. You thereby come up with a result that is unlike either. For this reason, poorly dubbed movies of foreign origin can be confusing. You are vaguely aware that the lips are saying one thing and you are hearing something else.

In one set of studies, Nicholls, Searle, and Bradshaw (2004) studied the McGurk effect with respect to lip-reading. The experimenters covered half of the speaker's mouth, while either matching or mismatching auditory and visual information. The experimenters found that, when the left side of the mouth was covered, there was little change in the occurrence of the McGurk effect. However, when the right side of the mouth was covered, the occurrence of the McGurk effect dropped dramatically. Then the researchers used an inverted video of the left side of the mouth, such that it appeared to be the right side of the mouth, and saw the McGurk effect rebound (Nicholls, Searle, & Bradshaw, 2004). These findings suggest that the right side, or what is perceived as the right side of the mouth, is attended to more in lip reading. Hence, lack of correspondence between what the right side of the mouth says and what is heard are the more likely to lead to the McGurk effect.

In normal conversation, we use lip reading to augment our perception of speech. It is particularly important in situations in which background noise may make speech perception more difficult. The motor theory accounts for this integration quite easily because articulatory information includes visual and auditory information. However, believers in other theories interpret these findings as support for more general perceptual processes. They believe these processes naturally integrate information across sensory modalities (Massaro, 1987; Massaro & Cohen, 1990).

Is a synthesis of these opposing views possible? Perhaps one reason for the complexity of this issue lies in the nature of speech perception itself. It involves both linguistic and perceptual attributes. From a purely perceptual perspective, speech is just a relatively complex signal that is not treated qualitatively differently from other signals. From a psycholinguistic perspective, speech is special because it lies within the domain of language, a special human ability. Indeed, cognitive psychology textbooks differ in terms of where speech perception is discussed. Sometimes it is discussed in the context of language, other times in the context of perception. Thus, the diversity of views on the nature of speech perception can be seen as reflecting the differences in how researchers treat speech. They view it either as regular acoustic signals or as more special phonetic messages (Remez, 1994).

Semantics and Syntax

Language is very difficult to put into words.

—Voltaire

Semantics

The opening of this chapter quoted Helen Keller's description of her first awareness that words had meanings. You probably do not remember the moment that words first came alive to you. But your parents surely do. In fact, one of the greatest joys of being a parent is watching your children's amazing discovery that words have meanings. In semantics, **denotation** is the strict dictionary definition of a word. **Connotation** is a word's emotional overtones, presuppositions, and other nonexplicit meanings. Taken together, denotation and connotation form the meaning of a word. Because connotations may vary between people, there can be variation in the meaning formed. Imagine the word *snake*. For many people, the connotation of *snake* is negative or dangerous. Others, say a biologist specializing in snakes (called a herpetologist), would have a very different and probably much more positive connotation for the word *snake*.

How do we understand word meanings in the first place? Recall from previous chapters that we encode meanings into memory through concepts. These include ideas, to which we may attach various characteristics and with which we may connect various other ideas, such as through propositions (Rey, 2003). They also include images and perhaps motor patterns for implementing particular procedures. Here, we are concerned only with concepts, particularly in terms of words as arbitrary symbols for concepts.

Actually, when we think of words as representing concepts, words are economical ways in which to manipulate related information. For example, when you think about the single word *desk*, you also may conjure all these things:

- All the instances of desks in existence anywhere
- Instances of desks that exist only in your imagination
- All the characteristics of desks
- All the things you might do with desks
- All the other concepts you might link to desks (e.g., things you put on or in desks or places where you might find desks)

Having a word for something helps us to add new information to our existing information about that concept. For example, you have access to the word *desk*. When you have new experiences related to desks or otherwise learn new things about desks, you have a word around which to organize all this related information.

Recall, too, the constructive nature of memory. Having word labels (e.g., "washing clothes," "peace march") has several effects. First, it facilitates the ease of understanding and remembering a text passage. Second, it enhances subjects' recall of the shape of a droodle. Third, it affects the accuracy of eyewitness testimony. Having words as concepts for things helps us in our everyday nonverbal interactions. For example, our concepts of *skunk* and of *dog* allow us more easily to recognize the difference between the two, even if we see an animal only for a moment (Ross & Spalding, 1994). This rapid recognition enables us to respond appropriately, depending on which we saw. Clearly, being able to comprehend the conceptual meanings of words is important. Just how do words combine to convey meaning, however?

Syntax

An equally important part of the psychology of language is the analysis of linguistic structure. *Syntax* is the systematic way in which words can be combined and sequenced to make meaningful phrases and sentences (Carroll, 1986). Whereas speech perception chiefly studies phonetic structure of language, syntax focuses on the study of the grammar of phrases and sentences. In other words, it considers the regularity of structure.

Although you have doubtless heard the word *grammar* before in regard to how people *ought* to structure their sentences, psycholinguists use the word *grammar* in a slightly different way. Specifically, **grammar** is the study of language in terms of noticing regular patterns. These patterns relate to the functions and relationships of words in a sentence. They extend as broadly as the level of discourse and as narrowly as the pronunciation and meaning of individual words. In your English courses, you may have been introduced to prescriptive grammar. This kind of grammar prescribes the "correct" ways in which to structure the use of written and spoken language. Of greater interest to psycholinguists is descriptive grammar, in which an attempt is made to describe the structures, functions, and relationships of words in language.

Consider an example of a sentence that illustrates the contrast between prescriptive and descriptive approaches to grammar: When Junior observes his father carrying upstairs an unappealing bedtime book, Junior responds, "Daddy, what did you bring that book that I don't want to be read to out of up for?" (Pinker, 1994, p. 97). Junior's utterance might shiver the spine of any prescriptive grammarian. But Junior's ability to produce such a complex sentence, with such intricate internal interdependencies, would please descriptive grammarians.

Why can syntax prompt such pleasure? First, the study of syntax allows analysis of language in manageable—and therefore relatively easily studied—units. Second, it offers limitless possibilities for exploration. There are virtually no bounds to the possible combinations of words that may be used to form sentences. Earlier, we referred to this property as the productivity of language. In English, as in any language, we can take a particular set of words (or morphemes, to be more accurate) and a particular set of rules for combining the items and produce a breathtakingly vast array of meaningful utterances. Suppose you were to go to the U.S. Library of Congress and randomly select any sentence from any book. You then searched for an identical sentence in the vast array of sentences in the books therein. Barring intentional quotations, you would be unlikely to find the identical sentence (Pinker, 1994).

Mark an asterisk next to the sentences that are not grammatical, regardless of whether the sentences are meaningful or accurate:

1. The student the book.
2. Bought the book.
3. Bought the student the book.
4. The book was bought by the student.
5. By whom was the book bought?
6. By student the bought book.
7. The student was bought by the book.
8. Who bought the book?
9. The book bought the student.
10. The book bought.

The Syntax Tendency

People demonstrate a remarkable knack for understanding syntactical structure. As the preceding demonstration showed, you, I, and other fluent speakers of a language can recognize syntactical structure immediately. We can do so whether particular sentences and particular word orders are or are not grammatical (Bock, 1990; Pinker, 1994). We can do so even when the sentences are meaningless. For example, we can evaluate Chomsky's sentence, "Colorless green ideas sleep furiously." Or we can evaluate a sentence composed of nonsense words, as in Lewis Carroll's poem "Jabberwocky," "'Twas brillig and the slithy toves did gyre and gimble in the wabe."

Also, just as we show semantic priming of word meanings in memory, we show syntactical priming of sentence structures. We spontaneously tend to use syntactical structures that parallel the structures of sentences we have just heard (Bock, 1990; Bock, Loebell, & Morey, 1992). For example, a speaker will be more likely to use a passive construction (e.g., "The student was praised by the professor") after hearing a passive construction. He or she will do so even when the topics of the sentences differ. Even children as young as age 4 described a series of new items with the same sentence structure as an experimenter used (Huttenlocher, Vasilyeva, & Shimpi, 2004).

Another example of syntactical priming can be seen through the use of sentence priming. In this type of experiment, participants are presented with a sentence. Participants are then presented with new sentences and asked to rate the degree to which they are grammatically correct. If a sentence has the same structure as the previously presented item, it is rated as more nearly grammatically correct (Luka & Barsalou, 2005), independent of its actual degree of grammatical correctness.

Other evidence of our uncanny aptitude for syntax is shown in the speech errors we produce (Bock, 1990). Even when we accidentally switch the placement of two words in a sentence, we still form grammatical, if meaningless or nonsensical, sentences. We almost invariably switch nouns for nouns, verbs for verbs, prepositions for prepositions, and so on. For example, we may say, "I put the oven in the cake." But we will probably not say, "I put the cake oven in the." We usually even attach (and detach) appropriate function morphemes to make the switched words fit their new

IN THE LAB OF STEVEN PINKER

Courtesy of Steven Pinker/
Photographer Rebecca Goldstein

My research tries to illuminate language by examining a single phenomenon with every technique imaginable. Regular verbs such as *walk/walked* form their past tense in a predictable way—by adding "-ed"—and people freely create new ones. When new verbs like *to spam* and *to diss* came into the language, no one ran to the dictionary to look up their past-tense forms; everyone knew they were *spammed* and *dissed*. In contrast, irregular verbs like *sing/sang* and *bring/brought* are idiosyncratic and have to be learned individually. A simple theory is that people produce regular forms by unconsciously applying a rule but produce irregular forms by dredging them up from memory. Because regular and irregular forms are equated for meaning (past) and length (one word), comparing them allows us to tease apart the roles of computational rules and memory lookup in language processing.

There are alternatives to this simple theory. Some connectionists believe that regular and irregular forms are stored in an associative memory that works by analogy, and some linguists believe they are both formed by rules. But a combination of methodologies suggests that the rule-plus-memory theory is correct.

Statistical linguistics: Irregular verbs are also the most frequently used verbs, such as *be, have, do, say,* and *make/just,* as one would expect if irregulars have to be memorized, because frequent items are easier to remember.

Experimental psychology: Common irregular verbs like *took* sound more natural and are faster to produce than uncommon irregular verbs like *strode,* suggesting they depend on memory traces that can be stronger or weaker. But this does not happen when we compare common regular verbs like *walked* with uncommon ones like *balked.* Presumably *balked* is generated on the fly by a rule, so the fact that it has a weak memory trace doesn't hurt it.

Developmental psychology: Children often make errors like *breaked* and *holded.* We analyzed 20,000 past-tense forms in transcripts of children's speech and found support for a simple explanation. Children's memory for irregular forms like *held* is unreliable, but once they have acquired the past-tense rule, they can apply it whenever memory fails and thus sometimes produce *holded.*

Linguistic theory: Why do irregular verbs sometimes show up in regular forms like *flied out* (in baseball) and *ringed the city with artillery?* The answer is that these are verbs built out of nouns ("to hit a fly," "to form a ring around"). Nouns cannot have stored past-tense forms, so memory is bypassed; the similar forms *flew* and *rang* are ignored, and the rule is applied instead.

Cognitive neuroscience: If regular forms are computed and irregular forms are memorized, they should be processed in different parts of the brain.

Indeed, patients with damage to the parts of the brain underlying word memory (from strokes or Alzheimer's disease) have more trouble producing irregular forms; patients with damage to the parts underlying grammar have more trouble with regular forms. Studies measuring event-related electrical potentials from the scalp show that irregular forms engage the parts of the brain that respond to words, whereas regular forms engage the parts that respond to grammatical combinations.

positions. For example, when meaning to say, "The butter knives are in the drawer," we may say, "The butter drawers are in the knife." Here, we change "drawer" to plural and "knives" to singular to preserve the grammaticality of the sentence. Consider even so-called agrammatic aphasics, who have extreme difficulties in both comprehending and producing language. Their substitution errors in speech seem to preserve syntactical categories (Butterworth & Howard, 1987; Garrett, 1992).

The preceding examples seem to indicate that we humans have some mental mechanism for classifying words according to syntactical categories. This classification mechanism is separate from the meanings for the words (Bock, 1990). When we compose sentences, we seem to parse the sentences. We assign appropriate syntactical categories (often called "parts of speech," e.g., noun, verb, article) to each component of the sentence. We then use the syntax rules for the language to construct grammatical sequences of the parsed components.

Using the following 10 words, create 5 strings of words that make grammatical sentences. Also create five sequences of words that violate the syntax rules of English grammar: *ball, basket, bounced, into, put, red, rolled, tall, the, woman.*

To complete the preceding task, you mentally classified the words into syntactical categories, even if you did not know the correct labels for the categories. You then arranged the words into grammatical sequences according to the syntactical categories for the words and your implicit knowledge of English syntax rules. You will see later in the chapter that most 4 year olds can demonstrate the same ability to parse words into categories and to arrange them into grammatical sentences. Of course, most 4 year olds probably cannot label the syntactical categories for any of the words.

INVESTIGATING COGNITIVE PSYCHOLOGY

Early in the twentieth century, linguists who studied syntax largely focused on how sentences could be analyzed in terms of sequences of phrases, such as noun phrases and verb phrases, which were mentioned previously. They also focused on how phrases could be parsed into various syntactical categories, such as nouns, verbs, and adjectives. Such analyses are of **phrase-structure grammars,** which analyze the structure of phrases as they are used. The rules governing the sequences of words are termed *phrase-structure rules.* To observe the interrelationships of phrases within a sentence, linguists often use tree diagrams, such as the ones shown in Figure 9.1. Various other models also have been proposed (e.g., relational grammar, Perlmutter, 1983a; lexical-functional grammar, Bresnan, 1982).

Tree diagrams help to reveal the interrelationships of syntactical classes within the phrase structures of sentences (Bock, 1990; Clegg & Shepherd, 2007; Wasow, 1989). In particular, such diagrams show that sentences are not merely organized chains of words, strung together sequentially. Rather, they are organized into hierarchical structures of embedded phrases. The use of tree diagrams helps to highlight many aspects of how we use language, including both our linguistic sophistication and our difficulties in using language. Look again at Figure 9.1. Focus on the two possible tree diagrams for one sentence, showing its two possible meanings. By observing tree diagrams of ambiguous sentences, psycholinguists can better pinpoint the source of confusion.

In 1957, Noam Chomsky revolutionized the study of syntax. He suggested that to understand syntax, we must observe not only the interrelationships among phrases within sentences but also the syntactical relationships between sentences. Specifically, Chomsky observed that particular sentences and their tree diagrams show peculiar relationships.

FIGURE 9.1

Phrase-structure grammars illustrate the hierarchies of phrases within sentences. (a) The sentence, "The girl looked at the boy with the red shirt" may be diagrammed as shown here. (b) Linguists usually abbreviate tree diagrams as shown here, in the abbreviated linguistic tree diagram of the sentence shown in panel a. Tree diagrams in panels c and d show the possible ways for analyzing the sentence, "The girl looked at the boy with the telescope."

Consider, for example, the following sentences:

S_1: Susie greedily ate the crocodile.

S_2: The crocodile was eaten greedily by Susie.

Oddly enough, a phrase-structure grammar would not show any particular relation at all between sentences S_1 and S_2 (Figure 9.2). Indeed, phrase-structure analyses of S_1 and S_2 would look almost completely different. Yet, the two sentences differ only in voice. The first sentence is expressed in the active voice and the second in the passive voice. Recall from Chapter 7 an important fact about propositions. They may be used for illustrating that the same underlying meanings can be derived through alternative means of representation. The preceding two sentences represent the same proposition: "ate (greedily) (Susie, crocodile)."

Consider another pair of paraphrased sentences:

S_3: The crocodile greedily ate Susie.

S_4: Susie was eaten greedily by the crocodile.

Phrase-structure grammar similarly would show no relationship between S_3 and S_4. What's more, phrase-structure grammar would show some similarities of surface structure between corresponding sentences in the first and second pairs (S_1 and S_3; S_2 and S_4). They clearly have quite different meanings, particularly to Susie and the crocodile. Apparently, an adequate grammar would address the fact that sentences with similar surface structures can have very different meanings.

This observation and other observations of the interrelationships among various phrase structures led linguists to go beyond merely describing various individual phrase structures. They began to focus their attention on the relationships among different phrase structures. Linguists may gain deeper understanding of syntax by studying the relationships among phrase structures that involve transformations of elements within sentences (Chomsky, 1957). Specifically, Chomsky suggested a way to augment the study of phrase structures. He proposed the study of **transformational grammar,** which involves the study of transformational rules that guide the ways in which underlying propositions can be rearranged to form various phrase structures.

A simple way of looking at Chomsky's transformational grammar is to say that "Transformations . . . are rules that map tree structures onto other tree structures" (Wasow, 1989, p. 170). For example, transformational grammar considers how the tree-structure diagrams in Figure 9.2 are interrelated. With application of the transformational rules, the tree structure of S_1 can be mapped onto the tree structure of S_2. Similarly, the structure of S_3 can be mapped onto the tree structure of S_4.

In transformational grammar, **deep structure** refers to an underlying syntactical structure that links various phrase structures through the application of various transformation rules. In contrast, **surface structure** refers to any of the various phrase structures that may result from such transformations. Many casual readers of Chomsky have misconstrued Chomsky's terms. They incorrectly inferred that deep structures signify profound underlying meanings for sentences, whereas surface structures refer only to superficial interpretations of sentences. Chomsky meant only to show that differing phrase structures may have a relationship that is not immediately ap-

FIGURE 9.2

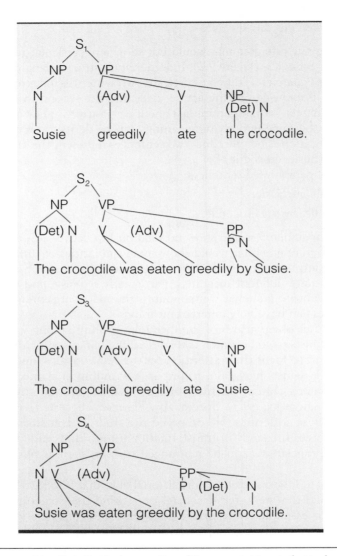

Phrase-structure grammars show surprising dissimilarities between S_1 and S_2, yet surprising similarities between S_1 and S_3 or between S_2 and S_4. Noam Chomsky suggested that to understand syntax, we also must consider a way of viewing the interrelationships among various phrase structures.

parent by using phrase-structure grammar alone. This notion would apply in the example of "Susie greedily ate the crocodile" and "The crocodile was eaten greedily by Susie." For detection of the underlying relationship between two phrase structures, transformation rules must be applied.

Relationships between Syntactical and Lexical Structures

Chomsky (1965, cited in Wasow, 1989) also addressed how syntactical structures may interact with lexical structures. In particular, Chomsky suggested that our mental lexicon contains more than the semantic meanings attached to each word (or morpheme). According to Chomsky, each lexical item also contains syntactical information. This syntactical information for each lexical item indicates three things. The first is the syntactical category of the item, such as noun versus verb. The second is the appropriate syntactical contexts in which the particular morpheme may be used, such as pronouns as subjects versus as direct objects. The third is any idiosyncratic information about the syntactical uses of the morpheme, such as the treatment of irregular verbs.

For example, there would be separate lexical entries for the word *spread* categorized as a noun and for *spread* as a verb. Each lexical entry also would indicate which syntactical rules to use for positioning the word. The rules that were applicable depend on which category was applicable in the given context. For example, as a verb, *spread* would not follow the article *the*. As a noun, however, spread would be allowed to do so. Even the peculiarities of syntax for a given lexical entry would be stored in the lexicon. For example, the lexical entry for the verb *spread* would indicate that this verb deviates from the normal syntactical rule for forming past tenses. This normal rule is to add *-ed* to the stem used for the present tense.

You may wonder why we would clutter up our mental lexicon with so much syntactical information. There is an advantage to attaching syntactical, context-sensitive, and idiosyncratic information to the items in our mental lexicon. If we add to the complexity of our mental lexicon, we can simplify drastically the number and complexity of the rules we need in our mental syntax. For example, by attaching the idiosyncratic treatment of irregular verbs (e.g., *spread* or *fall*) to our mental lexicon, we do not have to endure different syntactical rules for each verb. By making our lexicon more complex, we allow our syntax to be simpler. In this way, appropriate transformations may be simple and relatively context free. Once we know the basic syntax of a language, we easily can apply the rules to all items in our lexicon. We then can gradually expand our lexicon to provide increasing complexity and sophistication.

Not all cognitive psychologists agree with all aspects of Chomsky's theories (e.g., Bock, Loebell, & Morey, 1992; Garrett, 1992; Jackendoff, 1991). Many particularly disagree with his emphasis on syntax (form) over semantics (meaning). Nonetheless, several cognitive psychologists have proposed models of language comprehension and production that include key ideas of syntax. How do we link the elements in our mental lexicon to the elements in our syntactical structures? Various models for such bridging have been proposed (Bock, Loebell, & Morey, 1992; Jackendoff, 1991). According to some of these models, when we parse sentences by syntactical categories, we create slots for each item in the sentence. Consider, for example, the sentence, "Juan gave María the book from the shelf." There is a slot for a noun used as (1) a subject (Juan), (2) as a direct object (the book), (3) as an indirect object (María), and (4) as objects of prepositions (the shelf). There are also slots for the verb, the preposition, and the articles.

In turn, lexical items contain information regarding the kinds of slots into which the items can be placed. The information is based on the kinds of thematic roles the items can fill. **Thematic roles** are ways in which items can be used in the context of communication. Several roles have been identified. A first is that of agent, the "doer" of any action. A second is that of patient, the direct recipient of the action. A third role is that of the beneficiary, the indirect recipient of the action. A fourth role is the instrument, the means by which the action is implemented. A fifth role is location, the place where the action occurs. A sixth is the source, where the action originated. And a seventh is the goal, where the action is going (Bock, 1990; Fromkin & Rodman, 1988). According to this view of how syntax and semantics are linked, the various syntactical slots can be filled by lexical entries with corresponding thematic roles. For example, the slot of subject noun might be filled by the thematic role of agent. As a further example, nouns that can fill agent roles can be inserted into slots for subjects of phrases. Patient roles correspond to slots for direct objects. Beneficiary roles fit with indirect objects, and so on. Nouns that are objects of prepositions may be filled with various thematic roles. These include location, such as at the beach; source, such as from the kitchen; and goal, such as to the classroom. So far, we have concentrated on describing the structure and processes of language in its most developed state. How do we acquire this remarkable ability?

PRACTICAL APPLICATIONS OF COGNITIVE PSYCHOLOGY	Given what you now know about processes of speech perception, semantics, and syntax, think about ways to make your speech production easier for others to perceive. If you are speaking to someone whose primary language differs from yours, try slowing down your speech, exaggerating the length of time between words. Be sure to enunciate consonant sounds carefully, without making your vowel sounds too long. Use simpler sentence constructions. Break down lengthy and involved sentences into smaller units. Insert longer pauses between sentences to give the person time to translate the sentence into propositional form. Communication may feel more effortful but will probably be more effective.

Language Acquisition

In the past, debates about the acquisition of language centered on the same theme as debates about the acquisition of any ability—the nature versus nurture theme. However, current thinking about language acquisition has incorporated the understanding that acquiring language really involves a natural endowment modified by the environment (Bates & Goodman, 1999; Dehaene-Lambertz, Hertz-Pannier, & Dubois, 2006; Lightfoot, 2003; MacWhinney, 1999; Maratsos, 2003; Wexler, 1996). For example, the social environment, in which infants use their social capacities to interact with others, provides one source of information for language acquisition (Carpenter, Nagell, & Tomasello, 1998; Snow, 1999; Tomasello, 1999). Thus, the approach to studying language acquisition now revolves around discovering what abilities are innate and how the child's environment tempers these abilities. This process is aptly termed innately guided learning (see Elman & associates, 1996; Jusczyk, 1997). Before examining the nature-nurture debate, let's take a look at a series of stages that seems to be universal in language acquisition.

Stages of Language Acquisition

Around the world, people seem to acquire their primary language in pretty much the same sequence and in just about the same way. In recent years, research on the development of speech perception finds the same overall pattern of progression. This pattern is from more general to more specific abilities. That is, as infants we are initially able to distinguish among all possible phonetic contrasts. But over time we lose the ability to distinguish nonnative contrasts in favor of those used in our native language environment (see Jusczyk, 1997). Thus, some aspects of infants' speech perception and production abilities mirror each other. They develop from more general to more specific abilities. From day one, infants appear to be programmed to tune in to their linguistic environment with the specific goal of acquiring language. A current debate is whether this ability is especially used in learning concepts and their meanings, the connections between concepts and their meanings, or both (Fodor, 1997; Marcus, 1998; Pinker, 1999; Plunkett, 1998). Whatever may be the case, infants clearly have remarkably acute language-learning abilities. They show these abilities even from an early age (Marcus & associates, 1999; Pinker, 1997a, 1999).

For example, newborns seem to respond preferentially to their mothers' voices (Barker & Newman, 2004; DeCasper & Fifer, 1980). They also seem to respond motorically in synchrony with the speech of the caregivers who interact with them directly (Field, 1978; Martin, 1981; Schaffer, 1977; Snow, 1977; Stern, 1977). Infants also prefer to listen to someone speaking in what will be their native language over a future nonnative language. Perhaps they are focusing on the rhythmic structure of the language (Bertoncini, 1993; Mehler & associates, 1996). Suppose you were to videotape infants' motor responses while the infants were attending to someone speaking to them. Their movements would seem to be dancing in time with the rhythm of the speech. The emotional expression of infants also seems to be matched to that of their caregivers (Fogel, 1991). Infants are quite capable of interpreting and responding to emotional information, even when it is expressed by a stranger (Repacholi & Meltzoff, 2007). Furthermore, infants seem to be able to gather emotional information not only from facial expressions but also from tone of voice. In one study, experimenters examined 7-month-old infants' emotional understanding (Grossmann, Striano, & Friederici, 2006). The infants were presented with happy or angry faces paired with either a happy or angry voice. Sometimes the face and voice matched and sometimes they did not. When the expression and tone did not match, infants demonstrated confusion by looking longer at the faces (Grossmann, Striano, & Friederici, 2006). These findings indicate that infants are able to comprehend emotional facial expressions, emotional tone of voice, and whether or not they correspond.

Within the first years of life, we humans seem to progress through the following stages in producing language:

1. Cooing, which comprises mostly vowel sounds
2. Babbling, which comprises consonant as well as vowel sounds; to most people's ears, the babbling of infants growing up among speakers from different language groups sounds very similar (Oller & Eilers, 1998)

3. One-word utterances; these utterances are limited in both the vowels and the consonants they utilize (Ingram, 1999)
4. Two-word utterances and telegraphic speech
5. Basic adult sentence structure (present by about age 4 years), with continuing vocabulary acquisition (see Bloom, 2000, for a discussion of the mechanisms of this acquisition)

Consider these stages in more detail. Infants also have been known to produce sounds of their own. Most obviously, the communicative aspect of crying—whether intentional or not—works quite well. In terms of language acquisition, however, it is the cooing of infants that most intrigues linguists. **Cooing** is the infant's oral expression that explores the production of vowel sounds. The cooing of infants around the world, including deaf infants, is indistinguishable across babies and across languages. Infants are actually better than adults at being able to discriminate sounds that carry no meaning for them (Werker, 1989). They can make phonetic distinctions that adults have lost. Thus, there are things that extremely young children do better than adults.

During the cooing stage, hearing infants also can discriminate among all phones, not just the phonemes characteristic of their own language. For example, during this stage, both Japanese and American infants can discriminate the /l/ from the /r/ phoneme. However, as Japanese infants move into the next stage, they gradually lose this ability. By 1 year of age, Japanese infants—for whom the distinction does not make a phonemic difference—no longer make this discrimination (Eimas, 1985; Tsushima & associates, 1994).

Loss of discrimination ability is not limited to Japanese infants. Consider a skill of infants who grow up in homes where English is spoken. They are able to distinguish early in life between phonemes that are different in the Hindi language of India but that are not different in English (Werker, 1994; Werker & Tees, 1984). In English, the phonemes are allophones of the /t/ sound. In particular, the English-speaking infants are able to make the discrimination with roughly 95% accuracy at between 6 and 8 months of age. By 8 to 10 months, the infants' accuracy is down to 70%. By 10 to 12 months, it is down to a mere 20%. As they grow older, infants clearly lose the capacity to make discriminations that are not relevant to their language. Cooing is an important stage in language development. When examining children with cerebral palsy, researchers found that when cooing was delayed in onset, there was an increase in future language difficulties (Otapowicz & associates, 2005).

At the babbling stage, deaf infants no longer vocalize. The sounds produced by hearing infants change. **Babbling** is the infant's preferential production largely of those distinct phonemes—both vowels and consonants—that are characteristic of the infant's own language (Locke, 1994; Petitto & Marentette, 1991). Thus, the cooing of infants around the world is essentially the same. But infant babbling is more differentiated. As suggested previously, the ability of the infant to perceive, as well as to produce, nonphonemic phones recedes during this stage. An interesting instance of the specialization of babbling can be seen in the rare infants who can hear but who nevertheless are exposed to ASL as their primary language. These infants do demonstrate babbling but do so in a nonverbal way. Specifically, they form not only nonlinguistic hand movements but also linguistic ones, much like verbal infants do with spoken phonemes (Petitto & associates, 2004).

Eventually, the infant utters his or her first word. It is followed shortly by one or two more. Soon after, yet a few more follow. The infant uses these one-word utterances—termed *holophrases*—to convey intentions, desires, and demands. Usually, the words are nouns describing familiar objects that the child observes (e.g., *car, book, ball, baby, nose*) or wants (e.g., *Mama, Dada, juice, cookie*).

By 18 months of age, children typically have vocabularies of 3 to 100 words (Siegler, 1986). The young child's vocabulary cannot yet encompass all that the child wishes to describe. As a result, the child commits overextension errors. An **overextension error** is erroneously extending the meaning of words in the existing lexicon to cover things and ideas for which a new word is lacking. For example, the general term for a man may be "Dada"—which can be quite distressing to a new father in a public setting. The general term for any kind of four-legged animal may be "doggie." Young children have to overextend the meanings of the words they know. They have too few words in their vocabulary to do otherwise. How do they decide which words to use when overextending the meanings of the words they know?

A *feature hypothesis* suggests that children form definitions that include too few features (Clark, 1973). Thus, a child might refer to a cat as a dog because of a mental rule that if an animal has the feature of four legs, it is a "doggie." An alternative *functional hypothesis* (Nelson, 1973) suggests that children first learn to use words that describe important functions or purposes. For example, lamps give light. Blankets make us warm. According to this view, overextension errors result from functional confusions. A dog and a cat both do similar things and serve the same purposes as pets. So a child is likely to confuse them. The functional hypothesis usually has been viewed as an alternative to the feature hypothesis, but both mechanisms possibly could be at work in children's overextensions.

Gradually, between 1.5 and 2.5 years of age, children start combining single words to produce two-word utterances. Thus begins an understanding of syntax. These early syntactical communications seem more like telegrams than conversations. The articles, prepositions, and other function morphemes are usually left out. Hence, linguists refer to these early utterances with rudimentary syntax as telegraphic speech. **Telegraphic speech** can be used to describe two- or three-word utterances and even slightly longer ones, if they have omissions of some function morphemes. Examples of telegraphic speech include "want juice" and "mommy sit." These simple pairings of words convey a wealth of information about a child's intentions and needs.

Vocabulary expands rapidly. It more than triples from about 300 words at about 2 years of age to about 1000 words at about 3 years of age. Almost incredibly, by age 4 years children acquire the foundations of adult syntax and language structure (Table 9.3). By age 5 years, most children also can understand and produce quite complex and uncommon sentence constructions. By age 10 years, children's language is fundamentally the same as that of adults.

| TABLE 9.3 | Developmental Changes Associated with Language Acquisition |

Regardless of the language children acquire, children around the world seem to follow the same developmental pattern at about the same ages.

APPROXIMATE AGE	CHARACTERISTICS OF AGE	INTERACTION WITH INFORMATION PROCESSING
Prenatal First several months About the second 6 months after birth	Responsivity to human voices Cooing, which comprises largely vowel sounds Babbling, which comprises the distinct phonemes—vowels and consonants—that characterize the primary language of the infant	As sounds become more meaningful, the infant's perception of the sounds becomes more selective and the infant's ability to remember sounds increases.
About 1 to 3 years	One-word utterances Two-word utterances Telegraphic speech	As fluency and comprehension increase, the ability mentally to manipulate linguistic symbols increases, as does conceptual development; overextension errors occur when children try to apply their limited vocabulary to a variety of situations, but as children's vocabulary becomes more specialized, these errors occur less often.
About 3 to 4 years	Simple sentences that reflect tremendous expansion of vocabulary, as well as remarkably adept understanding of syntax, despite errors of overregularization	Vocabulary and concepts continue to expand in terms of both comprehension and fluency, and the child internalizes rules of syntax; overregularization errors offer insights into how children form rules about language structures.
About 4 years of age	Basic adult sentence structure; some increases in complexity of structure continue through adolescence; vocabulary continues to increase, although at a declining rate	Children's language patterns and strategies for language acquisition are studied in much the same ways as those for adults; however, their metacognitive strategies for acquiring vocabulary become increasingly sophisticated throughout childhood.

Nature and Nurture

Neither nature alone nor nurture alone adequately explains all aspects of language acquisition. Just how might nature then facilitate nurture in the process? Perhaps humans have a **language-acquisition device (LAD),** a biologically innate mechanism that facilitates language acquisition (Chomsky, 1965, 1972). That is, we humans seem to be biologically preconfigured to be ready to acquire language.

Several observations of humans support the notion that we are predisposed to acquire language. For one thing, human speech perception is quite remarkable, given the nature of auditory processing capacities for other sounds. Moreover, all children within a broad normal range of abilities and of environments seem to acquire language at an incredibly rapid rate. In fact, deaf children acquire sign language in about the same way and at about the same rate as hearing children acquire spoken language. If you have ever struggled to acquire a second language, you can appreciate the relative ease and speed with which young children seem to acquire their first language. This accomplishment is quite remarkable. Consider that children are offered a relatively modest quantity and variety of linguistic input (whether speech or signs) in relation to the highly sophisticated internalized language structures children create. Children seem to have a knack for acquiring an implicit understanding of the many rules of language structure. They also have a knack for applying those rules to new vocabulary and new contexts. However, many adults still can learn new languages quite well if placed in the right context, such as an immersion program. Their learning may be good, although they are likely to retain an accent that reflects the phonemes of their first language when they speak the new language. For example, a Spaniard learning English may speak English with a Spanish accent. In the same way, the American would be likely to speak Spanish with some degree of an American accent.

Further evidence of innate language abilities can be seen in our ability to segment spoken sentences into words. This ability is not only present for the language we speak, but also for foreign language and artificial language. In one experiment, participants listened to an artificial language. The participants were not given any information about the nature of the words. However, after listening to a stream of speech in the artificial language, in many cases participants were able to detect when words began and ended. Participants also later could recognize the words that were presented, even though they were artificial words (Saffran, Newport, & Aslin, 1996). The ability to segment words is also observed in infants as young as 6 months of age (Bortfeld & associates, 2005; Johnson & Jusczyk, 2001; Saffran, 2001). These abilities are likely to involve both familiarity of words and statistical probabilities. This second factor is a result of the frequency that specific phonemes follow one another in normal speech. These probabilities result in likely configurations of words in a new string of phonemes.

Metacognition is our understanding and control of our cognition (Scheck & Nelson, 2003). It provides one of our best aids in learning language. As adults, we have a great advantage in learning language. We have greater familiarity with the structure of language than we do when we are young. The extent to which metacognition helps, however, depends on how similar a new language is to the language or languages we already know. For example, most English-speaking adults find Spanish much easier to acquire than Russian. The reason is that the structure of Spanish is much more like that of English than is the structure of Russian. Chinese is still harder to acquire, on average, because it is even more different from English than is Russian.

Perhaps even more surprising, almost all children seem to acquire these aspects of language in the same progression and at more or less the same time. However, the linguistic environment clearly plays a role in the language-acquisition process. There seem to be *critical periods*—times of rapid development, during which a particular ability must be developed if it is ever to develop adequately—for acquiring these understandings of language (Newport, 2003; Scovel, 2000; Stromswold, 2000). No one knows exactly why critical periods occur. Perhaps young children are at an advantage in language learning because limitations in their perceptual and memory abilities render them more likely to process smaller chunks of speech information (Newport, 1991). These smaller chunks may make it easier for them to see the structure of language. This view has by no means been unanimously accepted, however (Rohde & Plaut, 1999). Nor has any other explanation been universally accepted for the existence of critical periods. During such periods, the environment plays a crucial role. For example, the cooing and babbling stages seem to be a critical period for acquiring a native speaker's discrimination and production of the distinctive phonemes of a particular language. During this critical period, the child's linguistic context must provide those distinctive phonemes.

There seems to be a critical period for acquiring a native understanding of a language's syntax, too. Perhaps the greatest support for this view comes from studies of adult users of ASL. Consider adults who have signed ASL for 30 years or more. Researchers could discernibly differentiate among those who acquired ASL before age 4 years, between ages 4 and 6 years, and after age 12 years. Despite 30 years of signing, those who acquired ASL later in childhood showed less profound understanding of the distinctive syntax of ASL (Meier, 1991; Newport, 1990).

Studies of linguistically isolated children seem to provide additional support for the notion of the interaction of both physiological maturation and environmental support. Consider the rare children who have been linguistically isolated. Those who are rescued at younger ages seem to acquire more sophisticated language structures than do those who are rescued when they are older. For instance, the child Genie, described in Chapter 1, was denied meaningful verbal interaction for the first 13 years of life. Another example is Victor, the wild boy of Aveyron, who was found after more than 3 years in the wilderness. Victor was never able to learn language despite extensive efforts at instruction (Newton, 2004). The research on critical periods for language acquisition is much more equivocal for the acquisition of additional languages, after acquiring a first one (Bahrick & associates, 1994; see also Chapter 10).

Two additional observations, which apply to all humans at all ages, also support the notion that nature contributes to language acquisition. First, humans possess several physiological structures that serve no purpose other than to produce speech (G. S. Dell, personal communication, November 1994). Second, myriad universal characteristics have been documented across the vast array of human languages. By 1963, a lone linguist documented 45 universal characteristics across 30 languages (e.g., Finnish, Hindi, Swahili, Quechua, and Serbian). Since then, hundreds of universal patterns have been documented across languages around the globe (see Pinker, 1994).

Neither nature nor nurture alone appears to determine language acquisition. According to the **hypothesis testing** view, children acquire language by mentally forming tentative hypotheses regarding language, based on their inherited facility for language acquisition, and then testing these hypotheses in the environment. Thus, nature and nurture work together. The implementation of this process is said to follow several operating principles (Slobin, 1971, 1985). In forming hypotheses, young children look for and attend to these things:

1. Patterns of changes in the forms of words
2. Morphemic inflections that signal changes in meaning, especially suffixes
3. Sequences of morphemes, including both the sequences of affixes and roots and the sequences of words in sentence

In addition, children learn to avoid exceptions. They also figure out various other patterns characteristic of their native tongue. Although not all linguists support the hypothesis-testing view, two phenomena support it. The first is overregularization, or using and sometimes overapplying rules. The second is language productivity, creating novel utterances based on some kind of understanding of how to do so.

A variant of the hypothesis-testing view is that while children are acquiring language, they do not pay attention to all aspects of language. Instead, children focus on the most perceptually salient aspects of language. These aspects happen to be the most meaningful in most cases (Newport, 1990). Although Newport's studies have focused on deaf children's acquisition of ASL, this phenomenon may apply to spoken language as well. Indeed, one study finds that hearing infants do attend to the salient acoustic cues in sentences that mark grammatically critical attributes of sentences (Hirsh-Pasek & associates, 1987).

Although few psychologists (if any) have asserted that language is entirely a result of nature, many researchers have emphasized the genetic component (e.g., Gilger, 1996; Pinker, 1994; Stromswold, 1998, 2000). Some focus on the environmental mechanisms that children use to acquire language. Three such mechanisms are imitation, modeling, and conditioning.

Imitation

In imitation, children do exactly what they see others do. Sometimes children do imitate the language patterns of others, especially their parents. The occurrence of imitation in children is related to vocabulary and socially insightful behavior (McEwen & associates, 2007). It is clear that imitation plays an important role in language learning. Imitation, however, would not in itself be sufficient for acquisition of language. Children must be doing something more. More often, children loosely follow what they hear. This phenomenon is referred to as *modeling*.

Modeling

Even amateur observers of children notice that children's speech patterns and vocabulary model the patterns and vocabulary of the people in their environment. From infancy, children listen to and try to imitate speech sounds they hear (Kuhl & Meltzoff, 1997). In fact, parents of very young children seem to go to great lengths to make it easy for children to attend to and to understand what they are saying. Almost without thinking, parents and other adults tend to use a higher pitch than usual. In this way, they exaggerate the vocal inflection of their speech. For example, they raise and lower pitch and volume more extremely than normal. They also use **child-directed speech**—simpler sentence constructions when speaking with infants and young children (Rice, 1989). This distinctive form of adult speech also has been termed *motherese*. For example, a mother might say to her baby, "Baby come to mama." In this way, she attempts to speak to the child in a way that the child will understand.

Through child-directed speech, adults seem to go out of their way to make language interesting and comprehensible to infants and other young children. Child-directed speech aids in the task of word segmentation, which is crucial to the learning of new words (Thiessen, Hill, & Saffran, 2005). This benefit is in part due to the use of diminutives, such as "doggy" and "birdie," in child-directed speech (Kemple, Brooks, & Gills, 2005). Their goal is to communicate successfully with their infants

(Acredolo & Goodwyn, 1998). In this way, they also make it possible for the infants to model aspects of the adults' behavior. Indeed, infants do seem to prefer listening to child-directed speech more than to other forms of adult speech (Fernald, 1985). These exaggerations serve at least two purposes. First, they seem to gain and hold infants' attention. Second, they signal the infants when to take turns in vocalizing and communicate affect (emotion-related information). Across cultures, parents seem to use this specialized form of speech. They further tailor it to particular circumstances. They use rising intonations to gain children's attention; falling intonations to comfort the children; and brief, discontinuous, rapid-fire explosions of speech to warn against prohibited behavior (Fernald & associates, 1989).

Parents even seem to model the correct format for verbal interactions. Early caregiver–child verbal interactions are characterized by verbal turn taking. The caregiver says something. She or he then uses vocal inflection to cue the infant to respond. The infant babbles, sneezes, burps, or otherwise makes some audible response. The caregiver then accepts whatever noises the infant makes as valid communicative utterances and replies. Next the infant further responds to the cue. The process continues on for as long as they both show interest in continuing.

Parents also seem to work hard to understand children's early utterances. In these utterances, one or two words may be used for conveying an entire array of concepts. As the child grows older and more sophisticated and acquires more language, parents gradually provide less linguistic support. They demand increasingly sophisticated utterances from the child. They initially seem to provide a scaffold from which the child can construct an edifice of language. As the child's language develops, the parents gradually remove the scaffolding.

Do parental models of language use provide the chief means by which children acquire language? The mechanism of imitation is quite appealing in its simplicity. Unfortunately, it does not explain many aspects of language acquisition. For example, suppose imitation is the primary mechanism. Why, in this case, do children universally begin by producing one-word utterances, then two-word and other telegraphic utterances, and later complete sentences? Why not start out with complete sentences? In addition, perhaps the most compelling argument against imitation alone relates to our linguistic productivity. Shakespeare may have been more productive than most of us. But each of us is quite innovative in the speech we produce. Most of the utterances we produce are ones that we have never heard or read before.

Yet another argument against imitation alone is a phenomenon that occurs when young children have acquired an understanding of how language usually works. **Overregularization** occurs when individuals apply the general rules of language to the exceptional cases that vary from the norm. For example, instead of imitating her parents' sentence pattern, "The mice fell down the hole, and they ran home," the young child might overregularize the irregular forms. She or he would then say, "The mouses falled down the hole, and they runned home." The fact that children say things like "mouses" and "runned" shows that the next mechanism to be considered—conditioning—could not tell the entire story of language acquisition.

Conditioning

The mechanism of conditioning is also exquisitely simple. Children hear utterances and associate those utterances with particular objects and events in their environment. They then produce those utterances and are rewarded by their parents and others for having spoken. Imagine the first time a child says "mama." The child's mother is likely to pick up the child and praise the child with lots of smiles and hugs. This behavior serves as a reinforcement to the child for saying "mama." Reinforcement increases the probability that behavior will be repeated, in general (talking) and in particular (saying "mama"). Initially children's utterances are not perfect, but through successive approximations, they come to speak just as well as native adult speakers of their language. The progression from babbling to one-word utterances to more complex utterances would seem to support the notion that children begin with simple associations. Their utterances gradually increase in complexity and in the degree to which they approximate adult speech.

As with imitation, the simplicity of the proposed conditioning mechanism does not suffice to explain actual language acquisition fully. For one thing, parents are much more likely to respond to whether the statement of the child is true or false than to the relative correctness of the child's grammar and pronunciation (Brown, Cazden, & Bellugi, 1969). Of course, parents sometimes do respond to the grammatical correctness of children's speech. But their responses only explain why children eventually stop overregularizing their speech. They do not explain why the children ever begin doing so. Also, just as linguistic productivity argues against imitation alone, it contradicts conditioning: Children constantly use novel utterances for which they have never previously been rewarded. They consistently apply the words and language structures they already know to novel situations and contexts for which they have never before received reinforcement. Thus, through the combined effects of innately given linguistic abilities and exposure to a linguistic environment, infants acquire a language automatically and seemingly effortlessly.

Beyond the First Years

The foregoing theories offer explanations of how children acquire the foundations of adult language structure by age 4 years or so. Indeed, 4-year-old language achievements are remarkable. But few of us would have difficulty recognizing that the vocabulary and the linguistic sophistication of 4 year olds differ from those of most older children and adults. What changes occur in children's use of language after age 4? And what do such changes imply regarding developmental changes in cognition?

To understand these changes, we explore both verbal comprehension and verbal fluency. In general, children's ability to comprehend language and to process information efficiently increases with age (Hunt, Lunneborg, & Lewis, 1975; Keating & Bobbitt, 1978). Older children also demonstrate greater verbal fluency than do younger children (Sincoff & Sternberg, 1988). We do not want to look only at increases in verbal comprehension and fluency abilities that develop with age. We also want to understand development by looking at the specific strategies a child of a given age uses to comprehend or generate verbal material. Much of what develops is not just verbal ability. It also is the ability to generate useful strategies for verbal comprehension and fluency. These strategies are at the intersection of language acquisition and metacognition. They are important aspects of human intelligence (Sternberg, 1985a).

An interesting aspect of research on strategies of verbal comprehension has been research on comprehension monitoring (Markman, 1977, 1979). This research hypothesizes that one of the ways in which we enhance our understanding of verbal information is to monitor what we hear and read. We thereby check it for accuracy, logic, and cohesiveness. To study the influence of comprehension monitoring, researchers observed children and adults and attempted to correlate comprehension-monitoring skills with assessments of overall comprehension.

Consider a typical experiment. Children between the ages of 8 and 11 years heard passages containing contradictory information. This description of how to make the dessert Baked Alaska is an example (Markman, 1979, p. 656):

> *To make it they put the ice cream in a very hot oven. The ice cream in Baked Alaska melts when it gets that hot. Then they take the ice cream out of the oven and serve it right away. When they make Baked Alaska, the ice cream stays firm and does not melt.*

Note that the passage contains a blatant internal contradiction. It says both that the ice cream melts and that it does not. Almost half of the young children who saw this passage did not notice the contradiction at all. Even when they were warned in advance about problems with the story, many of the youngest children still did not detect the inconsistency. Thus, young children are not very successful at comprehension monitoring. They are less than successful even when cued to be aware of inconsistencies in the text they read. An important aspect of development of all cognitive skills, including comprehension monitoring, is the improvement that people show in their use of these skills.

Animal Language

Some cognitive psychologists specialize in the study of nonhuman animals. Why would they study such animals, when humans are so readily available? There are several reasons.

First, nonhuman animals often are presumed to have somewhat simpler cognitive systems. It is therefore easier to model their behavior. These models can then be bootstrapped to the study of humans, as has happened most notably in the study of learning. For example, a model of conditioning that originally was proposed for nonhuman animals such as white rats has proven to be extremely useful in understanding human learning (Rescorla & Wagner, 1972). The model, when first proposed, was unique in suggesting that nonhuman animal cognition is more complex than had previously been thought. Robert Rescorla and Allan Wagner showed that classical conditioning depends not just on simple contiguity of an unconditioned and conditioned stimulus, but rather on the contingency involved in the situation. In other words, classical conditioning occurs when animals reduce uncertainty in a learning situation—when they learn the relation between occurrences of two kinds of stimuli. In sum, research on simpler animals often leads to important insights about human learning.

Second, nonhuman animals can be subject to procedures that would not be possible for human ones. For example, a rat may be sacrificed at the end of a learning experiment to study changes that have occurred in the brain as a result of learning. A rat may also be injected with drugs to examine a compound's effects on functioning. Such experimentation clearly cannot be completed on humans. All such studies, of course, must be subject to institutional approval for the ethics of experimentation before they are conducted.

Third, nonhuman animals that are not in the wild can serve as full-time subjects, or at least, regularly available subjects. They are typically there when the experimenter needs them. In contrast, college students and other humans have many other obligations, such as classes, homework, jobs, and personal commitments. Moreover, sometimes, even when they sign up for research, they fail to show up.

Fourth, an understanding of the comparative and evolutionary as well as developmental bases of human behavior requires studies of nonhuman animals of various kinds (Rumbaugh & Beran, 2003). If cognitive psychologists want to understand the origins of human cognition in the distant past, they need to study other kinds of animals besides humans.

Fifth and finally, the study of humans enables cognitive psychologists to explore which cognitive skills are uniquely human and which ones are shared with other animals. The philosopher René Descartes suggested that language is what qualitatively distinguishes human beings from other species. Was he right? Before we get into the particulars of language in nonhuman species, we should emphasize the distinction between communication and language. Few would doubt that nonhuman animals communicate in one way or another. What is at issue is whether they do so through what reasonably can be called a language. Whereas *language* is an organized means of combining words to communicate, *communication* more broadly encompasses not only the exchange of thoughts and feelings through language but also nonverbal expression. Examples include gestures, glances, distancing, and other contextual cues.

Primates—especially chimpanzees—offer our most promising insights into nonhuman language. Jane Goodall, the well-known investigator of chimpanzees in the wild, has studied diverse aspects of chimp behavior. One is vocalizations. Goodall considers many of them to be clearly communicative, although not necessarily indicative of language. For example, chimps have a specific cry indicating that they are about to be attacked. They have another for calling their fellow chimps together. Nonetheless, their repertoire of communicative vocalizations seems to be small, nonproductive (new utterances are not produced), limited in structure, lacking in structural complexity, and relatively nonarbitrary. It also is not spontaneously acquired. The chimps' communications thus do not satisfy our criteria for a language.

By using sign language, R. Allen and Beatrice Gardner were able to teach their tame chimp, Washoe, rudimentary language skills (Brown, 1973) beyond the stages a human toddler could reach. Subsequently, David Premack (1971) had even greater success with his chimpanzee, Sarah. She acquired a vocabulary of more than 100 words of various parts of speech and showed at least rudimentary linguistic skills. She modeled her trainer and was able to use the instruction she received to construct what appeared to be a rudimentary language of her own. Washoe died in 2007.

A less positive view of the linguistic capabilities of chimpanzees was taken by Herbert Terrace (1987), who raised a chimp named Nim Chimpsky, a takeoff on Noam Chomsky, the eminent linguist. Over the course of several years, Nim made more than 19,000 multiple-sign utterances in a slightly modified version of ASL. Most of his utterances consisted of two-word combinations.

Terrace's careful analysis of these utterances, however, revealed that most of them were repetitions of what Nim had seen. Terrace concluded that, despite what appeared to be impressive accomplishments, Nim did not show even the rudiments of syntactical expression. The chimp could produce single- or even multiple-word utterances, but not in a syntactically organized way. For example, Nim would alternate signing "Give Nim banana," "Banana give Nim," and "Banana Nim give," showing no preference for the grammatically correct form. Moreover, Terrace also studied films showing other chimpanzees supposedly producing language. He came to the same conclusion for them that he had reached for Nim. His position, then, is that although chimpanzees can understand and produce utterances, they do not have linguistic competence in the same sense that even very young humans do. Their communications lack structure, and particularly multiplicity of structure.

Susan Savage-Rumbaugh and her colleagues (Savage-Rumbaugh & associates, 1986, 1993) have found the best evidence yet in favor of language use among chimpanzees. Their pygmy chimpanzees spontaneously combined the visual symbols (such as red triangles and blue squares) of an artificial language the researchers taught them. They even appear to have understood some of the language spoken to them. One pygmy chimp in particular (Greenfield & Savage-Rumbaugh, 1990) seemed to possess remarkable skill, even possibly demonstrating a primitive grasp of language structure. It may be that the difference in results across groups of investigators is due to the particular kind of chimp tested or to the procedures used. The chimp's language may not meet all the constraints posed by the properties of language described at the beginning of the chapter. For example, the language used by the chimps is not spontaneously acquired. Rather, they learn it only through very deliberate and systematic programs of instruction. At this point, we just cannot be sure if the chimps truly show the full range of language abilities.

A famous exploration of language in a nonhuman can be seen in the gorilla Koko. Koko can use approximately 1000 signs and can communicate quite effectively with humans, expressing both desires and thoughts. Evidence also suggests that Koko is able to understand and use humor (Gamble, 2001). Koko also seems to be able to use language in a novel way, both combining signs in new ways and by forming entirely new signs. One of the most famous examples of this behavior was exhibited when Koko developed a new sign for "ring" by combining "finger" and "bracelet" (Hill, 1978).

Another famous incidence of nonhuman language can be seen in the case of an African Grey parrot named Alex. Alex could produce more than 200 words and express a variety of complex concepts, including *present* and *absent* and a zero-like concept (Pepperberg, 1999; Pepperberg & Gordon, 2005). Recent evidence also suggests that Alex was capable of novel combinations of words to form new ways of expressing concepts (Pepperberg, 2007). Alex died in 2007.

Whether nonhuman species can use language, it seems almost certain that the language facility of humans far exceeds that of other species we have studied. Noam Chomsky (1991) has stated the key question regarding nonhuman language quite eloquently: "If an animal had a capacity as biologically advantageous as language but somehow hadn't used it until now, it would be an evolutionary miracle, like finding an island of humans who could be taught to fly."

Key Themes

This chapter deals with a number of the major themes reviewed in Chapter 1.

First and foremost is the theme of nature versus nurture. To what extent is language the result of some innate language acquisition device and to what extent is it the result of experience? Earlier research during the times of behaviorism very heavily emphasized the role of nurture. Much modern research, since the work in the 1960s of Noam Chomsky, has emphasized the role of innate factors (nature). But clearly nature interacts with nurture. Children who receive minimal verbal experiences in their early years will be at a disadvantage in the development of language skills.

A second theme is that of rationalism versus empiricism. Most psychologists emphasize empirical techniques in their research. But linguists such as Chomsky have emphasized more rationalistic techniques. They analyze language, typically without formally collecting empirical data at all, at least in the cognitive psychologists' sense of what constitute such data. The stunning insights of Chomsky show that the two methods complement each other. Many insights can evolve from rationalism. They then can be tested by empirical methods.

A third theme is that of domain generality versus domain specificity. In particular, to what extent is language special? Is it a domain apart from other domains, or simply one more cognitive domain like any other? Many psychologists today believe that there is indeed something special about language. At the same time, cognitive processes operate on it so that people use their language in practically all the other domains in which they work. For example, many mathematical and physical problems are presented with words.

Say to any number of people, "In mud eels are, in clay none are." Ask them what you just said. Our experience is that almost no one can understand this sentence. The reason is that they are not applying the appropriate schema to understand your utterance. If you were to ask them to think of themselves as fish who don't want to be eaten by eels and then if you were to repeat this sentence, many will be able to understand what you say. (Our experience is that there are still some who will not be able to understand this utterance, so you will have to give them stronger hints.)

Summary

1. **What properties characterize language?**   There are at least six properties of language, the use of an organized means of combining words in order to communicate. (1) Language permits us to communicate with one or more people who share our language. (2) Language creates an arbitrary relationship between a symbol and its referent—an idea, a thing, a process, a relationship, or a description. (3) Language has a regular structure; only particular sequences of symbols (sounds and words) have meaning. Different sequences yield different meanings. (4) The structure of language can be analyzed at multiple levels (e.g., phonemic and morphemic). (5) Despite having the limits of a structure, language users can produce novel utterances; the possibilities for generating new utterances are virtually limitless. (6) Languages constantly evolve.

Language involves verbal comprehension—the ability to comprehend written and spoken linguistic input, such as words, sentences, and paragraphs. It also involves verbal fluency—the ability to produce linguistic output. The smallest units of sound produced by the human vocal tract are phones. Phonemes are the smallest units of sound that can be used to differentiate meaning in a given language. The smallest semantically meaningful unit in a language is a morpheme. Morphemes may be either roots or affixes—prefixes or suffixes. Affixes in turn may be either content morphemes, conveying the bulk of the word's meaning, or function morphemes, augmenting the meaning of the word. A lexicon is the repertoire of morphemes in a given language (or for a given language user). The study of the meaningful sequencing of words within phrases and sentences in a given language is syntax.

Larger units of language are embraced by the study of discourse.

2. **What are some of the processes involved in language?** In speech perception, listeners must overcome the influence of coarticulation (overlapping) of phonemes on the acoustic structure of the speech signal. Categorical perception is the phenomenon in which listeners perceive continuously varying speech sounds as distinct categories. It lends support to the notion that speech is perceived via specialized processes. The motor theory of speech perception attempts to explain these processes in relation to the processes involved in speech production. Those who believe speech perception is ordinary explain speech perception in terms of feature-detection, prototype, and Gestalt theories of perception.

Syntax is the study of the linguistic structure of sentences. Phrase-structure grammars analyze sentences in terms of the hierarchical relationships among words in phrases and sentences.

Transformational grammars analyze sentences in terms of transformational rules that describe interrelationships among the structures of various sentences. Some linguists have suggested a mechanism for linking syntax to semantics. By this mechanism, grammatical sentences contain particular slots for syntactical categories. These slots may be filled by words that have particular thematic roles within the sentences. According to this view, each item in a lexicon contains information regarding appropriate thematic roles, as well as appropriate syntactical categories.

3. **How do we acquire the ability to use language?** Humans seem to progress through stages in acquiring language. The first is cooing, which comprises all possible phones. The second is babbling, which comprises only the distinct phonemes that characterize the primary language of the infant.

The third is one-word utterances. The fourth is two-word utterances and telegraphic speech. And the fifth is basic adult sentence structure (present by about age 4 years). This progression includes changes in perception that reduce the number of phonemes that can be distinguished. After the cooing stage, the infant tunes in only to those phonemes of the native language environment.

During language acquisition, children engage in overextension errors, in which they extend the meaning of a word to encompass more concepts than the word is intended to encompass. Neither nature alone nor nurture alone can account for human language acquisition. The mechanism of hypothesis testing suggests an integration of nature and nurture. Children acquire language by mentally forming tentative hypotheses regarding language (based on nature) and then testing these hypotheses in the environment (based on nurture). Children are guided in the formation of these hypotheses by an innate language-acquisition device (LAD), which facilitates language acquisition. Over the course of development, language complexity, vocabulary, and even strategies for vocabulary acquisition become increasingly sophisticated.

Thinking about Thinking: Factual, Analytical, Creative, and Practical Questions

1. Describe the six key properties of language.

2. What evidence is there that both nature and nurture influence language acquisition?

3. In your opinion, why do some view speech perception as special, whereas others consider speech perception ordinary?

4. Compare and contrast the speech-is-ordinary and speech-is-special views, particularly in reference to categorical perception and phoneme restoration.

5. How do phrase-structure diagrams reveal the alternative meanings of ambiguous sentences?

6. Make up a sentence that illustrates several of the thematic roles mentioned in this chapter (i.e., agent, patient, beneficiary, instrument, location, source, and goal).

7. In this chapter, we saw that passive-voice sentences can be transformed into active-voice sentences using transformation rules. What are some other kinds of sentence structures that are related to one another? In your own words, state the transformation rules that would govern the changes from one form to another.

8. Give a sample of an utterance you might reasonably expect to hear from an 18-month-old child.

Key Terms

babbling	function morphemes	phrase-structure grammars
categorical perception	grammar	psycholinguistics
child-directed speech	hypothesis testing	semantics
coarticulation	language	surface structure
communication	language-acquisition device (LAD)	syntax
connotation	lexicon	telegraphic speech
content morphemes	morpheme	thematic roles
cooing	noun phrase	transformational grammar
deep structure	overextension error	verb phrase
denotation	overregularization	verbal comprehension
discourse	phoneme	verbal fluency

Explore CogLab by going to **http://coglab.wadsworth.com.** To learn more, examine the following experiments:

Categorical Perception
Identification
Discrimination

Suffix Effect
Lexical Decision

Annotated Suggested Readings

Bloom, P. (2000). *How children learn the meanings of words.* Cambridge, MA: MIT Press. A comprehensive and empirically supported account of vocabulary acquisition in young children.

Givens, D. G. (2002). *The nonverbal dictionary of gestures, signs & body language cues.* Spokane, WA: Center for Nonverbal Studies Press. This book provides a comprehensive explanation of nonverbal behaviors and cues, including, signals, signs, and body language.

Hillix, W. A., & Rumbaugh, D. M. (2004). *Animal bodies, human minds: Ape, dolphin, and parrot language skills.* New York: Kluwer Academic/Plenum. This book provides an overview of language in nonhuman animals. It contains detailed descriptions of research with many different animal species.

Language in Context

EXPLORING COGNITIVE PSYCHOLOGY

1. How does language affect the way we think?

2. How does our social context influence our use of language?

3. How can we find out about language by studying the human brain, and what do such studies reveal?

"My surgeon was a butcher."

"His house is a rat's nest."

"Her sermons are sleeping pills."

"He's a real toad, and he always dates real dogs."

"Abused children are walking time bombs."

"My boss is a tiger in board meetings but a real pussycat with me."

"Billboards are warts on the landscape."

"My cousin is a vegetable."

"John's last girlfriend chewed him up and spit him out."

Not one of the preceding statements is literally true. Yet fluent readers of English have little difficulty comprehending these metaphors and other nonliteral forms of language. How do we comprehend them? One of the reasons that we can understand nonliteral uses of language is that we can interpret the words we hear within a broader linguistic, cultural, social, and cognitive context. In this chapter, we first focus on the cognitive context of language. We look at how people use language in context to learn how to read and be proficient readers. Then, we look at how language and thought interact. Next, we discuss some uses of language in its social context. Finally, we examine some neuropsychological insights into language. Although the topics in this chapter are diverse, they all have one element in common. They address the issue of how language is used in the everyday contexts in which we need it to communicate with others and to make our communications as meaningful as we possibly can.

Reading: Bottom-Up and Top-Down Processes

Because reading is so complex, a discussion of how we engage in this process could be placed in any of a number of chapters in this book. At a minimum, reading involves language, memory, thinking, intelligence, and perception (Adams, 1990, 1999; Adams, Treiman, & Pressley, 1997; Garrod & Daneman, 2003; Just & Carpenter, 1987). In a typical day, we repeatedly encounter written language. Every day we see signs, billboards, labels, and notices. These items contain a wealth of information that helps us make decisions and understand situations. As a result, the ability to read is fundamental to our everyday lives.

People who have **dyslexia**—difficulty in deciphering, reading, and comprehending text—can suffer greatly in a society that puts a high premium on fluent reading (Benasich & Thomas, 2003; Coltheart, 2003; Galaburda, 1999; National Research Council, 1998; Shankweiler & associates, 1995; Spear-Swerling & Sternberg, 1996; Sternberg & Grigorenko, 1999; Sternberg & Spear-Swerling, 1999; Torgesen, 1997; Vellutino & associates, 1996). Problems in phonological processing, and thus in word identification, pose "the major stumbling block in learning to read" (Pollatsek & Rayner, 1989, p. 403; see also Grodzinsky, 2003; Rayner & Pollatsek, 2000). Several different processes may be impaired in dyslexia.

The first is phonological awareness. It refers to awareness of the sound structure of spoken language. A typical way of assessing phonological awareness is through a phoneme-deletion task. Children are asked to say, for example, "goat" without the "-t." Another task that is used is phoneme counting. Children might be asked how many different sounds there are in the word "fish." The correct answer is three.

A second process is phonological reading. It entails reading words in isolation. Teachers sometimes call this skill "word decoding" or "word attack." For measurement of the skill, children might be asked to read words in isolation. Some of the words might be quite easy; others, difficult. Individuals with dyslexia often have more trouble recognizing the words in isolation than in context. When given context, they use the context to figure out what the word means.

A third process is phonological coding in working memory. This process is involved in remembering strings of phonemes that are sometimes confusing. It might be measured by comparing working memory for confusable versus nonconfusable phonemes. For example, a child might be assessed for how well he or she remembers the string t, b, z, v, g versus o, x, r, y, q. Most people will have more difficulty with the first string. But individuals with dyslexia who have problems in phonological coding in working memory will have particular trouble.

A fourth process is lexical access. This process refers to one's ability to retrieve phonemes from long-term memory. The question here is whether one can quickly retrieve a word from long-term memory when it is seen. For example, if you see the word *pond*, do you immediately recognize the word as *pond*, or does it take you a while to retrieve it?

There are several different kinds of dyslexia. The most well-known kind is *developmental dyslexia*, which is difficulty in reading that starts in childhood and typically continues throughout adulthood. Most commonly, children with developmental dyslexia have difficulty in learning the rules that relate letters to sounds (Démonet, Taylor, & Chaix, 2004; Shaywitz & Shaywitz, 2005). A second kind of dyslexia is *acquired dyslexia*, which is typically caused by traumatic brain damage. A perfectly good reader who experiences a brain injury may acquire dyslexia (Coslett, 2003).

Developmental dyslexia is believed to have both biological and environmental causes. A major dispute in the field is the role of each (Sternberg & Spear-Swerling, 1999). People with developmental dyslexia often have been found to have abnormalities in certain chromosomes, most notably, 3, 6, and 15 (Paracchini, Scerri, & Monaco, 2007). However, educational interventions can help reduce the impairments in reading caused by dyslexia (Bakker, 2006).

Perceptual Issues in Reading

If you view your own text processing, you can see that the ability to read is truly re-markable. You somehow manage to perceive the correct letter when it is presented in a wide array of typestyles and typefaces. For example, you can perceive it correctly in capital and lowercase forms, and even in cursive forms. Such processes involve the perception of aspects of printed words relating to visual form. Such aspects are re-ferred to as *orthographic*. You then must translate the letter into a sound, creating a phonological code (relating to sound). This translation is particularly difficult in English because English does not always ensure a direct correspondence between a letter and a sound. George Bernard Shaw, playwright and lover of the English lan-guage, observed the illogicality of English spellings. He suggested that, in English, it would be perfectly reasonable to pronounce "ghoti" as "fish." You would pronounce the "gh" as in *rough*, the "o" as in *women*, and the "ti" as in *nation*. That brings up another perplexing "Englishism": How do you pronounce "ough"? Try the words *dough, bough, bought, through,* and *cough*—had *enough*?

After you somehow manage to translate all those visual symbols into sounds, you must sequence those sounds to form a word (Pollatsek & Miller, 2003). Then you need to identify the word and figure out what the word means. Ultimately you move on to the next word and repeat the process all over again. You continue this process with subsequent words to formulate a single sentence. You continue this process for as long as you read. Clearly, the normal ability to read is not at all sim-ple. About 36 million American adults have not yet learned to read at an eighth-grade level (Conn & Silverman, 1991). On the one hand, the statistics on low literacy and illiteracy should alarm us and provoke us to action. On the other hand, we may need to reconsider our possibly less-than-favorable appraisal of those who have not yet mastered the task of reading. To undertake such a challenge—at any age—is difficult indeed.

When learning to read, novice readers must come to master two basic kinds of perceptual processes: lexical processes and comprehension processes. **Lexical pro-cesses** are used to identify letters and words. They also activate relevant information in memory about these words. **Comprehension processes** are used to make sense of the text as a whole (and are discussed later in this chapter). The separation and inte-gration of both bottom-up and top-down approaches to perception can be seen as we consider the lexical processes of reading.

Lexical Processes in Reading

Fixations and Reading Speed

When we read, our eyes do not move smoothly along a page or even along a line of text. Rather, our eyes move in *saccades*—rapid sequential movements as they fixate on successive clumps of text. The fixations are like a series of "snapshots" (Pollatsek & Rayner, 1989). Fixations are of variable length (Carpenter & Just, 1981). Readers fixate for a longer time on longer words than on shorter words. They also fixate longer on less familiar words (i.e., words that appear less frequently in the English language) than on more familiar words (i.e., words of higher frequency). The last word of a sentence also seems to receive an extra long fixation time. This can be called "sentence wrap-up time" (Carpenter & Just, 1981).

Although most words are fixated, not all of them are. Readers fixate up to about 80% of the content words in a text. These words include nouns, verbs, and other words that carry the bulk of the meaning. (Function words, such as *the* and *of,* serve a supporting role to the content words.) Just what is the visual span of one of these fixations? It appears that we can extract useful information from a perceptual window of characters about four characters to the left of a fixation point and about 14 or 15 characters to the right of it. These characters include letters, numerals, punctuation marks, and spaces. Saccadic movements leap an average of about seven to nine characters between successive fixations. So some of the information we extract may be preparatory for subsequent fixation (Pollatsek & Rayner, 1989; Rayner & associates, 1995). When students speed-read, they show fewer and shorter fixations (Just, Carpenter, & Masson, 1982). But apparently their greater speed is at the expense of comprehension of anything more than just the gist of the passage (Homa, 1983).

Lexical Access

An important aspect of reading is **lexical access**—the identification of a word that allows us to gain access to the meaning of the word from memory. Most psychologists who study reading believe that lexical access is an interactive process. It combines information from multiple levels of processing, such as the features of letters, the letters themselves, and the words comprising the letters (Morton, 1969). Consider some of the basics of an interactive-activation model (Rumelhart & McClelland, 1981, 1982). The hypothesis of this model is that activation of particular lexical elements occurs at multiple levels. Moreover, activity at each of the levels is interactive.

The model distinguishes among three levels of processing following visual input. These are the feature level, the letter level, and the word level. The model assumes that information at each level is represented separately in memory. Information passes from one level to another bidirectionally. In other words, processing occurs in each of two directions. First, it is bottom-up, starting with sensory data and working up to higher levels of cognitive processing. Second, it is top-down, starting with high-level cognition operating on prior knowledge and experiences related to a given context (Figure 10.1). The interactive view implies that not only do we use the sensorially perceptible features of letters, say, to help us identify words. We also use the features we already know about words to help us identify letters. For this reason, the model is referred to as "interactive." Moreover, the top-down aspect of the model allows for generalized context effects (see also Plaut & associates, 1996).

Other theorists have suggested alternatives to Rumelhart and McClelland's model (e.g., Meyer & Schvaneveldt, 1976; Paap & associates, 1982), but the distinctions among interactive models go beyond the scope of this introductory text. Support for word-recognition models involving discrete levels of processing comes from studies of cerebral processing (Petersen & associates, 1988; Posner & associates, 1988, 1989). Studies that map brain metabolism indicate that different regions of the brain become activated during passive visual processing of word forms, as opposed to semantic analysis of words or even spoken pronunciation of the words. These studies involve the use of techniques such as positron emission tomography (PET) and functional magnetic resonance imaging (fMRI), discussed in Chapter 2.

FIGURE 10.1

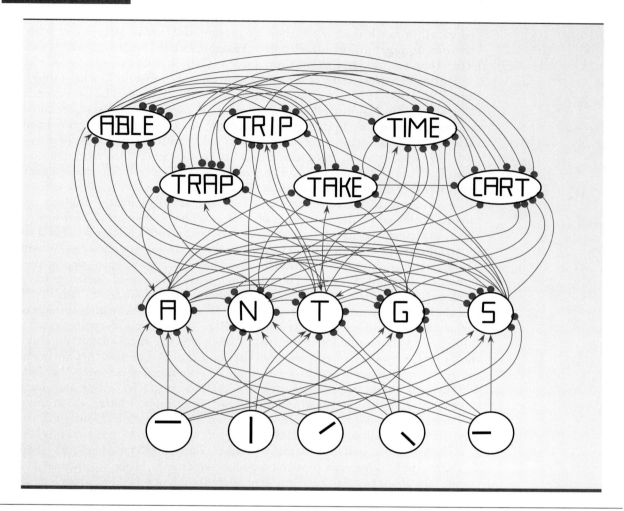

David Rumelhart and James McClelland used this figure to illustrate how activation at the feature level, the letter level, and the word level may interact during word recognition. In this figure, lines terminating in arrows prompt activation, and lines terminating in dots (blue circles) prompt inhibition. For example, the feature for a solid horizontal bar at the top of a letter leads to activation of the T character but to inhibition of the N character. Similarly, at the letter level, activation of T as the first letter leads to activation of TRAP and TRIP but to inhibition of ABLE. Going from the top down, activation of the word TRAP leads to inhibition of A, N, G, and S as the first letter but to activation of T as the first letter. From Richard E. Meyer, "The Search for Insight: Grappling with Gestalt Psychology's Unanswered Questions," in The Nature of Insight, edited by R. J. Sternberg and J. E. Davidson. © 1995 MIT Press. Reprinted with permission from MIT Press.

In addition to neuropsychological support, at least two of the word-recognition models have been simulated on computers (the McClelland and Rumelhart model and the model proposed by Paap & associates, 1982). Both models aptly predicted a word-superiority effect as well as a pseudoword-superiority effect. The word-superiority effect is similar to the configural-superiority effect and the object-superiority effect (mentioned in regard to top-down influences on perception). In the **word-superiority effect,** letters are read more easily when they are embedded in words than when they are presented either in isolation or with letters that do not form words. People take substantially longer to read unrelated letters than to read letters that form a word (Cattell, 1886).

Further demonstrations of the effect were offered by Gerald Reicher (1969) and Daniel Wheeler (1970), so it sometimes is called the Reicher-Wheeler effect. Typically, the word-superiority effect is observed in an experimental paradigm known as the *lexical-decision task*. In this paradigm, a string of letters is presented very briefly. It then is either removed or covered by a *visual mask*, a pattern that wipes out the previously presented stimulus from iconic memory (see Chapter 5 for more information about the iconic memory store). The participant then is asked to make a decision about whether the string of letters is a word.

In studying the word-superiority effect, the standard lexical-decision task is modified to examine the processing of letters. When studying the word-superiority effect, experimenters present participants very briefly with either a word or a single letter, followed by a visual mask. The participant then is given a choice of two letters. The participants must decide which he or she just saw. For example, suppose the test stimulus is the word "WORK." The test stimulus would be one of the letters from the word. Suppose the test stimulus is "K"; the alternatives might be "D" and "K." The test alternatives would be presented as "_ _ _ D" and "_ _ _ K," which correspond to the target "WORK" and a similar word "WORD," respectively. Participants are then instructed to choose the letter they saw. Participants are more accurate in choosing the correct letter when it is presented in the context of a word than they are in choosing the correct letter when it is presented in isolation (Johnston & McClelland, 1973). Even letters in pronounceable pseudowords (e.g., "MARD") are identified more accurately than letters in isolation. However, strings of letters that cannot be pronounced as words (e.g., "ORWK") do not aid in identification (Grainger & associates, 2003; Pollatsek & Rayner, 1989).

There is also a "sentence-superiority effect" (Cattell, 1886; Perfetti, 1985; Perfetti & Roth, 1981). One way that the sentence-superiority effect is observed is that people take about twice as long to read unrelated words as to read words in a sentence (Cattell, 1886). The sentence-superiority effect can be seen in other paradigms as well. For example, suppose that a reader very briefly sees a degraded stimulus. The word *window,* for example, might be shown but in degraded form (Figure 10.2). When the word is standing by itself in this form, it is more difficult to recognize than when it is preceded by a sentence context. An example of such a context would be "There were several repair jobs to be done. The first was to fix the _____" (Perfetti, 1985). Having a meaningful context for a stimulus helps the reader to perceive it.

Also, apparently context effects work at both conscious and preconscious levels. At the conscious level, we have active control over the use of context to determine word meanings. At the preconscious level, the use of context is probably automatic and outside our active control (Stanovich, 1981; see also Posner & Snyder, 1975; Sereno, Brewer, & O'Donnell, 2003). A series of experiments involving the lexical-decision task offers evidence of context effects in making lexical decisions (Meyer &

FIGURE 10.2

0%   pepper   window

21% pepper   window

42% pepper   window

This figure shows instances of the word window and of the word pepper, in which each word is clearly legible, somewhat legible, or almost completely illegible. Percentages are percentages of degradation.

Schvaneveldt, 1971; Schvaneveldt, Meyer, & Becker, 1976). Participants seem to make lexical decisions more quickly when presented with strings of letters that commonly are associated pairs of words (e.g., "doctor" and "nurse" or "bread" and "butter"). They respond more slowly when presented with unassociated pairs of words, with pairs of nonwords, or with pairs involving a word and a nonword.

How well we read is determined largely by how well we reflect on and think about what we are reading. What is the relation between the language in which material is presented—either visually or verbally—and the thinking we do?

Language and Thought

One of the most interesting areas in the study of language is the relationship between language and the thinking human mind (Harris, 2003). Many different questions have been asked about this relationship. We consider only some of them here. Studies comparing and contrasting users of differing languages and dialects form the basis of this section.

Differences among Languages

Why are there so many different languages around the world? And how does using any language in general and using a particular language influence human thought? As you know, different languages comprise different lexicons. They also use different syntactical structures. These differences often reflect variations in the physical and cultural environments in which the languages arose and developed. For example, in terms of lexicon, the Garo of Burma distinguish among many different kinds of rice, which is understandable because they are a rice-growing culture. Nomadic Arabs have more than 20 different words for camels. These peoples clearly conceptualize rice and camels more specifically and in more complex ways than do people outside their cultural groups. As a result of these linguistic differences, do the Garo think about rice differently than we do? And do the Arabs think about camels differently than we do? Consider the way we discuss computers. We differentiate between many aspects of computers, include whether the computer is a desktop or a laptop, a pc or a Mac, or a Linux or Windows machine. A person from a culture that does not have access to computers would not require so many words or distinctions to describe these machines. We expect, however, specific performance and features for a given computer based on these distinctions. Clearly, we think about computers in a way that is different from people who have never encountered a computer.

The syntactical structures of languages differ too. Almost all languages permit some way in which to communicate actions, agents of actions, and objects of actions (Gerrig & Banaji, 1994). What differs across languages is the order of subject, verb, and object in a typical declarative sentence. Also differing is the range of grammatical inflections and other markings that speakers are obliged to include as key elements of a sentence. For example, in describing past actions in English, we indicate whether an action took place in the past by changing (inflecting) the verb form. For example, *walk* changes to *walked* in the past tense. In Spanish and German, the verb also must indicate whether the agent of action was singular or plural and whether it is being referred to in the first, second, or third person. In Turkish, the verb form must indicate past action, singular or plural, and the person. It also must indicate whether the action was witnessed or experienced directly by the speaker or was noted only indirectly. Do these differences and other differences in obligatory syntactical structures influence—or perhaps even constrain—the users of these languages to think about things differently because of the language they use while thinking?

Linguistic Relativity: The Sapir-Whorf Hypothesis

The concept relevant to this question is **linguistic relativity,** the assertion that the speakers of different languages have differing cognitive systems and that these different cognitive systems influence the ways in which people speaking the various languages think about the world. Thus, according to the relativity view, the Garo would think about rice differently than we do. For example, the Garo would develop more cognitive categories for rice than would an English-speaking counterpart. What would happen when the Garo contemplated rice? They purportedly would view it differently—and perhaps with greater complexity of thought—than would English speakers, who have only a few words for rice. Thus, language would shape thought. There is some evidence that word learning may occur, in part, as a result of infants' mental differentiation among various kinds of concepts (Carey, 1994; Xu & Carey, 1995, 1996). So it might make sense that infants who encounter different kinds of objects might make different kinds of mental differentiations. These differentiations would be a function of the culture in which the infants grew up.

The linguistic relativity hypothesis is sometimes referred to as the Sapir-Whorf hypothesis, after the two men who were most forceful in propagating it. Edward Sapir (1941/1964) said that "we see and hear and otherwise experience very largely as we do because the language habits of our community predispose certain choices of interpretation" (p. 69). Benjamin Lee Whorf (1956) stated this view even more strongly:

We dissect nature along lines laid down by our native languages. The categories and types that we isolate from the world of phenomena we do not find there because they stare every observer in the face; on the contrary, the world is presented in a kaleidoscopic flux of impressions which has to be organized by our minds—and this means largely by the linguistic systems in our minds. (p. 213)

The Sapir-Whorf hypothesis has been one of the most widely mentioned ideas in all of the social and behavioral sciences (Lonner, 1989). However, some of its implications appear to have reached mythical proportions. For example, "many social scientists have warmly accepted and gladly propagated the notion that Eskimos have multitudinous words for the single English word *snow*. Contrary to popular beliefs, Eskimos do *not* have numerous words for snow (Martin, 1986). No one who knows anything about Eskimo (or more accurately, about the Inuit and Yupik families of related languages spoken from Siberia to Greenland) has ever said they do" (Pullum, 1991, p. 160). Laura Martin, who has done more than anyone else to debunk the myth, understands why her colleagues might consider the myth charming. But she has been quite "disappointed in the reaction of her colleagues when she pointed out the fallacy; most, she says, took the position that true or not 'it's still a great example'" (Adler, 1991, p. 63). Apparently, we must exercise caution in our interpretation of findings regarding linguistic relativity.

Consider a milder form of linguistic relativism. It is that language may not determine thought, but that language certainly may influence thought. Our thoughts and our language interact in myriad ways, only some of which we now understand. Clearly, language facilitates thought. It even affects perception and memory. For some reason, we have limited means by which to manipulate nonlinguistic images (Hunt & Banaji, 1988). Such limitations make desirable the use of language to facilitate mental representation and manipulation. Even nonsense pictures ("droodles") are recalled and redrawn differently, depending on the verbal label given to the picture (Bower, Karlin, & Dueck, 1975).

To see how this phenomenon might work, look at Figure 10.3 right now. Suppose, instead of being labeled as it is, it had been titled "beaded curtain." You might have perceived it differently. However, once a particular label has been given, viewing the same figure from the alternative perspective is much harder (Glucksberg, 1988). Psychologists have used other ambiguous figures (see Chapter 4) and have found similar results. Figure 10.4 illustrates three other figures that can be given alternative labels. When participants are given a particular label, they tend to draw their recollection of the figure in a way more similar to the given label. For example, after viewing a figure of two circles connected by a single line, they will draw a figure differently as a function of whether it is labeled "eyeglasses" or "dumbbells." Specifically, the connecting line will either be lengthened or shortened depending on the label.

Language also affects in other ways how we encode, store, and retrieve information in memory. Remember the examples in Chapter 6 regarding the label "Washing Clothes"? It enhanced people's responses to recall and comprehension questions about text passages (Bransford & Johnson, 1972, 1973). In a similar vein, eyewitness testimony is powerfully influenced by the distinctive phrasing of questions posed to eyewitnesses (Loftus & Palmer, 1974). In a famous study, participants viewed an ac-

FIGURE 10.3

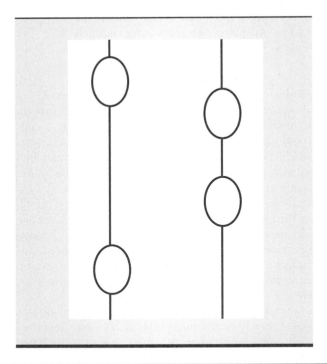

How does your label for this image affect your perception, your mental representation, and your memory of the image? From Psychology, *Fifth Edition by John Darley, et al. Copyright © 1998 Pearson Education. Reprinted by permission of John Darley.*

cident (Loftus & Palmer, 1974). Participants then were asked to describe the speeds of the cars before the accident. The word indicating impact was varied between participants. These words included *smashed, collided, bumped,* and *hit.* When the word *smashed* was used, the participants rated speed as significantly higher than when any of the other words were used. The connotation of the word *smash* thereby seems to bias participants to estimate a higher speed. Similarly, when participants were asked if they saw broken glass (after a week's delay), the participants who were questioned with the word *smashed* said "yes" much more frequently than any of the other participants (Loftus & Palmer, 1974). No other conditions varied between participants, so the difference in the description of the accident is presumably the result of the word choice.

Even when participants generated their own descriptions, the subsequent accuracy of their eyewitness testimony declined (Schooler & Engstler-Schooler, 1990). In other words, accurate recall actually declined following an opportunity to write a description of an observed event, a particular color, or a particular face. When given an opportunity to identify statements about an event, the actual color, or a face, participants were less able to do so accurately if they had previously described it. Paradoxically, when participants were allowed to take their time in responding, their performance was even less

FIGURE 10.4

Reproduced figure	Verbal label	Original figure	Verbal list	Reproduced figure
	Bottle		Stirrup	
	Crescent moon		Letter C	
	Eyeglasses		Dumbbells	

When the original figures (in the center) are redrawn from memory, the new drawings tend to be distorted to be more like the labeled figures. From Psychology, Fifth Edition *by John Darley, et al. Copyright © 1998 Pearson Education. Reprinted by permission of John Darley.*

accurate than when they were forced to respond quickly. In other words, given time to reflect on their answers, participants were more likely to respond in accord with what they had said or written than with what they had seen.

Is the Sapir-Whorf hypothesis relevant to everyday life? Almost certainly it is. If language constrains our thought, then we may fail to see solutions to problems because we do not have the right words to express these solutions. Consider the misunderstandings we have with people who speak other languages, such as what happens all the time at the United Nations. According to this view, the misunderstandings may result from the fact that the languages of the others parse the word differently than ours does. One must be grateful that extreme versions of the Sapir-Whorf hypothesis do not appear to be justified. Such versions would suggest that we are, figuratively, slaves to the words available to us.

Linguistic Universals

There has been some research that addresses **linguistic universals**—characteristic patterns across all languages of various cultures—and relativity. Recall from Chapter 9 that linguists have identified hundreds of linguistic universals related to phonology (the study of phonemes), morphology (the study of morphemes), semantics, and syntax. An area that illustrates much of this research well focuses on color names. These words provide an especially convenient way of testing for universals. Why? Because people in every culture can be expected to be exposed, at least potentially, to pretty much the same range of colors.

In actuality, different languages name colors quite differently. But the languages do not divide the color spectrum arbitrarily. A systematic pattern seems universally to govern color naming across languages. Consider the results of investigations of color terms across a large number of languages (Berlin & Kay, 1969; Kay, 1975). Two apparent linguistic universals about color naming have emerged across languages. First, all the languages surveyed took their basic color terms from a set of just 11 color names. These are *black, white, red, yellow, green, blue, brown, purple, pink, orange,* and *gray*. Languages ranged from using all 11 color names, as in English, to using just two of the names, as in the Dani tribe of Western New Guinea (Rosch Heider, 1972). Second, when only some of the color names are used, the naming of colors falls into a hierarchy of five levels. The levels are (1) black, white; (2) red; (3) yellow, green, blue; (4) brown; and (5) purple, pink, orange, gray. Thus, if a language names only two colors, they will be black and white. If it names three colors, they will be black, white, and red. A fourth color will be taken from the set of yellow, green, and blue. The fifth and sixth will be taken from this set as well. Selection will continue until all 11 colors have been labeled. The order of selection within the categories may, however, vary between cultures (Jameson, 2005).

Syntactical as well as semantic structural differences across languages may affect thought. For example, Spanish has two forms of the verb "to be"—*ser* and *estar*. However, they are used in different contexts. One investigator studied the uses of *ser* and *estar* in adults and in children (Sera, 1992).

When "to be" indicated the identity of something (e.g., in English, "This is José") or the class membership of something (e.g., "José is a carpenter"), both adults and children used the verb form *ser*. Moreover, both adults and children used different verb forms when "to be" indicated attributes of things. *Ser* was used to indicate permanent attributes (e.g., "Maria is tall"). *Estar* was also used to indicate temporary attributes (e.g., "Maria is busy"). Finally, when using forms of "to be" to describe the locations of objects, including of people, animals, and other things, both adults and children used *estar* (e.g., "Marie is on the chair"). However, when using forms of "to be" to describe the locations of events (e.g., meetings or parties), adults used *ser*, whereas children continued to use *estar*.

Sera (1992) interprets these findings as indicating two things. First, *ser* seems to be used primarily for indicating permanent conditions, such as identity; class inclusion; and relatively permanent, stable attributes of things. *Estar* seems to be used primarily for indicating temporary conditions, such as short-term attributes of things and the location of objects. These things often are subject to change from one place to another. Moreover, children treat the location of events in the same way as the location of objects. They view it as temporary and hence use *estar*. Adults, in contrast, differentiate between events and objects. In particular, adults consider the locations of events to be unchanging. Because they are permanent, they require the use of *ser*.

Other researchers have also suggested that young children have difficulty distinguishing between objects and events (e.g., Keil, 1979). Young children also find it difficult to recognize the permanent status of many attributes (Marcus & Overton, 1978). Thus, the developmental differences regarding the use of *ser* to describe the location of events may indicate developmental differences in cognition. Sera's work suggests that differences in language use may indeed indicate differences in thinking. However, her work leaves open an important psychological question. Do native Spanish speakers have a more differentiated sense of the temporary and the permanent than do native English speakers, who use the same verb form to express both senses of "to be"? Thus far, the answer is unclear.

Other languages also have been used in investigations of linguistic relativity. For example, in the Navaho language, the choice of verb depends on the shape of the object engaging in the action of the verb. In English, it does not (Carroll & Casagrande, 1958). Might the use of different verb forms for different shapes suggest that Navaho children would learn to perceive and organize information by shapes earlier than do children who speak English?

Early research indicated that young English-speaking children group objects by color before they group them by shape (Brian & Goodenough, 1929). In contrast, Navaho-speaking children are more likely than English-speaking Navaho children to classify objects on the basis of shape. However, these findings are problematic. The reason is that English-speaking children from Boston perform more like the Navaho-speaking Navaho children than like the English-speaking Navaho children (Carroll & Casagrande, 1958). Furthermore, other research comparing adults' and children's generalizations of novel nouns among novel objects finds that young English-speaking children actually will overuse shape in classifying objects (Smith, Jones, & Landau, 1996). What would happen for people who speak both languages being studied? Also consider another fact. Children who learn Mandarin Chinese tend to use more verbs than nouns. In contrast, children acquiring English or Italian tend to use more nouns than verbs (Tardif, 1996; Tardif, Shatz, & Naigles, 1997). Moreover, Korean-speaking children use verbs earlier than English-speaking children do. In contrast, English-speaking children have larger naming vocabularies earlier than do Korean-speaking children (Gopnik & Choi, 1995; Gopnik, Choi, & Baumberger, 1996).

What differences in thinking might such differences in acquisition imply? No one knows for sure.

An intriguing experiment assessed the possible effects of linguistic relativity by studying people who speak more than one language (Hoffman, Lau, & Johnson, 1986). In Chinese, a single term, *shì gÈ*, specifically describes a person who is "worldly, experienced, socially skillful, devoted to his or her family, and somewhat reserved" (p. 1098). English clearly has no comparable single term to embrace these diverse characteristics. Hoffman and his colleagues composed text passages in English and in Chinese describing various characters. They included the *shì gÈ* stereotype, without, of course, specifically using the term *shì gÈ* in the descriptions. The researchers then asked participants who were fluent in both Chinese and English to read the passages either in Chinese or in English. Then they rated various statements about the characters, in terms of the likelihood that the statements would be true of the characters. Some of these statements involved a stereotype of a *shì gÈ* person.

Their results seemed to support the notion of linguistic relativity. The participants were more likely to rate the various statements in accord with the *shì gÈ* stereotype when they had read the passages in Chinese than when they had read the passages in English. Similarly, when participants were asked to write their own impressions of the characters, their descriptions conformed more closely to the *shì gÈ* stereotype if they previously read the passages in Chinese. These authors do not suggest that it would be impossible for English speakers to comprehend the *shì gÈ* stereotype. Rather, they suggest that having that stereotype readily accessible facilitates its mental manipulation.

Research on linguistic relativity is a good example of the dialectic in action. Before Sapir and Whorf, the issue of how language constrains thought was not salient in the minds of psychologists. Sapir and Whorf then presented a thesis that language largely controls thought. After they presented their thesis, a number of psychologists tried to show the antithesis. This is that they were wrong and that language did not control thought. Today, many psychologists believe in a synthesis. This is that language has some influence on thought but not nearly so extreme an influence as Sapir and Whorf believed.

The question of whether linguistic relativity exists, and if so, to what extent, remains open. There may be a mild form of relativity. In other words, language can influence thought. However, a stronger deterministic form of relativity is less likely. Based on the available evidence, language does not seem to determine differences in thought among members of various cultures Finally, it is probably the case that language and thought interact with each other throughout the life span (Vygotsky, 1986).

Bilingualism and Dialects

Suppose a person can speak and think in two languages. Does the person think differently in each language? Further, do **bilinguals**—people who can speak two languages—think differently from **monolinguals**—people who can speak only one language? (Multilinguals speak at least two and possibly more languages.) What differences, if any, emanate from the availability of two languages versus just one? Might bilingualism affect intelligence, positively or negatively?

Does bilingualism make thinking in any one language more difficult, or does it enhance thought processes? The data are somewhat self-contradictory (Hakuta, 1986). Different participant populations, different methodologies, different language groups, and different experimenter biases may have contributed to the inconsistency in the literature. Consider what happens when bilinguals are balanced bilinguals, who are roughly equally fluent in both languages, and when they come from middle-class backgrounds. In these instances, positive effects of bilingualism tend to be found (Andreou & Karapetsas, 2004; Bialystok, 2001a; Bialystok & associates, 2004). But negative effects may result under other circumstances (Bialystok, 2001b; Cummins, 1979; Ricciardelli, 1992). What might be the causes of this difference?

Courtesy of Dr. Michael Cole

Michael Cole is a professor of psychology and communication at the University of California, San Diego. He is well known for his contributions to cultural and cross-cultural cognitive psychology, having shown that tests that are valid in one culture cannot simply be translated and directly carried over to another culture and remain valid. During the past 20 years, Cole also has been seminal in reviving psychological interest in the work of Lev Vygotsky.

Let us distinguish between what might be called additive versus subtractive bilingualism (Cummins, 1976). In *additive bilingualism*, a second language is acquired in addition to a relatively well-developed first language. In *subtractive bilingualism*, elements of a second language replace elements of the first language. It appears that the additive form results in increased thinking ability. In contrast, the subtractive form results in decreased thinking ability (Cummins, 1976). In particular, there may be something of a threshold effect. Individuals may need to be at a certain relatively high level of competence in both languages for a positive effect of bilingualism to be found. Classroom teachers often discourage bilingualism in children (Sook Lee & Oxelson, 2006). Either through letters requesting only English be spoken at home, or through subtle attitudes and methods, many teachers actually encourage subtractive bilingualism (Sook Lee & Oxelson, 2006). Additionally, children from backgrounds with lower socioeconomic status (SES) may be more likely to be subtractive bilinguals than are children from the middle SES. Their SES may be a factor in their being hurt rather than helped by their bilingualism.

Researchers also distinguish between *simultaneous bilingualism,* which occurs when a child learns two languages from birth, and *sequential bilingualism,* which occurs when an individual first learns one language and then another (Bhatia & Ritchie, 1999). Either form of language learning can contribute to fluency. It depends on the particular circumstances in which the languages are learned (Pearson & associates, 1997). It is known, however, that infants begin babbling at roughly the same age. This happens regardless of whether they consistently are exposed to one or two languages (Oller & associates, 1997). In the United States, many people make a big deal of bilingualism, perhaps because relatively few Americans born in the United States of nonimmigrant parents learn a second language to a high degree of fluency. In other cultures, however, the learning of multiple languages is taken for granted. For example, in parts of India, people routinely may learn as many as four languages (Khubchandani, 1997). In Flemish-speaking Belgium, many people learn at least some French, English, and/or German. Often, they learn one or more of these other languages to a high degree of fluency.

A significant factor believed to contribute to acquisition of a language is age. Some researchers have suggested that nativelike mastery of some aspects of a second language are rarely acquired after adolescence. Other researchers disagree with this view (Bahrick & associates, 1994). They found that some aspects of a second language, such as vocabulary comprehension and fluency, seem to be acquired just as well after adolescence as before. Furthermore, these researchers found that even some aspects of syntax seem to be acquired readily after adolescence. These results are contrary to prior findings (Johnson & Newport, 1989, 1991; Newport, 1990). The mastery of nativelike pronunciation, however, seems to depend on early acquisition (Asher & Garcia, 1969; Oyama, 1976). It may seem surprising that learning completely novel phonemes in a second language may be easier than learning phonemes that are highly similar to the phonemes of the first language (Flege, 1991). In any case, there do not appear to be critical periods for second-language acquisition (Birdsong, 1999). The possible exception is the acquisition of native accent. Adults may appear to have a harder time learning second languages because they can retain their native language as their dominant language. Young children, in contrast, who typically need to attend school in the new language, may have to switch dominant language. They thus learn the new language to a higher level of mastery (Jia & Aaronson, 1999).

A recent study found that age of acquisition and proficiency in a language are negatively correlated (Mechelli & associates, 2004). This finding has been well documented (Birdsong, 2006). This does not mean that we cannot learn a new language later in life, but rather, that the earlier we learn it, the more likely we will become highly proficient in its use. The same researchers also found that learning a second language increased the gray matter in the left inferior parietal cortex (Mechelli & associates, 2004). This density was also positively correlated with proficiency. Thus, the more proficient a person is in a second language, the denser this area of the brain will be. Finally, it was noted that a negative correlation existed between age of acquisition and the density in the left inferior parietal cortex (Mechelli & associates, 2004). Taken together, these findings suggest that this area of the brain benefits from the learning of a second language and that, further, the earlier this learning occurs, the better it is both for brain density and for overall proficiency.

What kinds of learning experiences facilitate second-language acquisition? There is no single correct answer to that question (Bialystock & Hakuta, 1994). One reason is that each individual language learner brings distinctive cognitive abilities and knowledge to the language-learning experience. In addition, the kinds of learning experiences that facilitate second-language acquisition should match the context and uses for the second language once it is acquired.

For example, consider four different individuals. Caitlin, a young child, may not need to master a wealth of vocabulary and complex syntax to get along well with other children. If she can master the phonology, some simple syntactical rules, and some basic vocabulary, she may be considered fluent. Similarly, José needs only to get by in a few everyday situations, such as shopping, handling routine family business transactions, and getting around town. He may be considered proficient after mastering some simple vocabulary and syntax, as well as some pragmatic knowledge regarding context-appropriate manners of communicating. Kim Yee must be able to communicate regarding her specialized technical field. She may be considered proficient if she masters the technical vocabulary, a primitive basic vocabulary, and the rudiments of syntax. Sumesh is a student who studies a second language in an academic setting. Sumesh may be expected to have a firm grasp of syntax and a rather broad, if shallow, vocabulary. Each of these language learners may require different kinds of language experiences to gain the proficiency being sought. Different kinds of experiences may be needed to enhance their competence in the phonology, vocabulary, syntax, and pragmatics of the second language.

When speakers of one language learn other languages, they find the languages differentially difficult. For example, it is much easier, on average, for a native speaker of English to acquire Spanish as a second language than it is to acquire Russian. One reason is that English and Spanish share more roots than do English and Russian. Moreover, Russian is much more highly inflected than are English and Spanish. English and Spanish are more highly dependent on word order. The difficulty of learning a language as a second language, however, does not appear to have much to do with its difficulty as a first language. Russian infants probably learn Russian about as easily as U.S. infants learn English (Maratsos, 1998).

Single-System versus Dual-System Hypotheses

One way of approaching bilingualism is to apply what we have learned from cognitive-psychological research to practical concerns regarding how to facilitate acquisition of a second language. Another approach is to study bilingual individuals to see how bilingualism may offer insight into the human mind. For example, some cognitive psychologists have been interested in finding out how the two languages are represented in the bilingual's mind. The **single-system hypothesis** suggests that two languages are represented in just one system or brain region (see Hernandez & associates, 2001, for evidence supporting this hypothesis in early bilinguals). Alternatively, the **dual-system hypothesis** suggests that two languages are represented somehow in separate systems of the mind (De Houwer, 1995; Paradis, 1981). For instance, might German language information be stored in a physically different part of the brain than English language information? Figure 10.5 shows schematically the difference in the two points of view.

FIGURE 10.5

The single-system conceptualization hypothesizes that both languages are represented in a unified cognitive system. The dual-system conceptualization of bilingualism hypothesizes that each language is represented in a separate cognitive system.

One way to address this question is through the study of bilinguals who have experienced brain damage. Suppose a bilingual person has brain damage in a particular part of the brain. An inference consistent with the dual-system hypothesis would be that the individual would show different degrees of impairment in the two languages. The single-system view would suggest roughly equal impairment in the two languages. The logic of this kind of investigation is compelling. But the results are not. When recovery of language after trauma is studied, sometimes the first language recovers first, sometimes the second language recovers first. And sometimes recovery is about equal for the two languages (Albert & Obler, 1978; Marrero, Golden, & Espe Pfeifer, 2002; Paradis, 1977). Recovery of one or both languages seems contingent on age of acquisition of the second language and on preincident language proficiency, among other factors (Marrero, Golden, & Espe Pfeifer, 2002).

In a related situation, an early bilingual aphasic was trained in his native language but was given no training in his second language (Meinzer & associates, 2006). The researchers found significant recovery of the first language but no change in the individual's ability to use the second language (Meinzer & associates, 2006).

The conclusions that can be drawn from all this research are equivocal. Nevertheless, the results seem to suggest at least some duality of structure. A different method of study has led to an alternative perspective on bilingualism. Two investigators mapped the region of the cerebral cortex relevant to language use in two of their bilingual patients being treated for epilepsy (Ojemann & Whitaker, 1978). Mild electrical stimulation was applied to the cortex of each patient. Electrical stimulation tends to inhibit activity where it is applied. It leads to a reduced ability to name objects for which the memories are stored at the location being stimulated. The results for both patients were the same. They may help explain the contradictions in the literature. Some areas of the brain showed equal impairments for object-naming in both languages. But other areas of the brain showed differential impairment in one or the other language. The results also suggested that the weaker language was more diffusely represented across the cortex than was the stronger language. In other words, asking the question of whether two languages are represented singly or separately may be asking the wrong question. The results of this study suggest that some aspects of the two languages may be represented singly. Other aspects may be represented separately.

To summarize, two languages seem to share some, but not all, aspects of mental representation. Learning a second language is often a plus, but it is probably most useful if the individual learning the second language is in an environment in which the learning of the second language adds to rather than subtracts from the learning of the first language. Moreover, for beneficial effects to appear, the second language must be learned well. In the approach usually taken in schools, students may receive as little as 2 or 3 years of second-language instruction spread out over a few class periods a week. This approach probably will not be sufficient for the beneficial effects of bilingualism to appear. However, schooling does seem to yield beneficial effects on acquisition of syntax. This is particularly so when a second language is acquired after adolescence. Furthermore, individual learners should choose specific kinds of language-acquisition techniques to suit their personal attributes. These attributes include abilities, preferences, and personal goals for using the second language.

Language Mixtures and Change

Bilingualism is not a certain outcome of linguistic contact between different language groups. Sometimes when people of two different language groups are in prolonged contact with one another, the language users of the two groups begin to share some vocabulary that is superimposed onto each group's syntax. This superimposition results in what is known as a pidgin. Over time, this admixture can develop into a distinct linguistic form. It has its own grammar and hence becomes a creole. An example of a creole is the Haitian Creole language, spoken in Haiti. The Haitian Creole language is a combination of French and a number of West African languages and is one of many creoles. One linguist has studied the similarities across different creoles (Bickerton, 1990). He has postulated that modern creoles may resemble an evolutionarily early form of language, termed *protolanguage*. The existence of pidgins and creoles, and possibly a protolanguage, supports the universality notion discussed earlier. That is, linguistic ability is so natural and universal that given the opportunity, humans actually invent new languages quite rapidly.

Creoles and pidgins arise when two linguistically distinctive groups meet. The counterpart—a dialect—occurs when a single linguistic group gradually diverges toward somewhat distinctive variations. A **dialect** is a regional variety of a language distinguished by features such as vocabulary, syntax, and pronunciation. The study of dialects provides insights into such diverse phenomena as auditory discrimination, test development, and social discrimination. Many of the words we choose are a result of the dialect we use. The most well known example is the word choice for a soft drink. Depending on the dialect you use, you may order a soda, pop, or even a Coke.

Dialectical differences often represent harmless regional variations. They create few serious communication difficulties. But these can lead to some confusion. In the United States, for example, when national advertisers give toll-free numbers to call, they sometimes route the calls to the Midwest. They do so because they have learned that the Midwestern form of speech seems to be the most universally understood form within the country. Other forms, such as southern and northeastern ones, may be harder for people from diverse parts of the country to understand. And when calls are routed to other countries, such as India, there may be serious difficulties in achieving effective communication because of differences in dialect as well as accent. Many radio announcers try to learn something close to a standard form of English, often called "network English." In this way, they can maximize their comprehensibility to as many listeners as possible.

Sometimes, differing dialects are assigned different social statuses, such as *standard* forms having higher status than *nonstandard* ones. The distinction between standard and nonstandard forms of a language can become unfortunate when speakers of one dialect start to view themselves as speakers of a superior dialect. The view that one dialect is superior to another may lead one to make judgments about the speaker that are biased. This *linguicism*, or stereotype based on dialect, may be quite widespread and can cause many interpersonal problems (Zuidema, 2005). For example, we frequently make judgments about people's intelligence, competence, and morality based on the dialect they use (Wolfram, Adger, & Christian, 1999). Specifically a person who uses a nonstandard form may be judged to be less educated or less trustworthy than a person who uses a more standard form. Usually, the standard dialect is that of the class in society that has the most political or economic power. Virtually any thought can be expressed in any dialect.

Slips of the Tongue

Thus far, much of the discussion has assumed that people use—or at least attempt to use—language correctly. An area of particular interest to cognitive psychologists, however, is how people use language incorrectly. One way of using language incorrectly is through **slips of the tongue,** inadvertent linguistic errors in what we say. They may occur at any level of linguistic analysis: phonemes, morphemes, or larger units of language (Crystal, 1987; McArthur, 1992). In such cases, what we think and mean to say do not correspond to what we actually do say. Freudian psychoanalysts have suggested that in Freudian slips, the verbal slip reflects some unconscious processing that has psychological significance. The slips are alleged often to indicate repressed emotions. For example, a business competitor may say, "I'm glad to beat you," when what was overtly intended was, "I'm glad to meet you."

Most cognitive psychologists see things differently from the psychoanalytic view. They are intrigued by slips of the tongue because of what the lack of correspondence between what is thought and what is said may tell us about how language is produced. In speaking, we have a mental plan for what we are going to say. Sometimes, however, this plan is disrupted when our mechanism for speech production does not cooperate with our cognitive one. Often, such errors result from intrusions by other thoughts or by stimuli in the environment. Examples would be a radio talk show or a neighboring conversation (Garrett, 1980; Saito & Baddeley, 2004). Slips of the tongue may be taken to indicate that the language of thought differs somewhat from the language through which we express our thoughts (Fodor, 1975). Often we have the idea right, but its expression comes out wrong. Sometimes we are not even aware of the slip until it is pointed out to us. In the language of the mind, whatever it may be, the idea is right, although the expression represented by the slip is inadvertently wrong. This fact can be seen in the occasional slips of the tongue even in preplanned and practiced speech (Kawachi, 2002).

People tend to make various kinds of slips in their conversations (Fromkin, 1973; Fromkin & Rodman, 1988):

- In anticipation, the speaker uses a language element before it is appropriate in the sentence because it corresponds to an element that will be needed later in the utterance. For example, instead of saying, "an inspiring expression," a speaker might say, "an expiring expression."
- In perseveration, the speaker uses a language element that was appropriate earlier in the sentence but that is not appropriate later on. For example, a speaker might say, "We sat down to a bounteous beast" instead of a "bounteous feast."
- In substitution, the speaker substitutes one language element for another. For example, you may have warned someone to do something "after it is too late," when you meant "before it is too late."
- In reversal (also called "transposition"), the speaker switches the positions of two language elements. An example is the reversal that reportedly led *flutterby* to become *butterfly*. This reversal captivated language users so much that it is now the preferred form. Sometimes, reversals can be fortuitously opportune.
- They create spoonerisms, in which the initial sounds of two words are reversed and make two entirely different words. The term is named after the Reverend William Spooner, who was famous for them. Some of his choicest slips include, "You have hissed all my mystery lectures," and "Easier for a camel to go through the knee of an idol" (Clark & Clark, 1977).
- In malapropism, one word is replaced by another that is similar in sound but different in meaning (e.g., furniture dealers selling "naughty pine" instead of "knotty pine").
- Additionally, slips may occur because of insertions of sounds (e.g., "mischievi-ous" instead of "mischievous" or "drown*d*ed" instead of "drowned") or other linguistic elements. The opposite kind of slip involves deletions (e.g., sound deletions such as "prossing" instead of "processing"). Such deletions often involve blends (e.g., "blounds" for "blended sounds").

Each kind of slip of the tongue may occur at different hierarchical levels of linguistic processing (Dell, 1986). That is, it may occur at the acoustical level of phonemes, as in "bounteous beast" instead of "bounteous feast." It may occur at the semantic level of morphemes, as in "after it's too late" instead of "before it's too late." Or it may occur at even higher levels, as in "bought the bucket" instead of "kicked the bucket" or "bought the farm." The patterns of errors (e.g., reversals, substitutions) at each hierarchical level tend to be parallel (Dell, 1986). For example, in phonemic errors, initial consonants tend to interact with initial consonants, as in "tasting wime" instead of "wasting time." Final consonants tend to interact with final consonants, as in "bing his tut" instead of "bit his tongue." Prefixes often interact with prefixes, as in "expiring expression," and so on.

Also, errors at each level of linguistic analysis suggest particular kinds of insights into how we produce speech. Consider, for example, phonemic errors. A stressed word, which is emphasized through speech rhythm and tone, is more likely to influence other words than is an unstressed word (Crystal, 1987). Furthermore, even when sounds are switched, the basic rhythmic and tonal patterns usually are preserved. An example is the emphasis on "hissed" and the first syllable of "mystery" in the first spoonerism quoted here.

Even at the level of words, the same parts of speech tend to be involved in the errors we produce (e.g., nouns interfere with other nouns, and verbs with verbs; Bock, 1990; Bock, Loebell, & Morey, 1992). In the second spoonerism quoted here, Spooner managed to preserve the syntactical categories, the nouns *knee* and *idol*. He also preserved the grammaticality of the sentence by changing the articles from "*a* needle" to "*an* idol." Even in the case of word substitutions, syntactic categories are preserved. In speech errors, semantic categories, too, may be preserved. An example would be naming a category when intending to name a member of the category, such as "fruit" for "apple." Another example would be naming the wrong member of the category, such as "peach" for "apple." A last example would be naming a member of a category when intending to name the category as a whole, as in "peach" for "fruit" (Garrett, 1992). Data from studies of speech errors may help us better understand normal language processing. Another aspect of language that offers us a distinctive view is the study of metaphorical language.

Metaphorical Language

Until now, we have discussed primarily the literal uses of language. At least as interesting to poets and to many others are its omnipresent figurative uses. A notable example is the use of metaphors as a way of expressing thoughts. **Metaphors** juxtapose two nouns in a way that positively asserts their similarities, while not disconfirming their dissimilarities (e.g., The house was a pigsty). Related to metaphors are similes. **Similes** introduce the words *like* or *as* into a comparison between items (e.g., The child was as quiet as a mouse).

Metaphors contain four key elements. Two are the items being compared, a tenor and a vehicle. And two are ways in which the items are related. The *tenor* is the topic of the metaphor (e.g., house). The *vehicle* is what the tenor is described in terms of (e.g., pigsty). For example, consider the metaphor, "Billboards are warts on the landscape." The tenor is "billboards." The vehicle is "warts." The *ground* of the metaphor is the set of similarities between the tenor and the vehicle (e.g., both are messy). The *tension* of the metaphor is the set of dissimilarities between the two (e.g., people do not live in pigsties but do live in houses). We may conjecture that a key similarity (ground) between billboards and warts is that they are both considered unattractive. The dissimilarities (tension) between the two are many, including that billboards appear on buildings, highways, and other impersonal public locations. But warts appear on diverse personal locations on an individual.

Of the various theories that have been proposed to explain how metaphors work, the main traditional views have highlighted either the ways in which the tenor and the vehicle are similar or the ways in which they differ. For example, the traditional comparison view highlights the importance of the comparison. It underscores the comparative similarities and analogical relationship between the tenor and the vehicle (Malgady & Johnson, 1976; Miller, 1979; Ortony, 1979; cf. also Sternberg & Nigro, 1983). As applied to the metaphor, "Abused children are walking time bombs," the comparison view would underscore the similarity between the elements: their potential for explosion. In contrast, the anomaly view of metaphor emphasizes the dissimilarity between the tenor and the vehicle (Beardsley, 1962; Bickerton, 1969; Clark & Lucy, 1975; Gerrig & Healy, 1983; Lyons, 1977; Searle, 1979; van Dijk, 1975). The anomaly view would highlight the many dissimilarities between abused children and time bombs.

The domain-interaction view integrates aspects of each of the preceding views. It suggests that a metaphor is more than a comparison and more than an anomaly. According to this view, a metaphor involves an interaction of some kind between the domain (area of knowledge, such as animals, machines, plants) of the tenor and the domain of the vehicle (Black, 1962; Hesse, 1966). The exact form of this interaction differs somewhat from one theory to another. The metaphor often is more effective when two circumstances occur. First, the tenor and the vehicle share many similar characteristics (e.g., the potential explosiveness of abused children and time bombs). Second, the domains of the tenor and the vehicle are highly dissimilar (e.g., the domain of humans and the domain of weapons) (Tourangeau & Sternberg, 1981, 1982).

Consider another view—that metaphors are essentially a nonliteral form of class-inclusion statements (Glucksberg & Keysar, 1990). According to this view, the tenor of each metaphor is a member of the class characterized by the vehicle of the given metaphor. That is, we understand metaphors not as statements of comparison but as statements of category membership, in which the vehicle is a prototypical member of the category.

For example, suppose I say, "My colleague's partner is an iceberg." I am thereby saying that the partner belongs to the category of things that are characterized by an utter lack of personal warmth, extreme rigidity, and the ability to produce a massively chilling effect on anyone in the surrounding environment. For a metaphor to work well, the reader should find the salient features of the vehicle ("iceberg") to be unexpectedly relevant as features of the tenor ("my colleague's partner"). That is, the reader should be at least mildly surprised that prominent features of the vehicle may characterize the tenor. But after consideration, the reader should agree that those features do describe the tenor.

Metaphors enrich our language in ways that literal statements cannot match. Our understanding of metaphors seems to require not only some kind of comparison. It also requires that the domains of the vehicle and of the tenor interact in some way. Reading a metaphor can change our perception of both domains. It therefore can educate us in a way that is perhaps more difficult to transmit through literal speech.

Metaphors can enrich our speech in social contexts. For example, suppose we say to someone, "You are a prince." Chances are that we do not mean that the person is literally a prince. Rather, we mean that the person has characteristics of a prince. How, in general, do we use language to negotiate social contexts?

Language in a Social Context

The study of the social context of language is a relatively new area of linguistic research. One aspect of context is the investigation of **pragmatics,** the study of how people use language. It includes sociolinguistics and other aspects of the social context of language.

Under most circumstances, you change your use of language in response to contextual cues without giving these changes much thought. Similarly, you usually unselfconsciously change your language patterns to fit different contexts.

To get an idea of how you change your use of language in different contexts, suppose that you and your friend are going to meet right after work. Suppose also that something comes up. You must call your friend to change the time or place for your meeting. When you call your friend at work, your friend's supervisor answers and offers to take a message. Exactly what will you say to your friend's supervisor to ensure that your friend will know about the change in time or location? Suppose, instead, that the 4-year-old son of your friend's supervisor answers. Exactly what will you say in this situation? Finally, suppose that your friend answers directly. How will you have modified your language for each context, even when your purpose (underlying message) in all three contexts was the same?

INVESTIGATING COGNITIVE PSYCHOLOGY

For example, in speaking with a conversational partner, you seek to establish common ground, or a shared basis for engaging in a conversation (Clark & Brennan, 1991). When we are with people who share background, knowledge, motives, or goals, establishing common ground is likely to be easy and scarcely noticeable. When little is shared, however, such common ground may be hard to find.

Gestures and vocal inflections, which are forms of nonverbal communication, can help establish common ground. One aspect of nonverbal communication is *personal space*—the distance between people in a conversation or other interaction that is considered comfortable for members of a given culture. *Proxemics* is the study of interpersonal distance or its opposite, proximity. It concerns itself with relative distancing and the positioning of you and your fellow conversants. In the United States, 18 to 24 inches is considered about right (Hall, 1966). Scandinavians expect more distance. Middle Easterners, southern Europeans, and South Americans expect less (Sommer, 1969; Watson, 1970).

When on our own familiar turf, we take our cultural views of personal space for granted. Only when we come into contact with people from other cultures do we notice these differences. For example, when I was visiting Venezuela, I noticed my cultural expectations coming into conflict with the expectations of those around me. I often found myself in a comical dance. I would back off from the person with whom I was speaking. Meanwhile, that person was trying to move closer. Within a given culture, greater proximity generally indicates one or more of three things. First, the people see themselves in a close relationship. Second, the people are participating in a social situation that permits violation of the bubble of personal space, such as close dancing. Third, the "violator" of the bubble is dominating the interaction.

Even within our own culture, there are differences in the amount of personal space that is expected. For instance, when two colleagues are interacting, the personal space is much smaller than when an employee and supervisor are interacting (Dean, Willis, & Hewitt, 1975; Hall, 1966).

A related area of research concerns proxemics in virtual-reality environments. It has been noted that violations of personal space even in virtual environments causes discomfort (Wilcox & associates, 2006). When given the option, people whose personal space is violated in a virtual environment will move away (Bailenson & associates, 2003). Physical space is also maintained in video conferencing (Grayson & Coventry, 1998). Taken together, these findings indicate the importance of interpersonal space in all interactions. They also indicate that proxemics is important, even when one or more of the people are not physically present.

Speech Acts

Direct Speech Acts

Another key aspect of the way in which you use language depends on what purpose you plan to achieve with language. In the earlier example, you were using language to try to ensure that your friend would meet you at the new location and time. When you speak, what kinds of things can you accomplish?

Speech acts address the question of what you can accomplish with speech. All speech acts seem to fall into five basic categories, based on the purpose of the acts (Searle, 1975a; see also Harnish, 2003). In other words, there are essentially five things you can accomplish with speech—no more, no less. Table 10.1 identifies these categories and gives examples of each.

1. The first category of speech acts is representatives. A *representative* is a speech act by which a person conveys a belief that a given proposition is true. The speaker can use various sources of information to support the given belief. But the statement is nothing more, nor less, than a statement of belief. We can put in various qualifiers to show our degree of certainty. But we still are stating a belief, which may or may not be verifiable.

2. A second category of speech act is a directive. A *directive* represents an attempt by a speaker to get a listener to do something. Sometimes a directive is quite indirect. For example, almost any sentence structured as a question probably is serving a directive function. Any attempt to elicit assistance of any kind, however indirect, falls into this category.

3. A third category is a commissive. In uttering a *commissive*, the speaker is committing himself or herself to some future course of action. Promises, pledges, contracts, guarantees, assurances, and the like all constitute commissives.

4. A fourth category of speech act is an expressive. An *expressive* is a statement regarding the speaker's psychological state.

TABLE 10.1	Speech Acts

The five basic categories of speech acts encompass the various tasks that can be accomplished through speech (or other modes of using language).

SPEECH ACT	DESCRIPTION	EXAMPLE
Representative	A speech act by which a person conveys a belief that a given proposition is true	If I say that "The Marquis de Sade is a sadist," I am conveying my belief that the marquis enjoyed seeing others feel pain. I can use various sources of information to support my belief, including the fact that the word *sadist* derives from this marquis. Nonetheless, the statement is nothing more nor less than a statement of belief. Similarly, I can make a statement that is more directly verifiable, such as "As you can see here on this thermometer, the temperature outside is 31 degrees Fahrenheit."
Directive	An attempt by a speaker to get a listener to do something, such as supplying the answer to a question	I can ask my son to help me shovel snow in various ways, some of which are more direct than others, such as, "Please help me shovel the snow," or "It sure would be nice if you were to help me shovel the snow," or "Would you help me shovel the snow?" The different surface forms are all attempts to get him to help me. Some directives are quite indirect. If I ask, "Has it stopped raining yet?" I am still uttering a directive, in this case seeking information rather than physical assistance. In fact, almost any sentence structured as a question probably serves a directive function.
Commissive	A commitment by the speaker to engage in some future course of action	If my son responds, "I'm busy now, but I'll help you shovel the snow later," he is uttering a commissive, in that he is pledging his future help. If my daughter then says, "I'll help you," she too is uttering a commissive because she is pledging her assistance now. Promises, pledges, contracts, guarantees, assurances, and the like all constitute commissives.
Expressive	A statement regarding the speaker's psychological state	If I tell my son later, "I'm really upset that you didn't come through in helping me shovel the snow," that, too, would be an expressive. If my son says, "I'm sorry I didn't get around to helping you out," he would be uttering an expressive. If my daughter says, "Daddy, I'm glad I was able to help out," she is uttering an expressive.
Declaration (also termed *performative*)	A speech act by which the very act of making a statement brings about an intended new state of affairs	Suppose that you are called into your boss's office and told that you are responsible for the company losing $50,000 and then your boss says, "You're fired." The speech act results in your being in a new state—that is, unemployed. You might then tell your boss, "That's fine because I wrote you a letter yesterday saying that the money was lost because of your glaring incompetence, not mine, and I resign." You are again making a declaration.

5. The fifth kind of speech act is a declaration. A *declaration* is a speech act by which the very act of making a statement brings about an intended new state of affairs. When a cleric says, "I now pronounce you husband and wife," the speech act is a declaration. Once the speech act is accomplished, the marriage rite is completed. Declarations also are termed *performatives* (Clark & Clark, 1977).

The appealing thing about Searle's taxonomy is that it classifies almost any statement that might be made. It shows exhaustively, at least at one level, the different kinds of things speech can accomplish. It also shows the close relationship between language structure and language function.

Indirect Speech Acts

Sometimes speech acts are indirect, meaning that we accomplish our goals in speaking in an oblique fashion. One way of communicating obliquely is through **indirect requests,** through which we make a request without doing so straightforwardly (Gordon & Lakoff, 1971; Searle, 1975b). An example would be "Won't you please take out the garbage?"

There are four basic ways of making indirect requests: (1) asking or making statements about abilities, (2) stating a desire, (3) stating a future action, and (4) citing reasons. Examples of these forms of indirect requests are illustrated in Table 10.2. In each case, the indirect request is aimed at having a waitress tell the speaker where to find the restroom in a restaurant.

When are indirect speech acts interpreted literally, and when is the indirect meaning understood by the listener? When an indirect speech act such as "Must you open the window?" is presented in isolation, it usually first is interpreted literally, for example, as "Do you need to open the window?" (Gibbs, 1979). When the same speech act is presented in a story context that makes the indirect meaning clear, the sentence first is interpreted in terms of the indirect meaning. For instance, suppose a character in a story had a cold and asked, "Must you open the window?" It would be interpreted as an indirect request: "Do not open the window."

Subsequent work showed that indirect speech acts often anticipate what potential obstacles the respondent might pose. These obstacles are specifically addressed

TABLE 10.2	Indirect Speech Acts
One way of using speech is to communicate obliquely, rather than directly.	

TYPE OF INDIRECT SPEECH ACT	EXAMPLE OF AN INDIRECT REQUEST FOR INFORMATION
Abilities	If you say, "Can you tell me where the restroom is?" to a waitress at a restaurant, and she says, "Yes, of course I can," the chances are she missed the point. The question about her ability to tell you the location of the restroom was an indirect request for her to tell you exactly where it is.
Desire	"I would be grateful if you told me where the restroom is." Your statements of thanks in advance are really ways of getting someone to do what you want.
Future action	"Would you tell me where the restroom is?" Your inquiry into another person's future actions is another way to state an indirect request.
Reasons	You need not spell out the reasons to imply that there are good reasons to comply with the request. For example, you might imply that you have such reasons for the waitress to tell you where the restroom is by saying, "I need to know where the restroom is."

through the indirect speech act (Gibbs, 1986). For example, the question, "May I have?" addresses potential obstacles of permission. "Would you mind?" addresses potential obstacles regarding a possible imposition on the respondent. "Do you have." addresses potential obstacles regarding availability. Indirect requests that ask permission are judged to be the most polite (Clark & Schunk, 1980). Similarly, indirect requests that speak to an obligation (i.e., "Shouldn't you…?") are judged as the most impolite (Clark & Schunk, 1980). The responses to these requests typically match the requests in terms of politeness (Clark & Schunk, 1980).

Conversational Postulates

In speaking to each other, we implicitly set up a cooperative enterprise. Indeed, if we do not cooperate with each other when we speak, we often end up talking past rather than to each other. We thereby fail to communicate what we intended. Conversations thrive on the basis of a **cooperative principle,** by which we seek to communicate in ways that make it easy for our listener to understand what we mean (Grice, 1967; Mooney, 2004). According to Grice, successful conversations follow four maxims: the maxim of quantity, the maxim of quality, the maxim of relation, and the maxim of manner. (Examples of these maxims are provided in Table 10.3.)

According to the *maxim of quantity,* you should make your contribution to a conversation as informative as required but no more informative than is appropriate. For example, suppose that someone says to you, "Hi, how are you?" You subsequently enter into a 3-hour soliloquy on how your life is not quite what you were hoping it to be. Here, you are violating the maxim of quantity. The social convention is to answer with a short response, even if you might like to go into greater detail. Sometimes we violate the maxim of quantity for a specific end. Suppose I have been seeking a chance to tell the chairperson of our department about problems I see with our educational program. The chairperson is taking a big risk by asking me, "How are things going?" while hoping for only a short reply.

According to the *maxim of quality,* your contribution to a conversation should be truthful. You are expected to say what you believe to be the case. If you have ever sought directions when in a strange city, you know the extreme frustration that can result if people are not truthful in telling you that they do not know where to find a particular location. Irony, sarcasm, and jokes might seem to be exceptions to the maxim of quality, but they are not. The listener is expected to recognize the irony or sarcasm and to infer the speaker's true state of mind from what is said. Similarly, a joke often is expected to accomplish a particular purpose. It usefully contributes to a conversation when that purpose is clear to everyone.

According to the *maxim of relation,* you should make your contributions to a conversation relevant to the aims of the conversation. Sometimes, of course, people purposely violate this maxim. Suppose a romantic partner says to you, "I think we need to talk about our relationship." You reply, "The weather sure is beautiful today." You are violating the maxim to make the point that you do not want to talk about the relationship. When you do so, however, you are being uncooperative. Unless the two of you can agree on how to define the conversation, you will talk past each other and have a very frustrating conversation.

TABLE 10.3	Conversational Postulates	

To maximize the communication that occurs during conversation, speakers generally follow four maxims.

POSTULATE	MAXIM	EXAMPLE
Maxim of quantity	Make your contribution to a conversation as informative as required but no more informative than is appropriate.	If someone asks you the temperature outside and you reply, "It's 31.297868086298 degrees out there," you are violating the maxim of quantity because you are giving more information than was probably wanted. In the old TV series *Star Trek*, Mr. Spock, a "Vulcan" with a computer-like mind, elicits shrugs when he gives much more information in answer to a question than anyone would expect or want, as in the preceding answer to the temperature question.
Maxim of quality	Your contribution to a conversation should be truthful; you are expected to say what you believe to be the case.	Clearly, there are awkward circumstances in which each of us is unsure of just how much honesty is being requested, such as for the response to, "Honey, how do I look?" Under most circumstances, however, communication depends on an assumption that both parties to the communication are being truthful.
Maxim of relation	You should make your contributions to a conversation relevant to the aims of the conversation.	Almost any large meeting I attend seems to have someone who violates this maxim. This someone inevitably goes into long digressions that have nothing to do with the purpose of the meeting and that hold up the meeting. That reminds me of a story a friend once told me about a meeting he once attended, where . . .
Maxim of manner	You should try to avoid obscure expressions, vague utterances, and purposeful obfuscation of your point.	Nobel Prize–winning physicist Richard Feynman (1997) described how he once read a paper by a well-known sociologist, and he found that he could not make heads or tails of it. One sentence went something like this: "The individual member of the social community often receives information via visual, symbolic channels" (p. 281). Feynman concluded, in essence, that the sociologist was violating the maxim of manner when Feynman realized that the sentence meant, "People read."

According to the *maxim of manner,* you should be clear and try to avoid obscure expressions, vague utterances, and purposeful obfuscation of your point. To these four maxims noted by Grice, we might add an additional maxim: Only one person speaks at a time (Sacks, Schegloff, & Jefferson, 1974). Given that maxim, the situational context and the relative social positions of the speakers affect turn taking (Keller, 1976; Sacks, Schegloff, & Jefferson, 1974). Sociolinguists have noted many ways in which speakers signal to one another when and how to take turns. Sometimes people flaunt the conversational postulates to make a point. For example, suppose one says, "My parents are wardens." One is not providing full information (what, exactly, does it mean for one's parents to be wardens?). But the ambiguity is intentional. Or sometimes when a conversation on a topic is becoming heated, one purposely may switch topics and bring up an irrelevant issue. One's purpose in doing so is to get the conversation to another, safer topic. When we flaunt the postulates, we are sending an explicit message by doing so: The postulates retain their importance because their absence is so notable. People who suffer from autism have difficulty with both language and emotion. It is therefore not surprising that people with autism have particular difficulty in detecting violations of the Gricean maxims (Eales, 1993; Surian, 1996). Further discussion of language impairments in autism will be discussed later in the chapter.

Gender and Language

Within our own culture, do men and women speak a different language? Gender differences have been found in the content of what we say. Young girls are more likely to ask for help than are young boys (Thompson, 1999). Older adolescent and young adult males prefer to talk about political views, sources of personal pride, and what they like about the other person. In contrast, females in this age group prefer to talk about feelings toward parents, close friends, classes, and their fears (Rubin & associates, 1980). Also, in general, women seem to disclose more about themselves than do men (Morton, 1978).

Conversations between men and women are sometimes regarded as cross-cultural communication (Tannen, 1986, 1990, 1994). According to Tannen, young girls and boys learn conversational communication in essentially separate cultural environments through their same-sex friendships. As men and women, we then carry over the conversational styles we have learned in childhood into our adult conversations.

Tannen has suggested that male–female differences in conversational style largely center on differing understandings of the goals of conversation. These cultural differences result in contrasting styles of communication. These in turn can lead to misunderstandings and even breakups as each partner somewhat unsuccessfully tries to understand the other. Men see the world as a hierarchical social order in which the purpose of communication is to negotiate for the upper hand, to preserve independence, and to avoid failure (Tannen, 1990, 1994). Each man strives to one-up the other and to "win" the contest. Women, in contrast, seek to establish a connection between the two participants, to give support and confirmation to others, and to reach consensus through communication.

To reach their conversational goals, women use conversational strategies that minimize differences, establish equity, and avoid any appearances of superiority on the part of one or another conversant. Women also affirm the importance of and the commitment to the relationship. They handle differences of opinion by negotiating to reach a consensus that promotes the connection and ensures that both parties at least feel that their wishes have been considered. They do so even if they are not entirely satisfied with the consensual decision.

Men enjoy connections and rapport. But because men have been raised in a gender culture in which status plays an important role, other goals take precedence in conversations. Tannen has suggested that men seek to assert their independence from their conversational partners. In this way, they indicate clearly their lack of acquiescence to the demands of others, which would indicate lack of power. Men also prefer to inform (thereby indicating the higher status conferred by authority) rather than to consult (indicating subordinate status) with their conversational partners. The male partner in a close relationship thus may end up informing his partner of their plans. In contrast, the female partner expects to be consulted on their plans. When men and women are engaged in cross-gender communications, their crossed purposes often result in miscommunication because each partner misinterprets the other's intentions.

Tannen has suggested that men and women need to become more aware of their cross-cultural styles and traditions. In this way, they may at least be less likely to misinterpret one another's conversational interactions. They are also both more likely to achieve their individual aims, the aims of the relationship, and the aims of the other people and institutions affected by their relationship. Such awareness is important not only in conversations between men and women. It is also important in conversations among family members in general (Tannen, 2001). Tannen may be right. But at present, converging operations are needed, in addition to Tannen's sociolinguistic case-based approach, to pin down the validity and generality of her interesting findings.

Gender differences in the written use of language have also been observed. For instance, in formal writing, female writers tend to use more pronouns and male writers use more noun specifiers (Argamon & associates, 2003). Also, females use more "involved" and males use more "informational" features (Argamon & associates, 2003). However, these findings are not conclusive. A study examining blogs noted that the type of blog, more than the gender of the author, dictated the writing style (Herring & Paolillo, 2006).

PRACTICAL APPLICATIONS OF COGNITIVE PSYCHOLOGY

Think about how your gender influences your conversational style. Construct some ways to communicate more effectively with people of the opposite sex. How might your speech acts and conversational postulates differ? If you are a man, do you tend to use and prefer directives and declarations over expressives and commissives? If you are a woman, do you use and prefer expressives and commissives over directives and declarations? If so, speaking to people of the opposite sex can lead to misinterpretations of meaning based on differences in style. For example, when you want to get another person to do something, it may be best to use the style that more directly reflects the other person's style. In this case, you might use a directive with men ("Would you go to the store?") and an expressive with women ("I really enjoy going shopping."). Also, remember that your responses should match the other person's expectations regarding how much information to provide, honesty, relevance, and directness. The art of effective communication really involves listening carefully to another person, observing body language, and interpreting the person's goals accurately. This can be accomplished only with time, effort, and sensitivity.

Discourse and Reading Comprehension

The preceding sections discussed some of the more general aspects of social uses of language. This section discusses more specifically the processes involved in understanding and using language in the social context of discourse. Discourse involves communicative units of language larger than individual sentences—in conversations, lectures, stories, essays, and even textbooks (Di Eugenio, 2003). Just as grammatical sentences are structured according to systematic syntactical rules, passages of discourse are structured systematically.

The following series of sentences is taken from a short story by O. Henry (William Sydney Porter, 1899–1953) titled "The Ransom of Red Chief." Actually, the following sequence of sentences is incorrect. Without knowing anything else about the story, try to figure out the correct sequence of sentences.

1. The father was respectable and tight, a mortgage financier and a stern, upright collection-plate passer and forecloser.
2. We selected for our victim the only child of a prominent citizen named Ebenezer Dorset.
3. We were down South in Alabama—Bill Driscoll and myself—when this kidnapping idea struck us.
4. Bill and me figured that Ebenezer would melt down for a ransom of two thousand dollars to a cent.

Hint: O. Henry was a master of irony, and by the end of the story the would-be kidnappers paid the father a hefty ransom to take back his son so that they could quickly escape from the boy.

The sequence used by O. Henry, ex-convict and expert storyteller, was 3, 2, 1, 4. Is that the order you chose? How did you know the correct sequence for these sentences?

INVESTIGATING COGNITIVE PSYCHOLOGY

By adulthood, most of us have a firm grasp of how sentences are sequenced into a discourse structure. From our knowledge of discourse structure, we can derive meanings of sentence elements that are not apparent by looking at isolated sentences. To see how some of these discourse-dependent elements work, read the sentences about Rita and Thomas in the "Investigating Cognitive Psychology" box. Then answer the questions that follow them.

Rita gave Thomas a book about problem solving. He thanked her for the book. She asked, "Is it what you wanted?" He answered enthusiastically, "Yes, definitely." Rita asked, "Should I get you the companion volume on decision making?" He responded, "Please do."

In the second and third sentences, who were the people and things being referred to with the pronouns "He," "her," "She," and "it"? Why was the noun "book" preceded by the article "a" in the first sentence and by the article "the" in the second one? How do you know what Thomas's answer, "Yes, definitely," means? What is the action being requested in the response, "Please do"?

INVESTIGATING COGNITIVE PSYCHOLOGY

Cognitive psycholinguists who analyze discourse particularly are intrigued by how we are able to answer the questions posed in the preceding example. When grasping the meanings of pronouns (e.g., *he, she, him, her, it, they, them, we, us*), how do we know to whom (or to what) the pronouns are pointing? How do we know the meanings of ellipsed utterances (e.g., "Yes, definitely")? What does the use of the definite article *the* (as opposed to the indefinite article *a*) preceding a noun signify to listeners regarding whether a noun was mentioned previously? How do you know what event is being referenced by the verb *do?* The meanings of pronouns, ellipses, definite articles, event references, and other local elements within sentences usually depend on the discourse structure within which these elements appear (Grosz, Pollack, & Sidner, 1989).

Often, for understanding discourse we rely not only on our knowledge of discourse structure. We also rely on our knowledge of a broad physical, social, or cultural context within which the discourse is presented (Cook & Gueraud, 2005; van Dijk, 2006). For example, observe how your understanding of the meaning of a paragraph is influenced by your existing knowledge and expectations. For example, this cognitive psychology textbook will be easier to read, on average, if you have taken an introductory psychology course than if you have not taken such a course. When reading the sentences in the "Investigating Cognitive Psychology" box that follows, pause between sentences and think about what you know and what you expect, based on your knowledge.

INVESTIGATING COGNITIVE PSYCHOLOGY	1. Susan became increasingly anxious as she prepared for the upcoming science exam. (What do you know about Susan?) 2. She had never written an exam before, and she wasn't sure how to construct an appropriate test of the students' knowledge. (How have your beliefs about Susan changed?) 3. She was particularly annoyed that the principal had even asked her to write the exam. 4. Even during a teachers' strike, a school nurse should not be expected to take on the task of writing an examination. (How did your expectations change over the course of the four sentences?) In the preceding example, your understanding at each point in the discourse was influenced by your existing knowledge and expectations based on your own experiences within a particular context. Thus, just as prior experience and knowledge may aid us in lexical processing of text, they also may aid us in comprehending the text itself. What are the main reading comprehension processes? The process of reading comprehension is so complex that many entire courses and myriad volumes are devoted exclusively to the topic, but we focus here on just a few processes. These include semantic encoding, acquiring vocabulary, comprehending ideas in text, creating mental models of text, and comprehending text based on context and point of view.

Semantic Encoding: Retrieving Word Meaning from Memory

Semantic encoding is the process by which we translate sensory information into a meaningful representation that we perceive. This representation is based on our understanding of the meanings of words. In lexical access we identify words, based on letter combinations. We thereby activate our memory in regard to the words. In semantic encoding we take the next step and gain access to the meaning of the word stored in memory. Sometimes we cannot semantically encode the word because its meaning does not already exist in memory. We then must find another way in which to derive the meanings of words, such as from noting the context in which we read them.

To engage in semantic encoding, the reader needs to know what a given word means. Knowledge of word meanings (vocabulary) very closely relates to the ability to comprehend text. People who are knowledgeable about word meanings tend to be good readers and vice versa. A reason for this relationship appears to be that readers simply cannot understand text well unless they know the meanings of the component words. For example, in one study, recall of the semantic content of a passage differed by 8% between two groups of participants when the two groups differed in their passage-relevant vocabulary knowledge by 9% (Beck, Perfetti, & McKeown, 1982). In children, vocabulary size is positively related to performance on a number of semantic-understanding tasks, including retelling (both written and oral), decoding ability, and the ability to draw inferences across sentences (Hagtvet, 2003). A number of studies suggest that in order to grasp meaning of a sample of text with ease, one should know approximately 95% of the vocabulary (Nation, 2001; Read, 2000). Still other studies suggest that, for one to enjoy reading a text, one needs to understand about 98% of the vocabulary (Hu & Nation, 2000).

People with larger vocabularies are able to access lexical information more rapidly than are those with smaller vocabularies (Hunt, 1978). Verbal information often is presented rapidly—whether in listening or in reading. The individual who can gain access to lexical information rapidly is able to process more information per unit of time than can one who can only gain access to such information slowly.

Acquiring Vocabulary: Deriving Word Meanings from Context

Another way in which having a larger vocabulary contributes to text comprehension is through learning from context. Whenever we cannot semantically encode a word because its meaning is not already stored in memory, we must engage in some kind of strategy to derive meaning from the text. In general, we must either search for a meaning, using external resources (such as dictionaries or teachers), or formulate a meaning. We formulate the meaning based on the existing information stored in memory, using context cues with which to do so.

People learn most of their vocabulary indirectly. They do so not by using external resources but by figuring out the meanings of the *flidges* from the surrounding information (Werner & Kaplan, 1952).

For example, if you tried to look up the word *flidges* in the dictionary, you did not find it there. From the structure of the sentence you probably figured out that *flidges* is a noun. From the surrounding context you probably figured out that it is a noun having something to do with words or vocabulary. In fact, *flidges* is a nonsense word I used as a placeholder for the word *words* to show how you would gain a fairly good idea of a word's meaning from its context.

One set of experimenters explored children's ability to learn the meanings of new words through both direct instruction and through context (Cain, Oakhill, & Lemmon, 2004). The experimenters found that in children with low reading comprehension, ability to figure out meanings of words from context was impaired. However, through direct instruction, children with low reading comprehension, but good vocabularies, could learn the meanings of new words just as well as children with high reading comprehension (Cain, Oakhill, & Lemmon, 2004).

Investigators had adult participants learn meanings of words from sentence contexts (van Daalen-Kapteijns & Elshout-Mohr, 1981; see also Sternberg & Powell,

IN THE LAB OF RICHARD GERRIG

Timothy Peterson

The movie has come to the end. As the theater lights come up, it takes you a few moments to detach yourself from the world the movie created and return to your own here and now. That experience of moving from one world to another is what we try to capture in our lab. Much of the research we do has been devoted to understanding the cognitive processes that allow people to have such powerful experiences in which they are transported to narrative worlds.

One particular type of research has focused on people's mental responses to ongoing narratives. Suppose the movie you just viewed had a scene that suggested that the hero was imperiled if he entered a particular room. You might very well have heard yourself think, "Don't go through the door!" We call these types of thoughts *participatory responses* because people are reacting as if, in certain respects, they are genuine participants in the narrative world.

Narratives provide people with opportunities to encode a variety of participatory responses (Polichak & Gerrig, 2002). During the last few years, David Rapp and I (Rapp & Gerrig, 2002, 2006) have documented the impact of a particular type of participatory response: circumstances in which readers express mental preferences in favor of one of two potential outcomes. Suppose, for example, you are reading a story in which a character, Stu, is turning the key to start his car. In one version of the story, Stu needs to get to a hospital to help his pregnant wife through her delivery. In a second version of the story, Stu is quite drunk. That additional material should have an impact on the preference you encode when you get to the moment at which Stu turns the key.

Our experiments are somewhat more elaborate because we are particularly interested in how readers' preferences interact with the additional knowledge they bring to a situation. In Stu's case, that additional knowledge centers on the prior likelihood that the car will start. In one version of the story, he has just gotten a tune-up; in the other version, the car is in disrepair. The combination of these factors lead readers to narrative moments at which, for example, they have reason to believe that Stu's car won't start but they sorely hope that it will (so that he can get to his wife). Under exactly those circumstances, readers find it difficult to assimilate the likely outcome, "The car absolutely refused to start."

Although our experiments are concerned with readers' participatory responses to texts, they also have broader implications for everyday life. You often find yourself in circumstances in which what you prefer—"I want to win the lottery"—clashes with what you know about the situation—"My chances are one in a million." When you find yourself in such circumstances, it's easy to tell yourself a story with your preferred ending. You can picture yourself checking the winning numbers, discovering that you've won, and starting your celebration! Once you've transported yourself to that highly pleasurable narrative world, how hard is it to restore yourself to reality?

References

Polichak, J. W., & Gerrig, R. J. (2002). "Get up and win!": Participatory responses to narratives. In T. C. Brock, J. J. Strange, & M. C. Green (Eds.), *Narrative impact: Social and cognitive foundations* (pp. 71–95). Mahwah, NJ: Erlbaum.

Rapp, D. N., & Gerrig, R. J. (2002). Readers' reality-driven and plot-driven analyses in narrative comprehension. *Memory & Cognition, 30,* 779–788.

Rapp, D. N., & Gerrig, R. J. (2006). Predilections for narrative outcomes: The impact of story contexts and reader preferences. *Journal of Memory and Language, 54,* 54–67.

1983). They found that high- and low-verbal participants (i.e., people with large or small vocabularies, respectively) learn word meanings differently. High-verbal participants perform a deeper analysis of the possibilities for a new word's meaning than do low-verbal participants. In particular, the high-verbal participants used a well-formulated strategy for figuring out word meanings. The low-verbal participants seemed to have no clear strategy at all.

Comprehension of Ideas in Text: Propositional Representations

What factors influence our comprehension of what we read? Walter Kintsch has developed a model of text comprehension based on his observations (Kintsch, 1990; Kintsch & van Dijk, 1978). According to the model, as we read we try to hold as much information as possible in working (active) memory to understand what we read. However, we do not try to store the exact words we read in working (active) memory. Rather, we try to extract the fundamental ideas from groups of words. We then store those fundamental ideas in a simplified representational form in working memory.

The representational form for these fundamental ideas is the proposition. Propositions were defined in more detail in Chapter 7. For now it suffices to say that a proposition is the briefest unit of language that can be independently found to be true or false. For example, the sentence, "Penguins are birds, and penguins can fly" contains two propositions. You can verify independently whether penguins are birds and whether penguins can fly. In general, propositions assert either an action (e.g., flying) or a relationship (e.g., membership of penguins in the category of birds).

According to Kintsch, working memory holds propositions rather than words. Its limits are thus taxed by large numbers of propositions, rather than by any particular number of words (Kintsch & Keenan, 1973). When a string of words in text requires us to hold a large number of propositions in working memory, we have difficulty comprehending the text. When information stays in working memory a longer time, it is better comprehended and better recalled subsequently. Because of the limits of working memory, however, some information must be moved out of working memory to make room for new information.

According to Kintsch, propositions that are thematically central to the understanding of the text will remain in working memory longer than propositions that are irrelevant to the theme of the text passage. Kintsch calls the thematically crucial propositions *macropropositions*. He further calls the overarching thematic structure of a passage of text the *macrostructure*. In an experiment testing his model, Kintsch and an associate asked participants to read a 1300-word text passage (Kintsch & van Dijk, 1978). The participants then had to summarize the key propositions in the passage immediately, at 1 month, or at 3 months after reading the passage. What happened after 3 months? Participants recalled the macropropositions and the overall macrostructure of the passage about as well as could participants who summarized it immediately after reading it. However, the propositions providing nonthematic details about the passage were not recalled as well after 1 month and not at all well after 3 months.

Representing the Text in Mental Models

Once words are semantically encoded or their meaning is derived from the use of context, the reader still must create a mental model of the text that is being read. This model simulates the world being described rather than the particular words being used to describe it (Craik, 1943; see Johnson-Laird, 1989). A mental model may be viewed as a sort of internal working model of the situation described in the text as the reader understands it. In other words, the reader creates some sort of mental representation that contains within it the main elements of the text. They are represented in a way that is relatively easy to grasp or at least that is simpler and more concrete than the text itself. For example, suppose that you read the sentence, "The loud bang scared Alice." You may form a picture of Alice becoming scared on hearing a loud noise. Or you may access propositions stored in memory regarding the effects of loud bangs.

A given passage of text or even a given set of propositions (to refer back to Kintsch's model) may lead to more than one mental model (Johnson-Laird, 1983). For example, you may need to modify your mental model. Whether you do depends on whether the next sentence is "She tried to steer off the highway without losing control of the car" or "She ducked to avoid being shot." In representing the loud bang that scared Alice, more than one mental model is possible. If you start out with a different model than the one required in a given passage, your ability to comprehend the text depends on your ability to form a new mental model. You can hold only a limited number of mental models at any given time (Johnson-Laird, Byrne, & Schaeken, 1992). Therefore, when one of the models is incorrect, it must be rejected to make room for new models.

Note that to form mental models, you must make at least tentative inferences (preliminary conclusions or judgments) about what is meant but not said. In the first case, you are likely to assume that a tire blew out. In the second case, you may infer that someone is shooting a gun. Note that neither of these things is stated explicitly. The construction of mental models illustrates that, in addition to comprehending the words themselves, we also need to understand how words combine into meaningfully integrated representations of narratives or expositions. Passages of text that lead unambiguously to a single mental model are easier to comprehend than are passages that may lead to multiple mental models (Johnson-Laird, 1989).

Inferences can be of different kinds. One of the most important kinds is a bridging inference (Haviland & Clark, 1974). This is an inference a reader (or listener) makes when a sentence seems not to follow directly from the sentence preceding it. In essence, what is new in the second sentence goes one step too far beyond what is given in the previous sentences. Consider, for example, two pairs of two sentences:

1. John took the picnic out of the trunk. The beer was warm.
2. John took the beer out of the trunk. The beer was warm.

Readers took about 180 milliseconds longer to read the first pair of sentences than the second. Haviland and Clark suggested a reason for this greater processing time. It was that, in the first pair, information needed to be inferred (the picnic included beer) that was directly stated in the second pair.

Although most researchers emphasize the importance of inference making in reading and forms of language comprehension (e.g., Graesser & Kreuz, 1993), not all researchers agree. According to the minimalist hypothesis, readers make inferences based only on information that is easily available to them. They do so only when they need to make such inferences to make sense of adjoining sentences (McKoon & Ratcliff, 1992a). I believe that the bulk of the evidence regarding the minimalist position indicates that it is itself too minimalist. Readers appear to make more inferences than this position suggests (Suh & Trabasso, 1993, Trabasso & Suh, 1993).

Comprehending Text Based on Context and Point of View

What we remember from a given passage of text often depends on our point of view. For example, suppose that you were reading a text passage about the home of a wealthy family. It described many of the features of the house, such as a leaky roof, a fireplace, and a musty basement. It also described the contents of the house, such as valuable coins, silverware, and television set. How might your encoding and comprehension of the text be different if you were reading it from the point of view of a prospective purchaser of the home as opposed to the viewpoint of a prospective cat burglar? In a study using just such a passage, people who read the passage from the viewpoint of a cat burglar remembered far more about the contents of the home. In contrast, those who read from the viewpoint of a homebuyer remembered more about the condition of the house (Anderson & Pichert, 1978). In fact, varying the retrieval situations or cues can cause different details to be remembered. Researchers found that differing retrieval instructions did not affect accuracy but did affect the specific details recalled (Gilbert & Fisher, 2006).

To summarize, our comprehension of what we read depends on several abilities. First is gaining access to the meanings of words, either from memory or on the basis of context. Second is deriving meaning from the key ideas in what we read. Third is forming mental models that simulate the situations about which we read. And fourth is extracting the key information from the text, based on the contexts in which we read and on the ways in which we intend to use what we read.

Thus far we have discussed the social and cognitive contexts for language. Language use interacts with, but does not completely determine, the nature of thought. Social interactions influence the ways in which language is used and comprehended in discourse and reading. Next, we highlight some of the insights we have gained by studying the physiological context for language. Specifically, how do our brains process language?

Neuropsychology of Language

Recall from Chapter 2 that some of our earliest insights into brain localization related to an association between specific language deficits and specific organic damage to the brain, as first discovered by Marc Dax, Paul Broca, and Carl Wernicke (see also Brown & Hagoort, 1999; Garrett, 2003). Broca's aphasia and Wernicke's aphasia are particularly well-documented instances in which brain lesions affect linguistic functions (see Chapter 2). Let's consider these and related syndromes in more detail.

Aphasia

Aphasia is an impairment of language functioning caused by damage to the brain (Caramazza & Shapiro, 2001; Garrett, 2003; Hillis & Caramazza, 2003). There are several types of aphasias (Figure 10.6).

Wernicke's aphasia is caused by damage to Wernicke's area of the brain (see Chapter 2). It is characterized by notable impairment in the understanding of spoken words and sentences. It also typically involves the production of sentences that have the basic

FIGURE 10.6

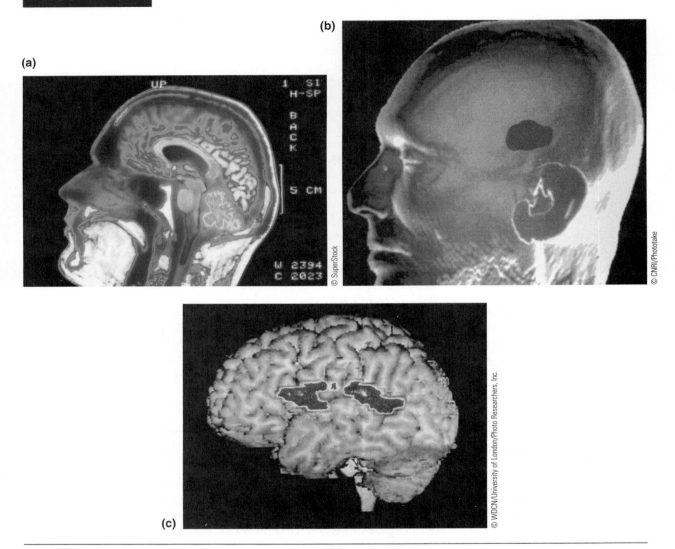

Brain scans comparing the brain of (a) a normal patient with brains of patients with (b) Wernicke's aphasia and (c) Broca's aphasia.

structure of the language spoken but that make no sense. They are sentences that are empty of meaning. Two examples are "Yeah, that was the pumpkin furthest from my thoughts" and "the scroolish prastimer ate my spanstakes" (Hillis & Caramazza, 2003, p. 176). In the first case, the words makes sense, but not in the context they are presented. In the second case, the words themselves are neologisms, or newly created words. Treatment for patients with this type of aphasia frequently involves supporting and encouraging nonlanguage communication (Altschuler & associates, 2006).

Broca's aphasia is caused by damage to Broca's area of the brain (see Chapter 2). It is characterized by the production of agrammatical speech at the same time that verbal comprehension ability is largely preserved. It thus differs from Wernicke's aphasia in two key respects. First is that speech is agrammatical rather than grammatical, as in Wernicke's. Second is that verbal comprehension is largely preserved. An example of a production by a patient with Broca's aphasia is "Stroke . . . Sunday . . . arm, talking—bad" (Hillis & Caramazza, 2003, p. 176). The gist of the intended sentence is maintained, but the expression of it is badly distorted. Broca's area is important for speech production, regardless of the format of the speech. In particular, Broca's area is activated during imagined or actual sign production (Campbell, MacSweeney, & Waters, 2007; Horwitz & associates, 2003).

Global aphasia is the combination of highly impaired comprehension and production of speech. It is caused by lesions to both Broca's and Wernicke's areas. Aphasia following a stroke frequently involves damage to both Broca's and Wernicke's areas. In one study, researchers found 32% of aphasias immediately following a stroke involved both Broca's and Wernicke's areas (Pedersen, Vinter, & Olsen, 2004).

Anomic aphasia involves difficulties in naming objects or in retrieving words. The patient may look at an object and simply be unable to retrieve the word that corresponds to the object. Sometimes, specific categories of things cannot be recalled, such as names of living things (Warrington & Shallice, 1984).

Autism

Autism is a developmental disorder characterized by abnormalities in social behavior, language, and cognition (Jarrold & Happé, 2003; Pierce & Courchesne, 2003). It is biological in its origins, although the genes responsible for it have not been conclusively identified (Lamb & associates, 2000). Children with autism show abnormalities in many areas of the brain, including the frontal and parietal lobes, as well as the cerebellum, brainstem, corpus callosum, basal ganglia, amygdala, and hippocampus. The disease was first identified in the middle of the twentieth century (Kanner, 1943). It is five times more common in males than in females. The incidence of diagnosed autism has increased rapidly over recent years. Between the years of 2000 and 2004, the frequency of diagnosis of autism increased 14% (Chen & associates, 2007). Autism is diagnosed today in approximately 60 out of every 10,000 children (Fombonne, 2003). This rate corresponds to about 1 out of every 165 children being diagnosed with an autism-spectrum disorder. The increase in recent times may be a result of a number of causes, including changes in diagnosing strategies or environmental pollution (Jick & Kaye, 2003; Windham & associates, 2006). Children with autism usually are identified by around 14 months of age, when they fail to show expected normal patterns of interactions with others. Children with autism display repetitive movements and stereotyped patterns of interests and activities (Pierce & Courchesne, 2003). Often they repeat the same motion, over and over again, with no obvious purpose to the movement. When they interact with someone, they are more likely to view their lips than their eyes. About half of children with autism fail to develop functional speech. What speech they do develop tends to be characterized by *echolalia*, meaning they repeat, over and over again, speech they have heard. Sometimes the repetition occurs several hours after the original use of the words by someone else (Pierce & Courchesne, 2003).

There are a variety of theories of autism. One recent theory suggests that autism can be understood in terms of sex differences in the wiring of the human brain. According to this theory (Baron-Cohen, 2003), male brains are, on average, stronger than female ones at understanding and building systems. These systems can be concrete ones, such as those involved in building machinery, or they can be abstract ones, such as those in politics or writing or music. Females' brains, in contrast, are stronger at empathizing and communicating. According to Baron-Cohen, autism results from an extreme male brain. This brain is almost totally inept in empathy and communication but very strong in systematizing. As a result, autistic individuals sometimes can perform tasks that require a great deal of systematization, such as figuring out the day corresponding to a date well in the future. As it happens, autism is also much more common among males than among females. Although this theory has not been conclusively proven, it is intriguing and currently undergoing further investigation.

Another theory of autism is that of executive dysfunction (Ozonoff & associates, 1994). This theory describes well the repetitive motion observed in autism, as well as difficulties in planning, mental flexibility, and self-monitoring (Hill, 2004). The executive dysfunction theory views autism as associated with dysfunction in the frontal lobes.

Lesion Studies and Event-Related Potentials Research

Through studies of patients with brain lesions, researchers have learned a great deal about the relations between particular areas of the brain (the areas of lesions observed in patients) and particular linguistic functions (the observed deficits in the brain-injured patients). For example, we can broadly generalize that many linguistic functions are located primarily in the areas identified by Broca and Wernicke. Damage to Wernicke's area, in the posterior of the cortex, is now believed to entail more grim consequences for linguistic function than does damage to Broca's area, closer to the front of the brain (Kolb & Whishaw, 1990). Also, lesion studies have shown that linguistic function is governed by a much larger area of the posterior cortex than just the area identified by Wernicke. In addition, other areas of the cortex also play a role. Examples are association-cortex areas in the left hemisphere and a portion of the left temporal cortex. Moreover, recent imaging studies of the post-traumatic recovery of linguistic functioning find that neurological language functioning appears to redistribute to other areas of the brain. These areas include analogous areas in the right hemisphere and some frontal areas. Thus, damage to the major left hemisphere areas responsible for language functioning sometimes can lead to enhanced involvement of other areas as language functioning recovers. It is as if previously dormant or overshadowed areas take over the duties left vacant (Cappa, & associates, 1997). Finally, some subcortical structures (e.g., the basal ganglia and the posterior thalamus) also are involved in linguistic function (Kolb & Whishaw, 1990).

Geschwind (1970) proposed a model, sometimes known as the Geschwind-Wernicke model, for how language is processed by the brain. According to this model, speech sounds signaling language travel to the inner ear. The auditory nerve then carries these signals to the primary auditory cortex of the temporal lobe. From there, the signal travels to an association area of the brain at a region in which the temporal, occipital, and parietal lobes join. There sense is made from what was said.

In other words, meaning is assigned at this point. From there, the processed information travels to Wernicke's area. It then moves on to Broca's area. Although the model as originally formulated localized language comprehension in Wernicke's area and language production in Broca's area, this view is now known to be an oversimplification. Wernicke's area seems to have some involvement in language production and Broca's area in language comprehension (Zurif, 1990).

Event-related potentials, or ERPs (see Chapter 2), also can be used to study the processing of language in the brain. For one thing, a certain ERP called N400 (a negative potential 400 milliseconds after stimulus onset) typically occurs when individuals hear an anomalous sentence (Dambacher & Kliegl, 2007; Kutas & Hillyard, 1980). Thus, if people are presented a sequence of normal sentences but also anomalous sentences (such as "The leopard is a very good napkin"), the anomalous sentences will elicit the N400 potential. Moreover, the more anomalous a sentence is, the greater the response shown in another ERP, P600 (a positive potential 600 milliseconds after the stimulus onset; Kutas & Van Patten, 1994). The P600 effect seems to be more related to syntactic violations, whereas the N400 effect is more related to semantic violations (Friederici & associates, 2004).

Another method used to examine brain functioning is fMRI. Through these methods, dominance of the left hemisphere is observed for most language users (Anderson & associates, 2006; Gaillard & associates, 2004). Men and women appear to process language differently, at least at the phonological level (Shaywitz, 2005). An fMRI study of men and women asked participants to perform one of four tasks:

1. Indicate whether a pair of letters was identical.
2. Indicate whether two words have the same meaning.
3. Indicate whether a pair of words rhymes.
4. Compare the lengths of two lines (a control task).

The researchers found that when both male and female participants were performing the letter-recognition and word-meaning tasks, they showed activation in the left temporal lobe of the brain. When they were performing the rhyming task, however, different areas were activated for men versus women. Only the inferior (lower) frontal region of the left hemisphere was activated for men. The inferior frontal region of both the left and right hemispheres was activated in women. These results suggested that men localized their phonological processing more than did women.

Some intriguing sex differences emerge in the ways that linguistic function appears to be localized in the brain (Kimura, 1987). Men seem to show more left-hemisphere dominance for linguistic function than the women show. Women show more bilateral, symmetrical patterns of linguistic function. Furthermore, the brain locations associated with aphasia seemed to differ for men and women. Most aphasic women showed lesions in the anterior region, although some aphasic women showed lesions in the temporal region. In contrast, aphasic men showed a more varied pattern of lesions. Aphasic men were more likely to show lesions in posterior regions rather than in anterior regions. One interpretation of Kimura's findings is that the role of the posterior region in linguistic function may be different for women than it is for men. Another interpretation relates to the fact that women show less lateralization of linguistic function. Women may be better able to compensate for any possible loss of function due to lesions in the left posterior hemisphere through functional offsets in the right posterior hemisphere. The possibility that there also may be subcortical sex differences in linguistic function further complicates the ease of interpreting Kimura's findings. (Recall also the earlier discussion of communication differences between men and women.)

Kimura (1981) also has studied hemispheric processing of language in people who use sign language rather than speech to communicate. She found that the locations of lesions that would be expected to disrupt speech also disrupt signing. Further, the hemispheric pattern of lesions associated with signing deficits is the same pattern shown with speech deficits. That is, all right-handers with signing deficits show left-hemisphere lesions, as do most left-handers. But some left-handers with signing deficits show right-hemisphere lesions (see also Pickell & associates, 2005). This finding supports the view that the brain processes both signing and speech similarly in terms of their linguistic function. It refutes the view that signing involves spatial processing or some other nonlinguistic form of cognitive processing.

There is some evidence that the brain mechanisms responsible for language learning are different from those responsible for the use of language by adults (Stiles & associates, 1998). In general, the left hemisphere seems to be better at processing well-practiced routines. The right hemisphere is better at dealing with novel stimuli. A possibly related finding is that individuals who have learned language later in life show more right-hemisphere involvement (Neville, 1995). Perhaps the reason is that language remains somewhat more novel for them than for others. These finding points out that one cannot precisely map linguistic or other kinds of functioning to hemispheres in a way that works for all people. Rather, the mappings differ somewhat from one person to another (Zurif, 1995).

Despite the many findings that have resulted from studies of brain-injured patients, there are three key difficulties in drawing conclusions based only on studies of patients with lesions:

1. Naturally occurring lesions are often not easily localized to a discrete region of the brain, with no untoward effects on other regions. For example, when hemorrhaging or insufficient blood flow (such as impairment due to clotting) causes lesions, the lesions also may affect other areas of the brain. Thus, many patients who show cortical damage also have suffered some damage in subcortical structures. This may confound the findings of cortical damage.

2. Researchers are able to study the linguistic function of patients only after the lesions have caused damage. Typically they are unable to document the linguistic function of patients prior to the damage.

3. Because it would be unethical to create lesions merely to observe their effects on patients, researchers are able to study the effects of lesions only in those areas where lesions happen to have occurred naturally. Other areas therefore are not studied.

Other Methods

Although lesion studies are valuable, researchers also investigate brain localization of linguistic function via other methods. One example is evaluating the effects on linguistic function that follow electrical stimulation of the brain (Ojemann, 1982; Ojemann & Mateer, 1979). Through stimulation studies, researchers have found that stimulation of particular points in the brain seems to yield discrete effects on particular linguistic functions (such as the naming of objects) across repeated, successive trials. For example, in a given person, repeated stimulation of one particular point might lead to difficulties in recalling the names of objects on every trial. In contrast, stimulation of another point might lead to incorrect naming of objects. In addition, information regarding brain locations in a specific individual may not apply across individuals. Thus, for a given individual, a discrete point of stimulation may seem to affect only one particular linguistic function. But across individuals, these particular localizations of function vary widely. The effects of electrical stimulation are transitory. Linguistic function returns to normal soon after the stimulation has ceased. These brain-stimulation studies also show that many more areas of the cortex are involved in linguistic function than was thought previously. One study examined electrical stimulation of the brains of bilingual speakers. The researchers found different areas of the brain were active when using the primary versus the secondary language to name items. There was, however, some overlap of active areas with the two languages (Lucas, McKhann, & Ojemann, 2004).

Using electrical-stimulation techniques, sex differences in linguistic function can be identified. There is a somewhat paradoxical interaction of language and the brain (Ojemann, 1982). Although females generally have superior verbal skills to males, males have a proportionately larger (more diffusely dispersed) language area in their brains than do females. Counterintuitively, therefore, the size of the language area in the brain may be inversely related to the ability to use language. This interpretation seems further bolstered by Ojemann's findings with bilinguals, mentioned earlier. These findings regard the diffuse distribution of the nondominant language versus the more concentrated localization of the dominant language.

Yet another avenue of research involves the study of the metabolic activity of the brain and the flow of blood in the brain during the performance of various verbal tasks. For example, preliminary metabolic and blood-flow studies of the brain have indicated that many areas of the brain appear to be involved simultaneously during linguistic processing (Petersen & associates, 1988). However, most studies confirm the left hemisphere bias indicated by lesion studies (see Cabeza & Nyberg, 1997). Through these kinds of studies, researchers can examine multiple simultaneous cerebral processes involved in various linguistic tasks.

For all right-handed individuals and for most left-handed people, the left hemisphere of the brain seems clearly implicated in syntactical aspects of linguistic processing. It is essential to speech and to signing. The left hemisphere also seems to be essential to the ability to write. However, the right hemisphere seems capable of quite a bit of auditory comprehension. This is so particularly in terms of semantic processing, as well as some reading comprehension and post-traumatic linguistic recovery. The right hemisphere also seems to be important in several of the subtle nuances of linguistic comprehension and expression. Examples are understanding and expressing vocal inflection and gesture and comprehending metaphors and other nonliteral aspects of language (e.g., jokes and sarcasm; Kolb & Whishaw, 1990).

Finally, some subcortical structures, especially the basal ganglia and the posterior thalamus, seem to be involved in linguistic function. The thalamus seems to be involved in linguistic function, particularly in coordinating the activities of the cortical areas involved in speech (Hughlings-Jackson, 1866/1932; Penfield & Roberts, 1959). Investigators have linked lesions in the thalamus to specific difficulties in speaking (e.g., perseveration or impairment of speed, fluency, or naming—Ojemann, 1975). Also, the thalamus may play a role in activating the cortex for understanding and remembering language. Because of the difficulty of studying subcortical structures, the specific role of the thalamus and other subcortical structures is not yet well defined (Kolb & Whishaw, 1990).

Much of this chapter has revealed the many ways in which language and thought interact. The following chapter focuses on problem solving and creativity. But it also further reveals the interconnectedness of the ways in which we use language and the ways in which we think.

Key Themes

This chapter deals with several of the themes highlighted in Chapter 1.

A first theme is that of validity of causal inference versus ecological validity. Some researchers study language comprehension and production in controlled laboratory settings. For example, studies of phonology are likely to occur in a laboratory where it is possible to gain precise experimental control of stimuli. But work on language and thought often is done in remote parts of the world where tight experimental controls are only a dream. Studies of language usage in remote African villages, for example, cannot be done with tight controls, although some control is possible. As always, a combination of methodologies best enables cognitive psychologists to understand psychological phenomena to their fullest.

A second theme is that of biological versus behavioral methods. Lesion studies are a particularly good example of a combination of the two methodologies. On the one hand, they require a deep understanding of the nature of the brain and the parts of the brain affected by particular lesions. On the other hand, researchers examine behavior to understand how the particular lesions, and by inference, parts of the brain, are related to behavioral functioning.

A third theme is structure versus process. To understand any linguistic phenomena, one must analyze thoroughly the structure of the language under investigation.

One can then investigate the processes that are used to comprehend and produce this language. Without an understanding of both structure and process, it would be impossible to fully understand language and thought.

Suppose you are on a camping trip and are sitting around the campfire at night, admiring the numerous stars in the sky. Suppose you were to say to someone the following metaphorical question, "Would you like to see the sun paint a picture across the morning sky?" What does this question mean? Some people might say that it means that you are asking if they would like to wake up early to see how beautiful the sunrise will be the next morning. Some people might say that it means that it is getting late and that you should go to sleep to wake up early to see the beautiful sunrise. Now, suppose you ask this same question not on a camping trip but in a sleazy bar. What do you think the utterance will mean in that context?

Read the following passage:

Aoccdrnig to a rseearch at an Elingsh uinervtisy, it dseon't mttaer in waht oredr the ltteers in a wrod are, the olny iprmoatnt tihng is that the frist and lsat ltteres are at the rghit pclae. The rset can be a toatl mses and you can sitll raed it wouthit porbelm. Tihs is bcuseae we do not raed ervey lteter by itslef but the wrod as a wlohe.

Although most people cannot read the above passage as quickly as they can if all the letters are in the right order, they still can understand what the passage says.

Summary

1. **How do perceptual processes interact with the cognitive processes of reading?** The reading difficulties of people with dyslexia often relate to problems with the perceptual aspects of reading.

   Reading comprises two basic kinds of processes: (1) lexical processes, which include sequences of eye fixations and lexical access; and (2) comprehension processes.

2. **How does language affect the way we think?** According to the linguistic relativity view, cognitive differences that result from using different languages cause people speaking the various languages to perceive the world differently. However, the linguistic universals view stresses cognitive commonalities across different language users. No single interpretation explains all the available evidence regarding the interaction of language and thought.

   Research on bilinguals seems to show that environmental considerations also affect the interaction of language and thought. For example, additive bilinguals have established a well-developed primary language. The second language adds to their linguistic and perhaps even their cognitive skills. In contrast, subtractive bilinguals have not yet firmly established their primary language when portions of a second language partially displace the primary language. This displacement may lead to difficulties in verbal skills. Theorists differ in their views as to whether bilinguals store two or more languages separately (dual-system hypothesis) or together (single-system hypothesis). Some aspects of multiple languages possibly could be stored separately and others unitarily. Creoles and pidgins arise when two or more distinct linguistic groups come into contact. A dialect appears when a regional variety of a language becomes distinguished by features such as distinctive vocabulary, grammar, and pronunciation.

   Slips of the tongue may involve inadvertent verbal errors in phonemes, morphemes, or larger units of language. Slips of the tongue include anticipations, perseverations, reversals (including spoonerisms), substitutions, insertions, and deletions. Alternative views of metaphor include the comparison view, the anomaly view, the domain-interaction view, and the class-inclusion view.

3. **How does our social context influence our use of language?** Psychologists, sociolinguists, and others who study pragmatics are interested in how language is used within a social context. Their research looks into various aspects of nonverbal as well as verbal communication. Speech acts com-

prise representatives, directives, commissives, expressives, and declarations. Indirect requests, ways of asking for something without doing so straightforwardly, may refer to abilities, desires, future actions, and reasons. Conversational postulates provide a means for establishing language as a cooperative enterprise. They comprise several maxims, including the maxims of quantity, quality, relation, and manner. Sociolinguists have observed that people engage in various strategies to signal turn taking in conversations.

Sociolinguistic research suggests that male–female differences in conversational style center largely on men's and women's differing understandings of the goals of conversation. It has been suggested that men tend to see the world as a hierarchical social order in which their communication aims involve the need to maintain a high rank in the social order. In contrast, women tend to see communication as a means for establishing and maintaining their connection to their communication partners. To do so, they seek ways to demonstrate equity and support and to reach consensual agreement.

In discourse and reading comprehension, we use the surrounding context to infer the reference of pronouns and ambiguous phrases. The discourse context also can influence the semantic interpretation of unknown words in passages and aid in acquiring new vocabulary. Propositional representations of information in passages can be organized into mental models for text comprehension. Finally, a person's point of view likewise influences what will be remembered.

4. **How can we find out about language by studying the human brain, and what do such studies reveal?** Neuropsychologists, cognitive psychologists, and other researchers have managed to link quite a few language functions with specific areas or structures in the brain. They observe what happens when a particular area of the brain is injured, is electrically stimulated, or is studied in terms of its metabolic activity. For most people, the left hemisphere of the brain is vital to speech. It affects many syntactical aspects and some semantic aspects of linguistic processing. For most people, the right hemisphere handles a more limited number of linguistic functions. They include auditory comprehension of semantic information, as well as comprehension and expression of some nonliteral aspects of language use. These aspects involve vocal inflection, gesture, metaphors, sarcasm, irony, and jokes.

Thinking about Thinking: Factual, Analytical, Creative, and Practical Questions

1. Based on the discussion of reading in this chapter, what practical suggestion could you recommend that might make reading easier for someone who is having difficulty reading?

2. Why are researchers interested in the number of color words used by different cultures?

3. Describe the five basic kinds of speech acts proposed by Searle.

4. How should cognitive psychologists interpret evidence of linguistic universals when considering the linguistic-relativity hypothesis?

5. Compare and contrast the kinds of understandings that can be gained by studying speech errors made by normal people with those that can be gained by studying the language produced by people who have particular brain lesions.

6. Write an example of a pidgin conversation between two people and a creole conversation, focusing on the differences between pidgins and creoles.

7. Draft an example of a brief dialogue between a male and a female in which each may misunderstand the other, based on their differing beliefs regarding the goals of communication.

8. Suppose that you are an instructor of English as a second language. What kinds of things will you want to know about your students to determine how much to emphasize phonology, vocabulary, syntax, or pragmatics in your instruction?

9. Give an example of a humorous violation of one of Grice's four maxims of successful conversation.

Key Terms

aphasia

bilinguals

comprehension processes

cooperative principle

dialect

dual-system hypothesis

dyslexia

indirect requests

lexical access

lexical processes

linguistic relativity

linguistic universals

metaphors

monolinguals

pragmatics

similes

single-system hypothesis

slips of the tongue

speech acts

word-superiority effect

 Explore CogLab by going to **http://coglab.wadsworth.com.** To learn more, examine the following experiments:

Word Superiority

Annotated Suggested Reading

Tomasello, M. (1999). *The cultural origins of human cognition.* Cambridge, MA: Harvard University Press. This book discusses the role of culture in the evolution of human cognition, with special emphasis on language.

Problem Solving and Creativity

EXPLORING COGNITIVE PSYCHOLOGY

1. **What are some key steps involved in solving problems?**

2. **What are the differences between problems that have a clear path to a solution versus problems that do not?**

3. **What are some of the obstacles and aids to problem solving?**

4. **How does expertise affect problem solving?**

5. **What is creativity, and how can it be fostered?**

How do you solve problems that arise in your relationships with other people? How do you solve the "two-string" problem illustrated in Figure 11.1? How does anyone solve any problem for that matter? This chapter considers the process of solving problems, as well as some of the hindrances and aids to **problem solving,** an effort to overcome obstacles obstructing the path to a solution (Reed, 2000). At the conclusion of this chapter, we discuss creativity and its role in problem solving. Throughout the whole chapter, we discuss how people make the "mental

FIGURE 11.1

Imagine that you are the person standing in the middle of this room, in which two strings are hanging down from the ceiling. Your goal is to tie together the two strings, but neither string is long enough so that you can reach out and grab the other string while holding either of the two strings. You have available a few clean paintbrushes, a can of paint, and a heavy canvas tarpaulin. How will you tie together the two strings? From Richard E. Mayer, "The Search for Insight: Grappling with Gestalt Psychology's Unanswered Questions," in The Nature of Insight, *edited by R. J. Sternberg and J. E. Davidson. © 1995 MIT Press. Reprinted with permission from MIT Press.*

leaps" that lead them from having a set of givens to having a solution to a problem (Holyoak & Thagard, 1995).

The focus of this chapter is on individual problem solving. It is worth remembering, however, that working in groups often facilitates problem solving. The solutions reached by groups often are better than those reached by individuals (Williams & Sternberg, 1988). This benefit is seen most notably when the group members represent a variety of ability levels (Hong & Page, 2004). Therefore, we can ease our burden in problem solving not just by improving our problem-solving skills. We also can facilitate our problem-solving efforts by working with others who will bring their skills to bear on the problems we face. With a greater variety of skills there is also a greater benefit of collaboration.

The Problem-Solving Cycle

We engage in problem solving when we need to overcome obstacles to answer a question or to achieve a goal. If we quickly can retrieve an answer from memory, we do not have a problem. If we cannot retrieve an immediate answer, then we have a problem to be solved. This section describes the steps of the **problem-solving cycle,** which include problem identification, problem definition, strategy formulation, organization of information, allocation of resources, monitoring, and evaluation (shown in Figure 11.2; see Bransford & Stein, 1993; Hayes, 1989; Pretz, Naples, & Sternberg, 2003; Sternberg, 1986).

FIGURE 11.2

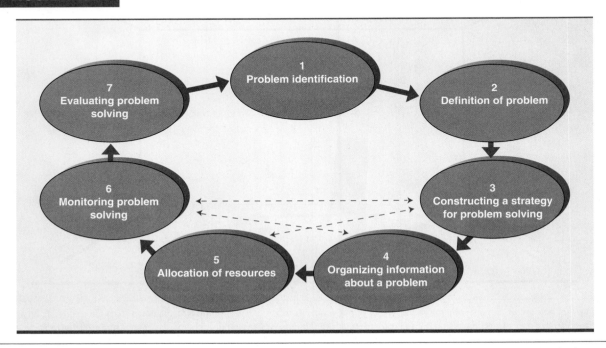

The steps of the problem-solving cycle include problem identification, problem definition, strategy formulation, organization of information, allocation of resources, monitoring, and evaluation.

In considering the steps, remember also the importance of flexibility in following the various steps of the cycle. Successful problem solving may involve occasionally tolerating some ambiguity regarding how best to proceed. Rarely can we solve problems by following any one optimal sequence of problem-solving steps. Moreover, we may go back and forth through the steps. We can change their order as need be, or even skip or add steps when it seems appropriate. How people solve problems depends partly on how they understand them (Whitten & Graesser, 2003). Consider an example of how understanding matters.

People are told the following about a drug (Stanovich, 2003; Stanovich & West, 1999):

- 150 people received the drug and were not cured.
- 150 people received the drug and were cured.
- 75 people did not receive the drug and were not cured.
- 300 people did not receive the drug and were cured.

Will they understand exactly what they were told? Many people believe that the drug in this instance is helpful. In fact, the drug described is not helpful at all. On the contrary, it is harmful. Only 50% of the people who received the drug were cured (i.e., 150 of 300). In contrast, 80% of the people who did not receive the drug were cured (300 of 375).

We also need to remember that our emotions can influence the ways in which we implement the problem-solving cycle (Schwarz & Skurnik, 2003). In groups with participants with high measured emotional intelligence—that is, the ability to identify emotions in others and regulate emotions in oneself—emotional processing can positively influence problem solving (Jordan & Troth, 2004). In mathematicians, the ability to regulate emotional state (among other factors) is related to higher problem-solving ability (Carlson & Bloom, 2005). Motivation also greatly affects how we solve problems and whether we ever complete them (Zimmerman & Campillo, 2003).

1. *Problem identification:* As odd as it sounds, identifying a situation as problematic is sometimes a difficult step. We may fail to recognize that we have a goal. For example, we might need to stay out of the path of an oncoming car we fail to observe. Or we might fail to recognize that our path to a goal is obstructed. An example would be needing to obtain more money because we lack enough to buy something we want. Or we might fail to recognize that the solution we had in mind does not work. For example, the job we expected to get might not now be available to us. If your problem is the need to write a term paper, you must first identify a question that your paper will address.

2. *Problem definition and representation:* Once we identify the existence of a problem, we still have to define and represent the problem well enough to understand how to solve it. Consider, for example, preparing to write your term paper. You must define your topic well enough to determine the research you will gather and your overall strategy for writing your paper. The problem-definition step is crucial. If you inaccurately define and represent the problem, you are much less able to solve it (Funke,

"Relax, honey. Change is good."

Sometimes we don't recognize an important problem that confronts us. © The New Yorker Collection 1993 Robert Mankoff from cartoonbank.com. All Rights Reserved.

1991; Hegarty, 1991). In fact, for the solution of the problem shown in Figure 11.1, this step is crucial to your finding the answer. That is, in solving the two-string problem, are you constraining your answer in ways that are limiting your ability to solve the problem?

3. *Strategy formulation:* Once the problem has been defined effectively, the next step is to plan a strategy for solving it. The strategy may involve **analysis**—breaking down the whole of a complex problem into manageable elements. Instead, or perhaps in addition, it may involve the complementary process of **synthesis**—putting together various elements to arrange them into something useful. In writing your term paper, you must analyze the components of your topic, research the various components, and then synthesize the topics into a rough draft of your paper. As in most dichotomies, one must be careful of drawing too much of a distinction (Kotovsky, 2003). People use analysis to help in synthesizing information. They also may use synthesis to help in analysis.

Another pair of complementary strategies involves divergent and convergent thinking. In **divergent thinking,** you try to generate a diverse assortment of possible alternative solutions to a problem. Once you have considered a variety of possibilities, however, you must engage in **conver-**

gent thinking to narrow down the multiple possibilities to converge on a single best answer. Sometimes, you merely find what you believe to be the most likely solution, which you will try first. When you came up with the topic for your paper, you first used divergent thinking to generate many possible topics. You then used convergent thinking to select the most suitable topic that interested you. In solving real-life problems, you may need both analysis and synthesis and both divergent and convergent thinking. There is no single ideal strategy for addressing every problem. Instead, the optimal strategy depends on both the problem and the problem solvers' personal preferences in problem-solving methods.

4. *Organization of information:* In this stage, you try to integrate all the information that you believe you will need to effectively do the task at hand. It might involve collecting references or even collecting your own ideas. This stage is critical to good problem solving. Sometimes, people fail to solve a problem not because they cannot solve it, but because they do not realize what information they have or how it fits together. Once a strategy (at least a tentative strategy) has been formulated, you are ready to organize the available information in a way that enables you to implement the strategy. Of course, throughout the problem-solving cycle you constantly are organizing and reorganizing the available information.

At this step, however, you organize the information strategically, finding a representation that best enables you to implement your strategy. For example, if your problem is to organize the information for your term paper, you may use an outline to organize your ideas. If your problem is to find a location, you may need to organize and represent the available information in the form of a map. If your problem is to earn a particular amount of money by a particular date, you may represent the available information in the form of a timetable for intervening dates by which you must have earned a particular portion of the total amount.

5. *Resource allocation:* In addition to our other problems, most of us face the problem of having limited resources. These resources include time, money, equipment, and space. Some problems are worth a lot of time and other resources. Others are worth very few resources. Moreover, we need to know when to allocate which resources. Studies show that expert problem solvers (and better students) tend to devote more of their mental resources to global (big-picture) planning than do novice problem solvers.

Novices (and poorer students) tend to allocate more time to local (detail-oriented) planning than do experts (Larkin & associates, 1980; Sternberg, 1981). For example, better students are more likely than poorer students to spend more time in the initial phase, deciding how to solve a problem, and less time actually solving it (Bloom & Broder, 1950). By spending more time in advance deciding what to do, effective students are less likely to fall prey to false starts, winding paths, and all kinds of errors.

When a person allocates more mental resources to planning on a large scale, he or she is able to save time and energy and to avoid frustration later on. Thus, when writing your term paper, you probably will spend much of your time conducting your research, organizing your notes, and planning your paper.

6. *Monitoring:* A prudent expenditure of time includes monitoring the process of solving the problem. Effective problem solvers do not set out on a path to a solution and then wait until they have reached the end of the path to check where they are (Schoenfeld, 1981). Rather, they check up on themselves all along the way to make sure that they are getting closer to their goal. If they are not, they reassess what they are doing. They may conclude that they made a false start, that they got off track somewhere along the way, or even that they see a more promising path if they take a new direction. If you are writing a term paper, you will want to be monitoring whether you are making good progress. If you are not making good progress, you will want to figure out why.

7. *Evaluation:* Just as you need to monitor a problem while you are in the process of solving it, you need to evaluate your solution after you have finished. Some of the evaluation may occur right away. The rest may occur a bit later or even much later. For example, after drafting your term paper, you probably will evaluate your draft. You will want to revise and edit it quite a few times before turning in your paper. Often key advances occur through the evaluation process. Through evaluation, new problems may be recognized. Moreover, the problem may be redefined, and new strategies may come to light. New resources may also become available, or existing ones may be used more efficiently. Hence, the cycle is completed when it leads to new insights and begins anew.

Types of Problems

Problems can be categorized according to whether they have clear paths to a solution (Davidson & Sternberg, 2003). **Well-structured problems** have clear paths to solutions. These problems also are termed *well-defined problems*. An example would be "How do you find the area of a parallelogram?" **Ill-structured problems** lack clear paths to solutions. These problems are also termed *ill-defined problems*. An example would be "How do you tie together two suspended strings, when neither string is long enough to allow you to reach the other string while holding either of the strings?" Of course, in the real world of problems, these two categories may represent a continuum of clarity in problem solving rather than two discrete classes with a clear boundary between the two. Nonetheless, the categories are useful in understanding how people solve problems. We next consider each of these kinds of problems in turn.

Well-Structured Problems

On tests in school, your teachers have asked you to tackle countless well-structured problems in specific content areas (e.g., math, history, geography). These problems had clear paths, if not necessarily easy paths, to their solutions—in particular, the application of a formula. In psychological research, cognitive psychologists might ask you to solve less content-specific kinds of well-structured problems. For example, cognitive psychologists often have studied a particular type of well-structured problem: the class of *move problems*, so termed because such problems require a series of moves to reach a final goal state. Perhaps the most well known of the move problems is one involving two antagonistic parties, whom we call "hobbits" and "orcs" in the "Investigating Cognitive Psychology" box.

INVESTIGATING COGNITIVE PSYCHOLOGY

Three hobbits and three orcs are on a river bank. The hobbits and orcs need to cross over to the other side of the river. They have for this purpose a small rowboat that will hold just two people. There is one problem, however. If the number of orcs on either river bank exceeds the number of hobbits on that bank, the orcs will eat the hobbits on that bank. How can all six creatures get across to the other side of the river in a way that guarantees that they all arrive there with the forest intact? Try to solve the problem before reading on.

The solution to the problem is shown in Figure 11.3. The solution contains several features worth noting. First, the problem can be solved in a minimum of eleven steps, including the first and last steps. Second, the solution is essentially *linear* in nature. There is just one valid move (connecting two points with a line segment) at most steps of problem solution. At all but two steps along the solution path, only one error can be made without violating the rules of the move problem: to go directly backward in the solution. At two steps, there are two possible forward-moving responses. But both of these lead toward the correct answer. Thus, again, the most likely error is to return to a previous state in the solution of the problem.

According to those who have studied the problem, people seem to make three main kinds of errors (Greeno, 1974; Simon & Reed, 1976; Thomas, 1974). They are (1) inadvertently moving backward, (2) making illegal moves, and (3) not realizing the nature of the next legal move. The first type of error is to revert to a state that is further from the end goal, for instance, moving all of the "orcs" and "hobbits" back to the first side of the river. The second kind of error is to make an illegal move—that is, a move that is not permitted according to the terms of the problem. For example, a move that resulted in having more than two individuals in the boat would be illegal. The third type of error involves becoming "stuck"—not knowing what to do next, given the current stage of the problem. An example would be realizing that you must bring one "orc" or "hobbit" back across the river to its starting point before you can move any of the remaining characters.

One method for studying how to solve well-defined problems is to develop computer simulations. Here, the researcher's task is to create a computer program that can solve these problems. By developing the instructions a computer must execute to solve problems, the researcher may better understand how humans solve similar kinds of problems. According to one model of problem solving (Newell & Simon, 1972), the problem solver (which may be using human or artificial intelligence) must view

FIGURE 11.3

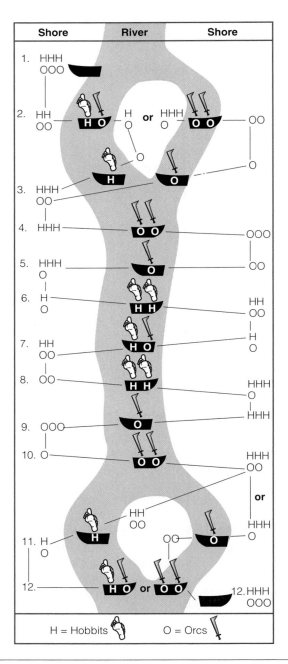

(Refer to the "Investigating Cognitive Psychology" box for an explanation of the solution.) What can you learn about your own methods of solving problems by seeing how you approached this particular problem? From In Search of the Human Mind by Robert J. Sternberg. Copyright © 1995 by Harcourt Brace & Company. Reproduced by permission of the publisher.

the initial problem state and the goal state within a problem space (Wenke & Frensch, 2003). A **problem space** is the universe of all possible actions that can be applied to solving a problem, given any constraints that apply to the solution of the problem. According to this model, the fundamental strategy for solving problems is to divide the problem task into a series of steps. These steps eventually will lead to the solution of the problem at hand. Each step involves a set of rules for procedures ("operations") that can be implemented. The set of rules is organized hierarchically into programs containing various internal levels of subprograms (called "routines" and "subroutines").

Many of the sublevel programs are **algorithms,** sequences of operations that may be repeated over and over again and that, in theory, guarantee the solution to a problem (Hunt, 1975; Sternberg, 2000). Generally, an algorithm continues until it satisfies a condition determined by a program. Suppose a computer is provided with a well-defined problem and an appropriate hierarchy (program) of operations organized into procedural algorithms. The computer can readily calculate all possible operations and combinations of operations within the problem space. It also can determine the best possible sequence of steps to take to solve the problem.

Unlike computers, however, the human mind does not specialize in high-speed computations of numerous possible combinations. The limits of our working memory prohibit us from considering more than just a few possible operations at one time (Hambrick & Engle, 2003; Kintsch & associates, 1999; see also Chapter 5). Newell and Simon recognized these limits and observed that humans must use mental shortcuts for solving problems. These mental shortcuts are termed **heuristics**—informal, intuitive, speculative strategies that sometimes lead to an effective solution and sometimes do not (Fischhoff, 1999; Holyoak, 1990; Korf, 1999; Stanovich, 2003; Sternberg, 2000). Suppose we store in long-term memory several simple heuristics that we can apply to a variety of problems. We thereby can lessen the burden on our limited-capacity working memory.

Newell and Simon observed that when problem solvers were confronted with a problem for which they could not immediately see an answer, effective problem solvers used the heuristic of means–ends analysis. In this strategy, the problem solver continually compares the current state and the goal state and takes steps to minimize the differences between the two states. Various other problem-solving heuristics include *working forward, working backward,* and *generate and test.* Table 11.1 illustrates how a problem solver might apply these heuristics to the aforementioned move problem (Greeno & Simon, 1988) and to a more common everyday problem (Hunt, 1994). Figure 11.4 shows a rudimentary problem space for the move problem. It illustrates that there may be any number of possible strategies for solving it.

You enter a bookstore seeking out a certain book, Hortense Hortigan's *Make a Million in a Month.* You are not sure where in the bookstore, if anywhere, you can find the book. What would be an algorithm for solving this problem? How about a heuristic?

The only algorithm that guarantees your discovering whether the book is in the bookstore is to check each book in the store. Eventually, you will either have found Hortigan's book or searched unsuccessfully through all titles. There are many possible heuristics you could apply, however. One is to ask a clerk for help. A second is to look

TABLE 11.1	Four Heuristics		
These four heuristics may be used in solving the move problem illustrated in Figures 11.3 and 11.4.			
HEURISTIC	**DEFINITION OF HEURISTIC**	**EXAMPLE OF HEURISTIC APPLIED TO THE MOVE PROBLEM (GREENO & SIMON, 1988)**	**EXAMPLE OF HEURISTIC APPLIED TO AN EVERYDAY PROBLEM: HOW TO TRAVEL BY AIR FROM YOUR HOME TO ANOTHER LOCATION USING THE MOST DIRECT ROUTE POSSIBLE (HUNT, 1994)**
Means–ends analysis	The problem solver analyzes the problem by viewing the end—the goal being sought—and then tries to decrease the distance between the current position in the problem space and the end goal in that space.	Try to get as many people on the far bank and as few people on the near bank as possible.	Try to minimize the distance between home and the destination.
Working forward	The problem solver starts at the beginning and tries to solve the problem from the start to the finish.	Evaluate the situation carefully with the six people on one bank and then try to move them step by step to the opposite bank.	Find the possible air routes leading from home toward the destination, and take the routes that seem most directly to lead to the destination.
Working backward	The problem solver starts at the end and tries to work backward from there.	Start with the final state—having all hobbits and all orcs on the far bank—and try to work back to the beginning state.	Find the possible air routes that reach the destination, and work backward to trace which of these routes can be most directly traced to originate at home.
Generate and test	The problem solver simply generates alternative courses of action, not necessarily in a systematic way, and then notices in turn whether each course of action will work.	This method works fairly well for the move problem because at most steps in the process, there is only one allowable forward move, and there are never more than two possibilities, both of which eventually will lead to the solution.	Find the various possible alternative routes leading from home, then see which of these routes might be used to end up at the destination. Choose the most direct route. Unfortunately, given the number of possible combinations of routes for air travel, this heuristic may not be very helpful.

through an index of books in the store, if one is available. A third is to start your search in more plausible sections (financial or self-help), only then moving to less plausible sections; and so on. Notice, however, that if you use the heuristics and do not find the book, you cannot be certain the book is not there. For example, it may be misplaced or not yet in the index.

FIGURE 11.4

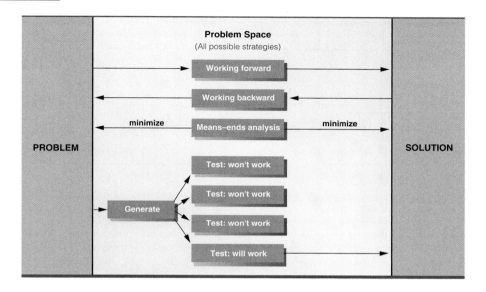

A problem space contains all the possible strategies leading from the initial problem state to the solution (the goal state). This problem space, for example, shows four of the heuristics that might be used in solving the move problem illustrated in Figure 11.3. From In Search of the Human Mind by Robert J. Sternberg. Copyright © 1995 by Harcourt Brace & Company. Reproduced by permission of the publisher.

Isomorphic Problems

Sometimes, two problems are **isomorphic;** that is, their formal structure is the same, and only their content differs. Sometimes, as in the case of the hobbits and orcs problem and a similar missionaries and cannibals problem, in which cannibals eat missionaries when they outnumber them, the isomorphism is obvious. Similarly, you can readily detect the isomorphism of many games that involve constructing words from jumbled or scrambled letters. Figure 11.5 also shows a different set of isomorphic problems. They illustrate some of the puzzles associated with isomorphic problems.

It often is extremely difficult to observe the underlying structural isomorphism of problems (Reed, 1987; Reed, Dempster, & Ettinger, 1985). It is also difficult to be able to apply problem-solving strategies from one problem to another. For example, it may not be clear how an example from a textbook applies to another problem (e.g., one on a test). Problem solvers are particularly unlikely to detect isomorphisms when two problems are similar but not identical in structure. Further, when the content or the surface characteristics of the problems differ sharply, detecting the isomorphism of the structure of problems is harder. For example, school-aged children may find it difficult to see the structural similarity between various word problems that are framed within different story situations. Similarly, physics students may have difficulty seeing the structural similarities among various physics problems when different kinds of materials are used. The problem of recognizing isomorphisms across varying contexts returns us to the recurring difficulties in problem representation.

FIGURE 11.5

(a)

| 1 | 2 | 3 | 4 | 5 | 6 | 7 | 8 | 9 |

(b)

```
  X | X | X
 ---+---+---
  X | O | O
 ---+---+---
  O | X | O
```

(c)

```
  6 | 1 | 8
 ---+---+---
  7 | 5 | 3
 ---+---+---
  2 | 9 | 4
```

Compare the problems illustrated in the games of (a) number scrabble, (b) tic-tac-toe, and (c) magic square. Number scrabble is based on equations. Which triples of numbers satisfy the equation X + Y + Z = 15? Tic-tac-toe requires one to produce three X's or three O's in a row, column, or diagonal. The magic square requires one to place numbers in the tic-tac-toe board so that every row, column, and major diagonal adds up to 15. In what ways are these problems isomorphic? How do their differences in presentation affect the ease of representing and solving these problems?

Problems of Problem Representation

What is the key reason that some problems are easier to solve than their isomorphisms? Consider the various versions of a problem known as the Tower of Hanoi. In this problem, the problem solver must use a series of moves to transfer a set of rings (usually three) from the first of three pegs to the third of the three pegs, using as few moves as possible (Figure 11.6). Researchers presented this same basic problem in many different isomorphic forms (Kotovsky, Hayes, & Simon, 1985). They found that some forms of the problem took up to 16 times as long to solve as other forms. Although many factors influenced these findings, a major determinant of the relative ease of solving the problem was how the problem was represented. For example, in the form shown in Figure 11.6, the physically different sizes of the discs facilitated the mental representation of the restriction against moving larger discs onto smaller discs. Other forms of the problem did not. There are many variations of this task, involving differing rules and restrictions (Chen, Tian, & Wang, 2007).

Problems such as the Tower of Hanoi challenge problem-solving skills, in part through their demands on working memory. One study finds that there is a relationship between working-memory capacity and the ability to solve analytic problems (Fleck, 2007). Other researchers had experimental participants do what they called the "Tower of London" task, which was very similar to the Tower of Hanoi (Welsh, Satterlee-Cartmell, & Stine, 1999). In this task, the goal was to move a set of colored balls across different-sized pegs in order to match a target configuration. As in the Tower of Hanoi, there were constraints on which balls could be moved at a given time. They also gave participants two tests of working-memory capacity. They found

FIGURE 11.6

There are three discs of unequal sizes, positioned on the leftmost of three pegs so that the largest disc is at the bottom, the middle-sized disc is in the middle, and the smallest disc is on the top. Your task is to transfer all three discs to the rightmost peg, using the middle peg as a stationing area as needed. You may move only one disc at a time, and you may never move a larger disc on top of a smaller disc. From Intelligence Applied: Understanding and Increasing Your Intellectual Skills *by Robert J. Sternberg. Copyright © 1986 by Harcourt Brace & Company. Reproduced by permission of the publisher.*

that the measures of working-memory capacity accounted for between 25% and 36% of the variance in how successful participants were in solving the problem. Interestingly, mental-processing speed, sometimes touted as a key to intelligence (see Chapter 13) showed no correlation with success in solution.

Recall the two-string problem, posed at the outset of this chapter. The solution to the "two-string problem" is shown in Figure 11.7. As this figure shows, the two-string problem can be solved. However, many people find it extremely difficult to arrive at the solution. Many never do, no matter how hard they try. People who find the problem insoluble often err at Step 2 of the problem-solving cycle, after which they never recover. That is, by defining the problem as being one in which they must be able to move toward one string while holding another, they impose on themselves a constraint that makes the problem virtually insoluble. Unfortunately, all of us are subject to misdefining problems from time to time, as the case of the two-string problem shows.

Ill-Structured Problems and the Role of Insight

The two-string problem is an example of an ill-structured problem. In fact, although we occasionally may misrepresent well-structured problems, we are much more likely to have difficulty representing ill-structured problems. Before we explain the nature of ill-structured problems, try to solve a couple more such problems. The following problems illustrate some of the difficulties created by the representation of ill-structured problems (after Sternberg, 1986). Be sure to try all three problems before you read about their solutions.

FIGURE 11.7

Many people assume that they must find a way to move themselves toward each string and then bring the two strings together. They fail to consider the possibility of finding a way to get one of the strings to move toward them, such as by tying something to one of the strings, then swinging the object as a pendulum, and grabbing the object when it swings close to the other string. There is nothing in the problem that suggests that the person must move, rather than that the string may move. Nevertheless, most people presuppose that the constraint exists. By placing an unnecessary and unwarranted constraint on themselves, people make the problem insoluble. From Richard E. Mayer, "The Search for Insight: Grappling with Gestalt Psychology's Unanswered Questions," in The Nature of Insight, *edited by R. J. Sternberg and J. E. Davidson. Copyright © 1995 by MIT Press. Reprinted by permission.*

1. Haughty Harry and several other job seekers were looking for work as carpenters. The site supervisor handed each applicant two sticks (a 1″ × 2″ × 60″ stick and a 1″ × 2″ × 43″ stick) and a 2″ C-clamp. This situation is represented in Figure 11.8. The opening of the clamp is wide enough so that both sticks can be inserted and held together securely when the clamp is tightened. The supervisor ushered the job applicants into a room 12′ 3″ × 13′ 5″, with an 8′ ceiling. Mounted on the ceiling were two 1′ × 1′ beams, dividing the ceiling into thirds lengthwise. She told the applicants that she would hire the first applicant who could build a hat rack capable of supporting her hard hat, using just the two sticks and the C-clamp. She could hire only one person. So she recommended that the applicants not try to help one another. What should Harry do?

FIGURE 11.8

Using just the materials shown here, how can you construct a hat rack in the room shown in this figure? From Richard E. Mayer, "The Search for Insight: Grappling with Gestalt Psychology's Unanswered Questions," in The Nature of Insight, *edited by R. J. Sternberg and J. E. Davidson. Copyright © 1995 MIT Press. Reprinted with permission from MIT Press.*

2. A woman who lived in a small town married 20 different men in that same town. All of them are still living, and she never divorced any of them. Yet she broke no laws. How could she do this?

3. You have loose black and brown socks in a drawer, mixed in a ratio of five black socks for every brown one. How many socks do you have to take out of that drawer to be assured of having a pair of the same color?

Both the two-string problem and each of the three preceding problems are ill-structured problems. There are no clear, readily available paths to solution. By definition, ill-structured problems do not have well-defined problem spaces. Problem solvers have difficulty constructing appropriate mental representations for modeling these problems and their solutions. For such problems, much of the difficulty is in constructing a plan for sequentially following a series of steps that inch ever closer to their solution. In one study, both domain knowledge and justification skills proved to be important for solving both ill- and well-structured problems (Shin, Jonassen, & McGee, 2003). However, additional cognitive and affective factors, including attitudes toward science and regulation of cognition, are also important for the solving of ill-structured problems (Shin, Jonassen, & McGee, 2003). These three particular ill-structured problems are termed *insight problems*. To solve each problem you need to see the problem in a novel way. In particular, you need to see it differently from how you would probably see the problem at first, and differently from how you would probably solve problems in general. That is, you must restructure your representation of the problem to solve it.

Insight is a distinctive and sometimes seemingly sudden understanding of a problem or of a strategy that aids in solving the problem. Often, an insight involves reconceptualizing a problem or a strategy for its solution in a totally new way. Insight often involves detecting and combining relevant old and new information to gain a novel view of the problem or of its solution. Although insights may feel as though they are sudden, they are often the result of much prior thought and hard work. Without this work, the insight would never have occurred. Insight can be involved in solving well-structured problems, but it more often is associated with the rocky and twisting path to solution that characterizes ill-structured problems. For many years, psychologists interested in problem solving have been trying to figure out the true nature of insight.

Recent efforts have been made to map the neural activity associated with insight. Using fMRI methods, researchers found that the right hippocampus is critical in the formation of an insightful solution (Luo & Niki, 2003). (As you may remember from Chapters 2 and 5, the hippocampus is integral to the formation of new memories. Therefore it makes sense that the hippocampus would be involved in the formation of an insightful solution, as this process involves combining of relevant information stored in memory.) Another study demonstrated a spike of activity in the right anterior temporal area immediately before an insight is formed (Jung-Beeman & associates, 2004). This area is active during all types of problem solving, as it involves making connections among distantly related items (Jung-Beeman & associates, 2004). This spike in activity, however, suggests a sudden understanding of relationships within a problem that leads to a solution.

Neural correlates measured even before an individual sees a problem can predict if insight will occur. In one study, during the preparation prior to viewing of a problem, participants who would later generate an insightful solution had substantial activation in the frontal lobes, whereas those who would not generate an insightful solution had comparable activation in the occipital lobes (Kounios & associates, 2006). These findings suggest, first, that certain problem solvers are more likely to use insight than others. Second, they suggest that insight involves some advanced planning that occurs before a problem is even presented.

To understand some of the alternative views on insightful problem solving, you may find it useful knowing the solutions to the preceding insight problems. Consider first the hat-rack problem. Harry was unable to solve the problem before Sally quickly whipped together a hat rack like the one shown in Figure 11.9. To solve the problem, Sally had to redefine her view of the materials in a way that allowed her to conceive of a C-clamp as a hat holder.

The woman who was involved in multiple marriages is a minister. The critical element for solving this problem is to recognize that the word *married* may be used to describe the performance of the marriage ceremony. So the minister married the 20 men but did not herself become wedded to any of them. To solve this problem, you had to redefine your interpretation of the term *married*. Others have suggested yet additional possibilities. For example, perhaps the woman was an actress and only married the men in her role as an actress. Or perhaps the woman's multiple marriages were annulled so she never technically divorced any of the men.

FIGURE 11.9

Were you able to modify your definition of the materials available in a way that helped you solve the problem? From Intelligence Applied: Understanding and Increasing Your Intellectual Skills *by Robert J. Sternberg. Copyright © 1986 by Harcourt Brace & Company. Reproduced by permission of the publisher.*

As for the socks, you need only to take out three socks to be assured of having a pair of the same color. The ratio information is irrelevant. Whether the first two socks you withdraw match in color, the third certainly will match at least one of the first two.

Early Gestaltist Views

Gestalt psychologists emphasized the importance of the whole as more than a collection of parts. In regard to problem solving, Gestalt psychologists held that insight problems require problem solvers to perceive the problem as a whole. Gestalt psychologist Max Wertheimer (1945/1959) wrote about **productive thinking,** which involves insights that go beyond the bounds of existing associations. He distinguished it from *reproductive thinking,* which is based on existing associations involving what is already known. According to Wertheimer, insightful (productive) thinking differs fundamentally from reproductive thinking. In solving the insight problems given in this chapter, you had to break away from your existing associations and see each problem in an entirely new light. Productive thinking also can be applied to well-structured problems.

Wertheimer's colleague Wolfgang Köhler (1927) studied insight in nonhuman primates, particularly a caged chimpanzee named Sultan (Figure 11.10). In Köhler's view, the ape's behavior illustrated insight. To Köhler and other Gestaltists, insight is a special process. It involves thinking that differs from normal, linear information processing.

Gestalt psychologists described examples of insight. They speculated on a few ways in which the special process of insight might occur: It might result from (1)

FIGURE 11.10

In the study depicted here, Gestalt psychologist Wolfgang Köhler placed an ape in an enclosure with a few boxes. At the top of the cage, just out of reach, was a bunch of bananas. After the ape unsuccessfully tried to jump and to stretch to reach the bananas, the ape showed sudden insight: The ape realized that the boxes could be stacked on top of one another to make a structure tall enough to reach the bunch of bananas.

extended unconscious leaps in thinking, (2) greatly accelerated mental processing, or (3) some kind of short-circuiting of normal reasoning processes (Perkins, 1981). Unfortunately, the early Gestaltists did not provide convincing evidence for any of these mechanisms. Nor did they specify exactly what insight is. Therefore, we need to consider alternative views as well.

The Nothing-Special View

According to the nothing-special view, insight is merely an extension of ordinary perceiving, recognizing, learning, and conceiving (Langley & associates, 1987; Perkins, 1981; Weisberg, 1986, 1995). They suggested that Gestalt psychologists failed to pin down insight because there is no special thinking process called "insight." Additionally, sometimes people seem to have solved so-called insight problems without experiencing any sudden mental restructuring of the problem. At other times, people seem to show sudden mental restructuring of so-called routine problems (Weisberg, 1995). Insights are merely significant products of ordinary thinking processes.

The Neo-Gestaltist View

Some researchers have found that insightful problem solving can be distinguished from noninsightful problem solving in two ways (Metcalfe, 1986; Metcalfe & Wiebe, 1987). For one thing, when given routine problems to solve, problem solvers show remarkable accuracy in their ability to predict their own success in solving a problem prior to any attempt to solve it. In contrast, when given insight problems, problem solvers show poor ability to predict their own success prior to trying to solve the problems. Not only were successful problem solvers pessimistic about their ability to solve insight problems, but unsuccessful problem solvers were often optimistic about their ability to solve them.

In addition, the investigators used a clever methodology to observe the problem-solving process while participants were solving routine versus insight problems. At 15-second intervals, participants paused briefly to rate how close ("warm") versus far ("cold") they felt they were to reaching a solution. Consider first what happened for routine problems, such as algebra, Tower of Hanoi, and deductive reasoning problems. Participants showed incremental increases in their feelings of warmth as they drew closer to reaching a correct solution. For insight problems, however, participants showed no such incremental increases. Figure 11.11 shows a comparison of participants' reported feelings of warmth for solving algebra problems versus insight problems. In solving insight problems, participants showed no increasing feelings of warmth until moments before abruptly realizing the solution and correctly solving the problem. Metcalfe's findings certainly seem to support the Gestaltist view that there is something special about insightful problem solving, as distinct from noninsightful, routine problem solving. The specific nature and underlying mechanisms of insightful problem solving have yet to be addressed by this research, however.

The Three-Process View

Yet another view of insight has focused specifically on the possible mechanisms for insightful problem solving (Davidson, 1995, 2003; Davidson & Sternberg, 1984). According to this view, insights are of three kinds. The three kinds correspond to three different processes: selective encoding, selective comparison, and selective combination. These processes may be used either with insight or with little insight.

Selective-encoding insights involve distinguishing relevant from irrelevant information. Recall from earlier chapters that encoding involves representing information in memory. All of us have available much more information than we possibly can handle. Thus, each of us must select the information that is important for our purposes. At the same time, we must filter out the unimportant or irrelevant information. Selective encoding is the process by which this filtering is done. For example, when you are taking notes during a lecture, you must selectively encode which points are crucial. You need to identify which points are supportive and explanatory and which are not necessary.

Selective-comparison insights involve novel perceptions of how new information relates to old information. The creative use of analogies is a form of selective comparison. When solving important problems, we almost always need to call on our existing knowledge. We then need to compare that information with our new knowledge of the current problem. Insights of selective comparison are the basis for this relating. For example, suppose that you must master a whole list of new terms for your cognitive psychology class. For some of the terms, you may be able to compare the new terms with synonymous words that you already know. For others, you may be able to expand on and elaborate words you already know to define the new terms.

Selective-combination insights involve taking selectively encoded and compared snippets of relevant information and combining that information in a novel, productive way. Often, for us just to identify analytically the important information for solving a problem is not enough. We also must figure out how to synthesize the

FIGURE 11.11

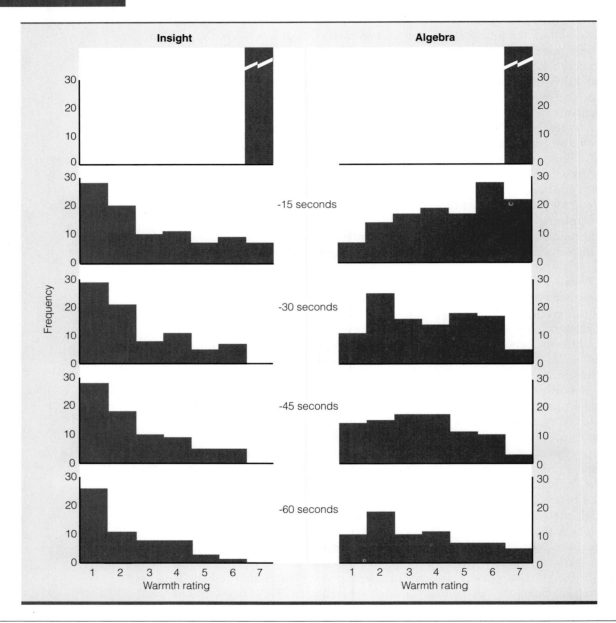

When Janet Metcalfe presented participants with routine problems and insight problems, they showed clear differences in their feelings of warmth as they approached a solution to the problems. These frequency histograms (bar graphs in which the area of each bar indicates the frequency for the given interval of time) show comparative feelings of warmth during the four 15-second intervals prior to solving the problems. When solving insight problems, participants showed no incremental increases in feelings of warmth, whereas when solving routine problems, participants showed distinct incremental increases in feelings of warmth. Routine problems included algebra problems such as "$(3x^2 + 2x + 10)(3x) = .$" Insight problems included problems such as "A prisoner was attempting escape from a tower. He found in his cell a rope which was half long enough to permit him to reach the ground safely. He divided the rope in half and tied the two parts together and escaped. How could he have done this?" (From Metcalfe & Wiebe, 1987, pp. 242, 245.)

information. For example, to solve either the hat-rack problem or the two-string problem, you had to find a way to put together the available materials in a novel way. To write a term paper, you must synthesize your research notes in a way that addresses the central question in your paper.

Additional Insights into Insight

There is yet another view of routine versus insightful problem solving (Smith, 1995a). One can distinguish between the insight experience and insight. An insight experience is a special process involving an abrupt mental restructuring. Insight is an understanding that may involve either the special insight experience or normal cognitive processes that occur incrementally, rather than suddenly. Thus, routine problems may demand insight, but they may not require the insight experience. Insight problems, however, require the insight experience. According to Smith, therefore, insights need not be sudden "ah-ha" experiences. They may and often do occur gradually and incrementally over time.

When an insightful solution is needed but not forthcoming, sleep may help produce a solution. In both mathematical problem solving and solution of a task that requires understanding underlying rules, sleep has been shown to increase the likelihood that an insight will be produced (Stickgold & Walker, 2004; Wagner & associates, 2004).

Unfortunately, insights—like many other aspects of human thinking—can be both startlingly brilliant and dead wrong. How do we fall into mental traps that lead us down false paths as we try to reach solutions?

Obstacles and Aids to Problem Solving

Several factors can hinder problem solving.

Mental Sets, Entrenchment, and Fixation

One factor that can hinder problem solving is **mental set**—a frame of mind involving an existing model for representing a problem, a problem context, or a procedure for problem solving. Another term for mental set is *entrenchment*. When problem solvers have an entrenched mental set, they fixate on a strategy that normally works well in solving many problems but that does not work well in solving this particular problem. For example, in the two-string problem, you may fixate on strategies that involve moving yourself toward the string, rather than moving the string toward you. In the oft-marrying minister problem, you may fixate on the notion that to marry someone is to become wedded to the person.

Mental sets also can influence the solution of rather routine problems. For example, consider "water-jar" problems (Luchins, 1942). In water-jar problems, participants are asked how to measure out a certain amount of water using three different jars. Each jar holds a different amount of water. Table 11.2 shows the problems used by Luchins.

If you are like many people solving these problems, you will have found a formula that works for all the remaining problems. You fill up Jar B. Then you pour out of it

TABLE 11.2	Luchins's Water-Jar Problems

How do you measure out the right amount of water using Jars A, B, and C? You need to use up to three jars to obtain the required amounts of water (measured in numbers of cups) in the last column. Columns A, B, and C show the capacity of each jar. The first problem, for example, requires you to get 20 cups of water from just two of the jars, a 29-cup one (Jar A) and a 3-cup one (Jar B). Easy: Just fill Jar A, and then empty out 9 cups from this jar by taking out 3 cups three times, using Jar B. Problem 2 isn't too hard, either. Fill Jar B with 127 cups, then empty out 21 cups using Jar A, and then empty out 6 cups, using Jar C twice. Now try the rest of the problems yourself. (After Luchins, 1942.)

	JARS AVAILABLE FOR USE			
PROBLEM NUMBER	A	B	C	REQUIRED AMOUNT (CUPS)
1	29	3	0	20
2	21	127	3	100
3	14	163	25	99
4	18	43	10	5
5	9	42	6	21
6	20	59	4	31
7	23	49	3	20
8	15	39	3	18
9	28	76	3	25
10	18	48	4	22
11	14	36	8	6

Abraham S. Luchins (1942), "Mechanization in Problem Solving: The Effect of Einstellung," *Psychological Monographs*, Vol. 54, No. 6 (Whole Number 248). Copyright © 1942 by Dr. Abraham S. Luchins. Reprinted by permission.

the amount of water you can put into Jar A. Then you twice pour out of it the amount of water you can put into Jar C. The formula, therefore, is $B - A - 2C$. However, Problems 7 through 11 can be solved in a much simpler way. One need use just two of the jars. For example, Problem 7 can be solved by $A - C$. Problem 8 can be solved by $A + C$, and so on. People who are given Problems 1 through 6 to solve generally continue to use the $B - A - 2C$ formula in solving Problems 7 through 11. Consider, in Luchins's original experiment, those participants who solved the first set of problems. Between 64% and 83% of them went on to solve the last set of problems by using the less simple strategy. What happened to the control participants, who were not given the first set of problems? Only 1% to 5% failed to apply the simpler solutions to the last set of problems. They had no established mental set that interfered with their seeing things in a new and simpler way.

Another type of mental set involves fixation on a particular use (function) for an object. Specifically, **functional fixedness** is the inability to realize that something known to have a particular use may also be used for performing other functions (German & Barrett, 2005). Functional fixedness prevents us from solving new problems by using old tools in novel ways. Becoming free of functional fixedness is what first allowed people to use a reshaped coat hanger to get into a locked car. It is also what first allowed thieves to pick simple spring door locks with a credit card. Another type of mental set is considered an aspect of social cognition. **Stereotypes** are beliefs that members of a social group tend more or less uniformly to have particular types of characteristics. We seem to learn many stereotypes during childhood. For example, cross-cultural studies of children show their increasing knowledge about—and use of—gender stereotypes across the childhood years (Neto, Williams, & Widner, 1991; Seguino, 2007). Stereotype awareness, for a variety of groups, develops in most children between the ages of 6 and 10 (McKown & Weinstein, 2003). Stereotypes often arise in the same way that other kinds of mental sets develop. We observe a particular instance or set of instances of some pattern. We then may overgeneralize from those limited observations. We may assume that all future instances similarly will demonstrate that pattern. Of course, when the stereotypes are used to target particular scapegoats for societal mistreatment, grave social consequences result for the targets of stereotypes. The targets are not the only ones to suffer from stereotypes, however. Like other kinds of mental sets, stereotypes hinder the problem-solving abilities of the individuals who used them. These people limit their thinking by using set stereotypes.

Negative and Positive Transfer

Often, people have particular mental sets that prompt them to fixate on one aspect of a problem or one strategy for problem solving to the exclusion of other possible relevant ones. They are carrying knowledge and strategies for solving one kind of problem to a different kind of problem. **Transfer** is any carryover of knowledge or skills from one problem situation to another (Detterman & Sternberg, 1993; Gentile, 2000). Transfer can be either negative or positive. **Negative transfer** occurs when solving an earlier problem makes it harder to solve a later one. Sometimes an early problem gets an individual on a wrong track. For example, police may have difficulty solving a political crime because such a crime differs so much from the kinds of crime that they typically deal with. Or when presented with a new tool, a person may operate it in a way similar to the way in which he or she operated a tool with which he or she was already familiar (Besnard & Cacitti, 2005). **Positive transfer** occurs when the solution of an earlier problem makes it easier to solve a new problem. That is, sometimes the transfer of a mental set can be an aid to problem solving. For instance, one may transfer early math skills, such as addition, to advanced math problems of the kinds found in algebra or physics (Bassok & Holyoak, 1989; Chen & Daehler, 1989).

From a broad perspective, positive transfer may be considered to involve the transfer of factual knowledge or skills from one setting to another. For example, you may apply your general knowledge about psychology and your study skills acquired during a lifetime of studying for tests to the problem of studying for an examination in cognitive psychology. More narrowly, however, during positive transfer, you effectively apply a strategy or a type of solution that worked well for one particular problem or set of problems when you are trying to solve an analogous problem. How do people realize that particular problems are analogous and can be solved through positive transfer of strategies or even of solutions?

Transfer of Analogies

Researchers designed some elegant studies of positive transfer involving analogies (Gick & Holyoak, 1980, 1983). To appreciate their results, you need to become familiar with a problem first used by Karl Duncker (1945), often called the "radiation problem." It is described in the "Investigating Cognitive Psychology" box.

IN THE LAB OF K. ANDERS ERICSSON

For as long as I can remember I have been fascinated by individual differences in thinking and problem solving. In particular I wondered if it would be possible for regular persons, like myself, to learn from experts and exceptional thinkers, such as scientists and chess masters. Would it be possible to find out how they attained their performance so I could improve my abilities by adopting their methods of study and practice?

Most of the descriptions of the development of experts' and other types of exceptional individuals' thinking come from informal interviews with these experts and contain subjective descriptions of events that happened many years ago. Scientists, however, have to be skeptical of these types of introspective descriptions that cannot be verified or even reproduced with scientific methods.

In my research lab we have invited expert performers, such as musicians, chess players, and athletes, to reproduce their superior performance under controlled conditions, so we can compare their performance to those of less skilled individuals on the same tasks (Ericsson & Ward, 2007; Ericsson & Williams, 2007). We instruct the experts to give verbal expression to their thoughts as they perform—that is, "think aloud"—or report their thoughts immediately after their task performance is completed. (See Ericsson, 2003b, 2006a, for a description of the fundamental differences between "thinking aloud" and introspection.) Using these types of verbal reports, along with specially designed experiments, we and other colleagues have been able to uncover the complex skills and thought processes that mediate the superior performance in people with exceptional memory (Ericsson, 2003a). We have been particularly interested in how experts, such as chess masters, musicians, athletes, and mental calculators, have acquired memory skills to allow them to plan, monitor, and evaluate complex sequences of actions (Ericsson, 2006a).

In my laboratory we interview the experts about their current practice methods and how their performance in the domain developed; often their reported information can be verified by their parents and teachers or by public records from competitions. Perhaps the most general, and intriguing, finding is that experts' superior performance is closely linked to their more extended and, particularly, goal-directed practice activities. Future expert performers primarily differ from their peers in their engagement in special practice activities that help them to increase beyond their current performance by repetition and gradual refinement through problem solving (deliberate practice) (Ericsson, 2006b). In domains such as music, sports and chess, the best performers start early and have spent up to 4 hours each day for many years engaged in deliberate practice—this amounts to many thousands of hours more than their less accomplished peers. Detailed analysis of the expert performers' deliberate practice in sports and music has also uncovered types of intense training activities that are capable of modifying physical characteristics of the body, such as increasing the degree of myelinization of nerve circuits in the brain, increasing number of capillaries supplying blood to critical muscles, and enlarging the chambers of the heart (Ericsson, 2006b). Research on expert performance has produced new insights into the cognitive structures and physiological adaptations that can be attained after thousands of hours of deliberate efforts to improve. The scientific study of the lives and practice methods of expert performers appears to be a very promising area in increasing our knowledge about what is humanly possible when individuals are motivated to reach their highest levels of achievement.

References

Ericsson, K. A. (2003a). Exceptional memorizers: Made, not born. *Trends in Cognitive Sciences, 7,* 233–235.

Ericsson, K. A. (2003b). Valid and non-reactive verbalization of thoughts during performance of tasks: Toward a solution to the central problems

IN THE LAB OF K. ANDERS ERICSSON—cont'd

of introspection as a source of scientific data. *Journal of Consciousness Studies, 10*(9–10), 1–18.

Ericsson, K. A. (2006a). Protocol analysis and expert thought: Concurrent verbalizations of thinking during experts' performance on representative task. In K. A. Ericsson, N. Charness, P. Feltovich, & R. R. Hoffman (Eds.), *Cambridge handbook of expertise and expert performance* (pp. 223–242). Cambridge, UK: Cambridge University Press.

Ericsson, K. A. (2006b). The influence of experience and deliberate practice on the development of superior expert performance. In K. A. Ericsson, N. Charness, P. Feltovich, & R. R. Hoffman

(Eds.), *Cambridge handbook of expertise and expert performance* (pp. 685–706). Cambridge, UK: Cambridge University Press.

Ericsson, K. A., & Ward, P. (2007). Capturing the naturally occurring superior performance of experts in the laboratory: Toward a science of expert and exceptional performance. *Current Directions in Psychological Science, 16*(6), 346–350.

Ericsson, K. A., & Williams, A. M. (2007). Capturing naturally occurring superior performance in the laboratory: Translational research on expert performance. *Journal of Experimental Psychology: Applied, 13*(3), 115–123.

Imagine that you are a doctor treating a patient with a malignant stomach tumor. You cannot operate on the patient because of the severity of the cancer. But unless you destroy the tumor somehow, the patient will die. You could use high-intensity X-rays to destroy the tumor. Unfortunately, the intensity of X-rays needed to destroy the tumor also will destroy healthy tissue through which the rays must pass. X-rays of lesser intensity will spare the healthy tissue, but they will be insufficiently powerful to destroy the tumor. Your problem is to figure out a procedure that will destroy the tumor without also destroying the healthy tissue surrounding the tumor.

INVESTIGATING COGNITIVE PSYCHOLOGY

Duncker had in mind a particular insightful solution as the optimal one for this problem. Figure 11.12 shows the solution pictorially.

Prior to presenting Duncker's radiation problem, participants received another, easier problem. This particular problem was called the "military problem" (Holyoak, 1984, p. 205). It is described in the "Investigating Cognitive Psychology" box.

A general wishes to capture a fortress located in the center of a country. There are many roads radiating outward from the fortress. All have been mined. Although small groups of men can pass over the roads safely, any large force will detonate the mines. A full-scale direct attack is therefore impossible. What should the general do?

INVESTIGATING COGNITIVE PSYCHOLOGY

Table 11.3 shows the correspondence between the radiation and military problems. It turns out to be quite close, although not perfect. The question is whether producing a group-convergence solution to the military problem helped participants in solving the radiation problem. Consider participants who received the military problem with the convergence solution and then were given a hint to apply it in some way to the radiation problem. About 75% of the participants reached the correct

FIGURE 11.12

The solution to the X-ray problem involves dispersion. The idea is to direct weak X-radiation toward the tumor from a number of different points outside the body. No single set of rays would be strong enough to destroy either the healthy tissue or the tumor. However, the rays would be aimed so that they all converged at one spot within the body—the spot that houses the tumor. This solution actually is used today in some X-ray treatments, except that a rotating source of X-rays is used for dispersing rays. From In Search of the Human Mind *by Robert J. Sternberg. Copyright © 1995 by Harcourt Brace & Company. Reproduced by permission of the publisher.*

solution to the radiation problem. This figure compared with less than 10% of the participants who did not receive the military story first but instead received no prior story or only an irrelevant one.

In another experiment, participants were not given the convergence solution to the military problem. They had to figure it out for themselves. About 50% of the participants generated the convergence solution to the military problem. Of these, 41% went on to generate a parallel solution to the radiation problem. That is, positive transfer was *weaker* when participants produced the original solution themselves than when the solution to the first problem was given to them (41%, as compared with 75%).

The investigators found that the usefulness of the military problem as an analogue to the radiation problem depended on the induced mental set with which the problem solver approached the problems. Consider what happened when participants were asked to memorize the military story under the guise that it was a story-recall experiment and then were given the radiation problem to solve. Only 30% of participants produced the convergence solution to the radiation problem. The investiga-

TABLE 11.3	Correspondence between the Radiation and the Military Problems

What are the commonalities between the two problems, and what is an elemental strategy that can be derived by comparing the two problems? (After Gick & Holyoak, 1983.)

Military Problem

Initial State Goal: Use army to capture fortress
   Resources: Sufficiently large army
   Constraint: Unable to send entire army along one road
Solution Plan: Send small groups along multiple roads simultaneously
Outcome: Fortress captured by army

Radiation Problem

Initial State Goal: Use rays to destroy tumor
   Resources: Sufficiently powerful rays
   Constraint: Unable to administer high-intensity rays from one direction only
Solution Plan: Administer low-intensity rays from multiple directions simultaneously
Outcome: Tumor destroyed by rays

Convergence Schema

Initial State Goal: Use force to overcome a central target
   Resources: Sufficiently great force
   Constraint: Unable to apply full force along one path alone
Solution Plan: Apply weak forces along multiple paths simultaneously
Outcome: Central target overcome by force

M. L. Gick and K. J. Holyoak (1983), "Schema Induction and Analogical Transfer," *Cognitive Psychology*, Vol. 15, p. 1–38. Reprinted by permission of Elsevier.

PRACTICAL APPLICATIONS OF COGNITIVE PSYCHOLOGY

These suggestions can be used directly to help you solve everyday problems. If you have an assignment due at some later date, take the time immediately on being given the assignment to plan a course of action. For example, in writing a term paper, scan the outlines of future readings in the course. Find the general topic that interests you. Then get some idea of how much information is available on your topic. Do not get too involved in the details. This procedure can help you narrow down the focus. Choosing a topic you are relatively unfamiliar with is generally a good option for shorter paper assignments. In this way, you will learn something new. Moreover, you will be more likely to have entrenched ideas or fixations concerning topics of higher familiarity. However, try positively to transfer major themes across different topics. For example, the nature-nurture issue often plays out in diverse topics in psychology. Finally, put the topic to the side for a while. Allow the course material to integrate itself with your existing knowledge and with your developing topic ideas. Then, about 2 to 3 weeks before the paper is due, start working on a draft that you can set aside again for a few days before final polishing. Overall, the total amount of distributed time involved in completing an assignment this way will be only slightly more than if you cram the work into a few days before the paper is due, but the quality of the paper is almost sure to be better.

tors also found that positive transfer improved if two, rather than just one, analogous problems were given in advance of the radiation problem. Researchers have expanded these findings to encompass problems other than the radiation problem. They found that when the domains or the contexts for the two problems were more similar, participants were more likely to see and apply the analogy (see Holyoak, 1990).

Similar patterns of data were found with various types of problems involving electricity (Gentner & Gentner, 1983). Related results also have emerged in studies of mathematical insight (Davidson & Sternberg, 1984; Novick & Holyoak, 1991). Perhaps the most crucial aspect of these studies is that people have trouble noticing the analogy unless they explicitly are told to look for it. Consider studies involving physics problems. Positive transfer from solved examples to unsolved problems was more likely among students who specifically tried to understand *why* particular examples were solved as they were, as compared with students who sought only to understand *how* particular problems were solved as they were (Chi & associates, 1989). Based on these findings, we generally need to be looking for analogies to find them. We often will not find them unless we explicitly seek them.

People sometimes do not recognize the surface similarities of problems (Bassok, 2003). Other times they are fooled by surface similarities into believing two different kinds of problems are the same (Bassok, Wu, & Olseth, 1995; Gentner, 2000; Gentner & Markman, 1997). Sometimes even experienced problem solvers are led astray. They believe that similar surface structures indicate comparable deep structures. For example, problem solvers may use the verbal content rather than the mathematical operations required in a mathematical problem to classify the problem as being of a certain kind (Blessing & Ross, 1996). So, in a way, it can make sense to err on the side of caution. Often, it is best not to immediately assume that two problems that look like they are essentially the same necessarily are (Ben-Zeev, 1996).

Intentional Transfer: Searching for Analogies

In looking for analogies, we need to be careful not to be misled by associations between two things that are analogically irrelevant. For example, one study investigated children's solutions to verbal analogies of the form "A is to B as C is to X" (Sternberg & Nigro, 1980). The children are given multiple-choice options for X. Children often will choose an answer that is associatively close but analogically incorrect. (In representing analogies, a single colon [:] indicates the "is to" expression and a double colon [::] is used to indicate the "as" expression.) For example, in the analogy LAWYER : CLIENT :: DOCTOR : (a. NURSE, b. PATIENT, c. MEDICINE, d. MD), children might choose option a because NURSE is more strongly associated with DOCTOR than is the correct answer, PATIENT.

As children age, their ability to form and use analogies improves. In one study, children were presented a picture that illustrated the solution to a problem. They then attempted to solve an analogous problem (Chen, 2003). As you might expect, the younger children had more difficulty with this task than did the older children (Chen, 2003). However, the older children who were relatively successful in solving these analogous problems were only 5 years old (Chen, 2003)! These findings illustrate that the ability to form and use analogies, at least at a rudimentary level, develops quite early.

Analogies between problems involve mappings of relationships between problems (Gentner, 1983, 2000). The actual content attributes of the problems are irrelevant. In other words, what matters in analogies is not the similarity of the content but how closely their structural systems of relationships match. Because we are accustomed to considering the importance of the content, we find it difficult to push the content to the background. It also is difficult to bring form (structural relationships) to the foreground. For example, the differing content makes the analogy between the military problem and the radiation problem hard to recognize and impedes positive transfer from one problem to the other.

The opposite phenomenon is **transparency,** in which people see analogies where they do not exist because of similarity of content. In making analogies, we need to be sure we are focusing on the relationships between the two terms being compared, not just their surface content attributes. For example, in studying for final exams in two psychology courses, you may need different strategies when studying for a closed-book essay exam than for an open-book, multiple-choice exam. Transparency of content may lead to negative transfer between nonisomorphic problems if care is not taken to avoid such transfer.

Incubation

For solving many problems, the chief obstacle is not the need to find a suitable strategy for positive transfer. Rather, it is to avoid obstacles resulting from negative transfer. **Incubation**—putting the problem aside for a while without consciously thinking about it—offers one way in which to minimize negative transfer. It involves taking a pause from the stages of problem solving. For example, suppose you find that you are unable to solve a problem. None of the strategies you can think of seem to work. Try setting the problem aside for a while to let it incubate. During incubation, you must not consciously think about the problem. You do, however, allow for the possibility that the problem will be processed subconsciously. Some investigators of problem solving have even asserted that incubation is an essential stage of the problem-solving process (e.g., Cattell, 1971; von Helmholtz, 1896). Others have failed to find experimental support for the phenomenon of incubation (e.g., Baron, 1988). Nevertheless, extensive anecdotal support for it has been offered (e.g., Poincaré, 1913). Still other investigators suggest that incubation may be particularly helpful in solving insight problems (e.g., Smith, 1995a). As discussed previously, when a participant sleeps after becoming "stuck" on an insight problem, he or she is more likely to find an insightful solution than is someone who does not sleep (Stickgold & Walker, 2004; Wagner & associates, 2004).

Several possible mechanisms for the beneficial effects of incubation have been proposed, such as the following:

1. When we no longer keep something in active memory, we let go of some of the unimportant details. We keep only the more meaningful aspects in memory. From these meaningful aspects, we then are free to reconstruct them anew. Fewer of the limitations of the earlier mental set remain (Anderson, 1975).

2. As time passes, more recent memories become integrated with existing memories (Anderson, 1985). During this reintegration, some associations of the mental set may weaken.

3. As time passes, new stimuli—both internal and external—may activate new perspectives on the problem. These stimuli may weaken the effects of the mental set (Bastik, 1982). In one experiment, participants were asked to solve a difficult problem; while the problem was still unsolved, participants were asked to complete a distractor task (Christensen & Schunn, 2005). For some participants, during this task an analogous cue relating to the unsolved problem was presented (Christensen & Schunn, 2005). Participants were later given a chance to solve the original problem (Christensen & Schunn, 2005). Even without being informed of this relationship, participants were able to use this information to answer the problem more efficiently (Christensen & Schunn, 2005).

4. An internal or external stimulus may lead the problem solver to see an analogy between the current problem and another problem. As a result, the problem solver can either readily find a comparable solution or perhaps even simply apply a known solution (Langley & Jones, 1988; Seifert & associates, 1995).

5. Consider what happens when problem solvers are in a low state of cortical arousal, such as in the shower, in bed, or taking a walk. Increases in attention span—and perhaps working-memory capacity—may allow increasingly remote cues to be perceived and held in active memory simultaneously. The person, while relaxed, may toy with cues that otherwise might be perceived as irrelevant or distracting when in a high state of cortical arousal. For example, the cues might be ignored while trying actively to solve the problem (Luria, 1973, 1984). Some of the preceding mechanisms also may interact. Such interaction may be through the process of spreading activation or through some sort of priming effect.

The benefits of incubation can be enhanced in two ways (Kaplan & Davidson, 1989). First, invest enough time in the problem initially. Explore all aspects of the problem. Investigate several possible avenues of solving it and form a plan for approaching the problem. Second, allow sufficient time for incubation to permit your old associations resulting from negative transfer to weaken somewhat. A drawback of incubation is that it takes time. If you have a deadline for problem solution, you must begin solving the problem early enough to meet the deadline. This includes the time you need for incubation.

Neuropsychology of Planning in Problem Solving

One way to invest enough initial time in a problem is through the formation of a plan of action for the problem. As previously discussed, planning saves time and improves performance. In one study employing variants of the Tower of Hanoi, as participants gained facility with this type of problem, they showed increased planning times (Gunzelmann & Anderson, 2003). This observation was made in the context of a study of improved behavioral problem solving as evidenced by a decrease in the total number of moves (Gunzelmann & Anderson, 2003). These results highlight the importance of planning for efficient problem solving.

Recall from Chapter 2 that the frontal lobes are involved in high-level cognitive processes. It is therefore not surprising that the frontal lobes and in particular the prefrontal cortex are essential for planning for complex problem-solving tasks (Unterrainer & Owen, 2006). A number of studies using a variety of neuropsychological methods, including functional magnetic resonance imaging (fMRI) and positron emission tomography (PET), have highlighted activation in this region of the brain during problem solving (Unterrainer & Owen, 2006). Additionally, both the left and right prefrontal areas are active during the planning stage of complex problem solving (Newman & associates, 2003). During problem solving, when a participant gives an incorrect response, he or she reveals greater bilateral prefrontal activation than is associated with a correct response (Unterrainer & associates, 2004). This finding would suggest that if the initial plan fails, problem solvers must devise a new plan, thereby activating the prefrontal cortex.

Further evidence for the importance of the prefrontal regions in problem solving can be seen in cases of traumatic brain injury. Both problem solving and planning ability decline following traumatic brain injury (Catroppa & Anderson, 2006). In fact, when examining the problem-solving ability of patients with traumatic brain injury, those patients who performed best were ones with limited damage to the left prefrontal regions (Cazalis & associates, 2006).

In the Tower of London task (which is essentially the Tower of Hanoi task), other areas, including the premotor cortex and the parietal regions, were also activated (Newman & associates, 2003; Unterrainer & Owen, 2006). This additional activation is likely the result of the need for attention and planning for movement. Other researchers have noted that, in addition to the prefrontal regions, the same areas active during use of visual spatial working memory are also active during solution of the Tower of London (Baker & associates, 1996).

Expertise: Knowledge and Problem Solving

Even people who do not have expertise in cognitive psychology recognize that knowledge, particularly expert knowledge, greatly enhances problem solving. Expertise is superior skills or achievement reflecting a well-developed and well-organized knowledge base. What interests cognitive psychologists is the reason that expertise enhances problem solving. Why can experts solve problems in their field more successfully than can novices? Do experts know more problem-solving algorithms, heuristics, and other strategies? Do experts know better strategies? Or do they just use these strategies more often? What do experts know that makes the problem-solving process more effective for them than for novices in a field? Is it all talent or just acquired skill?

Organization of Knowledge

A team of researchers set out to discover what experts know and do (Chase & Simon, 1973). They sought to determine what distinguishes expert from novice chess players. In one of their studies, they had expert and novice players briefly view a display of a chessboard with the chess pieces on it, and the players then had to recall the positions of the chess pieces on the board. In general, the experts performed quite a bit better than the novices. But they performed better only if the positions of the chess pieces on the board made sense in terms of an actual game of chess (see also De Groot, 1965; Vicente & De Groot, 1990). If the pieces were distributed around the board randomly, experts recalled the positions of the pieces no better than did the novices (Figure 11.13).

In a related study, beer experts and beer novices experienced tasting a series of beers (Valentin & associates, 2007). Both groups could sort the beers equally well. However, the beer experts performed better on subsequent recognition tasks (Valentin & associates, 2007). These findings suggest that there was no difference in perceptual abilities between the experts and the novices, but there was a difference in memory between these two groups (Valentin & associates, 2007). The researchers concluded that the beer experts had a superior framework for encoding and retrieving the new beer information (Valentin & associates, 2007).

Knowledge can interact with understanding in problem solving (Whitten & Graesser, 2003). Consider a study investigating how knowledge interacts with coherence of a text. Investigators presented children with biology texts (McNamara & associates, 1996). Half the children in the study had high levels of domain knowledge about biology and half had low levels. In addition, half the texts were highly coherent, meaning that they made clear how the various concepts in the text related to each other. The other half of the texts were of low coherence, meaning that they were more difficult to read because the ideas did not flow smoothly. Readers then had to do a variety of problem-solving tasks based on what they had read. As the authors predicted, participants with low domain knowledge performed better when the texts were highly coherent. This finding suggests that, in general, learners do better when they are presented new material in a coherent way. Surprisingly, however, the high-knowledge group performed better when the texts were of low rather than high coherence. The authors of the study suggested that high-knowledge readers may have been, essentially, on automatic pilot when reading the high-coherence texts, not paying much attention because they thought they knew what was in the texts. The low-coherence texts forced them to pay attention. These results point out the importance of attentional processes when people solve problems. This is particularly relevant in domains in which they are expert and in which they therefore may not feel they have to pay attention.

Elaboration of Knowledge

The work with arrays of chess pieces suggested that what differentiated the experts from the novices was in the amount, organization, and use of knowledge. In the chess study there were two tasks. One involved a random array of pieces and the other a meaningful arrangement of pieces. Both chess tasks required the experts to use heuristics for storing and retrieving information about the positions of the pieces on the chess-board. The key difference was that chess experts had stored and organized in memory tens of thousands of particular board positions. When they saw sensible board positions, they could use the knowledge they had in memory to help them. They were able to remember the various board positions as integrated, organized chunks of information. As you may recall from Chapter 5, the ability to chunk infor-

FIGURE 11.13

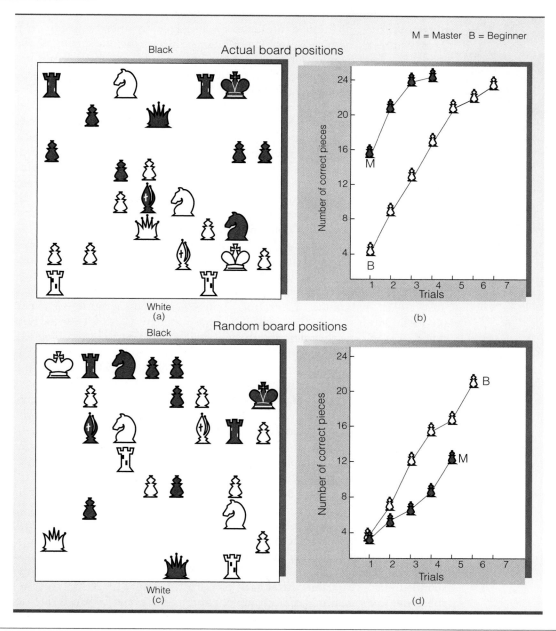

When experts and novices were asked to recall realistic patterns of chess pieces, as in panel a, experts demonstrated much better performance, as shown in panel b. However, when experts and novices were asked to recall random arrangements of chess pieces, as shown in panel c, experts performed no better than novices, as shown in panel d. From William G. Chase and Herbert A. Simon (1973), "The Mind's Eye in Chess," in Visual Information Processing, *edited by William G. Chase. Reprinted by permission of Elsevier.*

Michelene Chi is a professor of psychology at the University of Pittsburgh. She is most well known for showing that the organization of experts' knowledge in their domain of expertise allows them to represent this knowledge more profoundly than can novices. She also has shown that the initial organization of a learner's knowledge can be fundamentally flawed so that it prevents the learner from understanding the true meaning of a concept.

mation into meaningful units allows for superior memory and capacity. For random scatterings of pieces on the board, however, the knowledge of the experts was of no use. The experts had no advantage over the novices. Like the novices, they had to try to memorize the distinctive interrelations among many discrete pieces and positions. This requires the storage of many more items, thus taxing one's memory abilities.

Other work demonstrates that retrieval processes involving recognition of board arrangements are instrumental in grand master–level chess players' success when compared with novices' play (Gobet & Simon, 1996a, 1996b, 1996c). Even when grand masters are time-constrained so that look-ahead processes are curtailed, their constrained performance does not differ substantially from their unconstrained playing. Thus, an organized knowledge system is relatively more important to experts' performance in chess than even the processes involved in predicting future moves.

Other studies have examined experts in different domains. Examples of such domains are the game of Go (Reitman, 1976), radiology (Lesgold & associates, 1988), and physics (Larkin & associates, 1980). These studies revealed the same thing again and again. What differentiated experts from novices were their schemas for solving problems within their own domains of expertise (Glaser & Chi, 1988). The schemas of experts involve large, highly interconnected units of knowledge. They are organized according to underlying structural similarities among knowledge units. In contrast, the schemas of novices involve relatively small and disconnected units of knowledge. They are organized according to superficial similarities (Bryson & associates, 1991). This same observation applies to various activities of experts versus novices. One is in how they classify various problems (Chi, Glaser, & Rees, 1982). Another is in how they describe the essential nature of various problems (Larkin & associates, 1980). And a third is in how they determine and describe a solution method for various problems (Chi, Glaser, & Rees, 1982). One study exploring problem-solving strategies in both expert and novice mathematicians noted a difference in the use of visual depictions (Stylianou & Silver, 2004). The researchers observed that novice problem solvers use a visual representation to solve problems that have an obvious spatial component, such as geometry problems (Stylianou & Silver, 2004). However, expert problem solvers used visual representations to solve a wide range of mathematical problems (Stylianou & Silver, 2004), whether or not they had an obvious spatial component. The ability to apply a visual representation to a variety of problems allows greater flexibility and an increased likelihood that a solution will be found.

An interesting study looked at the role of knowledge in understanding and interpreting a news broadcast regarding a baseball game (Hambrick & Engle, 2002). A total of 181 adults having a wide range of knowledge about baseball listened to radio broadcasts recorded by a professional baseball announcer. The announcements sounded like a real game. After each broadcast, memory for changes in the status of the game were measured. For example, participants would be asked questions about which bases were occupied after each player's turn at bat and about the numbers of outs and of runs scored during the inning. Baseball knowledge accounted for more than half the reliable variation in participants' performance. Working memory capacity also mattered, but not nearly so much as knowledge. Thus, people can remember things better and solve problems with what they remember better if they have a solid knowledge base with which to work.

Setting Up the Problem

Another difference between experts and novices can be observed by asking problem solvers to report aloud what they are thinking as they are attempting to solve various problems (Bryson & associates, 1991; De Groot, 1965; Lesgold, 1988). Observers can compare various aspects of problem solving. One includes the statements made by problem solvers, so-called *verbal protocols*. An interesting effect of verbal protocols is that they can lead to increased problem-solving ability. In one study, when participants spoke aloud or wrote about their problem-solving strategy in a way that centered on the objects of the problem, an improvement in quality of solutions was observed (Steif & associates, 2006). In another study, problem-solving ability was enhanced when participants wrote a description of their problem-solving strategy as compared with when they spoke about their strategy (Pugalee, 2004). Thus, it seems that, for novice problem solvers, communicating their problem-solving strategy improves performance.

Another difference between expert and novice problem solvers is the time spent on various aspects of problems, and the relationship between problem-solving strategies and the solutions reached. Experts appear to spend proportionately more time determining how to represent a problem than do novices (Lesgold, 1988; Lesgold & associates, 1988), but they spend much less time than do novices actually implementing the strategy for solution.

The differences between experts and novices in their expenditure of time can be viewed in terms of the focus and direction of their problem solving. Experts seem to spend relatively more time than do novices figuring out how to match the given information in the problem with their existing schemas. In other words, they try to compare what they know about the problem with how the information they have matches what they already know, based on their expertise. Once experts find a correct match, they quickly can retrieve and implement a problem strategy. Thus, experts seem to be able to work forward from the given information ("What do I know?") to find the unknown information ("What do I need to find out?"). They implement the correct sequence of steps, based on the strategies they have retrieved from their schemas in long-term memory (Chi & associates, 1982).

Consider, for example, the ways an expert doctor and a novice medical student might handle a patient with a set of symptoms. The novice is not sure what to make of the symptoms. He somewhat haphazardly orders a long and expensive series of medical tests. He is hoping that with a more nearly complete set of symptomatic information, he may be able to make a correct diagnosis. The more experienced doctor, however, is more likely to immediately recognize the symptoms as fitting into a diagnostic pattern or one of a small number of patterns. This doctor orders only a small number of highly targeted tests. She is able to choose the correct diagnosis from among the limited number of possibilities. She then moves on to treat the diagnosed illness.

In contrast, novices seem to spend relatively little time trying to represent the problem. Instead, they choose to work backward from the unknown information to the given information. That is, they go from asking what they need to find out to asking what information is offered and what strategies do they know that can help them find the missing information. Often, novices use means–ends analysis (see Hunt, 1994). Thus, novices often consider more possible strategies than experts consider (see Holyoak, 1990). For experts, means–ends analysis of problems serves only as a backup strategy. They turn to it only if they are unable to retrieve an appropriate strategy, based on their existing schemas.

Thus, experts have not only more knowledge but also better-organized knowledge. They use their knowledge more effectively. Furthermore, the schemas of experts involve not only greater declarative knowledge about a problem domain. They also involve more procedural knowledge about strategies relevant to that domain. Perhaps because of their better grasp of the strategies required, experts more accurately predict the difficulty of solving problems than do novices (Lesgold & Lajoie, 1991). Experts also monitor their problem-solving strategies more carefully than do novices (Schoenfeld, 1981).

Automatic Expert Processes

Through practice in applying strategies, experts may automatize various operations. They can retrieve and execute these operations easily while working forward (see VanLehn, 1989). They use two important processes. One is *schematization*, which involves developing rich, highly organized schemas. The other is *automatization*, which involves consolidating sequences of steps into unified routines that require little or no conscious control. Through these two processes, experts may shift the burden of solving problems from limited-capacity working memory to infinite-capacity long-term memory. They thereby become increasingly efficient and accurate in solving problems. The freeing of their working-memory capacity may better enable them to monitor their progress and their accuracy during problem solving. Novices, in contrast, must use their working memory for trying to hold multiple features of a problem and various possible alternative strategies. This effort may leave novices with less working memory available for monitoring their accuracy and their progress toward solving the problem.

A good example of how automatization enhances performance can be seen in studies of reading ability. Consider the issue of expertise in reading. Why would some people, particularly children learning to read, be better than others at reading? Reading is believed by some to involve two distinct processes (Wagner & Stanovich, 1996). The first is a process of conversion from the *orthographic* (relating to visual appearance of letters) code to the *phonological* (relating to the sounds of the language) code. The second is a phonology-based word recognition process. Extensive exposure to text can enhance the orthographic-to-phonological conversion process by increasing automaticity at this level of processing. Thus, a portion of the differences in reading ability appears to be the result of increased automaticity in the conversion of orthographic to phonological encoding of words through increased reading practice (see Samuels, 1999, pp. 176–179; Sternberg & Wagner, 1982). Automaticity can also be seen in mathematics, where low-level skills, such as counting and adding, become automatic (Tronsky, 2005). These skills reduce the working-memory load and allow for higher-level mathematical procedures to be complete.

However, the automaticity of experts actually may hinder problem solving. This can occur when experts are tackling problems that differ structurally from the problems they normally encounter (Frensch & Sternberg, 1989). Initially, novices may perform better than experts when the problems appear structurally different from the norm. Eventually, however, the performance of experts generally catches

TABLE 11.4	What Characterizes Expertise?
Although many aspects of expertise remain to be explored, several characteristics of expert problem solving have been discovered.	

EXPERTS	NOVICES
Have large, rich schemas containing a great deal of declarative knowledge about domain	Have relatively impoverished schemas containing relatively less declarative knowledge about domain
Have well-organized, highly interconnected units of knowledge in schemas	Have poorly organized, loosely interconnected, scattered units of knowledge
Spend proportionately more time determining how to represent a problem than in searching for and executing a problem strategy	Spend proportionately more time searching for and executing a problem strategy than in determining how to represent a problem
Develop sophisticated representation of problems based on structural similarities among problems	Develop relatively poor and naive representation of problems based on superficial similarities among problems
Work forward from given information to implement strategies for finding unknown	Work backward from focusing on unknown to finding problem strategies that make use of given information
Generally choose a strategy based on elaborate schema of problem strategies; use means–ends analysis only as a backup strategy for handling unusual, atypical problems	Frequently use means–ends analysis as a strategy for handling most problems; sometimes choose a strategy based on knowledge of problem strategies
Schemas contain a great deal of procedural knowledge about problem strategies relevant to domain	Schemas contain relatively little procedural knowledge about problem strategies relevant to domain
Have automatized many sequences of steps within problem strategies	Show little or no automatization of any sequences of steps within problem strategies
Show highly efficient problem solving; when time constraints are imposed, solve problems more quickly than novices	Show relatively inefficient problem solving; solve problems less quickly than experts
Accurately predict the difficulty of solving particular problems	Do not accurately predict the difficulty of solving particular problems
Carefully monitor own problem-solving strategies and processes	Show poor monitoring of own problem-solving strategies and processes
Show high accuracy in reaching appropriate solutions	Show much less accuracy than experts in reaching appropriate solutions
When confronting highly unusual problems with atypical structural features, take relatively more time than novices both to represent the problem and to retrieve appropriate problem strategies	When confronting highly unusual problems with atypical structural features, novices take relatively less time than experts both to represent the problem and to retrieve problem strategies
When provided with new information that contradicts initial problem representation, show flexibility in adapting to a more appropriate strategy	Show less ability to adapt to new information that contradicts initial problem representation and strategy

up to and surpasses that of novices (Frensch & Sternberg, 1989; Lesgold, 1988). Perhaps this difference results from the experts' richly developed schemas and their enhanced self-monitoring skills. Table 11.4 summarizes the various characteristics of expert problem solving.

Innate Talent and Acquired Skill

Although a richly elaborated knowledge base is crucial to expertise in a domain, there remain differences in performance that are not explainable in terms of knowledge level alone. There is considerable debate as to whether differences between novices and experts and among different experts themselves are due either to innate talent or to the quantity and quality of practice in a domain. Many espouse the "practice makes perfect" point of view (see Ericsson, 1996, 1999, 2003; Ericsson, Krampe, & Tesch-Römer, 1993; Ericsson & Lehmann, 1996; Sloboda, 1996; Sloboda & associates, 1996; Sternberg, 1998). The practice should be deliberate, or focused. It should emphasize acquisition of new skills and applications rather than mindless repetition of what the developing expert already knows how to do. However, some take an alternative approach. This approach acknowledges the importance of practice in building a knowledge and skill base. It also underscores the importance of something like talent. Indeed, the interaction between innate abilities modified by experience is widely accepted in the domain of language acquisition (as discussed in Chapter 9) as well as other domains. Certainly, some skill domains are heavily dependent on nurture. For example, wisdom is partly knowledge based. The knowledge one uses to make wise judgments is necessarily a result of experience (Baltes & Smith, 1990).

Experts in some domains perform at superior levels by virtue of prediction skills. For example, expert typists move their fingers toward keys corresponding to the letters they will need to type more quickly than do novice typers (Norman & Rumelhart, 1983). Indeed, the single best predictor of typing speed is how far ahead in the text a typist looks when typing (Ericsson, 2003). The farther ahead he or she looks, the better the typist is able to have fingers in position as needed. When typists are not allowed to look ahead in their typing, the advantage of expert typists is largely eliminated (Salthouse, 1984). Expert sign-language users show variations in sign production in preparation for the next sign (Yang & Sarkar, 2006; see also Chapter 9). Rather than produce one sign in isolation, these signers are looking ahead. Looking ahead allows experts to produce signs more quickly than do novices. Expert musicians, too, are better able to sight-read than novices by virtue of their looking farther ahead in the music so they can anticipate what notes will be coming up (Sloboda, 1984). Even in sports, such as tennis, experts are superior to novices in part by virtue of their being able to predict the trajectory of an approaching ball more rapidly and accurately than novices (Abernethy, 1991).

Another characteristic of experts is that they tend to use a more systematic approach to difficult problems within their domain of expertise than do novices. For example, one study compared strategies used by problem solvers in a simulated biology laboratory (Vollmeyer, Burns, & Holyoak, 1996). The investigators found that better problem solvers were more systematic in their approach to the lab than were poorer problem solvers. For example, in seeking an explanation of a biological phenomenon, they were more likely to hold one variable constant while varying other variables.

Many scientists in the field of expertise prefer to minimize the contributions of talent to expertise by locking talent in the trunk of "folk" psychology (Sternberg, 1996a). This tendency is not surprising, given two factors. The first is the widespread use of the term *talent* outside the scientific community. The second is the lack of an adequate, testable definition of talent.

Genetic heritage seems to make some difference in the acquisition of at least some kinds of expertise. Studies of the heritability of reading disabilities, for example, seem to point to a strong role for genetic factors in people with a reading disability (see De-Fries & Gillis, 1993; Olson, 1999). Furthermore, differences in the phonological awareness required for reading ability could be a factor in reading for which individual differences are at least partially genetic (Wagner & Stanovich, 1996). In general, even if the role of practice is found to account for much of the expertise shown in a given domain, the contributions of genetic factors to the remaining portion of expertise could make some difference in a world of intense competition (Shiffrin, 1996).

A common trait among experts in various skills is that they put in tremendous numbers of hours of deliberate practice to perfect their skills.

The application of expertise to problem solving generally involves converging on a single correct solution from a broad range of possibilities. A complementary asset to expertise in problem solving involves creativity. Here, an individual extends the range of possibilities to consider never-before-explored options. In fact, many problems can be solved only by inventing or discovering strategies to answer a complex question.

Creativity

How can we possibly define creativity as a single construct that unifies the work of Leonardo da Vinci and Marie Curie, of Vincent Van Gogh and Isaac Newton, and of Toni Morrison and Albert Einstein? There may be about as many narrow definitions of creativity as there are people who think about creativity (Figure 11.14). However, most investigators in the field of creativity would broadly define **creativity** as the process of producing something that is both original and worthwhile (Csikszentmihalyi, 1999, 2000; Lubart & Mouchiroud, 2003; Runco, 1997, 2000; Sternberg & Lubart, 1996). The *something* could take many forms. It might be a theory, a dance, a chemical, a process or procedure, a story, a symphony, or almost anything else.

What does it take to create something original and worthwhile? What are creative people like? Almost everyone would agree that creative individuals show creative productivity. They produce inventions, insightful discoveries, artistic works, revolutionary paradigms, or other products that are both original and worthwhile. Conventional wisdom suggests that highly creative individuals also have creative lifestyles. These lifestyles are characterized by flexibility, nonstereotyped behaviors, and nonconforming attitudes. What characteristics do cognitive psychologists notice in creative individuals? The answer to this question depends on the perspective of the psychologist you ask. This section of this chapter describes a number of different approaches to creativity. They include psychometric and cognitive approaches; personality and motivational approaches; and social, societal, and historical approaches to understanding creativity. The chapter concludes with a couple of integrative perspectives. These perspectives attempt to incorporate key features of the other approaches to creativity.

It's How Much You Produce

Do creative individuals simply produce more? We have yet to develop a method for detecting highly creative individuals at a glance, but highly creative individuals seem to share several characteristics. Psychologists who take a psychometric (*-metric,* "measurement") approach emphasize performance on tasks involving specific aspects of creativity (Guilford, 1950). These tasks involve *divergent production*—the generation of a diverse assortment of appropriate responses. Therefore, creativity reflects simply the ability to create more.

For example, creative individuals often have high scores on tests of creativity. Examples of such a test are the Torrance Tests of Creative Thinking (Torrance, 1974, 1984). They measure the diversity, numerosity, and appropriateness of responses to

FIGURE 11.14

CREATIVITY IS...

DIGGING DEEPER

CREATIVITY IS...

LOOKING TWICE

CREATIVITY IS...

LISTENING FOR SMELLS

CREATIVITY IS...

~~TALKING~~ LISTENING TO A CAT

CROSSING OUT MISTAKES

Here are some original and worthwhile ways of defining creativity. How do you define creativity? From "The Nature of Creativity as Manifest in its Testing," by E.P. Torrance in THE NATURE OF CREATIVITY, *edited by Robert J. Sternberg. Copyright © 1988 by Cambridge University Press. Reprinted by permission of Cambridge University Press and E.P. Torrance.*

open-ended questions. An example of such a question is to think of all the possible ways in which to use a paper clip or a ballpoint pen. Torrance's test also assesses creative figural responses. For example, a person might be given a sheet of paper displaying some circles, squiggles, or lines. The test would assess how many different ways the person had used the given shapes to complete a drawing. Assessment of the Torrance test would consider particularly how much the person had used unusual or richly elaborated details in completing a figure.

It's What You Know

Other psychological researchers have focused on creativity as a cognitive process by studying problem solving and insight (Finke, 1995; Langley & Jones, 1988; Smith, 1995a, 1995b; Weisberg, 1988, 1995, 1999). Are creative people smarter than the rest of us? Some researchers believe that what distinguishes remarkably creative individuals from less remarkable people is their expertise and commitment to their creative endeavor (Weisberg, 1988, 1995, 1999). Highly creative individuals work long and

What do creative people such as these have in common?

hard. They study the work of their predecessors and their contemporaries. They thereby become thoroughly expert in their fields. They then build on and diverge from what they know to create innovative approaches and products (Weisberg, 1988, 1995, 1999). To these researchers, creativity in itself is nothing special. The processes involved in creativity are used by all of us every day in solving problems. What differentiates the remarkable from the mundane is the extraordinary content on which these ordinary processes operate. This notion feeds back to those discussed previously in expertise. Indeed, creativity often is treated as related to expertise. One study examined the creativity of projects completed by design students. The researchers found that the greater the knowledge amassed by a student, the greater, on average, the creativity of the project (Christiaans & Venselaar, 2007).

Not every cognitive psychologist agrees with the nothing-special view of creative insight. For example, to one investigator, "insight is what distinguishes . . . the inspiring from the denigrating, the magical from the mediocre" (Finke, 1995, p. 255). According to this view, there are two types of creative thinking. First, in convergent insight, the individual converges on a unifying pattern or structure within a scattered assortment of data. Second, in divergent insight, the individual diverges from a particular form or structure to explore what kinds of uses may be found for it. Divergent insight may be used to understand various creative endeavors (Finke, 1995). They include architectural design, physical or biological models, product development, or scientific invention.

Other investigators focus on creativity as it is manifested in scientific insight (Langley & Jones, 1988). These researchers suggest that memory processes such as spreading activation (see Chapter 8) and thinking processes such as analogical reasoning (see Chapter 12) account for much of scientific insight. Another investigator distinguishes between scientific insight and the insight experience (Smith, 1995a, 1995b). He has suggested that the abruptness of the insight experience may result from a sudden release from a mental rut (a mental set such as functional fixedness). This sudden release may be more likely to arise after a period of incubation in a context other than the context in which the individual became fixated on the problem.

Some computer programs that can do work, such as composing music (Johnson-Laird, 1988) or rediscovering scientific principles (Langley & associates, 1987), can be viewed as creative. The question one always need ask with these programs is whether their accomplishments truly are comparable to those of creative humans and whether the processes they use to be creative are the same as those used by humans (Boden, 1999). For example, Langley and colleagues' (1987) programs *rediscover* scientific ideas rather than discover them for the first time. Even Deep Blue, the computer program that beat world-champion chess player Gary Kasparov, did so not by playing chess more creatively than Kasparov. Rather, it won through its enormous powers of rapid computation.

It's Who You Are

Other psychologists have turned their focus away from cognition to consider the role of personality and motivation in creativity. Is there a creative personality—either you have it or you don't? Consider the importance of personal style:

> . . . *openness to new ways of seeing, intuition, alertness to opportunity, a liking for complexity as a challenge to find simplicity, independence of judgment that questions assumptions, willingness to take risks, unconventionality of thought that allows odd connections to be made, keen attention, and a drive to find pattern and meaning—these, coupled with the motive and the courage to create."* (Barron, 1988, p. 95)

Also important is the role of personal philosophy in creativity (Barron, 1988). This includes flexible beliefs and broadly accepting attitudes toward other cultures, other races, and other religious creeds. Some investigators have focused on the importance of motivation in creative productivity (e.g., Amabile, 1996; Collins & Amabile, 1999; Hennessey & Amabile, 1988). One may differentiate intrinsic motivation, which is internal to the individual, from extrinsic motivation, which is external to the individual. For example, intrinsic motivators might include sheer enjoyment of the creative process or personal desire to solve a problem. Extrinsic motivators might include a desire for fame or fortune. Intrinsic motivation is essential to creativity. Extrinsic motivators actually may impede creativity under many but not all circumstances (Amabile, 1996; Ruscio, Whitney, & Amabile, 1998). Curiously, in one experiment, extrinsic rewards for novel performance led to an increase in both creativity and intrinsic motivation (Eisenberger & Shanock, 2003). Conversely, extrinsic rewards for normal performance resulted in a decrease in both creativity and intrinsic motivation (Eisenberger, & Shanock, 2003).

In a review of the literature, certain traits seem consistently to be associated with creative individuals (Feist, 1998, 1999). In particular, creative individuals tend to be more open to new experiences, self-confident, self-accepting, impulsive, ambitious, driven, dominant, and hostile than less creative individuals. They also are less conventional.

It's Where You Are

Some researchers focus on the importance of external factors that contribute to creativity. Do you have to be in the right place at the right time? "We cannot study creativity by isolating individuals and their works from the social and historical milieu in which their actions are carried out . . . what we call creative is never the result of individual action alone" (Csikszentmihalyi, 1988, p. 325). In regard to the context for creativity, we should note two contexts (Csikszentmihalyi, 1996): the domain and the field. The domain comprises existing knowledge in a particular area of creative endeavor, such as particle physics or painting. The field comprises the social context surrounding creativity. It includes both the collegial network in the domain and the broader social and public institutions of the society.

One can seek to understand creativity by going beyond the immediate social, intellectual, and cultural context to embrace the entire sweep of history (Simonton, 1988, 1994, 1997, 1999). Creative contributions, almost by definition, are unpredictable because they violate the norms established by the forerunners and the contemporaries of the creator. Among the many attributes of creative individuals are the abilities to make serendipitous discoveries and to pursue such discoveries actively (Simonton, 1994).

Evolutionary thinking also can be used to study creativity (Cziko, 1998; Simonton, 1998). Underlying such models is the notion that creative ideas evolve much as organisms do. The idea is that creativity occurs as an outcome of a process of blind variation and selective retention (Campbell, 1960). In blind variation, creators first generate an idea. They have no real sense of whether the idea will be successful (selected for) in the world of ideas. As a result, their best bet for producing lasting ideas is to go for a large quantity of ideas. Some of these ideas then will be valued by their field. That is, they will be selectively retained by virtue of their being labeled as creative.

All of the Above

Consider an integrated view of what characterizes creative individuals (Gardner, 1993a; Policastro & Gardner, 1999). Like some case-study researchers (e.g., Gruber, 1974/1981; Gruber & Davis, 1988), Gardner (1993a) used in-depth study of seven creative individuals. Like Simonton, he attempted to relate these creative individuals to the historical context in which they developed and worked. He noted that great creators seemed to be in the right place at the right time for revolutionary change in their chosen domain. Like Csikszentmihalyi, Gardner studied how both the domain (e.g., physics, politics, music) and the field (e.g., collaborators, mentors, rivals) influence the way in which the creative individual demonstrates creativity. In addition, he studied both the kinds of early experiences leading to creative achievement and the development of creativity across the life span.

Creative individuals tended to have moderately supportive but rather strict and relatively chilly (i.e., not warmly affectionate and nurturing) early family lives. Most showed an early interest in their chosen field, but most were not particularly noteworthy. They generally tended to show an early interest in exploring uncharted territory; but only after gaining mastery of their chosen field, after about a decade of practicing their craft, did they have their initial revolutionary breakthrough. Most creators seemed to have obtained at least some emotional and intellectual support at the time of their breakthrough. However, following this initial breakthrough (and sometimes before), highly creative individuals generally dedicated all their energies to their work. They sometimes abandoned, neglected, or exploited close relationships during adulthood. About a decade after their initial creative achievement, most of the creators Gardner studied made a second breakthrough. It was more comprehensive and more integrative but less revolutionary. Whether a creator continued to make significant contributions depended on the particular field of endeavor. Poets and scientists were less likely to do so than musicians and painters.

An alternative integrative theory of creativity suggests that multiple individual and environmental factors must converge for creativity to occur (Sternberg & Lubart, 1991, 1993, 1995, 1996). What distinguishes the highly creative individual from the only modestly creative one is the confluence of multiple factors, rather than extremely high levels of any particular factor or even the possession of a distinctive trait. This theory is termed the *investment theory of creativity*. The theme unifying these various factors is that the creative individual takes a buy-low, sell-high approach to ideas (Sternberg & Lubart, 1995, 1996). In buying low, the creator initially sees the hidden potential of ideas that are presumed by others to have little value. The creative person then focuses attention on this idea. It is, at the time of the creator's interest, unrecognized or undervalued by contemporaries. But it has great potential for creative development. The creator then develops the idea into a meaningful, significant creative contribution until at last others also can recognize the merits of the idea. Once the idea has been developed and its value is recognized, the creator then sells high. He or she moves on to other pursuits and looks for the hidden potential in other undervalued ideas. Thus, the creative person influences the field most by always staying a step ahead of the rest.

Despite the diversity of views, most researchers would agree that most of the preceding individual characteristics and environmental conditions are necessary. None alone would be sufficient. In fact, extraordinary creative productivity may be as rare as it is precisely because so many variables must come together, in the right amounts, in a single person. A further complication is that many of these variables do not show a linear relationship to creativity. If the relation were linear, an increase in a particular characteristic or condition always would be associated with an increase in creativity. The contrary appears to be true. Many seem to show paradoxical effects and other nonlinear relationships.

Neuroscience of Creativity

The examination of creative thought and production has lead researchers to identify brain regions that are active during creativity. The prefrontal regions are especially active during the creative process, regardless of whether the creative thought is effortful or spontaneous (Dietrich, 2004).

In addition to the prefrontal area, other regions have also been identified as important for creativity. In one study, participants were given a list of words that were either semantically related or unrelated (Bechtereva & associates, 2004). The participants were then asked to make up a story using all of these words. Forming a story from a list of unrelated words should require more creativity than using a list of semantically related words. These researchers noted that Brodmann's area 39 was active during the unrelated-list story production but not during production of stories with the list of related words. Previous research has indicated that this and related Brodmann's areas are involved in verbal working memory, task switching, and imagination (Blackwood & associates, 2000; Collette & associates, 2001; Sohn & associates, 2000; Zurowski & associates, 2002). Taken together, these findings indicate that creativity involves many conscious processes.

Types of Creative Contributions

According to one set of investigators, creative contributions may be of eight kinds (Sternberg, 1999; Sternberg, Kaufman, & Pretz, 2001, 2002). The eight types of creative contributions include the following:

1. *Replication*. The creative contribution represents an effort to show that a given field is where it should be.

2. *Redefinition*. The creative contribution represents an effort to redefine where the field currently is. The current status of the field is thus seen from a new point of view.

3. *Forward movement*. The creative contribution represents an attempt to move the field forward in the direction in which it already is moving, and the contribution takes the field to a point where others are ready for the field to go.

4. *Advance forward movement*. The creative contribution represents an attempt to move the field forward in the direction it is already going. But the contribution moves beyond where others are ready for the field to go.

5. *Redirection*. The creative contribution represents an attempt to move the field from where it is toward a new and different direction.

6. *Redirection from a point in the past*. The creative contribution represents an attempt to move the field back to where it once was (a reconstruction of the past) so that the field may move onward from that point.

7. *Starting over*. The creative contribution represents an attempt to move the field to a different and as yet not reached starting point. It then moves the field in a different direction from that point.

8. *Integration*. The creative contribution represents an attempt to move the field by putting together aspects of two or more past kinds of creative contributions that formerly were viewed as distinct or even opposed. Now they are seen as synthesized (Sternberg, 1999).

The eight types of creative contributions described are viewed as qualitatively distinct. However, within each type, there can be quantitative differences. For example, a forward incrementation may represent a fairly small step forward or a substantial leap for a given field. A starting over may restart an entire field or just a small area of it. Moreover, a given contribution may overlap categories.

The eight kinds of creative contributions may differ in the extent of the creative contribution they make. But there is no *a priori* way of evaluating the *amount* of creativity on the basis of the *type* of creative contribution. Certain types of creative contributions probably tend, on average, to be greater in amounts of novelty than are others. For example, replications tend, on average, not to be highly novel. But creativity also involves the quality of work, and the type of creative contribution a work makes does not necessarily predict the quality of the work.

When people have new ideas, they have to use their reasoning skills to analyze these ideas and ultimately to decide if the ideas are truly creative. How do they do such reasoning and decision making? These issues are discussed in the next chapter.

Line up six toothpicks. Ask a friend to make four equilateral triangles with these six toothpicks without breaking the toothpicks into pieces. Most people will not be able to do this task because they will try to make the four triangles on a single plane. When they give up, make a single triangle flat on the table with three of the toothpicks, then with the other three toothpicks make a pyramid by joining the three toothpicks at the top and having the sides connect with the intersections of the three toothpicks on the table. Your friend was fixated on the plane of the alignment of the toothpicks. See if any of your friends can figure out this problem if you give them the toothpicks standing up in a toothpick holder.	**INVESTIGATING COGNITIVE PSYCHOLOGY**

Key Themes

This chapter highlights several of the themes first presented in Chapter 1.

The first theme is domain generality versus domain specificity. Early work on problem solving, such as that by Allen Newell and Herbert Simon and their colleagues, emphasized the domain generality of problem solving. These investigators sought to write computer routines, such as the General Problem Solver, that would solve a broad array of problems. Later theorists have more emphasized domain specificity in problem solving. They have especially called attention to the need for a broad knowledge base to solve problems successfully.

A second theme is validity of causal inference versus ecological validity. Most studies of creativity have occurred in laboratory settings. For example, Paul Torrance gave students paper-and-pencil tests of creative thinking administered in classrooms. In contrast, Howard Gruber has been interested only in creativity as it occurred in natural settings, such as when Darwin generated his many ideas behind the theory of evolution.

A third theme is basic versus applied research. The field of creativity has generated many insights regarding fundamental processes used in creative thought. But the field has also spawned a large industry of "creativity enhancement"—programs designed to make people more creative. Some of these programs utilize insights of basic research. Others represent little more than the intuitions of their inventors. It is important that training be based, where possible, on psychological theory and research rather than guesswork.

Summary

1. **What are some key steps involved in solving problems?**   Problem solving involves mentally working to overcome obstacles that stand in the way of reaching a goal. The key steps of problem solving are problem identification, problem definition and representation, strategy construction, organization of information, allocation of resources, monitoring, and evaluation. In everyday experiences, these steps may be implemented very flexibly. Various steps may be repeated, may occur out of sequence, or may be implemented interactively.

2. **What are the differences between problems that have a clear path to a solution versus problems that do not?**   Although well-structured problems may have clear paths to solution, the route to solution still may be difficult to follow. Some well-structured problems can be solved using algorithms. They may be tedious to implement but are likely to lead to an accurate solution if applicable to a given problem. Computers are likely to use algorithmic problem-solving strategies. Humans are more likely to use rather informal heuristics (e.g., means–ends analysis, working forward, working backward, and generate and test) for solving problems. When ill-structured problems are solved, the choice of an appropriate problem representation powerfully influences the ease of reaching an accurate solution. Additionally, in solving ill-structured problems, people may need to use more than a heuristic or an algorithmic strategy; insight may be required.

   Many ill-structured problems cannot be solved without the benefit of insight. There are several alternative views of how insightful problem solving takes place. According to the Gestaltist and the neo-Gestaltist views, insightful problem solving is a special process. It comprises more than the sum of its parts and may be evidenced by the suddenness of realizing a solution. According to the nothing-special view, insightful problem solving is no different from any other kind of problem solving. And according to the three-process view, insight involves a special use of three processes: selective encoding, selective combination, and selective comparison.

3. **What are some of the obstacles and aids to problem solving?**   A mental set (also termed entrenchment) is a strategy that has worked in the past but that does not work for a particular problem that needs to be solved in the present.

   A particular type of mental set is functional fixedness. It involves the inability to see that something that is known to have a particular use also may be used for serving other purposes. Transfer may be either positive or negative. It refers to the carryover of problem-solving skills from one problem or kind of problem to another. Positive transfer across isomorphic problems rarely occurs spontaneously, particularly if the problems appear to be different in content or in context. Incubation follows a period of intensive work on a problem. It involves laying a problem to rest for a while and then returning to it. In this way, subconscious work can continue on the problem while the problem is consciously ignored.

4. **How does expertise affect problem solving?**   Experts differ from novices in both the *amount* and the *organization of knowledge* that they bring to bear on problem solving in the domain of their expertise. For experts, many aspects of problem solving may be governed by automatic processes.

   Such automaticity usually facilitates the expert's ability to solve problems in the given area of expertise. When problems involve novel elements requiring novel strategies, however, the automaticity of some procedures actually may impede problem solving, at least temporarily. Expertise in a given domain is viewed mostly from the practice-makes-perfect perspective. However, many point out that the notion of talent should not be ignored and probably contributes much to the differences between different experts.

5. What is creativity, and how can it be fostered? Creativity involves producing something that is both original and worthwhile. Several factors characterize highly creative individuals. One is extremely high motivation to be creative in a particular field of endeavor (e.g., for the sheer enjoyment of the creative process). A second is both nonconformity in violating any conventions that might inhibit the creative work and dedication in maintaining standards of excellence and self-discipline related to the creative work. A third factor is deep belief in the value of the creative work, as well as willingness to criticize and improve the work. A fourth is careful choice of the problems or subjects on which to focus creative attention. A fifth is thought processes characterized by both insight and divergent thinking. A sixth factor is risk taking. A seventh factor is extensive knowledge of the relevant domain. And an eighth factor is profound commitment to the creative endeavor. In addition, the historical context and the domain and field of endeavor influence the expression of creativity.

Thinking about Thinking: Factual, Analytical, Creative, and Practical Questions

1. Describe the steps of the problem-solving cycle and give an example of each step.

2. What are some of the key characteristics of expert problem solvers?

3. What are some of the insights into problem solving gained through studying computer simulations of problem solving? How might a computer-based approach limit the potential for understanding problem solving in humans?

4. Compare and contrast the various approaches to creativity.

5. Design a problem that would require insight for its solution.

6. Design a context for problem solving that would enhance the ease of reaching a solution.

7. Given what we know about some of the hindrances to problem solving, how could you minimize those hindrances in your handling of the problems you face?

8. Given some of the ideas regarding creativity presented in this chapter, what can you do to enhance your own creativity?

Key Terms

algorithms
analysis
convergent thinking
creativity
divergent thinking
functional fixedness
heuristics
ill-structured problems
incubation

insight
isomorphic
mental set
negative transfer
positive transfer
problem solving
problem-solving cycle
problem space
productive thinking

selective-combination insights
selective-comparison insights
selective-encoding insights
stereotypes
synthesis
transfer
transparency
well-structured problems

CogLab Explore CogLab by going to **http://coglab.wadsworth.com.**
To learn more, examine the following experiments:

Monty Hall

Annotated Suggested Readings

Davidson, J. E., & Sternberg, R. J. (Eds.). (2003). *The psychology of problem solving.* New York: Cambridge University Press. A complete review of contemporary literature on problem solving.

Stickgold, R., & Walker, M. (2004). To sleep, perchance to gain creative insight? *Trends in Cognitive Science,* 8(5), 191–192. This is a study emphasizing the importance of sleep in problem solving and creativity.

Decision Making and Reasoning

EXPLORING COGNITIVE PSYCHOLOGY

1. **What are some of the strategies that guide human decision making?**

2. **What are some of the forms of deductive reasoning that people may use, and what factors facilitate or impede deductive reasoning?**

3. **How do people use inductive reasoning to make causal inferences and to reach other types of conclusions?**

4. **Are there any alternative views of reasoning?**

INVESTIGATING COGNITIVE PSYCHOLOGY

Linda is 31 years old, single, outspoken, and very bright. She majored in philosophy. As a student, she was deeply concerned with issues of discrimination and social justice and also participated in antinuclear demonstrations.

Based on the preceding description, list the likelihood that the following statements about Linda are true:

(a) Linda is a teacher in elementary school.
(b) Linda works in a bookstore and takes yoga classes.
(c) Linda is active in the feminist movement.
(d) Linda is a psychiatric social worker.
(e) Linda is a member of the League of Women Voters.
(f) Linda is a bank teller.
(g) Linda is an insurance salesperson.
(h) Linda is a bank teller and is active in the feminist movement.

(Tversky & Kahneman, 1983, p. 297).

If you are like 85% of the people Tversky and Kahneman studied, you rated the likelihood of item h above as greater than the likelihood of item f. Stop for a minute, however. Imagine a huge convention hall filled with the entire population of bank tellers. Now think about how many of them would be at a hypothetical booth for feminist bank tellers—a subset of the entire population of bank tellers. If Linda is at the booth for feminist bank tellers, she must, by definition, be in the convention hall of bank tellers. Hence, the likelihood that she is at the booth (i.e., she is a feminist bank teller) cannot logically be greater than the likelihood that she is in the convention hall (i.e., she is a bank teller). Nonetheless, given the description of Linda, we intuitively feel more likely to find her at the booth than in the convention hall. This intuitive feeling is an example of a **fallacy**—erroneous reasoning—in judgment and reasoning.

In this chapter we consider many ways in which we make judgments and decisions and use reasoning to draw conclusions. The first section deals with how we make choices and judgments. **Judgment and decision making** are used to select from among choices or to evaluate opportunities. An example would be choosing the car that would please you the most for the amount of money you have. The second section addresses various forms of reasoning. The goal of reasoning is to draw conclusions deductively from principles or inductively from evidence. An example of deductive reasoning would be applying the general laws of physics to reach conclusions regarding the mechanics of a particular car engine. An example of inductive reasoning would be reading consumer-oriented statistics to find out the reliability, economy, and safety of various cars.

Judgment and Decision Making

In the course of our everyday lives, we constantly are making judgments and decisions. One of the most important decisions you may have made is that of whether and where to go to college. Once in college, you still need to decide on which courses to take. Later on, you may need to choose a major field of study. You make decisions about friends and dates, about how to relate to your parents, and about how to spend money. How do you go about making these decisions?

Classical Decision Theory

The earliest models of how people make decisions are referred to as "classical decision theory." Most of these models were devised by economists, statisticians, and philosophers, not by psychologists. Hence, they reflect the strengths of an economic perspective. One such strength is the ease of developing and using mathematical models for human behavior. Among the early models of decision making crafted in the twentieth century was *economic man and woman*. This model assumed three things. First, decision makers are fully informed regarding all possible options for their decisions and of all possible outcomes of their decision options. Second, they are infinitely sensitive to the subtle distinctions among decision options. Third, they are fully rational in regard to their choice of options (Edwards, 1954; see also Slovic, 1990). The assumption of infinite sensitivity means that people can evaluate the difference between two outcomes, no matter how subtle the distinctions among options may be. The assumption of rationality means that people make their choices to maximize something of value, whatever that something may be.

Consider an example of how this model works. Suppose that a decision maker is considering which of two job offers to accept. Assume that both provide the same starting salaries. Suppose also that people at Company A have a 50% chance of getting a 20% salary increase the first year. People at Company B have a 90% chance of getting a 10% salary increase the first year. The decision maker will calculate the expected value for each option, which is the probability times the corresponding value (utility), which here is the increase in salary (0.50 0.20 = 0.10; 0.90 × 0.10 = 0.09). For all of the potential benefits (additive calculations) and costs (subtractive calculations) of each job, the person would perform similar calculations. He or she would then choose the job with the highest expected value. In other words, he or she would pick the one offering the highest calculated benefit at the lowest calculated cost. Assuming all other things are equal, we should choose Company A. A great deal of economic research has been based on this model.

An alternative model makes greater allowance for the psychological makeup of each individual decision maker. According to *subjective expected utility theory*, the goal of human action is to seek pleasure and avoid pain. According to this theory, in making decisions people will seek to maximize pleasure (referred to as positive utility) and to minimize pain (referred to as negative utility). In doing so, however, each of us uses calculations of two things. One is **subjective utility,** which is a calculation based on the individual's judged weightings of utility (value), rather than on objective criteria. The second is **subjective probability,** which is a calculation based on the individual's estimates of likelihood, rather than on objective statistical computations.

Ponder an example of how this model works. In deciding which of two job offers to accept, different people would give different subjective positive or negative utilities to each feature of each job offer. Consider someone with a husband and four children. She might give a higher positive utility to benefits such as health insurance, dental care, vacation time, paid holidays, and so on, than would a single person who is strongly career oriented. Similarly, the woman with a family might assign a higher negative utility to the warning that a job involves a lot of travel requiring the person to be out of state for many days each month.

Two job seekers also might assign differing subjective probabilities to various potential positive or negative utilities. A pessimist probably would expect a higher likelihood of negative utilities and a lower likelihood of positive utilities than would an optimist. Hence, according to subjective expected utility theory, each person will go through a series of steps. First the person will multiply each subjective probability by each subjective positive utility for each job offer. Then he or she will subtract the calculation of the subjective probability of each subjective negative utility. Finally, he or she will reach a decision based on the relative expected values obtained from these calculations. The alternative that has the highest expected value is chosen. Subjective utility theory takes into account the many subjective variables that arise when people are involved. But theorists soon noticed that human decision making is more complex than even this modified theory implies.

For most decisions, there is no one perfect option that will be selected by all people. How, then, can we predict the optimal decision for a particular person? According to subjective expected utility theory, we need know only the person's subjective expected utilities. These are based on both subjective estimates of probability and subjective weightings of costs and benefits. We then can predict the optimal decision for that person. This prediction is based on the belief that people seek to reach well-reasoned decisions based on five factors. The first factor is consideration of all possible known alternatives, given that unpredictable alternatives may be available. The second is use of a maximum amount of available information, given that some relevant information may not be available. The third is careful, if subjective, weighing of the potential costs (risks) and benefits of each alternative. The fourth is careful (although subjective) calculation of the probability of various outcomes, given that certainty of outcomes cannot be known. And the fifth is a maximum degree of sound reasoning, based on considering all the aforementioned factors. Now, answer the following question. When was the last time you implemented the five preceding aspects of optimal decision making, even allowing for limits on your knowledge and for unpredictable elements? Probably not recently.

Satisficing

As early as the 1950s some researchers were beginning to challenge the notion of unlimited rationality. Not only did these researchers recognize that we humans do not always make ideal decisions and that we usually include subjective considerations in our decisions. They also suggested that we humans are not entirely and boundlessly rational in making decisions. In particular, we humans are not necessarily irrational. Rather, we show **bounded rationality**—we are rational, but within limits (Simon, 1957).

Perhaps we typically use a decision-making strategy he termed satisficing (Simon, 1957). In **satisficing,** we consider options one by one, and then we select an option as soon as we find one that is satisfactory or just good enough to meet our minimum level of acceptability. We do not consider all possible options and then carefully compute which of the entire universe of options will maximize our gains and minimize our losses. Thus, we will consider the minimum possible number of options needed to arrive at a decision that we believe will satisfy our minimum requirements. Some evidence suggests that when there are limited working-memory resources available, the use of satisficing for making decisions may be increased (Chen & Sun, 2003). Of course, satisficing is only one of several suboptimal strategies people can use.

The appropriateness of this strategy will vary with the circumstance in which one finds oneself. For example, satisficing might be a poor strategy for diagnosing a disease. This strategy is useful in a number of other situations, however. Suppose, for example, that you are looking for a used car. There are probably a staggering number of used-car lots near where you live. You probably have neither the time nor the inclination to

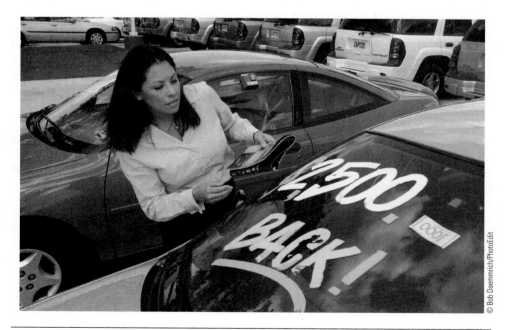

According to Herbert Simon, people often satisfice when they make important decisions, such as which car to buy. They decide for the first acceptable alternative that comes along.

Amos Tversky, now deceased, was the Davis-Brack professor of behavioral science at Stanford University. Tversky was best known for his work on human judgment and decision making, including work with Daniel Kahneman on heuristics and biases in judgment under conditions of uncertainty. Tversky also made major contributions to the study of similarity and psychological measurement.

visit them all. Such extensive visits would allow you to pick the car that seems best on all the many dimensions on which you might judge a car. So you go to one lot to see what is available. If you see a car there that you find satisfactory in terms of your major criteria for making the purchase, you buy it. If you do not find a car there that is good enough, you move on to the next lot. You keep looking only until you find a car that meets your needs. Then you buy it. On the one hand, you have probably not picked the optimal car of all those available. On the other hand, you have not spent 4 months looking through all the lots in town.

You also may use satisficing when considering research topics for a term project or paper. There are countless possible topics. You probably can consider quite a few, but then you need to settle on a satisfactory or even pretty good topic without continuing your exploration indefinitely. A decision maker may find that an uncomfortably high number of options have failed to reach the initial minimum level of acceptability. He or she may then decide to adjust the minimum level deemed adequate for satisficing. For example, suppose I decide that I want to buy a new luxury car with an excellent consumer track record and high fuel efficiency for less than $3000. I may end up having to adjust my minimum level of acceptability way downward.

Elimination by Aspects

We sometimes use a different strategy when faced with far more alternatives than we feel that we reasonably can consider in the time we have available (Tversky, 1972a, 1972b). In such situations, we do not try to manipulate mentally all the weighted attributes of all the available options. Rather, we use a process of elimination by aspects. In **elimination by aspects,** we eliminate alternatives by focusing on aspects of each alternative, one at a time. In particular, we focus on one aspect (attribute) of the various options. We form a minimum criterion for that aspect. We then eliminate all options that do not meet that criterion. For the remaining options, we then select a second aspect for which we set a minimum criterion by which to eliminate additional options. We continue using a sequential process of elimination of options by considering a series of aspects until a single option remains (Dawes, 2000).

For example, in choosing a car to buy we may focus on total price as an aspect. We may choose to dismiss factors such as maintenance costs, insurance costs, or other factors that realistically might affect the money we will have to spend on the car in addition to the sale price. Once we have weeded out the alternatives that do not meet our criterion, we choose another aspect. We set a criterion value and weed out additional alternatives. We continue in this way. We weed out more alternatives, one aspect at a time, until we are left with a single option. In practice, it appears that we may use some elements of elimination by aspects or satisficing to narrow the range of options to just a few. Then we use more thorough and careful strategies. Examples would be those suggested by subjective expected utility theory. They can be useful for selecting among the few remaining options (Payne, 1976).

We often use mental shortcuts and even biases that limit and sometimes distort our ability to make rational decisions. One of the key ways in which we use mental shortcuts centers on our estimations of probability. Consider, for example, some of the strategies used by statisticians when calculating probability. They are shown in Table 12.1.

TABLE 12.1	Rules of Probability

Hypothetical Example	**Calculation of Probability**
Lee is one of 10 highly qualified candidates applying for one scholarship. What are Lee's chances of getting the scholarship?	Lee has a 0.1 chance of getting the scholarship.
If Lee is one of 10 highly qualified scholarship students applying for one scholarship, what are Lee's chances of *not* getting the scholarship?	$1 - 0.1 = 0.9$ Lee has a 0.9 chance of not getting the scholarship.
Lee's roommate and Lee are among 10 highly qualified scholarship students applying for one scholarship. What are the chances that one of the two will get the scholarship?	$0.1 + 0.1 = 0.2$ There is a 0.2 chance that one of the two roommates will get the scholarship.
Lee owns four pairs of shoes—blue, white, black, and brown.	$0.25 \times 0.2 = 0.05$
Lee rotates randomly among the pairs of shoes he wears. What are the chances that one of the two roommates will be awarded the scholarship and that Lee will be wearing black shoes at the time?	There is a 0.05 chance that one of the two roommates will be awarded the scholarship and that Lee will be wearing black shoes at the time of the announcement.

You easily may be able to calculate the simple probability that a given cost or benefit will occur (shown on the first row of the table). You also can calculate the simple probability that a given cost or benefit will not occur (shown on the second line of the table). However, the calculations of combined probabilities for the occurrence or nonoccurrence of various costs and benefits can be quite cumbersome (see the third and fourth rows of the table).

Another probability is *conditional probability*. It is the likelihood of one event, given another. For example, you might want to calculate the likelihood of receiving an "A" for a cognitive psychology course, given that you receive an "A" on the final exam. The formula for calculating conditional probabilities in light of evidence is known as Bayes's theorem. It is quite complex, so most people do not use it in everyday-reasoning situations. Nonetheless, such calculations are essential to evaluating scientific hypotheses, forming realistic medical diagnoses, analyzing demographic data, and performing many other real-world tasks. (For a highly readable explanation of Bayes's theorem, see Eysenck & Keane, 1990, pp. 456–458. For a detailed description of Bayes's theorem from a cognitive psychological perspective, see Osherson, 1990.)

Naturalistic Decision Making

Many researchers contend that decision making is a complex process that cannot be adequately reproduced in the laboratory. This is because real decisions are frequently made in situations where there are high stakes. For instance, the mental state and cognitive pressure experienced by an ER doctor encountering a patient is difficult to reproduce outside a clinical setting. This criticism has led to the development of a field of study that is based on decision making in natural environments. Much of the research completed in this area is from professional settings, such as hospitals or nuclear plants (Carroll, Hatakenaka, & Rudolph, 2006; Galanter & Patel, 2005; Roswarski, & Murray, 2006). These situations share a number of features, including encountering ill-structured problems, changing situations, high risk, time pressure, and sometimes, a team environment (Orasanu & Connolly, 1993). A number of models are used to explain performance in these high-stakes situations. These models allow for the consideration of cognitive, emotional, and situational factors of skilled decision makers; they also provide a framework for advising future decision makers (Klein, 1997; Lipshitz & associates, 2001). For instance, Orasanu (2005) developed recommendations for training astronauts to be successful decision makers by evaluating what makes current astronauts successful. Naturalistic decision making can be applied to a broad range of behaviors and environments. These applications can include individuals as diverse as badminton players, railroad controllers, and NASA astronauts (Farrington-Darby & associates, 2006; Macquet & Fleurance, 2007; Orasanu, 2005; Patel, Kaufman, & Arocha, 2002).

Group Decision Making

Working as a group can enhance the effectiveness of decision making, just as it can enhance the effectiveness of problem solving. Many companies combine individuals into teams to improve decision making (Cannon-Bowers & Salas, 1998). By forming decision-making teams, the group benefits from the expertise of each of the members. There is also an increase in resources and ideas (Salas, Burke, & Cannon-Bowers, 2000). Another benefit of group decision making is improved group memory over individual memory (Hinsz, 1990). Groups that are successful in decision making exhibit a number of similar characteristics, including the following: the group is small; it has open communication; and members share a common mind set, identify with the group, and agree on acceptable group behavior (Shelton, 2006).

In juries, members share more information during decision making when the group is made up of diverse members (Sommers, 2006). The juries are thereby in a position to make better decisions. Furthermore, in examining decision making in public policy groups, it has been noted that interpersonal influence is important (Jenson, 2007). Group members frequently employed tactics to affect other members' decisions (Jenson, 2007). The most frequently used and influential tactics were inspirational and rational appeals. However, there are some disadvantages associated with group decision making. Of these disadvantages, one of the most explored is groupthink. *Groupthink* is a phenomena characterized by premature decision making that is generally the result of group members attempting to avoid conflict (Janis, 1971). Groupthink frequently results in suboptimum decision making that avoids nontraditional ideas (Esser, 1998). One major cause of groupthink is anxiety (Chapman, 2006). When group members are anxious, they are less likely to explore new options and will likely try to avoid further conflict.

What conditions lead to groupthink? Janis cited three kinds: (1) An isolated, cohesive, and homogeneous group is empowered to make decisions; (2) objective and impartial leadership is absent, within the group or outside it; and (3) high levels of stress impinge on the group decision-making process. The groups responsible for making foreign-policy decisions are excellent candidates for groupthink. They are usually like minded. Moreover, they frequently isolate themselves from what is going on outside their own group. They generally try to meet specific objectives and believe they cannot afford to be impartial. Also, of course, they are under very high stress because the stakes involved in their decisions can be tremendous.

Six Symptoms of Groupthink

Janis further delineated six symptoms of groupthink. (1) In *closed-mindedness*, the group is not open to alternative ideas. (2) In *rationalization*, the group goes to great lengths to justify both the process and the product of its decision making, distorting reality where necessary in order to be persuasive. (3) In the *squelching of dissent*, those who disagree are ignored, criticized, or even ostracized. (4) In the *formation of a "mindguard"* for the group, one person appoints himself or herself the keeper of the group norm and ensures that people stay in line. (5) In *feeling invulnerable*, the group believes that it must be right, given the intelligence of its members and the information available to them. (6) In *feeling unanimous*, members believe that everyone unanimously shares the opinions expressed by the group. Defective decision making results from groupthink, which in turn is due to examining alternatives insufficiently, examining risks inadequately, and seeking information about alternatives incompletely.

Consider how groupthink might arise in a decision when college students decide to damage a statue on the campus of a football rival to teach a lesson to the students and faculty in the rival university. The students rationalize that damage to a statue really is no big deal. Who cares about an old ugly statue anyway? When one group member dissents, other members quickly make him feel disloyal and cowardly. His dissent is squelched. The group's members feel invulnerable. They are going to damage the statue under the cover of darkness, and the statue is never guarded. They are sure they will not be caught. Finally, all the members agree on the course of action. This apparent feeling of unanimity convinces the group members that far from being out of line, they are doing what needs to be done.

Antidotes for Groupthink

Janis has prescribed several antidotes for groupthink. For example, the leader of a group should encourage constructive criticism, be impartial, and ensure that members seek input from people outside the group. The group should also form subgroups that meet separately to consider alternative solutions to a single problem. It is important that the leader take responsibility for preventing spurious conformity to a group norm.

In 1997, members of the Heaven's Gate cult in California committed mass suicide in the hope of meeting up with extraterrestrials in a spaceship trailing the Hale-Bopp comet. Although this group suicide is a striking example of conformity to a destructive group norm, similar events have occurred throughout human history, such as the suicide of more than 900 members of the Jonestown, Guyana, religious cult in 1978. Worse was the murder in 2000 of hundreds of individuals in Uganda by leaders of a cult that the individuals had joined. And even in the twenty-first century, suicide bombers are killing themselves and others in carefully planned attacks.

Heuristics and Biases

People make many decisions based on biases and heuristics (shortcuts) in their thinking (Kahneman & Tversky, 1972, 1990; Stanovich, Sái, & West, 2004; Tversky & Kahneman, 1971, 1993). These mental shortcuts lighten the cognitive load of making decisions, but they also allow for a much greater chance of error.

Representativeness

Before you read about representativeness, try the following problem from Kahneman and Tversky (1972).

INVESTIGATING COGNITIVE PSYCHOLOGY	All the families having exactly six children in a particular city were surveyed. In 72 of the families, the exact order of births of boys and girls was G B G B B G (G, girl; B, boy). What is your estimate of the number of families surveyed in which the exact order of births was B G B B B B?

Most people judging the number of families with the B G B B B B birth pattern estimate the number to be less than 72. Actually, the best estimate of the number of families with this birth order is 72, the same as for the G B G B B G birth order. The expected number for the second pattern would be the same because the gender for each birth is independent (at least, theoretically) of the gender for every other birth. For any one birth, the chance of a boy (or a girl) is one of two. Thus, any particular pattern of births is equally likely $(1/2)^6$, even B B B B B B or G G G G G G.

Why do many of us believe some birth orders to be more likely than others? In part, the reason is that we use the heuristic of representativeness. In **representativeness,** we judge the probability of an uncertain event according to (1) how obviously it is similar to or representative of the population from which it is derived and (2) the degree to which it reflects the salient features of the process by which it is generated (such as randomness) (see also Fischhoff, 1999; Johnson-Laird, 2000, 2004). For example, people believe that the first birth order is more likely because (1) it is more representative of the number of females and males in the population and (2) it looks more random than the second birth order. In fact, of course, either birth order is equally likely to occur by chance.

Similarly, suppose people are asked to judge the probability of flips of a coin yielding the sequence H T H H T H (H, heads; T, tails). Most people will judge it as higher than they will if asked to judge the sequence H H H H T H. If you expect a sequence to be random, you tend to view as more likely a sequence that "looks random." Indeed, people often comment that the numbers in a table of random numbers "don't look random." The reason is that people underestimate the number of runs of the same number that will appear wholly by chance. We frequently reason in terms of whether something appears to represent a set of accidental occurrences, rather than actually considering the true likelihood of a given chance occurrence. This tendency makes us more vulnerable to the machinations of magicians, charlatans, and con artists. Any of them may make much of their having predicted the realistic probability of a nonrandom-looking event. For example, the odds are 9 to 1 that two people in a

People often mistakenly believe in the gambler's fallacy. They think that if they have been unlucky in their gambles, it is time for their luck to change. In fact, success or failure in past gambles has no effect on the likelihood of success in future ones.

Research shows that the "hot hand" effect is in our minds, not in the players' games. Making a past shot does not increase the player's chance of making future shots.

group of 40 (e.g., in a classroom or a small nightclub audience) will share a birthday (the same month and day, not necessarily the same year). In a group of 14 people, there are better than even odds that two people will have birthdays within a day of each other (Krantz, 1992).

Another example of the representativeness heuristic is the gambler's fallacy. *Gambler's fallacy* is a mistaken belief that the probability of a given random event, such as winning or losing at a game of chance, is influenced by previous random events. For example, a gambler who loses five successive bets may believe that a win is therefore more likely the sixth time. He feels that he is "due" to win. In truth, of course, each bet (or coin toss) is an independent event. It has an equal probability of winning or losing. The gambler is no more likely to win on the 6th bet than on the 1st—or on the 1001st.

A related fallacy is the misguided belief in the "hot hand" or the "streak shooter" in basketball. Apparently, both professional and amateur basketball players, as well as their fans, believe that a player's chances of making a basket are greater after making a previous shot than after missing one. However, the statistical likelihoods (and the actual records of players) show no such tendency (Gilovich, Vallone, & Tversky, 1985). Shrewd players will take advantage of this belief and will closely guard opponents immediately after they have made baskets. The reason is that the opposing players will be more likely to try to get the ball to these perceived "streak shooters."

That we frequently rely on the representativeness heuristic may not be terribly surprising. It is easy to use and often works. For example, suppose we have not heard a weather report prior to stepping outside. We informally judge the probability that it will rain. We base our judgment on how well the characteristics of this day (e.g., the month of the year, the areas in which we live, and the presence or absence of clouds in the sky) represent the characteristics of days on which it rains. Another reason that we often use the representativeness heuristic is that we mistakenly believe that small samples (e.g., of events, of people, of characteristics) resemble in all respects the whole population from which the sample is drawn (Tversky & Kahneman, 1971). We particularly tend to underestimate the likelihood that the characteristics of a small sample (e.g., the people whom we know well) of a population inadequately represent the characteristics of the whole population.

We also tend to use the representativeness heuristic more frequently when we are highly aware of anecdotal evidence based on a very small sample of the population. This reliance on anecdotal evidence has been referred to as a "man-who" argument (Nisbett & Ross, 1980). When presented with statistics, we may refute those data with our own observations of, "I know a man who . . ." For example, faced with statistics on coronary disease and high-cholesterol diets, someone may counter with, "I know a man who ate whipped cream for breakfast, lunch, and dinner and lived to be 110 years old. He would have kept going but he was shot through his perfectly healthy heart by a jealous lover."

One reason that people misguidedly use the representativeness heuristic is because they fail to understand the concept of base rates. **Base rate** refers to the prevalence of an event or characteristic within its population of events or characteristics. In everyday decision making, people often ignore base-rate information, but it is important to effective judgment and decision making. In many occupations, the use of base-rate information is essential for adequate job performance. For example, suppose a doctor were told that a 10-year-old boy was suffering chest pains. The doctor would be much less likely to worry about an incipient heart attack than if told that a 50-year-old man had the identical symptom. Why? Because the base rate of heart attacks is much higher in 50-year-old men than in 10-year-old boys. Of course, people use other heuristics as well. People can be taught how to use base rates to improve their decision making (Gigerenzer, 1996; Koehler, 1996).

Availability

Most of us at least occasionally use the **availability heuristic,** in which we make judgments on the basis of how easily we can call to mind what we perceive as relevant instances of a phenomenon (Tversky & Kahneman, 1973; see also Fischhoff, 1999; Sternberg, 2000). For example, consider the letter *R*. Are there more words in the English language that begin with the letter *R* or that have *R* as their third letter? Most respondents say that there are more words beginning with the letter *R* (Tversky & Kahneman, 1973). Why? Because generating words beginning with the letter *R* is easier than generating words having *R* as the third letter. In fact, there are more English-language words with *R* as their third letter. The same happens to be true of some other letters as well, such as *K*, *L*, *N*, and *V*.

The availability heuristic also has been observed in regard to everyday situations. In one study, married partners individually stated which of the two partners performed a larger proportion of each of 20 different household chores (Ross & Sicoly, 1979). These tasks included mundane chores such as grocery shopping or preparing breakfast. Each partner stated that he or she more often performed about 16 of the 20 chores. Suppose each partner was correct. Then, to accomplish 100% of the work in a household, each partner would have to perform 80% of the work. Similar outcomes emerged from questioning of members of college basketball teams and joint participants in laboratory tasks. For all participants, the greater availability of their own actions made it seem that each had performed a greater proportion of the work in joint enterprises.

Although clearly 80% + 80% does not equal 100%, we can understand why people may engage in using the availability heuristic when it confirms their beliefs about themselves. However, people also use the availability heuristic when its use leads to a logical fallacy that has nothing to do with their beliefs about themselves. Two groups of participants were asked to estimate the number of words of a particular form that would be expected to appear in a 2000-word passage. For one group the form was _ _ _ _ing (i.e., seven letters ending in -ing). For the other group the form was _ _ _ _ _n_ (i.e., seven letters with n as the second-to-the-last letter). Clearly, there cannot be more seven-letter words ending in -ing than seven-letter words with n as the second-to-the-last letter. But the greater availability of the former led to estimates of probability that were more than twice as high for the former, as compared with the latter (Tversky & Kahneman, 1983). This example illustrates how the availability heuristic might lead to the conjunction fallacy. In the *conjunction fallacy*, an individual gives a higher estimate for a subset of events (e.g., the instances of -ing) than for the larger set of events containing the given subset (e.g., the instances of n as the second-to-the-last letter). This fallacy also is illustrated in the chapter-opening vignette regarding Linda.

The representativeness heuristic may also induce individuals to engage in the conjunction fallacy during probabilistic reasoning (Tversky & Kahneman, 1983; see also Dawes, 2000). Tversky and Kahneman asked college students:

> *Please give your estimate of the following values: What percentage of the men surveyed [in a health survey] have had one or more heart attacks? What percentage of the men surveyed both are over 55 years old and have had one or more heart attacks? (p. 308)*

The mean estimates were 18% for the former and 30% for the latter. In fact, 65% of the respondents gave higher estimates for the latter (which is clearly a subset of the former).

However, people do not always engage in the conjunction fallacy. Only 25% of respondents gave higher estimates for the latter question than for the former when the questions were rephrased as frequencies rather than as percentages. In other words, the questions were in terms of numbers of individuals within a given sample of the population. Also, the researchers found that the conjunction fallacy was less likely when the conjunctions are defined by the intersection of concrete classes than by a combination of properties. For example, they were less likely for types of objects or individuals such as dogs or beagles than they were for features of objects or individuals such as conservatism or feminism (Tversky & Kahneman, 1983). Although classes and properties are equivalent from a logical standpoint, they generate different mental representations (Stenning & Monaghan, 2004). Different rules and relations are used in each of the two cases. Thus, the formal equivalence of properties to classes is not intuitively obvious to most people (Tversky & Kahneman, 1983).

A variant of the conjunction fallacy is the *inclusion fallacy*. In the inclusion fallacy, the individual judges a greater likelihood that every member of an inclusive category has a particular characteristic than that every member of a subset of the inclusive category has that characteristic—that is, dogs (inclusive) and beagles (subset) (Shafir, Osherson, & Smith, 1990). For example, participants judged a much greater likelihood that "every single lawyer" (i.e., every lawyer) is conservative than that every single labor-union lawyer is conservative. According to the researchers, we tend to judge the likelihood that the members of a particular class (e.g., lawyers) or subclass (e.g., labor-union lawyers) of individuals will demonstrate a particular characteristic (e.g., conservatism) based on the perceived typicality (i.e., representativeness) of the given characteristic for the given category. For example, based on the characteristics of Sony televisions, participants were asked to judge features of either Sony camcorders or bicycles (Joiner & Loken, 1998). Participants committed the inclusion fallacy more for the camcorders than for the bicycles (Joiner & Loken, 1998). This is likely because, in this case, camcorders are more representative of the type of product produced by Sony. We should, however, judge likelihood based on statistical probability.

Heuristics such as representativeness and availability do not always lead to wrong judgments or poor decisions. Indeed, we use these mental shortcuts because they are so often right. For example, one of the factors that leads to the greater availability of an event is in fact the greater frequency of the event. However, availability also may be influenced by recency of presentation (as in implicit-memory cueing, mentioned in Chapter 5), unusualness, or distinctive salience of a particular event or event category for the individual. Nonetheless, when the available information is not biased for some reason, the instances that are most available are generally the most common ones. Examples of biased coverage might be sensationalized press coverage, extensive advertising, recency of an uncommon occurrence, or personal prejudices. We generally make decisions in which the most common instances are the most relevant and valuable ones. In such cases, the availability heuristic is often a convenient shortcut with few costs. However, when particular instances are better recalled because of biases (e.g., your views of your own behavior, in comparison with that of other people), the availability heuristic may lead to less than optimal decisions.

Other Judgment Phenomena

A heuristic related to availability is the *anchoring-and-adjustment heuristic*, by which people adjust their evaluations of things by means of certain reference points called *end-anchors*. Before you read on, quickly (in less than 5 seconds) calculate in your head the answer to the following problem:

$$8 \times 7 \times 6 \times 5 \times 4 \times 3 \times 2 \times 1$$

Now, quickly calculate your answer to the following problem:

$$1 \times 2 \times 3 \times 4 \times 5 \times 6 \times 7 \times 8$$

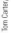

Although riding in a car is statistically much more risky than riding in a plane, people often feel less safe in a plane, in part because of the availability heuristic. People hear about every major U.S. plane crash that takes place, but they hear about relatively few car accidents.

Two groups of participants estimated the product of one or the other of the preceding two sets of eight numbers (Tversky & Kahneman, 1974). The median (middle) estimate for the participants given the first sequence was 2250. For the participants given the second sequence, the median estimate was 512. (The actual product is 40,320 for both.) The two products are the same, as they must be because the numbers are exactly the same (applying the commutative law of multiplication). Nonetheless, people provide a higher estimate for the first sequence than for the second. The reason is that their computation of the anchor—the first few digits multiplied by each other—renders a higher estimate from which they make an adjustment to reach a final estimate.

Another consideration in decision theory is the influence of *framing effects,* in which the way that the options are presented influences the selection of an option (Tversky & Kahneman, 1981). For instance, we tend to choose options that demonstrate risk aversion when we are faced with an option involving potential gains. That is, we tend to choose options offering a small but certain gain rather than a larger but uncertain gain, unless the uncertain gain is either tremendously greater or only modestly less than certain. The example in the "Investigating Cognitive Psychology" box is only slightly modified from one used by Tversky and Kahneman (1981).

INVESTIGATING COGNITIVE PSYCHOLOGY	Suppose that you were told that 600 people were at risk of dying of a particular disease. Vaccine A could save the lives of 200 of the people at risk. For Vaccine B, there is a 0.33 likelihood that all 600 people would be saved, but there is a 0.66 likelihood that all 600 people will die. Which option would you choose?

We tend to choose options that demonstrate risk seeking when we are faced with options involving potential losses. That is, we tend to choose options offering a large but uncertain loss rather than a smaller but certain loss, unless the uncertain loss is either tremendously greater or only modestly less than certain. The next "Investigating Cognitive Psychology" box provides an interesting example.

INVESTIGATING COGNITIVE PSYCHOLOGY	Suppose that for the 600 people at risk of dying of a particular disease, if Vaccine C is used, 400 people will die. However, if Vaccine D is used, there is a 0.33 likelihood that no one will die and a 0.66 likelihood that all 600 people will die. Which option would you choose?

In the preceding situations, most people will choose Vaccine A and Vaccine D. Now, compare the number of people whose lives will be lost or saved by using Vaccines A or C. Similarly, compare the number of people whose lives will be lost or saved by using Vaccines B or D. In both cases, the expected value is identical. Our predilection for risk aversion versus risk seeking leads us to quite different choices based on the way in which a decision is framed, even when the actual outcomes of the choices are the same.

Another judgment phenomenon is **illusory correlation,** in which we tend to see particular events or particular attributes and categories as going together because we are predisposed to do so (Hamilton & Lickel, 2000). In the case of events, we may see spurious cause-effect relationships. In the case of attributes, we may use personal prejudices to form and use stereotypes (perhaps as a result of using the representativeness heuristic). For example, suppose we expect people of a given political party to show particular intellectual or moral characteristics. The instances in which people show those characteristics are more likely to be available in memory and recalled more easily than are instances that contradict our biased expectations. In other words, we perceive a correlation between the political party and the particular characteristics.

Illusory correlation even may influence psychiatric diagnoses based on projective tests such as the Rorschach and the Draw-a-Person tests (Chapman & Chapman, 1967, 1969, 1975). Researchers suggested a false correlation in which particular responses would be associated with particular diagnoses. For example, they suggested that people diagnosed with paranoia tend to draw people with large eyes more than do people with other diagnoses. In fact, diagnoses of paranoia were no more likely to be linked to depictions of large eyes than were any other diagnoses. However, what happened when individuals expected to observe a correlation between the particular responses and the associated diagnoses? They tended to see the illusory correlation, although no actual correlation existed.

Another common error is **overconfidence**—an individual's overvaluation of her or his own skills, knowledge, or judgment. For example, people answered 200 two-alternative statements, such as "Absinthe is (a) a liqueur, (b) a precious stone." (Absinthe is a licorice-flavored liqueur.) People were asked to choose the correct answer and to state the probability that their answer was correct (Fischhoff, Slovic, & Lichtenstein, 1977). People were overconfident. For example, when people were 100% confident in their answers, they were right only 80% of the time. In general, people tend to overestimate the accuracy of their judgments (Kahneman & Tversky, 1996). Why are people overconfident? One reason is that people may not realize how little they know. A second reason is that they may realize what they are assuming when they call on the knowledge they have. A third reason may be their ignorance of the fact that their information comes from unreliable sources (Carlson, 1995; Griffin & Tversky, 1992).

Because of overconfidence, people often make poor decisions. These decisions are based on inadequate information and ineffective decision-making strategies. Why we tend to be overconfident in our judgments is not clear. One simple explanation is that we prefer not to think about being wrong (Fischhoff, 1988).

An error in judgment that is quite common in people's thinking is the *sunk-cost fallacy* (Dupuy, 1998, 1999; Nozick, 1990). This is the decision to continue to invest in something simply because one has invested in it before and one hopes to recover one's investment. For example, suppose you have bought a car. It is a lemon. You already have invested thousands of dollars in getting it fixed. Now you have another major repair on it confronting you. You have no reason to believe that this additional repair really will be the last in the string of repairs. You think how much money you have spent on repairs. You reason that you need to do the additional repair to justify the amount you already have spent on repairs. So you do the repair rather than buy a new car. You have just committed the sunk-cost fallacy. The problem is that you already have lost the money on those repairs. Throwing more money into the repairs will not get that money back. Your best bet may well be to view the money already spent on repairs as a "sunk cost." You then buy a new car. Similarly, suppose you go

Baruch Fischhoff is a professor of social and decision sciences and a professor of engineering and public policy at Carnegie-Mellon University. He has studied psychological processes such as hindsight bias, risk perception, and value elicitation. He also has done policy-making work in areas such as risk and environmental management.

on a vacation. You intend to stay on vacation for 2 weeks. You are having a miserable time. You are trying to decide whether to go home a week early. Should you go home a week early? You decide not to. In this way, you attempt to justify the investment you already have made in the vacation. Again, you have committed the sunk-cost fallacy. Instead of viewing the money simply as lost on an unfortunate decision, you have decided to throw more money away. But you do so without any hope that the vacation will get any better.

Taking *opportunity costs* into account is important when judgments are made. These are the prices paid for availing oneself of certain opportunities. For example, suppose you see a great job offer in San Francisco. You always wanted to live there. You are ready to take it. Before you do, you need to ask yourself a question. What other things will you have to forego to take advantage of this opportunity? An example might be the chance, on your budget, of having more than 500 square feet of living space. Another might be the chance to live in a place where you probably do not have to worry about earthquakes. Any time you take advantage of an opportunity, there are opportunity costs. They may, in some cases, make what looked like a good opportunity look like not such a great opportunity at all. Ideally, you should try to look at these opportunity costs in an unbiased way.

Finally, a bias that often affects all of us is **hindsight bias**—when we look at a situation retrospectively, we believe we easily can see all the signs and events leading up to a particular outcome (Fischhoff, 1982; Wasserman, Lempert, & Hastie, 1991). For example, suppose people are asked to predict the outcomes of psychological experiments in advance of the experiments. People rarely are able to predict the outcomes at better than chance levels. However, when people are told of the outcomes of psychological experiments, they frequently comment that these outcomes were obvious. They say the outcomes easily would have been predicted in advance. Similarly, when intimate personal relationships are in trouble, people often fail to observe signs of the difficulties until the problems reach crisis proportions. By then, it may be too late to save the relationship. In retrospect, however, people may slap their foreheads. They ask themselves, "Why didn't I see it coming? It was so obvious! I should have seen the signs."

Much of the work on judgment and decision making has focused on the errors we make. Human rationality is limited. Still, human irrationality also is limited (Cohen, 1981). We do act rationally in many instances. Also, each of us can improve our decision making through practice. We are most likely to do so if we obtain specific feedback regarding how to improve our decision-making strategies. Another key way to improve decision making is to gain accurate information for the calculation of probabilities. Then we must use probabilities appropriately in decision making. In addition, although subjective expected utility theory may offer a limited description of actual human decision making, it is far from useless. It offers a good prescription for enhancing the effectiveness of decision making when confronting a decision important enough to warrant the time and mental effort required (Slovic, 1990). Furthermore, we can try to avoid overconfidence in our intuitive guesses regarding optimal choices. Yet another way to enhance our decision making is to use careful reasoning in drawing inferences about the various options available to us.

The work on heuristics and biases shows the importance of distinguishing between intellectual competence and intellectual performance as it manifests itself in daily life. Even experts in the use of probability and statistics can find themselves falling into faulty patterns of judgment and decision making in their everyday lives. People may be intelligent in a conventional, test-based sense. Yet they may show exactly the same biases and faulty reasoning that someone with a lower test score would show. People often fail to fully utilize their intellectual competence in their daily life. There even can be a wide gap between the two. Thus, if we wish to be intelligent in our daily lives and not just on tests, we have to be street smart. In particular, we must be mindful of applying our intelligence to the problems that continually confront us.

Heuristics do not always lead us astray. Sometimes, they are amazingly simple ways of drawing sound conclusions. For example, a simple heuristic, *take the best,* can be amazingly effective in decision situations (Gigerenzer & Goldstein, 1996; Gigerenzer, Todd, & the ABC Research Group, 1999; Marsh, Todd, & Gigerenzer, 2004). The rule is simple. In making a decision, identify the single most important criterion to you for making that decision. For example, when you choose a new automobile, the most important factor might be good gas mileage, safety, or appearance. This heuristic would seem on its face to be inadequate. In fact, it often leads to very good decisions. It produces even better decisions, in many cases, than far more complicated heuristics. Thus, heuristics can be used for good as well as for bad decision making. Indeed, when we take people's goals into account, heuristics often are amazingly effective (Evans & Over, 1996).

The take-the-best heuristic belongs to a class of heuristics called fast-and-frugal heuristics (FFH). As the name implies, this class of heuristics is based on a small fraction of information and decisions using the heuristics are made rapidly. These heuristics set a standard of rationality that considers constraints including, time, information, and cognitive capacity (Bennis & Pachur, 2006). Further, these models consider the lack of optimum solutions and environments in which the decision is taking place. As a result, these heuristics provide a good description of decision making during sports (Bennis & Pachur, 2006). Other researchers have noted that FFHs can form a comprehensive description of how people behave in a variety of contexts. These behaviors vary from lunch selections to how physicians decide whether to prescribe medication for depression (Scheilbehenne, Miesler, & Todd, 2007; Smith & Gilhooly, 2006).

Neuroscience of Decision Making

As in problem solving, the prefrontal cortex, and particularly the anterior cingulate cortex, is active during the decision-making process (Barraclough, Conroy, & Lee, 2004; Kennerley & associates, 2006; Rogers & associates, 2004). Explorations of decision making in monkeys have noted activation in the parietal regions of the brain (Platt & Glimcher, 1999). The amount of gain associated with a decision also affects the amount of activation observed in the parietal region (Platt & Glimcher, 1999).

Examination of decision making in drug abusers identified a number of areas involved in risky decisions. Researchers found decreased activation in the left pregenual anterior cingulate cortex of drug abusers (Fishbein & associates, 2005). These findings suggest that, during decision making, the anterior cingulate cortex is involved in consideration of potential rewards. Another interesting effect seen in this area is observed in participants who have difficulty with a decision. In one study, participants made decisions concerning whether an item was old or new and which of two items

IN THE LAB OF GERD GIGERENZER

Courtesy of Dr. Gerd Gigerenzer/
Photographer: Dietmar Gust

Which city has a larger population, San Diego or San Antonio? Two-thirds of University of Chicago undergraduates got the answer right: San Diego. Then we asked German students who knew very little about San Diego, and many of whom had never even heard of San Antonio (Goldstein & Gigerenzer, 2002). What proportion of the German students do you think got the answer right? 100%. How can it be that people who know less about a subject get more correct answers? The answer is that the German students used the recognition heuristic. For the present case, this heuristic says:

If one of two objects is recognized and the other is not, then infer that the recognized object has the higher value with respect to the criterion.

Note that the American students could not use the recognition heuristic—they had heard of both cities. They had to rely on recall knowledge (i.e., facts) rather than recognition. The recognition heuristic can only be used by people who have a sufficient degree of ignorance, that is, who recognize only some objects—but not all. In such cases, the less-is-more effect can result; that is, less knowledge can lead to more accurate judgments. Similar surprising results have been obtained in predicting the outcome of British soccer games (e.g., Manchester United versus Shrewsbury Town) by people in England as opposed to Turkey. The recognition heuristic is also used in the supermarket when customers must choose among several similar products, preferring one whose name they have heard of. This heuristic is exploited by advertisements, like those of Bennetton, which give no information about the product but simply try to increase name recognition. Finally, the recognition heuristic has also been successful on the stock market, where it managed to outperform major mutual funds and the Dow in picking stock investments (Borges & associates, 1999).

The recognition heuristic does not always apply, however, nor can it always make correct inferences. The effectiveness of the apparently simplistic heuristic depends on its ecological rationality: its ability to exploit the structure of the information in natural environments. The heuristic is successful when ignorance—specifically, a lack of recognition—is systematically rather than randomly distributed, that is, when it is strongly correlated with the criterion. Experimental studies indicate that 90% or more of the participants rely on the recognition heuristic in situations in which it is ecologically rational.

In the Center for Adaptive Behavior and Cognition (ABC) at the Max Planck Institute for Human Development, we study not only this heuristic but a whole adaptive toolbox of heuristics. Part of the fun in the lab springs from the interdisciplinary nature of the ABC group. Psychologists collaborate with economists, mathematicians, computer scientists, and evolutionary biologists, among others. Using multiple methods, we attempt to open the adaptive toolbox.

The adaptive toolbox is, in two respects, a Darwinian metaphor for decision making. First, evolution does not follow a grand plan, but results in a patchwork of solutions for specific problems. The same goes for the toolbox: Its heuristics are domain specific, not general. Second, the heuristics in the adaptive toolbox are not good or bad, rational or irrational, per se, only relative to an environment, just as adaptations are context-bound. In these two restrictions lie their potential: Heuristics can perform astonishingly well when used in a suitable environment. The rationality of the adaptive toolbox is not logical, but rather ecological.

The ABC program aims at providing the building blocks, or, if you like, the ABC's of cognitive heuristics for choice, categorization, inference, estimation, preference, and other tasks. These heuristics are fast because they involve little computation, frugal because they search only for little information, and robust because their simplicity makes it likely they can be generalized effectively to new environments. Herbert Simon once introduced the metaphor of a pair of scissors to exemplify what we call ecological rationality. One blade is the mind, the other the environment. To understand cognition, we study the match between the structure of cognitive heuristics and the environment. Studying one blade alone, as much of cognitive science today does, will not reveal why and how cognition works.

was larger (Fleck & associates, 2006). Decisions that were rated lowest in confidence and that took the most time to answer were associated with higher activation of the anterior cingulate cortex. These findings suggest that this area of the brain is involved in the comparison and weighing of possible solutions.

Reasoning

Judgment and decision making involve evaluating opportunities and selecting one choice over another. A related kind of thinking is reasoning. **Reasoning** is the process of drawing conclusions from principles and from evidence (Leighton, 2004a, 2004b; Leighton & Sternberg, 2004; Sternberg, 2004; Wason & Johnson-Laird, 1972). In reasoning, we move from what is already known to infer a new conclusion or to evaluate a proposed conclusion.

Reasoning is often divided into two types: deductive and inductive reasoning. **Deductive reasoning** is the process of reasoning from one or more general statements regarding what is known to reach a logically certain conclusion (Johnson-Laird, 2000; Rips, 1999; Williams, 2000). It often involves reasoning from one or more general statements regarding what is known to a specific application of the general statement. In contrast, **inductive reasoning** is the process of reasoning from specific facts or observations to reach a likely conclusion that may explain the facts. The inductive reasoner then may use that probable conclusion to attempt to predict future specific instances (Johnson-Laird, 2000). The key feature distinguishing inductive from deductive reasoning is that in inductive reasoning, we never can reach a logically certain conclusion. We only can reach a particularly well-founded or probable conclusion.

Deductive Reasoning

Deductive reasoning is based on logical propositions. A **proposition** is basically an assertion, which may be either true or false. Examples are "Cognitive psychology students are brilliant," "cognitive psychology students wear shoes," or "cognitive psychology students like peanut butter." In a logical argument, **premises** are propositions about which arguments are made. Cognitive psychologists are interested particularly in propositions that may be connected in ways that require people to draw reasoned conclusions. That is, deductive reasoning is useful because it helps people connect various propositions to draw conclusions. Cognitive psychologists want to know how people connect propositions to draw conclusions. Some of these conclusions are well reasoned. Others are not. Much of the difficulty of reasoning is in even understanding the language of problems (Girotto, 2004). Some of the mental processes used in language understanding, and the cerebral functioning underlying them, are used in reasoning too (Lawson, 2004).

Conditional Reasoning

One of the primary types of deductive reasoning is **conditional reasoning,** in which the reasoner must draw a conclusion based on an if-then proposition. The conditional if-then proposition states that if antecedent condition p is met, then consequent event q follows. For example, "If students study hard, then they score high on their exams." Under some circumstances, if you have established a conditional proposition, then you

TABLE 12.2	Conditional Reasoning: Deductively Valid Inferences and Deductive Fallacies

Two kinds of conditional propositions lead to valid deductions, and two others lead to deductive fallacies.

TYPE OF ARGUMENT		**CONDITIONAL PROPOSITION**	**EXISTING CONDITION**	**INFERENCE**
Deductively valid inferences	*Modus ponens*	$p \rightarrow q$ If you are a mother, then you have a child.	p You are a mother.	∴ q Therefore, you have a child.
	Modus tollens	$p \rightarrow q$ If you are a mother, then you have a child.	¬ q You do not have a child.	∴ ¬ p Therefore, you are not a mother.
Deductive fallacies	Denying the antecedent	$p \rightarrow q$ If you are a mother, then you have a child.	¬ p You are not a mother.	∴ ¬ q Therefore, you do not have a child.
	Affirming the consequent	$p \rightarrow q$ If you are a mother, then you have a child.	q You have a child.	∴ p Therefore, you are a mother.

may draw a well-reasoned conclusion. The usual set of conditional propositions from which you can draw a well-reasoned conclusion is "If p, then q. p. Therefore, q." This inference illustrates deductive validity. That is, it follows logically from the propositions on which it is based. The following is also logical: "If students eat pizza, then they score high on their exams. They eat pizza. Therefore, they score high on their exams." As you may have guessed, deductive validity does not equate with truth. You can reach deductively valid conclusions that are completely untrue with respect to the world. Whether the conclusion is true depends on the truthfulness of the premises. In fact, people are more likely mistakenly to accept an illogical argument as logical if the conclusion is factually true. For now, however, we put aside the issue of truth and focus only on the **deductive validity,** or logical soundness, of the reasoning.

One set of propositions and its conclusion is the argument "If p, then q. p. Therefore, q," which is termed a *modus ponens* argument. In the modus ponens argument, the reasoner affirms the antecedent. For example, take the argument "If you are a husband, then you are married. Harrison is a husband. Therefore, he is married." The set of propositions for the *modus ponens* argument is shown in Table 12.2. In addition to the *modus ponens* argument, you may draw another well-reasoned conclusion from a conditional proposition, given a different second proposition: "If p, then q. Not q. Therefore, not p." This inference is also deductively valid. This particular set of propositions and its conclusion is termed a *modus tollens* argument, in which the reasoner denies the consequent. For example, we modify the second proposition of the argument to deny the consequent: "If you are a husband, then you are married. Harrison is not married. Therefore, he is not a husband." Table 12.2 shows two conditions in which a well-reasoned conclusion can be reached. It also shows two conditions in which such a conclusion cannot be reached. As the examples illustrate, some inferences based on conditional reasoning are fallacies. They lead to conclusions that are not deductively valid. When using conditional propositions, we cannot reach a deductively valid conclusion based either on denying the antecedent condition or on affirming the consequent. Let's return to the proposition, "If you are a husband, then you are married." We would not be able to confirm or to refute the proposition based on denying the antecedent: "Joan is not a husband. Therefore, she is not married." Even if we ascertain that Joan is not a husband, we cannot conclude that she is not married. Similarly, we cannot deduce a valid conclusion by affirming the consequent: "Joan is married. Therefore, she is a husband." Even if Joan is married, her spouse may not consider her a husband.

Conditional reasoning can be studied in the laboratory using a "selection task" (Wason, 1968, 1969, 1983; Wason & Johnson-Laird, 1970, 1972). Participants are presented with a set of four two-sided cards. Each card has a numeral on one side and a letter on the other side. Face up are two letters and two numerals. The letters are a consonant and a vowel. The numbers are an even number and an odd number. For example, participants may be faced with the following series of cards: S 3 A 2. Each participant then is told a conditional statement. An example would be "If a card has a consonant on one side, then it has an even number on the other side." The task is to determine whether the conditional statement is true or false. One does so by turning over the exact number of cards necessary to test the conditional statement. That is, the participant must not turn over any cards that are not valid tests of the statement. But the participant must turn over all cards that are valid tests of the conditional proposition.

Table 12.3 illustrates the four possible tests participants might perform on the cards. Two of the tests (affirming the antecedent and denying the consequent) are both necessary and sufficient for testing the conditional statement. That is, to evaluate the deduction, the participant must turn over the card showing a consonant to see whether it has an even number on the other side. He or she thereby affirms the antecedent (the *modus ponens* argument). In addition, the participant must turn over the card showing an odd number (i.e., not an even number) to see whether it has a vowel (i.e., not a consonant) on the other side. He or she thereby denies the consequent (the *modus tollens* argument). The other two possible tests (denying the antecedent and affirming the consequent) are irrelevant. That is, the participant need not turn over the card showing a vowel (i.e., not a consonant). To do so would be to deny the antecedent. He or she also need not turn over the card showing an even number (i.e., not a odd number). To do so would be to affirm the consequent. Most participants knew to test for the *modus ponens* argument. However, many participants failed to test for the *modus tollens* argument. Some of these participants instead tried to deny the antecedent as a means of testing the conditional proposition.

Most people of all ages (at least starting in elementary school) appear to have little difficulty in recognizing and applying the *modus ponens* argument. However, few people spontaneously recognize the need for reasoning by means of the *modus tollens* argument. Many people do not recognize the logical fallacies of denying the antecedent or affirming the consequent, at least as these fallacies are applied to abstract reasoning problems (Braine & O'Brien, 1991; O'Brien, 2004; Rips, 1988, 1994; Rumain,

TABLE 12.3	Conditional Reasoning: Wason's Selection Task

In the Wason selection task, Peter Wason presented participants with a set of four cards, from which the participants were to test the validity of a given proposition. This table illustrates how a reasoner might test the conditional proposition $(p \rightarrow q)$, "If a card has a consonant on one side (p), then it has an even number on the other side (q)."

PROPOSITION BASED ON WHAT SHOWS ON THE FACE OF THE CARD	TEST	TYPE OF REASONING	
p A given card has a consonant on one side (e.g., "S," "F," "V," or "P")	∴ q Does the card have an even number on the other side?	Based on *modus ponens*	Deductively valid inferences
¬ q A given card does not have an even number on one side. That is, a given card has an odd number on one side (e.g., "3," "5," "7," or "9").	∴ ¬ p Does the card *not* have a consonant on the other side? That is, does the card have a vowel on the other side?	Based on *modus tollens*	
¬ p A given card does not have a consonant on one side. That is, a given card has a vowel on one side (e.g., "A," "E," "I," or "O").	∴ ¬ q Does the card *not* have an even number on the other side? That is, does the card have an odd number on the other side?	Based on denying the antecedent	Deductive fallacies
q A given card has an even number on one side (e.g., "2," "4," "6," or "8").	∴ p Does the card have a consonant on the other side?	Based on affirming the consequent	

Connell, & Braine, 1983). In fact, some evidence suggests that even people who have taken a course in logic fail to demonstrate deductive reasoning across various situations (Cheng & associates, 1986). Even training aimed directly at improving reasoning leads to mixed results. After training aimed at increasing reasoning, there is a significant increase in the use of mental models and rules (Leighton, 2006). However, after this training, there may be only a moderate increase in the use of deductive reasoning (Leighton, 2006). Most people do demonstrate conditional reasoning under two kinds of circumstances. The first is conditions that minimize possible linguistic ambiguities. The second is conditions that activate schemas that provide a meaningful context for the reasoning.

Why might both children and adults fallaciously affirm the consequent or deny the antecedent? Perhaps they do because of invited inferences that follow from normal discourse comprehension of conditional phrasing (Rumain, Connell, & Braine, 1983). For instance, suppose that my publisher advertises, "If you buy this textbook, then we will give you a $5 rebate." Consider everyday situations. You probably correctly infer that if you do not buy this textbook, the publisher will not give you a $5 rebate. However, formal deductive reasoning would consider this denial of the antecedent to be fallacious. The statement says nothing about what happens if you do *not* buy the textbook. Similarly, you may infer that you must have bought this textbook (affirm the consequent) if you received a $5 rebate from the publisher. But the statement says nothing about the range of circumstances that lead you to receive the $5 rebate. There may be other ways to receive it. Both inferences are fallacious according to formal deductive reasoning, but both are quite reasonable invited inferences in everyday situations. It helps when the wording of conditional-reasoning problems either explicitly or implicitly disinvites these inferences. Both adults and children are then much less likely to engage in these logical fallacies.

The demonstration of conditional reasoning also is influenced by the presence of contextual information that converts the problem from one of abstract deductive reasoning to one that applies to an everyday situation. For example, participants received both the Wason selection task and a modified version of the Wason selection task (Griggs & Cox, 1982). In the modified version, the participants were asked to suppose that they were police officers. As officers, they were attempting to enforce the laws applying to the legal age for drinking alcoholic beverages. The particular rule to be enforced was "If a person is drinking beer, then the person must be over 19 years of age." Each participant was presented with a set of four cards: (1) "drinking a beer," (2) "drinking a Coke," (3) "16 years of age," and (4) "22 years of age." The participant then was instructed to "Select the card or cards that you definitely need to turn over to determine whether or not the people are violating the rule" (p. 414). On the one hand, none of Griggs and Cox's participants had responded correctly on the abstract version of the Wason selection task. On the other hand, a remarkable 72% of the participants correctly responded to the modified version of the task.

A more recent modification of this task has shown that beliefs regarding plausibility influence whether people choose the *modus tollens* argument. This is one's denying the consequent by checking to see whether a person who is not older than 19 years of age is not drinking beer. Specifically, people are far more likely to try to deny the consequent when the test involves checking to see whether an 18 year old is drinking beer than checking to see whether a 4 year old is drinking beer. Nevertheless, the logical argument is the same in both cases (Kirby, 1994). How do people use deductive reasoning in realistic situations? Two investigators have suggested that, rather than using formal inference rules, people often use pragmatic reasoning schemas (Cheng & Holyoak, 1985). **Pragmatic reasoning schemas** are general organizing principles or rules related to particular kinds of goals, such as permissions, obligations, or causations. These schemas sometimes are referred to as *pragmatic rules*. These pragmatic rules are not as abstract as formal logical rules. Yet they are sufficiently general and broad so that they can apply to a wide variety of specific situations. Prior beliefs, in other words, matter in reasoning (Evans & Feeney, 2004).

Alternatively, one's performance may be affected by *perspective effects*—that is, whether one takes the point of view of the police officers or of the people drinking the alcoholic beverages (Almor & Sloman, 1996; Staller, Sloman, & Ben-Zeev, 2000). So it may not be permissions *per se* that matter. Rather, what may matter are the perspectives one takes when solving such problems.

Thus, consider situations in which our previous experiences or our existing knowledge cannot tell us all we want to know. Pragmatic reasoning schemas help us deduce what might reasonably be true. Particular situations or contexts activate particular schemas. For example, suppose that you are walking across campus. You see someone who looks extremely young. Then you see the person walk to a car. He unlocks it, gets in, and drives away. This observation would activate your permission schema for driving. "If you are to be permitted to drive alone, then you must be at least 16 years old." You might now deduce that the person you saw is at least 16 years old. In one experiment, 62% of participants correctly chose *modus ponens* and *modus tollens* arguments but not the two logical fallacies when the conditional-reasoning task was presented in the context of permission statements. Only 11% did so when the task was presented in the context of arbitrary statements unrelated to pragmatic reasoning schemas (Cheng & Holyoak, 1985).

Researchers conducted an extensive analysis comparing the standard abstract Wason selection task with an abstract form of a permission problem (Griggs & Cox, 1993). The standard abstract form might be "If a card has an 'A' on one side, then it must have a '4' on the other side. The abstract permission form might be "If one is to take action 'A,' then one must first satisfy precondition 'P.'" Performance on the abstract permission task was still superior (49% correct overall) to performance on the standard abstract task (only 9% correct overall). This was so even when the authors added to the standard abstract task a statement that framed the task in a checking context. An example would be "Suppose you are an authority checking whether or not certain rules are being followed." The permission form was still better if a rule-clarification statement was added. An example of this would be "In other words, in order to have an 'A' on one side, a card must first have a '4' on the other side." And the permission form was better even for explicit negations. For example, "NOT A" and "NOT 4" would be used instead of implicit negations for "A" and "4"—namely, "B" and "7." Thus, although both the standard selection task and the permission-related task involve deductive reasoning, the two tasks actually appear to pose different problems (Griggs & Cox, 1993; Manktelow & Over, 1990, 1992). Pragmatic reasoning schemas do not, therefore, fully explain all aspects of conditional reasoning (Braine & O'Brien, 1991; Braine, Reiser, & Rumain, 1984; Rips, 1983, 1988, 1994). Indeed, people do not always use rules of reasoning at all (Garcia-Madruga & associates, 2000; Johnson-Laird & Savary, 1999; Smith, Langston, & Nisbett, 1992).

An altogether different approach to conditional reasoning takes an evolutionary view of cognition (Cummins, 2004). According to this view, we should consider what kinds of thinking skills would provide a naturally selective advantage for humans in adapting to our environment across evolutionary time (Cosmides, 1989; Cosmides & Tooby, 1996). To gain insight into human cognition, we should look to see what kinds of adaptations would have been most useful in the distant past. So we hypothesize on how human hunters and gatherers would have thought during the millions of years of evolutionary time that predated the relatively recent development of agriculture and the very recent development of industrialized societies.

How has evolution influenced human cognition? Humans may possess something like a schema-acquisition device (Cosmides, 1989). According to Cosmides, it facilitates our ability to quickly glean important information from our experiences. It also helps us to organize that information into meaningful frameworks. In her view, these schemas are highly flexible. But they also are specialized for selecting and organizing the information that will most effectively aid us in adapting to the situations we face. According to Cosmides, one of the distinctive adaptations shown by human hunters and gatherers has been in the area of social exchange. Hence, evolutionary development of human cognition should facilitate the acquisition of schemas related to social exchange.

According to Cosmides, there are two kinds of inferences in particular that social-exchange schemas facilitate. One kind is inferences related to cost-benefit relationships. The other kind is inferences that help people detect when someone is cheating in a particular social exchange. Across nine experiments, participants demonstrated deductive reasoning that confirmed the predictions of social-exchange theory, rather than predictions based on permissions-related schemas or on abstract deductive-reasoning principles (Cosmides, 1989).

Syllogistic Reasoning

In addition to conditional reasoning, the other key type of deductive reasoning is syllogistic reasoning, which is based on the use of syllogisms. **Syllogisms** are deductive arguments that involve drawing conclusions from two premises (Maxwell, 2005; Rips, 1994, 1999). All syllogisms comprise a major premise, a minor premise, and a conclusion. Unfortunately, sometimes the conclusion may be that no logical conclusion may be reached based on the two given premises.

Linear Syllogisms

In a syllogism, each of the two premises describes a particular relationship between two items and at least one of the items is common to both premises. The items may be objects, categories, attributes, or almost anything else that can be related to something. Logicians designate the first term of the major premise as the subject. The common term is the middle term (which is used once in each premise). The second term of the minor premise is the predicate.

In a linear syllogism, the relationship among the terms is linear. It involves a quantitative or qualitative comparison. Each term shows either more or less of a particular attribute or quantity. Suppose, for example, that you are presented with the problem in the "Investigating Cognitive Psychology" box.

You are smarter than your best friend. Your best friend is smarter than your roommate. Which of you is the smartest?	**INVESTIGATING COGNITIVE PSYCHOLOGY**

Each of the two premises describes a linear relationship between two items; Table 12.4 shows the terms of each premise and the relationship of the terms in each premise. The deductive-reasoning task for the linear syllogism is to determine a relationship between two items that do not appear in the same premise. In the preceding linear syllogism, the problem solver needs to infer that you are smarter than your roommate to realize that you are the smartest of the three.

When the linear syllogism is deductively valid, its conclusion follows logically from the premises. We correctly can deduce with complete certainty that you are the

TABLE 12.4	Linear Syllogisms

What logical deduction can you reach based on the premises of this linear syllogism? Is deductive validity the same as truth?

	First Term (Item)	**Linear Relationship**	**Second Term (Item)**
Premise A Premise B Conclusion: Who is smartest?	You Your best friend _____	are smarter than is smarter than is/are the smartest of the three.	your best friend. your roommate.

smartest of the three. Your roommate or your best friend may, however, point out an area of weakness in your conclusion. Even a conclusion that is deductively valid may not be objectively true. Of course, it is true in this example.

How do people solve linear syllogisms? Several different theories have been proposed. Some investigators have suggested that linear syllogisms are solved spatially, through mental representations of linear continua (DeSoto, London, & Handel, 1965; Huttenlocher, 1968). The idea here is that people imagine a visual representation laying out the terms on a linear continuum. For example, the premise "You are smarter than your roommate" might be represented mentally as an image of a vertical continuum. Your name is above your roommate's. The linear continuum usually is visualized vertically, although it can be visualized horizontally. When answering the question, people consult this continuum and choose the item in the correct place along the continuum.

Other investigators have proposed that people solve linear syllogisms using a semantic model involving propositional representations (Clark, 1969). For example, the premise "You are smarter than your roommate" might be represented as [smarter (you, your roommate)]. According to this view, people do not use images at all but rather combine semantic propositions.

A third view is that people use a combination of spatial and propositional representations in solving the syllogisms (Sternberg, 1980). According to this view, people use propositions initially to represent each of the premises. They then form mental images based on the contents of these propositions. Model testing has tended to support the combination (or mixture) model over exclusively propositional or exclusively spatial representations (Sternberg, 1980).

None of the three models appear to be quite right, however. They all represent performance averaged over many individuals. Rather, there seem to be individual differences in strategies, in which some people tend to use a more imaginal strategy and others tend to use a more propositional strategy (Sternberg & Weil, 1980). This result points out an important limitation of many psychological findings: Unless we consider each individual separately, we risk jumping to conclusions based on a group average that does not necessarily apply to each person individually (see Siegler, 1988). Whereas most people may use a combination strategy, not everyone does. The only way to find out which each person uses is to examine each individual.

Categorical Syllogisms

Probably the most well-known kind of syllogism is the categorical syllogism. Like other kinds of syllogisms, categorical syllogisms comprise two premises and a conclusion. In the case of the **categorical syllogism,** the premises state something about the category memberships of the terms. In fact, each term represents all, none, or some of the members of a particular class or category. As with other syllogisms, each premise contains two terms. One of them must be the middle term, common to both premises. The first and the second terms in each premise are linked through the categorical membership of the terms. That is, one term is a member of the class indicated by the other term. However the premises are worded, they state that some (or all or none) of the members of the category of the first term are (or are not) members of the category of the second term. To determine whether the conclusion follows logically from the premises, the reasoner must determine the category memberships of the terms. An example of a categorical syllogism would be as follows:

All cognitive psychologists are pianists.

All pianists are athletes.

Therefore, all cognitive psychologists are athletes.

Logicians often use circle diagrams to illustrate class membership. They make it easier to figure out whether a particular conclusion is logically sound. The conclusion for this syllogism does in fact follow logically from the premises. This is shown in the circle diagram in Figure 12.1. However, the conclusion is false because the premises are false. For the preceding categorical syllogism, the subject is cognitive psychologists, the middle term is pianists, and the predicate is athletes. In both premises, we asserted that all members of the category of the first term were members of the category of the second term.

Statements of the form "All A are B" sometimes are referred to as *universal affirmatives* because they make a positive (affirmative) statement about all members of a class (universal). In addition, there are three other kinds of possible statements in a categorical syllogism. One kind comprises *universal negative statements* (e.g., "No cognitive psychologists are flutists"). A second kind is *particular affirmative statements* (e.g., "Some cognitive psychologists are left-handed"). The last kind is *particular negative statements* (e.g., "Some cognitive psychologists are not physicists"). These are summarized in Table 12.5.

In all kinds of syllogisms, some combinations of premises lead to no logically valid conclusion. In categorical syllogisms, in particular, we cannot draw logically valid conclusions from categorical syllogisms with two particular premises or with two negative premises. For example, "Some cognitive psychologists are left-handed. Some left-handed people are smart." Based on these premises, you cannot conclude even that some cognitive psychologists are smart. The left-handed people who are smart might not be the same left-handed people who are cognitive psychologists. We just don't know. Consider a negative example: "No students are stupid. No stupid people eat pizza." We cannot conclude anything one way or the other about whether students eat pizza based on these two negative premises. As you may have guessed, people appear to have more difficulty (work more slowly and make more errors) when trying to deduce conclusions based on one or more particular premises or negative premises.

FIGURE 12.1

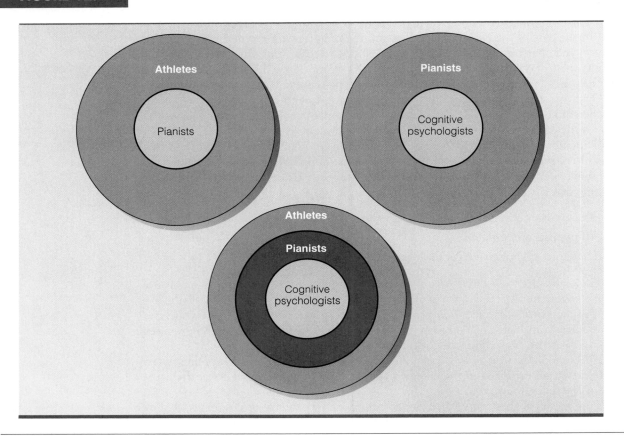

Circle diagrams may be used to represent categorical syllogisms such as the one shown here: "All pianists are athletes. All cognitive psychologists are pianists. Therefore, all cognitive psychologists are athletes." From In Search of the Human Mind *by Robert J. Sternberg. Copyright © 1995 by Harcourt Brace & Company. Reproduced by permission of the publisher.*

Various theories have been proposed as to how people solve categorical syllogisms. One of the earliest theories was the atmosphere bias (Begg & Denny, 1969; Woodworth & Sells, 1935). There are two basic ideas of this theory. The first is that if there is at least one negative in the premises, people will prefer a negative solution. The second is that if there is at least one particular in the premises, people will prefer a particular solution. For example, if one of the premises is "No pilots are children," people will prefer a solution that has the word *no* in it. Nonetheless, it does not account very well for large numbers of responses.

Other researchers focused attention on the conversion of premises (Chapman & Chapman, 1959). Here, the terms of a given premise are reversed. People sometimes believe that the reversed form of the premise is just as valid as the original form. The idea here is that people tend to convert statements like "If A, then B" into "If B, then

TABLE 12.5	Categorical Syllogisms: Types of Premises

The premises of categorical syllogisms may be universal affirmatives, universal negatives, particular affirmatives, or particular negatives.

TYPE OF PREMISE	FORM OF PREMISE STATEMENTS	DESCRIPTION	EXAMPLES	REVERSIBILITY*
Universal affirmative	All A are B.	The premise positively (affirmatively) states that all members of the first class (universal) are members of the second class.	All men are males.	All males are men. ≠ **Nonreversible** All A are B. All B are A.
Universal negative	No A are B. (Alternative: All A are *not* B.)	The premise states that none of the members of the first class are members of the second class.	No men are females. *or* All men are not females.	No men are females = No females are men. ↔Reversible↔ No A are B = No B are A.
Particular affirmative	Some A are B.	The premise states that only some of the members of the first class are members of the second class.	Some females are women.	Some females are women. ≠ Some women are females. **Nonreversible** Some A are B. ≠ Some B are A.
Particular negative	Some A are not B.	The premise states that some members of the first class are not members of the second class.	Some women are not females.	Some females are not women. ≠ **Nonreversible** Some A are not B. ≠ Some B are not A.

*In formal logic, the word *some* means "some and possibly all." In common parlance, and as used in cognitive psychology, *some* means "some and not all." Thus, in formal logic, the particular affirmative also would be reversible. For our purposes, it is not.

A." They do not realize that the statements are not equivalent. These errors are made by children and adults alike (Markovits, 2004).

A more widely accepted theory is based on the notion that people solve syllogisms by using a semantic (meaning-based) process based on mental models (Espino & associates, 2005; Johnson-Laird, 1997; Johnson-Laird & associates, 1999; Johnson-Laird, Byrne, & Schaeken, 1992; Johnson-Laird & Savary, 1999; Johnson-Laird & Steedman, 1978). This view of reasoning as involving semantic processes based on mental models may be contrasted with rule-based ("syntactic") processes, such as those characterized by formal logic. A **mental model** is an internal representation of information that corresponds analogously with whatever is being represented (see Johnson-Laird, 1983). Some mental models are more likely to lead to a deductively valid conclusion than are others. In particular, some mental models may not be effective in disconfirming an invalid conclusion.

For example, in the Johnson-Laird study, participants were asked to describe their conclusions and their mental models for the syllogism, "All of the artists are beekeep-

Philip Johnson-Laird is a professor of psychology at Princeton University. He is best known for his work on mental models, deductive reasoning, and creativity. In particular, Johnson-Laird has shown how the concept of mental models can be applied toward understanding a wide variety of psychological processes.

ers. Some of the beekeepers are clever." One participant said, "I thought of all the little . . . artists in the room and imagined they all had beekeeper's hats on" (Johnson-Laird & Steedman, 1978, p. 77). Figure 12.2 shows two different mental models for this syllogism. As the figure shows, the choice of a mental model may affect the reasoner's ability to reach a valid deductive conclusion. Because some models are better than others for solving some syllogisms, a person is more likely to reach a deductively valid conclusion by using more than one mental model.

In the figure, the mental model shown in part *a* may lead to the deductively invalid conclusion that some artists are clever. By observing the alternative model in part *b*, we can see an alternative view of the syllogism. It shows that the conclusion that some artists are clever may not be deduced on the basis of this information alone. Specifically, perhaps the beekeepers who are clever are not the same as the beekeepers who are artists.

Two types of representations of syllogisms are often used by logicians. As mentioned previously, circle diagrams are often used to represent categorical syllogisms. In circle diagrams, you can use overlapping, concentric, or nonoverlapping circles to represent the members of different categories (see Figures 12.1 and 12.2). An alternative representation often used by logicians is a truth table. It can be used to represent the truth value of various combinations of propositions, based on the truth value of each of the component propositions. People can learn how to improve their reasoning by being taught how to circle diagrams or truth tables (Nickerson, 2004).

According to this view, the difficulty of many problems of deductive reasoning relates to the number of mental models needed for adequately representing the premises of the deductive argument (Johnson-Laird, Byrne, & Schaeken, 1992). Arguments that entail only one mental model may be solved quickly and accurately. However, to infer accurate conclusions based on arguments that may be represented by multiple alternative models is much harder. Such inferences place great demands on working memory (Gilhooly, 2004). In these cases, the individual must simultaneously hold in working memory each of the various models. Only in this way can he or she reach or evaluate a conclusion. Thus, limitations of working-memory capacity may underlie at least some of the errors observed in human deductive reasoning (Johnson-Laird, Byrne, & Schaeken, 1992).

In two experiments, the role of working memory was studied in syllogistic reasoning (Gilhooly & associates, 1993). In the first, syllogisms were simply presented either orally or visually. Oral presentation placed a considerably higher load on working memory because participants had to remember the premises. In the visual-presentation condition, participants could look at the premises. As predicted, performance was lower in the oral-presentation condition. In a second experiment, participants needed to solve syllogisms while at the same time performing another task. Either the task drew on working-memory resources or it did not. The researchers found that the task that drew on working-memory resources interfered with syllogistic reasoning. The task that did not draw on these resources did not.

As children get older, their effective use of working memory increases. So their ability to use mental models that draw on working-memory resources also increases. Researchers asked children of different ages to look at cards with objects displayed on them, such as shirts and trousers of different colors (Barrouillet & Lecas, 1998). Then they were given premises, such as "If you wear a white shirt, you wear green trousers."

FIGURE 12.2

Philip Johnson-Laird and Mark Steedman hypothesized that people use various mental models analogously to represent the items within a syllogism. Some mental models are more effective than others, and for a valid deductive conclusion to be reached, more than one model may be necessary, as shown here. (See text for explanation.)

They were asked to indicate which combinations of cards were consistent with the premises. For example, cards with white shirts and green trousers would be consistent with this premise, but so would shirts and trousers of other colors because the statement also implies that if you do not wear green trousers, you do not wear a white shirt. Older children, who were able to hold more combinations in working memory, chose more different card combinations to represent the premises.

Other factors also may contribute to the ease of forming appropriate mental models. People seem to solve logical problems more accurately and more easily when the terms have high imagery value (Clement & Falmagne, 1986). This situation probably facilitates their mental representation. Similarly, when propositions showed high relatedness in terms of mental images, participants could more easily and accurately solve the problems and judge the accuracy of the conclusions. An example would be one premise about dogs and the other about cats, rather than one about dogs and the other about tables. For example, it would be relatively easy to solve a high-imagery, high-relatedness syllogism, such as "Some artists are painters. Some painters use black paint." It would be relatively hard to solve a low-imagery, low-relatedness syllogism, such as "Some texts are prose. Some prose is well-written." High imagery value and high relatedness may make it easier for reasoners to come up with counterexamples that reveal an argument to be deductively invalid (Clement & Falmagne, 1986).

Some deductive-reasoning problems comprise more than two premises. For example, transitive-inference problems, in which problem solvers must order multiple terms, can have any number of premises linking large numbers of terms. Mathematical and logical proofs are deductive in character and can have many steps as well.

Further Aids and Obstacles to Deductive Reasoning

In deductive reasoning, as in many other cognitive processes, we engage in many heuristic shortcuts. They sometimes lead to inaccurate conclusions. In addition to these shortcuts, we often are influenced by biases that distort the outcomes of our reasoning.

Heuristics in syllogistic reasoning include *overextension errors*. In these errors, we overextend the use of strategies that work in some syllogisms to syllogisms in which the strategies fail us. For example, although reversals work well with universal negatives, they do not work with other kinds of premises. We also experience *foreclosure effects* when we fail to consider all the possibilities before reaching a conclusion. For example, we may fail to think of contrary examples when inferring conclusions from particular or negative premises. In addition, premise-phrasing effects may influence our deductive reasoning. Examples would be the sequence of terms or the use of particular qualifiers or negative phrasing. Premise-phrasing effects may lead us to leap to a conclusion without adequately reflecting on the deductive validity of the syllogism.

Biases that affect deductive reasoning generally relate to the content of the premises and the believability of the conclusion. They also reflect the tendency toward *confirmation bias*. In confirmation bias, we seek confirmation rather than disconfirmation of what we already believe. Suppose the content of the premises and a conclusion seem to be true. In such cases, reasoners tend to believe in the validity of the conclusion, even when the logic is flawed (Evans, Barston, & Pollard, 1983).

Confirmation bias can be detrimental and even dangerous in some circumstances. For instance, in an emergency room, if a doctor assumes that a patient has condition X, the doctor may interpret the set of symptoms as supporting the diagnosis without fully considering all alternative interpretations (Pines, 2005). This shortcut can result in inappropriate diagnosis and treatment, which can be extremely dangerous. Other circumstances where the effects of confirmation bias can be observed are in police investigations, paranormal beliefs, and stereotyping behavior (Ask & Granhag, 2005; Biernat & Ma, 2005; Lawrence & Peters, 2004). To a lesser extent, people also show the opposite tendency to disconfirm the validity of the conclusion when the conclusion or the content of the premises contradicts the reasoner's existing beliefs (Evans, Barston, & Pollard, 1983; Janis & Frick, 1943). This is not to say that people fail to consider logical principles when reasoning deductively. In general, explicit attention to the premises seems more likely to lead to valid inferences. Explicit attention to irrelevant information more often leads to inferences based on prior beliefs regarding the believability of the conclusion (Evans, Barston, & Pollard, 1983).

To enhance our deductive reasoning, we may try to avoid heuristics and biases that distort our reasoning. We also may engage in practices that facilitate reasoning. For example, we may take longer to reach or to evaluate conclusions. Effective reasoners also consider more alternative conclusions than do poor reasoners (Galotti, Baron, & Sabini, 1986). In addition, training and practice seem to increase performance on reasoning tasks. The benefits of training tend to be strong when the training relates to pragmatic reasoning schemas (Cheng & associates, 1986) or to such fields as law and medicine (Lehman, Lempert, & Nisbett, 1987). The benefits are weaker for abstract logical problems divorced from our everyday life (see Holland & associates, 1986; Holyoak & Nisbett, 1988).

One factor that affects syllogistic reasoning is mood. When people are in a sad mood, they tend to pay more attention to details (Schwarz & Skurnik, 2003). Hence, perhaps surprisingly, they tend to do better in syllogistic reasoning tasks when they are in a sad mood than when they are in a happy mood (Fiedler, 1988; Melton, 1995). People in a neutral mood tend to show performance in between the two extremes.

Even without training you can improve your own deductive reasoning through developing strategies to avoid making errors. Make sure you are using the proper strategies in solving syllogisms. Remember that reversals only work with universal negatives. Sometimes translating abstract terms to concrete ones (e.g., the letter C to cows) can help. Also, take the time to consider contrary examples and create more mental models. The more mental models you use for a given set of premises, the more confident you can be that if your conclusion is not valid, it will be disconfirmed. Thus, the use of multiple mental models increases the likelihood of avoiding errors. The use of multiple mental models also helps you to avoid the tendency to engage in confirmation bias. Circle diagrams also can be helpful in solving deductive-reasoning problems.

PRACTICAL APPLICATIONS OF COGNITIVE PSYCHOLOGY

Inductive Reasoning

With deductive reasoning, reaching logically certain—deductively valid—conclusions is at least theoretically possible. In inductive reasoning, which is based on our observations, reaching any logically certain conclusion is not possible. The most that we can strive to reach is only a strong, or highly probable, conclusion (Johnson-Laird, 2000; Thagard, 1999).

For example, suppose that you notice that all the people enrolled in your cognitive psychology course are on the dean's list (or honor roll). From these observations, you could reason inductively that all students who enroll in cognitive psychology are excellent students (or at least earn the grades to give that impression). However, unless you can observe the grade-point averages of all people who ever have taken or ever will take cognitive psychology, you will be unable to prove your conclusion. Further, a single poor student who happened to enroll in a cognitive psychology course would disprove your conclusion. Still, after large numbers of observations, you might conclude that you had made enough observations to reason inductively.

The fundamental riddle of induction is how we can make any inductions at all. As the future has not happened, how can we predict what it will bring? There is also an important so-called new riddle of induction (Goodman, 1983). Given possible alternative futures, how do we know *which one* to predict? For example, in the number series problem 2, 4, 6, ?, most people would replace the question mark with an 8. But we cannot know for sure that the correct number is 8. A mathematical formula could be proposed that would yield any number at all as the next number. So why choose the pattern of ascending even numbers (2x, where *x* is increasing integers)? Partly we choose it because it seems simple to us. It is a less complex formula than others we might choose. And partly we choose it because we are familiar with it. We are used to ascending series of even numbers. But we are not used to other complex series in which 2, 4, 6, may be embedded, such as 2, 4, 6, 10, 12, 14, 18, 20, 22, and so forth.

In this situation and in many others requiring reasoning, you were not given clearly stated premises or obvious, certain relationships between the elements. Such information could lead you to deduce a surefire conclusion. In its absence, you cannot deduce a logically valid conclusion at all. At these times, an alternative kind of reasoning is needed. Inductive reasoning involves reasoning where there is no logically certain conclusion. Often it involves reasoning from specific facts or observations to a general conclusion that may explain the facts.

Inductive reasoning forms the basis of the empirical method. In it, we cannot logically leap from saying, "All observed instances to date of X are Y" to saying, "Therefore, all X are Y." It is always possible that the next observed X will not be a Y. Furthermore, regardless of the number of observations or the soundness of the reasoning, no inductively based conclusions can be proved. Such conclusions only can be supported, to a greater or lesser degree, by available evidence. Thus, we return to the need to consider probability. The inductive reasoner must state any conclusions about a hypothesis in terms of likelihoods. Examples are "There is a 99% chance of rain tomorrow," or "The probability is only 0.05 that the null hypothesis is correct in asserting that these findings are a result of random variation."

Cognitive psychologists probably agree on at least two of the reasons why people use inductive reasoning. First, it helps them to become increasingly able to make sense out of the great variability in their environment. Second, it also helps them to predict events in their environment, thereby reducing their uncertainty. Thus, cognitive psychologists seek to understand the *how* rather than the *why* of inductive reasoning. We may (or may not) have some innate schema-acquisition device. But we certainly are not born with all the inferences we manage to induce. We already have implied that inductive reasoning often involves the processes of generating and testing hypotheses. We may further figure out that we reach inferences by generalizing some broad understandings from a set of specific instances. As we observe additional instances, we may further broaden our understanding. Or we may infer specialized exceptions to the general understandings. For example, after observing quite a few birds, we may infer that birds can fly. But after observing penguins and ostriches, we may add to our generalized knowledge specialized exceptions for flightless birds.

During generalization, we observe that particular properties vary together across diverse instances of a concept, or we may observe that particular procedures covary across different events. We then can induce some general principles for those co-variations. The great puzzle of inductive reasoning is how we manage to infer useful general principles based on the huge number of observations of covariation to which we are constantly exposed. Humans do not approach induction with mind-staggering computational abilities to calculate every possible covariation. Nor can we derive inferences from just the most frequent or the most plausible of these covariations. Rather, we seem to approach this task as we approach so many other cognitive tasks. We look for shortcuts. Inductive reasoners, like other probabilistic reasoners, use heuristics. Examples are representativeness, availability, the law of large numbers, and the unusualness heuristic. When using the unusualness heuristic, we pay particular attention to unusual events. When two unusual events co-occur or occur in proximity to one another, we tend to assume that the two events are connected in some way. For example, we might infer that the former unusual event caused the latter one (Holyoak & Nisbett, 1988).

Reaching Causal Inferences

One approach to studying inductive reasoning is to examine **causal inferences**—how people make judgments about whether something causes something else (Cheng, 1997, 1999; Cheng & Holyoak, 1995; Koslowski, 1996; Spellman, 1997). One of the first investigators to propose a theory of how people make causal judgments was John Stuart Mill (1887). He proposed a set of canons—widely accepted heuristic principles on which people may base their judgments. For example, one of Mill's canons is the *method of agreement*. It involves making separate lists of the possible causes that are present and those that are absent when a given outcome occurs. If, of all the possible causes, only one is present in all instances of the given outcome, the observer can conclude inductively that the one cause present in all instances is the true cause. That is, despite all the differences among possible causes, there is agreement in terms of one cause and one effect.

For example, suppose a number of people in a given community contracted hepatitis. The local health authorities would try to track down all the various possible means by which each of the hepatitis sufferers had contracted the disease. Now suppose it turned out that they all lived in different neighborhoods, shopped at different grocery stores, had different physicians and dentists, and otherwise led very different lives but that they all ate in the same restaurant on a given night. The health authorities probably inductively would conclude that they contracted hepatitis while eating at that restaurant.

Another of Mill's canons is the *method of difference*. In this method, you observe that all the circumstances in which a given phenomenon occurs are just like those in which it does not occur except for one way in which they differ. For example, suppose that a particular group of students all live in the same dormitory, eat the same food in the same dining halls, sleep on the same schedule, and take all the same classes. But some of the students attend one discussion group, and other students attend another. The students in discussion group A get straight As. But the students in discussion group B get straight Cs. We could conclude inductively that something is happening in the discussion groups to lead to this difference. Does this method sound familiar? If the observer manipulated the various aspects of this method, the method might be

TABLE 12.6	Market Analyst Observations Regarding Cosmetics Manufacturers	
Based on the information given here, how would you determine causality?		
Company 1	The office staff of the company organized and joined a union. The company's major product was under suspicion as a carcinogen.	There was a drastic drop in the value of the company's stock.
Company 2	The office staff of the company did not organize and join a union. The company's major product was under suspicion as a carcinogen.	There was a drastic drop in the value of the company's stock.
Company 3	Illegal campaign contributions were traced to the company's managers. The company's major product was not under suspicion as a carcinogen.	There was no drastic drop in the value of the company's stock.

called an empirical experiment: You would hold constant all the variables but one. You would manipulate this variable to observe whether it is distinctively associated with the predicted outcome. In fact, inductive reasoning may be viewed as hypothesis testing (Bruner, Goodnow, & Austin, 1956).

One study investigated causal inference by giving people scenarios such as the one shown in Table 12.6 (Schustack & Sternberg, 1981). Participants were to use the information describing the consequences for each company. They needed to figure out whether a company's stock values would drop if the company's major product were under suspicion as a carcinogen. People used four pieces of information to make causal judgments, as shown in Table 12.7. Specifically, they tended to confirm that an event was causal in one of two ways. The first was based on the joint presence of the possibly causal event and the outcome. The second was based on the joint absence of the possibly causal event and the outcome. They tended to disconfirm the causality of a particular antecedent event in two ways as well. One was based on the presence of the possibly causal event but the absence of the outcome. The other was based on the absence of the possibly causal event but the presence of the outcome. In these ways, people can be quite rational in making causal judgments. However, we do fall prey to various common errors of inductive reasoning. One common error of induction relates to the law of large numbers. Under some circumstances, we recognize that a greater number of observations strengthens the likelihood of our conclusions. At other times, however, we fail to consider the size of the sample we have observed when assessing the strength or the likelihood of a particular inference. In addition, most of us tend to ignore base-rate information. Instead, we focus on unusual variations or salient anecdotal ones. Awareness of these errors can help us improve our decision making.

Perhaps our greatest failing is one that extends to psychologists, other scientists, and nonscientists: We demonstrate confirmation bias, which may lead us to errors such as illusory correlations (Chapman & Chapman, 1967, 1969, 1975). Furthermore, we frequently make mistakes when attempting to determine causality based on correlational evidence alone. As has been stated many times, correlational evidence cannot indicate the direction of causation. Suppose we observe a correlation between Factor A and Factor B. We may find one of three things. First, it may be that Factor

TABLE 12.7	Four Bases for Inferring Causality

Even nonlogicians often use available information effectively when assessing causality.

CAUSAL INFERENCE	BASIS FOR INFERENCE	EXPLANATION	EXAMPLE
Confirmation	The joint presence of the possibly causal event and the outcome	If an event and an outcome tend to co-occur, people are more likely to believe that the event causes the outcome.	If some other company had a major product suspected to be a carcinogen and its stock went down, that pairing of facts would increase people's belief that having a major product labeled as a carcinogen depresses stock values.
Confirmation	The joint absence of the possibly causal event and the outcome	If the outcome does not occur in the absence of the possibly causal event, then people are more likely to believe that the event causes the outcome.	If other companies' stocks have not gone down when they had no products labeled as carcinogens, then the absence of both the carcinogens among the major products and the stock drops is at least consistent with the notion that having a product labeled as a carcinogen might cause stocks to drop.
Disconfirmation	The presence of the possibly causal event but the absence of the outcome	If the possibly causal event is present but not the outcome, then the event is seen as less likely to lead to the outcome.	If other companies have had major products labeled as carcinogens but their stocks have not gone down, people would be more likely to conclude that having a major product labeled as a carcinogen does not lead to drops in stock prices.
Disconfirmation	The absence of the possibly causal event but the presence of the outcome	If the outcome occurs in the absence of the possibly causal event, then the event is seen as less likely to lead to the outcome. (This rule is one of Mill's canons.)	If other companies have had stock prices drop without having products labeled as carcinogens, people would be less likely to infer that having a product labeled as a carcinogen leads to decreases in stock prices.

A causes Factor B. Second, it may be that Factor B causes Factor A. Third, some higher order Factor C may be causing both Factors A and B to occur together.

A related error occurs when we fail to recognize that many phenomena have multiple causes. For example, a car accident often involves several causes. For example, it may have originated with the negligence of several drivers, rather than just one. Once we have identified one of the suspected causes of a phenomenon, we may commit what is known as a *discounting error*. We stop searching for additional alternative or contributing causes.

Confirmation bias can have a major effect on our everyday lives. For example, we may meet someone, expecting not to like him. As a result, we may treat him in ways that are different from how we would treat him if we expected to like him. He then may respond to us in less favorable ways. He thereby "confirms" our original belief that he is not likable. Confirmation bias thereby can play a major role in schooling. Teachers often expect little of students when they think them low in ability. The students then give the teachers little. The teachers' original beliefs are thereby "confirmed" (Sternberg, 1997). This effect is referred to as a *self-fulfilling prophecy* (Harber & Jussim, 2005).

Research has investigated the relationship between covariation (correlation) information and causal inferences (Ahn & associates, 1995; Ahn & Bailenson, 1996). For some information to contribute to causal inferences, the information necessarily must be correlated with the event. But this covariation information is not sufficient to imply causality. The researchers proposed that the covariation information also must provide information about a possible causal mechanism for the information to contribute to causal inferences. Consider their example. In attempting to determine the cause of Jane's car accident last night, one could use purely covariation information. An example would be "Jane is more likely than most to have a car accident" and "car accidents were more likely to have occurred last night." However, people prefer information specifically about causal mechanisms (Ahn & associates, 1995). An example would be "Jane was not wearing her glasses last night" and "the road was icy," in making causal attributions over information that only covaries with the car accident event. Both these latter pieces of information about Jane's car accident can be considered covariation information, but the descriptions provide additional causal mechanism information.

In Chapter 8, we discussed the theory-based model of concepts. People's theories affect not only the concepts they have but also the causal inferences they make with these concepts. Consider a set of studies investigating how clinical psychologists make inferences about patients who come to them with various kinds of disorders. Typically, they use the *Diagnostic and Statistical Manual of Mental Disorders* (fourth edition; *DSM-IV*, American Psychiatric Association, 1994) to make such diagnoses. The *DSM-IV* is *atheoretical*. In other words, it is based on no theory. In five experiments, clinicians were asked to diagnose patients with disorders that were either causally central or causally peripheral to the clinicians' own theories of disorders. Participants were more likely to diagnose a hypothetical patient as having a disorder if that disorder was more causally central to the clinicians' own belief system. In other words, the clinicians' own implicit theories trumped the *DSM-IV* in their diagnosing.

The theory-based model of categorization posits that concepts are represented as theories, not feature lists. Thus, it is interesting that the *DSM-IV* established atheoretical guidelines for mental disorder diagnosis. Five experiments investigated how clinicians handled an atheoretical nosology (Kim & Ahn, 2002). The investigators used a variety of methods to ascertain clinicians' implicit personal theories of disorders. In this way, it was possible to discover the clinicians' causal theories of disorders. Then the clinicians' responses on diagnostic and memory tasks were measured. Of particular interest here is how the clinicians decided whether a patient had a particular disorder. Did they primarily use the *DSM-IV*, the standard reference manual in the field? Or did they use their own causal theories of disorders? Participants were more likely to diagnose a hypothetical patient with a disorder if that patient had causally central rather than causally peripheral symptoms according to their theory of the disorder. In other words, the more causally central to their own implicit theory a diagnosis was, the more likely they were to give that diagnosis in response to a set of symptoms. Their memory for causally central symptoms was also better than their memory for symptoms they saw as causally peripheral. Clinicians are thus driven to use their own implicit causal theories, even if they have had decades of practice with the atheoretical *DSM*. This set of studies provides strong support for the theory-based notion of concepts discussed in Chapter 8. But it also shows that these theories do not just "sit" in the head. They are actively used when we do causal reasoning. Even experts prefer their causal theories over a standard reference work in their field *(DSM-IV)*.

An alternative view is that people act as naive scientists in positing unobservable theoretical causal power entities to explain observable covariations (Cheng, 1997). Thus, people are somewhat rational in making causal attributions based on the right kinds of covariation information.

Categorical Inferences

On what basis do people draw inferences? People generally use both bottom-up strategies and top-down strategies for doing so (Holyoak & Nisbett, 1988). That is, they use both information from their sensory experiences and information based on what they already know or have inferred previously. Bottom-up strategies are based on observing various instances and considering the degree of variability across instances. From these observations, we abstract a prototype (see Chapters 6 and 9). Once a prototype or a category has been induced, the individual may use focused sampling to add new instances to the category. He or she focuses chiefly on properties that have provided useful distinctions in the past. Top-down strategies include selectively searching for constancies within many variations and selectively combining existing concepts and categories.

Reasoning by Analogy

Inductive reasoning may be applied to a broader range of situations than those requiring causal or categorical inferences. For example, inductive reasoning may be applied to reasoning by analogy. Consider an example analogy problem: "Fire is to asbestos as water is to (a) vinyl, (b) air, (c) cotton, (d) faucet." In reasoning by analogy, the reasoner must observe the first pair of items ("fire" and "asbestos" in this example) and must induce from those two items one or more relations (in this case, surface resistance because surfaces coated with asbestos can resist fire). The reasoner then must apply the given relation in the second part of the analogy. In the example analogy, the reasoner chooses the solution to be "vinyl" because surfaces coated with vinyl can resist water.

Some investigators have used reaction-time methodology to figure out how people solve induction problems. For example, using mathematical modeling I was able to break down the amounts of time participants spent on various processes of analogical reasoning. I found that most of the time spent in solving simple verbal analogies is spent in encoding the terms and in responding (Sternberg, 1977). Only a small part actually is spent in doing reasoning operations on these encodings.

The difficulty of encoding can become even greater in various puzzling analogies. For example, in the analogy RAT : TAR :: BAT : (a. CONCRETE, b. MAMMAL, c. TAB, d. TAIL), the difficulty is in encoding the analogy as one involving letter reversal rather than semantic content for its solution. In a problematic analogy such as AUDACIOUS : TIMOROUS :: MITIGATE : (a. ADUMBRATE, b. EXACERBATE, c. EXPOSTULATE, d. EVISCERATE), the difficulty is in recognizing the meanings of the words. If reasoners know the meanings of the words, they probably will find it relatively easy to figure out that the relation is one of antonyms. (Did this example audaciously exacerbate your difficulties in solving problems involving analogies?)

An application of analogies in reasoning can be seen in politics. It has been noted that analogies can help governing bodies come to conclusions (Breuning, 2003). It has also been argued that these analogies can be effectively used to conveying the justification of the decision to the public (Breuning, 2003). However, the use of analogies is not always successful. For example, the failure to reach a diplomatic outcome in Kosovo in 1999 may have been due to the selection and use of an inappropriate analogy (Hehir, 2006). These findings highlight both the utility and possible pitfalls of using analogies in political deliberation.

In 2007, opponents of President Bush used an analogy to Vietnam to argue for withdrawing from Iraq. They asserted that the failure of U.S. policies to lead to a conclusive victory were analogous between Vietnam and Iraq. Bush then turned the tables, using an analogy to Vietnam to argue that withdrawal from Iraq could lead to mass slaughter, as he asserted happened in Vietnam after the Americans left. Thus, analogies can end up being largely in the eye of the beholder rather than in the actual elements being compared.

Development of Inductive Reasoning

Young children do not have the same inductive-reasoning skills as do older children. For example, 4 year olds appear not to induce generalized biological principles about animals when given specific information about individual animals (Carey, 1987). By age 10 years, however, children are much more likely to do so. For example, if 4 year olds are told that both dogs and bees have a particular body organ, they still assume that only animals that are highly similar either to dogs or to bees have this organ and that other animals do not. In contrast, 10 year olds would induce that if animals as dissimilar as dogs and bees have this organ, many other animals are likely to have this organ as well. Also, 10 year olds would be much more likely than 4 year olds to induce biological principles that link humans to other animals.

Along the same lines, when 5 year olds learn new information about a specific kind of animal, they seem to add the information to their existing schemas for the particular kind of animal but not to modify their overall schemas for animals or for biology as a whole (see Keil, 1989, 1999). However, first- and second-graders have shown an ability to choose and even to spontaneously generate appropriate tests for gathering indirect evidence to confirm or disconfirm alternative hypotheses (Sodian, Zaitchik, & Carey, 1991).

Even children as young as 3 years seem to induce some general principles from specific observations, particularly those principles that pertain to taxonomic categories for animals (Gelman, 1984/1985; Gelman & Markman, 1987). For example, preschoolers were able to induce principles that correctly attribute the cause of phenomena (such as growth) to natural processes rather than to human intervention (Gelman & Kremer, 1991; Hickling & Gelman, 1995). In related work, preschoolers were able to reason correctly that a blackbird was more likely to behave like a flamingo than like a bat because blackbirds and flamingos are both birds (Gelman & Markman, 1987). Note that in this example, preschoolers are going against their perception that blackbirds look more like bats than like flamingos, basing their judgment instead on the fact that they are both birds (although the effect is admittedly strongest when the term *bird* also is used in regard to both the flamingo and the blackbird). Sobel and Kirkham (2006) extended these findings to 24-month-old children. Additionally, these experimenters demonstrated reasoning in children as young as 8 months. Infants in this study were able to predict the spatial location of a future event based on the observation of previous events.

Although the purpose of words is largely to express meaning—for example, to indicate a dog by the use of the word *dog* or a flamingo by the use of the word *flamingo*—there is some evidence that the process is not wholly one directional. Sometimes, children use words whose meanings they do not understand and only gradually acquire the correct meaning after they have started to use the words (Kessler Shaw, 1999). Nelson (1999) refers to this phenomenon as "use without meaning."

Other work supports the view that preschoolers may make decisions based on induced general principles rather than on perceptual appearances. For example, they may induce taxonomic categories based on functions (such as means of breathing) rather than on perceptual appearances (such as apparent weight) (Gelman & Markman, 1986). When given information about the internal parts of objects in one category, preschoolers also induced that other objects in the same category were likely to have the same internal parts (Gelman & O'Reilly, 1988; see also Gelman & Wellman, 1991).

However, when inducing principles from discrete information, young preschoolers were more likely than older children to emphasize external, superficial features of animals than to give weight to internal structural or functional features. Also, given the same specific information, older children seem to induce richer inferences regarding biological properties than do younger children (Gelman, 1989).

It is important to maintain both forms of knowledge, appearance based and principled, for flexible use across different situations and domains (Wellman & Gelman, 1998). Knowledge about deep internal functional relationships is important for inducing properties of objects. But similarity in appearance is also important under other circumstances. Knowledge acquisition develops via the use of framework theories, or models, for drawing inferences about the environment in various domains (such as physics, psychology, and biology) (Wellman & Gelman, 1998). Numerous studies demonstrate children's early and rapid acquisition of expertise in understanding physical objects and causal relations among events, psychological entities and casual-explanatory reasoning, and biological entities and forces. The changes in reasoning about factors in these domains appear to show enhanced understanding of the relation between appearances and deeper functional principles. Thus, children use foundational knowledge within different domains to build framework understandings of the world.

An Alternative View of Reasoning

By now you have reasonably inferred that cognitive psychologists often disagree—sometimes rather heatedly—about how and why people reason as they do. An alternative perspective on reasoning has been proposed. It is that two complementary systems of reasoning can be distinguished. The first is an associative system, which involves mental operations based on observed similarities and temporal contiguities (i.e., tendencies for things to occur close together in time). The second is a rule-based system, which involves manipulations based on the relations among symbols (Sloman, 1996).

The associative system can lead to speedy responses that are highly sensitive to patterns and to general tendencies. Through this system we detect similarities between observed patterns and patterns stored in memory. We may pay more attention to salient features (e.g., highly typical or highly atypical ones) than to defining features of a pattern. This system imposes rather loose constraints that may inhibit the selection of patterns that are poor matches to the observed pattern. It favors remembered patterns that are better matches to the observed pattern. An example of associative reasoning is use of the representativeness heuristic. Another example is the belief-bias effects in syllogistic reasoning. This effect occurs when we agree more with syllogisms that affirm our beliefs, whether or not these syllogisms are logically valid. An example of the workings of the associative system may be in the *false-consensus effect*. Here, people believe that their own behavior and judgments are more common and more appropriate than those of other people (Ross, Greene, & House, 1977). Suppose people have an opinion on an issue. They are likely to believe that because it is their opinion, it is likely to be shared and believed to be correct by others. Of course, there is some diagnostic value in one's own opinions. It is quite possible that others do indeed believe what one believes (Dawes & Mulford, 1996; Krueger, 1998). On the whole, however, associating others' views with our own simply because they are our own is a questionable practice.

The rule-based system usually requires more deliberate, sometimes painstaking procedures for reaching conclusions. Through this system, we carefully analyze relevant features (e.g., defining features) of the available data, based on rules stored in memory. This system imposes rigid constraints that rule out possibilities that violate the rules. Evidence of rule-based reasoning are several. First, we can recognize logical arguments when they are explained to us. Second, we can recognize the need to make categorizations based on defining features despite similarities in typical features. For example, we can recognize that a coin with a 3-inch diameter, which looks exactly like a quarter, must be a counterfeit. Third, we can rule out impossibilities, such as cats conceiving and giving birth to puppies. Fourth, we can recognize many improbabilities. For example, it is unlikely that the U.S. Congress will pass a law that provides annual salaries to all full-time college students. According to Sloman, we need both complementary systems. We need to respond quickly and easily to everyday situations, based on observed similarities and temporal contiguities. Yet we also need a means for evaluating our responses more deliberately.

The two systems may be conceptualized within a connectionist framework (Sloman, 1996). The associative system is represented easily in terms of pattern activation and inhibition, which readily fits the connectionist model. The rule-based system may be represented as a system of production rules (see Chapter 11).

An alternative connectionist view suggests that deductive reasoning may occur when a given pattern of activation in one set of nodes (e.g., those associated with a particular premise or set of premises) entails or produces a particular pattern of activation in a second set of nodes (Rips, 1994). Similarly, a connectionist model of inductive reasoning may involve the repeated activation of a series of similar patterns across various instances. This repeated activation then may strengthen the links among the activated nodes. It thereby leads to generalization or abstraction of the pattern for a variety of instances.

Connectionist models of reasoning and the various other approaches described in this chapter offer diverse views of the available data regarding how we reason and make judgments. At present, no one theoretical model explains all the data well. But each model explains at least some of the data satisfactorily. Together, the theories help us understand human intelligence, the topic of the next and final chapter.

Consider this passage from Shakespeare's *Macbeth:*

First Apparition: *Macbeth! Macbeth! Beware Macduff; Beware the thane of Fife. Dismiss me: enough. . . .*

Second Apparition: *Be bloody, bold, and resolute; laugh to scorn the power of man, for none of woman born shall harm Macbeth.*

Macbeth: *Then live, Macduff: what need I fear of thee? But yet I'll make assurance double sure, and take a bond of fate: thou shalt not live; that I may tell pale-hearted fear it lies, and sleep in spite of thunder.*

In this passage, Macbeth mistakenly took the Second Apparition's vision to mean that no man could kill him, so he boldly decided to confront Macduff. However, as we all know, Macduff was born by abdominal (Cesarean) delivery, so he did not fall into the category of men who could not harm Macbeth. Macduff eventually killed Macbeth because Macbeth came to a wrong conclusion based on the Second Apparition's premonition. The First Apparition's warning about Macduff should have been heeded.

Suppose you are trying to decide between buying an SUV or a subcompact car. You would like the room of the SUV, but you would like the fuel efficiency of the subcompact car. Whichever one you choose, did you make the right choice? This is a difficult question to answer because most of our decisions are made under conditions of uncertainty. Thus, let us say that you bought the SUV. You can carry a number of people, you have the power to pull a trailer easily up a hill, and you sit higher so your road vision is much better. However, every time you fill up the gas tank, you are reminded of how much fuel this vehicle takes. On the other hand, let us say that you bought the subcompact car. When picking up friends at the airport, you have difficulty fitting all of them and their luggage; you cannot pull trailers up hills (or at least, not very easily); and you sit so low that when there is an SUV in front of you, you can hardly see what is on the road. However, every time you fill up your gas tank or hear someone with an SUV complaining about how much it costs to fill up his or her tank, you see how little you have to pay for gas. Again, did you make the right choice? There are no right nor wrong answers to most of the decisions we make. We use our best judgment at the time of our decisions and think that they are more right than wrong as opposed to definitively right or wrong.

Neuroscience of Reasoning

As in both problem solving and decision making, the process of reasoning involves the prefrontal cortex (Bunge & associates, 2004). Further, reasoning involves brain areas associated with working memory, such as the basal ganglia (Melrose, Poulin, & Stern, 2007). The basal ganglia are involved in a variety of functions, including cognition and learning. This area is also associated with the prefrontal cortex through a variety of connections (Melrose, Poulin, & Stern, 2007). Furthermore, the contribution of working-memory systems is to be expected, as reasoning involves the integration of information. Exploration of conditional reasoning through event-related potential (ERP) methods revealed an increased negativity in the anterior cingulate cortex approximately 600 milliseconds and 2000 milliseconds after task presentation (Qui & associates, 2007). This negativity suggests increased cognitive control, as would be expected in a reasoning task.

In one study exploring moral reasoning in persons who show antisocial behaviors indicative of poor moral reasoning, malfunctions were noted in several areas within the prefrontal cortex, including the dorsal and ventral regions (Raine & Yang, 2006). Additionally, impairments in the amygdala, hippocampus, angular gyrus, anterior cingulated, and temporal cortex were also observed. Recall that the anterior cingulate is involved in decision making and the hippocampus is involved in working memory. Therefore, it is to be expected that malfunctions in these areas would result in deficiencies in reasoning.

Key Themes

Several of the themes discussed in Chapter 1 are relevant to this chapter.

A first theme is rationalism versus empiricism. Consider, for example, errors in syllogistic reasoning. One way of understanding such errors is in terms of the particular logical error made, independently of the mental processes the reasoner has used. For example, affirming the consequent is a logical error. One need do no empirical research to understand at the level of symbolic logic the errors that have been made. Moreover, deductive reasoning is itself based on rationalism. A syllogism such as "All toys are chairs. All chairs are hot dogs. Therefore, all toys are hot dogs" is logically valid but factually incorrect. Thus, deductive logic can be understood at a rational level, independently of its empirical content. But if we wish to know psychologically why people make errors or what is factually true, then we need to combine empirical observations with rational logic.

A second theme is domain generality versus domain specificity. The rules of deductive logic apply equally in all domains. One can apply them, for example, to abstract or to concrete content. But research has shown that, psychologically, deductive reasoning with concrete content is easier than reasoning with abstract content. So although the rules apply in exactly the same way generally across domains, ease of application is not psychologically equivalent across those domains.

A third theme is nature versus nurture. Are people preprogrammed to be logical thinkers? Piaget, the famous Swiss cognitive-developmental psychologist, believed so. He believed that the development of logical thinking follows an inborn sequence of stages that unfold over time. According to Piaget, there is not much one can do to alter either the sequence or timing of these stages. But research has suggested that the sequence Piaget proposed does not unfold as he thought. For example, many people never reach his highest stage, and some children are able to reason in ways he would not have predicted they would be able to reason until they were older. So once again, nature and nurture interact.

Summary

1. **What are some of the strategies that guide human decision making?** Early theories were designed to achieve practical mathematical models of decision making and assumed that decision makers are fully informed, infinitely sensitive to information, and completely rational. Subsequent theories began to acknowledge that humans often use subjective criteria for decision making, that chance elements often influence the outcomes of decisions, that humans often use subjective estimates for considering the outcomes, and that humans are not boundlessly rational in making decisions. People apparently often use satisficing strategies, settling for the first minimally acceptable option, and strategies involving a process of elimination by aspects to weed out an overabundance of options.

One of the most common heuristics most of us use is the representativeness heuristic. We fall prey to the fallacious belief that small samples of a population resemble the whole population in all respects. Our misunderstanding of base rates and other aspects of probability often leads us to other mental shortcuts as well, such as in the conjunction fallacy and the inclusion fallacy. Another common heuristic is the availability heuristic, in which we make judgments based on information that is readily available in memory, without bothering to seek less available information. The use of heuristics such as anchoring and adjustment, illusory correlation, and framing effects also often impair our ability to make effective decisions.

Once we have made a decision (or better yet, another person has made a decision) and the outcome of the decision is known, we may engage in hindsight bias, skewing our perception of the earlier evidence in light of the eventual outcome. Perhaps the most serious of our mental biases, however, is overconfidence, which seems to be amazingly resistant to evidence of our own errors.

2. **What are some of the forms of deductive reasoning that people may use, and what factors facilitate or impede deductive reasoning?** Deductive reasoning involves reaching conclusions from a set of conditional propositions or from a syllogistic pair of premises. Among the various types of syllogisms are linear syllogisms and categorical syllogisms. In addition, deductive reasoning may involve complex transitive-inference problems or mathematical or logical proofs involving large numbers of terms. Also, deductive reasoning may involve the use of pragmatic reasoning schemas in practical, everyday situations.

In drawing conclusions from conditional propositions, people readily apply the *modus ponens* argument, particularly regarding universal affirmative propositions. Most of us have more difficulty, however, in using the *modus tollens* argument and in avoiding deductive fallacies such as affirming the consequent or denying the antecedent, particularly when faced with propositions involving particular propositions or negative propositions. In solving syllogisms, we have similar difficulties with particular premises and negative premises and with terms that are not presented in the customary sequence. Frequently, when trying to draw conclusions, we overextend a strategy from a situation in which it leads to a deductively valid conclusion to one in which it leads to a deductive fallacy. We also may foreclose on a given conclusion before considering the full range of possibilities that may affect the conclusion. These mental shortcuts may be exacerbated by situations in which we engage in confirmation bias (tending to confirm our own beliefs).

We can enhance our ability to draw well-reasoned conclusions in many ways, such as by taking time to evaluate the premises or propositions carefully and by forming multiple mental models of the propositions and their relationships. We also may benefit from training and practice in effective deductive reasoning. We are particularly likely to reach well-reasoned conclusions when such conclusions seem plausible and useful in pragmatic contexts, such as during social exchanges.

3. **How do people use inductive reasoning to reach causal inferences and to reach other types of conclusions?** Although we cannot reach logically certain conclusions through inductive reasoning, we can at least reach highly probable conclusions through careful reasoning. More than a century ago, John Stuart Mill recommended that people use various canonical strategies for reaching inductive conclusions. When making categorical inferences, people tend to use both top-down and bottom-up strategies. Processes of inductive reasoning generally form the basis of scientific study and hypothesis testing as a means to derive causal inferences. In addition, in reasoning by analogy people often spend more time encoding the terms of the problem than in performing the inductive reasoning. It appears that people sometimes may use reasoning based on formal rule systems, such as by applying rules of formal logic, and sometimes use reasoning based on associations, such as by noticing similarities and temporal contiguities.

4. **Are there any alternative views of reasoning?** Steven Sloman has suggested that people have two distinct systems of reasoning: an associative system that is sensitive to observed similarities and temporal contiguities and a rule-based system that involves manipulations based on relations among symbols.

Thinking about Thinking: Factual, Analytical, Creative, and Practical Questions

1. Describe some of the heuristics and biases people use while making judgments or reaching decisions.

2. What are the two logical arguments and the two logical fallacies associated with conditional reasoning, as in the Wason selection task?

3. Which of the various approaches to conditional reasoning seems best to explain the available data? Give reasons for your answer.

4. Some cognitive psychologists question the merits of studying logical formalisms such as linear or categorical syllogisms. What do you think can be gained by studying how people reason in regard to syllogisms?

5. Based on the information in this chapter, design a way to help college students more effectively apply deductive reasoning to the problems they face.

6. Design a question, such as the ones used by Kahneman and Tversky, which requires people to estimate subjective probabilities of two different events. Indicate the fallacies that you may expect to influence people's estimates or tell why you think people would give realistic estimates of probability.

7. Suppose that you need to rent an apartment. How would you go about finding one that most effectively meets your requirements and your preferences? How closely does your method resemble the methods described by subjective expected utility theory, by satisficing, or by elimination by aspects?

8. Give two examples showing how you use rule-based reasoning and associative reasoning in your everyday experiences.

Key Terms

availability heuristic	fallacy	proposition
base rate	hindsight bias	reasoning
bounded rationality	illusory correlation	representativeness
categorical syllogism	inductive reasoning	satisficing
causal inferences	judgment and decision making	subjective probability
conditional reasoning	mental model	subjective utility
deductive reasoning	overconfidence	syllogism
deductive validity	pragmatic reasoning schema	
elimination by aspects	premises	

 Explore CogLab by going to **http://coglab.wadsworth.com.** To learn more, examine the following experiments:

Risky Decisions   Wason Selection Task

Typical Reasoning

Annotated Suggested Readings

Leighton, J. P., & Sternberg, R. J. (Eds.). (2004). *The nature of reasoning*. New York: Cambridge University Press. A complete review of contemporary theories and research on reasoning.

Sobel, D. M., & Kirkham, N. Z. (2006). Blickets and babies: the development of causal reasoning in toddlers and infants. *Developmental Psychology*, 42(6), 1103–1115. An approachable study examining reasoning in infants.

Human and Artificial Intelligence

EXPLORING COGNITIVE PSYCHOLOGY

1. What are the key issues in measuring intelligence? How do different researchers and theorists approach the issues?

2. What are some information-processing approaches to intelligence?

3. What are some alternative views of intelligence?

4. How have researchers attempted to simulate intelligence using machines such as computers?

5. Can intelligence be improved, and if so, how?

6. How does intelligence develop in adults?

INVESTIGATING COGNITIVE PSYCHOLOGY

Before you read about how cognitive psychologists view intelligence, try responding to a few tasks that require you to use your own intelligence:

1. Candle is to tallow as tire is to (a) automobile, (b) round, (c) rubber, (d) hollow.
2. Complete this series: 100%, 0.75, ½; (a) whole, (b) one eighth, (c) one fourth.
3. The first three items form one series. Complete the analogous second series that starts with the fourth item:

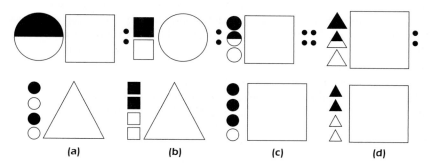

(a) (b) (c) (d)

4. You are at a party of truth-tellers and liars. The truth-tellers always tell the truth, and the liars always lie. You meet someone new. He tells you that he just heard a conversation in which a girl said she was a liar. Is the person you met a liar or a truth-teller?

Each of the preceding tasks is believed, at least by some cognitive psychologists, to require some degree of intelligence. (The answers are at the end of this section.) Intelligence is a concept that can be viewed as tying together all of cognitive psychology. Just what is intelligence? In a recent article, researchers identified approximately 70 different definitions of intelligence (Legg & Hutter, 2007). In 1921, when the editors of the *Journal of Educational Psychology* asked 14 famous psychologists that question, the responses varied but generally embraced these two themes. First, intelligence involves the capacity to learn from experience. Second, it involves the ability to adapt to the surrounding environment. Sixty-five years later, twenty-four cognitive psychologists with expertise in intelligence research were asked the same question

(Sternberg & Detterman, 1986). They, too, underscored the importance of learning from experience and adapting to the environment. They also broadened the definition to emphasize the importance of *metacognition*—people's understanding and control of their own thinking processes. Contemporary experts also more heavily emphasized the role of culture. They pointed out that what is considered intelligent in one culture may be considered stupid in another culture (Serpell, 2000). To summarize, **intelligence** is the capacity to learn from experience, using metacognitive processes to enhance learning, and the ability to adapt to the surrounding environment. It may require different adaptations within different social and cultural contexts.

According to the *Oxford English Dictionary,* the word *intelligence* entered our language in about the twelfth century. Today, we can look up intelligence in numerous dictionaries, but most of us still have our own implicit (unstated) ideas about what it means to be smart. That is, we have our own *implicit theories* (usually unstated conceptions) of intelligence. We use our implicit theories in many social situations. For example, we use them when we meet people and evaluate their intelligence. We also use them when we describe people we know as being very smart or not so smart.

Within our implicit theories of intelligence, we also recognize that intelligence has somewhat different meanings in different contexts. A smart salesperson may show a different kind of intelligence than a smart neurosurgeon or a smart accountant. Each of them may show a different kind of intelligence than a smart choreographer, composer, athlete, or sculptor. Often, we use our implicit and context-relevant definitions of intelligence to make assessments of intelligence. Is your mechanic smart enough to find and fix the problem in your car? Is your physician smart enough to find and treat your health problem? Is this attractive person smart enough to hold your interest in a conversation?

Implicit theories of intelligence may differ from one culture to another. For example, there is evidence that Chinese people in Taiwan include interpersonal and intrapersonal (self-understanding) skills as part of their conception of intelligence (Yang & Sternberg, 1997). Rural Kenyan conceptions of intelligence encompass moral as well as cognitive skills (Grigorenko & associates, 2001). Thus, what might count as a comprehensive assessment of intelligence could differ from one culture to another (Sternberg & Kaufman, 1998). Even within the United States, many people today have started viewing as important not only the cognitive aspects of intelligence but also the emotional aspects of intelligence. **Emotional intelligence** is "the ability to perceive and express emotion, assimilate emotion in thought, understand and reason with emotion, and regulate emotion in the self and others" (Mayer, Salovey, & Caruso, 2000, p. 396). There is good evidence for the existence of some kind of emotional intelligence (Cherniss & associates, 2006; Ciarrochi, Forgas, & Mayer, 2001; Mayer & Salovey, 1997; Salovey & Sluyter, 1997), although the evidence is mixed (Davies, Stankov, & Roberts, 1998; Waterhouse, 2006). The concept of emotional intelligence has also become very popular in recent years (Goleman, 1995, 1998). Some evidence suggests that emotional intelligence is a strong predictor of successful adaptation to new environments (e.g., college or a foreign country) and of success in one's chosen field (Gabel, Dolan, & Cerdin, 2005; Parker & associates, 2006; Stein & Book, 2006). A related concept is that of social intelligence. *Social intelligence* is the ability to understand and interact with other people (Goleman, 2007; Kihlstrom & Cantor, 2000).

Further, as discussed, there are a number of cultural differences in the definition of intelligence. These differences have led to a field of study within intelligence research that examines understanding of cultural differences in the definition of intelligence. This field explores what is termed *cultural intelligence,* or CQ (Sternberg & Grigorenko, 2006). This term is used to describe a person's ability to adapt to a variety of challenges in diverse cultures (Ang, Dyne, & Koh, 2006; Sternberg & Grigorenko, 2006; Triandis, 2006). Research also shows that personality variables are related to intelligence (Ackerman, 1996). Taken together, this evidence suggests that a comprehensive definition of intelligence incorporates many facets of intellect.

Explicit definitions of intelligence also frequently take on an assessment-oriented focus. In fact, some psychologists have been content to define intelligence as whatever it is that the tests measure (Boring, 1923). This definition, unfortunately, is circular. According to it, the nature of intelligence is what is tested. But what is tested must necessarily be determined by the nature of intelligence. Moreover, what different tests of intelligence measure is not always the same thing. Different tests measure somewhat different constructs (Daniel, 1997, 2000; Kaufman, 2000; Kaufman & Lichtenberger, 1998). So it is not feasible to define intelligence by what tests measure, as though they all measured the same thing. By the way, the answers to the questions in the chapter opener are as follows:

1. Rubber. Candles are frequently made of tallow, just as tires are frequently made of (c) rubber.

2. 100%, 0.75, and ½ are quantities that successively decrease by ¼; to complete the series, the answer is (c) one fourth, which is a further decrease by ¼.

3. The first series was a circle and a square, followed by two squares and a circle, followed by three circles and a square; the second series was three triangles and a square, which would be followed by (b), four squares and a triangle.

4. The person you met is clearly a liar. If the girl about whom this person was talking were a truth-teller, she would have said that she was a truth-teller. If she were a liar, she would have lied and said that she was a truth-teller also. Thus, regardless of whether the girl was a truth-teller or a liar, she would have said that she was a truth-teller. Because the man you met has said that she said she was a liar, he must be lying and hence must be a liar.

Measures and Structures of Intelligence

Contemporary measurements of intelligence usually can be traced to one of two very different historical traditions. One tradition concentrated on lower-level, psychophysical abilities. These include sensory acuity, physical strength, and motor coordination. The other focused on higher-level, judgmental abilities. We traditionally describe these abilities as related to thinking (Neçka & Orzechowski, 2005). Stop for a moment to think about yourself and your close associates. How would you assess yourself and your associates in terms of intelligence? When you make these assessments, do psychophysical abilities seem more important? Or do judgment abilities seem more important to you?

Francis Galton (1822–1911) believed that intelligence is a function of psychophysical abilities. For several years, Galton maintained a well-equipped laboratory where visitors could have themselves measured on a variety of psychophysical tests. These tests measured a broad range of psychophysical skills and sensitivities. One example was weight discrimination, the ability to notice small differences in the weights of objects. Another example was pitch sensitivity, the ability to hear small differences between musical notes. A third example was physical strength (Galton, 1883). One of the many enthusiastic followers of Galton attempted to detect links among the assorted tests (Wissler, 1901). He hoped such links would unify the various dimensions of psychophysically based intelligence. But he detected no unifying associations. Moreover, the psychophysical tests did not predict college grades. Thus, the psychophysical approach to assessing intelligence soon faded almost into oblivion. Nevertheless, it would reappear many years later in a somewhat different guise.

An alternative to the psychophysical approach was developed by Alfred Binet (1857–1911). He and his collaborator, Theodore Simon, also attempted to assess intelligence, but their goal was much more practical than purely scientific. Binet had been asked to devise a procedure for distinguishing normal learners from learners who are mentally retarded (Binet & Simon, 1916). Thus, Binet and his collaborator set out to measure intelligence as a function of the ability to learn within an academic setting. In Binet's view, judgment is the key to intelligence; the key, according to Binet, is not psychophysical acuity, strength, or skill.

For Binet (Binet & Simon, 1916), intelligent thought (mental judgment) comprises three distinct elements: direction, adaptation, and criticism. Think about how you are intelligently using these elements yourself at this moment: Direction involves knowing what has to be done and how to do it; adaptation refers to customizing a strategy for performing a task and then monitoring that strategy while implementing it; and criticism is your ability to critique your own thoughts and actions. The importance of direction and adaptation certainly fits with contemporary views of intelligence, and Binet's notion of criticism actually seems prescient, considering the current appreciation of metacognitive processes as a key aspect of intelligence.

Initially, when Binet and Simon developed their intelligence test, they were interested in some means of comparing the intelligence of a given child with that of other children of the same chronological (physical) age. For their purposes, they sought to determine each child's *mental age*—the average level of intelligence for a person of a given age. Thus, a mental age of 7 refers to the level of thinking reached by an average 7-year-old child. Mental ages worked just fine for comparing a given 7-year-old child with other 7-year-old children, but the use of mental ages made it difficult to compare relative intelligence in children of differing chronological ages.

William Stern (1912) suggested instead that we evaluate people's intelligence by using an *intelligence quotient* (IQ): a ratio of mental age (MA) divided by chronological age (CA), multiplied by 100 (Figure 13.1). This ratio can be expressed mathematically as follows: IQ 5 (MA/CA)(100). Thus, if Joan's mental age of 5 equals her chronological age of 5, then her intelligence is average and her IQ is 100 because (5/5)(100) = 100. When mental age exceeds chronological age, the ratio will lead to an IQ score above 100, and when chronological age exceeds mental age, the ratio will lead to an IQ score below 100. Intelligence scores that are expressed in terms of a ratio of mental age to chronological age are termed *ratio IQs*.

For various reasons, ratio IQs, too, proved inadequate. For example, increases in mental age slow down at about age 16 years. An 8-year-old child with a mental age of 12 years is pretty smart. However, do you feel sure that a 40-year-old adult with a

FIGURE 13.1

This figure shows a normal distribution as it applies to IQ, including identifying labels that are sometimes used to characterize different levels of IQ. It is important not to take these labels too seriously because they only are loose characterizations, not scientific descriptions of performance. From Intelligence Applied: Understanding and Increasing Your Intellectual Skills by Robert J. Sternberg, copyright © 1986 by Harcourt Brace & Company, reproduced by permission of the publisher.

mental age of 60 is similarly intelligent, although the ratio IQ is the same for the 8-year-old child and the 40-year-old adult? What does a mental age of 60 mean? Today, psychologists rarely use IQs based on mental ages. Instead, researchers have turned to measurement comparisons based on assumed normal distributions of test scores within large populations. Scores based on deviations from the middle score in a normal distribution of scores on a test of intelligence are termed *deviation IQs*. Many cognitive theorists believe that IQs provide only incomplete measurement of intelligence, as is discussed later.

Lewis Terman of Stanford University built on Binet and Simon's work in Europe and constructed the earliest version of what has come to be called the Stanford-Binet Intelligence Scale (Terman & Merrill, 1937, 1973; Thorndike, Hagen, & Sattler, 1986; Table 13.1). For years, the Stanford-Binet test was the standard for intelligence tests, and it still is used widely. The competitive Wechsler scales, named for their creator, David Wechsler, are probably even more widely used, however.

There are three levels of the Wechsler intelligence scales, including the third edition of the Wechsler Adult Intelligence Scale (WAIS-III), the fourth edition of the Wechsler Intelligence Scale for Children (WISC-IV), and the Wechsler Preschool and Primary Scale of Intelligence (WPPSI). The Wechsler tests yield three scores. They are a verbal score, a performance score, and an overall score. The verbal score is based on tests such as vocabulary and verbal similarities. In verbal similarities, the test-taker has to say how two things are similar. The performance score is based on several tests. One is picture completion, which requires identification of a missing part in a picture of an object. Another is picture arrangement, which requires rearrangement of a scrambled set of cartoon-like pictures into an order that tells a coher-

TABLE 13.1	The Stanford-Binet Intelligence Scale

The sample questions used throughout this chapter are not actual questions from any of the scales; they are intended only to illustrate the types of questions that might appear in each of the main content areas of the tests. How would you respond to these questions? What do your responses indicate about your intelligence?

CONTENT AREA	EXPLANATION OF TASKS/QUESTIONS	EXAMPLE OF A POSSIBLE TASK/QUESTION
Verbal Reasoning		
Vocabulary comprehension	Define the meaning of a word. Show an understanding of why the world works as it does.	What does the word *diligent* mean? Why do people sometimes borrow money?
Absurdities	Identify the odd or absurd feature of a picture.	(Recognize that ice hockey players do not ice skate on lakes into which swimmers in bathing suits are diving.)
Verbal relations	Tell how three of four items are similar to one another yet different from the fourth item.	(Note that an apple, a banana, and an orange can be eaten, but a mug cannot be.)
Quantitative Reasoning		
Number series	Complete a series of numbers.	Given the numbers 1, 3, 5, 7, 9, what number would you expect to come next?
Quantitative	Solve simple arithmetic-word problems.	If Maria has six apples, and she wants to divide them evenly among herself and her two best friends, how many apples will she give to each friend?
Figural/Abstract Reasoning		
Pattern analysis	Figure out a puzzle in which the test-taker must combine pieces representing parts of geometric shapes, fitting them together to form a particular geometric shape.	Fit together these pieces to form a (geometric shape).
Short-Term Memory		
Memory for sentences Memory for digits Memory for objects	Listen to a sentence, then repeat it back exactly as the examiner said it. Listen to a series of digits (numbers), then repeat the numbers either forward or backward or both. Watch the examiner point to a series of objects in a picture, then point to the same objects in exactly the same sequence in which the examiner did so.	Repeat this sentence back to me: "Harrison went to sleep late and awoke early the next morning." Repeat these numbers backward: "9, 1, 3, 6." (Point to the carrot, then the hoe, then the flower, then the scarecrow, then the baseball.)

ent story. The overall score is a combination of the verbal and the performance scores. Table 13.2 shows the types of items from each of the Wechsler adult-scale subtests, which you may wish to compare with those of the Stanford-Binet.

Wechsler, like Binet, had a conception of intelligence that went beyond what his own test measured. Wechsler clearly believed in the worth of attempting to measure

TABLE 13.2	The Wechsler Adult Intelligence Scale

Based on the content areas and the kinds of questions shown here, how does the Wechsler differ from the Stanford-Binet?

CONTENT AREA	EXPLANATION OF TASKS/QUESTIONS	EXAMPLE OF A POSSIBLE TASK/QUESTION
Verbal Scale		
Comprehension	Answer questions of social knowledge.	What does it mean when people say, "A stitch in time saves nine"? Why are convicted criminals put into prison?
Vocabulary	Define the meaning of a word.	What does *persistent* mean? What does *archaeology* mean?
Information	Supply generally known information.	Who is Laura Bush? What are six New England states?
Similarities	Explain how two things or concepts are similar.	In what ways are an ostrich and a penguin alike? In what ways are a lamp and a heater alike?
Arithmetic	Solve simple arithmetic-word problems.	If Paul has $14.43, and he buys two sandwiches, which cost $5.23 each, how much change will he receive? How many hours will it take to travel 1200 miles if you are traveling 60 miles per hour?
Digit span	Listen to a series of digits (numbers), then repeat the numbers either forward, backward, or both.	Repeat these numbers backward: "9, 1, 8, 3, 6." Repeat these numbers, just as I am telling you: "6, 9, 3, 2, 8."
Performance Scale		
Object assembly	Put together a puzzle by combining pieces to form a particular common object.	Put together these pieces to make something.
Block design	Use patterned blocks to form a design that looks identical to a design shown by the examiner.	Assemble the blocks at the left to match the design at the right.
Picture completion	Tell what is missing from each picture.	What is missing from this picture?
Picture arrangement	Put a set of cartoon-like pictures into chronological order so that they tell a coherent story.	Arrange these pictures in an order that tells a story, and then tell what is happening in the story.
Digit symbol	When given a key matching particular symbols to particular numerals, use the sequence of symbols to transcribe from symbols to numerals using the key.	Look carefully at the key, showing which symbols correspond to which numerals. In the blanks, write the correct numeral for the symbol above each blank.

intelligence. But he did not limit his conception of intelligence to test scores. Wechsler believed that intelligence is central in our everyday lives. Intelligence is not represented just by a test score or even by what we do in school. We use our intelligence not just in taking tests and in doing homework. We also use it in relating to people, in performing our jobs effectively, and in managing our lives in general.

A related intelligence test is the Wechsler Adult Intelligence Scale revised as a Neurological Instrument (WAIS-R NI) (Kaplan & associates, 1991). This tool is used to assess the intellectual abilities of people with brain injury. Among a number of differences between this scale and the WAIS, the key difference is the normative group to which the test taker is compared. In the WAIS-R NI, the normative group comprises people with brain injury. Therefore, this tool can be used to assess how the intellectual abilities of a person with brain injury compare with other people with brain injuries. This allows one to gage the severity of the injury.

A focus on the measurement of intelligence is only one of several approaches to theory and research on intelligence. At least two of the key issues in the approach to studying intelligence have arisen in earlier chapters of this book in regard to other topics in cognitive psychology. One is whether cognitive psychologists should focus on the measurement of intelligence or on the processes of intelligence. A second is that of what underlies intelligence: a person's genetic inheritance, a person's acquired attributes, or some kind of interaction between the two.

Psychologists interested in the structure of intelligence have relied on factor analysis as the indispensable tool for their research. **Factor analysis** is a statistical method for separating a construct—intelligence in this case—into a number of hypothetical factors or abilities that the researchers believe to form the basis of individual differences in test performance. The specific factors derived, of course, still depend on the specific questions being asked and the tasks being evaluated.

Factor analysis is based on studies of correlation. The idea is that the more highly two tests are correlated, the more likely they are to measure the same thing. In research on intelligence, a factor analysis might involve these steps. First, give a large number of people several different tests of ability. Second, determine the correlations among all those tests. Third, statistically analyze those correlations to simplify them into a relatively small number of factors that summarize people's performance on the tests. The investigators in this area generally have agreed on and followed this procedure. Yet the resulting factorial structures of intelligence have differed among different theorists. Among the many competing factorial theories, the main ones probably have been those of Spearman, Thurstone, Guilford, Cattell, Vernon, and Carroll. Figure 13.2 contrasts four of these theories.

Spearman: The "g" Factor

Charles Spearman (1863–1945) usually is credited with inventing factor analysis (Spearman, 1927). Using factor-analytic studies, Spearman concluded that intelligence can be understood in terms of two kinds of factors. A single general factor pervades performance on all tests of mental ability. A set of specific factors is involved in performance on only a single type of mental-ability test (e.g., arithmetic computations). In Spearman's view, the specific factors are of only casual interest because of the narrow applicability of these factors. To Spearman, the general factor, which he

FIGURE 13.2

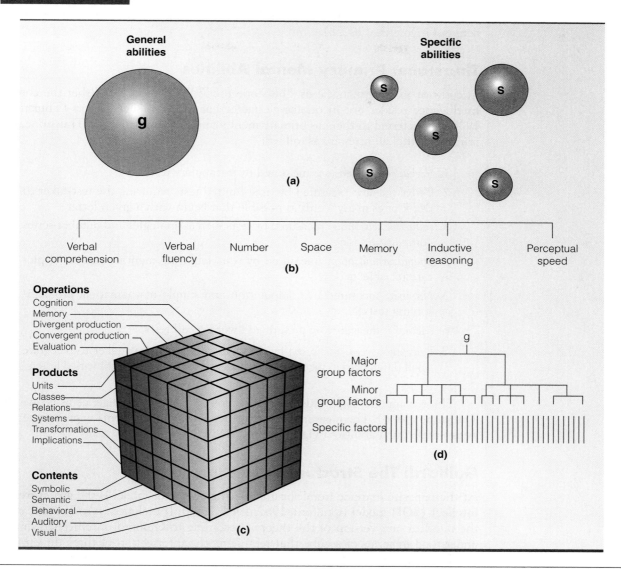

Although Spearman, Thurstone, Guilford, and Vernon all used factor analysis to determine the factors underlying intelligence, they all reached different conclusions regarding the structure of intelligence. Which model most simply yet comprehensively describes the structure of intelligence as you understand it? How do particular models of intelligence shape our understanding of intelligence? From In Search of the Human Mind by Robert J. Sternberg, copyright © 1995 by Harcourt Brace & Company. Reproduced by permission of the publisher.

labeled "**g,**" provides the key to understanding intelligence. Spearman believed "g" to be the result of "mental energy." Many psychologists still believe Spearman's theory to be essentially correct (e.g., Jensen, 1998, 2005; Lykken, 2005; see essays in Sternberg & Grigorenko, 2002b).

Thurstone: Primary Mental Abilities

In contrast to Spearman, Louis Thurstone (1887–1955) concluded that the core of intelligence resides not in one single factor but in seven such factors (Thurstone, 1938). He referred to them as primary mental abilities. According to Thurstone, the primary mental abilities are as follows:

1. *Verbal comprehension:* measured by vocabulary tests
2. *Verbal fluency:* measured by time-limited tests requiring the test-taker to think of as many words as possible that begin with a given letter
3. *Inductive reasoning:* measured by tests such as analogies and number-series completion tasks
4. *Spatial visualization:* measured by tests requiring mental rotation of pictures of objects
5. *Number:* measured by computation and simple mathematical problem-solving tests
6. *Memory:* measured by picture and word-recall tests
7. *Perceptual speed:* measured by tests that require the test-taker to recognize small differences in pictures or to cross out the *as* in strings of varied letters

These components provide a direct means to measure intelligence as defined by Thurstone (1938). The measure of intelligence is still used by some experimenters to assess intellectual abilities (Vigil-Colet & Morales-Vives, 2005).

Guilford: The Structure of Intellect

At the opposite extreme from Spearman's single g-factor model is the **structure-of-intellect (SOI) model** (Guilford, 1967, 1982, 1988). It includes up to 150 factors of the mind in one version of the theory. According to Guilford, intelligence can be understood in terms of a cube that represents the intersection of three dimensions (see Figure 13.2). The dimensions are operations, contents, and products. According to Guilford, operations are simply mental processes, such as memory and evaluation. Evaluation involves making judgments, such as determining whether a particular statement is of fact or opinion. Contents are the kinds of terms that appear in a problem. Examples are semantic (words) and visual (pictures). Products are the kinds of responses required. They include units (single words, numbers, or pictures), classes (hierarchies), and implications (see Figure 13.2).

Several psychologists have believed that Guilford posited more factors than he could prove (e.g., Eysenck, 1967; Horn & Knapp, 1973). Perhaps Guilford's most valuable contribution was to suggest that we consider various kinds of mental operations, contents, and products in our views and our assessments of intelligence.

Cattell, Vernon, and Carroll: Hierarchical Models

A more parsimonious way of handling a number of factors of the mind is through a hierarchical model of intelligence. One such model proposed that general intelligence comprises two major subfactors. They are fluid ability and crystallized ability. Fluid ability is speed and accuracy of abstract reasoning, especially for novel problems. Crystallized ability is accumulated knowledge and vocabulary (Cattell, 1971). Subsumed within these two major subfactors are other, more specific factors. A similar view is a general division between practical-mechanical and verbal-educational abilities (Vernon, 1971).

A more recent model is a hierarchy comprising three strata (Carroll, 1993). Stratum I includes many narrow, specific abilities (e.g., spelling ability, speed of reasoning). Stratum II includes various broad abilities (e.g., fluid intelligence, crystallized intelligence). And Stratum III is just a single general intelligence, much like Spearman's g. Of these strata, the most interesting is the middle stratum, which is neither too narrow nor too all encompassing.

In addition to fluid intelligence and crystallized intelligence, Carroll includes in the middle stratum several other abilities. They are learning and memory processes, visual perception, auditory perception, facile production of ideas (similar to verbal fluency), and speed (which includes both sheer speed of response and speed of accurate responding). Carroll's model is probably the most widely accepted of the psychometric models. Whereas the factor-analytic approach it exemplifies has tended to emphasize the structures of intelligence, the information-processing approach has tended to emphasize the operations of intelligence.

Information Processing and Intelligence

Information-processing theorists are interested in studying how people mentally manipulate what they learn and know about the world (Hunt, 2005). The ways in which various information-processing investigators study intelligence differ primarily in terms of the complexity of the processes being studied (Stankov, 2005). Researchers have considered both the speed and the accuracy of information processing to be important factors in intelligence.

Process-Timing Theories

Inspection time is the amount of time it takes you to inspect items and make a decision about them. It is measured through an inspection-time experimental paradigm (Nettelbeck, 1987; Nettelbeck & Lally, 1976; Nettelbeck & Rabbitt, 1992; see also Deary, 2000; Deary & Stough, 1996; Neubauer & Fink, 2005). Here is a typical use of the paradigm. For each of a number of trials, a computer monitor displays a fixation cue (a dot in the area where a target figure will appear) for 500 milliseconds. There is then a pause of 360 milliseconds. Following this period, the computer presents the target stimulus for a particular interval of time. Finally, it presents a visual mask (a stimulus that erases the trace in iconic memory).

The target stimulus typically comprises two vertical lines of unequal length. For example, one might be 25 millimeters and the other 35 millimeters. The two lines are

Earl Hunt is professor emeritus at the University of Washington. He has done major work on computer-simulation models of inductive reasoning, on the nature of intelligence, and on drug-induced alterations of memory and reasoning.

aligned at the top by a horizontal crossbar. The shorter of the two lines may appear on either the right or the left side of the stimulus. The visual mask is a pair of lines that are thicker and longer than the two lines of the target stimulus. The task is to inspect the target stimulus and then indicate the side on which the shorter line appeared. One indicates the left-hand stimulus by pressing a left-hand button on a keypad connected to a computer that records the responses. One indicates the right-hand stimulus by pressing the right-hand button.

The key variable is the length of time for the presentation of the target stimulus, not the speed of responding by pressing the button. Nettelbeck defined inspection time operationally. It is the length of time for presentation of the target stimulus after which the participant still responds with at least 90% accuracy in indicating the side on which the shorter line appeared. He found that shorter inspection times correlate with higher scores on intelligence tests (e.g., various subscales of the WAIS) among differing populations of participants (Nettelbeck, 1987). Other investigators have confirmed this finding (e.g., Deary & Stough, 1996).

Choice Reaction Time

Some investigators have proposed that intelligence can be understood in terms of speed of neuronal conduction (e.g., Jensen, 1979, 1998). In other words, the smart person is someone whose neural circuits conduct information rapidly. When Arthur Jensen proposed this notion, direct measures of neural-conduction velocity were not readily available. So Jensen primarily studied a proposed proxy for measuring neural-processing speed. The proxy was *choice reaction time*—the time it takes to select one answer from among several possibilities.

Consider a typical choice-reaction-time paradigm. The participant is seated in front of a set of lights on a board (Figure 13.3). When one of the lights flashes, he or

---

FIGURE 13.3

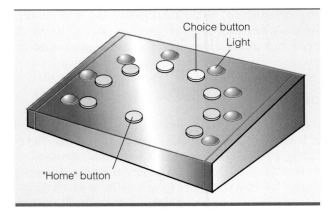

To measure choice reaction time, Jensen used an apparatus like the one shown here. Reprinted with permission of The Free Press, a division of Simon & Schuster Adult Publishing Group, from Bias in Mental Testing by Arthur R. Jensen. Copyright © 1980 by Arthur R. Jensen. All rights reserved.

she extinguishes it by pressing as rapidly as possible a button beneath the correct light. The experimenter would then measure the participant's speed in performing this task.

Participants with higher IQs are faster than participants with lower IQs in their reaction time (RT) (Jensen, 1982). In this particular version of the task, RT is defined as the time between when a light comes on and the finger leaves the home (central) button. In some studies, participants with higher IQs also showed a faster movement time (MT). MT is defined as the time between letting the finger leave the home button and hitting the button under the light. These findings may be due to increased central nerve-conduction velocity, although at present this proposal remains speculative (Reed & Jensen, 1991, 1993).

Various findings regarding choice reaction time may be influenced by extraneous factors. They include the number of response alternatives and the visual-scanning requirements of Jensen's apparatus. In this case, RT as measured would not be a result of speed of reaction time alone (Bors, MacLeod, & Forrin, 1993). In particular, manipulating the number of buttons and the size of the visual angle of the display (how much of the visual field it consumes) can reduce the correlation between IQ and reaction time (Bors, MacLeod, & Forrin, 1993). Thus, the relation between reaction time and intelligence is unclear.

Lexical-Access Speed and Speed of Simultaneous Processing

Some investigations have focused on *lexical-access speed*—the speed with which we can retrieve information about words (e.g., letter names) stored in our long-term memories (Hunt, 1978). This speed can be measured with a letter-matching, reaction-time task first proposed by Posner and Mitchell in 1967 (Hunt, 1978).

Participants are shown pairs of letters, such as "A A," "A a," or "A b." For each pair, they indicate whether the letters constitute a match in name (e.g., "A a" match in name of letter of the alphabet but "A b" do not). They also are given a simpler task. In it, they are asked to indicate whether the letters match physically (e.g., "A A" are physically identical, whereas "A a" are not). The variable of interest is the difference between their speed for the first set of tasks, involving name matching, and their speed for the second set, involving matching of physical characteristics. The difference in reaction time between the two kinds of tasks is said to provide a measure of speed of lexical access. This score is based on a *subtraction* of name-match minus physical-match reaction time. The subtraction controls for mere perceptual-processing time. Students with lower verbal ability take longer to gain access to lexical information than do students with higher verbal ability (Hunt, 1978).

Intelligence is also related to people's ability to divide their attention (Hunt & Lansman, 1982). For example, suppose that participants are asked to solve mathematical problems and simultaneously to listen for a tone and press a button as soon as they hear it. We can expect that they both would solve the math problems effectively and respond quickly to hearing the tone. According to Hunt and Lansman, more intelligent people are better able to timeshare between two tasks and to perform both effectively.

In sum, process-timing theories attempt to account for differences in intelligence by appealing to differences in the speed of various forms of information processing. Inspection time, choice reaction time, and lexical access timing all have been found to correlate with measures of intelligence. These findings suggest that, on average, higher intelligence may be related to the speed of various information-processing abilities. More intelligent people encode information more rapidly into working memory. They access information in long-term memory more rapidly. And they respond more rapidly. Why would more rapid encoding, retrieval, and responding be associated with higher intelligence test scores? Do rapid information processors learn more?

Is there a link between age-related slowing of information processing and (1) initial encoding and recall of information and (2) long-term retention (Nettelbeck & associates, 1996; see also Bors & Forrin, 1995)? It appears that the relation between inspection time and intelligence may not be related to learning. In particular, there is a difference between initial recall and actual long-term learning (Nettelbeck & associates, 1996). Initial recall performance is mediated by processing speed. Older, slower participants showed deficits. Longer-term retention of new information, preserved in older participants, is mediated by cognitive processes other than speed of processing. These processes include rehearsal strategies. Thus, speed of information processing may influence initial performance on recall and inspection time tasks, but speed is not related to long-term learning. Perhaps faster information processing aids participants in performance aspects of intelligence test tasks, rather than contributing to actual learning and intelligence. Clearly, this area requires more research to determine how information-processing speed relates to intelligence.

Working Memory

Recent work suggests that a critical component of intelligence may be working memory. Indeed, some investigators have argued that intelligence may be little more than working memory (Kyllonen & Christal, 1990). In one study, participants read sets of passages and, after they had read the passages, tried to remember the last word of each passage (Daneman & Carpenter, 1983). Recall was highly correlated with verbal ability. In another study, participants performed a variety of working memory tasks. In one task, for example, the participants saw a set of simple arithmetic problems, each of which was followed by a word or a digit. An example would be "Is $(3 \times 5) - 6 = 7$? TABLE" (Turner & Engle, 1989; see also Hambrick, Kane, & Engle, 2005). The participants saw sets of from two to six such problems and solved each one. After solving the problems in the set, they tried to recall the words that followed the problems. The number of words recalled was highly correlated with measured intelligence.

There are indications that a measure of working memory can provide almost perfect prediction of scores on tests of general ability (Colom & associates, 2004; see also Kane, Hambrick, & Conway, 2005). Other researchers have demonstrated a significant but smaller relationship between working memory and general intelligence (e.g., Ackerman, Beier, & Boyle, 2005). Thus, it appears that the ability to store and manipulate information in working memory may be an important aspect of intelligence. It is probably not all there is to intelligence, however.

Componential Theory and Complex Problem Solving

Cognitive approaches for studying information processing can be applied to more complex tasks, such as analogies, series problems (e.g., completing a numerical or figural series), and syllogisms (Sternberg, 1977, 1983, 1984; see Chapter 12). The idea is to take the kinds of tasks used on conventional intelligence tests and to isolate components of intelligence. *Components* are the mental processes used in performing these tasks, such as translating a sensory input into a mental representation, transforming one conceptual representation into another, or translating a conceptual representation into a motor output (Sternberg, 1982). Many investigators have elaborated on and expanded this basic approach (Lohman, 2000, 2005; Wenke, Frensch, & Funke, 2005).

Componential analysis breaks down people's reaction times and error rates on these tasks in terms of the processes that make up the tasks. This kind of analysis revealed that people may solve analogies and similar tasks by using several component processes. Among them are several processes. A first is encoding the terms of the problem. A second is inferring relations among at least some of the terms. A third is mapping the inferred relations to other terms, which would be presumed to show similar relations. And a fourth is applying the previously inferred relations to the new situations.

Consider the analogy LAWYER : CLIENT :: DOCTOR : (a. PATIENT, b. MEDICINE). To solve this analogy, you need to *encode* each term of the problem. This includes perceiving a term and retrieving information about it from memory. You then *infer* the relationship between lawyer and client. In particular, the former provides professional services to the latter. You then *map* the relationship in the first half of the analogy to the second half of the analogy. Here, you note that it will involve that same relationship. Finally, you *apply* that inferred relationship to generate the final term of the analogy. This leads to the appropriate response of PATIENT. Figure 13.4 shows how componential analysis would be applied to an analogy problem, A is to B as C is to D, where D is the solution. Studying these components of information processing reveals more than measuring mental speed alone.

FIGURE 13.4

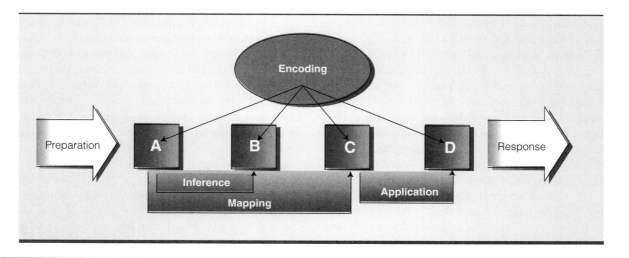

In the solution of an analogy problem, the problem solver must first encode the problem A is to B as C is to D. The problem solver then must infer the relationship between A and B. Next, the problem solver must map the relationship between A and B to the relationship between C and each of the possible solutions to the analogy. Finally, the problem solver must apply the relationship to choose which of the possible solutions is the correct solution to the problem.

IN THE LAB OF RANDALL ENGLE

Courtesy of Dr. Randall Engle

From the earliest days of the field, psychologists have been searching for measures that reflect elemental aspects of our cognitive abilities and limitations and the nature of individual differences in those abilities and limitations. One of the measures thought to best reflect crucial cognitive abilities was the memory span task, the number of digits or words that could be recalled perfectly in order after a single presentation. The digit version of this task was first proposed as a measure of central importance to cognition in the mid-1800s, and visitors to the 1893 World's Fair in Chicago paid to have their digit span measured by a group of early psychologists. However, for a task that is supposed to reflect a central cognitive ability, the digit span task does not correlate well with most higher-order cognitive tasks, at least among a normal, healthy adult population. However, some slight modification in those tasks leads to a rather drastic change in the predictive validity of measures of memory span or working memory capacity.

In my lab, my students and I are intrigued by questions about elemental cognitive abilities. We are specifically interested in the psychological nature of those abilities, how to measure them, how to design better measures for them, when those elemental abilities are important and when they are not important in real-world or feral cognition, and the brain mechanisms and experiential factors that affect these abilities. Recently we have begun to realize that, although these measures reflect an important abiding aspect of fluid intelligence and have a quality of trait about them, they also reflect a rather ephemeral state of the person that is affected by conditions such as sleep deprivation, depression, and social threat.

Let's back up those assertions with some details. We and others have found that, unlike simple digit span tasks, complex memory span tasks provide measures that satisfy the two key criteria for any psychological measurement. They are reliable, in that they tend to be consistent across time and administrations,

and they are valid, in that they predict a wide array of higher-order cognitive measures. These complex spans typically consist of interleaved tasks. For example, in the operation span task, the person being tested would solve a simple arithmetic string, such as: Is $3 \times 3 - 1 = 7$? After giving an answer to that question, they would then see a letter, such as F. After a series of three to seven such items, the person sees a set of question marks that indicates he or she is to recall all the letters in that series of items. The number of letters recalled is the critical score, though people are strongly encouraged to be as accurate with the arithmetic as possible. It turns out to not be very important whether the test includes the arithmetic component or requires the person to read and verify a sentence or mentally rotate a visual pattern. The simple act of interleaving some attention-demanding task with the items to be recalled leads to a measure that reflects something important about our cognitive abilities. In several large studies that used a statistical technique called structural-equation modeling, my lab has shown that a variety of such tasks tend to reflect a common construct, called a latent variable, regardless of whether those tasks are verbal or spatial. Further, that latent variable tends to be quite predictive of measures of fluid intelligence that were designed to be relatively culturally fair. We have argued that these complex working memory measures reflect an ability to control our attention, particularly when attention will tend to be drawn to irrelevant thoughts coming from the environment or retrieved from memory. In one of our studies, we had participants fixate on a cross in the center of a computer screen. At some point, a box would flicker on one side of the screen or the other. When that happened, the participant was to immediately move their eyes to a box on the *other* side of the screen. We measured eye movements so we could detect even slight and rapid errors of movement to the flickering box. This task is exceedingly simple but demanding. Millions of years of evolution have predisposed all animals to attend to things like flicker that suggest movement because those things might eat us or we could eat them. Re-

IN THE LAB OF RANDALL ENGLE—cont'd

sisting this powerful predisposed response requires strong control over our attention system. We found that individuals who scored well on the complex span measures made many fewer errors of glancing toward the flickering box. The lab and our associates at other universities have shown that these complex span measures tend to be reliable over months and months; in addition, they predict performance on a wide range of higher-order cognitive tasks, including many educationally relevant tasks such as reading comprehension but also many lower-order tasks such as the Stroop task. Previously, people have thought of cognitive abilities as a trait or something that is "fixed" for individuals. Interestingly, we have recently shown that the complex span measures are also highly sensitive to the effects of sleep deprivation. The operation span task was a very good predictor of the number of errors that highly experienced pilots made on a sophisticated flight simulator after 20 to 30 hours of sleep deprivation. We would argue that sleep deprivation leads to a temporary decline in the effectiveness of the brain systems responsible for attention or cognitive control and that will lead to errors on all tasks that require such control, both cognitive and emotional. Another real world example of the impact of external factors on cognitive abilities is the recent demonstration of the impact on the social psychology phenomenon called stereotype threat. Stereotype threat is the underperformance of a group based on their belief that the group is not as good at a task as another group. For example, women aren't as good as men at math. A reduction in cognitive control as measured by complex span measures is responsible for this debilitating effect on such measures as math tests for women or intelligence tests for minorities. These findings indicate that the complex span measures such as operation span and reading span might reflect a trait (fixed) variable of the individual but also reflect a current state (moderated) variable as well. The aspect of fluid intelligence we have called working memory capacity or attention control reflect both trait and state variables, which makes understanding any individual's performance at a given time a complex undertaking indeed. The goal of my lab is to continue to better understand and measure these concepts, as well as understand how they impact individuals and groups in their daily lives.

There are significant correlations between speed in executing these processes and performance on other, traditional intelligence tests. However, a more intriguing discovery is that participants who score higher on traditional intelligence tests take longer to encode the terms of the problem than do less intelligent participants. But they make up for the extra time by taking less time to perform the remaining components of the task. In general, more intelligent participants take longer during *global planning*—encoding the problem and formulating a general strategy for attacking the problem (or set of problems). But they take less time for *local planning*—forming and implementing strategies for the details of the task (Sternberg, 1981).

The advantage of spending more time on global planning is the increased likelihood that the overall strategy will be correct. Thus, when taking more time is advantageous, brighter people may take longer to do something than will less bright people. For example, the brighter person might spend more time researching and planning for writing a term paper but less time in the actual writing of it. This same differential in time allocation has been shown in other tasks as well. An example would be in solving physics problems (Larkin & associates, 1980; see Sternberg, 1979, 1985a). That is, more intelligent people seem to spend more time planning for and encoding the problems they face. But they spend less time engaging in the other components of task performance. This may relate to the previously mentioned metacognitive attribute many include in their notions of intelligence.

Researchers have also studied information processing of people engaged in complex problem-solving situations. Examples are playing chess and performing logical derivations (Newell & Simon, 1972; Simon, 1976). For example, a simple, brief task might require the participants first to view an arithmetic or geometric series. Then they must figure out the rule underlying the progression. And finally they must guess what numeral or geometric figure might come next. More complex tasks might include some of the tasks mentioned in Chapter 11 (e.g., the water jugs problems; see Estes, 1982). Can performance on these or other tasks be analyzed at a biological level?

An Integrative Approach

An integrative approach would combine models of various kinds of cognitive functioning as bases for intelligence. In such an approach, four sources of individual differences in intelligence might be detected (Ackerman, 1988, 2005). These are (1) breadth of declarative knowledge, (2) breadth of procedural skills, (3) capacity of working memory, and (4) speed of processing. The advantage of this approach is that it does not try to localize individual differences in intelligence as coming from one source. Rather, multiple sources are involved.

Biological Bases of Intelligence

The human brain is clearly the organ that serves as a biological basis for human intelligence. Early studies, such as those of Karl Lashley, studied the brain to find biological indices of intelligence and other aspects of mental processes. They were a resounding failure, despite great efforts. As tools for studying the brain have become more sophisticated, however, we are beginning to see the possibility of finding physiological indicators of intelligence. Some investigators believe that we will soon have clinically useful psychophysiological indices of intelligence (e.g., Matarazzo, 1992). But widely applicable indices will be much longer in coming. In the meantime, the biological studies we now have are largely correlational. They show statistical associations between biological and psychometric or other measures of intelligence. They do not establish causal relations.

One line of research looks at the relationship of brain size or volume to intelligence (see Jerison, 2000; Vernon & associates, 2000; Witelson, Beresh, & Kiga, 2006). The evidence suggests that, for humans, there is a modest but significant statistical relationship between brain size and intelligence. However, it is difficult to know what to make of this relationship. Greater brain size may cause greater intelligence, greater intelligence may cause greater brain size, or both may be dependent on some third factor. Moreover, it is probably at least as important how efficiently the brain is used than what its size is. For example, on average, men have larger brains than women. But women, on average, have better connections through the corpus callosum of the two hemispheres of the brain. So it is not clear which sex would be, on average, at an advantage. Probably neither would be. It is important to note that the relationship between brain size and intelligence does not hold across species (Jerison, 2000). Rather, what holds seems to be a relationship between intelligence and brain size, relative to the rough general size of the organism.

For now, some of the current studies offer some appealing possibilities. For example, complex patterns of electrical activity in the brain, which are prompted by specific stimuli, appear to correlate with scores on IQ tests (Barrett & Eysenck, 1992).

Several studies initially suggested that speed of conduction of neural impulses may correlate with intelligence, as measured by IQ tests (McGarry-Roberts, Stelmack, & Campbell, 1992; Vernon & Mori, 1992). A follow-up study, however, failed to find a strong relation between neural-conduction velocity and intelligence (Wickett & Vernon, 1994). In this study, conduction velocity was measured by neural-conduction speeds in a main nerve of the arm. Intelligence was measured by a Multidimensional Aptitude Battery. Surprisingly, neural-conduction velocity appears to be a more powerful predictor of IQ scores for men than for women. So sex differences may account for some of the differences in the data (Wickett & Vernon, 1994). Additional studies on both males and females are needed.

More recent work suggests it may be the flexibility of neural circuitry, rather than speed of conduction, that is key (Newman & Just, 2005). Hence, we would want to study not just speed but neural circuitry. An alternative approach to studying the brain suggests that neural efficiency may be related to intelligence. Such an approach is based on studies of how the brain metabolizes glucose (a simple sugar required for brain activity) during mental activities. (See Chapter 2 for more on positron emission tomography and other brain-imaging techniques.) Higher intelligence correlates with reduced levels of glucose metabolism during problem-solving tasks (Haier & associates, 1992; Haier & Jung, 2007). That is, smarter brains consume less sugar and hence expend less effort than do less smart brains doing the same task. Furthermore, cerebral efficiency increases as a result of learning on a relatively complex task involving visuospatial manipulations, the computer game Tetris (Haier & associates, 1992). As a result of practice, more intelligent participants not only show lower cerebral glucose metabolism overall but also show more specifically localized metabolism of glucose. In most areas of their brains, smarter participants show less glucose metabolism. But in selected areas of their brains, believed to be important to the task at hand, they show higher levels of glucose metabolism. Thus, more intelligent participants may have learned how to use their brains more efficiently. They carefully focus their thought processes on a given task.

Other research, however, suggests that the relationship between glucose metabolism and intelligence may be more complex (Haier & associates, 1995; Larson & associates, 1995). On the one hand, one study confirmed the earlier findings of increased glucose metabolism in less smart participants, in this case, participants who were mildly retarded (Haier & associates, 1995). On the other hand, another study found, contrary to the earlier findings, that smarter participants had increased glucose metabolism relative to their average comparison group (Larson & associates, 1995).

There was a problem with earlier studies. It was that the tasks participants received were not matched for difficulty level across groups of smart and average individuals. The study by Larson and colleagues used tasks that were matched to the ability levels of the smarter and average participants. They found that the smarter participants used more glucose. Moreover, the glucose metabolism was highest in the right hemisphere of the more intelligent participants performing the hard task. These results again suggest selectivity of brain areas. What could be driving the increases in glucose metabolism? Currently, the key factor appears to be subjective task difficulty. In earlier studies, smarter participants simply found the tasks to be too easy. Matching task difficulty to participants' abilities seems to indicate that smarter participants increase glucose metabolism when the task demands it. The preliminary findings in this area will need to be investigated further before any conclusive answers arise.

Some neuropsychological research suggests that performance on intelligence tests may not indicate a crucial aspect of intelligence. This is the ability to set goals, to plan how to meet them, and to execute those plans (Dempster, 1991). Specifically, people with lesions on the frontal lobe of the brain frequently perform quite well on standardized IQ tests. These tests require responses to questions within a highly structured situation. But they do not require much in the way of goal setting or planning. These tests frequently use what could be classified as crystallized intelligence. Damage to the posterior regions of the brain seems to have negative effects on measures of crystallized intelligence (Gray & Thompson, 2004; Kolb & Whishaw, 1996; Piercy, 1964). In patients with frontal lobe damage, impairments in fluid intelligence is observed (Duncan, Burgess, & Emslie, 1995; Gray, Chabris, & Braver, 2003; Gray & Thompson, 2004). This result should come as no surprise, given that the frontal lobes are involved in reasoning, decision making, and problem solving (see Chapters 10 and 11). Other research highlights the importance of the parietal regions for performance on general and fluid intelligence tasks (Lee & associates, 2006). Intelligence involves the ability to learn from experience and to adapt to the surrounding environment. Thus, the ability to set goals and to design and implement plans cannot be ignored. An essential aspect of goal setting and planning is the ability to attend appropriately to relevant stimuli. Another related ability is that of ignoring or discounting irrelevant stimuli.

The discovered importance of the frontal and parietal regions in intelligence tasks has led to the development of an integrated theory of intelligence that highlights the importance of these areas. This theory, called the parietal-frontal integration theory (P-FIT), stresses the importance of interconnected brain regions in determining differences in intelligence. The regions this theory focuses on are the Brodmann areas, the prefrontal cortex, the inferior and superior parietal lobule, the anterior cingulate, and portions of the temporal and occipital lobes (Jung & Haier, 2007). P-FIT theory describes patterns of brain activity in people with different levels of intelligence; it cannot, however, explain what makes a person intelligent or what intelligence is.

We cannot realistically study a brain or its contents and processes in isolation without also considering the entire human being. We must consider the interactions of that human being with the entire environmental context within which the person acts intelligently. Hence, many researchers and theorists urge us to take a more contextual view of intelligence. Furthermore, some alternative views of intelligence attempt to broaden the definition of intelligence to be more inclusive of people's varied abilities.

Alternative Approaches to Intelligence

Cultural Context and Intelligence

According to **contextualism,** intelligence must be understood in its real-world context. The context of intelligence may be viewed at any level of analysis. It may be focused narrowly, as on the home and family environment, or it may be extended broadly, to entire cultures. For example, even cross-community differences have been correlated with differences in performance on intelligence tests. Such context-related differences include those of rural versus urban communities, low versus high proportions of teenagers to adults within communities, and low versus high socioeconomic status of communities (see Coon, Carey, & Fulker, 1992). Contextualists have been intrigued particularly by the effects of cultural context on intelligence.

Contextualists consider intelligence to be inextricably linked to culture. They view intelligence as something that a culture creates to define the nature of adaptive performance in that culture. It further accounts for why some people perform better than others on the tasks that the culture happens to value (Sternberg, 1985a). Theorists who endorse this model study just how intelligence relates to the external world in which the model is being applied and evaluated. In general, definitions and theories of intelligence will more effectively encompass cultural diversity by broadening in scope. Before exploring some of the contextual theories of intelligence, we will look at what prompted psychologists to believe that culture might play a role in how we define and assess intelligence.

There have been many definitions of culture (e.g., Brislin, Lonner, & Thorndike, 1973; Kroeber & Kluckhohn, 1952). *Culture* is defined here as "the set of attitudes, values, beliefs and behaviors shared by a group of people, communicated form one generation to the next via language or some other means of communication (Barnouw, 1985)" (Matsumoto, 1994, p. 4). The term *culture* can be used in many ways and has a long history (Benedict, 1946; Boas, 1911; Mead, 1928/2001; see Matsumoto, 1996; Sternberg, 2004). Berry and colleagues (1992) described six uses of the term: descriptively to characterize a culture, historically to describe the traditions of a group, normatively to express rules and norms of a group, psychologically to emphasize how a group learns and solves problems, structurally to emphasize the organizational elements of a culture, and genetically to describe cultural origins.

One reason to study culture and intelligence is that they are so inextricably interlinked. Indeed, Tomasello (2001) has argued that culture is what, in large part, separates human from animal intelligence. Humans have evolved as they have, he believes, in part because of their cultural adaptations, which in turn develop from their ability, even in infancy from about 9 months onward, to understand others as intentional agents.

Many research programs demonstrate the potential hazards of single-culture research. For example, Greenfield (1997) found that it means a different thing to take a test among Mayan children than it does among most children in the United States. The Mayan expectation is that collaboration is permissible and that it is rather unnatural *not* to collaborate. Such a finding is consistent with the work of Markus and Kitayama (1991), which suggests different cultural constructions of the self in individualistic versus collectivistic cultures. Indeed, Nisbett (2003) has found that some cultures, especially Asian ones, tend to be more dialectical in their thinking, whereas other cultures, such as European and North American ones, tend to be more linear. Similarly, people from Asian cultures tend to take a different viewpoint than Westerners when approaching a new object (Nisbett & Masuda, 2003). In general, people from Western cultures tend to process objects independently of the context, whereas people from many Eastern cultures process objects in conjunction with the surrounding context (Nisbett & Miyamoto, 2005). In fact, some evidence suggests that culture influences many cognitive processes, including intelligence (Lehman, Chiu, & Schaller, 2004). As a result, individuals in different cultures may construct concepts in quite different ways, rendering results of concept-formation or identification studies in a single culture suspect (Atran, 1999; Coley & associates, 1999; Medin & Atran, 1999). Thus, groups may think about what appears superficially to be the same phenomenon—whether a concept or the taking of a test—differently. What appear to be differences in general intelligence may in fact be differences in cultural properties (Helms-Lorenz, Van de Vijver, & Poortinga, 2003). Helms-Lorenz and colleagues (2003) have argued that measured differences in intellectual performance may result from differences in cultural complexity; but complexity of a culture is extremely hard to define, and what appears to be simple or complex from the point of view of one culture may appear different from the point of view of another.

People in different cultures may have quite different ideas of what it means to be smart. For example, one of the more interesting cross-cultural studies of intelligence was performed by Michael Cole and his colleagues (Cole & associates, 1971). These investigators asked adult members of the Kpelle tribe in Africa to sort terms representing concepts. Consider what happens in Western culture when adults are given a sorting task on an intelligence test. More intelligent people typically will sort hierarchically. For example, they may sort names of different kinds of fish together. Then they place the word *fish* over that. They place the name *animal* over *fish* and over *birds*, and so on. Less intelligent people will typically sort functionally. They may sort *fish* with *eat*, for example. Why? Because we eat fish. Or they may sort *clothes* with *wear* because we wear clothes. The Kpelle sorted functionally. They did so even after investigators unsuccessfully tried to get the Kpelle spontaneously to sort hierarchically.

Finally, in desperation, one of the experimenters (Glick) asked a Kpelle to sort as a foolish person would sort. In response, the Kpelle quickly and easily sorted hierarchically. The Kpelle had been able to sort this way all along. They just had not done it because they viewed it as foolish. And they probably considered the questioners rather unintelligent for asking such stupid questions.

The Kpelle people are not the only ones who might question Western understandings of intelligence. In the Puluwat culture of the Pacific Ocean, for example, sailors navigate incredibly long distances. They use none of the navigational aids that sailors from technologically advanced countries would need to get from one place to another (Gladwin, 1970). Suppose Puluwat sailors were to devise intelligence tests for us and our fellow Americans. We and our compatriots might not seem very intelligent. Similarly, the highly skilled Puluwat sailors might not do well on American-crafted tests of intelligence. These and other observations have prompted quite a few theoreticians to recognize the importance of considering cultural context when intelligence is assessed.

A study provides an example a little closer to home regarding the effects of cultural differences on intelligence tests (Sarason & Doris, 1979). It tracked the IQs of an immigrant population: Italian Americans. Less than a century ago, first-generation Italian-American children showed a median IQ of 87 (low average; range 76–100). Their IQs were relatively low even when nonverbal measures were used and when so-called mainstream American attitudes were considered. Some social commentators and intelligence researchers of the day pointed to heredity and other nonenvironmental factors as the basis for the low IQs. Today, some commentators do the same for other minority groups (Herrnstein & Murray, 1994).

For example, a leading researcher of the day, Henry Goddard, pronounced that 79% of immigrant Italians were "feebleminded." He also asserted that about 80% of immigrant Jews, Hungarians, and Russians were similarly unendowed (Eysenck & Kamin, 1981). Goddard (1917) also asserted that moral decadence was associated with this deficit in intelligence. He recommended that the intelligence tests he used be administered to all immigrants and that all those he deemed substandard selectively be excluded from entering the United States. But subsequent generations of Italian-American students who take IQ tests today show slightly above-average IQs (Ceci, 1991). Other immigrant groups that Goddard had denigrated have shown similar "amazing" increases. Even the most fervent hereditarians would be unlikely to attribute such remarkable gains in so few generations to heredity. Cultural assimilation, including integrated education, seems a much more plausible explanation.

The preceding arguments may make it clear why it is so difficult to come up with a test that everyone would consider **culture-fair**—equally appropriate and fair for members of all cultures. If members of different cultures have different ideas of what it means to be intelligent, then the very behaviors that may be considered intelligent in one culture may be considered unintelligent in another. Take, for example, the concept of mental quickness. In mainstream U.S. culture, quickness usually is associated with intelligence. To say someone is "quick" is to say that the person is intelligent. Indeed, most group tests of intelligence are strictly timed. Even on individual tests of intelligence, the test-giver times some responses of the test-taker. For example, one set of researchers observed a positive relationship between measures of quickness and scores on the Graduate Record Examinations (GREs) (Powers & Kaufman, 2004). Many information-processing theorists and even psychophysiological theorists focus on the study of intelligence as a function of mental speed.

In many cultures of the world, however, quickness is not at a premium. In these cultures, people may believe that more intelligent people do not rush into things. Even in our own culture, no one will view you as brilliant if you rush things that should not be rushed. For example, it generally is not smart to decide on a marital partner, a job, or a place to live in the 20 to 30 seconds you normally might have to solve an intelligence-test problem. Thus, there exist no perfectly culture-fair tests of intelligence, at least at present. How then should we consider context when assessing and understanding intelligence?

Several researchers have suggested that providing culture-relevant tests is possible (e.g., Baltes, Dittmann-Kohli, & Dixon, 1984; Jenkins, 1979; Keating, 1984). **Culture-relevant tests** measure skills and knowledge that relate to the cultural experiences of the test-takers can be offered. Baltes and his colleagues, for example, have designed tests measuring skill in dealing with the pragmatic aspects of everyday life. Designing culture-relevant tests requires creativity and effort, but it is probably not impossible. For example, one study investigated memory abilities—one aspect of intelligence as our culture defines it—in our culture versus the Moroccan culture (Wagner, 1978). It found that the level of recall depended on the content that was being remembered. Culture-relevant content was remembered more effectively than nonrelevant content. For example, when compared with Westerners, Moroccan rug merchants were better able to recall complex visual patterns on black-and-white photos of Oriental rugs. Sometimes tests just are not designed to minimize the effects of cultural differences. In such cases, the key to culture-specific differences in memory

© George Holton/Photo Researchers, Inc.

Intricate patterns on Moroccan rugs were more easily remembered by Moroccan rug merchants than by Westerners. In contrast, Westerners more easily remembered information unfamiliar to Moroccan rug merchants.

may be the knowledge and use of metamemory strategies, rather than actual structural differences in memory (e.g., memory span and rates of forgetting) (Wagner, 1978).

Research has shown that rural Kenyan school children have substantial knowledge about natural herbal medicines they believe fight illnesses. Western children, of course, would not be able to identify any of these medicines (Sternberg & associates, 2001; Sternberg & Grigorenko, 1997). In short, making a test culturally relevant appears to involve much more than just removing specific linguistic barriers to understanding.

Similar context effects appear in children's and adults' performance on a variety of tasks. Three kinds of context affect performance (Ceci & Roazzi, 1994). The first is the social context. An example would be whether a task is considered masculine or feminine. The second is the mental context. An example would be whether a visuo-spatial task involves buying a home or burgling it. The third is the physical context. Here, an example would be whether a task is presented at the beach or in a laboratory. For example, 14-year-old boys performed poorly on a task when it was couched as a cupcake-baking task, but they performed well when it was framed as a battery-charging task (Ceci & Bronfenbrenner, 1985). Brazilian maids had no difficulty with proportional reasoning when hypothetically purchasing food, but they had great difficulty with it when hypothetically purchasing medicinal herbs (Schliemann & Magalhües, 1990). Brazilian children whose poverty had forced them to become street vendors showed no difficulty in performing complex arithmetic computations when selling things, but they had great difficulty performing similar calculations in a classroom (Carraher, Carraher, & Schliemann, 1985). Thus, test performance may be affected by the context in which the test terms are presented. The extent to which the context of performance resembles the context of learning of an intelligent action may partially determine the extent to which the behavior shows transfer from the first situation to the second (Barnett & Ceci, 2005).

In these studies, the investigators looked at the interaction of cognition and context. Several investigators have proposed theories that seek explicitly to examine this interaction within an integrated model of many aspects of intelligence. Such theories view intelligence as a complex system and are discussed in the next two sections.

Gardner: Multiple Intelligences

Howard Gardner (1983, 1993b, 1999, 2006) has proposed a **theory of multiple intelligences,** in which intelligence comprises multiple independent constructs, not just a single, unitary construct. However, instead of speaking of multiple abilities that together constitute intelligence (e.g., Thurstone, 1938), this theory distinguishes eight distinct intelligences that are relatively independent of each other (Table 13.3). Each is a separate system of functioning, although these systems can interact to produce what we see as intelligent performance. Looking at Gardner's list of intelligences, you might want to evaluate your own intelligences, perhaps rank ordering your strengths in each.

Howard Gardner is a professor of education and adjunct professor of psychology at Harvard University. He is best known for his theory of multiple intelligences and for showing how the theory can be applied in educational settings. He has also done important work in neuropsychology and in the psychology of creativity.

TABLE 13.3	Gardner's Eight Intelligences

On which of Howard Gardner's eight intelligences do you show the greatest ability? In what contexts can you use your intelligences most effectively? (After Gardner, 1999.)

TYPE OF INTELLIGENCE	TASKS REFLECTING THIS TYPE OF INTELLIGENCE
Linguistic intelligence	Used in reading a book; writing a paper, a novel, or a poem; and understanding spoken words
Logical-mathematical intelligence	Used in solving math problems, in balancing a checkbook, in solving a mathematical proof, and in logical reasoning
Spatial intelligence	Used in getting from one place to another, in reading a map, and in packing suitcases in the trunk of a car so that they all fit into a compact space
Musical intelligence	Used in singing a song, composing a sonata, playing a trumpet, or even appreciating the structure of a piece of music
Bodily-kinesthetic intelligence	Used in dancing, playing basketball, running a mile, or throwing a javelin
Interpersonal intelligence	Used in relating to other people, such as when we try to understand another person's behavior, motives, or emotions
Intrapersonal intelligence	Used in understanding ourselves—the basis for understanding who we are, what makes us tick, and how we can change ourselves, given our existing constraints on our abilities and our interests
Naturalist intelligence	Used in understanding patterns in nature

From *Multiple Intelligences* by Howard Gardner. Copyright © 1993 by Howard Gardner. Reprinted by permission of Basic Books, a member of Perseus Books, L.L.C.

In some respects, Gardner's theory sounds like a factorial one. It specifies several abilities that are construed to reflect intelligence of some sort. However, Gardner views each ability as a separate intelligence, not just as a part of a single whole. Moreover, a crucial difference between Gardner's theory and factorial ones is in the sources of evidence Gardner used for identifying the eight intelligences. Gardner used converging operations, gathering evidence from multiple sources and types of data.

In particular, the theory uses eight "signs" as criteria for detecting the existence of a discrete kind of intelligence (Gardner, 1983, pp. 63–67):

1. Potential isolation by brain damage. The destruction or sparing of a discrete area of the brain (e.g., areas linked to verbal aphasia) may destroy or spare a particular kind of intelligent behavior.

2. The existence of exceptional individuals (e.g., musical or mathematical prodigies). They demonstrate extraordinary ability (or deficit) in a particular kind of intelligent behavior.

3. An identifiable core operation or set of operations (e.g., detection of relationships among musical tones). It is essential to performance of a particular kind of intelligent behavior.

4. A distinctive developmental history leading from novice to master. It is accompanied by disparate levels of expert performance (i.e., varying degrees of expressing this type of intelligence).

5. A distinctive evolutionary history. Increases in intelligence plausibly may be associated with enhanced adaptation to the environment.

6. Supportive evidence from cognitive-experimental research. An example would be task-specific performance differences across discrete kinds of intelligence (e.g., visuospatial tasks versus verbal tasks). They would need to be accompanied by cross-task performance similarities within discrete kinds of intelligence (e.g., mental rotation of visuospatial imagery and recall memory of visuospatial images).

7. Supportive evidence from psychometric tests indicating discrete intelligences (e.g., differing performance on tests of visuospatial abilities versus on tests of linguistic abilities).

8. Susceptibility to encoding in a symbol system (e.g., language, math, musical notation) or in a culturally devised arena (e.g., dance, athletics, theater, engineering, or surgery as culturally devised expressions of bodily-kinesthetic intelligence).

Gardner does not dismiss entirely the use of psychometric tests. But the base of evidence used by Gardner does not rely on the factor analysis of various psychometric tests alone. In thinking about your own intelligences, how fully integrated do you believe them to be? How much do you perceive each type of intelligence as depending on any of the others?

Gardner's view of the mind is modular. Modularity theorists believe that different abilities—such as Gardner's intelligences—can be isolated as emanating from distinct portions or modules of the brain. Thus, a major task of existing and future research on intelligence is to isolate the portions of the brain responsible for each of the intelligences. Gardner has speculated as to at least some of these locales, but hard evidence for the existence of these separate intelligences has yet to be produced. Furthermore, some scientists question the strict modularity of Gardner's theory (Nettelbeck & Young, 1996). Consider the phenomenon of preserved specific cognitive functioning in autistic savants. Savants are people with severe social and cognitive deficits but with corresponding high ability in a narrow domain. They suggest that such preservation fails as evidence for modular intelligences. The narrow long-term memory and specific aptitudes of savants may not really be intelligent (Nettelbeck & Young, 1996). Thus, there may be reason to question the intelligence of inflexible modules.

Sternberg: The Triarchic Theory

Whereas Gardner emphasizes the separateness of the various aspects of intelligence, I tend to emphasize the extent to which they work together in my triarchic theory of human intelligence (Sternberg, 1985a, 1988, 1996b, 1999). According to the **triarchic theory of human intelligence,** intelligence comprises three aspects, dealing with the relation of intelligence (1) to the internal world of the person, (2) to experience, and (3) to the external world. Figure 13.5 illustrates the parts of the theory and their interrelations.

How Intelligence Relates to the Internal World

The internal part of the theory emphasizes the processing of information. Information processing can be viewed in terms of three different kinds of components. First are metacomponents—higher-order executive processes (i.e., metacognition) used to plan,

FIGURE 13.5

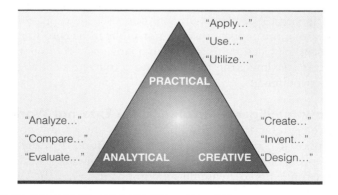

According to Robert Sternberg, intelligence comprises analytical, creative, and practical abilities. In analytical thinking, we try to solve familiar problems by using strategies that manipulate the elements of a problem or the relationships among the elements (e.g., comparing, analyzing); in creative thinking, we try to solve new kinds of problems that require us to think about the problem and its elements in a new way (e.g., inventing, designing); and in practical thinking, we try to solve problems that apply what we know to everyday contexts (e.g., applying, using).

monitor, and evaluate problem solving. Second are performance components—lower-order processes used for implementing the commands of the metacomponents. And third are knowledge-acquisition components—the processes used for learning how to solve the problems in the first place. The components are highly interdependent.

Suppose that you were asked to write a term paper. You would use metacomponents for higher-order decisions. Thus, you would use them to decide on a topic, plan the paper, monitor the writing, and evaluate how well your finished product succeeds in accomplishing your goals for it. You would use knowledge-acquisition components for research to learn about the topic. You would use performance components for the actual writing. In practice, the three kinds of components do not function in isolation. Before actually writing the paper, you first would have to decide on a topic. Then you would have to do some research. Similarly, your plans for writing the paper might change as you gather new information. It may turn out that there is not enough information on particular aspects of the chosen topic. This scarcity of information may force you to shift your emphasis. Your plans also may change if particular aspects of the writing go more smoothly than others.

How Intelligence Relates to Experience

The theory also considers how prior experience may interact with all three kinds of information-processing components. That is, each of us faces tasks and situations with which we have varying levels of experience. They range from a completely novel task, with which we have no previous experience, to a completely familiar task, with which we have vast, extensive experience. As a task becomes increasingly familiar, many aspects of the task may become *automatic*. They require little conscious effort for determining what step to take next and how to implement that next step. A novel task makes demands on intelligence different from those of a task for which automatic procedures have been developed.

According to the triarchic theory, relatively novel tasks—such as visiting a foreign country, mastering a new subject, or acquiring a foreign language—demand more of a person's intelligence. A completely unfamiliar task may demand so much of the person as to be overwhelming. Suppose, for example, you were visiting a foreign country. You probably would not profit from enrolling in a course with unfamiliar abstract subject matter taught in a language you do not understand. The most intellectually stimulating tasks are those that are challenging and demanding but not overwhelming.

How Intelligence Relates to the External World

The triarchic theory also proposes that the various components of intelligence are applied to experience to serve three functions in real-world contexts. The first is adapting ourselves to our existing environments. The second is shaping our existing environments to create new environments. And the third is selecting new environments. You use adaptation when you learn the ropes in a new environment and try to figure out how to succeed in it. For example, when you first start college, you probably try to figure out the explicit and implicit rules of college life. You then try to use these rules to succeed in the new environment. You also shape your environment. For example, you may decide what courses to take and what activities to pursue. You even may try to shape the behavior of those around you, perhaps by starting a new campus organization or by running for student government. Finally, if you are unable either to adapt yourself or to shape your environment to suit you, you might consider selecting another environment. For example, you might transfer to a different college.

According to the triarchic theory, people may apply their intelligence to many different kinds of problems. For example, some people may be more intelligent in the face of abstract, academic problems. Others may be more intelligent in the face of concrete, practical problems. An intelligent person does not necessarily excel in all aspects of intelligence. Rather, intelligent people know their strengths and weaknesses. They find ways in which to capitalize on their strengths and either to compensate for or to correct their weaknesses. For example, a person who is strong in psychology but not in physics might choose as a physics project the creation of a physics aptitude test (which I did when I took physics). The point is to make the most of your strengths and to find ways to improve on or at least to live comfortably with your weaknesses.

We performed a comprehensive study testing the validity of the triarchic theory and its usefulness in improving performance. We predicted that matching students' instruction and assessment to their abilities would lead to improved performance (Sternberg & associates, 1996; Sternberg & associates, 1999). Students were selected for one of five ability patterns: high only in analytical ability, high only in creative ability, high only in practical ability, high in all three abilities, or not high in any of the three abilities. Then students were assigned at random to one of four instructional groups. They emphasized either memory-based, analytical, creative, or practical learning. Then the memory-based, analytical, creative, and practical achievement of all students was assessed. We found that students who were placed in an instructional condition that matched their strength in terms of pattern of ability outperformed students who were mismatched. Thus, the prediction of the experiment was confirmed. For example, a high-analytical student being placed in an instructional condition that emphasized analytical thinking outperformed a high-analytical student being placed in an instructional condition that emphasized practical thinking.

Teaching students to use all of their analytic, creative, and practical abilities has resulted in improved school achievement for every students, whatever their ability pattern (Grigorenko, Jarvin, & Sternberg, 2002; Sternberg & Grigorenko, 2004; Sternberg, Torff, & Grigorenko, 1998). One important consideration in light of such findings is the need for changes in the assessment of intelligence (Sternberg & Kaufman, 1996). Current measures of intelligence are somewhat one-sided. They measure mostly analytical abilities. They involve little or no assessment of creative and practical aspects of intelligence (Sternberg & associates, 2000; Wagner, 2000). A more well-rounded assessment and instruction system could lead to greater benefits of education for a wider variety of students—a nominal goal of education.

One attempt to accomplish this goal can be seen through the Rainbow Project. In the Rainbow Project, students completed the SAT and additional assessments. These additional assessments included measures of creative and practical as well as of analytical abilities (Sternberg & the Rainbow Project Collaborators, 2006). The addition of these supplemental assessments resulted in superior prediction of college grade point average (GPA) as compared with scores on the SAT and high school GPA. In fact, the new tests doubled the prediction of first-year college GPA obtained just by the SAT. Moreover, the new assessments substantially reduced differences in scores among members of diverse ethnic groups.

Thus far, we have described various models of human intelligence. These models do not, in themselves, state whether intelligence can be taught or improved through instruction. A number of investigators have addressed this issue, however. Can intelligence actually be modified with instruction, and if so, how? What strategies are effective, and which ones, less so? Consider the answers.

PRACTICAL APPLICATIONS OF COGNITIVE PSYCHOLOGY	Robert L. Williams developed a test he called the BITCH Test (Black Intelligence Test of Cultural Homogeneity). Many "standard" intelligence tests rely heavily on vocabulary (e.g., The Shipley Test, a major section on the Wechsler intelligence tests). Williams scored very poorly on an intelligence test when he was in high school, so he was advised not to to college but to develop trade skills. Because Williams knew he had "street smarts," he ignored this advice, went to college, and eventually earned his Ph.D. To demonstrate that knowledge of vocabulary does not capture all of what goes into intelligence, Williams' BITCH test asked people to define various "Black" terms of the time, such as "alley apple," "deuce-and-a-quarter," and "Mother's Day." Not surprisingly, most Blacks did better on this test than their White counterparts. The items on the test were culturally relevant to most Blacks at the time (many of the terms are outdated now), and they were culturally irrelevant to most Whites.

Improving Intelligence: Effective, Ineffective, and Questionable Strategies

Human intelligence is highly malleable. It can be shaped and even increased through various kinds of interventions (Detterman & Sternberg, 1982; Grotzer & Perkins, 2000; Perkins & Grotzer, 1997; Sternberg & associates, 1996; Sternberg & associates, 1997). Moreover, the malleability of intelligence has nothing to do with the extent to which intelligence has a genetic basis (Sternberg, 1997). An attribute (such as height) can be partly or even largely genetically based and yet can be environmentally malleable.

The Head Start program was initiated in the 1960s. It was to be a way of providing preschoolers with an edge on intellectual abilities and accomplishments when they started school. Long-term follow-ups have indicated that by mid-adolescence, children who participated in the program were more than a grade ahead of matched controls who did not receive the program (Lazar & Darlington, 1982; Zigler & Berman, 1983). The children in the program also scored higher on a variety of tests of scholastic achievement. They were also less likely to need remedial attention. And they were less likely to show behavioral problems. Although such measures are not truly measures of intelligence, they show strong positive correlations with intelligence tests.

An alternative to intellectual enrichment outside the home may be to provide an enriched home environment. A particularly successful project has been the Abecedarian Project. It showed that the cognitive skills and achievements of lower socioeconomic status children could be increased through carefully planned and executed interventions (Ramey & Ramey, 2000). For instance, children who took part in the

Abecedarian program completed more years of postsecondary education than did their nonexperimental peers (Campbell & associates, 2002). In another study utilizing portions of the Abecedarian program with low-birth-weight children, early intervention also produced improvements in a number of skills, including ones measured in math and reading tasks (McCormick & associates, 2006).

A number of training programs have also shown some success. One such program is Reuven Feuerstein's (1980) Instrumental Enrichment program. It involves training in a variety of abstract-reasoning skills. It appears to be particularly effective for improving the skills of performers who have mental disabilities. Another program, the Odyssey program (see Adams, 1986), was shown to be effective in raising the intellectual performance of Venezuelan children of junior high school age. The Philosophy for Children program (Lipman, Sharp, & Oscanyan, 1980) was also shown to teach logical thinking skills to children throughout the primary and secondary levels of schooling. Aspects of the Intelligence Applied program (Sternberg, 1986; Sternberg & Grigorenko, 2002a; Sternberg, Kaufman, & Grigorenko, 2008) for teaching intellectual skills have been shown to be effective. It can improve both insight skills (Davidson & Sternberg, 1984) and the ability to learn meanings of words from context, a primary means for acquiring new vocabulary (Sternberg, 1987a). Practical intelligence also can be taught (Gardner & associates, 1994; Sternberg, Okagaki, & Jackson, 1990).

INVESTIGATING COGNITIVE PSYCHOLOGY

Several factors in the early (preschool) home environment appear to be correlated with high IQ scores (Bradley & Caldwell, 1984). They are emotional and verbal responsivity of the primary caregiver and the caregiver's involvement with the child, avoidance of restriction and punishment, organization of the physical environment and activity schedule, provision of appropriate play materials, and opportunities for variety in daily stimulation. Further, Bradley and Caldwell found that these factors more effectively predicted IQ scores than did socioeconomic status or family-structure variables. It should be noted, however, that the Bradley-Caldwell study is correlational. It therefore cannot be interpreted as indicating causality. Furthermore, their study pertained to preschool children. Children's IQ scores do not begin to predict adult IQ scores well until age 4 years. Moreover, before age 7 years, the scores are not very stable (Bloom, 1964). Other work has suggested that factors such as maternal social support and interactive behavior may play a key role in the instability of scores on tests of intellectual ability between ages 2 and 8 years (Pianta & Egeland, 1994).

The Bradley and Caldwell data should not be taken to indicate that demographic variables have little effect on IQ scores. On the contrary, throughout history and across cultures, many groups of people have been assigned pariah status as inferior members of the social order. Across cultures, these disadvantaged groups (e.g., native Maoris versus European New Zealanders) have shown differences in tests of intelligence and aptitude (Steele, 1990; Zeidner, 1990). Such was the case of the Burakumin tanners in Japan. In 1871, they were granted emancipation but not full acceptance into Japanese society. On the one hand, they show poor performance and underprivileged status in Japan. On the other hand, those who immigrate to

America—and are treated like other Japanese immigrants—perform on IQ tests and in school achievement at a level comparable to that of their fellow Japanese Americans (Ogbu, 1986).

Similar positive effects of integration were shown on the other side of the world. In Israel, the children of European Jews score much higher on IQ tests than do children of Arabic Jews. The exception is when the children are reared on kibbutzim. Here, the children of all national ancestries are raised by specially trained caregivers, in a dwelling separate from their parents. When these children shared the same child-rearing environments, there were no national-ancestry–related differences in IQ (Smilansky, 1974).

Altogether, there is now abundant evidence that a variety of factors can affect intellectual skills. One factor is people's environments (Ceci, Nightingale, & Baker, 1992; Reed, 1993; Sternberg & Wagner, 1994). Another is their motivation (Collier, 1994; Sternberg & Ruzgis, 1994). A third is their training (Feuerstein, 1980; Sternberg, 1987b). Thus, the controversial claims made by Herrnstein and Murray (1994) in their book, *The Bell Curve*, regarding the futility of intervention programs, are unfounded. One needs to consider all the evidence in favor of the possibility of improving cognitive skills. Likewise, Herrnstein and Murray's appeal to "a genetic factor in cognitive ethnic differences" (Herrnstein & Murray, 1994, p. 270) seems dicey in light of the direct evidence against such genetic differences (see Sternberg, 1996b). It appears to result in part from a misunderstanding of the heritability of traits in general.

Heredity certainly plays a role in individual differences in intelligence (Loehlin, Horn, & Willerman, 1997; Plomin, 1997), as does the environment (Sternberg & Grigorenko, 1999; Wahlsten & Gottlieb, 1997). Genetic inheritance may set some kind of upper limit on how intelligent a person may become. However, we now know that for any attribute that is partly genetic, there is a *reaction range*. This is the range of broad limits of possibilities in which an attribute can be expressed in various ways. Thus, each person's intelligence can be developed further within this broad range of potential intelligence (Grigorenko, 2000). We have no reason to believe that people now reach their upper limits in the development of their intellectual skills. To the contrary, the evidence suggests that we can do quite a bit to help people become more intelligent (for further discussion of these issues, see Mayer, 2000a; Sternberg, 1995; see also Neisser & associates, 1996).

Another study that examined the malleability of intelligence examined a different aspect, namely, students' beliefs about this malleability. Blackwell, Trzesniewski, and Dweck (2007) examined junior high school students and their beliefs about the nature of intelligence. The belief that intelligence is malleable predicted an improvement in mathematics achievement over the following 2 years (Blackwell, Trzesniewski, & Dweck, 2007). However, the students who believed that intelligence is fixed showed no significant change over this same time frame (Blackwell, Trzesniewski, & Dweck, 2007). In a second study, students whose math grades were declining were taught about the malleability of intelligence (Blackwell, Trzesniewski, & Dweck, 2007). The grades of students who received this training stopped declining. Furthermore, the students became more motivated in the classroom. However, the students who did not receive this training continued to show declines in their grades (Blackwell, Trzesniewski, & Dweck, 2007). These findings indicate that not only is intelligence malleable, but also it is greatly affected by our expectations.

Ultimately, we can help people to become more intelligent. To do so, we help them to better perceive, learn, remember, represent information, reason, decide, and solve problems. In other words, what we do is help them improve the cognitive functions that have been the focus of this book. The connection between improving intelligence and improving cognition is not a casual one. On the contrary, human cognition forms the core of human intelligence. Thus intelligence is a construct that helps us unify all the diverse aspects of cognition. Cultural and other contextual factors may influence the expression of our intelligence. For example, behavior that is considered intelligent in one culture may be considered unintelligent in another culture. But the cognitive processes underlying behavior are largely the same. In every culture people need to learn, to reason, to solve problems, and so on. Thus, when we study cognitive psychology, we are learning about the fundamental core of human intelligence that helps people the world over adapt to their environmental circumstances. And these processes apply, no matter how different those circumstances may be. No wonder, then, that the study of cognition is so fundamental to psychology in particular and to the understanding of human behavior in general.

Development of Intelligence in Adults

Intelligence, of course, develops with age (Anderson, 2005). Do scores on cognitive-ability tests continue to increase indefinitely? The available data suggest that they may not (Berg, 2000). Although crystallized intelligence is higher, on average, for older adults than for younger adults, fluid intelligence is higher, on average, for younger adults than for older ones (Horn & Cattell, 1966). At the college level, then, both fluid and crystallized abilities are increasing. Later in life, however, the picture often changes.

For example, the performance of older adults on many information-processing tasks appears to be slower, particularly on complex tasks (Bashore, Osman, & Hefley, 1989; Cerella, 1990, 1991; Poon, 1987; Schaie, 1989). In general, crystallized cognitive abilities seem to increase throughout the life span, whereas fluid cognitive abilities seem to increase up until the 20s or 30s or possibly 40s and slowly decrease thereafter. The preservation of crystallized abilities suggests that long-term memory and the structure and organization of knowledge representation are preserved across the life span (Salthouse, 1992, 1996, 2005). Moreover, many adults find ways of compensating for later deficits in skills so that their actual performance is unaffected. For example, older typists may type less quickly but look further ahead in their typing to compensate for the loss of processing speed (Salthouse, 1996). Or if they are forgetful, they may write notes to themselves more often than they did when they were younger.

Although psychometric researchers disagree about the age when fluid intelligence starts to decline, many researchers agree that eventually some decline does indeed occur, on average. The rate and extent of decline varies widely across people. Some cognitive abilities also seem to decline under some circumstances but not others, on average. For example, effectiveness of performance on some problem-solving tasks appears to show age-related decline (Denny, 1980), although even brief training appears to improve scores on problem-solving tasks for older adults (Rosenzweig &

Bennett, 1996; Willis, 1985). Other research implicates declines in executive functioning as a reason for decreased performance on intelligence tests (Taconnat & associates, 2007).

Not all cognitive abilities decline, however. For example, one book (Cerella & associates, 1993) devotes 20 chapters to describing studies showing little or no intellectual decline in various areas of cognition, including object and word perception, language comprehension, and problem solving. Some researchers (e.g., Schaie & Willis, 1986) have found that some kinds of learning abilities seem to increase, and others (Graf, 1990; Labouvie-Vief & Schell, 1982; Perlmutter, 1983b) have found that the ability to learn and remember meaningful skills and information shows little decline. Also, even in a single domain, such as memory, decreases in one kind of performance may not imply decreases in another. For example, although short-term memory performance seems to decline (Hultsch & Dixon, 1990; West, 1986), long-term memory (Bahrick, Bahrick, & Wittlinger, 1975) and recognition memory (Schonfield & Robertson, 1966) remain quite good.

Some researchers (e.g., Schaie, 1974, 1996) even question much of the evidence for intellectual decline. For one thing, our views of memory and aging may be confounded by reports of pathological changes that occur in some older adults. Such changes do not result from general intellectual decline but from specific neurophysiological disorders. These neurophysiological disorders, such as Alzheimer's disease, are fairly uncommon even among the most elderly. Preventive screening tools for Alzheimer's disease, which capitalize on differences in typical aging adult abilities, currently are being investigated with mixed success (Mirmiran, von Someren, & Swaab, 1996). Cognitive abilities seem to decline most in the last 10 years before death. The amount of decline occurring in these later years is, in part, predicted by intelligence test scores early in life (Bourne & associates, 2007).

Another qualification on findings of decline in older age is the frequent use of cross-sectional research designs, which involve testing different cohorts (generations) of individuals at the same time. Such designs tend to overestimate the extent of decline of cognitive abilities. For unknown reasons, more recent generations of individuals show higher cognitive abilities—at least as measured by IQ (Flynn, 1984, 1987)—than do earlier generations. Consequently, the lower IQs of the older individuals may be a generational effect rather than an aging effect. Indeed, longitudinal research designs, which test the same individuals repeatedly over an extended period, suggest less decline in mental abilities with age. These studies, however, may underestimate the extent of decline resulting from selective dropout. The less able participants drop out of the study over the years, perhaps because they find the taking of the cognitive tests to be discouraging or even humiliating.

Although the debate about intellectual decline with age continues, positions have converged somewhat. For instance, there is a consensus (Cerella, 1990, 1991; Kliegl, Mayr, & Krampe, 1994; Salthouse, 1994, 1996) that some slowing of the rate of cognitive processing occurs across the span of adulthood, and the evidence of slowing remains even when the experimental methodology and analyses rule out the disproportionate representation of demented adults among the elderly (Salthouse, Kausler, & Saults, 1990). Among the general factors that have been suggested as contributing to age-related slowing of cognitive processing have been a generalized decline in central nervous system functioning (Cerella, 1991), a decline in working-memory capacity

(Salthouse, 1993), a decline in attentional resources (see Horn & Hofer, 1992), and a decline in the functioning of the frontal lobes (Bugg & associates, 2006).

Slowed processing might lead to cognitive deficits through two speed-related issues in cognitive functioning—limited time and simultaneity (Salthouse, 1996). Slowed processing may prevent certain operations from being computed. Such operations may need to occur within a limited amount of time. The operations may need to overlap because of storage limitations. For example, auditory memory exhibits rapid decay, leading to the necessity for rapid classification of auditory signals. Slowing of upper-level processing can result in incomplete or inaccurate processing of auditory signals. Given the semi-parallel nature of much of cognitive processing along with the nature of synaptic transmission, that speed would be an issue is not surprising—such processing is very time dependent.

In addition to these general factors, many cognitive-developmental psychologists have suggested that specific factors also affect age-related changes in cognitive processing. The specific factors differentially may affect various cognitive tasks. For example, specific factors include greater slowing of higher-order cognitive processes than of sensory-motor processes (Cerella, 1985). They also include differential slowing of high- versus low-complexity tasks (Kliegl, Mayr, & Krampe, 1994). A further cognitive factor is greater slowing for tasks requiring coordinative complexity (requiring simultaneous processing of multiple stimuli) than for sequential complexity (requiring sequential processing of multiple stimuli; Mayr & Kliegl, 1993). A final factor is greater age-related decline in processes of information retrieval than in processes of encoding (see Salthouse, 1992). In addition, priming effects and tasks requiring implicit memory seem to show little or no evidence of decline (Mitchell & Bruss, 2003). But tasks involving explicit memory do show age-related decline (see Salthouse, 1992).

Based on existing research, three basic principles of cognitive development in adulthood have been suggested (Dixon & Baltes, 1986). First, fluid abilities and other aspects of information processing may decline in late adulthood. But this decline is balanced by stabilization and even advancement of well-practiced and pragmatic aspects of mental functioning (crystallized abilities). Second, despite the age-related decline in information processing, sufficient reserve capacity allows at least temporary increases in performance, especially if the older adult is motivated to perform well. Third, when adults lose some of the speed and physiology-related efficiency of information processing, they often compensate, in a given task, with other knowledge and expertise-based information-processing skills (Salthouse, 1991, 1996; see also Salthouse & Somberg, 1982). In other words, older adults develop practical strategies to retain relatively high levels of functioning (Berg & associates, 1998; Berg, Meegan, & Deviney, 1998; Sternberg, Grigorenko, & Oh, 2001). They also can draw on practical knowledge that younger people may not have (Berg, 2000; Colonia-Willner, 1998; Torff & Sternberg, 2001).

Although the evidence regarding age-related differences in the selection of cognitive strategies is mixed, there appear to be no age-related differences in self-monitoring of cognitive processes (see Salthouse, 1992). So it would appear that older adults may be able to effectively utilize information regarding how to enhance their cognitive performance. Also, when task performance is based more on accuracy than on speed, older adults may at least partly compensate for speed deficits with increased carefulness and persistence (see Horn & Hofer, 1992). Further, at all times throughout the life span, there is considerable *plasticity*—modifiability—of abilities (Baltes, 1997; Baltes & Willis, 1979; Garlick, 2002; Mirmiran, von Someren, & Swaab, 1996; Rosenzweig & Bennett, 1996). None of us is stuck at a particular level of performance. Each of us can improve.

In recent years, some psychologists have become particularly interested in the development of wisdom in adulthood (see Sternberg, 1990). Most theorists have argued that wisdom increases with age, although there are exceptions (Meacham, 1990). Psychologists' definitions of wisdom have been diverse. Some (Baltes & associates, 1995; Baltes & Smith, 1990; Baltes & Staudinger, 2000) define *wisdom* as exceptional insight into human development and life matters, including exceptionally good judgment and advice and commentary about difficult life problems. Furthermore, wisdom can be seen as reflecting a positive gain in culture-based cognitive pragmatics (meaningful uses of cognitive skills) in the face of the more physiologically controlled losses in cognitive mechanics (Baltes, 1993). Other research has found six factors in people's conceptions of wisdom. They are reasoning ability, sagacity (shrewdness), learning from ideas and from the environment, judgment, expeditious use of information, and perspicacity (intensely keen awareness, perception, and insight) (Sternberg, 1985b). In wisdom, to know what you do not know is also important (Meacham, 1983, 1990). Whatever the definition (Moshman, 1998), the study of wisdom represents an exciting new direction for discovering what abilities may be developed during later adulthood at the same time that fluid abilities or the mechanical aspects of information processing may be flagging.

Adults are sometimes called on to do tasks that challenge their intelligence in ways that are quite specific. For example, pilots use their intelligence to make decisions that, for their passengers as well as themselves, can be matters of life and death. Psychology can be used to help design cockpits that optimize the conditions for their making these decisions. Research shows that cockpits in which there is a high degree of similarity of colors of various elements, or in which background elements are moving, interfere with pilots' ability to read instrumentation (Nikolic, Orr, & Sarter, 2004). The branch of psychology that helps in the intelligent design of instruments, such as cockpit instruments, is called "human-factors" psychology. The errors pilots make can be of various kinds. For example, they may make a slip, in which they intend to do one thing but do another; or they may show a lapse, in which case they fail to attend to a signal that needs attention (Sarter & Alexander, 2000). Human-factors psychologists study not just the instrumentation but also the ways workers react to it. Their goal is to optimize the human–machine interaction as a whole.

Artificial Intelligence: Computer Simulations

Can a Computer Program Be "Intelligent"?

Much of the early information-processing research centered on work based on computer simulations of human intelligence as well as computer systems that use optimal methods to solve tasks. Programs of both kinds can be classified as examples of *artificial intelligence (AI)*, or intelligence in symbol-processing systems such as computers (see Schank & Towle, 2000). Computers cannot actually think. They must be programmed to behave as though they are thinking. That is, they must be programmed to simulate cognitive processes. In this way, they give us insight into the details of how people process information cognitively. Essentially, computers are just pieces of hardware—physical components of equipment—that respond to instructions. Other kinds of hardware (other pieces of equipment) also respond to instructions. For example, if you can figure out how to give the instructions, a DVR (digital video recorder) will respond to your instructions and will do what you tell it to do.

What makes computers so interesting to researchers is that they can be given highly complex instructions, known as computer programs or even more commonly as software. Programs tell the computer how to respond to new information.

Before we consider any intelligent programs, we need to consider seriously the issue of what, if anything, would lead us to describe a computer program as being "intelligent."

The Turing Test

Probably the first serious attempt to deal with the issue of whether a computer program can be intelligent was made by Alan Turing (1963), based on ideas Turing first presented in 1950. Specifically, Turing devised a test by which a human could assess the intelligence of a respondent (see Chapter 1). The basic idea behind the Turing Test is whether an observer can distinguish the performance of a computer from that of a human. For the test to work, everyone must agree that the human is intelligent in at least some degree. In the specific form proposed by Turing, the test is conducted with a computer, a human respondent, and an interrogator. The interrogator has two different "conversations" with an interactive computer program. The goal of the interrogator is to figure out which of two parties is a person communicating through the computer and which is the computer itself. The interrogator can ask the two parties any questions at all. However, the computer will try to fool the interrogator into believing that it is human. The human, in contrast, will be trying to show the interrogator that he or she truly is human. The computer passes the Turing Test if an interrogator is unable to distinguish the computer from the human.

The test of indistinguishability of computer from human commonly is used in assessing the intelligence of a computer program. The test is not usually performed in quite the way described by Turing. For example, outputs of some kind generated by a computer might be scanned and assessed for their comparability to human performance. In some cases, human data from a problem-solving task are compared with computer-generated data. The degree of relation between them is then evaluated. For example, suppose a computer solves number-series problems such as 1, 4, 9, 16, . . . (where each number is the next larger perfect square). The response times and error patterns of the computer can be compared with those of human participants who have solved the same problems (Kotovsky & Simon, 1973; Simon & Kotovsky, 1963). Of course, the response times of the computer are typically much faster than those of humans, but the researchers are less interested in overall reaction times than in patterns of reaction times. In other words, what matters is not whether computers take more or less time on each problem than do humans. Rather, it is whether the problems that take the computer relatively longer to solve also take human participants relatively longer.

Sometimes, the goal of a computer model is not to match human performance but to exceed it. In this case, maximum AI, rather than simulation of human intelligence, is the goal of the program. The criterion of whether computer performance matches that of humans is no longer relevant. Instead, the criterion of interest is that of how well the computer can perform the task assigned to it. Computer programs that play chess, for example, typically play in a way that emphasizes "brute force." The programs evaluate extremely large numbers of possible moves. Many of them are moves humans would never even consider evaluating (Berliner, 1969; Bernstein, 1958). Using brute force, the IBM program "Deep Blue" beat world champion Gary Kasparov in a 1997 chess match. The same brute-force method is used in programs that play checkers (Samuel, 1963). These programs generally are evaluated in terms of how well they can beat each other or, even more importantly, human contenders playing against them.

Having considered some issues of what constitutes an intelligent computer program, we now turn to some of the actual programs. The discussion of these programs will give you an idea of how AI research has evolved. It will also show you how AI models have influenced the work of cognitive psychologists. As the preceding examples have shown, many early AI programs focused on problem solving.

Early Programs

One of the very earliest intelligent programs was the Logic Theorist (LT) (Newell, Shaw, & Simon, 1957b). It was designed to discover proofs for theorems in elementary symbolic logic.

A successor to the LT was called the General Problem Solver (GPS) (Newell, Shaw, & Simon, 1957a). This program used a method of solving problems called *means–ends analysis*. It involves solving problems by successively reducing the difference between the present status (where you are now) and the goal status (where you want to be; see Chapter 11). Figure 13.6 shows a schematic **flow chart**—a model path for reaching a goal or solving a problem. The flow chart shows how GPS can transform one object (or one problem state) into another using means–ends analysis.

FIGURE 13.6

In developing GPS, Allen Newell, Clifford Shaw, and Herbert Simon suggested a flow chart for implementing a means–ends analysis to reach a goal.

Means–ends analysis can be applied to a wide range of problems. An example would be the "MOVE" problems described in Chapter 11, in which hobbits and orcs needed to cross a river using just one two-person boat. GPS, as it was formulated back in the 1950s and 1960s, could apply the heuristic to problems such as proving logic theorems or to some of the other problems described in Chapter 11. The GPS program and the LT program were typical of the early work carried out at Carnegie-Mellon University. But the Newell-Simon group at Carnegie was not the only group busy trying to create intelligent programs. At MIT, a group led primarily by Marvin Minsky also was interested in creating AI programs. The MIT programs differed from the Carnegie programs in their greater emphasis on the retrieval of semantic information—that is, the use of meaningful verbal information (Minsky, 1968). For example, by the early 1970s, MIT Researcher Terry Winograd (1972) had developed SHRDLU. This program commanded a robot arm manually to manipulate various blocks in a "block world." Figure 13.7 shows examples of the kinds of elements that inhabit the block world of SHRDLU.

Whereas SHRDLU processes information in terms of a block world, other programs operate in very different worlds. One of the more interesting is that of the psychotherapist, on the one hand, and the patient, on the other.

FIGURE 13.7

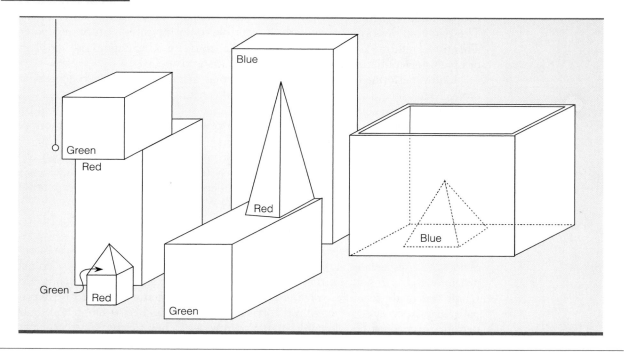

Terry Winograd's robot was programmed to operate within a three-dimensional block world containing elements such as the blocks shown here. From Understanding Natural Languages *by Terry Winograd. Copyright © 1972 by Terry Winograd. Reprinted by permission of Elsevier.*

Two programs that operate in the world of psychotherapy are ELIZA and PARRY. The former takes on the role of a nondirective psychotherapist. The latter takes on the role of a paranoid patient of a psychotherapist. The goal of the nondirective therapist is to elicit a patient's feelings. The therapist then reflects these feelings back to the patient and helps the patient understand and figure out what to do about these feelings. Consider, for example, a segment of an interaction between ELIZA and a patient working with ELIZA, as shown in Table 13.4. In this segment, ELIZA seems to show clinical insight about her patient. However, ELIZA is not as bright as she appears here. She uses key words and phrases in the interlocutor's (patient's) remarks to choose her own remarks. She does not understand in any larger sense what the patient is saying. Indeed, the creator of ELIZA chose the domain of nondirective psychotherapy because he believed simulating the responses of a nondirective psychotherapist would be relatively easy (Weizenbaum, 1966). He avoided simulating people in other occupations who more directively show their knowledge and expertise in their interactions with others.

If therapists can be simulated, why not patients? Kenneth Colby (1963), a trained psychiatrist, created a simulation of a paranoid patient who is especially concerned that the Mafia is after him. The workings of the program are shown in the segment of dialogue reproduced in Table 13.4. Colby's simulation of a paranoid is not just a set of responses that "sounds paranoid." Rather, the simulation is generated from a theory of the neurotic process of a paranoid. The primary intention of the paranoid is to determine another person's intentions. Messages from the other are scanned to assist in this determination. Messages are classified as malevolent, benevolent, or neutral. The paranoid person is particularly susceptible to an interpretation of malevolence. This interpretation can emanate from a belief that the other intends either physical or psychological harm to the person who is paranoid.

Colby performed a somewhat more formal evaluation of his program than is typical. He asked a group of 33 psychiatrists to read transcripts of "interviews" with PARRY and with actual paranoid patients. None of the psychiatrists were told that a computer model was involved. Roughly half of them rated the model as more paranoid than actual patients.

Colby's program differs fundamentally from many others. It simulates not just abstract cognitive processes but also a belief system. Another program by Colby uses cognitive therapy for the treatment of mild depression. It involves both a text and dialogue mode of interaction with a person (Colby, 1995).

Programs That Simulate Expertise

Unlike the East Coast research at Yale, MIT, and Carnegie-Mellon, AI research on the West Coast, especially at Stanford, tended to emphasize **expert systems:** computer programs that can perform the way an expert does in a fairly specific domain. No attempt was made to more globally model human intelligence or even to extend the particular expert systems, even in theory. Rather, the researchers attempted to simulate performance in just one domain, often a narrow one. They sought a level of expertise that surpasses what would be possible for a program that was fairly domain general.

For example, several programs were developed to diagnose various kinds of medical disorders. Such programs are obviously of enormous potential significance, given the very high costs (financial and personal) of incorrect diagnoses. Probably the

TABLE 13.4	Programs That Simulate Belief Systems: ELIZA and PARRY

Joseph Weizenbaum's ELIZA was developed to simulate a nondirective psychotherapist, and Kenneth Colby's PARRY was developed to simulate a paranoid patient. What might happen if PARRY were to seek psychotherapeutic guidance from ELIZA? (Adapted from Weizenbaum, 1966, and from Colby, 1963.)

ELIZA*	**PARRY†**
Men are all alike.	Why are you in the hospital?
IN WHAT WAY?	I SHOULDN'T BE HERE.
They're always bugging us about something or other.	Who brought you here?
CAN YOU THINK OF A SPECIFIC EXAMPLE?	THE POLICE.
Well, my boyfriend made me come here.	What trouble did you have with the police?
YOUR BOYFRIEND MADE YOU COME HERE.	COPS DON'T DO THEIR JOB.
He says I'm depressed much of the time.	What do they do instead?
I AM SORRY TO HEAR THAT YOU ARE DEPRESSED.	COPS ARREST THE WRONG PEOPLE.
It's true. I am unhappy.	They arrest the right ones sometimes.
DO YOU THINK COMING HERE WILL HELP YOU NOT TO BE UNHAPPY?	THE LAW SHOULD GET THOSE ITALIAN CROOKS.
I need some help, that much seems certain.	Are you Italian?
WHAT WOULD IT MEAN TO YOU IF YOU GOT SOME HELP?	MY BACKGROUND IS BRITISH BUT I WAS BORN IN THIS COUNTRY.
Perhaps I could learn to get along with my mother.	Do you know any Italian crooks?
TELL ME MORE ABOUT YOUR FAMILY.	I TRY TO AVOID THE UNDERWORLD.
My mother takes care of me.	Are you afraid of the underworld?
WHO ELSE IN YOUR FAMILY TAKES CARE OF YOU?	THE MAFIA ARE THE WORST GANGSTERS.
My father.	Are you connected with the Mafia?
YOUR FATHER?	YOU KNOW, THEY KNOW ME.
You are like my father in some ways.	How do they know you?
WHAT RESEMBLANCE DO YOU SEE?	THEY SPY ON ME.
You are not very aggressive, but I think you don't want me to notice that.	Why do they?
WHAT MAKES YOU THINK I AM NOT VERY AGGRESSIVE?	THEY WANT TO GET FALSE EVIDENCE TO FRAME ME.
You don't argue with me.	What do they have against you?
WHY DO YOU THINK I DON'T ARGUE WITH YOU?	THEY ARE OUT TO GET ME.
You are afraid of me.	What for?
DOES IT PLEASE YOU TO THINK THAT I AM AFRAID OF YOU?	I HAVE INCRIMINATING EVIDENCE AGAINST THE MAFIA.
My father is afraid of everybody.	Are you sure of all this?
WHAT ELSE COMES TO MIND WHEN YOU THINK OF YOUR FATHER?	YOU DON'T BELIEVE ME?
Bullies.	I am doing my best.
DOES THAT HAVE ANYTHING TO DO WITH THE FACT THAT YOUR BOYFRIEND MADE YOU COME HERE?	(SILENCE ON THE "PATIENT'S" PART)
	(Silence on the psychiatrist's part)
	CAN'T YOU THINK OF A DECENT QUESTION TO ASK?
	You seem hostile to me.
	SOME OF YOUR REMARKS ANNOY ME.
	I am sorry.
	FORGET THE EXCUSES, YOU GUYS ARE ALL ALIKE.

*J. Weizenbaum (1966) "Eliza—A Computer Program for the Study of Natural Language Communication Between Man & Machine," *Communications of the Association for Computing Machinery,* Vol. 9, p. 36–45. © 1966 Association of Computing Machinery. Reprinted by permission.
†"Computer Simulation of a Neurotic Process," by Perry Colby. In Tomkins/Messick, *Computer Simulation and Personality.* Copyright © 1963 by John Wiley & Sons, Inc.

TABLE 13.5	A Program That Simulates Expertise: MYCIN
At Stanford, the development of expert systems, such as the one excerpted here, has been a focus of AI research.	

If:	The gram stain of the organism is gramneg [i.e., not a particular type of microorganism], The morphology of the organism is rod, and The aerobicity of the organism is anaerobic.
Then:	There is suggestive evidence (.6) that the identity of the organism is bacteroides.

From *Computer Based Medical Consultations* by E. H. Shortliffe. Copyright © 1974 by Elsevier Science Publishing.

most well-known and certainly the oldest of these programs is MYCIN (Buchanan & Shortliffe, 1984; Shortliffe, 1976). MYCIN can be used for detecting and potentially even treating certain bacterial infections. Table 13.5 shows a fragment of a system of statements used by MYCIN, translated to be readable by humans. Note that the program gives an indication of its certainty (0.6) regarding the identification of the offending microorganism as being bacteroides. The 0.6 is not, strictly speaking, a probability. But it is on a scale where 0 indicates total lack of certainty regarding truth and 1 indicates total certainty. MYCIN contains roughly 500 rules (if-then statements). It can deal with about 100 different kinds of bacterial infections.

MYCIN has been tested for its validity in making diagnoses and treatment suggestions. MYCIN's performance compared favorably with that of faculty members in the Stanford School of Medicine. MYCIN outperformed medical students and residents in the same school (Yu & associates, 1984). Earlier, it had been shown to be quite effective in prescribing medication for meningitis. Thus, within its relatively narrow domain of expertise, MYCIN is clearly an impressive expert system.

Other expert systems also have been created for medical diagnosis. For example, INTERNIST (Miller, Pople, & Myers, 1982) diagnoses a broader spectrum of diseases than does MYCIN. Within its broader domain, its diagnostic powers do not measure up to those of an experienced internist. This program illustrates what sometimes is termed the *bandwidth-fidelity problem.* The broader the bandwidth of a radio or other receiver, the poorer its fidelity (faithfulness, reliability) tends to be. Similarly, the wider the spectrum of problems to which an AI program addresses itself, the less reliable it is likely to be in solving any one of those kinds of problems.

Other expert systems solve other types of problems, including some of the problems found by scientists. For example, DENDRAL, another early expert system developed at Stanford, helps scientists identify the molecular structure of newly discovered organic compounds (Buchanan & associates, 1976).

A number of recent projects exploring expert intelligence are of interest to cognitive psychologists. One of these projects, Cyc, has involved development of a system capable of learning (Matuszek & associates, 2005). The three components of this project are the knowledge base, the inference engine, and the natural language system (Matuszek & associates, 2005). By continuously adding to its knowledge base, Cyc, through its inference engine, is able to mimic at least some aspects of common sense.

Questions about the Intelligence of Intelligent Programs

Artificially intelligent programs such as the ones described here are not without their critics, of course. Consider some of the main objections that have been raised in regard to some of the aforementioned programs. Experts differ as to how much credence they give to these various objections. Ultimately, each of us needs to evaluate the objections for ourselves.

Serial Processing

Some of the objections to AI pertain to the limitations of the existing hardware and software designs. For one thing, human brains can process many sources of information simultaneously. However, because of the architectural structure of computer hardware, most computers (virtually all early computers, and even most contemporary ones) can handle only one instruction at a time. Hence, models based on computer simulations have tended to depend on serial processing (step-by-step, one-at-a-time) of information. However, with various computers linked into neural networks of computers, computers now may simulate parallel processing (multiple steps being performed simultaneously). Hence, the serial-processing limitation no longer applies to all computer-based models of AI.

Absence of Intuition

Another of the limitations of AI relates to a different characteristic of human intelligence: intuition. Some have argued that whereas computers can be good and competent manipulators of symbols according to prepackaged algorithms, they lack intuition (Dreyfus & Dreyfus, 1990). To these investigators, intuition is found in the kinds of hunches that distinguish genuine experts from those with book knowledge. Intuition does not necessarily involve the expertise that will enable people to exploit their knowledge maximally when confronted with a difficult situation. Basically, the Dreyfuses are arguing that computers excel in the mathematical and deductive aspect of thinking but not in the intuitive one.

For example, some years ago, a United Airlines DC-10 airliner crash-landed. All three of its hydraulic systems were severed by debris from an engine that was torn off in midair. It hit the tail of the plane, where the three hydraulic systems were interlinked. The pilot of the DC-10 radioed to technical headquarters for guidance as to what to do when all three hydraulic systems go down. The technical experts were unable to help the crew. They had never encountered the situation before and had no guidelines to follow. The crew, nevertheless, working on intuition, managed to steer the plane roughly by varying engine thrust. The news media and others applauded the pilot and his crew for their intuitions as to what to do in the face of a very thorny problem. In this instance, there were no guidelines, and no computer program had been written to solve the problem. As a result of these intuitions, roughly two thirds of the passengers in the plane survived a crash landing in Sioux City, Iowa.

The argument that computers cannot show intuitive intelligence does not go unchallenged. Several researchers interested in human problem solving (see Chapter 11) have studied computer simulations of problem solving. Their research has led them to infer that at least some characteristics of intuition can be modeled on computers. For example, one set of programs (the "Bacon" programs) simulates the processes involved in various important scientific discoveries in the past (Langley & associates, 1987). The investigators behind the programs argued that their programs do display intuition. Moreover, they argued that there is nothing mystical about intuition. Rather, according to these researchers, intuition can be understood in terms of the same information-processing mechanisms that are applied to conventional forms of problem solving. Intuition can be characterized in part through AI, when it is conceptualized as involving the subconscious recognition of patterns (Frantz, 2003).

Along a similar line, other investigators simulated large parts of a theory of how we reason inductively (Holland & associates, 1986). Their programs were inductive ones, going beyond the information given in a problem to come up with a solution that is not deductively determined by the problem elements. One can easily argue that such programs are intuitive, at least in some sense. They go beyond the information given. Other programs also make inferences that go well beyond the simple facts stored in their databases.

Applications of Artificial Intelligence

A recent application of AI can be seen in a competition sponsored by the Defense Advanced Research Projects Agency (DARPA). The program, originally called the DARPA Grand Challenge, requires groups to develop an automated vehicle (DARPA, 2007). Early versions of this project have had some success and have led to more challenging versions each year that it had been conducted. The most recent version of this challenge is the DARPA Urban Challenge, which requires the vehicle independently to perform in an urban environment including traffic (DARPA, 2007). This challenge does not permit drivers or control via a remote. As a result, these vehicles must integrate artificial intelligence capable of assessing and reacting to new environments.

Another application of AI can be seen in the Mars rovers. The designers integrate AI into these rovers, enabling them to make (some) mission decisions and be self-reliant (Bluck, 2004). The application of AI to these projects has led to independent machines capable of performing complex operations in variable environments. Clearly, these applications are major improvements over the original attempts at AI.

Intelligence versus the Appearance of Intelligence

A philosopher has raised an objection to the basic idea that computers can be considered truly intelligent (Searle, 1980). To make his objection, he uses what is known as the "Chinese Room" problem. Imagine that Searle, the philosopher, is locked in a room. He is given a large batch of Chinese writing to translate. He knows no Chinese at all. However, suppose that, in addition to the Chinese writing, Searle is given a second batch of Chinese script. He also receives a set of rules for translating the Chinese into English. Next, Searle is given a third batch. It gives him a set of rules for formulating responses to questions that were raised in the first batch of Chinese writing. Searle then responds to the original batch of writing with a response that makes sense and is in perfect Chinese. Presumably, over time, Searle could become extremely good at manipulating the rules. His responses would be every bit as good as those of a native Chinese speaker who understood exactly what was being asked. However, in fact, Searle still knows no Chinese at all. He is simply following a set of rules.

According to Searle, programs that seem to understand various kinds of inputs and to respond in a seemingly intelligent way (such as Winograd's SHRDLU) are like Searle in the Chinese room. The computers understand the input being given to them no better than Searle understands Chinese. They are simply operating according to a set of preprogrammed rules. Searle's notion is that the computer does not really see and understand the connections between input and output. Rather, it uses pre-established connections that make it seem intelligent on the surface. To Searle, these programs do not demonstrate AI. They only appear to show intelligence.

Predictably, AI researchers have not competed with each other to be the first to accept Searle's argument. They generally have not been eager to acknowledge any folly in their attempts to model AI. A number of researchers have offered responses to Searle's charge that the computer is not anything like what it is cracked up to be. One scientist, for example, argued that Searle's use of the rule systems in the second and third batches of input is, in fact, intelligent (Abelson, 1980). He further argued that children learning a language also at first apply rules rather blindly. Only later do they come to understand the rules and how they are being used. Others argue that the system as a whole (comprising Searle as well as the set of instructions) does indeed exhibit understanding. In addition, some computer programs even have shown an ability to simulate at least a modest degree of skill development and knowledge acquisition. Nevertheless, existing computer programs do not begin to approach our human ability to enhance our own intelligence.

Key Themes

This chapter addresses several of the themes described in Chapter 1.

First and most prominent, perhaps, is the nature-nurture theme. This theme has played a major part in intelligence research since the nineteenth century. Investigators are in general agreement that nature plays a role. Intelligence is partially heritable. The estimates of heritability actually increase with age. The older you are, the more nature plays a role and the less nurture plays a role. This may be because of differential effects of early rearing environments that start to wear off. But the kind of environment an individual has affects the extent to which people can utilize and make the most of their genetic potential. Moreover, research shows that environment can affect biology. The brain changes as a result of learning experiences.

A second theme is validity of causal inference versus ecological validity. Some studies of intelligence have been done in the laboratory. Others, especially studies of practical intelligence and cultural studies of intelligence, have more often been done in the field. For example, studies of practical intelligence in rural Kenya simply cannot be done in a highly controlled setting. Both kinds of studies enhance our knowledge of intelligence. They complement each other.

A third theme is basic versus applied research. In the twentieth century, much of the early research done on intelligence was applied. It was designed to create, standardize, and validate intelligence tests. But later in the twentieth century, researchers started to realize that they had very little idea of the cognitive processes that contribute to performance on the tests. So more basic research ensued in which investigators tried to understand these cognitive processes. The research suggested that the tests gave useful information. But other kinds of tests also emerged as useful for understanding human intelligence and individual differences in it.

PRACTICAL APPLICATIONS OF COGNITIVE PSYCHOLOGY	What is your dominant cognitive style? Defining your preferred way of interacting with the environment could help you perform better in school or on the job. The "Thinking about Thinking" section at the end of each of the chapters in this text was designed to appeal to different cognitive styles to more meaningfully integrate the information in each chapter. Which questions were more appealing to you or helped you most? Analytical questions asked you to compare, analyze, or evaluate ideas; creative questions asked you to design or create; and practical questions asked you to apply information to other situations. Try to apply your knowledge in all three ways for the most effective and flexible use.

Summary

1. **What are the key issues in intelligence research? How do different researchers and theorists respond to those issues?** An early issue in the study of intelligence centered on how to measure intelligence. Francis Galton and his followers emphasized psychophysical acuity. Binet and his followers emphasized judgment. Two common themes that run through the definitions of intelligence proposed by many experts are the capacity to learn from experience and the ability to adapt to the environment. In addition, the importance of metacognition and of cultural context increasingly are recognized by researchers and theorists of intelligence. Nonetheless, psychologists often disagree regarding the relative importance of context (nurture) versus inheritance (nature) in determining intelligence. Also, different researchers disagree regarding whether to focus on studying the structures of intelligence (e.g., Spearman, Thurstone, Cattell) or the processes of intelligence (e.g., Hunt, Jensen, Simon). Some researchers (e.g., Gardner, Sternberg) also have focused on trying to integrate the various approaches to intelligence into comprehensive systems models of intelligence. One approach to intelligence is to understand it in terms of factor analysis. This is a statistical technique that seeks to identify latent sources of individual differences in performance on tests. There are several principal factor-analytic models of the mind.

   One is the g-factor model of Spearman. Another is the primary mental abilities model of Thurstone. A third is the structure-of-intellect (SOI) model of Guilford. And a fourth comprises the hierarchical models of Cattell, of Vernon, and of Carroll, among others.

2. **What are some information-processing approaches to intelligence?** An alternative approach to intelligence is to understand it in terms of information processing. Information-processing theorists have sought to understand intelligence in terms of a number of constructs and tasks. They include inspection time, choice reaction time, speed of lexical access, the ability to divide attention successfully, the components of reasoning and problem solving, and complex problem solving that can be simulated via computers. A related approach is the biological model. It uses increasingly sophisticated means of viewing the brain while the brain is engaged in intel-

ligent behaviors. Preliminary findings suggest that speed of neural conduction may play a role in intelligence. Particularly intriguing are findings suggesting that neural efficiency and specialization of cerebral function may be influential in intelligent cognitive processing.

3. **What are some alternative views of intelligence?** Another main approach to understanding intelligence (based on an anthropological model) is a contextual approach. According to this approach, intelligence is viewed as wholly or partly determined by cultural values. Contextual theorists differ in the extent to which they believe that the meaning of intelligence differs from one culture to another. What is considered to be intelligent behavior is, to some extent, culturally relative. The same behavior that is considered to be intelligent in one culture may be considered unintelligent in another culture. To create a test of intelligence that is culture-fair—that is, equally fair for members of different cultures—is difficult, and perhaps impossible. Members of different cultures have different conceptions of what constitutes intelligent behavior.

   Systems models of intelligence seek to go beyond cultural content. Gardner's theory of multiple intelligences specifies that intelligence is not a unitary construct. Rather, there are multiple intelligences, each relatively independent of the others. Sternberg's triarchic theory of human intelligence conceives of intelligence in terms of information-processing components. They are applied to experience to serve the functions of adaptation to the environment, shaping of the environment, and selection of new environments.

4. **Can intelligence be improved, and if so, how?** Intellectual skills can be taught. Thus, intelligence is malleable rather than fixed. Researchers largely agree that some improvements are possible. They disagree regarding both the degree to which they believe that such improvements can be achieved and the means by which to do so.

5. **How does intelligence continue to develop in adults?** Intelligence continues to change in adulthood. Crystallized abilities appear to increase fairly steadily. Fluid abilities sometimes decline, especially within the last 10 years before death. A number of researchers have investigated wisdom, which can be seen as an extension of intelligence. Wisdom involves knowledge of the pragmatics of life. Wise people, according to some theorists, seek a common good.

6. **How have researchers attempted to simulate intelligence using machines such as computers?** AI research is conducted on the premise that having machines simulate intelligence is both possible and valuable. The Turing Test is designed to evaluate the extent to which particular AI programs have succeeded in simulating humanlike intelligence.

   Critics of AI, however, question both the possibility and the worth of trying to get machines to simulate human intelligence. They sometimes use the "Chinese Room" problem to illustrate a distinction between simulated intelligence and true understanding. Arguments can be made to support either perspective. Many now-classic AI programs have been developed. Among the earliest ones are the Logic Theorist, which proves theorems in symbolic logic, and the General Problem Solver, which solves various kinds of problems using means–ends analysis. A later program was SHRDLU. It simulated a robot performing various operations in a block world, such as placing one block on top of another or placing a block in a box. Programs that modeled belief systems include ELIZA. It was designed to simulate a nondirective psychotherapist.

   Another is PARRY, designed to simulate the thinking of a paranoid psychiatric patient. Expert systems, programs designed to demonstrate expertise, include MYCIN, which diagnoses certain bacterial diseases by analyzing the results of blood tests. They also include DENDRAL, which analyzes the structure of organic compounds.

Thinking about Thinking: Factual, Analytical, Creative, and Practical Questions

1. Briefly summarize the key strands of AI research and name an example of a program in each strand.

2. What are some of the main reasons that intelligence tests have been devised and used?

3. In what ways is the theory of multiple intelligences different from factor-analytic theories of intelligence?

4. What are some of the strengths and limitations of the information-processing approach to intelligence?

5. How would you design a program to improve intelligence (as you define the concept)?

6. Design an experiment that would link a physiological approach to a cognitive approach to intelligence.

7. How might any of the structural approaches to intelligence lead to practical applications?

8. Contextualists underscore the importance of viewing intelligence within a given context. What are some aspects of your social, mental, or physical context that you consider important to the expression of your intelligence?

Key Terms

contextualism

culture-fair

culture-relevant tests

emotional intelligence

expert systems

factor analysis

flow chart

"g" factor

intelligence

structure-of-intellect (SOI) model

theory of multiple intelligences

triarchic theory of human intelligence

Annotated Suggested Readings

Gray, J. R., & Thompson, P. M. (2004). Neurobiology of intelligence: science and ethics. *Nature Neuroscience Reviews, 5,* 471–482. Provides a review of neuroscience studies examining intelligence.

Lehman, D. R., Chiu, C.-Y., & Schaller, M. (2004). Psychology and culture. *Annual Review of Psychology, 55,* 689–714. Provides a review of cultural effects on psychological processes.

Sternberg, R. J., & Pretz, J. E. (Eds.). (2005). *Cognition and intelligence.* New York: Cambridge University Press. A comprehensive review of the relation between cognition and intelligence, covering virtually all aspects of cognition addressed in this book.

Glossary

accessibility—the degree to which we can gain access to the available information

ACT—Adaptive Control of Thought. In his ACT model, John Anderson synthesized some of the features of serial information-processing models and some of the features of semantic-network models. In ACT, procedural knowledge is represented in the form of production systems. Declarative knowledge is represented in the form of propositional networks

ACT-R—a model of information processing that integrates a network representation for declarative knowledge and a production-system representation for procedural knowledge

agnosia—a severe deficit in the ability to perceive sensory information

algorithms—sequences of operations that may be repeated over and over again and that, in theory, guarantee the solution to a problem

Alzheimer's disease—a disease of older adults that causes dementia as well as progressive memory loss

amacrine cells—along with horizontal cells, they make single lateral connections among adjacent areas of the retina in the middle layer of cells

amnesia—severe loss of explicit memory

amygdala—plays an important role in emotion, especially in anger and aggression

analogue codes—a form of knowledge representation that preserves the main perceptual features of whatever is being represented for the physical stimuli we observe in our environment

analysis—breaking down the whole of a complex problem into manageable elements

anterograde amnesia—the inability to remember events that occur after a traumatic event

aphasia—an impairment of language functioning caused by damage to the brain

arousal—a degree of physiological excitation, responsivity, and readiness for action, relative to a baseline

artifact categories—groupings that are designed or invented by humans to serve particular purposes or functions

artificial intelligence (AI)—the attempt by humans to construct systems that show intelligence and, particularly, the intelligent processing of information; intelligence in symbol-processing systems such as computers

associationism—examines how events or ideas can become associated with one another in the mind to result in a form of learning

attention—the active cognitive processing of a limited amount of information from the vast amount of information available through the senses, in memory, and through cognitive processes; focus on a small subset of available stimuli

autobiographical memory—refers to memory of an individual's history

automatic processes—involves no conscious control

automatization—the process by which a procedure changes from being highly conscious to being relatively automatic; also termed proceduralization

availability—the presence of information stored in long-term memory

availability heuristic—cognitive shortcut that occurs when we make judgments on the basis of how easily we can call to mind what we perceive as relevant instances of a phenomenon

axon—the part of the neuron through which intraneuronal conduction occurs (via the action potential) and at the terminus of which is located the terminal buttons that release neurotransmitters

babbling—the infant's preferential production largely of those distinct phonemes—both vowels and consonants—that are characteristic of the infant's own language

base rate—refers to the prevalence of an event or characteristic within its population of events or characteristics

basic level—degree of specificity of a concept that seems to be a level within a hierarchy that is preferred to other levels; sometimes termed natural level

behaviorism—a theoretical outlook that psychology should focus only on the relation between observable behavior, on the one hand, and environmental events or stimuli, on the other

bilinguals—people who can speak two languages

binaural presentation—presenting the same two messages, or sometimes just one message, to both ears simultaneously

binocular depth cues—based on the receipt of sensory information in three dimensions from both eyes

bipolar cells—make dual connections forward and outward to the ganglion cells, as well as backward and inward to the third layer of retinal cells

blindsight—traces of visual perceptual ability in blind areas

bottom-up theories—data-driven (i.e., stimulus-driven) theories

bounded rationality—belief that we are rational, but within limits

brain—the organ in our bodies that most directly controls our thoughts, emotions, and motivations

brainstem—connects the forebrain to the spinal cord

categorical perception—discontinuous categories of speech sounds

categorical syllogism—a deductive argument in which the relationship among the three terms in the two premises involves categorical membership

category—a concept that functions to organize or point out aspects of equivalence among other concepts based on common features or similarity to a prototype

causal inferences—how people make judgments about whether something causes something else

central executive—both coordinates attentional activities and governs responses

cerebellum—controls bodily coordination, balance, and muscle tone, as well as some aspects of memory involving procedure-related movements; from Latin, "little brain"

cerebral cortex—forms a 1- to 3-millimeter layer that wraps the surface of the brain somewhat like the bark of a tree wraps around the trunk

cerebral hemispheres—the two halves of the brain

change blindness—the inability to detect changes in objects or scenes that are being viewed

characteristic features—qualities that describe (characterize or typify) the prototype but are not necessary for it

child-directed speech—the use of simpler sentence constructions when speaking with infants and young children

coarticulation—occurs when phonemes or other units are produced in a way that overlaps them in time

cocktail party problem—the process of tracking one conversation in the face of the distraction of other conversations

cognitive maps—internal representations of our physical environment, particularly centering on spatial relationships

cognitive psychology—the study of how people perceive, learn, remember, and think about information

cognitive science—a cross-disciplinary field that uses ideas and methods from cognitive psychology, psychobiology, artificial intelligence, philosophy, linguistics, and anthropology

cognitivism—the belief that much of human behavior can be understood in terms of how people think

communication—exchange of thoughts and feelings

comprehension processes—used to make sense of the text as a whole

concept—an idea about something that provides a means of understanding the world

conditional reasoning—occurs when the reasoner must draw a conclusion based on an if-then proposition

cones—one of the two kinds of photoreceptors in the eye; less numerous, shorter, thicker, and more highly concentrated in the foveal region of the retina than in the periphery of the retina than are rods (the other type of photoreceptor); virtually nonfunctional in dim light, but highly effective in bright light and essential to color vision

conjunction search—looking for a particular combination (conjunction: joining together) of features

connectionist models—according to connectionist models, we handle very large numbers of cognitive operations at once through a network distributed across incalculable numbers of locations in the brain

connotation—a word's emotional overtones, presuppositions, and other nonexplicit meanings

consciousness—includes both the feeling of awareness and the content of awareness

consolidation—the process of integrating new information into stored information

constructive—prior experience affects how we recall things and what we actually recall from memory

constructive perception—the perceiver builds (constructs) a cognitive understanding (perception) of a stimulus; he or she uses sensory information as the foundation for the structure but also uses other sources of information to build the perception

content morphemes—the words that convey the bulk of the meaning of a language

context effects—the influences of the surrounding environment on perception

contextualism—belief that intelligence must be understood in its real-world context

contralateral—from one side to another

controlled processes—accessible to conscious control and even require it

convergent thinking—attempt to narrow down the multiple possibilities to converge on a single best answer

converging operations—the use of multiple approaches and techniques to address a problem

cooing—the infant's oral expression that explores the production of vowel sounds

cooperative principle—principle in conversation that holds that we seek to communicate in ways that make it easy for our listener to understand what we mean

core—refers to the defining features something must have to be considered an example of a category

corpus callosum—a dense aggregate of neural fibers connecting the two cerebral hemispheres

creativity—the process of producing something that is both original and worthwhile

culture-fair—equally appropriate and fair for members of all cultures

culture-relevant tests—measure skills and knowledge that relate to the cultural experiences of the test-takers

decay—occurs when simply the passage of time causes an individual to forget

decay theory—asserts that information is forgotten because of the gradual disappearance, rather than displacement, of the memory trace

declarative knowledge—knowledge of facts that can be stated

deductive reasoning—the process of reasoning from one or more general statements regarding what is known to reach a logically certain conclusion

deductive validity—logical soundness

deep structure—refers to an underlying syntactic structure that links various phrase structures through the application of various transformation rules

defining feature—a necessary attribute

dendrites—the branchlike structures of each neuron that extend into synapses with other neurons and that receive neurochemical messages sent into synapses by other neurons

denotation—the strict dictionary definition of a word

dependent variable—a response that is measured and is presumed to be the effect of one or more independent variables

depth—the distance from a surface, usually using your own body as a reference surface when speaking in terms of depth perception

dialect—a regional variety of a language distinguished by features such as vocabulary, syntax, and pronunciation

dichotic presentation—presenting a different message to each ear

direct perception theory—belief that the array of information in our sensory receptors, including the sensory context, is all we need to perceive anything

discourse—encompasses language use at the level beyond the sentence, such as in conversation, paragraphs, stories, chapters, and entire works of literature

dishabituation—change in a familiar stimulus that prompts us to start noticing the stimulus again

distracters—nontarget stimuli that divert our attention away from the target stimulus

distributed practice—learning in which various sessions are spaced over time

divergent thinking—when one tries to generate a diverse assortment of possible alternative solutions to a problem

divided attention—the prudent allocation of available attentional resources to coordinate the performance of more than one task at a time

dual-code theory—belief suggesting that knowledge is represented both in images and in symbols

dual-system hypothesis—suggests that two languages are represented somehow in separate systems of the mind

dyslexia—difficulty in deciphering, reading, and comprehending text

ecological validity—the degree to which particular findings in one environmental context may be considered relevant outside that context

electroencephalograms (EEGs)—recordings of the electrical frequencies and intensities of the living brain, typically recorded over relatively long periods

elimination by aspects—occurs when we eliminate alternatives by focusing on aspects of each alternative, one at a time

emotional intelligence—the ability to perceive and express emotion, assimilate emotion in thought, understand and reason with emotion, and regulate emotion in the self and others

empiricist—one who believes that we acquire knowledge via empirical evidence

encoding—refers to how you transform a physical, sensory input into a kind of representation that can be placed into memory

encoding specificity—what is recalled depends on what is encoded

episodic buffer—a limited-capacity system that is capable of binding information from the subsidiary systems and from long-term memory into a unitary episodic representation

episodic memory—stores personally experienced events or episodes

event-related potential—an electrophysiological response to a stimulus, whether internal or external

exemplars—typical representatives of a category

expert systems—computer programs that can perform the way an expert does in a fairly specific domain

explicit memory—when participants engage in conscious recollection

factor analysis—a statistical method for separating a construct into a number of hypothetical factors or traits that the researchers believe form the basis of individual differences in test performance

fallacy—erroneous reasoning

feature search—simply scanning the environment for a particular feature or features

feature-integration theory—explains the relative ease of conducting feature searches and the relative difficulty of conducting conjunction searches

figure-ground—what stands out from versus what recedes into the background

flashbulb memory—a memory of an event so powerful that the person remembers the event as vividly as if it were indelibly preserved on film

flow chart—a model path for reaching a goal or solving a problem

fovea—a part of the eye located in the center of the retina that is largely responsible for the sharp central vision people use in activities such as reading or watching television or movies

frontal lobe—associated with motor processing and higher thought processes, such as abstract reasoning

function morphemes—a morpheme that adds detail and nuance to the meaning of the content morphemes or helps the content morphemes fit the grammatical context

functional fixedness—the inability to realize that something known to have a particular use may also be used for performing other functions

functional magnetic resonance imaging (fMRI)—a neuroimaging technique that uses magnetic fields to construct a detailed representation in three dimensions of levels of activity in various parts of the brain at a given moment

functional-equivalence hypothesis—belief that although visual imagery is not identical to visual perception, it is functionally equivalent to it

functionalism—seeks to understand what people do, and why they do it

ganglion cells—a kind of neuron usually situated near the inner surface of the retina of the eye; receive visual information from photoreceptors by way of bipolar cells and amacrine cells; send visual information from the retina to several different parts of the brain, such as the thalamus and the hypothalamus

Gestalt approach to form perception—based on the notion that the whole differs from the sum of its individual parts

Gestalt psychology—states that we best understand psychological phenomena when we view them as organized, structured wholes

"g" factor—general ability

grammar—the study of language in terms of noticing regular patterns

habituation—involves our becoming accustomed to a stimulus so that we gradually pay less and less attention to it

heuristics—informal, intuitive, speculative strategies that sometimes lead to an effective solution and sometimes do not

hindsight bias—when we look at a situation retrospectively, we believe we easily can see all the signs and events leading up to a particular outcome

hippocampus—plays an essential role in memory formation

horizontal cells—along with amacrine cells, they make single lateral connections among adjacent areas of the retina in the middle layer of cells

hypermnesia—a process of producing retrieval of memories that seem to have been forgotten

hypothalamus—regulates behavior related to species survival: fighting, feeding, fleeing, and mating; also active in regulating emotions and reactions to stress

hypotheses—tentative proposals regarding expected empirical consequences of the theory

hypothesis testing—a view of language acquisition that asserts that children acquire language by mentally forming tentative hypotheses regarding language, based on their inherited facility for language acquisition and then testing these hypotheses in the environment

hypothetical constructs—concepts that are not themselves directly measurable or observable but that serve as mental models for understanding how a psychological phenomenon works

iconic store—a discrete visual sensory register that holds information for very short periods

ill-structured problems—problems that lack well-defined paths to solution

illusory correlation—occurs when we tend to see particular events or particular attributes and categories as going together because we are predisposed to do so

imagery—the mental representation of things that are not currently being sensed by the sense organs

implicit memory—when we recollect something but are not consciously aware that we are trying to do so

incubation—putting the problem aside for a while without consciously thinking about it

independent variable—a variable that is varied or purposefully manipulated and that affects one or more dependent variables

indirect requests—the making of a request without doing so straightforwardly

inductive reasoning—the process of reasoning from specific facts or observations to reach a likely conclusion that may explain the facts

infantile amnesia—the inability to recall events that happened when we were very young

insight—a distinctive and sometimes seemingly sudden understanding of a problem or of a strategy that aids in solving the problem

intelligence—the capacity to learn from experience, using metacognitive processes to enhance learning, and the ability to adapt to the surrounding environment

interference—occurs when competing information causes an individual to forget something

interference theory—refers to the view that forgetting occurs because recall of certain words interferes with recall of other words

introspection—looking inward at pieces of information passing through consciousness

ipsilateral transmission—on the same side

isomorphic—the formal structure is the same, and only the content differs

jargon—specialized vocabulary commonly used within a group, such as a profession or a trade

judgment and decision making—used to select from among choices or to evaluate opportunities

knowledge representation—the form for what you know in your mind about things, ideas, events, and so on that exist outside your mind

Korsakoff's syndrome—produces loss of memory function

language—the use of an organized means of combining words in order to communicate

language acquisition device (LAD)—a biologically innate mechanism that facilitates language acquisition

law of Prägnanz—tendency to perceive any given visual array in a way that most simply organizes the disparate elements into a stable and coherent form

levels-of-processing framework—postulates that memory does not comprise three or even any specific number of separate stores but rather varies along a continuous dimension in terms of depth of encoding

lexical access—the identification of a word that allows us to gain access to the meaning of the word from memory

lexical processes—used to identify letters and words

lexicon—the entire set of morphemes in a given language or in a given person's linguistic repertoire

limbic system—important to emotion, motivation, memory, and learning

linguistic relativity—the assertion that speakers of different languages have differing cognitive systems and that these different cognitive systems influence the ways in which people speaking the various languages think about the world

linguistic universals—characteristic patterns across all languages of various cultures

lobes—divide the cerebral hemispheres and cortex into four parts

localization of function—refers to the specific areas of the brain that control specific skills or behaviors

long-term store—very large capacity, capable of storing information for very long periods, perhaps even indefinitely

magnetic resonance imaging (MRI) scan—a technique for revealing high-resolution images of the structure of the living brain by computing and analyzing magnetic changes in the energy of the orbits of nuclear particles in the molecules of the body

magnetoencephalography (MEG)—an imaging technique that measures the magnetic fields generated by electrical activity in the brain by highly sensitive measuring devices

massed practice—learning in which sessions are crammed together in a very short space of time

medulla oblongata—brain structure that controls heart activity and largely controls breathing, swallowing, and digestion

memory—the means by which we retain and draw on our past experiences to use this information in the present

mental models—knowledge structures that individuals construct to understand and explain their experiences; an internal representation of information that corresponds analogously with whatever is being represented

mental rotation—involves rotationally transforming an object's visual mental image

mental set—a frame of mind involving an existing model for representing a problem, a problem context, or a procedure for problem solving

metacognition—our understanding and control of our cognition; our ability to think about and control our own processes of thought and ways of enhancing our thinking

metamemory—strategies involve reflecting on our own memory processes with a view to improving our memory

metaphor—two nouns juxtaposed in a way that positively asserts their similarities, while not disconfirming their dissimilarities

mnemonic devices—specific techniques to help you memorize lists of words

mnemonist—someone who demonstrates extraordinarily keen memory ability, usually based on the use of special techniques for memory enhancement

modular—divided into discrete modules that operate more or less independently of each other

monocular depth cues—can be represented in just two dimensions and observed with just one eye

monolinguals—people who can speak only one language

morpheme—the smallest unit that denotes meaning within a particular language

multimode theory—proposes that attention is flexible; selection of one message over another message can be made at any of various different points in the course of information processing

myelin—a fatty substance coating the axons of some neurons that facilitates the speed and accuracy of neuronal communication

natural categories—groupings that occur naturally in the world

negative transfer—occurs when solving an earlier problem makes it harder to solve a later one

nervous system—the organized network of cells (neurons) through which an individual receives information from the environment, processes that information, and then interacts with the environment

networks—a web of relationships (e.g., category membership, attribution) between nodes

neurons—individual nerve cells

neurotransmitters—chemical messengers used for interneuronal communication

nodes—the elements of a network

nodes of Ranvier—gaps in the myelin coating of myelinated axons

nominal kind—the arbitrary assignment of a label to an entity that meets a certain set of prespecified conditions

noun phrase—syntactic structure that contains at least one noun (often, the subject of the sentence) and includes all the relevant descriptors of the noun

object-centered representation—the individual stores a representation of the object, independent of its appearance to the viewer

occipital lobe—associated with visual processing, the primary motor cortex, which specializes in the planning, control, and execution of movement, particularly of movement involving any kind of delayed response

optic ataxia—impaired visual control of the arm in reaching out to a visual target

optic nerve—the nerve that transmits information from the retina to the brain

overconfidence—an individual's overvaluation of her or his own skills, knowledge, or judgment

overextension error—erroneously extending the meaning of words in the existing lexicon to cover things and ideas for which a new word is lacking

overregularization—occurs when individuals apply the general rules of language to the exceptional cases that vary from the norm

parallel distributed processing (PDP) models or connectionist models—the handling of very large numbers of cognitive operations at once through a network distributed across incalculable numbers of locations in the brain

parallel processing—occurs when multiple operations are executed all at once

parietal lobe—associated with somatosensory processing

perception—the set of processes by which we recognize, organize, and make sense of the sensations we receive from environmental stimuli

perceptual constancy—occurs when our perception of an object remains the same even when our proximal sensation of the distal object changes

phoneme—is the smallest unit of speech sound that can be used to distinguish one utterance in a given language from another

phonological loop—briefly holds inner speech for verbal comprehension and for acoustic rehearsal

photopigments—chemical substances that absorb light, thereby starting the complex transduction process that transforms physical electromagnetic energy into an electrochemical neural impulse; rods and cones contain different types of photopigments; different types of photopigments absorb differing amounts of light and may detect different hues

photoreceptors—the third layer of the retina contains the photoreceptors, which transduce light energy into electrochemical energy.

phrase-structure grammar—syntactical analysis of the structure of phrases as they are used

pons—serves as a kind of relay station because it contains neural fibers that pass signals from one part of the brain to another

positive transfer—occurs when the solution of an earlier problem makes it easier to solve a new problem

positron emission tomography (PET) scans—measure increases in glucose consumption in active brain areas during particular kinds of information processing

pragmatic reasoning schemas—general organizing principles or rules related to particular kinds of goals, such as permissions, obligations, or causations

pragmatics—the study of how people use language

pragmatists—ones who believe that knowledge is validated by its usefulness

premises—propositions about which arguments are made

primacy effect—refers to superior recall of words at and near the beginning of a list

primary motor cortex—region of the cerebral cortex that is chiefly responsible for directing the movements of all muscles

primary somatosensory cortex—receives information from the senses about pressure, texture, temperature, and pain

prime—a node that activates a connected node; this activation is known as the priming effect

priming—the facilitation of one's ability to utilize missing information; occurs when recognition of certain stimuli is affected by prior presentation of the same or similar stimuli

priming effect—the resulting activation of the node

proactive interference—occurs when the interfering material occurs before, rather than after, learning of the to-be-remembered material

problem solving—an effort to overcome obstacles obstructing the path to a solution

problem-solving cycle—includes problem identification, problem definition, strategy formulation, organization of information, allocation of resources, monitoring, and evaluation

problem space—the universe of all possible actions that can be applied to solving a problem, given any constraints that apply to the solution of the problem

procedural knowledge—knowledge of procedures that can be implemented

production—the generation and output of a procedure

production system—an ordered set of productions in which execution starts at the top of a list of productions, continues until a condition is satisfied, and then returns to the top of the list to start anew

productive thinking—involves insights that go beyond the bounds of existing associations

proposition—basically an assertion, which may be either true or false

propositional theory—belief suggesting that knowledge is represented only in underlying propositions, not in the form of images or of words and other symbols

prototype—a sort of average of a class of related objects or patterns, which integrates all the most typical (most frequently observed) features of the class

prototype theory—suggests that categories are formed on the basis of a (prototypical, or averaged) model of the category

psycholinguistics—the psychology of our language as it interacts with the human mind

rationalist—one who believes that the route to knowledge is through logical analysis

reasoning—the process of drawing conclusions from principles and from evidence

recall—to produce a fact, a word, or other item from memory

recency effect—refers to superior recall of words at and near the end of a list

recognition—to select or otherwise identify an item as being one that you learned previously

recognition-by-components (RBC) theory—the belief that we quickly recognize objects by observing the edges of objects and then decomposing the objects into geons

reconstructive—involving the use of various strategies (e.g., searching for cues, drawing inferences) for retrieving the original memory traces of our experiences and then rebuilding the original experiences as a basis for retrieval

rehearsal—the repeated recitation of an item

representativeness—occurs when we judge the probability of an uncertain event according to (1) its obvious similarity to or representation of the population from which it is derived and (2) the degree to which it reflects the salient features of the process by which it is generated (such as randomness)

reticular activating system (RAS)—a network of neurons essential to the regulation of consciousness (sleep, wakefulness, arousal, and even attention to some extent and to such vital functions as heartbeat and breathing); also called reticular formation

retina—a network of neurons extending over most of the back (posterior) surface of the interior of the eye. The retina is where electromagnetic light energy is transduced—that is, converted—into neural electrochemical impulses

retrieval (memory)—refers to how you gain access to information stored in memory

retroactive interference—caused by activity occurring after we learn something but before we are asked to recall that thing; also called retroactive inhibition

retrograde amnesia—occurs when individuals lose their purposeful memory for events prior to whatever trauma induces memory loss

rods—light-sensitive photoreceptors in the retina of the eye that provide peripheral vision and the ability to see objects at night or in dim light; rods are not color sensitive

satisficing—occurs when we consider options one by one, and then we select an option as soon as we find one that is satisfactory or just good enough to meet our minimum level of acceptability

schemas—mental frameworks for representing knowledge that encompass an array of interrelated concepts in a meaningful organization

script—a structure that describes appropriate sequences of events in a particular context

search—refers to a scan of the environment for particular features—actively looking for something when you are not sure where it will appear

selective attention—choosing to attend to some stimuli and to ignore others

selective-combination insight—involves taking selectively encoded and compared snippets of relevant information and combining that information in a novel, productive way

selective-comparison insight—involves novel perceptions of how new information relates to old information

selective-encoding insight—involves distinguishing relevant from irrelevant information

semantic memory—stores general world knowledge

semantic network—a web of interconnected elements of meaning

semantics—the study of meaning in a language

sensory adaptation—a lessening of attention to a stimulus that is not subject to conscious control

sensory store—capable of storing relatively limited amounts of information for very brief periods

septum—is involved in anger and fear

serial processing—means by which information is handled through a linear sequence of operations, one operation at a time

short-term store—capable of storing information for somewhat longer periods but also of relatively limited capacity

signal—a target stimulus

signal detection—the detection of the appearance of a particular stimulus

signal-detection theory (SDT)—a theory of how we detect stimuli that involves four possible outcomes of the presence or absence of a stimulus and our detection or nondetection of a stimulus

simile—introduces the word *like* or *as* into a comparison between items

single-system hypothesis—suggests that two languages are represented in just one system

slips of the tongue—inadvertent linguistic errors in what we say

soma—the cell body of a neuron that is the part of the neuron essential to the life and reproduction of the cell

speech acts—addresses the question of what you can accomplish with speech

split-brain patients—people who have undergone operations severing the corpus callosum

spreading activation—excitation that fans out along a set of nodes within a given network

statistical significance—indicates the likelihood that a given set of results would be obtained if only chance factors were in operation

stereotypes—beliefs that members of a social group tend more or less uniformly to have particular types of characteristics

storage (memory)—refers to how you retain encoded information in memory

Stroop effect—demonstrates the psychological difficulty in selectively attending to the color of the ink and trying to ignore the word that is printed with the ink of that color

structuralism—seeks to understand the structure (configuration of elements) of the mind and its perceptions by analyzing those perceptions into their constituent components

structure-of-intellect (SOI)—Guilford's model for a three-dimensional structure of intelligence, embracing various contents, operations, and products of intelligence

subjective probability—a calculation based on the individual's estimates of likelihood, rather than on objective statistical computations

subjective utility—a calculation based on the individual's judged weightings of utility (value), rather than on objective criteria

surface structure—a level of syntactic analysis that involves the specific syntactical sequence of words in a sentence and any of the various phrase structures that may result

syllogisms—deductive arguments that involve drawing conclusions from two premises

symbolic representation—meaning that the relationship between the word and what it represents is simply arbitrary

synapse—a small gap between neurons that serves as a point of contact between the terminal buttons of one or more neurons and the dendrites of one or more other neurons

syntax—refers to the way in which users of a particular language put words together to form sentences

synthesis—putting together various elements to arrange them into something useful

telegraphic speech—can be used to describe two- or three-word utterances and even slightly longer ones, if they have omissions of some function morphemes

templates—highly detailed models for patterns we potentially might recognize

temporal lobe—associated with auditory processing

terminal buttons—knobs at the end of each branch of an axon; each button may release a chemical neurotransmitter as a result of an action potential

thalamus—relays incoming sensory information through groups of neurons that project to the appropriate region in the cortex

thematic roles—ways in which items can be used in the context of communication

theory—an organized body of general explanatory principles regarding a phenomenon

theory of multiple intelligences—belief that intelligence comprises multiple independent constructs, not just a single, unitary construct

theory-based view of meaning—holds that people understand and categorize concepts in terms of implicit theories, or general ideas they have regarding those concepts

tip-of-the-tongue phenomenon—experience of trying to remember something that is known to be stored in memory but that cannot readily be retrieved

top-down theories—driven by high-level cognitive processes, existing knowledge, and prior expectations

transcranial magnetic stimulation (TMS)—technique that temporarily disrupts the normal activity of the brain in a limited area. This technique requires placing a coil on a person's head and then allowing an electrical current to pass though it. The current generates a magnetic field. This field disrupts the small area (usually no more than a cubic centimeter) beneath it. The researcher can then look at cognitive functioning when the particular area is disrupted

transfer—any carryover of knowledge or skills from one problem situation to another

transformational grammar—involves the study of transformational rules that guide the ways in which underlying propositions can be rearranged to form various phrase structures

transparency—occurs when people see analogies where they do not exist because of similarity of content

triarchic theory of human intelligence—belief that intelligence comprises three aspects, dealing with the relation of intelligence (1) to the internal world of the person, (2) to experience, and (3) to the external world

verb phrase—syntactic structure that contains at least one verb and whatever the verb acts on, if anything

verbal comprehension—the receptive ability to comprehend written and spoken linguistic input, such as words, sentences, and paragraphs

verbal fluency—the expressive ability to produce linguistic output

viewer-centered representation—an individual stores the way the object looks to him or her

vigilance—refers to a person's ability to attend to a field of stimulation over a prolonged period, during which the person seeks to detect the appearance of a particular target stimulus of interest

visuospatial sketchpad—briefly holds some visual images

well-structured problems—problems that have well-defined paths to solution

word-superiority effect—letters are read more easily when they are embedded in words than when they are presented either in isolation or with letters that do not form words

working memory—holds only the most recently activated portion of long-term memory, and it moves these activated elements into and out of brief, temporary memory storage

References

Abelson, R. P. (1980). Searle's argument is just a set of Chinese symbols. *Behavioral and Brain Sciences, 3,* 424–425.

Abernethy, B. (1991). Visual search strategies and decision-making in sport. *International Journal of Sport Psychology, 22,* 189–210.

Abrams, D. M., & Strogatz, S. H. (2003). Modeling the dynamics of language death. *Nature, 424,* 900.

Ackerman, P. (1988). Determinants of individual differences during skill acquisition: Cognitive abilities and information processing. *Journal of Experimental Psychology: General, 117,* 288–318.

Ackerman, P. (2005). Ability determinants of individual differences in skilled performance. In R. J. Sternberg & J. E. Pretz (Eds.), *Cognition and intelligence* (pp. 142–159). New York: Cambridge University Press.

Ackerman, P. L. (1996). A theory of adult intellectual development: Process, personality, interests, and knowledge. *Intelligence, 22,* 227–257.

Ackerman, P. L., Beier, M. E., & Boyle, M. O. (2005). Working memory and intelligence: The same or different constructs? *Psychological Bulletin, 131*(1), 30–60.

Ackil, J. K., & Zaragoza, M. S. (1998). Memorial consequences of forced confabulation: Age differences in susceptibility to false memories. *Developmental Psychology, 34,* 1358–1372.

Acredolo, L. P., & Goodwyn, S. W. (1998). *Baby signs: How to talk with your baby before your baby can talk.* Chicago: NTB/Contemporary Publishers.

Adams, M. J. (Ed.). (1986). *Odyssey: A curriculum for thinking* (Vols. 1–6). Watertown, MA: Charlesbridge Publishing.

Adams, M. J. (1990). *Beginning to read: Thinking and learning about print.* Cambridge, MA: MIT Press.

Adams, M. J. (1999). Reading. In R. A. Wilson & F. C. Keil (Eds.), *The MIT encyclopedia of the cognitive sciences* (pp. 705–707). Cambridge, MA: MIT Press.

Adams, M. J., Treiman, R., & Pressley, M. (1997). Reading, writing and literacy. In I. Sigel & A. Renninger (Eds.), *Handbook of child psychology* (5th ed., vol. 4). *Child psychology in practice* (pp. 275–357). New York: Wiley.

Adler, J. (1991, July 22). The melting of a mighty myth. *Newsweek, 63.*

Adolphs, R. (2003). Amygdala. In L. Nadel (Ed.), *Encyclopedia of cognitive science* (Vol. 1 pp. 98–105). London: Nature Publishing Group.

Adolphs, R., Sears, L., & Piven, J. (2001). Abnormal processing of social information from faces in autism. *Journal of Cognitive Neuroscience, 13,* 232–240.

Adolphs, R., Tranel, D., Damasio, H., & Damasio, A. (1994). Impaired recognition of emotion in facial expressions following bilateral damage to the human amygdala. *Nature, 372,* 669–672.

Agulera, A., Selgas, R., Codoceo, R., & Bajo, A. (2000). Uremic anorexia: A consequence of persistently high brain serotonin levels? The tryptophan/serotonin disorder hypothesis. *Peritoneal Dialysis, 20*(6), 810–816.

Ahn, W. K., & Bailenson, J. N. (1996). Causal attribution as a search for underlying mechanisms. An explanation of the conjunction fallacy and the discounting principle. *Cognitive Psychology, 31,* 82–123.

Ahn, W. K., Kalish, C. W., Medin, D. L., & Gelman, S. A. (1995). The role of covariation versus mechanism information in causal attribution. *Cognition, 54,* 299–352.

Akhtar, N. & Montague, L. (1999). Early lexical acquisition: The role of cross-situational learning. *First Language, 19,* 347–358.

Al'bertin, S. V., Mulder, A. B., & Wiener, S. I. (2003). The advantages of electrophysiological control for the localization and selective lesioning of the nucleus accumbens in rats. *Neuroscience and Behavioral Physiology, 33*(8), 805–809.

Albert, M. L., & Obler, L. (1978). *The bilingual brain: Neuro-psychological and neurolinguistic aspects of bilingualism.* New York: Academic Press.

Allain, P., Berrut, G., Etcharry-Bouyx, F., Barre, J., Dubas, F., & Le Gal, D. (2007). Executive functions in normal aging: An examination of script sequencing, script sorting, and script monitoring. *The Journals of Gerontology Series B: Psychological Sciences and Social Sciences, 62,* 187–190.

Almor, A., & Sloman, S. A. (1996). Is deontic reasoning special? *Psychological Review, 103,* 503–546.

Altschuler, E. L., Multari, A., Hirstein, W., & Ramachandran, V. S. (2006). Situational therapy for Wernicke's aphasia. *Medical Hypotheses, 67*(4), 713–716.

Amabile, T. M. (1996). *Creativity in context.* Boulder, CO: Westview.

Amabile, T. M., & Rovee-Collier, C. (1991). Contextual variation and memory retrieval at six months. *Child Development, 62*(5), 1155–1166.

American Psychiatric Association. (1994). *Diagnostic and statistical manual of mental disorders* (4th ed.). Washington, DC: Author.

Anaki, D., Kaufman, Y., Freedman, M., & Moscovitch, M. (2007). Associative (prosop) agnosia without (apparent) perceptual deficits: A case–study. *Neuropsychologia, 45*(8), 1658–1671.

The anatomy of a head injury. Retrieved December 29, 2004, from http://www.ahs.uwaterloo.ca/~cahr/headfall.html

Anderson, A. K., & Phelps, E. A. (2001). Lesions of the human amygdala impair enhanced perception of emotionally salient events. *Nature, 411,* 305–309.

Anderson, B. F. (1975). *Cognitive psychology.* New York: Academic Press.

Anderson, D. P., Harvey, A. S., Saling, M. M., Anderson, V., Kean, M., Abbott, D. F., et al. (2006). fMRI lateralization of expressive language in children with cerebral lesions. *Epilepsia 47*(6), 998–1008.

Anderson, J. R. (1972). FRAN: A simulation model of free recall. In G. H. Bower (Ed.), *The psychology of learning and motivation* (Vol. 5, pp. 315–378). New York: Academic Press.

Anderson, J. R. (1976). *Language, memory, and thought.* Hillsdale, NJ: Erlbaum.

Anderson, J. R. (1980). Concepts, propositions, and schemata: What are the cognitive units? *Nebraska Symposium on Motivation, 28,* 121–162.

Anderson, J. R. (1983). *The architecture of cognition.* Cambridge, MA: Harvard University Press.

Anderson, J. R. (1985). *Cognitive psychology and its implications.* New York: Freeman.

Anderson, J. R. (1991). The adaptive nature of human categorization. *Psychological Review, 98,* 409–429.

Anderson, J. R. (1993). *Rules of the mind.* Hillsdale, NJ: Erlbaum.

Anderson, J. R. (1996). ACT: A simple theory of complex cognition. *American Psychologist, 51,* 355–365.

Anderson, J. R., Bothell, D., Byrne, M. D., Douglass, S., Lebiere, C., & Qin, Y. (2004). An integrated theory of the mind. *Psychological Review, 111*(4),1036–1060.

Anderson, J. R., & Bower, G. H. (1973). *Human associative memory.* New York: Wiley.

Anderson, J. R., Budiu, R., & Reder, L. M. (2001). A theory of sentence memory as part of a general theory of memory. *Journal of Memory & Language, 45,* 277–367.

Anderson, J. R., & Fincham, J. M. (1996). Categorization and sensitivity to correlation. *Journal of Experimental Psychology: Learning, Memory, and Cognition, 22,* 259–277.

Anderson, M. (2005). Marrying intelligence and cognition. In R. J. Sternberg & J. E. Pretz (Eds.), *Cognition and intelligence* (pp. 268–287). New York: Cambridge University Press.

Anderson, R. C., & Pichert, J. W. (1978). Recall of previously unrecallable information following a shift in perspective. *Journal of Verbal Learning and Verbal Behavior, 17,* 1–12.

Anderson, S. W., Rizzo, M., Skaar, N., Stierman, L., Cavaco, S., Dawson, J., et al. (2007). Amnesia and driving. *Journal of Clinical and Experimental Neuropsychology, 29*(1), 1–12.

Andreou, G., & Karapetsas, A. (2004). Verbal abilities in low and highly proficient bilinguals. *Journal of Psycholinguistic Research, 33*(5), 357–364.

Ang, S., Dyne, L. V., & Koh, C. (2006). Personality correlates of the four-factor model of cultural intelligence. *Group & Organization Management, 31*(1), 100–123.

Anglin, J. M. (1993). Vocabulary development: A morphological analysis. *Monographs of the Society for Research in Child Development, 58,* (No. 10).

Appel, L. F., Cooper, R. G., McCarrell, N., Sims-Knight, J., Yussen, S. R., & Flavell, J. H. (1972). The development of the distinction between perceiving and memorizing. *Child Development, 43,* 1365–1381.

Ardekani, B. A., Nierenberg, J., Hoptman, M., Javitt, D., & Lim, K. O. (2003). MRI study of white matter diffusion anisotropy in schizophrenia. *Brain Imaging, 14*(16), 2025–2029.

Argamon, S., Koppel, M., Fine, J., & Shimoni, A. S. (2003). Gender, genre, and writing style in formal written texts. *Text, 23*(3), 321–346.

Armstrong, S. L., Gleitman, L. R., & Gleitman, H. (1983). What some concepts might not be. *Cognition, 13,* 263–308.

Asher, J. J., & Garcia, R. (1969). The optimal age to learn a foreign language. *Modern Language Journal, 53*(5), 334–341.

Ask, K., & Granhag, A. (2005). Motivational sources of confirmation bias in criminal investigations: The need for cognitive closure. *Journal of Investigative Psychology and Offender Profiling, 2*(1), 43–63.

Atkinson, R. C., & Shiffrin, R. M. (1968). Human memory: A proposed system and its control processes. In K. W. Spence & J. T. Spence (Eds.), *The psychology of learning and motivation: Vol. 2. Advances in research and theory.* New York: Academic Press.

Atkinson, R. C., & Shiffrin, R. M. (1971). The control of short-term memory. *Scientific American, 225,* 82–90.

Atran, S. (1999). Itzaj Maya folkbiological taxonomy: Cognitive universals and cultural particulars. In D. L. Medin & S. Atran (Eds.), *Folkbiology* (pp. 119–213). Cambridge, MA: MIT Press.

Attention deficit hyperactivity disorder. (http://www.nimh.nih.gov/Publicat/ADHD.cfm, retrieved 8/11/04).

Averbach, E., & Coriell, A. S. (1961). Short-term memory in vision. *Bell System Technical Journal, 40,* 309–328.

Ayers, M. S., & Reder, L. M. (1998). A theoretical review of the misinformation effect: Predictions from an activation-based memory model. *Psychonomic Bulletin & Review, 5,* 1–21.

Ayotte, J., Peretz, I., Rousseau, I., Bard, C., & Bojanowski, M. (2000). Patterns of music agnosia associated with middle cerebral artery infarcts. *Brain, 123,* 1926–1938.

Bachevalier, J., & Mishkin, M. (1986). Visual recognition impairment follows ventromedial but not dorsolateral frontal lesions in monkeys. *Behavioral Brain Research, 20*(3), 249–261.

Backhaus, J., Junghanns, K., Born, J., Hohaus, K., Faasch, F., & Hohagen, F. (2006). Impaired declarative memory consolidation during sleep in patients with primary insomnia: Influence of sleep architecture and nocturnal cortisol release. *Biological Psychiatry, 60*(12), 1324–1330.

Baddeley, A. D. (1966). Short-term memory for word sequences as function of acoustic, semantic, and formal similarity. *Quarterly Journal of Experimental Psychology, 18,* 362–365.

Baddeley, A. D. (1984). The fractionation of human memory. *Psychological Medicine, 14*(2), 259–264.

Baddeley, A. D. (1989). The psychology of remembering and forgetting. In T. Butler (Ed.), *Memory: History, culture and the mind.* London: Basil Blackwell.

Baddeley, A. D. (1990a). *Human memory.* Hove, England: Erlbaum.

Baddeley, A. D. (1990b). *Human memory: Theory and practice.* Needham Heights, MA: Allyn & Bacon.

Baddeley, A. D. (1992). Working memory. *Science, 255,* 556–559.

Baddeley, A. D. (1993). Verbal and visual subsystems of working memory. *Current Biology, 3,* 563–565.

Baddeley, A. D. (1995). Working memory. In M. S. Gazzaniga (Ed.), *The cognitive neurosciences* (pp. 755–764). Cambridge, MA: MIT Press.

Baddeley, A. D. (1997). *Human memory: Theory and practice* (rev. ed.). Hove, UK: Erlbaum.

Baddeley, A. D. (1998). *Human memory: Theory and practice* (rev. ed.). Needham Heights, MA: Allyn & Bacon.

Baddeley, A. D. (1999). Memory. In R. A. Wilson & F. C. Keil (Eds.), *The MIT encyclopedia of the cognitive sciences* (pp. 514–517). Cambridge, MA: MIT Press.

Baddeley, A. D. (2000). Short-term and working memory. In E. Tulving & F. I. M. Craik (Eds.), *The Oxford handbook of memory* (pp. 77–92). New York: Oxford University Press.

Baddeley, A. D. (2000a). The episodic buffer: A new component of working memory. *Trends in Cognitive Sciences, 4,* 417–423.

Baddeley, A. D. (2000b). Short-term and working memory. In E. Tulving & F. I. M. Craik (Eds.), *The Oxford handbook of memory* (pp. 77–92). New York: Oxford University Press.

Baddeley, A. D. (2001). Is working memory still working? *American Psychologist, 56*(11), 851–864.

Baddeley, A. D., & Hitch, G. J. (1974). Working memory. In G. Bower (Ed.), *Advances in learning and motivation* (Vol. 8, pp. 47–90). New York: Academic Press.

Baddeley A. D., & Larsen J. D. (2007). The phonological loop unmasked? A comment on the evidence for a "perceptual-gestural" alternative. *The Quarterly Journal of Experimental Psychology, 60*(4), 497–504.

Baddeley, A. D., Thomson, N., & Buchanan, M. (1975). Word length and the structure of short-term memory. *Journal of Verbal Learning & Verbal Behavior, 14*(6), 575–589.

Baddeley, A. D., & Warrington, E. (1970). Amnesia and the distinction between long- and short-term memory. *Journal of Verbal Learning & Verbal Behavior, 9*(2), 176–189.

Badgaiyan, R. D., Schacter, D. L., & Alpert, N. M. (1999). Auditory priming within and across modalities: Evidence from positron emission tomography. *Journal of Cognitive Neuroscience, 11*, 337–348.

Bahrick, H. P. (1984a). Fifty years of second language attrition: Implications for programmatic research. *Modern Language Journal, 68*(2), 105–118.

Bahrick, H. P. (1984b). Semantic memory content in permastore: Fifty years of memory for Spanish learned in school. *Journal of Experimental Psychology: General, 113*(1), 1–29.

Bahrick, H. P. (2000). Long-term maintenance of knowledge. In E. Tulving & F. I. M. Craik (Eds.), *The Oxford handbook of memory* (pp. 347–362). New York: Oxford University Press.

Bahrick, H. P., & Hall, L. K. (1991). Lifetime maintenance of high school mathematics content. *Journal of Experimental Psychology: General, 120*(1), 20–33.

Bahrick, H. P., Bahrick, L. E., Bahrick, A. S., & Bahrick, P. E. (1993). Maintenance of foreign language vocabulary and the spacing effect. *Psychological Science, 4*(5), 316–321.

Bahrick, H. P., Bahrick, P. O., & Wittlinger, R. P. (1975). Fifty years of memory for names and faces: A cross-sectional approach. *Journal of Experimental Psychology: General, 104*, 54–75.

Bahrick, H. P., Hall, L. K., Goggin, J. P., Bahrick, L. E., & Berger, S. A. (1994). Fifty years of language maintenance and language dominance in bilingual Hispanic immigrants. *Journal of Experimental Psychology: General, 123*(3), 264–283.

Bahrick, H. P., & Phelps, E. A. (1987). Retention of Spanish vocabulary over eight years. *Journal of Experimental Psychology: Learning, Memory, & Cognition, 13*, 344–349.

Bailenson, J. N., Blascovich, J., Beall, A. C., & Loomis, J. M. (2003). Interpersonal distance in immersive virtual environments, *Personality and Social Psychology Bulletin, 29*(7), 819–833.

Baker, S. C., Rogers, R. D., Owen, A. M., Frith, C. D., Dolan, R. J., Frackowiak, R. S. J., et al. (1996). Neural systems engaged by planning: A PET study of the Tower of London task. *Neuropsychologia, 34*, 515–526.

Bakker, D. J. (2006). Treatment of developmental dyslexia: a review. *Developmental Neurorehabilitation, 9*(1), 3–13.

Baliki, M., Katz, J., Chialvo, D. R., & Apkarian, A. V. (2005). Single subject pharmacological-MRI (phMRI) study: Modulation of brain activity of psoriatic arthritis pain by cyclooxygenase-2 inhibitor. *Molecular Pain, 1*, 1–32.

Balota, D. A., Cortese, M. J., Duchek, J. M., Adams, D., Roediger, H. L., McDermott, K. B., et al. (1999). Veridical and false memories in healthy older adults and in dementia and Alzheimer's types. *Cognitive Neuropsychology, 16*, 361–384.

Baltes, P. B. (1993). The aging mind: Potential and limits. *Gerontologist, 33*, 580–594.

Baltes, P. B. (1997). On the incomplete architecture of human ontogeny: Selection, optimization, and compensation as foundations of developmental theory. *American Psychologist, 52*, 366–380.

Baltes, P. B., Dittmann-Kohli, F., & Dixon, R. A. (1984). New perspectives on the development of intelligence in adulthood: Toward a dual-process conception and a model of selective optimization with compensation. In P. B. Baltes & O. G. Brim, Jr. (Eds.), *Life-span development and behavior* (Vol. 6, pp. 33–76). New York: Academic Press.

Baltes, P. B., & Smith, J. (1990). Toward a psychology of wisdom and its ontogenesis. In R. J. Sternberg (Ed.), *Wisdom: Its nature, origins, and development* (pp. 87–120). New York: Cambridge University Press.

Baltes, P. B., & Staudinger, U. M. (2000). Wisdom: A metaheuristic (pragmatic) to orchestrate mind and virtue toward excellence. *American Psychologist, 55*, 122–135.

Baltes, P. B., Staudinger, U. M., Maercker, A., & Smith, J. (1995). People nominated as wise: A comparative study of wisdom-related knowledge. *Psychology & Aging, 10*, 155–166.

Baltes, P. B., & Willis, S. L. (1979). Toward psychological theories of aging and development. In J. E. Birren & K. W. Schaie (Eds.), *Handbook of the psychology of aging*. New York: Van Nostrand Reinhold.

Banaji, M. R., & Crowder, R. G. (1989). The bankruptcy of everyday memory. *American Psychologist, 44*, 1185–1193.

Band, G. P. H., & Kok, A. (2000). Age effects on response monitoring in a mental-rotation task. *Biological Psychology, 51*, 201–221.

Bandler, R., & Shipley, M. T. (1994). Columnar organization in the midbrain periaqueductal gray: Modules for emotional expression? *Trends in Neuroscience, 17*, 379–389.

Bandura, A. (1977a). *Social learning theory*. Englewood Cliffs, NJ: Prentice-Hall.

Bandura, A. (1977b). *Social learning theory*. Englewood Cliffs, NJ: Prentice-Hall.

Bar, M. (2004). Visual objects in context. *Nature Reviews: Neuroscience, 5*, 617–629.

Barker, B. A., & Newman, R. S. (2004). Listen to your mother! The role of talker familiarity in infant streaming. *Cognition, 94*(2), B45–B53.

Barnett, S. M., & Ceci, S. J. (2005). The role of transferable knowledge in intelligence. In R. J. Sternberg & J. E. Pretz (Eds.), *Cognition and intelligence* (pp. 208–224). New York: Cambridge University Press.

Barnouw, V. (1985). *Culture and personality*. Chicago: Dorsey Press.

Baron, J. (1988). *Thinking and deciding*. New York: Cambridge University Press.

Baron-Cohen, S. (2003). *The essential difference: The truth about the male and female brain*. New York: Basic Books.

Baron-Cohen, S., Leslie, A. M., & Frith, U. (1985). Does the autistic child have a "theory of mind"? *Cognition, 21*, 37–46.

Baron-Cohen, S., Ring, H. A., Bullmore, E. T., Wheelwright, S., Ashwin, C., & Williams, S. C. R. (2000). The amygdala theory of autism. *Neuroscience Biobehavior Review, 24*, 355–364.

Barraclough, D. J., Conroy, M. L., & Lee, D. (2004). Prefrontal cortex and decision making in a mixed-strategy game. *Nature Neuroscience, 7*, 404–410.

Barrett, P. T., & Eysenck, H. J. (1992). Brain evoked potentials and intelligence: The Hendrickson paradigm. *Intelligence, 16*(3,4), 361–381.

Barron, F. (1988). Putting creativity to work. In R. J. Sternberg (Ed.), *The nature of creativity* (pp. 76–98). New York: Cambridge University Press.

Barrouillet, P., & Lecas, J. F. (1998). How can mental models account for content effects in conditional reasoning: A developmental perspective. *Cognition, 67*, 209–253.

Barsalou, L. W. (1983). Ad hoc categories. *Memory and Cognition, 11*, 211–227.

Barsalou, L. W. (1994). Flexibility, structure, and linguistic vagary in concepts: Manifestations of a compositional system of perceptual symbols. In A. F. Collins, S. E. Gathercole, M. A. Conway, & P. E. Morris (Eds.), *Theories of memory* (pp. 29–101). Hillsdale, NJ: Erlbaum.

Barsalou, L. W. (2000). Concepts: Structure. In A. E. Kazdin (Ed.), *Encyclopedia of psychology* (Vol. 2, pp. 245-248). Washington, DC: American Psychological Association.

Bartlett, F. C. (1932). *Remembering: A study in experimental and social psychology.* Cambridge, UK: Cambridge University Press.

Bashore, T. R., Osman, A., & Hefley, E. F. (1989). Mental slowing in elderly persons: A cognitive psychophysiological analysis. *Psychology & Aging, 4,* 235–244.

Bassok, M. (2003). Analogical transfer in problem solving. In J. E. Davidson & R. J. Sternberg (Eds.), *The psychology of problem solving* (pp. 343–369). New York: Cambridge University Press.

Bassok, M., & Holyoak, K. (1989). Interdomain transfer between isomorphic topics in algebra and physics. *Journal of Experimental Psychology: Learning,* 153–166.

Bassock, M., Wu, L., & Olseth, K. L. (1995). Judging a book by its cover: Interpretive effects of content on problem solving transfer. *Memory and Cognition, 23,* 354–367.

Bastik, T. (1982). *Intuition: How we think and act.* Chichester, UK: Wiley.

Bates, E., & Goodman, J. (1999). On the emergence of grammar from the lexicon. In B. MacWhinney (Ed.), *The emergence of language* (pp. 29–80). Mahwah, NJ: Erlbaum.

Baudouin, A., Vanneste, S. Pouthas, V., & Isingrini, M. (2006). Age-related changes in duration reproduction: Involvement of working memory processes. *Brain and Cognition, 62*(1), 17–23.

Bauer, P. J. (2005). Developments in declarative memory. Decreasing susceptibility to storage failure over the second year of life. *Psychological Science 16*(1), 41–47.

Bauer, P. J., & Van Abbema, D. L. (2003). Memory, development of. In L. Nadel (Ed.), *Encyclopedia of cognitive science* (Vol. 2, pp. 1090–1095). London: Nature Publishing Group.

Baumgartner, C. (2000). Clinical applications of magnetoencephalography. *Journal of Clinical Neurophysiology,17*(2), 175–176.

Bavelier, D., Newport, E. L., Hall, M. L., Supalla, T., & Boutla, M. (2006). Persistent difference in short-term memory span between sign and speech: Implications for cross-linguistic comparisons. *Psychological Science, 17*(12),1090–1092.

Baylis, G., Driver, J., & McLeod, P. (1992). Movement and proximity constrain miscombinations of colour and form. *Perception, 21*(2), 201–218.

Bearden, C. E., Glahn, D. C., Monkul, E. S., Barrett, J., Najt, P., Villarreal, V., et al. (2006). Patterns of memory impairment in bipolar disorder and unipolar major depression. *Psychiatry Research, 142*(2–3), 139–150.

Beardsley, M. (1962). The metaphorical twist. *Philosophical Phenomenological Research, 22,* 293–307.

Bechtereva, N. P., Korotkov, A. D., Pakhomov, S. V., Roudas, M. S., Starchenko, M. G., Medvedev, S. V. (2004). PET study of brain maintenance of verbal creative activity. *International Journal of Psychophysiology, 53,* 11–20.

Beck, D. M., Muggleton, N., Walsh, V., & Lavie, N. (2006). Right parietal cortex plays a critical role in change blindness. *Cerebral Cortex, 16*(5), 712–717.

Beck, I. L., Perfetti, C. A., & McKeown, M. G. (1982). Effects of long-term vocabulary instruction on lexical access and reading comprehension. *Journal of Educational Psychology, 74,* 506–521.

Begg, I., & Denny, J. (1969). Empirical reconciliation of atmosphere and conversion interpretations of syllogistic reasoning. *Journal of Experimental Psychology, 81,* 351–354.

Behrmann, M., Kosslyn, S. M., & Jeannerod, M. (Eds.). (1996). *The neuropsychology of mental imagery.* New York: Pergamon.

Bellezza, F. S. (1984). The self as a mnemonic device: The role of internal cues. *Journal of Personality and Social Psychology, 47,* 506–516.

Bellezza, F. S. (1992). Recall of congruent information in the self-reference task. *Bulletin of the Psychonomic Society, 30*(4), 275–278.

Belmont, J. M., & Butterfield, E. C. (1971). Learning strategies as determinants of memory deficiencies. *Cognitive Psychology, 2,* 411–420.

Benasich, A. A., & Thomas, J. J. (2003). Developmental disorders of language. In L. Nadel (Ed.), *Encyclopedia of cognitive science* (Vol. 1, pp. 959–967). London: Nature Publishing Group.

Benedict, R. (1946). *The crysanthemum and the sword.* Boston: Houghton Mifflin.

Benjamin, L. T., Jr., & Baker, D. B. (2004). Science for sale: Psychology's earliest adventures in American advertising. In J. D. Williams, W. N. Lee, & C. P. Haugtvedt (Eds.), *Diversity in advertising: Broadening the scope of research directions* (pp. 22–39). Mahwah, NJ: Lawrence Erlbaum.

Bennis, W. M., & Pachur, T. (2006). Fast and frugal heuristics in sports. *Psychology of Sport and Exercise, 7*(6), 611–629.

Ben-Zeev, T. (1996). When erroneous mathematical thinking is just as "correct": The oxymoron of rational errors. In R. J. Sternberg & T. Ben-Zeev (Eds.), *The nature of mathematical thinking* (pp. 55–79). Mahwah, NJ: Erlbaum.

Berg, C. A. (2000). Adult intellectual development. In R. J. Sternberg (Ed.), *Handbook of human intelligence.* Cambridge.

Berg, C. A., Meegan, S. P., & Deviney, F. P. (1998). A social contextual model of coping with everyday problems across the lifespan. *International Journal of Behavioral Development, 22,* 239–261.

Berg, C. A., Strough, J., Calderone, K. S., Sansone, C., & Weir, C. (1998). The role of problem definitions in understanding age and context effects on strategies for solving everyday problems. *Psychology and Aging, 13,* 29–44.

Bergerbest, D., Ghahremani, D. G., & Gabrieli, J. D. E. (2004). Neural correlates of auditory repetition priming: Reduced fMRI activation in the auditory cortex. *Journal of Cognitive Neuroscience, 16,* 966–977.

Berkow, R. (1992). *The Merck manual of diagnosis and therapy* (16th ed.). Rahway, NJ: Merck Research Laboratories.

Berlin, B., & Kay, P. (1969). *Basic color terms: Their universality and evolution.* Los Angeles: University of California Press.

Berliner, H. J. (1969, August). Chess playing program. *SICART Newsletter, 19,* 19–20.

Bernstein, A. (1958, July). A chess-playing program for the IBM704. *Chess Review,* 208–209.

Berry, D. (2002). Donald Broadbent. *The Psychologist, 15*(8), 402–405.

Berry, J. W., Poortinga, Y. H., Segall, M. H., & Dasen, P. R. (1992). *Cross-cultural psychology: Research and applications.* New York: Cambridge University Press.

Bertoncini, J. (1993). Infants' perception of speech units: Primary representation capacities. In B. B. De Boysson-Bardies, S. De Schonen, P. Jusczyk, P. MacNeilage, & J. Morton (Eds.), *Developmental neurocognition: Speech and face processing in the first year of life.* Dordrecht, Germany: Kluwer.

Besnard, D., & Cacitti, L. (2005). Interface changes causing accidents. An empirical study of negative transfer. *International Journal of Human-Computer Studies, 62*(1), 105–125.

Best, J. (2003). Memory mnemonics. In L. Nadel (Ed.), *Encyclopedia of cognitive science* (Vol. 2, pp. 1081–1084). London: Nature Publishing Group.

Bethell-Fox, C. E., & Shepard, R. N. (1988). Mental rotation: Effects of stimulus complexity and familiarity. *Journal of Experimental Psychology: Human Perception and Performance, 14*(1), 12–23.

Beyer, J. L., Ranga, K., & Krishnan, R. (2002). Volumetric brain imaging findings mood disorders. *Bipolar Disorders, 4*(2), 89–104.

Bhatia, T. T., & Ritchie, W. C. (1999). The bilingual child: Some issues and perspectives. In W. C. Ritchie & T. K. Bhatia (Eds.), *Handbook of child language acquisition* (pp. 569–646). San Diego: Academic Press.

Bialystok, E. (2001a). *Bilingualism in development: Language, literacy, and cognition.* New York: Cambridge University Press.

Bialystok, E. (2001b). Metalinguistic aspects of bilingual processing. *Annual Review of Applied Linguistics, 21,* 169–181.

Bialystok, E., Craik, F. I. M., Klein, R., & Viswanathan, M. (2004). Bilingualism, aging, and cognitive control: Evidence from the Simon task. *Psychology and Aging, 19*(2), 290–303.

Bialystok, E., & Hakuta, K. (1994). *In other words: The science and psychology of second-language acquisition.* New York: Basic Books.

Bickerton, D. (1969). Prolegomena to a linguistic theory of metaphor. *Foundations of Language, 5,* 36–51.

Bickerton, D. (1990). *Language and species.* Chicago: University of Chicago Press.

Biederman, I. (1972). Perceiving real-world scenes. *Science, 177*(4043), 77–80.

Biederman, I. (1987). Recognition-by-components: A theory of human image understanding. *Psychological Review, 94,* 115–147.

Biederman, I. (1993a). Geon theory as an account of shape recognition in mind and brain. *Irish Journal of Psychology, 14*(3), 314–327.

Biederman, I. (1993b). Visual object recognition. In A. I. Goldman (Ed.), *Readings in philosophy and cognitive science* (pp. 9–21). Cambridge, MA: MIT Press. (Original work published 1990)

Biederman, I., Glass, A. L., & Stacy, E. W. (1973). Searching for objects in real-world scenes. *Journal of Experimental Psychology, 97*(1), 22–27.

Biederman, I., Rabinowitz, J. C., Glass, A. L., & Stacy, E. W. (1974). On the information extracted from a glance at a scene. *Journal of Experimental Psychology, 103*(3), 597–600.

Biederman, J., & Faraone, S. V. (2005). Attention-deficit hyperactivity disorder. *The Lancet, 366*(9481), 237–248.

Biernat, M., & Ma, J. E. (2005). Stereotypes and the confirmability of trait concepts. *Personality and Social Psychology Bulletin, 31*(4), 483–495.

Binet, A., & Simon, T. (1916). *The development of intelligence in children* (E. S. Kite, Trans.). Baltimore: Williams & Wilkins.

Bingman, V. P., Hough II, G. E., Kahn, M. C., & Siegel, J. J. (2003). The homing pigeon hippocampus and space: In search of adaptive specialization. *Brain, Behavior and Evolution, 62*(2), 117–127.

Birdsong, D. (1999). Introduction: Whys and why nots of the critical period hypothesis for second language acquisition. In D. Birdsong (Ed.), *Second language acquisition and the critical period hypothesis* (pp. 1–22). Mahwah, NJ: Erlbaum.

Birdsong, D. (2006). Age and second language acquisition and processing: A selective overview. *Language Learning 56*(1), 9–49.

Bjorklund, D. F., Schneider, W., & Hernández Blasi, C. (2003). Memory. In L. Nadel (Ed.), *Encyclopedia of cognitive science* (Vol. 2, pp. 1059–1065). London: Nature Publishing Group.

Black, M. (1962). *Models and metaphors.* Ithaca, NY: Cornell University Press.

Blackwell, L. S., Trzesniewski, K. H., & Dweck, C. S. (2007). Implicit theories of intelligence predict achievement across an adolescent transition: A longitudinal study and an intervention. *Child Development, 78*(1), 246–263.

Blackwood, N. J., Howard, R. J., Fytche, D. H., Simmons, A., Bentall, R. P., Murray, R. M. (2000). Imaging attentional and attributional bias: An fMRI approach to the paranoid delusion. *Psychological Medicine, 30,* 873–883.

Blake, R. (2000). Vision and sight: Structure and function. In A. E. Kazdin (Ed.), *Encyclopedia of psychology* (pp. 177–178). Washington, DC: American Psychological Association.

Blake, W. C. A., McKenzie, K. J., & Hamm, J. P. (2002). Cerebral asymmetry for mental rotation: Effects of response hand, handedness and gender. *NeuroReport, 13*(15), 1929–1932.

Blakemore, S.-J., Smith, J., Steel, R., Johnstone, E. C., & Frith, C. D. (2000). The perception of self-produced sensory stimuli in patients with auditory hallucinations and passivity experiences: Evidence for a breakdown in self-monitoring. *Psychological Medicine, 30,* 1131–1139.

Blansjaar, B. A., Vielvoye, G. J., Van Dijk, J. Gert, & Rinders, R. J. (1992). Similar brain lesions in alcoholics and Korsakoff patients: MRI, psychometric and clinical findings. *Clinical Neurology & Neurosurgery, 94*(3), 197–203.

Blessing, S. B., & Ross, B. H. (1996). Content effects in problem categorization and problem solving. *Journal of Experimental Psychology: Learning, Memory, and Cognition, 22,* 792–810.

Block, N., Flanagan, O., & Güzeldere, G. (Eds.). (1997). *The nature of consciousness: Philosophical debates.* Cambridge, MA: MIT Press.

Bloom, B. S. (1964). *Stability and change in human characteristics.* New York: Wiley.

Bloom, B. S., & Broder, L. J. (1950). *Problem-solving processes of college students.* Chicago: University of Chicago Press.

Bloom, P. (2000). *How children learn the meanings of words.* Cambridge, MA: MIT Press.

Bluck, J. (2004). NASA develops robust artificial intelligence for planetary rovers. Retrieved September 5, 2007, from http://www.nasa.gov/vision/universe/roboticexplorers/robust_artificial_intelligence_jb.html

Boas, F. (1911). *The mind of primitive man.* New York: Macmillan.

Bock, K. (1990). Structure in language: Creating form in talk. *American Psychologist, 45*(11), 1221–1236.

Bock, K., Loebell, H., & Morey, R. (1992). From conceptual roles to structural relations: Bridging the syntactic cleft. *Psychological Review, 99*(1), 150–171.

Boden, M. A. (1999). Computer models of creativity. In R. J. Sternberg (Ed.), *Handbook of creativity* (pp. 351–372). New York: Cambridge University Press.

Bohannon, J. (1988). Flashbulb memories for the space shuttle disaster: A tale of two theories. *Cognition, 29*(2), 179–196.

Bolte, S., Hubl, D., Feineis-Matthews, S., Pruvulovic, D., Dierks, T., & Poustka, F. (2006). Facial affect recognition training in autism: Can we animate the fusiform gyrus? *Behavioral Neuroscience, 120*(1), 211–216.

Borges, B., Goldstein, D. G., Ortmann, A. & Gigerenzer, G. (1999). Can ignorance beat the stock market? In Gigerenzer, G., Todd, P. M., & the ABC Research Group (Eds.), *Simple heuristics that make us smart* (pp. 59–72). New York: Oxford University Press.

Boring, E. G. (1923, June 6). Intelligence as the tests test it. *New Republic,* 35–37.

Boring, E. G. (1942). *Sensation and perception in the history of experimental psychology.* New York: Appleton-Century-Crofts.

Boring, E. G. (1950). *A history of experimental psychology.* New York: Appleton-Century-Crofts.

Borkenau, P., & Mauer, N. (2006). Processing of pleasant, unpleasant, and neutral words in a lateralised emotional Stroop task. *Cognition & Emotion, 20*(6), 866–877.

Borovsky, D., & Rovee-Collier, C. (1990). Contextual constraints on memory retrieval at six months. *Child Development, 61*(5), 1569–1583.

Bors, D. A., & Forrin, B. (1995). Age, speed of information processing, recall, and fluid intelligence. *Intelligence, 20,* 229–248.

Bors, D. A., MacLeod, C. M., & Forrin, B. (1993). Eliminating the IQ–RT correlation by eliminating an experimental confound. *Intelligence, 17*(4), 475–500.

Bortfeld, H., Morgan, J. L., Golinkoff, R. M., & Rathbun, K. (2005). Mommy and me: Familiar names help launch babies into speech-stream segmentation. *Psychological Science, 16*(4), 298–304.

Bosco, A., Longoni, A. M., & Vecchi, T. (2004). Gender effects in spatial orientation: Cognitive profiles and mental strategies. *Applied Cognitive Psychology, 18*(5), 519–532.

Bothwell, R. K., Brigham, J. C., & Malpass, R. S. (1989). Cross-racial identification. *Personality & Social Psychology Bulletin, 15*(1), 19–25.

Bourguignon, E. (2000). Consciousness and unconsciousness: Cross-cultural experience. In A. E. Kazdin (Ed.), *Encyclopedia of psychology* (pp. 275–277). Washington, DC: American Psychological Association.

Bourne, V. J., Fox, H. C., Deary, I. J., & Whalley, L. J. (2007). Does childhood intelligence predict variation in cognitive change in later life? *Personality and Individual Differences, 42*(8), 1551–1559.

Bousfield, W. A. (1953). The occurrence of clustering in the recall of randomly arranged associates. *Journal of General Psychology, 49,* 229–240.

Bower, G. H. (1983). Affect and cognition. *Philosophical Transaction: Royal Society of London* (Series B), *302,* 387–402.

Bower, G. H., Black, J. B., & Turner, T. J. (1979). Scripts in memory for texts. *Cognitive Psychology, 11,* 177–220.

Bower, G. H., Clark, M. C., Lesgold, A. M., & Winzenz, D. (1969). Hierarchical retrieval schemes in recall of categorized word lists. *Journal of Verbal Learning and Verbal Behavior, 8,* 323–343.

Bower, G. H., & Gilligan, S. G. (1979). Remembering information related to one's self. *Journal of Research in Personality, 13,* 420–432.

Bower, G. H., Karlin, M. B., & Dueck, A. (1975). Comprehension and memory for pictures. *Memory & Cognition, 3,* 216–220.

Bowers, K. S., & Farvolden, P. (1996). Revisiting a century-old Freudian slip: From suggestion disavowed to the truth repressed. *Psychological Bulletin, 119,* 355–380.

Bowers, K. S., Regehr, G., Balthazard, C., & Parker, K. (1990). Intuition in the context of discovery. *Cognitive Psychology, 22,* 72–110.

Bradley, R. H., & Caldwell, B. M. (1984). 174 Children: A study of the relationship between home environment and cognitive development during the first 5 years. In A. W. Gottfried (Ed.), *Home environment and early cognitive development: Longitudinal research.* San Diego: Academic Press.

Braine, M. D. S., & O'Brien, D. P. (1991). A theory of if: A lexical entry, reasoning program, and pragmatic principles. *Psychological Review, 98*(2), 182–203.

Braine, M. D. S., Reiser, B. J., & Rumain, B. (1984). Some empirical justification for a theory of natural propositional logic. In G. H. Bower (Ed.), *The psychology of learning and motivation* (Vol. 18). New York: Academic Press.

Brambati, S. M., Termine, C., Ruffino, M., Danna, M., Lanzi, G., Stella, G., et al. (2006). Neuropsychological deficits and neural dysfunction in familial dyslexia. *Brain Research, 1113*(1), 174–185.

Bransford, J. D., & Johnson, M. K. (1972). Contextual prerequisites for understanding: Some investigations of comprehension and recall. *Journal of Verbal Learning and Verbal Behavior, 11,* 717–726.

Bransford, J. D., & Johnson, M. K. (1973). Considerations of some problems of comprehension. In W. G. Chase (Ed.), *Visual information processing* (pp. 383–438). New York: Academic Press.

Bransford, J. D., & Stein, B. S. (1993). *The ideal problem solver: A guide for improving thinking, learning, and creativity* (2nd ed.). New York: W. H. Freeman.

Braun, C. M. J., Godbout, L., Desbiens, C., Daigneault, S., Lussier, F., & Hamel-Hebert, I. (2004). Mental genesis of scripts in adolescents with attention deficit/hyperactivity disorder. *Child Neuropsychology, 10*(4), 280–296.

Braun, K. A., Ellis, R. & Loftus, E. F. (2002). Make my memory: How advertising can change our memories of the past. *Psychology and Marketing, 19,* 1–23.

Braun-LaTour, K. A., LaTour, M. S., Pickrell, J., & Loftus, E. F. (2004–05). How and when advertising can influence memory for consumer experience. *Journal of Advertising, 33,* 7–25.

Bregman, A. S. (1990). *Auditory scene analysis: The perceptual organization of sound.* Cambridge, MA: MIT Press.

Breier, J., Fletcher, J., Klaas, P., & Gray, L. (2004). Categorical perception of speech stimuli in children at risk for reading difficulty. *Journal of Experimental Child Psychology, 88*(2), 152–170.

Breier, J., Fletcher, J., Klaas, P., & Gray, L. (2005). The relation between categorical perception of speech stimuli and reading skills in children (A). *Journal of the Acoustical Society of America, 118*(3), 1963.

Brenneis, C. B. (2000). Evaluating the evidence: Can we find authenticated recovered memory? *Psychoanalytic Psychology, 17,* 61–77.

Brennen, T., Vikan, A., & Dybdahl, R. (2007). Are tip-of-the-tongue states universal? Evidence from the speakers of an unwritten language. *Memory, 15*(2), 167–176.

Bresnan, J. W. (Ed.). (1982). *The mental representation of grammatical relations.* Cambridge, MA: MIT Press.

Breuning, M. (2003). The role of analogies and abstract reasoning in decision-making: Evidence from the debate over Truman's proposal for development assistance. *International Studies Quarterly, 47*(2), 229–245.

Brewer, W. F. (1999). Schemata. In R. A. Wilson & F. C. Keil (Eds.), *The MIT encyclopedia of the cognitive sciences* (pp. 729–730). Cambridge, MA: MIT Press.

Brewer, W. F. (2003). Mental models. In L. Nadel (Ed.), *Encyclopedia of cognitive science* (Vol. 3, pp. 1–6). London: Nature Publishing Group.

Brian, C. R., & Goodenough, F. L. (1929). The relative potency of color and form perception at various ages. *Journal of Experimental Psychology, 12,* 197–213.

Briere, J., & Conte, J. R. (1993). Self-reported amnesia for abuse in adults molested as children. *Journal of Traumatic Stress, 6,* 21–31.

Brigden, R. (1933). A tachistoscopic study of the differentiation of perception. *Psychological Monographs, 44,* 153–166.

Brigham, J. C., & Malpass, R. S. (1985). The role of experience and contact in the recognition of faces of own and other-race persons. *Journal of Social Issues, 41*(3), 139–155.

Brislin, R. W., Lonner, W. J., & Thorndike, R. M. (Eds.). (1973). *Cross-cultural research methods*. New York: Wiley.

Broadbent, D. E. (1958). *Perception and communication*. Oxford, UK: Pergamon.

Broadbent, D. E., & Gregory, M. (1965). Effects of noise and of signal rate upon vigilance analyzed by means of decision theory. *Human Factors, 7,* 155–162.

Brooks, L. R. (1968). Spatial and verbal components of the act of recall. *Canadian Journal of Psychology, 22*(5), 349–368.

Brown, A. L. (1978). Knowing when, where, and how to remember: A problem of metacognition. In R. Glaser (Ed.), *Advances in instructional psychology* (Vol. 1, pp. 77–165). Hillsdale, NJ: Erlbaum.

Brown, A. L., Campione, J. C., Bray, N. W., & Wilcox, B. L. (1973). Keeping track of changing variables: Effects of rehearsal training and rehearsal prevention in normal and retarded adolescents. *Journal of Experimental Psychology, 101,* 123–131.

Brown, A. L., & DeLoache, J. S. (1978). Skills, plans, and self-regulation. In R. Siegler (Ed.), *Children's thinking: What develops?* (pp. 3–35). Hillsdale, NJ: Erlbaum.

Brown, C., & Laland, K. (2001). Social learning and life skills training for hatchery reared fish. *Journal of Fish Biology, 59*(3), 471–493.

Brown, C. M., & Hagoort, P. (Eds.) (1999). *Neurocognition of language*. Oxford, UK: Oxford University Press.

Brown, J. A. (1958). Some tests of the decay theory of immediate memory. *Quarterly Journal of Experimental Psychology, 10,* 12–21.

Brown, P., Keenan, J. M., & Potts, G. R. (1986). The self-reference effect with imagery encoding. *Journal of Personality & Social Psychology, 51*(5), 897–906.

Brown, R. (1965). *Social psychology*. New York: Free Press.

Brown, R. (1973). *A first language: The early stages*. Cambridge, MA: Harvard University Press.

Brown, R., Cazden, C. B., & Bellugi, U. (1969). The child's grammar from 1 to 3. In J. P. Hill (Ed.), *Minnesota Symposium on Child Psychology* (Vol. 2). Minneapolis: University of Minnesota Press.

Brown, R., & Kulik, J. (1977). Flashbulb memories. *Cognition, 5,* 73–99.

Brown, R., & McNeill, D. (1966). The "tip of the tongue" phenomenon. *Journal of Verbal Learning and Verbal Behavior, 5,* 325–337.

Brown, S. C., & Craik, F. I. M. (2000). Encoding and retrieval of information. In E. Tulving & F. I. M. Craik (Eds.), *The Oxford handbook of memory* (pp. 93–108). New York: Oxford University Press.

Bruce, D. (1991). Mechanistic and functional explanations of memory. *American Psychologist, 46*(1), 46–48.

Bruner, J. S. (1957). On perceptual readiness. *Psychological Review, 64,* 123–152.

Bruner, J. S., Goodnow, J. J., & Austin, G. A. (1956). *A study of thinking*. New York: Wiley.

Brungard, D. S., & Simpson, B. D. (2007). Cocktail party listening in a dynamic multitalker environment. *Perception & Psychophysics, 69*(1), 79–91.

Bryan, W. L., & Harter, N. (1899). Studies on the telegraphic language: The acquisition of a hierarchy of habits. *Psychological Review, 6,* 345–375.

Bryson, M., Bereiter, C., Scarmadalia, M., & Joram, E. (1991). Going beyond the problem as given: Problem solving in expert and novice writers. In R. J. Sternberg & P. A. Frensch (Eds.), *Complex problem solving: Principles and mechanisms* (pp. 61–84). Hillsdale, NJ: Erlbaum.

Buchanan, B. G., & Shortliffe, E. H. (1984). *Rule-based expert systems: The MYCIN experiments of the Stanford Heuristic Programming Project*. Reading, MA: Addison-Wesley.

Buchanan, B. G., Smith, D. H., White, W. C., Gritter, R., Feigenbaum, E. A., Lederberg, J., & Djerassi, C. (1976). Applications of artificial intelligence for chemical inference: XXII. Automatic rule formation in mass spectrometry by means of the meta-Dendral program. *Journal of the American Chemistry Society, 98,* 6168–6178.

Buckner, R. L. (2000a). Brain imaging techniques. In A. E. Kazdin (Ed.), *Encyclopedia of psychology* (Vol. 1, pp. 457–459). Washington, DC: American Psychological Association.

Buckner, R. L. (2000b). Neuroimaging of memory. In M. S. Gazzaniga (Ed.), *The new cognitive neurosciences* (2nd ed., pp. 817–828). Cambridge, MA: MIT Press.

Buckner, R. L. (2004). Memory and executive function in aging and AD multiple factors that cause decline and reserve factors that compensate. *Neuron, 44*(1), 195–208.

Buckner, R. L., Bandettini, P. A., O'Craven, K. M., Savoy, R. L., Petersen, E., Raichle, M. E., et al. (1996). Detection of cortical activation during averaged single trials of a cognitive task using functional magnetic resonance imaging. *Proceedings of the National Academy of Sciences, 93,* 14878–14883.

Budwig, N. (1995). *A developmental-functionalist approach to child language*. Mahwah, NJ: Erlbaum.

Bugg, J. M., Zook, N. A., DeLosh, E. L., Davalos, D. B., & Davis, H. P. (2006). Age differences in fluid intelligence: Contributions of general slowing and frontal decline. *Brain and Cognition, 62*(1), 9–16.

Bundesen, C. (1996). Formal models of visual attention: A tutorial review. In A. F. Kramer, M. G. H. Coles, & G. D. Logan (Eds.), *Converging operations in the study of visual selective attention* (pp. 1–43). Washington, DC: American Psychological Association.

Bundesen, C. (2000). Attention: Models of attention. In A. E. Kazdin (Ed.), *Encyclopedia of psychology* (Vol. 1, pp. 295–299). Washington, DC: American Psychological Association.

Bunge, S. A., Wendelken, C., Badre, D., & Wagner, A. D. (2004). Analogical reasoning and prefrontal cortex: Evidence for separable retrieval and integration mechanism. *Cerebral Cortex, 15*(3), 239–249.

Bunting, M. (2006). Proactive interference and item similarity in working memory. *Journal of Experimental Psychology: Learning, Memory and Cognition, 32*(2), 183–196.

Burgess, M. C. R, & Weaver, G. E. (2003). Interest and attention in facial recognition. *Perceptual and Motor Skills, 96*(2), 467–480.

Burgund, E. D., & Marsolek, C. J. (2000). Viewpoint-invariant and viewpoint-dependent object recognition in dissociable neural subsystems. *Psychonomic Bulletin & Review, 7,* 480–489.

Buschke, H., Kulansky, G., Katz, M., Stewart, W. F., Sliwinski, M. J., Eckholdt, H. M., et al. (1999). Screening for dementia with the Memory Impairment Screen. *Neurology, 52,* 231–238.

Butler, J., & Rovee-Collier, C. (1989). Contextual gating of memory retrieval. *Developmental Psychobiology, 22,* 533–552.

Butterfield, E. C., Wambold, C., & Belmont, J. M. (1973). On the theory and practice of improving short-term memory. *American Journal of Mental Deficiency, 77,* 654–669.

Butterworth, B., & Howard, D. (1987). Paragrammatisms. *Cognition, 26*(1), 1–37.

Byrne, R. M. J. (1996). A model theory of imaginary thinking. In J. Oakhill & A. Garnham (Eds.), *Mental models in cognitive science* (pp. 155–174). Hove, UK: Taylor & Francis.

Cabeza, R., Daselaar, S. M., Dolcos, F., Prince, S. E., Budde, M., & Nyberg, L. (2004). Task-independent and task-specific age effects on brain activity during working memory, visual attention and episodic retrieval. *Cerebral Cortex, 14,* 364–375.

Cabeza, R., & Nyberg, L. (1997). Imaging cognition: An empirical review of PET studies with normal subjects. *Journal of Cognitive Neuroscience, 9*(1), 1–26.

Cahill, L., Babinsky, R., Markowitsch, H. J., & McGaugh, J. L. (1995). The amygdala and emotional memory. *Nature, 377,* 295–296.

Cahill, L., Haier, R. J., Fallon, J., Alkire, M. T., Tang, C., Keator, D., Wu, J., & McGaugh, J. L. (1996). Amygdala activity at encoding correlated with long-term, free recall of emotional information. *Proceedings of the National Academy of Sciences, 93,* 8016–8021.

Cahill, L., & McGaugh, J. L. (1996). Modulation of memory storage. *Current Opinion in Neurobiology, 6,* 237–242.

Cain, D. P., Boon, F., & Corcoran, M. E. (2006). Thalamic and hippocampal mechanisms in spatial navigation: A dissociation between brain mechanisms for learning how versus learning where to navigate. *Brain Research, 170*(2), 241–256.

Cain, K., Oakhill, J., & Lemmon, K. (2004). Individual differences in the inference of word meanings from context: The influence of reading comprehension, vocabulary knowledge, and memory capacity. *Journal of Educational Psychology, 96*(4), 671–681.

Campbell, D. A. (1960). Blind variation and selective retention in creative thought as in other knowledge processes. *Psychological Review, 67,* 380–400.

Campbell, F. A., Ramey, C. T., Pungello, E., Sparling, J., & Miller-Johnson, S. (2002). Early childhood education: Young adult outcomes from the Abecedarian Project. *Applied Development Science, 6*(1), 42–57.

Campbell, R., MacSweeney, M., & Waters, D. (2007). Sign language and the brain: A review. *Journal of Deaf Studies and Deaf Education.* Advance Access published online June 29, 2007.

Canli, T., Desmond, J. E., Zhao, Z., & Gabrieli, J. D. (2002). Sex differences in the neural basis of emotional memories. *Proceedings of the National Academies of Sciences, 99,* 10789–10794.

Cannon-Bowers, J. A., & Salas, E. (1998). Individual and team decision making under stress: theoretical underpinnings. In J. A. Cannon-Bowers & E. Salas (Eds.), *Making decisions under stress: Implications for individual and team training* (pp. 17–38). Washington, DC: APA Press.

Cantor, J., & Engle, R. W. (1993). Working memory capacity as long-term memory activation: An individual differences approach. *Journal of Experimental Psychology: Learning, Memory, & Cognition, 19*(5), 1101–1114.

Capitani, E., Laiacona, M., Mahon, B., & Caramazza A. (2003). What are the facts of semantic category-specific deficits? A critical review of the clinical evidence. *Cognitive Neuropsychology, 20,* 213–261.

Cappa, S. F., Perani, D., Grassli, F., Bressi, S., Alberoni M., Franceschi M., et al. (1997). A PET follow-up study of recovery after stroke in acute aphasics. *Brain and Language, 56,* 55–67.

Caramazza, A., & Shapiro, K. (2001). Language categories in the brain: evidence from aphasia. In L. Rizzi & A. Belletti (Eds.), *Structures and beyond.* Oxford, UK: Oxford University Press.

Carey, S. (1987). *Conceptual change in childhood.* Cambridge, MA: Bradford Books.

Carey, S. (1994). Does learning a language require the child to reconceptualize the world? In L. Gleitman & B. Landau (Eds.), *The acquisition of the lexicon* (pp. 143–168). Cambridge, MA: Elsevier/MIT Press.

Carlson, E. R. (1995). Evaluating the credibility of sources: A missing link in the teaching of critical thinking. *Teaching of Psychology, 22,* 39–41.

Carlson, M. P., & Bloom, I. (2005). The cyclic nature of problem solving: An emergent multidimensional problem-solving framework. *Educational Studies in Mathematics, 58*(1), 45–75.

Carlson, N. R. (1992). *Foundations of physiological psychology* (2nd ed.). Boston: Allyn & Bacon.

Carlson, N. R. (2006). *Physiology of behavior* (9th ed.). Needham Heights, MA: Allyn-Bacon.

Carmichael, L., Hogan, H. P., & Walter, A. A. (1932). An experimental study of the effect of language on the reproduction of visually perceived form. *Journal of Experimental Psychology, 15,* 73–86.

Carpenter, M., Nagell, K., & Tomasello, M. (1998). Social cognition, joint attention, and communicative competence from 9 to 15 months of age. *Monographs of the Society for Research in Child Development, 63* (4, Serial No. 255).

Carpenter, P. A., & Just, M. A. (1981). Cognitive processes in reading: Models based on readers' eye fixations. In A. M. Lesgold & C. A. Perfetti (Eds.), *Interactive processes in reading* (pp. 177–213). Hillsdale, NJ: Erlbaum.

Carraher, T. N., Carraher, D., & Schliemann, A. D. (1985). Mathematics in the streets and in the schools. *British Journal of Developmental Psychology, 3,* 21–29.

Carroll, D. W. (1986). *Psychology of language.* Monterey, CA: Brooks/Cole.

Carroll, J. B. (1993). *Human cognitive abilities: A survey of factor-analytic studies.* New York: Cambridge University Press.

Carroll, J. B., & Casagrande, J. B. (1958). The function of language classification in behavior. In E. E. Maccoby, T. Newcomb, & E. L. Hartley (Eds.), *Readings in social psychology* (3rd ed., pp. 18–31). New York: Holt, Rinehart and Winston.

Carroll, J. S., Hatakenaka, S., & Rudolph, J. W. (2006). Naturalistic decision making and organizational learning in nuclear power plants: negotiating meaning between managers and problem investigation teams. *Organization Studies, 27*(7), 1037–1057.

Carver, L. J., & Bauer, P. J. (2001). The dawning of a past: The emergence of long-term explicit memory in infancy. *Journal of Experimental Psychology: General, 130*(4), 738–745.

Caryl, P. G. (1994). Early event-related potentials correlate with inspection time and intelligence. *Intelligence, 18*(1), 15–46.

Castellucci, V. F., & Kandel, E. R. (1976). Presynaptic facilitation as a mechanism for behavioral sensitization in *Aplysia. Science, 194,* 1176–1178.

Castle, L., Aubert, R. E., Verbrugge, R. R., Khalid, M., & Epstein, R. S. (2007). Trends in medication treatment for ADHD. *Journal of Attention Disorders, 10*(4), 335–342.

Catroppa, C., & Anderson, V. (2006). Planning, problem-solving and organizational abilities in children following traumatic brain injury: Intervention techniques. *Developmental Neurorehabilitation, 9*(2), 89–97.

Cattell, J. M. (1886). The influence of the intensity of the stimulus on the length of the reaction time. *Brain, 9,* 512–514.

Cattell, R. B. (1971). *Abilities: Their structure, growth, and action.* Boston: Houghton Mifflin.

Cave, K. R., & Wolfe, J. M. (1990). Modeling the role of parallel processing in visual search. *Cognitive Psychology, 22*(2), 225–271.

Cazalis, F., Feydy, A., Valabrègue, R., Pélégrini-Issac, M., Pierot, L., & Azouvi, P. (2006). fMRI study of problem-solving after severe traumatic brain injury. *Brain Injury, 20*(10), 1019–1028.

Ceci, S. J. (1991). How much does schooling influence general intelligence and its cognitive components? A reassessment of the evidence. *Developmental Psychology, 27*(5), 703–722.

Ceci, S. J., & Bronfenbrenner, U. (1985). Don't forget to take the cupcakes out of the oven: Strategic time-monitoring, prospective memory and context. *Child Development, 56,* 175–190.

Ceci, S. J., & Bruck, M. (1993). Suggestibility of the child witness: A historical review and synthesis. *Psychological Bulletin, 113*(3), 403–439.

Ceci, S. J., & Bruck, M. (1995). *Jeopardy in the courtroom.* Washington, DC: American Psychological Association.

Ceci, S. J., & Loftus, E. F. (1994). "Memory work": A royal road to false memories? *Applied Cognitive Psychology, 8,* 351–364.

Ceci, S. J., Nightingale, N. N., & Baker, J. G. (1992). The ecologies of intelligence: Challenges to traditional views. In D. K. Detterman (Ed.), *Current topics in human intelligence: Vol. 2. Is mind modular or unitary?* (pp. 61–82). Norwood, NJ: Ablex.

Ceci, S. J., & Roazzi, A. (1994). The effects of context on cognition: Postcards from Brazil. In R. J. Sternberg & R. K. Wagner (Eds.), *Mind in context: Interactionist perspectives on human intelligence* (pp. 74–101). New York: Cambridge University Press.

Cerella, J. (1985). Information processing rates in the elderly. *Psychological Bulletin, 98*(1), 67–83.

Cerella, J. (1990). Aging and information-processing rate. In J. E. Birren & K. W. Schaie (Eds.), *Handbook of the psychology of aging* (3rd ed., pp. 201–221). San Diego: Academic Press.

Cerella, J. (1991). Age effects may be global, not local: Comment on Fisk and Rogers (1991). *Journal of Experimental Psychology: General, 120*(2), 215–223.

Cerella, J., Rybash, J. M., Hoyer, W., & Commons, M. L. (1993). *Adult information processing: Limits on loss.* San Diego: Academic Press.

Chalmers, D. J. (1995). The puzzle of conscious experience. *Scientific American, 273,* 80–86.

Chalmers, D. J. (1996). *The conscious mind: In search of a fundamental theory.* New York: Oxford University Press.

Chambers, D., & Reisberg, D. (1985). Can mental images be ambiguous? *Journal of Experimental Psychology: Human Perception & Performance, 11*(3), 317–328.

Chambers, D., & Reisberg, D. (1992). What an image depicts depends on what an image means. *Cognitive Psychology, 24*(2), 145–174.

Chapman, J. P. (2006). Anxiety and defective decision making: An elaboration of the groupthink model. *Management Decision, 44*(10), 1391–1404.

Chapman, L. J., & Chapman, J. P. (1959). Atmosphere effect reexamined. *Journal of Experimental Psychology, 58,* 220–226.

Chapman, L. J., & Chapman, J. P. (1967). Genesis of popular but erroneous psychodiagnostic observations. *Journal of Abnormal Psychology, 72*(3), 193–204.

Chapman, L. J., & Chapman, J. P. (1969). Illusory correlation as an obstacle to the use of valid psychodiagnostic signs. *Journal of Abnormal Psychology, 74,* 271–280.

Chapman, L. J., & Chapman, J. P. (1975). The basis of illusory correlation. *Journal of Abnormal Psychology, 84*(5), 574–575.

Chase, W. G., & Simon, H. A. (1973). The mind's eye in chess. In W. G. Chase (Ed.), *Visual information processing* (pp. 215–281). New York: Academic Press.

Chechile, R. A. (2004). New multinomial models for the Chechile-Meyer task. *Journal of Mathematical Psychology, 48*(6), 364–384.

Chechile, R. A., & Soraci, S. A. (1999). Evidence for a multiple-process account of the generation effect, *Memory 7,* 483–508.

Cheesman, J., & Merikle, P. M. (1984). Priming with and without awareness. *Perception & Psychophysics, 36,* 387–395.

Chen, C.-Y., Liu, C.-Y., Su, W.-C., Huang, S.-L., & Lin, K.-M. (2007). Factors associated with the diagnosis of neurodevelopmental disorders: A population-based longitudinal study. *Pediatrics, 119*(2), 435–443.

Chen, X., Tian, B., & Wang, L. (2007). Santa Claus' towers of Hanoi. *Graphs and Combinatorics, 23*(1), 153–167.

Chen, Y., & Sun, Y. (2003). Age differences in financial decision-making: Using simple heuristics. *Educational Gerontology, 29*(7), 627–635.

Chen, Z. (2003). Worth one thousand words: Children's use of pictures in analogical problem solving. *Journal of Cognition and Development, 4*(4), 415–434.

Chen, Z., & Daehler, M. W. (1989). Positive and negative transfer in analogical problem solving. *Cognitive Development, 4,* 327–344.

Cheng, P. W. (1997). From covariation to causation: A causal power theory. *Psychological Review, 104,* 367–405.

Cheng, P. W. (1999). Causal reasoning. In R. A. Wilson & F. C. Keil (Eds.), *The MIT encyclopedia of the cognitive sciences* (pp. 106–108). Cambridge, MA: MIT Press.

Cheng, P. W., & Holyoak, K. J. (1985). Pragmatic reasoning schemas. *Cognitive Psychology, 17,* 391–416.

Cheng, P. W., & Holyoak, K. (1995). Complex adaptive systems as intuitive statisticians: Causality, contingency, and prediction. In H. L. Roitblat & J. A. Meyer (Eds.), *Comparative approaches to cognitive science* (pp. 271–302). Cambridge, MA: MIT Press.

Cheng, P. W., Holyoak, K. J., Nisbett, R. E., & Oliver, L. M. (1986). Pragmatic versus syntactic approaches to training deductive reasoning. *Cognitive Psychology, 17*(3), 391–416.

Cherniss, C., Extein, M., Goleman, D., & Weissberg, R. P. (2006). Emotional intelligence: what does research really indicate? *Educational Psychologist, 41*(4), 239–245.

Cherry, E. C. (1953). Some experiments on the recognition of speech with one and two ears. *Journal of the Acoustical Society of America, 25,* 975–979.

Chi, M. T. H., Bassok, M., Lewis, M., Reimann, P., & Glaser, R. (1989). Self-explanations: How students study and use examples in learning to solve problems. *Cognitive Science, 13,* 145–182.

Chi, M. T. H., Glaser, R., & Rees, E. (1982). Expertise in problem solving. In R. J. Sternberg (Ed.), *Advances in the psychology of expertise* (Vol. 1, pp. 7–76). Hillsdale, NJ: Erlbaum.

Chomsky, N. (1957). *Syntactic structures.* The Hague, Netherlands: Mouton.

Chomsky, N. (1959). Review of the book *Verbal behavior. Language, 35,* 26–58.

Chomsky, N. (1965). *Aspects of the theory of syntax.* Cambridge, MA: MIT Press.

Chomsky, N. (1972). *Language and mind* (2nd ed.). New York: Harcourt Brace Jovanovich.

Chomsky, N. (1991, March). [Quoted in] *Discover, 12*(3), 20.

Christensen, B. T., & Schunn, C. D. (2005). Spontaneous access and analogical incubation effects. *Creativity Research Journal, 17*(2–3), 207–220.

Christensen, T. C., Wood, J. V., & Barrett, L. F. (2003). Remembering everyday experience through the prism of self-esteem. *Personality and Social Psychology Bulletin, 29*(1), 51–62.

Christiaans, H., & Venselaar, K. (2007). Creativity in design engineering and the role of knowledge: Modelling the expert. *International Journal of Technology and Design Education, 15*(3), 217–236.

Churchland, P., & Sejnowski, T. (2004). *The computational brain.* Cambridge, MA: MIT Press.

Ciarrochi, J., Forgas, J. P., & Mayer, J. D. (Eds.) (2001). *Emotional intelligence in everyday life: A scientific inquiry*. Philadelphia: Psychology Press.

Clark, A. (2003). Perception, philosophical issues about. In L. Nadel (Ed.), *Encyclopedia of cognitive science* (Vol. 3, pp. 512–517). London: Nature Publishing Group.

Clark, E. V. (1973). What's in a word? On the child's acquisition of semantics in his first language. In T. E. Moore (Ed.), *Cognitive development and the acquisition of language*. New York: Academic Press.

Clark, E. V. (1993). *The lexicon in acquisition*. Cambridge, UK: Cambridge University Press.

Clark, E. V. (1995). Later lexical development and word formation. In P. Fletcher & B. MacWhinney (Eds.), *The handbook of child language* (pp. 393–412). Oxford, UK: Blackwell.

Clark, H. H. (1969). Linguistic processes in deductive reasoning. *Psychological Review, 76*, 387–404.

Clark, H. H., & Brennan, S. E. (1991). Grounding in communication. In L. B. Resnick, J. M. Levine, & S. P. Tansley (Eds.), *Perspectives on socially shared cognition* (pp. 127–149). Washington, DC: American Psychological Association.

Clark, H. H., & Chase, W. G. (1972). On the process of comparing sentences against pictures. *Cognitive Psychology, 3*, 472–517.

Clark, H. H., & Clark, E. V. (1977). *Psychology and language: An introduction to psycholinguistics*. New York: Harcourt Brace Jovanovich.

Clark, H. H., & Lucy, P. (1975). Understanding what is meant from what is said: A study in conversationally conveyed requests. *Journal of Verbal Learning and Verbal Behavior, 14*, 56–72.

Clark, H. H., & Schunk, D. H. (1980). Polite responses to polite requests. *Cognition, 8*, 111–143.

Clark, U. S., Oscar-Berman, M., Shagrin, B., & Pencina, M. (2007). Alcoholism and judgments of affective stimuli. *Neuropsychology, 21*(3), 346–362.

Clegg, A. B., & Shepherd, A. J. (2007). Benchmarking natural-language parsers for biological applications using dependency graphs. *BMC Bioinformatics, 8*(1), 24–41.

Clement, C. A., & Falmagne, R. J. (1986). Logical reasoning, world knowledge, and mental imagery: Interconnections in cognitive processes. *Memory & Cognition, 14*(4), 299–307.

Clinton, S. M., & Meador-Woodruff, J. H. (2004). Thalamic dysfunction in schizophrenia: Neurochemical, neuropathological, and in vivo imaging abnormalities. *Schizophrenia Research, 69*(2–3), 237–253.

Coane, J. H., McBride, D. M., Raulerson, B. A., & Jordan, J. S. (2007). False memory in a short-term memory task. *Experimental Psychology, 54*(1), 62–70.

Cohen, A. (2003). Selective attention. In L. Nadel (Ed.), *Encyclopedia of cognitive science* (Vol. 3, pp. 1033–1037). London: Nature Publishing Group.

Cohen, G. (1989). *Memory in the real world*. Hillsdale, NJ: Erlbaum.

Cohen, J. (1981). Can human irrationality be experimentally demonstrated? *Behavioral and Brain Sciences, 4*, 317–331.

Cohen, J. D., Romero, R. D., Servan-Schreiber, D., & Farah, M. J. (1994). Mechanisms of spatial attention: The relation of macrostructure to microstructure in parietal neglect. *Journal of Cognitive Neuroscience, 6*, 377–387.

Cohen, J. D., & Schooler, J. W. (Eds.) (1997). *Scientific approaches to consciousness*. Mahwah, NJ: Erlbaum.

Cohen, J. T., & Graham, J. D. (2003). A revised economic analysis of restrictions on the use of cell phones while driving. *Risk Analysis, 23*(1), 5–17.

Cohen, M. S., Kosslyn, S. M., Breiter, H. C., DiGirolamo, G. J., Thompson, W. L., Anderson, A. K., et al. (1996). Changes in cortical activity during mental rotation: A mapping study using functional MRI. *Brain, 119*, 89–100.

Cohen, N. J., Eichenbaum, H., Deacedo, B. S., & Corkin, S. (1985). Different memory systems underlying acquisition of procedural and declarative knowledge. *Annals of the New York Academy of Sciences, 444*, 54–71.

Cohen, N. J., McCloskey, M., & Wible, C. G. (1990). Flashbulb memories and underlying cognitive mechanisms: Reply to Pillemer. *Journal of Experimental Psychology: General, 119*(1), 97–100.

Cohen, N. J., & Squire, L. R. (1980). Preserved learning and retention of pattern-analyzing skill in amnesia: Dissociation of knowing how and knowing that. *Science, 210*(4466), 207–210.

Colby, K. M. (1963). Computer simulation of a neurotic process. In S. S. Tomkins & S. Messick (Eds.), *Computer simulation of personality: Frontier of psychological research* (pp. 165–180). New York: Wiley.

Colby, K. M. (1995). A computer program using cognitive therapy to treat depressed patients. *Psychiatric Services, 46*, 1223–1225.

Cole, M., Gay, J., Glick, J., & Sharp, D. W. (1971). *The cultural context of learning and thinking*. New York: Basic Books.

Coleman, J. (2003). Phonology, computational. In L. Nadel (Ed.), *Encyclopedia of cognitive science* (Vol. 3, pp. 650–654). London: Nature Group Press.

Coley, J. D., Atran, S., & Medin, D. L. (1997). Does rank have its privilege? Inductive inferences within folk biological taxonomies. *Cognition, 64*, 73–112.

Coley, J. D., Medin, D. L., Proffitt, J. B., Lynch, E., & Atran, S. (1999). Inductive reasoning in folkbiological thought. In D. L. Medin & S. Atran (Eds.), *Folkbiology* (pp. 205–232). Cambridge, MA: MIT Press.

Collette, F., Majerus, S., Van Der Linden, M., Dabe, P., Degueldre, C., Delfiore, G., et al. (2001). Contribution of lexico-semantic processes to verbal short-term memory tasks: A PET activation study. *Memory, 9*, 249–259.

Collie, A., Maruff, P., Shafiq-Antonacci, R., Smith, M., Hallup, M., Schofield, P. R., et al. (2001). Memory decline in healthy older people: Implications for identifying mild cognitive impairment. *Neurology, 56*, 1533–1538.

Collier, G. (1994). *Social origins of mental ability*. New York: Wiley.

Collier, M. (2005). Hume and cognitive science: The current status of the controversy over abstract ideas. *Phenomenology and the Cognitive Sciences, 4*(2), 197–207.

Collins, A. M., & Loftus, E. F. (1975). A spreading-activation theory of semantic processing. *Psychological Review, 82*, 407–429.

Collins, A. M., & Quillian, M. R. (1969). Retrieval time from semantic memory. *Journal of Verbal Learning and Verbal Behavior, 8*, 240–248.

Collins, M. A., & Amabile, T. M. (1999). Motivation and creativity. In R. J. Sternberg (Ed.), *Handbook of creativity* (pp. 297–312). New York: Cambridge University Press.

Colom, R., Rebollo, I., Palacios, A., Juan-Espinosa, M., & Kyllonen, P. C. (2004). Working memory is (almost) perfectly predicted by *g*. *Intelligence, 32*(3), 277–296.

Colonia-Willner, R. (1998). Practical intelligence at work: Relationship between aging and cognitive efficiency among managers in a bank environment. *Psychology and Aging, 13*, 45–57.

Coltheart, M. (2003). Dyslexia. In L. Nadel (Ed.), *Encyclopedia of cognitive science* (Vol. 1, pp. 1049–1052). London: Nature Publishing Group.

Committeri, G., Galati, G., Paradis, A., Pizzamiglio, L., Berthoz, A., & LeBihan, D. (2004). Reference frames for spatial cognition: Different brain areas are involved in viewer-, object-, and landmark-centered judgements about object location. *Journal of Cognitive Neuroscience, 16*(9), 1517–1535.

Conn, C., & Silverman, I., (Eds.). (1991). *What counts: The complete Harper's index.* New York: Henry Holt.

Conrad, R. (1964). Acoustic confusions in immediate memory. *British Journal of Psychology, 55,* 75–84.

Conway, A. R. A., Cowan, N., & Bunting, M. F. (2001). The cocktail party phenomenon revisited: The importance of working memory capacity. *Psychonomic Bulletin & Review, 8*(2), 331–335.

Conway, M. A. (1995). *Flashbulb memories.* Hove, England: Erlbaum.

Cook, A. E., & Gueraud, S. (2005). What have we been missing? The role of general world knowledge in discourse processing. *Discourse Processes, 39*(2–3), 265–278.

Coon, H., Carey, G., & Fulker, D. W. (1992). Community influences on cognitive ability. *Intelligence, 16*(2), 169–188.

Cooper, E. H., & Pantle, A. J. (1967). The total-time hypothesis in verbal learning. *Psychological Bulletin, 68,* 221–234.

Corballis, M. C. (1989). Laterality and human evolution. *Psychological Review, 96*(3), 49–50.

Corballis, M. C. (1997). Mental rotation and the right hemisphere. *Brain and Language, 57,* 100–121.

Corbetta, M., Miezin, F. M., Shulman, G. L., & Petersen, S. E. (1993). A PET study of visuospatial attention. *Journal of Neuroscience, 13*(3), 1202–1226.

Corcoran, D. W. J. (1971). *Pattern recognition.* Harmondsworth: Penguin.

Corcoran, J., & Dattalo, P. (2006). Parent involvement in treatment for ADHD: A meta-analysis of the published studies. *Research on Social Work Practice, 16*(6), 561–570.

Coren, S., & Girgus, J. S. (1978). *Seeing is deceiving: The psychology of visual illusions.* Hillsdale, NJ: Erlbaum.

Coslett, H. B. (2003). *Acquired dyslexia.* In K. M. Heilman & E. Valenstein (Eds.), *Clinical neuropsychology* (pp. 108–125). New York: Oxford University Press.

Cosmides, L. (1989). The logic of social exchange: Has natural selection shaped how humans reason? Studies with the Wason selection task. *Cognition, 31,* 187–276.

Cosmides, L., & Tooby, J. (1996). Are humans good intuitive statisticians after all? Rethinking some conclusions from the literature on judgment under uncertainty. *Cognition, 58,* 1–73.

Costello, C. G. (1967). The effects of an alien stimulus on reminiscence in pursuit rotor performance. *Psychonomic Science, 8*(8), 331–332.

Cowan, N. (1995). *Attention and memory: An integrated framework.* New York: Oxford University Press.

Cowan, N. (2001). The magical number 4 in short-term memory: A reconsideration of mental storage capacity. *Behavioral and Brain Sciences, 24.*

Cowan, N., Winkler, I., Teder, W., & Näätänen, R. (1993). Memory prerequisites of mismatch negativity in the auditory event-related potential (ERP). *Journal of Experimental Psychology: Learning, Memory, & Cognition, 19*(4), 909–921.

Craik, F. I. M., & Brown, S. C. (2000). Memory: Coding processes. In A. E. Kazdin (Ed.), *Encyclopedia of psychology* (Vol. 5, pp. 162–166). Washington, DC: American Psychological Association.

Craik, F. I. M., & Lockhart, R. S. (1972). Levels of processing: A framework for memory research. *Journal of Verbal Learning and Verbal Behavior, 11,* 671–684.

Craik, F. I. M., & Tulving, E. (1975). Depth of processing and the retention of words in episodic memory. *Journal of Experimental Psychology: General, 104,* 268–294.

Craik, K. (1943). *The nature of exploration.* Cambridge, UK: Cambridge University Press.

Crowder, R. G. (1976). *Principles of learning and memory.* Hillsdale, NJ: Erlbaum.

Crowder, R. G., & Green, R. L. (2000). Serial learning: Cognition and behavior. In E. Tulving & F. I. M. Craik (Eds.), *The Oxford handbook of memory* (pp. 125–136). New York: Oxford University Press.

Cruz, N. V., & Bahna, S. L. (2006). Do food or additives cause behavior disorders? *Psychiatric Annals, 36*(10), 724–732.

Crystal, D. (Ed.). (1987). *The Cambridge encyclopedia of language.* New York: Cambridge University Press.

Csikszentmihalyi, M. (1988). Society, culture, and person: A systems view of creativity. In R. J. Sternberg (Ed.), *The nature of creativity* (pp. 325–339). New York: Cambridge University Press.

Csikszentmihalyi, M. (1996). *Creativity: Flow and the psychology of discovery and invention.* New York: HarperCollins.

Csikszentmihalyi, M. (1999). Creativity. In R. A. Wilson & F. C. Keil (Eds.), *The MIT encyclopedia of the cognitive sciences* (pp. 205–206). Cambridge, MA: MIT Press.

Csikszentmihalyi, M. (2000). Creativity: An overview. In A. E. Kazdin (Ed.), *Encyclopedia of psychology* (Vol. 2, p. 342). Washington, DC: American Psychological Association.

Culham, J. C. (2003). Parietal cortex. In L. Nadel (Ed.), *Encyclopedia of cognitive science* (Vol. 3, pp. 451–457). London: Nature Publishing Group.

Cummins, D. D. (2004). The evolution of reasoning. In J. P. Leighton & R. J. Sternberg (Eds.), *The nature of reasoning* (pp. 339–374). New York: Cambridge University Press.

Cummins, J. (1976). The influence of bilingualism on cognitive growth: A synthesis of research findings and explanatory hypothesis. *Working Papers on Bilingualism, 9,* 1–43.

Cummins, J. (1979). Linguistic interdependence and the educational development of bilingual children. *Review of Educational Research 49,* 222–251.

Cummins, R., & Cummins, D. D. (Eds.). (2000). *Minds, brains, and computers: The foundations of cognitive science.* Singapore: Blackwell.

Cutler, B. L., & Penrod, S. D. (1995). *Mistaken identification: The eyewitness, psychology, and the law.* New York: Cambridge University Press.

Cutting, J., & Kozlowski, L. (1977). Recognizing friends by their walk: Gait perception without familiarity cues. *Bulletin of the Psychonomic Society, 9*(5), 353–356.

Cziko, G. A. (1998). From blind to creative: In defense of Donald Campbell's selectionist theory of human creativity. *Journal of Creative Behavior, 32,* 192–208.

D'Amico, A., & Guarnera, M. (2005). Exploring working memory in children with low arithmetical achievement. *Learning and Individual Differences, 15*(3),189–202.

D'Argembeau, A. Comblain, C., & Van der Linden, M. (2005). Affective valence and the self-reference effect: Influence of retrieval conditions. *British Journal of Psychology, 96*(4), 457–466.

Dakin, S. C., & Hess, R. F. (1999). Contour integration and scale combination processes in visual edge detection. *Spatial Vision, 12*, 309–327.

Damasio, A. R. (1985). Prosopagnosia. *Trends in Neurosciences, 8*, 132–135.

Damasio, H., Grabowski, T., Frank, R., Galaburda, A. M., & Damasio, A. R. (1994). The return of Phineas Gage: Clues about the brain from the skull of a famous patient. *Science, 264*, 1102–1105.

Dambacher, M., & Kliegl, R. (2007). Synchronizing timelines: Relations between fixation durations and N400 amplitudes during sentence reading. *Brain Research, 1155*(25), 147–162.

Daneman, M., & Carpenter, P. A. (1980). Individual differences in working memory and reading. *Journal of Verbal Learning and Verbal Behavior, 19*, 450–466.

Daneman, M., & Carpenter, P. A. (1983). Individual differences in integrating information between and within sentences. *Journal of Experimental Psychology: Learning, Memory, and Cognition, 9*, 561–583.

Daneman, M., & Tardif, T. (1987). Working memory and reading skill reexamined. In M. Coltheart (Ed.), *Attention and performance: Vol. 12. The psychology of reading* (pp. 491–508). Hove, UK: Erlbaum.

Daniel, M. H. (1997). Intelligence testing: Status and trends. *American Psychologist, 52*, 1038–1045.

Daniel, M. H. (2000). Interpretation of intelligence test scores. In R. J. Sternberg (Ed.), *Handbook of intelligence* (pp. 477–491). New York: Cambridge University Press.

DARPA: Urban Challenge. (2007). Retrieved September 5, 2007, from http://www.darpa.mil/grandchallenge/index.asp

Davidson, J. E. (1995). The suddenness of insight. In R. J. Sternberg & J. E. Davidson (Eds.), *The nature of insight* (pp. 125–155). Cambridge, MA: MIT Press.

Davidson, J. E. (2003). Insights about insightful problem solving. In J. E. Davidson & R. J. Sternberg (Eds.), *The psychology of problem solving* (pp. 149–175). New York: Cambridge University Press.

Davidson, J. E., & Sternberg, R. J. (1984). The role of insight in intellectual giftedness. *Gifted Child Quarterly, 28*, 58–64.

Davidson, J. E., & Sternberg, R. J. (Eds.). (2003). *The psychology of problem solving*. New York: Cambridge University Press.

Davidson, R. J., & Hugdahl, K. (Eds.) (1995). *Cerebral asymmetry*. Cambridge, MA: MIT Press.

Davies, M. (1999). Consciousness. In R. A. Wilson & F. C. Keil (Eds.), *The MIT encyclopedia of the cognitive sciences* (pp. 190–193). Cambridge, MA: MIT Press.

Davies, M., & Humphreys, G. W. (1993). *Consciousness: Psychological and philosophical essays*. Oxford, UK: Blackwell.

Davies, M., Stankov, L., & Roberts, R. D. (1998). Emotional intelligence: In search of an elusive construct. *Journal of Personality & Social Psychology, 75*, 989–1015.

Davis, M. P., Drecier, R., Walsh, D., Lagman, R., & LeGrand, S. B. (2004). Appetite and cancer-associated anorexia: A review. *Journal of Clinical Oncology, 22*(8), 1510–1517.

Dawes, R. (2000). Tversky, Amos. In A. Kazdin (Ed.), *Encyclopedia of psychology* (Vol. 8, pp. 127–128). Washington, DC: American Psychological Association.

Dawes, R. M., Mulford, M. (1996). The false consensus effect and overconfidence: Flaws in judgment or flaws in how we study judgment? *Organizational Behavior & Human Decision Processes, 65*(3), 201–211.

De Beni, R., Cornoldi, C., Larsson, M., Magnussen, S., & Ronnberg, J. (2007). Memory experts: Visual learning, wine tasting, orienteering and speech-reading. In S. Magnussen & T. Helstrup (Eds.), *Everyday memory* (pp. 201–227). New York: Psychology Press.

De Graef, P., Christiaens, D., & D'Ydewalle, G. (1990). Perceptual effects of scene context on object identification. *Psychological Research, 52*(4), 317–329.

De Groot, A. D. (1965). *Thought and choice in chess*. The Hague, Netherlands: Mouton.

De Houwer, A. (1995). Bilingual language acquisition. In P. Fletcher & B. MacWhinney (Eds.), *The handbook of child language* (pp. 219–250). Oxford, UK: Blackwell.

de la Iglesia, J. C. F., Buceta, M. J., & Campos, A. (2005). Prose learning in children and adults with Down syndrome: The use of visual and mental image strategies to improve recall. *Journal of Intellectual & Developmental Disability, 30*(4), 199–206.

De Lisi, R., & Cammarano, D. M. (1996). Computer experience and gender differences in undergraduate mental rotation performance. *Computers and Human Behavior, 12*(3), 351–361.

De Rosa, E., & Sullivan, E. V. (2003). Enhanced release from proactive interference in nonamnesic alcoholic individuals: Implications for impaired associative binding. *Neuropsychology, 17*(3), 469–481.

De Weerd, P. (2003a). Attention, neural basis of. In L. Nadel (Ed.), *Encyclopedia of cognitive science* (Vol. 1, pp. 238–246). London: Nature Publishing Group.

De Weerd, P. (2003b). Occipital cortex. In L. Nadel (Ed.), *Encyclopedia of cognitive science* (Vol. 3, pp. 408–414). London: Nature Publishing Group.

De Yoe, E. A., & Van Essen, D. C. (1988). Concurrent processing streams in monkey visual cortex. *Trends in Neurosciences, 11*, 219–226.

Dean, L. M., Willis, F. N., & Hewitt K. (1975). Initial interaction distance among individuals equal and unequal in military rank. *Journal of Personality and Social Psychology, 32*, 294–299.

Deary, I. J. (2000). Simple information processing and intelligence. In R. J. Sternberg (Ed.), *Handbook of intelligence* (pp. 267–284). New York: Cambridge University Press.

Deary, I. J., & Stough, C. (1996). Intelligence and inspection time: Achievements, prospects, and problems. *American Psychologist, 51*, 599–608.

DeCasper, A. J., & Fifer, W. P. (1980). Of human bonding: Newborns prefer their mothers' voices. *Science, 208*, 1174–1176.

Dedeogle, A., Choi, J., Cormier, K., Kowall, N. W., & Jenkins, B. G. (2004). Magnetic resonance spectroscopic analysis of Alzheimer's disease mouse brain that express mutant human APP shows altered neurochemical profile. *Brain Research, 1012*(1–2), 60–65.

Deeprose, C., Andrade, J., Harrison, D., & Edwards, N. (2005). Unconscious auditory priming during surgery with propofol and nitrous oxide anaesthesia: A replication. *British Journal of Anaesthesia, 94*(1), 57–62.

Deese, J. (1959). On the prediction of occurrence of particular verbal intrusions in immediate recall. *Journal of Experimental Psychology, 58*, 17–22.

Deffenbacher, J. L., Lynch, R. S., Filetti, L. B., Dahlen, E. R., & Oetting, E. R. (2003). Anger, aggression, risky behavior, and crash-related outcomes in three groups of drivers. *Behaviour Research and Therapy, 41*(3), 333–349.

Deffenbacher, K. A., Bornstein, B. H., Penrod, S. D., & McGorty, E. K. (2004). A meta-analytic review of the effects of high stress on eyewitness memory. *Law and Human Behavior, 28*(6), 697–706.

DeFries, J. C., & Gillis, J. J. (1993). Genetics of reading disability. In R. Plomin & G. McClearn (Eds.), *Nature, nurture & psychology* (pp. 121–145). Washington, DC: American Psychological Association.

Dehaene-Lambertz, G., Hertz-Pannier, L., & Dubois, J. (2006). Nature and nurture in language acquisition: Anatomical and functional brain-imaging studies in infants. *Trends in Neuroscience, 29*(7), 367–373.

Dell, G. S. (1986). A spreading-activation theory of retrieval in sentence production. *Psychological Review, 93*(3), 283–321.

Démonet, J.-F., Taylor, M. J., & Chaix, Y. (2004). Developmental dyslexia. *The Lancet, 363*(9419), 1451–1460.

Dempster, F. N. (1991). Inhibitory processes: A neglected dimension of intelligence. *Intelligence, 15*(2), 157–173.

Denis, M., Beschin, N., Logie, R. H., & Della Sala, S. (2002). Visual perception and verbal descriptions as sources for generating mental representations: Evidence from representational neglect. *Cognitive Neuropsychology, 19*(2), 97–112.

Denis, M., & Kosslyn, S. M. (1999). Scanning visual mental images: A window on the mind. *Cahiers de Psychologie Cognitive, 18*(4), 409–616.

Denny, N. W. (1980). Task demands and problem-solving strategies in middle-aged and older adults. *Journal of Gerontology, 35,* 559–564.

Desimone, R., & Duncan, J. (1995). Neural mechanisms of selective visual attention. *Annual Review of Neuroscience, 18,* 193–222.

DeSoto, C. B., London, M., & Handel, S. (1965). Social reasoning and spatial paralogic. *Journal of Personality and Social Psychology, 2,* 513–521.

Detre, J. A. (2004). fMRI: Applications in epilepsy. *Epilepsia 45*(4), 26–31.

Detterman, D. K., & Sternberg, R. J. (Eds.). (1982). *How and how much can intelligence be increased?* Norwood, NJ: Ablex.

Detterman, D. K., & Sternberg, R. J. (Eds.) (1993). *Transfer on trial: Intelligence, cognition, and instruction.* Norwood, NJ: Ablex.

Deutsch, J. A., & Deutsch, D. (1963). Attention: Some theoretical considerations. *Psychological Review, 70,* 80–90.

DeValois, R. L., & DeValois, K. K. (1980). Spatial vision. *Annual Review of Psychology, 31,* 309–341.

Dewhurst, S. A., Pursglove, R. C., & Lewis, C. (2007). Story contexts increase susceptibility to the DRM illusion in 5-year-olds. *Developmental Science, 10*(3), 374–378.

Di Eugenio, B. (2003). Discourse processing. In L. Nadel (Ed.), *Encyclopedia of cognitive science* (Vol. 1, pp. 976–983). London: Nature Publishing Group.

Diesendruck, G. (2005). The principles of conventionality and contrast in word learning: an empirical examination. *Developmental Psychology, 41*(3), 451–463.

Dietrich, A. (2004). The cognitive neuroscience of creativity. *Psychonomic Bulletin & Review, 11*(6), 1011–1026.

DiGirolamo, G. J., & Griffin, H. J. (2003). Consciousness and attention. In L. Nadel (Ed.), *Encyclopedia of cognitive science* (Vol. 1, pp. 711–717). London: Nature Publishing Group.

Ditchburn, R. W. (1980). The function of small saccades. *Vision Research, 20,* 271–272.

Dixon, R. A., & Baltes, P. B. (1986). Toward life-span research on the functions and pragmatics of intelligence. In R. J. Sternberg & R. K. Wagner (Eds.), *Practical intelligence: Nature and origins of competence in the everyday world* (pp. 203–235). New York: Cambridge University Press.

Dixon, T. L., & Maddox, K. B. (2005). Skin tone, crime news, and social reality judgments: Priming the stereotype of the dark and dangerous black criminal. *Journal of Applied Social Psychology, 35*(8), 1555–1570.

Dodd, M. D., & MacLeod, C. M. (2004). False recognition without intention learning. *Psychonomic Bulletin & Review, 11*(1), 137–142.

Dolan, M. (1995, February 11). When the mind's eye blinks. *Los Angeles Times,* pp. A1, A24, A25.

Donders, F. C. (1868/1869). Over de snelheid van psychische processen. Onderzoekingen gedaan in het Physiologisch Laboratorium der Utrechtsche Hoogeschool. [About the velocity of psychological processes: Studies done at the Physiological Laboratory of the University of Utrecht.] *Tweede reeks, II,* 92–120.

Dosher, B. A. (2003). Working memory. In L. Nadel (Ed.), *Encyclopedia of cognitive science* (Vol. 4, pp. 569–577). London: Nature Publishing Group.

Doyle, C. L. (2000). Psychology: Definition. In A. E. Kazdin (Ed.), *Encyclopedia of psychology* (Vol. 6, pp. 375–376). Washington, DC: American Psychological Association.

Drapier, D., Drapier, S., Sauleau, P., Derkinderen, P., Damier, P., Alain, H., et al. (2006). Pathological gambling secondary to dopaminergic therapy in Parkinson's disease. *Psychiatry Research, 144*(2–3), 241–244.

Dreyfus, H. L., & Dreyfus, S. E. (1990). Making a mind versus modelling the brain: Artificial intelligence back at a branch-point. In M. A. Boden (Ed.), *The philosophy of artificial intelligence: Oxford readings in philosophy* (pp. 309–333). Oxford, UK: Oxford University Press.

Dror, I. E., & Kosslyn, S. M. (1994). Mental imagery and aging. *Psychology and Aging, 9*(1), 90–102.

Dunbar, K. (2003). Scientific thought. In L. Nadel (Ed.), *Encyclopedia of cognitive science* (Vol. 3, pp. 1006–1009). London: Nature Publishing Group.

Duncan, E., & Bourg, T. (1983). An examination of the effects of encoding and decision processes on the rate of mental rotation. *Journal of Mental Imagery, 7*(2), 3–55.

Duncan, J. (1996). Cooperating brain systems in selective perception and action. In T. Inui & J. L. McClelland (Eds.), *Attention and performance XVI* (pp. 549–578). Cambridge, MA: MIT Press.

Duncan, J. (1999). Attention. In R. A. Wilson & F. C. Keil (Eds.), *The MIT encyclopedia of the cognitive sciences* (pp. 39–41). Cambridge, MA: MIT Press.

Duncan, J., Burgess, P., & Emslie, H. (1995). Fluid intelligence after frontal lobe lesions. *Neuropsychologia, 33,* 261–268.

Duncan, J., & Humphreys, G. W. (1989). Visual search and stimulus similarity. *Psychological Review, 96*(3), 433–458.

Duncan, J., & Humphreys, G. W. (1992). Beyond the search surface: Visual search and attentional engagement. *Journal of Experimental Psychology: Human Perception & Performance, 18*(2), 578–588.

Duncker, K. (1945). On problem-solving. *Psychological Monographs, 58*(5, Whole No. 270).

Dupuy, J. P. (1998). Rationality and self-deception. In J. P. Dupuy (Ed.), *Self-deception and paradoxes of rationality* (pp. 113–150). Stanford, CA: CSLI Publications.

Dupuy, J. P. (1999). Rational choice theory. In R. A. Wilson & F. C. Keil (Eds.), *The MIT encyclopedia of the cognitive sciences* (pp. 699–701). Cambridge, MA: MIT Press.

Durgin, F. H. (2000). Visual adaptation. In A. E. Kazdin (Ed.), *Encyclopedia of psychology* (Vol. 8, pp. 183–187). Washington, DC: American Psychological Association.

Eales, M. J. (1993). Pragmatic impairments in adults with childhood diagnoses of autism or developmental receptive language disorder. *Journal of Autism and Developmental Disorders, 23*(4), 593–617.

Easton, N., Marshall, F., Fone, K., & Marsden, C. (2007). Atomoxetine produces changes in cortico-basal thalamic loop circuits: Assessed by phMRI BOLD contrast. *Neuropharmacology, 52*(3), 812–826.

Ebbinghaus, H. (1885). *Uber das Gedächtnis.* Leipzig, Germany: Duncker and Humblot.

Eckstein, M. P., Shumozaki, S. S., & Abbey, C. K. (2000). The footprints of visual attention in the Posner cueing paradigm revealed by classification images. *Journal of Vision, 2*(1), 25–45.

Edelman, S., & Weinshall, D. (1991). A self-organizing multiple-view representation of 3D objects. *Biological Cybernetics, 64,* 209–219.

Edwards, W. (1954). The theory of decision making. *Psychological Bulletin, 51,* 380–417.

Egeth, H. (2000). Attention: An overview. In A. E. Kazdin (Ed.), *Encyclopedia of psychology* (Vol. 1, pp. 293–295). Washington, DC: American Psychological Association.

Egeth, H. E. (1993). What do we not know about eyewitness identification? *American Psychologist, 48*(5), 577–580.

Ehrlich, K. (1996). Applied mental models in human-computer interaction. In J. Oakhill & A. Garnham (Eds.), *Mental models in cognitive science* (pp. 313–339). Hillsdale, NJ: Erlbaum.

Eich, E. (1995). Searching for mood dependent memory. *Psychological Science, 6,* 67–75.

Eich, J. E. (1980). The cue-dependent nature of state-dependent retrieval. *Memory & Cognition, 8,* 157–158.

Eichenbaum, H. (1997). Declarative memory: Insights from cognitive neurobiology. *Annual Review of Psychology, 48,* 547–572.

Eichenbaum, H. (1999). Hippocampus. In R. A. Wilson & F. C. Keil (Eds.), *The MIT encyclopedia of the cognitive sciences* (pp. 377–378). Cambridge, MA: MIT Press.

Eichenbaum, H. (2002). *The cognitive neuroscience of memory.* New York: Oxford University Press.

Eimas, P. D. (1985). The perception of speech in early infancy. *Scientific American, 252,* 46–52.

Eisenberger, R., & Shanock, L. (2003). Rewards, intrinsic motivation, and creativity: a case study of conceptual and methodological isolation. *Creativity Research Journal, 15*(2–3), 121–130.

Eisenegger, C., Herwig, U., & Jancke, L. (2007). The involvement of primary motor cortex in mental rotation revealed by transcranial magnetic stimulation. *European Journal of Neuroscience, 25*(4), 1240–1244.

Eldridge, L. L., Knowlton, B. J., Furmanski, C. S., Bookheimer, S. Y., & Engel, S. A. (2000). Remembering episodes: A selective role for the hippocampus during retrieval. *Nature Neuroscience, 3*(11):1049–1052.

Ellenbogen, J. M., Payne, J. D., & Stickgold, R. (2006). The role of sleep in declarative memory consolidation: Passive, permissive, active or none? *Current Opinion in Neurobiology,16*(6), 716–722.

Elman, J. L., Bates, E. A., Johnson, M. H., Karmiloff-Smith, A., Parisi, D., & Plunkett, K. (1996). *Rethinking innateness: A connectionist perspective on development.* Cambridge, MA: MIT Press.

Emmorey, K. (1994). Sign language: A window into the brain, language, and cognition. In S. Ramachandran (Ed.), *Encyclopedia of human behavior* (Vol. 4, pp. 193–204). San Diego: Academic Press.

Engel, A. S., Rumelhart, D. E., Wandell, B. A., Lee, A. T., Gover, G. H., Chichilisky, E. J., et al. (1994). MRI measurement of language lateralization in Wada-tested patients. *Brain, 118,* 1411–1419.

Engle, R. W. (1994). Individual differences in memory and their implications for learning. In R. J. Sternberg (Ed.), *Encyclopedia of intelligence* (pp. 700–704). New York: Macmillan.

Engle, R. W., Cantor, J., & Carullo, J. J. (1992). Individual differences in working memory and comprehension: A test of four hypotheses. *Journal of Experimental Psychology: Learning, Memory, & Cognition, 18*(5), 972–992.

Epstein, W., & Rogers, S. (Eds.), (1995). *Handbook of perception and cognition: Vol. 5. Perception of space and motion.* San Diego: Academic Press.

Erdelyi, M., & Goldberg, B. (1979). Let's now sweep repression under the rug: Toward a cognitive psychology of repression. In J. F. Kihlstrom & F. J. Evans (Eds.), *Functional disorders of memory.* Hillsdale, NJ: Erlbaum.

Ericsson, K. A. (Ed.). (1996). *The road to excellence.* Mahwah, NJ: Erlbaum.

Ericsson, K. A. (1999). Expertise. In R. A. Wilson & F. C. Keil (Eds.), *The MIT encyclopedia of the cognitive sciences* (pp. 298–300). Cambridge, MA: MIT Press.

Ericsson, K. A. (2003). The acquisition of expert performance as problem solving: Construction and modification of mediating mechanisms through deliberate practice. In J. E. Davidson & R. J. Sternberg (Eds.), *The psychology of problem solving* (pp. 31–83). New York: Cambridge University Press.

Ericsson, K. A., Chase, W. G., & Faloon, S. (1980). Acquisition of a memory skill. *Science, 208,* 1181–1182.

Ericsson, K. A., Krampe, R. T., & Tesch-Römer, C. (1993). The role of deliberate practice in the acquisition of expert performance. *Psychological Review, 100,* 363–406.

Ericsson, K. A. & Lehmann, A. C. (1996). Expert and exceptional performance: Evidence on maximal adaptations on task constraints. *Annual Review of Psychology, 47,* 273–305.

Ericsson, K. A., & Simon, H. A. (1984). *Protocol analysis: Verbal reports as data.* Cambridge, MA: Bradford Books/MIT Press.

Espino, O., Santamaria, C., Meseguer, E., & Carreiras, M. (2005). Early and late processes in syllogistic reasoning: Evidence from eye-movements. *Cognition, 98*(1), B1–B9.

Esser J. K. (1998). Alive and well after 25 years: A review of groupthink research. *Organizational Behavioral and Human Decision Processes, 73*(23), 116–141.

Estes, W. K. (1982). Learning, memory, and intelligence. In R. J. Sternberg (Ed.), *Handbook of intelligence* (pp. 170–224). New York: Cambridge University Press.

Estes, W. K. (1994). *Classification and cognition.* New York: Oxford University Press.

Evans, J. St. B. T., Barston, J. I., & Pollard, P. (1983). On the conflict between logic and belief in syllogistic reasoning. *Memory and cognition, 11*(3), 295–306.

Evans, J. St. B. T., & Feeney, A. (2004). The role of prior belief in reasoning. In J. P. Leighton & R. J. Sternberg (Eds.), *The nature of reasoning* (pp. 78–102). New York: Cambridge University Press.

Evans, J. St. B. T., & Over, D. E. (1996). Rationality in the selection task: Epistemic utility versus uncertainty reduction. *Psychological Review, 103,* 356–363.

Eysenck, H. J. (1967). Intelligence assessment: A theoretical and experimental approach. *British Journal of Educational Psychology, 37,* 81–98.

Eysenck, H. J., & Kamin, L. (1981). *The intelligence controversy: H. J. Eysenck vs. Leon Kamin.* New York: Wiley.

Eysenck, M., & Byrne, A. (1992). Anxiety and susceptibility to distraction. *Personality & Individual Differences, 13*(7), 793–798.

Eysenck, M., & Calvo, M. G. (1992). Anxiety and performance: The processing efficiency theory. *Cognition & Emotion, 6*(6), 409–434.

Eysenck, M., & Graydon, J. (1989). Susceptibility to distraction as a function of personality. *Personality & Individual Differences, 10*(6), 681–687.

Eysenck, M., & Keane, M. T. (1990). *Cognitive psychology: A student's handbook.* Hove, UK: Erlbaum.

Fahle, M. (2003). Perceptual learning. In L. Nadel (Ed.), *Encyclopedia of cognitive science* (Vol. 3, pp. 548–552). London: Nature Publishing Group.

Farah, M. J. (1988a). Is visual imagery really visual? Overlooked evidence from neuropsychology. *Psychological Review, 95*(3), 307–317.

Farah, M. J. (1988b). The neuropsychology of mental imagery: Converging evidence from brain-damaged and normal subjects. In J. Stiles-Davis, M. Kritchevsky, & U. Bellugi (Eds.), *Spatial cognition: Brain bases and development* (pp. 33–56). Hillsdale, NJ: Erlbaum.

Farah, M. J. (1990). *Visual agnosia: Disorders of object recognition and what they tell us about normal vision.* Cambridge, MA: MIT Press.

Farah, M. J. (1992). Is an object an object an object? Cognitive and neuropsychological investigations of domain specifiity in visual object recognition. *Current Directions in Psychological Science, 1,* 164–169.

Farah, M. J. (1995). Dissociable systems for visual recogniiton: A cognitive neuropsycohlogy approach. In S. M. Kosslyn & D. N. Osherson (Eds.), *Visual cognition: An invitation to cognitive science* (Vol. 2). Cambridge, MA: MIT Press.

Farah, M. J. (1999). Object recognition, human neuropsychology. In R. A. Wilson & F. C. Keil (Eds.), *The MIT encyclopedia of the cognitive sciences* (pp. 615–618). Cambridge, MA: MIT Press.

Farah, M. J. (2000a). *The cognitive neuroscience of vision.* Malden, MA: Blackwell.

Farah, M. J. (2000b). The neural bases of mental imagery. In M. S. Gazzaniga (Ed.), *The new cognitive neurosciences* (2nd ed., pp. 965–974). Cambridge, MA: MIT Press.

Farah, M. J., Hammond, K. M., Levine, D. N., & Calvanio, R. (1988a). Visual and spatial mental imagery: Dissociable systems of representation. *Cognitive Psychology, 20*(4), 439–462.

Farah, M. J., Levinson, K. L., & Klein, K. L. (1995). Face perception and within category discrimination in prosopagnosia. *Neuropsychologia, 33,* 661–674.

Farah, M. J., Peronnet, F., Gonon, M. A., & Giard, M. H. (1988b). Electrophysiological evidence for a shared representational medium for visual images and visual percepts. *Journal of Experimental Psychology: General, 117*(3), 248–257.

Farah, M. J., & Ratcliff, G. (Eds.) (1994). *The neural bases of mental imagery.* Hillsdale, NJ: Erlbaum.

Farah, M. J., Wilson, K. D., Drain, H. M., & Tanaka, J. R. (1995). The inverted face inversion effect in prosopagnosia: Evidence for mandatory, face-specific, perceptual mechanisms. *Vision Research, 35,* 2089–2093.

Farah, M. J., Wilson, K. D., Drain, M., & Tanaka, J. (1998). What is "special" about face perception? *Psychological Review, 105,* 482–498.

Farrington-Darby, T., Wilson, J. R., Norris, B. J., & Clarke, T. (2006). A naturalistic study of railway controllers. *Ergonomics, 49*(12–13), 1370–1394.

Farthing, G. W. (1992). *The psychology of consciousness.* Englewood Cliffs, NJ: Prentice-Hall.

Farthing, G. W. (2000). Consciousness and unconsciousness: An overview. In A. E. Kazdin (Ed.), *Encyclopedia of psychology* (Vol. 2, pp. 268–272). Washington, DC: American Psychological Association.

Fawcett, J. W., Rosser, A. E., & Dunnett, S. B. (2001). *Brain damage, brain repair.* New York: Oxford University Press.

Feinberg, T. E., Schindler, R. J., Ochoa, E., Kwan, P. C., & Farah, M. H. (1994). Associative visual agnosia and alexia without prosopagnosia. *Cortex, 30*(3), 395–412.

Feist, G. J. (1998). A meta-analysis of personality in scientific and artistic creativity. *Personality and Social Psychology Review, 2,* 290–309.

Feist, G. J. (1999). The influence of personality on artistic and scientific creativity. In R. J. Sternberg (Ed.), *Handbook of creativity* (pp. 273–296). New York: Cambridge University Press.

Feldman, J. A., & Shastri, L. (2003). Connectionism. In L. Nadel (Ed.), *Encyclopedia of cognitive science* (Vol. 1, pp. 680–687). London: Nature Publishing Group.

Fernald, A. (1985). Four-month-old infants prefer to listen to motherese. *Infant Behavior and Development, 8,* 118–195.

Fernald, A., Taeschner, T., Dunn, J., Papousek, M., De Boysson-Bardies, B., & Fukui, I. (1989). A cross-cultural study of prosodic modification in mothers' and fathers' speech to preverbal infants. *Journal of Child Language, 16,* 477–501.

Feuerstein, R. (1980). *Instrumental enrichment: An intervention program for cognitive modifiability.* Baltimore: University Park Press.

Feynman, R. (1997). *Surely you're joking, Mr. Feynman: Adventures of a curious character.* New York: Norton.

Fiedler, K. (1988). Emotional mood, cognitive style, and behavior regulation. In K. Fiedler & J. Forgas (Eds.), *Affect, cognition, and social behavior* (pp. 100–119). Toronto: Hogrefe International.

Field, T. (1978). Interaction behaviors of primary versus secondary caregiver fathers. *Developmental Psychology, 14,* 183–184.

Finke, R. A. (1989). *Principles of mental imagery.* Cambridge, MA: MIT Press.

Finke, R. A. (1995). Creative insight and preinventive forms. In R. J. Sternberg & J. E. Davidson (Eds.), *The nature of insight* (pp. 255–280). Cambridge, MA: MIT Press.

Finke, R. A., Pinker, S., & Farah, M. J. (1989). Reinterpreting visual patterns in mental imagery. *Cognitive Science, 13*(3), 252–257.

Fiorio, M., Tinazzi, M., & Aglioti, S. M. (2006). Selective impairment of hand mental rotation in patients with focal hand dystonia. *Brain: A Journal of Neurology, 129*(1), 47–54.

Fiorio, M., Tinazzi, M., Ionta, S., Fiaschi, A., Moretto, G., Edwards, M. J., et al. (2007). Mental rotation of body parts and noncorporeal objects in patients with idiopathic cervical dystonia. *Neuropsychologia, 45*(10), 2346–2354.

Fischhoff, B. (1982). For those condemned to study the past: Heuristics and biases in hindsight. In D. Kahneman, P. Slovic, & A. Tversky (Eds.), *Judgment under uncertainty: Heuristics and biases* (pp. 335–351). Cambridge, UK: Cambridge University Press.

Fischhoff, B. (1988). Judgment and decision making. In R. J. Sternberg & E. E. Smith (Eds.), *The psychology of human thought* (pp. 153–187). New York: Cambridge University Press.

Fischhoff, B. (1999). Judgment heuristics. In R. A. Wilson & F. C. Keil (Eds.), *The MIT encyclopedia of the cognitive sciences* (pp. 423–425). Cambridge, MA: MIT Press.

Fischhoff, B., Slovic, P., & Lichtenstein, S. (1977). Knowing with certainty: The appropriateness of extreme confidence. *Journal of Experimental Psychology: Human Perception and Performance, 3*, 552–564.

Fischman, J. (2004, August 2). Vanishing minds: New research is helping Alzheimer's patients cope-and hope. *U.S. News & World Report, 137*, 3, 74–78.

Fishbein, D. H., Eldereth, D. L., Hyde, C., Matochik, J. A., London, E. D., Contoreggi, C., et al. (2005). Risky decision making and the anterior cingulate cortex in abstinent drug abusers and nonusers. *Brain Research Cognitive Brain Research, 23*(1), 119–136.

Fisher, R. P., & Craik, F. I. M. (1977). Interaction between encoding and retrieval operations in cued recall. *Journal of Experimental Psychology: Human Learning & Memory, 3*(6), 701–711.

Fisher, R. P., & Craik, F. I. M. (1980). The effects of elaboration on recognition memory. *Memory & Cognition, 8*(5), 400–404.

Fisk, A. D., & Schneider, W. (1981). Control and automatic processing during tasks requiring sustained attention: A new approach to vigilance. *Human Factors, 23*, 737–750.

Fivush, R., & Hamond, N. R. (1991). Autobiographical memory across the preschool years: Toward reconceptualizing childhood memory. In R. Fivush & N. R. Hamond (Eds.), *Knowing and remembering in young children* (pp. 223–248). New York: Cambridge University Press.

Flavell, J. H., Flavell, E. R., & Green, F. L. (1983). Development of the appearance–reality distinction. *Cognitive Psychology, 15*, 95–120.

Flavell, J. H., & Wellman, H. M. (1977). Metamemory. In R. V. Kail, Jr., & J. W. Hagen (Eds.), *Perspectives on the development of memory and cognition* (pp. 3–33). Hillsdale, NJ: Erlbaum.

Fleck, J. I. (2007). Working memory demands in insight versus analytic problem solving. *European Journal of Cognitive Psychology, 19*(2), 187–212.

Fleck, M. S., Daselaar, S. M., Dobbins, I. G., & Cabeza, R. (2006). Role of prefrontal and anterior cingulate regions in decision-making processes shared by memory and nonmemory tasks. *Cerebral Cortex 16*(11), 1623–1630.

Flege, J. (1991). The interlingual identification of Spanish and English vowels: Orthographic evidence. *Quarterly Journal of Experimental Psychology: Human Experimental Psychology, 43*, 701–731.

Flynn, J. R. (1984). The mean IQ of Americans: massive gains 1932 to 1978. *Psychological Bulletin, 95*, 29–51.

Flynn, J. R. (1987). Massive IQ gains in fourteen nations: What IQ tests really measure. *Psychological Bulletin, 95*, 29–51.

Fodor, J. A. (1973). *The modularity of mind.* Cambridge, MA: MIT Press.

Fodor, J. A. (1975). *The language of thought.* New York: Crowell.

Fodor, J. A. (1983). *The modularity of mind.* Cambridge, MA: MIT Press.

Fodor, J. A. (1994). Concepts-a pot-boiler. *Cognition, 50*, 95–113.

Fodor, J. A. (1997). Do we have it in us? (Review of Elman et al., *Rethinking innateness*). *Times Literary Supplement*, May 16, pp. 3–4.

Fodor, J., & Pylyshyn, Z. (1988). Connectionism and cognitive architecture: A critical analysis. *Cognition, 28*, 3–71.

Fogel, A. (1991). *Infancy: Infant, family, and society* (2nd ed.). St. Paul, MN: West.

Fombonne, E. (2003). The prevalence of autism. *Journal of the American Medical Association, 289*(1), 87–89.

Foulke, E., & Sticht, T. (1969). Review of research on the intelligibility and comprehension of accelerated speech. *Psychological Bulletin, 72*, 50–62.

Frackowiak, R. S. J., Friston, K. J., Frith, C. D., Dolan, R. J., & Mazziotta, J. C. (Eds.). (1997). *Human brain function.* San Diego: Academic Press USA.

Franklin, N., & Tversky, B. (1990). Searching imagined environments. *Journal of Experimental Psychology: General, 119*(1), 63–76.

Franks, J. J., & Bransford, J. D. (1971). Abstraction of visual patterns. *Journal of Experimental Psychology, 90*(1), 65–74.

Frantz, R. (2003). Herbert Simon. Artificial intelligence as a framework for understanding intuition. *Journal of Economic Psychology, 24*, 265–277.

Frean, M. (2003). Connectionist architectures: Optimization. In L. Nadel (Ed.), *Encyclopedia of cognitive science* (Vol. 1, pp. 691–697). London, England: Nature Publishing Group.

Frensch, P. A., & Sternberg, R. J. (1989). Expertise and intelligent thinking: When is it worse to know better? In R. J. Sternberg (Ed.), *Advances in the psychology of human intelligence* (Vol. 5, pp. 157–188). Hillsdale, NJ: Erlbaum.

Freud, S. (1953). *An aphasia.* London: Imago.

Friederici, A. D., Gunter, T. C., Hahne, A., & Mauth, K. (2004). The relative riming of syntactic and semantic processes in sentence comprehension. *Cognitive Neuroscience and Neuropsychology, 15*(1), 165–169.

Fromkin, V. A. (1973). *Speech errors as linguistic evidence.* The Hague, Netherlands: Mouton.

Fromkin, V. A., Krashen, S., Curtiss, S., Rigler, D., & Rigler, M. (1974). The development of language in Genie: A case of language acquisition beyond the "critical period," *Brain and Language, 1*(1), 81–107.

Fromkin, V. A., & Rodman, R. (1988). *An introduction to language* (4th ed.). Fort Worth, TX: Holt, Rinehart and Winston.

Frost, N. (1972). Encoding and retrieval in visual memory tasks. *Journal of Experimental Psychology, 95*, 317–326.

Funk, M., Brugger, P., & Wilkening, F. (2005). Motor processes in children's imagery: Developmental theory. *Psychological Review, 111*(2), 486–511.

Funke, J. (1991). Solving complex problems: Exploration and control of complex social systems. In R. J. Sternberg & P. A. Frensch (Eds.), *Complex problem solving: Principles and mechanisms* (pp. 159–183). Hillsdale, NJ: Erlbaum.

Gabel, R. S., Dolan, S. L., & Cerdin, J. L. (2005). Emotional intelligence as predictor of cultural adjustment for success in global assignments. *Career Development International, 10*(5), 375–395.

Gabrieli, J. D. E., Desmond, J. E., Demb, J. B., Wagner, A. D., Stone, M. V., Vaidya, C. J., et al. (1996). Functional magnetic resonance imaging of semantic memory processes in the frontal lobes. *Psychological Science, 7*, 278–283.

Gabrieli, J. D. E., Stebbins, G. T., Singh, J., Willingham, D. B., & Goetz, C. G. (1997). Intact mirror-tracing and impaired rotary-pursuit skill learning in patients with Huntington's disease: Evidence for dissociable memory systems in skill learning. *Neuropsychology, 11*(2), 272–281.

Gagliardo, A., Ioale, P., Odetti, F., Bingman, V. P., Siegel, J. J., & Vallortigara, G. (2001). Hippocampus and homing in pigeons: Left and right hemispheric differences in navigational map learning. *European Journal of Neuroscience, 13*(8), 1617–1624.

Gaillard, W. D., Balsamo, L., Xu, B., McKinney, C., Papero, P. H., Weinstein, S., et al. (2004). FMRI language task panel improves determination of language dominance. *Neurology, 63*, 1403–1408.

Gaillard, W. D., Sachs, B. C., Whitnah, J. R., Ahmad, Z., Balsamo, L. M., Petrella, J. R., et al. (2003). Developmental aspects of language processing: fMRI of verbal fluency in children and adults. *Human Brain Mapping, 18*(3), 176–185.

Gais, S., & Born, J. (2004). Low acetylcholine during slow-wave sleep is critical for declarative memory consolidation. *Neurosceince, 101*(7), 2140–2144.

Galaburda, A. M. (1999). Dyslexia. In R. A. Wilson & F. C. Keil (Eds.), *The MIT encyclopedia of the cognitive sciences* (pp. 249–251). Cambridge, MA: MIT Press.

Galaburda, A. M., & Rosen, G. D. (2003). Brain asymmetry. In L. Nadel (Ed.), *Encyclopedia of cognitive science* (Vol. 1, pp. 406–410). London: Nature Publishing Group.

Galanter, C. A., & Patel, V. L. (2005). Medical decision making: A selective review for child psychiatrists and psychologists. *Journal of Child Psychology and Psychiatry 46*(7), 675–689.

Galantucci, B., Fowler, C. A., & Turvey, M. T. (2006). The motor theory of speech perception reviewed. *Psychonomic Bulletin & Review, 13*(3), 361–377.

Gallace, A., Auvray, M., Tan, H. Z., & Spence, C. (2006). When visual transients impair tactile change detection: A novel case of crossmodal change blindness? *Neuroscience Letters, 398*, 280–285.

Galotti, K. M., Baron, J., & Sabini, J. P. (1986). Individual differences in syllogistic reasoning: Deduction rules or mental models? *Journal of Experimental Psychology: General, 115*(1), 16–25.

Galton, F. (1883). *Inquiry into human faculty and its development.* London: Macmillan.

Gamble, J. (2001). Humor in apes. *Humor, 14*(2), 163–179.

Ganel, T., & Goodale, M. A. (2003). Visual control of action but not perception requires analytical processing of object shape. *Nature, 426*, 664–667.

Ganel, T., Valyear, K. F., Goshen-Gottstein, Y., & Goodale, M. A. (2005). The involvement of the "fusiform face area" in processing facial expression. *Neuropsychologia, 43*(11), 1645–1654.

Ganellen, R. J., & Carver, C. S. (1985). Why does self-reference promote incidental encoding? *Journal of Experimental Social Psychology, 21*(3), 284–300.

Ganis, G, Thomspson, W. L., & Kosslyn, S. M. (2004). Brain areas underlying visual mental imagery and visual perception: An fMRI study. *Cognitive Brain Research, 20*, 226–241.

Garcia-Madruga, J. A., Moreno, S., Carriedo, N., & Gutierrez, F. (2000). Task, premise order, and strategies in Rips's conjunction-disjunction and conditionals problems. In W. Schaeken & G. De Vooght (Eds.), *Deductive reasoning and strategies* (pp. 49–71). Mahwah, NJ: Erlbaum.

Gardner, H. (1983). *Frames of mind: The theory of multiple intelligences.* New York: Basic Books.

Gardner, H. (1985). *The mind's new science: A history of the cognitive revolution.* New York: Basic Books.

Gardner, H. (1993a). *Creating minds: An anatomy of creativity seen through the lives of Freud, Einstein, Picasso, Stravinsky, Eliot, Graham, and Gandhi.* New York: HarperCollins.

Gardner, H. (1993b). *Multiple intelligences: The theory in practice.* New York: Basic Books.

Gardner, H. (1999). *Intelligence reframed.* New York: Basic Books.

Gardner, H. (2006). *Multiple intelligences: New horizons.* New York: Basic Books.

Gardner, H., Krechevsky, M. Sternberg, R. J., & Okagaki, L. (1994). Intelligence in context: Enhancing students' practical intelligence for school. In K. McGilly (Ed.), *Classroom lessons: Integrating cog-*

nitive theory and classroom practice (pp. 105–127). Cambridge, MA: Bradford Books.

Garlick, D. (2002). Understanding the nature of the general factor of intelligence: The role of individual differences in neural plasticity as an explanatory mechanism. *Psychological Review, 109*(1), 116–136.

Garnham, A. (1987). *Mental models as representations of discourse and text.* Chichester, UK: Ellis Horwood.

Garnham, A., & Oakhill, J. V. (1996). The mental models theory of language comprehension. In B. K. Britton & A. C. Graesser (Eds.), *Models of understanding text* (pp. 313–339). Hillsdale, NJ: Erlbaum.

Garrett, M. F. (1980). Levels of processing in sentence production. In B. Butterworth (Ed.), *Language production: Vol. 1. Speech and talk* (pp. 177–210). London: Academic Press.

Garrett, M. F. (1992). Disorders of lexical selection. *Cognition, 42*(1–3), 143–180.

Garrett, M. F. (2003). Language and brain. In L. Nadel (Ed.), *Encyclopedia of cognitive science* (Vol. 2, pp. 707–717). London: Nature Group Press.

Garrod, S., & Daneman, M. (2003). Reading, psychology of. In L. Nadel (Ed.), *Encyclopedia of cognitive science* (Vol. 3, pp. 848–854). London: Nature Publishing Group.

Garry, M., & Loftus, E. F. (1994). Pseudomemories without hypnosis. *International Journal of Clinical and Experimental Hypnosis, 42*, 363–378.

Garry, M., Manning, C. G., Loftus, E. F., & Sherman, S. J. (1996). Imagination inflation: Imaging a childhood event inflates confidence that it occurred. *Psychonomic Bulletin & Review, 3*, 208–214.

Gasser, M. (2003). Language learning, computational models of. In L. Nadel (Ed.), *Encyclopedia of cognitive science* (Vol. 2, pp. 747–753). London: Nature Group Press.

Gauthier, I., Curran, T., Curby, K. M., & Collins, D. (2003). Perceptual interference supports a non-modular account of face processing. *Nature Neuroscience, 6*, 428–432.

Gauthier, I., Skudlarski, P., Gore, J. C., & Anderson, A. W. (2000). Expertise for cars and birds recruits brain areas involved in face recognition. *Nature Neuroscience, 3*, 191–197.

Gauthier, I., Tarr, M. J., Anderson, A. W., Skudlarski, P., Gore, J. C. (1999). Activation of the middle fusiform "face area" increases with expertise in recognizing novel objects. *Nature Neuroscience, 2*(6), 568–573.

Gazzaniga, M. S. (1985). *The social brain: Discovering the networks of the mind.* New York: Basic Books.

Gazzaniga, M. S. (1995). Principles of human brain organization derived from split-brain studies. *Neuron, 14*, 217–228.

Gazzaniga, M. S. (Ed.). (1995b). *The cognitive neurosciences.* Cambridge, MA: MIT Press.

Gazzaniga, M. S. (Ed.). (2000). *The new cognitive neurosciences* (2nd ed.). Cambridge, MA: MIT Press.

Gazzaniga, M. S., & Hutsler, J. J. (1999). Hemispheric specialization. In R. A. Wilson & F. C. Keil (Eds.), *The MIT encyclopedia of the cognitive sciences* (pp. 369–372). Cambridge, MA: MIT Press.

Gazzaniga, M. S., Ivry, R. B., & Mangun, G. (1998). *Cognitive neuroscience: The biology of the mind.* New York: Norton.

Gazzaniga, M. S., Ivry, R. B., & Mangun, G. R. (2002). *Cognitive neuroscience: The biology of the mind* (2nd ed.). New York: Norton.

Gazzaniga, M. S., & LeDoux, J. E. (1978). *The integrated mind.* New York: Plenum.

Gazzaniga, M. S., & Sperry, R. W. (1967). Language after section of the cerebral commissures. *Brain*, 90(1), 131–148.

Gelman, S. A. (1985). Children's inductive inferences from natural kind and artifact categories. (Doctoral dissertation, Stanford University, 1984). *Dissertation Abstracts International*, 45(10B), 3351–3352.

Gelman, S. A. (1989). Children's use of categories to guide biological inferences. *Human Development*, 32(2), 65–71.

Gelman, S. A. (2003). *The essential child: Origins of essentialism in everyday thought*. New York: Oxford University Press.

Gelman, S. A. (2004). Psychological essentialism in children. *Trends in Cognitive Sciences*, 8, 404–409.

Gelman, S. A., & Kremer, K. E. (1991). Understanding natural causes: Children's explanations of how objects and their properties originate. *Child Development*, 62(2), 396–414.

Gelman, S. A., & Markman, E. M. (1986). Categories and induction in young children. *Cognition*, 23, 183–209.

Gelman, S. A., & Markman, E. M. (1987). Young children's inductions from natural kinds: The role of categories and appearances. *Child Development*, 58(6), 1532–1541.

Gelman, S. A., & O'Reilly, A. W. (1988). Children's inductive inferences within superordinate categories: The role of language and category structure. *Child Development*, 59(4), 876–887.

Gelman, S. A., & Wellman, H. M. (1991). Insides and essence: Early understandings of the non-obvious. *Cognition*, 38(3), 213–244.

Gentile, J. R. (2000). Learning, transfer of. In A. E. Kazdin (Ed.), *Encyclopedia of psychology* (Vol. 5, pp. 13–16). Washington, DC: American Psychological Association.

Gentner, D. (1983). Structure-mapping: A theoretical framework for analogy. *Cognitive Science*, 7, 155–170.

Gentner, D. (2000). Analogy. In R. A. Wilson & F. C. Keil (Eds.), *The MIT encyclopedia of the cognitive sciences* (pp. 17–20). Cambridge, MA: MIT Press.

Gentner, D., & Gentner, D. R. (1983). Flowing waters or teeming crowds: Mental models of electricity. In D. Gentner & A. Stevens (Eds.), *Mental models*. Hillsdale, NJ: Erlbaum.

Gentner, D., & Markman, A. B. (1997). Structure-mapping in analogy and similarity. *American Psychologist*, 52, 45–56.

Georgopoulos, A. P., Lurito, J. T., Petrides, M., & Schwartz, A. B., Massey, J. T. (1989). Mental rotation of the neuronal population vector. *Science*, 243(4888), 234–236.

Georgopoulos, A. P., & Pellizzer, G. (1995). The mental and the neural: Psychological and neural studies of mental rotation and memory scanning. *Neuropsychologia*, 33, 1531–1547.

German, T. P., & Barrett, H. C. (2005). Functional fixedness in a technologically sparse culture. *Psychological Science*, 16(1), 1–5.

Gernsbacher, M. A., & Kaschak, M. P. (2003a). Language comprehension. In L. Nadel (Ed.), *Encyclopedia of cognitive science* (Vol. 2, pp. 723–726). London: Nature Group Press.

Gernsbacher, M. A., & Kaschak, M. P. (2003b). Psycholinguistics. In L. Nadel (Ed.), *Encyclopedia of cognitive science* (Vol. 3, pp. 783–786). London: Nature Group Press.

Gerrig, R. J., & Banaji, M. R. (1994). Language and thought. In R. J. Sternberg (Ed.), *Thinking and problem solving* (pp. 235–261). New York: Academic Press.

Gerrig, R. J., & Healy, A. F. (1983). Dual processes in metaphor understanding: Comprehension and appreciation. *Journal of Experimental Psychology: Learning, Memory, & Cognition*, 9, 667–675.

Geschwind, N. (1970). The organization of language and the brain. *Science*, 170, 940–944.

Gibbs, R. W. (1979). Contextual effects in understanding indirect requests. *Discourse Processes*, 2, 1–10.

Gibbs, R. W. (1986). What makes some indirect speech acts conventional? *Journal of Memory and Language*, 25, 181–196.

Gibson, E. J. (1991). The ecological approach: A foundation for environmental psychology. In R. M. Downs, L. S. Liben, & D. S. Palermo (Eds.), *Visions of aesthetics, the environment & development: The legacy of Joachim F. Wohlwill* (pp. 87–111). Hillsdale, NJ: Erlbaum.

Gibson, E. J. (1992). How to think about perceptual learning: Twenty-five years later. In H. L. Pick, Jr., P. W. van den Broek, & D. C. Knill (Eds.), *Cognition: Conceptual and methodological issues* (pp. 215–237). Washington, DC: American Psychological Association.

Gibson, J. J. (1950). *The perception of the visual world*. Boston: Houghton Mifflin.

Gibson, J. J. (1966). *The senses considered as perceptual systems*. New York: Houghton Mifflin.

Gibson, J. J. (1979). *The ecological approach to visual perception*. Boston: Houghton Mifflin.

Gibson, J. J. (1994). The visual perception of objective motion and subjective movement. *Psychological Review*, 101(2), 318–323. (Original work published 1954)

Gick, M. L., & Holyoak, K. J. (1980). Analogical problem solving. *Cognitive Psychology*, 12, 306–355.

Gick, M. L., & Holyoak, K. J. (1983). Schema induction and analogical transfer. *Cognitive Psychology*, 15, 1–38.

Gigerenzer, G. (1996). On narrow norms and vague heuristics: A reply to Kahneman and Tversky. *Psychological Review*, 103, 592–596.

Gigerenzer, G., & Goldstein, D. G. (1996). Reasoning the fast and frugal way: Models of bounded rationality. *Psychological Review*, 103, 650–669.

Gigerenzer, G., Todd, P. M., & the ABC Research Group (1999). *Simple heuristics that make us smart*. New York: Oxford University Press.

Gilbert, J. A. E., & Fisher, R. P. (2006). The effects of varied retrieval cues on reminiscence in eyewitness memory. *Applied Cognitive Psychology*, 20(6), 723–739.

Gilboa, A., Winocur, G., Rosenbaum, S., Poreh, A., Gao, F., Black, S., et al. (2006). Hippocampal contributions to recollection in retrograde and anterograde amnesia. *Hippocampus*, 16(11), 966–980.

Gilger, J. W. (1996). How can behavioral genetic research help us understand language development and disorders? In M. L. Rice (Ed.), *Toward a genetics of language* (pp. 77–110). Mahwah, NJ: Erlbaum.

Gilhooly, K. J. (2004). Working memory and reasoning. In J. P. Leighton & R. J. Sternberg (Eds.), *The nature of reasoning* (pp. 49–77). New York: Cambridge University Press.

Gilhooly, K. J., Logie, R. H., Wetherick, N. E., & Wynn, V. (1993). Working memory and strategies in syllogistic reasoning tasks. *Memory and Cognition*, 21, 115–124.

Gillam, B. (2000). Perceptual constancies. In A. E. Kazdin (Ed.), *Encyclopedia of psychology* (Vol. 6, pp. 89–93). Washington, DC: American Psychological Association.

Gilovich, T., Vallone, R., & Tversky, A. (1985). The hot hand in basketball: On the misperception of random sequences. *Cognitive Psychology*, 17(3), 295–314.

Girelli, L., Sandrini, M., Cappa, S., & Butterworth, B. (2001). Number-Stroop performance in normal aging and Alzheimer's-type dementia. *Brain Cognition*, 46(1–2), 144–149.

Girotto, V. (2004). Task understanding. In J. P. Leighton & R. J. Sternberg (Eds.), *The nature of reasoning* (pp. 103–125). New York: Cambridge University Press.

Givens, D. G. (2002). *The nonverbal dictionary of gestures, signs & body language cues*. Spokane, WA: Center for Nonverbal Studies Press.

Gladwin, T. (1970). *East is a big bird*. Cambridge, MA: Harvard University Press.

Glaser, R., & Chi, M. T. H. (1988). Overview. In M. T. H. Chi, R. Glaser, & M. Farr (Eds.), *The nature of expertise* (pp. xv–xxxvi). Hillsdale, NJ: Erlbaum.

Glenberg, A. M. (1977). Influences of retrieval processes on the spacing effect in free recall. *Journal of Experimental Psychology: Human Learning & Memory, 3*(3), 282–294.

Glenberg, A. M. (1979). Component-levels theory of the effects of spacing of repetitions on recall and recognition. *Memory & Cognition, 7*(2), 95–112.

Glenberg, A. M. (1997). What memory is for. *Behavioral and Brain Sciences, 20*, 1–55.

Glenberg, A. M., Meyer, M., & Lindem, K. (1987). Mental models contribute to foregrounding during text comprehension. *Journal of Memory & Language, 26*(1), 69–83.

Gloor, P. (1997). *The temporal lobe and limbic system*. New York: Oxford University Press.

Gluck, M. A. (Ed.) (1996). Computational models of hippocampal function in memory. Special issue of *Hippocampus, 6*, 6.

Glucksberg, S. (1988). Language and thought. In R. J. Sternberg & E. E. Smith (Eds.), *The psychology of human thought* (pp. 214–241). New York: Cambridge University Press.

Glucksberg, S., & Danks, J. H. (1975). *Experimental psycholinguistics*. Hillsdale, NJ: Erlbaum.

Glucksberg, S., & Keysar, B. (1990). Understanding metaphorical comparisons: Beyond similarity. *Psychological Review, 97*(1), 3–18.

Gobet, F., & Jackson, S. (2002). In search of templates. *Cognitive Systems Research, 3*(1), 35–44.

Gobet, F., & Simon, H. A. (1996a). Recall of random and distorted chess positions: Implications for the theory of expertise. *Memory and Cognition, 24*, 493–503.

Gobet, F., & Simon, H. A. (1996b). Roles of recognition processes and look-ahead search in time-constrained expert problem solving: Evidence from grand-master-level chess. *Psychological Science, 7*, 52–55.

Gobet, F., & Simon, H. A. (1996c). Templates in chess memory: A mechanism for recalling several boards. *Cognitive Psychology, 31*, 1–40.

Godbout, L., Cloutier, P., Bouchard, C., Braun, C. M. J., & Gagnon, S. (2004). Script generation following frontal and parietal lesions. *Journal of Clinical and Experimental Neuropsychology, 26*(7), 857–873.

Goddard, H. H. (1917). Mental tests and immigrants. *Journal of Delinquency, 2*, 243–277.

Godden, D. R., & Baddeley, A. D. (1975). Context-dependent memory in two natural environments: On land and underwater. *British Journal of Psychology, 66*, 325–331.

Goff, L. M., & Roediger, H. L. (1998). Imagination inflation for action events: Repeated imaginings lead to illusory recollections. *Memory and Cognition, 26*, 20–33.

Goldstein, D. G., & Gigerenzer, G. (2002). Models of ecological rationality: The recognition heuristic. *Psychological Review, 109*(1), 75–90.

Goldstone, R. L. (2003). Perceptual organizatoin in vision: Behavioral and neural perspectives. In R. Kimchi & M. Behrmann (Eds.), *Perceptual organization in vision: Behavioral and neural perspectives* (pp. 233–280). Mahwah, NJ: Erlbaum.

Goleman, D. (1995). *Emotional intelligence*. New York: Bantam.

Goleman, D. (1998). *Working with emotional intelligence*. New York: Bantam.

Goleman, D. (2007). *Social intelligence*. New York: Bantam.

Gollan, T. H., & Brown, A. S. (2006). From tip-of-the-tongue (TOT) data to theoretical implications in two steps: When more TOTs means better retrieval. *Journal of Experimental Psychology: General, 135*(3), 462–483.

Goodale, M. A. (2000). Perception and action. In A. E. Kazdin (Ed.), *Encyclopedia of psychology* (Vol. 6, pp. 86–89). Washington, DC: American Psychological Association.

Goodale, M. A. (2000a). Perception and action. In A. E. Kazdin (Ed.), *Encyclopedia of psychology* (Vol. 6, pp. 86–89). Washington, DC: American Psychological Association.

Goodale, M. A. (2000b). Perception and action in the human visual system. In M. Gazzaniga (Ed.), *The new cognitive neurosciences* (pp. 365–378). Cambridge, MA: MIT Press.

Goodale, M. A., & Milner, A. D. (2004). *Sight unseen: An exploration of conscious and unconscious vision*. New York: Oxford University Press.

Goodale, M. A., & Westwood, D. A. (2004). An evolving view of duplex vision: Separate but interacting cortical pathways for perception and action. *Current Opinion in Neurobiology, 14*, 203–211.

Goodman, N. (1983). *Fact, fiction, and forecast* (4th ed). Cambridge, MA: Harvard University Press.

Gopnik, A., & Choi, S. (1995). Names, relational words, and cognitive development in English and Korean speakers: Nouns are not always learned before verbs. In M. Tomasello & W. E. Merriman (Eds.), *Beyond names for things: Young children's acquisition of verbs* (pp. 83–90). Hillsdale, NJ: Erlbaum.

Gopnik, A., Choi, S., & Baumberger, T. (1996). Cross-linguistic differences in early semantic and cognitive development. *Cognitive Development, 11*, 197–227.

Gordon, D., & Lakoff, G. (1971). Conversational postulates. In *Papers from the Seventh Regional Meeting, Chicago Linguistic Society* (pp. 63–84). Chicago: Chicago Linguistic Society.

Graesser, A. C., & Kreuz, R. J. (1993). A theory of inference generation during text comprehension. *Discourse Processes, 16*, 145–160.

Graf, P. (1990). Life-span changes in implicit and explicit memory. *Bulletin of the Psychonomic Society, 28*, 353–358.

Graf, P., Mandler, G., & Haden, P. E. (1982). Simulating amnesic symptoms in normal subjects. *Science, 218*(4578), 1243–1255.

Grainger, J., Bouttevin, S., Truc, C., Bastien, M., & Ziegler, J. (2003). Word superiority, pseudoword superiority, and learning to read: A comparison of dyslexic and normal readers. *Brain and Language, 87*(3), 432–440.

Grant, E. R., & Ceci, S. J. (2000). Memory: Constructive processes. In A. E. Kazdin (Ed.), *Encyclopedia of psychology* (Vol. 5, pp. 166–169). Washington, DC: American Psychological Association.

Gray, J. A., & Wedderburn, A. A. I. (1960). Grouping strategies with simultaneous stimuli. *Quarterly Journal of Experimental Psychology, 12*, 180–184.

Gray, J. R., Chabris, C. F., & Braver, T. S. (2003). Neural mechanisms of general fluid intelligence. *Nature Neuroscience Reviews, 6*, 316–322.

Gray, J. R., & Thompson, P. M. (2004). Neurobiology of intelligence: Science and ethics. *Nature Neuroscience Reviews, 5*, 471–482.

Grayson, D., & Coventry, L. (1998). The effects of visual proxemic information in video mediated communication. *SIGCHI, 30*(3). In Y. Wilks (Ed.), *Machine conversations.* Amsterdam, Netherlands: Kluwer.

Green, D. W. (1998). Mental control of the bilingual lexico-semantic system. *Bilingualism: Language and Cognition, 1*(2), 67–81.

Greenberg, R., & Underwood, B. J. (1950). Retention as a function of stage of practice. *Journal of Experimental Psychology, 40,* 452–457.

Greene, J. A., & Azevedo, R. (2007). Adolescents' use of self-regulatory processes and their relation to qualitative mental model shifts while using hypermedia. *Journal of Educational Computing Research, 36*(2), 125–148.

Greenfield, P. M. (1997). You can't take it with you: Why abilities assessments don't cross cultures. *American Psychologist, 52,* 1115–1124.

Greenfield, P. M., & Savage-Rumbaugh, S. (1990). Grammatical combination in Pan paniscus: Processes of learning and invention in the evolution and development of language. In S. Parker & K. Gibson (Eds.), *"Language" and intelligence in monkeys and apes: Comparative developmental perspectives.* New York: Cambridge University Press.

Greeno, J. G. (1974). Hobbits and orcs: Acquisition of a sequential concept. *Cognitive Psychology, 6,* 270–292.

Greeno, J. G., & Simon, H. A. (1988). Problem solving and reasoning. In R. C. Atkinson, R. Herrnstein, G. Lindzey, & R. D. Luce (Eds.), *Stevens' handbook of experimental psychology* (Rev. ed., pp. 589–672). New York: Wiley.

Greenwald, A. G., & Banaji, M. (1989). The self as a memory system: Powerful, but ordinary. *Journal of Personality & Social Psychology, 57*(1), 41–54.

Gregory, R. L. (1980). Perceptions as hypotheses. *Philosophical Transactions of the Royal Society of London, Series B, 290,* 181–197.

Grice, H. P. (1967). William James Lectures, Harvard University, published in part as "Logic and conversation." In P. Cole & J. L. Morgan (Eds.), *Syntax and semantics: Vol. 3. Speech acts* (pp. 41–58). New York: Seminar Press.

Griffin, D., & Tversky, A. (1992). The weighing of evidence and the determinants of confidence. *Cognitive Psychology, 24,* 411–435.

Griggs, R. A., & Cox, J. R. (1982). The elusive thematic-materials effect in Wason's selection task. *British Journal of Psychology, 73,* 407–420.

Griggs, R. A., & Cox, J. R. (1993). Permission schemas and the selection task. *The Quarterly Journal of Experimental Psychology, 46A*(4), 637–651.

Grigorenko, E. L. (2000). Heritability and intelligence. In R. J. Sternberg (Ed.), *Handbook of intelligence* (pp. 53–91). New York: Cambridge University Press.

Grigorenko, E. L., Geissler, P. W., Prince, R., Okatcha, F., Nokes, C., Kenny, D. A., et al. (2001). The organization of Luo conceptions of intelligence: A study of implicit theories in a Kenyan village. *International Journal of Behavioral Development, 25,* 367–378.

Grigorenko, E. L., Jarvin, L., & Sternberg, R. J. (2002). School-based tests of the triarchic theory of intelligence: Three settings, three samples, three syllabi. *Contemporary Educational Psychology, 27,* 167–208.

Grodzinsky, Y. (2003). Language disorders. In L. Nadel (Ed.), *Encyclopedia of cognitive science* (Vol. 2, pp. 740–746). London: Nature Group Press.

Grossman, L., & Eagle, M. (1970). Synonymity, antonymity, and association in false recognition responses. *Journal of Experimental Psychology, 83,* 244–248.

Grossmann, T., Striano, T., & Friederici, A. D. (2006). Crossmodal integration of emotional information from face and voice in the infant brain. *Developmental Science, 9*(3), 309–315.

Grosz, B. J., Pollack, M. E., & Sidner, C. L. (1989). Discourse. In M. I. Posner (Ed.), *Foundations of cognitive science* (pp. 437–468). Cambridge, MA: MIT Press.

Grotzer, T. A., & Perkins, D. N. (2000). Teaching intelligence: A performance conception. In R. J. Sternberg (Ed.), *Handbook of intelligence* (pp. 492–515). New York: Cambridge University Press.

Gruber, H. E. (1981). *Darwin on man: A psychological study of scientific creativity* (2nd ed.). Chicago: University of Chicago Press. (Original work published 1974.)

Gruber, H. E., & Davis, S. N. (1988). Inching our way up Mount Olympus: The evolving-systems approach to creative thinking. In R. J. Sternberg (Ed.), *The nature of creativity* (pp. 243–270). New York: Cambridge University Press.

Guilford, J. P. (1950). Creativity. *American Psychologist, 5*(9), 444–454.

Guilford, J. P. (1967). *The nature of human intelligence.* New York: McGraw Hill.

Guilford, J. P. (1982). Cognitive psychology's ambiguities: Some suggested remedies. *Psychological Review, 89,* 48–59.

Guilford, J. P. (1988). Some dangers in the structure-of-intellect model. *Educational & Psychological Measurement, 48,* 1–4.

Gunzelmann, G., & Anderson, J. R. (2003). Problem solving: Increased planning with practice. *Cognitive System Research, 4*(1), 57–76.

Haber, R. N. (1983). The impending demise of the icon: A critique of the concept of iconic storage in visual information processing. *Behavioral and Brain Sciences, 6*(1), 1–54.

Hagtvet, B. E. (2003). Listening comprehension and reading comprehension in poor decoders: Evidence for the importance of syntactic and semantic skills as well as phonological skills. *Reading and Writing: An Interdisciplinary Journal, 16*(6), 505–539.

Haier, R. J., Chueh, D., Touchette, P., Lott, I., Buchbaum, M. S., MacMillan, D., et al. (1995). Brain size and cerebral glucose metabolic rate in nonspecific mental retardation and Down syndrome. *Intelligence, 20,* 191–210.

Haier, R. J., & Jung, R. E. (2007). Beautiful minds (i.e., brains) and the neural basis of intelligence. *Behavioral and Brain Sciences, 30*(2), 174–178.

Haier, R. J., Siegel, B., Tang, C., Abel, L., & Buchsbaum, M. S. (1992). Intelligence and changes in regional cerebral glucose metabolic rate following learning. *Intelligence, 16*(3–4), 415–426.

Hakuta, K. (1986). *Mirror of language.* New York: Basic Books.

Halford, G. S. (1993). *Children's understanding: The development of mental models.* Hillsdale, NJ: Erlbaum.

Hall, E. T. (1966). *The hidden dimension: Man's use of space in public and private.* Garden City, N.Y.: Doubleday.

Hall, G. B. C., Szechtman, H., & Nahmias, C. (2003). Enhanced salience and emotion recognition in autism: A PET study. *American Journal of Psychiatry, 160,* 1439–1441.

Halpin, J. A., Puff, C. R., Mason, H. F., & Marston, S. P. (1984). Self-reference and incidental recall by children. *Bulletin of the Psychonomic Society, 22,* 87–89.

Hambrick, D. Z., & Engle, R. W. (2002). Effects of domain knowledge, working memory capacity, and age on cognitive performance: An investigation of the knowledge-is-power hypothesis. *Cognitive Psychology, 44*, 339–387.

Hambrick, D. Z., & Engle, R. W. (2003). The role of working memory in problem solving. In J. E. Davidson & R. J. Sternberg (Eds.), *The psychology of problem solving* (pp. 176–206). New York: Cambridge University Press.

Hambrick D. Z., Kane, M. J., & Engle, R. W. (2005). The role of working memory in higher-level cognition. In R. J. Sternberg & J. E. Pretz (Eds.), *Cognition and intelligence* (pp. 104–121). New York: Cambridge University Press.

Hamilton, D. L., & Lickel, B. (2000). Illusory correlation. In A. E. Kazdin (Ed.), *Encyclopedia of psychology* (Vol. 4, pp. 226–227). Washington, DC: American Psychological Association.

Hamm, A. O., Weike, A. I., Schupp, H. T., Treig, T., Dressel, A., & Kessler, C. (2003). Affective blindsight: Intact fear conditioning to a visual cue in a cortically blind patient. *Brain, 126*(2), 267–275.

Hampson, P. J., Marks, D. F., & Richardson, J. T. E. (1990). *Imagery: Current developments.* London: Routledge.

Hampton, J. A. (1995). Testing the prototype theory of concepts. *Journal of Memory and Language, 32*, 68–708.

Hampton, J. A. (1997a). Emergent attributes of combined concepts. In T. B. Ward, S. M. Smith, & J. Vaid (Eds.), *Conceptual structures and processes: Emergence, discovery, and change* (pp. 83–110). Washington, DC: American Psychological Association.

Hampton, J. A. (1997b). Psychological representations of concepts. In M. A. Conway & S. E. Gathercole (Eds.), *Cognitive models of memory* (pp. 81–110). Hove, UK: Psychology Press.

Hampton, J. A. (1999). Concepts. In R. A. Wilson & F. C. Keil (Eds.), *The MIT encyclopedia of the cognitive sciences* (pp. 177–179). Cambridge, MA: MIT Press.

Hancock, T. W., Hicks, J., Marsh, R. L., & Ritschel, L. (2003). Measuring the activation level of critical lures in the Deese-Roediger-McDermott paradigm. *American Journal of Psychology, 116*, 1–14.

Harber, K. D., & Jussim, L. (2005). Teacher expectations and self-fulfilling prophecies: Knowns and unknowns, resolved and unresolved controversies. *Personality and Social Psychological Review, 9*(2), 131–155.

Harnish, R. M. (2003). Speech acts. In L. Nadel (Ed.), *Encyclopedia of cognitive science* (Vol. 4, pp. 150–156). London: Nature Publishing Group.

Harris, C. L. (2003). Language and cognition. In L. Nadel (Ed.), *Encyclopedia of cognitive science* (Vol. 2, pp. 717–722). London: Nature Group Press.

Hasselmo, M. E. (2006). The role of acetylcholine in learning and memory. *Current Opinion in Neurobiology, 16*(6), 710–715.

Hausknecht, K. A., Acheson, A., Farrar, A. M., Kieres, A. K., Shen, R. Y., Richards, J. B., et al. (2005). Prenatal alcohol exposure causes attention deficits in male rats. *Behavioral Neuroscience, 119*(1), 302–310.

Haviland, S. E., & Clark, H. H. (1974). What's new? Acquiring new information as a process in comprehension. *Journal of Verbal Learning and Verbal Behavior, 13*, 512–521.

Haxby, J. V., Gobbini, M. I., Furye, M. L., Ishai, A., Schouten, J. L., & Pietrini, P. (2001). Distributed and overlapping representations of faces and objects in ventral temporal cortex. *Science, 293*, 2425–2430.

Haxby, J. V., Gobbini, M. I., & Montgomery, K. (2004). Spatial and temporal distribution of face and object representations in the human brain. In M. S. Gazzaniga (Ed.), *The cognitive neurosciences* (3rd ed., pp. 889–904). Cambridge, MA: MIT Press.

Haxby, J. V., Ungerleider, L. G., Horwitz, B., Maisog, J. M., Rappaport, S. L., & Grady, C. L. (1996). Face encoding and recognition in the human brain. *Proceedings of he National Academy of Sciences USA, 98*, 922–927.

Haxby, J. V., Ungerleider, L. G., Horwitz, B., Rapoport, S., & Grady, C. L. (1995). Hemispheric differences in neural systems for face working memory: A PET-rCBF study. *Human Brain Mapping, 3*, 68–82.

Hayes, J. R. (1989). *The complete problem solver* (2nd ed.). Hillsdale, NJ: Erlbaum.

He, Z., & Nakayama, K. (1992). Apparent motion determined by surface layout not by disparity or three-dimensional distance. *Nature, 367*(6459), 173–175.

Head injuries. Retrieved December 29, 2004, from http://kidshealth.org/parent/firstaid_safe/emergencies/head_injury.html

Heaps, C., & Nash, M. (1999). Individual differences in imagination inflation. *Psychonomic Bulletin & Review, 6*, 313–318.

Heaton, J. M. (1968). *The eye: Phenomenology and psychology of function and disorder.* London: Tavistock.

Hebb, D. O. (1949). *The organization of behavior: A neuropsychological theory.* New York: Wiley.

Hegarty, M. (1991). Knowledge and processes in mechanical problem solving. In R. J. Sternberg & P. A. Frensch (Eds.), *Complex problem solving: Principles and mechanisms* (pp. 159–183). Hillsdale, NJ: Erlbaum.

Hehir, A. (2006). The impact of analogical reasoning on US foreign policy towards Kosova. *Journal of Peace Research, 43*(1), 67–81.

Heindel, W. C., Butters, N., & Salmon, D. P. (1988). Impaired learning of a motor skill in patients with Huntington's disease. *Behavioral Neuroscience, 102*(1), 141–147.

Heiser, M., Iacoboni, M., Maeda, F., Marcus, J., & Mazziotta, J. C. (2003). The essential role of Broca's area in imitation. *European Journal of Neuroscience 17*(5), 1123–1128.

Hellige, J. B. (1993). *Hemispheric asymmetry.* Cambridge, MA: Harvard University Press.

Hellige, J. B. (1995). Hemispheric asymmetry for components of visual information processing. In R. J. Davidson & K. Hugdahl (Eds.), *Brain asymmetry.* Cambridge, MA: MIT Press.

Helms-Lorenz, M., Van de Vijver, F. J. R., & Poortinga, Y. H. (2003). Cross-cultural differences in cognitive performance and Spearman's hypothesis: g or c? *Intelligence, 31*, 9–29.

Henley, N. M. (1969). A psychological study of the semantics of animal terms. *Journal of Verbal Learning and Verbal Behavior, 8*, 176–184.

Hennessey, B. A., & Amabile, T. M. (1988). The conditions of creativity. In R. J. Sternberg (Ed.), *The nature of creativity* (pp. 11–38). New York: Cambridge University Press.

Henry, J. D., MacLeod, M. S., Phillips, L. H., & Crawford, J. R. (2004). A meta-analytic review of prospective memory and aging. *Psychology and Aging, 19*(1), 27–39.

Henry, L. A., & Gudjonsson, G. H. (2003). Eyewitness memory, suggestibility, and repeated recall sessions in children with mild and moderate intellectual disabilities. *Law and Human Behavior, 27*(5), 481–505.

Hernandez, A. E., Dapretto, M., Mazziotta, J., & Bookheimer, S. (2001). Language switching and language representation in Spanish-English bilinguals: An fMRI study. *Neuroimage, 14*, 510–520.

Herring, S. C., & Paolillo, J. C. (2006). Gender and genre variation in weblogs. *Journal of Sociolinguistics, 10*(4), 439–459.

Herrnstein, R., & Murray, C. (1994). *The bell curve: Intelligence and class structure in American life*. New York: Free Press.

Hertzog, C., Vernon, M. C., & Rypma, B. (1993). Age differences in mental rotation task performance: The influence of speed/accuracy tradeoffs. *Journal of Gerontology, 48*(3), 150–156.

Herz, R. S., & Engen, T. (1996). Odor memory: Review and analysis. *Psychonomic Bulletin and Review, 3*, 300–313.

Hesse, M. (1966). *Models and analogies in science*. South Bend, IN: University of Notre Dame Press.

Hickling, A. K., & Gelman, S. A. (1995). How does your garden grow? Early conceptualization of seeds and their place in the plant growth cycle. *Child Development, 66*, 856–867.

Hickok, G., & Poeppel, D. (2000). Towards a functional neuroanatomy of speech perception. *Trends in Cognitive Sciences, 4*, 131–138.

Hill, E. L. (2004). Evaluating the theory of executive dysfunction in autism. *Developmental Review, 24*, 189–233.

Hill, J. H. (1978). Apes and language. *Annual Review of Anthropology, 7*, 89–112.

Hillis, A. E., & Caramazza, A. (2003). Aphasia. In L. Nadel (Ed.), *Encyclopedia of cognitive science* (Vol. 1, pp. 175–184). London: Nature Publishing Group.

Hillix, W. A., & Rumbaugh, D. M. (2004). *Animal bodies, human minds: Ape, dolphin, and parrot language skills*. New York: Kluwer Academic/Plenum Publishers.

Himmelbach, M., & Karnath, H. O. (2005). Dorsal and ventral stream interaction: Contributions from optic ataxia. *Journal of Cognitive Neuroscience, 17*, 632–640.

Hinsz, V. B. (1990). Cognitive and consensus processes in group recognition memory. *Journal of Personality and Social Psychology, 59*(4), 705–718.

Hinton, G. E. (1979). Some demonstrations of the effects of structural descriptions in mental imagery. *Cognitive Science, 3*, 231–251.

Hinton, G. E. (Ed.). (1991). *Connectionist symbol processing*. Cambridge, MA: MIT Press.

Hinton, G. E., & Shallice, T. (1991). Lesioning an attractor network: Investigations of acquired dyslexia. *Psychological Review, 98*, 74–95.

Hintzman, D. L. (1978). *The psychology of learning and memory*. San Francisco: Freeman.

Hirsh-Pasek, K., Kemler Nelson, D. G., Jusczyk, P. W., Cassidy, K. W., Druss, B., & Kennedy, L. (1987). Clauses are perceptual units for young infants. *Cognition, 26*, 269–286.

Hirtle, S. C., & Jonides, J. (1985). Evidence of hierarchies in cognitive maps. *Memory & Cognition, 13*(3), 208–217.

Hirtle, S. C., & Mascolo, M. F. (1986). Effect of semantic clustering on the memory of spatial locations. *Journal of Experimental Psychology: Learning, Memory, & Cognition, 12*(2), 182–189.

Hochberg, J. (1978). *Perception* (2nd ed.). Englewood Cliffs, NJ: Prentice-Hall.

Hoff, E., & Naigles, L. (1999). *Fast mapping is only the beginning: Complete word learning requires multiple exposures*. Paper presented at the VIIIth International Congress for the Study of Child Language. July 12–16. San Sebastian, Spain.

Hoffding, H. (1891). *Outlines of psychology*. New York: Macmillan.

Hoffman, C., Lau, I., & Johnson, D. R. (1986). The linguistic relativity of person cognition: An English–Chinese comparison. *Journal of Personality and Social Psychology, 51*, 1097–1105.

Holland, J. H., Holyoak, K. J., Nisbett, R. E., & Thagard, P. R. (1986). *Induction processes of inference, learning, and discovery*. Cambridge, MA: MIT Press.

Holmes, D. (1991). The evidence for repression: an examination of sixty years of research. In J. L. Singer (Ed.), *Repression and dissociation: Implications for personality theory, psychopathology and health* (pp. 85–102). Chicago: University of Chicago Press.

Holt, J. (1964). *How children fail*. New York: Pitman.

Holyoak, K. J. (1984). Analogical thinking and human intelligence. In R. J. Sternberg (Ed.), *Advances in the psychology of human intelligence* (Vol. 2, pp. 199–230). Hillsdale, NJ: Erlbaum.

Holyoak, K. J. (1990). Problem solving. In D. N. Osherson & E. E. Smith (Eds.), *An invitation to cognitive science: Vol. 3. Thinking* (pp. 116–146). Cambridge, MA: MIT Press.

Holyoak, K. J., & Nisbett, R. E. (1988). Induction. In R. J. Sternberg & E. E. Smith (Eds.), *The psychology of human thought* (pp. 50–91). New York: Cambridge University Press.

Holyoak, K. J., & Thagard, P. (1995). *Mental leaps*. Cambridge, MA: MIT Press.

Homa, D. (1983). An assessment of two extraordinary speed-readers. *Bulletin of the Psychonomic Society, 21*, 115–118.

Honey, G., & Bullmore, E. (2004). Human pharmacological MRI. *Trends in Pharmacological Sciences, 2*(7), 366–374.

Hong, L., & Page, S. E. (2004). Groups of diverse problem solvers can outperform groups of high-ability problem solvers. *Proceedings of the National Academy of Sciences of the United States of America, 101*(46), 16385–16389.

Horn, J. L., & Cattell, R. B. (1966). Refinement and test of the theory of fluid and crystallized ability intelligences. *Journal of Educational Psychology, 57*, 253–270.

Horn, J. L., & Hofer, S. M. (1992). Major abilities and development in the adult period. In R. J. Sternberg & C. A. Berg (Eds.), *Intellectual development* (pp. 44–99). New York: Cambridge University Press.

Horn, J. L., & Knapp, J. R. (1973). On the subjective character of the empirical base of Guilford's structure-of-intellect model. *Psychological Bulletin, 80*, 33–43.

Hornung, O. P., Regen, F., Danker-Hopfe, H., Schredl, M., & Heuser, I. (2007). The relationship between REM sleep and memory consolidation in old age and effects of cholinergic medication. *Biological Psychiatry, 61*(6), 750–757.

Horwitz, B., Amunts, K., Bhattacharyya, R., Patkin, D., Jeffries, K., Zilles, K., et al. (2003). Activation of Broca's area during the production of spoken and signed language: A combined cytoarchitectonic mapping and PET analysis. *Neuropsychologia, 41*, 1868–1876.

Howard, M., Cowell, P., Boucher, P., Broks, P., Mayes, A., Farrant, A., et al. (2000). Convergent neuroanatomical and behavioural evidence of an amygdala hypothesis of autism. *Neuroreport 11*, 2931–2935.

Hu, M., & Nation, P. (2000). Unknown vocabulary density and reading comprehension. *Reading in a Foreign Language, 13*(1), 403–430.

Hubbard, T. L. (1995). Environmental invariants in the representation of motion: Implied and representational momentum, gravity, friction, and centripetal force. *Psychonomic Bulletin and Review, 2*, 322–338.

Hubel, D., & Wiesel, T. (1963). Receptive fields of cells in the striate cortex of very young, visually inexperienced kittens. *Journal of Neurophysiology, 26*, 994–1002.

Hubel, D., & Wiesel, T. (1968). Receptive fields and functional architecture of the monkey striate cortex. *Journal of Physiology, 195*, 215–243.

Hubel, D. H., & Wiesel, T. N. (1979). Brain mechanisms of vision. *Scientific American, 241*, 150–162.

Hughlings-Jackson, J. (1932). In J. Taylor (Ed.), *Selected writings of John Hughlings-Jackson*. London: Hodder and Stoughton. (Original work published 1866)

Hultsch, D. F., & Dixon, R. A. (1990). Learning and memory in aging. In J. E. Birren & K. W. Schaie (Eds.), *Handbook of the psychology of aging* (3rd ed., pp. 258–274). San Diego: Academic Press.

Humphreys, M., Bain, J. D., & Pike, R. (1989). Different ways to cue a coherent memory system: A theory for episodic, semantic, and procedural tasks. *Psychological Review, 96*(2), 208–233.

Hunt, E. B. (1975). *Artificial intelligence*. New York: Academic Press.

Hunt, E. B. (1978). Mechanics of verbal ability. *Psychological Review, 85*, 109–130.

Hunt, E. B. (1994). Problem solving. In R. J. Sternberg (Ed.), *Handbook of perception and cognition: Vol. 12. Thinking and problem solving* (pp. 215–232). New York: Academic Press.

Hunt, E. B. (2005). Information processing and intelligence. In R. J. Sternberg & J. E. Pretz (Eds.), *Cognition and intelligence* (pp. 1–25). New York: Cambridge University Press.

Hunt, E. B., & Banaji, M. (1988). The Whorfian hypothesis revisited: A cognitive science view of linguistic and cultural effects on thought. In J. W. Berry, S. H. Irvine, & E. Hunt (Eds.), *Indigenous cognition: Functioning in cultural context*. Dordrecht, The Netherlands: Martinus Nijhoff Publishers.

Hunt, E. B., & Lansman, M. (1982). Individual differences in attention. In R. J. Sternberg (Ed.), *Advances in the psychology of human intelligence* (Vol. 1, pp. 207–254). Hillsdale, NJ: Erlbaum.

Hunt, E. B., & Love, T. (1972). How good can memory be? In A. W. Melton & E. Martin (Eds.), *Coding processes in human memory*. Washington, DC: V. H. Winston & Sons.

Hunt, E. B., Lunneborg, C., & Lewis, J. (1975). What does it mean to be high verbal? *Cognitive Psychology, 7*, 194–227.

Huttenlocher, J. (1968). Constructing spatial images: A strategy in reasoning. *Psychological Review, 75*, 550–560.

Huttenlocher, J., Hedges, L. V., & Duncan, S. (1991). Categories and particulars: Prototype effects in spatial location. *Psychological Review, 98*(3), 352–376.

Huttenlocher, J., & Presson, C. C. (1973). Mental rotation and the perspective problem. *Cognitive Psychology, 4*, 277–299.

Huttenlocher, J., & Presson, C. C. (1979). The coding and transformation of spatial information. *Cognitive Psychology, 11*(3), 375–394.

Huttenlocher, J., Vasilyeva, M., & Shimpi, P. (2004). Syntactic priming in young children. *Journal of Memory and Language, 50*(2), 182–195.

Inagaki, H., Meguro, K., Shimada, M., Ishizaki, J., Okuzumi, H., & Yamadori, A. (2002). Discrepancy between mental rotation and perspective-taking abilities in normal aging assessed by Piaget's three-mountain task. *Journal of Clinical and Experimental Neuropsychology, 24*(1), 18–25.

Indefrey, P., & Levelt, W. J. M. (2000). The neural correlates of language production. In M. Gazzaniga (Ed.), *The new cognitive neurosciences* (2nd ed., pp. 845–865). Cambridge, MA: MIT Press.

Ingram, D. (1999). Phonological acquisition. In M. Barrett (Ed.), *The development of language* (pp. 73–98). East Sussex, UK: Psychology Press.

Intons-Peterson, M. J. (1983). Imagery paradigms: How vulnerable are they to experimenters' expectations? *Journal of Experimental Psychology: Human Perception & Performance, 9*(3), 394–412.

Intons-Peterson, M. J. (1992). Components of auditory imagery. In D. Reisberg (Ed.), *Auditory imagery* (pp. 45–71). Hillsdale, NJ: Erlbaum.

Intons-Peterson, M. J., Russell, W., & Dressel, S. (1992). The role of pitch in auditory imagery. *Journal of Experimental Psychology: Human Perception & Performance, 18*(1), 233–240.

Isaacowitz, D. M., Wadlinger, H. A., Goren, D., & Wilson, H. R. (2006a). Is there an age-related positivity effect in visual attention? A comparison of two methodologies. *Emotion, 6*, 511–516.

Isaacowitz, D. M, Wadlinger, H. A., Goren, D., & Wilson, H. R. (2006b). Selective preference in visual fixation away from negative images in old age? An eye-tracking study: Correction. *Psychology and Aging, 21*, 221.

Ishii, R., Shinosaki, K., Ikejiri, Y., Ukai, S., Yamashita, K., Iwase, M., et al. (2000). Theta rhythm increase in left superior temporal cortex during auditory hallucinations in schizophrenia: A case report. *NeuroReport, 28*, 11–14.

Izquierdo, I., & Medina, J. H. (1997). Memory formation: The sequence of biochemical events in the hippocampus and its connection to activity in other brain structures. *Neurobiology of Learning and Memory, 68*, 285–316.

Jackendoff, R. (1991). Parts and boundaries. *Cognition, 41*(1–3), 9–45.

Jacobson, R. R., & Lishman, W. A. (1990). Cortical and diencephalic lesions in Korsakoff's syndrome: A clinical and CT scan study. *Psychological Medicine, 20*(1), 63–75.

Jacoby, L. L. (1991). A process dissociation framework: Separating automatic from intentional uses of memory. *Journal of Memory and Language, 30*, 513–541.

Jacoby, L. L., Lindsay, D. S., & Toth, J. P. (1992). Unconscious influences revealed: Attention, awareness, and control. *American Psychologist, 47*, 802–209.

James, T. W., Humphrey, G. K., Gati, J. S., Servos, P., Menon, R. S., & Goodale, M. A. (2002). Haptic study of three-dimensional objects activates extrastriate visual areas. *Neuropsychologia, 40*, 1706–1714.

James, W. (1970). *The principles of psychology* (Vol. 1). New York: Holt. (Original work published 1890.)

Jameson, K. A. (2005). Culture and cognition: What is universal about the representation of color experience. *Journal of Cognition and Culture, 5*(3), 293–347.

Janis, I. L. (1971). Groupthink. *Psychology Today 5*(43–46), 74–76.

Janis, I. L., & Frick, F. (1943). The relationship between attitudes toward conclusions and errors in judging logical validity of syllogisms. *Journal of Experimental Psychology, 33*, 73–77.

Jansiewicz, E. M., Newschaffer, C. J., Denckla, M. B., & Mostofsky, S. H. (2004). Impaired habituation in children with attention deficit hyperactivity disorder. *Cognitive & Behavioral Neurology, 17*(1), 1–8.

Jarrold, C., Baddeley, A. D., & Hewes, A. K. (2000). Verbal short-term memory deficits in Down syndrome: A consequence of problems in rehearsal? *The Journal of Child Psychology and Psychiatry and Allied Disciplines, 41*, 233–244.

Jarrold, C., & Happé, F. (2003). Autism, psychology of. In L. Nadel (Ed.), *Encyclopedia of cognitive science* (Vol. 1, pp. 283–286). London: Nature Publishing Group.

Jenkins, J. J. (1979). Four points to remember: A tetrahedral model of memory experiments. In L. S. Cermak & F. I. M. Craik (Eds.), *Levels of processing in human memory* (pp. 429–446). Hillsdale, NJ: Erlbaum.

Jensen, A. R. (1979). *g*: Outmoded theory or unconquered frontier? *Creative Science and Technology, 2*, 16–29.

Jensen, A. R. (1982). The chronometry of intelligence. In R. J. Sternberg (Ed.), *Advances in the psychology of human intelligence.* (Vol. 1, pp. 255–310). Hillsdale, NJ: Erlbaum.

Jensen, A. R. (1998). *The g factor.* Westport, CT: Praeger/Greenwood.

Jensen, A. R. (2005). Mental chronometry and the unification of differential psychology. In R. J. Sternberg & J. E. Pretz (Eds.), *Cognition and intelligence* (pp. 26–50). New York: Cambridge University Press.

Jenson, J. L. (2007). Getting one's way in policy debates: Influence tactics used in group decision-making settings. *Public Administration Review, 67*(2), 216–227.

Jerde, T. E., Soechting, J. F., & Flanders, M. (2003). Coarticulation in fluent fingerspelling. *The Journal of Neuroscience, 23*(3), 2383.

Jerison, H. J. (2000). The evolution of intelligence. In R. J. Sternberg (Ed.), *Handbook of intelligence* (pp. 216–244). New York: Cambridge University Press.

Jernigan, T. L., Schafer, K., Butters, N., & Cermak, L. S. (1991). Magnetic resonance imaging of alcoholic Korsakoff patients. *Neuropsychopharmacology, 4*(3), 175–186.

Jia, G., & Aaronson, D. (1999). Age differences in second language acquisition: The dominant language switch and maintenance hypothesis. In A. Greenhill, H. Littlefield, & C. Tano, *Proceedings of the 23rd Annual Boston University Conference on Language Development* (pp. 301–312). Somerville, MA: Cascadilla Press.

Jick, H., & Kaye, J. A. (2003). Epidemiology and possible causes of autism. *Pharmacotherapy, 23*(12), 1524–1530.

Johnson, E. K., & Jusczyk, P. W. (2001). Word segmentation by 8-month-olds: When speech cues count more than statistics. *Journal of Memory and Language, 44*(4), 548–567.

Johnson, J. S., & Newport, E. L. (1989). Critical period effects in second language learning: The influence of maturational state on the acquisition of English as a second language. *Cognitive Psychology, 21,* 60–99.

Johnson, J. S., & Newport, E. L. (1991). Critical period effects on universal properties of language: The status of subjacency in the acquisition of a second language. *Cognition, 39*(3), 215–258.

Johnson, M. K. (1996). Fact, fantasy, and public policy. In D. J. Herrmann, C. McEvoy, C. Hertzog, P. Hertel, & M. K. Johnson (Eds.), *Basic and applied memory research: Theory in context* (Vol. 1). Mahwah, NJ: Erlbaum.

Johnson, M. K., Foley, M. A., Suengas, A. G., & Raye, C. L. (1988). Phenomenal characteristics of memories for perceived and imagined autobiographical events. *Journal of Experimental Psychology: General, 117*(4), 371–376.

Johnson, M. K., & Hasher, L. (1987). Human learning and memory. *Annual Review of Psychology, 38,* 631–668.

Johnson, M. K., Hashtroudi, S., & Lindsay, D. S. (1993). Source monitoring. *Psychological Bulletin, 114,* 3–28.

Johnson, M. K., Nolde, S. F., & De Leonardis, D. M. (1996). Emotional focus and source monitoring. *Journal of Memory and Language, 35,* 135–156.

Johnson, M. K., & Raye, C. L. (1981). Reality monitoring. *Psychological Review, 88,* 67–85.

Johnson, M. K., & Raye, C. L. (1998). False memories and confabulation. *Trends in Cognitive Sciences, 2,* 137–145.

Johnson-Laird, P. N. (1983). *Mental models.* Cambridge, MA: Harvard University Press.

Johnson-Laird, P. N. (1988). Freedom and constraint in creativity. In R. J. Sternberg (Ed.), *The nature of creativity* (pp. 202–219). New York: Cambridge University Press.

Johnson-Laird, P. N. (1989). Mental models. In M. I. Posner (Ed.), *Foundations of cognitive science* (pp. 469–499). Cambridge, MA: MIT Press.

Johnson-Laird, P. N. (1995). Mental models, deductive reasoning, and the brain. In M. S. Gazzaniga (Ed.), *The cognitive neurosciences* (pp. 999–1008). Cambridge, MA: MIT Press.

Johnson-Laird, P. N. (1997). Rules and illusions: A critical study of Rips's *The psychology of proof: Minds and machines, 7,* 387–407.

Johnson-Laird, P. N. (1999). Mental models. In R. A. Wilson & F. C. Keil (Eds.), *The MIT encyclopedia of the cognitive sciences* (pp. 525–527). Cambridge, MA: MIT Press.

Johnson-Laird, P. N. (2000). Thinking: Reasoning. In A. Kazdin (Ed.), *Encyclopedia of psychology* (Vol. 8, pp. 75–79). Washington, DC: American Psychological Association.

Johnson-Laird, P. N. (2001). Mental models and deduction. *Trends in Cognitive Sciences, 5*(10), 434–442.

Johnson-Laird, P. N. (2004). Mental models and reasoning. In J. P. Leighton & R. J. Sternberg (Eds.), *The nature of reasoning* (pp. 169–204). New York: Cambridge University Press.

Johnson-Laird, P. N., Byrne, R. M. J., & Schaeken, W. (1992). Propositional reasoning by model. *Psychological Review, 99*(3), 418–439.

Johnson-Laird, P. N., & Goldvarg, Y. (1997). How to make the impossible seem possible. In *Proceedings of the Nineteenth Annual Conference of the Cognitive Science Society* (pp. 354–357), Stanford, CA. Hillsdale, NJ: Erlbaum.

Johnson-Laird, P. N., Legrenzi, P., Girotto, V., Legrenzi, M. S., & Caverni, J. P. (1999). Naïve probability: A model theory of extensional reasoning. *Psychological Review, 106,* 62–88.

Johnson-Laird, P. N., & Savary, F. (1999). Illusory inference: A novel class of erroneous deductions. *Cognition, 71,* 191–229.

Johnson-Laird, P. N., & Steedman, M. (1978). The psychology of syllogisms. *Cognitive Psychology, 10,* 64–99.

Johnston, J. C., & McClelland, J. L. (1973). Visual factors in word perception. *Perception & Psychophysics, 14,* 365–370.

Johnston, W. A., & Heinz, S. P. (1978). Flexibility and capacity demands of attention. *Journal of Experimental Psychology: General, 107,* 420–435.

Joiner, C., & Loken, B. (1998). The inclusion effect and category-based induction. *Journal of Consumer Psychology, 7*(2), 101–129.

Jolicoeur, P. (1985). The time to name disoriented natural objects. *Memory & Cognition, 13*(4), 289–303.

Jolicoeur, P., & Kosslyn, S. M. (1985a). Demand characteristics in image scanning experiments. *Journal of Mental Imagery, 9*(2), 41–49.

Jolicoeur, P., & Kosslyn, S. M. (1985b). Is time to scan visual images due to demand characteristics? *Memory & Cognition, 13*(4), 320–332.

Jolicoeur, P., Snow, D., & Murray, J. (1987). The time to identify disoriented letters: Effects of practice and font. *Canadian Journal of Psychology, 41*(3), 303–316.

Jones, G., & Ritter, F. E. (2003). Production systems and rule-based inference. In L. Nadel (Ed.), *Encyclopedia of cognitive science* (Vol. 3, pp. 741–747). London: Nature Publishing Group.

Jones, P. E. (1995). Contradictions and unanswered questions in the Genie case: A fresh look at the linguistic evidence. *Language & Communication, 15*(3), 261–280.

Jordan, K., & Huntsman, L. A. (1990). Image rotation of misoriented letter strings: Effects of orientation cuing and repetition. *Perception & Psychophysics, 48*(4), 363–374.

Jordan, K., Wustenberg, T., Heinze, H. J., Peters, M., & Jancke, L. (2002). Women and men exhibit different cortical activation patterns during mental rotation tasks. *Neuropsychologia, 40*(13), 2397–2408.

Jordan, P. J., & Troth, A. C. (2004). Managing emotions during team problem solving: Emotional intelligence and conflict resolution. *Human Performance, 17*(2), 195–218.

Jung, R. E., & Haier, R. J. (2007). The parieto-frontal integration theory (P-FIT) of intelligence: Converging neuroimaging evidence. *Behavioral and Brain Sciences, 30*(2), 135–154.

Jung-Beeman, M., Bowden, E. M., Haberman, J., Frymiare, J. L., Arambel-Liu, S., Greenblatt, R., et al. (2004). Neural activity when people solve verbal problems with insight. *Public Library of Science Biology, 2*(4), e97.

Jusczyk, P. W. (1997). *The discovery of spoken language.* Cambridge, MA: MIT Press.

Jusczyk, P. W. (2003). Phonology and phonetics, acquisition of. In L. Nadel (Ed.), *Encyclopedia of cognitive science* (Vol. 3, pp. 645–650). London: Nature Group Press.

Just, M. A., & Carpenter, P. A. (1985). Cognitive coordinate systems: Accounts of mental rotation and individual differences in spatial ability. *Psychological Review, 92*(2), 137–172.

Just, M. A., & Carpenter, P. A. (1987). *The psychology of reading and language comprehension.* Boston: Allyn and Bacon.

Just, M. A., Carpenter, P. A., & Masson, M. E. J. (1982). *What eye fixations tell us about speed reading and skimming* (EyeLab Tech. Rep.). Pittsburgh: Carnegie-Mellon University.

Kahneman, D. (1973). *Attention and effort.* Englewood Cliffs, NJ: Prentice-Hall.

Kahneman, D., & Tversky, A. (1972). Subjective probability: A judgment of representativeness. *Cognitive Psychology, 3,* 430–454.

Kahneman, D., & Tversky, A. (1990). Prospect theory: An analysis of decision under risk. In P. K. Moser (Ed.), *Rationality in action: Contemporary approaches* (pp. 140–170). New York: Cambridge University Press.

Kahneman, D., & Tversky, A. (1996). On the reality of cognitive illusions. *Psychological Review, 103,* 582–591.

Kail, R. V. (1991). Controlled and automatic processing during mental rotation. *Journal of Experimental Child Psychology, 51*(3), 337–347.

Kail, R. V. (1997). Processing time, imagery, and spatial memory. *Journal of Experimental Child Psychology, 64,* 67–78.

Kail, R. V., & Bisanz, J. (1992). The information-processing perspective on cognitive development in childhood and adolescence. In R. J. Sternberg & C. A. Berg (Eds.), *Intellectual development* (pp. 229–260). New York: Cambridge University Press.

Kail, R. V., & Park, Y. S. (1990). Impact of practice on speed of mental rotation. *Journal of Experimental Child Psychology, 49*(2), 227–244.

Kail, R. V., Pellegrino, J. W., & Carter, P. (1980). Developmental changes in mental rotation. *Journal of Experimental Child Psychology, 29,* 102–116.

Kalisch, R., Salome, N., Platzer, S., Wigger, A., Czisch, M., Sommer, W., et al. (2004). High trait anxiety and hyporeactivity to stress of the dorsomedial prefrontal cortex: A combined phMRI and Fos study in rats. *Neuroimage, 23,* 382–391.

Kane, M. J., Hambrick, D. Z., & Conway, A. R. A. (2005). Working memory capacity and fluid intelligence are strongly related constructs: Comment on Ackerman, Beier, and Boyle (2005). *Psychology Bulletin, 131*(1), 66–71.

Kanner, L. (1943). Autistic disturbances of affective contact. *Nervous Child, 2,* 217–250.

Kanwisher, N., Chun, M. M., McDermott, J., & Ledden, P. J. (1996). Functional imaging of human visual recognition. *Cognitive Brain Research, 5,* 55–67.

Kanwisher, N., McDermott, J., & Chun, M. M. (1997). The fusiform face area: A module in human extrastriate cortex specialized for face perception. *Journal of Neuroscience, 17,* 4302–4311.

Kanwisher, N., Woods, R., Ioacoboni, M., & Mazziotta, J. (1997). A locus in human extrastriate cortex for visual shape analysis. *Journal of Cognitive Neuroscience, 9,* 133–142.

Kaplan, C. A., & Davidson, J. E. (1989). *Incubation effects in problem solving.* Unpublished manuscript.

Kaplan, E., Fein, D., Morris, R., & Delis, D. C. (1991). *WAIS-R NI manual.* San Antonio: The Psychological Corporation.

Kaplan, G. B., Sengor, N. S., Gurvit, H., & Guzelis, C. (2007). Modelling the Stroop effect: A connectionist approach. *Neurocomputing, 70*(7–9), 1414–1423.

Karni, A., Tanne, D., Rubenstein, B. S., Askenasy, J. J. M., & Sagi, D. (1994). Dependence on REM sleep of overnight improvement of a perceptual skill. *Science, 265,* 679.

Kass, S. J., Ahlers, R. H., & Dugger, M. (1998). Eliminating gender differences through practice in an applied visual spatial task. *Human Performance, 11*(4), 337–349.

Katz, A. N. (1987). Self-reference in the encoding of creative-relevant traits. *Journal of Personality, 55,* 97–120.

Katz, A. N. (2000). Mental imagery. In A. E. Kazdin (Ed.), *Encyclopedia of psychology* (Vol. 5, pp. 187–191). Washington, DC: American Psychological Association.

Katz, J. J. (1972). *Semantic theory.* New York: Harper & Row.

Katz, J. J., & Fodor, J. A. (1963). The structure of a semantic theory. *Language, 39,* 170–210.

Kaufman, A. S. (2000). Tests of intelligence. In R. J. Sternberg (Ed.), *Handbook of intelligence* (pp. 445–476). New York: Cambridge University Press.

Kaufman, A. S., & Lichtenberger, E. O. (1998). Intellectual assessment. In C. R. Reynolds (Ed.), *Comprehensive clinical psychology: Vol. 4. Assessment* (pp. 203–238). Tarrytown, NY : Elsevier Science.

Kaufmann, L., & Nuerk, H. C. (2006). Interference effects in a numerical Stroop paradigm in 9- to 12-year-old children with ADHD-C. *Child Neuropsychology, 12*(3), 223–243.

Kawachi, K. (2002). Practice effects on speech production planning: Evidence from slips of the tongue in spontaneous vs. preplanning speech in Japanese. *Journal of Psycholinguistic Research, 31*(4), 363–390.

Kay, P. (1975). Synchronic variability and diachronic changes in basic color terms. *Language in Society, 4,* 257–270.

Keane, M. T. (1994). Propositional representations. In M. W. Eysenck (Ed.), *The Blackwell dictionary of cognitive psychology.* Cambridge, MA: Blackwell.

Kearins, J. M. (1981). Visual spatial memory in Australian aboriginal children of desert regions. *Cognitive Psychology, 13*(3), 434–460.

Keating, D. P. (1984). The emperor's new clothes: The "new look" in intelligence research. In R. J. Sternberg (Ed.), *Advances in the psychology of human intelligence* (Vol. 2, pp. 1–45). Hillsdale, NJ: Erlbaum.

Keating, D. P., & Bobbitt, B. L. (1978). Individual and developmental differences in cognitive-processing components of mental ability. *Child Development, 49,* 155–167.

Keil, F. C. (1979). *Semantic and conceptual development.* Cambridge, MA: Harvard University Press.

Keil, F. C. (1989). *Concepts, kinds, and cognitive development*. Cambridge, MA: MIT Press.

Keil, F. C. (1999). Cognition, content, and development. In M. Bennett (Ed.), *Developmental psychology: Achievements and prospects* (pp. 165–184). Philadelphia: Psychology Press.

Keil, F. C., & Batterman, N. (1984). A characteristic-to-defining shift in the development of word meaning. *Journal of Verbal Learning and Verbal Behavior, 23*, 221–236.

Keller, E. (1976). Gambits. *TESL Talk, 7*(2), 18–21.

Keller, H. (1988). *The story of my life*. New York: Signet. (Original work published 1902)

Kelly, S. W., Griffiths, S., & Frith, U. (2002). Evidence for implicit sequence learning in dyslexia. *Dyslexia, 8*(1), 43–52.

Kemple, V., Brooks, P. J., & Gills, S. (2005). Diminutives in child-directed speech supplement metric with distributional word segmentation cues. *Psychonomic Bulletin & Review, 12*(1), 145–151.

Kennerley, S. W., Walton, M. E., Behrens, T. E. J., Buckley, M. J., & Rushworth, M. F. S. (2006). Optimal decision making and the anterior cingulate cortex. *Nature Neuroscience, 9*, 940–947.

Kensinger, E. A., Brierley, B., Medford, N., Growdon, J. H., & Corkin, S. (2002). Effects of normal aging and Alzheimer's disease on emotional memory. *Emotion, 2*, 118–134.

Kensinger, E. A., & Corkin, S. (2003). Alzheimer's disease. In L. Nadel (Ed.), *Encyclopedia of cognitive science* (Vol. 1, pp. 83–89). London: Nature Publishing Group.

Kentridge, R. W. (2003). Blindsight. In L. Nadel (Ed.), *Encyclopedia of cognitive science* (Vol. 1, pp. 390–397). London: Nature Publishing Group.

Keppel, G., & Underwood, B. J. (1962). Proactive inhibition in short-term retention of single items. *Journal of Verbal Learning and Verbal Behavior, 1*, 153–161.

Kerr, N. (1983). The role of vision in "visual imagery" experiments: Evidence from the congenitally blind. *Journal of Experimental Psychology: General, 112*(2), 265–277.

Kessler Shaw, L. (1999). *Acquiring the meaning of* know *and* think. Unpublished doctoral dissertation. City University of New York Graduate Center.

Khubchandani, L. M. (1997). Bilingual education for indigenous groups in India. In J. Cummins & D. Corson (Eds.), *Encyclopedia of language and education: Vol. 5. Bilingual education* (pp. 67–76). Dordrecht, Netherlands: Kluwer.

Kihara, K., & Yoshikawa, S. (2001). The comparison between mental image manipulation and distinctive feature scan on recognition memory of faces. *Japanese Journal of Psychology, 72*(3), 234–239.

Kihlstrom, J. F., & Cantor, N. (2000). Social intelligence. In R. J. Sternberg (Ed.), *Handbook of intelligence* (pp. 359–379). New York: Cambridge University Press.

Kilingberg, T. Forssberg, H., & Westerberg, H. (2002). Training of working memory in children with ADHD. *Journal of Clinical and Experimental Neuropsychology, 24*(6), 781–791.

Kim, N. S., & Ahn, W. K. (2002). Clinical psychologists' theory-based representations of mental disorders predict their diagnostic reasoning and memory. *Journal of Experimental Psychology: General, 131*, 451–476.

Kimura, D. (1981). Neural mechanisms in manual signing. *Sign Language Studies, 33*, 291–312.

Kimura, D. (1987). Are men's and women's brains really different? *Canadian Psychology, 28*(2), 133–147.

Kintsch, W. (1990). The representation of knowledge and the use of knowledge in discourse comprehension. In C. Graumann & R. Dietrich (Eds.), *Language in the social context*. Amsterdam: Elsevier.

Kintsch, W., Healy, A. F., Hegarty, M., Pennington, B. F., & Salthouse, T. A. (1999). Models of working memory: Eight questions and some general issues. In A. Miyake & P. Shah (Eds.), *Models of working memory: Mechanisms of active maintenance and executive control* (pp. 412–441). New York: Cambridge University Press.

Kintsch, W., & Keenan, J. M. (1973). Reading rate and retention as a function of the number of propositions in the base structure of sentences. *Cognitive Psychology, 5*, 257–274.

Kintsch, W., & van Dijk, T. A. (1978). Toward a model of text comprehension and production. *Psychological Review, 85*(5), 363–394.

Kirby, K. N. (1994). Probabilities and utilities of fictional outcomes in Wason's selection task. *Cognition, 51*(1), 1–28.

Klein, G. (1997). Developing expertise in decision making. *Thinking & Reasoning, 3*(4), 337–352.

Klein, S. B., & Kihlstrom, J. F. (1986). Elaboration, organization, and the self-reference effect in memory. *Journal of Experimental Psychology: General, 115*(1), 26–38.

Kliegl, R., Mayr, U., & Krampe, R. T. (1994). Time–accuracy functions for determining process and person differences: An application to cognitive aging. *Cognitive Psychology, 26*(2), 134–164.

Kloos, H., & Sloutsky, V. (2004). Are natural kinds psychologically distinct from nominal kinds? Evidence from learning and development. *Proceedings of the Meeting of the Cognitive Science Society*, Chicago, IL.

Koehler, J. J. (1996). The base rate fallacy reconsidered: Descriptive, normative, and methodological challenges. *Behavioral and Brain Sciences, 19*, 1–53.

Köhler, S., Kapur, S., Moscovitch, M., Winocur, G., & Houle, S. (1995). Dissociation of pathways for object and spatial vision in the intact human brain. *Neuroreport, 6*, 1865–1868.

Köhler, W. (1927). *The mentality of apes*. New York: Harcourt Brace.

Köhler, W. (1940). *Dynamics in psychology*. New York: Liveright.

Kolb, B., & Whishaw, I. Q. (1985). *Fundamentals of human neuropsychology* (2nd ed.). New York: Freeman.

Kolb, B., & Whishaw, I. Q. (1990). *Fundamentals of human neuropsychology* (3rd ed.). New York: Freeman.

Kolb, I., & Whishaw, B. (1996). *Fundamentals of human neuropsychology*. New York: W. H. Freeman.

Kolodner, J. L. (1983). Reconstructive memory: A computer model. *Cognitive Science, 7*(4), 281–328.

Komatsu, L. K. (1992). Recent views on conceptual structure. *Psychological Bulletin, 112*(3), 500–526.

Korf, R. (1999). Heuristic search. In R. A. Wilson & F. C. Keil (Eds.), *The MIT encyclopedia of the cognitive sciences* (pp. 372–373). Cambridge, MA: MIT Press.

Koriat, A., & Goldsmith, M. (1996a). Memory metaphors and the everyday–laboratory controversy: The correspondence versus the storehouse conceptions of memory. *Behavioral and Brain Sciences, 19*, 167–228.

Koriat, A., & Goldsmith, M. (1996b). Monitoring and control processes in the strategic regulation of memory accuracy. *Psychological Review, 103*, 490–517.

Kornblum, H. I., Araujo, D. M., Annala, A. J., Tatsukawa, K. J., Phelps, M. E., & Cherry, S. R. (2000). In vivo imaging of neuronal activation and plasticity in the rat brain by high resolution positron emission tomography (microPET). *Nature Biotechnology, 18,* 655–660.

Koslowski, B. (1996). *Theory and evidence: The development of scientific reasoning.* Cambridge, MA: MIT Press.

Kosslyn, S. M. (1975). Information representation in visual images. *Cognitive Psychology, 7*(3), 341–370.

Kosslyn, S. M. (1976). Using imagery to retrieve semantic information: A developmental study. *Child Development, 47*(2), 434–444.

Kosslyn, S. M. (1981). The medium and the message in mental imagery: A theory. *Psychological Review, 88*(1), 46–66.

Kosslyn, S. M. (1983). *Ghosts in the mind's machine: Creating and using images in the brain.* New York: Norton.

Kosslyn, S. M. (1990). Mental imagery. In D. N. Osherson, S. M. Kosslyn, & J. M. Hollerbach (Eds.), *Visual cognition and action: Vol. 2. An invitation to cognitive science* (pp. 73–97). Cambridge, MA: MIT Press.

Kosslyn, S. M. (1994a). Computational theory of imagery. In M. W. Eysenck (Ed.), *The Blackwell dictionary of cognitive psychology* (pp. 177–181). Cambridge, MA: Blackwell.

Kosslyn, S. M. (1994b). Image and brain: The resolution of the imagery debate. Cambridge, MA: MIT Press.

Kosslyn, S. M., Ball, T. M., & Reiser, B. J. (1978). Visual images preserve metric spatial information: Evidence from studies of image scanning. *Journal of Experimental Psychology: Human Perception and Performance, 4,* 47–60.

Kosslyn, S. M., & Koenig, O. (1992). *Wet mind: The new cognitive neuroscience.* New York: Free Press.

Kosslyn, S. M., & Osherson, D. N. (Eds.) (1995). *An invitation to cognitive science: Vol. 2. Visual cognition* (2nd ed.). Cambridge, MA: MIT Press.

Kosslyn, S. M., & Pomerantz, J. R. (1977). Imagery, propositions, and the form of internal representations. *Cognitive Psychology, 9*(1), 52–76.

Kosslyn, S. M., & Rabin, C. S. (1999). Imagery. In R. A. Wilson & F. C. Keil (Eds.), *The MIT encyclopedia of the cognitive sciences* (pp. 387–389). Cambridge, MA: MIT Press.

Kosslyn, S. M., Seger, C., Pani, J. R., & Hillger, L. A. (1990). When is imagery used in everyday life? A diary study. *Journal of Mental Imagery, 14*(3–4), 131–152.

Kosslyn, S. M., & Sussman, A. L. (1995). Roles of memory in perception. In M. S. Gazzaniga (Ed.), *The cognitive neurosciences* (pp. 1035–1042). Cambridge, MA: MIT Press.

Kosslyn, S. M., & Thompson, W. L. (2000). Shared mechanisms in visual imagery and visual perception: Insights from cognitive neuroscience. In M. S. Gazzaniga (Ed.), *The new cognitive neurosciences* (2nd ed., pp. 975–986). Cambridge, MA: MIT Press.

Kosslyn, S. M., Thompson, W. L., Kim, J. J., & Alpert, N. M. (1995). Topographical representations of mental images in primary visual cortex. *Nature, 378,* 496–498.

Kotovsky, K. (2003). Problem solving—large/small, hard/easy, conscious/nonconscious, problem-space/problem-solver: The issue of dichotomization. In J. E. Davidson & R. J. Sternberg (Eds.), *The psychology of problem solving* (pp. 373–383). New York: Cambridge University Press.

Kotovsky, K., Hayes, J. R., & Simon, H. A. (1985). Why are some problems hard? Evidence from the tower of Hanoi. *Cognitive Psychology, 17,* 248–294.

Kotovsky, K., & Simon, H. A. (1973). Empirical tests of a theory of human acquisition of concepts for sequential events. *Cognitive Psychology, 4,* 399–424.

Kounios, J., Frymiare, J. L., Bowman, E. M., Fleck, J. I., Subramaniam, K., Parrish, T. B., et al. (2006). The prepared mind: Neural activity prior to problem presentation predicts subsequent solution by sudden insight. *Psychological Science, 17*(10), 882–890.

Kraemer, D. J. M., Macrae, C. N., Green, A. E., & Kelley, W. M. (2005). Musical imagery: Sound of silence activates auditory cortex. *Nature, 434*(7030), 158.

Krantz, L. (1992). *What the odds are: A-to-Z odds on everything you hoped or feared could happen.* New York: Harper Perennial.

Kreuger, J. (1998, October). The bet on bias: A foregone conclusion? *Psychology, 9.*

Kringelbach, M. L., Jenkinson, N., Green, A. L., Owen, S. L. F., Hansen, P. C., Cornelissen, P. L., et al. (2007). Deep brain stimulation for chronic pain investigated with magnetoencephalography. *NeuroReport, 18* (3), 223–228.

Kroeber, A. L., & Kluckhohn, C. (1952). *Culture: A critical review of concepts and definitions.* Cambridge, MA: Peabody Museum.

Kruschke, J. K. (2003). Concept learning and categorization: Models. In L. Nadel (Ed.), *Encyclopedia of cognitive science* (Vol. 1, pp. 646–652). London: Nature Publishing Group.

Kuhl, P. K. (1991). Human adults and infants show a "perceptual magnet effect" for the prototypes of speech categories, monkeys do not. *Perception & Psycholinguistics, 50,* 93–107.

Kuhl, P. K., & Meltzoff, A. N. (1997). Evolution, nativism, and learning in the development of language and speech. In M. Gopnik (Ed.), *The inheritance and innateness of grammars* (pp. 7–44). New York: Oxford University Press.

Kunzendorf, R. (Ed.) (1991). *Mental imagery.* New York: Plenum.

Kuperberg, G. R., Sitnikova, T., Goff, D., & Holcomb, P. J. (2006). Making sense of sentences in schizophrenia: Electrophysiological evidence for abnormal interactions between semantic and syntactic processing. *Journal of Abnormal Psychology, 115*(2), 251–265.

Kutas, M., & Hillyard, S. A. (1980). Reading senseless sentences: Brain potentials reflect semantic incongruity. *Science, 207,* 203–205.

Kutas, M., & Van Patten, C. (1994). Psycholinguistics electrified: Event-related brain potential investigations. In M. A. Gernsbacher (Ed.), *Handbook of psycholinguistics* (pp. 83–143). San Diego: Academic Press.

Kyllonen, P. C., & Christal, R. E. (1990). Reasoning ability is (little more than) working-memory capacity?! *Intelligence, 14,* 389–433.

LaBerge, D. (1975). Acquisition of automatic processing in perceptual and associative learning. In P. M. A. Rabbit & S. Dornic (Eds.), *Attention and performance.* London: Academic Press.

LaBerge, D. (1976). Perceptual learning and attention. In W. Estes (Ed.), *Handbook of learning and cognitive processes: Vol. 4. Attention and memory.* Hillsdale, NJ: Erlbaum.

LaBerge, D. (1990). Attention. *Psychological Science, 1*(3), 156–162.

LaBerge, D., & Brown, V. (1989). Theory of attentional operations in shape identification. *Psychological Review, 96*(1), 101–124.

LaBerge, D., Carter, M., & Brown, V. (1992). A network simulation of thalamic circuit operations in selective attention. *Neural Computation, 4*(3), 318–331.

LaBerge D., & Samuels, S. J. (1974). Toward a theory of automatic information processing in reading. *Cognitive Psychology, 6*(2), 293–323.

Labouvie-Vief, G., & Schell, D. A. (1982). Learning and memory in later life. In B. B. Wolman (Ed.), *Handbook of developmental psychology.* Englewood Cliffs, NJ: Prentice-Hall.

Ladavas, E., del Pesce, M., Mangun, G. R., & Gazzaniga, M. S. (1994). Variations in attentional bias of the disconnected cerebral hemispheres. *Cognitive Neuropsychology, 11*(1), 57–74.

Ladefoged, P., & Maddieson, I. (1996). *The sounds of the world's languages*. Cambridge, UK: Blackwell.

Laland, K. N. (2004). Social learning strategies. *Learning & Behavior, 32*(1), 4–14.

Lamb, J. A., Moore, J., Bailey, A., & Monaco, A. P. (2000). Autism: Recent molecular genetic advances. *Human Molecular Genetics, 9,* 861–868.

Lander, K., & Metcalfe, S. (2007). The influence of positive and negative facial expressions on face familiarity. *Memory, 15*(1), 63–69.

Langer, E. J. (1989). *Mindfulness*. New York: Addison-Wesley.

Langer, E. J. (1997). *The power of mindful learning*. Needham Heights, MA: Addison-Wesley.

Langlais, P. J., Mandel, R. J., & Mair, R. G. (1992). Diencephalic lesions, learning impairments, and intact retrograde memory following acute thiamine deficiency in the rat. *Behavioural Brain Research, 48*(2), 177–185.

Langley, P., & Jones, R. (1988). A computational model of scientific insight. In R. J. Sternberg (Ed.), *The nature of creativity* (pp. 117–201). New York: Cambridge University Press.

Langley, P., Simon, H. A., Bradshaw, G. L., & Zytkow, J. M. (1987). *Scientific discovery: Computational explorations of the creative process*. Cambridge, MA: MIT Press.

Lanze, M., Weisstein, N., & Harris, J. R. (1982). Perceived depth versus structural relevance in the object-superiority effect. *Perception & Psychophysics, 31*(4), 376–382.

LaPointe, L. L. (2005). Feral children. *Journal of Medical Speech-Language Pathology, 13*(1), vii–ix.

Larkin, J. H., McDermott, J., Simon, D. P., & Simon, H. A. (1980). Expert and novice performance in solving physics problems. *Science, 208,* 1335–1342.

Larsen, R. J., Mercer, K. A., & Balota, D. A. (2006). Lexical characteristics of words used in emotional Stroop experiments. *Emotion, 6*(1), 62–72.

Larson, G. E., Haier, R. J., LaCasse, L. & Hazen, K. (1995). Evaluation of a "mental effort" hypothesis for correlation between cortical metabolism and intelligence. *Intelligence, 21,* 267–278.

Lashley, K. S. (1950). In search of the engram. *Symposia of the Society for Experimental Biology, 4,* 454–482.

Lawrence, E., & Peters, E. (2004). Reasoning in believers in the paranormal. *Journal of Nervous & Mental Disease, 192*(11), 727–733.

Lawson, A. E. (2004). Reasoning and brain function. In J. P. Leighton & R. J. Sternberg (Eds.), *The nature of reasoning* (pp. 12–48). New York: Cambridge University Press.

Lazar, I., & Darlington, R. (1982). Lasting effects of early education: A report from the consortium for longitudinal studies. *Monographs of the Society for Research in Child Development, 47*(2–3, Serial No. 195).

Leahey, T. H. (2003). *A history of psychology: Main currents in psychological thought*. Upper Saddle River, NJ: Prentice-Hall.

Lederer, R. (1991). *The miracle of language*. New York: Pocket Books.

Ledoux, J. (1996). *The emotional brain*. New York: Simon & Schuster.

Lee, D., & Chun, M. M. (2001). What are the units of visual short-term memory, objects or spatial locations? *Perception & Psychophysics, 63,* 253–257.

Lee, K. H., Choi, Y. Y., Gray, J. R., Cho, S. H., Chae, J.-H., Lee, S., et al. (2006). Neural correlates of superior intelligence: Stronger recruitment of posterior parietal cortex. *Neuroimage, 29*(2), 578–586.

Legg, S., & Hutter, M. (2007). A collection of definitions of intelligence. *Frontiers in Artificial Intelligence and Applications, 157,* 17–24.

Lehman, D. R., Chiu, C. Y. P., & Schaller, M. (2004). Psychology and culture. *Annual Review of Psychology, 55,* 689–714.

Lehman, D. R., Lempert, R., & Nisbett, R. E. (1987). *The effects of graduate education on reasoning: Formal discipline and thinking about everyday-life events*. Unpublished manuscript, University of British Columbia.

Leicht, K. L., & Overton, R. (1987). Encoding variability and spacing repetitions. *American Journal of Psychology, 100*(1), 61–68.

Leighton, J. P. (2004a). The assessment of logical reasoning. In J. P. Leighton & R. J. Sternberg (Eds.), *The nature of reasoning*. New York: Cambridge University Press.

Leighton, J. P. (2004b). Defining and describing reason. In J. P. Leighton & R. J. Sternberg (Eds.), *The nature of reasoning* (pp. 3–11). New York: Cambridge University Press.

Leighton, J. P. (2006). Teaching and assessing deductive reasoning skills. *The Journal of Experimental Education, 74*(2), 107–136.

Leighton, J. P., & Sternberg, R. J. (Eds). (2004). *The nature of reasoning*. New York: Cambridge University Press.

Lennox, B. R., Park, S. B. G., Medley, I., Morris, P. G., & Jones, P. B. (2000). The functional anatomy of auditory hallucinations in schizophrenia. *Psychiatry Research: Neuroimaging, 100*(1), 13–20.

Leopold, D. A., O'Toole, A. J., Vetter, T., & Blanz, V. (2001). Prototype-referenced shape encoding revealed by high-level aftereffects. *Nature Neuroscience, 4,* 89–94.

Lesgold, A. M. (1988). Problem solving. In R. J. Sternberg & E. E. Smith (Eds.), *The psychology of human thought* (pp. 188–213). New York: Cambridge University Press.

Lesgold, A. M., & Lajoie, S. (1991). Complex problem solving in electronics. In R. J. Sternberg & P. A. Frensch (Eds.), *Complex problem solving: Principles and mechanisms* (pp. 287–316). Hillsdale, NJ: Erlbaum.

Lesgold, A. M., Rubinson, H., Feltovich, P., Glaser, R., Klopfer, D., & Wang, Y. (1988). Expertise in a complex skill: Diagnosing x-ray pictures. In M. T. H. Chi, R. Glaser, & M. Farr (Eds.), *The nature of expertise*. Hillsdale, NJ: Erlbaum.

Levin, D. T., & Simons, D. J. (1997). Failure to detect changes in attended objects in motion pictures. *Psychonomic Bulletin & Review, 4,* 501–506.

Levy, J. (1974). Cerebral asymmetries as manifested in split-brain man. In M. Kinsbourne & W. L. Smith (Eds.), *Hemispheric disconnection and cerebral function*. Springfield, IL: Charles C. Thomas.

Levy, J. (2000). Hemispheric functions. In A. E. Kazdin (Ed.), *Encyclopedia of psychology* (Vol. 4, pp. 113–115). Washington, DC: American Psychological Association.

Levy, J., Trevarthen, C., & Sperry, R. W. (1972). Perception of bilateral chimeric figures following hemispheric deconnexion. *Brain, 95*(1), 61–78.

Lewis, R. L. (2003). Psycholinguistics, computational. In L. Nadel (Ed.), *Encyclopedia of cognitive science* (Vol. 3, pp. 787–794). London: Nature Group Press.

Liberman, A. M., Cooper, F. S., Shankweiler, D. P., & Studdert-Kennedy, M. (1967). Perception of the speech code. *Psychological Review, 74,* 431–461.

Liberman, A. M., Harris, K. S., Hoffman, H. S., & Griffith, B. C. (1957). The discrimination of speech sounds within and across phoneme boundaries. *Journal of Experimental Psychology, 54,* 358–368.

Liberman, A. M., & Mattingly, I. G. (1985). The motor theory of speech perception revised. *Cognition, 21,* 1–36.

Lightfoot, D. W. (2003). Language acquisition and language change. In L. Nadel (Ed.), *Encyclopedia of cognitive science* (Vol. 2, pp. 697–700). London: Nature Group Press.

Lindsay, D. S., & Johnson, M. K. (1991). Recognition memory and source monitoring. *Bulletin of the Psychonomic Society, 29,* 203–205.

Lindsay, D. S., & Read, J. D. (1994). Psychotherapy and memories of childhood sexual abuse: A cognitive perspective. *Applied Cognitive Psychology, 8,* 281–338.

Linton, M. (1982). Transformations of memory in everyday life. In U. Neisser (Ed.), *Memory observed: Remembering in natural contexts.* San Francisco: Freeman.

Lipman, M., Sharp, A. M., & Oscanyan, F. S. (1980). *Philosophy in the classroom.* Philadelphia: Temple University Press.

Lipshitz, R., Klein, G., Orasanu, J., & Salas, E. (2001). Taking stock of naturalistic decision making. *Journal of Behavioral Decision Making, 14*(5), 331–352.

Little, D. R., Lewandowsky, S., & Heit, E. (2006). Ad hoc category restructuring. *Memory & Cognition, 34*(7), 1398–1413.

Locke, J. L. (1994). Phases in the child's development of language. *American Scientist, 82,* 436–445.

Lockhart, R. S. (2000). Methods of memory research. In E. Tulving & F. I. M. Craik (Eds.), *The Oxford handbook of memory* (pp. 45–58). New York: Oxford University Press.

Lodi, R., Tonon, C., Vignatelli, L., Iotti, S., Montagna, P., Barbiroli, B., et al. (2004). In vivo evidence of neuronal loss in the hypothalamus of narcoleptic patients. *Neurology, 63,* 1513–1515.

Loehlin, J. C., Horn, J. M., & Willerman, L. (1997). Heredity, environment, and IQ in the Texas Adoption Project. In R. J. Sternberg & E. L. Grigorenko (Eds.), *Intelligence, heredity, and environment* (pp. 105–125). New York: Cambridge University Press.

Loftus, E. F. (1975). Leading questions and the eyewitness report. *Cognitive Psychology, 7,* 560–572.

Loftus, E. F. (1977). Shifting human color memory. *Memory & Cognition, 5,* 696–699.

Loftus, E. F. (1993a). Psychologists in the eyewitness world. *American Psychologist, 48*(5), 550–552.

Loftus, E. F. (1993b). The reality of repressed memories. *American Psychologist, 48*(5), 518–537.

Loftus, E. F. (1998). Imaginary memories. In M. A. Conway, S. E. Gathercole, & C. Cornoldi (Eds.), *Theory of memory II* (pp. 135–145). Hove, UK: Psychology Press.

Loftus, E. F., & Ketcham, K. (1991). *Witness for the defense: The accused, the eyewitness, and the expert who puts memory on trial.* New York: St. Martin's Press.

Loftus, E. F., & Ketcham, K. (1994). *The myth of repressed memory.* New York: St. Martin's Press.

Loftus, E. F., & Loftus, G. R. (1980). On the permanence of stored information in the human brain. *American Psychologist, 35,* 409–420.

Loftus, E. F., Miller, D. G., & Burns, H. J. (1978). Semantic integration of verbal information into a visual memory. *Journal of Experimental Psychology: Human Learning and Memory, 4,* 19–31.

Loftus, E. F., Miller, D. G., & Burns, H. J. (1987). Semantic integration of verbal information into a visual memory. In L. S. Wrightsman, C. E. Willis, S. M. Kassin (Eds.), *On the witness stand: Vol. 2. Controversies in the courtroom* (pp. 157–177). Newbury Park, CA: Sage.

Loftus, E. F., & Palmer, J. C. (1974). Reconstruction of automobile destruction: An example of the interaction between language and memory. *Journal of Verbal Learning and Verbal Behavior, 13,* 585–589.

Logan, G. (1988). Toward an instance theory of automatization. *Psychological Review, 95*(4), 492–527.

Logan, G. D. (1996). The CODE theory of visual attention: An integration of space-based and object-based attention. *Psychological Review, 103,* 603–649.

Logie, R. H., Della Sala, S., Beschin, N., & Denis, M. (2005). Dissociating mental transformations and visuo-spatial storage in working memory: Evidence from representational neglect. *Memory, 13*(3–4), 430–434.

Logie, R. H., & Denis, M. (1991). *Mental images in human cognition.* Amsterdam: North Holland.

Logothetis, N. K. (2004). Functional MRI in monkeys: A bridge between human and animal brain research. In M. S. Gazzaniga (Ed.), *The cognitive neurosciences,* (Vol. 3, pp. 957–969). Cambridge, MA: MIT Press.

Lohman, D. F. (2000). Complex information processing and intelligence. In R. J. Sternberg (Ed.), *Handbook of intelligence* (pp. 285–340). New York: Cambridge University Press.

Lohman, D. F. (2005). Reasoning abilities. In R. J. Sternberg & J. E. Pretz (Eds.), *Cognition and intelligence* (pp. 225–250). New York: Cambridge University Press.

Lonner, W. J. (1989). The introductory psychology text: Beyond Ekman, Whorf, and biased IQ tests. In D. M. Keats, D. Munro, & L. Mann (Eds.), *Heterogeneity in cross-cultural psychology* (pp. 4–22). Amsterdam: Swets & Zeitlinger.

Lou, H. C., Henriksen, L., & Bruhn, P. (1984). Focal cerebral hypoperfusion in children with dyphasia and/or attention deficit disorder. *Archives of Neurology, 41*(8), 825–829.

Love, B. C. (2003). Concept learning. In L. Nadel (Ed.), *Encyclopedia of cognitive science* (Vol. 1, pp. 646–652). London: Nature Publishing Group.

Luaute, J., Halligan, P., Rode, G., Rossetti, Y., & Boisson, D. (2006). Visuo-spatial neglect: A systematic review of current interventions and their effectiveness. *Neuroscience & Biobehavioral Reviews, 30*(7), 961–982.

Lubart, T. I., & Mouchiroud, C. (2003). Creativity: A source of difficulty in problem solving. In J. E. Davidson & R. J. Sternberg (Eds.), *The psychology of problem solving* (pp. 127–148). New York: Cambridge University Press.

Lucas, T. H., McKhann, G. M., & Ojemann, G. A. (2004). Functional separation of languages in the bilingual brain: A comparison of electrical stimulation language mapping in 25 bilingual patients and 117 monolingual control patients. *Journal of Neurosurgery, 101,* 449–457.

Luchins, A. S. (1942). Mechanization in problem solving. *Psychological Monographs, 54*(6, Whole No. 248).

Luck, S. J., Hillyard, S. A., Mangun, G. R., & Gazzaniga, M. S. (1989). Independent hemispheric attentional systems mediate visual search in split-brain patients. *Nature, 342*(6249), 543–545.

Luck, S. J., Hillyard, S. A., Mouloua, M., & Hawkins, H. L. (1996). Mechanisms of visual-spatial attention-resource allocation or uncertainty reduction? *Journal of Experimental Psychology: Human Perception and Performance, 22,* 725–737.

Luck, S. J., & Vogel, E. K. (1997). The capacity of visual working memory for features and conjunctions. *Nature, 390,* 279–281.

Luka, B. J., & Barsalou, L. W. (2005). Structural facilitation: Mere exposure effects for grammatical acceptability as evidence for syntactic priming in comprehension. *Journal of Memory and Language, 52* (3), 436–459.

Luo, J., & Niki, K. (2003). Function of hippocampus in "insight" of problem solving. *Hippocampus, 13*(3), 316–323.

Lupton, L. (1998). Fluency in American sign language. *Journal of Deaf Studies and Deaf Education, 3*(4), 320–328.

Luria, A. R. (1968). *The mind of a mnemonist*. New York: Basic Books.

Luria, A. R. (1973). *The working brain*. London: Penguin.

Luria, A. R. (1976). *Basic problems of neurolinguistics*. The Hague, Netherlands: Mouton.

Luria, A. R. (1984). *The working brain: An introduction to neuropsychology* (B. Haigh, Trans.). Harmondsworth, UK: Penguin. (Original work published 1973)

Lycan, W. (2003). Perspectival representation and the knowledge argument. In Q. Smith & A. Jokic (Eds.), *Consciousness. New philosophical perspectives*. Oxford, UK: Oxford University Press.

Lykken, D. (2005). Mental energy. *Intelligence, 33*(4), 331–335.

Lynne H., Yukako U., & McKinney M. (2002). Savings in the relearning of second language vocabulary: The effects of time and proficiency. *Language Learning 52*(4), 653–678.

Lyons, J. (1977). *Semantics*. New York: Cambridge University Press.

Mace, W. M. (1986). J. J. Gibson's ecological theory of information pickup: Cognition from the ground up. In T. J. Knapp & L. C. Robertson (Eds.), *Approaches to cognition: Contrasts and controversies* (pp. 137–157). Hillsdale, NJ: Erlbaum.

MacKay, D., James, L., Taylor, J., & Marian, D. (2006). Amnesic H. M. exhibits parallel deficits and sparing in language and memory: Systems versus binding theory accounts. *Language and Cognitive Processes, 21.*

MacKay, D. G. (2006). Aging, memory, and language in amnesic H. M. *Hippocampus, 16*(5), 491–494.

Mackworth, N. H. (1948). The breakdown of vigilance during prolonged visual search. *Quarterly Journal of Experimental Psychology, 1,* 6–21.

MacLeod, C. (1991). Half a century of research on the Stroop effect: An integrative review. *Psychological Bulletin, 109*(2), 163–203.

MacLeod, C. M. (1996). How priming affects two-speeded implicit tests of remembering: Naming colors versus reading words. *Consciousness and Cognition: An International Journal, 5,* 73–90.

Macquet, A. C., & Fleurance, P. (2007). Naturalistic decision-making in expert badminton players. *Ergonomics, 50*(9), 1433–1450.

MacWhinney, B. (1999). *The emergence of language*. Mahwah, NJ: Erlbaum.

Madden, D. J. (2007). Aging and visual attention. *Current Directions in Psychological Science, 16*(2), 70–74.

Madden, D. J., Spaniol, J. Whiting, W. L., Bucur, B., Provenzale, J. M., Cabeza, R., et al. (2007). Adult age differences in the functional neuroanatomy of visual attention: A combined fMRI and DTI study. *Neurobiology of Aging, 28*(3), 459–476.

Maguire, E. A., Frackowiak, S. J., & Frith, C. D. (1996). Learning to find your way: A role for the human hippocampal formation. *Proceedings: Biological Sciences, 263*(1377), 1745–1750.

Malgady, R., & Johnson, M. K. (1976). Modifiers in metaphors: Effects of constituent phrase similarity on the interpretation of figurative sentences. *Journal of Psycholinguistic Research, 5,* 43–52.

Malonek, D., & Grinvald, A. (1996). Interactions between electrical activity and cortical microcirculation revealed by imaging spectroscopy: Implication for functional brain mapping. *Science, 272,* 551–554.

Malsbury, C. W. (2003). Hypothalamus. In L. Nadel (Ed.), *Encyclopedia of cognitive science* (Vol. 2, pp. 445–451). London: Nature Publishing Group.

Malt, B. C., & Smith, E. E. (1984). Correlated properties in natural categories. *Journal of Verbal Learning and Verbal Behavior, 23,* 250–269.

Mangun, G. R., & Hillyard, S. A. (1990). Electrophysiological studies of visual selective attention in humans. In A. B. Scheibel & A. F. Wechsler (Eds.), *Neurobiology of higher cognitive function* (pp. 271–295). New York: Guilford.

Mangun, G. R., & Hillyard, S. A. (1991). Modulations of sensory-evoked brain potentials indicate changes in perceptual processing during visual-spatial priming. *Journal of Experimental Psychology: Human Perception & Performance, 17*(4), 1057–1074.

Mangun, G. R., Plager, R., Loftus, W., Hillyard, S. A., Luck, S. J., Clark, V., et al. (1994). Monitoring the visual world: Hemispheric asymmetries and subcortical processes in attention. *Journal of Cognitive Neuroscience, 6,* 265–273.

Mani, K., & Johnson-Laird, P. N. (1982). The mental representation of spatial descriptions. *Memory & Cognition, 10*(2), 181–187.

Manktelow, K. I., & Over, D. E. (1990). Deontic thought and the selection task. In K. J. Gilhooly, M. T. G. Keane, & G. Erdos (Eds.), *Lines of thinking* (Vol. 1, pp. 153–164). London: Wiley.

Manktelow, K. I., & Over, D. E. (1992). Obligation, permission, and mental models. In V. Rogers, A. Rutherford, & P. Bibby (Eds.), *Models in the mind* (pp. 249–266). London: Academic Press.

Manns, J. R., & Eichenbaum, H. (2006). Evolution of declarative memory. *Hippocampus, 16*(9), 795–808.

Mantyla, T. (1986). Optimizing cue effectiveness: Recall of 500 and 600 incidentally learned words. *Journal of Experimental Psychology: Learning, Memory, & Cognition, 12,* 66–71.

Maratsos, M. P. (1998). The acquisition of grammar. In D. Kuhn & R. S. Siegler (Eds.), *Handbook of child psychology: Vol. 2: Cognition, perception, and language* (5th ed., pp. 421–466). New York: Wiley.

Maratsos, M. P. (2003). Language acquisition. In L. Nadel (Ed.), *Encyclopedia of cognitive science* (Vol. 2, pp. 691–696). London: Nature Group Press.

Marcel, A. J. (1983a). Conscious and unconscious perception: An approach to the relations between phenomenal experience and perceptual processes. *Cognitive Psychology, 15*(2), 238–300.

Marcel, A. J. (1983b). Conscious and unconscious perception: Experiments on visual masking and word recognition. *Cognitive Psychology, 15*(2), 197–237.

Marcel, A. J. (1986). Consciousness and processing: Choosing and testing a null hypothesis. *Brain and Behavioral Sciences, 9,* 40–41.

Marcel, A. J., & Bisiach, E. (Eds.) (1988). *Consciousness in contemporary science*. New York: Oxford University Press.

Marcus, D., & Overton, W. (1978). The development of gender constancy and sex role preferences. *Child Development, 49,* 434–444.

Marcus, G. F. (1998). Rethinking eliminative connectionism. *Cognitive Psychology, 37,* 243–282.

Marcus, G. F., Vijayan, S., Bandi Rao, S., & Vishton, P. M. (1999). Rule learning by seven-month-old infants. *Science, 283,* 77–80.

Maril, A., Wagner, A. D., & Schacter, D. L. (2001). On the tip of the tongue: An event-related fMRI study of semantic retrieval failure and cognitive conflict. *Neuron, 31* (4), 653–660.

Markman, A. B. (2003). Conceptual representations in psychology. In L. Nadel (Ed.), *Encyclopedia of cognitive science* (Vol. 1, pp. 670–673). London: Nature Publishing Group.

Markman, A. B., & Ross, B. H. (2003). Category use and category learning. *Psychological Bulletin, 129,* 592–613.

Markman, E. M. (1977). Realizing that you don't understand: A preliminary investigation. *Child Development, 48,* 986–992.

Markman, E. M. (1979). Realizing that you don't understand: Elementary school children's awareness of inconsistencies. *Child Development, 50,* 643–655.

Markovits, H. (2004). The development of deductive reasoning. In J. P. Leighton & R. J. Sternberg (Eds.), *The nature of reasoning* (pp. 313–338). New York: Cambridge University Press.

Markowitsch, H. J. (2000). Neuroanatomy of memory. In E. Tulving & F. I. M. Craik (Eds.), *The Oxford handbook of memory* (pp. 465–484). New York: Oxford University Press.

Markus, H. R., & Kitayama, S. (1991). Culture and the self: Implications for cognition, emotion, and motivation. *Psychological Review, 98,* 224–253.

Marmor, G. S. (1975). Development of kinetic images: When does the child first represent movement in mental images? *Cognitive Psychology, 7,* 548–559.

Marmor, G. S. (1977). Mental rotation and number conservation: Are they related? *Developmental Psychology, 13,* 320–325.

Marr, D. (1982). *Vision.* San Francisco: Freeman.

Marrero, M. Z., Golden, C. J., & Espe Pfeifer, P. (2002). Bilingualism, brain injury, and recovery: Implications for understanding the bilingual and for therapy. *Clinical Psychology Review, 22*(3), 465–480.

Marsh, B., Todd, P. M., & Gigerenzer, G. (2004). Cognitive heuristics: Reasoning the fast and frugal way. In J. P. Leighton & R. J. Sternberg (Eds.), *The nature of reasoning* (pp. 273–287). New York: Cambridge University Press.

Martin, J. A. (1981). A longitudinal study of the consequences of early mother–infant interaction: A microanalytic approach. *Monographs of the Society for Research in Child Development, 46*(203, Serial No. 190).

Martin, L. (1986). Eskimo words for snow: A case study in the genesis and decay of an anthropological example. *American Psychologist, 88,* 418–423.

Martin, M. (1979). Local and global processing: The role of sparsity. *Memory & Cognition, 7,* 476–484.

Martinez-Conde, S., Macknik, S. L., & Hybel, D. (2004). The role fixational eye movements in visual perception. *Nature Reviews: Neuroscience, 5,* 229–240.

Massaro, D. W. (1987). *Speech perception by ear and eye: A paradigm for psychological inquiry.* Hillsdale, NJ: Erlbaum.

Massaro, D. W., & Cohen, M. M. (1990). Perception of synthesized audible and visible speech. *Psychological Science, 1,* 55–63.

Masuda, T., & Nisbett, R. E. (2006). Culture and change blindness. *Cognitive Science: A Multidisciplinary Journal, 20*(2), 381–399.

Matarazzo, J. D. (1992). Biological and physiological correlates of intelligence. *Intelligence, 16*(3,4), 257–258.

Matlin, M. W., & Underhill, W. A. (1979). Selective rehearsal and selective recall. *Bulletin of the Psychonomic Society, 14*(5), 389–392.

Matsui, M., Sumiyoshi, T., Yuuki, H., Kato, K., & Kurachi, M. (2006). Impairment of event schema in patients with schizophrenia: Examination of script for shopping at supermarket. *Psychiatry Research, 143*(2–3), 179–187.

Matsumoto, D. (1994). *People: Psychology from a cultural perspective.* Pacific Grove, CA: Brooks Cole.

Matsumoto, D. (1996). *Culture and psychology.* Pacific Grove, CA: Brooks Cole.

Matthews, R. J. (2003). Connectionism and systematicity. In L. Nadel (Ed.), *Encyclopedia of cognitive science* (Vol. 1, pp. 687–690). London: Nature Publishing Group.

Matuszek, C., Witbrock, M., Kahlert, R. C., Cabrel, J., Schneider, D. Shah, P., et al. (2005). Searching for common sense populating Cyc from the web. *Proceedings of the Twentieth National Conference on Artificial Intelligence,* Pittsburgh, PA.

Maunsell, J. H. (1995). The brain's visual world: Representation of visual targets in cerebral cortex. *Science, 270,* 764–769.

Maxwell, R. J. (2005). Expanding the universe of categorical syllogisms: A challenge for reasoning researchers. *Behavior Research Methods, 37*(4), 560–580.

Mayer, J. D., & Salovey, P. (1997). What is emotional intelligence? In P. Salovey & D. Sluyter (Eds.), *Emotional development and emotional intelligence: Implications for educators* (pp. 3–31). New York: Basic.

Mayer, J. D., Salovey, P., & Caruso, D. (2000). Emotional intelligence. In R. J. Sternberg (Ed.), *Handbook of intelligence* (pp. 396–420). New York: Cambridge University Press.

Mayer, R. E. (2000a). Concepts: Conceptual change. In A. E. Kazdin (Ed.), *Encyclopedia of psychology* (Vol. 2, pp. 253–255). Washington, DC: American Psychological Association.

Mayer, R. E. (2000b). Intelligence and education. In R. J. Sternberg (Ed.), *Handbook of intelligence* (pp. 519–533). New York: Cambridge University Press.

Mayes, A. R., & Hunkin, N. M. (2003). Amnesia. In L. Nadel (Ed.), *Encyclopedia of cognitive science* (Vol. 1, pp. 90–97). London: Nature Publishing Group.

Mayr, U., & Kliegl, R. (1993). Sequential and coordinative complexity: Age-based processing in figural transformations. *Journal of Experimental Psychology: Learning, Memory, & Cognition, 19*(6), 1297–1320.

McAlister, A., & Peterson, C. (2007). A longitudinal study of child siblings and theory of mind development. *Cognitive Development, 22*(2), 258–270.

McArthur, T. (Ed.). (1992). *The Oxford companion to the English language.* New York: Oxford University Press.

McBride, D. (2007). Methods for measuring conscious and automatic memory: A brief review. *Journal of Consciousness Studies, 14*(1–2), 198–215.

McBride, D. M., & Dosher, B. A. (2002). A comparison of conscious and automatic memory processes for picture and word stimuli: A process dissociation analysis. *Consciousness & Cognition: An International Journal, 11*(3), 423–460.

McCann, R. S., & Johnston, J. C. (1992). Locus of single-channel bottleneck in dual-task interference. *Journal of Experimental Psychology: Human Perception & Performance, 18*(2), 471–484.

McCarthy, G., Blamire, A. M., Puce, A., Nobe, A. C., Bloch, G., Hyder, F., et al. (1994). Functional magnetic resonance imaging of human prefrontal cortex activation during a spatial working memory task. *Proceedings of the National Academy of Sciences, USA, 90,* 4952–4956.

McClelland, J. L., & Elman, J. L. (1986). The TRACE model of speech perception. *Cognitive Psychology, 18,* 1–86.

McClelland, J. L., McNaughton, B. C., & O'Reilly, R. C. (1995). Why there are complementary learning systems in the hippocampus and neocortex: Insights from the successes and failures of connectionist models of learning and memory. *Psychological Review, 102*, 419–457.

McClelland, J. L., & Rogers, T. T. (2003). The parallel distributed processing approach to semantic cognition. *Nature Reviews: Neuroscience, 4*, 1–14.

McClelland, J. L., & Rumelhart, D. E. (1981). An interactive activation model of context effects in letter perception: Part 1. An account of basic findings. *Psychological Review, 88*, 483–524.

McClelland, J. L., & Rumelhart, D. E., (1985). Distributed memory and the representation of general and specific information. *Journal of Experimental Psychology: General, 114*(2), 159–188.

McClelland, J. L., & Rumelhart, D. E. (1988). *Explorations in parallel distributed processing: A handbook of models, programs, and exercises.* Cambridge, MA: MIT Press.

McClelland, J. L., Rumelhart, D. E., & the PDP Research Group (1986). *Parallel distributed processing: Explorations in the microstructure of cognition: Vol. 2. Psychological and biological models.* Cambridge, MA: MIT Books.

McCormick, D. A., & Thompson, R. F. (1984). Cerebellum: Essential involvement in the classically conditioned eyelid response. *Science, 223*, 296–299.

McCormick, M. C., Brooks-Gunn, J., Buka, S. L., Goldman, J., Yu, J., Salganik, M., et al. (2006). Early intervention in low birth weight premature infants: Results at 18 years of age for the infant health and development program. *Pediatrics, 117*(3), 771–780.

McDermott, K. B. (1996). The persistence of false memories in list recall. *Journal of Memory and Language, 35*, 212–230.

McEwen, F., Happe, F., Bolton, P., Rijsdijk, F., Ronald, A., Dworzynski, K., et al. (2007). Origins of individual differences in imitation: Links with language, pretend play, and social insightful behavior in two-year-old twins. *Child Development, 78*(2), 474–492.

McGarry-Roberts, P. A., Stelmack, R. M., & Campbell, K. B. (1992). Intelligence, reaction time, and event-related potentials. *Intelligence, 16*(3,4), 289–313.

McGarva, A. R., Ramsey, M., & Shear, S. A. (2006). Effects of driver cell phone use on driver aggression. *Journal of Social Psychology, 146*(2), 133–146.

McGaugh, J. L. (1999). Memory storage, modulation of. In R. A. Wilson & F. C. Keil (Eds.), *The MIT encyclopedia of the cognitive sciences* (pp. 522–524). Cambridge, MA: MIT Press.

McGaugh, J. L., Cahill, L., & Roozendall, B. (1996). Modulation of memory storage. *Current Opinion in Neurobiology, 6*, 237–242.

McGurk, H., & MacDonald, J. (1976). Hearing lips and seeing voices. *Nature, 264*, 746–748.

McKenna, J., Treadway, M., & McCloskey, M. E. (1992). Expert psychological testimony on eyewitness reliability: Selling psychology before its time. In P. Suedfeld & P. E. Tetlock (Eds.), *Psychology and social policy* (pp. 283–293). New York: Hemisphere.

McKenzie, W. A., & Tiberghien, G. (2004). Context effects in recognition memory: The role of familiarity and recollection. *Consciousness and Cognition, 13*(1), 20–38.

McKoon, G., & Ratcliff, R. (1980). Priming in item recognition: The organization of propositions in memory for text. *Journal of Verbal Learning and Verbal Behavior, 19*, 369–386.

McKoon, G., & Ratcliff, R. (1992a). Inference during reading. *Psychological Review, 99*, 440–466.

McKoon, G., & Ratcliff, R. (1992b). Spreading activation versus compound cue accounts of priming: Mediated priming revisited. *Journal of Experimental Psychology: Learning, Memory, & Cognition, 18*(6), 1155–1172.

McKown, C., & Weinstein, R. S. (2003). The development and consequences of stereotype consciousness in middle childhood. *Child Development 74*(2), 498–515.

McLeod, P., Plunkett, K., & Rolls, E. T. (1998). *Introduction to connectionist modelling of cognitive processes.* Oxford, UK: Oxford University Press.

McNamara, D. S., Kintsch, E., Songer, N. B., & Kintsch, W. (1996). Learning from text: Effect of prior knowledge and text coherence. *Discourse Processes, 30*, 201–236.

McNamara, T. P. (1992). Theories of priming: I. Associative distance and lag. *Journal of Experimental Psychology: Learning, Memory, & Cognition, 18*(6), 1173–1190.

McNamara, T. P., Hardy, J. K., & Hirtle, S. C. (1989). Subjective hierarchies in spatial memory. *Memory & Cognition, 17*(4), 444–453.

McNamara, T. P., Ratcliff, R., & McKoon, G. (1984). The mental representation of knowledge acquired from maps. *Journal of Experimental Psychology: Learning, Memory, & Cognition, 10*(4), 723–732.

McNeil, J. E., & Warrington, E. K. (1993). Prosopagnosia: A face specific disorder. *Quarterly Journal of Experimental Psychology: Human Experimental Psychology, 46*, 1–10.

Meacham, J. (1982). A note on remembering to execute planned actions. *Journal of Applied Developmental Psychology, 3*, 121–133.

Meacham, J. A. (1983). Wisdom and the context of knowledge: Knowing that one doesn't know. In D. Kuhn & J. A. Meacham (Eds.), *On the development of developmental psychology* (pp. 111–134). Basel, Switzerland: Karger.

Meacham, J. A. (1990). The loss of wisdom. In R. J. Sternberg (Ed.), *Wisdom: Its nature, origins, and development* (pp. 181–211). New York: Cambridge University Press.

Meacham, J. A., & Singer, J. (1977). Incentive in prospective remembering. *Journal of Psychology, 97*, 191–197.

Mead, M. (1928/2001). *Coming of age in Samoa: A psychological study of primitive youth for Western civilisation.* New York: Harper Perennial Classics.

Meade, M. L., Watson, J. M., Balota, D. A., & Roediger, H. L. (2007). The roles of spreading activation and retrieval mode in producing false recognition in the DRM paradigm. *Journal of Memory and Language, 56*(3), 305–320.

Mechelli, A., Crinion, J. T., Nippeney, U., O'Doherty, J., Ashburner, J., Frackowiak, R. S., et al. (2004). Neurolinguistics: Structural plasticity in the bilingual brain. *Nature, 431*(7010), 757.

Medin, D. L. (1998). Concepts and conceptual structure. In P. Thagard (Ed.), *Mind readings* (pp. 93–126). Cambridge, MA: MIT Press.

Medin, D. L., & Aguilar, C. (1999). Categorization. In R. A. Wilson & F. C. Keil (Eds.), *The MIT encyclopedia of the cognitive sciences* (pp. 104–106). Cambridge, MA: MIT Press.

Medin, D. L., & Atran, S. (Eds.) (1999). *Folkbiology.* Cambridge, MA: MIT Press.

Medin, D. L., & Heit, E. (1999). Categorization. In D. Rumelhart & B. Martin (Eds.), *Handbook of cognition and perception* (pp. 99–143). New York: Academic Press.

Medin, D. L., Lynch, J., & Solomon, H. (2000). Are there kinds of concepts? *Annual Review of Psychology, 51*, 121–147.

Medin, D. L., Proffitt, J. B., & Schwartz, H. C. (2000). Concepts: An overview. In A. E. Kazdin (Ed.), *Encyclopedia of psychology* (Vol. 2, pp. 242–245). Washington, DC: American Psychological Association.

Mehler, J., Dupoux, E., Nazzi, T., & Dahaene-Lambertz, G. (1996). Coping with linguistic diversity: The infant's viewpoint. In J. L. Morgan & K. Demuth (Eds.), *Signal to Syntax: Bootstrapping from speech to grammar in early acquisition* (pp. 101–116). Mahwah, NJ: Erlbaum.

Meier, R. P. (1991). Language acquisition by deaf children. *American Scientist, 79*, 60–76.

Meinzer, M., Obleser, J., Flaisch, T., Eulitz, C., & Rockstroh, B. (2006). Recovery from aphasia as a function of language therapy in an early bilingual patient demonstrated by fMRI. *Neuropsychologia, 45*(6), 1247–1256.

Mejia-Arauz, R., Rogoff, B., & Paradise, R. (2005). Cultural variation in children's observation during a demonstration. *International Journal of Behavioral Development, 29*(4), 282–291.

Melnyk, L., & Bruck, M. (2004). Timing moderates the effects of repeated suggestive interviewing on children's eyewitness memory. *Applied Cognitive Psychology, 18*(5), 613–631.

Melrose, R. J., Poulin, R. M., & Stern, C. E. (2007). An fMRI investigation of the role of the basal ganglia in reasoning. *Brain Research, 1142,* 146–158.

Melton, R. J. (1995). The role of positive affect in syllogism performance. *Personality and Social Psychology Bulletin, 21,* 788–794.

Memon, A., Holliday, R., & Hill, C. (2006). Pre-event stereotypes and misinformation effects in young children. *Memory, 14*(1), 104–114.

Merikle, P. (2000). Consciousness and unconsciousness: Processes. In A. E. Kazdin (Ed.), *Encyclopedia of psychology* (Vol. 2, pp. 272–275). Washington, DC: American Psychological Association.

Mervis, C. B., Catlin, J., & Rosch, E. (1976). Relationships among goodness-of-example, category norms, and word frequency. *Bulletin of the Psychonomic Society, 7,* 268–284.

Metcalfe, J. (1986). Feeling of knowing in memory and problem solving. *Journal of Experimental Psychology: Learning, Memory, & Cognition, 12*(2), 288–294.

Metcalfe, J. (2000). Metamemory: Theory and data. In E. Tulving & F. I. M. Craik (Eds.), *The Oxford handbook of memory* (pp. 197–211). New York: Oxford University Press.

Metcalfe, J., & Wiebe, D. (1987). Intuition in insight and noninsight problem solving. *Memory & Cognition, 15*(3), 238–246.

Metzinger, T. (Ed.) (1995). *Conscious experience.* Paderborn: Schoningh.

Meyer, A. S., & Wheeldon, L. R. (2003). Phonological encoding of words. In L. Nadel (Ed.), *Encyclopedia of cognitive science* (Vol. 3, pp. 627–629). London: Nature Group Press.

Meyer, D. E., & Schvaneveldt, R. W. (1971). Facilitation in recognizing pairs of words: Evidence of a dependence between retrieval operations. *Journal of Experimental Psychology, 90*(2), 227–234.

Meyer, D. E., & Schvaneveldt, R. W. (1976). Meaning, memory structure, and mental processes. *Science, 192*(4234), 27–33.

Middleton, F. A., & Helms Tillery, S. I. (2003). Cerebellum. In L. Nadel (Ed.), *Encyclopedia of cognitive science* (Vol. 1, pp. 467–475). London: Nature Publishing Group.

Mignot, E., Taheri, S., & Nishino, S. (2002). Sleep with the hypothalamus: Emerging therapeutic targets for sleep disorders. *Nature Neuroscience 5,* 1071–1075.

Mill, J. S. (1887). *A system of logic.* New York: Harper & Brothers.

Miller, G. A. (1956). The magical number seven, plus or minus two: Some limits on our capacity for processing information. *Psychological Review, 63,* 81–97.

Miller, G. A. (1979). Images and models, similes and metaphors. In A. Ortony (Ed.), *Metaphor and thought* (pp. 202–250). New York: Cambridge University Press.

Miller, G. A., Galanter, E. H., & Pribram, K. H. (1960). *Plans and the structure of behavior.* New York: Holt, Rinehart and Winston.

Miller, G. A., & Gildea, P. M. (1987). How children learn words. *Scientific American, 257*(3), 94–99.

Miller, R. A., Pople, H., & Myers, J. (1982). INTERNIST, an experimental computer-based diagnostic consultant for general internal medicine. *New England Journal of Medicine, 307*(8), 494.

Mills, C. J. (1983). Sex-typing and self-schemata effects on memory and response latency. *Journal of Personality & Social Psychology, 45*(1), 163–172.

Milner, B. (1968). Disorders of memory loss after brain lesions in man: Preface-material-specific and generalized memory loss. *Neuropsychologia, 6*(3), 175–179.

Milner, B. (1972). Disorders of learning and memory after temporal lobe lesions in man. *Clinical Neurosurgery, 19,* 421–446.

Milner, B., Corkin, S., & Teuber, H. L. (1968). Further analysis of the hippocampal amnesic syndrome: 14-year follow-up study of H. M. *Neuropsychologia, 6,* 215–234.

Milner, B., Squire, L. R., & Kandel, E. R. (1998). Cognitive neuroscience and the study of memory. *Neuron, 20*(3), 445–468.

Minsky, M. (Ed.). (1968). *Semantic information processing.* Cambridge, MA: MIT Press.

Mirmiran, N., von Someren, E. J. W., & Swaab, D. F. (1996). Is brain plasticity preserved during aging and in Alzheimer's disease? *Behavioral Brain Research, 78,* 43–48.

Mishkin, M., & Appenzeller, T. (1987). The anatomy of memory. *Scientific American, 256*(6), 80–89.

Mishkin, M., & Petri, H. L. (1984). Memories and habits: Some implications for the analysis of learning and retention. In L. R. Squire & N. Butters (Eds.), *Neurophysiology of memory* (pp. 287–296). New York: Guilford.

Mishkin, M., Ungerleider, L. G., & Macko, K. A. (1983). Object vision and spatial vision: Two cortical pathways. *Trends in Neurosciences, 6*(10), 414–417.

Mitchell, D. B., & Bruss, P. J. (2003). Age differences in implicit memory: Conceptual, perceptual, or methodological? *Psychology and Aging, 18*(4), 807–822.

Moar, I., & Bower, G. H. (1983). Inconsistency in spatial knowledge. *Memory & Cognition, 11*(2), 107–113.

Modell, H. I., Michael, J. A., Adamson, T., Goldberg, J., Horwitz, B. A., Bruce, D. S., et al. (2000). Helping undergraduates repair faulty mental models in the student laboratory. *Advances in Physiological Education, 23,* 82–90.

Mohammed, A. K., Jonsson, G., & Archer, T. (1986). Selective lesioning of forebrain noradrenaline neurons at birth abolishes the improved maze learning performance induced by rearing in complex environment. *Brain Research, 398*(1), 6–10.

Monk, C. S., Gunderson, V. M., Grant, K. S., & Mechling, J. L. (1996). A demonstration of the memory savings effect in infant monkeys. *Developmental Psychology, 32*(6), 1051–1055.

Mooney, A. (2004). Co-operation, violations and making sense. *Journal of Pragmatics, 36*(5), 899–920.

Moore, C. M., & Egeth, H. (1997). Perception without attention: Evidence of grouping under conditions of inattention. *Journal of Experimental Psychology: Human Perception and Performance, 23,* 339–352.

Morawski, J. (2000). Psychology: Early twentieth century. In A. E. Kazdin (Ed.), *Encyclopedia of psychology* (Vol. 6, pp. 403–410). Washington, DC: American Psychological Association.

Moray, N. (1959). Attention in dichotic listening: Affective cues and the influence of instructions. *Quarterly Journal of Experimental Psychology, 11,* 56–60.

Morris, C. D., Bransford, J. D., & Franks, J. (1977). Levels of processing versus transfer appropriate processing. *Journal of Verbal Learning & Verbal Behavior, 16*(5), 519–533.

Morton, J. (1969). Interaction of information in word recognition. *Psychological Review, 76,* 165–178.

Morton, T. U. (1978). Intimacy and reciprocity of exchange: A comparison of spouses and strangers. *Journal of Personality and Social Psychology, 36,* 72–81.

Moscovitch, M. (2003). Memory consolidation. In L. Nadel (Ed.), *Encyclopedia of cognitive science* (Vol. 2, pp. 1066–1081). London: Nature Publishing Group.

Moscovitch, M., & Craik, F. I. M. (1976). Depth of processing, retrieval cues, and uniqueness of encoding as factors in recall. *Journal of Verbal Learning and Verbal Behavior, 15,* 447–458.

Moscovitch, M., Winocur, G., & Behrmann, M. (1997). What is special about face recognition? Nineteen experiments on a person with visual object agnosia and dyslexia but normal face recognition. *Journal of Cognitive Neuroscience, 9,* 555–604.

Moshman, E. (1998). Cognitive development beyond childhood. In W. Damon (Ed.-in-Chief), D. Kuhn, & R. S. Siegler (Vol. Eds.), *Handbook of child psychology: Vol. 2. Cognitive Development* (pp. 947–978). New York: Wiley.

Motter, A. E., de Moura, A. P. S., Lai, Y. C., & Dasgupta, P. (2002). Topology of the conceptual network of language. *Physical Review E: Statistical, Nonlinear, and Soft Matter Physics, 65,* 065102.

Motter, B. (1999). Attention in the animal brain. In R. A. Wilson & F. C. Keil (Eds.), *The MIT encyclopedia of the cognitive sciences* (pp. 41–43). Cambridge, MA: MIT Press.

Mufwene, S. S. (2004). Language birth and death. *Annual Review of Anthropology, 33,* 201–222.

Mulligan, N. W. (2003). Memory: Implicit versus explicit. In L. Nadel (Ed.), *Encyclopedia of cognitive science* (Vol. 2, pp. 1114–1120). London: Nature Publishing Group.

Munhall, K. G. (2003). Phonology, neural basis of. In L. Nadel (Ed.), *Encyclopedia of cognitive science* (Vol. 3, pp. 655–658). London: Nature Group Press.

Münte, T. F., Altenmüller, E., & Jäncke, L. (2002). The musician's brain as a model of neuroplasticity. *Nature Reviews: Neuroscience, 3,* 473–478.

Murdock, B. B. (2003). Memory models. In L. Nadel (Ed.), *Encyclopedia of cognitive science* (Vol. 2, pp. 1084–1089). London: Nature Publishing Group.

Murdock, B. B., Jr. (1961). Short-term retention of single paired-associates. *Psychological Reports, 8,* 280.

Murphy, G. L. (1993). Theories and concept formation. In I. Van Mechelen, J. A. Hampton, R. S. Michalski, & P. Theuns (Eds.), *Categories and concepts: Theoretical views and inductive data analysis* (pp. 173–200). London: Academic Press.

Murphy, K., McKone, E., & Slee, J. (2003). Dissociations between implicit and explicit memory in children: The role of strategic processing and the knowledge base. *Journal of Experimental Child Psychology, 84*(2), 124–165.

Murray, E. A. (2003). Temporal cortex. In L. Nadel (Ed.), *Encyclopedia of cognitive science* (Vol. 4, pp. 353–360). London: Nature Publishing Group.

Näätänen, R. (1988a). Implications of ERP data for psychological theories of attention. *Biological Psychology, 26*(1–3), 117–163.

Näätänen, R. (1988b). Regional cerebral blood-flow: Supplement to event-related potential studies of selective attention. In G. C. Galbraith, M. L. Kietzman, & E. Donchin (Eds.), *Neurophysiology and psychophysiology: Experimental and clinical applications* (pp. 144–156). Hillsdale, NJ: Erlbaum.

Näätänen, R. (1990). The role of attention in auditory information processing as revealed by event-related potentials and other brain measures of cognitive function. *Behavioral & Brain Sciences, 13*(2), 201–288.

Näätänen, R. (1992). *Attention and brain function.* Hillsdale, NJ: Erlbaum.

Nagell, K., Olguin, R. S., & Tomasello, M. (1993). Processes of social learning in the tool use of chimpanzees (Pan troglodytes) and human children (Homo sapiens). *Journal of Comparative Psychology, 107*(2), 174–186.

Nairne, J. S., & Crowder, R. G. (1982). On the locus of the stimulus suffix effect. *Memory & Cognition, 10,* 350–357.

Nakayama, K. (1990). Visual inference in the perception of occluded surfaces (Summary). *Proceedings of the 125th Annual Conference of the Cognitive Science Society* (p. 1019). Hillsdale, NJ: Erlbaum.

Nation, P. (2001). *Learning vocabulary in another language.* Cambridge, UK: Cambridge University Press.

National Research Council. (1998). *Preventing reading difficulties in young children.* Washington, DC: National Academy Press.

Naus, M. J. (1974). Memory search of categorized lists: A consideration of alternative self-terminating search strategies. *Journal of Experimental Psychology, 102,* 992–1000.

Naus, M. J., Glucksberg, S., & Ornstein, P. A. (1972). Taxonomic word categories and memory search. *Cognitive Psychology, 3,* 643–654.

Naveh-Benjamin, M., & Ayres, T. J. (1986). Digit span, reading rate, and linguistic relativity. *Quarterly Journal of Experimental Psychology: Human Experimental Psychology, 38*(4), 739–751.

Navon, D. (1977). Forest before trees: The precedence of global features in visual perception. *Cognitive Psychology, 9,* 353–383.

Navon, D., & Gopher, D. (1979). On the economy of the human-processing system. *Psychological Review, 86,* 214–255.

Neçka, E., & Orzechowski, J. (2005). Higher-order cognition and intelligence. In R. J. Sternberg & J. E. Pretz (Eds.), *Cognition and intelligence* (pp. 122–141). New York: Cambridge University Press.

Neely, J. H. (2003). Priming. In L. Nadel (Ed.), *Encyclopedia of cognitive science* (Vol. 3, pp. 721–724). London: Nature Publishing Group.

Neisser, U. (1967). *Cognitive psychology.* New York: Appleton-Century-Crofts.

Neisser, U. (1978). Memory: What are the important questions? In M. M. Gruneberg, P. Morris, & R. Sykes (Eds.), *Practical aspects of memory* (pp. 3–24). London: Academic Press.

Neisser, U. (1982). Snapshots or benchmarks? In U. Neisser (Ed.), *Memory observed: Remembering in natural contexts.* San Francisco: Freeman.

Neisser, U. (1999). *Memory observed* (rev. ed.). New York: Worth.

Neisser, U., & Becklen, R. (1975). Selective looking: Attending to visually specified events. *Cognitive Psychology, 7*(4), 480–494.

Neisser, U., Boodoo, G., Bouchard, T. J., Boykin, W. A., Brody, N., Ceci, S. J., et al. (1996). Intelligence: Knowns and unknowns. *American Psychologist, 51*, 77–101.

Neisser, U., & Harsch, N. (1993). Phantom flashbulbs: False recollections of hearing the news about Challenger. In E. Winograd & U. Neisser (Eds.), *Affect and accuracy in recall: Studies of "flashbulb" memories* (pp. 9–31). New York: Cambridge University Press.

Nelkin, N. (1996). *Consciousness and the origins of thought.* Cambridge, UK: Cambridge University Press.

Nelson, K. (1973). Structure and strategy in learning to talk. *Monograph of the Society for Research in Child Development, 38*(Serial No. 149).

Nelson, K. (1999). Language and thought. In M. Bennett (Ed.), *Developmental psychology* (pp. 185–204). Philadelphia: Psychology Press.

Nelson, K., & Fivush, R. (2004). The emergence of autobiographical memory: A social cultural *Neuropsychologia, 40*, 964–969.

Nelson, T. O., & Narens, L. (1994). Why investigate metacognition? In J. Metcalfe & A. P. Shimamura (Eds.), *Metacognition—knowing about knowing* (pp. 1–26). Cambridge, MA: MIT Press.

Nelson, T. O., & Rothbart, R. (1972). Acoustic savings for items forgotten from long-term memory. *Journal of Experimental Psychology, 93*, 357–360.

Neto, F., Williams, J. E., & Widner, S. C. (1991). Portuguese children's knowledge of sex stereotypes: Effects of age, gender, and socioeconomic status. *Journal of Cross-Cultural Psychology, 22*(3), 376–388.

Nettelbeck, T. (1987). Inspection time and intelligence. In P. A. Vernon (Ed.), *Speed of information-processing and intelligence* (pp. 295–346). Norwood, NJ: Ablex.

Nettelbeck, T., & Lally, M. (1976). Inspection time and measured intelligence. *British Journal of Psychology, 67*, 17–22.

Nettelbeck, T., & Rabbitt, P. M. A. (1992). Aging, cognitive performance, and mental speed. *Intelligence, 16*(2), 189–205.

Nettelbeck, T., Rabbitt, P. M. A., Wilson, C., & Batt, R. (1996). Uncoupling learning from initial recall: The relationship between speed and memory deficits in old age. *British Journal of Psychology, 87*, 593–607.

Nettelbeck, T., & Young, R. (1996). Intelligence and savant syndrome: Is the whole greater than the sum of the fragments? *Intelligence, 22*, 49–67.

Neubauer, A. C., & Fink, A. (2005). Basic information processing and the psychophysiology of intelligence. In R. J. Sternberg & J. E. Pretz (Eds.), *Cognition and intelligence* (pp. 68–87). New York: Cambridge University Press.

Neumann, P. G. (1977). Visual prototype formation with discontinuous representation of dimensions of variability. *Memory & Cognition, 5*(2), 187–197.

Neville, H. J. (1995). Developmental specificity in neurocognitive development in humans. In M. S. Gazzaniga (Ed.), *The cognitive neurosciences* (pp. 219–231). Cambridge, MA: MIT Press.

Newell, A., Shaw, J. C., & Simon, H. A. (1957a). Empirical explorations of the logic theory machine: A case study in heuristics. *Proceedings of the Western Joint Computer Conference, 230–240.*

Newell, A., Shaw, J. C., & Simon, H. A. (1957b). Problem solving in humans and computers. *Carnegie Technical, 21*(4), 34–38.

Newell, A., & Simon, H. A. (1972). *Human problem solving.* Englewood Cliffs, NJ: Prentice-Hall.

Newman, R. S. (2005). The cocktail party effect in infants revisited: Listening to one's name in noise. *Developmental Psychology, 41*(2), 352–362.

Newman, S. D., Carpenter, P. A., Varma, S., & Just, M. A. (2003). Frontal and parietal participation in problem solving in the Tower of London: fMRI and computational modeling of planning and high-level perception. *Neuropsychologia, 41*, 1668–1682.

Newman, S. D., & Just, M. A. (2005). The neural bases of intelligence. In R. J. Sternberg & J. E. Pretz (Eds.), *Cognition and intelligence* (pp. 88–103). New York: Cambridge University Press.

Newport, E. L. (1990). Maturational constraints on language learning. *Cognitive Science, 14*, 11–28.

Newport, E. L. (1991). Constraining concepts of the critical period of language. In S. Carey & R. Gelman (Eds.), *The epigenesis of mind: Essays on biology and cognition* (pp. 111–130). Hillsdale, NJ: Erlbaum.

Newport, E. L. (2003). Language development, critical periods in. In L. Nadel (Ed.), *Encyclopedia of cognitive science* (Vol. 2, pp. 737–740). London: Nature Group Press.

Newton, M. (2004). *Savage girls and wild boys: A history of feral children.* London: Faber and Faber.

Nicholls, M. E. R., Searle, D. A., & Bradshaw, J. L. (2004). Read my lips. Asymmetries in the visual expression and perception of speech revealed through the McGurk effect. *Psychological Science, 15*(2), 138–141.

Nickerson, R. S. (2004). Teaching reasoning. In J. P. Leighton & R. J. Sternberg (Eds.), *The nature of reasoning* (pp. 410–442). New York: Cambridge University Press.

Nickerson, R. S. (2005). Technology and cognition amplification. In R. J. Sternberg & D. Preiss (Eds), *Intelligence and technology: The impact of tools on the nature and development of human abilities* (pp. 3–27). Mahwah, NJ: Erlbaum.

Nijboer, T. C. W., van der Smagt, M., van Zandvoort, M. J. E., & de Haan, E. H. F. (2007). Colour agnosia impairs the recognition of natural but not of non-natural scenes. *Cognitive Neuropsychology, 24*(2), 152–161.

Nijboer, T. C. W., van Zandvoort, M. J. E., & de Haan, E. H. F. (2007). A familial factor in the development of colour agnosia. *Neuropsychologia, 45*(8), 1961–1965.

Nikolic, M. I., Orr, J. M., & Sarter, N. B. (2004). Why pilots miss the green box: How display context undermines attention capture. *International Journal of Aviation Psychology, 14*, 39–52.

NINDS stroke information page. Retrieved December 27, 2004, from http://www.ninds.nih.gov/disorders/stroke/stroke.htm

Nisbett, R. E. (2003). *The geography of thought: Why we think the way we do.* New York: The Free Press.

Nisbett, R. E., & Masuda, T. (2003). Culture and point of view. *Proceedings of the National Academy of Science of the United States, 100*(19), 11163–11170.

Nisbett, R. E., & Miyamoto, Y. (2005). The influence of culture: Holistic versus analytic perception. *Trends in Cognitive Science, 9*(10), 467–473.

Nisbett, R. E., & Ross, L. (1980). *Human inference: Strategies and shortcomings of social judgment.* Englewood Cliffs, NJ: Prentice-Hall.

Nisbett, R. E., & Wilson, T. D. (1977). Telling more than we can know: Verbal reports on mental processes. *Psychological Review, 84*, 231–259.

Norman, D. A. (1968). Toward a theory of memory and attention. *Psychological Review, 75*, 522–536.

Norman, D. A. (1976). *Memory and attention: An introduction to human information processing* (2nd ed.). New York: Wiley.

Norman, D. A. (1988). *The design of everyday things.* New York: Doubleday.

Norman, D. A., & Rumelhart, D. E. (1975). *Explorations in cognition*. San Francisco: Freeman.

Norman, D. A., & Rumelhart, D. E. (1983). Studies of typing from the LNR research group. In W. E. Cooper (Ed.), *Cognitive aspects of skilled typing* (pp. 45–65). New York: Springer-Verlag.

Norman, K. A., & Schacter, D. L. (1997). False recognition in younger and older adults: Exploring the characteristics of illusory memories. *Memory and Cognition, 25*, 838–848.

Nosofsky, R. M., & Palmeri, T. J. (1997). An exemplar-based random walk model of speeded classification. *Psychological Review, 104*, 266–300.

Nosofsky, R. M., Palmeri, T. J., & McKinley, S. C. (1994). Rule-plus-exception model of classification learning. *Psychological Review, 101*, 53–79.

Novick, L. R., & Holyoak, K. J. (1991). Mathematical problem solving by analogy. *Journal of Experimental Psychology: Learning, Memory and Cognition, 17*(3), 398–415.

Nozick, R. (1990). Newcomb's problem and two principles of choice. In P. K. Moser (Ed.), *Rationality in action: Contemporary approaches.* (pp. 207–234). New York: Cambridge University Press.

Nyberg, L., & Cabeza, R. (2000). Brain imaging of memory. In E. Tulving & F. I. M. Craik (Eds.), *The Oxford handbook of memory* (pp. 501–520). New York: Oxford University Press.

Nyberg, L., Cabeza, R. & Tulving, E. (1996). PET studies of encoding and retrieval: The HERA model. *Psychonomic Bulletin and Review, 3*, 135–148.

O'Brien, D. P. (2004). Mental-logic theory: What it proposes, and reasons to take this proposal seriously. In J. P. Leighton & R. J. Sternberg (Eds.), *The nature of reasoning* (pp. 205–233). New York: Cambridge University Press.

O'Kane, G., Kensinger, E. A., & Corkin, S. (2004). Evidence for semantic learning in profound amnesia: An investigation with patient H.M. *Hippocampus, 14*(4), 417–425.

O'Keefe, J. (2003). Hippocampus. In L. Nadel (Ed.), *Encyclopedia of cognitive science* (Vol. 1, pp. 336–347). London: Nature Publishing Group.

O'Keefe, J. A., & Nadel, L. (1978). *The hippocampus as a cognitive map*. New York: Oxford University Press.

O'Leary, D. S., Block, R. I., Koeppel, J. A., Schultz, S. K., Magnotta, V. A., Ponto, L. B., et al. (2007). Effects of smoking marijuana on focal attention and brain blood flow. *Human Psychopharmacology: Clinical and Experimental, 22*(3), 135–148.

O'Regan, J. K. (2003). Change blindness. In L. Nadel (Ed.), *Encyclopedia of cognitive science* (Vol. 1, pp. 486–490). London: Nature Publishing Group.

O'Reilly, R. C. (1996). Biologically plausible error-driven learning using local activation differences: The generalized recirculation algorithm. *Neural Computation, 8*, 895–938.

O'Toole, A. J., Jiang, F., Abdi, H., & Haxby, J. V. (2005). Partially distributed representations of objects and faces in ventral temporal cortex. *Journal of Cognitive Neuroscience, 17*, 580–590.

Ogbu, J. U. (1986). The consequences of the American caste system. In U. Neisser (Ed.), *The school achievement of minority children*. Hillsdale, NJ: Erlbaum.

Ojemann, G. A. (1975). The thalamus and language. *Brain and Language, 2*, 1–120.

Ojemann, G. A. (1982). Models of the brain organization for higher integrative functions derived with electrical stimulation techniques. *Human Neurobiology, 1*, 243–250.

Ojemann, G. A., & Mateer, C. (1979). Human language cortex: Localization of memory, syntax, and sequential motor–phoneme identification systems. *Science, 205*, 1401–1403.

Ojemann, G. A., & Whitaker, H. A. (1978). The bilingual brain. *Archives of Neurology, 35*, 409–412.

Oller, D. K., & Eilers, R. E. (1998). Interpretive and methodological difficulties in evaluating babbling drift. *Parole, 7/8*, 147–164.

Oller, D. K., Eilers, R. E., Urbano, R., & Cobo-Lewis, A. B. (1997). Development of precursors to speech in infants exposed to two languages. *Journal of Child Language, 24*, 407–425.

Olshausen, B., Andersen, C., & Van Essen, D. C. (1993). A neural model of visual attention and invariant pattern recognition. *Journal of Neuroscience, 13*, 4700–4719.

Olson, R. K. (1999). Genes, environment, and reading disabilities. In R. J. Sternberg & L. Spear-Swerling (Eds.), *Perspectives on learning disabilities: Biological, cognitive, contextual*. Boulder, CO: Westview Press.

Orasanu, J. (2005). Crew collaboration in space: A naturalistic decision-making perspective. *Aviation, Space and Environmental Medicine, 76*(Suppl 6), B154–B163.

Orasanu, J., & Connolly, T. (1993). The reinvention of decision making. In G. E. Klein, J. Orasanu, R. Calderwood, & C. E. Zsambok (Eds.), *Decision making in action: Models and methods* (pp. 3–20). Norwood, NJ: Ablex.

Ortony, A. (1979). The role of similarity in similes and metaphors. In A. Ortony (Ed.), *Metaphor and thought* (pp. 186–201). New York: Cambridge University Press.

Osherson, D. N. (1990). Judgment. In D. N. Osherson & E. E. Smith (Eds.), *An invitation to cognitive science: Vol. 3. Thinking* (pp. 55–87). Cambridge, MA: MIT Press.

Otapowicz, D., Sobaniec, W., Kulak, W., & Okurowska-Zwada, B. (2005). Time of cooing appearance and further development of speech in children with cerebral palsy. *Annales Academiae Medicae Bialostocensis, 50*(1), 78–81.

Oxford English Dictionary (2nd ed.). (1989). Oxford, England: Clarendon Press.

Oyama, S. (1976). A sensitive period for the acquisition of a nonnative phonological system. *Journal of Psycholinguistic Research, 5*(3), 261–283.

Ozonoff, S., Strayer, D. L., McMahon, W. M., & Filloux, F. (1994). Executive function abilities in autism and Tourette syndrome: An information-processing approach. *Journal of Child Psychology and Psychiatry, 35*, 1015–1032.

Paap, K. R., Newsome, S. L., McDonald, J. E., & Schvaneveldt, R. W. (1982). An activation-verification model for letter and word recognition: The word-superiority effect. *Psychological Review, 89*(5), 573–594.

Paavilainen, P., Tiitinen, H., Alho, K., & Näätänen R. (1993). Mismatch negativity to slight pitch changes outside strong attentional focus. *Biological Psychology, 37*(1), 23–41.

Packard, M. G., Cahill, L., & McGaugh, J. L. (1994). Amygdala modulation of hippocampal-dependent and caudate nucleus-dependent memory processes. *Proceedings of the National Academy of Sciences, U.S.A., 91*, 8477–8481.

Paivio, A. (1969). Mental imagery in associative learning and memory. *Psychological Review, 76*(3), 241–263.

Paivio, A. (1971). *Imagery and verbal processes*. New York: Holt, Rinehart and Winston.

Palmer, J. C. (1990). Attentional limits on the perception and memory of visual information. *Journal of Experimental Psychology: Human Perception & Performance, 16*(2), 332–350.

Palmer, S. E. (1975). The effects of contextual scenes on the identification of objects. *Memory & Cognition, 3*, 519–526.

Palmer, S. E. (1977). Hierarchical structure in perceptual representation. *Cognitive Psychology, 9*, 441–474.

Palmer, S. E. (1992). Modern theories of Gestalt perception. In G. W. Humphreys (Ed.), *Understanding vision: An interdisciplinary perspective-readings in mind and language* (pp. 39–70). Oxford, UK: Blackwell.

Palmer, S. E. (1999a). Gestalt perception. In R. A. Wilson & F. C. Keil (Eds.), *The MIT encyclopedia of the cognitive sciences* (pp. 344–346). Cambridge, MA: MIT Press.

Palmer, S. E. (1999b). *Vision science: Photons to phenomenology*. Cambridge, MA: MIT Press.

Palmer, S. E. (2000). Perceptual organization. In A. E. Kazdin (Ed.), *Encyclopedia of psychology* (Vol. 6, pp. 93–97). Washington, DC: American Psychological Association.

Palmer, S. E., & Rock, I. (1994). Rethinking perceptual organization: The role of uniform connectedness. *Psychonomic Bulletin & Review, 1*, 29–55.

Palmeri, T. J. (2003). Automaticity. In L. Nadel (Ed.), *Encyclopedia of cognitive science* (Vol. 1, pp. 290–301). London: Nature Publishing Group.

Paracchini, S., Scerri, T., & Monaco, A. P. (2007). The genetic lexicon of dyslexia. *Annual Review of Genomics and Human Genetics, 8*, 57–79.

Paradis, M. (1977). Bilingualism and aphasia. In H. A. Whitaker & H. Whitaker (Eds.), *Studies in neurolinguistics* (Vol. 3). New York: Academic Press.

Paradis, M. (1981). Neurolinguistic organization of a bilingual's two languages. In J. E. Copeland & P. W. Davis (Eds.), *The seventh LACUS forum*. Columbia, SC: Hornbeam Press.

Parker, A. J. (2007). Binocular depth perception and the cerebral cortex. *Nature Reviews: Neuroscience, 8*(6), 379–391.

Parker, A. J., Cumming, B. G., & Dodd, J. V. (2000). Binocular neurons and the perception of depth. In M. Gazzaniga (Ed.), *The new cognitive neurosciences* (pp. 263–278). Cambridge, MA: MIT Press.

Parker, J. D. A., Duffy, J. M., Wood, L. M., Bond, B. J., & Hogan, M. J. (2006). Academic achievement and emotional intelligence: Predicting the successful transition from high school to university. *Journal of The First-Year Experience & Students in Transition, 17*(1), 67–78.

Parkin, A. J. (1991). Recent advances in the neuropsychology of memory. In J. Weinman & J. Hunter (Eds.), *Memory: Neurochemical and abnormal perspectives* (pp. 141–162). London: Harwood Academic Publishers.

Parsons, O. A., & Nixon, S. J. (1993). Neurobehavioral sequelae of alcoholism. *Neurologic Clinics, 11*(1), 205–218.

Pashler, H. (1994). Dual-task interference in simple tasks: Data and theory. *Psychological Bulletin, 116*(2), 220–244.

Pashler, H. (1998). *The psychology of attention*. Cambridge, MA: MIT Press.

Pashler, H. E., & Johnston, J. (1998). Attentional limitations in dual task performance. In H. Pashler (Ed.), *Attention* (pp. 155–189). East Sussex, UK: Psychology Press.

Passafiume, D., Di Giacomo, D., & Carolei, A. (2006). Word-stem completion task to investigate semantic network in patients with Alzheimer's disease. *European Journal of Neurology, 13*(5), 460–464.

Patel, V. L., Kaufman, D. R., & Arocha, J. F. (2002). Methodological review: Emerging paradigms of cognition in medical decision-making. *Journal of Biomedical Infomatics, 35*, 52–75.

Pavlov, I. P. (1955). *Selected works*. Moscow: Foreign Languages Publishing House.

Payne, J. (1976). Task complexity and contingent processing in decision making: An information search and protocol analysis. *Organizational Behavior and Human Performance, 16*, 366–387.

Payne, J. D., Nadel, L., Allen, J. J. B., Thomas, K. G. F., & Jacobs, W. J. (2002). The effects of experimentally induced stress on false recognition. *Memory, 10*(1), 1–6.

Peacocke, C. (1998). Conscious attitudes, attention and self-knowledge. In C. Wright, B. C. Smith, & C. Macdonald (Eds.), *Knowing our own minds* (pp. 63–98). Oxford, UK: Oxford University Press.

Pearson, B. Z., Fernandez, S. C., Lewedeg, V., & Oller, D. K. (1997). The relation of input factors to lexical learning by bilingual infants. *Applied Psycholinguistics, 18*, 41–58.

Pedersen, P. M., Vinter, K., & Olsen, T. S. (2004). Aphasia after stroke: Type severity and prognosis the Copenhagen aphasia study. *Cerebrovascular Disease, 17*(1), 35–43.

Peigneux, P., Laureys, S., Fuchs, S., Collette, F., Perrin, F. Reggers, J., et al. (2004). Are spatial memories strengthened in the human hippocampus during slow wave sleep? *Neuron, 44*(3), 535–545.

Penfield, W. (1955). The permanent record of the stream of consciousness. *Acta Psychologica, 11*, 47–69.

Penfield, W. (1969). Consciousness, memory, and man's conditioned reflexes. In K. H. Pribram (Ed.), *On the biology of learning* (pp. 129–168). New York: Harcourt, Brace & World.

Penfield, W., & Roberts, L. (1959). *Speech and brain mechanisms*. Princeton, NJ: Princeton University Press.

Pennebaker, J. W., & Memon, A. (1996). Recovered memories in context: Thoughts and elaborations on Bowers and Farvolden. *Psychological Bulletin, 119*, 381–385.

Pepperberg, I. M. (1999). *The Alex Studies: Cognitive and communicative abilities of grey parrots*. Cambridge, MA: Harvard University Press.

Pepperberg, I. M. (2007). Grey parrots do not always 'parrot': The roles of imitation and phonological awareness in the creation of new labels from existing vocalizations. *Language Sciences, 29*(1), 1–13.

Pepperberg, I. M., & Gordon, J. D. (2005). Number comprehension by a grey parrot (*Psittacus erithacus*), including a zero-like concept. *Journal of Comparative Psychology, 119*(2), 197–209.

Peretz, I. (1996). Can we lose memory for music? A case of music agnosia in a nonmusician. *Journal of Cognitive Neuroscience, 8*(6), 481–496.

Peretz, I., Kolinsky, R., Tramo, M., Labrecque, R., Hublet, C., Demeurisse, G., & Belleville, S. (1994). Functional dissociations following bilateral lesions of auditory cortex. *Brain, 117*, 1283–1301.

Perfetti, C. A. (1985). *Reading ability*. New York: Oxford University Press.

Perfetti, C. A., & Roth, S. F. (1981). Some of the interactive processes in reading and their role in reading skill. In A. M. Lesgold & C. A. Perfetti (Eds.), *Interactive processes in reading* (pp. 269–297). Hillsdale, NJ: Erlbaum.

Perkins, D. N. (1981). *The mind's best work*. Cambridge, MA: Harvard University Press.

Perkins, D. N., & Grotzer, T. A. (1997). Teaching intelligence. *American Psychologist, 52,* 1125–1133.

Perlmutter, D. (Ed.). (1983a). *Studies in relational grammar* (Vol. 1). Chicago: University of Chicago Press.

Perlmutter, M. (1983b). Learning and memory through adulthood. In M. W. Riley, B. B. Hess, & K. Bond (Eds.), *Aging in society: Selected reviews of recent research.* Hillsdale, NJ: Erlbaum.

Perner, J. (1998). The meta-intentional nature of executive functions and theory of mind. In P. Carruthers & J. Boucher (Eds.), *Language and thought* (pp. 270–283). Cambridge, UK: Cambridge University Press.

Perner, J. (1999). Theory of mind. In M. Bennett (Ed.), *Developmental psychology: Achievements and prospects* (pp. 205–230). Philadelphia: Psychology Press.

Peru, A., & Zapparoli, P. (1999). A new case of representational neglect. The Italian *Journal of Neurological Sciences, 20*(4), 392–461.

Petersen, S. E., Fox, P. T., Posner, M. I., Mintun, M., & Raichle, M. E. (1988). Positron emission tomographic studies of the cortical anatomy of single-word processing. *Nature, 331*(6157), 585–589.

Petersen, S. E., Fox, P. T., Posner, M. I., Mintun, M., & Raichle, M. E. (1989). Positron emission tomographic studies of the processing of single words. *Journal of Cognitive Neuroscience, 1*(2), 153–170.

Peterson, L. R., & Peterson, M. J. (1959). Short-term retention of individual verbal items. *Journal of Experimental Psychology, 58,* 193–198.

Peterson, M. A. (1999). What's in a stage name? *Journal of Experimental Psychology: Human Perception and Performance, 25,* 276–286.

Peterson, M. A., Kihlstrom, J. F., Rose, P. M., & Glisky, M. L. (1992). Mental images can be ambiguous: Reconstruals and reference-frame reversals. *Memory & Cognition, 20*(2), 107–123.

Petitto, L., & Marentette, P. F. (1991). Babbling in the manual mode: Evidence for the ontogeny of language. *Science, 251*(5000), 1493–1499.

Petitto, L. A., Holowka, S., Sergio, L. E., Levy, B., & Ostry, D. J. (2004). Baby hands that move to the rhythm of language: Hearing babies acquiring sign language babble silently on the hands. *Cognition, 93*(1), 43–73.

Pezdek, K. (2003). Event memory and autobiographical memory for the events of September 11, 2001. *Applied Cognitive Psychology, 17*(9), 1033–1045.

Pezdek, K. (2006). Memory for the events of September 11, 2001. In L.-G. Nilsson & N. Ohta (Eds.), *Memory and society: Psychological perspectives* (pp. 73–90). New York: Psychology Press.

Pezdek, K., Blandon-Gitlin, I., & Moore, C. M. (2003). Children's face recognition memory: More evidence for the cross-race effect. *Journal of Applied Psychology, 88*(4), 760–763.

Phaf, R. H., & Kan, K. J. (2007). The automaticity of emotional Stroop: A meta-analysis. *Journal of Behavior Therapy and Experimental Psychiatry, 38*(2), 184–199.

Phelps, E. A. (1999). Brain versus behavioral studies of cognition. In R. J. Sternberg (Ed.), *The nature of cognition* (pp. 295–322). Cambridge, MA: MIT Press.

Phelps, E. A. (2004). Human emotion and memory: Interactions of the amygdala and the hippocampal complex. *Current Opinions in Neurobiology, 14,* 198–202.

Phelps, E. A. (2006). Emotion and cognition: Insights from studies of the human amygdala. *Annual Review of Psychology, 57,* 27–53.

Piaget, J. (1928). *Judgment and reasoning in the child.* London: Routledge & Kegan Paul.

Piaget, J. (1952). *The origins of intelligence in children.* New York: International Universities Press.

Piaget, J. (1955). *The language and thought of the child.* New York: Meridian Books.

Pianta, R. C., & Egeland, B. (1994). Predictors of instability in children's mental test performance at 24, 48, and 96 months. *Intelligence, 18*(2), 145–163.

Pickell, H., Klima, E., Love, T., Krichevsky, M., Bellugi, U., & Hickok, G. (2005). Sign language aphasia following right hemisphere damage in a left-hander: A case of reversed cerebral dominance in a deaf signer? *Neurocase, 11*(3), 194–203.

Picton, T. W., & Mazaheri, A. (2003). Electroencephalography. In L. Nadel (Ed.), *Encyclopedia of cognitive science* (Vol. 1, pp. 1083–1087). London: Nature Publishing Group.

Pierce, K., & Courchesne, E. (2003). Austism. In L. Nadel (Ed.), *Encyclopedia of cognitive science* (Vol. 1, pp. 278–283). London: Nature Publishing Group.

Piercy, M. (1964). The effects of cerebral lesions on intellectual function: A review of current research trends. *British Journal of Psychiatry 110,* 310–352.

Pillemer, D., & White, S. H. (1989). Childhood events recalled by children and adults. In H. W. Reese (Ed.), *Advances in child development and behavior,* (Vol. 22, pp. 297–340). New York: Academic Press.

Pines, J. M. (2005). Profiles in patient safety: Confirmation bias in emergency medicine. *Academic Emergency Medicine, 13*(1), 90–94.

Pinker, S. (1980). Mental imagery and the third dimension. *Journal of Experimental Psychology: General, 109*(3), 354–371.

Pinker, S. (1985). Visual cognition: An introduction. In S. Pinker (Ed.), *Visual cognition* (pp. 1–63). Cambridge, MA: MIT Press.

Pinker, S. (1994). *The language instinct.* New York: William Morrow.

Pinker, S. (1997a). *How the mind works.* New York: Norton.

Pinker, S. (1997b). Letter to the editor. *Science, 276,* 1177–1178.

Pinker, S. (1999). *Words and rules.* New York: Basic Books.

Pisoni, D. B., Nusbaum, H. C., Luce, P. A., & Slowiaczek, L. M. (1985). Speech perception, word recognition and the structure of the lexicon. *Speech Communication, 4,* 75–95.

Platek, S. M., Keenan, J. P., Gallup, G. G., & Geroze, B. M. (2004). Where am I? The neurological correlates of self and other. *Cognitive Brain Research, 19,* 114–122.

Platt, M. L., & Glimcher, P. W. (1999). Neural correlates of decision variables in parietal cortex. *Nature, 400,* 233–238.

Plaut, D. C. (2000). Connectionism. In A. E. Kazdin (Ed.), *Encyclopedia of psychology* (pp. 265–268). Washington, DC: American Psychological Association.

Plaut, D. C., McClelland, J. L., Seidenberg, M. S., & Patterson, K. (1996). Understanding normal and impaired word reading: Computational principles in quasi-regular domains. *Psychological Review, 103,* 56–115.

Plaut, D. C., & Shallice, T. (1994). *Connectionist modelling in cognitive neuropsychology: A case study.* Hillsdale, NJ: Erlbaum.

Plomin, R. (1997). Identifying genes for cognitive abilities and disabilities. In R. J. Sternberg & E. L. Grigorenko (Eds.), *Intelligence, heredity, and environment* (pp. 89–104). New York: Cambridge University Press.

Plunkett, K. (1998). Language acquisition and connectionism. *Language and Cognitive Processes, 13,* 97–104.

Poggio, T., & Edelman, S. (1990). A network that learns to recognize three-dimensional objects. *Nature, 343,* 263–266.

Poincaré, H. (1913). *The foundations of science.* New York: Science Press.

Policastro, E., & Gardner, H. (1999). From case studies to robust generalizations: An approach to the study of creativity. In R. J.

Sternberg (Ed.), *Handbook of creativity* (pp. 213–225). New York: Cambridge University Press.

Pollatsek, A., & Miller, B. (2003). Reading and writing. In L. Nadel (Ed.), *Encyclopedia of cognitive science* (Vol. 3, pp. 841–847). London: Nature Publishing Group.

Pollatsek, A., & Rayner, K. (1989). Reading. In M. I. Posner (Ed.), *Foundations of cognitive science* (pp. 401–436). Cambridge, MA: MIT Press.

Pomerantz, J. R. (1981). Perceptual organization in information processing. In M. Kubovy & J. R. Pomerantz (Eds.), *Perceptual organization* (pp. 141–180). Hillsdale, NJ: Erlbaum.

Pomerantz, J. R. (2003). Perception: Overview. In L. Nadel (Ed.), *Encyclopedia of cognitive science* (Vol. 3, pp. 527–537). London: Nature Publishing Group.

Poon, L. W. (1987). *Myths and truisms: Beyond extant analyses of speed of behavior and age.* Address to the Eastern Psychological Association Convention.

Posner, M., & Keele, S. W. (1968). On the genesis of abstract ideas. *Journal of Experimental Psychology, 77*(3, Pt. 1), 353–363.

Posner, M. I. (1969). Abstraction and the process of recognition. In G. H. Bower & J. T. Spence (Eds.), *The psychology of learning and motivation: Vol. 3. Advances in learning and motivation.* New York: Academic Press.

Posner, M. I. (1992). Attention as a cognitive and neural system. *Current Directions in Psychological Science, 1*(1), 11–14.

Posner, M. I. (1995). Attention in cognitive neuroscience: An overview. In M. Gazzaniga (Ed.), *The cognitive neurosciences* (pp. 615–624). Cambridge, MA: MIT Press.

Posner, M. I., Boies, S., Eichelman, W., & Taylor, R. (1969). Retention of visual and name codes of single letters. *Journal of Experimental Psychology, 81,* 10–15.

Posner, M. I., & Dehaene, S. (1994). Attentional networks. *Trends in Neurosciences, 17*(2), 75–79.

Posner, M. I., & DiGirolamo, G. J. (1998). Conflict, target detection and cognitive control. In R. Parasuraman (Ed.), *The attentive brain.* Cambridge, MA: MIT Press.

Posner, M. I., DiGirolamo, G. J., & Fernandez-Duque, D. (1997). Brain mechanisms of cognitive skills. *Consciousness and Cognition, 6,* 267–290.

Posner, M. I., & Fernandez-Duque, D. (1999). Attention in the human brain. In R. A. Wilson & F. C. Keil (Eds.), *The MIT encyclopedia of the cognitive sciences* (pp. 43–46). Cambridge, MA: MIT Press.

Posner, M. I., Goldsmith, R., & Welton, K. E., Jr. (1967). Perceived distance and the classification of distorted patterns. *Journal of Experimental Psychology, 73*(1), 28–38.

Posner, M. I., & Keele, S. W. (1967). Decay of visual information from a single letter. *Science, 158*(3797), 137–139.

Posner, M. I., & Petersen, S. E. (1990). The attention system of the human brain. *Annual Review of Neuroscience, 13,* 25–42.

Posner, M. I., Petersen, S. E., Fox, P. T., & Raichle, M. E. (1988). Localization of cognitive operations in the human brain. *Science, 240*(4859), 1627–1631.

Posner, M. I., & Raichle, M. E. (1994). *Images of mind.* New York: Freeman.

Posner, M. I., & Rothbart, M. K. (2007). Research on attention networks as a model for the integration of psychological science. *Annual Review of Psychology, 58,* 1–23.

Posner, M. I., Sandson, J., Dhawan, M., & Shulman, G. L. (1989). Is word recognition automatic? A cognitive-anatomical approach. *Journal of Cognitive Neuroscience, 1,* 50–60.

Posner, M. I., & Snyder, C. R. R. (1975). Attention and cognitive control. In R. Solso (Ed.), *Information processing and cognition: The Loyola Symposium* (pp. 55–85). Hillsdale, NJ: Erlbaum.

Posner, M. I., Snyder, C. R. R., & Davidson, B. J. (1980). Attention and the detection of signals. *Journal of Experimental Psychology: General, 109*(2), 160–174.

Postle, B. R., Brush, L. N., & Nick, A. M. (2004). Prefrontal cortex and the mediation of proactive interference in working memory. *Cognitive Affective Behavioral Neuroscience, 4*(4), 600–608.

Powers, D. E., & Kaufman, J. C. (2004). Do standardized tests penalize deep-thinking, creative, or conscientious students? Some personality correlates of Graduate Record Examinations test scores. *Intelligence, 32*(2), 145–153.

Premack, D. (1971). Language in chimpanzees? *Science, 172,* 808–822.

Pretz, J. E., Naples, A. J., & Sternberg, R J. (2003). Recognizing, defining, and representing problems. In J. E. Davidson & R. J. Sternberg (Eds.), The *psychology of problem solving* (pp. 3–30). New York: Cambridge University Press.

Prince, S. E., Tsukiura, R., & Cabeza, R. (2007). Distinguishing the neural correlates of episodic memory encoding and semantic memory retrieval. *Psychological Science, 18*(2), 144–151.

Prinzmetal, W. P. (1995). Visual feature integration in a world of objects. *Current Directions in Psychological Science, 4,* 90–94.

Proffitt, D. R., Stefanucci, J., Banton, T., & Epstein, W. (2003). The role of effort in perceiving distance. *Psychological Science, 14,* 106–112.

Proffitt, D. R., Stefanucci, J., Banton, T., & Epstein, W. (2006). Reply to Hutchinson & Loomis. *Spanish Journal of Psychology, 9,* 340–342.

Pugalee, D. K. (2004). A comparison of verbal and written descriptions of students' problem solving processes. *Educational Studies in Mathematics, 55*(1–3), 27–47.

Pullum, G. K. (1991). *The Great Eskimo vocabulary hoax and other irreverent essays on the study of language.* Chicago: University of Chicago Press.

Pylyshyn, Z. (1973). What the mind's eye tells the mind's brain: A critique of mental imagery. *Psychological Bulletin, 80,* 1–24.

Pylyshyn, Z. (1978). Imagery and artificial intelligence. In C. W. Savage (Ed.), *Minnesota studies in the philosophy of science: Vol. 9. Perception and cognition issues in the foundations of psychology* (pp. 19–56). Minneapolis: University of Minnesota Press.

Pylyshyn, Z. (1981). The imagery debate: Analogue media versus tacit knowledge. *Psychological Review, 88*(1), 16–45.

Pylyshyn, Z. (1984). *Computation and cognition.* Cambridge, MA: MIT Press.

Qui, J., Li, H., Huang, X., Zhang, F., Chen, A., Luo, Y., et al. (2007). The neural basis of conditional reasoning: An event-related potential study. *Neuropsychologia, 45*(7), 1533–1539.

Ragland, J. D., Moelter, S. T., McGrath, C., Hill, S. K., Gur, R. E., Bilker, W. B., et al. (2003). Levels-of-processing effect on word recognition in schizophrenia. *Biological Psychiatry, 54*(11), 1154–1161.

Raichle, M. E. (1998). Behind the scenes of function brain imaging: A historical and physiological perspective. *Proceedings of the National Academy of Sciences, 95,* 765–772.

Raichle, M. E. (1999). Positron emission tomography. In R. A. Wilson & F. C. Keil (Eds.), *The MIT encyclopedia of the cognitive sciences* (pp. 656–659). Cambridge, MA: MIT Press.

Raine, A., & Yang, Y. (2006). Neural foundations to moral reasoning and antisocial behavior. *Social Cognitive and Affective Neuroscience, 1*(3), 203–213.

Rajah, M. N., & McIntosh, A. R. (2005). Overlap in the functional neural systems involved in semantic and episodic memory retrieval. *Journal of Cognitive Neuroscience, 17*(3), 470–482.

Ralph, M. A. L., Lowe, C., & Rogers, T. T. (2007). Neural basis of category-specific semantic deficits for living things: Evidence from semantic dementia, HSVE and a neural network. *Brain, 130*(4), 1127–1137.

Ramachandra, P., Tymmala, R. M., Chu, H. L., Charles, L., & Truwit, W. A. H. (2003). Application of diffusion tensor imaging to magnetic-resonance-guided brain tumor resection. *Pediatric Neurosurgery, 39*(1), 39–43.

Ramey, C. T., & Ramey, S. L. (2000). Intelligence and public policy. In R. J. Sternberg (Ed.), *Handbook of intelligence* (pp. 534–548). New York: Cambridge University Press.

Ramus, F., Rosen, S., Dakin, S., Day, B. L., Castellote, J. M., White, S., et al. (2003). Theories of developmental dyslexia: Insights from a multiple case study of dyslexic adults. *Brain, 126*(4), 841–865.

Rao, R. P. N. (2003). Attention, models of. In L. Nadel (Ed.), *Encyclopedia of cognitive science* (Vol. 1, pp. 231–237). London: Nature Publishing Group.

Ratcliff, R. (1990). Connectionist models of recognition memory: Constraints imposed by learning and forgetting functions. *Psychological Review, 97*(2), 285–308.

Ratcliff, R., & McKoon, G. (1986). More on the distinction between episodic and semantic memories. *Journal of Experimental Psychology: Learning, Memory, & Cognition, 12*(2), 312–313.

Rayner, K., & Pollatsek, A. (2000). Reading. In A. E. Kazdin (Ed.), *Encyclopedia of psychology* (Vol. 7, pp. 14–18). Washington, DC: American Psychological Association.

Rayner, K., Sereno, S. C., Lesch, M. F., & Pollatsek, A. (1995). Phonological codes are automatically activated during reading: Evidence from an eye movement priming paradigm. *Psychological Science, 6*, 26–31.

Read, J. D. (2000). *Assessing vocabulary.* Cambridge, UK: Cambridge University Press.

Reason, J. (1990). *Human error.* New York: Cambridge University Press.

Reber, P. J., Knowlton, B. J, & Squire, L. R. (1996). Dissociable properties of memory systems: Differences in the flexibility of declarative and nondeclarative knowledge. *Behavioral Neurosciences, 110*, 861–871.

Reed, S. (1972). Pattern recognition and categorization. *Cognitive Psychology, 3*(3), 382–407.

Reed, S. (1974). Structural descriptions and the limitations of visual images. *Memory & Cognition, 2*(2), 329–336.

Reed, S. K. (1987). A structure-mapping model for word problems. *Journal of Experimental Psychology: Learning, Memory, & Cognition, 13*(1), 125–139.

Reed, S. K. (2000). Thinking: Problem solving. In A. E. Kazdin (Ed.), *Encyclopedia of psychology* (Vol. 8, pp. 71–75). Washington, DC: American Psychological Association.

Reed, S. K., Dempster, A., & Ettinger, M. (1985). Usefulness of analogous solutions for solving algebra word problems. *Journal of Experimental Psychology: Learning, Memory, & Cognition, 11*(1), 106–125.

Reed, T. E. (1993). Effect of enriched (complex) environment on nerve conduction velocity: New data and review of implications for the speed of information processing. *Intelligence, 17*(4), 533–540.

Reed, T. E., & Jensen, A. R. (1991). Arm nerve conduction velocity (NCV), brain NCV, reaction time, and intelligence. *Intelligence, 15*, 33–47.

Reed, T. E., & Jensen, A. R. (1993). Choice reaction time and visual pathway nerve conduction velocity both correlate with intelligence, but appear not to correlate with each other: Implications for information processing. *Intelligence, 17*, 191–203.

Reeder, G. D., McCormick, C. B., & Esselman, E. D. (1987). Self-referent processing and recall of prose. *Journal of Educational Psychology, 79*, 243–248.

Reicher, G. M. (1969). Perceptual recognition as a function of meaningfulness of stimulus material. *Journal of Experimental Psychology, 81*, 275–280.

Reisberg, D., Culver, L. C., Heuer, F., & Fischman, D. (1986). Visual memory: When imagery vividness makes a difference. *Journal of Mental Imagery, 10*(4), 51–74.

Reisberg, D., Smith, J. D., Baxter, D. A., & Sonenshine, M. (1989). "Enacted" auditory images are ambiguous: "Pure" auditory images are not. *Quarterly Journal of Experimental Psychology: Human Experimental Psychology, 41*(3–A), 619–641.

Reisberg, D., Wilson, M. A., & Smith, J. D. (1991). Auditory imagery and inner speech. In R. H. Logie & M. Denis (Eds.), *Advances in psychology: Vol. 80. Mental images in human cognition* (pp. 59–81). Amsterdam: North-Holland.

Reitman, J. S. (1971). Mechanisms of forgetting in short-term memory. *Cognitive Psychology, 2*, 185–195.

Reitman, J. S. (1974). Without surreptitious rehearsal, information in short-term memory decays. *Journal of Verbal Learning and Verbal Behavior, 13*, 365–377.

Reitman, J. S. (1976). Skilled perception in Go: Deducing memory structures from inter-response times. *Cognitive Psychology, 8*, 336–356.

Remez, R. E. (1994). A guide to research on the perception of speech. In M. A. Gernsbacher (Ed.), *Handbook of psycholinguistics* (pp. 145–172). San Diego: Academic Press.

Rempel-Clower, N., Zola, S. M., Squire, L. R., & Amaral, D. G. (1996). Three cases of enduring memory impairment following bilateral damage limited to the hippocampal formation. *Journal of Neuroscience, 16*, 5233–5255.

Rensink, R. A., O'Regan, J. K., & Clark, J. J. (1997). To see or not to see: The need for attention to perceive changes in scenes. *Psychological Science, 8*, 368–373.

Repacholi, B. M., & Meltzoff A. N. (2007). Emotional eavesdropping: Infants selectively respond to indirect emotional signals. *Child Development, 78*(2), 503–521.

Resches, M., & Perez Pereira, M. (2007). Referential communication abilities and Theory of Mind development in preschool children. *Journal of Child Language, 34*(1), 21–52.

Rescorla, R. A. (1967). Pavlovian conditioning and its proper control procedures. *Psychological Review, 74*, 71–80.

Rescorla, R. A., & Wagner, A. R. (1972). A theory of Pavlovian conditioning: Variations in the effectiveness of reinforcement and non-reinforcement. In A. H. Black & W. F. Prokasy (Eds.), *Classical conditioning: Vol. 2. Current research and theory.* New York: Appleton-Century-Crofts.

Rey, G. (2003). Language of thought. In L. Nadel (Ed.), *Encyclopedia of cognitive science* (Vol. 2, pp. 753–760). London: Nature Group Press.

Rhodes, G., Byatt, G., Michie, P. T., & Puce, A. (2004). Is the fusiform face area specialized for faces, individuation, or expert individuation? *Journal of Cognitive Neuroscience, 16*(2), 189–203.

Ricciardelli, L. A. (1992). Bilingualism and cognitive development in relation to threshold theory. *Journal of Psycholinguistic Research, 21*(4), 301–316.

Rice, M. L. (1989). Children's language acquisition. *American Psychologist, 44*, 149–156.

Richardson, J. T. E. (1994). Gender differences in mental rotation. *Perceptual Motor Skills, 78*(2), 435–448.

Richardson-Klavehn, A., & Bjork, R. A. (1988). Measures of memory. *Annual Review of Psychology, 39*, 475–543.

Richardson-Klavehn, A. R., & Bjork, R. A. (2003). Memory, long-term. In L. Nadel (Ed.), *Encyclopedia of cognitive science* (Vol. 2, pp. 1096–1105). London: Nature Publishing Group.

Riggs, L. A., Ratliff, F., Cornsweet, J. C., & Cornsweet, T. N. (1953). The disappearance of steadily fixated visual test objects. *Journal of the Optical Society of America, 43*, 495–501.

Rips, L. J. (1983). Cognitive processes in propositional reasoning. *Psychological Review, 90*(1), 38–71.

Rips, L. J. (1988). Deduction. In R. J. Sternberg & E. E. Smith (Eds.), *The psychology of human thought* (pp. 116–152). New York: Cambridge University Press.

Rips, L. J. (1989). Similarity, typicality, and categorization. In S. Vosniadou & A. Ortony (Eds.), *Similarity and analogical reasoning* (pp. 21–59). New York: Cambridge University Press.

Rips, L. J. (1994). Deductive reasoning. In R. J. Sternberg (Ed.), *Handbook of perception and cognition: Thinking and problem solving* (pp. 149–178). New York: Academic Press.

Rips, L. J. (1999). Deductive reasoning. In R. A. Wilson & F. C. Keil (Eds.), *The MIT Encyclopedia of the cognitive sciences* (pp. 225–226). Cambridge, MA: MIT Press.

Ro, T., & Rafal, R. (2006). Visual restoration in cortical blindness: Insights from natural and TMS-induced blindsight. *Neuropsychological Rehabilitation, 16*(4), 377–396.

Roberson-Nay, R., McClure, E. B., Monk, C. S., Nelson, E. E., Guyer, A. E., Fromm, S. J., et al. (2006). Increased amygdala activation during successful memory encoding in adolescent major depressive disorder: An fMRI study. *Biological Psychiatry, 60*(9), 966–973.

Roberts, A. C., Robbins, T. W., & Weiskrantz, L. (1996). Executive and cognitive functions of the pre-frontal cortex. *Philosophical Transactions of the Royal Society (London), B, 351,* (1346).

Roberts, J. E., & Bell, M. A. (2000a). Sex differences on a computerized mental rotation task disappear with computer familiarization. *Perceptual and Motor Skills, 91,* 1027–1034.

Roberts, J. E., & Bell, M. A. (2000b). Sex differences on a mental rotation task: Variations in electroencephalogram hemispheric activation between children and college students. *Developmental Neuropsychology, 17*(2), 199–223.

Roberts, J. E., & Bell, M. A. (2003). Two- and three-dimensional mental rotation tasks lead to different parietal laterality for men and women. *International Journal of Psychophysiology, 50,* 235–246.

Robinson, S. R. (2005). Conjugate limb coordination after experience with an interlimb yoke: Evidence for motor learning in the rat fetus. *Developmental Psychobiology, 47*(4), 328–344.

Roca, I. M. (2003a). Phonetics. In L. Nadel (Ed.), *Encyclopedia of cognitive science* (Vol. 3, pp. 619–625). London: Nature Group Press.

Roca, I. M. (2003b). Phonology. In L. Nadel (Ed.), *Encyclopedia of cognitive science* (Vol. 3, pp. 637–645). London: Nature Group Press.

Rock, I. (1983). *The logic of perception.* Cambridge, MA: MIT Press.

Rockland, K. S. (2000). Brain. In A. E. Kazdin (Ed.), *Encyclopedia of psychology* (Vol. 1, pp. 447–455). Washington, DC: American Psychological Association.

Rode, G., Rossetti, Y., Perenin, M.-T., & Boisson, D. (2004). Geographic information has to be spatialised to be neglected: a representational neglect case. *Cortex, 40*(2), 391–397.

Rodrigue, K. M., Kennedy, K. M., & Raz, N. (2005). Aging and longitudinal change in perceptual-motor skill acquisition in healthy adults. *Journals of Gerontology: Series B: Psychological Sciences and Social Sciences, 60*(4), 174–181.

Rodriguez, A., & Bohlin, G. (2005) Are maternal smoking and stress during pregnancy related to ADHD symptoms in children? *Journal of Child Psychology and Psychiatry, 46*(3), 246–254.

Roediger, H. L. (1980a). The effectiveness of four mnemonics in ordering recall. *Journal of Experimental Psychology: Human Learning & Memory, 6*(5), 558–567.

Roediger, H. L., & McDermott, K. B. (1993). Implicit memory in normal human subjects. In F. Boller & J. Grafman (Eds.), *Handbook of neuropsychology* (Vol. 8, pp. 63–131). Amsterdam: Elsevier.

Roediger, H. L., & McDermott, K. B. (2000). Distortions of memory. In E. Tulving & F. I. M. Craik (Eds.), *The Oxford handbook of memory* (pp. 149–162). New York: Oxford University Press.

Roediger, H. L., III. (1980b). Memory metaphors in cognitive psychology. *Memory & Cognition, 8*(3), 231–246.

Roediger, H. L., III, Balota, D. A., & Watson, J. M. (2001). Spreading activation and arousal of false memories. In H. L. Roediger III, J. S. Nairne, I. Neath, & A. M. Surprenant (Eds.), *The nature of remembering* (pp. 95–115). Washington, DC: American Psychological Association.

Roediger, H. L., III., & McDermott, K. B. (1995). Creating false memories: Remembering words not presented in lists. *Journal of Experimental Psychology: Learning, Memory, and Cognition, 21,* 803–814.

Rogers, R. D., Ramnani, N., Mackay, C., Wilson, J. L., Jezzard, P., Carter, C. S., et al. (2004). Distinct portions of anterior cingulate cortex and medial prefrontal cortex are activated by reward processing in separable phases of decision-making cognition. *Biological Psychiatry, 55*(6), 594–602.

Rogers, T. B., Kuiper, N. A., & Kirker, W. S. (1977). Self-reference and the encoding of personal information. *Journal of Personality & Social Psychology, 35*(9), 677–688.

Rogers, Y., Rutherford, A, & Bibby, P. A. (Eds.) (1992). *Models in the mind: Theory, perspective and application.* London: Academic Press.

Rogoff, B. (1986). The development of strategic use of context in spatial memory. In M. Perlmutter (Ed.), *Perspectives on intellectual development.* Hillsdale, NJ: Erlbaum.

Rohde, D. L. T., & Plaut, D. C. (1999). Language acquisition in the absence of explicit negative evidence: How important is starting small? *Cognition, 72,* 67–109.

Roozendaal, B. (2002). Stress and memory: Opposing effects of glucocorticoids on memory consolidation and memory retrieval. *Neurobiology of Learning and Memory, 78,* 578–595.

Roozendaal, B. (2003). Systems mediating acute glucocorticoid effects on memory consolidation and retrieval. *Progress in Neuro-Psychopharmacology and Biological Psychiatry, 27*(8), 1213–1223.

Rosch, E. H. (1975). Cognitive representations of semantic categories. *Journal of Experimental Psychology: General, 104,* 192–233.

Rosch, E. H. (1978). Principles of categorization. In E. Rosch & B. B. Lloyd (Eds.), *Cognition and categorization.* Hillsdale, NJ: Erlbaum.

Rosch, E. H., & Mervis, C. B. (1975). Family resemblances: Studies in the internal structure of categories. *Cognitive Psychology, 7,* 573–605.

Rosch, E. H., Mervis, C. B., Gray, W. D., Johnson, D. M., & Boyes-Braem, P. (1976). Basic objects in natural categories. *Cognitive Psychology, 8,* 382–439.

Rosch Heider, K. G. (1972). Universals in color naming and memory. *Journal of Experimental Psychology, 93*(1), 10–20.

Rosen, B. R., Buckner, R. L., & Dale, A. M. (1998). Event-related fMRI: Past, present, and future. *Proceedings of the National Academy of Sciences USA, 95,* 773–780.

Rosenzweig, M. R. (2003). Memory, neural basis of: Cellular and molecular mechanisms. In L. Nadel (Ed.), *Encyclopedia of cognitive science* (Vol. 2, pp. 1105–1109). London: Nature Publishing Group.

Rosenzweig, M. R. & Bennett, E. L. (1996). Psychobiology of plasticity: Effects of training and experience on brain and behavior. *Behavior and Brain Research, 78,* 57–65.

Rosenzweig, M. R., & Leiman, A. L. (1989). *Physiological psychology* (2nd ed.). New York: Random House.

Ross, B. H. (1997). The use of categories affects classification. *Journal of Memory and Language, 37,* 165–192.

Ross, B. H. (2000). Concepts: Learning. In A. E. Kazdin (Ed.), *Encyclopedia of psychology* (Vol. 2, pp. 248–251). Washington, DC: American Psychological Association.

Ross, B. H., & Spalding, T. L. (1994). Concepts and categories. In R. J. Sternberg (Ed.), *Handbook of perception and cognition: Vol. 12. Thinking and problem solving* (pp. 119–148). New York: Academic Press.

Ross, L., Greene, D., & House, P. (1977). The false consensus effect: An egocentric bias in social perception and attribution processes. *Journal of Experimental Social Psychology, 13*(3), 279–301.

Ross, M., & Sicoly, F. (1979). Egocentric biases in availability and attribution. *Journal of Personality and Social Psychology, 37,* 322–336.

Rostain, A. L., & Tamsay, J. R. (2006). A combined treatment approach for adults with ADHD—results of an open study of 43 patients. *Journal of Attention Disorders, 10*(2), 150–159.

Roswarski, T. E., & Murray, M. D. (2006). Supervision of students may protect academic physicians from cognitive bias: A study of decision making and multiple treatment alternatives in medicine. *Medical Decision Making, 26*(2), 154–161.

Rouder, J. N., & Ratcliff, R. (2004). Comparing categorization models. *Journal of Experimental Psychology: General, 133*(1), 63–82.

Rouder, J. N., & Ratcliff, R. (2006). Comparing exemplar- and rule-based theories of categorization. *Current Directions in Psychological Science, 15*(1), 9–13.

Rovee-Collier, C., Borza, M. A., Adler, S. A., & Boller, K. (1993). Infants' eyewitness testimony: Effects of postevent information on a prior memory representation. *Memory & Cognition, 21*(2), 267–279.

Rovee-Collier, C., & DuFault, D. (1991). Multiple contexts and memory retrieval at three months. *Developmental Psychobiology, 24*(1), 39–49.

Rubin, D. C. (1982). On the retention function for autobiographical memory. *Journal of Verbal Learning and Verbal Behavior, 19,* 21–38.

Rubin, D. C. (Ed.). (1996). *Remembering our past: Studies in autobiographical memory.* New York: Cambridge University Press.

Rubin, Z., Hill, C. T., Peplau, L. A., & Dunkel-Schetter, C. (1980). Self-disclosure in dating couples: Sex roles and the ethic of openness. *Journal of Marriage and the Family, 42,* 305–317.

Rudkin, S. J., Pearson, D. G., & Logie, R. H. (2007). Executive processes in visual and spatial working memory tasks. *Quarterly Journal of Experimental Psychology, 60*(1), 79–100.

Rudner, M., Fransson, P., Ingvar, M., Nyberg, L., & Rönnberg J. (2007). Neural representation of binding lexical signs and words in the episodic buffer of working memory. *Neuropsychologia, 45*(10), 2258–2276.

Ruffman, T., Perner, J., Naito, M., Parkin, L., & Clements, W. A. (1998). Older (but not younger) siblings facilitate false belief understanding. *Developmental Psychology, 34,* 161–174.

Rugg, M. D. (Ed.) (1997). *Cognitive neuroscience.* Hove East Sussex, UK: Psychology Press.

Rugg, M. D., & Allan, K. (2000). Event-related potential studies of memory. In E. Tulving & F. I. M. Craik (Eds.), *The Oxford handbook of memory* (pp. 521–538). New York: Oxford University Press.

Rumain, B., Connell, J., & Braine, M. D. S. (1983). Conversational comprehension processes are responsible for reasoning fallacies in children as well as adults: If is not the biconditional. *Developmental Psychology, 19*(4), 471–481.

Rumbaugh, D. M., & Beran, M. J. (2003). Language acquisition by animals. In L. Nadel (Ed.), *Encyclopedia of cognitive science* (Vol. 2, pp. 700–707). London: Nature Group Press.

Rumelhart, D. E., & McClelland, J. L. (1981). Interactive processing through spreading activation. In A. M. Lesgold & C. A. Perfetti (Eds.), *Interactive processes in reading* (pp. 37–60). Hillsdale, NJ: Erlbaum.

Rumelhart, D. E., & McClelland, J. L. (1982). An interactive activation model of context effects in letter perception: Part 2. The contextual enhancement effect and some tests and extensions of the model. *Psychological Review, 89,* 60–94.

Rumelhart, D. E., McClelland, J. L., & the PDP Research Group. (1986). *Parallel distributed processing. Explorations in the microstructure of cognition: Vol. 1. Foundations.* Cambridge, MA: MIT Press.

Rumelhart, D. E., & Norman, D. A. (1988). Representation in memory. In R. C. Atkinson, R. J. Herrnstein, G. Lindzey, R. D. Luce (Eds.), *Stevens' handbook of experimental psychology: Vol. 2. Learning and cognition* (2nd ed., pp. 511–587). New York: Wiley.

Rumelhart, D. E., & Ortony, A. (1977). The representation of knowledge in memory. In R. C. Anderson, R. J. Spiro, & W. E. Montague (Eds.), *Schooling and the acquisition of knowledge* (pp. 99–135). Hillsdale, NJ: Erlbaum.

Runco, M. A. (Ed.) (1997). *Creativity research handbook* (Vols. 1–3). Cresskill, NJ: Hampton Press.

Runco, M. A. (2000). Creativity: Research on the process of creativity. In A. E. Kazdin (Ed.), *Encyclopedia of psychology* (Vol. 2, pp. 342–346). Washington, DC: American Psychological Association.

Ruscio, J., Whitney, D. M., & Amabile, T. M. (1998). Looking inside the fishbowl of creativity: Verbal and behavioral predictors of creative performance. *Creativity Research Journal, 11,* 243–263.

Russell, J. A., & Ward, L. M. (1982). Environmental psychology. *Annual Review of Psychology, 33,* 651–688.

Russell, W. R., & Nathan, P. W. (1946). Traumatic amnesia. *Brain, 69,* 280–300.

Rychlak, J. F., & Struckman, A. (2000). Psychology: Post-World War II. In A. E. Kazdin (Ed.), *Encyclopedia of psychology* (Vol. 6, pp. 410–416). Washington, DC: American Psychological Association.

Ryle, G. (1949). *The concept of mind.* London: Hutchinson.

Saarinen, J. (1987a). Perception of positional relationships between line segments in eccentric vision. *Perception, 16*(5), 583–591.

Saarinen, T. F. (1987b). *Centering of mental maps of the world* (discussion paper). University of Arizona, Tucson: Department of Geography and Regional Development.

Sacks, H., Schegloff, E. A., & Jefferson, G. (1974). A simplest systematics for the organization of turn-taking for conversation. *Language, 50*, 696–735.

Saffran, J. R. (2001). Words in a sea of sounds: The output of infant statistical learning. *Cognition, 81*, 149–169.

Saffran, J. R., Newport, E. L., & Aslin, R. N. (1996). Word segmentation: The role of distributed cues. *Journal of Memory and Language, 35*, 606–621.

Saito, S., & Baddeley, A. D. (2004). Irrelevant sound disrupts speech production: Exploring the relationship between short-term memory and experimentally induced slips of the tongue. *The Quarterly Journal of Experimental Psychology A: Human Experimental Psychology, 57A*(7), 1309–1340.

Salas, E., Burke, C. S., & Cannon-Bowers, J. A. (2000). Teamwork: Emerging principles. *International Journal of Management Reviews, 2*(4), 305–379.

Salat, D. H., Van der Kouwe, A. J. W., Tuch, D. S., Quinn, B. T., Fischl, B., Dale, A. M., et al. (2006). Neuroimaging H. M.: A 10-year follow-up examination. *Hippocampus, 16*(11), 936–945.

Salovey, P., & Sluyter, D. J. (Eds.) (1997). *Emotional development and emotional intelligence: Implications for educators*. New York: Basic Books.

Salthouse, T. A. (1984). Effects of age and skill in typing. *Journal of Experimental Psychology: General, 113*, 345–371.

Salthouse, T. A. (1991). Expertise as the circumvention of human processing limitations. In K. A. Ericsson & J. Smith (Eds.), *Toward a general theory of expertise: Prospects and limits* (pp. 286–300). New York: Cambridge University Press.

Salthouse, T. A. (1992). The information-processing perspective on cognitive aging. In R. J. Sternberg & C. A. Berg (Eds.), *Intellectual development* (pp. 261–277). New York: Cambridge University Press.

Salthouse, T. A. (1993). Influence of working memory on adult age differences in matrix reasoning. *British Journal of Psychology, 84*(2), 171–199.

Salthouse, T. A. (1994). The nature of the influence of speed on adult age differences in cognition. *Developmental Psychology, 30*(2), 240–259.

Salthouse, T. A. (1996). The processing-speed theory of adult age differences in cognition. *Psychological Review, 103*, 403–428.

Salthouse, T. A. (2005). From description to explanation in cognitive aging. In R. J. Sternberg & J. E. Pretz (Eds.), *Cognition and intelligence* (pp. 288–305). New York: Cambridge University Press.

Salthouse, T. A., Kausler, D. H., & Saults, J. S. (1990). Age, self-assessed health status, and cognition. *Journal of Gerontology, 45*(4), P156–P160.

Salthouse, T. A., & Somberg, B. L. (1982). Skilled performance: Effects of adult age and experience on elementary processes. *Journal of Experimental Psychology: General, 111*(2), 176–207.

Samuel, A. G. (1981). Phonemic restoration: Insights from a new methodology. *Journal of Experimental Psychology: General, 110*, 474–494.

Samuel, A. L. (1963). Some studies in machine learning using the game of checkers. In E. A. Feigenbaum & J. Feldman (Eds.), *Computers and thought* (pp. 71–105). New York: McGraw-Hill.

Samuels, J. J. (1999). Developing reading fluency in learning disabled students. In R. J. Sternberg & L. Spear-Swerling (Eds.), *Perspectives on learning disabilities: Biological, cognitive, contextual* (pp. 176–189). Boulder, CO: Westview Press.

Sandell, J. (2000). Vision and sight: Behavioral and functional aspects. In A. E. Kazdin (Ed.), *Encyclopedia of psychology* (Vol. 8, pp. 178–180). Washington, DC: American Psychological Association.

Sapir, E. (1964). *Culture, language and personality*. Berkeley, CA: University of California Press. (Original work published 1941)

Sarason, S. B., & Doris, J. (1979). *Educational handicap, public policy, and social history*. New York: Free Press.

Sarter, M., Bruno, J. P., & Berntson, G. G. (2003). Reticular activating system. In L. Nadel (Ed.), *Encyclopedia of cognitive science* (Vol. 3, pp. 963–967). London: Nature Publishing Group.

Sarter, N. B., & Alexander, H. M. (2000). Error types and related error detection mechanisms in the vaiation domain: An analysis of aviation safety reporting system incident reports. *International Journal of Aviation Psychology, 10*, 189–206.

Savage-Rumbaugh, S., McDonald, K., Sevcik, R. A., Hopkins, W. D., & Rubert, E. (1986). Spontaneous symbol acquisition and communicative use by pygmy chimpanzees *(Pan paniscus)*. *Journal of Experimental Psychology: General, 115*, 211–235.

Savage-Rumbaugh, S., Murphy, J., Sevcik, R., Brakke, K., Williams, S., & Rumbaugh, D. M. (1993). Language comprehension in ape and child. *Monographs of the Society for Research in Child Development, 58*(3–4, Serial No. 233).

Scaggs, W. E., & McNaughton, B. L. (1996). Replay of neuronal firing sequences in rat hippocampus during sleep following spatial experience. *Science, 271*, 1870–1873.

Schacter, D. L. (1989a). Memory. In M. I. Posner (Ed.), *Foundations of cognitive science* (pp. 683–725). Cambridge, MA: MIT Press.

Schacter, D. L. (1989b). On the relation between memory and consciousness: Dissociable interactions and conscious experience. In H. L. Roediger & F. I. M. Craik (Eds.), *Varieties of memory and consciousness: Essays in honor of Endel Tulving*. Hillsdale, NJ: Erlbaum.

Schacter, D. L. (1995a). Implicit memory. In M. S. Gazzaniga (Ed.), *The cognitive neurosciences* (pp. 815–824). Cambridge, MA: MIT Press.

Schacter, D. L. (1995b). Memory distortion: History and current status. In D. L. Schacter, J. T. Coyle, G. D. Fischbach, M. M. Mesulam, & L. E. Sullivan (Eds.), *Memory distortions* (pp. 1–43). Cambridge, MA: Harvard University Press.

Schacter, D. L. (2000). Memory: Memory systems. In A. E. Kazdin (Ed.), *Encyclopedia of psychology* (Vol. 5, pp. 169–172). Washington, DC: American Psychological Association.

Schacter, D. L. (2001). *The seven sins of memory: How the mind forgets and remembers*. Boston: Houghton Mifflin.

Schacter, D. L., Chiu, C. Y. P., & Ochsner, K. N. (1993). Implicit memory: A selective review. *Annual Review of Neuroscience, 16*, 159–182.

Schacter, D. L., & Church, B. A. (1992). Auditory priming: Implicit and explicit memory for words and voices. *Journal of Experimental Psychology: Learning, Memory and Cognition, 18*(5), 915–930.

Schacter, D. L., & Curran, T. (2000). Memory without remembering and remembering without memory: Implicit and false memories. In M. S. Gazzaniga (Ed.), *The new cognitive neurosciences* (2nd ed., pp. 829–840). Cambridge, MA: MIT Press.

Schacter, D. L., & Graf, P. (1986a). Effects of elaborative processing on implicit and explicit memory for new associations. *Journal of Experimental Psychology: Learning, Memory, & Cognition, 12*(3), 432–444.

Schacter, D. L., & Graf, P. (1986b). Preserved learning in amnesic patients: Perspectives from research on direct priming. *Journal of Clinical & Experimental Neuropsychology, 8*(6), 727–743.

Schacter, D. L., Verfaellie, M., & Pradere, D. (1996). The neuropsychology of memory illusions: False recall and recognition in amnesic patients. *Journal of Memory and Language, 35,* 319–334.

Schaeken, W., Johnson-Laird, P. N., & D'Ydewalle, G. (1996). Mental models and temporal reasoning. *Cognition, 60,* 205-234.

Schaffer, H. R. (1977). *Mothering.* Cambridge, MA: Harvard University Press.

Schaie, K. W. (1974). Translations in gerontology-from lab to life. *American Psychologist, 29,* 802–807.

Schaie, K. W. (1989). Perceptual speed in adulthood: Cross-sectional and longitudinal studies. *Psychology and Aging, 4,* 443–453.

Schaie, K. W. (1996). *Intellectual development in adulthood: The Seattle longitudinal study.* New York: Cambridge University Press.

Schaie, K. W., & Willis, S. L. (1986). Can decline in intellectual functioning in the elderly be reversed? *Developmental Psychology, 22,* 223–232.

Schank, R. C., & Abelson, R. P. (1977). *Scripts, plans, goals, and understanding.* Hillsdale. NJ: Erlbaum.

Schank, R. C., & Towle, B. (2000). Artificial intelligence. In R. J. Sternberg (Ed.), *Handbook of intelligence* (pp. 341–356). New York: Cambridge University Press.

Scheck, P., & Nelson, T. O. (2003). Metacognition. In L. Nadel (Ed.), *Encyclopedia of cognitive science* (Vol. 3, pp. 11–15). London: Nature Publishing Group.

Scheibehenne, B., Miesler, L., & Todd, P. M. (2007). Fast and frugal food choices: Uncovering individual decision heuristics. *Appetite, 49*(3), 578–589.

Schindler, I., Clavagnier, S., Karnath, H. O., Derex, L., & Perenin, M. T. (2006). A common basis for visual and tactile exploration deficits in spatial neglect? *Neuropsychologia, 44*(8), 1444–1451.

Schliemann, A. D., & Magalhües, V. P. (1990). *Proportional reasoning: From shops, to kitchens, laboratories, and, hopefully, schools.* Proceedings of the Fourteenth International Conference for the Psychology of Mathematics Education, Oaxtepec, Mexico.

Schmidt, H. G., Peech, V. H., Paas, F., & Van Breukelen, G. J. P. (2000). Remembering the street names of one's childhood neighbourhood: A study of very long-term retention. *Memory, 8*(1), 37–49.

Schmidt, S. R., & Bohannon, J. N. (1988). In defense of the flashbulb-memory hypothesis: A comment on McCloskey, Wible, & Cohen (1988). *Journal of Experimental Psychology: General, 117*(3), 332–335.

Schneider, W., & Bjorklund, D. F. (1998). Memory. In W. Damon (Ed.-in-Chief), D. Kuhn, & R. S. Siegler (Vol. Eds.), *Handbook of child psychology: Vol. 2. Cognitive development* (pp. 467–521). New York: Wiley.

Schneider, W., & Shiffrin, R. M. (1977). Controlled and automatic human information processing. *Psychological Review, 84,* 1–66.

Schoenfeld, A. H. (1981). *Episodes and executive decisions in mathematical problem solving.* Paper presented at the annual meeting of the American Educational Research Association, Los Angeles, CA.

Schonbein, W., & Bechtel, W. (2003). History of computational modeling and cognitive science. *Encyclopedia of Cognitive Science.* London, England: Nature Publishing Group.

Schonfield, D., & Robertson, D. A. (1966). Memory storage and aging. *Canadian Journal of Psychology, 20,* 228–236.

Schooler, J. W. (1994). Seeking the core: The issues and evidence surrounding recovered accounts of sexual trauma. *Consciousness and Cognition, 3,* 452–469.

Schooler, J. W., & Engstler-Schooler, T. Y. (1990). Verbal overshadowing of visual memories: Some things are better left unsaid. *Cognitive Psychology, 22,* 36–71.

Schustack, M. W., & Sternberg, R. J. (1981). Evaluation of evidence in causal inference. *Journal of Experimental Psychology: General, 110,* 101–120.

Schvaneveldt, R. W., Meyer, D. E., & Becker, C. A. (1976). Lexical ambiguity, semantic context, and visual word recognition. *Journal of Experimental Psychology: Human Perception & Performance, 2*(2), 243–256.

Schwartz, B. L., & Metcalfe, J. (1994). Methodological problems and pitfalls in the study of human metacognition. In J. Metcalfe & A. P. Shimamura (Eds.), *Metacognition: Knowing about knowing* (pp. 93–114). Cambridge, MA: MIT Press.

Schwartz, D. L. (1996). Analog imagery in mental model reasoning: Depictive models. *Cognitive Psychology, 30,* 154–219.

Schwartz, D. L., & Black, J. B. (1996). Analog imagery in mental model reasoning: Depictive models. *Cognitive Psychology, 30,* 154–219.

Schwarz, N., & Skurnik, I.(2003). Feeling and thinking: Implications for problem solving. In J. E. Davidson & R. J. Sternberg (Eds.), *The psychology of problem solving* (pp. 263–290). New York: Cambridge University Press.

Schweickert, R., & Boruff, B. (1986). Short-term memory capacity: Magic number or magic spell? *Journal of Experimental Psychology: Learning, Memory, & Cognition, 12*(3), 419–425.

Scovel, T. (2000). A critical review of the critical period research. *Annual Review of Applied Linguistics, 20,* 213–223.

Scoville, W. B., & Milner, B. (1957). Loss of recent memory after bilateral hippocampal lesions. *Journal of Neurology, Neurosurgery, and Psychiatry, 20,* 11–19.

Seal, M. L., Aleman, A., & McGuire, P. K. (2004). Compelling imagery, unanticipated speech and deceptive memory: Neurocognitive models of auditory verbal hallucinations in schizophrenia. *Cognitive Neuropsychiatry, 9*(1–2), 43–72.

Searle, J. R. (1975a). Indirect speech acts. In P. Cole & J. L. Morgan (Eds.), *Syntax and semantics: Speech acts* (Vol. 3, pp. 59–82). New York: Seminar Press.

Searle, J. R. (1975b). A taxonomy of elocutionary acts. In K. Gunderson (Ed.), *Minnesota studies in the philosophy of language* (pp. 344–369). Minneapolis: University of Minnesota Press.

Searle, J. R. (1979). *Expression and meaning: Studies in the theory of speech acts.* Cambridge, UK: Cambridge University Press.

Searle, J. R. (1980). Minds, brains, and programs. *Behavioral and Brain Sciences, 3,* 417–424.

Seguino, S. (2007). *Plus ça change?* Evidence on global trends in gender norms and stereotypes. *Feminist Economics, 13*(2), 1–28.

Sehulster, J. R. (1989). Content and temporal structure of autobiographical knowledge: Remembering twenty five seasons at the Metropolitan Opera. *Memory and Cognition, 17,* 290–606.

Seidenberg, M. S., & McClelland, J. L. (1989). A distributed, developmental model of word recognition and naming. *Psychological Review, 96,* 523–568.

Seifert, C. M., Meyer, D. E., Davidson, N., Palatano, A. L., & Yaniv, I. (1995). Demystification of cognitive insight: Opportunistic assimilation and the prepare-mind perspective. In R. J. Sternberg & J. E. Davidson (Eds.), *The nature of insight* (pp. 65–124). Cambridge, MA: MIT Press.

Seigel, J. J., Nitz, D., Bingman, V. P. (2005). Spatial-specificity of single-units in the hippocampal formation of freely moving homing pigeons. *Hippocampus, 15*(1), 26–40.

Seizova-Cajic, T. (2003). The role of perceived relative position in pointing to objects apparently shifted by depth-contrast. *Spatial Vision, 6*(3–4), 325–346.

Selfridge, O. G. (1959). Pandemonium: A paradigm for learning. In D. V. Blake & A. M. Uttley (Eds.), *Proceedings of the Symposium on the Mechanization of Thought Processes* (pp. 511–529). London: Her Majesty's Stationery Office.

Selfridge, O. G., & Neisser, U. (1960). Pattern recognition by machine. *Scientific American, 203*, 60–68.

Selkoe, D. J. (2002). Alzheimer's disease is a synaptic failure. *Science, 298*, 789–791.

Seo, D. C., & Torabi, M. R. (2004). The impact of in-vehicle cell-phone use on accidents or near-accidents among college students. *Journal of American College Health, 53*(3), 101–107.

Sera, M. D. (1992). To be or to be: Use and acquisition of the Spanish copulas. *Journal of Memory and Language, 31*, 408–427.

Sereno, S. C., Brewer, C. C., & O'Donnell, P. J. (2003). Context effects in word recognition: evidence for early interactive processing. *Psychological Science 14*(4), 328–333.

Serniclaes, W., Ventura, P., Morais, J., & Kolinsky, R. (2005). Categorical perception of speech sounds in illiterate adults. *Cognition, 9*(2), B35–B44.

Serpell, R. (2000). Intelligence and culture. In R. J. Sternberg (Ed.), *Handbook of intelligence* (pp. 549–577). New York: Cambridge University Press.

Shafir, E. B., Osherson, D. N., & Smith, E. E. (1990). Typicality and reasoning fallacies. *Memory & Cognition, 18*(3), 229–239.

Shallice, T. (1979). Neuropsychological research and the fractionation of memory systems. In L. G. Nilsson (Ed.), *Perspectives on memory research*. Hillsdale, NJ: Erlbaum.

Shallice, T., & Warrington, E. (1970). Independent functioning of verbal memory stores: A neuropsychological study. *Quarterly Journal of Experimental Psychology, 22*(2), 261–273.

Shankweiler, D., Crain, D. S., Katz, L., Fowler, A. E., Liberman, A. M., Brady, S. A., et al. (1995). Cognitive profiles of reading-disabled children: Comparison of language skills in phonology, morphology, and syntax. *Psychological Science, 6*, 149–156.

Shannon, C., & Weaver, W. (1963). *The mathematical theory of communication*. Urbana, IL: University of Illinois Press.

Shapiro, P., & Penrod, S. (1986). Meta-analysis of facial identification studies. *Psychological Bulletin, 100*(2), 139–156.

Shapley, R., & Lennie, P. (1985). Spatial frequency analysis in the visual system. *Annual Review of Neuroscience, 8*, 547–583.

Shastri, L. (2003). Spreading-activation networks. In L. Nadel (Ed.), *Encyclopedia of cognitive science* (Vol. 4, pp. 211–218). London: Nature Publishing Group.

Shaywitz, S. E. (2005). *Overcoming dyslexia*. New York: Knopf.

Shaywitz, S. E., & Shaywitz, B. A. (2005). Dyslexia (specific reading disability). *Biological Psychiatry, 57*(11), 1301–1309.

Shear, J. (Ed.) (1997). *Explaining consciousness: The hard problem.* Cambridge, MA: MIT Press.

Shelton, S. T. (2006). Jury decision making: Using group theory to improve deliberation. *Politics & Policy, 34*(4), 706–725.

Shepard, R. N. (1984). Ecological constraints on internal representation. Resonant kinematics of perceiving, imaging, thinking, and dreaming. *Psychological Review, 91*, 417–447.

Shepard, R. N., & Metzler, J. (1971). Mental rotation of three-dimensional objects. *Science, 171*(3972), 701–703.

Shepherd, G. (Ed.) (1998). *The synaptic organization of the brain.* New York; Oxford University Press.

Shepherd, G. M. (2004). *The synaptic organization of the brain* (5th ed.). New York: Oxford University Press.

Shiffrin, R. M. (1973). Information persistence in short-term memory. *Journal of Experimental Psychology, 100*, 39–49.

Shiffrin, R. M. (1996). Laboratory experimentation on the genesis of expertise. In K. A. Ericsson (Ed.), *The road to excellence* (pp. 337–347). Mahwah, NJ: Erlbaum.

Shiffrin, R. M., & Schneider, W. (1977). Controlled and automatic human information processing: II. Perceptual learning, automatic attending, and a general theory. *Psychological Review, 84*, 127–190.

Shimamura, A. P., & Squire, L. R. (1986). Korsakoff's syndrome: A study of the relation between anterograde amnesia and remote memory impairment. *Behavioral Neuroscience, 100*(2), 165–170.

Shin, N., Jonassen, D. H., & McGee, S. (2003). Predictors of well-structured and ill-structured problem solving in astronomy simulation. *Journal of Research in Science Teaching, 40*(1), 6–33.

Shoben, E. J. (1984). Semantic and episodic memory. In R. W. Wyer, Jr., & T. K. Srull (Eds.), *Handbook of social cognition* (Vol. 2, pp. 213–231). Hillsdale, NJ: Erlbaum.

Shore, D. I., & Klein, R. M. (2000). The effects of scene inversion on change blindness. *Journal of General Psychology, 127*, 27–43.

Shortliffe, E. H. (1976). *Computer-based medical consultations: MYCIN.* New York: American Elsevier.

Shulman, H. G. (1970). Encoding and retention of semantic and phonemic information in short-term memory. *Journal of Verbal Learning and Verbal Behavior, 9*, 499–508.

Siegler, R. S. (1986). *Children's thinking.* Englewood Cliffs, NJ: Prentice-Hall.

Siegler, R. S. (1988). Individual differences in strategy choices: Good students, not-so-good students, and perfectionists. *Child Development, 59*(4), 833–851.

Silverman, I., & Eals, M. (1992). Sex differences in spatial abilities: Evolutionary theory and data. In J. Barkow, L. Cosmides, & J. Tooby (Eds.), *The adapted mind* (pp. 533–549). New York: Oxford.

Simon, H. A. (1957). *Administrative behavior* (2nd ed.). Totowa, NJ: Littlefield, Adams.

Simon, H. A. (1976). Identifying basic abilities underlying intelligent performance of complex tasks. In L. B. Resnick (Ed.), *The nature of intelligence* (pp. 65–98). Hillsdale, NJ: Erlbaum.

Simon, H. A. (1999a). Problem solving. In R. A. Wilson & F. C. Keil (Eds.), *The MIT encyclopedia of the cognitive sciences* (pp. 674–676). Cambridge, MA: MIT Press.

Simon, H. A. (1999b). Production systems. In R. A. Wilson & F. C. Keil (Eds.), *The MIT encyclopedia of the cognitive sciences* (pp. 676–678). Cambridge, MA: MIT Press.

Simon, H. A., & Kotovsky, K. (1963). Human acquisition of concepts for sequential patterns. *Psychological Review, 70*, 534–546.

Simon, H. A., & Reed, S. K. (1976). Modeling strategy shifts in a problem-solving task. *Cognitive Psychology, 8*, 86–97.

Simons, D. J. (1996). In sight, out of mind: When object representations fail. *Psychological Science, 5*, 301–305.

Simons, D. J. (2000). Attentional capture and inattentional blindness. *Trends in Cognitive Science, 4*, 147–155.

Simons, D. J., & Ambinder, M. S. (2005). Change blindness theory and consequences. *Current Directions in Psychological Science, 14*(1), 44–48.

Simons, D. J, & Levin, D. T. (1997). Change blindness. *Trends in Cognitive Science, 1,* 261–267.

Simons, D. J., & Levin, D. T. (1998). Failure to detect changes to people during a real-world interaction. *Psychonomic Bulletin & Review, 5,* 644–649.

Simonton, D. K. (1988). Creativity, leadership, and chance. In R. J. Sternberg (Ed.), *The nature of creativity* (pp. 386–426). New York: Cambridge University Press.

Simonton, D. K. (1994). *Greatness: Who makes history and why.* New York: Guilford.

Simonton, D. K. (1997). Creativity in personality, developmental, and social psychology: Any links with cognitive psychology? In T. B. Ward, S. M. Smith, & J. Vaid (Eds.), *Creative thought: Conceptual structures and processes* (pp. 309–324). Washington, DC: American Psychological Association.

Simonton, D. K. (1998). Donald Campbell's model of the creative process: Creativity as blind variation and selective retention. *Journal of Creative Behavior, 32,* 153–158.

Simonton, D. K. (1999). Creativity from a historiometric perspective. In R. J. Sternberg (Ed.), *Handbook of creativity* (pp. 116–133). New York: Cambridge University Press.

Sincoff, J. B., & Sternberg, R. J. (1988). Development of verbal fluency abilities and strategies in elementary-school-age children. *Developmental Psychology, 24,* 646–653.

Skinner, B. F. (1957). *Verbal behavior.* New York: Appleton-Century-Crofts.

Skotko, B. G., Kensinger, E. A., Locascio, J. J., Einstein, G., Rubin, D. C., Tupler, L. A., et al. (2004). Puzzling thoughts for H. M.: Can new semantic information be anchored to old semantic memories? *Neuropsychology, 18*(4), 756–769.

Slobin, D. I. (1971). Cognitive prerequisites for the acquisition of grammar. In C. A. Ferguson & D. I. Slobin (Eds.), *Studies of child language development.* New York: Holt, Rinehart and Winston.

Slobin, D. I. (Ed.). (1985). *The cross-linguistic study of language acquisition.* Hillsdale, NJ: Erlbaum.

Sloboda, J. A. (1984). Experimental studies in music reading: A review. *Music Perception, 22,* 222–236.

Sloboda, J. A. (1996). The acquisition of musical performance expertise: Deconstructing the "talent" account of individual differences in musical expressivity. In K. A. Ericsson (Ed.), *The road to excellence* (pp. 107–127). Mahwah, NJ: Erlbaum.

Sloboda, J. A., Davidson, J. W., Howe, M. J. A., & Moore, D. G. (1996). The role of practice in the development of performing musicians. *British Journal of Psychology, 87,* 287–309.

Sloman, S. A. (1996). The empirical case for two systems of reasoning. *Psychological Bulletin, 119,* 3–22.

Slovic, P. (1990). Choice. In D. N. Osherson & E. E. Smith (Eds.), *An invitation to cognitive science: Vol. 3. Thinking* (pp. 89–116). Cambridge, MA: MIT Press.

Smilansky, B. (1974). Paper presented at the meeting of the American Educational Research Association, Chicago.

Smith, C. (1996). Sleep states, memory phases, and synaptic plasticity. *Behavior and Brain Research, 78,* 49–56.

Smith, C., Bibi, U., & Sheard, D. E. (2004). Evidence for the differential impact of time and emotion on personal and event memo-ries for September 11, 2001. *Applied Cognitive Psychology, 17*(9), 1047–1055.

Smith, E. E. (1988). Concepts and thought. In R. J. Sternberg & E. E. Smith (Eds.), *The psychology of human thought* (pp. 19–49). New York: Cambridge University Press.

Smith, E. E. (1995a). Concepts and categorization. In E. E. Smith & D. N. Osherson (Eds.), *An invitation to cognitive science: Vol. 3. Thinking* (2nd ed., pp. 3–33). Cambridge, MA: MIT Press.

Smith, E. E., & Jonides, J. (1995). Working memory in humans: Neuropsychological evidence. In M. Gazzaniga (Ed.), *The cognitive neurosciences* (pp. 1009–1020). Cambridge, MA: MIT Press.

Smith, E. E., Langston, C., & Nisbett, R. E. (1992). The case for rules in reasoning. *Cognitive Science, 16*(1), 1–40.

Smith, E. E., & Medin, D. L. (1981). *Categories and concepts.* Cambridge, MA: Harvard University Press.

Smith, E. E., Osherson, D. N., Rips, L. J., & Keane, M. (1988). Combining prototypes: A modification model. *Cognitive Science, 12,* 485–527.

Smith, E. E., Shoben, E. J., & Rips, L. J. (1974). Structure and process in semantic memory: A featural model for semantic decisions. *Psychological Review, 81,* 214–241.

Smith, J. D. (2005). Wanted: A new psychology of exemplars. *Canadian Journal of Experimental Psychology, 59*(1), 47–53.

Smith, J. D., Reisberg, D., & Wilson, M. A. (1992). Subvocalization and auditory imagery: Interactions between the inner ear and inner voice. In D. Reisberg (Ed.), *Auditory imagery* (pp. 95–119). Hillsdale, NJ: Erlbaum.

Smith, L. B., & Gilhooly, K. (2006). Regression versus fast and frugal models of decision-making: The case of prescribing for depression. *Applied Cognitive Psychology, 20*(2), 265–274.

Smith, L. B., Jones, S. S., & Landau, B. (1996). Naming in young children: A dumb attentional mechanism? *Cognition, 60,* 143–171.

Smith, S. M. (1995b). Getting into and out of mental ruts: A theory of fixation, incubation, and insight. In R. J. Sternberg & J. E. Davidson (Eds.), *The nature of insight* (pp. 229–251). Cambridge, MA: MIT Press.

Smolensky, P. (1999). Connectionist approaches to language. In R. A. Wilson & F. C. Keil (Eds.), *The MIT encyclopedia of the cognitive sciences* (pp. 188–190). Cambridge, MA: MIT Press.

Snow, C. (1999). Social perspectives on the emergence of language. In B. MacWhinney (Ed.), *The emergence of language* (pp. 257–276). Mahwah, NJ: Erlbaum.

Snow, C. E. (1977). The development of conversation between mothers and babies. *Journal of Child Language, 4,* 1–22.

Snow, J. C., & Mattingley, J. B. (2003). Perception, unconscious. In L. Nadel (Ed.), *Encyclopedia of cognitive science* (Vol. 3, pp. 517–526). London: Nature Publishing Group.

Sobel, D. M., & Kirkham, N. Z. (2006). Blickets and babies: The development of causal reasoning in toddlers and infants. *Developmental Psychology, 42*(6), 1103–1115.

Sodian, B., Zaitchik, D., & Carey, S. (1991). Young children's differentiation of hypothetical beliefs from evidence. *Child Development, 62*(4), 753–766.

Sohn, M. H., Ursu, S., Anderson, J. R., Stenger, V. A., & Carter, C. S. (2000). Inaugural article: The role of prefrontal cortex and posterior parietal cortex in task switching. *Proceedings of the National Academy of Science, 97,* 13448–13453.

Solso, R., & McCarthy, J. E. (1981). Prototype formation of faces: A case of pseudomemory. *British Journal of Psychology, 72,* 499–503.

Sommer, R. (1969). *Personal space*. Englewood Cliffs, NJ: Prentice-Hall.

Sommers, S. R. (2006). On racial diversity and group decision making: Identifying multiple effects of racial composition on jury deliberations. *Journal of Personality and Social Psychology, 90*(4), 597–612.

Sook Lee, J., & Oxelson, E. (2006). "It's not my job": K–12 teacher attitudes towards students' heritage language maintenance. *Bilingual Research Journal, 30*(2), 453–477.

Sotak, C. (2002). Diffusion tensor imaging and axonal mapping—state of the art. *NRM in Biomedicine, 15*(7–8), 561–569.

Sparr, S. A., Jay, M., Drislane, F. W., & Venna, N. (1991). A historical case of visual agnosia revisited after 40 years. *Brain, 114*(2), 789–790.

Spear, N. E. (1979). Experimental analysis of infantile amnesia. In J. E. Kihlstrom & F. J. Evans (Eds.), *Functional disorders of memory*. Hillsdale, NJ: Erlbaum.

Spearman, C. (1927). *The abilities of man*. New York: Macmillan.

Spear-Swerling, L., & Sternberg, R. J. (1996). *Off-track: When poor readers become learning disabled*. Boulder, CO: Westview.

Spelke, E., Hirst, W., & Neisser, U. (1976). Skills of divided attention. *Cognition, 4*, 215–230.

Spellman, B. A. (1997). Crediting causality. *Journal of Experimental Psychology: General, 126*, 1–26.

Sperling, G. (1960). The information available in brief visual presentations. *Psychological Monographs: General and Applied, 74*, 1–28.

Sperry, R. W. (1964). The great cerebral commissure. *Scientific American, 210*(1), 42–52.

Squire, L. R. (1982). The neuropsychology of human memory. *Annual Review of Neuroscience, 5*, 241–273.

Squire, L. R. (1986). Mechanisms of memory. *Science, 232*(4578), 1612–1619.

Squire, L. R. (1987). *Memory and the brain*. New York: Oxford University Press.

Squire, L. R. (1992). Memory and the hippocampus: A synthesis of findings with rats, monkeys, and humans. *Psychological Review, 99*, 195–231.

Squire, L. R. (1993). The organization of declarative and nondeclarative memory. In T. Ono, L. R. Squire, M. E. Raichle, D. I. Perrett, & M. Fukuda (Eds.), *Brain mechanisms of perception and memory: From neuron to behavior* (pp. 219–227). New York: Oxford University Press.

Squire, L. R., (1999). Memory, human neuropsychology. In R. A. Wilson & F. C. Keil (Eds.), *The MIT encyclopedia of the cognitive sciences* (pp. 521–522). Cambridge, MA: MIT Press.

Squire, L. R., Cohen, N. J., & Nadel, L. (1984). The medial temporal region and memory consolidations: A new hypothesis. In H. Weingardner & E. Parker (Eds.), *Memory consolidation*. Hillsdale, NJ: Erlbaum.

Squire, L. R., & Knowlton, B. J. (2000). The medial temporal lobe, the hippocampus, and the memory systems of the brain. In M. Gazzaniga (Ed.), *The new cognitive neurosciences* (2nd ed., pp. 765–780). Cambridge, MA: MIT Press.

Squire, L. R., Knowlton, B. J., & Musen, G. (1993). The structure and organization of memory. *Annual Review of Psychology, 44*, 453–495.

Squire, L. R., & Zola-Morgan, S. (1991). The medial temporal lobe memory system. *Science, 253*, 1380–1386.

Squire, L. R., Zola-Morgan, S., Cave, C. B., Haist, F., Musen, G., & Suzuki, W. P. (1990). Memory: Organization of brain systems and cognition. In D. E. Meyer & S. Kornblum (Eds.), *Attention and performance: Vol. 14. Synergies in experimental psychology, artificial intelligence, and cognitive neuroscience* (pp. 393–424). Cambridge, MA: MIT Press.

Staller, A., Sloman, S. A., & Ben-Zeev, T. (2000). Perspective effects in non-deontic version of the Wason selection task. *Memory and Cognition, 28*, 396–405.

Standing, L., Conezio, J., & Haber, R. N. (1970). Perception and memory for pictures: Single-trial learning of 2500 visual stimuli. *Psychonomic Science, 19*, 73–74.

Stankiewicz, B. J. (2003). Perceptual systems: The visual model. In L. Nadel (Ed.), *Encyclopedia of cognitive science* (Vol. 3, pp. 552–560). London: Nature Publishing Group.

Stankov, L. (2005). Reductionism versus charting. In R. J. Sternberg & J. E. Pretz (Eds.), *Cognition and intelligence* (pp. 51–67). New York: Cambridge University Press.

Stanovich, K. E. (1981). Attentional and automatic context effects in reading. In A. M. Lesgold & C. A. Perfetti (Eds.), *Interactive processes in reading* (pp. 241–267). Hillsdale, NJ: Erlbaum.

Stanovich, K. E. (2003). The fundamental computational biases of human cognition: Heuristics that (sometimes) impair decision making and problem solving. In J. E. Davidson & R. J. Sternberg (Eds.), *The psychology of problem solving* (pp. 291–342). New York: Cambridge University Press.

Stanovich, K. E., Sái, W. C., & West, R. F. (2004). Individual differences in thinking, reasoning, and decision making. In J. P. Leighton & R. J. Sternberg (Eds.), *The nature of reasoning* (pp. 375–409). New York: Cambridge University Press.

Stanovich, K. E., & West, R. F. (1999). Individual differences in reasoning and the heuristics and biases debate. In P. L. Ackerman, P. C. Kyllonen, & R. D. Roberts (Eds.), *Learning and individual differences: Process, trait, and content determinants* (pp. 389–411). Washington, DC: American Psychological Association.

Starr, M S., & Rayner, K. (2003). Language comprehension, methodologies for studying. In L. Nadel (Ed.), *Encyclopedia of cognitive science* (Vol. 2, pp. 730–736). London: Nature Group Press.

Steedman, M. (2003). Language, connectionist and symbolic representations of. In L. Nadel (Ed.), *Encyclopedia of cognitive science* (Vol. 2, pp. 765–771). London: Nature Group Press.

Steele, C. (1990, May). A conversation with Claude Steele. *APS Observer*, pp. 11–17.

Steffanaci, L. (1999). Amygdala, primate. In R. A. Wilson & F. C. Keil (Eds.), *The MIT encyclopedia of the cognitive sciences* (pp. 15–17). Cambridge, MA: MIT Press.

Steif, P. S., Fay, A. L., Kara, L. B., & Spencer, S. E. (2006). Work in progress: Improving problem solving performance in statics through body-centric talk. *ASEE/IEEE Frontiers in Education Conference*.

Stein, S. J., & Book, H. E. (2006). *The EQ Edge: Emotional intelligence and your success*. Mississuaga, Ontario, Canada: John Wiley & Sons.

Stenning, K., & Monaghan, P. (2004). Strategies and knowledge representation. In J. P. Leighton & R. J. Sternberg (Eds.), *The nature of reasoning* (pp.129–168). New York: Cambridge University Press.

Steriade, M., Jones, E. G., & McCormick, D. A. (1997). *Thalamus, organization and function* (Vol. 1). New York: Elsevier.

Stern, D. (1977). *The first relationship: Mother and infant*. Cambridge, MA: Harvard University Press.

Stern, W. (1912). *Psychologische Methoden der Intelligenz-Prüfung*. Leipzig, Germany: Barth.

Sternberg, R. J. (1977). *Intelligence, information processing, and analogical reasoning: The componential analysis of human abilities*. Hillsdale, NJ: Erlbaum.

Sternberg, R. J. (1979, September). Beyond IQ: Stalking the IQ quark. *Psychology Today*, pp. 42–54.

Sternberg, R. J. (1980). Representation and process in linear syllogistic reasoning. *Journal of Experimental Psychology: General, 109*, 119–159.

Sternberg, R. J. (1981). Intelligence and nonentrenchment. *Journal of Educational Psychology, 73*, 1–16.

Sternberg, R. J. (Ed.). (1982). *Handbook of human intelligence*. New York: Cambridge University Press.

Sternberg, R. J. (1983). Components of human intelligence. *Cognition, 15*, 1–48.

Sternberg, R. J. (Ed.). (1984). *Human abilities: An information-processing approach*. San Francisco: Freeman.

Sternberg, R. J. (1985a). *Beyond IQ: A triarchic theory of human intelligence*. New York: Cambridge University Press.

Sternberg, R. J. (1985b). Implicit theories of intelligence, creativity, and wisdom. *Journal of Personality and Social Psychology, 49*, 607–627.

Sternberg, R. J. (1986). *Intelligence applied: Understanding and increasing your intellectual skills*. San Diego: Harcourt Brace Jovanovich.

Sternberg, R. J. (1987a). Most vocabulary is learned from context. In M. McKeown (Ed.), *The nature of vocabulary acquisition* (pp. 89–105). Hillsdale, NJ: Erlbaum.

Sternberg, R. J. (1987b). Teaching intelligence: The application of cognitive psychology to the improvement of intellectual skills. In J. B. Baron & R. J. Sternberg (Eds.), *Teaching thinking skills: Theory and practice* (pp. 182–218). New York: W. H. Freeman.

Sternberg, R. J. (1988). *The triarchic mind*. New York: Viking.

Sternberg, R. J. (Ed.). (1990). *Wisdom: Its nature, origins, and development*. New York: Cambridge University Press.

Sternberg, R. J. (1995). For whom the bell curve tolls: A review of *The Bell Curve*. *Psychological Science, 6*, 257-261.

Sternberg, R. J. (1996a). Costs of expertise. In K. A. Ericsson (Ed.), *The road to excellence* (pp. 347–355). Mahwah, NJ: Erlbaum.

Sternberg, R. J. (1996b). Myths, countermyths, and truths about human intelligence. *Educational Researcher, 25*(2), 11–16.

Sternberg, R. J. (1997). *Successful intelligence*. New York: Simon & Schuster.

Sternberg, R. J. (1998). Abilities are forms of developing expertise. *Educational Researcher, 27*(3), 11–20.

Sternberg, R. J. (1999). A dialectical basis for understanding the study of cognition. In R. J. Sternberg (Ed.), *The nature of cognition* (pp. 51–78). Cambridge, MA: MIT Press.

Sternberg, R. J. (2000). Thinking: An overview. In A. Kazdin (Ed.), *Encyclopedia of psychology* (Vol. 8, pp. 68–71). Washington, DC: American Psychological Association.

Sternberg, R. J. (2004). What do we know about the nature of reasoning? In J. P. Leighton & R. J. Sternberg (Eds.), *The nature of reasoning* (pp. 443–455). New York: Cambridge University Press.

Sternberg, R. J., & Detterman, D. K. (Eds.). (1986). *What is intelligence? Contemporary viewpoints on its nature and definition*. Norwood, NJ: Ablex.

Sternberg, R. J., Ferrari, M., Clinkenbeard, P. R., & Grigorenko, E. L. (1996). Identification, instruction, and assessment of gifted children: A construct validation of a triarchic model. *Gifted Child Quarterly, 40*, 129–137.

Sternberg, R. J., Forsythe, G. B., Hedlund, J., Horvath, J., Snook, S., Williams, W. M., et al. (2000). *Practical intelligence in everyday life*. New York: Cambridge University Press.

Sternberg, R. J., & Grigorenko, E. L. (1997, Fall). The cognitive costs of physical and mental ill health: Applying the psychology of the developed world to the problems of the developing world. *Eye on Psi Chi, 2*(1), 20–27.

Sternberg, R. J., & Grigorenko, E. L. (1999). *Our labeled children: What every parent and teacher needs to know about learning disabilities*. Somerville, MA: Perseus.

Sternberg, R. J., & Grigorenko, E. L. (Eds.) (2002a). *Intelligence applied* (2nd ed.). New York: Oxford University Press.

Sternberg, R. J., & Grigorenko, E. L. (Eds.) (2002b). *The general factor of intelligence: How general is it?* Mahwah, NJ: Erlbaum.

Sternberg, R. J., & Grigorenko, E. L. (2004). Successful intelligence in the classroom. *Theory into Practice, 43*(4), 274–280.

Sternberg, R. J., & Grigorenko, E. L. (2006). Cultural intelligence and successful intelligence. *Group & Organization Management, 31*(1), 27–39.

Sternberg, R. J., Grigorenko, E. L., Ferrari, M., & Clinkenbeard, P. (1999). A triarchic analysis of an aptitude-treatment interaction. *European Journal of Psychological Assessment, 15*, 1–11.

Sternberg, R. J., Grigorenko, E. L., & Oh, S. (2001). The development of intelligence at midlife. In M. E. Lachman (Ed.), *Handbook of midlife development* (pp. 217–247). New York: Wiley.

Sternberg, R. J., & Kaufman, J. C. (1996). Innovation and intelligence testing: The curious case of the dog that didn't bark. *European Journal of Psychological Assessment, 12*, 175–182.

Sternberg, R. J., & Kaufman, J. C. (1998). Human abilities. *Annual Review of Psychology, 49*, 479–502.

Sternberg, R. J., Kaufman, J. C., & Grigorenko, E. L. (2008). *Applied intelligence*. New York: Cambridge University Press.

Sternberg, R. J., Kaufman, J. C., & Pretz, J. E. (2001). The propulsion model of creative contributions applied to the arts and letters. *Journal of Creative Behavior, 35*, 75–101.

Sternberg, R. J., Kaufman, J. C., & Pretz, J. E. (2002). *The creativity conundrum: A propulsion model of kinds of creative contributions*. New York: Psychology Press.

Sternberg, R. J., & Lubart, T. I. (1991). An investment theory of creativity and its development. *Human Development, 34*, 1–31.

Sternberg, R. J., & Lubart, T. I. (1993). Investing in creativity. *Psychological Inquiry, 4*(3), 229–232.

Sternberg, R. J., & Lubart, T. I. (1995). *Defying the crowd*. New York: Free Press.

Sternberg, R. J., & Lubart, T. I. (1996). Investing in creativity. *American Psychologist, 51*, 677–688.

Sternberg, R. J., & Nigro, G. (1980). Developmental patterns in the solution of verbal analogies. *Child Development, 51*, 27–38.

Sternberg, R. J., & Nigro, G. (1983). Interaction and analogy in the comprehension and appreciation of metaphors. *Quarterly Journal of Experimental Psychology, 35A*, 17–38.

Sternberg, R. J., Nokes, K., Geissler, P. W., Price, R., Okatcha, F., Bundy, D. A., et al. (2001). The relationship between academic and practical intelligence: A case study in Kenya. *Intelligence, 29*, 401–418.

Sternberg, R. J., Okagaki, L., & Jackson, A. (1990). Practical intelligence for success in school. *Educational Leadership, 48*, 35–39.

Sternberg, R. J., Powell, C., McGrane, P. A., & McGregor, S. (1997). Effects of a parasitic infection on cognitive functioning. *Journal of Experimental Psychology: Applied, 3*, 67–76.

Sternberg, R. J., & Powell, J. S. (1983). Comprehending verbal comprehension. *American Psychologist, 38*, 878–893.

Sternberg, R. J., & The Rainbow Project Collaborators (2006). The Rainbow Project: Enhancing the SAT through assessments of analytical, practical and creative skills. *Intelligence, 34*(4), 321–350.

Sternberg, R. J., & Ruzgis, P. (Eds.). (1994). *Personality and intelligence*. New York: Cambridge University Press.

Sternberg, R. J., & Spear-Swerling, L. (Eds.) (1999). *Perspectives on learning disabilities*. Boulder, CO: Westview.

Sternberg, R. J., Torff, B., & Grigorenko, E. L. (1998). Teaching for successful intelligence raises school achievement. *Phi Delta Kappan, 79*(9), 667–669.

Sternberg, R. J., & Wagner, R. K. (1982, July). Automization failure in learning disabilities. *Topics in Learning and Learning Disabilities, 2*, 1–11.

Sternberg, R. J., & Wagner, R. K. (Eds.). (1994). *Mind in context: Interactionist perspectives on human intelligence*. New York: Cambridge University Press.

Sternberg, R. J., & Weil, E. M. (1980). An aptitude–strategy interaction in linear syllogistic reasoning. *Journal of Educational Psychology, 72*, 226–234.

Sternberg, S. (1966). High-speed memory scanning in human memory. *Science, 153*, 652–654.

Sternberg, S. (1969). Memory-scanning: Mental processes revealed by reaction-time experiments. *American Scientist, 4*, 421–457.

Stevens, A., & Coupe, P. (1978). Distortions in judged spatial relations. *Cognitive Psychology, 10*, 422–437.

Stevens, K. N., & Blumstein, S. E. (1981). The search for invariant acoustic correlates of phonetic features. In P. K. Eimas & J. L. Miller (Eds.), *Perspectives on the study of speech* (pp. 1–38). Hillsdale: Erlbaum.

Stevenson, R. J. (1993). *Language, thought, and representation*. New York: Wiley.

Stickgold, R., & Walker, M. (2004). To sleep, perchance to gain creative insight? *Trends in Cognitive Science, 8*(5), 191–192.

Stiles, J., Bates, E. A., Thal, D., Trauner, D., & Reilly, J. (1998). Linguistic, cognitive, and affective development in children with pre- and perinatal focal brain injury: A ten-year overview from the San Diego longitudinal project. In C. Rovee-Collier, L. Lipsitt, & H. Hayne (Eds.), *Advances in infancy research* (Vol. 12, pp. 131–164). Stamford, CT: Ablex.

Strayer, D. L., Drews, F. A., & Crouch, D. J. (2006). A comparison of the cell phone driver and the drunk driver. *Human Factors, 48*(2), 381–391.

Strayer, D. L., & Johnston, W. A. (2001). Driven to distraction: Dual-task studies of simulated driving and conversing on a cellular telephone. *Psychological Science,12*, 462–466.

Stromswold, K. (1998). The genetics of spoken language disorders. *Human Biology, 70*, 297–324.

Stromswold, K. (2000). The cognitive neuroscience of language acquisition. In M. Gazzaniga (Ed.), *The new cognitive neurosciences* (2nd ed., pp. 909–932). Cambridge, MA: MIT Press.

Stroop, J. R. (1935). Studies of interference in serial verbal reactions. *Journal of Experimental Psychology, 18*, 624–643.

Stuss, D. T., & Floden, D. (2003). Frontal cortex. In L. Nadel (Ed.), *Encyclopedia of cognitive science* (Vol. 2, pp. 163–169). London: Nature Publishing Group.

Stuss, D. T., Shallice, T., Alexander, M. P., & Picton, T. W. (1995). A multidisciplinary approach to anterior attention functions. In J. Grafman, K. J. Holyoak, & F. Boller (Eds.), *Structure and functions of the human prefrontal cortex*. New York: New York Academy of Sciences.

Stylianou, D. A., & Silver, E. A. (2004). The role of visual representations in advanced mathematical problem solving: An examination of expert–novice similarities and differences. *Mathematical Thinking and Learning, 6*(4), 353–387.

Sugrue, K., & Hayne, H. (2006). False memories produced by children and adults in the DRM paradigm. *Applied Cognitive Psychology, 20*(5), 625–631.

Suh, S., & Trabasso, T. (1993). Inferences during reading: Converging evidence from discourse analysis, talk-aloud protocols, and recognition priming. *Journal of Memory and Language, 32*, 279–300.

Sun, R. (2003). Connectionist implementation and hybrid systems. In L. Nadel (Ed.), *Encyclopedia of cognitive science* (Vol. 1, pp. 697–703). London: Nature Publishing Group.

Sundgren, P. C., Dong, Q., Gómez-Hassan, D., Mukherji, S. K., Maly, P., & Welsh, R. (2004). Diffusion tensor imaging of the brain: Review of clinical applications. *Neuroradiology, 46*(5), 339–350.

Surian, L. (1996). Are children with autism deaf to Gricean maxims? *Cognitive Neuropsychiatry, 1*(1), 55–72.

Sutton, J. (2003). Memory, philosophical issues about. In L. Nadel (Ed.), *Encyclopedia of cognitive science* (Vol. 2, pp. 1109–1113). London: Nature Publishing Group.

Swanson, J. M., Volkow, N. D., Newcorn, J., Casey, B. J., Moyzis, R., Grandy, D., & Posner, M. (2003). Attention deficit hyperactivity disorder. In L. Nadel (Ed.), *Encyclopedia of cognitive science* (Vol. 1, pp. 226–231). London: Nature Publishing Group.

Taatgen, N. A., & Lee, F. L. (2003). Production compilation: A simple mechanism to model complex skill acquisition. *Human Factors, 45*(1), 61–77.

Taconnat, L., Clarys, D., Vanneste, S., Bouazzaoui, B., & Isingrini, M. (2007). Aging and strategic retrieval in a cued-recall test: The role of executive functions and fluid intelligence. *Brain and Cognition, 64*(1), 1–6.

Takano, Y., & Okubo, M. (2003). Mental rotation. In L. Nadel (Ed.), *Encyclopedia of cognitive science* (Vol. 3, pp. 7–10). London: Nature Publishing Group.

Talasli, U. (1990). Simultaneous manipulation of propositional and analog codes in picture memory. *Perceptual and Motor Skills, 70*(2), 403–414.

Tanaka, J. W., & Taylor, M. (1991). Object categories and expertise: Is the basic level in the eye of the beholder? *Cognitive Psychology, 23*, 457–482.

Tannen, D. (1986). *That's not what I meant! How conversational style makes or breaks relationships*. New York: Ballantine.

Tannen, D. (1990). *You just don't understand: Women and men in conversation*. New York: Ballantine.

Tannen, D. (1994). *Talking from 9 to 5: How women's and men's conversational styles affect who gets heard, who gets credit, and what gets done at work*. New York: Morrow.

Tannen, D. (2001). *I only say this because I love you: How the way we talk can make or break family relationships throughout our lives*. New York: Random House.

Tardif, T. (1996). Nouns are not always learned before verbs: Evidence from Mandarin speakers' early vocabularies. *Developmental Psychology, 32*, 492–504.

Tardif, T., Shatz, M., & Naigles, L. (1997). Caregiver speech and children's use of nouns versus verbs: A comparison of English, Italian, and Mandarin. *Journal of Child Language, 24*, 535–565.

Tarr, M. J. (1995). Rotating objects to recognize them: a case study on the role of viewpoint dependency in the recognition of three-dimensional objects. *Psychonomic Bulletin and Review, 2,* 55–82.

Tarr, M. J. (1999). Mental rotation. In R. A. Wilson & F. C. Keil (Eds.), *The MIT encyclopedia of the cognitive sciences* (pp. 531–533). Cambridge, MA: MIT Press.

Tarr, M. J. (2000). Pattern recognition. In A. Kazdin (Ed.), *Encyclopedia of psychology* (Vol. 6, pp. 66–71). Washington, DC: American Psychological Association.

Tarr, M. J., & Bülthoff, H. H. (1995). Is human object recognition better described by geon structural descriptions or by multiple views? Comment on Biederman and Gerhardstein (1993). *Journal of Experimental Psychology: Human Perception and Performance, 21,* 1494–1505.

Tarr, M. J., & Bülthoff, H. H. (1998). Image-based object recognition in man, monkey, and machine. *Cognition, 67,* 1–20.

Tarr, M. J., & Cheng, Y. D. (2003). Learning to see faces and objects. *Trends in Cognitive Sciences, 7,* 23–30.

Taylor, H., & Tversky, B. (1992a). Descriptions and depictions of environments. *Memory & Cognition, 20*(5), 483–496.

Taylor, H., & Tversky, B. (1992b). Spatial mental models derived from survey and route descriptions. *Journal of Memory & Language, 31*(2), 261–292.

Taylor, J. (2002). Paying attention to consciousness. *Trends in Cognitive Science, 6*(5), 206–210.

Taylor, M. J., & Baldeweg, T. (2002). Application of EEG, ERP and intracranial recordings to the investigation of cognitive functions in children. *Developmental Science, 5*(3), 318–334.

Temple, C.M., & Richardson, P. (2004). Developmental amnesia: A new pattern of dissociation with intact episodic memory. *Neuropsychologia 42*(6), 764–781.

Terman, L. M., & Merrill, M. A. (1937). *Measuring intelligence.* Boston: Houghton Mifflin.

Terman, L. M., & Merrill, M. A. (1973). *Stanford–Binet Intelligence Scale: Manual for the third revision.* Boston: Houghton Mifflin.

Terrace, H. (1987). *Nim.* New York: Columbia University Press.

Thagard, P. (1995). *Mind: Introduction to cognitive science.* Cambridge, MA: MIT Press.

Thagard, P. (1999). Induction. In R. A. Wilson & F. C. Keil (Eds.), *The MIT encyclopedia of the cognitive sciences* (pp. 399–400). Cambridge, MA: MIT Press.

Thagard, P. (2003). Conceptual change. In L. Nadel (Ed.), *Encyclopedia of cognitive science* (Vol. 1, pp. 666–670). London: Nature Publishing Group.

Theeuwes, J. (1992). Perceptual selectivity for color and form. *Perception & Psychophysics, 51*(6), 599–606.

Thiessen, E. D., Hill, E. A., & Saffran, J. R. (2005). Infant-directed speech facilitates word segmentation. *Infancy, 7*(1), 53–71.

Thomas, J. C., Jr. (1974). An analysis of behavior in the hobbits–orcs problem. *Cognitive Psychology, 6,* 257–269.

Thomas, N. J. T. (2003). Mental imagery, philosophical issues about. In L. Nadel (Ed.), *Encyclopedia of cognitive science* (Vol. 2, pp. 1147–1153). London: Nature Publishing Group.

Thomas, S. J., Johnstone, S. J., & Gonsalvez, C. J. (2007). Event-related potentials during an emotional Stroop task. *International Journal of Psychophysiology, 63*(3), 221–231.

Thompson, R. B. (1999). Gender differences in preschoolers' help-eliciting communication. *The Journal of Genetic Psychology, 160,* 357–368.

Thompson, R. F. (1987). The cerebellum and memory storage: A response to Bloedel. *Science, 238,* 1729–1730.

Thompson, R. F. (2000). Memory: Brain systems. In A. E. Kazdin (Ed.), *Encyclopedia of psychology* (Vol. 5, pp. 175–178). Washington, DC: American Psychological Association.

Thompson, R. F., & Krupa, D. J. (1994). Organization of memory traces in the mammalian brain. *Annual Review of Neuroscience, 17,* 519–549.

Thomsen, T., Hugdahl, K., Ersland, L., Barndon, R., Lundervold, A., Smievoll, A. I., et al. (2000). Functional magnetic resonance imaging (fMRI) study of sex differences in a mental rotation task. *Medical Science Monitor, 6*(6), 1186–1196.

Thorndike, E. L. (1905). *The elements of psychology.* New York: Seiler.

Thorndike, R. L., Hagen, E. P., & Sattler, J. M. (1986). *Stanford–Binet Intelligence Scale: Guide for administering and scoring the fourth edition.* Chicago: Riverside.

Thorndyke, P. W. (1981). Distance estimation from cognitive maps. *Cognitive Psychology, 13,* 526–550.

Thorndyke, P. W. (1984). Applications of schema theory in cognitive research. In J. R. Anderson & S. M. Kosslyn (Eds.), *Tutorials in learning and memory* (pp. 167–192). San Francisco: Freeman.

Thorndyke, P. W., & Hayes-Roth, B. (1982). Differences in spatial knowledge acquired from maps and navigation. *Cognitive Psychology, 14,* 580–589.

Thurstone, L. L. (1938). *Primary mental abilities.* Chicago: University of Chicago Press.

Thurstone, L. L., & Thurstone, T. G. (1962). *Tests of primary abilities* (Rev. ed.). Chicago: Science Research Associates.

Titchener, E. B. (1910). *A textbook of psychology.* New York: Macmillan.

Toichi, M., & Kamio, Y. (2002). Long-term memory and levels-of-processing in autism. *Neuropsychologia 7*(40), 964–969.

Tolman, E. C. (1932). *Purposive behavior in animals and men.* New York: Appleton-Century-Crofts.

Tolman, E. C., & Honzik, C. H. (1930). "Insight" in rats. *University of California Publications in Psychology, 4,* 215–232.

Tomasello, M. (1999). *The cultural origins of human cognition* (hardback). Cambridge, MA: Harvard University Press.

Tomasello, M. (2001). *The cultural origins of human cognition* (hardback). Cambridge, MA: Harvard University Press.

Torff, B., & Sternberg, R. J. (2001). Intuitive conceptions among learners and teachers. In B. Torff & R. J. Sternberg (Eds.), *Understanding and teaching the intuitive mind: Student and teacher learning* (pp. 3–26). Mahwah, NJ: Erlbaum.

Torgesen, J. K. (1997). The prevention and remediation of reading disabilities: Evaluating what we know from research. *Journal of Academic Language Therapy, 1,* 11–47.

Torrance, E. P. (1974). *The Torrance tests of creative thinking: Technical norms manual.* Bensenville, IL: Scholastic Testing Services.

Torrance, E. P. (1984). *Torrance tests of creative thinking: Streamlined (revised) manual, Figural A and B.* Bensenville, IL: Scholastic Testing Services.

Tourangeau, R., & Sternberg, R. J. (1981). Aptness in metaphor. *Cognitive Psychology, 13,* 27–55.

Tourangeau, R., & Sternberg, R. J. (1982). Understanding and appreciating metaphors. *Cognition, 11,* 203–244.

Townsend, J. T. (1971). A note on the identifiability of parallel and serial processes. *Perception and Psychophysics, 10,* 161–163.

Trabasso, T., & Suh, S. (1993). Understanding text: achieving explanatory coherence through on-line inferences and mental operations in working memory. *Discourse Processes, 16,* 3–34.

Treadway, M., McCloskey, M., Gordon, B., & Cohen, N. J. (1992). Landmark life events and the organization of memory: Evidence from functional retrograde amnesia. In S. A. Christianson (Ed.), *The handbook of emotion and memory: Research and theory* (pp. 389–410). Hillsdale, NJ: Erlbaum.

Treisman, A. M. (1960). Contextual cues in selective listening. *Quarterly Journal of Experimental Psychology, 12,* 242–248.

Treisman, A. M. (1964a). Monitoring and storage of irrelevant messages in selective attention. *Journal of Verbal Learning and Verbal Behavior, 3,* 449–459.

Treisman, A. M. (1964b). Selective attention in man. *British Medical Bulletin, 20,* 12–16.

Treisman, A. M. (1986). Features and objects in visual processing. *Scientific American, 255*(5), 114B–125.

Treisman, A. M. (1990). Visual coding of features and objects: Some evidence from behavioral studies. In National Research Council (Ed.), *Advances in the modularity of vision: Selections from a symposium on frontiers of visual science* (pp. 39–61). Washington, DC: National Academy Press.

Treisman, A. M. (1991). Search, similarity, and integration of features between and within dimensions. *Journal of Experimental Psychology: Human Perception & Performance, 17,* 652–676.

Treisman, A. M. (1992). Perceiving and re-perceiving objects. *American Psychologist, 47,* 862–875.

Treisman, A. M. (1993). The perception of features and objects. In A. Baddeley & C. L. Weiskrantz (Eds.), *Attention: Selection, awareness, and control* (pp. 5–35). Oxford, UK: Clarenden.

Treisman, A. M., & Sato, S. (1990). Conjunction search revisited. *Journal of Experimental Psychology: Human Perception and Performance, 16,* 459–478.

Treue, S. (2003). Visual attention: The where, what, how and why of saliency. *Current Opinion in Neurobiology, 13,* 428–432.

Triandis, H. C. (2006). Cultural intelligence in organizations. *Group & Organization Management, 31*(1), 20–26.

Tronsky, L. N. (2005). Strategy use, the development of automaticity, and working memory involvement in complex multiplication. *Memory & Cognition, 33*(5), 927–940.

Tsushima, T., Takizawa, O., Saski, M., Siraki, S., Nishi, K., Kohno, M., et al. (1994). Discrimination of English /r-l/ and w-y/ by Japanese infants at 6–12 months: Language specific developmental changes in speech perception abilities. Paper presented at International Conference on Spoken Language Processing, 4. Yokohama, Japan.

Tulving, E. (1962). Subjective organization in free recall of "unrelated" words. *Psychological Review, 69,* 344–354.

Tulving, E. (1972). Episodic and semantic memory. In E. Tulving & W. Donaldson (Eds.), *Organization of memory.* New York: Academic Press.

Tulving, E. (1983). *Elements of episodic memory.* New York: Oxford University Press.

Tulving, E. (1984). Precis: Elements of episodic memory. *Behavioral and Brain Sciences, 7,* 223–268.

Tulving, E. (1985). How many memory systems are there? *American Psychologist, 40*(4), 385–398.

Tulving, E. (1986). What kind of a hypothesis is the distinction between episodic and semantic memory? *Journal of Experimental Psychology: Learning, Memory, & Cognition, 12*(2), 307–311.

Tulving, E. (1989, July/August). Remembering and knowing the past. *American Scientist, 77,* 361–367.

Tulving, E. (2000a). Concepts of memory. In E. Tulving & F. I. M. Craik (Eds.), *The Oxford handbook of memory* (pp. 33–44). New York: Oxford University Press.

Tulving, E. (2000b). Memory: An overview. In A. E. Kazdin (Ed.), *Encyclopedia of psychology* (Vol. 5, pp. 161–162). Washington, DC: American Psychological Association.

Tulving, E., & Craik, F. I. M. (Eds.) (2000). *The Oxford handbook of memory.* New York: Oxford University Press.

Tulving, E., Kapur, S., Craik, F. I.M., Moscovitch, M., & Houle, S. (1994). Hemispheric encoding/retrieval asymmetry in episodic memory: Positron emission tomography findings. *Proceedings of the National Academy of Sciences, 91,* 2016–2020.

Tulving, E., & Pearlstone, Z. (1966). Availability versus accessibility of information in memory for words. *Journal of Verbal Learning and Verbal Behavior, 5,* 381–391.

Tulving, E., & Schacter, D. L. (1994). *Memory systems 1994.* Cambridge, MA: MIT Press.

Tulving, E., Schacter, D. L., & Stark, H. A. (1982). Priming effects in word-fragment completion are independent of recognition memory. *Journal of Experimental Psychology: Learning, Memory, & Cognition, 8*(4), 336–342.

Tulving, E., & Thomson, D. M. (1973). Encoding specificity and retrieval processes in episodic memory. *Psychological Review, 80,* 352–373.

Tunney, N., Taylor, L. F., Higbie, E. J., & Haist, F. (2002). Declarative memory and motor learning in the older adult. *Physical & Occupational Therapy in Geriatrics, 20*(2), 21–42.

Turing, A. (1950). Computing machinery and intelligence. *Mind, 59,* 433–460.

Turing, A. M. (1963). Computing machinery and intelligence. In E. A. Feigenbaum & J. Feldman (Eds.), *Computers and thought.* New York: McGraw-Hill.

Turner, A. M., & Greenough, W. T. (1985). Differential rearing effects on rat visual cortex synapses: I. Synaptic and neuronal density and synapses per neuron. *Brain Research, 329,* 195–203.

Turner, M. L., & Engle, R. W. (1989). Is working-memory capacity task dependent? *Journal of Memory and Language, 28,* 127–154.

Turtle, J., & Yuille, J. (1994). Lost but not forgotten details: Repeated eyewitness recall leads to reminiscence but not hypermnesia. *Journal of Applied Psychology, 79,* 260–271.

Turvey, M. T. (2003). Perception: The ecological approach. In L. Nadel (Ed.), *Encyclopedia of cognitive science* (Vol. 3, pp. 538–541). London: Nature Publishing Group.

Tversky, A. (1972a). Choice by elimination. *Journal of Mathematical Psychology, 9*(4), 341–367.

Tversky, A. (1972b). Elimination by aspects: A theory of choice. *Psychological Review, 79,* 281–299.

Tversky, A., & Kahneman, D. (1971). Belief in the law of small numbers. *Psychological Bulletin, 76*(2), 105–110.

Tversky, A., & Kahneman, D. (1973). Availability: A heuristic for judging frequency and probability. *Cognitive Psychology, 5,* 207–232.

Tversky, A., & Kahneman, D. (1974). Judgment under uncertainty: Heuristics and biases. *Science, 185,* 1124–1131.

Tversky, A., & Kahneman, D. (1981). The framing of decisions and the psychology of choice. *Science, 211,* 453–458.

Tversky, A., & Kahneman, D. (1983). Extensional versus intuitive reasoning: The conjunction fallacy in probability judgment. *Psychological Review, 90*(4), 293–315.

Tversky, A., & Kahneman, D. (1993). Belief in the law of small numbers. In G. Keren & C. Lewis (Eds.), *A handbook for data analysis in the behavioral sciences: Methodological issues* (pp. 341–349). Hillsdale, NJ: Erlbaum.

Tversky, B. (1981). Distortions in memory for maps. *Cognitive Psychology, 13*(3), 407–433.

Tversky, B. (1991). Distortions in memory for visual displays. In S. R. Ellis, M. Kaiser, & A. Grunewald (Eds.), *Spatial instruments and spatial displays* (pp. 61–75). Hillsdale, NJ: Erlbaum.

Tversky, B. (2000). Mental models. In A. E. Kazdin (Ed.), *Encyclopedia of psychology* (Vol. 5, pp. 191–193). Washington, DC: American Psychological Association.

Tversky, B., & Schiano, D. J. (1989). Perceptual and conceptual factors in distortions in memory for graphs and maps. *Journal of Experimental Psychology: General, 118*, 387–398.

Tye, M. (1995). *Ten problems of consciousness: A representational theory of the phenomenal mind.* Cambridge, MA: MIT Press.

Ugurbil, K. (1999). Magnetic resonance imaging. In R. A. Wilson & F. C. Keil (Eds.), *The MIT encyclopedia of the cognitive sciences* (pp. 505–507). Cambridge, MA: MIT Press.

Underwood, B. J. (1957). Interference and forgetting. *Psychological Review, 64*, 49–60.

Ungerleider, L., & Mishkin, M. (1982). Two cortical visual systems. In D. J. Ingle, M. A. Goodale, & R. J. W. Mansfield (Eds.), *Analysis of visual behavior* (pp. 549–586). Cambridge, MA: MIT Press.

Ungerleider, L. G. (1995). Functional brain imaging studies of cortical mechanisms for memory. *Science, 270*, 760–775.

Ungerleider, L. G., & Haxy, J. V. (1994). "What" and "where" in the human brain. *Current Opinion in Neurobiology, 4*, 157–165.

Unsworth, N., Schrock, J. C., & Engle, R. W. (2004). Working memory capacity and the antisaccade task: Individual differences in voluntary saccade control. *Journal of Experimental Psychology: Learning, Memory, and Cognition, 30*, 1302–1321.

Unterrainer, J. M., & Owen, A. M. (2006). Planning and problem solving: From neuropsychology to functional neuroimaging. *Journal of Physiology Paris, 99* (4–6), 308–317.

Unterrainer, J. M., Rahm, B., Kaller, C. P., Ruff, C. C., Spreer, J., Krause, B. J., et al. (2004). When planning fails: Individual differences and error-related brain activity in problem solving. *Cerebral Cortex, 14*(12), 1390–1397.

Usher, J. A., & Neisser, U. (1993). Childhood amnesia and the beginnings of memory for four early life events. *Journal of Experimental Psychology: General, 122*(2), 155–165.

Vakil, S., Sharot, T., Markowitz, M., Aberbuch, S., & Groswasser, Z. (2002). Script memory for typical and atypical actions: Controls versus patients with severe closed-head injury. *Brain Injury, 17*(10), 825–833.

Valentin, D., Chollet, S., Beal, S., & Patris, B. (2007). Expertise and memory for beers and beer olfactory compounds. *Food Quality and Preference, 18*, 776–785.

van Daalen-Kapteijns, M., & Elshout-Mohr, M. (1981). The acquisition of word meanings as a cognitive learning process. *Journal of Verbal Learning & Verbal Behavior, 20*(4), 386–399.

Van der Heijden, A. H. C. (1992). *Selective attention in vision.* London: Routledge.

van der Leij, A., de Jong, P. F., & Rijswijk-Prins, H. (2001). Characteristics of dyslexia in a Dutch family. *Dyslexia, 7*(3), 105–123.

van Dijk, T. A. (1975). Formal semantics of metaphorical discourse. *Poetics, 4*, 173–198.

van Dijk, T. A. (2006). Discourse, context and cognition. *Discourse Studies, 8*(1), 159–177.

Van Garderen, D. (2006). Spatial visualization, visual imagery, and mathematical problem solving of students with varying abilities. *Journal of Learning Disabilities, 39*(6), 496–506.

Van Selst, M., & Jolicoeur, P. (1994). Can mental rotation occur before the dual-task bottleneck? *Journal of Experimental Psychology: Human Perception and Performance, 20*, 905–921.

van Zoest, W., & Donk, M. (2004). Bottom-up and top-down control in visual search. *Perception, 33*, 927–937.

VanLehn, K. (1989). Problem solving and cognitive skill acquisition. In M. I. Posner (Ed.), *Foundations of cognitive science* (pp. 526–579). Cambridge, MA: MIT Press.

VanLehn, K. (1990). *Mind bugs: The origins of procedural misconceptions.* Cambridge, MA: MIT Press.

VanRullen R., & Thorpe S. J. (2001). Is it a bird? Is it a plane? Ultrarapid visual categorisation of natural and artifactual objects. *Perception 30*(6), 655–668.

Vargha-Khadem, F., Gadian, D. G., Watkins, K. E., Connelly, A., Van Paesschen, W., & Mishkin, M. (1997). Differential effects of early hippocampal pathology on episodic and semantic memory. *Science, 277*(5324), 376–380.

Vellutino, F. R., Scanlon, D. M., Sipay, E., Small, S., Pratt, A., Chen, R., et al. (1996). Cognitive profiles of difficult-to-remediate and readily remediated poor readers: Early intervention as a vehicle for distinguishing between cognitive and experiential deficits as basic causes of specific reading disability. *Journal of Educational Psychology, 88*, 601–638.

Velmans, M. (Ed.) (1996). *Science of consciousness: Psychological, neuropsychological, and clinical reviews.* London: Routledge.

Verdolini-Marston, K., & Balota, D. A. (1994). Role of elaborative and perceptual integrative processes in perceptual–motor performance. *Journal of Experimental Psychology: Learning, Memory and Cognition, 20*(3), 739–749.

Vernon, P. A., & Mori, M. (1992). Intelligence, reaction times, and peripheral nerve conduction velocity. *Intelligence, 16*(3–4), 273–288.

Vernon, P. A., Wickett, J. C., Bazana, P. G., & Stelmack, R. M. (2000). The neuropsychology and psychophysiology of human intelligence. In R. J. Sternberg (Ed.), *Handbook of intelligence* (pp. 245–264). New York: Cambridge University Press.

Vernon, P. E. (1971). *The structure of human abilities.* London: Methuen.

Vicente, K. J., & DeGroot, A. D. (1990). The memory recall paradigm: straightening out the historical record. *American Psychologist, 45*, 285–287.

Vigil-Colet, A., & Morales-Vives, F. (2005). How impulsivity is related to intelligence and academic achievement. *The Spanish Journal of Psychology, 8*(2), 199–204.

Vignal, J., Maillard, L., McGonigal, A., & Chauvel, P. (2007). The dreamy state: Hallucinations of autobiographic memory evoked by temporal lobe stimulation and seizures. *Brain, 130*(1), 88–99.

Vignolo, L. A. (2003). Music agnosia and auditory agnosia: Dissociation in stroke patients. *The Neuroscience and Music, 999*(50), 50–57.

Visual disabilities: Color-blindness. Retrieved December 28, 2004, from http://www.webaim.org/techniques/visual/colorblind

Vitevitch, M. S. (2003). Change deafness: The inability to detect changes between two voices. *Journal of Experimental Psychology: Human Perception and Performance, 29*(2), 333–342.

Vogel, E. K., Woodman, G. F., & Luck, S. J. (2001). Storage of features, conjunctions, and objects in visual working memory. *Journal of Experimental Psychology: Human Perception and Performance, 27,* 92–114.

Vogel, J. J., Bowers, C. A., & Vogel, D. S. (2003). Cerebral lateralization of spatial abilities: A meta-analysis. *Brain Cognition, 52*(2), 197–204.

Vogels, T. P., Rajan, K., & Abbott, L. F. (2005). Neural network dynamics. *Annual Review of Neuroscience, 28,* 357–376.

Vollmeyer, R., Burns, B. D., & Holyoak, K. J. (1996). The impact of goal specificity on strategy use and the acquisition of problem structure. *Cognitive Science, 20,* 75–100.

von Bohlen und Halbach, O., & Dermietzel, R. (2006). *Neurotransmitters and neuromodulators: Handbook of receptors and biological effects.* New York: Wiley.

Von Eckardt, B. (1993). *What is cognitive science?* Cambridge, MA: MIT Press.

Von Eckardt, B. (1999). Mental representation. In R. A. Wilson & F. C. Keil (Eds.), *The MIT encyclopedia of the cognitive sciences* (pp. 527–529). Cambridge, MA: MIT Press.

Von Eckardt, B. (2005). *What is cognitive science?* Cambridge, MA: Bradford.

von Frisch, K. (1962). Dialects in the language of the bees. *Scientific American, 207,* 79–87.

von Frisch, K. (1967). Honeybees: Do they use direction and distance information provided by their dances? *Science, 158,* 1072–1076.

von Helmholtz, H. (1896). *Vorträge und Reden.* Braunschweig, Germany: Vieweg und Sohn.

von Helmholtz, H. L. F. (1962). *Treatise on physiological optics* (3rd ed., J. P. C. Southall, Ed. and Trans.). New York: Dover. (Original work published 1909)

Voon, V., Thomsen, T., Miyasaki, J. M., de Souza, M., Shafro, A., Fox, S. H., et al. (2007). Factors associated with dopaminergic drug-related pathological gambling in Parkinson disease. *Archives of Neurology, 64*(2), 212–216.

Vygotsky, L. S. (1986). *Thought and language.* Cambridge, MA: MIT Press.

Wagenaar, W. (1986). My memory: A study of autobiographic memory over the past six years. *Cognitive Psychology, 18,* 225–252.

Wagner, A. R., & Rescorla, R. A. (1972). Inhibition in Pavlovian conditioning: Application of a theory. In R. A. Boakes & M. S. Halliday (Eds.), *Inhibition and learning.* New York: Academic Press.

Wagner, D. A. (1978). Memories of Morocco: The influence of age, schooling, and environment on memory. *Cognitive Psychology, 10,* 1–28.

Wagner, R. K. (2000). Practical intelligence. In R. J. Sternberg (Ed.), *Practical intelligence in everyday life.* New York: Cambridge University Press.

Wagner, R. K., & Stanovich, K. E. (1996). Expertise in reading. In K. A. Ericsson (Ed.), *The road to excellence* (pp. 159–227). Mahwah, NJ: Erlbaum.

Wagner, U., Gais, S., Haider, H., Verleger, R., & Born, J. (2004). Sleep inspires insight. *Letters to Nature, 427,* 352–355.

Wahlsten, D., & Gottlieb, G. (1997). The invalid separation of effects of nature and nurture: Lessons from animal experimentation. In R. J. Sternberg & E. L. Grigorenko (Eds.), *Intelligence, heredity, and environment* (pp. 163–192). New York: Cambridge University Press.

Walker, M. P., Brakefield, T., Hobson, J. A., & Stickgold, R. (2003). Dissociable stages of human memory consolidation and reconsolidation. *Nature, 425*(6958), 616–620.

Walker, P. M., & Tanaka, J. W. (2003). An encoding advantage for own-race versus other-race faces. *Perception, 32,* 1117–1125.

Walpurger, V., Hebing-Lennartz, G., Denecke, H., & Pietrowsky, R. (2003). Habituation deficit in auditory event-related potentials in tinnitus complainers. *Hearing Research, 181*(1–2), 57–64.

Walsh, V., & Pascual-Leone, A. (2005). *Transcranial magnetic stimulation: A neurochronometrics of mind.* Cambridge, MA: MIT Press.

Warner, J. (2004). Rubbernecking distracts more than phone. Retrieved August 11, 2004, from http://content.health.msn.com/content/article/62/71477.htm

Warren, R. M. (1970). Perceptual restoration of missing speech sounds. *Science, 167,* 392–393.

Warren, R. M., Obusek, C. J., Farmer, R. M., & Warren, R. P. (1969). Auditory sequence: Confusion of patterns other than speech or music. *Science, 164,* 586–587.

Warren, R. M., & Warren, R. P. (1970). Auditory illusions and confusions. *Scientific American, 223,* 30–36.

Warrington, E. (1982). The double dissociation of short- and long-term memory deficits. In L. S. Cermak (Ed.), *Human memory and amnesia.* Hillsdale, NJ: Erlbaum.

Warrington, E., & Shallice, T. (1972). Neuropsychological evidence of visual storage in short-term memory tasks. *Quarterly Journal of Experimental Psychology, 24*(1), 30–40.

Warrington, E., & Shallice, T. (1984). Category specific semantic impairments. *Brain, 107,* 829–853.

Warrington, E., & Weiskrantz, L. (1970). Amnesic syndrome: Consolidation or retrieval? *Nature, 228*(5272), 628–630.

Warrington, E. K, & Shallice, T. (1972). Neuropsychological evidence of visual storage in short-term memory tasks. *The Quarterly Journal of Experimental Psychology, 24,* 30–40.

Wason, P. C. (1968). Reasoning about a rule. *Quarterly Journal of Experimental Psychology, 20*(3), 273–281.

Wason, P. C. (1969). Regression in reasoning? *British Journal of Psychology, 60*(4), 471–480.

Wason, P. C. (1983). Realism and rationality in the selection task. In J. St. B. T. Evans (Ed.), *Thinking and reasoning: Psychological approaches* (pp. 44–75). Boston: Routledge & Kegan Paul.

Wason, P. C., & Johnson-Laird, P. (1970). A conflict between selecting and evaluating information in an inferential task. *British Journal of Psychology, 61*(4), 509–515.

Wason, P. C., & Johnson-Laird, P. N. (1972). *Psychology of reasoning: Structure and content.* London: B. T. Batsford.

Wasow, T. (1989). Grammatical theory. In M. I. Posner (Ed.), *Foundations of cognitive science* (pp. 208–243). Cambridge, MA: MIT Press.

Wasserman, D., Lempert, R. O., & Hastie, R. (1991). Hindsight and causality. *Personality & Social Psychology Bulletin, 17*(1), 30–35.

Waterhouse, L. (2006). Multiple intelligences, the Mozart effect, and emotional intelligence: A critical review. *Educational Psychologist, 41*(4), 207–225.

Waterman, A. H., Blades, M., & Spencer, C. (2001) Interviewing children and adults: The effect of question format on the tendency to speculate. *Applied Cognitive Psychology, 15*(5), 521–531.

Waters, G. S., & Caplan, D. (2003). Language comprehension and verbal working memory. In L. Nadel (Ed.), *Encyclopedia of cognitive science* (Vol. 2, pp. 726–730). London: Nature Group Press.

Watkins, M. J., & Tulving, E. (1975). Episodic memory: When recognition fails. *Journal of Experimental Psychology: General, 104,* 5–29.

Watson, O. M. (1970). *Proxemic behavior: A cross-cultural study.* The Hague, Netherlands: Mouton.

Wattenmaker, W. D. (1995). Knowledge structures and linear separability: integrating information in object and social categorization. *Cognitive Psychology, 28*, 274–328.

Waugh, N. C., & Norman, D. A. (1965). Primary memory. *Psychological Review, 72*, 89–104.

Weaver, C. A. (1993). Do you need a "flash" to form a flashbulb memory? *Journal of Experimental Psychology: General, 122*(1), 39–46.

Weaver, K. E., & Stevens, A. A. (2007). Attention and sensory interactions within the occipital cortex in the early blind: An fMRI study. *Journal of Cognitive Neuroscience, 19*(2), 315–330.

Webster, M. A., Kaping, D., Mizokami, Y., & Duhamel, P. (2004). Adaptation to natural face categories. *Nature, 428*, 557–561.

Wegner, D. M. (1997a). When the antidote is the poison: Ironic mental control processses. *Psychological Science, 8*, 148–153.

Wegner, D. M. (1997b). Why the mind wanders. In J. D Cohen & J. W. Schooler (Eds.), *Scientific approaches to consciousness* (pp. 295–315). Mahwah, NJ: Erlbaum.

Wegner, D. M. (2002). *The illusion of conscious will*. Cambridge, MA: Bradford Books.

Weinberger, D. R., Mattay, V., Callicott, J. Kotrla, K., Santha, A., van Gelderen, P., et al. (1996). fMRI applications in schizophrenia research. *Neuroimage, 4*(3), 118–126.

Weingartner, H., Rudorfer, M. V., Buchsbaum, M. S., & Linnoila, M. (1983). Effects of serotonin on memory impairments produced by ethanol. *Science, 221*, 442–473.

Weisberg, R. W. (1986). *Creativity: Genius and other myths*. New York: Freeman.

Weisberg, R. W. (1988). Problem solving and creativity. In R. J. Sternberg (Ed.), *The nature of creativity* (pp. 148–176). New York: Cambridge University Press.

Weisberg, R. W. (1995). Prolegomena to theories of insight in problem solving: A taxonomy of problems. In R. J. Sternberg & J. E. Davidson (Eds.), *The nature of insight* (pp. 157–196). Cambridge, MA: MIT Press.

Weisberg, R. W. (1999). Creativity and knowledge: A challenge to theories. In R. J. Sternberg (Ed.), *Handbook of creativity* (pp. 226–250). New York: Cambridge University Press.

Weiskrantz, L. (1986). Some aspects of memory functions and the temporal lobes. *Acta Neurologica Scandinavica, 74*(Suppl 109), 69–74.

Weiskrantz, L. (1994). Blindsight. In M. W. Eysenck (Ed.), *The Blackwell dictionary of cognitive psychology*. Cambridge, MA: Blackwell.

Weisstein, N., & Harris, C. S. (1974). Visual detection of line segments: An object-superiority effect. *Science, 186*, 752–755.

Weizenbaum, J. (1966). ELIZA-A computer program for the study of natural language communication between man and machine. *Communications of the Association for Computing Machinery, 9*, 36–45.

Welbourne, S. R., & Ralph, M. A. L. (2007). Using parallel distributed processing models to simulate phonological dyslexia: The key role of plasticity-related recovery. *Journal of Cognitive Neuroscience, 19*, 1125–1139.

Wellman, H. M., & Gelman, S. A. (1998). Knowledge acquisition in foundational domains. In W. Damon (Ed.-in-Chief), D. Kuhn, & R. S. Siegler (Vol. Eds.), *Handbook of child psychology: Vol. 2. Cognitive development* (pp. 523–573). New York: Wiley.

Wells, G. L. (1993). What do we know about eyewitness identification? *American Psychologist, 48*, 553–571.

Wells, G. L., & Loftus, E. G. (1984). *Eyewitness testimony: Psychological perspectives*. New York: Cambridge University Press.

Wells, G. L., Luus, C. A. E., & Windschitl, P. D. (1994). Maximizing the utility of eyewitness identification evidence. *Current Directions in Psychological Science, 6*, 194–197.

Welsh, M. C., Satterlee-Cartmell, T., & Stine, M. (1999). Towers of Hanoi and London: Contribution of working memory and inhibition to performance. *Brain & Cognition, 41*, 231–242.

Wenke, D., & Frensch, P. A. (2003). Is success or failure at solving complex problems related to intellectual ability? In J. E. Davidson & R. J. Sternberg (Eds.), *The psychology of problem solving* (pp. 87–126). New York: Cambridge University Press.

Wenke, D., Frensch, P. A., & Funke, J. (2005). Complex problem solving and intelligence. In R. J. Sternberg & J. E. Pretz (Eds.), *Cognition and intelligence* (pp. 160–187). New York: Cambridge University Press.

Werker, J. F. (1989). Becoming a native listener. *American Scientist, 77*, 54–59.

Werker, J. F. (1994). Cross-language speech perception: Developmental change does not involve loss. In J. C. Goodman & H. L. Nusbaum (Eds.), *The development of speech perception: The transition from speech sounds to spoken words* (pp. 93–120). Cambridge, MA: MIT Press.

Werker, J. F., & Tees, R. L. (1984). Cross-language speech perception: Evidence for perceptual reorganization during the first year of life. *Infant Behavior and Development, 7*, 49–63.

Werner, H., & Kaplan, E. (1952). The acquisition of word meanings: A developmental study. *Monographs of the Society for Research in Child Development*, No. 51.

Wertheimer, M. (1959). *Productive thinking* (Rev. ed.). New York: Harper & Row. (Original work published 1945)

West, R. L. (1986). Everyday memory and aging. *Developmental Neuropsychology, 2*(4), 323–344.

Wexler, K. (1996). The development of inflection in a biologically based theory of language acquisition. In M. L. Rice (Ed.), *Toward a genetics of language* (pp. 113–144). Mahwah, NJ: Erlbaum.

Whalen, P. J. (1998). Fear, vigilance, and ambiguity: Initial neuroimaging studies of the human amygdala. *Current Directions in Psychological Science, 7*(6), 177–188.

What is achromatopsia? Retrieved March 21, 2007, from http://www.achromat.org/what_is_achromatopsia.html

What you need to know about brain tumors. Retrieved December 29, 2004, from http://www.cancer.gov/cancertopics/wyntk/brain

Wheeldon, L. R., Meyer, A. S., & Smith, M. (2003). Language production, incremental. In L. Nadel (Ed.), *Encyclopedia of cognitive science* (Vol. 2, pp. 760–764). London: Nature Group Press.

Wheeler, D. D. (1970). Processes in word recognition. *Cognitive Psychology, 1*, 59–85.

Whitten, S., & Graesser, A. C. (2003). Comprehension of text in problem solving. In J. E. Davidson & R. J. Sternberg (Eds.), *The psychology of problem solving* (pp. 207–229). New York: Cambridge University Press.

Whorf, B. L. (1956). In J. B. Carroll (Ed.), *Language, thought and reality: Selected writings of Benjamin Lee Whorf*. Cambridge, MA: MIT Press.

Wickens, D. D., Dalezman, R. E., & Eggemeier, F. T. (1976). Multiple encoding of word attributes in memory. *Memory & Cognition, 4*(3), 307–310.

Wickett, J. C., & Vernon, P. (1994). Peripheral nerve conduction velocity, reaction time, and intelligence: An attempt to replicate Vernon and Mori. *Intelligence, 18*, 127–132.

Wiedenbauer, G., Schmid, J., & Jansen-Osmann, P. (2007). Manual training of mental rotation. *European Journal of Cognitive Psychology, 19*(1), 17–36.

Wilcox, L. M., Allison, R. S., Elfassy, S., & Grelik, C. (2006). Personal space in virtual reality. ACM *Transactions on Applied Perception (TAP), 3*(4), 412–428.

Williams, M. (1970). *Brain damage and the mind.* London: Penguin.

Williams, R. N. (2000). Epistemology. In A. E. Kazdin (Ed.), *Encyclopedia of psychology* (Vol. 3, pp. 225–232). Washington, DC: American Psychological Association.

Williams, W. M., & Sternberg, R. J. (1988). Group intelligence: Why some groups are better than others. *Intelligence, 12,* 351–377.

Willis, S. L. (1985). Towards an educational psychology of the older adult learner: Intellectual and cognitive bases. In J. E. Birren & K. W. Schaie (Eds.), *Handbook of the psychology of aging* (2nd ed.). New York: Van Nostrand Reinhold.

Wilson, B. A. (2003). Brain damage, treatment and recovery from. In L. Nadel (Ed.), *Encyclopedia of cognitive science* (Vol. 1, pp. 410–416). London: Nature Publishing Group.

Wilson, M. A., & Emmorey, K. (2006). No difference in short-term memory span between sign and speech. *Psychological Science, 17*(12), 1093–1094.

Wilson, M. A., & McNaughton, B. L. (1994). Reactivation of hippocampal ensemble memories during sleep. *Science, 265,* 676–679.

Wilson, T. D. (2002). *Strangers to ourselves: Discovering the adaptive unconscious.* Cambridge, MA: Belknap.

Wilt, J. K., & Proffitt, D. R. (2005). See the ball; hit the ball: Apparent ball size is correlated with batting average. *Psychological Science, 16,* 937–938.

Wilt, J. K., Proffitt, D. R., & Epstein, W. (2004). Perceiving distance: A role of effort and intent. *Perception, 33,* 577–590.

Windham, G. C., Zhang, L., Gunier, R., Croen, L. A., & Grether, J. K. (2006). Autism spectrum disorders in relation to distribution of hazardous air pollutants in the San Francisco bay area. *Environmental Health Perspective, 114*(9), 1438–1444.

Winograd, T. (1972). *Understanding natural language.* New York: Academic Press.

Wisniewski, E. J. (1997). When concepts combine. *Psychonomic Bulletin and Review, 4,* 167–183.

Wisniewski, E. J. (2000). Concepts: Combinations. In A. E. Kazdin (Ed.), *Encyclopedia of psychology* (Vol. 2, pp. 251-253). Washington, DC: American Psychological Association.

Wisniewski, E. J., & Medin, D. L. (1994). On the interaction of theory and data in concept learning. *Cognitive Science, 18,* 221–281.

Wissler, C. (1901). The correlation of mental and physical tests. *Psychological Review, Monograph Supplement 3*(6).

Witelson, S. F., Beresh, H., & Kiga, D. L. (2006). Intelligence and brain size in 100 postmortem brains: Sex, lateralization and age factors. *Brain, 129*(2), 386–398.

Witelson, S. F., Kigar, D. L., & Walter, A. (2003). Cerebral commissures. In L. Nadel (Ed.), *Encyclopedia of cognitive science* (Vol. 1, pp. 476–485). London: Nature Publishing Group.

Wittgenstein, L. (1953). *Philosophical investigations.* New York: Macmillan.

Wolfe, J. M. (1994). Guided search 2.0: A revised model of visual search. *Psychonomic Bulletin & Review, 1,* 202–238.

Wolfe, J. M., Butcher, S. J., Lee, C., & Hyle, M. (2003). Changing your mind: On the contributions of top-down and bottom up guidance in visual search for feature singletons. *Journal of Experimental Psychology: Human Perception and Performance, 29*(2), 483–502.

Wolford, G., Miller, M. B., & Gazzaniga, M. (2000) The left hemisphere's role in hypothesis formation. *The Journal of Neuroscience, 20*(64), 1–4.

Wolfram, W., Adger, C. T., & Christian, D. (1999). Dialects in schools and communities. Mahwah, NJ: Erlbaum.

Wolkowitz, O. M., Tinklenberg, J. R., & Weingartner, H. (1985). A psychopharmacological perspective of cognitive functions: II. Specific pharmacologic agents. *Neuropsychobiology, 14*(3), 133–156.

Woodward, A. L., & Markman. E. M. (1998). Early word learning. In D. Kuhn & R. S. Siegler (Eds.), *Handbook of child psychology: Vol. 2. Cognition, perception, and language* (5th ed., pp. 371–420). New York: Wiley.

Woodward, T. S., Dixon, M. J., Mullen, K. T. Christensen, K. M., & Bub, D. N. (1999). Analysis of errors in color agnosia: a single-case study. *Neurocase, 5*(2), 95–108.

Woodworth, R. S., & Sells, S. B. (1935). An atmosphere effect in formal syllogistic reasoning. *Journal of Experimental Psychology, 18,* 451–460.

Xu, F, & Carey, S. (1995). Do children's first object names map onto adult-like conceptual representations? In D. MacLaughlin & S. McEwen (Eds.), *Proceedings of the 19th Annual Boston University Conference on Language Development* (pp. 679–688). Somerville, MA: Cascadilla Press.

Xu, F., & Carey, S. (1996). Infants' metaphysics: The case of numerical identity. *Cognitive Psychology, 30,* 111–153.

Xu, Y. (2005). Revisiting the role of the fusiform face area in visual expertise. *Cerebral Cortex. 15*(8), 1234–1242.

Yamauchi, T., & Markman. A. B. (1998). Category learning by inference and classification. *Journal of Memory and Language, 39,* 124–148.

Yang, R., & Sarkar, S. (2006). Detecting coarticulation in sign language using conditional random fields. *Proceedings of the 18th International Conference on Pattern Recognition, 2,* 108–112.

Yang, S. Y., & Sternberg, R. J. (1997). Taiwanese Chinese people's conceptions of intelligence. *Intelligence, 25,* 21–36.

Yantis, S. (1993). Stimulus-driven attentional capture. *Current Directions in Psychological Science, 2*(5), 156–161.

Yap, R. L., & van der Leij, A. (1994). Testing the automatization deficit hypothesis of dyslexia via a dual-task paradigm. *Journal of Learning Disabilities, 27*(10), 660–665.

Yonelinas, A. P. (2001). Consciousness, control, and confidence: The 3 Cs of recognition memory. *Journal of Experimental Psychology: General, 130*(3), 361–379.

Young, A. W. (2003). Prosopagnosia. In L. Nadel (Ed.), *Encyclopedia of cognitive science* (Vol. 3, pp. 768–771). London: Nature Publishing Group.

Yovel, G., & Kanwisher, N. (2004). Face perception: Domain specific, not process specific. *Neuron, 44*(5), 889–898.

Yu, J., & Bellezza, F. S. (2000). Process dissociation as source monitoring. *Journal of Experimental Psychology: Learning, Memory, and Cognition, 26*(6), 1518–1533.

Yu, V. L., Fagan, L. M., Bennet, S. W., Clancey, W. J., Scott, A. C., Hannigan, J. F., et al. (1984). An evaluation of MYCIN's advice. In B. G. Buchanan & E. H. Shortliffe (Eds.), *Rule-based expert systems.* Reading, MA: Addison-Wesley.

Yuille, J. C. (1993). We must study forensic eyewitnesses to know about them. *American Psychologist, 48*(5), 572–573.

Zaidel, E. (1983). A response to Gazzaniga: Language in the right hemisphere, convergent perspectives. *American Psychologist, 38*(5), 542–546.

Zaragoza, M. S., McCloskey, M., & Jamis, M. (1987). Misleading post-event information and recall of the original event: Further evidence against the memory impairment hypothesis. *Journal of Experimental Psychology: Learning, Memory, & Cognition, 13*(1), 36–44.

Zeidner, M. (1990). Perceptions of ethnic group modal intelligence scores: Reflections of cultural stereotypes or intelligence test scores? *Journal of Cross-Cultural Psychology, 21,* 214–231.

Zhang, M., Weisser, V. D., Stilla, R., Prather, S. C., & Sathian, K. (2004). Multisensory cortical processing of object shape and its relation to mental imagery. *Cognitive, Affective, & Behavioral Neuroscience, 4*(2), 251–259.

Zhao, L., & Chubb, C. (2001). The size-tuning of the face-distortion after-effect. *Vision Research, 41,* 2979–2994.

Zigler, E., & Berman, W. (1983). Discerning the future of early childhood intervention. *American Psychologist, 38,* 894–906.

Zihl, J., von Cramon, D., & Mai, N. (1983). Selective disturbance of movement vision after bilateral brain damage. *Brain, 106,* 313–340.

Zimmerman, B. J., & Campillo, M. (2003). Motivating self-regulated problem solvers. In J. E. Davidson & R. J. Sternberg (Eds.), *The psychology of problem solving* (pp. 233–262). New York: Cambridge University Press.

Zinchenko, P. I. (1962). *Neproizvol'noe azpominanie* [Involuntary memory] (pp. 172–207). Moscow: USSR APN RSFSR.

Zinchenko, P. I. (1981). Involuntary memory and the goal-directed nature of activity. In J. V. Wertsch, *The concept of activity in Soviet psychology.* Armonk, NY: Sharpe.

Zola, S. M., & Squire, L. R. (2000). The medial temporal lobe and the hippocampus. In E. Tulving & F. I. M. Craik (Eds.), *The Oxford handbook of memory* (pp. 485–500). New York: Oxford University Press.

Zola-Morgan, S. M., & Squire, L. R. (1990). The primate hippocampal formation: Evidence for a time-limited role in memory storage. *Science, 250,* 228–290.

Zoltan, B. (1996). *Vision, perception, & cognition: A manual for the evaluation and treatment of the neurologically impaired adult* (pp. 109–111). Thorofare, NJ: Slack Incorporated.

Zuidema, L. A. (2005). Myth education: Rationale and strategies for teaching against linguistic prejudice: Literacy educators must work to combat prejudice by dispelling linguistic myths. *Journal of Adolescent & Adult Literacy, 48*(8), 666–675.

Zurif, E. B. (1990). Language and the brain. In D. N. Osherson & H. Lasnik (Eds.), *Language* (pp. 177–198). Cambridge, MA: MIT Press.

Zurif, E. B. (1995). Brain regions of relevance to syntactic processing. In L. R. Gleitman & M. Liberman (Eds.), *Language: An invitation to cognitive science* (Vol. 1, 2nd ed., pp. 381–398). Cambridge, MA: MIT Press.

Zurowski, B., Gostomzyk, J., Gron, G., Weller, R., Schirrmeister, H., Neumeier, B., et al. (2002). Dissociating a common working memory network from different neural substrates of phonological and spatial stimulus processing. *Neuroimage, 15,* 45–57.

Zwaan, R. A., Magliano, J. P., & Graesser, A. C. (1995). Dimensions of situation model construction in narrative comprehension. *Journal of Experimental Psychology: Learning, Memory, and Cognition, 21,* 386–397.

Zwaan, R. A., & Radvansky, G. A. (1998). Situation models in language comprehension and memory. *Psychological Bulletin, 123,* 62–185.

Name Index

Subject Index